WORLD LITERATURE CRITICISM

1500 to the Present

WORLD LITERATURE CRITICISM

1500 to the Present

*A Selection of
Major Authors from
Gale's Literary
Criticism Series*

Lee-Poe

JAMES P. DRAPER, Editor

Gale Research Inc. · *DETROIT* · *LONDON*

STAFF

James P. Draper, *Editor*

Laurie DiMauro, Tina Grant, Paula Kepos, Jelena Krstović, Daniel G. Marowski, Roger Matuz, James E. Person, Jr., Joann Prosyniuk, David Segal, Joseph C. Tardiff, Bridget Travers, Lawrence Trudeau, Thomas Votteler, Sandra L. Williamson, Robyn V. Young, *Contributing Editors*

Catherine Falk, Grace Jeromski, Michael W. Jones, Andrew M. Kalasky, David Kmenta, Marie Lazzari, Zoran Minderović, Sean René Pollock, Mark Swartz, *Contributing Associate Editors*

Jennifer Brostrom, David J. Engelman, Andrea Gacki, Judith Galens, Christopher Giroux, Ian A. Goodhall, Alan Hedblad, Elizabeth P. Henry, Christopher K. King, Kyung-Sun Lim, Elisabeth Morrison, Kristin Palm, Susan M. Peters, James Poniewozik, Eric Priehs, Bruce Walker, Debra A. Wells, Janet Witalec, Allyson J. Wylie, *Contributing Assistant Editors*

Jeanne A. Gough, *Permissions & Production Manager*

Linda M. Pugliese, *Production Supervisor*
Paul Lewon, Lorna Mabunda, Maureen Puhl, Camille Robinson, Jennifer VanSickle, *Editorial Associates*
Donna Craft, Brandy C. Johnson, Sheila Walencewicz, *Editorial Assistants*

Victoria B. Cariappa, *Research Manager*

Maureen Richards, *Research Supervisor*
Mary Beth McElmeel, Tamara C. Nott, *Editorial Associates*
Andrea B. Ghorai, Daniel J. Jankowski, Julie K. Karmazin, Robert S. Lazich, *Editorial Assistants*

Sandra C. Davis, *Permissions Supervisor* (*Text*)
Maria L. Franklin, Josephine M. Keene, Michele M. Lonoconus, Denise M. Singleton, Kimberly F. Smilay, *Permissions Associates*
Rebecca A. Hartford, Shalice Shah, Nancy K. Sheridan, *Permissions Assistants*

Margaret A. Chamberlain, *Permissions Supervisor* (*Pictures*)
Pamela A. Hayes, *Permissions Associate*
Amy Lynn Emrich, Karla Kulkis, Nancy M. Rattenbury, Keith Reed, *Permissions Assistants*

Mary Beth Trimper, *Production Manager*
Mary Winterhalter, *Production Assistant*

Arthur Chartow, *Art Director*
C. J. Jonik, *Keyliner*
Kathleen A. Hourdakis, Mary Krzewinski, *Graphic Designers*

∞™ This book is printed on acid-free paper that meets the minimum requirements of American National Standard for Information Sciences— Permanence Paper for Printed Library Materials, ANSI Z39.48-1984.

ISBN 0-8103-8361-6 (6-volume set)
A CIP catalogue record for this book is available from the British Library

Printed in the United States of America

Published simultaneously in the United Kingdom
by Gale Research International Limited
(An affiliated company of Gale Research Inc.)

Table of Contents

Introduction

A Comprehensive Information Source
on World Literature

World Literature Criticism, 1500 to the Present (WLC) presents a broad selection of the best criticism of works by major writers of the past five hundred years. Among the authors included in *WLC* are sixteenth-century Spanish novelist Miguel de Cervantes and English dramatist William Shakespeare; seventeenth-century English poet John Milton and dramatist Aphra Behn; eighteenth-century Anglo-Irish novelist Jonathan Swift, English essayist Samuel Johnson, and French Enlightenment masters Jean-Jacques Rousseau and Voltaire; acclaimed nineteenth-century writers Jane Austen, William Blake, Emily Brontë, Lewis Carroll, Charles Dickens, Fyodor Dostoyevsky, Frederick Douglass, Gustave Flaubert, Edgar Allan Poe, Mary Shelley, Robert Louis Stevenson, William Wordsworth, and Emile Zola; and major twentieth-century authors W. H. Auden, James Baldwin, Albert Camus, Arthur Conan Doyle, Ralph Ellison, F. Scott Fitzgerald, Ernest Hemingway, James Joyce, Franz Kafka, Toni Morrison, Sylvia Plath, J. D. Salinger, Gertrude Stein, John Steinbeck, Virginia Woolf, and Richard Wright. The scope of *WLC* is wide: more than 225 writers representing dozens of nations, cultures, and time periods.

Coverage

This six-volume set is designed for high school, college, and university students, as well as for the general reader who wants to learn more about literature. *WLC* was developed in response to strong demand by students, librarians, and other readers for a one-stop, authoritative guide to the whole spectrum of world literature. No other compendium like it exists in the marketplace. About 95% of the entries in *WLC* were selected from Gale's acclaimed Literary Criticism Series and completely updated for publication here. Typically, the revisions are extensive, ranging from new author introductions to wide changes in the selection of criticism. A few entries—about 5%— were prepared especially for *WLC* in order to furnish the most comprehensive coverage possible.

Inclusion Criteria

Authors were selected for inclusion in *WLC* based on the advice of leading experts on world literature as well as on the recommendation of a specially formed advisory panel made up of high school teachers and high school and public librarians from throughout the United States. Additionally, the most recent major curriculum studies were closely examined, notably Arthur N. Applebee, *A Study of Book-Length Works Taught in High School English Courses* (1989); Arthur N. Applebee, *A Study of High School Literature Anthologies* (1991); and Doug Estel, Michele L. Satchwell, and Patricia S. Wright, *Reading Lists for College-Bound Students* (1990). All of these resources were collated and compared to produce a reference product that is strongly curriculum driven. To ensure that *WLC* will continue to meet the needs of students and general readers alike, an effort was made to identify a group of important new writers in addition to the most studied authors.

Scope

Each author entry in *WLC* presents a historical survey of critical response to the author's works. Typically, early criticism is offered to indicate initial responses, later selections document any rise or decline in literary reputations, and retrospective analyses provide modern views. Every endeavor has been made to include seminal essays on each author's work along with commentary providing current perspectives. Interviews and author statements are also included in many entries. Thus, *WLC* is both timely and comprehensive.

Organization of Author Entries

Information about authors and their works is presented through ten key access points:

- The **Descriptive Table of Contents** guides readers through the range of world literature, offering summary sketches of authors' careers and achievements.

- In each author entry, the **Author Heading** cites the name under which the author most commonly wrote, followed by birth and, where appropriate, death dates. Uncertain birth or death dates are indicated by question marks. Name variations, including full birth names when available, are given in parentheses in the caption below the **Author Portrait**.

- The **Biographical and Critical Introduction** contains background information about the life and works of the author. Emphasis is given to four main areas: 1) biographical details that help reveal the life, character, and personality of the author; 2) overviews of the major literary interests of the author—for example, novel writing, autobiography, poetry, social reform, documentary, etc.; 3) descriptions and summaries of the author's best-known works; and 4) critical commentary about the author's achievement, stature, and importance. The concluding paragraph of the **Biographical and Critical Introduction** directs readers to other Gale series containing information about the author.

- Every *WLC* entry includes an **Author Portrait**. Many entries also contain **Illustrations**—including holographs, title pages of works, letters, or pictures of important people, places, and events in the author's life—that document the author's career.

- The **List of Principal Works** is chronological by date of first book publication and identifies the genre of each work. For non-English-language authors whose works have been translated into English, the title and date of the first English-language edition are given in brackets beneath the foreign-language listing. Unless otherwise indicated, dramas are dated by first performance rather than first publication.

- **Criticism** is arranged chronologically in each author entry to provide a useful perspective on changes in critical evaluation over the years. Most entries contain a detailed, comprehensive study of the author's career as well as book reviews, studies of individual works, and comparative examinations. To ensure timeliness, current views are most often presented, but not to the exclusion of important early pieces. For the purpose of easy identification, the critic's name and the date of the critical work are given at the beginning of each piece of criticism. Unsigned criticism is preceded by the title of the source in which it appeared. Within the criticism, titles of works by the author are printed in boldface type. Publication information (such as publisher names and book prices) and certain numerical references (such as footnotes or page and line references to specific editions of works) have been deleted at the editor's discretion to provide smoother reading of the text.

■ Critical essays are prefaced by **Explanatory Notes** as an additional aid to readers of *WLC*. These notes may provide several types of valuable information, including: 1) the reputation of the critic; 2) the importance of the work of criticism; 3) the commentator's approach to the author's work; 4) the purpose of the criticism; and 5) changes in critical trends regarding the author. In some cases, **Explanatory Notes** cross-reference the work of critics within an entry who agree or disagree with each other.

■ A complete **Bibliographical Citation** of the original essay or book follows each piece of criticism.

■ An annotated list of **Sources for Further Study** appears at the end of each entry and suggests resources for additional study. These lists were specially compiled to meet the needs of high school and college students. Additionally, most of the sources cited are available in typical small and medium-size libraries.

■ Many entries contain a **Major Media Adaptations** section listing important non-print treatments and adaptations of the author's works, including feature films, TV mini-series, and radio broadcasts. This feature was specially conceived for *WLC* to meet strong demand from students for this type of information.

Other Features

WLC contains three distinct indexes to help readers find information quickly and easily:

■ The **Author Index** lists all the authors appearing in *WLC*. To ensure easy access, name variations and changes are fully cross-indexed.

■ The **Nationality Index** lists all authors featured in *WLC* by nationality. For expatriate authors and authors identified with more than one nation, multiple listings are offered.

■ The **Title Index** lists in alphabetical order all individual works by the authors appearing in *WLC*. English-language translations of original foreign-language titles are cross-referenced to the foreign titles so that all references to a work are combined in one listing.

Citing *World Literature Criticism*

When writing papers, students who quote directly from *WLC* may use the following general forms to footnote reprinted criticism. The first example is for material drawn from periodicals, the second for material reprinted from books:

Gary Smith, "Gwendolyn Brooks's 'A Street in Bronzeville,' the Harlem Renaissance and the Mythologies of Black Women," *MELUS*, Vol. 10, No. 3 (Fall 1983), 33-46; excerpted and reprinted in *World Literature Criticism, 1500 to the Present*, ed. James P. Draper (Detroit: Gale Research, 1992), pp. 459-61.

Frederick R. Karl, *American Fictions, 1940/1980: A Comprehensive History and Critical Evaluation* (Harper & Row, 1983); excerpted and reprinted in *World Literature Criticism, 1500 to the Present*, ed. James P. Draper (Detroit: Gale Research, 1992), pp. 541-46.

Acknowledgments

The editor wishes to acknowledge the valuable contributions of the many librarians, authors, and scholars who assisted in the compilation of *WLC* with their responses to telephone and mail inquiries. Special thanks are offered to the members of *WLC*'s advisory board, whose names are listed opposite the title page.

Comments Are Welcome

The editor hopes that readers will find *WLC* to be a useful reference tool and welcomes comments about the work. Send comments and suggestions to: Editor, *World Literature Criticism, 1500 to the Present*, Gale Research Inc., Penobscot Building, Detroit, MI 48226-4094.

WORLD LITERATURE CRITICISM

1500 to the Present

Harper Lee

1926-

(Full name Nelle Harper Lee) American novelist.

INTRODUCTION

*I*n her first and only novel to date, *To Kill a Mockingbird* (1960), Lee drew upon her childhood experiences as the daughter of a Southern lawyer to portray the moral awakening of two children in Maycomb, Alabama during the 1930s. Recalling her experiences as a six-year-old girl from an adult perspective, Jean Louise Finch, nicknamed "Scout," describes the circumstances that involve her widowed father, Atticus, and his legal defense of Tom Robinson, a local black man falsely accused of raping a white woman. In the three years surrounding the trial, Scout and her older brother, Jem, witness the unjust consequences of prejudice and hate while experiencing the value of courage and integrity through the example of their father. *To Kill a Mockingbird* achieved immediate popular acclaim; Lee won the 1961 Pulitzer Prize for literature by its merits, and in 1962 it was adapted by Horton Foote into an Academy Award-winning film. Although occasionally faulted as melodramatic, *To Kill a Mockingbird* is widely regarded as one of the most sensitive and revealing portraits of the American South in contemporary literature. R. A. Dave contended: "[The novel's] small world assumes a macrocosmic dimension and expands into immensity, holding an epic canvas against which is enacted a movingly human drama of the jostling worlds— of children and adults, of innocence and experience, of kindness and cruelty, of love and hatred, of humour and pathos, and above all of appearance and reality— all taking the reader to the root of human behaviour."

Lee was born in Monroeville, Alabama. Her father, Amasa Coleman Lee, a lawyer in that town, served as her model for the character of Atticus Finch in *To Kill a Mockingbird*. After a year at Huntingdon College, she enrolled at the University of Alabama in 1945 to study law. She spent one year at Oxford University as an exchange student. During her college years, Lee contributed satires, editorial columns, and reviews to several campus publications. She left Alabama six months before she was to receive her law degree. She worked for a time as an airline reservation clerk in New York City before eventually devoting her full time to writing. *To Kill a Mockingbird* won almost unanimous critical acclaim when it first appeared, and it has since been translated into a dozen languages. Lee now lives in Monroeville, where she has long been at work on a second novel.

To Kill a Mockingbird opens with the mature voice of Scout recalling her upbringing in Maycomb, "a tired old town" reluctant to surrender its past traditions to progressive change. Cared for by Calpurnia, a black housekeeper, Scout and her brother are rarely allowed to leave their street, except to meet their father on his way home from the courthouse. Although Atticus belongs to one of the area's oldest families, he is an individualist whose struggle to raise his children as tolerant members of society forms the central conflict of *To Kill a Mockingbird*. However, the journey of Scout and Jem toward understanding begins in their own world when they meet seven-year-old Dill Harris, a diminutive, mischievous summertime visitor to Maycomb whom Lee based upon young Truman Capote, a childhood companion. Dill suggests to Scout and Jem that they make Arthur ("Boo") Radley, the town recluse, come outside his family house, in which he has remained—unseen by the outside world—ever since his arrest and subsequent release from jail for an adolescent prank fifteen years earlier. Believing rumors that Boo dines on raw squirrels and roams their street by night, the children dare one another to approach the Radley porch or to peer inside Boo's window. Critics have observed that the behavior of the children toward Boo subtly reflects the dynamics of racial prejudice in which fear, rather than knowledge, dictate behavior.

In the fall, Dill departs and school begins, forcing Scout and Jem to abandon their pursuit of Boo. As a first grade student, Scout starts "off on the wrong foot" with her teacher, Miss Caroline, after attempting to explain why the son of a proud local sharecropper refuses Miss Caroline's offer of a quarter to buy his lunch. Scout resolves never to return to school after Miss Caroline decrees that she may no longer read with her father, as it will interfere with her education. When Atticus later divines the reason for her unhappiness, he asks Scout to first consider the viewpoint of Miss Caroline, a novice teacher, before judging her actions, hoping that Scout will apply this stratagem to future conflicts. Critics often interpret the contrast between Miss Caroline and Atticus as the first of Lee's many ironic comments upon the ineffectiveness of institutional education.

Months later, Scout and Jem discover chewing gum hidden in a tree on the Radley property, the first of many objects to appear there, including polished pennies, a pocket knife, a broken watch, and two carved dolls resembling Scout and Jem. Other mysterious events transpire; for instance, after Jem abandons his entangled pants on the Radley fence after attempting to spy on Boo, he returns one night later to find them crudely sewn and neatly folded. Yet the mystery of Boo is soon overshadowed by Atticus's involvement in Tom Robinson's case. In the months preceding the trial, Scout and Jem endure the taunts of classmates whose parents object to their father's defense of blacks. Atticus instructs his children to ignore their insults, sensing in Scout and Jem an innate sense of truth that may be nurtured or corrupted by the example of adults, a conviction that several commentators perceived as Lee's personal belief. Atticus hopes that by observing his defense of Tom, his children will not succumb to the prevailing prejudices of the community.

For Christmas, Atticus gives Jem and Scout their first air rifles, cautioning that "it's a sin to kill a mockingbird" because the birds "don't do one thing but sing their hearts out for us." The children view their father's own disinterest in guns as proof of his often frustrating staidness, but their opinions change when they learn that Atticus once earned a reputation as "the deadest shot in Maycomb County" after killing a rabid dog on their street. Their concept of heroism formed by this incident is subsequently tempered when Atticus asks Jem to read to their neighbor, Mrs. Dubose, a recovering morphine addict. When Mrs. Dubose dies, Atticus tells his son that in witnessing her struggle Jem saw "what real courage is, instead of getting the idea that courage is a man with a gun in his hand. It's when you know you're licked before you begin but you begin anyway and you see it through no matter what." According to commentators, Atticus fulfills this ideal in his defense of Tom.

The next spring, Calpurnia takes Scout and Jem to her church while their father is away on business. Like Atticus, Calpurnia is perceived as a link between the races by virtue of her humanistic compassion and moral courage. Through her example and that of the other members of the church, the Finch children gain a new understanding of black people—particularly Tom Robinson—as human beings. Following the service, Scout asks if she may visit Calpurnia at her house, but abandons the idea when Atticus's sister, Alexandria, arrives unexpectedly. Alexandria endeavors to counteract what she perceives as the negative effect of her brother's liberal views on his children. Primarily concerned with class, family breeding, and, in Scout's case, ladylike manners, Alexandria embodies traditional Southern mores as embraced by Maycomb society.

Dill returns shortly after Alexandria's appearance, but the joy of his arrival is overshadowed by tensions surrounding the transferal of Tom from the state penitentiary to the county jail for his trial. On the eve of the hearing, a threatened lynching is narrowly averted when Scout, having followed Atticus to the jail along with Jem and Dill, recognizes a schoolmate's father in the crowd and politely inquires about her friend. Made self-conscious by her innocent questions, the group disperses. On the day of the trial, townsfolk crowd the courtroom to hear the testimony of Mayella Ewell, the alleged rape victim, who lives in abject poverty with her numerous siblings and her shiftless father, Bob. Both she and Bob claim that Tom attacked her after being asked inside their fence to break up an old chifforobe for firewood. During cross-examination, however, Atticus proves their accusations false before reconstructing the actual incident with Tom on the witness stand. At the climax of the trial, Atticus charges the jury to put aside prejudices and fulfill their duty as participants in a democratic judicial system. After a two-hour deliberation, the jury finds Tom guilty.

Critics generally agree that Lee's narrative falters at this point, as Scout and Jem attempt to comprehend the verdict amid what has been characterized as contrived speeches against racism by adults. After the trial, the children's disbelief gives way to shock when Tom is killed during a prison escape attempt. Few whites express outrage at his death, apart from Atticus and the publisher of the local newspaper, who compares the incident to "the senseless slaughter of songbirds by hunters and children." Although the controversy subsides in the fall, Bob Ewell, discredited in court by Atticus, begins to threaten the Finches and finally attacks Scout and Jem with a knife as they walk home from the school Halloween pageant at night. Trapped inside her wire costume, which was crushed about her during the confused, violent scuffle with Ewell, Scout, dazed, sees a stranger carry off her injured brother but soon realizes that it was Boo, whom she later instinctively recognizes standing in Jem's room. The monster of neighborhood legend is revealed to be a shy, childish man who saved Scout and Jem—but killed Ewell in the process. When Atticus and the sheriff decide not to expose Boo's deed to the town, Scout agrees, reasoning that it would be "like shootin' a mockingbird." Commentators maintain that this image of the songbird unites the characters of Tom and Boo, who both emerge as innocent victims of a prejudiced community. After walking Boo home, Scout stands on the Radley porch and, seeing the tree where their unseen friend once deposited gifts, believes that now she has nothing more to learn "except possibly algebra."

Following the publication of *To Kill a Mockingbird,* some reviewers dismissed the narrative voice of Scout as unconvincing for a girl not yet ten years of age. However, subsequent critics have recognized Lee's rendering of a child's perspective through an adult's evaluation as among the most technically expert in contemporary literature. According to commentators, Lee adroitly exposes the turbulence underlying southern society and psychology while presenting the possibility of its elimination through the understanding of individuals. Edgar H. Shuster asserted: "The achievement of Harper Lee is not that she has written another novel about race prejudice, but rather that she has placed race prejudice in a perspective which allows us to see it as an aspect of a larger thing; as something that arises from phantom contacts, from fear and lack of knowledge; and finally as something that disappears with the kind of knowledge or 'education' that one gains through learning what people are really like when you 'finally see them.' "

(For further information about Lee's life and works, see *Concise Dictionary of American Literary Biography, 1941-1968; Contemporary Authors,* Vols. 13-16; *Contemporary Literary Criticism,* Vols. 12, 60; *Dictionary of Literary Biography,* Vol. 6: *American Novelists Since World War II;* and *Something about the Author,* Vol. 11.)

CRITICAL COMMENTARY

FRED ERISMAN

(essay date 1973)

[In the following excerpt, Erisman explains how Lee presents her vision of a "New South" in *To Kill a Mockingbird,* especially through the character of Atticus Finch. It is "in the several Maycomb townspeople who see through the fog of the past, and who act not from tradition but from principle," he claims, that Lee places her hope for "the possible salvation of the South."]

When Mark Twain stranded the steamboat *Walter Scott* on a rocky point in Chapter 13 of *Huckleberry Finn,* he rounded out an attack on Southern romanticism begun in *Life on the Mississippi.* There, as every reader knows, he asserted that Sir Walter Scott's novels of knighthood

Principal Work

To Kill a Mockingbird (novel) 1960

absurd past that is dead." This premise does not stop with Twain. W. J. Cash, writing almost sixty years later, continues the assertion, observing that the South, already nostalgic in the early nineteenth century, "found perhaps the most perfect expression for this part of its spirit in the cardboard medievalism of the Scotch novels." As recently as 1961, W. R. Taylor, in *Cavalier and Yankee,* several times alludes to Scott as he traces the development of the myth of the planter aristocracy.

For these three men, and for many like them, Southern romanticism has been a pernicious, backward-looking belief. It has, they imply, mired the South in a stagnant morass of outdated ideas, from which there is little chance of escape. A more hopeful view, however, appears in Harper Lee's novel of Alabama life, *To Kill a Mockingbird* (1960). Miss Lee is well aware of traditional Southern romanticism and, indeed, agrees that it was and is a pervasive influence in the South; one of the subtlest allusions in the entire novel comes in Chapter 11, as the Finch children read *Ivanhoe* to the dying but indomitable Southern lady, Mrs. Henry Lafayette Dubose. At the same time, she sees in the New South—the South of 1930-1935—the dawning of a newer and more vital form of romanticism. She does not see this newer romanticism as widespread, nor does she venture any sweeping predictions as to its future. Nevertheless, in *To Kill a Mockingbird,* Miss Lee presents an Emersonian view of Southern romanticism, suggesting that the South can move from the archaic, imported romanticism of its past toward the more reasonable, pragmatic, and native romanticism of a Ralph Waldo Emerson. If the movement can come to maturity, she implies, the South will have made a major step toward becoming truly regional in its vision.

As Miss Lee unfolds her account of three years in the lives of Atticus, Jem, and Scout Finch, and in the history of Maycomb, Alabama, she makes clear the persistence of the old beliefs. Maycomb, she says, is "an old town, . . . a tired old town," even "an ancient town." A part of southern Alabama from the time of the first settlements, and isolated and largely untouched by the Civil War, it was, like the South, turned inward upon itself by Reconstruction. Indeed, its history parallels that of the South in so many ways that it emerges as a microcosm of the South. This quality is graphically suggested by the Maycomb County courthouse, which dominates the town square:

The Maycomb County courthouse was faintly reminiscent of Arlington in one respect: the concrete pillars supporting its south roof were too heavy for their light burden. The pillars were all that remained standing when the original courthouse burned in 1856. Another courthouse was built around them. It is better to say, built in spite of them. But for the south porch, the Maycomb County courthouse was early Victorian, presenting an unoffensive vista when seen from the north. From the other side, however, Greek revival columns clashed with a big nineteenth-century clock tower housing a rusty unreliable instrument, a view indicating a people determined to preserve every physical scrap of the past.

Miss Lee's courthouse, inoffensive from the north but architecturally appalling from the south, neatly summarizes Maycomb's reluctance to shed the past. It is, like the South, still largely subject to the traditions of the past.

The microcosmic quality of Maycomb suggested by its courthouse appears in other ways, as well. The town's social structure, for example, is characteristically Southern. Beneath its deceptively placid exterior, Maycomb has a taut, well-developed caste system designed to separate whites from blacks. If Maycomb's caste system is not so openly oppressive as that of John Dollard's "Southerntown" (where "caste has replaced slavery as a means of maintaining the essence of the old status order in the South"), it still serves the same end—to keep the blacks in their place. The operations of this system are obvious. First Purchase African M. E. Church, for example, "the only church in Maycomb with a steeple and bell," is subjected to minor but consistent desecration: "Negroes worshiped in it on Sundays and white men gambled in it on weekdays." The whites, moreover, clearly expect deferential behavior of the blacks. . . . The Finch children, attending church with Calpurnia, their black housekeeper, are confronted with doffed hats and "weekday gestures of respectful attention." And, in the most telling commentary of all upon the pervasive pressures of the caste system, when Calpurnia accompanies Atticus Finch to convey the news of Tom Robinson's death, she must ride in the back seat of the automobile.

Even more indicative of Maycomb's characteristically Southern caste system is the power of the sexual taboo, which has been called "the strongest taboo of the system." This is dramatized by the maneuverings during Tom Robinson's trial of allegedly raping Mayella Ewell, a central episode in the novel. Although Tom's infraction of the black man-white woman code is demonstrated to have been false, he is nonetheless condemned. The caste taboo outweighs empirical evidence. As Atticus says later of the jury, "Those are twelve reasonable men in everyday life, Tom's jury, but you saw something come between them and reason. . . . There's something in our world that makes men lose their heads—they couldn't be fair if they tried." Despite the presence of a more than reasonable doubt as to his guilt, despite the discrediting of the Ewells, the chief witnesses for the prosecution, Tom Robinson is condemned. As Atticus points out, the entire prosecution is based upon "the assumption—the evil assumption—that *all* Negroes lie, that *all* Negroes are basically immoral beings, that *all* Negro men are not to be trusted around our women." Tom's conviction is mute testimony to the strength of that caste-oriented assumption.

Another illustration of Maycomb's archetypal Southernness that is as typical as its caste system is the ubiquitous system of class distinctions among the whites. Miss Lee's characters fall readily into four classes, ranging from the "old aristocracy" represented by Atticus Finch's class-conscious sister, Alexandra, to the poor white trash represented by Bob Ewell and his brood, who have been "the disgrace of Maycomb for three generations." In presenting the interaction of these classes, she gives a textbook demonstration of the traditional social stratification of the American South.

The upper-class-consciousness so manifest in Aunt Alexandra appears most strongly in her regard for "family", a concern that permeates Part II of *To Kill a Mockingbird.* Like the small-town aristocrats described in Allison Davis's *Deep South,* she has a keen appreciation of the "laterally extended kin group." Although the complex interrelationships of Maycomb society are generally known to the Finch children, it is Aunt Alexandra who drives home their social significance. . . . In her insistence that family status be preserved, Aunt Alexandra typifies the family-oriented aristocrat of the Old South.

No less well developed is Miss Lee's emphasis upon the subtleties of class distinction. In this, too, she defines Maycomb as a characteristically Southern community. It has its upper class, in Aunt Alexandra, in the members of the Missionary Society, and in the town's professional men—Atticus, Dr. Reynolds, Judge Taylor, and so on. It has its middle class, in the numerous faceless and often nameless individuals who flesh out Miss Lee's story—Braxton Underwood, the owner-editor of *The Maycomb Tribune,* or Mr. Sam Levy, who shamed the Ku Klux Klan in 1920 by proclaiming that "he'd sold 'em the very sheets on their backs." It has its lower class, generically condemned by Aunt Alexandra as "trash", but sympathetically presented in characters like Walter Cunningham, one of the Cunninghams of Old Sarum, a breed of men who "hadn't taken anything from or off of anybody since they migrated to the New World." Finally, it has its dregs, the Ewells, who, though more slovenly than the supposedly slovenliest of the blacks, still possess the redeeming grace of a white skin. These distinctions Aunt Alexandra reveres and protects, as when she remarks, "You can scrub Walter Cunningham till he shines, you can put him in shoes and a new suit, but he'll never be like Jem. . . . Because—he—is—trash." For Aunt Alexandra, the class gap between the Finches and the Cunninghams is one that can never be bridged.

The existence of a caste system separating black from white, or of a well-developed regard for kin-group relations, or of a system of class stratification is, of course, not unique. But, from the simultaneous existence of these three systems, and from the way in which they dominate Maycomb attitudes, emerges the significance of Maycomb's antiquity. It is a representation of the Old South, still clinging, as in its courthouse, to every scrap of the past. Left alone, it would remain static, moldering away as surely as John Brown's body. So too, Miss Lee suggests, may the South. This decay, however, can be prevented. In her picture of the New South and the New Southerner, Miss Lee suggests how a decadently romantic tradition can be transformed into a functional romanticism, and how, from this change, can come a revitalizing of the South.

The "New South" that Harper Lee advocates is new only by courtesy. In one respect—the degree to which it draws upon the romantic idealism of an Emerson—it is almost as old as the Scottish novels so lacerated by Mark Twain; in another, it is even older, as it at times harks back to the Puritan ideals of the seventeenth century. By the standards of the American South of the first third of the twentieth century, however, it is new, for it flies in the face of much that traditionally characterizes the South. With Emerson, it spurns the past, looking instead to the reality of the present. With him, it places principled action above self-interest, willingly accepting the difficult consequences of a right decision. It recognizes, like both Emerson and the Puritans, the diversity of mankind, yet recognizes also that this diversity is unified by a set of "higher laws" that cannot be ignored. In short, in the several Maycomb townspeople who see through the fog of the past, and who act not from tradition but from principle, Miss Lee presents the possible salvation of the South.

Foremost among these people is Atticus Finch, attorney, the central character of Miss Lee's novel. Though himself a native of Maycomb, a member of one of the oldest families in the area, and "related by blood or marriage to nearly every family in the town," Atticus is not the archetypal Southerner that his sister has become. Instead, he is presented as a Southern version of Emersonian man, the individual who vibrates to his own iron string, the one man in the town that the community trusts "to do right," even as they deplore his peculiarities. Through him, and through Jem and Scout, the children he is rearing according to his lights, Miss Lee presents her view of the New South.

That Atticus Finch is meant to be an atypical Southerner is plain; Miss Lee establishes this from the beginning, as she reports that Atticus and his brother are the first Finches to leave the family lands and study elsewhere. This atypical quality, however, is developed even further. Like Emerson, Atticus recognizes that his culture is retrospective, groping "among the dry bones of the past . . . [and putting] the living generation into masquerade out of its faded wardrobe." He had no hostility toward his past; he is not one of the alienated souls so beloved of Southern Gothicists. He does, though, approach his past and its traditions with a tolerant skepticism. His attitude toward "old family" and "gentle breeding" has already been suggested. A similar skepticism is implied by his repeated observation that "you never really understand a person until you consider things from his point of view . . . until you climb into his skin and walk around in it." He understands the difficulties of Tom Robinson, although Tom Robinson is black; he understands the difficulties of a Walter Cunningham, though Cunningham is—to Aunt Alexandra—"trash"; he understands the pressures being brought to bear upon his children because of his own considered actions. In each instance he acts according to his estimate of the merits of the situation, striving to see that each receives justice. He is, in short, as Edwin Bruell has suggested, "no heroic type but any graceful, restrained, simple person like one from Attica." Unfettered by the corpse of the past, he is free to live and work as an individual.

This freedom to act he does not gain easily. Indeed, he, like Emerson's nonconformist, frequently finds himself whipped by the world's displeasure. And yet, like Emerson's ideal man, when faced by this harassment and displeasure, he has "the habit of magnanimity and religion to treat it godlike as a trifle of no concernment." In the development of this habit he is aided by a strong regard for personal principle, even as he recognizes the difficulty that it brings to his life and the lives of his children. This is established early in the novel, with the introduction of the Tom Robinson trial. When the case is brought up by Scout, following a fight at school, Atticus responds, " 'If I didn't [defend Tom Robinson] I couldn't hold up my head in town, I couldn't represent this county in the legislature, I couldn't even tell you or Jem not to do something again. . . . Scout, simply by the nature of the work, every lawyer gets at least one case in his lifetime that affects him personally. This one's mine, I guess'." He returns to this theme later, observing that " 'This case . . . is something that goes to the essence of a man's conscience—Scout, I couldn't go to church and worship God if I didn't try to help that man'." Scout points out that opinion among the townspeople runs counter to this, whereupon Atticus replies, " 'They're certainly entitled to think that, and they're entitled to

full respect for their opinions . . . but before I can live with other folks I've got to live with myself. The one thing that doesn't abide by majority rule is a person's conscience'." No careful ear is needed to hear the echoes of Emerson's "Nothing can bring you peace but yourself. Nothing can bring you peace but the triumph of principles." In his heeding both principle and conscience, whatever the cost to himself, Atticus is singularly Emersonian.

The Emersonian quality of Atticus's individualism is emphasized in two additional ways—through his awareness of the clarity of the childhood vision . . . , and through his belief in the higher laws of life. The first of these appears at least three times throughout the novel. Early in the Tom Robinson sequence, an attempted lynching is thwarted by the sudden appearance of the Finch children, leading Atticus to observe, " 'So it took an eight-year-old child to bring 'em to their senses, didn't it? . . . Hmp, maybe we need a police force of children . . . you children last night made Walter Cunningham stand in my shoes for a minute. That was enough'." The view is reinforced by the comments of Dolphus Raymond, the town drunk, who sees in the children's reaction to the trial the unsullied operations of instinct. And, thus suggested, it is made explicit by Atticus himself, as, following Tom Robinson's conviction, he tells Jem: " 'If you had been on that jury, son, and eleven other boys like you, Tom would be a free man. . . . So far nothing in your life has interfered with your reasoning process'." The point could not be more obvious; in the unsophisticated vision of the child is a perception of truth that most older, tradition-bound people have lost. Atticus, like Emerson's lover of nature, has retained it, and can understand it; it only remains for that vision to be instilled in others.

Linked to this belief is Atticus's recognition of the diversity of man and his faith in the higher laws—although, significantly, his higher laws are not the abstruse, cosmic laws of Emerson, but the practical laws of the courts. Atticus, by his own confession, is no idealist, believing in the absolute goodness of mankind. In his courtroom argument he acknowledges his belief that " 'there is not a person . . . who has never told a lie, who has never done an immoral thing, and there is no man living who has never looked upon a woman without desire'." To this he adds his recognition of the randomness of life: " 'Some people are smarter than others, some people have more opportunity because they're born with it, some men make more money than others, some ladies make better cakes than others— some people are born gifted beyond the normal scope of most men'." At the same time, he also believes that these flawed, diverse people are united by one thing— the law. There is, he says, " 'one way in this country in which all men are created equal—there is one human institution that makes a pauper the equal of a Rockefeller, the stupid man the equal of an Einstein, and the ignorant man the equal of any college president. That institution, gentlemen, is a court'." In this, his climactic speech to the jury, Atticus makes clear his commitment. Like the Puritans, he assumes the flawed nature of man, but, like Emerson, he looks to the higher laws—those of the court and of the nation—that enable man to transcend his base diversity and give him the only form of equality possible in a diverse society. Like the Emerson of the "Ode to Channing," he argues:

> Let man serve law for man;
> Live for friendship, live for love;
> For truth's and harmony's behoof;
> The state may follow how it can.

Atticus will, indeed, serve law for man, leaving the state—his contemporaries—to follow how it can. He, at least, has absolved him to himself.

Throughout *To Kill a Mockingbird,* Harper Lee presents a dual view of the American South. On the one hand, she sees the South as still in the grip of the traditions and habits so amply documented by Davis, Dollard, and others—caste division along strictly color lines, hierarchical class stratification within castes, and exaggerated regard for kin-group relations within particular classes, especially the upper and middle classes of the white caste. On the other hand, she argues that the South has within itself the potential for progressive change, stimulated by the incorporation of the New England romanticism of an Emerson, and characterized by the pragmatism, principles, and wisdom of Atticus Finch. If, as she suggests, the South can exchange its old romanticism for the new, it can modify its life to bring justice and humanity to all of its inhabitants, black and white alike.

In suggesting the possibility of a shift from the old romanticism to the new, however, Miss Lee goes even further. If her argument is carried to its logical extension, it becomes apparent that she is suggesting that the South, by assimilating native (though extraregional) ideals, can transcend the confining sectionalism that has dominated it in the past, and develop the breadth of vision characteristic of the truly regional outlook. (pp. 122-33)

Miss Lee sees such a development as a distinct possibility. Maycomb, in the past isolated and insulated, untouched by even the Civil War, is no longer detached from the outside world. It is, as Miss Lee suggests through the Finch brothers' going elsewhere to study, beginning to seek for what it does not possess. (This quest, however, is no panacea, as Miss Lee implies with the character of the pathetically inept Miss Caroline Fisher, the first-grade teacher from North Alabama, who introduces the "Dewey Decimal System" to revolutionize the Maycomb County School System.) Moreover, Maycomb is being forced to respond to events touching the nation and the world. The Depression is a real thing, affecting the lives of white and black alike; the merchants of Maycomb are touched by the fall of the National Recovery Act; and Hitler's rise to power and his persecution of the Jews make the power of Nazism apparent even to the comfortable Christians of the town. Maycomb, in short, like the South it represents, is becoming at last a part of the United States; what affects the nation affects it, and the influence of external events can no longer be ignored.

The organic links of Maycomb with the world at large extend even further, as Miss Lee goes on to point out the relationship between what happens in Maycomb and the entirety of human experience. The novel opens and closes on a significant note—that life in Maycomb, despite its Southern particularity, is an integral part of human history. This broadly regional vision appears in the first paragraphs of the novel, as the narrator, the mature Scout, reflects upon the events leading up to the death of Bob Ewell:

> I maintain that the Ewells started it all, but Jem, who was four years my senior, said it started long before that. He said it began the summer Dill came to us, when Dill first gave us the idea of making Boo Radley come out.

> I said if he wanted to take a broad view of the thing, it really began with Andrew Jackson. If General Jackson hadn't run the Creeks up the creek, Simon Finch would never have paddled up the Alabama, and where would we be if he hadn't? We were far too old to settle an argument with a fist-fight, so we consulted Atticus. Our father said we were both right.

The theme of this passage—that events of long ago and far away can have consequences in the present—is echoed at the novel's end. Tom Robinson is dead, Bob Ewell is dead, Boo Radley has emerged and submerged, and Scout, aged nine, is returning home. The view from the Radley porch evokes a flood of memories, which, for the first time, fall into a coherent pattern for her: the complex interaction of three years of children's play and adult tragedy is revealed in a single, spontaneous moment of intuitive perception. "Just standing on the Radley porch was enough," she says. "As I made my way home, I felt very old. . . . As I made my way home, I thought what a thing to tell Jem tomorrow. . . . As I made my way home, I thought Jem and I would get grown but there wasn't much else left for us to learn, except possibly algebra." She has learned, with Emerson, that "to the young mind every thing is individual. . . . By and by, it finds how to join two things and see in them one nature; then three, then three thousand; and so, tyrannized over by its own unifying instinct, it goes on tying things together . . . [discovering] that these objects are not chaotic, and are not foreign, but have a law which is also a law of the human mind." When the oneness of the world dawns upon a person, truly all that remains is algebra.

Miss Lee's convictions could not be more explicit. The South, embodied here in Maycomb and its residents, can no longer stand along and apart. It must recognize and accept its place in national and international life, and it must accept the consequences for doing so. It must recognize and accept that adjustments must come, that other ways of looking at things are perhaps better than the traditional ones. Like Emerson's individual, it must be no longer hindered by the name of goodness, but must explore if it is goodness. If, to a perceptive and thoughtful observer, the old ways have lost their value, new ones must be found to supplant them; if, on the other hand, the old ways stand up to the skeptical eye, they should by all means by preserved. This Atticus Finch has done, and this he is teaching his children to do. By extension, the South must do the same, cultivating the good that it possesses, but looking elsewhere for the good that it lacks. . . . If the South can learn this fundamental lesson, seeking its unique place in relation to human experience, national experience, and world experience, all that will remain for it, too, will be algebra. (pp. 134-36)

Fred Erisman, "The Romantic Regionalism of Harper Lee," in *The Alabama Review,* Vol. XXVI, No. 2, April, 1973, pp. 122-36.

R. A. DAVE
(essay date 1974)

[In the excerpt below, Dave asserts that Lee's novel succeeds by effectively fusing a fictional work with a moral theme, claiming that "we hardly feel any tension between the novelist's creativity and social criticisms."]

To Kill a Mockingbird is quite an ambiguous title, the infinitive leaving a wide scope for a number of adverbial queries—how, when, where, and, of course, *why*—all leading to intriguing speculation and suspense. One is left guessing whether it is a crime-thriller or a book on bird-hunting. Look at it any way, the title hurts the reader's sensibility and creates an impression that something beautiful is being bruised and broken. It is only after he plunges into the narrative and is swept off into its current that he starts gathering the significance of the title. After buying the gift of an air gun for his little son, Atticus says: 'I would rather you shot at tin cans in the backyard, but I know you will go after birds . . . but remember, it's a sin to kill a mockingbird.' And when Scout asks Miss Maudie about it, for

that is the only time when she ever heard her father say it is a sin to do something, she replies saying:

'Your father is right. Mockingbirds don't do one thing but make music for us to enjoy. They don't eat up people's gardens, don't nest in corncribs, they don't do one thing but sing their hearts out for us. That's why it is a sin to kill a mockingbird.'

And as the words 'it's a sin to kill a mockingbird' keep on echoing into our ears, we are apt to see on their wings the mockingbirds that will sing all day and even at night without seeming to take time to hunt for worms or insects. At once the moral undertones of the story acquire symbolical expression and the myth of the mockingbird is seen right at the thematic centre of the story. The streets of Maycomb were deserted, the doors and windows were instantaneously shut the moment Calpurnia sent round the word about the dog, gone mad in February not in August. . . . There was hush all over. 'Nothing is more deadly than a deserted waiting street. The trees were silent, the mockingbirds were silent.' During moments of peril, such as these, even the mockingbirds do not sing! That the little girl should see in the dog's march to death some motivation of 'an invisible force' is as significant as her being struck by the silence of the mockingbirds. We have several such moments of eloquent silence in the novel. But what is more disturbing is the behaviour of the neighbours, who open their 'windows one by one' only after the danger was over. Atticus could protect them against a mad dog: he could not protect the innocent victim against their madness! As the Finch children along with their friend Dill waver at the portals of the Radley House on their way to solve the Boo mystery, we again hear the solitary singer:

High above us in the darkness a solitary mocker poured out his repertoire in blissful unawareness of whose tree he sat in, plunging from the shrill kee, kee of the sunflower bird to the irascible qua-ack of a bluejay, to the sad lament of Poor Will, Poor Will, Poor Will.

And when they shoot Tom Robinson, while lost in his unavailing effort to scale the wall in quest of freedom, Mr. Underwood, the editor of *The Montgomery Advertiser,* 'likened Tom's death to the senseless slaughter of songbirds by hunters and children.' As we find the mockingbird fluttering and singing time and again, the whole of Maycomb seems to be turning before our eyes into a wilderness full of senseless slaughter. The mockingbird motif, as effective as it is ubiquitous, and a continual reminder of the thematic crux, comes alive in the novel with all its associations of innocence, joy, and beauty.

The mockingbird myth is there in American literature and folklore. In Walt Whitman's "Out of the Cradle Endlessly Rocking", we have a tender tale of mockingbirds, the tale of love and longing and loss. . . . The mockingbird myth is most powerfully used by Whitman, who travels back and forth on the waves of childhood memories with a mist of tears through which 'a man, yet by these tears a little boy again', sings a reminiscence. The mockingbird symbol in the novel acquires a profound moral significance. For, unlike the world of tender love and longing of Walt Whitman's Alabama birds, Harper Lee's Alabama presents a bleak picture of a narrow world torn by hatred, injustice, violence and cruelty, and we lament to see 'what man has made of man'. It brings out forcefully the condition of Negro subculture in the white world where a Negro, as dark as a mockingbird, is accepted largely as a servant or at best as an entertainer. But apart from the symbolical identity, *To Kill a Mockingbird* has an astonishing technical kinship with Whitman's "Out of the Cradle Endlessly Rocking". Both, Whitman and Harper Lee, recollect childhood memories after many years have gone by. In both, the poem and the novel, we see a parabolic pattern. After years, the narrator goes back into the past, swimming across a flood of memories, and then comes back floating onwards towards the present moment and beyond. The way childhood memories impinge on adult consciousness, turning 'a man, yet by these tears a little boy again', gives a new dimension to the autobiographical mode, and heightens dramatically the reported impressions by the fact that what happens to the artist's consciousness is more important than the actual happening itself. In the novel, Harper Lee installs herself avowedly as the narrator and depicts not only the external world of action, but the internal world of character also. (pp. 311-13)

Harper Lee has a remarkable gift of story-telling. Her art is visual, and with cinematographic fluidity and subtlety we see a scene melting into another scene without jolts of transition. Like Browning's poet, Harper Lee is a 'maker-see'. She unfolds the wide panorama of Maycomb life in such a way that we, the readers, too, get transported in that world within world and watch helplessly, though not quite hopelessly, the bleak shadows of the adult world darkening the children's dream world.

To Kill a Mockingbird is autobiographical not merely in its mode of expression but also in quite a personal sense. If David Copperfield is Charles Dickens and Stephen Dedalus in *A Portrait of the Artist as a Young Man* is James Joyce, Jean Louise Finch (Scout) is unmistakably Harper Lee. If we examine the internal evidence, we can easily infer that in 1935, while Hitler was persecuting the Jews in Germany and Tom Robinson was being tried in Maycomb, Jean Finch Scout, the narrator, was 'not yet nine'; perhaps she was born, like her creator, in 1926. The identification between the narrator and the novelist is apparent. The novel with its autobiographical mode strikes a psychological balance

between the past, the present, and the future. The writer projects herself into the story as Scout in the present. What she narrates is the past. And as the past is being unfolded the reader wonders how the writer's retrospect will lead her on to the future, which is a continual mystery. This evokes in the novel considerable suspense. We follow the trial of Tom Robinson and the ostracising of the Finch family, holding our breath. But unlike David Copperfield who casts a backward glance over a long-travelled road or Stephen Dedalus who grows from childhood to youth and to manhood seeking aesthetic vision and development in exile, Scout Finch concentrates on a single phase, a moment of crisis in which childhood innocence was shattered by the terrifying experiences of the adult world.

It is a memory tale told by a little girl, Jean Louise Finch, called Scout in the novel. She becomes a mirror of experience and we see reflected in her the Maycomb world. Her memories recollected in imaginative tranquility become a dramatised action and the fiction gets an extraordinary gloss of veracity. A white girl's accusation of her rape by a Negro causes a huge upheaval that rocks 'the very old and tired town of Maycomb'. It all began the summer when Scout was six and her brother Jem ten. We find the Finch family caught in the storm of the white, popular reaction, but braving it all with remarkable steadfastness, courage and fortitude. The two motherless children and their father face the ordeal so heroically that it lifts the story from the probable melodramatic and sentimental doldrums and makes *To Kill a Mockingbird,* which is a winter's tale, a heroic one told in a lyric way. Apart from the mockingbird symbol which is pervasive, we have several other symbols. When it snows in Maycomb, after years and years, the county school declares a holiday, and we see the Finch children trying to make a snow-man. But there is more mud than snow:

> 'Jem, I ain't ever heard of a nigger snowman,' I said.
> 'He won't be black long,' he grunted.

And he tries to cover it with some snow-flakes, making it white. But at night Miss Maudie's house is on fire, and Scout watches 'our absolute Morphodite go black and crumble'. The snow-man turning alternately white and black suggests how frail and skin-deep is the colour. Besides, Miss Maudie's flowers, too, caught in the flames, symbolise innocence in the grip of fire. And as we see the yellow flames leaping up in a snowy, dark night we have the symbols of the white snow and the coloured flames standing for cold hatred and fiery wrath that might lead to the crack of the world as visualised by Robert Frost in his poem "Fire and Ice." Symbolism lends poetic touch to the novel that depicts not only the external world of action but also the internal world of character. For, here the novelist registers the impact of the central action not so much on the pro-

In this scene, Scout assures Boo Radley: "You can pet him, Mr. Arthur, he's asleep. You couldn't if he was awake, though, he wouldn't let you . . . " From the movie *To Kill a Mockingbird,* starring Gregory Peck, Mary Badham, and Robert Duvall as Boo Radley.

tagonist as on the others. Both Boo Radley locked in his own home for fifteen long years for some trifling adolescent pranks so that his father could find the vanity fair of the society congenial, and Tom Robinson sentenced to death for a rape he never committed, are kept as invisible as the crimes they never committed. Two such innocent victimisations paralleled with each other intensify the tragic view of the world and recall the terrifying prognosis: 'So shall the world go on: to good men malignant, to bad men benign.' What happens to the innocent victims, who are largely shut out from us like beasts in a cage, is really not as important as the way it stirs the world around. The novel that opens with the theme of persecution taking us back to the ancestor, Simon Finch, who sailed across the Atlantic to escape religious persecution in England, keeps the victims generally off the stage, invisible while the prolonged tensions between the protagonist minority and the antagonist majority shake the small world of Maycomb with an ever increasing emotional and moral disturbance. In this oblique handling of the central theme

we have, what Virginia Woolf describes as 'a luminous halo, a semi-transparent envelope'. It is an effective artistic device. All this is presented through the fascinating, though disturbing, flash-backs, and the continual backthrust intensifies the unforgettableness of the narrator's experience.

Maycomb is a microcosm, and the novelist's creative fecundity has peopled it well. We have a cross-section of humanity: men and women, young and old, good and bad, white and black. *To Kill a Mockingbird* presents a memorable portrait gallery. Generally it is the evil characters that are better portrayed than the good, Satan rather than God. But Harper Lee's emotional and moral bias seems to put her more at ease with good people than bad. The wicked characters tend to be hazy whereas the good characters stand out prominently throbbing with life. Bob Ewell and his allies are just paper-figures. Again, the women in the novel are better delineated than the men with the probable exception of Atticus. But her highest achievement in characterisation is manifest in children who at once spring to life. If the successful delineation of children characters is a mark of creative genius, Harper Lee has attained a notable success. Unlike her grown-up characters who easily tend to be caricatures seen in concave and convex mirrors, these children are wonderfully true to life. We have some most unforgettable vignettes. . . . [Think] of Dill getting sick of the trial and breaking down. It is Mr Raymond, the man 'who perpetrated fraud against himself by drinking Coca Cola in a whiskey bag' who says:

> 'Let him get a little older and he won't get sick and cry. Maybe things will strike him as being—not quite right, say, but he won't cry, not when he gets a few years on him.'

And we have the sad juxtaposition of the two worlds. We have children—Jem, Scout, Dill and the whole lot of them with an insatiable sense of wonder and curiosity. It is they who are bewildered by the ways of the grown-up world and confronted with the most disturbing problems like 'What exactly is a Nigger-lover Atticus?' 'What is rape, Cal?' When Tom Robinson is adjudged to be guilty, it is their young hearts that we see bleeding:

> I shut my eyes. Judge Taylor was polling the jury: 'Guilty . . . guilty . . . guilty . . . guilty . . . ' I pecked at Jem: his hands were white from gripping the balcony rail, and his shoulders jerked as if each 'guilty' was a separate stab between them.

And here is Atticus, the defence counsel, the hero of the trial scene, but for whom the trial would have seemed as if out of Kafka's world. At least the phantasmal jury and the accusers all seem to have been people who should not have surprised even Joseph K. The trial was over, but not so the heartquakes of the young, although they knew, as Scout points out, 'in the secret courts of men's hearts Atticus had no case'.

'Atticus—' said Jem bleakly.

He turned the door way. 'What, son?'

'How could they do it, how could they?'

'I don't know, but they did it. They've done it before and they did it tonight and they'll do it again, and when they do, it seems that only children will weep. Goodnight.'

Atticus is the protagonist, reticent, dignified and distant. When the entire white world seems to have lost its head, it is he who remains sane and firm. He is a wonderful combination of strength and tenderness. He is a stoic and can withstand the ostracism and persecution with almost superhuman courage and fortitude. He is a widower but treats his motherless children with so much affection and understanding that they call him 'Atticus'. They are about his only friends in a world in which he is lonely. It is in the trial scene that we see Atticus at his best, exposing the falsehood and meanness of the white world intent on destroying an innocent Negro. If Jean Scout, the daughter, keeps the wheel of the story turning, Atticus is the axle. He is a man who seems to have been made to approximate to Newman's idea of a gentleman. He never inflicts pain on others, but strives to relieve them of it even at the cost of his own and his children's suffering. It is a highly idealised character. He stands up like a lighthouse, firm, noble, and magnanimous.

But the children and Atticus, with a few other probable exceptions like Calpurnia and Sheriff Tate, and the victims are about the only normal fold in the novel. These Maycomb women are quite funny. They are the comic characters in a tragic world; they play the chorus in the novel. Here is Aunt Alexandra, 'analogous to Mount Everest . . . she was cold and there', betraying the novelist's eye for the ridiculous:

> She was not fat, but solid, and she chose protective garments that drew up her bosom to giddy heights, inched in her waist, flared out her rear, and managed to suggest that Aunt Alexandra's was once an hourglass figure. From any angle it was formidable.

We have 'Miss Stephanie Crawford, that English channel of gossip', and Miss Dubose who was horrible: 'Her face was horrible. Her face was the color of a dirty pillow-case, and the corners of her mouth glistened.' But Calpurnia, the nurse, who reminds us of Dilsey in Faulkner's *The Sound and the Fury*, and Miss Maudie are the only two women who have beneath their tough exteriors abundant humanity. Calpurnia, who leads a double-life, takes Jem and Scout to the Negro church the way Dilsey takes Benjy to the Easter service in Faulkner. Here we are in the church; the novelist has almost actually taken us in:

> The warm bitter sweet smell of clean Negro welcomed us as we entered the churchyard—Hearts of Love hair-dressing mingled with asafoetida, snuff, Hoyt's Cologne, Brown's Mule, peppermint, and lilac talcum.

But there is a counterpoint. Lula, a Negro, protests against the visit of the white children; and Calpurnia retorts: 'It's the same God, ain't it?' Calpurnia has brought up these motherless children. It is the persons like Atticus and Calpurnia who try to bridge the chasm dividing the whites from the blacks. But it is in Miss Maudie that we have a most remarkable woman. When her house is burnt up, she replies to Jem with robust optimism: 'Always wanted a smaller house, Jem Finch . . . Just think, I'll have more room for my azaleas now.' When the whole of Maycomb is madly excited over Tom's trial, without ever realising that it was not so much Tom as the white world on trial, Miss Maudie does not lose her head: 'I am not. 'Tis morbid watching a poor devil on trial for his life. Look at all those folks, it's like a Roman carnival.' When children put all sorts of queer questions about Arthur Radley, she replies pat:

'Stephanie Crawford even told me, once she woke up in the middle of the night and found him looking in the window at her. I said what did you do, Stephanie, move over in the bed and make room for him? That shut her up awhile.'

She tells the Finch children:

'You are too young to understand it . . . but sometimes the Bible in the hand of one man is worse than a whiskey bottle in the hand—oh, of your father.'

And here is the heart of the matter—the dichotomy between appearance and reality. Things are not what they seem. Both Arthur Radley and Tom Robinson, who are punished for no crimes they ever committed, are the representatives of all innocent victims. In fact, Radley stitching Jem's pants torn during the children's pranks against himself, leaving gifts for the children in the tree hole, throwing a blanket round Scout while she stood shivering in a dark, cold night watching the house on fire, and finally saving children's lives from the fatal attack of Bob Ewell, is more human than most of the Maycomb fold. He is not the blood-thirsty devil as pictured in the popular fantasy. And so is Tom, who was driven only by compassion to respond to Mayella's request for help. She had assaulted him. There was no rape. But in the court Bob Ewell shamelessly 'stood up and pointed his finger at Tom Robinson: "I see that black nigger yonder ruttin' on my Mayella."' Ewell and evil are almost homophones. They are filthy parasites, a blot on society. This shows how culture has nothing to do with colour. The novelist's moral and emotional identification with the whole problem is so great that the verdict of the trial upsets her, too. For a moment she seems to be losing her grip on the story. The characters are on the brink of losing their identity, and the novelist, in her righteous anger, is on the point of reducing them to mere mouthpieces. For even the children stunned by the judgment fumble for words, and for a while the narrative is in danger of getting lost in the doldrums of discussion—dull, heavy, futile. This can be understood in the context of her having patterned the story after the model of a morality play with a distinct line of demarcation between good and evil, right and wrong, beautiful and ugly. Like Ewell, Cunningham, too, betrays his character through connotation. The finch, the family name of Atticus, means a songbird like the mockingbird. It is the Finch family that pits itself against evil in defence of good. Jem Calways (sounds like Gem) and Scout are names that do not fail to evoke a sense of value and selfless service,

whereas Jean, which is a variation of Joan, distantly clicks into our memory that angelical girl, Joan of Arc, battling for a great cause.

To Kill a Mockingbird is a regional novel. Like Jane Austen, who does not care to go beyond the district of Bath, or Thomas Hardy who hardly, if ever, takes his story out of the confines of Wessex, Harper Lee sticks to Maycomb in Alabama. The small world assumes a macrocosmic dimension and expands into immensity, holding an epic canvas against which is enacted a movingly human drama of the jostling worlds—of children and adults, of innocence and experience, of kindness and cruelty, of love and hatred, of humour and pathos, and above all of appearance and reality—all taking the reader to the root of human behaviour. Time does not have a stop in Harper Lee's world, but it moves on lazily. The cycle of seasons keeps on turning with the ever-returning summer, and life in Maycomb, 'a tired old town', flows on in all its splendour and ugliness, joys and sorrows. Harper Lee, in her firm determination to keep away from the contemporary trend of experimentation without ever succumbing to the lure of following the footsteps of novelists like Hemingway and Faulkner, returns to the nineteenth century tradition of the well-made novel with immense facility. If she at all betrays any influence, it is from the past rather than the present—Jane Austen's morality and regionalism, Mark Twain's blending of humour and pathos in the jostling worlds, Dickens's humanitarianism and characterisation, Harriet Stowe's sentimental concern for the coloured folk. If by modernism we mean whatever that is anti-traditional, Harper Lee is not a modern, though a contemporary novelist. The contemporaneity of *To Kill a Mockingbird* is incidental, its universality essential. She tells the story with astonishing zest and yet a leisureliness characteristic of the past age. For instance, about a century divides *To Kill a Mockingbird* from Harriet Stowe's *Uncle Tom's Cabin* but there is no fundamental difference either about the content or the technique of the novels. In both we see an astonishing streak of sentimentality, an irresistible love of melodrama and the same age-old pity for the underdog. But Harper Lee has an unusual intensity of imagination which creates a world more living than the one in which we live, so very solid, so easily recognisable. It all looks so effortless, so very uncontrived. But it is painful to see the way the harsh realities impinge mercilessly on the juvenile world of innocence. Harper Lee has an intense ethical bias and there is about the novel a definite moral fervour.

The novelist, in an unmistakable way, has viewed one of the most fundamental human problems with the essentially Christian terms of reference, and we see emerging from the novel a definite moral pattern embodying a scale of values. As we notice the instinctive humanising of the world of things we are also impressed by the way Harper Lee can reconcile art and morality. For *To Kill a Mockingbird* is not a work of propaganda, it is a work of art, not without a tragic view of life. The novelist has been able to combine humour and pathos in an astonishing way. But comedy and tragedy are, in the final analysis, two sides of the same coin. The novel bubbling with life and overflowing with human emotions is not without a tragic pattern involving a contest between good and evil. Atticus in his failure to defend the Negro victim, eventually hunted down while scaling the wall in quest of freedom, the innocent victim, and Arthur Boo, who is endowed with tender human emotions and compassion, but is nearly buried alive in the Radley House, which is a veritable sepulchre, simply because his father loved to wallow in the vanity fair, and the suffering Finch children, they all intensify the sense of waste involved in the eternal conflict. 'The hero of a tragedy,' observes Freud in *Totem and Taboo,* 'had to suffer; this is today still the essential content of a tragedy.' By that norm, *To Kill a Mockingbird* could be seen to hover on the frontier of a near-tragedy. The tragic mode is no longer a monopoly of the theatre. Like the epic that precedes it, the novel that succeeds it, too, can easily order itself into a comic or a tragic pattern. . . . *To Kill a Mockingbird* has the unity of place and action that should satisfy an Aristotle although there is no authority of the invisible here as in a Greek tragedy. With Atticus and his family at the narrative centre standing like a rock in a troubled sea of cruelty, hatred and injustice, we have an imitation of an action which is noble and of a certain magnitude. And the story, that is closed off on the melancholy note of the failure of good, also is not without its poetic justice through the nemesis that destroys the villain out to kill the Finch children. In fact, twice before the final catastrophe the story seems to be verging on its end. The first probable terminal is chapter twenty-one, when Tom is convicted and sentenced; the second is chapter twenty-six, when Tom is shot dead—not killed but set free from the coils of life, as it were—and there is nothing really left. But the novelist wants to bring the story to a rounded-off moral end. Like a symphony it starts off on a new movement after touching the lowest, almost inaudible key, and we have the crescendo of its finale. Here is exploration, or at least an honest attempt at exploration, of the whole truth which is lost in the polarities of life. But Harper Lee who lets us hear in the novel the 'still, sad music of humanity' is immensely sentimental. Her love for melodrama is inexhaustible. Hence, although her view of human life is tragic, the treatment is sentimental, even melodramatic. However, though not a tragedy, it is since *Uncle Tom's Cabin* one of the most effective expressions of the voice of protest against the injustice to the Negro in the white world. Without militant championship of 'native sons' writing in a spirit of commitment, here is a woman novelist transmuting the raw material

of the Negro predicament aesthetically. . . . As we read *To Kill a Mockingbird,* a thesis novel, we notice an unfailing moral order arising out of the flux of experience which is the evolution of human consciousness elaborated through the structure of events, without ever raising the age-old problem of art and morality. There is a complete cohesion of art and morality. And therein lies the novelist's success. She is a remarkable story-teller. The reader just glides through the novel abounding in humour and pathos, hopes and fears, love and hatred, humanity and brutality—all affording him a memorable human experience of journeying through sunshine and rain at once. *To Kill a Mockingbird* is indeed a criticism of life and that, too, a most disturbing criticism, but we hardly feel any tension between the novelist's creativity and social criticism and the tale of heroic struggle lingers in our memory as an unforgettable experience while its locale, Maycomb County—'*Ad Astra per Aspera:* from mud to the stars'—stretches itself beyond our everyday horizon as an old familiar world. (pp. 314-23)

R. A. Dave, " 'To Kill a Mockingbird': Harper Lee's Tragic Vision," in *Indian Studies in American Fiction,* M. K. Naik, S. K. Desai, S. Mokashi-Punekar, eds., The Macmillan Company of India Limited, 1974, pp. 311-23.

WILLIAM T. GOING
(essay date 1975)

[In the following excerpt, Going praises Lee's first-person narrative techniques and her treatment of the themes of childhood and the law in *To Kill a Mockingbird*. This excerpt contains revisions specially made by the critic for *World Literature Criticism*.]

One of the things about [T. S.] Stribling that disturbed Robert Penn Warren in 1934 when he was writing about the new Pulitzer Prize winner was that the author "has never been interested in the dramatic possibilities of a superior white man brought into conflict with his native environment," a matter that has challenged many serious Southern novelists like William Faulkner and Caroline Gordon. A quarter of a century later Miss Lee has done precisely that for the Alabama scene [in *To Kill a Mockingbird*]. Even though it is usually easier to write about the spectacular, wicked man, Harper Lee has chosen the more difficult task of writing about the quiet, good man. Other novelists have been concerned with this type of man—the thoughtful, well-educated Southerner at quiet odds with his environment like the minor character Gavin Stevens in Faulkner's *Intruder in the Dust.* But Lee has made him the central figure and hero of her novel and succeeded at the same time in writing an exciting and significant story.

The epigraph from Charles Lamb—"Lawyers, I suppose, were once children"—indicates the two aspects of *Mockingbird,* childhood and the law. The plot can be simply stated: Atticus Finch, one of Maycomb's leading attorneys, is the court-appointed defender of Tom Robinson, accused of raping Mayella Ewell, a daughter of the town's notorious poor white-trash family. In this struggle he is unsuccessful—at least the all-white jury finds Tom guilty, and he is killed escaping from prison before Atticus can gain a hearing on the appeal. But to a certain extent the case is not altogether lost; certain precedents have been set. Instead of a young lawyer who defends only for the record's sake Judge Taylor appoints a distinguished lawyer who chooses to fight obvious lies and racial hatred so that he and his children—and ultimately Maycomb itself—can remain honest and honorable people. No one except Atticus Finch ever kept a jury out so long on a case involving a Negro. And in the process of the trial Atticus's children have matured in the right way—at least in his eyes.

The struggle of the children toward maturity, however, occupies more space than Atticus's struggle to free Tom, the central episode. Through their escapades and subsequent entanglements with their father and neighbors like Miss Maudie Atkinson, Mrs. Henry Lafayette Dubose, and particularly the legends about Boo Radley, the town's boogie man, Jem and Scout learn what it means to come to a humane maturity. In Part I, an evocation of the happy days of summer play, the process is begun. With their friend Dill Harris from Meridian they enact the weird stories about Boo Radley—how he sits in his shuttered house all day and wanders about in the shadows of night looking in people's windows, how he once drove the scissors into his father's leg, how as a not-too-bright adolescent he had terrorized the county with a "gang" from Old Sarum. Might he even be dead in that solemn, silent house, the children wonder. Miss Maudie gives, as always, a forthright answer to that question: "I know he's alive, Jean Louise, because I haven't seen him carried out yet." Although Atticus forbids these "Boo Radley" games, the children go on playing. . . . (pp. 23-4)

In the midst of these juvenile Gothic masques the children begin to learn something about the difference between gossip and truth. When Jem tears his pants and is forced to leave them behind on the wire fence during their night expedition to peek through the Radleys' shutters, he later finds them crudely mended, pressed, and hanging over the fence. When Miss Maudie's house burns during a cold night, all the neighborhood turns out to help and to watch. Scout, who is told to come no closer than the Radleys' gate, discovers that

during the confusion a blanket has been thrown round her shoulders. Jem realizes that this thoughtful act was not performed by Mr. or Mrs. Radley, who have long been dead, and he saw Mr. Nathan, Boo's brother and "jailer," helping haul out Miss Maudie's mattress. It could have been only Boo.

One of the most interesting features of *Mockingbird* is the skill with which Lee weaves these two struggles about childhood and the law together into one thematic idea. . . . [She] does a neat workmanlike job of dovetailing her plots. When Scout attends her first day at school, the morning session is devoted to explaining the Cunningham family to Miss Caroline so that she will understand why she must not lend Walter any lunch money. The Cunninghams are poor but proud. When the Sunday night lynching party arrives at the jail, it is Jem and Scout, who, having slipped off from home, see their father calmly reading a newspaper by the light at the jail door, sitting in one of his office chairs. Hiding in the doorway of the Jitney Jungle, Scout rushes forward in time to disconcert the Cunningham mob by asking innocent questions about Walter, her classmate—her father had always taught her to talk to folks about the things that would interest them.

The afternoon session of Scout's first day at school had been taken up with Burris Ewell and his dirt and defiance of Miss Caroline. It is Burris's father who brings the charge of rape against Tom Robinson.

This neatness that makes for economy of character portrayal is successful when it avoids the appearance of too convenient coincidental circumstances—a fault that *Mockingbird* does not entirely escape. But in the more important aspect of thematic development the novel is successful. Carson McCullers and Truman Capote have written with insight about Southern childhood, and William Faulkner has traced the legal and moral injustices done the Negro just as Eudora Welty has underlined the quiet patience of the Negro's acceptance of his bleak world. Harper Lee has united these two concepts into the image of a little child—schooled in basic decencies by her father even though "ladylike" manners of the superficial sort that Aunt Alexandra admires are sometimes lacking—who turns the tide to stop the Sunday night lynching. After the trial when Jem cannot comprehend the injustice done Tom Robinson by the jury, he asks his father, "How could they do it, how could they?" Atticus replies, "I don't know, but they did it. They've done it before and they did it tonight and they'll do it again and when they do it—seems that only the children weep."

Almost all readers will agree that the first two-thirds of *Mockingbird* is excellent fiction; the difference of opinion will probably turn upon the events after the trial. The major incident here is the school pageant about the history of Maycomb County as written by Mrs. Merriweather; the performance is the town's attempt at "organized activity" on Halloween. On their way home from the pageant, Ewell attacks the Finch children to get even with Atticus for making him appear a complete and guilty fool at Tom's trial. Scout is saved from the knife by her wire costume representing a Maycomb County ham; Jem receives a painful broken arm. And Ewell is killed with his own knife by Boo Radley, who again lurks opportunely in the shadows. Later that night after visits from the doctor and the sheriff when Scout is allowed to walk home with Mr. Arthur, she stands for a moment on the Radley porch seeing the knothole in the tree where Boo had once left them pitiful little presents of chewing gum and Indianhead pennies. She half realizes as a child of nine, and now as an adult she more fully realizes, what their childish antics must have meant to a lonely, "imprisoned," mentally limited man like Mr. Arthur, and she recalls her father's word to Jem that "you never really know a man until you *stand* in his shoes and walk around in them. Just standing on the Radley porch was enough."

Thematically the aftermath of the injustice done Tom and the growing up of a boy and girl are brought together in the Halloween episode. The structural problem of joining Boo Radley and Tom Robinson into some sort of juxtaposition is solved, but the slapstick comedy of the school pageant and the grotesque coincidental tragedy and subsequent salvation are perilously close to the verge of melodrama. . . . To keep this section of *Mockingbird* from seeming altogether an anticlimax to the trial of Tom, it should at least have been denominated Part III. Then the story would have been set off into its three components of School and Summer Play, Tom Robinson's Trial, and Halloween Masquerade. Such a device would distribute the thirty-one chapters into the equal grouping of Lee's apparent planning, and at the same time it would not force the Halloween tragi-comedy to seem quite so close to the climactic trial.

It is strange that the structural *forte* of *Mockingbird,* the point of view of the telling, is either misunderstood or misinterpreted by most of the initial reviewers of the novel. Phoebe Adams in the *Atlantic Monthly* calls it "frankly and completely impossible, being told in the first person by a six-year-old girl with the prose and style of a well-educated adult." Richard Sullivan in the *Chicago Tribune* [see Sources for Further Study] is puzzled and only half understands: "The unaffected young narrator uses adult language to render the matter she deals with, but the point of view is cunningly restricted to that of a perceptive, independent child, who doesn't always understand fully what's happening, but who conveys completely, by implication, the weight and burden of the story." More careful reviewers like Granville Hicks in the *Saturday Review* and

F. H. Lyell in the *New York Times* are more perceptive. The latter states the matter neatly: "Scout is the narrator, reflecting in maturity on childhood events of the mid-Thirties."

Maycomb and the South, then, are all seen through the eyes of Jean Louise, who speaks from the mature and witty vantage of an older woman recalling her father as well as her brother and their childhood days. This method is managed with so little ado that the average reader slips well into the story before he realizes that the best evidence that Atticus has reared an intellectually sophisticated daughter is that she remembers her formative years in significant detail and then narrates them with charm and wisdom. She has become the good daughter of a good man, who never let his children know what an expert marksman he was until he was forced to kill a mad dog on their street. Atticus did not like to shoot for the mere sport of it lest he kill a mockingbird like Tom Robinson or Boo Radley; and mockingbirds must be protected for their songs' sake.

This modification of a Jamesian technique of allowing the story to be seen only through the eyes of a main character but to be understood by the omniscient intelligence of Henry James is here exploited to bold advantage. The reader comes to learn the true meaning of Maycomb through the eyes of a child who now recollects with the wisdom of maturity. Along with Scout and Jem we may at first be puzzled why Atticus insists that Jem read every afternoon to old Mrs. Henry Lafayette Dubose in atonement for his cutting the tops off her camellia bushes after she taunted him about his father's being "no better than the niggers and trash he works for." But we soon learn with Scout that Atticus believed Jem would become aware of the real meaning of courage when he was forced to aid a dying old woman in breaking the narcotic habit she abhorred.

Jean Louise's evolving perception of the social milieu in her home town as she grows up in it and as she recalls her own growing up involves the reader in an understanding of the various strata of Maycomb society and its Southern significance. After Jem has brooded about the trial, he explains to Scout that

"There's four kinds of folks in the world. There's the ordinary kind like us and the neighbors, there's the kind like the Cunninghams out in the woods, the kind like the Ewells down at the dump, and the Negroes."

"What about the Chinese, and the Cajuns down yonder in Baldwin County?"

"I mean in Maycomb County. The thing about it is, our kind of folks don't like the Cunninghams, and the Cunninghams don't like the Ewells, and the Ewells hate and despise the colored folks."

I told Jem if that was so, then why didn't Tom's jury, made up of folks like the Cunninghams, acquit Tom to spite the Ewells?

After considerable debate Scout concludes, "Naw, Jem, I think there's just one kind of folks. Folks."

This naively sophisticated sociological rationalization is far more valid and persuasive in its two-pronged approach. As mature readers we realize its mature validity; as observers of children we delight in their alert reactions to the unfolding events. The convolutions of the "mind of Henry James" have given way to the immediacy and pithy wisdom of Jean Louise's first-person narration.

Though Harper Lee may not have solved all her problems of style in the dual approach of child eyes and mature heart, *Mockingbird* demonstrates the powerful effect and economy of a well-conceived point of view. . . . (pp. 25-9)

Lee, in a sense, has actually revealed more of Alabama history from the Simon Finches of old Saint Stephens to distrusted Republicans like the Misses Barber from Clanton than does Stribling in [*The Store*], his much longer historical novel. The spirit of history is as important as the events of history, and Lee presents Miss Caroline as an outsider from Winston County because she represents to this Maycomb community what every South Alabama child knew about north Alabama: a place "full of Liquor Interests, Big Mules, steel companies, Republicans, professors, and other persons of no background." Lee has mastered an eclectic technique of a meaningful point of view along with validity of idea and freshness of material. She echoes Faulkner in her deep concern for the inchoate tragedy of the South, and like him she is not afraid to pursue the Gothic shadows of Edgar Allan Poe. But her eclecticism is her own: she has told a story of racial injustice from the point of view of thoughtful children with "open, unprejudiced, well-furnished minds of their own," as the *New York Times* has phrased it. And in Atticus Finch she has created the most memorable portrait in recent fiction of the just and equitable Southern liberal. (pp. 30-1)

William T. Going, "Store and Mockingbird: Two Pulitzer Novels about Alabama," in his *Essays on Alabama Literature,* The University of Alabama Press, 1975, pp. 9-31.

SOURCES FOR FURTHER STUDY

Bruell, Edwin. "Keen Scalpel on Racial Ills." *English Journal* 53 (December 1964): 656-61.

> Examines Lee's use of irony in *To Kill a Mockingbird.*

Deitch, Joseph. "Harper Lee: Novelist of the South." *Christian Science Monitor* 3 (October 1961): 6.

> Discusses Lee and *To Kill a Mockingbird.*

Ford, Nick Aaron. "Battle of the Books: A Critical Survey of Significant Books by and about Negroes Published in 1960." *Phylon* XXII, No. 2 (Summer 1961): 119-34.

> Analyzes Lee's presentation of convincing characters, rather than stereotyped Southerners, in *To Kill a Mockingbird.*

"Mocking Bird Call." *Newsweek* 57 (9 January 1961): 83.

> Interview with Lee.

Schuster, Edgar H. "Discovering Theme and Structure in the Novel." *English Journal* 52 (October 1963): 506-11.

> A classroom approach to teaching the theme and structure of *To Kill a Mockingbird.*

Sullivan, Richard. "Engrossing First Novel of Rare Excellence." *Chicago Sunday Tribune* (17 July 1960): 1.

> Favorable review of *To Kill a Mockingbird,* calling it "a novel of strong contemporary national significance."

C. S. Lewis

1898-1963

(Full name Clive Staples Lewis; also wrote under pseudonyms Clive Hamilton, Nat Whilk, and N. W. Clerk) Irish-born English novelist, essayist, critic, autobiographer, poet, short story writer, writer of miscellaneous prose, and diarist.

INTRODUCTION

*L*ewis is considered one of the most accomplished and influential literary scholars and imaginative writers of the twentieth century. A formidable logician and Christian polemicist, he was also a highly regarded writer of fantasy literature. Among the imaginative works for which he is best known are *The Screwtape Letters* (1942), the series of children's books collectively called The Chronicles of Narnia (1950-56), and the science-fiction trilogy comprising *Out of the Silent Planet* (1938), *Perelandra* (1943), and *That Hideous Strength* (1945). The conflicts presented therein evoke the cosmic struggle between good and evil, and evidence the Christian vision which informs both his literary and critical works.

A respected authority on medieval and Renaissance literature, Lewis was a traditionalist in his approach to life and literature who opposed the modern movement in literary criticism toward biographical and psychological interpretation. Instead, he practiced and propounded a theory of criticism which stresses the importance of the author's intent, rather than the reader's presuppositions and prejudices. In his Christian polemics, notably *Mere Christianity* (1952) and *The Abolition of Man* (1943), Lewis's renowned wit and reason serve to defend the Christian faith and to attack the modern social/religious trend which equates change—no matter how foolish or destructive—with progress. Lewis's books continue to attract a growing readership and are the subject of increasing critical study.

Born in 1898 in Belfast, Lewis was the younger son of an Ulster solicitor. Along with his brother Warren, he was raised in a nominally Christian home and educated in England, with both boys acquiring in their youth and teens a lifelong passion for reading works of Norse myth and romantic imagination. At school, C. S. Lewis abandoned all personal religious faith, though he continued to enjoy works permeated with Christian thought, notably the fiction of a writer whose work he encountered in his mid-teens, George MacDonald. To prepare for his college entrance examinations, he was tutored by W. T. Kirkpatrick, a skilled logician who sharpened the younger man's mind in the skills of logical argument. (Many years later, Lewis gave credit to Kirkpatrick as one of the strongest of his early teachers and influences.) Having won a scholarship to University College, Oxford, Lewis studied there for a short time before World War I interrupted his education; he served in the British infantry on the Western Front, where he was badly wounded in 1918. While recovering from his wounds over several months, Lewis first read the essays of G. K. Chesterton, whose work proved a signal influence upon his later life and work. Having been demobilized, he reentered University College, where over four years he earned three Firsts: in Classical Moderations, in Literae Humaniores ("Greats"), and in English Language and Literature. In 1919 he published his first book—a volume of myth-laden poetry, Spirits in Bondage—and met Owen Barfield, who became a lifelong close friend and, for the first ten years of their friendship, an informal debating opponent of sorts. During those years, the time of their self-styled "Great War" of philosophy, Barfield proved crucial to opening Lewis's mind to the vital role of myth in the making of language, the absurdity of "chronological snobbery" (briefly defined by Lewis as "the uncritical assumption that whatever has gone out of date is on that account discredited"), and the possibility of the supernatural's existance.

In 1925, Lewis was elected Fellow and Tutor in English at Magdalen College, Oxford, where he lectured and tutored for the next 29 years. While he kept rooms at Magdalen during term, on weekends and between terms he resided in Headington Quarry (just outside Oxford) at "The Kilns," a house he shared with Warren and with the mother and sister of one of his World War I service chums who had died in the war. As he began work as a tutor and lecturer, Lewis found himself increasingly hard pressed to keep out of his thoughts and words some sort of objective, ultimately transcendent reference point when discussing matters to which values of quality or truth are assigned. He also found it troubling that the authors to whose works he was most closely drawn—Edmund Spenser, John Milton, MacDonald, and Chesterton, among others—shared a common Christian vision, which permeated their works. In addition, some of the Oxford colleagues Lewis admired most, including his fellow don J. R. R. Tolkien, were themselves Christians—and were thus partakers in a belief system Lewis considered irrational and untenable to the enlightened modern mind. By 1929 he had grudgingly embraced a vague theism, though he remained wary of the claims of Christianity.

As Lewis later explained in his autobiography Surprised by Joy (1955), this question was settled one September evening in 1931 during a nightlong discussion with his friends Tolkien and H. V. D. Dyson, who convinced him that to believe in the God of Christianity was to enter into the enjoyment of a myth—a myth which happened to be true, grounded in history. Lewis's belief in the God of traditional Judaism and Christianity dates from that conversation with Tolkien and Dyson, while his conversion to Christianity came three days later.

During the 1930s and early 1940s, Lewis published numerous essays on a variety of scholarly topics, most notably The Allegory of Love (1936) and several imaginative works, including his science-fantasy novels Out of the Silent Planet, Perelandra, and That Hideous Strength—works known collectively as the Ransom Trilogy after their central character, Dr. Elwin Ransom. Lewis arose to prominence as a Christian speaker and writer in the early years of World War II with his broadcast talks over BBC radio to besieged British troops and civilians and with the publication of The Screwtape Letters (1942), a collection of witty fictional letters written by a "senior temptor" among Hell's hierarchy of demons to a novice temptor, offering advice aimed at ensuring the damnation of the trainee's human target. On the eve of World War II, Lewis also became the center of a loosely knit circle of like-minded, traditionalist authors and scholars known as the Oxford Christians (or "Inklings"), who met weekly—though some attended far less frequently—in his rooms at Magdalen to talk and to read works-in-progress to each other for appraisal and enjoyment. Besides Lewis and his brother, the Inklings included Tolkien, Barfield, Dyson, Charles Williams, R. E. Havard, Nevill Coghill, and Colin Hardie, among others; with Lewis, Tolkien, and Williams considered the central group. The novelist and Arthurian poet Williams, whose vision and works posited the ceaseless interaction between the natural and and supernatural worlds, influenced Lewis's theology and fiction to some extent during the 1940s, especially the apocalyptic That Hideous Strength and the Dantean fantasy The Great Divorce (1945), a work described by Sheldon Vanauken as "a miniature Divine Comedy" in which Lewis makes Heaven "not only utterly believable but infinitely desirable . . . the most difficult of all things." As the war in Europe raged, the Lewis brothers opened The Kilns as a shelter for several children evacuated from London because of bombing raids by the Nazi Luftwaffe. Four young wartime evacuees later served as the protagonists in his children's story The Lion, the Witch and the Wardrobe (1950), the first of his acclaimed seven-volume Chronicles of Narnia.

By the mid 1950s, Lewis was an established authority on medieval and Renaissance literature, an outspoken foe of literary Modernism (he maintained a longtime quarrel with T. S. Eliot—whose early poetry he abhorred—though the two became friends near the end of their lives), a respected Christian apologist, an accomplished writer of children's books, and a widely read popular novelist. Scholars have speculated that for these last three accomplishments especially, he was repeatedly denied further advancement at Oxford, where it was expected that dons would confine their writings to their respective areas of academic expertise and direct their written studies to a college readership. The same year he published his acclaimed contribution to the Oxford History of English Literature, *English Literature in the Sixteenth Century Excluding Drama* (1954), Lewis left Oxford to fill the newly created chair of Professor of Medieval and Renaissance Language and Literature at Magdalene College, Cambridge—though he kept his home at The Kilns and maintained close contact with his Oxford friends. In 1956 he married Joy Davidman, an American suffering from cancer, who died four years later. Lewis's short book *A Grief Observed* (1961) records his thoughts in the aftermath of his wife's death, and is considered a moving, honest account of faith tested severely. In the early 1960s Lewis's own health failed. Suffering from the effects of toxemia stemming from renal failure, the result of an enlarged prostate, he resigned his position at Cambridge in mid-1963 and died of a heart attack at The Kilns, attended by Warren, on November 22—the same day fellow author Aldous Huxley and President John F. Kennedy died.

Just as the interplay of reason and imagination was instrumental in the conversion of Lewis to theism and subsequently to Christianity, so did it characterize the body of writings which flowed from his pen in the following years. Propelled by the conviction that reason is related to truth, and imagination connects with meaning, Lewis communicated his ideas in myth, satire, and fantasy, which appealed to the imagination, and in didactic logical treatises, whose arguments addressed the mind. And though critics have distinguished between these genres and assigned his works to one category or another, many have acknowledged the interplay between them within individual works. In *C. S. Lewis: Defender of the Faith* (1967), Richard B. Cunningham observed: "His literary technique, even in his didactic writing where he relies so heavily on reason and logic, also depends for its impact on the myths, allegories, metaphors, analogies, epigrams, and illustrations provided by his imagination."

Lewis's first scholarly work was *The Allegory of Love*. According to Margaret Patterson Hannay in *C. S. Lewis* (1981), the work "introduces the reader first to the phenomenon of courtly love, then to the literary form of allegory, before presenting detailed studies of medieval allegory. . . . The book thus traces the form of allegorical love poetry from the late eleventh century to the late sixteenth century. Lewis argues that romantic love, something we assume as part of the nature of reality, is a relatively new phenomenon, unknown in classical, biblical, or early medieval times." *The Allegory of Love* includes "the best critical treatment in English of Chaucer's psychological romance, *Troilus and Criseyde*," Charles A. Brady noted in *America*. And a *Times Literary Supplement* contributor stated, "This is plainly a great book—one which is destined to outlive its particular conclusions as few works of literary scholarship contrive to do. . . . The book is itself an allegory of love, a scholarly romance, in which a journey among works of poetry, many of them neglected, among erotic and scholastic treatises, most of them little read, is woven together into an imaginative and self-subsistent whole, and made available to the literate common reader as this material had never been before." The high scholarly stature Lewis achieved with *The Allegory of Love* was maintained by such later works as *A Preface to "Paradise Lost"* (1942), *English Literature in the Sixteenth Century Excluding Drama, An Experiment in Criticism* (1954), *The Discarded Image* (1964), and his periodical essays.

Many of his academic colleagues wished Lewis had restricted himself to scholarly pursuits, but he sought a wider audience. His *Screwtape Letters,* Chronicles of Narnia, and science-fiction trilogy, among other works, for adults achieved that goal. While Christian ideas undergird these works, they also contain mythic and literary themes, such as Greek and Roman fables and the Arthurian legends. Writing on the trilogy in *Extrapolation,* A. K. Nardo found that "as the reader travels with Ransom into Deep Heaven, he too is introduced to worlds where myth comes true and where what are merely artificial constructs to delineate kinds of poetry on earth become living realities in the heroic world of Mars and the pastoral world of Venus. Through identification with Ransom, the reader tastes what, Lewis seems to believe, is almost impossible in the modern world: pure epic and pure lyric experiences." And Brady considered the "Miltonic grandeur of conception [in *Out of the Silent Planet* and *Perelandra*] the greatest exercise of pure imagination in immediately contemporary literature." Of the trilogy's final volume, Eugene McGovern, writing in *Dictionary of Literary Biography,* observed: "Lewis packs *That Hideous Strength* with scenes from college politics, bureaucracy, journalism, and married life, and he has much to say about academic ambition, education, equality and obedience, language and abuses of it, scientism and social science, vivisection, magic, the legend of King Arthur, and medieval cosmology. . . . All of this is kept under an impressive control, with the many discursive elements never interfering with the narrative."

The Screwtape Letters contains some of the best-known descriptions of the bureaucracy of Hell in twentieth-century literature. As the title indicates, the novel's form is a series of letters: all are from Uncle Screwtape, a senior devil, to his nephew, Wormwood, a junior tempter, who is endeavoring to lure a malleable young man to damnation. But the devils find themselves in competition with the Church and with a young Christian woman, whom the demons find "nauseating." Leonard Bacon wrote in the *Saturday Review of Literature* that "whatever you may think of the theses of Mr. Lewis . . . the fact remains that [*The Screwtape Letters*] is a spectacular and satisfactory nova in the bleak sky of satire." A *Commonweal* reviewer felt that while Lewis's "comments on marriage seem inadequate, the author exhibits a remarkable knowledge of human nature." And P. W. Wilson recounted in the *New York Times* Thomas More's observation that the devil " 'cannot endure to be mocked,' and which, if correct, means that somewhere in the inferno there must be considerable annoyance."

Lewis's seven-volume series for children, The Chronicles of Narnia, is considered by some his best-loved popular work. While the stories rely heavily on Christian ideas, traces of Greek and Roman mythology also surface in its pages. Some critics have mistaken parts of the stories—in particular the first volume, *The Lion, the Witch, and the Wardrobe* (1950)—for a direct allegory of Christ's death and resurrection. But in his *Of Other Worlds: Essays and Stories,* Walter Hooper contains Lewis's comments, denying allegorical intent, on his initial creation of the fantastic country of Narnia: "Everything began with images; a faun carrying an umbrella, a queen on a sledge, a magnificent lion. At first there wasn't even anything Christian about them; that element pushed itself in of its own accord." In the same volume, Lewis recollects how he planned the stories to communicate with readers who were uninterested in God, writing: "I thought I saw how stories of this kind could steal past a certain inhibition which had paralysed much of my own religion in childhood. Why did one find it so hard to feel as one was told one ought to feel about God or about the sufferings of Christ? I thought the chief reason was that one was told one ought to. . . . But supposing that by casting all these things into an imaginary world, stripping them of their stained-glass and Sunday school associations, one could make them for the first time appear in their real potency? Could one not thus steal past those watchful dragons? I thought one could."

Despite the books' continual popularity with children, Lewis was not altogether successful with adults. According to *Use of English* contributor Peter Hollindale, "The structure of power in Narnia, with Aslan at its head, is enforced by battle, violence, retributive justice, pain and death. Anything which challenges the power is either evil or stupid, and frequently both." And Penelope Lively in another issue of the same periodical

saw an "underlying savagery that . . . makes the books . . . sinister, and the more so because this is what emerges as the most convincing thing about them." Perhaps the problem some critics had with the powerful Aslan, the talking lion who is the series' Christ-figure, was the author's conception of goodness. Walter Hooper, in *Imagination and the Spirit: Essays in Literature and the Christian Faith* (1971), described this as "none of the mushy, goody-goody sort of thing we sometimes find in people we feel we ought to like, but cannot. Here, in this magnificent Lion, is absolute goodness beyond anything we could imagine. Qualities we sometimes think of as opposites meet in him and blend." Lewis reconciled many apparent opposites in presenting Aslan's character, where ferocity mingled with tenderness, and sternness was followed by humor.

Frequently controversial but as popular now as during his lifetime, Lewis has excited as much criticism as praise. Helen Gardner said of Lewis: "He aroused warm affection, loyalty, and devotion in his friends, and feelings of almost equal strength among innumerable persons who knew him only through his books. But he also aroused strong antipathy, disapproval, and distaste among some of his colleagues and pupils, and among some readers. It was impossible to be indifferent to him." In his belief that "man does not 'make himself,' " he appeared a reactionary to many twentieth-century minds. Patrick J. Callahan explained in *Science Fiction: The Other Side of Realism—Essays on Modern Fantasy and Science Fiction* (1971), Lewis's conviction that man's "reason is capable of apprehending a rational universe, and thus, that there is a natural moral order. Such a stance places him in opposition to all principles of infinite human progress, to all philosophies of the superman. Lewis would accept Blake's maxim that 'in trying to be more than man, we become less.' "

Whether one approaches Lewis through the land Narnia, the mythic worlds described in the Ransom Trilogy, the satiric letters of Screwtape to his nephew Wormwood, the witty but thoroughly logical theological works, or the critical literary studies which established him as a noted scholar, one finds that each path leads to an encounter with the faith that thoroughly shaped Lewis's life and writing. Phrases such as "apostle to the skeptics" and "defender of the faith" testify to the influence of Lewis's thought upon readers beginning in the mid-twentieth century and continuing through to the present.

(For further information about Lewis's life and works, see *Children's Literature Review,* Vol. 3; *Contemporary Authors,* Vols. 81-84; *Contemporary Authors New Revision Series,* Vol. 33; *Contemporary Literary Criticism,* Vols. 1, 3, 6, 14, 27; *Dictionary of Liter-*

ary Biography, Vols. 3, 15; and *Something about the Author*, Vol. 13.)

CRITICAL COMMENTARY

J. R. R. TOLKIEN
(letter date 1938)

[Tolkien is famous as the author of the mythopoeic Lord of the Rings trilogy (1954-56) and its prequel, *The Hobbit* (1938). With Lewis, Charles Williams, and others, he was a central member of the Oxford Christians, or Inklings, a group of like-minded writers and friends who met weekly to discuss literature and read works-in-progress to each other. Tolkien had conservative literary tastes; like Lewis, he disliked nearly all of the formal developments in twentieth-century writing, his preferences tending instead toward the traditional epic. Lewis submitted his novel *Out of the Silent Planet* to Tolkien's publisher, Stanley Unwin, for publication, and in March 1938 Unwin sent Tolkien an excerpt from a reader's report, which disparaged as "bunk" the inhabitants of Lewis's planet Malacandra. Having asked Tolkien his thoughts on *Out of the Silent Planet*, Unwin received the following reply.]

Lewis is a great friend of mine, and we are in close sympathy (witness his two reviews of my *Hobbit*): this may make for understanding, but it may also cast an unduly rosy light. Since you ask for my opinion, here it is.

I read [*Out of the Silent Planet*] in the original MS. and was so enthralled that I could do nothing else until I had finished it. My first criticism was simply that it was too short. I still think that criticism holds, for both practical and artistic reasons. Other criticisms, concerning narrative style (Lewis is always apt to have rather creaking stiff-jointed passages), inconsistent details in the plot, and philology, have since been corrected to my satisfaction. The author holds to items of linguistic invention that do not appeal to me (Malacandra, Maledil—eldila, in any case, I suspect to be due to the influence of the *Eldar* in the Silmarillion—and Pfifltriggi); but this is a matter of taste. After all your reader found my invented names, made with cherished care, eye-splitting. But the linguistic inventions and the philology on the whole are more than good enough. All the part about language and poetry—the glimpses of its Malacandrian nature and form—is very well done, and extremely interesting, far superior to what one usually gets from travellers in untravelled regions. The language difficulty is usually slid over or fudged. Here it

not only has verisimilitude, but also underlying thought.

I was disturbed by your reader's report. I am afraid that at the first blush I feel inclined to retort that anyone capable of using the word 'bunk' will inevitably find matter of this sort—bunk. But one must be reasonable. I realize of course that to be even moderately marketable such a story must pass muster on its surface value, as a *vera historia* of a journey to a strange land. I am extremely fond of the genre, even having read *Land under England* with some pleasure (though it was a weak example, and distasteful to me in many points). I thought *Out of the Silent Planet* did pass this test very successfully. The openings and the actual mode of transportation in time or space are always the weakest points of such tales. They are well enough worked here, but there should be more narrative given to adventure on Malacandra to balance and justify them. The theme of three distinct rational species *(hnau)* requires more attention to the third species, *Pfifltriggi*. Also the central episode of the visit to Eldilorn is reached too soon, artistically. Also would not the book be in fact practically rather short for a narrative of this type?

But I should have said that the story had for the more intelligent reader a great number of philosophical and mythical implications that enormously enhanced without detracting from the surface 'adventure'. I found the blend of *vera historia* with *mythos* irresistible. There are of course certain satirical elements, inevitable in any such traveller's tale, and also a spice of satire on other superficially similar works of 'scientific' fiction—such as the reference to the notion that higher intelligence will inevitably be combined with ruthlessness. The underlying myth is of course that of the Fall of the Angels (and the fall of man on this our silent planet); and the central point is the sculpture of the planets revealing the erasure of the sign of the Angel of this world. I cannot understand how any one can say this sticks in his gullet, unless (a) he thinks this particular myth 'bunk', that is not worth adult attention (even on a mythical plane); or (b) the use of it unjustified or perhaps unsuccessful. The latter is perhaps arguable—though I dissent—but at any rate the critique should have pointed out the existence of the myth. Oyarsa is not of course a 'nice kind scientific God', but something so profoundly different that the difference seems to

Principal Works

Spirits in Bondage: A Cycle of Lyrics [as Clive Hamilton] (poetry) 1919

Dymer [as Clive Hamilton] (poetry) 1926

The Pilgrim's Regress: An Allegorical Apology for Christianity, Reason and Romanticism (allegory) 1933

The Allegory of Love: A Study in Medieval Tradition (essays) 1936

*Out of the Silent Planet (novel) 1938

The Personal Heresy: A Controversy [with E. M. W. Tillyard] (essays) 1939

The Problem of Pain (essay) 1940

†Broadcast Talks (broadcasts) 1942

A Preface to "Paradise Lost" (essay) 1942

The Screwtape Letters (fictional letters) 1942

The Abolition of Man: Reflections on Education with Special Reference to the Teaching of English in the Upper Forms of Schools (essay) 1943

†Christian Behaviour: A Further Series of Broadcast Talks (broadcasts) 1943

*Perelandra (novel) 1943; also published as The Voyage to Venus (Perelandra), 1953

†Beyond Personality: The Christian Idea of God (broadcasts) 1944

George MacDonald: An Anthology [editor] (aphorisms) 1945; also published as George MacDonald: 365 Readings, 1986

The Great Divorce: A Dream (novel) 1945

*That Hideous Strength: A Modern Fairy-Tale for Grown-Ups (novel) 1945

[The Tortured Planet (That Hideous Strength) (abridged edition), 1946]

Miracles: A Preliminary Study (essay) 1947; revised edition, 1960

‡The Lion, the Witch, and the Wardrobe: A Story for Children (novel) 1950

‡Prince Caspian: The Return to Narnia (novel) 1951

‡The Voyage of the "Dawn Treader" (novel) 1952

‡The Silver Chair (novel) 1953

English Literature in the Sixteenth Century Excluding Drama (nonfiction) 1954; also published as Poetry and Prose in the Sixteenth Century, 1990

‡The Horse and His Boy (novel) 1954

‡The Magician's Nephew (novel) 1955

Surprised by Joy: The Shape of My Early Life (autobiography) 1955

‡The Last Battle: A Story for Children (novel) 1956

Till We Have Faces: A Myth Retold (novel) 1956

Reflections on the Psalms (essay) 1958

The Four Loves (essay) 1960

The World's Last Night, and Other Essays (essays) 1960

A Grief Observed [as N. W. Clerk] (journal) 1961

The Discarded Image: An Introduction to Medieval and Renaissance Literature (essays) 1964

Letters to Malcolm: Chiefly on Prayer (fictional letters) 1964

Poems (poetry) 1964

Letters of C. S. Lewis (letters) 1966

God in the Dock: Essays on Theology and Ethics (essays, letters) 1970; also published as Undeceptions: Essays on Theology and Ethics, 1971

They Stand Together: The Letters of C. S. Lewis to Arthur Greeves, 1914-1963 (letters) 1979

On Stories, and Other Essays in Literature (essays) 1982; also published as Of This and Other Worlds, 1982

Boxen: The Imaginary World of the Young C. S. Lewis (juvenilia) 1985

All My Road before Me: The Diary of C. S. Lewis (1922-1927) (diary) 1991

*These novels comprise what is popularly called the Deep-Space Trilogy (or the Ransom Trilogy).

†Revised, these three works were published together as Mere Christianity in 1952.

‡These seven novels comprise The Chronicles of Narnia.

have been unnoticed, namely an Angel. Yet even as a nice kind scientific God I think he compares favourably with the governing potentates of other stories of this kind. His name is not invented, but is from Bernardus Silvestris, as I think is explained at the end of the book (not that I think that this learned detail matters, but it is as legitimate as pseudo-scientific learning). In conclusion I might say that in designating the *Pfifltriggi* as the 'workers' your reader also misses the point, and is misled by current notions that are not applicable. But I have probably said more than enough. I at any rate should have bought this story at almost any price if I had found it in print, and loudly recommended it as a

'thriller' by (however and surprisingly) an intelligent man. (pp. 32-4)

J. R. R. Tolkien, in a letter to Stanley Unwin on March 4, 1938, in his *The Letters of J. R. R. Tolkien,* edited by Humphrey Carpenter with Christopher Tolkien, George Allen & Unwin (Publishers) Ltd., 1981, pp. 32-5.

ALISTAIR COOKE
(essay date 1944)

[Cooke is respected worldwide as one of the most perceptive and eloquent popular interpreters of American life and history. He is best known to Americans as the host of the television series "Masterpiece Theatre" and as the author/narrator of "America: A Personal History of the United States," upon which he based his *Alistair Cooke's America* (1976). In the following excerpt from a review, Cooke dismisses Lewis's *Perelandra* and *Christian Behavior* as the reflections of a straitlaced Puritan-type.]

There must be profound reasons why wars spawn so many quack religions and Messiahs, but to discover them would require an exhaustive psychological study of the relations of war and peace to personal insecurity. On a lower level, we may wonder at the alarming vogue of Mr. C. S. Lewis, whose harmless fantasies about the kingdoms of Good and Evil (*Out of the Silent Planet, The Screwtape Letters* and now *Perelandra*) have had a modest literary success, while multitudes of readers, and in Britain radio listeners, succumb to the charm of his more direct treatises on Christian conduct.

It may be that a war in which our own shining ideology is so blurred by political trickery, cowardice and double-talk, puts a desperate premium on believers from 'way back, so that we gain confidence from hearing them preach as gospel what we have heard ourselves saying faintly since September, 1939. . . . It must be the same impulse that has pitchforked Mr. Lewis into the limelight, for in doubting times completely unremarkable minor prophets are pressed into making a career of reassurance.

In the days before radio, Mr. Lewis' little volume [*Christian Behavior*] would have been reviewed politely in the well bred magazines and no harm would have been done. But the chief danger of these homilies on behavior is their assumption of modesty. They are talks given over the radio by an Oxford don fairly recently converted to Christianity. From the way they were received in Britain, and from the eagerness of American networks to have Mr. Lewis shed the light on our own dark continent, it may be assumed that the personal values of several million Britons and Americans stand in imminent danger of the befuddlement at which Mr. Lewis is so transparently adroit. Mr. Lewis has a real radio talent. . . . He knows it is the first task of radio to make difficult ideas honestly clear. Since his subject is morality, or as he calls it "directions for running the human machine," and since this is the topic above all others that has exercised the finest agonies of the saints, and the best skill of poets, philosophers and psychiatrists since the beginning of time, he is tackling about the toughest assignment ever known to radio. He has to explain the Beatitudes in words of one syllable.

These noble limitations, of which he seems so conscientiously aware, would throw a better man than Mr. Lewis. That they produce in him a persuasive pseudo-simplicity, giving smooth reassurance on questions that are for most men matters of profound concern, would be unimportant if the radio did not encourage its acceptance as the sort of redemption we have all been waiting for. The exposition of every fundamental human problem from "Social morality" to "Marriage" and "Charity," comes out with a patness that murders the issues it pretends to clarify. Thus you learn (though it doesn't help) that in making a moral choice "two things are involved. One is the act of choosing. The other is the various feelings, impulses and so on which his psychological outfit presents him with, and which are the *raw material* of his choice." (What do you choose with?) Mr. Lewis' use of italics here is quite characteristic. It is a frantic make-weight used to tip the scales of an argument that will not conform to the easy balance he has arranged ahead of time. Talking of the sin of Pride, he says, "The other, and less bad, vices come from the devil working on us through our animal nature. But this doesn't come through our animal nature at all. It comes *direct* from Hell." How much more intriguingly might this discussion have been prolonged if Mr. Lewis could have arranged for it to come *indirectly.* These italics remind me of the British use of such adverbs as definitely, really, *ac*tually—they are testy emphases masking indecision about something that should be plain enough.

But the vortex in which Mr. Lewis flounders, while keeping up the same simple pretense of doing an easy and muscular crawl, is sex and marriage. He allows that as a bachelor it is possible he may be prejudiced, but his deep distaste (and fear?) of the whole subject reduces him to the convictions that because a young man might by a single act "populate a small village," the appetite "is in ludicrous and preposterous excess of its function"; that there is something "wrong" with the "sexual instinct" of present-day humans; that being in love was never intended to last; and that extra-marital sex is monstrous because "it isolates one kind of union from all the other kinds of union which were intended to go along with it" (by the same reasoning, it must be equally irresponsible to lunch with friends you don't live with). This is exactly, Mr. Lewis might be appalled to discover, the Puritan's view of sex, as it is the rake's. This frightened dualism is further demonstrated by a brilliant Freudian slip, revealing an unconscious identification of two nouns that bare Mr. Lewis' worst suspicions: he says, "If anyone thinks that Christians regard unchastity as *the* great vice, he is quite wrong. The sins of the flesh are bad, but they are the least bad of all sins. All the worst pleasures are purely spiritual." No wonder "pleasures" is not in italics. For this idea can lead only to Mr. Lewis' secret fear that unchastity is the best pleasure.

Perelandra appears superficially to be a bracing holiday from these grave matters, for it is another adventure of Dr. Ransom in search of his unearthly utopia. But it is the natural, and arid, counterpart of *Christian Behavior,* for it is a fantasy compensation for Mr. Lewis' deep dissatisfaction with mankind and the world he inhabits. . . . In *Perelandra,* which is Mr. Lewis' name for the more embarrassing planet Venus, Dr. Ransom-Lewis swims in oceans of unsalted water ("It was drinkable"!), rushes deliciously into gaping valleys, wins the battle of Temptation against the spirit of evil (not a gigantic cat but as grisly, and known as the Un-Man), and—if it is not too bold a word—conceives bliss in the scene of himself standing in an enchanted wood discussing loneliness and death (he had traveled from earth in a coffin) with a beautiful girl who is "totally naked" but sexless, because on Perelandra they blessedly do not know about sex.

It is at this point that an earthly book-reviewer must uncross his gross legs and tiptoe out, leaving Mr. Lewis to the absorbed serenity of his dreams. (pp. 578-80)

Alistair Cooke, "Mr. Anthony at Oxford," in *The New Republic,* Vol. 110, No. 17, April 27, 1944, pp. 578-80.

KATHRYN ANN LINDSKOOG
(essay date 1957)

[Lindskoog is an American educator and essayist. She met Lewis in 1956, a year before she completed her Master's thesis, *The Lion of Judah in Never-Never Land*—a study of The Chronicles of Narnia which was not published for the general public until 1973. Lewis himself read her finished thesis and praised her scholarship, writing, "You are in the center of the target everywhere. For one thing, you know my work better than anyone else I've met: certainly better than I do myself. . . . But secondly you (alone of the critics I've met) realize the connection or even the unity of all the books—scholarly, fantastic, theological—and make me appear a single author; not a man who impersonates half a dozen authors which is what I seem to most." Lindskoog is also the author of *C. S. Lewis: Mere Christian* (1973) and *The C. S. Lewis Hoax* (1988), a controversial polemic that has hotly divided Lewis scholars. (In

the last-named volume, she purports to show that Lewis's literary estate has been, since Lewis's death, controlled by a conniving opportunist who has distorted and otherwise falsified the Lewis canon.) In the following excerpt from her first study of Lewis's work, she offers an overview of the philosophy underlying The Chronicles of Narnia and illustrates how it is expressed in the individual volumes of that series.]

[C. S. Lewis's] Narnian series hinges upon the acceptance of supernatural phenomena. . . . (p. 33)

There are, of course, skeptics in these books. In *The Lion, the Witch and the Wardrobe* the children did not accept Lucy's tale about discovering Narnia when they first heard it. They consulted the wise old professor about her strange story. They complained that when they looked in the wardrobe there was nothing there, asserting that if things are real they're there all the time. "Are they?" the Professor said. The time element also bothered the children. During less than one minute, Lucy claimed to have spent several hours in Narnia. "That is the very thing that makes her story so likely to be true," said the Professor. He explained that if there really was a door in his house that led to some other world, it would be very likely that the other world had a separate time of its own so that however long one stayed there it would never take up any time on earth. (pp. 33-4)

When the children had had actual experiences with the supernatural, the concept of other worlds was much easier to accept. Once they had been out of their own world, they could conceive of many others with comparative facility. The idea came to Digory in *The Magician's Nephew:* "Why, if we can get back to our own world by jumping into *this* pool, mightn't we get somewhere else by jumping into one of the others? Supposing there was a world at the bottom of every pool!" (p. 34)

The philosophy underlying this structure of multiple natures is clearly explained in a speculative passage in *Miracles.* . . . Lewis begins with the supernaturalist's belief that a Primary Thing exists independently and has produced our composition of space, time, and connected events which we call nature. There might be other natures so created which we don't know about. Lewis is not referring here to other solar systems or galaxies existing far away in our own system of space and time, because those would be a part of our nature in spite of their distance. Only if other natures were not spatiotemporal at all, or if their space and time had no relation to our own, could we call them different natures. This is important in Lewis's literary theory:

No merely physical strangeness or merely spatial distance will realize that idea of otherness which is what we are always trying to grasp in a story about voyaging through space: you must go into another dimension. To construct plausible and moving 'other worlds' you must draw on the only real 'other world' we know, that of the spirit.

The only relationship to our system would be through common derivation from a single supernatural force. Here Lewis resorts to the figure of authorship discussed by Dorothy Sayers in *The Mind of the Maker.* The only relationship between events in one novel and events in another is the fact that they were written by the same author, which causes a continuity in his mind only.

There could be no connection between the events in one nature and the events in another, by virtue of the character of the two systems. But perhaps God would choose to bring the two natures into partial contact at some point. This would not turn the two natures into one, because they would still lack the total reciprocity of one nature, and this spasmodic interlocking would arise, not from within them, but from a divine act. Thus, each of the two natures would be "supernatural" to the other. But in an even more absolute sense, their contact itself would be supernatural, because it would

Lewis's longtime friend and influence, Owen Barfield, in a photograph dating from the early 1920s—the years of his "Great War" with Lewis. Inset: Barfield at age ninety, in 1989.

be not only outside of a particular nature but beyond any and every nature.

When this philosophical speculation is geared to a childhood level of interests, delightful possibilities for story situations appear. One of these, [introduced by the prince of Narnia to a young English guest aboard the "Dawn Treader," is] the concept of our world being known elsewhere as a myth. . . . (pp. 34-6)

Just as our world bears aspects of a fairy-tale world from the Narnian point of view, so the Narnian world is rich with figures of earthly folklore. . . .

In Narnia, giants, centaurs, dryads, fauns, dwarfs, sea serpents, mermaids, dragons, monopods, and pirates live in an environment of castles, caves, magic whistles, golden chessmen, and enchanted gardens. The implication is that all elements of myth as we know them are shadows of a foreign reality. (p. 37)

C. S. Lewis is known for opposing the spirit of modern thought with the unpopular Christian doctrines of sin and evil. He considers evil not as a nebulous abstraction but as a destructive immanence which should be openly recognized and not complacently ignored, even though such recognition is disquieting. This principle is the major element in Lewis's otherwise happy concept of nature. In his own words, "We find ourselves in a world of transporting pleasures, ravishing beauties, and tantalising possibilities, but all constantly being destroyed, all coming to nothing. Nature has all the air of a good thing spoiled." In *The Magician's Nephew* original sin enters Narnia: " . . . before the new, clean world I gave you is seven hours old, a force of evil has already entered it; waked and brought hither by this son of Adam." . . .

Throughout the rest of the series, this element of evil manifests itself in Narnia in various forms, always subjugating and trying to destroy the goodness in nature. (p. 38)

In *The Silver Chair* [a] witch has assumed power . . . by suppression of the glad natural order of the world beneath the surface of the earth, reminiscent of Wagner's Nibelheim. There she enchanted merry dwarfs from the deep land of Bism and brought them up near the surface of the earth to Shallowlands to work for her in a state of glum amnesia. She is planning a great invasion of Narnia. The idea of invasions and battles is basic to those books.

"Enemy-occupied territory—that is what this world is," Lewis plainly states in *Mere Christianity.* Yet he consciously avoids slipping into dualism, which he defines as "the belief that there are two equal and independent powers at the back of everything, one of them good and the other bad, and that this universe is the battlefield in which they fight out an endless War." . . . (pp. 39-40)

Lewis makes it clear in *The Lion, the Witch and*

the Wardrobe that the power of evil is inferior to the power of good. The power of good is that of the great King. . . . (pp. 40-1)

The limitations of evil are discussed in *Mere Christianity,* where Lewis states, as he does in *The Screwtape Letters,* that wickedness is the pursuit of something good in the wrong way. One can be good for the sake of goodness even when it hurts, but one cannot be bad for the sake of badness. One is cruel for the pleasure or usefulness of it, not for the sake of cruelty itself. Badness cannot be bad in the way that goodness is good, for badness is only spoiled goodness. . . . (p. 42)

Spoiled goodness is illustrated in the beginning of sin in Narnia, as related in *The Magician's Nephew.* Digory had been sent to a distant garden to fetch a silver apple. On the gate was written this verse:

Come in by the gold gates or not at all,
Take of my fruit for others or forbear.
For those who steal or those who climb my wall
Shall find their heart's desire and find despair. . . .
(pp. 42-3)

Digory was just turning to go back to the gates when he stopped for one last look and received a terrible shock. There stood the Witch, throwing away the core of an apple which she had eaten. The juice had made a horrid dark stain around her mouth. Digory guessed that she must have climbed in over the wall. He began to see the truth in the last line of the verse, because "the Witch looked stronger and prouder than ever . . . but her face was deadly white, white as salt." . . .

The King explained the result of this act to the children later. The Witch had fled from the garden to the North of the World, where she was growing stronger in dark Magic. She would not dare to return to Narnia so long as the tree was flourishing there, because its fragrance had become a horror to her. "That is what happens to those who pluck and eat fruits at the wrong time and in the wrong way," the King concluded. "The fruit is good, but they loathe it ever after." . . . (p. 43)

The preponderance of dark magic and witches in Lewis's books gives the impression that he is greatly concerned with demonology. However, the overall tone of his work echoes the glad assurance of St. Paul, "For I am sure that neither death, nor life, nor angels, nor principalities, nor things present, nor things to come, nor powers, nor height, nor depth, nor anything else in all creation will be able to separate us from the love of God in Christ Jesus our Lord" (Romans 8:38).

In contrast to the everlasting quality of God's love, which is his principal message, Lewis reminds us that the physical world is in a process of disintegration. He seems to agree with the concept of Sir James Jeans,

that "If the inanimate universe moves in the direction we suppose, biological evolution moves like a sailor who runs up the rigging in a sinking ship."

In Lewis's opinion, the modern conception of progress, as popularly imagined, is simply a delusion, supported by no evidence. Darwinism gives no support to the belief that natural selection, working upon chance variations, has a general tendency to produce improvement. Lewis asserts that there is no general law of progress in biological history. He calls the idea of the world slowly ripening to perfection a myth, not a generalization from experience. He feels that this myth distracts us from our real duties and our real interests.

This attitude is illustrated by the depressing picture of [the dying world of Charn] given in *The Magician's Nephew.* . . . (pp. 43-5)

In *The Last Battle* Jill declares, "*Our* world is going to have an end some day. Perhaps this one won't . . . wouldn't it be lovely if Narnia just went on and on . . . ?"

"Nay," she was answered, "all worlds draw to an end; except Aslan's own country." (p. 46)

The destruction of Narnia began with the invasion of commerce and the plunder of nature by greedy men. The idyllic forest was ruthlessly destroyed in a sacrilegious turmoil by crowds of imported workers, before the rightful owners realized what was happening. This is an exact parallel to the development of the near-fatal dangers in Lewis's adult book about Britain, *That Hideous Strength.*

The actual end of Narnia was a dramatic pageant of mythical splendour. It concluded with the moon being sucked into the sun, and the world freezing forever in total darkness. Here Lewis follows the tradition of the North rather than the conventional Christian concept of destruction by fire. Peter, High King of Narnia, was given the key to the door of heaven, and locked out the cold.

Lewis's response to nature, then, is threefold. First is romantic appreciation and idealization. Second is analysis leading to an acceptance of the supernatural and to speculation about it. Third is moral awareness of the force of evil in nature and of the temporal quality of our world. Each of these responses is basic to Lewis's Christian philosophy and is an important influence upon his books for children. Nature is more than a background setting for the action of his characters. "Either there is significance in the whole process of things as well as in human activity, or there is no significance in human activity itself." (pp. 46-7)

Kathryn Ann Lindskoog, in her *The Lion of Judah in Never-Never Land: The Theology of C. S. Lewis Expressed in His Fantasies for Children,* William B. Eerdmans Publishing Co., 1973, 141 p.

PETER KREEFT
(essay date 1969)

[Kreeft is an American educator and lay Roman Catholic writer. In the latter capacity, he is part of an informal circle that includes Thomas Howard, Sheldon Vanauken, and Dom Julian Stead, scholars and authors who share a common interest in the thought of the Oxford Inklings and are themselves proponents of Christian orthodoxy. In the following excerpt from a study first published in 1969, Kreeft examines the views and roles of fantasy and myth in the fiction of Lewis.]

The fact that a Christian apologist's writing highly imaginative fiction surprises many people, surprises Lewis. "I do not think the resemblance between the Christian and the merely imaginative experience is accidental. I think that all things, in their way, reflect heavenly truth, the imagination not least." However, it may be thought that the resemblance between fantasy and Christianity lies in their both being forms of escapism; Lewis therefore offers a critical defense of the former as well as the latter:

(1) Fantasy is escapism only in the sense in which all fiction is escapism from present fact. To attack fantasy is to attack fiction; to defend fiction is to defend fantasy. Lewis's defense is

that we seek an enlargement of our being. We want to be more than ourselves. Each of us by nature sees the whole world from one point of view. . . . to acquiesce in this particularity on the sensuous level—in other words, not to discount perspective—would be lunacy. . . . but we want to escape the illusions of perspective on higher levels too. . . . the man who is contented to be only himself, and therefore less a self, is in prison. (*An Experiment in Criticism*)

Far from dulling or emptying the actual world, fantasy deepens it: A man "does not despise real woods all real woods a little enchanted" (**"On Three Ways of Writing for Children"**).

(2) Fantasy is in its own way realistic: "Nature has that in her which compels us to invent giants: and only giants will do." Talking beasts are "masks for Man, cartoons, parodies by Nature formed to reveal us." It is so-called realism, not fantasy, that fosters wishful thinking, escapism, and deception: "I never expected the real world to be like the fairy tales. I think that I did expect school to be like the school stories" (*ibid.*).

(3) Fantasy is a traditionally human form; for

until quite modern times, nearly all stories were [nonrealistic]. . . . Just as all except bores relate in conversation not what is normal but what is exceptional—you mention having seen a giraffe in Petty Cury, but don't mention having seen an undergraduate—so authors told of the exceptional. (*An Experiment in Criticism*)

Therefore "I side impenitently with the human race against the modern reformer. Let there be wicked kings and beheadings, battles and dungeons, giants and dragons, and let villains be soundly killed at the end of the book" (**"On Three Ways of Writing for Children"**).

(4) Fantasy is not by nature fit only for children:

The whole association of fairy tale and fantasy with childhood is local and accidental. I hope everyone has read Tolkien's essay on Fairy Tales, which is perhaps the most important contribution to the subject that anyone has yet made. If so, you will know already that, in most places and times, the fairy tale has not been specially made for, nor exclusively enjoyed by, children. It has gravitated to the nursery when it became unfashionable in literary circles, just as unfashionable furniture gravitated to the nursery in Victorian houses.

Critics who treat *adult* as a term of approval, instead of as a merely descriptive term, cannot be adult themselves. To be concerned about being grown up, to admire the grown up because it is grown up, to blush at the suspicion of being childish; these things are the marks of childhood and adolescence.

The modern view seems to me to involve a false conception of growth. They accuse us of arrested development because we have not lost a taste we had in childhood. But surely arrested development consists not in refusing to lose old things but in failing to add new things? . . . a tree grows because it adds rings; a train doesn't grow by leaving one station behind and puffing on to the next. . . . if to drop parcels and to leave stations behind were the essence and virtue of growth, why should we stop at the adult? Why should not *senile* be equally a term of approval? (*Ibid.*)

Lewis's fiction is not merely fantasy, however; he is one of the few writers who dares to concoct a myth. "*Out of the Silent Planet, Perelandra,* and *That Hideous Strength* were issued as 'novels,' but in reality they are three installments of one myth," observes Chad Walsh. What does this mean?

First of all, for Lewis "myth" is not an antonym to "truth." There is a kind of truth to a good myth that is different from, but no less true—more true, in fact—than fact: a fairy tale may be truer than a statistic. We can understand this kind of truth only from the experience of reading or hearing a great myth, like Lewis's or Tolkien's: when you close the covers of the book and look once again outside your apartment window, it seems overwhelmingly evident to you that you have not turned from fiction to reality but vice versa, from the more to the less real. A "willing suspension of disbelief" is required not for the world inside the myth but for the world outside it. How can we account for this power to move the intellectual will to believe unless the myth possesses some kind of truth? Tolkien explains it thus: "If he [the literary artist] indeed achieves a quality that can fairly be described by the dictionary definition: 'inner consistency of reality,' it is difficult to conceive how this can be, if the work does not in some way partake of reality" ("On Fairy Stories").

Lewis's explanation, in *Perelandra,* is itself mythical. Ransom finds that what is myth in one world is fact in another; that on pre-fallen Perelandra the distinction between myth and fact has not occurred; and that

> There is an environment of minds as well as of space. The universe is one—a spider's web wherein each mind lives along every line, a vast whispering gallery where (save for the direct action of Maleldil) though no news travels unchanged yet no secret can be rigorously kept. In the mind of the fallen Archon under whom our planet groans, the memory of Deep Heaven and the Gods with whom he once consorted is still alive. Nay, in the very matter of our world, the traces of the celestial commonwealth are not quite lost. Memory passes through the womb and hovers in the air. The Muse is a real thing. A faint breath, as Virgil says, reaches even the late generations. Our mythology is based on a solider reality than we dream: but it is also at an almost infinite distance from that base.

But how is a good myth *more* real than "the real world"? Lewis's Platonic definition of symbolism in *The Allegory of Love* is the clue:

> It is of the very nature of thought and language to represent what is immaterial in picturable terms. What is good or happy has always been high like the heavens and bright like the sun. Evil and misery were deep and dark from the first. . . . To ask how these married pairs of sensible and insensibles first came together would be of great folly; the real question is how they ever came apart. . . . This fundamental equivalence between the immaterial and the material may be used by the mind in two ways. . . . on the one hand you can start with an immaterial fact, such as the passions which you actually experience, and can then invent *visibilia* to express them. . . . this is allegory. . . . but there is another way of using the equivalence, which is almost the opposite of allegory, and which I would call sacramentalism or symbolism. If our passions, being immaterial, can be copied by material inventions, then it is possible that our material world in its turn is the copy of an invisible world. . . . The attempt to read that something else through its sensible imitations,

to see the archetype in the copy, is what I mean by symbolism or sacramentalism. . . . The allegorist leaves the given—his own passions—to talk of that which is confessedly less real, which is a fiction. The symbolist leaves the given to find that which is more real. To put the difference in another way, for the symbolist it is we who are the allegory.

(pp. 47-50)

Lewis's own mythical achievements are three: his understanding of the nature of myth as such, in passages of literary criticism such as the preceding; his empathy with the medieval cosmological myth in *The Discarded Image;* and his creative use of the medieval myth as a foundation for his own mythic fiction. We must now consider this last area.

Lewis is best known for his overtly religious fiction. But *The Screwtape Letters, The Great Divorce,* and *The Pilgrim's Regress* are all allegorical rather than mythical, and really belong to apologetics more than to fiction. About his science fiction trilogy, however, he maintains that "a simple sense of wonder extraordinary things going on, were the motive forces behind the creation. . . . I've never started from a message or a moral. . . . the story itself should force its moral upon you" (**"Unreal Estates"**). Unlike most science fiction writers, Lewis writes not merely about other *worlds* but about *other* worlds: he is a master of this genre's peculiar virtue, the ability to expand our experience. One very small but typical example of this must suffice: the taste of fruit on Perelandra:

> It was so different from every other taste that it seemed mere pedantry to call it a taste at all. It was like the discovery of a totally new *genus* of pleasures, something unheard of among men, out of all reckoning, beyond all covenant. For one draught of this on earth wars would be fought and nations betrayed. It could not be classified. He could never tell us, when he came back to the world of men, whether it was sharp or sweet, savoury or voluptuous, creamy or piercing. 'Not like that' was all he could ever say to such inquiries. . . . It appeared to him better not to taste again. Perhaps the experience had been so complete that repetition would be a vulgarity—like asking to hear the same symphony twice in a day.

A more general "expansion of experience" is his conception of "outer space" as full rather than empty:

> Now, with a certainty which never after deserted him, he saw the planets—the 'earths' he called them in his thought—as mere holes or gaps in the living heaven. . . . formed not by addition to but by subtraction from the surrounding brightness. . . . unless. . . . he groped for the idea. . . . unless visible light is also a hole or gap, a mere diminution of something else. Something that is to bright unchanging heaven as heaven is to the dark, heavy earths. . . . How indeed should it be otherwise, since out of this ocean the worlds and all their life

had come? He had thought it barren: he saw now that it was the womb of the worlds. . . . space was the wrong name. Older thinkers had been wiser when they named it simply the heavens. (*Out of the Silent Planet*)

Though the works are novels and the protagonists men, the most successful element in the trilogy are the eldils. Lewis has done to angels what Tolkien has done to elves; as he himself observes, "nothing less like the 'angel' of popular art could well be imagined." (pp. 51-2)

Till We Have Faces is not a myth in this cosmic sense, though it is labeled "a myth [Cupid and Psyche] retold." It is a "realistic" (historical) novel of conflicting myths: that of the Greek god of light, Apollonian reason, and that of Ungit the dark god of Dionysian blood and mystery. The god of light is not heavy enough, and Ungit is proved the wiser. Though we must avoid what Lewis calls "the personal heresy" (reading the writing through the writer rather than vice versa), we may note an obvious resemblance to Lewis's own rationalism-romanticism dilemma, his preference for the romantic, and his catalytic resolution through a higher revelation. The last is the point of this book. Someone is said to have asked Bertrand Russell what he would say to God if after death he found that God really existed. Russell replied that he would ask Him why He hadn't given us a little more evidence. To this excellent question Lewis gives a surprisingly "developmental" answer. "I saw well why the gods do not speak to us openly, nor let us answer. Till that word can be dug out of us, why should they hear the babble that we think we mean? How can they meet us face to face till we have faces?"

The Chronicles of Narnia constitute another mythic cosmos, simpler but even more successful, to my mind, than that of the science fiction trilogy. These seven books are written for children, and the protagonists are children; but by Lewis's own critical dictum any children's story that cannot be read by adults with pleasure and profit is not a good children's story either, but a patronization, an attempt "to regale the child with things calculated to please it but regarded by yourself with indifference or contempt. The child, I am certain, would see through that." Lewis respects children, as many modern children do not. . . . (pp. 53-4)

The Narnia books are called "dangerous" by Kathleen Nott (no one more unsympathetic to Lewis than she has yet seen print) because they contain not only little digs at modern foibles such as the one above but also an overall theological allegory, frustrating to the parent who likes the story but fears the child may pick up some religious ideas subconsciously. (As Lewis himself found out, "a young atheist cannot be too careful of his reading.") Even Tolkien finds them "too allegorical." Yet their moral is not *imposed*. Lewis practises

what he preaches, which is to let "the pictures tell you their own moral. For the moral inherent in them will rise from whatever spiritual roots you have succeeded in striking during the whole course of your life" (**"On Three Ways of Writing for Children"**).

Perhaps this is why the Narnia books succeed with many readers to whom his formally apologetic essays and even his overtly religious allegories fail. Or perhaps, as Lewis says,

the reason why the Passion of Aslan (lion-symbol of Christ) sometimes moves people more than the real story in the Gospels is. . . . that it takes them off their guard. In reading the real story, the fatal knowledge that one *ought* to feel in a certain way often inhibits the feeling. (*Letters*)

Or again, perhaps the simple change of names from "God" to "Aslan" or "Maleldil" lets us see behind the obscuring and encrusting veil not only of dull familiarity and religious associations but also that most convenient of all idols, the *word* "God."

Narnia's cosmos is true in the same mythic sense as that of the trilogy: it holds together as a world in itself, integral, consistent, and "astonishingly underivative." There is so much reality *in* it that the question of the reality outside it and of its relations to that latter reality need not even arise. A few chapter titles of the seven books, randomly arranged, will convey something of the atmosphere: "Deep Magic from the Dawn of Time"; "the Spell of the Utter East"; and "The Deplorable Word," which if spoken would destroy all of the speaker's world, leaving only himself. Lewis dares to describe without preciousness "a retired star," "drinkable light," and the wall at the world's end where the sky comes down to the earth. *The Last Battle*, last and greatest of the seven, simply bursts its bounds; never, I believe, has there been a children's story like it. Like its Arthurian predecessor (its title is from Malory's famous last chapter), its theme is the archetypal End of the World, End of the Old Order. The Giant Time wakes, the sky falls, and Aslan calls home the stars in a reversal of the progression of Creation (which Lewis has also dared to describe in *The Magician's Nephew*). The plot leading to such a denouement parallels that of *That Hideous Strength:* men usurping the place of God "have pulled down Deep Heaven upon their heads." The problem, however, is that of *Till We Have Faces:* the divine silence; and the fear is that of *A Grief Observed:* the Cosmic Sadist, "this horrible fear that Aslan has come and is not like the Aslan we have believed in and hoped for. . . . it is as if the sun rose one day and were a black sun. . . . this is the end of all things." But its concluding Heaven is as deep as the pit from which it is the rescue: total despair leads to total Joy. More than any other, this book is the apotheosis of Lewis's works. Its themes are his major themes; its medium is his most successful medium; and its personality is his personality.

Despite Lewis's own critical dictum that evaluative criticism, and especially adverse criticism, is one of the most difficult and least rewarding literary tasks, I should like to venture some general judgments on his fiction. By conventional standards, the greatest weakness of Lewis's fiction is certainly his characterization. He is at his best in the least intimate and personal scenes; he describes his villains better than his heroes, damnation better than salvation, strange men better than ordinary men, inhabitants of other planets better than those of earth, and even *eldils* better than human beings. He seems like the feudal French peasant who knew more of the geography of Hell than of France. A further problem is his rationalism. A style as suitable to apologetic essays as Lewis's can hardly be suitable to fiction. Because Lewis's writing is so very rational, one gets the impression that his characters are all very rational. Worse, he often gives reasons instead of motives, rarely attempting to even acknowledge the existence of subconscious motivation, and often seems to *use* his characters as bearers of philosophical points, often by means of rational, expository conversations, rather than as objects of the author's interest for their own sake.

Such a basic charge can be met only by an equally basic defense, and Lewis has one: he is writing a different *kind* of novel than is usually written today. . . . Lewis does not write "realism" but epic—"higher realism." Stella Gibbons says:

> I wish that Lewis could have written a 'straight' novel in a modern setting, but perhaps his mind, soaked since boyhood in saga and myth, could find no patience with modern people and their small dramas. He seems to have been perpetually haunted by the realities lying behind appearances. ("Imaginative Writing" in *Light on C. S. Lewis*)

In this type of Spenserian, Platonic, archetypal, mythic fiction,

> the plot, as we call it, is only really a net whereby to catch something else. The real theme may be, and perhaps usually is, something that has no sequence in it, something other than a process and much more like a state or quality. Giantship, otherness, the desolation of space, are examples that have crossed our path. The titles of some stories illustrate the point very well. *The Well at the World's End*—can a man write a story to that title? ("**On Stories**")

Thus *Perelandra* is not about Ransom, or his adventures, or the Fall, but about Perelandra; and *That Hideous Strength* is about that hideous strength! Lewis burns his archetypes into our brains like Ingmar Bergman's visual images: what reader can forget *Perelandra*'s Eden of floating islands, or in *That Hideous Strength* the anti-utopia of a planet-wide machine sterile of all organic life, a lunar "freedom from Nature"? (pp. 54-8)

[In] the large Lewis's combination of romanticism with rationalism, imagination with philosophy, is a rich one, yet in the small, in such details as the didactic conversations, the reader often feels lectured to. Lewis never fully resolved his basic dualism of rationalism and romanticism: his philosophy is better put in his philosophical works and his fiction is best when the philosophy is so implicit in the simple beauty of the story or setting that extraction is impossible.

Finally, in minimizing Lewis's characterizations we must not forget his supreme success: few writers of fiction *or* apologetics, and far fewer writers of both, have portrayed as compellingly attractive a God as Lewis has dared to portray. No God farther from the God of undersexed seminarians could be imagined: regal, male, and glorious. Like Aslan, "of course he isn't *safe*. But he's good." (pp. 58-9)

Peter Kreeft, in his *C. S. Lewis: A Critical Essay,* 1969. Reprint by Christendom College Press, 1988, 48 p.

OWEN BARFIELD
(lecture date 1977)

[Barfield is considered by many scholars to be one of the most underrated men of letters in twentieth-century English literature. Lewis himself called him the "wisest and best of my unofficial teachers." Barfield was one of Lewis's best longtime friends, the two having met late in 1919 at Oxford. For years they engaged in what they later termed "The Great War": a running debate on Anthroposophy, naturalism versus supernaturalism, language and its relation to myth, and the nature of truth. Barfield has written many essays about his friend's life and work, many of which were collected in *Owen Barfield on C. S. Lewis* (1990). In the following excerpt from a lecture delivered at Wheaton College in 1977, Barfield identifies and examines the dichotomous "logical Lewis," writer of works defending objectivity and Christianity, and "imaginative Lewis," author of poems and novels.]

Pilate's famous question "What is truth?" can be interpreted in two very different ways. It can be taken as asking: What is the truth—about this or that question—and how are we to ascertain it? Or it can be taken, much more underminingly, as asking: What does one mean by "truth"? Is there such a thing? Is there really any difference between truth and error? I think it is true to say that the world in which C. S.

Lewis grew up, and in which he lived out his life, was one in which the second interpretation was insidiously ousting the first. Moreover, it was tending more and more to be answered, by a few deliberately and consciously, but by an ever-increasing number only half-consciously, in the negative. What Pyrrhonist philosophy, of one kind or another, was doing for the few, the popularization of a psychology that presupposed the Darwinian concept of an exclusively biological evolution was doing for the many. Reductionism (or, as we used to call it, materialism), subjectivism, relativism were coming more and more into the open, growing more and more influential in determining the general climate of opinion. As Lewis put it in an article, **"The Poison of Subjectivism"** in 1943:

> After studying his environment man has begun to study himself. Up to that point, he had assumed his own reason and through it seen all other things. Now, his own reason has become the object: it is as if we took out our eyes to look at them. Thus studied his own reason appears to him as the epiphenomenon which accompanies chemical or electrical events in a cortex which is itself the by-product of a blind evolutionary process. His own logic, hitherto the King whom events in all possible worlds must obey, becomes merely subjective. There is no reason for supposing that it yields truth.

There you have all three of them: reductionism, subjectivism, relativism, and the relation between them, assembled together in a pithy nutshell.

They are still influential enough, goodness knows, but if they are a little less so today, I believe we owe that in some measure to Lewis. No one saw more clearly what was going on. The one thing he never tired of doing, or would not let himself tire of doing, was to expose the appallingly muddled thinking on which all three of them rest, by way of a battery of very simple, very lucid, and totally unanswerable arguments reinforced by equally simple and vigorous metaphors.

I will not attempt to give a list of the books and articles in which examples of this exposure are to be found (*The Abolition of Man* is one of my favorites), because they keep on cropping up in almost all his non-fictional writings. I will, however, cite very briefly two actual examples. On the particular brand of subjectivism which we owe to the doctrines of psychoanalysis, there is the chapter entitled "Parrot Disease" in *The Pilgrim's Regress*, where the jailer is examining his captives:

> 'Come, come', said the jailer. 'You must know your catechism by now. You, there' (and he pointed to a prisoner little older than a boy whose name was Master Parrot), 'What is argument?'

> 'Argument', said Master Parrot, 'is the attempted rationalization of the arguer's desires.'

> 'Very good', replied the jailer, 'but you should turn out your toes and put your hands behind your back. That is better. Now: what is the proper answer to an argument proving the existence of the Landlord?'

> 'The proper answer is, You say that because you are a Steward.'

> 'Good boy. But hold your head up . . . '

And finally (I am shortening a little):

> 'Good. Now just one more. What is the answer turning on the belief that two and two make four?'

> 'The answer is, You say that because you are a mathematician.'

> 'You are a very good boy,' said the jailer . . . '

On relativism and reductionism (that is to say, on philosophical, as opposed to psychological, subjectivism) this, from the essay *"De Futilitate,"* will do as well as any:

> I asked whether in general human thought could be set aside as irrelevant to the real universe and merely subjective. . . . The answer is that at least one kind of thought—logical thought—cannot be subjective and irrelevant to the real universe: for unless thought is valid we have no reason to believe in the real universe. We reach our knowledge of the universe only by inference. The very object to which our thought is supposed to be irrelevant depends on the relevance of our thought. A universe whose only claim to be believed in rests on the validity of inference must not start telling us that inference is invalid. That would really be a bit too nonsensical.

It was this nonsensical foundation beneath most of what most of his contemporaries were taking for granted that Lewis excelled in laying bare. Over and over again, but each time in slightly different language, he pointed out that, as soon as that foundation is clearly affirmed, instead of being cloudily assumed, it undermines itself. You cannot *prove* that there is no such thing as proof, or (without imbecility) *argue* that argument is merely a biological process. You cannot hold it *true* that there is no such thing as truth. He forced us to do what most of us are unwilling to do, to apply the thing we are saying at the moment, not only to everything else in the world, but also to the thing we are saying and the fact that we are saying it. His simple but infallible modus operandi was to step quietly around to the back of his reductionist opponent and trip him up from behind. I remember telling him, when I first realized how very much this was his forte as a controversialist, that he was like Sir Andrew Aguecheek, because he "had the back-trick simply the best of any man in Illyria."

A little earlier I described his arguments—one might also say his argument—as "totally unanswerable." And I did so, because, to any mind capable of sustaining attention long enough to understand it, it is self-evident or obvious. But he lived in a world in which fewer and fewer minds were any longer capable of such sustained attention. It was this fact which made George Orwell remark of the times we live in: "We have now sunk to a depth at which re-statement of the obvious is the first duty of intelligent men." And I can think of no writer, living or dead (for Socrates was not a writer), who has performed that duty more faithfully or so brilliantly as C. S. Lewis. (pp. 90-3)

Yet all this was only one side of his mind. Besides the Lewis of *The Abolition of Man,* **"The Poison of Subjectivism,"** the **"Reply to Professor Haldane,"** and so forth, there is, as you know, the Lewis of those much underrated *Poems,* of the planetary novels, of *Till We Have Faces,* and the seven **"Narnia"** tales for children. Besides combatively logical Lewis, there is gently imaginative Lewis. And they do sometimes seem like two completely different men—so divergent, I sometimes feel, that it required something approaching a third Lewis to discover an area in which they could come together and work more or less in harmony. Of course there *was* that third Lewis: the Lewis of literary scholarship and literary criticism, the Lewis of *The Personal Heresy, A Preface to Paradise Lost, The Allegory of Love, History of English Literature in the Sixteenth Century,* and such essays as **"Psycho-analysis and Literary Criticism."**

Am I right, I wonder (and you will form your own opinions as to that), in the strong feeling I have that this proclivity for speaking, I would even say for *thinking,* almost as two different men, when the subjects are different, was Lewis's distinctive characteristic? Other great men have distinguished themselves in more than one genre. But when, to take a supreme example, we read Goethe, we have no difficulty in feeling that it is the same Goethe speaking, whether it be a lyric poem, or *Faust,* or literary or aesthetic criticism, or even in the domain of science. Am I right in feeling that it is not quite the same when we read Lewis? And if I am right, how important is it?

There is one genre on which he left an indelible mark, which I have not yet mentioned, and that is Christian apologetics. It is of course in the nature of apologetics to be polemical, eristic, hard-hitting, logical. We would not have it otherwise. Is that all I mean when I record the feeling I have that in *Miracles, Mere Christianity, The Problem of Pain* the voice we hear is exclusively the voice of Lewis number one? I believe not. They might have been worse, that is, less effective, or they might have been better had it been otherwise. That is a question on which I decline to make up my mind. But I believe it was so. Lewis number two, imaginative Lewis, was indeed a servant of the Word, hardly less than logical Lewis, but only in different places, in

different books, in *Till We Have Faces,* in the **"Narnia"** books. His irradiating presence is hardly felt in *Mere Christianity* or *Miracles.* (pp. 93-5)

The use of imagination is one thing; a theory of imagination is another. A theory of imagination must concern itself, whether positively or negatively, with its relation to truth. Is it, for instance, or can it be, a vehicle of revelation? Is it the human faculty through which the world around us may acquire, or recover, its true nature as a theophany, or is its exercise merely one among many permissible recreations for creaturely minds? Well, it is almost the same as the good old question, Is it objective or subjective? That is certainly not a question to which it can be said that Lewis never addressed his mind. Indeed, he and I had a special, and rather protracted, tussle over it, when we were both young. It *is* a question in which he lost interest at the time of his conversion, or perhaps a little before it. If he no longer denied, as he had done at the time of the tussle, that imagination had a positive relation to truth, he was disinclined to give any attention to it. There is a rather halfhearted suggestion in the two final paragraphs of *The Abolition of Man* that imaginal, as opposed to analytical, thinking may prove in the end to have some relation even to scientific truth; but, as far as I know, that is the only occasion when such a possibility is touched on. I am inclined to attribute this conspicuous reticence to two causes, both of them connected with the dichotomy I have stressed.

It sometimes happens at the end of a lecture that some infuriating person in the audience gets up and asks point-blank, and in the crudest possible terms, the very question to which the whole lecture was intended to be a profound and subtle answer, and incidentally the shortest possible answer such a searching question permits of. If someone were to ask me at the point of a pistol, and with ten seconds to answer in: What was Lewis's relation to imagination? I should reply (supposing I had my wits enough about me to meet the challenge): He was in love with it. And being in love (which is not quite coterminous with "having sex") has been observed to entail a strong impulse to protect the beloved object from contamination, a kind of horror at the contrast between her perfections and the harsh world of reality. (pp. 97-8)

Lewis had within him this loving impulse to protect and insulate imagination, so that it could continue to live its own pure and chaste life; to insulate it, therefore, from having anything whatever to do with *fact.* "May it not be that there is something in belief which is hostile to perfect imaginative enjoyment?" he asks in the essay **"Is Theology Poetry?"** and elsewhere he suggests that, if there had been no myths, the poets would have had to invent them. My memory tells me that, once you are alert to it, you find indications of that protective impulse in many places in his writings.

That, then, I would put as the first explanation of his marked reticence on the issue of imagination's relation to truth. The second is rather more complex. Imaginative, or, better, imaginal, statements differ from logical or discursive statements in a number of ways, for which the late Philip Wheelwright invented the useful portmanteau epithet "soft-focus." For instance, they are concerned with the resemblance between one shape or pattern and another, rather than with a logical nexus between one idea and another. Moreover, the shapes and patterns are not fixed. They are apt to change into each other by a process of development. Their syntax, so to speak, is one of metamorphosis, rather than of sequence and aggregation. This is very noticeable in the case of myths, which I suppose are the archetypal instances of imaginal statement. It is no accident that one of the principal encyclopedias of Greek mythology is Ovid's long poem entitled *Metamorphoses.*

It is obvious that the statements occurring in the literature of myth and symbol and metaphor are generally not "true" in the literal sense, are not taken, that is, as a chain of affirmative propositions. The question is, can they be true in any sense? Another way of putting this would be to ask: Is imagination one way of *thinking,* and therefore of acquiring knowledge, or is it something else altogether? Here the trouble is that, if it *is* treated as a way of thinking, then the kind of thinking it is bears a strong superficial resemblance to that blur of confused impressions into which, as I said, Lewis found the intellectual world as a whole degenerating under the influence of subjectivism and relativism—a sort of mishmash, in which nothing is definitely anything, because everything is also everything else, or in the act of becoming so; the kind of mishmash he illustrated so effectively in the utterances of Wither in *That Hideous Strength.* Lewis, I am sure, felt this resemblance acutely and for that reason, when any question was at issue bearing on truth or knowledge, he preferred to leave out imagination altogether.

It is characteristic of images that they interpenetrate one another. Indeed, more than half the art of poetry consists in helping them to do so. That is just what the terms of logic, and the notions we employ in logical or would-be logical thinking, must *not* do. *There,* interpenetration becomes the slovenly confusion of one determinate meaning with another determinate meaning, and there, its proper name is not interpenetration, but equivocation; there, "we must speak by the card, or equivocation will undo us," as Hamlet said; for equivocation is the first step on the road to mishmash. I believe Lewis's just hatred of his sworn foe, mishmash, led him beyond mere reticence on the subject of imagination and into a strong repugnance to the idea of interpenetration of any sort, whether material or psychic or spiritual. Compare the imagery of Dante's *Paradiso* with the imagery Lewis employs for his dream of heav-

en in *The Great Divorce.* The beings in Dante's heaven are constantly presented in terms of light, of lights mirroring each other, entering each other, interpenetrating each other, in-dwelling each other, after the manner of luminous beams. In the heaven of *The Great Divorce* what is remorselessly emphasized is the impenetrable *solidity* of everything and everybody. There is indeed a realm where the opposite obtains, where *nothing* is solid, and whose inhabitants have the capacity of ultimately interpenetrating, or absorbing, or slithering into, one another. But for Lewis, and I think also for his friend Charles Williams, the name of this particular part of the spiritual world was hell. I am thinking now mainly of *The Screwtape Letters,* but also of parts of the dialogue between Ransom and Merlin in *That Hideous Strength.* (pp. 98-100)

In the domain of Christian apologetics it was, as I have said, logical Lewis who had the upper hand, imaginative Lewis being kept so far out of sight that the author is sometimes accused, though not by intelligent critics, of fundamentalism. But his religious utterances were not all apologetic, and in the end it was in his Christian reflections, I feel (if I may borrow the phrase from Walter Hooper's book title), even more than in his work on English literature, that the two Lewises I have particularly distinguished came nearest to joining hands. The posthumous *Letters to Malcolm: Chiefly on Prayer* is to my mind irradiated by imaginative Lewis here and there in a way that the other books referred to are not. Much earlier, he had disclosed on one particular occasion the movement—dare I say the forward movement?—of his mind which made this possible. I refer to the sermon **"Transposition,"** which he preached at Mansfield College, Oxford, in 1949. It is quite short, and in it he begins by directing attention to one particular instance where the problem of meaning, or the relation between apparent meaninglessness and actual meaning, arises in an acute form; namely, the phenomenon of glossolalia, or "speaking with tongues." Hysteria, or the Holy Spirit bearing witness with our spirit? Mishmash, or valid, though nonlogical, communication? Sometimes one and sometimes the other? If so, how are we to distinguish the one from the other?

Reductionism, with which I began, may be assailed in two different ways, or from two opposite directions. It may be assailed from below, by exposing its inherent absurdity. This was the direction to which logical Lewis usually confined himself, and we have seen how he excelled at it. It may also be assailed from above, and this is the direction from which that ragged and irregular army of hermeneutists, phenomenologists, symbolists—I mean all those people I tried to point to, who have been interesting themselves in imagination and its concomitants during the last forty years or so—have tried to assail it. This is the direction from which logical Lewis assails it in **"Transposition."** His argument is that "what is happening in the lower medium can be understood only if we know the higher medium." Confronted with a picture in two dimensions, only a mind which had some experience or knowledge of the real world of three dimensions could discern that what the picture represents is not a copy, but a kind of *transposition,* of such a real world. He gives other examples. Throughout the sermon he uses his own concepts, his own vocabulary. For instance, what the soldiers of that irregular army would call "a man without imagination" he calls "the observer who knows only the lower medium," and he adds that the world of such a man must necessarily be "all fact and no meaning." It took me some time to realize that, whatever else it is as well, **"Transposition"** can be seen as a theory of imagination. Read it carefully and you will find all the proper ingredients—metamorphosis, interpenetration of meanings, interpenetration of mind and body, of spirit and soul. Lewis's eye is on the ball, even if he prefers to call it a "pill" or a "sphere." . . . I am not sure whether there is anything like it anywhere else in Lewis's writing, but that little sermon **"Transposition"** amounts in my view to a theory of imagination, in which imagination is not mentioned. (pp. 101-03)

Owen Barfield, in his *Owen Barfield on C. S. Lewis,* edited by G. B. Tennyson, Wesleyan University Press, 1989, 171 p.

CORBIN SCOTT CARNELL

(essay date 1990)

[Carnell is an American educator, essayist, and authority on the works of Lewis and J. R. R. Tolkien. In the following excerpt, he provides a broad overview of Lewis's accomplishment as a novelist.]

Just how good is C. S. Lewis as a novelist? Does he belong in the canon? Does his clearly Christian orientation offend too many readers for him to be included in straight literature courses?

Any reader, even one who does not like Lewis, will have to grant that he is a superb story-teller. With a few details and not many words he can create a setting, a mood, an absorbing conflict, a suspenseful tale. The fact that he can write successfully for children (few can!) is proof of his story-telling gifts. But evaluating Lewis is confusing, for he has at least five fictional styles. There is first the naive, Disney-like charm of *Out of the Silent Planet:*

At that moment the sound of an opening door made him turn his head. An oblong of dazzling light ap-

peared behind him and instantly vanished as the door closed again, having admitted the bulky form of a . . . man. . . . The mere presence of a human being, with its offer of at least some companionship, broke down the tension in which his nerves had long been resisting a bottomless dismay. He found, when he spoke, that he was sobbing.

"Weston! Weston!" he gasped. "What is it? It's not the moon, not that size. It can't be, can it?"

"No," replied Weston, "it's the Earth." (ch. 3)

The style here is reminiscent of H. G. Wells and Arthur C. Clarke. It is Lewis's simplest style in writing for adults.

Second, there is the musical, poetic texture of *Perelandra:*

There was great silence on the mountain top and Ransom also had fallen down before the human pair. When at last he raised his eyes from the four blessed feet, he found himself involuntarily speaking though his voice was broken and his eyes dimmed. "Do not move away, do not raise me up," he said. "I have never before seen a man or a woman. I have lived my life among shadows and broken images." . . .

"All is gift," the voice said. "I am Oyarsa not by His gift alone but by our foster mother's, not by hers alone but by yours, not by yours alone but by my wife's—nay in some sort, by gift of the very beasts and birds. Through many hands, enriched by many different kinds of love and labor, the gift comes to me. It is the Law. The best fruits are plucked for each by some hand that is not his own." . . .

"Blessed be He." (ch. 17)

Here the style is like the most poetic passages in D. H. Lawrence or Joyce. It verges continually on poetry and is a joy to read aloud.

And there is yet a third and very different style in *That Hideous Strength,* where Lewis writes a bit like C. P. Snow and also George Orwell as he describes the conflict between the St. Anne's community and the demonic N.I.C.E.

The woman who had laughed rose hastily from her chair. The man seated next to her heard her murmur in his ear, "Vood wooloo." He took in the meaningless syllables and her unnatural expression in one moment. Both for some reason infuriated him. He rose to help her to move back her chair with one of those gestures of savage politeness which often, in modern society, serve instead of blows. He wrenched the chair, in fact, out of her hand. She screamed, tripped on a ruck in the carpet and fell. The man on the other side of her saw her fall and saw the first man's expression of fury, "Bot are you blammit?" he roared. (ch. 16)

The almost journalistic lack of ornament and the straightforwardness of this writing is clearly different from Lewis's other books. He seems almost to assume the astringent and tense nature of the setting in the style.

Furthermore, *Till We Have Faces* (Lewis's last novel) has a primitive, mythic flavor:

> The great change came when he [the priest] proposed to set up an image of her—a woman-shaped image in the Greek fashion—in front of the old shapeless stone. I think he would have got rid of the stone altogether, but it is, in a manner, Ungit herself and the people would have gone mad if she were moved. . . . It had to be brought, not indeed from the Greek-lands themselves, but from lands where men had learned of the Greeks. I was rich now and I helped him with silver. (ch. 20)

The simplicity here is misleading for there is a multilayered rendering of mythic archetypes throughout *Till We Have Faces* (e.g., the plague-stricken land, the beautiful and innocent Psyche, the ugly but intelligent heroine, the wise teacher in the Fox). The simplicity is born not of a desire to streamline but rather a desire to capture in the sparse everyday detail the weight of mythic experience and awareness, which can be more themselves because they do not compete with realistic complexity.

And there is yet a fifth style in the Narnia books, where in simple words and easily remembered details Lewis tells seven beautiful stories. (That the Narnia story details are easy to remember is clear when you compare those books with Tolkien's *The Hobbit,* which some children have difficulty with because of the wealth of detail.) Note this typical passage from *The Lion, the Witch, and the Wardrobe:*

> There was no trace of the fog now. The sky became bluer and bluer and now there were white clouds hurrying across it from time to time. In the wide glades there were primroses. A light breeze sprang up which scattered drops of moisture from the swaying branches and carried cool, delicious scents against the faces of the travellers. The trees began to come fully alive. . . .
>
> "This is no thaw," said the Dwarf. suddenly stopping. "This is *spring.* What are we to do? Your winter has been destroyed, I tell you! This is Aslan's doing."
>
> "If either of you mention that name again," said the Witch, "he shall be instantly killed." (ch. 11)

This is clearly the fairy tale world. To inject the complexity of twentieth century Realism would dilute the fantasy narrative Lewis is creating here and yet it would be a mistake to say that any of his fiction neglects or nullifies reality. Rather it is the reality of Joseph Campbell's monomyth and the rich world of Jungian archetypes, some would say a higher reality than what is aimed for in the Realism of Sinclair Lewis or Arnold Bennett.

One has to give Lewis high marks on plot. Each of his narratives has a clear shape, with skillful management of exposition, suspense, climax, and denouement. A possible exception is *That Hideous Strength,* which gets off to a slow start, but this slow beginning could be defended on the grounds that the novel is at first a story of academic life and a certain deliberation is appropriate. Lewis does not do as well on character, for he seldom gives us round characters; exceptions are Ransom, Orual, and Lucy, but he tends to handle character as Aldous Huxley and George Orwell do—as ancillary to ideas, for they also write novels of ideas.

And it can be argued that Lewis creates the kinds of characters he needs. Weston in *Out of the Silent Planet* is hardly a round character but Lewis is using him to represent science run amuck and he does not need a round character for that. The Green Lady in *Perelandra* presents problems when one asks if her character is flat or round. She is not of the fallen human species so it is pointless to examine her as if she were. She is a genuinely mythic personage, rich in imaginative detail yet not quite human.

In *That Hideous Strength* Fairy Hardcastle, Frost, and Wither are deliberately flat characters, representing various aspects of evil which arise out of wrong thinking and wrong purposes. In *Till We Have Faces* we are clearly in the world of pre-realist mythic narrative. There is much convincing detail, but Lewis is weaving a myth, not writing a realistic novel. As for the Chronicles of Narnia, here Lewis is creating realism only to the extent that he wants his writing to be vivid and convincing. He is again moving in the world of fantasy and myth where archetypes are more important than twentieth century Realism.

The character which shows the most development is of course Elwin Ransom, who has three novels to grow in. He changes from the retiring, rather sedentary professor at the beginning of *Silent Planet* to the athletically involved and courageous hero of *Perelandra* to the kingly authority who presides over the St. Anne's community in *Hideous Strength.* Ransom's adventures make him a more outgoing and physically disciplined person as well as a man in whom the spirit has made great progress. This progress involves receiving an inconsolable wound in the subterranean caves of Perelandra, which gives him a pain that can only one day be healed by his return to Perelandra.

It is difficult for a fiction writer to handle every aspect of fiction well. Even the greatest novelists have flaws. James Joyce can become hopelessly obscure at times, Virginia Woolf too abstruse, D. H. Lawrence too preachy. Perhaps Lewis would defend his work on the grounds that if he had created many round characters his work would have become unwieldy, because he is committed to exploring ideas first and foremost.

I think Lewis can be defended on the charges against his kind of characterization, but there is a more serious charge against which it is harder to mount a defense. And this charge is that he is too unsubtle in his didacticism. Could Lewis's liking for novelists like George MacDonald and H. G. Wells have so accustomed him to a didactic pointing of the narrative that he was unaware of his lack of subtlety? He once argued that a writer could put any amount of Christianity in his work if he wanted, but that it should be latent rather than a manifest message. Does he live up to his own standard? I find readers' measure of his subtlety varies widely. (pp. 1-3)

The whole problem of didacticism in fiction is complex. We accept Joyce's advocacy of art for art's sake. We accept Virginia Woolf 's dicta about the capacity of art to transcend the commonplace and to glorify life. Yet some balk at the orthodox Christianity in Lewis. Actually the space trilogy and *Till We Have Faces* are not overtly Christian. Except for one reference in *Silent Planet* to Maleldil the Young (who is clearly Christ), one could read these novels only as promoting supernaturalism and in the case of *Till We Have Faces* the Christian doctrine of substituted love, or what Charles Williams called Coinherence.. . . .

It is certainly true that readers differ widely in the amount of teaching they will tolerate or welcome in fiction. Some want no ethical insights that are easily observed; indeed if a preachment, however subtle, emerges, those readers will then devalue the work. Others are disappointed if there is not some teaching, perhaps even overt. Though most of us would prefer that the teaching be subtle and latent, most of us would also agree that to be literature, there has to be instruction or insight. We see too much of the merely pleasurable in popular literature, music, and film. One gets hungry for some honest insights, for some reassurance that there is a moral order to which so much of our experience resonates.

What might Lewis have done differently? Given his priorities, I would have to say very little. He might have been more subtle, excluding, for example, the reference to Maleldil the Young in the space trilogy. The Narnia books would have to stay as they are, for they are designed to teach and given the childlike mind, the teaching does not seem to intrude. I have known many college students who said that when they read the Chronicles of Narnia they got none of the Christianity. They detected an outlook which values loyalty, obedience to duly constituted authority, compassion, and courage, but even when Aslan gives his life for the traitor Edmund in *The Lion, The Witch, and the Wardrobe*, they did not hear the Christian echoes. So complete is the work of secularization in young people today they simply do not detect Christianity very readily. Thus Lewis could well reply that writing in a post-Christian age he had to be more religiously explicit than he would have been in the Middle Ages, for example.

On balance, how good is Lewis as a fiction writer? I would say he is good or better than Aldous Huxley, who is also a novelist of ideas. He is as good as H. G. Wells, and more imaginative. He is as good as Barbara Pym and better than Irish Murdoch, though she is more prolific. Only an anti-religious bias can deny Lewis a place in the canon of worthwhile minor writers of twentieth century British fiction. He is not one of the giants (as a novelist—he is a giant as a thinker). He is not a Joyce or a Lawrence. But neither is Huxley or Orwell and they continue to be taught.

There is no question about Lewis's place in the canon of writers for children. The immediate success of his Narnia stories and their continuing popularity—not only among children but among teachers and parents—attest to his success in this genre. The recent very satisfying adaptation of *The Lion, the Witch, and the Wardrobe* for television by the BBC also shows that Lewis knew how to tap the wellsprings of imagination for children of all ages. (p. 4)

Corbin Scott Carnell, "C. S. Lewis as a Novelist," in *CSL: The Bulletin of the New York C. S. Lewis Society*, Vol. 21, No. 7, May, 1990, pp. 1-4.

SOURCES FOR FURTHER STUDY

Como, James T., ed. *C. S. Lewis at the Breakfast Table and Other Reminiscences*. New York: Macmillan, 1979, 299 p.

Anecdotal biographical essays by Lewis's friends and associates, and by scholars of his works; including John Wain, Derek Brewer, Eugene McGovern, and many others. A full primary bibliography, compiled by Walter Hooper, is provided.

Edwards, Bruce L., ed. *The Taste of the Pineapple: Essays on C. S. Lewis as Reader, Critic, and Imaginative Writer*.

Bowling Green, Ohio: Bowling Green State University Press, 1988, 246 p.

> Collection of critical essays by such scholars as Thomas Howard, Joe McClatchey, David H. Stewart, and others.

Gibb, Jocelyn, ed. *Light on C. S. Lewis.* London: Geoffrey Bles, 1965, 160 p.

> Essays on Lewis's life and work by Owen Barfield, Kathleen Raine, J. A. W. Bennett, and several others.

Howard, Thomas. *C. S. Lewis: Man of Letters.* San Francisco: Ignatius Press, 1990, 259 p.

> Convincing critical study of Lewis's long fiction, with individual chapters devoted to examinations of The Chronicles of Narnia, *Out of the Silent Planet, Perelandra, That Hideous Strength,* and *Till We Have Faces.* This work was originally published in 1980 as *The Achievement of C. S. Lewis.*

Sayer, George. *Jack: C. S. Lewis and His Times.* San Francisco: Harper & Row, Publishers, 1988, 278 p.

> Acclaimed biography of Lewis that draws heavily upon *The Lewis Papers,* a privately published family history written by Lewis's brother, Warren. Written by a longtime friend of Lewis, *Jack* is considered by some critics the best biography of the subject written to date.

Schakel, Peter J., and Huttar, Charles A. *Word and Story in C. S. Lewis.* Columbia: University of Missouri Press, 1991, 316 p.

> Collection of sixteen critical essays on language and narrative in Lewis's work, with an afterword by Owen Barfield. Contributing essayists include Stephen Medcalf, Gregory Wolfe, Donald E. Glover, Jared C. Lobdell, Michael Murrin, Colin Manlove, and others.

Sinclair Lewis

1885-1951

(Full name Harry Sinclair Lewis; also wrote under pseudonym Tom Graham) American novelist, short story writer, essayist, critic, dramatist, journalist, and poet.

INTRODUCTION

*O*ne of the leading American novelists of the 1920s, Lewis created some of the most effective satires in American literature. Along with the noted critic and essayist H. L. Mencken, he vengefully attacked the dullness, the smug provincialism, and the socially enforced conformity of the American middle class. Lewis's fame rests upon five satiric novels published during the 1920s: *Main Street* (1920), *Babbitt* (1922), *Arrowsmith* (1925), *Elmer Gantry* (1927), and *Dodsworth* (1929). In these works, he created grotesque yet disturbingly recognizable caricatures of middle-class Americans with a skill for which he is often likened to Charles Dickens. In 1930 Lewis was awarded the Nobel Prize in literature, becoming the first American to be so honored.

.   Lewis was born in the small town of Sauk Centre, Minnesota, and was raised to follow the traditions of his middle-class, Protestant home town. As scholars have observed, throughout his early life Lewis was torn between two conflicting desires. The first was to conform to the standards of sameness, of respectability, and of financial advancement as dictated by his family and by the town. Opposing this desire to be a "Regular Guy" was Lewis's need to acknowledge his own nonconformist nature and ambitions: his agnosticism, his literary inclinations, and his general rebellion against the village's preference for unquestioning adherence to established standards of thought, faith, and aesthetics. After writing news stories and working at various odd jobs in the offices of Sauk Centre's two newspapers during his teens, Lewis—to the townsfolks' disapproval—left the Midwest to attend a university in the East. During his years at Yale, which included periods of travel and temporary employment, he read voraciously and published a number of light stories and poems. For a time Lewis worked as the furnaceman at Upton Sinclair's Helicon Hall, a socialist communal experiment in Englewood, New Jersey, and then went on to graduate from Yale in 1908. He married writer Grace Hegger and drifted about America for the next few years, writing and selling short stories to *The Saturday Evening Post* and other popular journals. A prolific writer with an abundant imagination, Lewis even sold ideas for stories to novelist Jack London during London's final years.

For the most part, Lewis's early short stories and novels reflect what the author termed the "Sauk-Centricities" of his own nature; they are conventional, optimistic, lightly humorous, and were written for a middle-class audience. Of Lewis's apprentice fiction, critics generally cite two works that foreshadow the skill and themes of the author's novels of the 1920s: *The Job* (1917), a novel that evidences traces of harsh realism as it tells of a small-town woman's struggle for success as a businesswoman in a large city; and the story "I'm a Stranger Here Myself," which narrates the adventures of a smug, narrow-minded Midwestern couple who condescend to leave "God's Country" for a vacation in Florida. These works marked the first significant sign of Lewis's discontent with writing about what William Dean Howells termed "the more smiling aspects of life, which are the more American." In 1920 Lewis published *Main Street,* the novel he had long intended to write in revolt against the sentimental myth of the American small town.

With *Main Street* Lewis assumed the leadership of the movement known as "the revolt from the village" in American literature, culminating a tradition begun by Mark Twain, Harold Frederic, Edgar Lee Masters, and Sherwood Anderson, among others. The partly autobiographical novel portrays the frustrations of Carol Kennicott's idealistic crusades to bring elements of liveliness and culture to her new husband's home town of Gopher Prairie, Minnesota, an ugly little settlement populated by an appalling collection of blustering, inarticulate oafs and prying, vicious shrews. To *Main Street*'s early readers and critics, the work was perceived as an indictment of traditional nineteenth-century values, which were completely unacceptable in the jaded, sophisticated climate of the Jazz Age. The new generation, fresh from witnessing the mechanized mass-slaughter of World War I, was ready for literature that would reflect its rejection of genteel optimism, blind nationalism, and traditional religion, and it welcomed Lewis's next two novels as it had earlier embraced *Main Street.* Of Lewis's five major satires, *Babbitt* and *Arrowsmith* are widely considered his most accomplished works. In *Babbitt,* Lewis skewered the loud, hypocritical American businessman as well as members of America's public service organizations and booster clubs, with their endless, vapid speeches and inane rituals. In the character of businessman

George F. Babbitt, Lewis created a literary archetype equal in stature to Mark Twain's Huckleberry Finn. *Arrowsmith* tells of the battles of a humanitarian scientist to conduct medical research against the beckoning forces of fame, commercialism, and material comforts. Widely acclaimed as one of America's most significant voices of the postwar era, Lewis won the 1926 Pulitzer Prize in fiction for *Arrowsmith,* but refused to accept the award, claiming that it was intended only for champions of American wholesomeness. Evidence from Lewis's letters suggests that another, less idealistic reason for his refusal was his anger that Edith Wharton's *The Age of Innocence* had been chosen over *Main Street* as winner of the 1921 Pulitzer Prize.

In 1927 storms both of protest and of acclamation erupted at the appearance of Lewis's "preacher novel," *Elmer Gantry.* An all-out attack on Fundamentalist Protestantism as practiced by such flamboyant evangelists as Billy Sunday and Aimee Semple McPherson, the book was praised by Mencken and several other major critics as a fair-minded exposé revealing the essential fraudulence of Christianity and the gullibility of its adherents. The majority of critics, however, have joined Walter Lippmann in judging *Elmer Gantry* to be a deeply flawed novel, one in which Lewis's satiric intent is crushed beneath his hatred of the faith he had rejected as a young man. A year after the publication of this, the weakest but most controversial of his five major novels, Lewis, who had divorced his first wife, married the distinguished journalist Dorothy Thompson. Thompson was a major influence on Lewis's work and thought for the rest of his life. In 1930 the couple traveled to Stockholm, where Lewis received the Nobel Prize for his literary achievement. In his now-famous acceptance speech, Lewis blasted the entire American literary tradition up until roughly his own era, and then hailed the rising new generation of the nation's writers, praising Ernest Hemingway, John Dos Passos, Thomas Wolfe, and several others. Lewis's own artistic stature had reached its zenith with the appearance in 1929 of *Dodsworth,* a novel in which a harried, disillusioned American businessman seeks peace of mind through travel in Europe. Considered one of the best of Lewis's satires, *Dodsworth* nonetheless marked the end of his preeminence as a major novelist; he never again wrote with the skill and power exhibited in his landmark satires of the 1920s.

Critics continue to speculate about the reasons for Lewis's literary decline during the last two decades of his life. Of all the theories offered, from his failure to complete a proposed novel on American labor to the possibility of his having strained to compete professionally with his wife, it is fairly certain that the Great Depression had the most damaging effect on his talent; for with much of the American middle class jobless and impoverished, Lewis lost both his reading audience and the target of his satiric jibes. During the rest of his career, Lewis periodically lectured, taught university writing courses, contributed book reviews to various magazines, and turned out a succession of relatively undistinguished novels. Among these, three contain traces of the early satiric skill and have received more favorable critical treatment than the others: they are *It Can't Happen Here* (1935), which documents a plausible fascist takeover of America from within; *Cass Timberlane* (1945), a blow aimed at the institution of marriage; and *Kingsblood Royal* (1947), which attacks racial bigotry. Lewis was living in Italy, where he had just completed *World So Wide* (1951)—a novel which resurrects businessman Sam Dodsworth of the author's earlier work—when he died of heart disease.

A common concern among critics of Lewis's work is the ambivalent attitude expressed throughout the author's mature fiction toward the American middle class. In a recurrently cited example, Carol Kennicott of *Main Street* is alternately depicted as a sensitive, intelligent woman and as a pretentious, naive whiner. Her husband Will is likewise portrayed as at once a practical, warm, and loving man and as a bellicose lout. Speaking of *Main Street* in a conversation with Charles Breasted, Lewis acknowledged his longstanding love/hate relationship with small-town America, admitting that Carol is a portrait of himself: "always groping for something she isn't capable of attaining, always dissatisfied, always restlessly straining to see what lies just over the horizon, intolerant of her surroundings, yet lacking any clearly defined vision of what she really wants to do or

to be." Lewis's lack of a clear vision of life and his impatient nature are often noted as crucial to understanding the weakness of his fiction: the occasionally shrill tone, the sometimes overly harsh exaggerations of society's foibles, and the bleak outlook that remains even after the fooleries of the "booboisie" are exposed. In praise of Lewis's ability, critics note his superb skill at caricaturing and mimicking the appearance and speech of the common American. And although Lewis's work is not today the subject of extensive critical discussion, in the author's time he performed the role of American gadfly with a power unequalled except by Thomas Paine, Mark Twain, and H. L. Mencken, according to critic Sheldon Norman Grebstein. His five major satires not only introduced such definitive terms as "Main Street," "Babbitt," and "Babbittry" into common usage, but they also paved the way for much of the self-critical realistic fiction of mid-century American literature. As Lewis's biographer, Mark Schorer, has written: "In any strict literary sense, he was not a great writer, but without his writing one cannot imagine modern American literature."

(For further information about Lewis's life and works, see *Concise Dictionary of American Literary Biography, 1917-1929; Contemporary Authors,* Vol. 104; *Dictionary of Literary Biography,* Vol. 9: *American Novelists, 1910-1945; Dictionary of Literary Biography Documentary Series,* Vol. 1; *Major Twentieth-Century Writers;* and *Twentieth-Century Literary Criticism,* Vols. 4, 13, 23, 39.)

CRITICAL COMMENTARY

H. L. MENCKEN
(essay date 1921)

[One of the most influential intellectuals in America from the era of World War I until the early years of the Great Depression, Mencken is best known as a social and literary critic. He was one of Lewis's closest friends, and throughout the 1920s he praised Lewis's books as resounding indictments of America's provincial ignorance and stupidity. In the following excerpt from an essay that first appeared in 1921 in *The Smart Set,* he praises *Main Street* for its "packed and brilliant detail," declaring it "an attempt, not to solve the American cultural problem, but simply to depict with great care a group of typical Americans."]

Authors with their pockets full of best-seller money are bitten by high ambition, and strive heroically to scram-

ble out of the literary Cloaca Maxima. Now and then one of them succeeds, bursting suddenly into the light of the good red sun with the foul liquors of the depths still streaming from him, like a prisoner loosed from some obscene dungeon. . . . A few months ago I recorded the case of Zona Gale, emerging from her stew of glad books with *Miss Lulu Bett.* Now comes another fugitive, his face blanched by years in the hulks, but his eyes alight with high purpose. His name is Sinclair Lewis, and the work he offers is a novel called *Main Street.* . . .

This *Main Street* I commend to your polite attention. It is, in brief, good stuff. It presents characters that are genuinely human, and not only genuinely human but also authentically American; it carries them through a series of transactions that are all interesting and plausible; it exhibits those transactions thought-

Principal Works

Hike and the Aeroplane [as Tom Graham] (novel) 1912

Our Mr. Wrenn: The Romantic Adventures of a Gentle Man (novel) 1914

The Trail of the Hawk: A Comedy of the Seriousness of Life (novel) 1915

The Job (novel) 1917

Free Air (novel) 1919

Main Street: The Story of Carol Kennicott (novel) 1920

Babbitt (novel) 1922

Arrowsmith (novel) 1925; also published as Martin Arrowsmith, 1925

Mantrap (novel) 1926

Elmer Gantry (novel) 1927

The Man Who Knew Coolidge: Being the Soul of Lowell Schmaltz, Constructive and Nordic Citizen (novel) 1928

Cheap and Contented Labor: The Picture of a Southern Mill Town in 1929 (essay) 1929

Dodsworth (novel) 1929

Ann Vickers (novel) 1933

Work of Art (novel) 1934

It Can't Happen Here (novel) 1935

Jayhawker [with Lloyd Lewis] (drama) 1935

Selected Short Stories of Sinclair Lewis (short stories) 1935

The Prodigal Parents (novel) 1938

Bethel Merriday (novel) 1940

Gideon Planish (novel) 1943

Cass Timberlane (novel) 1945

Kingsblood Royal (novel) 1947

The God Seeker (novel) 1949

World So Wide (novel) 1951

From Main Street to Stockholm: Letters of Sinclair Lewis, 1919-1930 (letters) 1952

The Man from Main Street: Selected Essays and Other Writings, 1904-1950 (essays and criticism) 1953

---

fully and acutely, in the light of the social and cultural forces underlying them; it is well written, and full of a sharp sense of comedy, and rich in observation, and competently designed. Superficially, the story of a man and his wife in a small Minnesota town, it is actually the typical story of the American family—that is, of the family in its first stage, before husband and wife have become lost in father and mother. The average American wife, I daresay, does not come quite so close to downright revolt as Carol Kennicott, but that is the only exaggeration, and we may well overlook it. Otherwise, she and her Will are triumphs of the national normalcy—she with her vague stirrings, her unintelligible yearnings, her clumsy gropings, and he with his magnificent obtuseness, his childish belief in meaningless phrases, his intellectual deafness and nearsightedness, his pathetic inability to comprehend the turmoil that goes on within her. Here is the essential tragedy of American life, and if not the tragedy, then at least the sardonic farce; the disparate cultural development of male and female, the great strangeness that lies between husband and wife when they begin to function as members of society. The men, sweating at their sordid concerns, have given the women leisure, and out of that leisure the women have fashioned disquieting discontents. To Will Kennicott, as to most other normal American males, life remains simple; do your work, care for your family, buy your Liberty Bonds, root for your home team, help to build up your lodge, venerate the flag. But to Carol it is far more complex and challenging. She has become aware of forces that her hus-

band is wholly unable to comprehend, and that she herself can comprehend only in a dim and muddled way. The ideas of the great world press upon her, confusing her and making her uneasy. She is flustered by strange heresies, by romantic personalities, by exotic images of beauty. To Kennicott she is flighty, illogical, ungrateful for the benefits that he and God have heaped upon her. To her he is dull, narrow, ignoble.

Mr. Lewis depicts the resultant struggle with great penetration. He is far too intelligent to take sides—to turn the thing into a mere harangue against one or the other. Above all, he is too intelligent to take the side of Carol, as nine novelists out of ten would have done. He sees clearly what is too often not seen—that her superior culture is, after all, chiefly bogus—that the oafish Kennicott, in more ways than one, is actually better than she is. Her war upon his Philistinism is carried on with essentially Philistine weapons. Her dream of converting a Minnesota prairie town into a sort of Long Island suburb, with overtones of Greenwich Village and the Harvard campus, is quite as absurd as his dream of converting it into a second Minneapolis, with overtones of Gary, Ind., and Paterson, N.J. When their conflict is made concrete and dramatic by the entrance of a *tertium quid*, the hollowness of her whole case is at once made apparent, for this *tertium quid* is a Swedish trousers-presser who becomes a moving-picture actor. It seems to me that the irony here is delicate and delicious. This, then, is the end-product of the Maeterlinck complex! Needless to say, Carol lacks the courage to decamp with her Scandinavian. Instead, she descends to sheer banality. That is, she departs for Washington, becomes a war-worker, and rubs noses with the suffragettes. In the end, it goes without saying, she returns to Gopher Prairie and the hearth-stone of her Will. The fellow is at least honest. He offers her no ignominious compromise. She comes back under the old rules, and is presently nursing a baby. Thus the true idealism of the Republic, the idealism of its Chambers of Commerce, its Knights of Pythias, its Rotary Clubs and its National Defense Leagues, for which Washington froze at Valley Forge and Our Boys died at Châ-teau-Thierry—thus this genuine and unpolluted article conquers the phoney idealism of Nietzsche, Edward W. Bok, Dunsany, George Bernard Shaw, Margaret Anderson, Mrs. Margaret Sanger, Percy Mackaye and the I.W.W.

But the mere story, after all, is nothing; the virtue of the book lies in its packed and brilliant detail. It is an attempt, not to solve the American cultural problem, but simply to depict with great care a group of typical Americans. This attempt is extraordinarily successful. The figures often remain in the flat; the author is quite unable to get that poignancy into them which Dreiser manages so superbly; one seldom sees into them very deeply or feels with them very keenly. But in their externals, at all events, they are done with uncommon skill. In particular, Mr. Lewis represents their speech vividly and accurately. It would be hard to find a false note in the dialogue, and it would be impossible to exceed the verisimilitude of the various extracts from the Gopher Prairie paper, or of the sermon by a Methodist dervish in the Gopher Prairie Wesleyan cathedral, or of a speech by a boomer at a banquet of the Chamber of Commerce. Here Mr. Lewis lays on with obvious malice, but always he keeps within the bounds of probability, always his realism holds up. It is, as I have said, good stuff. I have read no more genuinely amusing novel for a long while. (pp. 279-82)

H. L. Mencken, "Sinclair Lewis: The Story of An American Family," in his *H. L. Mencken's "Smart Set" Criticism*, edited by William H. Nolte, Cornell University Press, 1968, pp. 279-82.

VIRGINIA WOOLF

(essay date 1925)

[Woolf was an English novelist, essayist, and critic. In the following excerpt from a 1925 *Saturday Review of Literature* essay, she cites *Babbitt* as evidence that Lewis is a great social critic and satirist and asserts that the limit of his achievement was dictated by the "meagre" subject matter of American culture.]

[It is] by its hardness, its efficiency, its compactness that Mr. Lewis's work excels. . . . [His] books, one is inclined to say, are all shell; the only doubt is whether he has left any room for the snail. At any rate *Babbitt* completely refutes the theory that an American writer, writing about America, must necessarily lack the finish, the technique, the power to model and control his material which one might suppose to be the bequest of an old civilisation to its artists. In all these respects, *Babbitt* is the equal of any novel written in English in the present century. . . . [But study] of Mr. Lewis more and more convinces us that the surface appearance of downright decision is deceptive; the outer composure hardly holds together the warring elements within; the colours have run.

For though *Babbitt* would appear as solid and authentic a portrait of the American business man as can well be painted, certain doubts run across us and shake our conviction. But, we may ask, where all is so masterly, self-assured, and confident, what foothold can there be for doubt to lodge upon? To begin with we doubt Mr. Lewis himself: we doubt, that is to say, that he is nearly as sure of himself or of his subject as he would have us believe. For he . . . is writing with one eye on Europe, a division of attention which the reader is quick to feel and resent. He . . . has the American self-consciousness, though it is masterfully suppressed and allowed only to utter itself once or twice in a sharp cry of bitterness ("Babbitt was as much amused by the antiquated provincialism as any proper Englishman by any American"). But the uneasiness is there. He has not identified himself with America; rather he has constituted himself the guide and interpreter between the Americans and the English, and, as he conducts his party of Europeans over the typical American city (of which he is a native) and shows them the typical American citizen (to whom he is related) he is equally divided between shame at what he has to show and anger at the Europeans for laughing at it. Zenith is a despicable place, but the English are even more despicable for despising it. (pp. 118-19)

Mr. Lewis it would seem was meant by nature to take his place with Mr. [H. G.] Wells and Mr. [Arnold] Bennett, and had he been born in England would undoubtedly have proved himself the equal of these two famous men. Denied, however, the richness of an old civilisation—the swarm of ideas upon which the art of Mr. Wells has battened, the solidity of custom which has nourished the art of Mr. Bennett—he has been forced to criticise rather than to explore, and the object of his criticism—the civilisation of Zenith—was unfortunately too meagre to sustain him. (pp. 121-22)

Virginia Woolf, "American Fiction," in her *The Moment and Other Essays*, 1947. Reprint by Harcourt Brace Jovanovich, Inc., 1948, pp. 113-27.

JAMES BRANCH CABELL
(essay date 1930)

[Cabell's novels, which combine extremes of lavish romance and degraded reality, idealistic fantasy and jaded disillusionment, are among the outstanding oddities in American fiction. His most enduring achievement, *The Biography of Manuel* (1904-29), belongs to a tradition of fantasy literature that includes Edmund Spenser's *The Faerie Queene* (1590-96) and Jonathan Swift's *Gulliver's Travels* (1726). In the following excerpt, Cabell praises Lewis as the creator of exaggerated literary types and likens him, in this respect, to Charles Dickens.]

I perceive some merit in Sinclair Lewis, even though I fail to detect it upon the grounds usually advanced. People who ought to know a great deal better will tell you that Sinclair Lewis has portrayed many aspects of our American life. In fact, when *Babbitt* and *Main Street* were but lately included in the library presented to President Herbert C. Hoover, it was upon the tactless ground, as stated by one of the selectors, that "the reading of them will help a man to understand the temperament of the American people." I put aside the ineluctable inference—as being an over-blunt if unintentional criticism of our first British President's conduct in office,—and I remark merely that I do not think the statement itself is true.

I shall come back to that. Meanwhile, in whatsoever milieu, Mr. Lewis throughout the deceased 'twenties dealt incessantly with one single problem: whether or not it is better to do that which seems expected? As long ago as in the autumn of 1920, in *Main Street*, the question was raised whether Carol Kennicott should or should not conform to what Gopher Prairie expected? The question was given perhaps its most nearly classic form in *Babbitt*, wherein the protagonist fidgets before this problem, of conforming or of not conforming, in connection with well-nigh all departments of life as it is led in Zenith the Zip City. Then Mr. Lewis turned to the especial variant of the same problem as it concerns the scientist, in *Arrowsmith;* in *Elmer Gantry* he brought the minister of the gospel face to face with this problem; and finally, in 1929, he confronted Sam Dodsworth with the problem (already touched upon in *Mantrap*) of conforming or of not conforming to that which seemed expected in—of all avocations—the pursuit of pleasure. (pp. 61-2)

Mr. Lewis does not ever answer [the] question outright: but he does very insistently compel his readers to cast about for an answer. Time and again Sinclair Lewis has exalted the bravery if not precisely the wisdom of individualism by the roundabout method of depicting the conformist. There is, he has discovered, a great deal of humbug and stupidity and viciousness going about masked as the correct thing to do in every walk of life as life speeds in Winnemac, the home of manly men and of womanly women and of other Regular Guys. And Mr. Lewis portrays with loving abhorrence superb monsters, now and then a bit suggestive of human beings, who make the very best (in an entirely utilitarian sense) of this humbug and of this stupidity and of this viciousness, to enhance their own moral standing and bank accounts.

I said, he portrays. Yet Sinclair Lewis is far too opulently gifted to have to plagiarize his manly men and his womanly women from the life about him. He has turned instead—compelled it may be by those freakish planets which ruled over the date of his birth,—to commemorate a more striking race, [that of Charles Dickens]. (p. 63)

In every book by Dickens the backbone of all is optimism and a fixed faith that by-and-by justice and candor will prevail. (p. 65)

The doctrine of Mr. Lewis would seem to run quite the other way. In book after book he has presented one or another individualist at least as truly heroic as ever was young Martin Chuzzlewit [in Dickens's *The Life and Adventures of Martin Chuzzlewit*], and an individualist who, in opposing the solicitations of the elvish burghers of Winnemac, remains theoretically in the right, but who ends as a rule in material ruin and who ends always in defeat. I shall not labor this point, because Mr. Lewis himself does not make much of it. He does but indicate, by sketching lightly the career of a Frank Shallard or of a Max Gottlieb, the truism that in Winnemac as elsewhere the opponent of any communal folly is in for a bad time of it. These adventurers find that the old recipe, of not conforming to that which the goblins urge them to do, is of no least avail to deliver them from the goblins of Winnemac. Instead, the Rev. Dr. Elmer Gantry and the Honorable Almus Pickerbaugh are with them to the very end, in some not unfriendly bewilderment as to why the poor mutt should have opposed the *mores* of Winnemac when he could so easily have made use of these fantasies to enhance his moral standing and his bank account.

This is a tragedy, I repeat, which Mr. Lewis does but indicate. His real interest turns other-whither as though bewitched by the quaintness of the commonplace. It remains fascinated by the conformist and by the droll ways of his goblin flourishing (wherein timidity turns to sound money and lies become limousines) at the cost of intellectual and spiritual ruin. The individualist is lost in a world made over-safe for democracy; and the conformist becomes not worth saving. That is the doctrine which informs all the derisive apologues

Sinclair Lewis has fetched out of Winnemac. That is, in one sense, the powder which speeds his every shot at our polity. In another sense it is the powder disguised in the succulent jam of his caricatures.

So it has been throughout the ten years since Mr. Lewis first toyed with his pet problem in Gopher Prairie. He then told us, with a mendacity which time and his later books have coöperated to expose, that Gopher Prairie was a small town in Minnesota. We all know now that Gopher Prairie—like Zenith and Monarch and Sparta and Banjo Crossing, and like every other place that Mr. Lewis has written about since 1920,—is a portion of the grotesque and yet always rather sinister, strange goblin land of Winnemac.

I delight in Winnemac and in all its citizenry: yet it is, as I have suggested, with very much the same pleasure I derive from Dickens. That pleasure is, to the one side, somewhat the pleasure I get from the "Mr. and Mrs." cartoons in the Sunday paper and from Amos and Andy over the radio, and (to the other side) from a great deal of Molière and Swift and Aristophanes and Lucian,—the pleasure, that is, of seeing a minim of reality exaggerated into Brobdingnagian incredibility. There is apparent in each that single grain of truth which has budded, through more or less skilled and patient gardening, into this gaudy efflorescence of the impossible. The seed explains the flowering: but it is the flowering which counts, and which charms. So when I hear Sinclair Lewis classed as a "realist," it is with something of the same wonderment in which I have heard that he lives, along with Messrs. Dreiser and Cabell and Anderson, in a never lifting atmosphere of despair and frustration. (pp. 66-9)

If you can believe in the "realism" of Sinclair Lewis it will give you a great deal more of comfort than does any other "realism." For my part, I can but protest that I very heartily enjoy his books without any more believing in Almus Pickerbaugh and Elmer Gantry and the other hobgoblins as persons whom one may hope to encounter in our imperfect world than I can believe (after any such literal fashion) in Joe and Vi, or in Jefferson Brick and Colonel Diver, or, for that matter, in Bottom and Caliban.

Meanwhile if, as one hears freely nowadays, Sinclair Lewis is obsolescent, and his books are doomed, the trouble is not merely that the United States is due to lose one of its most interesting commonwealths, in the State of Winnemac. For one really wonders what in the world is to be done about George Follansbee Babbitt? Just eight years ago this Babbitt emigrated from 401 pages of a novel into the racial consciousness of mankind. He is one of those satisfying large symbols which at long intervals some author hits upon, and which promptly take on a life that is not confined to the books wherein they first figured. Babbitt is in train, I think, to become one of those myths which rove forev-

er through the irrational Marches of Antan, and about which writers not yet born will weave their own pet stories as inevitably as writers will continue to concern themselves with Faust and Don Juan and the Brown God Pan. (pp. 69-71)

James Branch Cabell, "Goblins in Winnemac," in his *Some of Us: An Essay in Epitaphs,* Robert M. McBride & Company, 1930, pp. 59-73.

GRANVILLE HICKS
(essay date 1935)

[In 1933 Hicks published his famous Marxist study *The Great Tradition: An Interpretation of American Literature since the Civil War.* Throughout the 1930s, he argued for a more socially engaged brand of literature that confronts rather than provides refuge from the realities of society. In the following excerpt from *The Great Tradition*, he examines what he perceives as the strengths and weaknesses of Lewis's vision and work.]

In Sinclair Lewis we have to reckon with a different kind of talent, neither Dreiser's massiveness nor Anderson's penetration. Lewis is the shrewd reporter, armed with the skepticism and frankness of his generation, the shrewd reporter with a chip on his shoulder. For six years he wrote books in which he gave free play neither to his powers of observation nor to his acute exasperation with his complacent contemporaries. *Main Street* . . . he wrote deliberately, as a foreword shows, to expose "our comfortable tradition and sure faith," to "betray himself as an alien cynic," and to "distress the citizens by speculating whether there may not be other faiths." Its success pointed to the existence of other persons not quite convinced that "Main Street is the climax of civilization."

Once he had abandoned himself to his temperament and his talents, Lewis took his place among the recorders of the contemporary scene. With systematic zeal he has described the small town, the prosperous mid-western city, and the great metropolis, and he has written of business, medicine, the church, and social work. If what one wants is the detailed, accurate record of the way people live, Lewis is the most satisfying of our authors. What Carol Kennicott saw in Gopher Prairie might be seen in thousands of American communities; the day in Babbitt's life that Lewis so minutely records has been duplicated in the lives of tens of thousands of small business men; it is to the keeping of such doctors as Martin Arrowsmith met in Wheatsylvania, Nautilus, and the McGurk Institute that our lives are entrusted. About the middle stratum of the population, the moderately prosperous professional and business men, Lewis has written with a keenness of eye and an alertness of ear that any novelist might envy him.

In the books of these three authors we have the best that the middle generation has contributed to the study of the contemporary scene. They have brought our literature closer to the center of American life, and we can rejoice in Dreiser's strength, Lewis's shrewdness, and Anderson's sensitivity. But can we be satisfied with their work? We are grieved, of course, by such things as Dreiser's clumsiness, Anderson's frequent obscurity, Lewis's reliance on mimicry; but these are superficial faults, lamentable but chiefly significant as symptoms of more serious failures. Dreiser seems always to be heavily stalking some secret that constantly eludes him. The brilliant flash of Anderson's imagination illuminates a tiny spot in a black night of mystery. Lewis's amusing chatter fails to conceal his blind helplessness. (pp. 230-31)

Sinclair Lewis, though he became interested in socialism many years ago, has not joined Dreiser and Anderson in endorsing the Communist Party. In *Ann Vickers* the heroine recognizes a certain validity in the communist position, but she is irritated by the fanaticism of a party member she knows, and in any case her life is too full for her to limit herself to a particular program. Lewis is rather like her. In his own way he perfectly illustrates the middle-class contradiction. . . . The side of him that secretly sympathizes with Will Kennicott and George Babbitt lends authority to his portraits, and the side of him that damns them gives his books their salt.

Criticism and satire imply the conception of a better way of life. Lewis knows what he would like to destroy—provincialism, complacency, hypocrisy, intellectual timidity, and similar faults—but he has only the vaguest idea of what kind of society he would like to see in existence. Carol Kennicott's attempts to reform Gopher Prairie are not only futile; they reveal standards almost as inadequate as those of the villagers. George Babbitt's only guides, as he goes along the path of revolt, are the old-fashioned liberalism of Seneca Doane and the dull bohemianism of the Bunch. Beside Elmer Gantry's foul hypocrisy Lewis can place only the weak modernism of Frank Shallard and the sentimental piety of Father Pengilly; he is as incapable of revealing the strength of the church as he is of expounding the nature of honest, intelligent atheism. Dodsworth returns from Europe, freed from subservience to both the narrow American idea of success and the narrow European idea of culture; and he returns to build better houses—an experiment in constructive capitalism in which Jack London's Elam Harnish had already anticipated him. Ann Vickers, who wants a career and has one, finds happiness in a man and a baby. The man, Judge Dolphin, seems to be Lewis's ideal, a straight-

shooting he-man who plays the game; and he is one of the few characters in Lewis's books that are completely unconvincing. Only once, in all his novels, has Lewis succeeded in creating a worthy antagonist to the myriad of petty-minded men he has described: in *Arrowsmith* Max Gottlieb's devotion to pure science is both convincing and admirable.

Arrowsmith is Lewis's strongest and most unified novel. In *Main Street* and *Babbitt* he showed his keenness of eye and ear and his sharpness of tongue; but the very effectiveness of his satire compelled him to speak in positive as well as negative terms, and in *Arrowsmith* he succeeded in doing so. Lewis's discovery of the scientific method as a possible alternative to the confusion of the age was, as has been noted, characteristic of the middle generation. And for the moment his assumptions worked. But pure science operates in too narrow a field to provide a theory and an attitude for a social critic, and Lewis could not establish the relevance of science to his own interests. He was thus forced back into his old confusion, and his superficiality became increasingly apparent. *Elmer Gantry, Dodsworth,* and *Ann Vickers* are inferior to *Main Street, Babbitt,* and *Arrowsmith. Ann Vickers* not only is less unified than *Arrowsmith,* which in its general outlines it resembles; it shows less interest in the characteristic details of American life and is less convincing in the handling of detail; its satire is diffused, and Lewis's old power of indignation is felt only in the description of Copperhead Gap Penitentiary; the ending is a peculiarly painful confession of surrender to standards the satirist has pretended to scorn. Lewis's virtues were never enough, and he is losing those virtues.

Not only is the absence of adequate comprehension itself a weakness in the work of Dreiser, Anderson, and Lewis; it accounts for many of their other faults. . . . Lewis, acute as he is in noting revealing mannerisms and tricks of speech, has only created two or three rounded personalities.

However, with all their faults, these three writers are far more important than Mrs. Wharton, Miss Cather, Hergesheimer, and Cabell. Not only have they achieved more; their failures have more significance for the future of American literature than the successes of the others. Their work was a natural development of the tendencies of the muckrakers. Less concerned with specific reforms, they had the same interest in the dominant tendencies of American life. And they made real advances over the muckrakers: they ended the tyranny of boarding school standards; they substituted the fresh, natural speech of the people for the language of books; they created a certain number of convincing and representative men and women. The novel grew in their hands, but the great central problem— emphasized by the failures of all the realists from Howells on—was left unsolved. (pp. 234-37)

Lewis at Villa La Costa, Florence, 1950.

Granville Hicks, "Two Roads," in his *The Great Tradition: An Interpretation of American Literature since the Civil War,* revised edition, Macmillan Publishing Company, 1935, pp. 207-56.

MARK SCHORER

(essay date 1969)

[Schorer wrote many essays on Lewis as well as his definitive biography. In the following excerpt from an essay first published in 1969 in *Landmarks of American Writing,* he closely examines the compositional technique of *Babbitt.*]

It has been fashionable since some time before his death in 1951 to say that Sinclair Lewis' fiction has nothing now to say to Americans, and nothing to say any longer that is centrally relevant to American life. Americans no longer talk like Lewis' characters, it is asserted, if indeed they ever did. Sinclair Lewis is dead! To the bulk of his twenty-one novels and to almost the

entire mass of his shorter fiction, the charge is probably applicable enough, but to three or four or possibly even five novels, above all, to *Babbitt,* it is not. (p. 105)

Main Street was published in 1920. This story about the sluggish backwaters of American village life was published in the year that officially announced American village life to have become a backwater. The 1920 census showed that at some point between 1915 and that year American society had crossed a line from what had been a rural to what had become an urban society. Sometime between those years, the old majority of farmers and villagers had become the minority, and the residents of cities comprised the new majority. *Babbitt* opens in April 1920. It is concerned not only with the new urban society but also with certain new urban attitudes that attach to American commercial culture: the idea of "boosting," for example, that aggressive promotion of special civic interests that finally finds its apotheosis in our enormous system of Public Relations; and that idea of business "service" to the community, which bears the same relationship to the actual practices of commercialism as the idea of "the white man's burden" bears to the actualities of imperialism and colonialism. Yet it shows us, too, how the residents of Zenith, booming the city, profess still much of the rural faith of their fathers, and how from this conflict between old and newer attitudes proceed frustration, guilt, despair of a watered kind, at last emptiness. (pp. 107-08)

Babbitt is a satiric prelude to a decade of dizzying and often mindless economic expansion, the epic of our "boom" years, and it remains today the major documentation in literature of American business culture in general. We can no longer say, as Woodrow Wilson said in 1900, that "The history of a nation is only the history of its villages written large." By 1920, we substitute for *village* the name of *Zenith.*

As we see Zenith looming beyond Gopher Prairie, so we see Gopher Prairie still in the process of receding in Zenith. On the first page "the mist took pity on the fretted structures of earlier generations: the Post Office with its shingle-tortured mansard, the red brick minarets of hulking old houses. . . . " There is the explicit contrast between Babbitt and his father-in-law, Henry Thompson, between "the old-fashioned, lean Yankee, rugged, traditional stage type of American business man, and Babbitt, the plump, smooth, efficient, up-to-the-minute and otherwise perfected modern." The ironic limitations of this contrast are underlined in the discussion of small towns at the Babbitts' first dinner party in the novel, when the talk of the whole company, consisting of the emptiest banalities and comprising a pure parody of any interchange that could be called conversation, laments the absence of meaningful conversation and "culture" in the "hick towns" that Chum

---

Major Media Adaptations: Motion Pictures

Newly Rich, 1931. Paramount. [Adaptation of "Let's Play King"] Director: Norman Taurog. Cast: Mitzi Green, Edna May Oliver, Louise Fazenda, Jackie Searl, Bruce Line, Virginia Hammond, Dell Henderson.

Arrowsmith, 1932. United Artists. Director: John Ford. Cast: Ronald Colman, Helen Hayes, Myrna Loy, Richard Bennett, Beulah Bondi, A. C. Anson.

Ann Vickers, 1933. RKO. Director: John Cromwell. Cast: Irene Dunne, Walter Huston, Conrad Nagel, Bruce Cabot, Edna May Oliver, Sam Hardy, Mitchell Lewis.

Babbitt, 1934. Warner. Director: William Keighley. Cast: Guy Kibbee, Aline MacMahon, Claire Dodd, Maxine Doyle, Glen Boles, Minna Gombell, Alan Hale, Berton Churchill, Russell Hicks, Nan Grey.

Dodsworth, 1936. United Artists. Director: William Wyler. Cast: Walter Huston, Mary Astor, David Niven, Ruth Chatterton, Paul Lukas, Gregory Gaye, Maria Ouspenskaya, Odette Myrtil, Spring Byington, John Payne.

I Married a Doctor, 1936. Warner. [Adaptation of *Main Street*] Director: Archie L. Mayo. Cast: Pat O'Brien, Josephine Hutchinson, Ross Alexander, Guy Kibbee, Louise Fazenda, Olin Howland, Margaret Irving, Alma Lloyd, Grace Stafford, Ray Mayer.

Untamed, 1940. Paramount. [Adaption of *Mantrap*] Director: George Archainbaud. Cast: Ray Milland, Patricia Morison, Akim Tamiroff, William Frawley, Jane Darwell, Esther Dale, J. M. Kerrigan, Eily Malyon.

This Is the Life, 1944. Universal. [Adaptation of "Angela is 22"] Director: Felix Feist. Cast: Donald O'Connor, Susanna Foster, Peggy Ryan, Louise Allbritton, Patric Knowles, Dorothy Peterson, Jonathan Hale, Eddie Quillan, Otto Hoffman, Frank Jenks.

Cass Timberlane, 1947. MGM. Director: George Sidney. Cast: Spencer Tracy, Lana Turner, Zachary Scott, Mary Astor, Tom Drake, Albert Dekker, Selena Royle, Josephine Hutchinson, Margaret Lindsay, John Litel, Mona Barrie.

Elmer Gantry, 1960. United Artists. Director: Richard Brooks. Cast: Burt Lancaster, Shirley Jones, Jean Simmons, Arthur Kennedy, Dean Jagger, Edward Andrews, Patti Page, John McIntire.

Frink, "a Famous Poet and a distinguished advertising agent," has just been touring.

Physically, the culture has become predominantly urban; but psychologically it is in large part still stubbornly rural, perhaps even more profoundly provincial than before. . . . [The] whole aim of the documentation of *Babbitt* is to demonstrate that with the cultural shift, the slavery of the individual has become even more rigid, that freedom exists only in impossibly infantile, whimpering dreams.

I have twice used the word *documentation,* and quite intentionally. *Babbitt* is the first of Lewis' novels that rests on what was henceforth to be his characteristic method of "research." His preceding five novels had shown traces of similar "research," but now it becomes nearly systematic. He established a *pied-à-terre* ["base of operations"] at the Queen City Club in Cincinnati, Ohio, and if Zenith is modeled on any one city, it is this one. Here he consolidated his researches, and his gray notebooks were already fat with his notation.

The method involved a series of steps. First, he chose a subject and a "field" within it to be mastered—not, as for most novelists, a character situation or a mere theme, but a social area (a sub-class within the middle class) that could be studied and "worked up"—in this instance, the world of the small businessman and within that, real estate. Then, armed with his notebooks, he mingled with the kind of people that the fiction would mainly concern. In Pullman cars and smokers, in the lobbies of side-street hotels, in athletic clubs, in a hundred junky streets he watched and listened, and then meticulously copied into his notebooks whole catalogs of expressions drawn from the American lingo, elaborate lists of proper names, every kind of physical detail. Once his story was determined, he drew intricately detailed maps, and maps not only of the city in which the story was set but of the houses in which his actions would take place, floor plans with furniture precisely located, streets and the kind and color of dogs that walked on them. Once his chief characters were settled upon, he wrote out full biographies of all of them. From this body of material, he would then write out a summary of his story, and from this, a much more extended "plan," as he called it, with every scene sketched in, the whole sometimes nearly as long as the book that would come from it. A first draft would then follow, usually much longer than the final version, and then a long process of revision and cutting, and at last the publishable text. (pp. 109-10)

The immediate result is not surprising even though the ultimate effect may be. The immediate result is a fictional approximation of the social anthropologist's field report. A year after the publication of *Babbitt,* when asked about its origins, Lewis said that all he could remember was that the original name of the protagonist was Pumphrey and that "I planned to make the whole novel 24 hours in his life, from alarm clock to alarm clock. The rest came more or less unconsciously." . . . The name *Pumphrey* remained as that of a minor character—"Professor Joseph K. Pumphrey, owner of the Riteway Business College and instructor in Public Speaking, Business English, Scenario Writing, and Commercial Law"—and the original structural conception remained in the first seven chapters, in which we do indeed follow George Babbitt from dreaming sleep to dreaming sleep. But that is only one-fourth of the whole novel.

The remainder, twenty-seven chapters, did not come about "unconsciously," as their obviously planned substance makes very clear. They are, rather than "unconscious," a quite highly conscious, indeed systematic series of set pieces, each with its own topic, and all together giving us an almost punctilious analysis of the sociology of American commercial culture and middle-class life. Over halfway through the novel, mingling with these set pieces, the first of three "plots" begins.

These twenty-seven chapters could well have carried, in the convention of earlier fiction, subject titles. Chapters Eight and Nine, in which the Babbitts entertain at dinner in their Floral Heights house, could have been called Domestic Manners of the Americans. The next two chapters might have been headed Marital Relations and Pullman Car Customs. Chapter Twelve is about Leisure: baseball, golf, the movies, bridge, motoring. Chapter Thirteen takes up the phenomenon of the annual Trade Association Convention and, since it ends with some adult but immature louts in a brothel, Juvenile Delinquency. Chapter Fourteen has to do with Political and Professional Oratory, and Fifteen, with Class Structure. The next two chapters devote themselves to Religion, and Eighteen, to Family Relations. The first of the three separate "plots" begins in the next chapter, Nineteen, and delaying discussion of these for a moment, we may observe that the general topics remaining are the weekly Service Club Lunch, the Bachelor, the Barber Shop, Labor Relations, the Speakeasy, and "Crank" Religion. It is a very thorough canvassing of an entire milieu, and its nearly anthropological intention is made evident in such a sentence as "Now this was the manner of obtaining alcohol under the reign of righteousness and prohibition," the sentence that introduces Babbitt's visit to a bootlegger.

If the canvas that these pieces comprise is surprisingly complete, their ordering is nevertheless quite haphazard. They might have been presented in almost any other sequence, and that is because there is no genuine plot or coherent, causative march of dramatic events from beginning to end and that would necessarily have determined their order. Their fragmentariness is in part overcome by the fact that it is the single figure of Babbitt who moves through all of them in the course of his mounting discontent, revolt, his retreat and relapse into resignation. (pp. 111-12)

It is Babbitt's tragedy that he can never be anything but Babbitt, even though he has a glimmering recognition of what it is about being Babbitt that he does not always like. . . . The terror and loneliness that he feels in his brief taste of freedom (and that freedom itself consists largely of a very "mechanical" bit of adultery) arise from the fact that when he is free he is nothing at all. His only self is the self that exists solely within the circle of conformity.

Since the publication of *Babbitt,* everyone has learned that conformity is the great price that our predominantly commercial culture exacts of American life. But when *Babbitt* was published, this was its revelation to Americans, and this was likewise how the novel differed from all novels about business that had been published before it.

American literature had a rich if brief tradition of the business novel. Henry James, William Dean Howells, Charles and Frank Norris, Jack London, David Graham Phillips, Robert Herrick, Upton Sinclair, Edith Wharton, Theodore Dreiser, Ernest Poole, Booth Tarkington—all these writers and others as well had been concerned with the businessman, and after James and Howells, only Tarkington was to find in him any of the old, perdurable American virtues. Business was synonymous with ethical corruption; the world of business was savagely competitive, brutally aggressive, murderous. The motivation of the businessman was power, money, social prestige, in that order. But the businessman in all this fiction was the tycoon, the powerful manufacturer, the vast speculator, the fabulous financier, the monarch of enormous enterprises, the arch-individual responsible only to himself. He was the equivalent in the developing industrial world of the old, aggressively independent frontiersman. And his concern was with production, if only of more money from money.

After the First World War and our shift to an urban culture, the tycoon may still have been the most colorful and dramatic figure in the business myth, but he was no longer by any means the characteristic figure, and *Babbitt* discovers that difference. If George F. Babbitt has vague hankerings after the old frontier independence, his incompetence in that role is made plain enough by his ridiculous vacation excursions into Maine. His is the shriveled office world of the small businessman, and more particularly, of the small middleman. If his morals are no better, his defections are anything but spectacular: a little cheating in a deal, a little lie to one's wife, a little stealthy fornication that one pretends did not occur. Not in the least resembling the autocratic individualist, he is always the compromising conformist. No producer himself, his success depends on public relations. He does not rule; he "joins" to be safe. He boosts and boasts with his fellows, sings and cheers and prays with the throng, derides all difference, denounces all dissent—and all to climb with the crowd. With the supremacy of public relations, he abolishes human relations. And finally, therefore, without at all knowing it, he abolishes all but a wretched remnant of his own humanity.

All this Sinclair Lewis' novel gave back to a culture that was just becoming aware that it would not be able to tolerate what it was in the process of making itself. And his novel did it with a difference. The older novels, generally speaking, were solemn or grandly melodramatic denunciations of monstrous figures of aggressive evil. *Babbitt* was raucously satirical of a crowd of ninnies and buffoons who, if they were vindictive and petty, were also absurd. Yet, along with all that, Babbitt himself was pathetic. How could the novel possibly have failed? It did not. It was one of the greatest international successes in all publishing history.

The European response was unadulterated delight: this was the way—crass, materialistic, complacent, chauvinistic—that Europe had always known America to be, and now an American had made the confession to the world. In the United States the response was, understandably, more diluted. Among those who were either unimpressed or outraged, there was, however, a small complaint on the score of the deficiencies of *Babbitt* as a novel. No one, for example, observed the slack structure, or the repetitiousness of point in the long series of sociological demonstrations. Edith Wharton, in her letter of congratulations to Lewis, did recognize that he seemed to depend on an excess of slang, on nearly endless imitation of midwestern garrulity; but this did not bother others. Had anyone complained, for example, that in his use of public addresses of one sort or another, Lewis' pleasure in mimicry threatened to carry him far beyond the demands of his fiction, it could have been pointed out that here is a very integral part of his satire. Elocution is an old American institution, and a windy, mindless rhetoric has been of its essence, as the oratory at the conventions of either of our chief political parties still painfully reminds us. Lewis' use of elocution adds a swelling note to the already loud *blat-blat* of the public voice that roars and rattles through the novel, and if Lewis lets Babbitt admire Chan Mott because he "can make a good talk even when he hasn't got a doggone thing to say," he is also making an observation on the empty and noisy restlessness of American life.

It was not generally the writing, nor even Lewis' satiric exposure of American commercial culture in itself that disturbed those readers who were disturbed, but rather their failure to find in the novel anything beyond this grossness. With George Santayana, who was otherwise impressed by the novel, they saw "no suggestion of the direction . . . in which salvation may come." The complaint was to say of Lewis, in effect, what Lewis had himself said of Babbitt, that he was "without a canon [of value] which would enable him to speak with authority." If Babbitt, with his faint sense that the values of excellence, joy, passion, wisdom, do indeed exist somewhere, but had not the slightest notion of how to pursue them, did Sinclair Lewis?

It became a commonplace to say of Lewis that he

was himself too much a George F. Babbitt to lift his sights to values beyond Babbitt's own. In many ways the charge is just. But Lewis is different from Babbitt in one supreme way: he *observed* him, and Babbitt had not been observed before; thus he *created* him; and Babbitt endures in our literature as in our life, where Sinclair Lewis enabled all of us to see him for the first and for an enduring time.

He endures with a special kind of solidity and vitality. He is so inexhaustibly *there.* This achievement obviously derives from Lewis' technique. That mass of social notation that we have remarked, notation that Lewis pursued with all the naturalist's compulsiveness, is yet, in the end, not at all a naturalistic performance. It shares rather in the realm of what today we call Pop Art. Take any very mundane item from our daily lives—a Campbell's Soup can, for example; observe it in the most exact and even microscopic detail; then enlarge it; then repeat it over and over in the monotonous design; and at last something *not* naturalistic but rather grotesque and even monstrous emerges, and something in the end much more substantial than the absurdity from which it is constructed.

It was this quality that Constance Rourke had in mind in 1931 when she singled Lewis out among his contemporaries: "With one exception none of those definitive novelists have appeared who make an aspect of contemporary life their own and leave it with the color of their imagination upon it forever afterward. The exception of course is Sinclair Lewis. . . ." The term *novelist* in the usual sense was not quite right for him. She gave him, and we do still, the larger title: *fabulist.* (pp. 113-16)

Mark Schorer, "Sinclair Lewis: 'Babbitt'," in *The Merrill Studies in "Babbitt,"* edited by Martin Light, Charles E. Merrill Publishing Company, 1971, pp. 105-16.

ANTHONY CHANNELL HILFER
(essay date 1969)

[In the following excerpt, Hilfer offers a close textual and thematic analysis of *Main Street* and *Babbitt,* asserting that each indicates small-town values without suggesting a constructive alternative.]

Many critics see *Main Street* and Lewis' other novels only as sociological and historical events: superficial and intrinsically valueless reflections of a widespread discontent with old values. Lewis is attacked for the very faults his fiction satirizes: the banality and Babbittry that he does, in truth, partially share with his characters. Lewis lacks very obviously the psychological penetration and the subjective sensibility that modern criticism does well to value. His characters are, it is true, all surface, no depth, but Lewis' talent lies precisely in the incisiveness and suggestiveness of his delineations of the social surface, his unmasking of the dominant middle class. As a sociological satirist, Lewis deserves critical attention and respect.

Lewis' best novels are sociological in content and, to a large extent, in form. Mark Schorer notes, "With Lewis, the subject, the social section, always came first; systematic research, sometimes conducted by research assistants and carrying Lewis himself into 'the field' like any cultural anthropologist, followed; the story came last, devised to carry home and usually limping under the burden of data." Lewis conceived of novels in sociological terms. *Main Street* is a fictional study of the small town, *Babbitt* is a study of the "businessman," later novels deal with a social worker (*Ann Vickers*), with organized "philanthropy" (*Gideon Planish*), and the "race problem" (*Kingsblood Royal*). The structure of his novels is often sociological. The first seven chapters of *Babbitt,* for instance, are based on the businessman's day—a standard sociological method—followed by twenty-seven chapters built around sociological topics that reflect various aspects of bourgeois manners and mores. Finally, the intended and actual importance of *Main Street* and *Babbitt* is as cultural critiques.

Lewis even makes half-hearted efforts toward the fairness and objectivity that sociologists strive for, but Lewis is not fair and not objective; like Mencken he uses sociology as a satirical weapon. In one sense, Gopher Prairie and Babbitt are sociological ideal types. The most general and essential qualities of small towns and of businessmen are abstracted and then put together in the concrete image of the ideal type: Gopher Prairie is the typical town; Babbitt, the archetypal businessman. But the image is stacked, and tendentious; the portraits are caricatures. (pp. 158-59)

Main Street is a sociological caricature unmasking the small town. (p. 160)

In sociological manner, Lewis attacks false stereotypes of the small town. The stereotype of the hick town populated by comic farmers with whiskers is, Lewis notes, forty years out of date. The 1920 small town differs from the city mostly in negative terms: it has the same standardized products but with less a variety, the same social and political orthodoxies but with less dissent. The more popular stereotype is that "the American village remains the one sure abode of friendship, honesty, and clean sweet marriageable girls." To this favorable stereotype, Lewis opposes his caricature: Gopher Prairie, a sketch unifying the physiognomy of the town into a single expression of mechanical and fatuous dullness.

The ideas behind Lewis' image come from several sources. Like Van Wyck Brooks, Lewis was what might be termed an aesthetic socialist in the tradition of Ruskin and Morris. The physical ugliness of the village, from this point of view, reflects its dearth of spiritual values. Church, school, and post office are all shabby, but the bank is an "ionic temple of marble. Pure, exquisite, solitary." . . . Lewis overrates bank architecture, but the spiritual stature of finance as contrasted to church and state is clearly established. As an aesthetic socialist, Lewis blames the ugliness of the town on its lack of a guiding and unifying spiritual ideal—the *sine qua non* of all great architecture in the view of the Victorian culture critics. In Brooksian fashion, Lewis blames the hangover of pioneer values for the "planlessness, the flimsy temporariness of the buildings." . . . The town is a frontier outpost that has lost its vigor and its contact with nature without gaining culture.

Main Street also has the Brooksian buried life, though treated with gross and clumsy clichés. The Vida Sherwin of *Main Street* is an unintentional parody of Masters and Anderson. "She lived an engrossed useful life, and seemed as cool and simple as an apple. But secretly she was creeping among fears, longing, and guilt. She knew what it was, but she dared not name it. She hated even the sound of the word 'sex'." (pp. 161-62)

Lewis did not have to have read Brooks to pick up such ideas. They were in the air though Brooks was their most influential exponent. Such is the case with Thorstein Veblen, as well, but it is hard to believe Lewis' later claim that he had never read Veblen. *The Job,* an earlier novel, seems to reflect Veblen, as do *Main Street* and *Babbitt.* At any rate, Lewis' characters read Veblen: Carol Kennicott and Miles Bjornstam are Veblen readers. . . . When Carol decides that the most properly subversive thing she could do would be "asking people to define their jobs," . . . she is talking Veblen's language. Much of Veblen's writings consist of vituperative redefinitions of economic functions which unmask the merchant class as exploitative and parasitic. Lewis makes it clear that Gopher Prairie lives off the farmers whom the town despises, overcharges, and cheats.

The central influence on *Main Street,* as later on *Babbitt* and *Elmer Gantry,* was H. L. Mencken. For what most bothers Carol is not the ugliness of the town, not its injustice, but the soul-destroying intellectual conformity that leads to a pervasive and inescapable dullness.

Percy Boynton has commented that the reader has difficulty remembering individual characters by the end of the book. The characters are indistinguishable because, though some are kinder or better-natured, they all think in the same clichés. The sociology of the book is Mencken's and Sumner's: the group mind thinks in stock formulas and is controlled by group conventions. (pp. 162-63)

The townspeople completely lack the sympathetic and the critical imagination. They are as unable to conceive of the possibility of anyone outside their own class having a mind or emotions as they are to conceive of the possibility that any value of the in-group might be wrong. They are in mental prisons, able to see the world only through the narrow slits of self-interest and accepted ideas. In such a world, critical thought cannot exist, and conversation consists either of the ritual chanting of orthodoxies or of gossip about personalities. As for personality, the villagers discuss it at the lowest level of superficiality. Someone's personality is forever fixed and tagged by some ancient joke or scandal about him or by some peculiarity of manner or physique.

This anatomy of provincialism still holds fairly true: provincial people are closed-minded and unable to cope with objective thought. Worse yet, they really believe in the mythology of the small town: that it is decent, moral, democratic, honest, God's own country, etc. This is what most irritates Lewis' heroine, Carol Kennicott. The villagers have faith in their superiority to the undemocratic East, but in reality the town is a "sterile oligarchy." . . . The final straw for Carol is the town's boosting campaign: "she could, she asserted, endure a shabby but modest town; the town shabby but egomaniac she could not endure." . . . Like most satirists Lewis was less irritated by the dreariness of his targets than by their complacent pride in their dreariness. His satire is an attack on the pride of what seemed to be a village civilization newly inflated to a world power. . . . (pp. 163-64)

Lewis, then, exaggerates the actual power of the American small town but not its mythic significance. He attacks widespread American provincialism at its symbolic source. The popularity of *Main Street* is not hard to account for; the myth it deflates was—like all combinations of pride, hypocrisy, smugness, and meanness—ripe for unmasking and a vast amount of irritation was released by the public exposure of what everyone really knew.

Lewis' anatomy of provincialism is accurate but it is also old hat. No one is likely to be surprised by anything in *Main Street.* Lewis has become so assimilated as to become almost obsolescent. This could not happen to an author who *renders* human experience, but *Main Street* is largely editorial; we are told about, rather than shown, the town. Its gossips and dullards never come to life even in their deadness so that the weakest passages in the novel are those in which Lewis has dialogue or action. Even at the level of abstract editorializing, Lewis' ideas are trite and obvious. His exposure of small towns never cuts to the bone as Mark Twain's often does. There is a more intense vision of human meanness in two or three passages of "The Man That Corrupted Hadleyburg" than in all of Lewis' overstuffed novel.

Lewis' banal style is another element contributing to the loss of favor his writings have suffered. He should, however, be granted the virtues of his vices: his personal superficiality is mirrored in his style, but so is his intense nervous vitality; his writing is thin but electric.

Even 1920 readers were irritated by Carol Kennicott, though many thought Lewis intended her to seem ridiculous. Some modern readers like to suppose, conversely, that Lewis has no idea of his heroine's defects; Lewis is properly shown up by such a reading. In fact, not only Lewis but Carol herself is aware of her faults. The pattern of the book is made up of her self-assertions followed by her self-doubtings. She thoroughly realizes the absurdity of many of her ideas, and Lewis' irony can hardly be doubted in his descriptions of her belief in a "rather vaguely conceived sweetness and light" . . . or of her desire to "conquer the world—almost entirely for the world's own good." . . . Nevertheless, Lewis does overrate his heroine and in some ways he is reflected in her. He overrates her, however, not through failing to realize her silliness but because of his indulgence toward it. He did not expect as much from a heroine as most readers do. (Perhaps the reader's irritation is slightly priggish, for that matter.) Some critics seemed to feel that Carol should be content with Gopher Prairie simply because she herself was no genius but that is to miss the point of the book. Carol does not condemn the ignorance of Gopher Prairie so much as its complacency in ignorance nor its stupidity so much as its resistance to knowledge. Carol has the one quality Lewis most admires: she wants to know, she stays loose, she refuses to renounce her freedom to criticize and to wonder. This is what gives her a life in the novel which the other characters, fixed in their provincial orthodoxies, lack.

Freedom is, in fact, the main theme of Lewis' novels. At the beginning of *Main Street,* we find Carol in an attitude of "suspended freedom." . . . Since freedom was the one and only thing that Lewis really believed in, freedom can only exist in suspension; an absolute conviction enslaves. When someone asked Lewis if Carol were a self-portrait, he replied: "Yes . . . Carol is 'Red' Lewis: always groping for something she isn't capable of attaining, always dissatisfied, always restlessly straining to see what lies just over the horizon, intolerant of her surroundings, yet lacking any clearly defined vision of what she really wants to do or be." This commitment to a rootless and indefinable freedom is the key to Lewis' writings and career, the essential quality responsible for his success and failure. Lewis is nervous and alive, a man on the move, but he never gets anywhere. He is free to go but where to?

As far as the theme of freedom goes, *Babbitt* is a mere rewriting of *Main Street* though far superior in technique. In *Babbitt,* the protagonist is at the center of the world Lewis is attacking rather than on the periphery, illustrating the absurdities that Carol merely editorializes. Carol sees Gopher Prairie from the outside whereas Babbitt is the archetype of Zenith.

Zenith is something more than Gopher Prairie. As Lewis' unpublished introduction to *Babbitt* makes clear, Zenith is meant to represent the typical, small, boom city, a relatively unexploited literary subject. . . . (pp. 165-68)

Zenith is between the large city and the small village in more aspects than merely size. Gopher Prairie aspires to reach the heights of Zenith, but in all too many ways Zenith is merely a monstrously enlarged Gopher Prairie. Zenith is an anomaly: physically it is a city, but spiritually it is still a small town. . . . This along with the usual freedom-conformity conflict is the essential theme of *Babbitt:* the anomalous relationship of the American businessman with his small-town mass mind to the vastly powerful urban-industrial complex that he rules without understanding. It is a fictional variation on the themes of Thorstein Veblen's *The Theory of Business Enterprise* and a fictional anticipation of Ortega y Gasset's *The Revolt of the Masses.*

Lewis' image of the businessman and his relation to his culture begins in the early pages of *Babbitt* with a Veblen-like comparison of industrial power and the businessmen who take credit for it. Zenith at dawn is described in a passage emphasizing what Lewis believes to be the beauty and majesty of industrial power. The essential joke in the book is established with the description of the man who lives in "a city built—it seemed—for giants." . . .(pp. 168-69)

The businessman as baby is the dominant image that runs throughout *Babbitt.* The name itself suggests part of the image: Babbitt = baby, babble. Moreover, in addition to the details given in the quoted passage which establish the image of a baby—the pink head, the baby plumpness, the helpless hand—there are the later touches of Babbitt's "baby-blue pajamas," . . . his childishly petulant face, . . . and "the sleeveless dimity B.V.D. undershirt, in which he resembled a small boy humorlessly wearing a cheesecloth tabard at a civic pageant." . . . In this last image, Babbitt is less the baby than the pre-adolescent, but nowhere in the book does he seem to have wandered very far from the border of puberty. Even his wife is an indulgent mother, "as sexless as an anemic nun." . . . She calls him "Georgie boy." . . . (p. 169)

Babbitt does have sexual fantasies about a "fairy child," but if the fairy child sometimes seems to be a dream substitute for a flapper, at other times she is a childish playmate and sometimes, like Myra Babbitt, a

mother. . . . Even the fantasies expressive of Babbitt's "buried life" are adolescent.

Babbitt's world, like that of any small boy, is ruled by rituals of speech and behavior. The more commonplace the action, the more of a ritual it becomes. Even having the car filled with gasoline is a "rite." . . . Driving the car is both a rite and a game: "Babbitt . . . devoted himself to the game of beating trolley cars to the corner: a spurt, a tail-chase, nervous speeding between the huge yellow side of the trolley and the jagged row of parked motors, shooting past just as the trolley stopped—a rare game and valiant." . . .

Babbitt's relation then to the complex technological world around him is that of a baby surrounded by shiny toys. His small-town mind is quite as incapable of understanding the scientific principles underlying his world as Theron Ware's was to cope with the new theology. Babbitt's car, for instance, is a private fighter plane, a virility-substitute. Babbitt lives in a world of meaningless gadgetry, a world typified by the worship rather than the understanding of machinery. . . . (p. 170)

In a strange reversal of Kant, machines rather than people are regarded as ends in themselves, as with the electric cigar lighter that Babbitt buys: "It was a pretty thing, a nickeled cylinder with an almost silvery socket, to be attached to the dashboard of his car. It was not only, as the placard on the counter observed, 'a dandy little refinement, lending the last touch of class to a gentleman's auto,' but a priceless time-saver. By freeing him from halting the car to light a match, it would in a month or two easily save ten minutes." . . . The lighter is similar to Babbitt's own business function: he too is expensive, decorative, and modern but not very useful. As the small-towners of *Main Street* have a parasitic relationship with the farmers, so is Babbitt a mere parasite of modern industry.

The bathroom is the supreme architectural accomplishment of Babbitt's culture. At the end of his working day, we see Babbitt, "plump, smooth, pink," reverting unashamedly to babyhood in the bathtub. . . . The porcelain tub, the nickel taps, and the tiled walls of Babbitt's bathroom symbolize a civilization that is typified by all that is antiseptic, cellophane-wrapped, and standardized: a civilization separated from nature and inimical to human nature. (pp. 170-71)

The main difference between Zenith and Gopher Prairie, and between Babbitt and Doctor Kennicott, is just this predominance of the machine and the hygenic. (p. 171)

Zenith is merely a Gopher Prairie enlarged, mechanized, and cleaned up; Babbitt and his friends merely small-towners who are better dressed, closer shaved, slicker, and running on faster though equally mechanical rhythms. These men have graduated to the machine age only in the most superficial manner; their relation to the machine is merely that of superstitious worship and mindless, uncomprehending imitation. Essentially they are small-towners, mass minds, babies lost in a world of machines.

The world of Lewis' novel is machine made. It is characterized by images of glittering surfaces, meaningless hustle and bustle, inescapable noise, and standardized people. At times, Babbitt himself seems merely a mechanical cog in this world-machine, as, indeed, he imagines himself: "He felt superior and powerful, like a shuttle of polished steel darting in a vast machine." . . . Babbitt's very name has a mechanistic as well as babyish association: babbitt metal is an antifriction alloy used for bearings. Yet Babbitt, other-directed though he is, does not always avoid friction nor is he forever content as a cog in a machine. Babbitt is humanized not only by his childishness but also by a pathetic attempt at rebellion. . . . His buried emotional life attempts to assert itself.

A very unsatisfactory and abortive rebellion it is. Babbitt manages to make a brief escape to the Maine woods in an attempt to find solace in nature, in the manner of Thoreau, who was a central influence on Lewis' writing. Thoreau's influence shows in Babbitt's curious choice of the Maine woods as a refuge rather than the nearer wilds of Minnesota or Michigan; in Babbitt's realization that he is living "a life of barren heartiness" with its echo of "lives of quiet desperation"; and in the pervasive presence of a set of values in opposition to those of Babbitt's world—an organic, natural, inward existence, fronting the essential truths of life. Far from becoming transformed into a Midwestern Thoreau, Babbitt turns out to be a babe in the woods. He conceives of nature in terms of the childish adventure story and the motion picture: "Moccasins—sixgun—frontier town—gamblers—sleep under the stars—be a regular man." . . . Babbitt, corrupted by his culture, lacks the inner quietude, the ability to absorb experience without its being thrust upon him. Thoreau was able to discover nature by freeing his mind from the petty encumbrances of a busy and unimportant civilization. Babbitt, however, as a victim of the machine age "could never run away from Zenith and family and office, because in his own brain he bore the office and the family and every street and disquiet and illusion of Zenith." . . . If Thomas Wolfe could not go home again, Babbitt could never leave.

At home in Zenith, Babbitt's ineffectual rebellion continues. He becomes a liberal for a while on no better grounds than a conversation with a lawyer. He has an affair. But these efforts are merely impotent attempts to escape the vague dissatisfaction that haunts him throughout the novel. He has dim intimations of what he wants to escape from but no idea of what he wants to escape to. He cannot escape from his world of stan-

dardized and mechanical thought for he has nothing with which to replace it. In fact, he has no real alternative, for he is trapped not by outer circumstances so much as his own conditioned and inert mind.

Eventually, the near-fatal illness of Babbitt's wife allows him, rather gratefully, to return to the comfortable world of stereotypes and expected responses, free from the insupportable requirements of freedom. Accompanying his wife to the hospital, he burns his hand on the radiator. His wife immediately assumes her accustomed role and he his. . . . (pp. 172–74)

Still Babbitt does not wholly succumb. He keeps the spark of freedom alive by defending his son's elopement with a girl who is the embodiment of Babbitt's own wished-for fairy child. It is no accident that this ending is an almost exact repetition of *Main Street:* the unequipped rebel finally succumbs but with an inner defiance and hopes for a younger generation. Both novels begin well but begin to get a bit dull when it becomes apparent that neither the characters nor the plot is really going anywhere and that both are condemned to circle back to their starting point, with nothing gained and much energy lost. Lewis' own dilemma is exactly mirrored. Although his life was, in a sense, a continual flight from Sauk Center, he was never able to transcend the limiting dichotomies bequeathed him by his background. He has only two basic characters: the conformist and the nonconformist, the latter symbiotically dependent on the former since his only energy is in rejection. Even this rejection cannot become an absolute and transcendent gesture since total rejection would demand a reflexive conviction—and Lewis has none to offer.

It is questionable as to whether the actual limitations of freedom in American society are as strong as Lewis represents them to be in his novels. Genuinely critical thought may run into obstacles anywhere, but Lewis exaggerates the strength of the obstacles and the weakness of the rebels. Lewis himself, after all, was a successful rebel; he made rebellion pay to the extent that he even became honored in his own country, Sauk Center's "favorite son." But such success is denied his main characters as if to indicate his own apparent freedom was illusory. Lewis would likely defend himself on realistic grounds. When Floyd Dell complained that *Main Street* was too one-sided, not fairly representing the presence and strength of nonconformist elements, Lewis replied that Gopher Prairie was a much smaller town than the more mixed Port Royal of Dell's *Moon-Calf.* Similarly, a real estate man might find it difficult to be unorthodox, whereas a lawyer (like the liberal Seneca Doane, a minor character in *Babbitt*) has more leeway. The truth is that Lewis simply cannot imagine freedom within the social structure of America.

Moreover, Lewis cannot make up his mind about another of the major conflicts that runs through the novel, that of the mechanization of life. On the one hand, Babbitt and his cohorts are judged for having failed to measure up to the romantic possibilities of an industrial-technological world. They are in the wrong for not being adequately attuned to the machine world they live in. They are small-towners and provincials in their inability to truly comprehend the rich possibilities of a technological world. On the other hand, one of the key indictments against the Babbitt-world, just as against the Main Street world, is its mechanism, and Lewis indicts this in the traditional organic *vs.* mechanical formula of the Victorian culture critics (not to mention Van Wyck Brooks). Here the complaint is that the small-town mind is *too* mechanistic, too willing to submit to merely mechanical rhythms. If Lewis had any notion of how to reconcile these contradictions, it is not apparent in *Babbitt.* (pp. 175-76)

Anthony Channell Hilfer, "Sinclair Lewis: Caricaturist of the Village Mind," in his *The Revolt from the Village: 1915-1930,* University of North Carolina Press, 1969, pp. 158-76.

C. HUGH HOLMAN
(essay date 1973)

[Holman was an American detective novelist and literary scholar. In the following excerpt, he discusses Lewis's skill and technique as a satirist.]

Sinclair Lewis, America's first Nobel laureate in literature, was the summation and epitome of the satiric and comic reaction to what he labeled the "Village Virus." Indeed, the Nobel citation read: "The 1930 Nobel Prize in Literature is awarded to Sinclair Lewis for his powerful and vivid art of description and his ability to use wit and humor in the creation of original characters." . . . In the 1920's he turned his attention back to the country of his childhood and adolescence and produced five novels that, despite a number of obvious weaknesses, seem to have a secure place in our national literature. These novels are *Main Street,* a satiric portrait of a small town huddled on the Great Plains; *Babbitt,* a portrait of a representative businessman in a typical small city in the Middle West; *Arrowsmith,* a portrait of the scientist as saint, of a physician pursuing truth with unselfish and absolute commitment, and an attack on the society that tries to inhibit and pervert his search; *Elmer Gantry,* a savagely comic portrait of a dishonest and insincere minister and of the world in which he works; and *Dodsworth,* a mellower satire, this time of Americans seeking culture in Europe. He was to produce ten more novels before his death in 1951, but none of them had the energy, vitality, and originality of the five that established his fame and, in fact, said just

about all that he had to say of a world that he both loved and mocked for its painful inadequacies. Yet most of the novels published after *Dodsworth* remained grounded in the life of the Middle West, were couched in the language of the earlier works, and maintained many of the same attitudes, although mellowed by time, of his earlier years.

Lewis was originally taken as a realist, partly because his great power of mimicry gave an apparent authenticity to the speech of his characters and partly because the massive research which he did in getting the surface details of the daily lives of his people precisely right cast an air of great accuracy over the world he represented. But Sinclair Lewis was really a satirist and a humorist, and in his use of the devices and methods of the satirist and humorist lie both his greatest strengths and his chief weaknesses.

As a humorist he belongs clearly in the tradition of Yankee humor, that of the shrewd and knowing peddler or the crackerbox philosopher. For the most important person in Lewis's best work is Lewis himself. It is he who sees with great clarity, describes with deflating directness, mocks, sneers at, condemns. Everywhere in his novels—and particularly in *Main Street* and *Babbitt*—the reader is listening to the narrator-novelist and indeed is being invited to share with him his sense of the incongruity and falseness of the world being described. Thus the novels become extended comic and satiric essays, with narrative exempla to illustrate and underscore the points. The most common posture of the narrator is that of detached observer and sardonic critic. The characters are seen from the outside, their words checked against their deeds, their actions presented mockingly. When we enter their thoughts, it is seldom to explore them as fully realized characters but rather to pinpoint a motive or make ridiculous an aspiration or dream. For example, when Carol Kennicott, in *Main Street,* is putting out plants in a park near the railroad station, Lewis says: "Passengers looking from trains saw her as a village woman of fading prettiness, incorruptible virtue, and no abnormalities . . . and all the while she saw herself running garlanded through the streets of Babylon." Certainly the interior glimpse is not intended to make an exploration of psychological depths but to deflate and to mock. The original plan of *Babbitt* was that it should represent a typical day in the life of a typical businessman. That plan still survives in the first seven chapters, one-fourth of the total book, and it is only after this eventless and typical day that the casual plot of Babbitt's futile efforts at rebellion get underway. Lewis's statement about Elmer Gantry is not unusual: "He had been sitting with a Bible and an evening paper in his lap, reading one of them." Nor is the description of Gantry praying in the pulpit of his church: "He turned to include the choir, and for the first time he saw that there was a new singer, a girl with charming ankles and lively eyes, with whom he would certainly have to become well acquainted. But the thought was so swift that it did not interrupt the paean of his prayer." No, Lewis is not drawing extended psychographs of people; he is exhibiting specimens as though they were insects in a display case, and when he penetrates their skin it is primarily to make them squirm.

This narrator is superior to his subjects. In the five big novels he presents only two characters who are treated with full sympathy, Martin Arrowsmith and Sam Dodsworth, and one, Carol Kennicott of *Main Street,* whom he likes but frequently mocks. The superiority he feels toward his people is based on his greater knowledge and his distance from them but, most important of all, it is based on his moral sense. To find the standard against which to measure these people in establishing this judgment of their morality, Lewis looks toward the past. He finds it in the sturdy pioneers, whom he often celebrates. *Main Street* begins: "On a hill by the Mississippi where Chippewas camped two generations ago. . . . " And it goes on to say, "The days of pioneering, of lassies in sunbonnets, and bears killed with axes in piney clearings, are deader now than Camelot; and a rebellious girl is the spirit of that bewildered empire called the American Middlewest." *Arrowsmith* opens with the protagonist's great-grandmother, as a girl of fourteen, driving a wagon in the Ohio wilderness in the face of great adversity. It is what the towns and cities, the practices of business and the conventions of so-called polite society do to these pioneer virtues that Lewis is attacking, and it is the individualism and rugged independence which the pioneers exemplify to him whose passing he laments. It is little wonder that that most antisocial of American individualists, Henry David Thoreau, should have been one of his ideals.

This narrator is brash and even outrageous in his style. He flings at his satiric target not merely the customary satiric methods, but he brightens and sharpens his writing with vigorous metaphors. In *Elmer Gantry* he describes the workers in the "Charity Organization Society" as being "as efficient and as tender as vermin-exterminators," and he says of a saloon that "it had the delicacy of a mining camp minus its vigor." In *Main Street* he says that the people at a party "sat up with gaiety as with a corpse." (pp. 267-70)

Lewis is a satirist above all other things. While satire is often comic, its object is not to evoke mere laughter but laughter for a corrective purpose. It always has a target, an object which it attacks, such as pretense, falsity, deception, arrogance; and this target is held up to ridicule by the satirist's unmasking it. The satirist's vision is ultimately that of the cold-eyed realist, who penetrates shams and pretenses to reveal the truth. The simplest kind of satire is invective—that is,

forthright and abusive language directed against a target so that it makes a sudden revelation of a damaging truth. Another kind of direct satire is exaggeration, by which the good characteristics are reduced and the evil or ridiculous ones are increased. Indirect satire whereby characters render themselves ridiculous by their actions and their speech is more subtle. Lewis as a satirist is usually direct and blunt. His favorite devices are invective and caricature, and in his role of unabashed and self-conscious narrator he can apply these methods directly.

His invective can be devastating. He wrote of small-town ladies as "creamy-skinned fair women, smeared with grease and chalk, gorgeous in the skins of beasts and the bloody feathers of slain birds, playing bridge with puffy pink-nailed jeweled fingers, women who after much expenditure of labor and bad temper still grotesquely resemble their own flatulent lapdogs." He described a group of small-town citizens as a "Sunday-afternoon mob staring at monkeys in the Zoo, poking fingers and making faces and giggling at the resentment of the more dignified race." He described Gantry as being like his watch, "large, thick, shiny, with a near-gold case," and declared, "He was born to be a senator. He never said anything important, and he always said it sonorously." (p. 271)

Of course, this kind of invective leads very directly to caricature, in which the bad is exaggerated and the good reduced. For example Carol in *Main Street* went calling on Mrs. Lyman Cass, and Lewis wrote that she

> pounced on . . . the hook-nosed consort of the owner of the floor-mill. Mrs. Cass's parlor belonged to the crammed-Victorian school. . . . It was furnished on two principles: First, everything must resemble something else. A rocker had a back like a lyre, a near-leather seat imitating tufted cloth, and arms like Scotch Presbyterian lions; with knobs, scrolls, shields, and spear-points on unexpected portions of the chair. The second principle of the crammed-Victorian school was that every inch of the interior must be filled with useless objects.

Lewis then gives a detailed and hilarious listing of the contents of the parlor. The intention and the result is caricature.

Another kind of exaggeration results from a literal-minded reductio ad absurdum, as in the assertion that "the Maker of a universe with stars a hundred thousand light-years apart was interested, furious, and very personal about it if a small boy played baseball on Sunday afternoon." Lewis is a master of this kind of literal statement for satiric ends, as in "In the spring of '18 he was one of the most courageous defenders of the Midwest against the imminent invasion of the Germans." (p. 272)

One of the qualities of Lewis's work that is difficult to describe or analyze is the way in which he can take the speech of his people, weave it into a monologue or an address, and make of it a severe indictment of the speaker, and yet appear at no point to be exaggerating the normal talk of such men. . . . As Edgar Johnson has observed, "Burlesque there is in Lewis, but when we try to put a finger on it, in Babbitt's speech before the Real Estate Board, Luke Dawson's opinions on labor unions, or 'Old Jud's' Y.M.C.A. evangelism, it is embarrassingly apt to melt away and turn into realism. Mainly it is a matter of proportion rather than detail." (p. 273)

Lewis holds the Middle Western world up to Juvenalian laughter, points with unmistakable directness to its weaknesses and errors, and, as satirists have always done, seems to hope that seeing itself in the steel mirror of his description will make it repent and improve. Sometimes what he has to say is blunt and direct. In *Main Street* he declares of the small town:

> It is an unimaginatively standardized background, a sluggishness of speech and manners, a rigid ruling of the spirit by the desire to appear respectable. It is contentment . . . the contentment of the quiet dead, who are scornful of the living for their restless walking. It is negation canonized as the one positive virtue. It is the prohibition of happiness. It is slavery self-sought and self-defended. It is dullness made God.
>
> A savorless people, gulping tasteless food, and sitting afterward, coatless, and thoughtless, in rocking-chairs prickly with inane decorations, listening to mechanical music, saying mechanical things about the excellence of Ford automobiles, and viewing themselves as the greatest race in the world.

Here the outrage and anger are not masked, the comic cushion is not present. The point of view that leads the narrator through his long attack on the people of the books is present in red-faced anger. But such direct statement is unusual in Lewis.

Even at his most solemn moments, wit and the comic spirit usually cloak his rage. In a statement that is almost a declaration of faith for Lewis, he describes Martin Arrowsmith as preaching to himself "the loyalty of dissent, the faith of being very doubtful, the gospel of not bawling gospels, the wisdom of admitting the probable ignorance of one's self and of everybody else, and the energetic acceleration of a Movement for going very slow." In that series of witty paradoxes on a most serious subject Lewis is very much himself. If the paradox undercuts a little the seriousness of the portrait of Martin Arrowsmith, it enhances the role that Lewis the narrator wants to play. If his form is nearer essay than fiction, if his laughter is more embittered and angry than exuberant or outgoing, if his view of men and institutions is that of Juvenal and not Horace—that is merely another way of saying that he is of the Middle West and its towns and Main Streets, and while satiric laughter is an anodyne for what he feels there, he wants it to be more than an analgesic; he wants it to be a specific for the disease that causes the pain. If, as Mark Schorer has said, "he gave us a vigorous, perhaps a unique thrust into the imagination of ourselves," he intended the thrust to be therapeutic. If it has not been, then we are the poorer for its failure. (pp. 273-74)

C. Hugh Holman, "Anodyne for the Village Virus," in *The Comic Imagination in American Literature,* edited by Louis D. Rubin, Jr., Rutgers University Press, 1973, pp. 263-74.

SOURCES FOR FURTHER STUDY

Dooley, D. J. *The Art of Sinclair Lewis.* Lincoln: University of Nebraska Press, 1967, 286 p.

 Synopses and criticism of Lewis's works. This study is sprinkled with critical excerpts by other essayists.

Grebstein, Sheldon Norman. *Sinclair Lewis.* Boston: Twayne Publishers, 1962, 192 p.

 Comprehensive biographical and critical study.

Griffin, Robert J., ed. *Twentieth Century Interpretations of "Arrowsmith."* Englewood Cliffs, N.J.: Prentice-Hall, 1968, 119 p.

 Reprints twenty-two essays on *Arrowsmith* by such prominent critics as Stuart P. Sherman, Carl Van Doren, and Joseph Wood Krutch.

Light, Martin, ed. *The Merrill Studies in "Babbitt."* Columbus: Charles E. Merrill Publishing Co., 1971, 116 p.

 Reprints essays on *Babbitt* by such noted critics as Upton Sinclair, Maxwell Geismar, and Sheldon Norman Grebstein.

O'Connor, Richard. *Sinclair Lewis.* New York: McGraw-Hill Book Co., 1971, 144 p.

 Biographical and critical work which provides a moderately detailed study of Lewis's life, works, and critical reception.

Schorer, Mark. *Sinclair Lewis: An American Life.* New York: McGraw-Hill Book Co., 1961, 867 p.

 The definitive biography.

Vachel Lindsay

1879-1931

(Full name Nicholas Vachel Lindsay) American poet and essayist.

*L*indsay was a popular American poet of the early twentieth century who celebrated small-town Midwestern populism in strongly rhythmic poetry designed to be chanted aloud. Lindsay, in fact, gained recognition for his spirited public readings, and his frequently anthologized poems "General William Booth Enters into Heaven" and "The Congo" are notable for their vividness and vigor. While these poems secured recognition for Lindsay during his lifetime and typify the characteristics with which the poet's work is associated, their reception imposed limitations on his career, as audiences and critics concentrated on his exuberant showmanship and neglected his deep concern for beauty and democracy.

Lindsay was born in Springfield, Illinois, in a house designed by the architect of Abraham Lincoln's home, and in a room said to have been one in which Lincoln himself had slept. In this milieu, Lindsay developed a deep-rooted and abiding respect for Lincoln's love of the common people, which later directed the course of his artistic career. Lindsay's father, a struggling physician who fully expected his son to assume the duties of his practice, was humorless and a strict disciplinarian. Lindsay's mother, regarded by her neighbors variously as a social climber and an eccentric, was active in the local Campbellite church and in Springfield literary circles. She undertook her children's education until they were old enough to attend public school, introducing Lindsay and his two sisters to the fine arts, to classic English and Latin authors, and to a wealth of Greek, Roman, and Nordic legends. It was his mother who encouraged Lindsay in his early artistic pursuits, and to whom he turned for approval and support throughout much of his career. While Lindsay wrote poetry as early as childhood, art was his primary passion. Lindsay's mother, an artist herself, encouraged his artistic pursuits; however, she also supported her husband's insistence that Lindsay become established in a more secure occupation.

In 1897 Lindsay attended Hiram College, a small sectarian school in Ohio, where he showed little aptitude for medical studies, largely neglecting them for personal reading and writing. Despite his parents' advice that he persevere, the poet abandoned his medical education and, in 1901, enrolled at the Art Institute in Chicago, where the regimen of technical and anatomical studies made him equally unhappy. Lindsay discovered that while drawing gave him pleasure, a structured learning environment did not; he found, furthermore, that his actual artistic abilities, at least within such an environment, were minimal. Convinced that he would progress more rapidly at the New York School of Art, Lindsay enrolled there in 1903 to study painting with William Merritt Chase and his associate, Robert Henri. When approached by Lindsay to appraise one of his illustrated manuscripts, Henri, who both respected Lindsay and applauded his determination to succeed at painting as much as he doubted the likelihood of its occurring, candidly advised Lindsay to concentrate instead on writing poems, which he found more impressive than Lindsay's art. After following Henri's advice, Lindsay took his poetry to the New York streets in 1905, distributing copies of his verse among merchants and passersby for a nominal sum. A year later, Lindsay left the city for what was to be one of several tramping expeditions across the country, offering a sheet of his verses extolling beauty and democratic ideals in exchange for bed and board.

While Lindsay spent the summer of 1912 on the road, Harriet Monroe, a Chicago poet who was in the process of launching the periodical *Poetry,* published "General William Booth Enters into Heaven." The poem received wide attention and much praise from readers and critics alike, some of whom had before summarily rejected Lindsay's work. A collection of Lindsay's poetry, headed by "Booth," was published in 1913; and another collection which included "The Congo," a poem inspired both by the poet's fascination for Africa's spiritualism and Joseph Conrad's *Heart of Darkness,* was published the following year. In *General William Booth Enters into Heaven, and Other Poems* (1913) and *The Congo, and Other Poems* (1914), Lindsay attempted to reach a less educated and less culturally sophisticated audience than that addressed by other contemporary poets. He insisted that poetry is most effective when recited, and many of the poems were accompanied by marginal notations governing the specific volume and tone of voice to be used, among other directives. It had also occurred to Lindsay, in observing the overwhelming popularity of vaudeville, that despite his own reservations regarding this form of entertainment, certain of its elements might be employed to capture an audience's attention. Lindsay devised pieces referred to as "poem games," ritualistic enactments involving dancing and chanting which required the participation of an audience as well as specific players. These performances of "higher vaudeville" formed part of Lindsay's exhausting schedule of popular and lucrative public readings. Although at first encouraged by the enthusiastic response of his audiences and by their eager participation in his "poem games," Lindsay soon wearied of incessant public demand to hear "Booth" and "The Congo" to the exclusion of his other work. It also exasperated Lindsay that those dramatic elements employed to entice an audience succeeded, as well, in overshadowing the idealistic visions of beauty and democratic virtue underlying his art.

After the appearance of his first three volumes, Lindsay was both acclaimed as the people's poet and caricatured as a vagabond American minstrel whose resounding phrases were shouted to the clouds and stars as he strode across the Midwestern plains. Painfully aware of the frustrating limitations inherent in such a publicly allocated role, and conscious, too, of the dangers of fulfilling this caricature, Lindsay nevertheless found it impossible to give up the lucrative entertainer's circuit. Although he constantly had ideas for new works, his exacting schedule did not permit him to pursue most of these. While inwardly distressed over the shape his career was assuming, and while not a wealthy man, Lindsay did enjoy moderate success for several years. By the early 1920s, however, his popularity began to wane as widespread, optimistic faith in America's future was supplanted by pessimism bred of World War I and as traditional small-town and rural values were pilloried by more worldly cosmopolitans. Disparagement of Lindsay's work became widespread, shaking the poet's faith in himself. H. L. Mencken mockingly wrote of Lindsay that "what was new in him, at the start, was an echo of the barbaric rhythms of the Jubilee songs. But very soon the thing ceased to be a marvel, and of late his elephantine college yells have ceased to be amusing." In the last years of his life, Lindsay, who had married at forty-five and now had two children, experienced crushing debts, deteriorating health, and periods of unreasoning rage and paranoia which were directed, by turns, at his family, supporters, and a world he perceived as too urbane to embrace his unsophisticated and now unfashionable philosophies. In 1931, bitter and disappointed, Lindsay poisoned himself. He announced to those attendant on his death-bed: "They tried to get me; I got them first."

The rhythms of Lindsay's poetry are based on those of the Protestant camp meeting. Imbued with faith in the inherent goodness and efficacy of common people united in a democratic cause, Lindsay's poems encourage the continued efforts of people to better and beautify their lives and environments, as well as to celebrate both their realized and untapped abilities to do so. Many of his works also extol nature and a life lived close to the soil, and nearly all affirm God's immanence. Although some denigrate his ideals and unsophisticated style, many commentators agree that Lindsay's best efforts are found in his verses commemorating such little-known heroes as William Booth and John Chapman (Johnny Appleseed), whose lives evoked from Lindsay vivid portraits largely unmarred by the prosy moralization and commonplace thought found in many of his works. "General William Booth Enters into Heaven," for example, is a colorful, teeming panorama which escapes the tribute's customary restrictions; critics have noted that Booth, whose life of sacrifice and charitable labor admits him into heaven, is as vigorously and interestingly portrayed as are the unwashed and unwanted to whom he ministered. Critics have also found that Lindsay's fictionalized account in "Johnny Appleseed" of John Chapman, whose solitary odyssey to sow for the enrichment of future generations perhaps inspired the poet's own expeditions, is, like his other portrayals, made vivid by Lindsay's fusion of fact with myth. Lindsay embellished history with his own imaginative additions in these portraits to arouse the ambition of Americans to live up to the nation's heritage; his widely anthologized "Abraham Lincoln Walks at Midnight," for instance, departs from a staid representation or rigid documentary style to present a great leader who cannot rest peacefully in his grave because of worldwide strife and injustice.

Although Lindsay's work is no longer widely read, most commentators find his contribution to American poetry valuable because of his colorful depiction of American ideals and idealists, and his attempt to address certain sectors of society ignored by other artists. Like the figures he immortalized, Lindsay refused either to surrender his ideals to modern exigencies, or, in their preservation, to divorce them from the world. Rather, he perceived pursuits of democratic and aesthetic goals to be integral to life and, accordingly, took them to street corners, farmhouses, and rural meeting places. Lindsay's poetic legacy is valued for its vivid presentation of distinctly American characters and ideals.

(For further information about Lindsay's life and works, see *Concise Dictionary of American Literary Biography, 1865-1917*; *Dictionary of Literary Biography*, Vol. 54: *American Poets, 1880-1945*; *Contemporary Authors*, Vol. 114; *Something about the Author*, Vol. 40; and *Twentieth-Century Literary Criticism*, Vol. 17.)

CRITICAL COMMENTARY

LOUIS UNTERMEYER

(essay date 1919)

[A poet during his early career, Untermeyer is better known as an anthologist of poetry and short fiction and as a master parodist. In the following excerpt, he pronounces Lindsay's flamboyant technique daring and innovative.]

Striking as are the differences between Frost and Oppenheim, the diversity of our new American poets is even more emphasized by the contrasting work of Vachel Lindsay. His background, like Frost's, is definitely local; his impulse, like Oppenheim's, indefinitely religious. But his blend of these forces is peculiarly individualized and peculiarly national. A pagan by intention and a puritan by intuition. He is, as I think he desires to be, the minstrel turned missionary; a corn-fed Apollo singing to convert the heathen. This *flair* for reformation exhibits itself in many ways. It includes a rhymed explanation as to why Lindsay voted the socialist ticket, exhortative verses pleading for Prohibition, a Salvation Army tribute (with all the drums and tambourines) to General Booth Entering Heaven, and a jeremiad (running to the other extreme) addressed bluntly "to the United States Senate." But his first and most enduring concern is doubtless embodied in the doctrine which he has called "The New Localism," which is explained in his prose volume *Adventures While Preaching the Gospel of Beauty*, a thesis that will be found amplified and applied in his forthcoming *The Golden Book of Springfield*. I doubt if there is any man in America who has laboured longer and more earnestly than Lindsay to encourage the half-hearted beauty that hides and fears to declare itself in our dull and complacent villages and townships. His gay, intrepid spirit, his racy little prose pamphlets, his tramping journeys on which the sixteen-page *Rhymes to be Traded for Bread* (printed and distributed by himself) were given for a meal or a night's lodging—these, in themselves, compose a gospel of beauty more persuasive and potent than a hundred sermons. (pp. 65-6)

There is something curious, almost contradictory

Principal Works

Rhymes to Be Traded for Bread (poetry) 1912

General William Booth Enters into Heaven, and Other Poems (poetry) 1913

Adventures While Preaching the Gospel of Beauty (poetry) 1914

The Congo, and Other Poems (poetry) 1914

The Art of the Moving Picture (criticism) 1915; also published as The Art of the Moving Picture [revised edition], 1922

A Handy Guide for Beggars (poetry) 1916

The Chinese Nightingale, and Other Poems (poetry) 1917

The Golden Whales of California (poetry) 1920

Johnny Appleseed, and Other Poems (poetry) 1928

Selected Poems of Vachel Lindsay (poetry) 1963

Springfield Town Is Butterfly Town, and Other Poems for Children (poetry) 1969

Letters of Vachel Lindsay (letters) 1979

about a man leaving his home town to tell men they should return to their birthplaces. But this is precisely what Lindsay preached and did. One should know the earth but one should not be a gypsy forever. The vagabond, he insisted, should taste the scattered largesse of the world. But he should return home. And having returned, he should plant the seeds he had gathered abroad. (pp. 70-1)

With an appreciation of these matters, one approaches his first important volume of poetry, *General William Booth Enters into Heaven and Other Poems* . . . , with sympathetic understanding. Here one immediately encounters the curious blend of athletic exuberance, community pride and evangelism. Consider the first poem, which gives the book its title. Here is the apotheosis of a great social-religious movement; but it is not so much a tribute to the Salvation Army as it is a glorification of a spirit greater and far beyond it. From a technical standpoint, Lindsay's attempt to blend noise, novelty and an old ecstasy is highly successful—and almost fortuitous. The experiment of setting lofty lines and reverential sentiment to cheap and brassy music is daring and splendid; especially since, in its very tawdriness, the music of the verse gives back the flavor of those earnest and blatant gatherings. It is, in a more definitely revivalistic spirit, the first of those characteristic chants (with the germs of the "higher vaudeville") which Lindsay lifted to so individual a plane. . . . No more colorful and solemn noise has yet been heard in our living song.

The banjos rattled, and the tambourines

Jing-jing-jingled in the hands of Queens!

Such a scrap is as orchestral as a dozen pages of elaborate instrumentation. It is, in its brazen directness, another phase not only of the new spirit that has enlivened American poetry but of America itself.

It would be too much to expect the rest of the volume to live up to this amazing piece of work, and it does not. Lindsay the man is always a poet, but Lindsay the poet does not always write poetry. When he errs it is not, as one critic has pointed out, "on the side of the time-spirit"; when he fails it is not because he tries to express his age but because he expresses it badly. Frequently his verse rises from nothing more carefully constructed than a conviction, an anger, a crusade against the white-slave traffic or the corner saloon. Here his voice gets beyond his control; in his haste to deliver his message, he has no time to choose sharp and living words; he takes what comes first to hand—good, bad, indifferent—and hurries on, blurring the firm outline, losing the sense of leashed power without which no art-work can be ennobled. His aim is commendable but his volleys are erratic. In his anxiety to bang the bell, he sometimes shoots not only the target but the background to pieces. Such an effect is **"The Trap,"** with its glib didacticism and its stock-worn phrases. Such a poem also is the polemic **"To the United States Senate"** and one or two more. But these things are the poet in his dullest periods even though they be the propagandist in his most fiery moments. The excellent blend of both of them is achieved otherwise, notably in the dignified and sonorous [poem **"The Eagle That Is Forgotten"**]. (pp. 72-5)

This fused quality is to be seen, in a lighter vein, in **"Upon Returning to the Country Road,"** in **"Where is David, the Next King of Israel?"** and **"A Net to Snare the Moonlight."** In these we note the growth of fantasy and whimsical extravagance which, in the ensuing volumes, come to play so great a part in Lindsay's work. Touched with an elfin charm that is both good-humored and grotesque, they reach their highest pitch in **"The Light o' the Moon,"** a series in which different people and animals look upon the moon and each creature finds in it his own mood and disposition. (pp. 76-7)

This series is continued and amplified in the succeeding volume. (p. 78)

[*The Congo and Other Poems*] gives us Lindsay's mixture of rhymes, rag-time and religion in his best blend. Here the rubberstamp idioms, the trade jargons of poetry, are lost in a sudden sweep of infectious and impulsive rhythms. These chants which form the larger part of the volume may not be the most powerful poetry that Lindsay has written, but they are undoubtedly the most popular; they give people that primitive joy in syncopated sound that thrills them far more than critical didacticism or an ingenious theory of aesthetics.

These verses demand to be read aloud; they are fresh evidence of the fact that poetry is fundamentally an oral art, an art appealing to the ear rather than to the eye. And it is an experiment in widening the borders of this song-art that they must be regarded. In pleading for a consideration of the possibilities of its development, Lindsay calls attention (*via* Professor Edward Bliss Reed's volume *The English Lyric*) to the Greek lyrists who, accompanying themselves, composed their own accompaniments. "Here," he says, "is pictured a type of Greek work which survives in American vaudeville, where every line may be two-thirds spoken and one-third sung; the entire rendering, musical and elocutionary, depending upon the improvising power and sure instinct of the performer. . . . I respectfully submit these poems," continued Lindsay, "as experiments in which I endeavor to carry this vaudeville form back towards the old Greek precedent of the half-chanted lyric. In this case the one-third of music must be added by the instinct of the reader. He must be Iophon. And he can easily be Iophon if he brings to bear upon the piece what might be called the Higher Vaudeville imagination."

It must be admitted that, to bring out their full surge and swing, it is not only necessary to hear these poems chanted, but to hear them chanted by Lindsay himself. Once having heard his highly original declamations, it is impossible for any one to forget the tunes and *tempi*. Without this variation of manner and melody—the rich unction of certain phrases contrasting sharply with the metallic *staccato* of others, the abrupt changes from a slow, deliberate *andante* to the briskest and most burly of *allegros*—much of the verse is merely rumbling and repetitive. Lindsay does his best to help his readers by means of a running fire of stage-directions along the edge of each page. But it is difficult, for any but a trained musician, to achieve half the effects he calls for. In the speed and clatter of the verses, Lindsay's admonishing voice, coaching, as it were, from the side-lines, is often lost.

For all this, the title-poem is a complete success, even on the printed page. The same flaming sincerity that kindled **"General Booth Enters into Heaven"** turns what is noisy or extravagant in these lines to eloquence. The cold type warms with a savage, insistent beat; the roll and sweep, even without Lindsay's sonorous baritone, quicken passages prosy and almost perfunctory by themselves. (pp. 79-81)

"The Santa Fé Trail," which follows this poem, is the most daring experiment in the volume, and there are about a dozen excellent aesthetic reasons why it should be a complete failure. Strangely enough, it is a complete success. This delicate and light-hearted humoresque is sung to an orchestral accompaniment of race-horns, klaxons, trumpets, thundering motors, the mad tympani of open mufflers, and a list of cities blared

through the megaphone or shouted "like a train caller in a Union depot." And all this uproar whirls around fairy interludes and scraps of fancy which somehow are not drowned in the shrieking maelstrom. So strikingly does each contrast set off the other, that the effect of the whole is startling in loveliness no less than speed.

It is in the third poem (**"The Firemen's Ball"**) that Lindsay unconsciously reveals how this very power, when pushed beyond its limits, fails; how, as in this instance, it often falls into dogma and doggerel. The musical content shows this poet at his worst (although it is still a far cry from the futurism of Marinetti and the typographical tricks of his followers like Apollinaire and others); it is seven parts unlovely noise and three parts uninspired nonsense. This very increase of clangor defeats itself. Poe, many years ago, accomplished the magic of mere sound; but he did it by bringing to such poor rhymes as "Ulalume" and "The Bells," a subtle music that rang new changes under the insistent reiteration.

To return to **"The Firemen's Ball,"** its philosophy is even more questionable than the melody. It is its own amazing contradiction. From a roaring picture of a burning building, which is meant to symbolize the holocaust of life, Lindsay turns to the horrible (to him) glimpse of the firemen making love to their sweethearts (the baleful fires of passion mingling with the "lustful, insinuating music") and, as a grand finale, he gives us a rumbling, vague and negative Buddhistic sermon, quoting approvingly from a section of the Mahavagga that ends, "By absence of passion he is made free." The contradiction is in Lindsay's very treatment; he cannot get his spirit to believe in his theme. Even while he writes:

Life is a flame:—
Be cold as the dew
Would you win at the game,

his lines refuse to obey him and go leaping along. Lindsay in this, as well as in some of the other poems, is like a man dancing gaily on the top of a windy mountain, his eyes blazing, his whole body kindled with the energy of living—and shouting all the while, "We must abolish passion! Down with Life!"

It is hard to understand this unwillingness on Lindsay's part to understand passion. It is harder to understand why he misrepresents and misinterprets it. And it is all the more strange since this passionate *élan* is his most valuable possession. The passion for making drab villages beautiful (*vide* **"The Soul of the City," "I Heard Immanuel Singing"** and his early broadsides); the passion for peace, as evinced in the somewhat rhetorical but none the less earnest war poems at the end of *The Congo*; the passion for righting hideous wrongs—these are some of the passions that burn through Lindsay's work and illuminate his lines with their quickening flame. There are many times, indeed, when he reminds one of the revivalist turned socialist; he has the strangely mingled passions of both. (pp. 83-5)

I pass hurriedly over the unaccountable stupidities which have been injected into the volume: The mawkish tributes to the doll-like Mary Pickford, the flashing Blanche Sweet *et al,* the 'comic'-supplement humor of **"When Gassy Thompson Struck It Rich"**—and proceed to Lindsay's most recent volume. Here (*The Chinese Nightingale.* . .) we have a similar mixture of high-flying fantasy and dogged fact, of primitive emotionalism and evangelistic propaganda. The two volumes give the weird effect of Buddha dancing to a jazz band; of the doxology performed on a steam calliope; of the Twentieth Century Express running lightly over a child's flower garden; of The Reverend William Sunday and Bert Williams reciting the Beatitudes. The latter effect is particularly evoked by **"The Booker Washington Trilogy,"** most strikingly in the poem **"Simon Legree."** It would be interesting to see what genuine negro composers like Will Marion Cook, Rosamund Johnson or H. T. Burleigh could do with this poem. Or with the **"The Congo,"** using it as a symphony for full orchestra, reinforced by banjos, bones, marimbas, xylophones and a dark baritone solo. Or **"King Solomon and the Queen of Sheba"** as the libretto for an opulent, afro-oriental cantata. Here again one wishes for Lindsay's vocal delivery in order to receive the full flavor of these lines. But the person who can read them without feeling a good part of their racy imagery, vigor and humor, is dead not alone to poetry but to persuasion. No one can fail to enjoy the spectacle of the white poet speaking through the confused oratory of the old negro preacher, working up his audience and himself, and making desirable the very thing he set out to make horrible—Simon Legree being described, with loving envy, in a hell that sounds suspiciously like a poor slave's paradise. (pp. 86-7)

It is these original chants that have made many critics exaggerate Lindsay's standing as a bizarre innovator and minimize his importance as a serious creator. Most of his deprecators insist on discussing only the twenty per cent of his art that they think is the novelty. But even here, they are mistaken. They have taken a journalistic, almost a jejune attitude toward his work; and they fail to realize that when they assume he is lost in technical mazes (he has even been grouped, by two cataloguing critics, with the Imagists) he is distracted little by method and not at all by form. Technical discussions rage, he surmises, because most poets are twenty-five, which is the technical age. It is therefore somewhat distressing to an artist who has reached the maturity of thirty-nine years, to have his detractors protest at violations that he never committed. These critics assume that **"The Congo,"** for instance, is a new

form. It is not. It is, as Lindsay has retorted, one of the oldest, most orthodox, most over-conventionalized forms in the English language:—the Ode. It is a form which, says Lindsay, has been worn out and practically dropped because it degenerated into false and pompous apostrophes. One can doubtless find precedents for every line of **"The Congo"** in a long array of odes in English, which have not failed to be in print simply because they were originally intended to be sung. Many times the most successful odes are not specifically so labeled and this adds to the critics' confusion. It seems probable that Lanier thought he was inventing a new form when he wrote "The Marshes of Glynn" and that Coleridge was laboring under a similar delusion when he began "Kubla Khan" and "Christabel." Lindsay is not so self-deceived and it seems an ironic injustice that he should be accused of doing or, what is still more ludicrous, failing to do the very thing he has carefully avoided even trying to do.

The defects in this volume are of an entirely different caliber. He has, in a commendable effort to extend the borders of the ode, gone a few steps farther and (taking his cue, I suspect, from Dryden's "Alexander's Feast") has expanded the chant into what he calls "Poem-Games," which add an undercurrent of alien music and the services of a dancer to the elocutionist's art. "In the 'Poem-Games,' " the author writes in an introductory note, "the English word is still first in importance, the dancer comes second, the chanter third." But in order to keep the chanter from getting too far ahead of the dancer, the poet has been compelled to repeat insignificant and fugitive phrases, until the English word loses not only its importance but its import. For instance, observe how the rich and simple music of **"King Solomon"** has been attenuated and dragged out into tiresome commonplaces by the dull and devasting repetitions. Or see how so slight a piece of fooling as **"The Potatoes' Dance"** has been lengthened far beyond the poem's limits and the reader's interest. The opening lines will explain:

"Down cellar," said the cricket,
"Down cellar," said the cricket,
"Down cellar," said the cricket, . . .

(pp. 87-9)

Compare this doggerel to the amazing **"John Brown,"** which, lacking these verbal impediments, begins with a childlike catalog and runs through negro pomposity to a picturesque and powerful close.

But Lindsay is not only the lyric interpreter of the dark race. He can play on other instruments as well as the bones and calliope. In fact, some of his strummings on the lute are even more potent though less dynamic than his improvisations for brass band. Turn to the title poem and see how lightly the music evokes new hints of the ancient East. Forgetting programs or pronunciamentoes, Lindsay has let his whimsical mind loose among singing idols, "golden junks in a laughing river," rainbow fishes, explanatory nightingales, river-pirates, windbells, affable dragons, peacock landscapes and ghostly suggestions of a culture that was old when the Ming dynasty was young.

Elsewhere the mixture is less enticing. The evangelist seems to be in the ascendancy and the verse suffers in consequence. The war has undoubtedly brought out in Lindsay the usual religious reaction, but it is a somewhat ministerial fervor. Compared to the cosmic religion celebrated by James Oppenheim, it has a prim and parochial tang; it sounds frequently less like a surge of song than a Sunday sermon. The Chatauqua platform performer is a rôle to which Lindsay seems to be growing increasingly partial. This shifting of artistic bases recalls how difficult a position Lindsay maintained in his other volumes; how dexterously he balanced himself in a devotion to a liberal socialism on one hand and a strict prohibition on the other. So in this collection. Pulled one way as a poet by the imperious demands of Beauty and another way, as propagandist, by the moral dictates of the Uplift crusade; he shows a vacillation, almost pathetic, between a universal compulsion and, to be literal, local option. Any admirer of Lindsay will observe with distrust the growing emphasis on the sermonizing features of his work. Even his Heaven is uninviting; a Nirvana of communal kitchens, daily parades and a Beauty scrubbed and worshiped with prescribed regularity. In **"The Eagle That is Forgotten," "Sunshine"** and others of the poems already mentioned, there was a successful mingling of poet and pamphleteer. But in the present volume it is somewhat disturbing to witness Lindsay hitching his clipped Pegasus in front of the meeting-house, mounting the worn-out steps and going into the pulpit to deliver himself of such orotund banalities as **"God Send the Regicide," "Where is the Real Non-Resistant?"** and the still flatter wordiness of rhymes like:

When Bryan speaks, the sky is ours,
The wheat, the forests, and the flowers.
And who is here to say us nay?
Fled are the ancient tyrant powers.

When Bryan speaks, then I rejoice.
His is the strange composite voice
Of many million singing souls
Who make world-brotherhood their choice

When he forgets to preach, or when the preachment takes on a less predetermined and more unconscious tone (as in the highly-colored **"Tale of the Tiger Tree"** and the brightly ironic **"Here's to the Mice"**), he regains his power—a power with an artistic dignity that his revivalistic gusto scarcely reaches. It is a relief to turn to those poems in which Lindsay's native fancy is given full swing. To **"The Ghosts of the Buffaloes,"** where he takes the reader on a midnight scamper with

nothing more purposeful than the driving power of the imagination. Or to the **"The Prairie Battlements."** Here again he is not trying to prove anything or convince any one; he is concerned only with trying to snare a glimmering and elusive loveliness. No village improvement societies will embroider this on their banners; no anti-vice crusaders will take it up as a slogan. And yet I like to feel that the real Lindsay is in these unofficial and merely beautiful poems. Or witness these lines, a part of **"The Broncho That Would Not Be Broken":** . . .

"Nobody cares for you," rattled the crows,
As you dragged the whole reaper, next day, down the rows.
The three mules held back, yet you danced on your toes.
You pulled like a racer, and kept the mules chasing.
You tangled the harness with bright eyes side-glancing,
While the drunk driver bled you—a pole for a lance—
And the giant mules bit at you—keeping their places,
O broncho that would not be broken of dancing.

It is in this homely fantasy, this natural extravagance that Lindsay excels. It runs through things as delicate as the moon poems and as burly as **"Simon Legree"** with its fallacious moral and its rollicking high spirits. And it is this last quality which will keep Lindsay from accumulating too fat a churchliness. It is the whimsical buoyancy, the side-spring, the gay appraisal of beauty as he finds it in people, places and art (as he hopes to find it even in politics) that will keep Lindsay the missionary from superseding Lindsay the minstrel. A careless singer of democracy, he goes adventuring with one hand on his lyre and the other on his sword. And the tune that he whistles is *"Gaily the Troubadour—"*. (pp. 89-93)

Louis Untermeyer, "Vachel Lindsay," in his *The New Era in American Poetry*, 1919. Reprint by Scholarly Press, 1970, pp. 65-93.

MARIANNE MOORE

(essay date 1923)

[Moore was an American poet, translator, essayist, and editor. In the following excerpt, she commends Lindsay's vigor and preoccupation with humanitarianism but criticizes his lack of aesthetic discipline.]

The outstanding impression made by Mr Lindsay's collected poems is that the author pities the fallen, deplores misunderstandings, and is saddened that the spirit should so often be at the mercy of the body. One cannot but revere his instinctive charity and determination to make a benevolent ordering of the universe possible. . . . It is a fine courage that enables a writer to let himself loose in the religious revival sense of the term at the risk of being thought an unintentional clown. It is impossible not to respect Mr Lindsay's preoccupation with humanitarianism, but at the same time to deplore his lack of aesthetic rigour. In a lover of the chant, one expects a metronomelike exactness of ear; it is the exception, however, when the concluding lines of Mr Lindsay's stanzas are not like a top which totters, or a hoop which rolls crazily before it finally stops. We have:

Murdered in filth in a day,
Somehow by the merchant gay! . . .

It is difficult to enunciate the words in such lines as:

With my two bosomed blossoms gay
Like rivers sweet and steep,
Deep rock-clefts before my feet
You were a girl-child slight.

One is disaffected even in the mood of informal discursiveness by adjacent terminal words such as calculation, Appalachian; whole, jowl; ore, floor; trial, vile; fire, the higher; and

Join hands,
Poets,
Companions

is a metrical barbarism. Why, in a **"Dirge for a Righteous Kitten,"** "His shirt was always laundried well"? What of the prose lines, "A special tang for those who are tasty"? And in the phrase, "when the statue of Andrew Jackson . . . is removed," we have that popular weak misuse of the present tense which we have in such an expression as "I hope he gets there." There is a lack of neat thinking in such phrases as "Lining his shelves with books from everywhere" and "All in the name of this or that grim flag." There is inexactness of meaning in

The long handclasp you gave
Still shakes upon my hands.

(pp. 498-99)

As a visionary, as an interpreter of America, and as a modern primitive—in what are regarded as the three provinces of his power, Mr Lindsay is hampered to the point of self-destruction by his imperviousness to the need for aesthetic self-discipline. Many poets have thoughts that are similar, in which case, only heedlessness prevents the author of the less perfect product from giving place to the author of the stronger, and much of Mr Lindsay's collected work is unfortunate in thus provoking comparison with attested great-

ness. Unfortunate also, is the conscious altering of great familiar expressions:

The times are out of joint! O cursed spite!
The noble jester Yorick comes no more. . . .

(p. 500)

Although it was not intended that the poems should be read to oneself, they will, on occasion, be so read, and so surely as they are it is inevitable that the author will in certain respects be presented amiss. Certain repetitions suggest the pleonasm of the illiterate preacher who repeats a phrase in order to get time to formulate another:

Love is not velvet, not all of it velvet
When a million million years were done
And a million million years beside,

We have not that reinforcing of sentiment which we have in reiteration by Yeats:

She pulled the thread and bit the thread,
And made a golden gown.

In his essay on "Poetic Diction," Robert Bridges says, "the higher the poet's command of diction, the wider may be the field of his Properties; . . . and this is a very practical point, if a writer with no command of imaginative diction, should use such Properties as are difficult of harmonization, he will discredit both the Properties and the Diction." Despite the fact that Mr Lindsay's properties are abundant and often harmonious as in the fantasy of the gipsies:

Dressed, as of old, like turkey-cocks and zebras,
Like tiger-lilies and chameleons,

the grouping is often conspicuously self-destructive. One feels that

Percival and Bedivere
And Nogi side by side

distracted from the poet's meaning as do the statesmen, artists, and sages, in **"The Litany of the Heroes"**: Amenophis Fourth—Hamlet and Keats "in one"—Moses, Confucious, Alexander, Caesar, St Paul, "Augustine," Mohammed, St Francis, Dante, Columbus, Titian, Michael Angelo, Shakespeare, Milton, Napoleon, Darwin, Lincoln, Emerson, Roosevelt, Woodrow Wilson, Socrates. Like paintings in public buildings of the world's cultural and scientific progress, such groups sacrifice impact to inclusiveness. **"Johnny Appleseed"** is marred, one feels, by such phrases as "the bouncing moon," and

He laid him down sweetly, . . .
Like a bump on a log, like a stone washed white.

We rejoice in the resilience of imagination in the idea of a grasshopper as "the Brownies' racehorse," "the fairies' Kangaroo"; and in **"The Golden Whales of California,"** there is controlled extravagance in the enumeration of "the swine with velvet ears," "the sacred raisins," "the trees which climb so high the crows are dizzy," "the snake fried in the desert," but "the biggest ocean in the world," and the whales "whooping that their souls are free," suggest the tired European's idea of America. . . . (501-02)

Objecting further, it is impossible not to say that Mr Lindsay's phrases of negro dialect are a deep disappointment. A familiarity with negros and the fact that the adaptations are intentional cannot absolve such Aryan doggerel as:

> And we fell by the altar
> And we fell by the aisle,
> And found our Savior
> In just a little while.

Such lines are startlingly at variance with real negro parallelism as we have it in:

> Oh, Hell am deep 'n Hell am wide
> an' you can't touch bottom on either side

and are incompatible with that perfect fragment of negro cadence which Mr Lindsay has combined with it, "Every time I hear the spirit moving in my heart I'll pray." A stentorianly emphatic combining of the elements of the black genius and the white, but emphasizes their incompatability. . . . In stage directions, the most expert craftsmen such as Shaw and Yeats barely escape pedantry and one feels that however necessary to Mr Lindsay's conception of the spoken word particular information may be, when he asks us "to keep as lightfooted as possible," to read "orotund fashion," "with heavy buzzing bass," et cetera, one can but feel, unfairly or not, that he is subordinating a poorly endowed audience to wit which he proposes to furnish.

Some of Mr Lindsay's work would lead one to infer that "a man is out on three wide balls but walks on four good strikes." The literary reader tends not to be compensated by moral fervour for technical misapprehensions, but there is life in any kind of beauty and in these poems avoidance of grossness and the entirely vengeful, is fortifying. **"Why I Voted the Socialist Ticket"** is full of contagious vigour . . . but in his **"Curse for Kings,"** Mr Lindsay gives the effect of an emotional pacifism which is incompatible with earnestness.

"This whole book is a weapon in a strenuous battlefield," Mr Lindsay says; "practically every copy will be first opened on the lap of some person . . . trying to follow me as I recite as one follows the translation of the opera libretto." He is not to be refuted. There is a perhaps not very exact analogy between him in his *rôle* of undismayed, national interpreter, and a certain young eagle conveyed by American naval officers to the Philippines, styled "an American rooster," and pitted invariably with mortal consequence against Philippine gamecocks.

If a reader felt no responsibility for a writer, and were merely culling felicities, certain of Mr Lindsay's poems would undoubtedly give complete pleasure; disregarding as a whole the poem, **"How a Little Girl Danced,"** there is a fine accuracy in the lines:

> With foot like the snow, and with step like the rain.

There is suggested fragility in the poem game of yellow butterflies:

> They shiver by the shallow pools. . . .
> They drink and drink. A frail pretense!

There is beauty in **"The Dandelion";** especially also, in **"The Flower of Mending":**

> When moths have marred the overcoat
> Of tender Mr Mouse.

And the lines:

> Factory windows are always broken.
> Somebody's always throwing bricks,

are expertly captivating. Lincoln is not added to, but he is not travestied in **"Abraham Lincoln Walks at Midnight";** there is glory in the conception of Alexander Campbell stepping "from out the Brush Run Meeting House": and reality in **"Bryan":**

> With my necktie by my ear, I was stepping on my
>   dear. . . .
> The earth rocked like the ocean, the sidewalk was a
>   deck.
> The houses for the moment were lost in the wide
>   wreck.

We have in this poem, some of Gertrude Stein's power of "telling what you are being while you are doing what you are doing," and there is "blood within the rhyme" in:

> The banjos rattled and the tamborines
> Jing-jing-jingled in the hands of Queens.

(pp. 502-05)

Marianne Moore, "An Eagle in the Ring," in *The Dial,* Chicago, Vol. LXXV, No. 5, November, 1923, pp. 498-505.

ANN MASSA

(essay date 1968)

[In the following excerpt, Massa explores the relationship between Lindsay's artistic awareness and his social conscience.]

Lindsay was convinced of the existence of a national

malaise; and it was this conviction which diverted his artistic conscience into social channels. He was worried about amorality, conspicuous consumption, and urban eyesores. He was horrified by the perversion of electoral processes at city level, and by scandals at Federal Government level. Darwinistic indifference to social and financial inequalities appalled him; so did the jungle that awaited immigrants. Dedicated materialism was gaining adherence, while traditional standards of religion and morality, to which he subscribed, were slipping.

He was determined to stir up awareness of these alarming tendencies; and in the *War Bulletins* of 1909 (his privately printed monthly journal, which only ran to five issues) and in **'The Golden Whales of California'** . . . he fulminated against the almighty dollar. To counteract American 'deviationism' he put together his gospel of (oecumenical) Religion, (moral) Beauty, and (socialist) Equality; and through a series of poems on American history and myth—**'Our Mother Pocahontas', 'In Praise of Johnny Appleseed', 'Old, Old, Old Andrew Jackson', 'Abraham Lincoln Walks at Midnight', 'Bryan, Bryan, Bryan, Bryan', 'The Eagle That Is Forgotten'** (John Peter Altgeld), and **'Roosevelt'**—he tried to establish an American entity. It is in such social contexts that the bulk of Lindsay's writings become comprehensible. (p. 241)

Lindsay moved in the theological milieu of the reform impulse of the first two decades of the twentieth century. He had points of contact with the political theories of Herbert Croly, the economic panaceas of Henry George, the Social Gospel of Walter Rauschenbusch, and the muckraking activities of Henry Demarest Lloyd. But his diagnosis of the national *malaise* was too grim for him to affiliate himself with men whose vision of a root evil, and whose advocacy of one-stroke remedies—the readjustment of constitutional checks and balances, a Single Tax, the municipal ownership of utilities, trustbusting—sprang from basic confidence in a just off-course, easily righted America. Lindsay was not so sanguine. He considered America's problems were as much the formidable problems of mentality as the soluble ones of institutional defects. For him the American Dream had become 'a middle-class aspiration built on a bog of toil-sodden minds'.

In the 1920s his brand of pessimistic realism made him an even more alien figure. 'Arm yourself against the worst so that disappointment in humanity is impossible' he had noted in his diary; and he had too few expectations to be disillusioned by the 1914-18 war, or by the Peace of Versailles (in his eyes it was a step forward that the idea of international government had been given top-level airing). As an internationalist he found it hard to condone American isolationism and crudely domestic Presidential criteria; as a conscientious practitioner of the kind of Christian morality that

was preached in the Mid-west bible belt he could not come to terms with the decade's frenetic relaxation of taboos and its cultivation of materialism for its own sake.

But it was not solely in his capacity as an American citizen that Lindsay took it upon himself to criticize and protest; if the national need arose, the artist, as an individual with exceptional talents of perception and expression, had a duty to practise remedial art. Lindsay thus had a writer's concern with style and form; but the nature of his concern was idiosyncratic. He believed that a writer's duty was not to himself, but to his audience, which should be all-class and nation-wide. His artistic conscience told him to put matter and mass appeal before self-expression and aesthetics. Form was to follow the function of social utility.

In 1915 in *The Art of the Moving Picture,* and again in the 1922 edition, Lindsay hailed the motion picture as the most important artistic event of his lifetime. Not only could it lure people in for entertainment, and proceed to please whilst insidiously educating; it was an art form, with an art form's power to regenerate and refine. He tried to imitate it by making his writing a deceptive art for the people.

This stance was as extreme as art for art's sake, and as open to disputation. The logic of Lindsay's theory placed severe limitations on subtleties of construction and vocabulary; obliqueness was at a premium when the common man was the envisaged audience. For, while Lindsay believed in a dormant equality of taste, the American masses he was writing for were at the stage when 'they love best neither the words that explain, nor the fancies that are fine, nor the voice that is articulate with well-chosen speech'. They only responded to emotional, raucous modes of expression, and 'words must be chosen accordingly'.

It could be argued that Lindsay's disregard for traditional refinements of style, and for the Imagist experiments of the New Poetry, was less revolutionary and independent than it seemed. One of his talents was for the production of large, generous, rumbustious verse, which flowed along in spite of its imperfections, and without a great deal of stylistic reworking. A poet of emotion rather than one of intellectual discipline, he had a voracious appetite for recitation, both professionally (from 1913 to 1931) and in his leisure time at home. His conscientious response to duty, in fact, came easily, fulfilled his dramatic dimension, and involved genuine pleasure.

But talent and enjoyment did not guide his conscience; on the contrary, he almost failed to make the connexion. The national literary circuit acclaimed the choruses in **'The Congo'** of 'Boomlay, boomlay, boomlay, Boom', and 'Mumbo-Jumbo will hoo-doo you'; but Lindsay wondered whether he was writing poetry.

After all, he admitted, 'one composes it not by listening to the inner voice and following the gleam, but pounding the table and looking out of the window at electric signs'. Even a prize from *Poetry* in 1913 for **'General William Booth . . .'** did not still his doubts; it took the approval of William Butler Yeats to do that.

Lindsay and Yeats met at a dinner party given by Harriet Monroe for Yeats in Chicago in March 1914. Lindsay's recitation of **'The Congo'** was the sensation of the evening, and impressed Yeats. In after-dinner conversation with Lindsay he preached the virtues of folk-culture, and told Lindsay that all that survived in America of the much-to-be-desired 'primitive singing of poetry' and the Greek lyric chant was American vaudeville and Vachel Lindsay. The *imprimatur* reconciled Lindsay to his achievement; a man whose artistic conscience was avowedly a social conscience was bound to develop what he came to call 'The Higher Vaudeville'. (pp. 242-44)

To emphasize that his aim was more serious than vaudeville's, and to counteract its slapstick and revue connotations, Lindsay coined the phrase 'The Higher Vaudeville' to describe the poems he wrote in 'a sort of ragtime manner that deceives them [the American masses] into thinking they are at the vaudeville'. In spite of the rag-time manner he was 'trying to keep it to an art': it was a refined vaudeville, which sprang from his sensitive, critical response to American society, and his awareness of 'democracy [which] is itself a paradox'. Any beauty the Higher Vaudeville might describe or create was as paradoxical as democracy. . . .

One might usefully coin a . . . term, Higher Chautauqua, to convey what Lindsay was trying to achieve in the Higher Vaudeville, and throughout his writings. The Chautauqua movement (1875-*c.* 1925), which carried on the popular educational traditions of the lyceums with correspondence courses and tours of eminent speakers ranging from Phineas Taylor Barnum to William Rainey Harper, was a uniquely effective way of communicating with the adult population. Chautauqua's aim was mass morality and mass education, McGuffey-style; and Chautauqua's realistic and successful technique was to insert entertainments—minstrels, opera singers, circus acts—among its educational items, or even to disguise education as entertainment. (p. 246)

The Higher Vaudeville coincided with the pre-war heyday of Imagism, a movement which reflected precisely that dedication to form for form's sake, to the intrinsic worth of beautifully constructed, but comparatively unread and unheard poems, which Lindsay opposed. He scornfully called the imagists 'the Aesthetic Aristocracy', who 'were singing on an island to one another while the people perish'. Ezra Pound, *imagiste,* spoke for this school when he gleefully noted in July 1918 about the fourth volume of *The Little Review:* 'The response has been oligarchic; the plain man, in his gum overshoes, with his touching belief in W. J. Bryan, is not with us.' In the September issue, Lindsay was stung into an equally exaggerated, but telling response: 'I write for the good-hearted People of the Great Pure Republic.

He might be writing for the people; but was he reaching them? Lindsay found himself in a quandary. He had the message—but had he found the medium? Higher Vaudeville recitations brought in a large audience, and reached a new set of hearers (and sometimes readers): the American *bourgeoisie.* But Lindsay gradually realized that audiences enjoyed and remembered **'The Kallyope Yell'**, for instance, because that poem revived memories of steam and circus, and not because he had made the calliope an image of bathetic democracy in the lines

I am but the pioneer
Voice of the Democracy;
I am the gutter dream
I am the golden dream
Singing science, singing steam. . . .

As well as becoming dissatisfied with audience responses, Lindsay came to feel the difficulty of tying the Higher Vaudeville, a natural 'fun' medium, to serious topics; and he began to think of other media and other audiences. He was learning the hard way what Albert McLean noted about vaudeville, that 'cause and effect relationships were completely bypassed, the question of ultimate ends was never raised, and the problem of higher values could be submerged in waves of pathos and humor'. But up to 1920 he continued to operate within the limitations of his audiences; the acclaim he received from 1913 to 1920, however narrowly based, was exhilarating, and must have seemed to him to augur well for the popularization of his ideas through literature. However, in 1920 the tide swung against him. The Higher Vaudeville was no longer a novelty, and his unfashionable artistic conscience would not allow him to project universal dilemmas in personal terms, as Hemingway and Fitzgerald did so successfully. And in 1920 his message in its most studied form, *The Golden Book of Springfield,* flopped. Ironically, its failure was partly due to the logic of Higher Chautauqua. Lindsay was still orienting himself to an all-class audience, and tempered his discussion of social and political trends with a linking fantasy-cum-story. The end-product was an incongruous mixture of the sane and the silly, which irritated serious readers, and bored the rest. Stylistically, the sentiment and rhetoric which he could control in poetry ran away with him in prose. Digressions and exaggerations spilled over one another. But what uncomfortably persistent critique would have been acceptable in 1920, except Mencken's unique brand? Lindsay had picked the wrong moment to be preoccupied with what Americans ought to be: hedonism was about to set in. Today, the sombre fascination of Lindsay's perceptions redeems the book; an ironic reversal of the stylistic success of the Higher Vaudeville. In neither case was the medium the message.

Lindsay hung on to his belief in equality of taste; but he concluded that mass potential was more deeply buried than he had imagined, and mass crassness more deeply rooted. He decided to concentrate on élite audiences, who might read his books, and respond to his schemes: on teachers, students, journalists, businessmen and local dignitaries. Higher Chautauqua techniques were not applicable to these audiences; and he approached them differently. He prepared the ground by sending out a circular letter, 'The kind of visit I like to make'. The letter adjured journalists to teach his verses 'by running them in the newspaper with paraphrases and local applications by the editor'; and made it clear that Lindsay expected the English teachers to have his books 'in the school library or the public library the month beforehand. I mean nothing whatever to an audience unfamiliar with my work . . . I want every member of my audience to have at least some knowledge of these books. When he lectured on one particular book, 'Dear reader, either bring the book or stay away!' . . . At one time he made the half-serious suggestion that only those who could pass an examination on his books should be admitted to his recital/lectures.

Lindsay's attitude to his audience was barely recognizable as that of a creative writer seeking a hearing. He had come to think of himself as a teacher, and of his writings as textbooks. He had obviously become irritated and impatient, for he believed, however mistakenly, that he was offering a vital service to a public which would not avail itself of the service. An element of compensatory, personal arrogance was involved; but so was a generic, artistic arrogance. . . . (pp. 247-49)

To his contemporaries Lindsay's work seemed stagnant and retrospective, though in content, if not in style, it was naggingly valid. In one sense, however, he was an anachronism: he was a precursor and practitioner of present-day 'pop art'. He affirmed that popular taste—'the human soul in action'—was a neo-artistic perception; and he, as an artist, by acts of will, representation and reproduction, made this perception total art. Mass consensus had made Mary Pickford a folk-culture queen; and Lindsay repeatedly celebrated her national visual impact in a way comparable to Andy Warhol's statement-painting 'Marilyn Monroe', which consists of repeated rows of her face. The American collage of popcorn and yellow cabs, 'Arrow-collar heroes' and the Star Spangled Banner preoccupied him as realistically and sentimentally as it does many pop artists. And, just as pop artists let others finish their cre-

ations, and have them mass-produced, Lindsay, with the same mixture of arrogance and humility, urged other people to adapt and rewrite his work—though he was too far ahead of his times to be taken at his word.

Lindsay diverged from the main stream of pop art in that his aim was propaganda; pop artists tend to draw the line at comment. He was as much concerned to create as to accept popular culture, and he was interested in new media for the specific purposes of uplifting and educating the masses. Yet his enthusiastic support of the motion picture bears comparison with the pop-art theory of the interchangeability of words and pictures, and the communication potential of a nationally recognized alphabet of images. 'Edison is the new Gutenberg. He has invented the new printing', Lindsay wrote; and he went so far as to try his own hand at a new word/picture art which he called 'hieroglyphics': an entirely public art, an easily identified currency of national symbols. His nearest approximation of a successful hieroglyphic was the drawing of a lotus/rose . . . to celebrate the East/West symbolism of the Panama Canal; a pacific symbolism that would have found one American dissenter in T. R.! Motion pictures were hieroglyphics of a more complex sort. They were sculpture-in-motion, painting-in-motion, architecture-in-motion and furniture-in-motion; they were the American people in its envisaged likeness; they were the pop artist's multi-evocative images.

H. L. Mencken wrote of Lindsay's career that 'the yokels welcomed him, not because they were interested in his poetry, but because it struck them as an amazing and perhaps even a fascinatingly obscene thing for a sane man to go about the country on such bizarre and undemocratic business'. As usual, Mencken had a point amidst his hyperbole. Lindsay was implying not only mass deprivation, but temporary mass inferiority. He thus showed a certain lack of tact; and also, in failing to follow up the implications of the theory his conscience made him formulate, a lack of rationality. For instance, was abstract art necessarily selfish art? Did social insight always accompany creative ability? Was equality of taste desirable? Could any writer, without being an ideological weather-vane, consistently appeal to mass audiences which changed their tastes and *mores* in less than a generation?

Lindsay's failure to answer, perhaps even to pose, such questions made him react irrationally to his popularity with an audience which licked off the sugar coating, but left the rest of the pill. He had wanted to be like William Jennings Bryan—but resented being gaped at like a 'Bryan sensation' or 'like Tagore in his nightgown'. He felt he was being 'speculated in like pork'—but wasn't he himself pushing a commodity—his gospel and his urban blueprint—and making certain assumptions about the market? He was paying the penalty of his illogic; he was reacting with heart rather than mind. But his confusion and irateness were measures of his ambitious, earnest socioartistic conscience; and they were telling comments on his organization of himself as a writer. (pp. 250-52)

Ann Massa, "The Artistic Conscience of Vachel Lindsay," in *Journal of American Studies,* Vol. 2, No. 2, October, 1968, pp. 239-52.

PETER VIERECK
(essay date 1976)

[Viereck is a Pulitzer Prize-winning American poet, novelist, critic, and essayist. In the following excerpt, he links Lindsay with Dante as poets representative of their respective religious communities.]

The end of an outer material frontier to explore in the west and midwest has helped cause the increasing inner explorations of the spirit. Vachel Lindsay represents a transition: apparently still an outer explorer, an evoker of picturesque place-names and loud American voices in the fashion of an older school; yet in reality an inward voyager of the religious imagination and the aesthetic imagination. Lindsay remains the finest religious poet produced by America's most local native roots. He is the Dante of the Fundamentalists (A Yankee Doodle Dante).

The comparison of Lindsay with Dante is intended not in terms of greatness, whether of poetry or thought, but in terms of voicing one's roots. In their respective religious communities, each was the poet who best voiced his particular heritage. The contrasting views of man in those two heritages will broaden the second part of this discussion from Lindsay to American culture as a whole.

Lindsay is the Dante of America's only indigenous church: Fundamentalist Bible-belt revivalism. For that church he wrote major poetry of mystical vision, as well as the jingly junk (boom-lay-boom) for which he is better known. Carrying further, church for church and relic for relic, the analogy with the Florentine poet of Catholicism, we may summarize: Lindsay's Rome was Springfield, Illinois; his Holy Roman Emperor was the specter of Abe Lincoln; his Virgil-guide was Johnny Appleseed. His Beatrice was **"A Golden-Haired Girl in a Louisiana Town"**: "You are my love / If your heart is as kind / As your eyes are now." His martyred Saint Sebastian was Governor Altgeld (persecuted for saving the Haymarket anarchists from lynching). His angel hosts were the Anti-Saloon League and the Salvation Army, lovingly washing in the "blood of the lamb" the stenos and garage mechanics of Chicago.

To continue the analogy: Lindsay's version of the Deadly Sins, as a middleclass Fundamentalist schoolma'am might see them, were the beguiling depravities of "matching pennies and shooting craps," "playing poker and taking naps." These two lines are from **"Simon Legree,"** a combination of a Negro spiritual with a Calvinistic morality; the result of that combination can only be called: intoxicated with sobriety. Dante's medieval heretics partly corresponded to what Lindsay called "the renegade Campbellites," a Fundamentalist splinter-group secession:

O prodigal son, O recreant daughter,
When broken by the death of a child,
You called for the graybeard Campbellite elder,
Who spoke as of old in the wild . . .
An American Millennium . . .
When Campbell arose,
A pillar of fire,
The great high priest of the spring . . .

But then, in the same poem, comes the sudden self-mockery of:

And millennial trumpets poised, half-lifted,
Millennial trumpets that wait. . . .

Here the verb "wait," mocking the ever-unfulfilled prophecies of Fundamentalist revivalism, is the kind of slip that occurs accidentally-on-purpose. Such frequent semi-conscious slips represent Lindsay's protest against his self-imposed, self-deceiving role of trying to be more Fundamentalist than any Fundamentalist and more folkish than the real folk.

That self-imposed role, which ultimately became his shirt-of-Nessus, may have resulted from two tacit postulates. First, that poetry readers have no more right to laugh at the homespun Fundamentalist theology of the old American west than at the subtler but perhaps no more pious-hearted theology of Dante's day. Second, that the American small-town carnival deserved as much respect as Dante's medieval pageants; it was as fitting a literary theme; it was no less capable of combining the divine with the humdrum.

Once you concede these two postulates to Lindsay, all the rest seems to follow, including such lofty Lindsay invocations as: "Love-town, Troy-town Kalamazoo" and "Hail, all hail the popcorn stand." It follows that the Fundamentalist prophet, Alexander Campbell, should debate with the devil upon none other than "a picnic ground." It follows that real, tangible angels jostle Lindsay's circus-barkers and salesmen of soda pop. And certainly Lindsay has as much aesthetic right to stage a modern Trojan war, over love, between Osh Kosh and Kalamazoo as Homer between Greeks and Trojans. So far so good. But Lindsay often absurdly overstrains this aesthetic right, these old-world analogies. For example, he hails not an easily-hailed American *objet* like, say, Washington's monument but the popcorn stand.

Lindsay's motive for choosing the popcorn stand is not unconscious crudeness but conscious provocation. In effect he is saying: "By broadening the boundaries of aestheticism to include such hitherto-inacceptable Americana, my poetry is deliberately provoking, and thereby re-educating, all you supercilious eastern-seaboard-conditioned readers or Europe-conditioned readers."

But at the same time there is a suppressed saboteur within Lindsay, as within every exaggerated nationalist. That underground saboteur infiltrates Lindsay's poems via the most awkward-looking, absurdity-connoting letter in our alphabet, the letter "K." For whatever psychological reasons many Americans go into convulsions of laughter over the names of foreign towns like Omsk, Tomsk, Minsk, Pinsk, and nearer home, Hoboken, Yonkers, Keokuk, Sauk Center, not to mention those two Lindsay favorites, Osh Kosh and Kalamazoo. The core of each of those place-names is a throaty, explosive "K." (pp. 124-26)

Of course, no such deliberate linguistic analysis determined Lindsay's obsessive use of awkward town-names with "K." Rather, his use was determined by a blind instinct—a shrewdly blind instinct—for catching the very soul of spoken Americana. No one has ever equalled Lindsay's genius for manipulating the unconscious connotations of the colloquial, even though he perversely misused those connotations for the self-torturing purpose of provoking and then staring-down the ridicule of sophisticated audiences.

That willingness to provoke ridicule may produce his worst poems. Yet it is also the root of the moral courage producing his best poems, such as his elegy for Governor Altgeld of Illinois. Altgeld had defied a nineteenth-century kind of "McCarthyism" by his idealistic defense of slandered minorities. Political poetry, even courageous political poetry, is by itself merely a rhymed editorial, better written in prose, unless universalized beyond journalism and arid ideologies into the non-political realm of artistic beauty. Lindsay's Altgeld poem remains one of the great American elegies because it does achieve this humanizing process, transfiguring courage into lyric tenderness. . . . (p. 128)

However, more frequently the heroes Lindsay's poetry presents as the American equivalent of old-world Galahads are not exactly Altgelds. For example, the subtitle of his actual poem **"Galahad"** reads: "Dedicated to all Crusaders against the International and Interstate Traffic in Young Girls." The subtitle of his poem **"King Arthur's Men Have Come Again"** was equally earnest and uplifting, namely: "Written while a fieldworker in the Anti-Saloon League of Illinois." Of course, the moral heritage of rural Fundamentalism

particularly objects to alcohol, along with "playing poker and taking naps."

These twin odes to the Anti-Vice Squad and the Anti-Saloon League are bad poems not because the evil they denounce is unserious but because their treatment of that evil sounds like a mock-heroic parody. To explain such bad writing in so good a poet, let us suggest the hypothesis that Lindsay's mentality included a demon of self-destruction, forever turning the preacher into the clown. This compulsion forced Lindsay, again and again in his verse, to strip himself in public of every shred of what he most prized: human dignity. Perhaps this inner demon was related to the compulsion that finally made Lindsay choose not just any method of suicide but the most horribly painful method imaginable: swallowing a bottle of searing acid.

When a poet consistently exalts whatever heroes, place-names, and occupations sound most ludicrous to his modern poetry audience (for example, Lindsay was an avid exalter of college cheerleaders), it may be either because he has no ear for poetry or because he has an excellent ear knowingly misused. The first explanation is easily ruled out by the beauty of the above Altgeld elegy. Aside from the self-destructive aspect, there is an important messianic-pedagogic aspect making the second explanation the more plausible one. For example, by inserting the pedantic adjective "interstate" in front of "traffic in young girls" and thereby incongruously juxtaposing the prosaic Mann Act law with the poetic word "Galahad," Lindsay says in effect:

> If you accept my hick-fundamentalist approach to morality, which I happen to consider the only true and autochthonous American religion, then you must also accept its humorless terminology, its ridicule-provoking bigotries. What is more, you must accept them with a religious spirit exactly as earnest as that with which Homer and Dante accepted their own autochthonous religious traditions.

Thus considered, Lindsay's poetry is not mere clowning, whether intentional or unintentional, but—in his own revealing phrase—"the higher vaudeville." The adjective "higher" makes all the difference; it means a medieval vaudeville, a messianic circus, a homespun midwest equivalent of the medieval fool-in-Christ.

In refusing to be apologetic toward the old world about America's own kind of creativity, Lindsay does have a valid point. In refusing to allow European legends, heroes, place-names a greater claim on glamor than American ones, he again does have a valid point. Likewise when he establishes the American gift for finding loveliness in the exaggerated, the grotesque. But the self-sabotaging demon within him tends to push these valid points to extremes that strain even the most willing "suspension of disbelief."

When Lindsay fails to make us suspend our disbelief, the reason often is this: he is trying to link not two compatibles, such as prosaic object with prosaic rhetoric or fabulous object with fabulous rhetoric, but prosaic object with fabulous rhetoric. Modern university-trained readers of poetry react unsolemnly to: "Hail, all hail the popcorn stand." Why? Because of a gap I would define as: the Lindsay disproportion. The Lindsay disproportion is the gap between the heroic tone of the invocation and the smallness of the invoked object. But Lindsay's aim, rarely understood by modern readers, was to overcome that disproportion between tone and object by conjuring up a mystic grandeur to sanctify the smallness of American trivia. That mystic grandeur derived from his dream of America as a new world free from old-world frailty, free from original sin. His dream-America was infinitely perfectable, whatever its present faults. Even its most trivial objects were sacred because incarnating the old Rousseauistic dream of natural goodness of man and eternal progress.

Lindsay believed, or felt he ought to believe, in the impossible America invented by the French poet Chateaubriand and other European romantics. Later, much later (nature imitating art) that invented America was sung by Americans themselves, by Emerson and Whitman. In poetry this utopian American myth culminated in Lindsay's *Golden Book of Springfield* and Hart Crane's *The Bridge;* in politics it culminated in the Populist and Progressive movements of the west. (pp. 128-31)

Instead of pouncing with shoddy glee on the absurd aspects of the Lindsay disproportion between tone and object, let us reexamine more rigorously the Chateaubriand-style dream of America behind those absurd aspects. That American myth is part of a romantic, optimistic philosophy seriously maintained, whatever one may think of it, by great or almost-great minds like Rousseau and Emerson. Therefore, it is unjust to dismiss that same philosophy contemptuously in Lindsay merely because his name has less prestige than theirs. What is wrong-headed in him, is wrong-headed in his preceptors also. He and they dreamed of a new world miraculously reborn without the burden of past history. That unhistorical myth of America distinguishes Whitman and Lindsay from Hawthorne and Faulkner in literature. It distinguishes Jefferson from John Adams in political philosophy. It distinguishes Fundamentalist revivalism, with its millennium just around the corner, and the hope of quick redemption that Lindsay's poetry hailed in the Salvation Army, from Niebuhrian pessimism within the American Protestant religion. While Lindsay is the Dante of the Fundamentalists, he differs from the old-world Catholic Dante by substituting a romantic, optimistic view of man for the tragic view held by traditional Christianity as well as by Greek classicism.

On this issue American literature has two con-

flicting traditions, the first romantic and progressive, the second classical and conservative. The first heartily affirms American folklore, American democratic and material progress. That Whitman-Emerson literary tradition cracked up in Vachel Lindsay and Hart Crane. It cracked up not merely in their personal breakdowns and final suicides—let us not overstress mere biography—but in the aesthetic breakdown of the myth-making part of their poetry. The non-mythic part of their poetry, its pure lyricism, never did break down and in part remains lastingly beautiful.

A second American tradition is that of the literary pessimists, a new-world continuation of the great Christian pessimists of the old world, from Saint Augustine to Kierkegaard and Cardinal Newman. In America the second literary tradition is just as authentically American as the first one but has never received the same popular recognition, being less comforting. The most influential literary voices of our second tradition are Melville, Hawthorne, Henry Adams, William Faulkner. Its greatest political heritage comes from the Federalist papers and from the actual anti-Jeffersonian party of the Federalists, with their partly European source not in Rousseau but in Burke. Its most influential theological voices in America today are Paul Tillich and Reinhold Niebuhr. Note that all these literary, political, and theological voices are characterized by skepticism about man and mass and by awareness of the deep sadness of history. Therefore, their bulwark against man and mass and against the precariousness of progress is some relatively conservative framework of traditional continuity, whether in culture, literature, politics, or religion. (pp. 131-33)

The optimistic progress-affirming and folklore-affirming voices of Emerson and Whitman cracked up in their disciples Lindsay and Crane when the crushing of the individual in modern mechanization became simply too unbearable to affirm. The modern poet of progress may try to keep up his optimistic grin for his readers while the custard pie of "higher vaudeville" drips down his face. But past a certain point, he can no longer keep up the grin, whether psychologically in his private life or aesthetically in his public poetry. Our overadjusted standardization becomes just one custard pie too many for the unadjusted poet to affirm, no matter how desperately he tries to outshout his inner tragic insight by shouting (in Lindsay's case) "Hail, all hail the popcorn stand" and by hailing (in Crane's case) the Brooklyn Bridge as "the myth whereof I sing." Lindsay and Crane committed suicide in 1931 and 1932 respectively, in both cases in that depression era which seemed temporarily to end the boundless optimism of American material progress. (p. 134)

What is shoddy in the American myth is not affirmation itself; classic tragedy affirms ("Gaiety transfiguring all that dread"). What is shoddy is not the hard-won affirmation that follows tragic insight but the facile unearned optimism that leads only to disillusionment. Here is a prose example of how Lindsay's valid crusade against the adjective "standardized" collapses suddenly into a too-easy optimism:

> I have been looking out of standardized windows of "The Flat-Wheeled Pullman car." I have been living in standardized hotels, have been eating jazzed meals as impersonal as patent breakfast-food. . . . The unstandardized thing is the overwhelming flame of youth . . . an audience of one thousand different dazzling hieroglyphics of flame. . . . My mystic Springfield is here, also, in its fashion . . . a Springfield torn down and rebuilt from the very foundations, according to visions that might appear to an Egyptian . . . or any one else whose secret movie-soul was a part of the great spiritual movie. . . .

Note the typical Lindsay disproportion by which this moving passage ends with an appalling anticlimax, equating Hollywood's facile commercialized "visions" with the tragically-earned classic ones. Yet his best and worst writing are so intertwined that this "movie soul" gush is immediately followed by one of his finest prose passages about American democracy at its noblest:

> I believe that civic ecstasy can be so splendid, so unutterably afire, continuing and increasing with such apocalyptic zeal, that the whole visible fabric of the world can be changed. . . . And I say: change not the mass, but change the fabric of your own soul and your own visions, and you change all. . . .
>
> (p. 139)

Lindsay's authentic western Americana were never presented for their own sake, never merely as quaint antiques for the tourist trade. Rather, they were presented for the more serious purposes of either his Whitman-messianic aspect or his Ruskin-aesthetic aspect. . . . (pp. 140-41)

Part of Lindsay's aesthetic compulsion, giving him the uniqueness only possessed by major poets, lies in his juxtaposition of the delicate and the grotesque: for example, in his phrase "the flower-fed buffaloes of the spring," subject of one of his purest lyrics. Running through his diversities of titles and subject matter, note also the delicate and the grotesque color-juxtapositions of "the king of yellow butterflies" with "the golden whales of California" and the semantic juxtaposition of "harps in heaven" with "the sins of Kalamazoo." Such gargoyle tenderness is a genre of sensibility explored by few other poets beside Beddoes and Rimbaud, the poets with whom Lindsay's unfulfilled genius, beneath its tough loud disguises, properly belongs. (p. 141)

Delicacy is not a noun most modern readers associate with Lindsay. Yet his sense of cadence was so very delicate that it disguised itself defensively, his time and place being what they were, beneath ear-splitting auditory signposts. His signposts deliberately pointed in the wrong direction, the loud indelicate direction. Living where he did and believing the myth he believed, he needed to conceal his bitter, introverted sensitivity beneath the extroverted optimism of American folklore. That is, beneath a tone deliberately coarse, chummy, whooping, the whiz-bang claptrap of poems like **"The Kallyope Yell."** In such curiosities of our literature, no poet was ever more perversely skilful at sounding embarrassingly unskilful. No poet was ever more dexterous at sounding gauche. . . .

Consequently Lindsay's poetry is often defined as mere oratory, to be shouted aloud by a mob chorus. Part of him wanted this view to be held. Another part of him lamented: "I have paid too great a penalty for having a few rhymed orations. All I write is assumed to be loose oratory or even jazz, though I have never used the word 'jazz' except in irony." His best work, often his least known work, was produced by the part of him that once confessed: "All my poetry marked to be read aloud should be whispered . . . for the inner ear . . . whispering in solitude." (p. 142)

Like Yeats, Lindsay transforms sentimentality into true art by means of the accompanying antisentimentality of nervously sinewy rhythms. Note, for example, the craftsmanship with which the lean rhythmic rightness of these two Lindsay quatrains redeems their otherwise sentimental rhetoric:

> Why do I faint with love
> Till the prairies dip and reel?
> My heart is a kicking horse
> Shod with Kentucky steel.
> No drop of my blood from north
> Of Mason and Dixon's line
> And this racer in my breast
> Tears my ribs for a sign. . . .
>
> (p. 144)

Let us consider that extraordinary Bryan poem first aesthetically, then politically. Note the sensuous concreteness of imagery. Instead of characterizing Bryan's enemies with the abstract, unlyrical word "the rich," Lindsay says concretely: "Victory of letter files / And plutocrats in miles / With dollar signs upon their coats." His self-mocking sense of humor, the subtlely of his pseudo-crudity, explains the surrealist fantasy of pretending, with wonderful preposterousness, that plutocrats literally wear dollar signs on their coats. (p. 145)

In Lindsay's day, the midwest dream of messianic "civic ecstasy" in politics (really, Fundamentalist revivalism secularized) still had a touching youthful innocence; his Bryan poem, despite its doctrinaire social message, could still succeed in being movingly lyrical; American optimism was cracking but not yet cracked up. In contrast, the neo-Populist nationalism of our own day can find no voice, whether poetic or social-reformist, of Lindsay's cultural or moral stature. For meanwhile American standardization plus Ortega's "revolt of the masses" have transformed salvation-via-mob from innocent dream to sordid nightmare. And from genuine economic needs (such as Populist farmers exploited by railroads) to economic hypochondria. (p. 146)

From this salvation-via-mob dilemma, with its false choice between leftist and rightist mob-hatreds, Lindsay himself pointed the way out. The way out was love; not that philistine-humanitarian love of progress (so aptly refuted by Edmund Burke and Irving Babbitt) whose hug squashes individuals into an impersonal mass; but the creative lyric love that flows healingly from the inner integrity—the holy imagination—of great art. In short, when Lindsay did voice deeply enough the roots of the human condition, he became a fundamental poet, rather than merely the poet of the Fundamentalists. His poem **"The Leaden-Eyed"** describes perfectly the human price paid for unimaginative standardization and at the same time, through the very act of being lyrical, demands the rehumanizing of the machine age:

Not that they starve, but starve so dreamlessly,
Not that they sow, but that they seldom reap,
Not that they serve, but have no gods to serve,
Not that they die but that they die like sheep. . . .

Such a rehumanizing-through-creativity as Lindsay achieved at his best, seems the only way out from our age of the three impersonal M's: masses, machines, and mediocrity. This great, absurd, and holy poet of America's native religious roots merits the adjective "God-intoxicated" because he found the redeeming religious imagination everywhere, everywhere—in the absurd as well as in the high. . . . (p. 147)

Peter Viereck, "Vachel Lindsay: The Dante of the Fundamentalists," in *A Question of Quality: Popularity and Value in Modern Creative Writing,* edited by Louis Filler, Bowling Green University Popular Press, 1976, pp. 124-47.

JAMES DICKEY

(essay date 1979)

[Dickey, an American poet, novelist, and critic, is considered one of America's foremost contemporary writers. In the following excerpt, he argues for a reappraisal of Lindsay's works, discovering in the poet's career a unique and total commitment to the powers of invention.]

Though the small Midwestern towns of the early part of the century did not, for Sherwood Anderson's Hugh McVey in "Poor White," "burn and change in the light," they strangely and confidently did for Nicholas Vachel Lindsay . . . ; in fact, they were the light, glowing with every imaginable color, giving off the odd-angled and essential glimmers of New World "promise" from a smoldering bedrock communality, a combustion always latent, and always—especially under Lindsay's own ministrations—capable of leaping into full, vital flame, warming, entertaining and explaining us all. His birthplace, Springfield, Ill., was for him this quintessential town, the rapt, chanting keeper of the Christian-Populist flame, undevious and irresistible, in whose light all things look and sound as they are: obvious, clumsy, crazy, good-hearted, vigorous, outgoing and, above all, loud. Lindsay's **"Golden Book of Springfield"** is the Book of Books of this ideal, its Platonic frame and fire-cave.

Have we really buried foolish, half-talented, half-cracked Lindsay in the textbooks—the very oldest and most mistaken ones—of literary history? Have we settled him in the dust of provincial libraries, in the unimaginable oblivion of metropolitan bookvaults? Was there ever anything, really, in all his wandering, his "gospel of beauty," his "higher vaudeville"? In those forgotten audiences hungering for him and his readings, providing thunderous response to his poems? Or in his curious, exasperating, self-enchanted, canny, bulldozing and somehow devilish innocence? Can any of him be saved, or is it better to move on? (pp. 9, 17)

It seems to me . . . that Lindsay's career and example raise some interesting—if not exactly crucial—questions about the relation between the poet and his audience, and also about the desirability and danger of self-delusion in the artist. I have always felt that Lindsay provided a kind of focus by means of which we might, if we so choose, gauge such questions and to some extent resolve them, each privately. But beyond a few superficial assumptions gleaned from the author notes of anthologies, I have never, before reading [*Letters of Vachel Lindsay*], known much of what sort of man Lindsay actually was, or how he lived and worked, that he had studied medicine and trained as an artist before devoting himself mainly to poetry.

I use the word *worked* advisedly, for Lindsay was very consciously a *worker* in the cause of his version of poetry, and of some mysterious entity he and his Campbellite mother called "art": for example, his accounts of the means he used to get his poems and graphics—his "Christian cartoons"—before a public are not only enthralling in themselves but show a kind of crank ingenuity that is quite impressive and even heartening in its singlemindedness. One would like to have the guts, the *chutzpah,* to do some of the things he did to reach people, and these not in isolated instances but as a mere matter of course. (p. 17)

The letters after [the] early ones are an erratic reverse "Pilgrim's Progress" through successive states of eroding self-delusion, a raw account of the manner in which a man of compassion and of odd-ball, shamanistic insight was fashioned into a freak—or, better still, into a carnival geek. For Lindsay, what seemed at first to be the incredibly fecund native ground of the American village turned into a tangled, sterile wilderness of hamlet-studded, boob-haunted railroad track, once the mere novelty of his personal presence and his "message" had been worn off by over-exposure; just before his suicide at 52 in the house of his birth in "golden" Springfield, he confessed that both he and his "dream" had failed utterly, that he had wasted himself, and spoke of "my best years . . . simply used up in shouting."

If I had the power, I should like very much to save Lindsay, to hold on to at least some aspects of him, if for only one reason. He lived naturally in a condition that many greater poets never had, or if they had it, were embarrassed or diffident about it: a total commitment to his own powers of invention, a complete loss of himself in his materials. To his fantasies, to the absurd figures he made—not a whit more convincing than Disney's—by trying to mythologize American history and legend, he gave himself in unthinking abandon: He invited and gloried in seizure, and as a result was totally immersed in his creative element, no matter what might be the end result. Perhaps that is not much, but perhaps it is more than we think. The best of Lindsay's poetry seems to me unique, its innocence not only real but unified and valuable. The letters, too, make available the same kind of right-or-wrong totality, the hell-with-it and go-with-it. (pp. 17-18)

James Dickey, "The Geek of Poetry," in *The New York Times Book Review,* December 23, 1979, pp. 9, 17-18.

SOURCES FOR FURTHER STUDY

Enkvist, Nils Erik. "The Folk Elements in Vachel Lindsay's Poetry." *English Studies* 32, Nos. 1-6 (1951): 241-49.

  Examines the sources and treatment of American folk-lore, Negro history, and American Indian legend in Lindsay's work.

Massa, Ann. *Vachel Lindsay: Fieldworker for the American Dream.* Bloomington: Indiana University Press, 1970, 310 p.

  Biography that sympathetically details Lindsay's life and explores *The Golden Book of Springfield* at length.

Masters, Edgar Lee. *Vachel Lindsay: A Poet in America.* New York: Charles Scribner's Sons, 1935, 392 p.

  Biography that includes lengthy excerpts from Lindsay's journals and offers Masters's own insights on the poet's life and career.

Mencken, H. L. "Vachel Lindsay: The True Voice of Middle America." *The Courier* II, No. 4 (December 1962): 13-16.

  Proclaims Lindsay a representative voice of America and the only poet since Walt Whitman to display any notable originality.

Monroe, Harriet. "Vachel Lindsay." In her *Poets & Their Art,* pp. 21-8. New York: MacMillan, 1932.

  Favorable assessment of Lindsay's poetry, praising the poet's wisdom, humor, and insight.

Van Doren, Carl. "Salvation with Jazz: Vachel Lindsay." In his *Many Minds,* pp. 151-66. New York: Alfred A. Knopf, 1924.

  Overview of Lindsay's career, noting that "the potency of Mr. Lindsay's verse . . . shows how far he goes beyond mere noise and rhythm. He has pungent phrases, clinging cadences, dramatic energy, comic thrust, lyric seriousness, tragic intensity."

Jack London

1876-1916

(Full name John Griffith London) American novelist, short story writer, essayist, journalist, autobiographer, and dramatist.

INTRODUCTION

*L*ondon was a popular author whose fiction combined high adventure, socialism, mysticism, Darwinian determinism, and Nietzschean theories of race. Of the fifty books published during his career, *The Call of the Wild* (1903) is the most famous and widely read. London's fiction, particularly *The Call of the Wild, The Sea-Wolf* (1904), and *The Iron Heel* (1908), and the short stories "Love of Life," "To Build a Fire," and "Bâtard," are considered classics in American literature, and have often been compared with the stories of Joseph Conrad and Rudyard Kipling.

London was born in San Francisco to Flora Wellman, who had been abandoned by her common-law husband of one year. Nine months after the child's birth, Wellman married John London, for whom the infant was named. The family moved often, living on farms and attempting several business schemes at the insistence of London's mother, a proud, erratic, somewhat unstable woman whose actions went unchecked by her gentle but ineffective husband. After completing grammar school in Oakland, London worked in a cannery and as a longshoreman; he also became a nocturnal scavenger on San Francisco Bay, styling himself as the "Prince of the Oyster Pirates." While still in his teens he tramped around the country viewing the seamy side of life, which he later depicted in *The Road* (1907). In his spare time London read widely in literature and philosophy, and was most profoundly influenced by the works of Herbert Spencer, Karl Marx, Kipling, and Friedrich Nietzsche. At the age of nineteen he enrolled in high school, completing the course work in one year, then entered the University of California, where he also joined the Socialist Workers Party. Unable to finance more than one semester of college, he went to the Klondike during the gold rush of 1898. A year later he returned to San Francisco penniless, but with a wealth of memories that provided the raw material for his first collection of short stories, *The Son of the Wolf* (1900), which contains violent, colorful adventures about men and animals fighting for survival amidst the "white silence" of the pitiless Yukon wilds. These stories were immensely popular, and several other stories and novels set in Alaska followed, written in the simple, vigorous style that distinguishes London's work. *The Call of the Wild* and *White Fang* (1906), the most highly regarded of these Alaskan books, are characteristic in their exploration of the struggle between the conflicting calls of barbarity and civilization.

In 1900, confident that early success promised impending greatness, London married with the expectation that his wife would cure his wanderlust by providing a stable, well-disciplined family environment that would enable him to produce serious literary works. His wife, however, soon resented the weekly gatherings of intellectuals, hangers-on, and assorted "characters" that London arranged in order to amuse himself with games, pranks, and heated debate. In this setting London met the independent, talkative Charmian Kittredge. She fulfilled his ideal of the comrade-mate that he depicted in numerous stories and novels. After three years of marriage London and his wife separated, and London married Charmian within a day of his final divorce decree.

In addition to his popular and highly remunerative fiction, London also wrote for various magazines as a journalist. Among other assignments, he was a widely syndicated correspondent during the Russo-Japanese War of 1904-05. He continually sought first-hand experience for his writings, the most important instance being the period in 1902 when he wandered the slums of England disguised as a derelict; he later recorded his observations of poverty and degradation in *The People of the Abyss* (1903). The highest paid writer of his day, London earned more than a million dollars; but financial naiveté and poor judgment were compounded by mismanagement on the part of his employees. The thousands of dollars he poured into labor and materials for his boat, the *Snark,* and his dream home, Wolf House, are the most striking examples of his ill-advised faith in his business sense. The destruction of Wolf House, a case of suspected arson, was a devastating event from which London never recovered. In his last years, he was despondent about his failure to produce a male heir, and mounting financial obligations drove him to maintain the taxing thousand-word-a-day writing schedule he had established at the onset of his career. Suffering from constant pain and depression brought on by various maladies, including liver and intestinal disease, London tried to mask his symptoms with drugs and alcohol in order to keep up the self-imposed public image of the invincible man of action. It has been conjectured that his death from an overdose of painkiller was suicide.

The wide variety of experiences and readings that fed London's literary imagination produced the seemingly contradictory world views found in his works. His high regard for the writings of Charles Darwin and Nietzsche is demonstrated by the doctrines of rugged individualism and of the amoral *übermensch* ("superman") that dominate such early adventure stories as *The Call of the Wild* and *The Sea-Wolf. The Call of the Wild* differs drastically from the overly sentimental animal stories popular during London's early career, with his dog protagonist Buck existing unrestrained by the human emotions and morality that limited portrayal of the savagery of nature in other popular novels. Buck's brutality and complete avarice are at the same time repelling and alluring to readers who vicariously participate in his conquests without guilt. In later short story collections such as *South Sea Tales* (1911), London's evolutionary theory took on the sinister aspect of white supremacy reflected in characterizations of Nordic or Anglo-Saxon heroes as conquerors of "inferior" island races. Yet, at the time that London was writing these celebrations of the Great Blond Beast, he was also producing thoughtful socialist novels and essays in which he advocated the solidarity of the working class for the betterment of humanity. *The Iron Heel,* a futuristic dystopia, is the most notable example of his political fiction; in this work, London drew upon his experiences as a laborer and his reading of Marx to portray a vision of the rise of fascism in America. Marxist critic Leon Trotsky called the novel "astonishing" in its "prophetic vision of the methods by which the Iron Heel will sustain its domination over crushed mankind." As in most of his works, London projected his own political sympathies into the novel, making his protagonist a socialist leader who champions the cause of labor reform. These paradoxes in London's fiction mirror the contradictions of his personal and political life; he once told a reporter, "I am a white man first and a socialist second."

London also declared that such works as *The Sea-Wolf* and the autobiographical *Martin Eden* (1909) were written to refute the doctrines of individualistic supermen, an argument many critics have been unable to reconcile upon examination of the texts. In *The Sea-Wolf,* the Nietzschean sea captain, Wolf Larsen, bears London's nickname and his past and shares his favorite authors and philosophical beliefs. He also echoes London's insistence upon facing the reality that life is totally meaningless as opposed to accepting the comforts of moral convention and traditional religious faith. Many critics consider these and other criteria unmistakable evidence of London's admiration for Wolf Larsen. In *Martin Eden* on the other hand, London created what some critics regard as a self-conscious, self-pitying, romanticized portrait of the author as a young man. Early critics dismissed the novel as a minor work replete with embarrassing revelations and stylistic flaws, and regarded the protagonist's ultimate suicide as absurdly unaccountable. However, more recent critics view the suicide as a natural consequence of Eden's discovery of nihilistic truths he is emotionally unfit to face—not unlike the reaction of Wolf Larsen. Though each man secretly desires to return to a paradise of ignorance, the dark knowledge can only be escaped through "the long sickness" or death.

London believed that all great fiction blended fact with romantically rendered beauty, power, brutality, and other vigorous attributes. Accordingly, he romanticized autobiographical experiences in his works. Many critics believe that an egotistic narcissism drove him to project himself into the strongest, hardest working, most intelligent protagonists in his works, while the physically extraordinary, unconventional helpmates in such later novels as *The Valley of the Moon* (1913) and *The Little Lady of the Big House* (1916) idealize the qualities he most admired in his wife Charmian.

Most critics agree with H. L. Mencken's estimate that London's "too deadly industry" produced a "steady emission of half-done books" that the author did not rework. However, most also agree that despite stylistic clumsiness and didactic intent, there remain in London's works moments of brilliance. His innovative, simple style, descriptive skill, and adherence to the principles of Naturalism laid the ground work for such later writers as Sherwood Anderson, Ring Lardner, and Ernest Hemingway. In Earle Labor's estimation, London's stature as an artist derives from "his 'primordial vision'—the mythopoeic force which animates his finest creations and to which we respond without fully knowing why." Carl Sandburg defined the basis of the attraction when he stated: "The more civilized we become, the deeper is the fear that back in barbarism is something of the beauty and joy of life we have not brought with us." London's works offer this vicarious alternative, as Robert Barltrop observed, because "their material does not reflect—indeed, it provides an escape from—life as the mass of people know it."

(For further information about London's life and works, see *Concise Dictionary of American Literary Biography, 1865-1917*; *Dictionary of Literary Biography*, Vols. 8, 12, 78; *Short Story Criticism*, Vol. 4; *Something about the Author*, Vol. 18; and *Twentieth-Century Literary Criticism*, Vols. 9, 15, 39.)

CRITICAL COMMENTARY

MAXWELL GEISMAR
(essay date 1953)

[Geismar is one of America's most respected literary critics. In the following excerpt, he provides a survey of London's work.]

London's first collection of Arctic tales, *The Son of the Wolf*, in 1900, was dedicated to the last of the frontiersmen "who sought their heritage and left their bones among the shadows of the circle." (p. 144)

Against the background of abstract splendor, there were the deeds of men's heroism, or cruelty, or the meticulous descriptions of moral and physical deterioration as in the scurvy, when muscles and joints began to swell, the flesh turned black, and gums and lips took on the color of rich cream. In *"In A Far Country"* two tenderfeet from the Southland lose their sanity in the silent space of an Arctic winter—are betrayed finally by nature's apparitions. (pp. 144-45)

[The second collection, *The God of His Fathers*, presented] writing that was completely fresh in its time, offering a contrast to the sweetness and goodness of popular fiction in the 1900's. The cadence of [the] prose only became completely familiar to us, indeed, in the work of the postwar generation of the 1920's. The frenzied epic of the gold rush was summarized in a vista of broken and dying animals (beside which the famous horses in Stephen Crane's work were almost untouched). In these tales of cupidity, of fear, of hunger, of the grim humor of murder and death, too, the will to survive—all that was left here of men's appetites and joys—was often viewed as another kind of phobia, ironical, insane. And in the lament of a northern gambler who was bankrupt and pursued by the shapes and forms of his crimes, merely waiting for death in the same unchanging position, London made his theme explicit. "Life's a skin-game. . . . I never had half a chance. . . . I was faked in my birth and flimflammed with my mother's milk. The dice were loaded when she tossed the box, and I was born to prove the loss."

But there were few instances in the short stories where London's sense of character was up to the level of the emotions he described, or where in fact the excellent material was not finally circumscribed by a shallow set of moral values. After the hero of **"The Great**

Principal Works

The Son of the Wolf (short stories) 1900

The God of His Fathers and Other Stories (short stories) 1901

A Daughter of the Snows (novel) 1902

The Call of the Wild (novel) 1903

The Kempton-Wace Letters [with Anna Strunsky] (novel) 1903

The People of the Abyss (essay) 1903

The Sea-Wolf (novel) 1904

The Game (novel) 1905

War of the Classes (essays) 1905

White Fang (novel) 1906

Before Adam (novel) 1907

Love of Life and Other Stories (short stories) 1907

The Road (essays) 1907

The Iron Heel (novel) 1908

Martin Eden (novel) 1909

Lost Face (short stories) 1910

Revolution and Other Essays (essays) 1910

The Cruise of the "Snark" (essays) 1911

South Sea Tales (short stories) 1911

John Barleycorn (autobiography) 1913

The Valley of the Moon (novel) 1913

The Mutiny of the "Elsinore" (novel) 1914

The Strength of the Strong (short stories) 1914

The Scarlet Plague (novella) 1915

The Star Rover (novel) 1915

The Little Lady of the Big House (novel) 1916

The Turtles of Tasman (short stories and drama) 1916

The Red One (short stories) 1918

Island Tales (short stories) 1920

Letters (letters) 1965

Interrogation," like many northern adventurers, had taken an Indian wife, he was urged by his former sweetheart, Mrs. Sayther, to renounce a debased form of marriage. . . . And this anthropological widow couching her love call in the clichés of popular Darwinism, expressed the central point of view in London's collection of Indian stories, *Children of the Frost,* in 1902. Although Sitka Charley, the half-breed, had been one of London's heroes in the earlier series of tales, even he, respecting, almost venerating the white man's power, had yet to divine its secret essence, so we are told—the honor of the trail, and of the 'law.'

Whose law, what law? The white man's law, of course, or at least the law in Kipling's romances of the white man's fate, as adapted to an imperial American audience of the 1900's. (pp. 145-46)

[In **"The League of Old Men,"** an] aboriginal chieftain recorded a desperate compact to kill off the whites before the tribal life had disappeared completely. The judge, listening to this confession of crime and frustration, also has another view of race—his steel-shod, mail-clad race, the lawgiver and worldmaker among the families of men. "He saw it dawn red-flickering across the dark forests and sullen seas; he saw it blaze, bloody and red, to full and triumphant noon; and down the shaded slope he saw the blood-red sands dropping into night."

Darwin's grand principle of natural selection had been cut down here, even from the Anglo-Saxon 'law' of conquest and empire to a single law of slaughter in the progress of Nordics whose horizon was bathed in a river of blood. Nevertheless, the boss of the Yukon

in London's first novel, *A Daughter of the Snows,* in 1902, was another economic strong man and empire builder. Jacob Welse is a robber baron of the Arctic shore, a raw individualist of the icy waste, who combines private enterprise with the code of the frontier. . . . The Yukon scene of *A Daughter of the Snows* contained Bonanza Kings who were adventurers, outcasts, misfits, scoundrels from the four corners of the world; the life in the dance halls of Dawson with their gamblers and gay women; the odd democracy of the northern frontier with its extremes of fantastic wealth, gained overnight, and of ruin, suffering and death; the mixed society of miners, tradespeople, guides, badmen, hunters, trappers and police; the mixture and jumble of national types from the Americans, Russians and Scandinavians to the Indians, Eskimos and half-breeds. But all this—the true material of the novelist—was used only for 'local color,' a trite romance, a meretricious philosophy.

And London himself had realized his first novel was a failure while he was writing it. In the movement of a talent which was itself a mixture of extremes, spontaneous, poetic, erratic, unchartable, even while it had already been confined to the standards of popular fiction, he was on the edge of his first memorable work. (pp. 147-49)

[*The Call of the Wild*] was in fact a sort of prose-poem, a novella of a single mood, admirably sustained. The sketch of the great Chilkoot Divide, which stood between the salt water and the fresh, "and guards forbiddingly the sad and lonely North," set the tone; just as the early episode in which Buck was 'broken' into the "reign of primitive law," the first step in his education as a pack dog, starts his reversion to the wild. One notices how delicately London kept his story within the limits of credible animal behavior. The human beings are good or bad, efficient or useless, only to the degree that they affect the well-being of the dogs—and here indeed the brutes often rose to a stoic dignity not granted to the humans. (p. 149)

London carried us back—with an ease and sureness of perception that appeared also to be "without effort of discovery"—through the ages of fire and roof to the raw beginnings of animal creation. . . . The theory of racial instinct, of memory as inherited habit, that was at the start, through long aeons, a very conscious and alert process of behavior indeed—this theory, as developed by such figures as Samuel Butler, Bergson or Jung, was very clear here, of course. Similarly, the scene in which Buck finally deposed Spitz as the leader of the team, surrounded by the ring of huskies waiting to kill and eat the vanquished king, was a perfect instance of the 'son-horde' theory which Frazer traced in *The Golden Bough,* and of that primitive ritual to which Freud himself attributed both a sense of original sin and the fundamental ceremony of religious exorcism. But what is fascinating in *The Call of the Wild* is the brilliance of London's own intuitions (quite apart from any system of psychology) in this study of animal instincts which are the first, as they are the final biological response to the blind savagery of existence. (pp. 150-51)

If *The Call of the Wild* celebrated the animal instincts, indeed, *The Sea Wolf,* in 1904, still one of London's best known or best remembered novels, was the study of a cruel and to a large degree corrupt 'natural man.' The writer himself claimed the story was an argument against a rapacious individualism, and was one of his most widely misunderstood books. But there was a certain ambiguity between the 'conscious' moral of the artist and the true emotional center of his work. The popular audience at least was concerned with the portrait of a savage and tyrannical sea captain. Wolf Larsen was really a sort of nautical Nietzsche or a Lucifer of the sealing trade—vicious and proud spirit that he was, condemned by his own excess of vitality. He had "the mechanism of a primitive fighting beast," he was perfectly at home in the welter of violence that marked the sailing life of his period; he took pleasure and almost drew his life breath by tormenting and mastering the crew.

In addition, he has read Herbert Spencer and theorizes at some length about the meaning of life, immortality, social reform. Larsen is today, of course, through modern eyes, an empty and inflated figure; without the myth of the superman to bolster his rhetoric, his original fascination has collapsed. (p. 153)

[Heroes] and villains alike in the story all became puppets in a continuous play of shocks and horrors.

The true theme of *The Sea Wolf* was simply the reversion of a higher form of intelligence not so much to an animal as to a subhuman level. The consciousness of evil is the corrupting element; the novel's tone in the end is curiously close to that of entertainment. . . . Did the evidence of virility flow really through these channels of brutality? There was a practically schizophrenic split here between brutal Darwinian mating (or coupling) and the spiritual love, attendant upon a world of art and culture in London's mind, which was attributed to the novel's two upper-class figures, Humphrey Van Weyden and Maude Brewster. The closing sections of *The Sea Wolf* marked, indeed, the victory of a false idealism over what was essentially a false, and to some degree perverted materialism, and this was also a central issue in *The Kempton-Wace Letters,* which London had published a year earlier, in 1903.

The book was written in collaboration with Anna Strunsky, gifted daughter of a Russian Jewish family in San Francisco, who was herself a memorable personality in the intellectual life of the west coast and a strong influence on London's early work. She was Kempton in the exchange of letters, while London was Wace, and the theme of their argument was ostensibly that of love. But their discourses included Science, Socialism, Art and Life in a curious fusion of Victorian morals and frontier values in the 1900's. *The Kempton-Wace Letters* was an interesting record of the period—the climax of the Yellow Nineties on the Gold Coast—and in no other book of this period did London reveal his own 'program' and personal beliefs quite so clearly. (p. 155)

[One] realizes that throughout *The Kempton-Wace Letters* human behavior, . . . in London's mind was reduced, at best to an animal, but often to a merely mechanical level. Was the post-Darwinian view of man based on the main functions of nutrition and reproduction, and life itself a blind expression of an infinite fecundity? In London's own thought "the mere passion of begetting" and "the paltry romance of pursuit" had been reduced even further to a continuous letting-off steam, as it were—by a more or less inefficient valve system. (p. 157)

[*The People of the Abyss*] was the first of London's social documents. . . .

The book was a running account of experiences in such places as the "sweat-dens" of Frying-pan Alley, the casual ward at Whitechapel workhouse, or Spitalfields Garden where, in the shadow of Christ's Church, he found families of paupers and women who would sell themselves "for thru'pence, or tu'pence, or a loaf of stale bread." It was a diseased lung of England's capital, "an abscess, a great putrescent sore." Though the writing was light, breezy, human-interest stuff—a typical muckraking document, a catalogue of human misery—*The People of the Abyss* was an illuminating document. (p. 158)

London's next book of social criticism, his *War of the Classes,* in 1905, dealt in part with an impending battle for world supremacy among the nations. (p. 159)

[The book] was actually a collection of articles and socialist talks which had been written during the period of London's apprenticeship and early literary success. The tone of the volume was an odd mixture of the abstract or conceptual, and the evangelical or hortatory vein. But the tenets of London's revolutionary socialism were very different from the intellectual or 'leisure class' socialism in, say, the later work of William Dean Howells, and he was the first major fiction writer to proclaim these beliefs not only so clearly but so loudly. (p. 160)

In the moral underworld that was described in the pages of *War of the Classes,* the strike and the boycott, the black list and the lockout, led the way only to suborned judges and armies of private militias; and these in turn were the support of an industrial system whose primary condition of existence was that there should be less work than there were men to do work. (p. 161)

The Iron Heel was a blueprint for fascism in which London had joined the Freudian social pathology, as it were, with the evangelical Marxist dialectic; and compared with his instinct for the propagation of mass terror and consolidation of social barbarism in the native scene, a novel like Sinclair Lewis's *It Can't Happen Here* would appear naïve. Two years later, moreover, during the richest creative period in London's career, *Martin Eden* was another book famous in its own time.

The story was based on his early romance with Mabel Applegarth in San Francisco, a fatal romance for London at least. It was one of London's most completely personal works of fiction, authentic in tone from the opening scene of the suffering 'proletarian' hero in a drawing room of (to him) pure beauty and luxury. (pp. 168-69)

[The] coarse grain of the writing in *Martin Eden,* quite different from the prose of *The Iron Heel,* was exactly right for the emotional texture of the story. The best literary comparison is with the early D. H. Lawrence in *Sons and Lovers.* There is the same mixture of anger, frustration and sexual desire—but the theme of the novel is a typical one in our own letters. "Never had he been at such an altitude of living," Martin Eden says, in almost the same phrases that Thomas Wolfe used to describe the effect of Park Avenue society—that "enfabled Rock" of wealth and beauty and art—upon a later provincial hero; and there was the same confusion of the heroine's temperament with the values of her milieu. He did not think of her flesh as flesh, London said, but as an emanation of her spirit; and her spirit is, at the outset, almost purely that of the cultural environment which she represents. What was different, though, and lent power to *Martin Eden*—a power

of definition—was the sharp stress on social class in this drama of social ambition. (pp. 169-70)

Martin Eden is one of the angry books in American literature, very much in the manner of Richard Wright's *Black Boy,* and as in Wright's case, too, there were curious personal undertones in this acrid and feverish story of what appeared to be purely a social—or even a class—struggle. (p. 172)

The final volume in this phase of London's work, *Revolution and Other Essays,* in 1910, was an interesting contrast to his first collection of socialist essays, five years earlier. One notices the harsh tone of London's polemics. "Our statesmen sell themselves and their country for gold. . . . The world of graft! the world of betrayal!" Yet in **"The Yellow Peril,"** the economic issues of Asia were described in almost purely racist terms. (There was also his notorious remark of this period, when he was attacked for these views: "I am a white man first, a socialist second.") The true meaning of this increasingly dominant strain in his thinking was revealed in his praise of Kipling as the poet of the Anglo-Saxon race and the English empire. (p. 173)

The history of increasing corruption in a genuine talent is both painful and fascinating. . . . Some of London's most brilliant passages of prose will describe the sensations of drawing steadily closer to a moral, if not now a social abyss.

It was interesting, too, that in *The Game,* a story of boxing which London published in 1905 (along with *War of the Classes*), his view of the working classes for popular consumption stressed their sexual purity to the point of incredulity.

The hero was a champ; the heroine a soda fountain girl. They were altogether unreal, wooden characters in the middle class vein, very different from the working class people whom London knew and wrote about in his serious work. The high point of their tedious romance, very much like the barely disguised strip-tease act that London had used to redeem the faltering action in *Theft,* was when the peeping girl, smuggled into a boxing match, saw her young proletarian lover "naked save for the low canvas shoes and narrow hip-cloth of white."

As in some of Ellen Glasgow's early novels—in the fashion of the times—the Victorian taboo on direct sexuality led to a veiled sexuality, or a sexual sublimation that verged on pornography, almost everywhere in the story, despite the fact that London's athlete was presented as an absolutely pure young boy with an honest pride in his muscles. . . . There was the glorification of physical prowess and virility, the adulation of the masculine body, or the symbolic use of that "looking-glass" into which Martin himself, like any young Scott Fitzgerald figure, gazed and conversed with his own image so consistently—and was "both onlooker and participant." (pp. 178-79)

[*White Fang*], a converse to *The Call of the Wild*, dealt with a wolf-dog who was finally domesticated. But, more accurately, the earlier parable dealt with the rebirth of primitive instincts in the wilderness, the true life impulses. This one was concerned quite literally with the death impulses which apparently, in London's case as in Freud's, were dominant in nature itself—or at least were primary in the key episodes and prevailing imagery of London's second animal fable. (p. 181)

The cry of a brokenhearted youth—of an outcast in a world of horrors—is a familiar refrain in London's work. It was illuminating that the last memorable episode in the wolf-dog's apprenticeship should be that of the bulldog's grip on his throat. ("It made him frantic, this clinging, dragging weight. . . . It was like a trap.") While the bulldog's stumpy tail, in the blind horrors of nature and civilization alike, continued to wag vigorously. . . . The Clinging Death indeed! It was only when White Fang was rescued from these extremes of cruelty and terror, to become "the blessed wolf" of a gracious California estate in the Southland, a perfect pet of an aristocratic gentry, that London succumbed to the sentiment which spoiled another beautiful little parable of the instinctual life.

"From my earliest recollection my sleep was a period of terror," said the hero of *Before Adam,* published in the same year . . . , and this fantasy of prehistoric man carried on and developed the dark vein in London's middle period. (p. 183)

This portrait of childhood in the childhood of the race—the Lost Eden—is an Eden of Horrors, viewed ironically. In his evocation of an age of "perpetual insecurity," London tied together all the terrors of primitive life with the fears and terrors of childhood itself, which he attributed indeed to racial memory—and Weismann's germ-plasm theory—more than to personal neurosis. *Before Adam* is a prime instance of the Darwinian unconscious, so to say, rather than the Freudian. But Freud, as well as Marx owed much to the central revelation of evolutionary thinking; and we should not miss the brilliance of intuition which London himself used to transform the embryonic anthropology of his own period into the insights of art.

The central mood in [*Love of Life and Other Stories* and *Lost Face*], two more collections of tales, was also one of inhuman, but almost mechanical misery. (p. 187)

Burning Daylight, in 1910, was another bit of hack work, a poor novel about Alaska; and the romance of the Northland which had established London's fame was in its way the real trap of his literary career. The hero, Burning Daylight himself, was another explicit example of the Superman of the Snows, the Blond Brute of the North Pole, and later, returning to the California scene, the Lone Wolf of Western Finance. (p. 190)

"He had become cynical, bitter, brutal," London said about this spokesman for a central line of heroes. His enemies "feared and hated him, and no one loved him." As in the career of Martin Eden also, his single motivation was merely "lust for power in order to revenge." He was described as an enemy of his society and, though the novel has been praised by some left critics as authentic proletarian writing, the summary of American finance, of the press, politics, civic responsibility, and the masses of the people, was intended only to justify the views of London's hero. It was not so much social criticism as the reflection of a consuming sense of personal corruption. The guiding influence wasn't Marx but, so to speak, Narcissus; and from the prophet of the social abyss this was in the end an abysmal view of society. . . . "When all was said and done, it was a scurvy game. The dice were loaded. Those that died did not win, and all died. Who won? Not even Life, the stoolpigeon, the arch-capper for the game—Life, the ever flourishing graveyard, the everlasting funeral procession." (p. 191)

That was the underlying philosophy of the novel, and it was of course a more direct statement of the dominant symbolism and imagery in his fiction of this period. (p. 192)

In the beginning, [London's] realism, however circumspect in the final analysis, had revolutionized the tone of popular fiction in the 1900's. Now he capitulated cynically to the standards of the mass mind, and to the new vulgarity of a lower middle class audience that had been reached by the low-priced journals. . . . *Adventure,* in 1911, the first of London's South Sea stories, was a popular romance in this vein. The contrast in London's work was not merely between the Arctic scene and the warm, lush tropics; but, as almost always, between what he could have done with this material, and what he did do.

The hero of the novel ran a slave plantation in the Solomon islands. The blacks on whom he depended for profits were head-hunters, cannibals, savages of the lowest order, adorned with barbaric ornaments and endowed with a native cunning and cruelty. A wonderful scene for a storyteller (as Alaska was, too), granted the ways of the world, and balanced here by the savages' own methods of revenge. But one realizes that London compressed this material, too, into a stereotyped version of the white man's burden and the wily 'niggers.' There was the sadistic humor he extracted from the spectacle of the dog Satan, who had been trained to attack the Negro slaves; and the underground sexuality he suggested when the virtuous white heroine watched the naked black being whipped in public. (pp. 199-200)

The Night-Born, in 1913, took its title from Thoreau's lines. "The Society Islanders had their day-born gods, but they were not supposed to be of equal antiquity with the night-born gods." Most surely London himself was an example of primitive and supernatural strains in the artist—of the darker and ancient side of life, of the buried instincts that in his case hardly rose to the human level. Yet these stories of pathology, insanity, or crime, were for the most part converted into popular tales, again with false or sentimental endings. They were hardly so revealing as *John Barleycorn,* a key document in London's personal history that was published in the same year. The book was written ostensibly as a sermon on alcoholism. It is actually a close and illuminating kind of spiritual autobiography, and, as in all more or less personal statements of this writer, the drums rolled in a somber overture of disaster. (pp. 202-03)

[In] this twisted and tortured *apologia pro vita sua*—so remarkably honest and penetrating in parts to the point of narcissistic self-abasement—there were evasions and lacunae. And there were certain developments, still. *The Valley of the Moon,* also published in 1913, and received with higher critical acclaim than the "alcoholic memoirs," is less impressive today. Often described as an example of London's later proletarian fiction, it is actually another phase of his languishing interest in social problems, or his antipathy to them. The hero was a teamster; the early part of the novel was centered around a trucking strike in San Francisco, but the description of this area of society was vulgar and trite. The heroine's name was 'Saxon' and almost from the story's start there was a continual stress on the Anglo-Saxon Nordic White Supremacy of native American stock that seemed not only to be threatened (in London's mind) but practically extinct. . . . The novel was a weird concoction of a sexuality that verged on pornography, of distorted chauvinism, and of social-economic crises that were interpreted as racial phenomena. The real theme of *The Valley of the Moon* was indeed race, blood and soil. (pp. 206-07)

London's own model farm had become the center of his literary cosmos, in a tradition which extended to other prosperous literary hinds like Louis Bromfield, and from the center of his Ovidian meadows he threw out a strange melange of bucolic fears and superstitions. . . . Though he transferred the scene to an old-fashioned clipper ship in his next novel, *The Mutiny of the Elsinore,* in 1914, the central mood was identical, when he forced this story, too, into a procrustean mold of race and class. The decline of the clippers became a parable of "these degenerate sailing days." The "mass of human wreckage" that London found in the crew was another instance, not of an outmoded style of transportation, but of biological differentiation. (p. 208)

[The] theme of a diseased life force was repeated in *The Scarlet Plague,* in 1915, where the artist saw the source of evolutionary development only as "the abysmal fecundity." In *The Strength of the Strong,* a collection of stories published a year earlier, a new China, "rejuvenescent, fruitful, and militant," that had dominated Asia by the sheer force of her massive population, was annihilated by the methods of bacterial warfare. "Hundreds of millions of dead remained unburied and the germs multiplied themselves, and, toward the last, millions died daily of starvation." And the main action of *The Star Rover,* in 1915 also, took place within a strait jacket—from which the hero continued to defy the prison authorities who had, he thinks, wrongly condemned him. One of the last novels London wrote before his death, it was disorganized and broken in structure, an incredibly bad novel, but interesting in its descriptions of a curious psychological state. Supine, prostrate in the bosom of the strait jacket, London's Last Superman still proclaimed his innate superiority over those who were slowly breaking down his body but who are themselves the victims of his fantastic will to survive. He has perfected a form of trance and self-hypnotism during his periods of torture. He learns to make his body die, while in his delusionary fantasies he roves through the central epochs of history as the perfect egomaniac in a series of cruel and bloody catastrophes. (pp. 209-10)

In a literary cosmos that was now a world beyond pain, the final triumph was that of invincible, untouchable paranoia. . . .

[The style of *The Star Rover*]—an absolute frenzy of hyperbole and capital letters—was admirably suited to the grandiloquent thesis, the insane ecstasy. (p. 211)

The Little Lady of the Big House, in 1916, the last novel published before his death, had some autobiographical interest, too, in the final stage of London's life. Here, as in **"The Kanaka Surf "** in *On the Makaloa Mat,* a collection of tales published posthumously in 1919, the theme was the break-up of a marital relationship through the wife's infidelity. . . . The record of the rest of London's posthumous books is brief. (*The Turtles of Tasman,* 1916, contained an almost Lardnerian tale of "a high-grade feeb" who emphasized his superiority to the low-grade droolers and epileptics in a state mental institution.) *The Human Drift,* in 1917, was a collection of minor essays and sketches London had written earlier. *Jerry of the Islands* and *Michael, Brother of Jerry,* in the same year, were two supposed juveniles which concerned the adventures of "a nigger-chasing, adorable Irish terrier puppy" (*sic*) in the familiar setting of the Solomon islands. (pp. 212-13)

The broken tone of the stories in London's final period, the uneven style of his later work as a whole, with bad and good jumbled together, showed the haste and recklessness with which he had poured out this virtuosity. (p. 216)

Maxwell Geismar, "Jack London: The Short Cut," in his *Rebels and Ancestors: The American Novel, 1890-1915,* Houghton Mifflin, 1953, pp. 139-216.

JAMES I. McCLINTOCK
(essay date 1975)

[In the following excerpt, McClintock explores the development of London's story-writing technique.]

When London began dissecting the magazine fiction in order to find "the proper trend of style and literary art" which led to the publication of the Northland stories, one of the first techniques he discovered was the use of the reliable, omniscient narrative point of view. He dropped the loose first person point of view that allowed his stories like **"Typhoon," "In the Time of Prince Charley," "A Thousand Deaths"** and **"The Rejuvenation of Major Rathborn"** to ramble in chronicle fashion and began to utilize more narrative control in the Alaskan tales. Switching to the third person narrator brought him into line with the most commonly used narrative method employed by his contemporaries. But with it, he inherited its legacy of authorial intrusion, even though writers were learning to restrict narrative privilege. Many of his stories, particularly in his first two volumes, *The Son of the Wolf* and *The God of His Fathers,* employ an essay-exemplum type of construction reminiscent of earlier writers who prefixed rambling sermons to their stories. . . . He thought of his short stories as having a block form of introduction-story rather than as a single entity.

In these introductory essays, in order to give the text, London would pose as an Alaskan social historian **("The Wife of a King," "The God of His Fathers,"** and **"At the Rainbow's End")**; a modern philosopher **("In a Far Country")**; or psychologist **("The Son of the Wolf ")** among other roles. Then the illustrative story would follow. No doubt, this was the simplest method for presenting unequivocally the peculiarities of life in surroundings unfamiliar to the readers. Since London's first loyalty was to ideas and values, this uncomplicated form allowed him to present them so clearly that no reader could misunderstand. He never forgot his audience, and in these essay-exemplum stories, his didacticism led him to present views rather than to merely use them. Often the essays are superfluous, detachable moralizations whose import is implicit in the stories themselves. (pp. 15-16)

By discovering the omniscient narrator, London

did improve beyond his early first person experiments. Although he sometimes rambled or padded his materials in these introductory essays which characterize many of his early Klondike tales, he generally used only those ideas which were germane to his story. Still, he was violating the primary concern of the short story theorists, the movement towards a more dramatic story. But call as they would for economical story-telling, the critics were not fully understood by London or other practicing magazine writers. Theory remained, to some extent, divorced from practice. The omniscient narrator did not move unobtrusively behind stories; instead, the narrator continued to impose his personality upon the fiction. He was privy to his characters' minds and hearts, had access to all knowledge and cavalierly interrupted at will to pass judgment upon his characters, situations and life in general.

London's first Northland stories demonstrate that he was not an innovator in this regard. Even after the introductory essays, the narrator insistently performs many functions. The characters do not reveal themselves through their actions and speech; instead, the narrator intrudes to comment and evaluate. . . . Often these intrusions are epigrammatic summaries used to resolve one section of the story before going on to the next. Rather than being inconspicuous, they draw attention to themselves and exist for their own sakes as well as for structural purposes—for example, this aside to the reader from **"The Priestly Prerogative,"** one of the most flagrantly non-dramatic stories he ever wrote: "Some people are good, not for inherent love of virtue, but from sheer laziness. Those of us who know weak moments may understand." . . . Besides the precious, epigrammatic language, the intrusions are often particularly noticeable because of their exuberant, emotional or moralizing tone that draws attention to the highly personalized narrator who is indistinguishable from the author. (pp. 17-18)

[London] was learning "the art of omission" which he found most difficult but realized that its mastery meant the difference between a powerful story and one whose strength was dissipated. . . . [Dialogue] does begin to replace the narrator in some stories, but often it is a mere transplantation of the narrator's essay into the mouths of the characters, as, for example, Karen's discussion of "race affinity" in **"The Great Interrogation."** . . . But no matter how amateurishly executed, this is a step towards depersonalizing the narrator. Furthermore, London began to find techniques which would eliminate the author, or, at least, camouflage his operations. (pp. 19-20)

London hit upon a form of which Kipling was the master—the frame story. In these stories the narrator provides some kind of setting that permits a character to elicit a story from another, recalls some story told to him, or provides some motivation for a character to recall a personal experience. These frame stories represent London's first major movement towards a more dramatic form of story-telling. They begin early in his work, while he continued to produce the essay-exemplum form, and became a significantly large portion of his total canon. Significantly there are more frame stories in the second volume of his short stories than in the first, and more in the third than in the second. They are a modification of the essay-exemplum type since the frame takes the place of the essay, and the story within often illustrates some idea that is discussed in the frame section.

"**An Odyssey of the North**" is a well known London story which exemplifies his experimentation with this more dramatic type of story. An omniscient narrator begins by introducing the characters, familiar from earlier stories, and establishing the setting. The Malemute Kid and Prince take over the narrative functions through their dialogue and provide the frame. They discuss the various Northland types of men who are in their cabin, especially the mysterious visitor who is later revealed as Naass, the central figure who narrates the odyssey in the title. The initial part of the frame ends here. Finally, the tale within the story is told by Naass in the long first person narrative passage which is the central interest of this story. After Naass' tale, the "Odyssey of the North" concludes with the final part of the frame as the Kid and Prince ponder what they have heard. (pp. 20-1)

In his movement from the essay-exemplum form to the frame story, London was not only responding to a general dramatic trend reflected in the construction of magazine stories, but revealing his indebtedness to Kipling's example. Rothberg and other critics have documented the themes and materials shared by Kipling and London, and Joan London mentioned that Jack attempted to imitate Kipling's style. But no one has noticed the remarkable similarity of their short story structures. Moreover, Jack London's testimony that he studied the magazines when Kipling was in the first rank in order to find the proper short story form and techniques, his open and frequently mentioned admiration of Kipling, and the striking correspondences between the two authors' short story patterns, even plots, are strong evidence that London used Kipling's stories as models for his own. (pp. 21-2)

[London learned] to use the frame story adequately, and it allowed him to explore his ideas more thoroughly than the essay-exemplum type. In the essay-exemplum stories the narrator was constrained to speak in what can only be the author's authoritative voice rather than through a *persona.* Most of the explicit comments made by the narrator are awkwardly overbearing and dogmatic in their attempts to force ideas upon the reader and commit the story-teller to arriving at definite conclusions. But London's frame stories,

using a teller who is clearly distinguishable from London himself, allowed him to present more complicated social and moral situations. For example, in "**An Odyssey of the North**" Naass, an admirable and complex character-narrator, comes into conflict with two other idealized characters. The situation is morally complex since Naass's suffering and loyalty are emotionally equivalent to Unga's and Axel's love for each other, and equally justified. Yet the two sets of emotions are incompatible, and the story rightly remains unresolved. Because the point of view is not that absolutely omniscient and reliable author's, the dilemma can be left without final auctorial redress and pontifical judgment, making artistic uses of ambiguity and irony. And in the Northland tales as a group we find that the frame tale becomes a frequently employed form for presenting stories which deal with the conflict between civilization and primitive culture, the white man and the Indian, topics complex in their moral overtones. (pp. 24-5)

Sometime in late spring, 1900, only a year and a half after beginning his serious apprenticeship and after composing most of the stories eventually collected in *Son of the Wolf* and *God of His Fathers* and beginning to work on the *Children of the Frost* stories, Jack London began to recognize the need for a more satisfactory dramatic form that would encompass an entire story, rather than being limited to the story within another story. In the course of the next few months he developed his most sophisticated theory and practice of dramatic fiction. . . . (p. 25)

[In "**The Law of Life**"]London discovered that he could use a limited, rather than fully omniscient, third person point of view for a dramatic effect powerful in its simplicity. There is no essay in the beginning, and the setting is established in terms of the old man's awareness so that there is no awkward shift from narrative landscaping to action; therefore, the reader is not conscious of a direct bid for his attention. . . . The comments made by the narrator are tailored to the demands of character rather than inappropriately out of the range of the character's perceptions and are so appropriate in tone and style that no unusual emphasis draws attention away from the character's point of view.

Although none of the stories following "**The Law of Life**" in *The Children of the Frost* . . . are as rigorous in point of view nor in artistic simplicity, stories like "**Nam-Bok the Unverscious**," "**The Sunlanders**," and "**Keesh, the Son of Keesh**," (told "from the Indian's point of view, through the Indian's eyes as it were") do demonstrate that London was avoiding direct philosophical, social or psychological evaluations of character or setting in the voice of the narrator appealing directly to his audience.

London, then, was learning techniques which allowed him to be more economical and dramatic. The

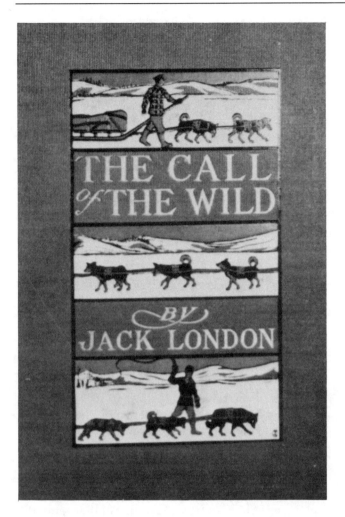

Front cover of London's best-known book.

Prerogative," fail to focus upon a single dramatic scene or central image. London did realize though that such scenes replace the author, or, more accurately, become the author in the sense that his emotional and intellectual experience can be embodied more compactly and forcefully through scene than through exposition. (p. 29)

Throughout the rest of his career, London continued to rely on the three major short story forms and the evocative style that he learned during these early, apprenticeship years. His social criticism stories and South Seas stories, the good ones as well as the potboilers, are cast in these familiar molds. At their best, the stories wed form, content and style while transcending formal and technical deficiencies by emphasizing central, powerful scenes. The essay-exemplum form remained a staple for presenting ideas dogmatically, particularly when introducing new ideas about strange lands or situations whether in the Northland, the South Seas, or among the "submerged tenth" in America. The frame stories allowed him to develop more complex ideas. The more dramatic forms and techniques were used for statements about basic human experiences which needed no explicit introduction, but demanded emotional impact, especially if the perspective were ironic. (p. 32)

James I. McClintock, in his *White Logic: Jack London's Short Stories,* Wolf House Books, 1975, 206 p.

logical extension of this movement toward depersonalizing the narrator voice is a scenic method which uses a stage-manager narrator who merely records what can be seen and heard but who does not enter the characters' minds, analyze their motives, nor explain the source and implications of the scenes. The product of such a method would be similar to a painting, a pictorial representation of a situation. (pp. 27-8)

[There] is an extremely important basic correlation between London's theory and his actual practice. From the beginning of his Klondike stories, he had relied upon dramatic scenes as the core around which the rest of the story coalesced. Although the story might contain narrative essays and other authorial interference, an evocative scene lay at the center of dramatic interest in the best of these stories. Even an early critic recognized the visual quality achieved in the *Children of the Frost* as a mark of distinguished writing and wrote that in **"The Master of Mystery,"** "the subject is so interesting and the treatment so powerfully simple and sincere that the picture stands out clear and flawless." The poorer stories, the ones that London himself disliked, such as **"The Wife of a King"** and **"A Priestly**

JAMES DICKEY
(essay date 1981)

[Considered one of America's foremost contemporary poets, Dickey is also an esteemed novelist and critic. In the following excerpt from an introduction to *The Call of the Wild, White Fang, and Other Stories,* he discusses the symbolic and personal significance of the wolf in the author's Arctic stories and other works.]

"Primeval" is a word often used to describe Jack London's work, his attitude toward existence, and his own life. From the beginning of the intensive self-education he undertook early in his adolescence through the end of his life at the age of forty, he prided himself on his "animality," and identified with his chosen totem beast, the wolf. His gullible friend, the California poet George Sterling, called him Wolf, he referred to his wife as Mate-Woman, named his ill-fated mansion in the Sonoma Valley Wolf House, and created his most memorable human character, Wolf Larsen, in *The Sea Wolf.* Larsen exemplifies all of the characteristics London admired most: courage, resourcefulness, ruthlessness, and above all, a strength of will that he partly bases on that of Milton's Satan in *Paradise Lost*. Larsen's favorite lines from Milton are "To reign is worth ambition, though in hell: / Better to reign in hell than serve in heaven," a sentiment with which London certainly concurred.

This attitude toward the *figure* of the wolf—a kind of Presence, an image, a symbolic and very personal representation of a mythologized human being—is pervasive throughout all of London's Arctic tales and is implied in many of his other fictions. The reader should willingly give himself over to this interpretation of the wolf, and conjure the animal up in the guise of the mysterious, shadowy, and dangerous figment that London imagines it to be. We should encounter the Londonian wolf as we would a spirit symbolic of the deepest forest, the most extremely high and forbidding mountain range, the most desolate snowfield: in short, as the ultimate wild creature, supreme in savagery, mystery, and beauty.

The mythic wolf that London "found" in his single winter spent in the Canadian North during the Klondike Gold Rush of 1897-98 and imbued with strangeness and ferocity bears in fact little resemblance to any true wolf ever observed. In studies by biologist Adolph Murie and researchers like L. David Mech and Boyce Rensberger, the wolf emerges as a shy and likable animal with a strong aversion to fighting. (pp. 7-8)

And yet London's wolf is very much a part of the consciousness of many people, and as the wolf's habitat continues to shrink under the pressure of oil pipelines and other industrial encroachments, its mystery and its savage spirituality increase, now that vulnerability has been added. We need London's mythical wolf almost as much as we need the wildernesses of the world, for without such ghost-animals from the depths of the human subconscious we are alone with ourselves.

That Jack London, the Klondike, the wolf, and the dog should have come together in exactly the circumstances that the gold-fever afforded seems not so much a merely fortunate conjunction of events but a situation tinged strongly with elements of predestination, of fate. Born in poverty only a little above the truly abject, London displayed almost from the beginning such a will to dominate as might have been envied by Satan himself, or for that matter, by Milton. (pp. 8-9)

During his later travels and his battles for survival in the economic wilderness, he came quickly to the belief that knowledge is indeed power. In his case, knowledge was more than the simple and too-abstract word "power" implied; it was muscle, blood, teeth, and stamina; it gave the force and direction that the will must take. When he landed in the Yukon in 1897, he had already read, with virtually superhuman vora-

ciousness, hundreds of books and articles, principally in the fields of sociology, biology, and philosophy. He was alive with ideas and a search for ultimate meaning that amounted to an obsessively personal quest, and shared with the pre-Socratic philosophers . . . a belief that the great All is single and can be known. As he moved farther into the winter wilderness of the northern latitudes, he came increasingly to the conclusion that the "white silence" of the North is the indifferently triumphant demonstration of the All, the arena where the knowable Secret could most unequivocally be apprehended and, as the conditions demanded, lived. The snowfields, mountains, forests, and enormous frozen lakes were to London only the strictest, most spectacular, and unarguable symbols of the universal abyss, the eternal mystery at the heart of nothingness, or the eternal nothingness at the heart of mystery, as Herman Melville saw it in *Moby Dick*. (pp. 9-10)

London's scattered but deeply *felt* reading had so imbued him with Darwinian principles that he looked on the landscape of the Yukon as a kind of metaphysical arena in which natural selection and the survival of the fittest were enacted unendingly, illustrating (though to no perceiver but the casual) the "Law." The North is a background that determines character and action, bringing out in men certain qualities from the psychic depths of the race of all living beings. London does not attempt, as Melville does, to strike through the "mask." The "mask" in London's tales is more the classic mask of the actor, the mask that each participant feels rising to his face from the setting of the drama, the frozen features that *rerum natura* has always reserved for it.

As George Orwell has remarked, London's instincts "lay toward acceptance of a 'natural aristocracy' of strength, beauty and talent." Few writers have dwelt with such fixation on superlatives: "the strongest," "the biggest," "the handsomest," "the most cunning," "the fiercest," "the most ruthless." One cannot read these stories without agreeing with Orwell that "there is something in London [that] takes a kind of pleasure in the whole cruel process. It is not so much an approval of the harshness of nature, as a mystical belief that nature *is* like that. 'Nature red in tooth and claw.' Perhaps fierceness is the price of survival. The young lady slay the old, the strong slay the weak, by an inexorable law." London insists, as Melville does not, that there is a morality inherent in the twin drives of animal evolution; brute survival and the desire of the species to reproduce itself are not primary but exclusive motivations.

In this savage theater of extremes, this vast stage of indifference, where "the slightest whisper seemed sacrilege," London felt himself to be a man speaking out of the void of cosmic neutrality and even to it and for it, wearing, really, no mask but his half-frozen face, from which issued in steam and ice the truth of existence: the way things are.

The actors are men and dogs. (pp. 10-11)

London's anthropomorphizing of animals is well known, and the instances in which he overindulges this tendency are frequent and sometimes absurd. He was no Rilke or Lawrence, seemingly able to project his own human point of observation into another entity, either living or inorganic, and *become* the contemplated Other. He could not and certainly would not have wanted to know, as Aldous Huxley said Lawrence did, "by personal experience, what it was like to be a tree or a daisy or a breaking wave or even the mysterious moon itself. He could get inside the skin of an animal and could tell you in the most convincing detail how it felt and how, dimly, inhumanly, it thought." London had no wish to negate himself in favor of becoming an animal; the London dog or wolf is presented not as itself but as London feels that *he* would feel if he were embodied in the form of a dog or a wolf. The self-dramatizing Nietzschean is always very much present. In the canine battle scenes, for example, London analyzes with an almost absurd and quite human confidence the various "tactics" employed by the participants.

> But Buck possessed a quality that made for greatness—imagination. He fought by instinct, but he could fight by head as well. He rushed, as though attempting the old shoulder trick, but at the last instant swept low to the snow and in. His teeth closed on Spitz's left fore leg. There was a crunch of breaking bone, and the white dog faced him on three legs. Thrice he tried to knock him over, then repeated the trick and broke the right fore leg.

Anyone who has ever seen dogs fighting knows that such subtleties as "the old shoulder trick" do not occur; if the affair is not merely one of a good deal of threatening noise, then one dog just goes for the other in any way possible. When London describes what dogs *do* rather than what they "think"—how they *look* when listening, how they appear when in repose, how they pace when restless or hungry—he is very good. When he makes a primitive philosopher of the dog in the same sense in which the author is himself a primitive philosopher, the result is less convincing. One believes of Bâtard that in five years "he heard but one kind word, received but one soft stroke of a hand, and then he did not know what manner of things they were." It is quite conceivable that a dog that had never received such treatment would not know how to respond. On the other hand, Buck's mystique of racial fulfillment, his metaphysical musculature, are . . . plainly impossible. . . . Likewise, White Fang's encounter with the Californian electric streetcars "that were to him colossal screaming lynxes" is not the product of a first-rate imagination. London merely knew that, since White Fang had lived in the Arctic and lynx-

es also lived there, and since lynxes sometimes make noises and streetcars also make them, he could feel justified in combining these items in a figure of speech the reader would be inclined to take as reasonable because neither reader nor lynx nor London nor streetcars could prove it was not. A moment's reflection, however, should disclose how farfetched the image is; the dog would simply have been bothered by the utter *unfamiliarity* of the machine, would simply have apprehended it as a large noise-making *something,* though assuredly no lynx.

White Fang was conceived as a "complete antithesis and companion piece to *The Call of the Wild.*" London averred that "I'm going to reverse the process. Instead of the devolution or decivilization of a dog, I'm going to give the evolution, the civilization of a dog—development of domesticity, faithfulness, love, morality, and all the amenities and virtues." Yet, why is *White Fang*—more than twice as long as *The Call of the Wild* and a good deal more virtue-bent in the human sense of intention, a story in which the animal protagonist ends not as the leader of a pack of wild wolves but crooning his "love-growl" amidst a chorus of city women rubbing his ears and calling him the Blessed Wolf—why is it so markedly inferior to the story of reversion? Largely, I think, because the events depicted in *The Call of the Wild* are closer to what one *wants* to see happen: because we desire the basic, the "natural," the *"what is"* to win and not the world of streetcars and sentimentalism that we have made. Thus, in a sense, if we accede to London's narrative we also are approving of God and his white, mocking malevolence, his "Law" maintaining sway over all the irrelevances and over-subtleties of mechanized life. We like the author for putting the perspective in this way, and especially in a way as forthright, inexorable, exciting, and involving as he commands.

The key to London's effectiveness is to be found in his complete absorption in the world he evokes. The author is *in* and committed to his creations to a degree very nearly unparalleled in the composition of fiction. The resulting go-for-broke, event-intoxicated, headlong wild-Irish prose-fury completely overrides a great many stylistic lapses and crudities that would ordinarily cause readers to smile. As Orwell notes, "the texture of the writing is poor, the phrases are worn and obvious, and the dialogue is erratic."

True, but it is nonetheless also true that London has at his best the ability to involve the reader in his story so thoroughly that nothing matters but *what* happens; in this sense he is basic indeed. His primary concern is action, with no pause to allow the savoring of verbal nuances or subtleties of insight. "La vérité, c'est dans la nuance," said Flaubert. London would have left that notion behind in the dog blood crystallizing on the ice floe, the eddying plume of a miner's frozen breath.

His style is in presenting what *is,* and that only. As a writer London is at his most compelling in "presentational immediacy"; the more the passage relates to the nerves and feelings of the body, the more effective it is. (pp. 12-15)

He is an artist of violent action, exemplifying what the American poet Allen Tate meant when he said: "I think of my poems as commentaries on those human situations from which there is no escape." Once caught in London's swirling, desperate, life-and-death violence, the reader has no escape either, for it is a vision of exceptional and crucial vitality. London's most characteristic tales have the graphic power of the best cinema. . . . [The] quintessential Jack London is in the on-rushing compulsiveness of his northern stories. Few men have more convincingly examined the connection between the creative powers of the individual writer and the unconscious drive to breed and to survive, found in the natural world. (p. 16)

James Dickey, in an introduction to *The Call of the Wild, White Fang, and Other Stories* by Jack London, edited by Andrew Sinclair, Penguin Books, 1981, pp. 7-16.

JOAN D. HEDRICK

(essay date 1982)

[Hedrick is an American educator and the author of *Solitary Comrade: Jack London and His Work.* In the following excerpt from that work, she examines London's apparent inability to integrate his political insight with his emotional limitations in such "socialist" works as *The Iron Heel.*]

After London established his literary reputation, he had more latitude in the material the editors would accept, and he experimented, especially in the period between 1905 and 1909, with stories that had a political point of view. It is fair to wonder if London did not bring a different consciousness to bear in the stories he wrote not for the literary marketplace but to further the cause of socialism. Three of these stories are especially revealing of London's relationship to the working class. They are **"The Apostate,"** . . . **"The Dream of Debs,"** . . . and **"South of the Slot."** . . . A fourth, **"The Strength of the Strong,"** . . . is notable for its eloquent expression of the goal of a cooperative commonwealth.

Much can be inferred about London's relation to his material by the persona that he adopts in the telling of his stories. **"The Strength of the Strong,"** like **"South of the Slot,"** is an extraordinarily controlled and well-wrought piece. In it London adopts the para-

ble form and with it a formal distance from his material. He employs a third-person narrator, but the events of the tale, which concern the rivalry between two primitive tribes, the Meat-Eaters and the Fish-Eaters, are told by Long-Beard, patriarch of the Fish-Eaters. This story-within-the-story technique further distances author and reader from the material, as does the story's unfolding in the dawn of human history. London's narrative stance in **"The Strength of the Strong"** is very like that characteristically adopted by Hawthorne in his allegories of the human heart: there is an evenhandedness in the portrayal of characters, and personality is subordinated to psychological and social types. This is appropriate to their exploration not of one person's consciousness but of the dynamics of social intercourse. (p. 169)

["**The Strength of the Strong"**] is perhaps London's finest expression of his socialist consciousness. The distancing achieved by his formal devices allows him to deal forthrightly with the institutions of his society. The parable is a disguise of sorts, but it is an accepted literary device through which dangerous and seditious views may be expressed. In that it is an accepted and "public" device, it differs from the private dream-language that characterizes London's more covert attempts to subvert his readers. The "public" quality of London's narrative stance is responsible for the high degree of control he exercises on his material. With complete awareness of what it is about, **"The Strength of the Strong"** juxtaposes what is with what should be. Yet it must be said that, like Hawthorne's allegories, this parable appeals primarily to the intellect, not the emotions. It lacks the power of *The Call of the Wild* and does not seem to engage London's and the reader's desires on the deepest level. Still, it is a more humanistic vision than London ordinarily brought to his stories of human beings, which perhaps has to do with the fact that the Fish-Eaters are suspended between the animal world and the modern world of industrial capitalism.

"The Apostate" is the most directly autobiographical of the four stories. Though London is predictably closer to his material, he still exercises a high degree of control over his story. Perhaps because the factory life of Johnny, a "work-beast," so clearly represented an earlier, discarded self, London was able both to understand his character and to feel distant from him. (pp. 170-71)

London could not have described Johnny's working-class life in such convincing detail had he not experienced the same mind-and-body-destroying factory rhythms; yet London attributes to his character a consciousness more limited than his own, and this discrepancy distances London from his creation. London's detachment is apparent in his description of Johnny as he walks away from his home and his job, never to return: "He did not walk like a man. He did not look like a man. He was a travesty of the human. It was a twisted and stunted and nameless piece of life that shambled like a sickly ape, arms loose-hanging, stoop-shouldered, narrow-chested, grotesque and terrible." . . . This description comes as a shock, even though the distortion of Johnny's body by his work has been completely accounted for. The reader can believe that the industrial labor has extorted a terrible human price; what is unacceptable and disturbing about London's description of Johnny as "a twisted and stunted and nameless piece of life" is that it seems to totally deny him humanity; he lacks even the glimmering illusions that made London's dray horse labor on. He is only a piece of flesh. In London's reduction of his character to this material basis he makes him less than human in the very moment that he asserts himself against the system that has dehumanized him. London can empathize with Johnny in his victory over his mother, but in this story neither Johnny nor his author break through to a fully human consciousness. Neither does the story transcend the immediate power relationships of the family to mount a critique of the social relations of capitalist production. (pp. 175-76)

In **"The Dream of Debs"** a general strike has paralyzed the whole country. . . . The major difference between this story and others in which London has portrayed the working class is that here they are superbly organized and disciplined, and, far from being beastly and degraded, they take destiny into their own hands and bring capital to their terms before the strike is over. . . . But the emotions that London might have brought to this collective struggle are singularly absent. London's use of an upper-class narrator who is victimized by the strike denies the reader direct participation in the working-class victory, and his dead-pan narration kills much of the vitality of the story. Clearly, as McClintock has suggested, London intended to satirize the limited consciousness of this Mr. Cerf, whose final comment on the events is that the "tyranny of organized labor is getting beyond human endurance," and "something must be done." But it is significant that London was unable to imagine himself part of this working-class struggle. In this dream of working-class triumph, London allied his consciousness with that of a deposed upper-class victim. (p. 176)

In **"South of the Slot"** London creates an alternative to the scenario he had worked out in *The Sea-Wolf*. In that novel the bourgeois narrator triumphed over Wolf Larsen by refusing to look at the reality of capitalist society. In **"South of the Slot,"** the working-class persona triumphs over the middle-class Freddie Drummond, and, because Bill Totts is engaged in a collective struggle, he is associated not with the pessimistic materialism of Wolf Larsen but with unity, strength, and emotional wholeness. It is perhaps the only happy ending London ever wrote that was not sentimental and

false, with the notable exception of *The Call of the Wild*. (p. 177)

If **"South of the Slot"** was Jack London's most self-aware socialist story, his most ambitious contribution to socialist literature was *The Iron Heel*. Insofar as *The Iron Heel* is compelling, its energy comes from what Trotsky called the "powerful intuition of the revolutionary artist." Ernest Everhard, the hero of this book, is able to see further than his contemporaries; before others are fully aware of the oligarchic tendencies of capitalism, Everhard prophecies the coming of the Iron Heel. London's power as a political visionary is the mainspring of a book that lacks novelistic interest yet deeply reveals the consciousness and identity of Jack London. (p. 188)

[By] focusing on the way *The Iron Heel* fails as a novel, we can perhaps better understand London's inability to integrate the political and the personal in his own consciousness. Better than any other single work, *The Iron Heel* reveals the radical disjunction between London's political insight and his emotional limitations. (p. 189)

The first scene in *The Iron Heel* is in outline precisely parallel to the opening scene of *Martin Eden;* the proletarian hero is brought to an upper-class home and introduced to the bourgeois heroine, who immediately falls in love with him. Both heroes make "a rather incongruous appearance." . . . The hero's powerful workingclass physique exercises its fascination on Avis. . . . Seated at dinner in the midst of Avis and her father, who is a university professor, and his preacher friends, who are skilled metaphysicians, Ernest not only knows how to use a knife and fork, he effortlessly triumphs in debate, and does it without even alluding to humiliations inflicted on him by his workingclass background. (pp. 192-93)

Everhard is the scientific socialist, reasoning from the world to his ideas about the world; the ministers are the metaphysicians, reasoning from their consciousness to the world. But never does London suggest to his readers what some of these "facts" of working-class life were, for specificity would puncture the daydream. The purpose of this scene is not to enlighten the readers to the realities of working-class life but to impress upon them the superiority of Ernest Everhard. "How the scene comes back to me!" exclaims Avis. "I can hear him now, with that war-note in his voice, flaying them with his facts, each fact a lash that stung and stung again. And he was merciless." . . . The pleasure that we are meant to take in this triumph is covertly sadomasochistic. Everhard's intellectual battles with the capitalist class and their flunkies are repeatedly described in terms of physical violence ("sometimes he exchanged the rapier for the club and went smashing amongst their thoughts right and left" . . .), and the pleasure Ernest takes in these victories is fraught with unhealthy and seemingly very unsocialistic emotions. Here he is at the Philomath Club, pausing in his blows to scrutinize the expression of his victim, Col. Van Gilbert, a tough corporation lawyer: "Ernest paused for a moment and regarded him thoughtfully, noting his face dark and twisted with anger, his panting chest, his writhing body, and his slim white hands nervously clenching and unclenching." . . . Though we are privy to these scenes suggestive of repressed sexuality, nowhere do we see Everhard expressing tender and sexual feelings toward Avis. The closest he comes to it is the "bold" look he gives her at their first meeting: " 'You pleased me,' he explained long afterward; 'and why should I not fill my eyes with that which pleases me?' " . . . Avis is delighted to be the object of his will, but her pleasure in his mastery is destined to be vicarious; in her erotic fantasies she prefers to see him mastering other men—in debate—to being herself sexually overpowered. . . . Her vicarious enjoyment of Ernest's powers makes her a perfect mate, for in the few scenes in which they are together, he is so exhausted from doing battle with the oligarchy that he is reduced to infantile dependence. . . .

> He paused and looked at me, and added:
> "Social evolution is exasperatingly slow, isn't it, sweetheart?"
> My arms were about him, and his head was on my breast. "Sing me to sleep," he murmured whimsically. "I have had a visioning, and I wish to forget." . . .

Reminiscent of the scene in *The Sea-Wolf* when Maud tucks Humphrey into bed, this passage may also be compared to the scene in *Lady Chatterley's Lover,* when Clifford, the impotent husband of Lawrence's heroine, allows himself to be bathed and cared for by Ivy Bolton. Clifford Chatterley, a gentleman-artist whose war wound has not permitted him to be a real husband to his wife, has by this late point in the novel transformed himself into a hard-driving industrialist who achieves extraordinary production from his miners. . . . The perverse and infantile emotional relationships that Lawrence ascribes to his capitalist are identical to the ones London, in a much less self-conscious way, ascribes to his revolutionary. Both Lawrence and London describe relationships in which sexual feelings are displaced onto work and then replaced by pregenital, narcissistic emotions. In this scenario women allow men to sink back into a state of blissful unawareness. Ernest Everhard, whose X-ray vision crowds his consciousness with more reality than ordinary men experience, has particular need of this escape from thought.

Thus London's revolutionary hero has a very unrevolutionary consciousness. The contradictions here are acute: Everhard builds his vision of a new society by pumping iron in the oppressive social relationships of the capitalist society he wishes to overthrow. London's awareness of the contradictions of manhood in capitalist society was neutralized by his ignorance of the contradictions of womanhood. Like Hemingway, he writes about "men without women." Even though London's heroes are sometimes with women, his understanding of them does not include their relationships with women. He is at his best when describing oppression in the male spheres of work, saloon, and prison. When he attempts to write about women's spheres, which he identifies with romantic love and the upper class, he is too aware of his own victimization to understand the peculiar ways in which women, too, are victims. Like Charmian London, Avis Everhard takes pride in her ability to make her husband happy. . . . Ernest is simply too tired to extend the revolutionary struggle into the politics of his domestic life. But if we were to reply to Avis's rhetorical question—what greater joy could have blessed her than to provide her husband forgetfulness—we might suggest that she urge him to struggle with the politics of his own sexuality. (pp. 193-96)

If Ernest Everhard was too weary to take up this subject, he was doubtless also too threatened. The feelings associated with sexual politics are so intense as to require great personal courage to face. The intensity of London's feelings—in particular the intensity of his unconscious revulsion from women—may be suggested by a revealing slip of the pen. This occurs just after Ernest's initial triumph over the churchmen at the Cunningham's dinner table, in which Avis's father took great delight. "After the guests had gone, father threw himself into a chair and gave vent to roars of Gargantuan laughter. Not since the death of my mother had I known him to laugh so heartily." . . . Clearly Avis means "not since *before* the death of my mother," but the elision conflates the two incidents, the death of the mother/wife and the confounding of the bourgeois metaphysicians. In this unconscious association, both events give rise to one long laugh of triumph. This slip may be compared to London's comments in *The Road* about the stories he made up about his past, for the consumption of his "marks." Invariably he presented himself as an orphan, and he delighted in disposing of his mother through deadly disease: "Heart disease was my favorite way of getting rid of my mother, though on occasion I did away with her by means of consumption, pneumonia, and typhoid fever." . . . London did not always wish death upon his mother figures, but, as Kevin Starr has observed, "The shaming of an upper class woman appears as a frequent motif in London's stories." (p. 196)

In one further way *The Iron Heel* is suggestive of Jack London's consciousness and identity. Chapter 19 is entitled "Transformation," and here the common naturalistic device of a radical change in class identity is employed in the service of a guerilla war against the

Iron Heel. Avis assumes the identity of a daughter of the oligarchy: she becomes Felice Van Verdighan. As a double agent, she gives secret signals to both the revolutionaries and the mercenaries of the oligarchy. "As agents-provocateurs, not alone were we able to travel a great deal, but our very work threw us in contact with the proletariat and with our comrades, the revolutionists. Thus we were in both camps at the same time, ostensibly serving the Iron Heel and secretly working with all our might for the Cause." . . . Her work "in both camps at the same time" is suggestive of the posture London maintained throughout much of his life, writing for the bourgeois press but attempting secretly

to subvert their principles. In order to accomplish this, Avis is commanded by Ernest, "You must make yourself over again so that even I would not know you—your voice, your gestures, your mannerisms, your carriage, your walk, everything." Avis obeys. . . . London even imagines surgeons trained in the revolutionary art of plastic surgery. . . . But if one must become the enemy in order to destroy him, is the game worth the candle? London seems never to have asked this question in *The Iron Heel,* but it derives his hero to suicide in *Martin Eden.* (pp. 198-99)

Joan D. Hedrick, in her *Solitary Comrade: Jack London and His Work,* The University of North Carolina Press, 1982, 265 p.

SOURCES FOR FURTHER STUDY

London, Charmian. *The Book of Jack London.* 2 Vols. New York: Century Co., 1921.

> An intimate portrait of London written by his second wife. His personal life is the focus of this biography, which includes extensive quotations from private conversations and numerous excerpts from London's correspondence.

London, Joan. *Jack London and His Times.* Seattle: University of Washington Press, 1939, 385 p.

> Describes the economic and political backdrop against which London pursued his literary career. The author, London's daughter, concentrates on the rise of industrialism, the concommitant popularization of socialist and labor politics, and the influence of both upon London's work.

Orwell, George. Introduction to *Love of Life, and Other Stories,* by Jack London. London: Paul Elek, 1946.

> Explores London's ambivalent attitude toward socialism and power as these themes appear in his fiction. Orwell concludes, of London and his work, that "if he had been a politically reliable person he would probably have left behind nothing of interest."

Ownbey, Ray Wilson, ed. *Jack London: Essays in Criticism.* Santa Barbara and Salt Lake City: Peregrine Smith, 1978, 126 p.

> A collection of critical essays by Clarice Stasz, Sam S. Baskett, Earle Labor, and others.

Tavernier-Courbin, Jacqueline. *Critical Essays on Jack London.* Boston: G. K. Hall, 1983, 298 p.

> Includes essays by Tavernier-Courbin, H. L. Mencken, Anatole France, Earle Labor, Susan Ward, and others. The collection is divided into sections on London's life, his works in general, specific works, and writing techniques.

Walcutt, Charles Child. "Jack London: Blond Beasts and Supermen." In his *American Literary Naturalism, A Divided Stream,* pp. 87-113. Minneapolis: University of Minnesota Press, 1956.

> Discusses London's adventure stories. Walcutt contends that because London found the struggle to survive implied in the theories of Darwin and Spenser so appealing, he cast primitive, strong-minded heroes as exaggeratedly self-conscious extensions of himself in his works. His moral idealism about social injustice equated the hero with courage and the villain with cowardice.

Robert Lowell

1917-1977

(Born Robert Traill Spence Lowell, Jr.) American poet, dramatist, editor, translator, critic, and novelist.

INTRODUCTION

Widely considered the most influential American poet of the mid-twentieth century, Lowell is acclaimed for his mastery of diverse forms, intense expression of personal concerns, and candid commentary on social and moral issues. Lowell's verse reflects his knowledge of European literary traditions as well as the social and literary history of his native New England; the former is evinced in his skillful use of such devices as assonance, alliteration, symbolism, and conventional verse structures, the latter by his exploration of Puritanism, democratic ideals, and the role of the artist in American society. Throughout his career, Lowell experimented with verse forms and styles, seeking through artistic expression to order and make meaning of experience, particularly dark and chaotic aspects of life. The sense of tension and vigor that distinguishes Lowell's verse derives, in part, from his use of highly-charged, concentrated phrasing, sudden bold epigrams, a profusion of details ranging from everyday objects and events to esoteric allusions, and blunt confrontations with personal and social conflicts.

Lowell was born into an established New England family whose ancestors include the literary figures Amy Lowell and James Russell Lowell. His social position, formal education, and literary reputation brought him into contact with many of the significant American poets of his time. At St. Mark's School in Massachusetts, where he was a student from 1930 to 1935, he began writing poetry under the guidance of academic poet Richard Eberhart. From 1935 to 1937 Lowell studied at Harvard University. There he encountered the poetry of William Carlos Williams, which later influenced Lowell's break in the 1950s from the conventional style of his early works to the openness of form and content of what critics refer to as his confessional verse—intense poems that concentrate on personal conflicts and failings. Critics have labeled this post-World War II trend the Confessional movement, and include Lowell, John Berryman, Sylvia Plath, and Anne Sexton, among others, as members.

Lowell's private life was marked by profound emotional and spiritual turmoil. He was nicknamed "Cal" in his school days after the infamous Roman emperor Caligula because of his manic behavior, and later suffered bouts of mental illness that resulted in hospitalization. His emotional instability, precarious personal and family relations, and reactions to what he perceived as the increasing disorder of modern life contributed to his inner turbulence. Such matters as his conversion to Roman Catholicism and ongoing marital difficulties are evidenced in some of his greatest works. Lowell also reacted strongly to the rapidly changing social and political climate of his time; his refusal to serve in World War II resulted in a one-year sentence in a federal penitentiary, of which he served about six months, and his objection to the Vietnam War led him to publicly decline an invitation to the White House Festival of the Arts in 1965. The intensity of Lowell's private life and his response to the world around him form the thematic core of his art. Hayden Carruth remarked: "[Lowell] was truly the figure of the embattled artist . . . , the artist fighting a degraded society, a cruel history, an absurd universe, and most of all a sense of lack in his own being, fighting in complete honesty and utterly refusing to compromise."

The poems in Lowell's first book, *Land of Unlikeness* (1944), reflect turbulent political events of World War II as well as Lowell's conversion to Roman Catholicism and his reaction to his Protestant heritage, often alluded to through religious symbolism. The collection earned Lowell moderate acclaim and recognition as an important new voice in modern poetry. His next collection, *Lord Weary's Castle* (1946), was awarded the Pulitzer Prize in poetry and firmly established Lowell's presence in American literature. In the most influential commentary on *Lord Weary's Castle,* Randall Jarrell observed that the oppositional pull between "that cake of custom in which all of us lie embedded" and "everything that is free or open, that grows or is willing to change" can be seen at the heart of Lowell's work. "The Quaker Graveyard in Nantucket," the book's most acclaimed poem and one of Lowell's most famous works, exemplifies these dual forces. Revolving around the recent death of Warren Winslow, Lowell's cousin who died while serving in the Navy, the poem displays Lowell's characteristic historical awareness as well as his acute sensitivity to the chaos and failures of the modern world. The piece features vividly evoked descriptions of the Cape Cod seascape, replete with symbolism and allusions that enrich Lowell's meditations on death and humanity's relationship with nature. *The Mills of the Kavanaughs* (1951), Lowell's next volume, is largely considered an ambitious although unsuccessful attempt to explore new poetic techniques. Written in the form of dramatic monologues, the poems in this collection are marked by highly rhetorical, symbolic language that is regarded by most critics as convoluted and burdensome.

Life Studies (1959) signals a breakthrough in both content and style, as Lowell turned to free verse and created the poetic voice of intense personal concentration that characterizes the best confessional poetry. In this work he incorporated the aesthetic of common speech introduced to him by William Carlos Williams and the clear, sharp imagism of Elizabeth Bishop. Lowell's profound emotional energy, the depth of his self-scrutiny, and his synthesis of private and public concerns marks this as one of the most influential volumes of post-World War II poetry. This collection contains "Skunk Hour," perhaps Lowell's best known poem. "Skunk Hour" begins with a description of a declining seaside town and its inhabitants—recognizable New England character types who acquire mythic qualities. Many critics liken the setting to various literary descriptions of the underworld and note that the poem takes place near Halloween. The speaker arrives in the second half of the poem, but finds the town deserted except for skunks searching for food. The image of skunks foraging in a symbolically desolate landscape has prompted diverse interpretations; some commentators argue that they represent waste and death, while others claim the image of a mother skunk and her kittens symbolizes endurance and rebirth.

In *For the Union Dead* (1964) Lowell continued in the confessional vein but placed increasing emphasis on the interplay of past and present, the social and the political, confronting spiritual hollowness and alienation in a technologically advanced modern society. The title poem of *For the Union Dead* begins with a description of the decaying South Boston Aquarium, which the speaker frequently visited in his youth; the building and several others in the cultural center surrounding the historically significant Statehouse of Massachusetts are being demolished. Attention focuses on a memorial at the Statehouse for Colonel Robert Gould Shaw and the soldiers he commanded—the first organized black army regiment, which fought in the Civil War. The appearance of a sudden shocking phrase, a common feature in Lowell's poems, occurs halfway through: "Their monument sticks like a fishbone / in the city's throat." The soldiers' struggles are ambiguously poised between heroism and absurd futility, underscored by references to World War II, an advertisement that exploits the image of the atomic bomb blast in Hiroshima, and a television news story concerning black schoolchildren caught in a social conflict over desegregation.

Throughout the remainder of his life Lowell wrote

and revised extensively, drawing on his strong sense of literary tradition as well as the problems in his private life and the world around him. His output during these years was considerable. *Notebook 1967-1968* (1969) is a combination of polished verse and spontaneous expression, much of which was revised and expanded into three separate volumes of unrhymed sonnets published in 1973: *For Lizzie and Harriet, The Dolphin,* and *History.* Most critical attention focuses on *The Dolphin,* which concerns an object of beauty that offers the speaker the ambivalent possibilities of paradise and loss of self. The poem addresses such actual events in Lowell's life as an extramarital affair, the birth of a child out of wedlock, divorce, and remarriage. *The Dolphin* also features a self-conscious depiction of the poet ordering material and attempting to come to terms with his actions, a process underscored in the famous concluding line—"My eyes have seen what my hand did"—that reflects Lowell's emotional candor and the confessional nature of his verse.

Despite the diverse changes in form that characterize his art, Lowell's drive to express his personal torment and the contemporary and historical struggles of the nation are thematically connected, resulting in a unified and distinguished body of work. Lowell's fusion of formal technique and personal concerns, his vision of the inextricability of the public and private selves, and the superior talent with which he crafted his work have established him as a central figure of postwar American society. Steven Gould Axelrod observed: "Lowell once commented that American literature looks like 'a bravado of perpetual revolution,' and so indeed does his own poetic career. . . . Yet for all its dynamism, his poetic oeuvre is unified. At its center is Lowell himself, discovering, altering, creating the conditions of his own existence."

For further information about Lowell's life and works, see *Contemporary Authors,* Vols. 9-12, 73-76 [obituary]; *Contemporary Authors New Revision Series,* Vol. 26; *Contemporary Authors Bibliographical Series,* Vol. 2; *Contemporary Literary Criticism,* Vols. 1, 2, 3, 4, 5, 8, 9, 11, 15, 37; and *Dictionary of Literary Biography,* Vol. 5: *American Poets Since World War II.*)

CRITICAL COMMENTARY

RANDALL JARRELL

(essay date 1947)

[Jarrell was a respected writer often linked, like Lowell, with the "Middle Generation" of American poets who gained prominence after World War II. His review of *Lord Weary's Castle* excerpted below is considered a seminal discussion of the concerns that dominate Lowell's early work.]

Many of the reviews of *Lord Weary's Castle* have been conscious that it is an event of the order of Auden's first book; I know no poetry since Auden's that is better than Robert Lowell's. Everybody who reads poetry will read it sooner or later. I hope that I can help readers by pointing out its distinguishing features, by tracing its development, and by analyzing the themes that unify it.

Underneath all these poems "there is one story and one story only": when this essential theme or subject is understood, the unity of attitudes and judgments underlying the variety of the poems becomes startlingly explicit. The poems understand the world as a sort of conflict of opposites. In this struggle one opposite is that cake of custom in which all of us lie imbedded like lungfish—the stasis or inertia of the complacent self, the satisfied persistence in evil that is damnation. In this realm of necessity the poems place everything that is closed, turned inward, incestuous, that blinds or binds: the Old Law, imperialism, militarism, capitalism, Calvinism, Authority, the Father, the rich who will "do everything for the poor except get off their backs." But struggling within this like leaven, falling to it like light, is everything that is free or open, that grows or is willing to change: here is the generosity or willingness or openness that is itself salvation; here is "accessibility to experience"; this is the realm of freedom, of the Grace that has replaced the Law, of the perfect liberator whom the poet calls Christ.

Consequently the poems can have two possible movements or organizations: they can move from what is closed to what is open, or from what is open to what is closed. The second of these organizations—which corresponds to an "unhappy ending"—is less common, though there are many good examples of it: **"The Exile's Return"**, with its menacing *Voi ch'entrate* that transforms the exile's old home into a place where even hope must be abandoned; that extraordinary treatment of the "Oedipus complex," **"Between the Porch and the Altar"**, with its four parts each ending in constriction and frustration, its hero who cannot get free of his mother, her punishments, and her world even by dying, but who sees both life and death in terms of her,

Principal Works

Land of Unlikeness (poetry) 1944

Lord Weary's Castle (poetry) 1946

The Mills of the Kavanaughs (poetry) 1951

Life Studies (poetry) 1959

For the Union Dead (poetry) 1964

The Old Glory (drama) 1965

Near the Ocean (poetry) 1967

Notebook 1967-1968 (poetry) 1969

Prometheus Bound (drama) 1969

The Dolphin (poetry) 1973

For Lizzie and Harriet (poetry) 1973

History (poetry) 1973

*The Poetry of Robert Lowell (recording) 1974

Selected Poems (poetry) 1976

Day by Day (poetry) 1978

Robert Lowell: A Reading (recording) 1978

Robert Lowell Reading His Own Poems (recording) 1978

*1968 Reading in New York City.

and thinks at the end that, sword in hand, the Lord "watches me for Mother, and will turn / The bier and baby-carriage where I burn."

But normally the poems move into liberation—even death is seen as liberation, a widening into darkness: that old closed system, **"Grandfather Arthur Winslow"**, dying of cancer in his adjusted bed, at the last is the child Arthur whom the swanboats once rode through the **"Public Garden"**, whom now "the ghost of risen Jesus walks the waves to run / Upon a trumpeting black swan / Beyond Charles River to the Acheron / Where the wide waters and their voyager are one." (Compare the endings of **"The Drunken Fisherman"** and **"Des Roma".**) **"The Death of the Sheriff "** moves from closure—the "ordered darkness" of the homicidal sheriff, the "loved sightless smother" of the incestuous lovers, the "unsearchable quicksilver heart / Where spiders stare their eyes out at their own / Spitting and knotted likeness"—up into the open sky, to those "light wanderers" the planets, to the "thirsty Dipper on the arc of night." Just so the cold, blundering, iron confusion of **"Christmas Eve Under Hooker's Statute"** ends in flowers, the wild fields, a Christ "once again turned wanderer and child." In Rebellion the son seals "an everlasting pact / With Dives to *contract* / The world that *spreads* in pain"; but at last he rebels against his father and his father's New England commercial theocracy, and "the world *spread.* When the clubbed flintlock broke my father's brain." The italicized words ought to

demonstrate how explicitly, at times, these poems formulate the world in the exact terms that I have used.

"Where the Rainbow Ends" describes in apocalyptic terms the wintry, Calvinist, capitalist—Lowell has Weber's attitude about the connection of capitalism and Calvinism—dead end of God's covenant with man, a frozen Boston where even the cold-blooded serpents "whistle at the cold." (Lowell often uses cold as a plain and physically correct symbol for what is constricted, static, turned in upon itself.) There "the scythers, Time and Death, / Helmed locusts, move upon the tree of breath," of the spirit of man; a bridge curves over Charles River like an ironic parody of the rainbow's covenant; both "the wild ingrafted olive and its root / Are withered" (these are Paul's terms for the Judaism of the Old Law and the Gentile Christianity grafted upon it); "every dove [the Holy Ghost, the bringer of the olive leaf to the Ark] is sold" for a commercialized, legalized sacrifice. The whole system seems an abstract, rationalized "graph of Revelations," of the last accusation and judgment brought against man now that "the Chapel's sharp-shinned eagle shifts its hold / On serpent-Time, the rainbow's epitaph." This last line means exactly what the last line in **"The Quaker Graveyard"**—"The Lord survives the rainbow of his will"—means; both are inexpressibly menacing, since they show the covenant as something that binds only us, as something abrogated merely by the passage of time, as a closed system opening not into liberation but into infinite and overwhelming possibility; they have something of the terror, but none of the pity, of Blake's "Time is the mercy of Eternity." (p. 24)

Lowell seems a strange opposite of the usual Catholic convert, who distrusts freedom as much as he needs bondage, and who sees the world as a liberal chaos which can be ordered and redeemed only by that rigid and final Authority to which men submit without question. Lowell reminds one more of those heretical enthusiasts, often disciplined and occasionally sanctified or excommunicated, who are more at home in the Church Triumphant than in the church of this world, which is one more state; a phrase like Lowell's "St. Peter, the distorted key" is likely to be appreciated outside the church and overlooked inside it, *ad maiorem gloriam* of Catholic poetry. In Lowell's poems the Son is pure liberation from the incestuous, complacent, inveterate evil of established society, of which the Law is a part—although the Father, Jehovah, has retained both the violence necessary to break up this inertia and a good deal of the menacing sternness of Authority as such. (It is interesting to compare the figure of the Uncle in early Auden, who sanctifies rebellion by his authority; the authority of Lowell's Christ is sanctified by his rebellion or liberation.)

Anyone who compares Lowell's earlier and later poems will see this movement from constriction to liberation as his work's ruling principle of growth. The grim, violent, sordid constriction of his earliest poems—most of them omitted from this book—seems to be temperamental, the Old Adam which the poet grew from and partially transcends; and a good deal of what was excessive in the wonderful rhetorical machine of a poem like **"The Quaker Graveyard at Nantucket"**, which catches and twists to pieces the helplessly enjoying reader, is gone from his latest poems, or else dramatically justified and no longer excessive. **"The Quaker Graveyard"** is a baroque work, like *Paradise Lost;* but the coiling violence of the rhetoric, the harshly stubborn intensity that accompanies its verbs and verbals, the clustering stresses learned from accentual verse, come from a man contracting every muscle, grinding his teeth together till his shut eyes ache. Lowell's later work has moved in the direction of the poem's quiet contrast-section, Walsingham; the denunciatory prophetic tone has disappeared, along with the early satiric effects that were one of the poet's weaknesses. The later poems depend less on rhetorical description than on dramatic speech; their wholes have escaped from the hypnotic bondage of the details. Often the elaborate rhetorical stanzas have changed into a novel sort of dramatic or narrative couplet, run-on but with heavily stressed rhymes. A girl's nightmare, in the late **"Katherine's Dream"**, is far more open, classical, and speech-like than the poet's own descriptive meditation in an earlier work like **"Christmas at Black Rock"**. It is important to understand this development; the reviews I have read have not realized that it exists.

Lowell has a completely unscientific, but thoroughly historical mind. (It is literary and traditional as well: he uses the past so effectively because he thinks so much as it did.) Lowell's present contains the past—especially Rome, the late Middle Ages, and New England—as an operative skeleton just under the skin. This is rare among contemporary poets, who look at the past as Blücher looked at London: "What a city to sack!" (p. 76)

Lowell is an extremely professional poet, and the degree of intensity of his poems is equaled by their degree of organization. Inside its elaborate stanzas the poem is put together like a mosaic: the shifts of movement, the varied pauses, the alternation in the length of sentences, the counterpoint between lines and sentences, are the outer form of a subject matter that has been given a dramatic, dialectical internal organization; and it is hard to exaggerate the strength and life, the constant richness and surprise of metaphor and sound and motion, of the language itself. The organization of Lowell's poems resembles that of traditional English poetry—especially when compared to that type of semi-imagist modern organization in which the things of the poem seem to marshal themselves like Dryden's

atoms—but often this is complicated by stream-of-consciousness, dream, or dramatic-monologue types of structure. This makes the poems more difficult, but it is worth the price—a great many of the most valuable dramatic effects cannot be attained inside a more logical or abstract organization. Lowell's poetry is a unique fusion of modernist and traditional poetry, and there exist conjoined in it certain effects that one would hitherto have thought mutually exclusive; however, it is essentially a post- or anti-modernist poetry, and as such is certain to be influential.

Lowell is wonderfully good at discovering powerful, homely, grotesque, but exactly appropriate particulars for his poems. "Actuality is something brute," said Peirce. "There is no reason in it. I instance putting your shoulder against a door and trying to force it open against an unseen, silent and unknown resistance." The things in Lowell's poems have, necessarily, been wrenched into formal shape, organized under terrific pressure, but they keep to an extraordinary degree their stubborn, unmoved toughness, their senseless originality and contingency: no poet is more notable for what, I have read, **"Duns Scotus"** calls *haeccitas*— the contrary, persisting, and singular thinginess of every being in the world; but this detailed factuality is particularly effective because it sets off, or is set off by, the elevation and rhetorical sweep characteristic of much of the best poetry of the past. Lowell is obviously a haptic rather than a visual type: a poem like **"Colloquy in Black Rock"** has some of the most extraordinary kinesthetic effects in English, perfect duplications of what is being described. It is impossible not to notice the weight and power of his lines—most others look a little threadbare or transparent beside them. Because of passages like

> In the great ash-pit of Jehoshaphat
> The bones cry for the blood of the white whale,
> The fat flukes arch and whack about its ears,
> The death-lance churns into the sanctuary, tears
> The gun-blue swingle, heaving like a flail,
> And hacks the coiling life out . . .

the smooth, calm, and flowing ease of some passages, the flat ease of the ordinary speech of others, have more than their usual effectiveness: the dead mistress of Propertius, a black nail dangling from a finger, Lethe oozing from her nether lip, in the end can murmur to the "apple-sweetened Anio":

> Anio, you will please
> Me if you whisper upon sliding knees:
> "Propertius, Cynthia is here:
> She shakes her blossoms when my waters clear."

The poems' wit is often the wit of things: the "poised relations sipping sherry / And tracking up the carpet," the "postgirl sounding her French horn" over the snows of Maine, the "stern Colonial magistrates and wards / of Charles the Second." The "corn-fed mouse / Reined in his bestial passions"; the "red-flanneled madmen looked through bars." One laughs out in church.

Lowell, at his best and latest, is a dramatic poet: he presents people, actions, speeches, things as they feel and look to people; the poet's generalizations are usually implied, and the poem's explicit generalizations are there primarily because they are dramatically necessary—it is not usually the poet who means them. He does not present themes or generalizations but a world—and the differences and similarities between it and the ordinary one bring home to us themes, generalizations, and the poet himself. There is never any exploitation of the "personality" of the poet; the *I* who stands meditating by Hooker's statue or the Quaker graveyard is closer to the different *I*'s of the dramatic monologues than to the man who wrote them. It is partly because of this that atheists are vexed by his Catholic views, and Catholics by his heretical ones, so much less than they normally would be.

But there are other reasons. The poet's rather odd and imaginative Catholicism is thoroughly suitable to his mind, which is so traditional and dramatic that no images from the sciences, next to none from philosophy, occur in his poems. Such a Catholicism is thoroughly suited to literature, since it *is* essentially literary, anthropomorphic, emotional. It is an advantage to the poet to have a frame of reference, terms of generalization, which are themselves human, emotional, and effective as literature. "Bodily Changes in Fear, Rage, and Hunger" may let the poet know more about the anger of Achilles, but it is hard for him to have to talk about adrenalin and the thalamus; and when the arrows of Apollo are transformed into "a lack of adequate sanitary facilities," everything is lost but understanding. (This helps explain the dependence of contemporary poetry on particulars, emotions, things—its generalizations, where they are most effective, are fantastic, though often traditionally so.) Naturally the terms of scientific explanation cannot have these poetic and emotional effects, since it is precisely by the exclusion of such effects that science has developed. Lowell's Catholicism represents effective realities of human behavior and desire, regardless of whether it is true, false, or absurd; and, as everyone must realize, it is possible to tell part of the truth about the world in terms that are false, limited, and fantastic—else how should we have told it? (pp. 76-7)

When I reviewed Lowell's first book [see excerpt above] I finished by saying, "Some of the best poems of the next years ought to be written by him." The appearance of *Lord Weary's Castle* makes me feel less like Adams or Leverrier than like a rainmaker who predicts rain, and gets a flood which drowns everyone in the

county. A few of these poems, I believe, will be read as long as men remember English. (p. 77)

Randall Jarrell, "From the Kingdom of Necessity," in *The Nation,* New York, Vol. 164, No. 3, January 18, 1947, pp. 74, 76-7.

ROBERT LOWELL WITH A. ALVAREZ
(interview date 1963)

[Alvarez, an important English authority on contemporary poetry, championed the verse of the Confessional poets. The interview below is considered particularly insightful for Lowell's remarks on his technique and development.]

[Alvarez]: *Your verse has changed a great deal, hasn't it? Most of the mannerisms of rhythm and imagery that you used in your early poems have disappeared, and yet you now have something much more personal. Is this how you see your own work?*

[Lowell]: When my second book came out the most interesting review of it was by Randall Jarrell [see excerpt dated 1947]. Though he liked the book, he made the point that I was doing things I could do best quite often, and I think he quoted Kipling—when you learn how to do something, don't do it again. I think you should always do something a little longer than you should, go on until it gives out. There was a long pause between the second and the third. I didn't want to go just cranking the same machine.

When your first poems came out you were a Catholic, weren't you? You've ceased to be one since. Has the change in style anything to do with this change in allegiance?

It may have. In the second book I wasn't a Catholic but I was using Catholic material from a non-Catholic point of view, a neutral one. In *Life Studies* I was very anxious to get a tone that sounded a little like conversation.

I felt that in **Life Studies** *you were setting your personal house in order, you were dealing with very personal material almost as you would in psychoanalysis. It seemed that, having left behind the dogmatic Catholic base and the dogmatic rhythms and symbols that went with it, you were trying to build a new base from which you could work.*

I had in the back of my mind something like the prose of a Chekhov short story. The poems came in two spurts. The first was more intense when two-thirds of the autobiographical poems were written. This was a period of, at most, three months. Then there was a second period which finished that group and filled in blank spaces.

I remember someone in The Review *saying that the prose section in your book [*"91 Revere Street"*] which unfortunately* *wasn't published in the English version—was often more concentrated than one or two of the poems about your relatives. Do you think that's a fair comment?*

There's a long first section in *Life Studies* called "Last Afternoon with Uncle Devereux Winslow" which was originally written in prose. I put it aside and I later cut things out and re-arranged it and made different transitions and put it into verse, so there is that connection and perhaps the style comes out of writing prose. But I'd say that the prose was an awful job to do. It took a long time and I think it could be less concentrated with more sting or something like that.

You don't find prose comes naturally?

I find it very hard. I like to revise and when you have something of thirty or forty pages written as carefully as a poem—and it was written that carefully—it's very hard.

Do you revise your poems much?

Usually. I think my record is a poem that was finished in one day. Usually it's a long time. I would have said that writing free verse you're more likely to get a few lines that are right in the beginning than you are in metre.

My own interpretation of **Life Studies** *is that the family poems cleared the ground and that, with the now very famous poems like* **"Man and Wife"**, **"Home After Three Months Away"**, *and* **"Waking in the Blue"**, *you own voice came up absolutely clear—they have this unmistakable Lowell rhythm.*

They are not written chronologically. Actually the first poem finished was **"Skunk Hour"** and I think the second was **"Man and Wife"**, though they were all going on at the same time. But the first nut to crack really was **"Skunk Hour"**— that was the hardest. I cast about . . . it was written backwards, more or less, and I added the first four stanzas after I'd finished it.

It came before these family poems?

Yes, actually it was the first, although the others were sort of started. I guess the first thing I had was a very imperfect version of **"Man and Wife"**, which I dropped, and then I wrote **"Skunk Hour"**. **"Skunk Hour"** was the first one completed. I was reading Elizabeth Bishop's poems very carefully at the time and imitating the loose formality of her style.

It seems to me that that poem is less successful in its opening lines. It suddenly gets down to what you're really talking about in the last part.

The opening's sort of cotton-nosed, it's supposed to let you sink into the poem and then it tenses up. I don't know whether it works or not. You dawdle in the first part and suddenly get caught in the poem.

Confessional verse as you write it isn't simply an outpouring, is it? It's very strict, although the rules are hard to find.

You're asking how a confessional poem that's a

work of art differs from someone's outpourings, sensational confessions for the newspapers or confessions to one's analyst. It seems to me there is some connection. When I was doing what might be called confessional poems there was a big chunk of something to be gotten out, but a great deal of it was very tame; the whole thing wasn't any very great story, but still there were things I wanted to say. Then the thing was the joy of composition, to get some music and imagination and form into it and to know just when to stop and what sort of language to put it in—it was pure joy writing it and I think it was pure technical joy, and poems are dull if you don't have that.

What about the technique? You were saying that you have a great love for William Carlos Williams, who I would say seems to be the antithetical poet to you. Has he had any effect?

I always liked Williams, since I was a young man. But I don't think I've ever written anything that's very much like him. He really is utterly carried away into the object, it intoxicated him in describing it, and his way of composition's so different from mine. He was an active doctor and he wrote in snatches; he developed a way of writing in which he could get things out very quickly. I find him a very artful poet, but his art was largely cutting what he poured out. My things are much more formal, much more connected with older English poetry; there's a sort of formal personality in myself. I think anyone could tell that my free verse was written by someone who'd done a lot of formal verse. I began writing in the thirties and the current I fell into was the southern group of poets—John Crowe Ransom and Allen Tate—and that was partly a continuation of Pound and Eliot and partly an attempt to make poetry much more formal than Eliot and Pound did: to write in metres but to make the metres look hard and make them hard to write. It was the period of the famous book *Understanding Poetry*, of analysing poems to see how they're put together; there was a great emphasis on craftsmanship. Out of that, though it came later, were poetry workshops and all that sort of thing. Well, that's in my blood very much, and about 1950 it was prevailing everywhere in America. There were poets trained that way, writing in the style, writing rather complicated, difficult, laboured poems, and it was getting very dry. You felt you had to get away from that at all costs. Yet still it's in one's blood. We're trained that way and I admire Tate and Ransom as much as ever. But in England that was the period of Auden and poetry was trying to express the times, politics, psychology, economics, the war and everything that somehow wasn't very strong with us. We had such poets and we had a lot of Auden imitators, but the strongest feeling seemed to be to get away from that and just write a poem. We talked a lot about form, craft, tragic experience and things like that.

On this question of Auden, you seem to feel apparently quite strongly about not being political.

Well, yes, and that's quite misleading because it now seems to me that Auden's glory is that he caught all those things with much greater power than any of the people of his group. He's made the period immortal, of waiting for the war. At that time it seemed so stifled in controversy that it wasn't possible for us. People tried it in our country.

What he got really was not the politics but the neurotic tension.

That's a better description. He caught the air and it was air in which events were hovering over your shoulder at every point, the second war was boiling into existence. Freud and Marx and a host of thinkers who were the most alive at that time—and still are in many ways—all do get into his poetry, and the idiom of those people waiting! I find that marvellous. I don't think this is a period of parties and politics the way the thirties were. Here and in America that all seems to have calmed down to something we imagine is more the way life ordinarily is. I don't meet people who are violently anti-Russian very often. That doesn't seem to be the air.

They still exist, though.

They exist, but they don't exist very much in the intellectual world. While in the thirties everybody was taking sides on something, usually very violently— violent conversions, violent Marxist positions, violent new deal, violent anti-new deal—things couldn't be more different now. The terrible danger now is of the great impersonal bureaucratic machinery rolling over everything and flattening out humanity. (pp. 36-40)

Robert Lowell and A. Alvarez, in an interview, in *The Review*, No. 8, August, 1963, pp. 36-40.

ROBERT LOWELL

(essay date 1964)

[In the essay excerpted below, which was originally published in *The Contemporary Poet as Artist and Critic*, Lowell discusses how he came to write "Skunk Hour," considered by some his most powerful poem.]

I. The Meaning

The author of a poem is not necessarily the ideal person to explain its meaning. He is as liable as anyone else to muddle, dishonesty and reticence. Nor is it his purpose to provide a peg for a prose essay. Meaning varies in importance from poem to poem, and from

style to style, but always it is only a strand and an element in the brute flow of composition. Other elements are pictures that please or thrill for themselves, phrases that ring for their music or carry some buried suggestion. For all this the author is an opportunist, throwing whatever comes to hand into his feeling for start, continuity, contrast, climax, and completion. It is imbecile for him not to know his intentions, and unsophisticated for him to know too explicitly and fully. (p. 131)

I am not sure whether I can distinguish between intention and interpretation. I think this is what I more or less intended. The first four stanzas [of "Skunk Hour"] are meant to give a dawdling more or less amiable picture of a declining Maine sea town. I move from the ocean inland. Sterility howls through the scenery, but I try to give a tone of tolerance, humor, and randomness to the sad prospect. The composition drifts, its direction sinks out of sight into the casual, chancy arrangements of nature and decay. Then all comes alive in stanzas V and VI. This is the dark night. I hoped my readers would remember John of the Cross's poem. My night is not gracious, but secular, puritan, and agnostical. An Existentialist night. Somewhere in my mind was a passage from Sartre or Camus about reaching some point of final darkness where the one free act is suicide. Out of this comes the march and affirmation, an ambiguous one, of my skunks in the last two stanzas. The skunks are both quixotic and barbarously absurd, hence the tone of amusement and defiance. "Skunk Hour" is not entirely independent, but the anchor poem in its sequence. (pp. 131-32)

II. How the Poem Was Written

"Skunk Hour" was begun in mid-August, 1957, and finished about a month later. In March of the same year, I had been giving readings on the West Coast, often reading six days a week and sometimes twice on a single day. I was in San Francisco, the era and setting of Allen Ginsberg, and all about very modest poets were waking up prophets. I became sorely aware of how few poems I had written, and that these few had been finished at the latest three or four years earlier. Their style seemed distant, symbol-ridden and willfully difficult. I began to paraphrase my Latin quotations, and to add extra syllables to a line to make it clearer and more colloquial. I felt my old poems hid what they were really about, and many times offered a stiff, humorless and even impenetrable surface. I am no convert to the "beats." I know well too that the best poems are not necessarily poems that read aloud. Many of the greatest poems can only be read to one's self, for inspiration is no substitute for humor, shock, narrative and a hypnotic voice, the four musts for oral performance. Still, my own poems seemed like prehistoric monsters dragged down into the bog and death by their ponderous armor. I was reciting what I no longer felt. What influenced me more than San Francisco and reading aloud was that for some time I had been writing prose. I felt that the best style for poetry was none of the many poetic styles in English, but something like the prose of Chekhov or Flaubert.

When I returned to my home, I began writing lines in a new style. No poem, however, got finished and soon I left off and tried to forget the whole headache. Suddenly, in August, I was struck by the sadness of writing nothing, and having nothing to write, of having, at least, no language. When I began writing **"Skunk Hour,"** I felt that most of what I knew about writing was a hindrance.

The dedication is to Elizabeth Bishop, because re-reading her suggested a way of breaking through the shell of my old manner. Her rhythms, idiom, images, and stanza structure seemed to belong to a later century. **"Skunk Hour"** is modeled on Miss Bishop's "The Armadillo," a much better poem and one I had heard her read and had later carried around with me. Both **"Skunk Hour"** and "The Armadillo" use short line stanzas, start with drifting description and end with a single animal.

This was the main source. My others were Hölderlin's "Brod und Wein," particularly the moon lines:

> Sich! und das Schattenbild unserer Erde, der Mond,
> kommet geheim nun auch; die Schwärmerische, die Nacht kommt
> "vohl" mit Sternen und "wohl" wenig bekummert um uns,

and so forth. I put this in long straggling lines and then added touches of Maine scenery, till I saw I was getting nowhere. Another source, probably undetectable now, was Annette von Droste-Hülshoff 's "Amletzten Tage des Jahres." She too uses a six-line stanza with short lines. Her second stanza is as follows:

> 's ist tiefe Nacht!
> Ob wohl ein Auge offen noch?
> In diesen Mauern ruttelt dein
> Verrinnen, Zeit! Mir schaudert; doch
> Es will die letzte Stunde sein
> Einsam durchwacht.

> Geschehen all

Here and elsewhere, my poem and the German poem have the same shudders and situation.

"Skunk Hour" was written backwards, first the last two stanzas, I think, and then the next to last two. Anyway, there was a time when I had the last four stanzas much as they now are and nothing before them. I found the bleak personal violence repellent. All was too close, though watching the lovers was not mine, but from an anecdote about Walt Whitman in his old age. I began to feel that real poetry came, not from fierce confessions, but from something almost mean-

ingless but imagined. I was haunted by an image of a blue china doorknob. I never used the doorknob, or knew what it meant, yet somehow it started the current of images in my opening stanzas. They were written in reverse order, and at last gave my poem an earth to stand on, and space to breathe. (pp. 132-34)

Robert Lowell, "On 'Skunk Hour'," in *Robert Lowell: A Collection of Critical Essays,* edited by Thomas Parkinson, Prentice-Hall, Inc., 1968, pp. 131-34.

GEOFFREY H. HARTMAN
(essay date 1965)

[A German-born American critic, Hartman established his reputation with studies of the English Romantic poets. In later works he challenged the "close reading" method advocated by New Criticism, preferring more intuitive approaches and praising poets like Lowell whose works encourage such readings. In the essay excerpted below, he discusses Lowell's change of style as revealed in *For the Union Dead.*]

The poet, approaching his fiftieth year, has changed his style [in *For the Union Dead*]: there are freer rhythms, unexpectedly gentle contours, and a partial return to imagistic reticence. This is a strange turn of events, since the early Lowell, in curious rivalry with Hart Crane, took Eliot as a point of departure toward a complete reversal of direction. As thoroughly accusative as Eliot's poetry is evasive, *Lord Weary's Castle* raised the image to the power of a direct, admonitory emblem. The needles of a Christmas tree "nail us to the wall," "Time and the grindstone and the knife of God" assail us by their overt and cumulative presence, and verbal flushes learned from Hopkins obtrude: "The search-guns click and spit and split up timber / And nick. . . . " Lowell's newest poetry, however, is balanced in tone and elliptical in movement: its energy is more hidden, its exclamations almost musical.

There are difficulties in evaluating this change of style. Perhaps the best that can be done is to balance the gain and the loss. To start with the loss: Lowell had recovered and mechanized an aspect of medieval style, the "definition poem." Now some of the definiteness is gone. The strange and splendid harshness, the pointed shards of images, the aggressive apostrophes—they have given way to a new and casual compactness. Lowell is also, perhaps, affected by a European or "international" style which seems to have reached American poetry in the sixties. The Hopkinsian, or over-energetic, use of language is being abandoned for a quieter and naiver mode. Has Lowell succumbed to this *dolce stil nuovo* in such poems as **"The Lesson"**?

No longer to lie reading *Tess of the d'Urbervilles,*
while the high mysterious squirrels
rain small green branches on our sleep!

This, surely, is "imitating," and to the point of parody. But Lowell's earlier stylistic appropriations are at least equally apparent in these new poems, and with ominous rather than whimsical overtones, as in **"Beyond the Alps"** (from *Life Studies* and expanded here) where a classical dawn comes with unclassical violence:

the blear-eyed ego kicking in my berth
lay still, and saw Apollo plant his heels
on terra firma through the morning's thigh.

This is the Lowell one knows best, who associates birth with labor and violence. Things "bleed with dawn." And because this Lowell remains so essential in *For The Union Dead,* it is hard to consider the muted style as very significant. If Lowell's poetry moves more haltingly between sentiments and stanzas, his images continue to be entries in a doomsday book: they come nearer and nearer to us, threatening our detachment, massing with prophetic intensity. Is the intermingling, then, of a subtler style, purely experimental, purely a technique? "Each drug that numbs," he says in **"Soft Wood,"** "alerts another nerve to pain." Perhaps it is a spice or drug of this kind.

I would argue that the style of *For The Union Dead* reveals a genuine spiritual change, a revision of thought on the deepest and most internal level. Let us begin with what remains constant in Lowell. The major concern of this book is, as ever, pain: pain and anguish at temporality. That "chilling sensation of here and now, of exact contemporaneity" which Elizabeth Bishop had praised is strongly present. Lowell's attitude toward time is paradoxical: time is the accuser, yet time is inauthentic. Time eyes us through objects that loom large, or through "unforgivable" landscapes, yet everything converges to no effect, like waves breaking harmlessly and sight blurring. Time, and also memory, are the "back-track of the screw"; yet their pressure—the pressure essentially of religious expectation—is unremitting. "Even new life is fuel," Lowell says ironically.

No ease from the eye
of the sharp-shinned hawk in the birdbook there,
with reddish brown buffalo hair
on its shanks, one ascetic talon
clasping the imperial sky.
It says:
an eye for an eye
a tooth for a tooth.

The *lex talionis* here referred to is an imperative laid by consciousness on itself, and requires us to be perpet-

ually on guard, open to every sight. Our verdict on temporal matters should be that they are "true and insignificant" (**"Hawthorne"**). Instead, because of an American or Puritan tension between trivia and magnalia, life becomes a restless search for evidence, a satanic "going to and fro" in the earth.

If time is inauthentic, can a poet do more than record or "accuse" this to-and-fro? What genuine visionariness is possible? The question has a bearing on Lowell's development and on his present change of style. His earliest poetry strives for vision, but there is no vision except a methodical *hastening of the end.* In the poetry that precedes *Life Studies,* darkness calls to darkness: Nature appears as a world of portents rising against the dominion of man, and the poet harshly welcomes the suggested reversal. His visionary method is a kind of *temporicide,* and his poetical method sets spiritual symbol against daily event. He is not a reconciling poet. The very grinding together of natural experience and supernatural emblem is part of a harshness directed against temporality.

But in *Life Studies,* and even more so in [*For the Union dead*], Lowell resists methodical darkness. He is like Faustus at midnight who cries, *"Lente, lente currite noctis equi."* There is a first retreat from darkness, and into life, when poetry becomes more confessional—a sharp-eyed census of the unreconcilable elements in life. The retreat, however, is very imperfect. For realism easily becomes expressionism, while Lowell's indicative mood tends to indite rather than describe. "The man is killing time," he writes in **"The Drinker."** Or, in the title poem of *For The Union Dead,* which turns on several apocalyptic emblems: "The ditch is nearer." This nearing, this investing of experience with doom, this dark gloating even, this aggressive parody of at-one-ment in the grim images and the massing of the very words ("The Duce's lynched, bare, booted skull still spoke") is the temptation as well as energy of his vision.

It is, however, the special distinction of *For The Union Dead* to retreat even further from darkness by taking this retreat for subject. Here poetry itself, by virtue of its style—that subtler style—holds back the darkening mind. A presumption of restraint is felt at every level. Lowell is more successful in avoiding the intrusive literary or apocalyptic symbol, though whales still rear their blubber and spiders march. A poem like **"The Drinker,"** with its discreet, almost neutral ending, is utterly different from **"The Drunken Fisherman"** (*Lord Weary's Castle* which outsped even Donne's imagination of ruin. The new portrait of **"Jonathan Edwards"** is unusually urbane in tone and meandering. Natural experience and supernatural emblem may even blend, as when Exodus 12 quietly supports the "red ear of Indian maize . . . splashed on the door" in **"The Old Flame,"** a poem dealing with the old pass-

Caricature of Lowell by David Levine.

ing into the new. That Lowell should admit newness is itself new, though an ironic image of "the plow / groaning up hill—/ a red light, then a blue . . . " flickers in memory and disturbs the idea of a definitive progress. **"Water,"** another memory study, shows him in the very act of restraining a darkening yet consolatory movement of the mind. . . . (pp. 277-79)

The greatest of these memory studies, and the most difficult, is the title poem. Its precarious forward motion reflects the problem of the prophetic mind. There is a consistent "drawing back" from certain conclusions or imaginations. I do not like everything in **"For the Union Dead"**; the continuity, for example, is aggressively casual. Yet its vibrant and vital imprisonment of apocalyptic themes is totally effective in evoking great but repressed powers—powers waiting for "the blesséd break." Chief among these is the power of both Negro and white to take the initiative in civil rights, though the rights struggle is in an eccentric rather than central position. The poem centers, if at all, in several "places" (civil rights, Boston, urbanization, the slippage of time) and is held together in Lowell fashion by an elliptical biography and an ideal. The ideal, that of service, finds its clearest expression in Lowell's inversion of a Christian paradox: service, leadership, is to "choose life and die"; and dying into life is what *Life Studies* already taught. The poem ends with a further inversion of a Christian theme, with a parody of Revelation. Servility instead of service and the omen of a monstrous backlash flood the aquarium of memory:

The Aquarium is gone. Everywhere,
giant finned cars nose forward like fish;
a savage servility
slides by on grease.

This is still the poet of **"The Quaker Graveyard,"** but quietly, consciously, in the eye of the storm. (p. 280)

Geoffrey H. Hartman, "The Eye of the Storm," in *Partisan Review,* Vol. XXXII, No. 2, Spring, 1965, pp. 277-80.

___

M. L. ROSENTHAL
(essay date 1967)

[Rosenthal is an American poet, editor, and critic whose survey studies *The Modern Poets: A Critical Introduction* (1960) and *The New Poets: American and British Poetry Since World War II* (1967) are considered excellent overviews of contemporary verse. The excerpt below from the latter book focuses on poems in *Life Studies*.]

The term 'confessional poetry' came naturally to my mind when I reviewed Robert Lowell's *Life Studies* in 1959, and perhaps it came to the minds of others just as naturally. Whoever invented it, it was a term both helpful and too limited, and very possibly the conception of a confessional school has by now done a certain amount of damage. (p. 25)

Because of the way Lowell brought his private humiliations, sufferings, and psychological problems into the poems of *Life Studies,* the word 'confessional' seemed appropriate enough. Sexual guilt, alcoholism, repeated confinement in a mental hospital (and some suggestion that the malady has its violent phase)—these are explicit themes of a number of the poems, usually developed in the first person and intended without question to point to the author himself. Accompanying these poems are the long prose-section "91 Revere Street" and a group of related poems presenting the Lowell family background in a manner at once nostalgic, bitter, and psychologically knowledgeable. The mixture of love and loathing, humor and horror, had the impact of a purely personal release, and the softer and more genial notes in the book went mostly unnoticed at first. Lowell had not published a book for eight years before *Life Studies* appeared, and so the term 'confessional' served also to distinguish the new work from the earlier and at the same time to suggest that everything before had been largely a preparation for this development. In a larger, more impersonal context, these poems seemed to me one culmination of the

Romantic and modern tendency to place the literal Self more and more at the center of the poem.

In examining Lowell's poetry, therefore, it will be helpful to concentrate on *Life Studies* as his chief volume so far, though we may also look back, if briefly, to *Lord Weary's Castle* (1946) and *The Mills of the Kavanaughs* (1951) and ahead to *For the Union Dead* (1965). (*Land of Unlikeness,* his first book, was published in 1944, but its best poems were for the most part reprinted in *Lord Weary's Castle.*) The earlier collections show his power and enterprise. Their conception and emotional drive are inseparable from his artistry. The technique is rigorous, and poems like **"The Quaker Graveyard at Nantucket"** and **"Colloquy in Black Rock"** leave no doubt of their author's genius. But despite their explosive brilliance, the books are often musclebound. The awkwardly contained violence of *Lord Weary's Castle* struggles against tight rhymes and a general formal rigidity, as well as against elaborate, stifling overlays of religious and social symbolism, themselves fairly derivative. In the long monologues of *The Mills of the Kavanaughs,* an unspeakably tangled complex of special circumstances and contrived mythical allusiveness hampers the movement, though it provides a protective armor or disguise for Lowell's sensitive reachings out toward confessional statement.

Life Studies, however, is the volume in which the poet at last 'finds himself.' He does so literally, for in most of the poems he himself and his family are at the center, and his object is to catch himself in process of becoming himself. Equally important, in fact more so, he finds himself as a stylist. For the first time he can be casual, simple, and direct throughout a poem, and at the same time he can strike home more tellingly than ever when he wishes. Or, if he desires, he can be transparently clear and *gentle* in his emotional realizations, as he could not have been before. Thus, for instance, the first stanza of **"Grandparents"**:

> They're altogether otherworldly now,
> those adults champing for their ritual Friday
>   spin
> to pharmacist and five-and-ten in Brockton.
> Back in my throw-away and shaggy span
> of adolescence, Grandpa still waves his stick
> like a policeman;
> Grandmother, like a Mohammedan, still wears
>   her thick
> lavender mourning and touring veil;
> the Pierce Arrow clears its throat in a horse-
>   stall.
> Then the dry road dust rises to whiten
> the fatigued elm leaves—
> the nineteenth century, tired of children, is gone.
> They're all gone into a world of light; the farm's
>   my own.

I have chosen this passage just because it is in one

of the less dynamic poems of *Life Studies.* It can be observed without arousing a passion either to cheer it or to do battle with it, yet it is moving on precisely its own terms. The diction is straightforward, accurate but informal. The nostalgic humor of the first nine lines evokes a time in the 1930's when the speaker's grandparents were still alive and dominating his world. Their old-fashioned attitude toward the automobile is remembered with loving irony, darkened by the sadness of the first line. (They who were 'otherworldly' enough in the innocent rituals of their lives are now, in death, *'altogether'* so.) The final four lines of the stanza become consistently, though gently, serious. Their overtones, suggesting the death of an era as well as of two specific people, make themselves felt without calling special attention to the symbolism of white dust, fatigued elm leaves, or even the guilt of the young—their sense that the elders died to punish them deservedly. There is nothing here or in the two stanzas that follow to match the stiffer phrases and the more forced allusions of **"Mary Winslow,"** the elegiac poem in *Lord Weary's Castle* that begins:

> Her Irish maids could never spoon out mush
> Or orange-juice enough; the body cools
> And smiles as a sick child
> Who adds up figures, and a hush
> Grips at the poised relations sipping sherry
> And tracking up the carpets of her four
> Room kingdom. On the rigid Charles, in snow,
> Charon, the Lubber, clambers from his wherry,
> And stops her hideous baby-squawks and yells,
> Wit's clownish afterthought. . . .

Now **"Mary Winslow"** is hardly a *bad* poem. It begins as naturally and rightly as does the later **"Grandparents."** It has the same compassion without developing it as richly. Lowell brings to bear in it his amazing memory and eye, better than any anthropologist's, for relevant cultural details—though relevance for him is to the pity of the human condition. Both the poems are crowded with such details. **"Grandparents,"** however, is in better control of its own direction, for Lowell has outgrown his compulsion to push a symbolic scene so far in search of implication that he is almost led away from the central human insight. In the same way, it is less rhyme-ridden. Rhymes are every bit as operative, but they are far less conspicuous. There is only one exact rhyme ('stick'—'thick'); all the other rhymes are only approximate. [In a footnote, the critic adds: In 'span'—'policeman' we have a light rhyme (that is, a stressed syllable rhymed with an unstressed one). In any case, the *a* is pronounced differently in the two words.] Thus, seven of the thirteen lines quoted echo one another by ending in *n,* each time preceded by a vowel in a syllable that is sometimes stressed, sometimes unstressed. 'Veil' and 'stall' make another such off-rhyme. There is another, more sunken kind of rhyming, between 'now' in the first line and 'own' in the last, and between 'veil' and 'leaves,' for these two pairs are each for the most part simply variant arrangements of the same sounds. This kind of sound-patterning, which is naturally not limited simply to line-endings but saturates a good poem, is one of a poet's major means of reinforcing feeling and thought and of gaining organic structure. Another is the pattern of line-length and stresses. It is easy to see that while both poems are made up of lines tending toward a basic five-stress pattern but with many variations from it, **"Grandparents"** is more flexible, with a movement very close to that of normal, somewhat heightened speech.

These are the minutiae of the poem, no doubt, rather than its major qualities. But they seem inseparable from the general liberation of perspective, and of power to call upon his resources, developed by Lowell in the long period before *Life Studies* appeared. It is clear now that the shock of the autobiographical sections of that book did not come altogether, as it seemed in 1959, from their self-exposing frankness and the humiliating things said by the poet about his family, especially his father. It came at least as much from the redirection of energy, through the free mastery of these 'minutiae' for a particular purpose that now emerged, toward realizations so intense that at first reading they approached direct experience. Lowell had made a terrifying recovery of his own past, and with it of the lost realities of his parents' and grandparents' existence and of their surrounding life. This recovery did not really happen suddenly. The extraordinary passion of his earlier books is an expression of the search for it, and in *Lord Weary's Castle* we find an almost confessional poem like **"Rebellion"** and 'family' poems like **"In Memory of Arthur Winslow," "Winter in Dunbarton,"** and **"Mary Winslow."** None of these have quite the painful immediacy of *Life Studies*. They are denied the release that would at once have achieved this immediacy and resolved the artificial complexities of the early style. Charged with the same ultimate themes of humiliation, frustration, and unlocated guilt, the earlier books were nevertheless impersonal in a fashion that held the poet himself at arm's length from his true goal (like the early work of Robert Penn Warren).

"Grandparents" is 'terrifying' and 'painful' only in the ultimate sense of any sharp realization of loss. It is, as I have observed, gentler than many other poems in *Life Studies*. Still, it resembles them in its recovery of crucial family experience. Intensity and poignancy are cradled within the gentleness, and the recovery of the past is suddenly converted, in the closing stanzas, into a stricken sense of the present instant. In these stanzas, the lines grow generally shorter and include a number of exclamations, culminating in a cry of childish longing for Grandpa's return and in a reproachful

self-characterization. It is the method of *Life Studies* at its simplest that we see in this poem, which forms one brief movement in a series of parallel repossessions of the past, many far stormier. Risking sentimentality, Lowell does not quite avoid it, but the risk is essential to the self-discovery he is after:

> Never again
> to walk there, chalk our cues,
> insist on shooting for us both.
> Grandpa! Have me, hold me, cherish me!
> Tears smut my fingers. There
> half my life-lease later,
> I hold an *Illustrated London News*—;
> disloyal still,
> I doodle handlebar
> mustaches on the last Russian Czar.

The two confessional sections of *Life Studies*—the title-section of poems and the prose-section called "91 Revere Street"—form the bulk of the book. There are eight poems in addition. An opening group of four, which in a sense sums up the cultural and historical context within which the poet finds himself, precedes **"91 Revere Street."** The first two of these poems, **"Beyond the Alps"** and **"The Banker's Daughter,"** present the failure of the European traditions out of which our classical humanistic ideals were born. The third poem is a severe, tragically tinged, short satire on Eisenhower (**"Inauguration Day: January 1953"**); and the fourth is a savage, even manic poem called **"A Mad Negro Soldier Confined at Munich."** This last poem stands as one of the most cumulatively powerful pieces that Lowell has ever written. The progression of the four poems is clear. They move from a general critical summing-up of the state of the civilization—similar in conception though not in style or the specifics of political attitude to that made familiar to us by Pound and Eliot—to an equally harsh comment on the state of the Republic, and then to a close-up of the effect of the last war on one Negro soldier. This final poem in the introductory group shifts our attention from the madness of society to its embodiment in one man. We may assume an intended relationship between this progression and the prose account of his family background, his father's failure especially, that Lowell gives in "91 Revere Street."

We can see a comparable focusing and progression of intensity in the other nonconfessional group. It too consists of four poems, placed between the prose-section and the fifteen poems of the "Life Studies" section proper. As with the monologue of the 'mad Negro soldier,' these four poems present figures analogous to the ultimate protagonist of the book, Lowell himself. **"Ford Madox Ford"** and **"For George Santayana"** are sympathetic but candid portraits of the life-defeated Ford and the dauntless Santayana, 'unbelieving, unconfessed and unreceived.' **"To Delmore Schwartz"** is a beautifully engaging, ironic self-portrait of Lowell and his friend and fellow-poet Delmore Schwartz. **"Words for Hart Crane"** is the one poem among these in which Lowell is not himself the speaker, yet it is his strongest personal statement in the book. Hart Crane does the speaking, but of course the 'words' referred to in the title are supplied by Lowell, to underline his identification with Crane. The poem locates the dissident, lyrical, and Romantic traditions with which both men are to be associated: Catullus, Shelley, Whitman, the bohemian life of Paris and Greenwich Village. It insists that the poet's outcast state is a failure of America, irredeemable except through unqualified gestures of love:

Who asks for me, the Shelley of my age,
must lay his heart out for my bed and board.

It will already be evident, I hope, that although it was the naked, nearly exhibitionistic aspect of *Life Studies* that attracted the greatest attention when the book appeared, this was by no means its only importance. The reductive imitation by other poets of this one aspect results in very different effects from those in Lowell. What I should like to suggest now is the actual character of his achievement in the confessional sections (remembering the symbolic framework created by the eight poems I have just briefly described). (pp. 26-34)

We may usefully divide the "Life Studies" [poems] into five sections. [In a footnote, the critic observes: Lowell himself divides it into two more inclusive sections. Section I consists of the first eleven poems (family background and mental breakdown) and Section II of the concluding four (effect on his political experience, marriage, and ultimate relation to life).] The first section, consisting of three poems, has mainly to do with the child's relation to his grandparents. **"My Last Afternoon with Uncle Devereux Winslow"** introduces various motifs that cut through the whole sequence: the child's preference for his grandfather over his father and mother; psychoneurotic tendencies in the family; and an almost hysterically nostalgic pain at the loss of the past, epitomized in this instance in the lament for a young uncle that concludes the poem. After this fierce beginning, **"Dunbarton"** (the title refers to the site of the family graveyard) takes up the theme of the boy's special relationship with his grandfather: 'He was my Father. I was his son.' The feeling of betrayal of the real father dramatized in the opening lines of the first poem (" 'I won't go with you. I want to stay with Grandpa!' ") is sustained in this poem. What would ordinarily seem a delightful and normal relationship is given, if only whimsically, a pathological coloration:

I saw myself as a young newt,

neurasthenic, scarlet
and wild in the wild coffee-colored water.

In the mornings I cuddled like a paramour
in my Grandfather's bed,
while he scouted about the chattering greenwood stove.

"Grandparents," which puts the relationship in another perspective, horror at the irredeemability of the past, brings this opening movement to a sharply nostalgic close.

The second movement, or section, of "Life Studies" consists of six poems, all having to do with the poet's parents, particularly their deaths. The first of them, **"Commander Lowell 1887-1950,"** plunges us at once into the atmosphere of failure, neurosis, and shame remembered from the child's seventh year:

There were no undesirables or girls in my set,
when I was a boy at Mattapoisett—
only Mother, still her Father's daughter.
Her voice was still electric
with a hysterical, unmarried panic. . . .

Most of the poem, however, centers on the father—his failure to impress his fellows in 'the mob of ruling-class Bostonians,' his failure to gain distinction either in the Navy or out of it, his 'piker speculations' that cost him more and more money, his loss of his wife's confidence, his remembered early promise when

nineteen, the youngest ensign in his class,
he was 'the old man' of a gunboat on the
    Yangtze.

"Commander Lowell," taken by itself, seems full of condescension and contempt for 'poor Father,' 'smiling on all,' 'cheerful and cowed.' In **"Terminal Days at Beverly Farms,"** which follows it, the odor of humiliation is even stronger, but is tempered by the same elegiac pain and compassion that were shown in the poem about the death of Lowell's Uncle Devereux Winslow. In this poem we see Commander Lowell at Beverly Farms after his second stroke—'a two minute walk from the station' and 'half an hour by train from the Boston doctors.' His meekness is given a tragic dignity, and because the main source of pain in this poem is transferred from his failure as a man to the impersonal, invulnerable fact of his death, we see him as a victim of a universally sinister principle rather than as the cause of his son's psychosis. As we can see from the figures used to describe the realms of both nature and artifact, the objective world is now the true enemy:

They had no sea-view,
but sky-blue tracks of the commuters' railroad
    shone
like a double-barrelled shotgun
through the scarlet late August sumac,

multiplying like cancer
at their garden's border.

Two poignant afterbeats follow the finalities of these two poems. In **"Father's Bedroom"** and **"For Sale"** we linger over the neat details of the room in which the father died, over an inscription in one of his books that reminds us that he was a hero *manqué,* and over the 'empty, open, intimate' feeling of the cottage afterwards, 'waiting' to be sold. Quietly, at the very end of **"For Sale,"** the camera shifts its focus to the mother:

Ready, afraid
of living alone till eighty,
Mother mooned in a window,
as if she had stayed on a train
one stop past her destination.

And the camera remains fixed on her through the next two poems, **"Sailing Home from Rapallo"** and **"During Fever."** The first of these takes us to her death and burial four years later. The poet begins with his arrival in Italy to bring her body back to the cemetery in Dunbarton. The first stanza might have stood by itself, a brief 'Chinese' poem that at first seems unconvincing but is actually a sharp, affecting projection of a moment of realization:

Your nurse could only speak Italian,
but after twenty minutes I could imagine your
   final week,
and tears ran down my cheeks. . . .

Those tears are the only direct image of emotion in the poem. The next two stanzas present the gaudy colors of the *Golfo di Genova* coastline 'breaking into fiery flower' as the ship sails out in which 'Mother travelled first-class in the hold,' and then the freezing contrast of the family graveyard in midwinter, 'dour and dark against the blinding snowdrifts.' On the one hand,

The crazy yellow and azure sea-sleds
blasting like jack-hammers across
the *spumante*-bubbling wake of our liner. . . .

On the other hand,

A fence of iron spear-hafts
black-bordered its mostly Colonial grave-slates.

The dazzling opposition of two entirely different states of concrete existence would be too obvious an ironic effect were it not, in the first place, so anchored in Lowell's extraordinarily keen sense of place, and, more important, were it not so true to subjective experience in action. For this latter reason, as well, the overlay of still another kind of irony—that of the inescapable awareness of considerations of class and status, even in the wake of his mother's death—is absolutely, movingly relevant here. The mother, travelling 'first-

class' in a '*Risorgimento* black and gold casket,' is all the more pathetic for this somehow ridiculous fact in the midst of a riotously beautiful nature. This elegiacally tinged absurdity summons up another. After he describes Dunbarton in winter with such Anglo-Saxon somberness, Lowell intrudes one last note on his father:

The only 'unhistoric' soul to come here
was Father, now buried beneath his recent
unweathered pink-veined slice of marble.
Even the Latin of his Lowell motto:
Occasionem cognosce,
seemed too businesslike and pushing here,
where the burning cold illuminated
the hewn inscriptions of Mother's relatives:
twenty or thirty Winslows and Starks.
Frost had given their names a diamond edge. . . .

A brief concluding stanza, paralleling the opening one, adds two further items to the list of absurdities. These are at a level of irony that is simply recognition of life's (or death's) indifference to pride of self or personality. Mother's coffin has 'grandiloquent' lettering, but the name is misspelled 'LOVEL.' Her body 'was wrapped like *panetone* in Italian tinfoil.' One might well ask how an elegiac poem on the death of one's mother could end with these grotesque little items. The reply must be either that the strictly elegiac portion is confined to the first three lines, or that the poem begins with pity and grief for the mother's pain and ends with pity and grief for her degradation when death has reduced her to a mere object that can be put in a package and mislabeled. But there is another consideration: the arbitrariness with which these admittedly relevant and accurate details of humiliation have been selected for special attention from early on in the poem. It *is* a poem of humiliation, and to this fact even the elegiac motive is subordinated. The psychological confession implicit in these grotesque juxtapositions, the suggestion of a psychotic supersensitivity, has been grafted onto the elegiac elements and has produced a different kind of poem. The true elegy 'lets go,' liberated by a reconciliation, grave yet ultimately buoyant, with the deep rhythms and meanings of existence. This poem does not let go, except in the sense of conceding the intrinsic meaninglessness of both social and private presumptions about the self. It will take the whole sequence to reach an affirmation at all comparable with that of the traditional elegy, and the terms of reference will be quite different.

"During Fever" rounds out this second movement of the sequence much as **"Grandparents"** rounded out the first movement. It takes us into the present. The poet's little daughter is ill and apologetic for the fact ('"Sorry," she mumbles like her dim-bulb father, "sorry." ' The connection with 'her dim-bulb father's' humiliation at life's 'normal' sufferings illuminates a memory for him, and he addresses his mother in retrospect, recalling how

> as a gemlike undergraduate,
> part criminal and yet a Phi Bete,
> I used to barge home late. . . .
> Often with unadulterated joy,
> Mother, we bent by the fire
> rehashing Father's character—
> when he thought we were asleep,
> he'd tiptoe down the stairs
> and chain the door.

From this touching bit of family comedy the poem moves to a description of the mother's master-bedroom, with its three-colored 'nuptial bed' that was 'as big as a bathroom'—a description to be compared in its lush impression of womanly expectation with the sparse neatness and frustrated manly hopes evoked in **"Father's Bedroom."** Finally, we are taken in imagination (based again, though, on fact) to another scene and another, still earlier generation.

> Born ten years and yet an aeon
> too early for the twenties,
> Mother, you smile
> as if you saw your Father
> inches away yet hidden, as when he groused be-
>   hind a screen
> over a National Geographic Magazine,
> whenever young men came to court you
> back in those settled years of World War One.
> Terrible that old life of decency
> without unseemly intimacy
> or quarrels, when the unemancipated woman
> still had her Freudian papá and maids!

The exclamation is both flippant and serious. Guilt and repression lie behind the protagonist's present discontents, and he has passed on the guilt, at least, to his little daughter. The mother fades out of the sequence, a textbook case who has brought forth yet another textbook case, who has perhaps carried the process forward unto yet another generation. We have had three innocent-seeming scenes, each with its sinister implications—a design made up of echoes, putting the whole matter of the generations into perspective.

The deaths of Lowell's parents occurred in 1950 and 1954, between his thirty-third and thirty-seventh birthdays, so that the time of the long second movement of 'Life Studies' actually overlaps with that of the concluding movements. The latter seem to take place later, however, because in them our attention is fixed on the poet's own adult life, without reference to his parents. What we may call the third movement consists of two poems (**"Waking in the Blue"** and **"Home after Three Months Away"**) about his confinement in a mental hospital and one (**"Memories of West Street and Lepke"**) about his five-months imprisonment dur-

ing the war as a conscientious objector. Two poems follow, forming a fourth unit. They are **"Man and Wife,"** which seems to be about Lowell's second marriage, and **" 'To Speak of Woe That Is in Marriage,' "** which presents a tormented wife talking about her 'hopped up,' 'screwball' husband. The concluding poem in the sequence, **"Skunk Hour,"** stands out independently. It provides a self-loathing close-up for the speaker and with it a dominating image both for his own psychological state and prospects and for the poetic process we have been brought through in this book. The transference of attention in these last six poems from the older figures to Lowell himself makes for great gains in immediacy and concentration—the effect is of having been subjected to successive waves of mounting violence. (pp. 46-53)

Looking back over *Life Studies* for its stylistic dynamics, we can see that Lowell has made sophisticated use of the whole modern tradition of the poetic sequence. This tradition includes as its main representatives *Song of Myself*, *Spoon River Anthology*, *Hugh Selwyn Mauberley* and the *Cantos*, *The Waste Land* and *Four Quartets*, *The Bridge*, and *Paterson*. Lowell has deliberately forgone certain rhetorical heights that his forerunners stormed, and some of their more obvious exploitation of myth (and myth-making) as well. The opening poem, **"Beyond the Alps,"** though it hints of these heights and this exploitation, presents the protagonist on a train leaving Rome and its associations behind: 'I left the City of God where it belongs.' Not only the City of God, but the Classical past—'Minerva, the miscarriage of the brain'—is put behind him as he speeds toward his own theme of the disintegration of the modern embodied in his own life's history:

> Now Paris, our black classic, breaking up
> like killer kings on an Etruscan cup.

Nowhere in *Life Studies* is there eloquence for its own sake, or abstractly developed religious or philosophical symbolism. Lowell had displayed both in his earlier work, but this sequence is stripped down to the immediately relevant. The only, mild exceptions are the two opening poems, which suggest fairly simply the broader historical and cultural relevance of his close-ups of himself and his times, and the four 'documentary' interpretations of a few other modern writers, whose careers throw a clear light on the problems of Lowell himself. The 'myth' that Lowell creates is that of an America (and a contemporary civilization generally) whose history and present predicament are embodied in those of his own family and epitomized in his own psychological experience. It is easy to see how in so doing he parallels some of the important implications of Whitman, Pound, Eliot, Crane, and Williams, and also how he has received clues from these writers' most 'confessional' moments and from Masters's characters at their most disillusioned and nervously disturbed.

But though the stripped-down quality of the work limits its range in one sense, Lowell's virtuosity is such that we get a wide range indeed of effects, most of them functioning appropriately according to what is needed at the given point in the sequence. As his basic formal framework, he tends toward a free use of the heroic couplet, giving the rhymes a hammering emphasis that is supported by concrete, active verbs and well-placed alliteration. The stiffness and straining that often result do mar the earlier poems, and even in *Life Studies* the rhythm can run away with the feeling. In only one poem, though—**"The Banker's Daughter"**—does this runaway effect take over for very long. It is, indeed, a dramatic monologue in the earlier style, though it serves, as I have suggested, to broaden the context of allusion in the sequence. It serves, too, to foreshadow the brief, intense **" 'To Speak of Woe That Is in Marriage,' "** for it too has to do with an unspeakably brutal marriage relationship. The latter poem is equally emphatic and rhyme-dominated, but its brevity, simplicity, and colloquialism give it a far more natural and flexible character. The off-rhymes with which it begins and ends, and its intelligent placing of caesuras, as well as the excitement of what goes on *within* the lines (the sensuous, racy, suffering diction, and the speed of the idiomatic thinking), keep our attention on the whole sense and feeling as it moves along, rather than on the form apart from them. Even when the alliteration and rhymes are most effective, Lowell succeeds in keeping first things foremost:

> My hopped up husband drops his home disputes,
> and hits the streets to cruise for prostitutes,
> free-lancing out along the razor's edge.

Much of the power of these poems derives from Lowell's ability to employ these fundamental resources explosively or (to change the metaphor) to hold them in reserve like a taut bow ready to release the arrow. But given this ability, he modulates his effects in practice in many ways. The third poem, **"Inauguration Day: January 1953,"** is in short, four-stress lines, with the rhyme-scheme close to that of a Petrarchan sonnet. The first stanza, of nine lines, rises out of a depressed picture of the mechanical life of New York City in winter to an ironic mimicry of heroic motifs from the past:

> Cyclonic zero of the word,
> God of our armies, who interred
> Cold Harbor's blue immortals, Grant!
> Horseman, your sword is in the groove!

The second stanza, of five lines, begins with an enormous letdown: 'Ice, ice. Our wheels no longer move.' It ends with a bitter taunt to the nation and to President Eisenhower, elected to office at the height of the cold war and in the depths of the national paralysis of morale marked by the influence of Senator Joseph McCarthy:

> and the Republic summons Ike,
> the mausoleum in her heart.

"A Mad Negro Soldier Confined at Munich" follows, speeding manically after the subtly evoked depression of **"Inauguration Day."** Here there is no 'pure music' (even in a form of mockery). It is a highly colloquial dramatic monologue. With one dubious exception, the rhymes are all exact. The verbs are almost all highly charged—'floored,' 'punch,' 'fumes,' 'squawked' ('lieutenants squawked like chickens in her skirts'), and a half-dozen more of the same order. Stanzas two, three, and four gain enormous speed and pressure by the omission of caesuras and by the language used to show the sexual dimension of the speaker's dangerously excited condition. The metaphors of electric power in the fifth stanza bring this movement to its climax:

> Oh mama, mama, like a trolley-pole
> sparking at contact, her electric shock—
> the power-house! . . .
> The doctor calls our roll—
> no knives, no forks. We file before the
> clock. . . .

With equal swiftness, and without transition, the voice takes on a sophisticated but deadly ferocity in the final stanza. It has become the poet's voice speaking for the Negro soldier as later in the sequence it will speak for Hart Crane and still later, in the asylum and prison poems, for Lowell in his own person. (In some important respects, incidentally, John Berryman's *77 Dream Songs,* published in 1964, seems to pick up cues from this poem—especially in its assumption of the tone, and its inconsistent use of the idiom of American Negro speech and its shifting to an alternative self within what is presented as a continuous speech, in quotation-marks, by a single speaker.)

After this introductory group of poems, . . . the prose-section **"91 Revere Street"** transfers the spotlight to the poet himself, in the setting of his early family life. . . . I shall content myself now with a single observation having to do with the use of poetic effects in this section. These come mostly toward the end, in the songs and doggerel humor of Commander Billy Harkness, and in some of his boisterously metaphorical and self-indulgent prose. As the protagonist's embarrassment and shame, on his father's behalf, come more and more into the foreground, these forays of Captain Billy's are more and more in evidence. They add up to the drowning of Lowell senior's deeper but unrealized sensitivity as a man by the extrovert virility of his successful friend who, incidentally and innocently, is at the same time deriding the life of sensibility and its poetic manifestation in particular. Here we have an epitome of the alienating process. The four poems that follow, about Ford, Santayana, Schwartz (and Lowell himself), and Crane, show four results of this process, in a series of subjectivized documentary presentations.

The most brilliantly manipulated of these is **"To Delmore Schwartz,"** which fuses casually the compassionate and witty comment and narrative of the poems on Ford and Santayana (with their equally casual yet deft handling of rhyme, sound, and line) with a wild comedy and pain and a more telling imagery. It swings masterfully between shorter and longer lines, depending on the need of the moment, and at the very end breaks into a strange imagist poem, rhythmically tight yet in free verse, with cleverly placed rhymes. The changes of voice—Lowell's own, Schwartz's, Wordsworth's, and then Lowell's again in another mood—make for the liveliest dynamics in the book, encompassing the widest range of emotional tones. After it we have the sonnet **"Words for Hart Crane,"** far more concentrated and angry in its passion, in its 'alienated' derangement of a traditional form, and in its piling up of defiantly self-castigating detail.

The fifteen poems of Part IV ("Life Studies" proper) show a similar progression, in general, from a slower, more casually anecdotal, though always moving, style to the highly charged style of the closing pieces. The whole progression is in a sense foreshadowed in the four sections of **"My Last Afternoon with Uncle Devereux Winslow"**: the leisurely opening section; the bemused second section, so brief and 'odd' in its final effect but still in tune with the first part; the poignant close-up of Great Aunt Sarah in the third section, a little like Masters but more piquantly vivid than his portraits usually are; and then the terrifying ending, in which we see the dying young uncle through the eyes of the five-year-old child, guilty and omniscient as **"Agrippina in the Golden House of Nero."** The final fourteen lines are a triumph of projection of this vision. The rigid parallelism has the quality of a black-magic incantation; what appears at first to be humorous description is actually a hair-raising evocation of an apparition, or at least of a living man so near death that he might almost be a wax figure:

> He was as brushed as Bayard, our riding horse.
> His face was putty.
> His blue coat and white trousers
> grew sharper and straighter.
> His coat was a blue jay's tail,
> his trousers were solid cream from the top of the
> bottle.
> He was animated, hierarchical,
> like a ginger snap man in a clothes-press.
> He was dying of the incurable Hodgkin's
> disease. . . .

> My hands were warm, then cool, on the piles
> of earth and lime,
> a black pile and a white pile. . . .
> Come winter,
> Uncle Devereux would blend to the one color.

The next poem in which this kind of 'strangeness' is matched, with a similar grim, climactic effect, is **"Memories of West Street and Lepke."** Both poems prepare us for the startling ending of **"Skunk Hour,"** though not for the paradoxical confidence in the future that is part of the picture of the garbage-swilling mother skunk. Lowell has rung many changes within the clearly defined formal range he has allowed himself. I have tried to show enough of these to suggest the intimate relationship between the minutiae of these changes and what is going on in the sequence as a whole. *Life Studies* is perhaps the most functionally shaped and continuously communicative of the great poetic sequences. (pp. 60-6)

M. L. Rosenthal, "Robert Lowell and 'Confessional' Poetry," in his *The New Poets: American and British Poetry Since World War II,* Oxford University Press, 1967, pp. 25-78.

STEVEN GOULD AXELROD
(essay date 1978)

[An American educator, Axelrod wrote *Robert Lowell: Life and Art,* a critical study of Lowell's work from which the excerpt below was taken, and, with Helen Deese, coedited *Robert Lowell: A Collection of Critical Essays.* In the following excerpt, he examines Lowell's poetry of experience.]

Throughout his career, Lowell demonstrated an astonishing willingness and ability to make his writing new. "My books have changed," he once explained. "It doesn't really matter whether one style is better than the last. When it no longer serves, you must adventure." Despite this characteristic modesty, he was an ambitious poet, and like other American poets before him—Whitman, Pound, Williams, Eliot—he spoke with different voices. Each of his books embodies his struggle to find a way to say the thing he had then to say. None succeeds completely. The books, and the individual poems, are imperfect because not fully distinct from the indeterminacy of the life that produced them. Lowell's "failure," if we want to call it that, is an inextricable feature of his ambition, is indeed part of what his poems are about: his attempt to create a language in which he could more fully realize his being.

He thus stands firmly within the main line of American poetry. Roy Harvey Pearce has observed [in

Lowell commenting on sources of poetic inspiration:

Some bit of scenery or something you've felt. Almost the whole problem of writing poetry is to bring it back to what you really feel, and that takes an awful lot of maneuvering. You may feel the doorknob more strongly than some big personal event, and the doorknob will open into something that you can use as your own. A lot of poetry seems to me very good in the tradition but just doesn't move me very much because it doesn't have personal vibrance to it. I probably exaggerate the value of it, but it's precious to me. Some little image, some detail you've noticed—you're writing about a little country shop, just describing it, and your poem ends up with an existentialist account of your experience. But it's the shop that started it off. You didn't know why it meant a lot to you. Often images and often the sense of the beginning and end of a poem are all you have—some journey to be gone through between those things: you know that, but you don't know the details. And that's marvelous; then you feel the poem will come out. It's a terrible struggle, because what you really feel hasn't got the form, it's not what you can put down in a poem. And the poem you're equipped to write concerns nothing that you care very much about or have much to say on. Then the great moment comes when there's enough resolution of your technical equipment, your way of constructing things, and what you can make a poem out of, to hit something you really want to say. You may not know you have it to say.

Robert Lowell, Paris Review, *1961*.

The Continuity of American Poetry] that "American poems record the discovery, rediscovery, and again and again the rediscovery of the Fall into Existence—American Existence." Lowell's poetry microcosmically recapitulates that repeated rediscovery. Lowell once commented that American literature looks like "a bravado of perpetual revolution," and so indeed does his own poetic career. He successively appeared as the passionate young rhetorician-prophet of *Lord Weary's Castle* (1946); the Frost-or Browning-like storyteller of *The Mills of the Kavanaughs* (1951); the cold-eyed, witty memoirist of *Life Studies* (1959), narrating his family history with an art disguised as candor; the translator of *Imitations* (1961); the withered observer of *For the Union Dead* (1964); the playwright of *The Old Glory* (1964) and *Prometheus Bound* (1967); the Jeremiah of *Near the Ocean* (1966); the historian-on-the-run of *Notebook* (1970) and *History* (1973); the verse novelist-autobiographer of *The Dolphin* (1973), recounting his quest for an elusive creature of joy; and, finally, the aging and introspective diarist of *Day by Day* (1977). Yet for all its dynamism, his poetic oeuvre is unified.

At its center is Lowell himself, discovering, altering, creating the conditions of his own existence.

Although the style of Lowell's art changed radically over the years, its essentially experiential character remained constant. "The thread that strings it together," he remarked, "is my autobiography"; "what made the earlier poems valuable seems to be some recording of experience and that seems to be what makes the later ones." "Experience" does not mean only what "happened" to Lowell, for that formulation would place too much emphasis on an active but unilateral environment, and would reduce the experiencer's mind to the passive role of a transmitting lens. The mind itself is active, trembling to "caress the light." "Experience" more truly means the sum of the relations and interactions between psyche and environment. It grows from the Cartesian dualism of inner and outer, but through its interpenetrating energies abolishes the dualism. Just as experience mediates between self and world, partaking of both, so Lowell's poems mediate between himself and his world, and between his personal history and that of his readers. His poems are structures of experience. They both record his life and assume a life of their own; and as they transform the poet's life into the autonomous life of art, they reenter his life by clarifying and completing it.

In his first published essay, a review of Yvor Winters's *Maule's Curse* in the Kenyon College student journal *Hika*, Lowell revealed himself already to be centrally concerned with the relationship of art to experience. Just past his twenty-second birthday, he wrote that "literature can only dramatize life and world that is real to it. And literary reality must be judged on perception, consistency and moral seriousness." The crudities and cruelties of mortal life in this age, in any age, are difficult to bear, and artists and readers have therefore frequently conceived of art as a medium of escape, a "world elsewhere," a "beautiful illusion." Clearly, this conception of art never had the slightest interest for Lowell. From the beginning, he viewed art and life as being closely connected. In the *Hika* review he wrote, "When we ask [Winters] 'Is interpreted experience art?,' his answer is 'No, but what art is made from.'" Lowell soon came to ask the very same question of himself; his poetry is the history of his ever more sophisticated attempts at an answer.

In choosing poems from his early, privately printed book *Land of Unlikeness* to reprint two years later in his first commercial book *Lord Weary's Castle*, Lowell chose the poems that he felt were "more experienced," "more concrete." A decade later, in *Life Studies*, he rejected the impersonal and metrically regular mode of *Lord Weary's Castle* entirely because he found he "couldn't get [his] experience into tight metrical forms." In changing his style and subject matter, he turned away from the canons of Modernist formalism, precisely because Modernist esthetics, from Hulme, Eliot, and Pound on, tended to view the poem as a world of its own, lacking reference to the poet and culture that produced it. Lowell came to see that—at least for himself and perhaps for others—the relationship of art to human experience was too elemental for an "Impersonal theory of poetry," as Eliot called his own early theory, to do anything but block up the springs of inspiration. Lowell explained to Frederick Seidel in [a *Paris Review* interview in 1961] that "writing seems divorced from culture somehow. It's become too much something specialized that can't handle much experience. It's become a craft, purely a craft, and there must be some breakthrough back into life." *Life Studies,* a book about "direct experience and not symbols," was just such a breakthrough. All of Lowell's subsequent work centered around his quest for the craft and inspiration to bring even more experience into his art, and his related quest to account for the place art makes in experience.

Although art and experience continued to retain an important thin edge of distinctness for Lowell—art was experience that had been "worked up," imagined into form—the two came to have an increasingly complex interrelationship in his thought. His life made his writing possible, and the ability to write saved his life and gave it meaning. As much as Emerson, Lowell believed that "the man is only half himself, the other half is his expression"; as much as Henry James, he believed that art *"makes* life." He argued that for the American writer, "the arts should be 'all out'—you're in it, you're all out in it. . . . The artist finds new life in his art and almost sheds his other life." Over and over again his later poems return to the interrelatedness of "one life, one writing." One of the loveliest expressions of this idea occurs at the conclusion of *The Dolphin,* in which Lowell accepts responsibility for his book as he accepts responsibility for his life:

My eyes have seen what my hand did.

The hand has written that which the eyes have previously seen, that which the I has experienced. But also, the eyes have seen, the I has experienced and acknowledges, the hand as it writes.

Lowell did not write poems in hopes of achieving immortal fame, "grass on the minor slopes of Parnassus." His "open book," he suggests in *History,* amounts to no more than an "open coffin," doomed like his corporeal self to perish in time, though more slowly. Poetry had an entirely different value for Lowell, an existential value: it proved its maker was "alive." Thus he viewed himself as engaged in the quintessential labor of the American poet. For the difference between American and other writers, he once argued [in *Encounter,* February 1965], is that in America "the artist's exis-

tence becomes his art. He is reborn in it, and he hardly exists without it." (pp. 3-7)

Lowell's esthetic places his art at the center of American literary tradition. In his seminal essay on this topic, "The Cult of Experience in American Writing," Philip Rahv termed the affirmation of individual experience the "basic theme and unifying principle" of American writing. Rooted in Puritan antinomianism, fostered by Jeffersonian democratic idealism, and formulated most eloquently by Emerson, this theme preoccupies the American literary mind. . . . American literature, with Emerson as its prophet, understands the individual's existence-in-the-world as both the overwhelming problem and the source of redemption.

Thus, in the radically experiential and existential qualities of his poetry, Lowell continues the central quest of the American imagination. But his accomplishment is even more significant than that. He has made himself an Emersonian "reconciler" for our time. For despite the wholeness advocated by Emerson and exemplified in good measure by Whitman, experience in American literature has tended to fragment itself. Early in this century Van Wyck Brooks lambasted American culture for failing to achieve an organic conception of life. Rather, Brooks argued, American literature drifts chaotically between two extremes—the extremes, simply put, of understanding experience intellectually and understanding it through the emotions. Brooks applied to these extremes his celebrated labels "highbrow" and "lowbrow," and termed the failure of our writers to synthesize the two "a deadlock in the American mind." This kind of dualism may have originated, as Edwin Fussell has suggested, in America's divided loyalties between Old World and Western Frontier; or it may have originated in class difference. Whatever its source, some version of the highbrow-lowbrow dualism has been discerned by most students of American literature. Philip Rahv, for example, argued that American literature composes itself into a debate between "palefaces" and "redskins." The "palefaces" (Henry James, T. S. Eliot, and Allen Tate would belong to this party) produce a patrician art which is intellectual, symbolic, cosmopolitan, disciplined, cultured. The "redskins" (Walt Whitman and William Carlos Williams would tend to belong here) produce a plebeian art which is emotional, naturalistic, nativist, energetic, in some sense *un*cultured. . . . [Like] the very greatest of American poets, Lowell tried to diminish this split, to repair the "broken circuit" of American culture. His goal was not the middlebrow's bland insensitivity to *any* kind of experience, but rather the unified central vision of what Emerson termed "the complete man" among partial men.

To borrow one of his own metaphors, Lowell's poetry "clutches only life," for it is based on his belief that "art and the life blood of experience can't live without each other." . . . In his youthful period, under the direct tutelage of Allen Tate and the pervasive influence of T. S. Eliot, Lowell fit his personal experience into impersonal mythic patterns. He conceived of his life as being in service to the poetic idea, as needing to be depersonalized and transformed into art. He constructed verbal icons out of his experience, the most ambitious and powerful of these being **"The Quaker Graveyard in Nantucket."** In his second, "revolutionary" phase, he learned, under the approving eye of William Carlos Williams, to bring his undisguised personal experience to the forefront of his poetry. Exercising a brilliantly original art, he produced an album of "photographs" of experience, his Confessional masterpiece *Life Studies.* In the third, long period of his maturity, Lowell continued to explore the domain along the boundary where life meets art. He now conceived of experience as being more inward than in his *Life Studies* stage: not isolable events from the past but a fusion of immediate impressions with consciousness itself. Experience in this sense, as T. S. Eliot wrote long ago, is indefinable except that it is "more real than anything else." In the great poems of this period—**"For the Union Dead,"** the **"Near the Ocean"** sequence, and *The Dolphin*—Lowell revealed the truth of a human heart and mind, his own.

Lowell's poetry of experience presents both danger and opportunity. The very word "experience"—signifying a trial, a putting to the test, an experiment, in Lowell's phrase a "working through"—implies risk. There is point in the fact that "peril" lies half-hidden within it. Yet the peril is redeemed by the reward: a poetry that unites the values of artistic creation with more universal human values. Lowell's poems plunge into, and thereby affirm for himself and for us all, the infinite possibilities for human life in the actual world. They embody a complex process of clarifying and thus culminating his experience; and then, since poems are themselves real, they take their rightful place within experience, leaving author and reader alike altered. Lowell once said of Thoreau that the most wonderful and necessary thing about his life was the courageous hand that wrote it down. (pp. 8-12)

Steven Gould Axelrod, in his *Robert Lowell: Life and Art,* Princeton University Press, 1978, 286 p.

SOURCES FOR FURTHER STUDY

Altieri, Charles. "Robert Lowell and the Difficulty of Escaping Modernism." In his *Enlarging the Temple: New Directions in American Poetry During the 1960s,* pp. 53-77. Lewisburg, Pa: Buckness University Press, 1979.

> Concentrates on Lowell's verse up to the publication of *Notebook,* focusing on aesthetic and artistic implications of the changes and developments in Lowell's poetry.

Axelrod, Steven Gould, and Deese, Helen. *Robert Lowell: A Collection of Critical Essays.* Cambridge: Cambridge University Press, 1986, 269 p.

> Contains twelve essays that offers new approaches to Lowell's work. This collection is intended to "refocus attention on Lowell's texts" in order to counter but not repress the increasing attention paid to the poet's private life.

Hamilton, Ian. *Robert Lowell: A Biography.* New York: Random House, 1982, 527 p.

> Biography valued primarily for its wealth of factual detail.

Mazzaro, Jerome, ed. *Profile of Robert Lowell.* Columbus, Ohio: Charles E. Merrill Publishing Co., 1971, 104 p.

> Collects essays and interviews, many of which had not been previously available in book form.

Perloff, Marjorie G. *The Poetic Art of Robert Lowell.* Ithaca: Cornell University Press, 1973, 209 p.

> Broad discussion of Lowell's verse concentrating on imagery, genre, convention, syntax, and tone.

Williamson, Alan. *Pity the Monsters: The Political Vision of Robert Lowell.* New Haven, Conn.: Yale University Press, 1974, 221 p.

> Argues that Lowell's emphasis on uncertainties of existence, his skepticism, and his sympathy for the oppressed contributed to a strong moral and political vision appropriate to his era.

Bernard Malamud

1914-1986

American novelist and short story writer.

INTRODUCTION

*M*alamud is considered one of the most promi-nent figures in Jewish-American literature, a movement that originated in the 1930s and is known for its tragicomic elements. His stories and nov-els, in which reality and fantasy are frequently inter-laced, have been compared to parables, myths, and al-legories and often illustrate the importance of moral obligation. Although he draws upon his Jewish heritage to address the themes of sin, suffering, and redemp-tion, Malamud emphasizes human contact and com-passion over orthodox religious dogma. Malamud's characters, while often awkward and isolated from so-ciety, evoke both pity and humor through their attempts at survival and salvation. Sheldon J. Hershinow ob-served: "Out of the everyday defeats and indignities of ordinary people, Malamud creates beautiful parables that capture the joy as well as the pain of life; he ex-presses the dignity of the human spirit searching for freedom and moral growth in the face of hardship, in-justice, and the existential anguish of life."

Malamud was born in Brooklyn, New York, to Russian Jewish immigrants. His parents, whom he de-scribed as "gentle, honest, kindly people," were not highly educated and knew very little about literature or the arts: "There were no books that I remember in the house, no records, music, pictures on the wall." Mala-mud attended high school in Brooklyn and received his Bachelor's degree from the City College of New York in 1936. After graduation, he worked in a factory and as a clerk at the Census Bureau in Washington, D. C. Although he wrote in his spare time, Malamud did not begin writing seriously until the advent of World War II and the subsequent horrors of the Holocaust. He ques-tioned his religious identity and started reading about Jewish tradition and history. He explained: "I was con-cerned with what Jews stood for, with their getting down to the bare bones of things. I was concerned with their ethnicity—how Jews felt they had to live in order to go on living." In 1949, he began teaching at Oregon State University; he left this post in 1961 to teach creative writing at Bennington College in Vermont. He remained there until shortly before his death in 1986.

Malamud's first novel, *The Natural* (1952), is considered one of his most symbolic works. While the novel ostensibly traces the life of Roy Hobbs, an American baseball player, the work has underlying mythic elements and explores such themes as initiation and isolation. For instance, some reviewers cited evidence of the Arthurian legend of the Holy Grail; others applied T. S. Eliot's "wasteland" myth in their analyses. *The Natural* also foreshadows what would become Malamud's predominant narrative focus: a suffering protagonist struggling to reconcile moral dilemmas, to act according to what is right, and to accept the complexities and hardships of existence. Malamud's second novel, *The Assistant* (1957), portrays the life of Morris Bober, a Jewish immigrant who owns a grocery store in Brooklyn. Although he is struggling to survive financially, Bober hires a cynical anti-Semitic youth, Frank Alpine, after learning that the man is homeless and on the verge of starvation. Through this contact Frank learns to find grace and dignity in his own identity. Described as a naturalistic fable, this novel affirms the redemptive value of maintaining faith in the goodness of the human soul. Malamud's first collection of short stories, *The Magic Barrel* (1958), was awarded the National Book award in 1959. Like *The Assistant,* most of the stories in this collection depict the search for hope and meaning within the grim entrapment of poor urban settings and were influenced by Yiddish folktales and Hasidic traditions. Many of Malamud's best-known short stories, including "The Last Mohican," "Angel Levine," and "Idiots First," were republished in *The Stories of Bernard Malamud* in 1983.

A New Life (1961), considered one of Malamud's most realistic novels, is based in part on Malamud's teaching career at Oregon State University. This work focuses on an ex-alcoholic Jew from New York City who, in order to escape his reputation as a drunkard, becomes a professor at an agricultural and technical college in the Pacific Northwest. Interweaving the protagonist's quest for significance and self-respect with a satiric mockery of academia, Malamud explores the destructive nature of idealism, how love can lead to deception, and the pain of loneliness. Malamud's next novel, *The Fixer* (1966), is considered one of his most powerful works. The winner of both the Pulitzer Prize and the National Book Award, this book is derived from the historical account of Mendel Beiliss, a Russian Jew

who was accused of murdering a Christian child. Drawing upon Eastern European Jewish mysticism, *The Fixer* turns this terrifying story of torture and humiliation into a parable of human triumph. With *The Tenants* (1971), Malamud returns to a New York City setting, where the theme of self-exploration is developed through the contrast between two writers, one Jewish and the other black, struggling to survive in an urban ghetto. Within the context of their confrontations about artistic standards, Malamud also explores how race informs cultural identity, the purpose of literature, and the conflict between art and life. Alvin B. Kernan commented: "[*The Tenants*] is extraordinarily powerful and compelling in its realization of the view that is central to the conception of literature as a social institution: that literature and the arts are an inescapable part of society."

Malamud further addresses the nature of literature and the role of the artist in *Dubin's Lives* (1979). In this work, the protagonist, William Dubin, attempts to create a sense of worth for himself, both as a man and as a writer. A biographer who escapes into his work to avoid the reality of his life, Dubin bumbles through comically disastrous attempts at love and passion in an effort to find self-fulfillment. Malamud's next novel, *God's Grace* (1982), differs from his earlier works in scope and presentation of subject matter. Set in the near future immediately after a nuclear disaster which leaves only one human being alive, *God's Grace* explores the darkness of human morality, the nature of God, and the vanity and destruction associated with contemporary life. Critical reception to this work varied greatly. Some critics felt that the contrast between the serious moral fable and the protagonist's penchant for alternately conversing with God and a group of apes unique and challenging; others believed the structure of the novel did not support the seriousness and ambition of its themes. However, *God's Grace,* like all of his works, reveals Malamud's motivations as a writer and expresses his profound humanistic concerns. Malamud explained: "It seems to me that the writer's most important task, no matter what the current theory of man, or his prevailing mood, is to recapture his image as human being as each of us in his secret heart knows it to be."

(For further information about Malamud's life and works, see *Contemporary Authors,* Vols. 5-8, 118 [obituary]; *Contemporary Authors Bibliographical Series,* Vol. 1; *Contemporary Literary Criticism,* Vols. 1, 2, 3, 5, 8, 9, 11, 18, 27, 44; *Dictionary of Literary Biography,* Vols. 2, 28; and *Dictionary of Literary Biography Yearbook: 1980.*)

CRITICAL COMMENTARY

LESLIE A. FIELD AND JOYCE W. FIELD WITH BERNARD MALAMUD
(interview date 1973)

[The Fields are American editors who have published collected criticism on such writers as Thomas Wolfe and Bernard Malamud. In the following interview, which was conducted over a four-month period in 1973 through a series of letters, Malamud discusses his writing technique, his artistic ideals, and critical reaction to his fiction.]

[The Fields]: *It has been reported that you once said: "A Malamud character is someone who fears his fate, is caught up in it, yet manages to outrun it. He's the subject and object of laughter and pity." Could you elaborate on this statement? Do you still consider that it capsulizes recent important Malamud characters—for example, Fidelman, Yakov Bok, and Harry Lesser?*

[Malamud]: I can't work up any great enthusiasm for the statement but what I imagine it means is that my characters often outwit their predictable fates. I'd say that holds for Fidelman, Yakov Bok, and even Harry Lesser.

How did you happen to write a baseball novel?

Baseball players were the "heroes" of my American childhood. I wrote *The Natural* as a tale of a mythological hero because, between childhood and the beginning of a writing career, I'd been to college. I became interested in myth and tried to use it, among other things, to symbolize and explicate an ethical dilemma of American life. Roy Hobbs is as American as the White House lawyers involved in Watergate.

As you know, the "academic novel" has been a subject of critical commentary. It used to be said, for example, that every professor of English had at least one academic novel within him that was crying to get out. Would it be accurate to say that a novel such as **A New Life** *(although it obviously does much more than depict academic life) could not be written today because the campus is now a composite of a drastically altered set of symbols?*

This is an involved query concerning what to me was the simple act of writing a novel out of my experience. The "academic novel," as such, simply doesn't interest me.

One fairly popular view has it that the schlemiel *as metaphor or character in fiction is an uneasy transplant from East European Yiddish fiction to modern American fiction. As a matter of fact, two recent full-length books on the* schlemiel *conclude that the* schlemiel *as fictional character was able to work quite effectively for a Malamud and a Bellow up through the sixties. At that point these critics sound the death knell for the* schlemiel. *They say, for example, that an America which is going through (or has just gone through) Vietnam and civil strife, a country which is no longer considered a "winner," cannot accept with equanimity a fictional depiction of a "loser." How do you react to this commentary on the use of the* schlemiel *in fiction?*

With many apologies, I don't much care for the *schlemiel* treatment of fictional characters. Willy-nilly, it reduces to stereotypes people of complex motivations and fates—not to mention possibilities. The literary critic who wants to measure the quality and depth of a fictional character has better terms to use.

When you received the National Book Award for **The Fixer** *you said the novel was not simply a fictional retelling of the Beilis case of Czarist Russia, that it involved much more, that in some way it also owed much to a later horrible event in history—the Nazi Holocaust. Could you elaborate on this? Moreover, do you believe you could have used the Dreyfus case or the Sacco-Vanzetti case to express equally well what it was you had to say in* **The Fixer?**

My original desire was to write a novel based on the Sacco-Vanzetti case, but when I began to read on the subject I had the feeling that I couldn't invent a more dramatic story than the original. Since I was interested in how some men grow as men in prison I turned to the Beilis case, which my father had told me about when I was a boy. *The Fixer* is largely an invention. That is, I've tried to bring it as close to a folk tale as I could. However, in it I was able to relate feeling-fully to the situation of the Jews in Czarist Russia partly because of what I knew about the fate of the Jews in Hitler's Germany.

I. B. Singer has said he writes about devils, sprites, and evil spirits—about the supernatural in general—because he believes in the supernatural. Much earlier, Hawthorne explained that he wanted to find some "neutral ground" for his fiction. Your use of the supernatural has been compared to that of Singer and Hawthorne. Do you believe in the supernatural? Do you look for a "neutral ground" in your fiction as you order your supernatural or fantastic worlds? Or do some other explanations apply to this world of your fiction?

I don't believe in the supernatural except as I can invent it. Nor do I look for a "neutral ground" for my fiction. I write fantasy because when I do I am imaginative and funny and having a good time.

In one of your early, infrequent interviews, we believe you

Principal Works

The Natural (novel) 1952

The Assistant (novel) 1957

The Magic Barrel (short stories) 1958

A New Life (novel) 1961

Idiots First (short stories) 1963

The Fixer (novel) 1966

Pictures of Fidelman: An Exhibition (short stories) 1969

The Tenants (novel) 1971

Rembrandt's Hat (short stories) 1973

Dubin's Lives (novel) 1979

God's Grace (novel) 1982

The Stories of Bernard Malamud (short stories) 1983

said that Kafka was one of the modern authors who had influenced you. How?

He writes well. He moves me. He makes me want to write well and move my readers. Other writers have had a similar effect. I guess what I'm trying to say is that I am influenced by literature.

There has been much critical commentary concerning a statement you are alleged to have made: "All men are Jews." Did you ever actually make this statement? Do you believe it is true? It is, of course, a view one cannot take literally. In any event, would you elaborate on the "All men are Jews" statement?

I think I said "All men are Jews except they don't know it." I doubt I expected anyone to take the statement literally. But I think it's an understandable statement and a metaphoric way of indicating how history, sooner or later, treats all men.

Some have seen parallels between your work and painting, especially the spiral, mystical works of Chagall. This has been observed, for instance, in your short story "**The Magic Barrel.**" *Elsewhere readers have remarked on your concern with the plastic arts in general—in* **Pictures of Fidelman,** *for example. What influence has painting had on your fiction? Have you consciously tried to fuse one art form with another?*

It's true that I did make use of what might be called Chagallean imagery in **"The Magic Barrel."** I did so intentionally in that story, but I've not done it again in any other piece of fiction, and I feel that some critics make too much of Chagall as an image maker in my work. Chagall, as a painter, doesn't mean as much to me as Matisse, for instance. Painting helps me to see with greater clarity the multifarious world and to depict it simply.

Saul Bellow, Philip Roth, Bruce J. Friedman, and other contemporary American novelists have rejected the label "Jewish-American Writer." In one way or another you have also. Nevertheless, you, the other writers mentioned—and one could bring in addi-

tional writers such as Chaim Potok and Herbert Gold—are still being classified as Jewish-American writers by many scholars, critics, and readers. It is our impression that the responsible people who place you and others in this category do not intend to reduce your stature or disregard the universalism they see in your work. They have simply categorized or schematicized as scholars are prone to do, much as one labels Faulkner a Southern-American writer because the spirit of place (the South) imbues his work or Graham Greene an Anglo-Catholic writer because a certain spirit of a specific religion permeates much of his significant work. How do you respond to this categorizing of you and your work? Would you reject the term Jewish-American writer categorically?

The term is schematic and reductive. If the scholar needs the term he can have it, but it won't be doing him any good if he limits his interpretation of a writer to fit a label he applies.

Bellow pokes fun at this sort of thing by calling "Bellow-Malamud-Roth" the Hart, Schaffner and Marx of Jewish-American literature.

Whether or not you accept the label of Jewish-American writer, would you not agree that your writing reveals a special sense of a people's destiny that more often than not cannot be fully grasped in all its nuances and vibrations by those who are not fully sensitized to that people or its destiny? On one level, for example, it has been said that one must be a Russian in order to respond completely to the nineteenth-century notion of salvation through suffering that is dramatized so well by Dostoevsky. Or that only blacks can truly appreciate the plight of black America. Could one not also say that only those who understand the Yiddishkeit *of the characters or the Yiddish milieu are able to respond fully to the silent communication between a Morris Bober and a Brietbart or between a Yakov Bok and his father-in-law, and so on?*

I'm sensitive to Jews and Jewish life but so far as literature is concerned I can't say that I approve of your thesis: that one has to be of a certain nationality or color to "fully grasp" the "nuances and vibrations" of its fiction. I write on the assumption that any one sensitive to fiction can understand my work and *feel* it.

Much has been made of the prison motif in your work. Do you see the prison metaphor as one that aptly describes the dilemma of modern man? If so, could you elaborate on this?

It's a metaphor for the dilemma of all men throughout history. Necessity is the primary prison, though the bars are not visible to all. Then there are the man-made prisons of social injustice, apathy, ignorance. There are others, tight or loose, visible or invisible, according to one's predilection or vulnerability. Therefore our most extraordinary invention is human freedom.

It has been noted that if one is to interpret your work correctly, one must not weigh Judaic interpretations too heavily. One must rather look to the Christian symbolism or perhaps the Judaic-Christian. How do you respond to this?

I don't know whether there is a "correct" interpretation of my work. I hope not.

You yourself have said that in your fiction you are concerned with humanity, man's humanism. Could you explore this notion somewhat?

I don't think I ought to. People can read; they can read what I say. That's a lot more interesting than reading what I say I say.

Some have remarked that you are not interested in a novel of ideas as such, but in a depiction of human nature. Henry James, for example, was quite vocal in explaining his fictional approach (which he attributed to Turgenev's influence). That is, he would start out with a clearly defined character thrust into a specific situation. How that character responded to the situation became all-important. Do you believe your own fictional approach follows this Jamesian-Turgenev method?

Basically, that's it, but I don't think I would limit my "fictional approach" to the "Jamesian-Turgenev method." One learns from Shakespeare as well. My novels are close to plays. I had once, as a young writer, wanted to be a playwright.

The tension between life and art seems to be a major concern in your fiction. One could see it in some of your early work. And as recently as **The Tenants** *and* **Rembrandt's Hat** *it is obvious that this tension is still a significant part of your fiction. Of course* **Pictures of Fidelman** *is introduced by the epigraphs taken from Rilke and Yeats, and is followed by A. Fidelman's terse conclusion. Many would agree that life versus art is central to the Fidelman stories. Do you concur? Can you perhaps now probe in a bit more detail the life versus art theme as you see it?*

It isn't life versus art necessarily; it's life *and* art. On Fidelman's tombstone read: "I kept my finger in art." The point is I don't have large thoughts of life versus art; I try to deepen any given situation.

As one reads through your work one is tempted to continue pairing concepts, terms such as the life and art mentioned earlier. Another pair—love and redemption—comes to mind. The Frank Alpines and Yakov Boks, for example, apparently do redeem themselves. But terms such as love, humanity, belonging, compassion or rachmones *or* menschlechkeit *(and other terms as well) seem to slip in and out of one's consciousness in this context. In a variety of ways, you seem to demonstrate that love brings redemption to an individual. But both of these terms—love and redemption—are endowed by you with a multiplicity of meanings. Would this be a fair estimation? Or would you prefer one to place love and redemption into a narrower, perhaps more religious context?*

Yes, there are various ways. I wouldn't want to place love and redemption in a religious context, although acting out love and redemption may be a religious deed.

Characters in your fiction from time to time wrestle with their Jewishness. In response to a question, Morris Bober defines Jewishness. Bok ultimately feels he must rejoin his people. But these characters and others seem to adapt as minority people to the pluralistic societies they find themselves in—whether it be the United States, Russia, or Italy. One of our students recently noted that the current writers who frequently people their work with Jews—Bellow, Roth, I. B. Singer, etc.—*and who explore serious matters concerning Jewishness, probe or suggest a variety of possible identities. These may involve religion, assimilation, acculturation, bundism, social action, etc. But Zionism (specifically seeking one's Jewish identity in Israel) is quite conspicuous by its absence. As a matter of fact, this student further observed that the real (in-depth) American Zionist novel has not only not been written, but probably will never be undertaken by a major American writer. Do you agree? Why has Zionism played such a minor role for the Jewish characters who have populated so much of our fiction during the last two decades?*

I agree. Writing about Zionism wouldn't interest me. I'd rather write about Israel if I knew the country. I don't, so I leave it to the Israeli writers.

Not too long ago Robert Alter noted the black-white confrontations in Rabbit Redux, Mr. Sammler's Plane, *and* The Tenants. *In the latter two books, of course, the whites assumed another dimension because they were Jews. It is perhaps no coincidence that these books emerged at a time of great conflict between blacks and whites in this country and in certain pockets of the country between blacks and Jews. Do you yourself see a new relationship developing in the United States between blacks and Jews? If so, how do you define this relationship?*

It's impossible to predict—it may go one way; it may go another. A good deal depends on the efficacy of American democracy. If that works as it ought—guaranteeing blacks what they deserve as human beings—a larger share of our national wealth, equal opportunity under the law, their rights as men, the relationship of blacks and Jews and other minorities are bound to improve.

At one time you mentioned that even though a number of years separate your first Fidelman story from the last one, when you initially created Arthur Fidelman you had plans that went beyond **"The Last Mohican."** *Can you explain why it was that they became a series of separate stories ultimately woven into a novel rather than a novel more in the form of* **The Assistant** *or* **The Tenants**? *Also, the name Fidelman. Some critics have played around with the name as symbol. Few, however, have noted that it is also your mother's maiden name. Was this choice significant or incidental?*

Right after I wrote **"The Last Mohican"** in Rome in 1957, I worked out an outline of other Fidelman stories, the whole to develop one theme in the form of a picaresque novel. Why do it the same way all the time?

I used my mother's maiden name because I needed a name I liked.

Has your wife's Italian background contributed to your "Italian" stories in the same way that your Jewish background has contributed to your "Jewish" stories? We are talking here more of an Italian and Jewish context, characterization, and rhythm of place rather than simply settings and people that happen to be Italian and Jewish.

Yes. I met Italians in America through my wife before and after we were married, and because she had been to Italy and could speak Italian like a native, we decided to live in Rome with our children in 1956-7. Through her relatives and acquaintances I was almost at once *into* Italian life and got the feel of their speech, modes of behavior, style. When I go abroad I like to stay in one place as long as possible until I can define its quality.

Do you read much of the criticism of your fiction? How do you respond to literary criticism in general?

I read here and there in criticism about my work when it hits the eye. I don't go looking for it. I like imaginative interpretations of my books, whether I agree with them or not. I enjoy criticism that views the work in ways I haven't anticipated—that surprises me. I dislike crap—criticism, favorable or unfavorable, that really doesn't understand what the books are about. I do take seriously insightful criticism of individual works that affirm judgments, negative or positive, of my own.

Does teaching interfere with your writing of fiction or does it help and complement in some ways?

I devote little time to teaching now—a quarter of a program, one class in the spring. Teaching "interferes" only in cutting down writing time. On a day I teach I can't write. But teaching helps more than it hinders. It gets me out of my study and puts me in touch with people. And I like reading, and talking about books.

I'm not arguing that the academic life is the life for a writer—often it restricts experience and homogenizes it; but I am grateful that when I was earning little or nothing as a writer, because of teaching, when I wrote I wrote only what I wanted to write.

In **The Assistant** *your characters are frequently referred to as* the Poilesheh, the Swede, the Italyener, the Norwegian, the Greek *and even the Jew. In one sense it reminds one of Stephen Crane's use of* the youthful soldier, the cheerful soldier, the loud soldier, the spectral soldier, *etc. Were you attempting an ethnic view of twentieth-century urban America much as Crane may have tried to depict the world of the Civil War Soldier through a set of humors?*

No, I don't play those games. That's the way the Bobers talk.

Another reference to Stephen Crane, a variation. Are you very concerned with drawing prototypes and archetypes in your fiction as opposed to depicting realistic human beings? In other words, do you find yourself deliberately flattening out some of your characters much as a Stephen Crane would do or as a Cézanne would do in painting because you are at times much more interested in something beyond the depiction of a recognizable three-dimensional character?

I would never deliberately flatten a character to create a stereotype. Again—I'm not much one for preconceptions, theories—even E. M. Forster's "flats and rounds." Most of all I'm out to create real and passion-ate human beings. I do as much as I can with a character. I may not show him in full blast every moment, but before the end of a fiction he has had a chance to dance his dance.

It appears that you rarely develop children or young characters in your fiction, especially in your longer fiction. Children are in the background often in novels such as **The Natural** *and* **A New Life,** *but are almost nonexistent in other works. Have you been conscious of this characteristic of your fiction? Do you have any thoughts on this matter?*

I've got to leave something for my old age.

Would you agree that yours is basically a comic vision of life?

There is comedy in my vision of life. To live sanely one must discover—or invent it. Consider the lilies of the field; consider the Jewish lily that toils and spins.

Do you see a major shift in the point of view of your recent short stories collected in **Rembrandt's Hat** *as opposed to views you may have held when you wrote* **The Magic Barrel** *and* **Idiots First?** *There is still, of course, the concern with humanity or menschlechkeit. Is there more stoic acceptance in these stories?*

They're the stories of an older man than the one who wrote *The Magic Barrel* and *Idiots First*, possibly a man who knows more than he did ten or fifteen years ago.

Do you read more fiction or nonfiction these days? At any rate, could you give us some notion of your current reading?

I read a good deal of biography. I like some of the Latin American novelists I've been reading lately. I read too much half-ass American fiction and not enough good poetry. At the moment I'm rereading *Walden*. I'm also reading Jane Goodall's study of chimps, *In the Shadow of Man*. More than half of my reading centers around what I may need to know for my own writing.

Would you say something about your writing habits, the physical setting for your writing, and perhaps along the way give a few clues about your earliest writing experiences, etc?

I've answered this question in an interview with Israel Shenker in the *N. Y. Times*. It's not a question that I love to answer more than once. Young writers have a legitimate but exaggerated interest in the way other writers work. To them I'd say the way to work is the way you write best.

You've mentioned another novel you are working on now. Would you care to give us some idea of its direction and scope?

I don't believe, as Hemingway seemed to, that you hex a work-in-progress simply by talking about it. I'm writing another novel—a difficult one, just started, which may not see the light of day. If it does, the opening paragraph may read as follows:

"Although it isn't yet end of summer, William Dubin, at one moment of his walk in the country—rural into pastoral—beats his arms vigorously across chest and shoulders as though he had suddenly encountered cold, the clouds have darkened, and a snow-storm threatens. He had, in a way, been thinking of winter."

Can you think of other questions which have not been asked or which should be asked or which you would like asked? Perhaps you can supply answers for these unasked questions.

No, I've talked too much. (pp. 9-17)

Bernard Malamud, Leslie A. Field and Joyce W. Field, in an interview in *Bernard Malamud: A Collection of Critical Essays,* edited by Leslie A. Field and Joyce W. Field, Prentice Hall, Inc., 1975, pp. 8-17.

SHELDON NORMAN GREBSTEIN

(essay date 1973)

[Grebstein, an American critic and educator, has written numerous works on American literature and culture. In the following excerpt from an essay that first appeared in 1973, he assesses Malamud's contribution to the Jewish movement in American letters and provides an overview of themes and literary techniques in the author's early fiction.]

Malamud best represents the phenomenon of the Jewish Movement; not only is he one of its founders and major practitioners, he is probably its best single exemplar. In Malamud's work we most clearly perceive just those characteristics which define the entire Movement.

First and foremost, there is the theme of meaningful suffering, which in Malamud also implies the quest for moral resolution and self-realization. But the theme of suffering cannot alone sustain either a movement or a writer's career. We can take just so much bad news. Malamud's writing, like that of the Movement at large, is also richly comic. Paradoxically, the comedy is at once a mode of expression of the suffering and a way of easing it. With the Jew humor is an escape valve for dangerous pressures, a manner of letting out things too painful to be kept in. (Could it be that one of the reasons we have able black writers like Ellison and Baldwin but not a Black Movement, is the prevailing solemnity of these writers?) Finally, the Jewish writer speaks in a distinctive literary voice. With Bellow and at about the same time, Malamud invented and perfected a fresh literary idiom, a "Jewish style." This style consists of much more than the importation of Yiddish words and phrases into English, or a mere broken Yiddish-English dialect, long the staple of popular works presenting lovably silly Jewish stereotypes (*Abie's Irish Rose*). Rather, it is a significant development and expansion of the American colloquial style, established as a

vital literary medium by Mark Twain. The Jewish style is for the first time in our literary history a voice that conveys ethnic characteristics, a special sort of sensibility, and the quality of a foreign language, yet remains familiar and eloquent to non-Jews. Although dialects and dialect styles tend to be reductive, rendering their speakers either funny or absurd, Malamud's style can evoke either tragic dignity or comic foolishness, or, miraculously, both at once. (pp. 20-1)

His heroes all suffer deeply, but they are also secular men whose suffering is not always voluntary, undertaken wholly for exalted reasons, or blessed by great rewards. Malamud's real concern is for the social and moral aspects of suffering as they impinge upon personality. If his characters expect some recompense for their misery, they would like it in the here and now. In sum, although we have no conclusive biographical evidence to assess Malamud's personal religious commitment, the testimony of his work suggests him to be an agnostic humanist. Some of his own remarks support that deduction: "My premise is that we will not destroy each other. My premise is that we will live on. We will seek a better life. We may not become better, but at least we will seek betterment."

This is Malamud's real toughness, the factor that prevents his treatment of suffering from deteriorating into drippy melodrama or comfortable piety. He has a view of man which perceives the property of conscience, the seeking to be better, not as a divine mystery but as natural to humans as skin, hair, voice. Yet this basically optimistic concept of human nature is checked by an almost equally persistent view of man as greedy, treacherous, lustful, and often vicious. Cheerful idealist and hard-eyed realist peer out through the same bifocals.

Consequently, Malamud's depiction of suffering is ambivalent; in each of his major characters altruism and materialism combine as motives for self-sacrifice. (pp. 21-2)

[Although Malamud draws upon all the Yiddish] varieties of humor, I find the mode of fantastic comedy particularly interesting and successful. In this mode Malamud implies the immanence of a spiritual dimension or realm of human experience without committing himself to a specific faith, doctrine, or theology. In short, the fantastic and the metaphysical enter into Malamud's world as though they were fact, and he solidifies them and ties them to earth by depicting them in the same voice and with the same solidity of specification that he uses for grocery stores and Czarist prisons. One might say that this is Malamud's version of the quasi-religious folklore and superstition permeating *shtetl* life, and as much a fact of that life as its food and drink. . . . Malamud is thus the heir to rich Jewish traditions, and worthy heir that he is, he remakes them his way and reinvigorates them. (pp. 26-7)

Malamud's first novel *The Natural* is largely a work of fantastic comedy, and though a flawed book, there is such verve in it and such an abundance of talent, one might have predicted that this was to be Malamud's *métier*. In brief, Malamud transforms the national game of baseball, familiar to all and in which all are experts, into a contest among demigods and conducted as though it were a sacred ritual in a cosmic arena. This placing together of unlike pairs, baseball and the universe, already inspires a comic response. For the literary reader Malamud provides an extra dimension of incongruity by juxtaposing a sports story, rendered with the appropriate data and terminology, against a mythic context which draws upon the myths of the Quest Hero, the Fisher King, and, to some degree, the White Goddess. (pp. 27-8)

The pervasive dreariness of *The Assistant*, with its central locale of the dark store, is relieved and modulated by occasional but effective comic moments, notably one brief yet vivid episode of fantasy in which Morris Bober receives a visit from the devil and succumbs to his temptation. However, in keeping with the general method of the book, the agent of evil appears not in a spectacular scene but in a muted little encounter so close to credibility it can almost be taken as actual. . . . Malamud blends the fantastic with the realistic, for in such a novel as *The Assistant* the wholly bizarre and surrealistic would be an intrusion. (pp. 28-9)

The fantastic component in *The Fixer,* to some degree anticipated by the characters' dreams and visions in *The Assistant*, consists entirely of Yakov's dreams, fevers, and hallucinations during his long and dreadful confinement. But these, however farfetched, are often too painful to be comic. . . . Indeed, the bitterness of Jewish humor is nowhere better exemplified than in *The Fixer.* A prevailing source of comedy comprises examples of the incredible misconceptions and superstitions about the Jews held by the Russians, misconceptions for which the Jews, not the Russians, suffer. I doubt if a more horrendous humor exists in any culture than this sort, frequent in *The Fixer*. . . . (p. 30)

The comedy of *A New Life* and *Pictures of Fidelman* abandons fantasy almost entirely. Rather, these novels depend upon zany and often bawdy situations and employ the earthy humor, burlesque, and slapstick which derive from human lusts, mistakes, and misconduct. (p. 31)

Quite aside from the burlesque sexuality of *A New Life*, a matter which Malamud treats with decreasing emphasis and increased seriousness as the novel proceeds—and sex becomes love, and love becomes commitment—*A New Life* demands comment as the only instance to date of Malamud as satirist. Although the satire finally collapses under the weight of too much academic detail and too much debate, for a time Malamud's fantastic gift exhilarates his depiction

of Cascadia College and its English department. In this respect the novel's scene temporarily partakes in the great tradition of satire as fable: Gulliver's Lilliput, Martin Chuzzlewit's America, Sinclair Lewis's Zenith, all of them peopled not by *homo sapiens* but by goblins in human costume. The problem in *A New Life* is that the satire turns too grittily truthful, too near the quality of a *roman à clef,* and Levin, lovable and interesting as *shlemiel*-cum-lover, becomes something of a bore as academic crusader. Consequently, the novel is too playful to persuade entirely as realism and not playful enough to persuade as satire.

Pictures of Fidelman avoids that mistake. Although hardly Malamud's largest achievement, it is surely his most accomplished as a comic work. The humor arises from the antic misadventures in Italy of a world-be art student and painter. (pp. 31-2)

But as hilarious as such scenes are, Malamud grounds them upon certain hard actualities which keep the book from dissipating into mere ribald spoofing. There is the authentic context of the Italian locale: of cold, poverty, venality, a people scrabbling for the next meal, including Fidelman himself. Simultaneously, there is the presence of great art, part of the air breathed in Italy, and the irresistible appeal to attempt it oneself. Thus Fidelman's wild sexual encounters are played off against his increasingly desperate and futile attempts to become an artist. The incongruous juxtaposition in *Pictures of Fidelman* is, then, that between the coarsely sexual and the sublimely aesthetic.

Too, the novel may be viewed as a kind of comic *bildungsroman,* intermixed with the International Theme and structured as a picaresque story cycle. Fidelman arrives in Italy respectably dressed and with the worthy ambition to become an art critic. Then, just as in the first episode he is robbed of his attaché case containing the initial chapter of his projected book, and swindled out of his extra suit of clothes, the layers of his superficial identity are stripped away episode by episode in a series of comic but also bitter encounters, until he is no longer definable as a middle-class American Jew. Instead, he gains a more basic identity: craftsman and lover. Furthermore, he has travelled there the hard way, through privation, failure, humiliation, abuse, crime, and fakery—an experience which brings him in the book's surrealistic penultimate episode face to face with the devil. In Fidelman Malamud has created his own version of an enduring Jewish comic prototype, the *luftmensch* with feet of clay. We have known worse people. (pp. 32-3)

Malamud's chief distinction as an artist is his command of a particular literary idiom. This idiom not only bears Malamud's own signature, it has so permeated Jewish-American writing that the Movement itself is in some measure distinguished by it. Furthermore, the style is integral to [his] very themes and motifs. . . . In a fundamental sense the suffering and the comedy are embedded in the language, and their peculiar simultaneity or proximity, the sweetly tragic and the bitterly comic, must to a significant degree be attributed to the style. In his own way Malamud captures in English what has been called an untranslatable quality of Yiddish, the admixture of the jocular and the solemn, "the fusion of the sacred and the profane." (p. 33)

First, he avails himself of what is perhaps the most versatile and fluent of narrative modes, selective omniscience. In this mode the writer retains the objectivity, the freedom to move through time and space, and the power to know all, which are the great advantages of the traditional third-person outside narrator; yet by refraining from editorial intrusions and maintaining the focus on a single character or a few characters, the writer can shift into interior monologue or take a stance which allows him to perceive as through the character's eyes without any obvious break in the narrative seam or detection by the reader. This is, of course, a modern technique, and one at the service of many resourceful writers. It is the narrative perspective Malamud has employed in all his novels and, with rare exceptions, his stories as well. (pp. 33-4)

Malamud's best work is realistic, though it should be clear from the frequent and important presence of fantastic comedy that it breaks through strict categories. Indeed, although Malamud is a realist, as demonstrated in *The Assistant, The Fixer,* and the major part of *A New Life,* he is of the best sort: a symbolic realist. The Jewish sense of the Transcendent merged with the Actual expresses itself in Malamud's technique in a hard-rock verisimilitude, in which we smell garbage and know exactly how much money lies in the cash register or what a sadistic prison official does with his fingers when he searches a prisoner. At the same time, we are ever aware of the play of the human imagination upon experience and the inexhaustible intimations of the protean natural world. Symbols and emblems recur everywhere in Malamud's fiction, obtrusive only in the case of his first book, *The Natural,* and even there not inappropriate to a work with a frame of myth. Elsewhere they are wholly integrated.

[So, for example, in] *The Assistant,* the characters' movements in that work—quite normal in a building containing a cellar, a first-floor store, and living quarters above—assume symbolic purport. As already implied, these movements constitute a dramatic metaphor for the characters' moral conditions. Frank comes up from the cellar where he has been hiding, to the store, and then to a room on the floor above. This parallels his climb from bummery to decency. Conversely, Morris goes upstairs to sleep and dream, his only escape from his prison—the store. In his one concession to evil, he goes downstairs to set fire to his business but

is saved from this by Frank, who has already experienced what things are like in the cellar. (pp. 35-6)

[Malamud utilizes] heat and cold, light and dark, fragrance and stench, the indoors and the outdoors. . . . Too, throughout his work he consistently uses weather, season, climate, as corollary and symbolic context for his characters' actions and moral conditions. He also skillfully employs emblems: mirrors, books, articles of clothing, for example. Thus . . . there is always much more to see in Malamud's stories than what will happen next. (p. 36)

[Malamud's style is] three styles, or a confluence of styles.

First there is a "straight" or standard belletristic style; that is, a style composed of the same linguistic materials used by other modern writers, with a syntax familiar to all speakers of American English, and a diction drawn from the common vocabulary of standard-informal usage. . . . Lucid and vigorous, [this style] contains nothing intrinsically alien or exotic and little identifying it as specifically Malamudian if it were taken out of context and seen in isolation. (pp. 36-7)

A second Malamud style, that most unlike the standard belletristic, is a dialect style which deliberately evokes the sound of Yiddish. It demonstrates Malamud's familiarity with the old mother tongue. . . . It also demonstrates Malamud's skill at transliterating that tongue into a kind of English. However, Malamud can hardly be credited with inventing the dialect style or being the first to use Yiddish dialect as a literary medium. . . . In the twentieth century Yiddish dialect has been a staple of comedy and of comedians for decades, although very rare in serious writing. (pp. 37-8)

The third style, the most complex and resonant and that which Malamud has impressed with his own signature, is a mixed or fused style which combines both the belletristic and dialect styles yet is wholly neither. Malamud can be named the co-inventor of this style; he and Bellow began to use it at about the same time, in the early 1950's, though apparently without the conscious indebtedness of either one to the other. The fused style gathers additional force from the juxtaposition or combination of lyric, eloquent, soaring phrases (the belletristic) and homely idiom and vulgate (the dialect). The belletristic exalts the vulgate, infusing it with dignity and seriousness; the vulgate pulls down the belletristic from its literary eminence and makes it speak for ordinary men and coarse experience. The juxtaposition of the two also makes possible that remarkable bitter comedy we observe in Malamud, Bellow, and Roth. (pp. 38-9)

In *The Assistant,* to continue our concern with that novel a moment longer, each of the three styles appears in a variety of uses and combinations. The dialect style, for example, functions appropriately in the conversations of those characters for whom Yiddish was the language of their youth. . . . We also hear this style in certain interior monologues. Perhaps its most consistent use in the novel is to depict Ida, I suspect as a way to fix her into a kind of narrowness or limitation of vision. Of all the important characters, hers is the meanest worldview. (p. 40)

But what is so artistic about using a dialect style for a dialect character? We have the answer to that in Malamud's treatment of Morris, because, in contrast, Malamud shrewdly avoids the dialect style and renders him, whether by omniscient narration or interior monologue, either in the standard belletristic style or the fused style. This "straight" treatment of Morris reiterates his identity as an Everyman figure and comprises the stylistic equivalent to the novel's thesis that all men are, potentially, Jews. To depict him in the dialect style would be to insist upon his ethnic identity and thus to weaken the characterization. Morris's character gains depth, too, in that Malamud shows him as capable of different levels of speech, depending on the situation. To Ida he speaks strictly in Yiddish dialect, as to Karp and others; to Helen and Frank his speech remains homely but closer to standard and almost purged of its Yiddishisms; to Detective Minogue he speaks in a stilted but "correct" manner which reflects the strain he feels dealing with this man within a formal, official context.

On the other hand, Helen and Frank can be rendered in a style which at times borders on dialect in its loose colloquialism, yet without risk of stereotyping. As Helen's style is slightly more literary because of her aspirations and her education, so Frank's tends to be slangy, appropriate to his background as drifter. However, we perceive a subtle but progressive heightening of Frank's speech and interior monologue, as well as of the omniscient narration describing him, on those occasions when he delves into serious subjects either with Morris or Helen, and as his moral ascension continues. He achieves, in his best moments, a striking combination of literary eloquence and lowdown bluntness. (p. 41)

The Natural totally lacks Yiddish flavor, rightly so, yet the style is breezy and slangy—accurate to a world of baseball players. At the same time the earthy colloquialism sets up an artistically desirable tension against the novel's heavy mythic and allegorical machinery, with two beneficial effects: it provides an illusion of actuality; it produces a keen humor. *A New Life* is written largely in the fused style, again seemly to the subject and to the novel's hero, an urban Eastern Jew with an M.A. However, just as Levin's Jewishness overtly plays only a small role in the novel, the "Jewish" elements in his thought and speech are suppressed. . . . In this novel, too, the mixture of collo-

quial and belletristic materials generates a comic undercurrent.

The same comic potentiality, inherent in any style which employs idiom, helps to enliven *The Fixer* and prevent it from unbearable morbidity. (pp. 41-2)

First, [Malamud] establishes a continual contrast between the language of all the official proceedings, innately formal and bombastic, and the spontaneous simplicity and pungency of Yakov's own speech. Accordingly, there is posed the repeated incongruity between what is uttered by the various magistrates and functionaries, and the pithy, unaffected quality of what Yakov is saying inside his own head. The incongruity becomes even more absurd in that when Yakov replies to his persecutors, he usually does so in the same stilted manner they use. The result is a kind of chorus of voices. Second, the contrast of voices, of what is said and what is thought, communicates an authentic difference of tongues. . . . At the same time Malamud's voice, employing the fused style of an omniscient narrator outside the hero but never very far away, merges with Yakov's. Narrator and hero often become one in that both express themselves in the same way: lucidly, candidly, sometimes earthily, sometimes in short lyric flights. In sum, what Malamud does, linguistically, is to pit the good Jews (Malamud and Yakov) against the bad Russians. You can usually tell the bad guys by their bombast, if they have rank, or if lower class by their nasty, vulgar mouths. (p. 42)

Although the narrative [of *Pictures of Fidelman*] is largely rendered in the fused style, Malamud flies higher with the belletristic and dives lower with the vulgate than in any of his other work. He also takes greater chances with narrative perspective, shifting from objective to subjective narration more frequently and swiftly than ever before. He makes other rapid and varied shifts as well: from the conventional narrative past tense to the immediate present, from exposition to dialogue, from interior monologue or selective omniscience to direct impression. Technically the book is as wild and unpredictable as its hero's adventures. Indeed, chapter five is a technical *tour de force,* a packed and dazzling virtuoso demonstration of Malamud's range, a stylistic splurge. One can only describe it as a neo-Joycean, comitragic, surrealistic, stream-of-consciousness, visionary sequence, perhaps a burst of true madness in poor Fidelman but also containing a portion of almost coherent narrative which advances the story line. There is nothing remotely like it in Malamud's earlier writing. (p. 43)

Although for all its virtuosity and comic gusto *Pictures of Fidelman* is a much less estimable work than such solid accomplishments as *The Assistant* and *The Fixer,* this novel does make a number of important affirmations. For one thing, it affirms that despite Malamud's association with the Jewish Movement and his importance to it, his material is not restricted to the themes and prototypes characteristic to that Movement. It affirms that he retains the capacity to surprise us, a capacity always beyond the scope of a minor writer. It affirms, moreover, that Malamud continues to be devoted to the subject he believes the writer must treat as his mission: the richness of the development of human personality. Finally, it affirms that whether his treatment be somber or comic, his possibilities as a craftsman are far from exhausted. (pp. 43-4)

The Tenants appeared after this essay had been written, and too late to be included in it. However, from my first reading of the book I would amend my conclusions here in only one important respect: it seems to indicate that Malamud is capable of unmitigated pessimism, gloomier even than that in *The Fixer.* Or, we could take a little comfort from the ending of *The Tenants* by interpreting it as warning and object lesson to both Jew and Black: learn to get along, *or else.* In any case the novel confirms my belief that Malamud is still growing. (p. 44)

Sheldon Norman Grebstein, "Bernard Malamud and the Jewish Movement," in *Bernard Malamud: A Collection of Critical Essays,* edited by Leslie A. Field and Joyce W. Field, Prentice-Hall, Inc., 1975, pp. 18-44.

DAVID R. MESHER

(essay date 1975)

[In the following excerpt, Mesher provides an in-depth analysis of Malamud's short story "The Last Mohican," a work that the critic feels is "representative of [Malamud's] early period" and "is valuable for any analysis of the author's work in general."]

Bernard Malamud's first story in the Fidelman sequence, **"The Last Mohican,"** is a pivotal work in the author's writing. Since it utilizes themes and techniques found throughout Malamud's first three novels, *The Natural, The Assistant,* and *A New Life,* and in most of the stories collected in *The Magic Barrel* and in *Idiots First,* the story is representative of the author's early period; in addition, **"The Last Mohican"** is a seminal story for the motifs and concerns of some of Malamud's more recent fiction, including *The Tenants* and, most obviously, *Pictures of Fidelman.* The technique in the story of the double, for example, in which one character teaches the other self-knowledge, is similar to that of *The Assistant,* while the motif of the stolen manuscript reappears as a central component in the plot of *The Tenants.* Because it holds such a crucial place in Malamud's canon, a correct understanding of

"The Last Mohican" is valuable for any analysis of the author's work in general. (p. 397)

The story concerns Arthur Fidelman, who arrives in Italy intending to write "a critical study of Giotto, the opening chapter of which he had carried across the ocean." When he enters Rome, the art student is approached by the inimitable Shimon Susskind, a Jewish refugee. Though Fidelman gives him some money, Susskind is unsatisfied. " 'In your luggage,' he said vaguely, 'would you maybe have a suit you can't use. I could use a suit'." . . . Fidelman, budgeting to make his money last long enough to finish the book, refuses to give the refugee his spare suit. Nevertheless, Susskind continues to shadow Fidelman's movements and to plague his thoughts. The refugee is literally a *luftmentsh:* when the student asks him how he lives, Susskind replies, "I eat air." . . . After Susskind appears surreptitiously in Fidelman's room to renew his suit for the student's spare one, without success, Fidelman discovers his manuscript missing. He suspects the refugee, naturally, and searches Rome for him, but the formerly ubiquitous Susskind has disappeared. Fidelman finally locates him months later, selling Christian articles in front of St. Peter's, and follows him to "an overgrown closet containing bed and table" . . . , but not the manuscript. Finally, the answer comes to Fidelman as he dreams of a fresco by Giotto of Saint Francis of Assisi giving his cloak to a poor knight: "San Francesco dona le vesti al cavaliere povero." . . . Like Frank Alpine in *The Assistant,* Fidelman receives enlightenment from St. Francis, in this case through the agency of Giotto's art. Waking, the student immediately carries his suit to Susskind, reenacting the charity of the saint. Though the refugee suspects that the suit is being offered in trade for the manuscript, Fidelman assures Susskind that he wants "nothing at all" . . . , and leaves the rat's nest. . . . The relationship between art and life—a common theme in Malamud—is at least this clear from the story: one who cannot act charitably and humanely in life cannot really appreciate, or has not sufficiently understood, great art, which has compassion at its root. Giotto's painting of the charity of St. Francis was unintelligible to Fidelman while the student could refuse to consider giving his suit to an impoverished refugee; the spirit of that charity was missing from the manuscript and from the student himself until Susskind helped him to enlightenment. Fidelman sees this, and calls after the fleeing refugee, " 'Susskind, come back,' he shouted, half sobbing. 'The suit is yours. All is forgiven'." . . . The story ends with Susskind, having educated the student, running out of sight; Fidelman is left equipped with genuine compassion.

Few critics have presented readings similar to this, and none has pursued his beyond the story's literal level. Many more have misunderstood even these superficial aspects of Malamud's story. Sheldon Norman Grebstein, for example, describes Fidelman on arrival in Rome as "respectably dressed and with the worthy ambition to become an art critic." . . . The worthiness of being a critic is also dubious in **"The Last Mohican."** Fidelman only chooses that profession after he is "a self-confessed failure as a painter" . . . , and the movement of the story tends to restore his artistic powers; the relationship of the artist to life, central to all the Fidelman stories, does not apply to an art critic. (pp. 397-99)

The refugee's qualifications for teaching Fidelman self-knowledge arise from the characters' intimacy as doubles. This is clear from Susskind's first appearance: standing outside the Rome railroad station, "Fidelman experienced the sensation of suddenly seeing himself as he was, to the pinpoint, outside and in, not without bittersweet pleasure"; shortly afterwards, the student "became aware that there was an exterior source to the strange, almost tri-dimensional reflection of himself." . . . Not only does Susskind's presence show Fidelman his true, innermost self, but the double first appears beside the statue of another famous pair, Romulus and Remus. A further identification with Susskind is also found in the student's name: especially in Yiddish, there is little orthographical difference between "Fidel" and "peddle."

Susskind, much more in the story than just Fidelman's double, is hardly the "dirty, sponging, obnoxious immigrant," or the "shameless parasite," that some critics have described. This misunderstanding of Susskind's character may originate with Fidelman himself, who concludes from the insufficient evidence of the peddler's first "shalom" that he is "a schnorrer." . . . Accepting Fidelman's appraisal, however, is a critical error; Malamud has taken great pains in **"The Last Mohican"** to distinguish between peddling and begging. Susskind never begs in the story, nor is he ever termed a beggar by the narrator. . . . Susskind may seem to be asking for money, but in fact his questions are carefully worded not to ask for more, but to ask, hypothetically, why more shouldn't be forthcoming. If this is hairsplitting, it is Malamud's distinction as well as that of Susskind; those who have seen in the peddler the archetype of "Susskind the Beggar" have misunderstood both his character and his function in the story.

The difference between begging and accepting charity is finely delineated in the scene at the trattoria. At first, Susskind watches Fidelman eat "with rapt attention." . . . Initially, Susskind does not refuse the food; his first reply is one of acceptance. But acceptance with "thanks" is different from asking with "thanks yes." Asking is begging, and Susskind refuses to beg; when he must commit himself, if only by a simple "yes," the refugee goes hungry. Susskind even avoids

asking for the student's spare suit. "In your luggage," he questions Fidelman during their first meeting, "would you maybe have a suit you can't use. I could use a suit." . . . The refugee thus presents Fidelman with two premises: Fidelman has a spare suit, and Susskind needs one. The charitable conclusion, that the student should give Susskind his suit, is never voiced by the peddler. (pp. 399-400)

Susskind's identification as a peddler begins with his first name, Shimon, in English Simon. When Fidelman finally finds him after months of searching, Susskind is engaged in simony, "selling black and white rosaries to all who would buy." . . . Though the profession is inauspicious, and rather ill-suited for saving Fidelman's soul and heritage, Malamud's imagery elevates peddlers to the level of angels. Until Susskind is located selling rosaries, only two types of beings fly in the story: there are the "flights of angels" Fidelman sees one night after overtaxing his eyes in the Vatican museum . . . , and the "fly-by-night peddlers" amongst whom he searches for Susskind. . . . Fidelman, who travels to Rome by boat and train, never flies, but Susskind, who "had an odd way of standing motionless, like a cigar store Indian about to burst into flight" . . . , is consistently associated with flying and angels. (pp. 400-01)

Though Susskind does not beg, he does demand; he comes "instead of an angel," but he comes as a Jew. For Malamud, Jewish consciousness makes certain demands; and as Susskind tells him, Fidelman is responsible for them "because you are a man. Because you are a Jew." . . . Fidelman's primary problem is that he has rejected his own Jewish culture, but is unable to assimilate into that of the Italians. His gift of the suit at the end of the story is not merely a sign that he has understood Giotto's painting; by that point, he also understands—and accepts—himself and his people.

The conflict between Italian and Jewish history begins immediately upon Fidelman's arrival in Rome. Viewing the Baths of Diocletian, he mutters to himself, "Imagine all that history." . . . The word *imagine* is repeated three times in as many lines, drawing attention to the student's distance from the history of Rome. Later, walking along the banks of the Tiber, Fidelman defines history in his thoughts as "the remembrance of things unknown" . . . , playing on the translation of Proust's title. The history of the Jews is also present in the world of **"The Last Mohican,"** embodied by Shimon Susskind. Like a microcosmic Diaspora, Susskind lived in Israel "once" . . . , and has also fled from "Germany, Hungary, Poland. Where not?" . . . That history, however, bores Fidelman; he says to Susskind, "Ah, that's so long ago." . . . The remark contains a double irony, both parts at Fidelman's expense. Compared to the history of ancient Rome, of course, the recent horrors of Nazi persecutions, as represented by

Susskind the individual, hardly occurred "long ago." In contrast, the history of Susskind, representative of the Jewish people, is far longer than that of Rome, to which Fidelman is attracted because of its apparent antiquity. (p. 401)

Of all Jewish history, it seems only "Israel interested Fidelman" . . . ; the student identifies with Israeli victors, but refuses to acknowledge the centuries of Jewish victims. To Malamud, however, the lessons of persecution are at least as valuable as the rewards of success; Fidelman must therefore accept his heritage as a Jew to gain a full understanding of himself. To discuss this process of acceptance, we must return to Fidelman's search for Susskind.

After the refugee takes the manuscript, Fidelman is unable to work. The absence of his chapter exposes a vicious circularity in the student's character: he always "needed something solid behind him before he could advance, some worthwhile accomplishment upon which to build another." . . .

While searching to recover the chapter, Fidelman begins unconsciously to identify with his double, Susskind. He wears "a blue beret with his trench coat and a pair of black Italian shoes" . . . , which are, as Richman has noted, "the very clothes Susskind wears." He also searches in the ghetto, and even visits an Italian synagogue, where elements of Jewish and Italian history are intertwined in the beadle's story of a son "killed in the Ardeatine Caves." . . . When Fidelman finally does locate the peddler, he follows him "all the way home, indeed the ghetto," and returns later to search Susskind's hovel, "a pitch black freezing cave." . . . The destitution in which the refugee subsists appalls Fidelman; "from the visit he never fully recovered." . . . (p. 402)

Subsequently, Fidelman has his dream in which a Dantean "long-nosed brown shade, Virgilio Susskind" guides him through the underworld of his own subconscious. . . . The shade's taunt, "Why is art?" not only twists the title of Tolstoy's essay to force a perception of humanity on the student, but also poses a more personal question about the existence of Art Fidelman. The climax of the dream, Fidelman's vision of Giotto's painting, is an example of Malamud's genius in synthesizing his themes. The scene of St. Francis giving away his cloak integrates Susskind's need for the suit with Fidelman's desire for self-knowledge and appreciation of art. Moreover, the use of Giotto as the painter is simultaneously the central and yet the most understated element of the synthesis. The Italian word *giotto*, "foundry," is traditionally the etymological root of *ghetto*. The first official ghetto, proclaimed by Pope Paul IV in 1555, was "located on the malarial west bank of the Tiber, near the *giotto*, the gun factory." (pp. 402-03)

Malamud's ambiguous use of Giotto's name in place of its paronym is also reversed within the story; the beadle's advice to "look in the ghetto" . . . , foreshadows the student's dream of Giotto's fresco.

The story operates on several levels, connected by verbal ambiguities, on each of which Fidelman progresses from alienation to reconciliation, with art, humanity, his Jewish heritage, and himself; in each instance, Susskind's intervention, in a dream or otherwise, provides the fundamental stimulus for Fidelman's amelioration. Most critical misreadings have originated with an undue sense of parasitism. Similarly, in **"The Mourners"** (*The Magic Barrel*), **"The Death of Me"** (*Idiots First*), and *The Tenants,* readers have mistakenly seen Gruber, Marcus, and Levenspiel, respectively, as the innocent victims of ruthless demands perpetrated by someone only marginally connected to them, as an employee or a tenant. Susskind's association with Fidelman, either as a man or as a Jew, is even more tenuous; but in this story, and in the others, no one is victimized except by himself. Only under Susskind's tutelage can Fidelman regain "the remembrance of things unknown" in the Jewish past so essential to his own present.

Due emphasis must also be given to this story, and to all of Malamud's work, as universal art, transcending the issue of Jewishness. The author's statement that "all men are Jews," is particularly applicable to **"The Last Mohican,"** where all men are Shimon Susskind. Fidelman sees his search for the refugee as an attempt "to know man" . . . , and the cry when he is found—"ecco, Susskind!" . . . —reinforces the peddler's role as humanity personified. Ultimately, Fidelman's insight, by which he becomes himself and Everyman, is also available to the reader, both despite and because of Malamud's ethnocentric approach. (pp. 403-04)

David R. Mesher, "The Remembrance of Things Unknown: Malamud's 'The Last Mohican'," in *Studies in Short Fiction*, Vol. XII, No. 4, Fall, 1975, pp. 397-404.

SHELDON J. HERSHINOW
(essay date 1980)

[In the following excerpt, Hershinow examines the moralistic and humanistic elements of Malamud's fiction.]

Critics have thoroughly evaluated Malamud's work. Because his gift is multifaceted, different critics emphasize different aspects of his fiction. Jonathan Baumbach discusses Malamud as fantasist; F. W. Dupee evaluates him as a realist; Earl Wasserman writes of Malamud as symbolist; Charles Alva Hoyt and Jackson Benson explore Malamud's American romanticism; Robert Ducharme and Max Schultz examine his mythic technique; Earl Rovit treats him as a writer in the Jewish folk tradition; Ruth R. Wisse and Leslie A. Field examine Malamud's uses of the schlemiel; Sheldon Grebstein analyzes stylistic innovations. Most critics mention Malamud's humor and irony, as well as his humanistic affirmation and ethical concern. His mastery of ironic plotting and effect, his distinctive techniques and forms combine with his compassion for humanity and moral purpose to produce a complex vision of muted belief in the potential of the human spirit.

Regardless of each critic's particular interest in Malamud's fiction, virtually all agree that the most noticeable component is its moral vision. As a humanist, Malamud is committed to a position that is neither wholly Jewish, nor Christian, nor existential. Because his statements of moral purpose do not mention God, it seems safe to conclude that he does not believe in a supernatural deity, as such. Nor does his work fall within the Greek and Christian tradition of tragedy.

Dust jacket of Malamud's fourth novel, winner of both a Pulitzer Prize and a National Book Award.

However, in his writing Malamud draws on his understanding of all these traditions.

Early in his writing career, Malamud began to combine his humanistic moral vision with a sense of ethnic identity to create what might be called a "Jewish" humanism. The fusion of his moral concerns with the colorful ethnicity and ironic humor of immigrant Jews produced a distinctly urban comic vision that freed Malamud's inventiveness and his talent for fantasy without compromising his moral earnestness. The combination is so fortuitous that throughout his career Malamud has continued to explore the artistic possibilities of this vision. Drawing on his childhood memories of Yiddish-speaking Americans in New York City, Malamud created a whole arsenal of narrative and stylistic techniques that adapt the rhythms of Yiddish, a folktale-like use of fantasy, and the double vision of Jewish humor.

Writing in a parable mode that uses (to varying degrees) his own distinctive mix of realism, myth, fantasy, romance, comedy, and fairy tale, Malamud has continued to grow artistically. Always a writer willing to take risks, he has freely experimented with new themes and techniques, especially in his short stories. He has over the years developed considerable stylistic range and has often attempted to move beyond the pale of his "Jewish" humanism. These efforts are always interesting, frequently successful. Yet his great achievement, as an artist and as a moralist, has come from his success in creating a distinctive fictional world that is the embodiment of his "Jewish" humanism.

Central to Malamud's moral sensibility is his positive, pragmatic attitude toward suffering. When asked about suffering as a subject in his writing, Malamud replied, "I'm against it, but when it occurs why waste the experience?" His fiction suggests that life—at least for goodhearted, humane people—is a search to make unavoidable suffering meaningful. Nearly all of his novels center on the suffering that results from the conflict between human freedom and human limitations, with the stress on the latter rather than the former. Frank Alpine (*The Assistant*), Sy Levin (*A New Life*), Yakov Bok (*The Fixer*), Arthur Fidelman (*Pictures of Fidelman*), Roy Hobbs (*The Natural*), and Harry Lesser (*The Tenants*), all strive to escape an ignominious or unfulfilling past and to achieve a new life of comfort and fulfillment. All six are defeated in their ambition, but the first four achieve a new dignity, turning defeat into victory by assuming a burden of self-sacrifice. Frank Alpine assumes the living death of the deceased Morris Bober—running Morris's store and assuming the responsibility for his family—out of a deepened sense of commitment mixed with a sense of guilt and a vague hope of winning the love of Morris's daughter. Yakov Bok chooses prison over release for the sake of all Russian Jews. Sy Levin achieves a kind of unsought-after heroism by sacrificing his career for the principle of love, accepting responsibility for a love he no longer feels. Arthur Fidelman learns self-sacrifice born of love and compassion. Roy Hobbs, on the other hand, fails to learn from his suffering and yields to materialism by accepting a bribe (although the ending hints that he may now be able to begin a new life with Iris Lemon). Harry Lesser shuts himself off from humanity in a misguided attempt to achieve artistic self-actualization.

Malamud characteristically develops the idea of the regenerative power of suffering by using the Jew (specifically the schlemiel figure) as a symbol of conscience and moral behavior. In *The Assistant,* Frank Alpine comes to believe that, as a Jew, Morris Bober lives in order to suffer, but Morris tells him that we all suffer because we all live—it is one of the conditions of life. A Jew, Morris says, suffers for the Law, and the Law is "to do what is right, to be honest, to be good." After he accepts the burden of Morris's suffering, Frank Alpine's conversion to Judaism is merely the appropriate symbolic action—perhaps heavy-handed in its symbolism—to complete the statement of the novel. Yet the act does grow naturally from Frank's understanding of what it means to be a Jew—an understanding that is much like Malamud's own view of Jewishness as an avenue to the goals of humanism. In a celebrated statement, Malamud once said, "All men are Jews except they don't know it." By this he meant that the Jew can serve to represent the individual's existential situation as an isolated, displaced loner who has the potential for achieving moral transcendence through suffering that engenders insight and a commitment to love. All people, Malamud implies, have a common identity as ethical beings; for example, by the end of *The Assistant,* Frank Alpine has learned that indeed, metaphorically, "All men are Jews."

In Malamud's fiction, the Jew as a symbol of ethical man is joined by another pervasive symbol—that of life as a prison. When Morris Bober resents his bad fortune, he sees his grocery store as a "prison," a "graveyard," a "tomb." The store is the source of his bitterness, suffering, and frustration—evidence of the limitations of the human condition on earth—and at the same time it symbolizes Morris's very existence, embodying the source of his moral strength. *A New Life* moves Malamud even closer to an explicit existentialist viewpoint. Sy Levin chooses a future "chained" to Pauline Gilley. With her he might appear to be a free man, but really he will be locked inside "a windowless prison" that is "really himself, flawed ediface of failures, each locking up tight the one before." In other words, Levin has exercised the freedom to choose his own "prison." Similarly, Yakov Bok finds spiritual peace only after choosing to remain in the tsar's prison, with no guarantee of ever being released. Harry Lesser voluntarily entombs himself in what he likes to think

of as a "sacred cathedral" of art, but which turns out to be the prison of his own divided soul.

Yet one must ask whether Malamud's metaphoric use of the Jew to represent the good man struggling for a meaningful existence in the prison of life is convincing. Certainly the European Jews, throughout the Middle Ages and again in the nineteenth and twentieth centuries, experienced an extraordinary amount of suffering, but in elevating their hardship to the level of an ethical symbol, Malamud, in spite of his characteristic irony, sometimes borders on sentimentality. For example, near the end of *The Fixer* Yakov Bok's lawyer proclaims to his client, "You suffer for us all. . . . I would be honored to be in your place." Seen in this light, Malamud's famous statement, "All men are Jews," implies that it is the human lot to suffer, that suffering is potentially beneficial, and that we should therefore learn to accept our burdens and see in them the promise of growth and fulfillment.

Critics often talk about the theme of redemptive suffering in Malamud's works. This terminology can be misleading, since it has the effect of suggesting a specifically Christian view of salvation that is present but peripheral in Malamud's fiction. It should be emphasized that his vision has its roots in the Old Testament, while the Christian idea of salvation derives from the New Testament. This point is fundamental to an understanding of Malamud's work. In his fiction, he unrelentingly asks what might be called Old Testament questions: Why do good men suffer while evil men frequently prosper? Why should we be good, when there is no reward for goodness? How can we have faith when there are no signs to confirm our faith? Why should we love, if our love is met only with scorn? Malamud's perspective on these age-old questions is heavily influenced by the somewhat fatalistic Old Testament story of Job, a pious man who suffers unjustly without ever understanding why. He knows only that it is God's will that he suffer. To the man who suffers without any apparent reason, God's ways seem harsh and unjust, but Job does not attempt to rationalize this injustice; rather, he acknowledges this as part of the mystery of life. It is simply the way of the world; the sun shines as brightly on the wicked as it does on the good and just.

The suffering of Morris Bober and Yakov Bok is not redemptive in the Christian sense. For them as Jews, the concepts of heaven and hell do not offer a solution to the dilemma of existence. They have no sense of individual salvation; they do not believe that their suffering in this life will be rewarded in the next. Malamud's view is rather that goodness is its own reward while evil inflicts its own punishment. This is why love and compassion—and schlemiel heroes—are so important in Malamud's fiction. No suffering can be redeemed by any act of God or the State. The only "solution" possible for the problem of evil is for people to respect and nourish each other now, during this life. And only a schlemiel would choose the intangible spiritual rewards of goodness over the material benefits of narrow self-interest. Thus, Malamud's association of suffering with Jewishness is not merely sentimental. It also contains a hardheaded realism.

Suffering, however, does not interest Malamud for its own sake. It is, rather, a corollary to his real concern, one that can easily be missed: what he primarily wishes to explore and express is the sheer terror of existence in the twentieth century. The horrors of Verdun, the Great Depression, Dresden, Auschwitz, Hiroshima, Vietnam—the world's "uncertain balance of terror," as President Kennedy expressed it in his inaugural address—these have their counterparts in Malamud's fiction. Backdrops of Depression hardship, symbolic landscapes of garbage-filled back alleys and collapsing buildings, McCarthyism, and anti-Semitic injustice on a massive scale—these settings cast their dark shadows over all of Malamud's fictional world, serving as constant reminders that we are faced with malevolent forces so powerful that they threaten our very existence as thinking, feeling, moral beings. Thus it was understandable that Malamud should choose the Jews as symbols of suffering, for they have lived through the Holocaust, the most horrifying campaign of terror in human history. In Malamud's works the Jew becomes an isolated loner who represents the hopes, fears, and possibilities of twentieth-century humanity.

Suffering in Malamud's fiction, then, has two aspects, one somewhat sentimental, the other more fatalistic, full of terror. To the extent that Malamud's writing romanticizes suffering, it is dangerous and destructive. Morris Bober and Frank Alpine are masterful creations, but for people actually to submit to similar suffering in their own lives, acting on the belief that their suffering will somehow redeem them, would be fruitless and masochistic. Similarly, Yakov Bok becomes a powerful example of a human being's ability to grow spiritually in the face of injustice, but the hard fact is that most poor people unjustly imprisoned—even "political prisoners"—simply waste away without ever being allowed to serve the cause of justice, no matter how noble their suffering might be. But Malamud surely never intended anyone to take his metaphoric treatment of suffering literally, as a life model. Nonetheless, the literal implication is there. For the most part, however, the hardheaded attitude toward suffering prevails in Malamud's fiction. In this respect his writing provides a sort of strategy for living with the terror of modern life on an everyday basis. This is the source of both the power and the importance of his fiction. *The Assistant* and *The Fixer* are Malamud's strongest novels largely because they capture most effectively our existential sense of terror in the modern world.

Another source of power in Malamud's writing lies in the special relationship he creates between pairs of characters. One often thinks of his characters as coming in sets—Frank Alpine and Morris Bober, Harry Lesser and Willie Spearmint, Fidelman and Susskind, Finkle and Salzman, Gruber and Kessler, Mendel and Ginzburg, Harry Cohen and "Jewbird" Schwartz, Manischevitz and (Angel) Levine, Albert Gans and Rabbi Jonas Lifschitz. In general, one of three different kinds of relationship binds each pair together.

The first involves a character near the protagonist who represents his conscience and who, ultimately, challenges his humanity. The prototype is Susskind in **"Last Mohican."** Trying mightily to escape Susskind's "harassment," Fidelman simply cannot avoid the inevitable confrontation, for Susskind echoes a lost part of Fidelman, of his heritage and his conscience. He is forced, through Susskind's uncanny ability to track him down, to take inventory of his soul and to come to terms with himself. In this way Malamud uses Susskind and other symbolic conscience figures such as Morris Bober, Shmuel, and "Jewbird" Schwartz to dramatize the respective protagonist's spiritual conflict.

The relentless pursuit of one character by another in Malamud's fiction operates as a symbolic double image, representing two contradictory tendencies in each of us, the urge to flee and the determination to fight. The secret escapist urge to remain uninvolved with life competes with the call (often prompted by guilt) to a conscious and willed acceptance of responsibility.

The second kind of relationship that binds pairs of characters together, sometimes overlapping with the first, depends on a more destructive psychological process; namely, symbiotic victimization—the intense, often irrational relationship of two people who are bound together by a strange mixture of hate and compassion, intolerance and understanding, guilt and forgiveness, each needing the other in some way to achieve completeness.

The prototype for these symbiotic pairs appears in the early story, **"The Death of Me,"** which was first published in 1951 and later collected in *Idiots First.* Marcus, a tailor, has two assistants who both are fond of Marcus but despise each other for apparently complex reasons that Marcus cannot fully understand. Their feuding eventually erupts into a serious fight, in which the combatants injure each other with makeshift weapons. But they are not the only ones to suffer. Marcus becomes so upset by the atmosphere of dissension that he has a heart attack and dies. Malamud emphasizes the effects of the mutual hatred rather than probing deeply into its causes. **"The Death of Me"** portrays the same kind of larger moral consequence Malamud emphasizes in *The Tenants,* where Levenspiel and Irene—indeed, all of us—suffer from Harry and Willie's mutual self-destruction. The theme of symbiotic victimization describes the failure of men to nourish and sustain each other in the face of the terror of existence. In **"The Mourners,"** for example, the ironic ending turns on the reader's awareness that Gruber and Kessler remain isolated from each other in spite of their individual flashes of self-awareness.

The third kind of relationship draws its power from the primacy of family relationships; its impulse lies in the search for a father. Many of Malamud's protagonists are orphans (actual or symbolic), unconsciously searching for the male parent they lost or never had. Frank Alpine, Sy Levin, Yakov Bok, and Arthur Fidelman all receive nourishment and a degree of wisdom or compassion by accepting a surrogate father. Roy Hobbs, on the other hand, rejects the fatherly influence of Pop Fisher and suffers a moral defeat in so doing.

Although many cultures have legends and myths about orphans in search of fathers, Malamud's use of the theme, like his attitude toward suffering, has its roots firmly embedded in the Old Testament. Central to an understanding of the Old Testament as a Jewish epic history is the idea of the Jews as God's Chosen People. The patriarchal monotheism of the Jews derives from the conception of God as a stern father who made a covenant with the Hebrews to be their God if they would agree to worship him alone and to obey his commandments. This covenant was first entered into by the patriarch Abraham and later renewed by his heirs, Isaac and Jacob. However, being chosen was a mixed blessing, for failure to live up to God's high ethical standards brought frequent punishment and suffering to the Hebrews. As a result, the Jews, historically, developed a very special relationship with their God; bitterness and even hatred resided alongside praise and thankfulness. Strangely, to modern theism, the relationship was reciprocal: God needed the Jews almost as much as they needed him, because, according to Jewish folklore, although he had previously approached many other tribes with the offer of the holy contract, none but the Jews would accept his commandments.

In Malamud's writing, the archetypal theme of the search for a father has a spiritual dimension. Its prototype is the ancient Hebrews' relationship with their God. This special biblical influence is most explicitly revealed in **"Angel Levine,"** where Manischevitz must set aside his prejudices and be able to believe in Levine before the angel can perform a miracle. In accepting a spiritual father, Frank Alpine, Sy Levin, Yakov Bok, and Arthur Fidelman reenact Abraham's entering into a sacred covenant, which gives their lives an ethical meaning and provides them with a new sense of identity.

In his fiction Malamud considers the moral evolution of his characters. They grow in ethical depth through various kinds of suffering, intellectual as well as physical. Using such techniques as mirror images, symbiotic pairs of characters, and the double vision of Jewish humor, Malamud often succeeds in showing us the human soul, stripped bare of romantic dreams, pretense, and materialistic aspirations, in conflict with its own divided nature. It is no exaggeration to say that spiritual conflict dwells at the center of Malamud's moral universe. Freedom can be achieved, but only through moral awareness, which, paradoxically, binds a person to others in a web of commitments.

Each of the protagonists of Malamud's novels faces a trial of conscience or a spiritual test and triumphs only by accepting fatherly spiritual guidance or by listening to his own troubled conscience, an acceptance that must be accompanied by an expression of mercy, love, charity, or forgiveness. The three who pass the test—Frank Alpine, Sy Levin, and Yakov Bok—first find themselves in a desperate situation, try to escape, seek for justification, and reassure themselves about redemption. Their final experience, however, is purification, as they realize that justification for their actions will not come from God or any other external source—only from inside themselves. Weighed down by self-doubts, internal conflicts, and the corrupting temptation to seek material success, Alpine, Levin, and Bok each nonetheless wins a moral victory.

The implied lesson is, quite simply, that people can change. Their circumstances may remain the same but spiritually they transcend their surroundings. This recurring theme in Malamud's writing is simple but efficacious. For example, as a corollary Malamud implies that life is relative. A store can become a prison for one man and a means of deliverance for another. Things, in and of themselves, are neither good nor bad; they are what we make of them. In the world of Malamud's fiction compassion, love, and understanding—the humane values—rather than physical circumstances give meaning to one's life. It is a world that blends hope with despair, pain with possibility, and suffering with moral growth. Out of the everyday defeats and indignities of ordinary people, Malamud creates beautiful parables that capture the joy as well as the pain of life; he expresses the dignity of the human spirit searching for freedom and moral growth in the face of hardship, injustice, and the existential anguish of life in our time. (pp. 135-46)

Sheldon J. Hershinow, in his *Bernard Malamud,* Frederick Ungar Publishing Co., 1980, 165 p.

Malamud on his fiction:

I'm an American, I'm a Jew, and I write for all men. A novelist has to or he's built himself a cage. I write about Jews, when I write about Jews, because they set my imagination going. I know something about their history, the quality of their experience and belief, and of their literature, though not as much as I would like. Like many writers I'm influenced especially by the Bible, both Testaments. I respond in particular to the East European immigrants of my father's and mother's generation; many of them were Jews of the Pale as described by the classic Yiddish writers. And of course I've been deeply moved by the Jews of the concentration camps, and the refugees wandering from nowhere to nowhere. I'm concerned about Israel. Nevertheless, Jews like Rabbis Kahane and Korrf set my teeth on edge. Sometimes I make characters Jewish because I think I will understand them better as people, not because I am out to prove anything. That's a qualification. Still another is that I know that, as a writer, I've been influenced by Hawthorne, James, Mark Twain, Hemingway, more than I have been by Sholem Aleichem and I.L. Peretz, whom I read with pleasure. Of course I admire and have been moved by other writers, Dostoyevsky and Chekhov, for instance, but the point I'm making is that I was born in America and respond, in American life, to more than Jewish experience. I wrote for those who read.

Malamud, in a 1974 interview published in *Paris Review*, Spring, 1975.

ROBERT ALTER

(essay date 1983)

[Alter is an American critic and educator who specializes in modern Jewish writing. In the following excerpt, he discusses the thematic and structural aspects of Malamud's *The Stories of Bernard Malamud*, asserting that "[Malamud's] real gift is for the short story."]

[None of Bernard Malamud's] longer fictions has the absolute rightness of tone and invention of his best short stories [collected in *The Stories of Bernard Malamud*].

His real gift is for the short story, for the spare, rigorous etching of solitary figures caught in the stress of adversity. When Malamud translates such figures into the novel, whose ampler dimensions lead us to expect development, he has difficulty in making his personages go anywhere except deeper into disaster. The plots of his novels tend to devolve into extended fantasies—sometimes lurid, sometimes just depressing—of mutilation and interment. By contrast, his stronger stories exhibit exquisite artistic tact, a remarkable intuition for saying a great deal with the most minimal narrative gestures, and a delicacy of feeling about the characters that cannot be reduced to any simple technique. (p. 1)

[The typical protagonist]—the isolate pensioner as everyman—is more often than not a Yiddish-speaking immigrant Jew who seems to have known little in his life but hard work and hard times. He is typically beset with painful and humiliating ailments—hernia, bad back, weak heart, arthritis, a veritable cornucopia of the physical ills flesh is heir to. He is also typically on the brink, or below it, of poverty, counting pennies in the back of his rundown grocery store or in his dingy rented room, wondering where next month's rent will come from, perhaps dreaming sometimes of a sufficiency he knows he will never enjoy. (Malamud's vision is pre-eminently that of a writer whose formative years were spent in the Great Depression.) Finally, the characteristic Malamud protagonist often proves to be desperate for love. In several instances, it is a father whose love for a rebellious child has soured into a resentment bordering on hatred. In other stories, it is the pathetic love or mere erotic longing of an older man for a younger woman which will get him nothing but mockery and frustration.

As my composite portrait of the Malamudian hero may suggest, this is bleak and narrow stuff for the making of a fictional world, but in his stories Malamud has often been able to transform this material into the most arresting images of the human predicament. There is no single formula that will explain how this transformation takes place, but I think it has a good deal to do with the laconic lyricism with which his prose evokes loneliness and abandonment and poverty. For such subjects, too little stylistic elaboration would produce mere flatness, too much, insistent pathos or masochistic self-indulgence. But in his best stories Malamud works in a perfect middle register that elicits compassion through its very terseness. . . .

Rereading these stories, I am surprised to find that the tautness of the prose owes something to a writer radically removed from Malamud in sensibility and values—Ernest Hemingway. In his fondness for sequences of short sentences and monosyllabic words, the shifting of much of the emotional burden to strategically chosen physical objects rendered with flatly descriptive terms . . . , Malamud shows at least an affinity with the writing in perfect Hemingway achievements like "A Clean, Well-Lighted Place" and "Old Man at the Bridge." The difference, of course, is that Malamud does not hesitate to point directly to Davidov's limp and his weariness, or to Rosen's "wasted" appearance and "despairing" eyes, though he is prudent in simply stating these attributes of adversity and then allowing Rosen's dreadful room to speak for itself. Also unlike Hemingway is the interpolation of a bit of interior monologue. . . . (p. 35)

Perhaps one of Malamud's difficulties as a novelist has been that anxiety deployed over 300 or more pages begins to rasp, the anxious characters often driving themselves in the end to some orgy of self-immolation. In the short stories, however, where the writer can catch a revelatory moment of distress that intimates a lifetime, Malamud has been able to become the bard of anxiety, making the more successfully realized of his protagonists large and resonant in their smallness and their plaintive groans, allowing us as readers to see the fears and uncertainties of our lives figured, however grotesquely, in theirs.

The actual fictional rendering of these eternal flounderers is often a good deal less bleak than any summary of their predicament might lead one to suppose. In this regard, what I have said about the "Hemingwayesque" aspect of the style is a little misleading; though the prose is usually not very metaphorical and certainly avoids pyrotechnic effects, there are little eruptions of figurative perception that are funny or mysterious or magical, tokens of an imagination outside the grimy walls of the trap in which the protagonists are typically caught. . . .

[In] the most memorable of Malamud's stories there are often significant glimpses of a shimmering horizon of fantasy beyond the grim scenes of impoverishment and loneliness in the foreground. The fantasy can enter through an image, a dream, a hallucination, or occasionally through the configuration of the whole story, as in **"The First Seven Years"**; for all its realistic depiction of immigrant existence, it is a touching fairy tale of an apprentice winning the master's daughter, with an echo of the Bible (Jacob working seven years for Rachel) and perhaps a reminiscence of I. B. Singer. . . .

Of all these stories, it can be said that only Bernard Malamud could have written them. They are neither imitative nor imitable. Not every story in the selection is equally strong, and there are four or five pieces that strike me as flat or even abortive. But this volume includes stories like **"The First Seven Years," "The Magic Barrel," "The Last Mohican," "Idiots First"** and **"Angel Levine,"** which I think will be read as long as anyone continues to care about American fiction written in the 20th century. (p. 36)

Robert Alter, "Ordinary Anguish," in *The New York Times Book Review,* October 16, 1983, pp. 1, 35-6.

RICHARD GILMAN
(essay date 1986)

[An American critic and nonfiction writer, Gilman has published books on the American theater and has served as literary editor for such journals as *Commonweal* and *Partisan Review.* In the following excerpt, he analyzes Malamud's writings, particularly for their "humanistic values," and praises the author for his evocative short stories.]

Malamud was known for having had "compassion," "moral wisdom," a concern for the "ordinary man." True, but was that what made him a good writer? . . .

If anything, what we might call the humanistic values of his writing gave him an air of being a little out of date—earnest, kindly, thoughtful. His gaze was on the perennial, instead of conjuring with our confusions and chaos and inventing brilliantly in order to confront and combat them. He was a storyteller in an era when most of our best writers have been suspicious of straightforward narrative. Nobody thinks of him as an innovator, unless being among the first to bring the rhythms and intonations of Jewish, or Yiddish, speech to formal prose counts as innovation.

He himself contributed to the image of a somewhat old-fashioned, or unfashionable, champion of the spirit, a humanist in a literary era in which humanism is almost anomalous. Again and again he used the word "human" in the occasional interviews and speeches he gave: "My work . . . is an idea of dedication to the human. . . . If you don't respect man, you cannot respect my work. I'm in defense of the human." And he spoke of art as "sanctifying human life and freedom."

So what's to object, as he might have put it? Those lofty, sonorous phrases, more mottoes than anything else, left me uncomfortable when they came from him and leave me so when they come from others. It isn't enough to speak of defending the human or respecting man, or rather it sounds a bit self-serving and even pompous. Did he think it was what was expected of him? To shift the burden to us, isn't it naive to say that he "touched our hearts"? Bad fiction, melodramas, kitsch touch our hearts too, bring tears more reliably, certainly in greater floods, than does good writing.

It seems to me that Malamud was usually at his weakest when he sought or fell into too direct a way to our emotions, when he was most self-consciously "humane." I think of stories like **"Black Is My Favorite Color," "The Lady of the Lake,"** and **"The Loan,"** each brought down by predictable sentiment, and even more of novels such as *The Fixer,* at once heavy, pseudo-lyrical, and tendentious; *The Tenants,* where social painfulness isn't fully transmuted into imaginative truth; and *God's Grace,* embarrassingly cute in a mode of fantasy—jocose, biblically flavored science fiction—to which he wasn't suited.

To what, then, was he suited? to begin with, there is that swift rooting of so many of his protagonists in an occupation or a past. His opening words located his characters: "S. Levin, formerly a drunkard"; "Davidov, the census-taker"; "Manischevitz, a tailor"; "Fidelman, a self-confessed failure as a painter"; "Kessler, formerly an egg-candler." Having so placed them, relieved of the necessity to develop them, yet having granted them a specificity that kept them from being parabolic, he moved them quickly into position to experience their fates. These are destinies of self-recognition—ironic, painful, lugubrious, or threnodic—and they are, when all is working well, revelatory of the morally or psychically unknown, or not yet known. And along the way, there are the pleasures of the text, the little fates of language: . . .

From **"The Magic Barrel"**: "Life, despite their frantic yoo-hooings, had passed them by."

From **"The Girl of My Dreams"**: " . . . he pitied her, her daughter, the world. Who not?"

From **"The Death of Me"**: "His heart, like a fragile pitcher, toppled from the shelf and bump bumped down the stairs, cracking at the bottom." (p. 40)

From *Dubin's Lives:* "On the road a jogger trotted toward him, a man with a blue band around his head. He slowed down as Dubin halted. 'What are you running for?' the biographer asked him. 'All I can't stand to do. What about you?' 'Broken heart, I think.' 'Ah, too bad about that.' They trotted in opposing directions."

From somewhere: "exaltation went where exaltation goes."

He was neither a realist nor a fantasist. He was both. I don't mean he alternated between reality and fantasy, but that at his best the line between the two was obliterated. Observation gave way to imagining. Without strain, experience flowed into dream. In some stories characters and properties literally move up into the air, as in Chagall, with whose paintings these tales have been justly compared. "He heard an odd noise, as though of a whirring of wings, and when he strained for a wider view, could have sworn he saw a dark figure borne aloft on a pair of magnificent black wings" (**"Angel Levine"**). "He pictured, in her, his own redemption. Violins and lit candles revolved in the sky" (**"The Magic Barrel"**). Even a story like **"The Jewbird"** (to my mind perhaps his finest), a piece that appears all whimsy and allegorical effort, is anchored in pebbly actuality, an actuality into which the bird flies, scattering

meanings as he does feathers, an agent of our own self-knowledge.

In a culture where quantity is god it may seem demeaning to say that Bernard Malamud was a better short-story writer than novelist. Yet a case can be made that many great or good writers of fiction in English have been better makers of stories than of novels: Hawthorne, to go way back, Lawrence, Hemingway, Fitzgerald, Cheever, Flannery O'Connor. She wrote in a letter of 1958 about a short-story writer "who is better than any one of them, including myself. Go to the library [for] a book called *The Magic Barrel* by Bernard Malamud." (He was immensely pleased, for he greatly esteemed her.)

To be sure, the novels have their pleasures, but even in the best of them his predilection for the shorter form often shows itself, straining against what novels are supposed to be. Books as good as *The Assistant* and *Dubin's Lives* are, I think, more notable in some ways for their nearly self-contained sequences than for their architectonics and narrative continuity. He may have called *Pictures of Fidelman* an "Exhibition" because he saw that it would otherwise be taken for a novel (it was by most anyway) and faulted for its lack of development. It wasn't easy for him to follow a fiction through a long, complicated course to its end. His wish for those qualities of epiphany, of revelation and decisive verbal triumph, kept breaking through.

What makes his place in literature and our memories secure isn't his themes or subjects. It isn't his nobility of purpose, his compassion or moral understanding, in short, his humanism. Or rather it's not those qualities in themselves, as detached and detachable essences. One wants to say to the sentimental admirers of his fiction (as well as to those erstwhile admirers who found him growing "cold" in his later work) that imaginative writing isn't the exemplification of preexisting values and virtues. It is their discovery, against all odds, in the shocks and surprises of the unfolding tale. The imagination teaches us newly. It doesn't instruct us in what we already know, and it certainly doesn't grant us our comfortable, "humane" wishes.

"It's not easy to be moral," thinks Cronin, the protagonist of **"A Choice of Profession."** It's at least as difficult to shed moral light in fiction, where the recalcitrance of words, their pressure toward the familiar—and hence the unenlightening—is constant and unyielding.

"Creativity," Arthur Koestler wrote, "is the defeat of habit by originality." Habit was for Bernard Malamud, as for all true writers, the enemy from which you wrest the victories you can, replacing, through a series of miracles, the banalities or weariness of language with its grace. (pp. 40-1)

Richard Gilman, "Malamud's Grace," in *The New Republic,* Vol. 194, No. 19, May 12, 1986, pp. 40-1.

SOURCES FOR FURTHER STUDY

Astro, Richard and Benson, Jackson J., eds. *The Fiction of Bernard Malamud.* Corvallis: Oregon State University Press, 1977, 190 p.

> Collection of addresses, essays, and lectures presented at a Malamud symposium.

Cohen, Sandy. *Bernard Malamud and the Trial by Love.* Amsterdam: Rodopi, 1974, 132 p.

> Interpretive study of Malamud's canon.

Field, Leslie A., and Field, Joyce W., eds. *Bernard Malamud and the Critics.* New York: New York University Press, 1970, 353 p.

> Critical study that addresses such topics as the Jewish literary tradition and Malamud's use of myth and folklore. Includes essays by such critics as Samuel Irving Bellman, Peter L. Hayes, and Ben Siegal.

————. *Bernard Malamud: A Collection of Critical Essays.* Englewood Cliffs, N. J.: Prentice-Hall, 1975, 179 p.

> Collection of essays by such critics as Sam Bluefarb, Cynthia Ozick, and William Freedman. Topics include Malamud's use of irony, his depiction of the artist in *Pictures of Fidelman,* and critical response to *The Fixer.*

Richman, Sidney. *Bernard Malamud.* New York: Twayne, 1966, 160 p.

> Comprehensive analysis of Malamud's works.

Stern, Daniel. "The Art of Fiction LII." *Paris Review* 16, No. 61 (Spring 1975): 40-64.

> Interview in which Malamud discusses his childhood, his experiences as a creative writing teacher, his writing technique, and his reaction to literary criticism.

Thomas Mann

1875-1955

German novelist, short story writer, essayist, and critic.

INTRODUCTION

Mann, winner of the 1929 Nobel Prize in literature, is one of the foremost German novelists of the twentieth century. In his works, he presents a synthesis of aesthetic, philosophical, and social concerns, while combining elements of literary Realism and Symbolism with an ironic sensibility. Though his fiction typically reveals a somber and cerebral fascination with death and decay, most critics agree that beneath this complex surface Mann expresses a deep, often humorous sympathy for humanity and a desire to resolve what he sees as the dualities of life. Critics have frequently observed a thematic unity in Mann's work and often refer to his use of leitmotiv in this regard. His many recurring themes include the isolation of the artist in society, the relation of life and art, the nature of time, and the seduction of the individual by disease and death. Mann's accomplishment, admirers suggest, was to use fiction to conduct a lifelong exploration of philosophical issues, ranging from the role of a creative individual in society to the nature of Western culture. He wrote at a time when Europe was experiencing massive and shocking changes: new technology challenged traditional values and ways of life; mass social movements gained unprecedented importance; and Germany erupted with the horrors of Nazism. Reflecting in his work the doubts and fears of his era, Mann held the attention of millions of readers throughout the world.

Born in Lübeck, Germany, Mann was the son of a successful grain merchant. His mother, an accomplished musician, was born and raised in Brazil, and his older brother, Heinrich, was a noted writer. Mann's bourgeois background and the contrasting natures of his parents—his father was austere, his mother passionate—figured prominently in much of his fiction. Mann's first story, "Gefallen" (1894), was published in the prestigious journal *Die Gesellschaft* when he was nineteen years old. While this story displayed a marked Romantic influence, Mann abandoned the tenets of Romanticism in his later works and developed an ironic sensibility that became the signature of his art. Although health problems prevented him from serving in World War I, Mann remained involved in the conflict through his nationalistic political essays. Following the war he cultivated interests in the writings of Johann Wolfgang von Goethe, Sigmund Freud, Friedrich Nietzsche, and Arthur Schopenhauer, and published his novel *Der Zauberberg* (1924; *The Magic Mountain*), for which he was awarded the Nobel Prize in Literature in 1929. Despite his nationalism during World War I, Mann fervently opposed the growth of national socialism and fascism in the 1930s. In 1933, he left Germany and went into self-imposed exile, eventually settling in the United States. In 1952, Mann left the United States and migrated to Switzerland where he spent the remaining years of his life.

Commentators suggest that Mann's diverse influences—from dutiful burghers to the flamboyant Nietzsche—do not form a unified philosophy, or even a succession of philosophies. For many of Mann's admirers, his ability to pursue several different modes of thought at once is key to his appeal. As Henry Hatfield explained: "Mann's gift—or curse—of seeing both sides of almost everything and everyone was perhaps his most characteristic talent. It often made him irritating and unsatisfactory as a thinker, and particularly as a political essayist. But in the realm of fiction this 'dual perspective' on man gave his vision a stereoptic quality, and his characters a third dimension. His people are good *and* evil, perceptive *and* blind; they are extraordinarily real. . . . their very inconsistencies keep them alive and fascinating." Mann's double vision extends to his narrative style, as well, which is well known for its irony. His narrators tend to remain aloof; they undercut characters with bemused skepticism.

Mann's first major novel, *Buddenbrooks* (1901), about his German merchant ancestors, whom he thinly disguised as the Buddenbrook family, had few precedents in German literature. It was patterned on the naturalistic novels of Western Europe and Scandinavia, which used lavish detail to create the portrait of an individual, a family, or a society. Commentators suggest that *Buddenbrooks,* for all its meticulous realism, is based on a philosophical issue: can successive generations of a family become so emotionally sensitive, so preoccupied with personal concerns, that they become unable to survive in life? In Mann's other early fiction, typically novellas and short stories, he applied such a question to his own situation as a fledgling writer, showing the conflict between life and art. The tone of these stories is often cold and pessimistic: as Hatfield observed, " 'life' and its healthy representatives are dull or brutal or both; but the antagonists to 'life,' the isolated and introspective protagonists, are sick, psychologically maladjusted, and frequently grotesque."

In such works as "Tonio Kroeger" (1903), and *Der Tod in Venedig* (1912; *Death in Venice*), Mann made an explicit effort to resolve the controversy between art and life. Son of a North German merchant with a foreign-born wife, Tonio Kroeger invites comparison to Mann, his Italian-German name underscoring his divided sympathies. Kroeger finds a sense of purpose by accepting his ambiguous position in society: "It is precisely [Kroeger's] frustrated love for the Nordic-normal-bourgeois which gives him the inner tension that makes him creative," wrote Hatfield. "He will stand between [the art world and the middle class], a sympathetic if ironic mediator."

Death in Venice combines psychological realism and mythological symbolism to create a multidimensional story that explores the moral transformation undergone by the artist in quest of perfect beauty. The novella depicts the decline and ultimate collapse of Mann's artist-hero Gustave von Aschenbach, a renowned German author who, after years of living a morally and artistically ascetic life, surrenders to the sensual side of his nature during a sojourn in Venice. There, the sultry Venetian setting incites Aschenbach's homoerotic passion for Tadzio, a beautiful, godlike youth. As Aschenbach succumbs to long-repressed spiritual and physical desires, he loses control of his will, and his resulting degradation leads to his death. *Death in Venice* has prompted a vast array of interpretations. Some critics, including D. H. Lawrence, have suggested that the work is based on Mann's own homosexual fantasies. T. E. Apter, noting the story's focus on "death, passion and the debilitating effects of beauty," averred that Mann was repudiating the emotional excess he found in Richard Wagner's compositions. Martin Swales pointed out that Aschenbach's widespread popularity as a writer makes him "the spokesman of a generation"; thus Aschenbach's swing between emotional extremes—from strident repression to unthinking frenzy—seems an ominous diagnosis of European society on the eve of World War I. Europe, relatively peaceful and productive for a century, greeted the war in 1914 with what Swales calls "waves of collective enthusiasm."

Mann's 1924 novel *The Magic Mountain,* is considered a landmark of world literature, depicting the conflicting cultural and political trends that vexed all Europe in the opening decades of the twentieth century. Set in the years preceding World War I, *The Magic Mountain* takes place on a Swiss mountaintop in a tuberculosis sanatorium. Mann had visited such a place in 1912, when his wife was recovering from the disease. Mann's fictional sanatorium serves as a symbolic gathering place for the nations of Europe, for its patients include wealthy patrons from throughout the continent. As guests undergo the prescribed "rest cure," they lose their sense of the passing of time, for they are removed from the struggles of ordinary existence and turn to pastimes that range from games to endless philosophical discussions. As biographer Nigel Hamilton wrote, *"The Magic Mountain* restored [Mann] to his rightful standing: the master novelist of his age." Mann, wrote Joseph Wood Krutch, had "[told] the whole story of the modern mind," creating a unique work about the interaction between ideas and individual character. Commentators have reiterated such views for decades. *The Magic Mountain* "is Thomas Mann's most complex creation," wrote T. J. Reed, "the summa of his life, thought, and technical achievement to the age of fifty." Reed called the work "spiritual autobiography . . . intricate allegory . . . historical novel, an analysis of Mann and a declaration of principle for practical humanism."

To portray Germany's descent into evil, Mann revived the old German legend of Faust, a learned man who sold his soul to the devil in exchange for knowledge and supernatural power. Titling his work *Doktor Faustus* (1947, *Doctor Faustus*), Mann made his lead character Adrian Leverkuehn, a fictional German composer who lives from 1885 to 1940. Adrian's life particularly resembles that of Nietzsche, whose works Nazi propagandists falsely claimed as precursors of their own ideas about a master Germanic race. As with Nietzsche, Adrian suddenly collapses in insanity, and he spends the last ten years of his life being tended by his mother.

Mann spoke of *Doctor Faustus* as one of the most important and daring works of his career, calling it his "wildest" novel. But even commentators who respected the author's effort often found the book flawed. Mann's characteristic weaknesses—a love of length and complexity, a preoccupation with philoso-

phy—seemed, for many commentators, to have defeated his intention. "Among [Mann's] longer works," wrote Hatfield, *The Magic Mountain* "is formally more successful, and conveys a far greater sense of intellectual excitement," but *Doctor Faustus* is still much more than "an ambitious failure." Hatfield called the work an "end product"—a writer's final summation of his artistic vision. As with the "vast late works" of other authors, Hatfield averred, the novel is "only partially successful" but "contain[s] an enormous variety of riches."

After Mann died in 1955, critics sometimes recalled him as a friend of democracy and humanism—ignoring, perhaps, the complex and ambiguous nature of his work. "I once saw Thomas Mann plain," declared Alfred Kazin, contending that Mann used a "conservative social self " to mask "a mind so complex that his real opinions were always elusive." R. J. Hollingdale depicted Mann in Nietzschean terms, as the child of a Western civilization that had become unable to believe in God or anything else. In a world without values, Mann's novels were long because there was, in the critic's words, "no principle of selection." Mann preached no ideology because none was credible; irony was his "self-defence against the meaningless." For a world that *"really has no values,"* Hollingdale observed, Mann's "fictional world is a *true* mirror." He summarized Mann with a proverb: "As the mirror replied to the monster: 'There is nothing wrong with me, it is *you* who are distorted.' "

(For further information about Mann's life and works, see *Contemporary Authors*, Vols. 104, 128; *Dictionary of Literary Biography*, Vol. 66: *German Fiction Writers, 1885-1913*; *Major Twentieth-Century Writers*; *Short Story Criticism*, Vol. 5; and *Twentieth-Century Literary Criticism*, Vols. 2, 8, 14, 21, 35.)

CRITICAL COMMENTARY

ROBERT MORSS LOVETT

(essay date 1931)

[Lovett was an American literary critic, educator, and statesman. In the following excerpt, he praises various elements of Mann's artistry in *Buddenbrooks*, particularly the author's ability to blend realism and symbolism and his skillful use of irony.]

Buddenbrooks itself covers little more than fifty years,

but it brings into prominence four generations of the family whose name supplies its title. It focuses particular attention on the third of these four generations: Tom, Tony, and Christian, of whom Tom is the most important since in him the story of the Buddenbrooks is recapitulated. But Tom is a mere episode in that larger narrative which concerns the gradual dissolution of the family and the dissipation of the wealth acquired by its progenitors.

Principal Works

Buddenbrooks: Verfall einer Familie (novel) 1901
  [Buddenbrooks: The Decline of a Family, 1924]
Der Tod in Venedig (novella) 1912
  [Death in Venice, 1928]
Der Zauberberg (novel) 1924
  [The Magic Mountain, 1927]
Mario und die Zauberer: Ein Tragisches Reiseerlebnis
  (novella) 1930
  [Mario and the Magician, 1930]
Die Geschichten Jaakobs (novel) 1933
  [Joseph and His Brothers, 1934]
Der junge Joseph (novel) 1934
  [Young Joseph: Joseph and His Brothers II, 1935]
Joseph in Aegypten (novel) 1936
  [Joseph in Egypt: Joseph and His Brothers III, 1938]
Stories of Three Decades (short fiction) 1936
Lotte in Weimer (novel) 1939
  [The Beloved Returns, 1940]
Joseph der Ernaehrer (novel) 1943
  [Joseph the Provider: Joseph and His Brothers IV,
  1944]
Doktor Faustus: Das Leben des deutschen Tonsetzers
  Adrian Leverkuehn, erzaehlt von einem Freunde
  (novel) 1947
  [Doctor Faustus: The Life of the German Composer
  Adrian Leverkuehn as Told by a Friend, 1948]
Bekenntnisse des Hochstaplers Felix Krull: Der Me-
  moiren erster Teil (novel) 1954
  [Confessions of Felix Krull, Confidence Man: The
  Early Years, 1955]

To describe a novel as a story of decay is to suggest an emphasis on the morbid and unpleasant which is quite apart from the actual tone of Mann's book. The tragedy of dissolution is foreshadowed even in the heyday of Buddenbrook prosperity, but the process is effected in a manner which brings out the beauty inherent in decay, and reminds one that the term decadence implies an increase in refinement and sensibility as well as a decrease in vitality. The very style, even in translation, carries that suggestion of beauty in death which is called elegiac. It is a suggestion always, for in this, his first novel of importance, published in 1901, Thomas Mann established himself as a craftsman who accomplished his effects by means so subtle as to seem only a happy accident. He also established himself as perhaps the foremost contemporary writer of German prose, a position recognized by the award of the Nobel Prize in 1929.

A novel covering so many years and dealing with so many characters demands an unusually convincing background. This Mann has supplied in terms of the physical, the social, and the historical. Most of the action takes place in the little Hanseatic city of Lübeck, and before the book is finished the reader is comfortably familiar with its geography. One becomes acquainted with its climate as with its topography—its rain, its snow, its mist, the occasional burst of sun and heat, are an integrated part of the lives and deaths of the people who move through its pages. These include not only Buddenbrooks, but also the numerous families who compose the social stratification of Lübeck: the aristocratic Krögers, with whom the Buddenbrooks are intermarried, the upstart Hagenstroms and Köppens who are *nouveaux riches* and so inferior to the Langhals and Möllendorpfs. All this human background is unobtrusive, but it supplies that social third dimension which adds solidity to *Vanity Fair,* and even more strikingly to Proust's *A La Recherche du Temps Perdu.* The same unobtrusive presence of detail achieves the same sense of solidity with regard to the routine of daily life. One knows how the family mansion is furnished, what the characters wear, what they eat. This matter of menus is apt to be prominent in genealogical novels, since the dinner table is a natural gathering place of the family. The *Forsyte Saga* includes a surprising number of meals; and a comparison of the two novels would bear out the statement that perhaps no other typical scene is so helpful in suggesting the atmosphere and *mores* of a group.

The historical events which occur during the course of *Buddenbrooks* creep in as casually but as correctly as the gradual changes in fashion and manners. The Napoleonic epoch is still a lively memory to old Consul Buddenbrook and his contemporaries. The Revolution of '48 furnishes to his son an opportunity for displaying his solid bourgeois courage. To Tony it vouchsafes the slogans of liberalism which she employs long after the event is as remote as the lover who preached them is to her. The Austro-Prussian War brings to Lübeck the benefits of having sided with the winner, but strikes at the Buddenbrooks through their financial interests in Frankfort. The Danish and Franco-German conflicts, however, reach the town chiefly as an echo of distant marching and a painless flare of patriotism. War is thus a significant element in the background of the century.

Against this firm, though lightly indicated background, the more immediate drama of the Buddenbrooks is enacted. The structure of the novel depends on a series of family scenes, beginning with the joyous housewarming at the mansion on Mengstrasse—"Such plenty, such elegance! I must say you know how to do things!" Thus the ill-bred wine merchant, Köppen, proud to be admitted to the gathering, sounds the keynote of the occasion. Years later, the celebration of the family centenary furnishes a companion piece to this introductory group picture. Again the atmosphere is one of prosperity. The family has reached the pinnacle of its worldly position. But Tom, now acting patriarch, already feels within him the symptoms of decay; and during the festivities he is called out to receive a telegram announcing his disastrous failure in a wheat speculation. One feels that his ancestors, who had amassed the fortune which he inherited, would not have speculated; but if they had, they would have won. So the family scenes progress, each marking a step in the rise and fall of the collective hero's career; until at the final gathering, after the death of the last male Buddenbrook, his mother announces her decision to return to her girlhood home in Holland. She is the first member by marriage to resist the assimilative power of the clan; and its members are left, convicted and convinced of ruin, to seek in some mystical assurance the compensation for worldly decline.

Birth and death of necessity bulk large in the chronicles of a family. But it is significant that the death scenes are far more elaborated than the births; and that the one birth which is dwelt upon—that of little Hanno, last of the line—is in itself the threat of a death temporarily averted. Because he comes into the world ill equipped to cope with the life his lusty ancestors had relished, his birth is really a signal to prepare for the funeral. (pp. 83-7)

The death scenes throughout *Buddenbrooks* bear witness to Mann's consummate blending of realism and symbolism, and this is true whether they are taken singly or considered as a progression. For the earlier ones are easily passed over, while with the growing decadence of the family the demise of its members assumes an ever more tragic aspect. It is as if the author placed himself on the very line where the two types of writing merge, so that this book in itself demonstrates how realism may develop into symbolism, how the choice of significant naturalistic detail inevitably suggests a meaning beyond its concrete limits. He has not spared unpleasant physical trivia—the minute odors and sensations which can be made to endow a scene with reality. But neither has he overlooked symbolical values. Part of the horror of Tom's death rises from the fact that he who had been so immaculate in life was borne home to his death-bed coated with mud and slush, his white kid gloves streaked with filth. And when his son Hanno comes to die, we are made to feel that he has succumbed, not to the power of death, but to the weakness of his own grasp on life.

This blend of realism and symbolism makes itself felt in the constant use of physical detail, and of objects that serve almost as stage properties: the Buddenbrook hand, "too short but finely modeled," modified to an almost unearthly delicacy and whiteness in Tom, but still recognizable in Hanno; the leather-bound volume wherein are inscribed the family births, marriages, deaths, and important events as they occur. A reverent perusal of this record impresses upon Tony Buddenbrook the duty to family which must come before her individual happiness; and her submission is registered by inscribing in her own hand, wet with the tears she is weeping, her betrothal to the despised Grünlich. Little Hanno also peruses the book years later, and is moved to rule in, after his own name, the double line which signifies in book-keeping that an account is closed. When rebuked by his father, he stammers: "I thought—I thought—there was nothing else coming." Contrary to Mann's custom, the symbolism here is patent. And it is doubly significant, indicating the end of the family, and also, the commerical element which is inseparable from Buddenbrook history. (pp. 87-9)

Buddenbrooks is . . . explicit about the size of the family fortune, the various losses it suffers through marriage settlements and bad speculations. Because this is a commercial family, the state of its fortune serves as an index to its general state. When its possessions decline, its morale and its very hold on existence likewise deteriorate. Even the crimes which affect its standing are commercial crimes, the bankruptcy of Tony's husband, the embezzlement of her son-in-law.

In portraying his characters Mann has, for the most part, been content with classical methods. There is no attempt to limit the point of view, which shifts easily from one to another, though it is always given to some member of the family. Nor is there much stress on that exploring of the unconscious which recent psychological developments have brought so strongly to the fore, and which plays so large a part in *The Magic Mountain.*

The restraint which makes Mann's literary devices almost imperceptible is admirably illustrated in the case of Tom Buddenbrook, who is revealed as much through behavioristic as through analytical detail. His "Buddenbrook hand," and his death have been mentioned as examples of realism and symbolism. The modification of the hand may be taken to indicate the suppressed artistic impulses hinted at in his choice of a wife and openly expressed in his son. The strange deterioration which takes place within him so that he feels himself eaten away by a species of spiritual dry rot, is revealed through his growing obsession with details of wardrobe and toilet. As the inner man melts away he strengthens his armor of spotless elegance, till in the end he is but the exquisite shell of a man. Here Mann achieves a realistic and far more effective treatment of the theme which Henry James played upon more crudely and more fantastically in *The Private Life.*

The character of Tom is effective, just as the general technique of *Buddenbrooks* is effective, because it hovers on the border line between two types, and benefits by both. Apparently normal, he yet suffers from conflicts and suppressions which play a large part in abnormal psychology. One feels that he is straining against the bars which hold him to stolid decorum, and this sense of stress increases the poignancy of his characterization. The distance he has traveled between self-confident young manhood and his final state, is well brought out by two scenes which also illustrate Mann's masterful economy: the first, Tom's interview with his mistress, the little florist's assistant, when moved, but very much master of himself, he bids her a final good-by; the second, his suffering as he sits alone in his office listening to his wife and the handsome lieutenant making music in a room above—a prey to suspicions of a spiritual betrayal far more torturing than those based on physical infidelity.

Tom's evolution from assured and almost callous conservatism to anguished sensitivity is counterbalanced by that of Tony, who changes from an impetuous young girl into the spirit of conventionality and the personification of the family point of view. Her very conversation grows to be a compote of *clichés* in which the jargon of the Forty-eighters, sole vestige of her youthful revolt, clashes oddly with the bromides of the seventies and eighties, by which she shapes her life.

The family deterioration, recapitulated in Tom's character, takes final form in Hanno's physical weakness and artistic temperament. His tooth troubles, described with extreme realism, also serve as a symbol of general debility; and that his weakness stems directly from his father is emphasized by the fact that it is a decayed tooth which precipitates Tom's death. In addition, the teeth offer opportunity for implied comment on the rôle of dentistry in modern life, and the essential impotence of dentists, doctors, and all the agents of science to exercise that helpful control which is supposed to be their function. As for the aesthetic leanings suppressed in Tom and evident in Hanno, they too become symbols of decadence since they are wholly at odds with the sturdy commercialism which is the essence of the Buddenbrooks. The genius of the family has been the sort that could be reflected through rooms shining with comfort and cleanliness, opulent fur coats, and superabundance of good things to eat. When it descends to such a vessel as a frail, tearful boy with bad teeth, a weak digestion, and a burning love for music, it has declined indeed!

Because the point of view is limited to the family which is the group hero, the real touch of caricature is reserved for outsiders, such as Tony's second husband, Herr Permaneder from Munich, who is sketched with something of the good natured satire turned upon those beyond the pale. The Buddenbrooks are always sympathetically portrayed. Yet irony is never far from the surface, though so suavely insinuated that the reader feels it his own, developed from a strictly realistic representation of the material. Herein lies Mann's triumph. *Buddenbrooks* seems to take seriously the family and the family ideals; it almost does so. Nevertheless, by methods more veiled than innuendo, it does imply a satirical comment on pride of family, on provincial, and even national pride. One suspects, even though it is not hinted, that Tom's later preoccupation with clothes is a sly dig at the last Kaiser.

The irony strikes deeper, however, down to the very roots of human aspiration, both worldly and otherworldly. Its full force is for an instant released during Tom's one moment of vision, which gives the most eloquent passage in the book, and which by implication adds to the painfulness of his death when at last it comes. Dipping into a stray treatise on philosophy he seems to find an inkling of the strength he needs, and an assurance of some deeper portent in life itself. The assurance grows as he thinks it over during the night:

> "I shall live!" said Thomas Buddenbrook, almost aloud, and felt his breast shaken with inward sobs. "This is the revelation; that I shall live." . . . He wept, he pressed his face into the pillows and wept, shaken through and through, lifted up in transports by a joy without compare. . . .
>
> . . . He never succeeded in looking again into the precious volume—to say nothing of buying its other parts. His days were consumed by nervous pedantry: harassed by a thousand details, all of them unimportant, he was too weak-willed to arrive at a reasonable and fruitful arrangement of his time. Nearly two weeks after that memorable afternoon he gave it up—and ordered the maid-servant to fetch the book from the drawer in the garden table and replace it in the bookcase.

This might be, as it purports to be, merely an account of what happens. Yet it carries overtones of comment on Tom and his species as well as on the value of mystical assurances concerning the life everlasting. A similar chord is struck in the very last scene. The Buddenbrook women on the eve of the family's final disintegration, meet in a pathetic conclave that recalls by contrast the buoyant group with which the novel began. There are quiet tears but there is also courage; and Tony in a moment of exaltation asks whether there can be an after life in which may occur a joyous reunion of Buddenbrooks. Her kinswomen are silent—this is not their field. But Sesemi Weichbrodt, Tony's old teacher and the family's staunch friend, undertakes to answer:

> "*It is so!*" she said, with her whole strength; and looked at them all with a challenge in her eyes.
>
> She stood there, a victor in the good fight which all her life she had waged against the assaults of Reason: humpbacked, tiny, quivering with the strength of her convictions, a little prophetess, admonishing and inspired.

Does Thomas Mann see Sesemi as sublime or ridiculous, or a little of both? The essence of his art lies in leaving the question open. (pp. 90-6)

Robert Morss Lovett, " 'Buddenbrooks'," in his *Preface to Fiction: A Discussion of Great Modern Novels,* Thomas S. Rockwell, 1931, pp. 81-96.

MALCOLM COWLEY
(essay date 1936)

[Cowley was an American literary critic and editor. In the following excerpt from a review originally published in 1936, he suggests that *Stories from Three Decades* illustrates Mann's development from a symbolist to a socialist artist.]

The line that divides Symbolist or "art" novels from social novels is probably not so straight or definite as people seemed to think a few years ago, when the subject was being vehemently argued. It is a border without guards or customs officials, and doubtful travelers are privileged to stand with one foot in either country. They can even become leading citizens of both, as witness the example of Thomas Mann, who is probably more respected than any other living writer. During the last twenty-five years, Mann has gradually become a social novelist, in an admirable sense of the word, yet he has not abandoned the technique or the emotional color of the Symbolists. He has never made the gesture of violently deserting an ivory tower.

His career can be traced in *Stories of Three Decades,* an omnibus volume containing everything he has written for publication except his essays and his four big novels. The book includes two long stories, **"Death in Venice"** and **"Tonio Kröger,"** which Mann says in his introduction that he is inclined to reckon "not with my slighter but with my more important works." It includes two other long stories which, with much hesitation, I should be willing to place above Mann's favorites: these two are **"Tristan"** and **"Mario and the Magician." "Blood of the Walsungs,"** describing a family of rich, hateful, pitiable Jews, is a shorter story almost as good; so too is **"Disorder and Early Sorrow,"** in which all the hysteria of the German inflation is distilled into the tears of a six-year-old girl. There are stories still shorter than these last; there are episodes, sketches and a long, beautifully accurate biography of Mann's dog, recommended as corrective reading to people who believe that dog stories are childish. There is the first chapter of a novel, "Felix Krull," that Mann did not continue; and there is *Fiorenza,* a historico-philosophical drama that had some success on the stage, but not enough to make its author a professional

playwright. In all there are twenty-four pieces, written at every stage of his life—from the year 1896, when he was twenty-one, to the year 1929, when he won the Nobel Prize. In their chronological order they give a fairly clear picture of his development.

His early work was centered round the familiar Symbolist theme of the artist's solitude. "There are two worlds," Mann always seemed to be saying. "There is the world of happy, normal people, to be envied even for their stupidity, and there is the lonely world in which the artist tries to bridle his nightmares, but often lets them run away with him." Almost all his stories dealt either with artists or else with moral or physical cripples (and he tended to place all these people in the same category, little Herr Friedemann the hunchback, Detlev Spinell the dilettante and Felix Krull the swindler).

His nearest approach to a hero is Tonio Kröger, the young, successful, hard-working novelist; yet this autobiographical character is the one who says most forcibly that art is a product of decay and that artists by their calling are barred out of ordinary society. "Literature is not a calling, it's a curse," Tonio tells his good friend Lisabeta Ivanovna. "It begins by your feeling yourself set apart, in a curious sort of opposition to the nice, regular people; there is a gulf of ironic sensibility, of knowledge, skepticism, disagreement, between you and the others; it grows deeper and deeper, you realize that you are alone." Both the artists and their audience are "always and only the poor and suffering, never any of the others, the blue-eyed ones. . . . The kingdom of art increases and that of health and innocence declines on this earth." It is curious to find that Tonio does not feel in the least angry or contemptuous toward the world that half rejects him; in this respect he is unlike Joyce's Stephen Dedalus and Huysmans' des Esseintes and almost all the other Symbolist heroes. He really loves and envies the ordinary people, "the blue-eyed ones" who have no need of art. His good friend tells him, "You are really a bourgeois on the wrong path, a bourgeois *manqué.*"

"Tonio Kröger" is an unusual story, warm and open-hearted in mood, skillful in craftsmanship, the first work in which Mann learned to interweave his themes like a composer writing a symphony. Yet with the passage of years it is losing part of its effectiveness: the ideas behind it are beginning to seem localized in time and space. In writing it Mann did not foresee that the conflict between artist and bourgeois would not be an eternal subject, nor that it would soon become impossible to use the upper middle class as a symbol of health. He would soon be forced to go into his material more deeply.

That is exactly what he did in writing **"Death in Venice,"** which was finished eight years later. Ostensibly it is another story of the relation between life and art, between art and self-discipline. Gustav von Aschenbach, the hero, is a distinguished novelist who has sustained himself through fifty years by obeying his Prussian sense of duty. Then, in the late afternoon of his life, he yields to the dissipation that is, for Mann, both a symbol of art and a symbol of death. He finds that Venice is a plague-stricken city, but he has fallen in love with a beautiful Polish boy and refuses to go northward until it is too late for him to escape. The story is extraordinary for its musical structure and for the complicated suggestions it evokes. But among these suggestions is one of a historical nature. **"Death in Venice"** was published two years before the War, and Mann is inclined to believe that its popularity was due to its "intense timeliness"—the delirium in which Aschenbach foundered belonged to the mood of the day and was a prophecy of the general delirium in which Europe would shortly founder. Aschenbach was not merely a picture of the artist yielding to his vices: he came to represent a moment of the European mind.

I am trying to describe the process by which a Symbolist novelist developed into a social novelist without greatly changing his aims or his methods, but chiefly by broadening his human sympathies. In another story—it is the last in the volume and appeared in 1929—the point becomes much clearer. **"Mario and the Magician"** relates the misadventures of a German family at a little Italian watering place. They do not like Torre di Venere; the chip-on-the-shoulder nationalism of the Italian tourists makes their lives mildly but persistently disagreeable. Nevertheless they remain, by inertia, and get themselves involved in the dangerous affair of the Cavaliere Cipolla. This magician, as he advertises himself—this hypnotist, as he is in reality—proves to be crippled and hateful and compelling. At his one performance he overawes and insults the audience, forcing one man after another to obey him, and the audience likes it; even the German children laugh and clap without quite knowing what is taking place. But Cipolla goes too far and one of his victims shoots him down, thus clearing the air of hysteria and constraint.

"Mario and the Magician" is not on the face of it a political story, in spite of occasional references to Mussolini and Italian pride. It deals with one episode witnessed by an ordinary German family. Yet it conveys, more strongly than anything else I have read, the atmosphere of Europe in these days of dictatorship and mass insanity: it suggests in miniature the great meetings at the Sport Palace in Berlin where Hitler sways the crowd like wind-bowed aspens; it gives us the essence of the Blood Purge, the Saar Plebiscite, the Ethopian war—everything is there, if only in the germ, and it was there six years before most of it was printed in the morning papers. We should not demand that poets be prophets; this is not part of their trade. But

sometimes it happens that a writer, by going into his subject deeply, finds in it the spiritual tendencies that grew out of yesterday's events and will become the political tendencies of tomorrow. Thomas Mann, like Tolstoy, has done this more than once, and not for his country alone. In this age of crazy nationalisms, he is almost the last great European. (pp. 291-94)

Malcolm Cowley, "The Last Great European: Thomas Mann," in his *Think Back on Us: A Contemporary Chronicle of the 1930's*, edited by Henry Dan Piper, Southern Illinois University Press, 1967, pp. 291-94.

FREDERICK J. HOFFMAN
(essay date 1945)

[In the following excerpt, Hoffman examines Mann's use of Freudian concepts in his works.]

In the mature estimate of Thomas Mann, Freud's work stood out as a storm signal of science against the dangers of nineteenth-century irrationalism. Mann had not always thought thus of Freud, but was ultimately to accept psychoanalysis as a protection against irrational forces. Yet Freud also belongs to the group of nineteenth-century thinkers with whom we have come to associate the anti-intellectualism and irrationalism of our day. How can we explain this apparent inconsistency? Thomas Mann has done it for us. (pp. 209-10)

Mann associates Freud with the "romantic, anti-rational" tradition in Germany, with that part of German thought which did not flee the responsibilities and consequences of examining man's anti-rational nature but which sought with some success to appraise it. Freud's interest in sex, his so-called "pan-sexualism," has made him an explorer of the Unconscious, which "makes him understand life through disease," with the object not of accepting the disease but of curing the patient.

The mind of modern Germany's greatest writer was so well prepared by a lifelong study of his country's philosophic resources that he was to find in the work of Freud a note of hope for the future of humankind. For Mann's acceptance of any body of theory is contingent upon its service in fortifying the spirit and intellect; knowledge of the irrational is important only so far as it gives strength to the human mind. . . . The theories of psychoanalysis were therefore quite naturally a part of his penetrating and exhaustive study of the modern mind in *The Magic Mountain*. In fact, the position of the psychoanalyst in the International Sanatorium Berghof is portrayed with great care and some humor. He is Dr. Krokowski, whose lectures on love and disease are no small part of Sanatorium entertainment. (pp. 210-11)

The impression one gets of Dr. Krokowski is singular and strange. It is apparent that he is obsessed with a single idea, and that his sole concern is to explore its implications: the organic relationship of disease to love. (p. 211)

Love and chastity are in perpetual conflict, says the good doctor. Chastity usually wins the struggle. "Love was suppressed, held in darkness and chains, by fear, conventionality, aversion, or a tremulous yearning to be pure." The victory, however, proves to be a pyrrhic one. The suppressed love "would break through the ban of chastity, it would emerge—if in a form so altered as to be unrecognizable." The new form was illness. " 'Symptoms of disease are nothing but a disguised manifestation of the power of love; and all disease is only love transformed.' " . . .

For some years before the composition of *The Magic Mountain,* Thomas Mann had been interested in the relationship of the artist to society, and in the problem of genius and disease. The artist seemed a misfit in bourgeois society, and the sources of creation seemed almost directly opposed to social standards. It was part of Mann's debt to Schopenhauer that he recognized in the latter's work the important dependence of the artist upon suffering. (p. 212)

Each of Mann's earlier tales deals with one of two themes: the artist's painful isolation from bourgeois society, and the persistent function of disease (another mark of separation from the healthy bourgeoisie) in the work of genius. In pursuit of his themes, Mann listened with great interest to two spokesmen of the German Romantic tradition, Schopenhauer and Nietzsche. . . . From Nietzsche, Mann derived much that was of interest to his earlier career. The sense of the artist's being unusual, separate from the ordinary run of society, scornful of the reasonable life—this theme, developed to one or another degree of subtlety, combines with Schopenhauer's concept of the artist as an exceptional person, the principal sign of whose vocation is his capacity for suffering. Blind striving, the will to live, dominates the lives of all; it is for the artist, who observes this suffering from a painfully objective point of view, to wrest knowledge from will, and to render permanent his aesthetic comprehension of ideal states. (pp. 212-13)

The Magic Mountain is . . . a compendium of information about matters in anatomy and medicine. More than that, however, Mann thought to see in a study of disease something of a positive value. For it is disease that causes a shift of attention—provided the disease is not itself stupidly or deliberately willed, as in the case of Christian Buddenbrooks—from the superficial level of social observation and "busy-ness" to the inner nature of being. Disease also makes for greater sensitivity, a quality necessary to the full expression of genius. (p. 213)

It is necessary for the artist to go beneath the surface levels of rational life—and rational life is for the most part controlled by social institutions which limit opportunities for spiritual knowledge. Thus Mann, from his reading of Schopenhauer and Nietzsche and his observation of the powerful effect of Wagner's music, participates in the nineteenth-century romantic-irrational revolt against the sanctity of consciousness. It is possible also that this irrationalism was for Mann a fascinating thing, and that he believed the duty of art was to show the most pessimistic conclusions obtainable from it. Further, Mann's acceptance of the exceptional character of the artist, his portrayal of the artist's painful abnormalities, both social and psychological, gave such clear pictures of the artist as neurotic as *Death in Venice*—a story which was immediately claimed by psychoanalysts as a convincing demonstration of the association between the "artistic impulse and the erotic drive." (p. 214)

The Magic Mountain is a complex work of art. It cannot be said to have had any specific "therapeutic effect" upon its author. The real significance of the work may be summarized as follows: for the first time since the writing of *Buddenbrooks,* Mann was writing a novel on a grand scale. He had fairly well exhausted the aesthetic possibilities of the philosophies of Schopenhauer and Nietzsche, and it was through the peculiar nature of the setting of *The Magic Mountain* that all of his previous convictions were to be tested and compared with other notions and beliefs. . . . Mann suspected . . . that a simple explanation of the artist's position in terms of his physiological and psychological nature was insufficient justification for his life and work. He was still primarily interested in the artist because of his insight into the irrational wells of man's behavior. Knowledge of the "dark areas" of man's Unconscious, plus an understanding of the tension which exists between man's will and the agencies which attempt to control it—these were still the principal distinguishing marks of the aesthetic temperament, as Mann saw it. But it struck him that psychoanalysis was more than an open door to the irrational; it was a science of *control* whereby the irrational might be reformed and shaped to meet the vital needs of twentieth-century man. For one thing, psychoanalysis explained disease and its relationship to genius. [Hermann J.] Weigand points out that, though Dr. Krokowski is a far less likable person than Behrens, Mann's preference is ultimately for the ideas and theories of the former: " . . . he may be closer to an understanding of the relation obtaining between mind and body than a good physiologist and fine surgeon who is a capital fellow besides." (pp. 215-16)

[In] Mann's opinion, the virtue and value of psychoanalysis are that it is of and yet not of the "irrationalist drive of his times." It understands man's Unconscious, yet does not over-value it, or allow man to disappear within it, or to become a slave to his irrational passions. Indeed, this is Mann's hope: that psychoanalysis will not only contribute new insights to the artist, but will serve reason in the future with a powerful instrument of control over the irrational forces of our day. This is the burden of his extended statement, **"Freud's Position in the History of Modern Thought."** (pp. 216-17)

Thomas Mann was of all modern writers the only one to take a lively aesthetic interest in Freud's contributions to anthropology. Indeed, it may be said that the Joseph stories—though they are certainly not just one thing—are an aesthetic development of Freud's theories of the racial Unconscious. (p. 219)

The unity of universal myths and attitudes lies in the Unconscious, which insures a continuity of racial memory from one generation to the next. Subsequent legend or history duplicates or repeats, with some slight variation, the points of view, the taboos, even the incidents of the past, if they have been of sufficient psychological importance. There is, therefore, an unconscious legislative residue, upon which new generations, quite remote from the origins of taboos may draw for the government of their behavior. Thus a race may have its "regression," in much the same way as an individual does. Mann plays upon this theme with admirable subtlety and sympathy in the Joseph tetralogy. (p. 220)

Mann also finds in Freud's analysis of the Unconscious a suspension of the limitations of time itself and a reassertion of the life of man as a recurrent myth; that is, man is rarely influenced in his behavior by only the present—if indeed the present plays any part at all in determining his conduct—but by the past, or by the myth which is the pattern of the past. Man himself looks upon the chaos of the Unconscious with a dread which makes him "cover up his nakedness"; but each time he renounces a pattern of life (each time he surmounts a crisis, or is overcome by it) he dies. "To die: that means actually to lose sight of time, to travel beyond it, to exchange for it eternity and presentness, and therewith for the first time, life." Joseph himself dies and is reborn twice, as does Jacob as well. The myth holds security for such rebirth. . . . (p. 221)

The Joseph story opens with this latter idea as its theme: time has uneven measure; memory, "resting on oral tradition from generation to generation, was more direct and confiding, it flowed freer, time was a more unified and thus a briefer vista." Repetitions of historical incident, which are lived by personalities crucial to the survival of myth, can be explained psychologically. . . . (p. 222)

Mann at home in California, 1947.

Ultimately, Mann's wish is to show the increasing socialization of the human will, as it alters its purpose through recurring experience. Thus Joseph is to be used as a symbol of increasing social solidarity and cooperation, in the fourth novel of the series, *Joseph, the Provider.*

The "Freudian hope" . . . that the ego will be extended by the future work of psychoanalysis, the energies of the id harnessed to the social good—this is what Mann has in mind, in his projected fourth novel. We may safely suggest that Mann intends Joseph as the racial symbol of the ego, which will serve as a prototype of civilization.

One other interesting application of Freudian psychology is to be seen in the union of Biblical story and dream interpretation. Freud's insistence upon wish-fulfillment as the source of most personal dreams may appear to have been disregarded in Mann's analysis of the dreams of Joseph. Though Mann is concerned primarily with the problem of making the biblical story psychologically creditable, he is free to use the analyst's materials with some independence. In the early dreams of Joseph, as well as in those which he interprets for the Pharaoh, God's wish is fulfilled more than that of the dreamer. This is the peculiar quality of these dreams which makes them prophetic. Since, as Mann suggests in **"Freud and the Future,"** the subjective will plays a large role in dictating the nature of events which happen to it, it may not be altogether irregular that the wish-fulfillment is both God's and Joseph's. That Mann was aware of the nature and construction of human dreams, whose wish-fulfillment is obviously of a sexual nature, is brilliantly illustrated by his description of Mut-em-enet's dream at the very beginning of her relationship with Joseph. Within the limits of a single dream the story of Mut's seduction of Joseph is told, and the symbolism of the dream suggests a complete fulfillment of her unconscious wish. It is a brilliantly constructed dream pattern, well adjusted to the needs of the narrative, and certainly not in any way a violation of its purpose. (pp. 226-27)

Mann's acceptance of Freud leads to the development of a hopeful ethical and religious scheme, in which the irrational energies of the id are slowly being brought within the benevolent control of the ego and of all its social and political accessories. . . . Mann's firsthand acquaintance with Nazism . . . forced him to venture a serious reshaping of the relationship of art with morality. He had for some time been teaching the peculiar nature of the artist and pointing out his insight into the unconscious resources of man's behavior and energy. He did not change overnight from an "unpolitical man" to a political lecturer and special pleader. He turned to that form of irrationalism which he thought had most hope for the future of man. This, it seemed to him, is the science of psychoanalysis, especially as it is applied to the study of mythology and primitive religious thought and custom. (pp. 227-28)

Frederick J. Hoffman, "Kafka and Mann," in his *Freudianism and the Literary Mind,* Louisiana State University Press, 1945, pp. 181-229.

FRANK DONALD HIRSCHBACH

(essay date 1955)

[In the following excerpt, Hirschbach discusses the conflict between erotic passion and the rational control of individual will in *Death in Venice*.]

Seen from a naturalistic point of view, *Death in Venice* is the story of an aging, successful, highly sensitive writer who feels in need of a vacation, travels to Venice, remains there because of his passion for the fourteen-year old Polish boy, Tadzio, contracts cholera and dies of it. There are no incidents in the story which cannot be explained naturally. Everyone has encountered remarkable-looking people, such as the man whom Aschenbach meets at the streetcar stop in Munich. There is nothing astounding about an insolent and unlicensed

gondolier who flees when he fears the intervention of the police. A mix-up in baggage was probably a common occurrence in a pre-Fascist Italy in which the trains did not yet run on time.

A good many other elements contribute to the naturalistic tenor of the story. The names of real streets in Munich and Venice are employed. The works of the fictitious Gustav von Aschenbach bear a close resemblance to those already written or planned by Thomas Mann. The descriptions of people are drawn with great attention to detail (such as the false teeth of the old man on the steamer) and the unpleasant is described along with the pleasant. The use of the cholera element is in itself a naturalistic device.

When the story is read on a naturalistic level, Aschenbach's homosexual tendencies fit well into the picture. It would appear that Aschenbach has repressed these tendencies for many years, and we are constantly told about his tremendous self-discipline in sentences like "the pattern of self-discipline he had followed ever since his youth," "a proud, tenacious, well-tried will," "he had bridled and tempered his sensibilities", or later on when it is said:

Forgotten feelings, precious pangs of his youth, quenched long since by the stern service that had been his life, now returned so strangely metamorphosed . . .

It is the sight of a man, who in some way attracts Aschenbach, that is the innocent cause of his trip to Venice. Beginning with the chance meeting with the mysterious stranger in Munich, Aschenbach's will fights a losing battle with his desires. The use of such terms as "a longing inexplicable," "contagion", "vice, passion," "the embers of smouldering fire," "to strengthen . . . the ethically impossible" leave no doubt about the erotic character of his emotions which Aschenbach at first tries to characterize as merely "longing to travel."

Once in Venice, where he is unknown, his once-repressed desires fix upon a beautiful fourteen-year old boy, and from here on Aschenbach's reactions and actions are much the same as those of any undeclared lover. He pursues his beloved, gradually throwing all caution to the winds; he only feels happy when the object of his love is within his sight; he tries to exchange glances with him; he stands at his door at night; he feels the pangs of jealousy; and he finally even uses cosmetics in order to be pleasing to him. By the time that he reaches the high point of his passion for Tadzio he is almost completely unaware of the "impropriety" or unconventionality of his love, and even launches into a defense of homosexuality on the basis of historical fact.

When the story, on the other hand, is read on a symbolic level, it becomes the case study of the gradual deterioration and abdication of the human will and of the artistic will in the face of beauty. . . . Aschenbach's rise and greatness are due to a colossal effort of the will to subdue his natural inclinations. All his life he was said to be too busy with the tasks which his ego and his European conscience provided for him. His favorite term is "Durchhalten" ("Stick to it!"). . . . The hero of Aschenbach's writings is a masculine, intellectual and virginal youth who clenches his teeth and stands in silent defiance of the swords and spears that pierce his side. The picture is that of the martyr, Saint Sebastian; the ideal is that of Stefan George. Aschenbach's efforts are on one occasion labelled ecstasy of will ("Willensverzückung"), an achievement as well as a means to further achievement.

The irony and tragedy of Gustav Aschenbach lie in the fact that this iron will, which has carried him to such great heights, collapses utterly within a matter of weeks, and it collapses of itself. Tadzio, who might be regarded as the prime agent in Aschenbach's negation of the will, is in reality only the main station on a road which has begun long before. There are perhaps four other stations on this road, each symbolized by one of the strangers whom Aschenbach meets, three of them before his acquaintance with Tadzio is made. The stranger in Munich, set against the background of a cemetery, acts as the catalytic agent who sets off the reactions that lead to Aschenbach's downfall and death. This first stranger indirectly causes Aschenbach to have a daydream of symbolic import. He dreams of an exotic, tropical landscape, the type where cholera breeds. Thus, his death is forecast for a second time. But it is also the type of region where all living organisms, plants and animals alike, are able to grow and act free of inhibitions and restraints. During the dream Aschenbach feels his heart pounding with horror and mysterious desire. In Venice he seeks his dream landscape in a civilized setting.

The second stranger, the ancient adolescent on the steamer, "a painted and primped old scapegrace", represents the point to which a man can fall when he lets his urges overpower his will—a warning to Aschenbach, and yet the second stranger, who sidles up to him at the end of the trip and whispers a significant "Pray keep us in mind" into his ear, already sees an ally in the aging man.

The gondolier asserts his will over Aschenbach's will in a most decisive manner. Although Aschenbach has taken the gondola in order to make a steamship connection at San Marco, the gondolier takes him to the Lido. Twice during the trip Aschenbach tries to protest, but "the wisest thing—and how much the pleasantest!—was to let matters take their own course." Thus, Aschenbach is borne to his destination in a black barque which resembles a coffin.

Much is said in the story about the extraordinary beauty of the boy Tadzio. But his beauty is not perfect, and in fact, if he were not seen through the eyes of his lover, he would probably turn out to be just a very handsome boy of fourteen. He is the symbol of a passion which cannot come to any fruition and which Aschenbach does not really want to be fulfilled. If he and Tadzio were to become friends, if he had spoken to him, if he had a chance to observe Tadzio more intimately, no doubt his love would die and his will return.

After the gondola episode his will makes one last attempt to assert itself: the attempted flight from Venice. It is perfectly obvious that Aschenbach does not really wish to leave Venice, since he could have done so even without his baggage. After this, his will deteriorates step by step. His realization that it was Tadzio who kept him in Venice; his enraptured contemplation of Tadzio's body on the beach; his passivity toward the disease which later grows into complete carelessness; finally his use of cosmetics are all steps on the way to a total abdication of the will.

One is reminded of the devil in *Doctor Faustus,* who constantly changes shapes during his conversation with Leverkühn, when one encounters the fourth stranger, the guitar player. He has the prominent Adam's apple and the two furrows of the Munich stranger; he lets his tongue run from one corner of the mouth to the other like the stranger on the steamer; and he frequently bares his strong teeth like the gondolier. This fourth stranger no longer has any particular function except to signify the demon's complete victory over Aschenbach. His familiarity and his bawdy gestures symbolize that Aschenbach is now considered vanquished. Shortly before it had already been said:

> Mind and heart were drunk with passion, his footsteps guided by the demonic power whose pastime it is to trample on human reason and dignity.

After all the strangers have led their victim a little bit on his way to death, it is finally again Tadzio, "the pale and lovely Summoner" who leads the soul of the dying artist into the lower regions.

Aschenbach's downfall is projected within the frame of an erotic dream which he has shortly before his death. He dreams of a tremendous, communal sex orgy, in which humans and animals alike participate, a voluptuous adoration of the phallic symbol which he approaches with a combination of anxiety and desire and in which he finally takes full part. Here for the first time, Thomas Mann uses the term "the stranger god" for God's Mephistophelian counterpart, who rules the drives and urges within us.

Love and the uncontrolled contemplation of beauty play their part in this story of the gradual disintegration of the will: the will to create, the will to remain dignified, and finally the will to live. For death itself here becomes a symbol of the inevitable last step on the road to the renunciation of the will. (pp. 17-21)

Frank Donald Hirschbach, in his *The Arrow and the Lyre: A Study of the Role of Love in the Works of Thomas Mann,* Martinus Nijhoff, 1955, 195 p.

MARGUERITE YOURCENAR
(essay date 1962)

[In the excerpt below, Yourcenar discusses humanism and realism in Mann's works.]

[Mann's works are thoroughly] German in their resort to hallucination to penetrate outer reality, and likewise in their search for occult wisdom, the secrets of which, whispered or implied, hover between the lines as if intended to remain there virtually undisclosed. German, too, in their feeling for those great entities which have ever haunted Germanic thought, the Earth-Spirit, the Mothers, the Devil, and Death, a death more active and more virulent than elsewhere, mysteriously mingled with life itself, and sometimes endued with attributes of love. And last, these works are German in their strong symphonic structure, in the contrapuntal character of their parts as developed throughout more than half a century. But this Germanic substance has been permeated, like the country itself, with leaven from other lands: the heroes of *Death in Venice* and *The Magic Mountain* both owe their supreme revelation to the Greek mysteries; the learned convolutions of the *Joseph* tetralogy are impregnated with Jewish thought

(Talmudic, and sometimes Cabalistic, even more than Biblical). . . . (p. 185)

Mann's rock-crystal structures of allegory only gradually take form in the mother-solution which his meticulous realism provides, that veritably obsessed realism so characteristic of German vision; realism is also the bed for his nearly subterranean stream of myth and of dream. *Death in Venice,* opening with the detailed account of a stroll in suburban Munich and proceeding to give other realistic details (the schedule of trains and steamers, the barber's prattle in full, the conspicuous coloring of a tie), slowly fashions from the vexations and mishaps of a journey an allegoric Dance of Death; far below the surface, burning but inexhaustible, secretly born of some more ancient symbolism, flows the profound meditation of a man in prey of his own death, drawing both his love and his disaster from within. *The Magic Mountain* is a highly accurate description of a sanatorium in German Switzerland about the year 1912; it is also a medieval *summa,* an allegory of the City of the World; and last, it is a mythological epic of a Ulysses of the inner depths, of a voyager bound over to ogres and to larvae but ultimately reaching his modest Ithaca, a certain wisdom within himself. . . . Actuality, allegory, and myth merge in Mann's works; by some process of continuous circulation all these elements are constantly re-absorbed into life's ebb and flow, from which they are born.

The same complexity obtains in these novels in the matter of time, and of its corollary, place. Time is infinitely varied in Mann, since he draws in great part upon an historic or legendary past, both remote and near, and since whatever was contemporary in his narratives, just because they have been fashioned in the course of a long life, has been caught up in the turning of Time's wheel, and has slipped from the present to the past. His picture of post-1870 Germany in *Buddenbrooks,* and of pre-1914 Germany in *The Blood of the Walsungs* and in *Death in Venice,* the pre-1914 Germany as seen in retrospect in *The Magic Mountain,* the post-World War Germany of *The Black Swan,* and finally the ravaged Germany of *Doctor Faustus,* at the end of the Second World War, though separated from first to last by scarcely three quarters of a century, are as remote each from the other as all of them are from the Goethean setting of *The Beloved Returns.* . . . Occasionally these novels, though set in the past, have encroached upon the future, as when at the end of *The Magic Mountain* Joachim's ghost appears wearing a helmet from a war which has not yet taken place. . . . (p. 186-87)

Gradually Mann's spatial and temporal conceptions have been enlarged, if not changed, by his progression throughout half a century from realism in the literal sense of the term to realism in its full philosophic implications. The drama of *Buddenbrooks* was still set against a background of urban life, and moved with the town clocks of Lübeck. In *The Magic Mountain,* however, Hans Castorp's evocation of waves and sand along a distant Baltic shore suggests the beat and timeless particles of pure duration. The feverish tempo of the sanatorium, so exactly situated in an hour of universal history (just before the outbreak of the War of 1914), is gauged on the scale of geological time, like that of the mountain itself. (p. 187)

"I adore you, phantom of water and albumin, destined for dissection in the tomb." Such in effect, is Hans Castorp's strange avowal of love to Clavdia Chauchat. Mann is only formulating here, in terms of organic chemistry, views akin to those of the great humanist occultists of the Renaissance: man the microcosm, formed of the same substance and governed by the same laws as the cosmos, subject like matter itself to a series of partial or total transmutations, and connected with everything else by some highly developed capillary system. Such basically cosmic humanism is, of course, quite unconcerned with Platonic and Christian ideas of antinomy of soul and body, of the world of the mind and the world of the senses, of God and matter. It admits, therefore, neither of the process of rejection and conversion such as marks an Aldous Huxley's gradual approach to a concept of mystic universality, nor of that asceticism, on aesthetic grounds, which raises a Proust from contemplation of a world of imperfect and transitory reality to the vision of a world which is flawless and pure. Nor does it allow for that identification of the physiological with the repulsive which is so typical of Sartre, and of many other novelists of our time, for whom the Christian concept of the indignity of the flesh persists in a context otherwise shorn of Christian ideals. But the simple and reassuring notions of felicity, good health, and moral equilibrium, so important for the old, traditional humanism, are likewise alien to this humanism, which sounds the abyss. Desire, sickness, death, and evil, and, by a bold paradox, thought itself, slowly corroding its bodily support, all are ferments and solvents in a process of alchemical transmutation. . . . (p. 187-88)

His principal characters differ from many of those presented by the literature of our day in that they do not at first sight appear to be solitary and desocialized, cut off from ideological bases, or even questioning that such bases exist; nor are they launched in the absurd, or comfortably installed in some imaginary world. Instead, his heroes are first portrayed as inseparable from a class or a group, supported but also bound fast by social customs which they believe to be good, and which have been so, perhaps, but which are now no more than sclerotic remains of a life gone by; their initial state is much less one of despair than of a certain blind complacency. Only belatedly, and in fumbling fashion, will each one in turn try to penetrate beneath that petrified

crust, seeking to regain the world of vital energy to which he belongs, but which he cannot rejoin without sacrifice of his external man in actual or symbolic death. Indeed, Mann seems never to have eliminated wholly from his consciousness, and still less from his unconscious mind, some remnant of puritanical reprobation, or bourgeois timidity, in face of that adventure in self-discovery. . . . To the very last this drama of the artist in revolt against his middle-class environment, though the problem is frankly conventional, remains for Mann the symbol of a terrifying choice. . . . (p. 188)

Mann is closer to Goethe in line of descent than any of [his own] great contemporaries, possibly for the reason that merely in following his vocation as novelist he has found a counterbalance both to pure dream and to dogmatic systematization in the study and description of the individual, and decidedly average, man. The result is that often, even in the highly metaphysical aspects of his novels, a kind of pragmatism appears, not unlike that to which Goethe's Faust turns (in the *Second Part of Faust*) shortly before his death. Like Goethe, too, in his commentaries on his own Orphic poems, reducing almost ineffable truths expressed there to somewhat prosy exhortations toward a good life, Mann tends to exalt the homeliest and most exoteric virtues in that central massif of his work, *The Magic Mountain.* Honesty, modesty, and kindness are the qualities with which the hero Hans Castorp is endowed, with only enough courage and common sense added to keep those virtues from falling, as they so often do, into the service of existing prejudice or new and dangerous error. Even in *Doctor Faustus,* where the emphasis is placed upon excess inherent in the nature of genius, to the exclusion of every average virtue or vice, that weird adventure, pitched like Leverkühn's music itself at the furthest limits perceptible to human ears, is reported to us by the very commonplace character who serves as narrator. The merits of humdrum humanity must apparently be defended by Mann in the presence of genius. . . . (p. 200)

Even the style of Mann, somewhat slow in pace and at times heavily descriptive, carrying over into the dialogue the paraphrasis and courteous formulas of a bygone age, is less hermetic than exegetic. That cautious advance which takes up no new point until the preceding has been properly exhausted, that thesis which perpetually produces its own antithesis, reminds us of medieval scholasticism but also of Renaissance scholia. The ponderous, interpretative dialectic in *Doctor Faustus,* the half frenzied proliferation of analysis in the *Joseph* volumes . . . belong historically to a type of devious thinking which Mann inherits; his purpose is not to offer a rational explanation of a world too vast and complex for human categories, but to scrutinize it with what help our reason affords. As is to be expected, therefore, he tends in his writing to conserve the logical structure of language in its strictest form even at the sacrifice of realism in dialogue, and to preserve for discourse its classical rôle of intellectual rather than emotional medium of expression. (pp. 200-01)

The long circuitous course of Mann's writing is in keeping with the cautious deliberation of his approach to reality; he sees to it that the reader, like the character, advances gradually, and not on the surface level alone. Such skillfully delayed exposition is very different from the haughty obscurity of a poet like George, where half-revealed meanings flash with a diamond's fire, or from the triple-locked allegory of a Kafka. Carried one step further Mann's discursive commentary would be downright didacticism; he stops just short of that error by introducing myth; in myth, by its very nature, are fused all the complex elements which didactic explication would detail. Imbedded in the heavy ore of everyday existence, to be perceived there by none but watchful eyes, myth is for Mann only a more hidden, but more final, form of explanation.

Accustomed as we are to an almost academic definition of the term *humanism,* we may ask whether or not a mind so concerned with the irrational, and sometimes with the occult, so open to change and indeed almost to chaos, can still be called *humanist.* Assuredly it could not if we were to retain without qualification the old, strictly limited definition of a humanist, that is to say, of a scholar well versed in classical literature, with its central focus on the study of man. Nor even if we were to enlarge that definition to make it include, as is often done nowadays, the concept of a philosophy which is based on the worth and dignity of the human being (on what Shakespeare calls the infinite faculty of this masterpiece, man) would the appellation apply. For both these views suggest an element of optimism with regard to human kind, and possibly even an overvaluation of the species, which can scarcely be attributed to a writer so obsessed by the dubious aspects of the human personality, so concerned to portray man as a mere particle of the universe and a refraction of the whole. But Shakespeare's phrase, "how infinite in faculty," suggests still another form of humanism, one alert to what lies deeper within the human being than his ordinary deportment may betray; whether we will or no, those words lead us to depths in which we come into contact with forces stranger than are dreamt of in a philosophy where Nature is regarded as a simple entity. A humanism directed thus toward the shadowy and unexplained, even toward the occult, seems at first view opposed to traditional humanism, but it is rather the extreme extension of the latter, a kind of left wing humanism. Mann rightly belongs to that small, somewhat isolated group of thinkers, who are cautious and tortuous by nature, and often are cryptic by necessity; once emboldened they seem to venture in spite of

themselves, as if moved by some inner compulsion; though conservative in letting nothing be lost from the accumulated cultural riches of thousands of years, they tend nevertheless to the subversive in their continual reinterpretation of human thought and behavior. For such minds all arts and science, myth and dream, the known and the unknown, and human substance itself are objects of an investigation which will go on as long as mankind endures. (pp. 201-02)

Marguerite Yourcenar, "Humanism in Thomas Mann," translated by Grace Frick and the author, in *The Partisan Review Anthology,* edited by William Phillips and Philip Rahv, Holt, Rinehart and Winston, 1962, pp. 185-202.

HENRY HATFIELD

(essay date 1962)

[Hatfield is an American educator and critic. In the excerpt below, he offers an overview of Mann's major works.]

Among the major writers of this century, Thomas Mann appears at first glance as perhaps the most conservative. One finds few if any startling affirmations; rather, a slow, painful groping towards a synthesis, or more often a weighing of antithetical extremes. Nor is the reader likely to find Mann's work obviously experimental. Mann's world is often complicated but seldom private: his use of symbols is at least relatively simple; one need only think of Joyce, Kafka, or Eliot, and the contrast is clear enough. (p. 1)

If then there are new directions in Mann, they are not obviously indicated. They exist nevertheless; the cautious bourgeois is an explorer, as bourgeois often are. For all his deceptive air of conservatism, there is in Mann an almost Faustian urge to experiment, to go beyond. (pp. 1-2)

Regarded as a whole, Mann's career is a striking example of the "repeated puberty" which Goethe thought characteristic of the genius. In technique as well as in thought, he experimented far more daringly than is generally realized. In *Buddenbrooks* he wrote one of the last of the great "old-fashioned" novels, a patient, thorough tracing of the fortunes of a family. The novel, far from naturalistic in spirit, demonstrates his mastery of the techniques of naturalism and impressionism: elaborate accounts of the dinners, the bank balances, and the ailments of the Buddenbrooks alternate with swift evocations of mood. Primarily—and hence no doubt its enormous popularity—the novel tells a story, in a solid, conventional, unilinear way. From *The Magic Mountain* on, the secure ground of the nineteenth-century novel has been left for good. Daring experiments with the time sense, lack of interest, for long periods, in narration as such, and mythical associations are characteristic. In the climactic chapter of *The Beloved Returns* Mann uses the technique of the stream of consciousness, which he ventures to apply to the mind of Goethe. Still more audacious is the attempt, in *Doctor Faustus,* to render in words the spirit and the impact of both actual and imaginary works of music. All of the later novels are in some sense experimental. Mann says somewhere that the great novel transcends the limits of the genre; this, like so many of his general statements, probably refers primarily to his own work. (pp. 2-3)

In Mann's development of the symphonic novel, with a structure based on anticipation, repetition, and variation, there is the same tendency towards increased range of experimentation. The leitmotif, as Mann first used it, was nothing new in German literature. The repetition of a few words to characterize a given person or situation was a technique well understood by Otto Ludwig and Fontane; Mann might have hit upon it even without knowing Wagner. Gradually, almost imperceptibly, the leitmotif is used both more subtly and more extensively until in *Joseph* or *Doctor Faustus* a whole situation may be repeated, more or less varied; or a basic type of character returns under another name: Ishmael as Esau, Abraham as Jacob. Here as elsewhere Mann appears as a quiet revolutionary in literature; all the more effective, perhaps, for his outer conformity.

To emphasize only the new in Mann, however, would be grossly misleading. Few writers have been as conscious of tradition; few have stressed so insistently their relation to tradition. In Mann's case, the dominant early influences came from extra-literary sources: Schopenhauer, Wagner, Nietzsche, and later Freud. As Mann gradually shifted away from nineteenth-century romanticism and pessimism, he turned increasingly to an older strain in German culture, without completely repudiating his former guides. The figure of Goethe, both as man and artist, became increasingly significant to him. In varying ways, the major novels which follow *The Magic Mountain* reflect this significance. (pp. 3-4)

Mann's work stands out from the mass of contemporary German literature above all because of its combination of great intellectual range and distinction and finesse of style. . . . [It] is Mann's fusion of matter and manner which is unique. Beyond this, and more precisely, his flair for psychology, his use of a pattern of subtle relationships within the frame of each work, and his solid, careful craftsmanship further distinguish his writings. His psychological vision, sharpened by Nietzsche, the Russian and the French novel, and later by Freud, is of a keenness which the German novel has rarely equaled. (pp. 4-5)

One of the most basic of Mann's characteristics

is the conscientious thoroughness often attributed to the Germans in general. . . . The solidity, the undeniable distinction of Mann's work come in no small degree from this thoroughness. Yet the defects of this virtue are no less real for being obvious: sheer Wagnerian bulk, and a tendency to digressions which are not always fascinating in their own right. The chapter "Operationes Spirituales" in *The Magic Mountain* shows by example as well as by precept that endless intellectual gymnastics lead inevitably to mental fatigue.

Mann's self-consciousness, extraordinary even in our time, would seem to spring from the same psychological ground as his anxious attention to detail. All his works, to some degree, are "portraits of the artist," and even much of his criticism falls into the same category. . . . Mann had more right than most to quote Ibsen's dictum that writing means sitting in judgment on oneself. His castigation of the artist as parasite, criminal, and demagogue would have satisfied Plato at his most puritanical. Even Joseph, who is something of an artist, is also something of a rogue. Like his model Goethe, Mann characteristically exaggerates his sense of guilt in order to attain a sense of psychic relief. (pp. 6-7)

Whether literally artists or not, all Mann's heroes are of course "marked men," and marked, with very few exceptions, in a sinister sense. Generally they are threatened by illness of some sort; and Mann's deepest sympathy is with the "heroes of creative work," the *Leistungsethiker* who like Thomas Buddenbrook, Aschenbach, and Schiller work at "the edge of exhaustion" and often succumb to tasks beyond their strength. (p. 7)

The dualism implicit in Mann's view of the artist is basic in all of his thought. Convinced that monism is a "boring" philosophy, he divides the universe into a glittering series of polar opposites, of which the opposition of spirit to life is the most fundamental; the antithesis artist-*Bürger* is only a corollary. When one realizes that for "spirit" one can substitute art, death, illness, or love; for "life" nature, the normal, the material, or the naive, a certain looseness in Mann's mode of thought becomes obvious enough. This thinking in antitheses lends a dramatic flair: often two contrasted characters (or ideas) illuminate each other reciprocally. One thinks of Tonio Kröger and Hans Hansen, Naphta and Settembrini, Goethe and Schiller. Yet arbitrarily to declare certain ideas "polar opposites"—as in Mann's notorious contrast between *Kultur* and civilization—and then to play one against the other like a virtuoso, can lead to confusion and intellectual irresponsibility. In the *Reflections of a Non-Political Man,* for example, a *tour de force* of this type of thinking, the author often appears as a word-intoxicated man. (p. 8)

In *Tonio Kröger* and elsewhere, Mann speaks of a racial mixture—his North German father and a mother with Creole blood—as a force which produced a sharp split in his view of life, impelling him towards a certain dualism from the womb, as it were. More satisfying than this dubious biological theory is the explanation afforded by his intellectual and social position. The dichotomy in his own nature between the artist and the descendant of a patrician Lübeck family has been treated by Mann in numerous variations and discussed *ad nauseam* by his interpreters. At least equally significant, though relatively neglected, is the tension between the German romantic tradition and the European, cosmopolitan strain which runs throughout his work. On the one hand, Mann, by his own repeated statements, is the follower of a romantic, pessimistic, and deeply conservative tendency in German thought; musical rather than logical; and significantly enough, an admirer of such an enormously sentimental story as Storm's *Immensee.* Yet as the author of *Buddenbrooks* he is the pupil of European naturalism, as such of a predominantly logical, rationalistic, and "scientific" movement. Politically he is equally torn; his *Frederick and the Great Coalition* and other war books defend the Prussianism he had elsewhere treated ironically. The duel in *The Magic Mountain* symbolizes, among other things, the clash between the two sides of Mann's heritage. It will not do, of course, to construct an absolute antithesis between the German and the Western European. The greatest Germans are Europeans too; it is no accident that Joseph, Mann's most ambitious attempt at a synthesis of spirit and life, bears a certain resemblance to young Goethe. But the tension between the two elements remains. The *Joseph* stories mark the extreme of his flight from a Germany grown distasteful, while in *Doctor Faustus* there is a symbolic exile's return to the German scene, but a return marked by anguish.

For many reasons, then, Mann's view of the world is profoundly dualistic. Attracted to the "spirit" and to life, to art and the middle class, he seems to have found it equally difficult to cast in his lot finally with either side. In this dualism lies the source of Mann's irony: life is attracted to spirit, spirit to life; the artist longs, with "the least bit of scorn" for "the bliss of the ordinary." Mann's divided view of the world, which characteristically results in ambiguities and ambivalences, has irritated some readers. But his irony, like Voltaire's is "no cruel goddess." An ironic attitude towards human characters does not exclude real warmth towards them; one thinks of Toni Buddenbrook, Hans Castorp, and Serenus Zeitblom in *Doctor Faustus.*

Yet in the ironic treatment of ideas Mann is sometimes less happy. One grows impatient with his refusal to commit himself; what, for example, is one's attitude towards the values represented by Peeperkorn in *The Magic Mountain* supposed to be? Here too there has been a development. While ironies still abound, they become less decisive, intellectually. More and more, in his fiction as well as in his essays, Mann takes a humanistic and "Western" position. *Doctor Faustus,* in many ways a return to the German "side," shares its forthrightness with the later political essays. Despite its many ironies, it is unique among Mann's novels in the degree of its commitment to a fixed system of standards. (pp. 9-11)

Mann is too versatile, and above all too individual a writer to be assigned to any school or "-ism." His most representative works, from *Buddenbrooks* on, combine the strains of realism and symbolism, but gradually the latter has become dominant. From this point of view, as from others, *The Magic Mountain* is an apex and a turning point in his development. Employing a microscopic closeness of observation, it adds a new dimension to the realistic novel, while at the same time it marks Mann's major shift to the use of mythical patterns. Yet even in his later, most symbolic works, the accuracy of Mann's eye has not decreased. It would seem that his "dual perspective" on the world—his way of seeing persons and events dialectically, from two sides—gives his vision a stereoptic quality. . . .

In regarding Mann's literary career, which extended for something over sixty years, one is impressed even more by the sustained quality of Mann's work than by its range. Few novelists, and perhaps no other German novelist, have produced an integrated body of fiction in which the general level is so consistently maintained. (p. 162)

It is high time to discard the notion of Mann as a virtuoso performing endless variations on a single theme. The author of "nervous little sketches" and lyrical novellas experienced a rebirth like his own Joseph's before he could produce, in *The Magic Mountain,* one of the most imposing structures erected by the modern mind. The novels and stories of his "third career," from 1933 on, have in turn a character and physiognomy of their own. Some of these later and more experimental works betray a decrease in immediacy and freshness. Yet Mann's last works—the *Confessions of Felix Krull* and the essay on Schiller—are among his most vivid and effective. (p. 163)

Henry Hatfield, in his *Thomas Mann,* revised edition, New Directions, 1962, 196 p.

SOURCES FOR FURTHER STUDY

Apter, T. E. *Thomas Mann: The Devil's Advocate.* New York: New York University Press, 1979, 165 p.

> Contends that Mann believed "an investigation of evil's force and fascination would result in refreshing disgust with evil."

Heller, Erich. *Thomas Mann: The Ironic German.* Cleveland: World Publishing Co., 1961, 303 p.

> Comprehensive critical study of Mann's literary techniques.

Hollingdale, R. J. *Thomas Mann: A Critical Study.* Lewisburg, Pa.: Bucknell University Press, 1971, 203 p.

> Examines the "foundation" of Mann's fiction by studying six of its central preoccupations: ideology, decadence, irony, myth, crime, and sickness.

McWilliams, James R. *"Buddenbrooks."* In his *Brother Artist: A Psychological Study of Thomas Mann's Fiction,* pp. 15-49. Lanham, Md.: University Press of America, 1983.

> Asserts that "in *Buddenbrooks* Mann deals with a major eruption of material from the subconscious that embraced in a unified sequence the basic experiences, reactions, and judgments of his childhood. The result is a singularly great work."

Swales, Martin. *Thomas Mann: A Study.* London: Heinemann, 1980, 117 p.

> Critical biography, examining Mann's dominant themes and philosophical views.

Thomas, R. Hinton. *Thomas Mann: The Mediation of Art.* Oxford: Oxford University Press, 1963, 188 p.

> Critical study focusing on Mann's major works.

Katherine Mansfield

1888-1923

(Born Kathleen Mansfield Beauchamp; also wrote under pseudonym Boris Petrovsky) New Zealand short story writer, critic, and poet.

INTRODUCTION

*M*ansfield is a central figure in the development of the modern short story. An early practitioner of stream-of-consciousness narration, she applied this technique to create stories based on the illumination of character rather than the contrivances of plot. Her works treat such universal concerns as family and love relationships and the everyday experiences of childhood, and are noted for their distinctive wit, psychological acuity, and perceptive characterizations.

Mansfield was born into a prosperous family in Wellington, New Zealand, and attended school in England in her early teens. She returned home after completing her education, but was thereafter dissatisfied with colonial life, and at nineteen she persuaded her parents to allow her to return to England. Biographers believe that Mansfield either arrived in London pregnant as the result of a shipboard romance, or that she became pregnant after her arrival as the result of an affair with a man she had known in New Zealand. She entered into a hasty marriage with George Bowden, a young musician, and left him the next day, after which her mother arranged for her removal to a German spa, where she miscarried. Mansfield returned to England following a period of recuperation, during which she wrote the short stories comprising her first collection, *In a German Pension* (1911). Offering satiric commentary on the attitudes and behavior of the German people, these stories focus on themes relating to sexual relationships, female subjugation, and childbearing. Critics have found that these stories, although less technically accomplished than Mansfield's later fiction, evince her characteristic wit and perception—in particular her incisive grasp of female psychology—as well as her early experimentation with interior monologue. Determined to pursue a literary career, between 1911 and 1915 Mansfield published short stories and book reviews in such magazines as the *Athenaeum*, the *Blue Review*, the *New Age*, the *Open Window*, and *Rhythm*. In 1912 she met the editor and critic John Middleton Murry and was soon sharing the editorship of the *Blue Review* and *Rhythm* with him. The two began living together, and married in 1918, when Bowden finally consented to a divorce.

In 1915 Mansfield was reunited in London with her only brother, Leslie Heron Beauchamp, shortly before he was killed in a military training accident, and Beauchamp's visit is believed to have reinforced Mansfield's resolve to incorporate material drawn from her New Zealand background into her fiction. The collections *Bliss, and Other Stories* (1920) and *The Garden Party, and Other Stories* (1922)—the last that Mansfield edited and oversaw in production—contain many of her New Zealand stories, including "Prelude," "At the Bay," "The Garden Party," "The Voyage," and "A Doll's House," as well as other examples of her mature fiction. The success of these volumes established Mansfield as a major talent comparable to such contemporaries as Virginia Woolf and James Joyce. Never in vigorous health, Mansfield was severely weakened by tuberculosis in the early 1920s. Nonetheless, she worked almost continuously, writing until the last few months of her life, when she undertook a faith cure at a "psychical institute" in France. She died in 1923 at the age of thirty-four.

Early assessments of Mansfield were based largely on the romanticized image presented by Murry in extensively edited volumes of her private papers, as well as in reminiscences and critical commentary that he published after her death. His disposition of her literary estate is considered by some commentators to

have been exploitative: he profited from the publication of stories that Mansfield had rejected for publication, as well as notebook jottings, intermittent diaries, and letters. The idealized representation of Mansfield promulgated by Murry, termed the "cult of Katherine," is undergoing revision by modern biographers aided by new editions of her letters and journals.

Mansfield's best and most characteristic work is generally considered to be contained in *Bliss, and Other Stories* and *The Garden Party, and Other Stories*. These volumes collect many of Mansfield's highly regarded New Zealand stories as well as the widely reprinted and often discussed "Bliss," "The Daughters of the Late Colonel," "Je Ne Parle Pas Français," and "Miss Brill," which are considered among the finest short stories in the English language. These stories display some of Mansfield's most successful innovations with narrative technique, including interior monologue, stream of consciousness, and shifting narrative perspectives. They are commended for the facility with which Mansfield represented intricate balances within family relationships, her depictions of love relationships from both female and male points of view, and her portrayals of children, which are considered especially insightful. Mansfield is one of the few authors to attain prominence exclusively for short stories, and her works remain among the most widely read in world literature.

(For further information about Mansfield's life and works, see *Contemporary Authors*, Vol. 104; *Short Story Criticism*, Vol. 9; and *Twentieth-Century Literary Criticism*, Vols. 2, 8, 39.)

CRITICAL COMMENTARY

MALCOLM COWLEY
(essay date 1922)

[Cowley was a prominent American critic who wrote extensively on modern American literature. In the following excerpt, he assesses Mansfield's short fiction and discusses her second volume of short stories, *The Garden Party, and Other Stories*.]

There is no doubt that the stories of Katherine Mansfield are literature. That is, their qualities are literary qualities. No one would think of dramatizing these stories, of condensing them into pithy paragraphs, or of making them into a scenario for Douglas Fairbanks.

They do not dissolve into music, like Mallarmé, or materialize into sculpture like Heredia. The figures are not plastic; the landscapes are not painted, but described, and they are described, usually, through the eyes of a character, so that they serve both as a background and as a character study. In the same way Katherine Mansfield does not treat events, but rather the reflection of events in someone's mind. Her stories are literature because they produce effects which can be easily attained by no other art.

Nobody ever dies in one of her stories; nobody ever marries or is born. These pompous happenings occur off-stage, discreetly, a day before the curtain rises

Principal Works

In a German Pension (short stories) 1911

Prelude (short story) 1918

Bliss, and Other Stories (short stories) 1920

The Garden Party, and Other Stories (short stories) 1922

The Doves' Nest, and Other Stories (short stories) 1923

Poems (poetry) 1923

The Little Girl, and Other Stories (short stories) 1924; also published as Something Childish, and Other Stories, 1924

Journal of Katherine Mansfield (journal) 1927

The Letters of Katherine Mansfield. 2 vols. (letters) 1928

Novels and Novelists (criticism) 1930

The Short Stories of Katherine Mansfield (short stories) 1937

The Scrapbook of Katherine Mansfield (journal) 1939

Katherine Mansfield's Letters to John Middleton Murry: 1913-1922 (letters) 1951

The Urewera Notebook (journal) 1978

The Collected Letters of Katherine Mansfield. 2 vols. (letters) 1984-87

The Critical Writings of Katherine Mansfield (criticism) 1987

Letters between Katherine Mansfield and John Middleton Murry (letters) 1988

Poems of Katherine Mansfield (poetry) 1988

or a year after its descent; so do most other events on which her stories touch. . . . [There] is no plot; instead she tries to define a situation. That is why her stories give the effect of overflowing their frame; an event has a beginning and an end, but the consequences of a situation continue indefinitely like waves of sound or the familiar ripples of a pool. This is the effect produced by the best of her work, but actually it is nothing more than a moment out of the lives of her characters; a moment not of action but of realization, and a realization of one particular sort.

These stories, at least the fifteen contained in her second volume [*The Garden Party and Other Stories*], have a thesis: namely, that life is a very wonderful spectacle, but disagreeable for the actors. Not that she ever states it bluntly in so many words; blunt statement is the opposite of her method. (p. 230)

[The characters] discover life to be wonderful and very disagreeable. . . . The moment from their existence which Katherine Mansfield chooses to describe is the moment of this realization.

The method is excellent, and the thesis which it enforces is vague enough and sufficiently probable to be justified aesthetically. Only, there is sometimes a suspicion—I hate to mention it in the case of an author so delicate and so apparently just, but there is sometimes a suspicion that she stacks the cards. She seems to choose characters that will support her thesis. The unsympathetic ones are too aggressively drawn, and the good and simple folk confronted with misfortunes too undeviating; she doesn't treat them fairly. (p. 231)

[This] volume, compared with the first, adheres more faithfully to the technique of Chekhov, and the adherence begins to be dangerous. He avoided monotonousness only, and not always, by the immense range of his knowledge and sympathy. Katherine Mansfield's stories have no such range; they are literature, but they are limited. She has three backgrounds only: continental hotels, New Zealand upper-class society, and a certain artistic set in London. Her characters reduce to half a dozen types; when she deserts these she flounders awkwardly, and especially when she describes the Poorer Classes. Lacking a broad scope, she could find salvation in technical variety, but in her second volume she seems to strive for that no longer.

To read her first book was to make a voyage of adventure, or maybe even to open Chapman's Homer. She had borrowed a little from her English contemporaries, but not enough so that one could identify her sources. She has borrowed a great deal from Chekhov, but her characters were other and more familiar. In general the stories were her own experiments and successful experiments; that is why it was exhilarating to read them. One did not quite know what she would write next. . . . *The Garden Party* has answered that question. It is almost as good as **"Bliss,"** but not much different; from Katherine Mansfield it is immensely disappointing. (pp. 231-32)

Malcolm Cowley, "The Author of 'Bliss'," in *The Dial,* Chicago, Vol. 73, August 22, 1922, pp. 230-32.

DAVID DAICHES

(essay date 1936)

[Daiches is a prominent English scholar and critic. He is especially renowned for his in-depth studies of such writers as Robert Burns, Robert Louis Stevenson, and Virginia Woolf. In the following excerpt, he discusses Mansfield's fictional methods and principal aims as an author.]

The short stories of Katherine Mansfield, though not

many in number, contain some of the most sensitive writing in our literature. (p. 83)

She has imposed upon herself a much severer discipline than the majority of story-tellers dare to do; she writes only to tell the truth—not the truth for the outsider, for the observer who watches the action from the street corner, but the truth for the characters themselves and so the real meaning of the situation.

A situation can have "meaning" from many different points of view. The point of view may be ethical, or aesthetic, or dependent on any scheme of values the author wishes to apply. Katherine Mansfield consciously and deliberately avoided any such external approach. For her the meaning of the situation meant its potentialities for change in the lives of the characters, in so far as such a change had reference to aspects of experience known and appreciated by feeling and suffering begins in general. There is always this ultimate reference to life in its wider aspect, though it does not take the form of the description of the most impressive or superficially the most "significant" elements in life. It is not the course of the action itself that has this connection, but, in so many cases, this element of *change* which links up her stories with general human activity. The varying and unstable qualities of human emotions and the very essence of these qualities are illustrated by the point, the dynamic element in the story which is brought out in the presentation. It is a point the mere *observer* would miss—some subtle change of emotional atmosphere or realisation by the characters of something new, something different and cogent, though they might not themselves be aware of what it is. Thus the "truth of the idea" meant to Katherine Mansfield the meaning of the situation for those concerned in it, and this had implications far beyond the individual instance, though these implications were not stressed or commented on: this meaning she nearly always saw as involving some kind of change. (pp. 84-6)

In **"The Garden Party"** the story rests on the change from the party atmosphere to the atmosphere of sudden death in the carter's cottage, and the *meaning* of that change. All the other elements, the description, the dialogue, the character sketching, are subordinated to this. (p. 87)

[With] Katherine Mansfield much . . . depends on the actual presentation of the story. Neither she nor her characters make lengthy comment; the meaning of the situation is never *stated,* but implied. Her endeavour is to put the story in a position to illuminate itself; the parts throw light on the whole and the whole throws light on the parts so that, for example, the change at the end puts new meaning into what has gone before, putting everything into a new perspective which we had not been aware of until we arrived at the end. (pp. 91-2)

That she had a tendency in [a sentimental] direc-

tion is shown by occasional false touches throughout her work. . . .

As a rule Katherine Mansfield manages to bring out the significance of a situation with greater economy and a surer touch. (p. 93)

Objective truth was always Katherine Mansfield's aim in her stories. She wished to become the supreme recorder, free from all personal bias and even interest. . . . Yet sometimes the reader is left a little in doubt whether the story is told in terms of the thought of the observer or the observed. The meaning of the situation is the meaning for those concerned in it, but occasionally we find the writer herself entering into the situation for an instant. (pp. 94-5)

We find this occasionally throughout the stories—the spectator becoming too interested to hold aloof and allowing her own consciousness to enter. It is just because her approach is usually so objective that we notice those occasions where, only for a moment, she allows the subjective element to enter. Of course, in pure description the author must talk to some extent in her own person, but once the characters are set going and the story is told in terms of *their* minds any intrusion by the author is dangerous. There are few authors who intrude so rarely as Katherine Mansfield, who, when she does intrude, does it in this almost imperceptible way, substituting her own imagination directly just for a sentence or two. . . . (pp. 95-6)

Only in her less successful moments does Katherine Mansfield give us some notion of the difficulty of the achievement involved in her successful work. Her writing at its best has a purity rare in literature. . . . She wrote no more than she saw, but she saw so much in the least human activity that she never needed to do more than record her observations. (pp. 96-7)

Katherine Mansfield's method lies somewhere between the traditional one and that of Joyce and other modern writers. She refuses to sacrifice her powers of independent observation, but at the same time she takes note of nothing which is not in the highest sense relevant to the situation she is presenting. She frees herself by a deliberate effort from any irrelevant emotion or pre-supposition. (p. 106)

Sometimes Katherine Mansfield succumbs to the temptation of substituting her own clear vision for the blindness of those whose reactions she is portraying. But she never does this sufficiently to interfere with the reality of the story or with that creation of atmosphere which is one of her greatest achievements. (p. 108)

Katherine Mansfield's development was the result of increased consciousness of what she wanted to achieve in her writing. She was not one of those writers who improve with practice automatically. (p. 113)

The time has come when we can look back on Katherine Mansfield's work and place it in its true perspective. We can see it now as one of the greatest contributions to the development of the art of the short story ever made. Her work has shown new possibilities for the small-scale writer, and by the uniqueness of its achievement points the way to a new critical approach to that age-long problem, the relation of "art" to "life." No writer in either the creative or the critical field has yet shown himself of the calibre to profit to the full from this twofold contribution to literature. (pp. 113-14)

David Daiches, "The Art of Katherine Mansfield," in his *New Literary Values: Studies in Modern Literature,* 1936. Reprint by Oliver and Boyd, 1968, pp. 83-114.

ELIZABETH BOWEN
(essay date 1956)

[Bowen, an Anglo-Irish fiction writer and critic, wrote novels and short stories that display great stylistic control and subtle insight in the portrayal of human relationships. She is also noted for her series of supernatural stories set in London during World War II. In the following excerpt from a 1956 essay, she comments on the diversity and innovative nature of Mansfield's short fiction.]

"Katherine Mansfield's death, by coming so early, left her work still at the experimental stage." This could be said—but would it be true? To me, such a verdict would be misleading. First, her writing already *had* touched perfection a recognizable number of times; second, she would have been bound to go on experimenting up to the end, however late that had come. One cannot imagine her settling down to any one fixed concept of the short story—her art was, by its very nature, tentative, responsive, exploratory. There are no signs that she was casting about to find a formula: a formula would, in fact, have been what she fled from. Her sense of the possibilities of the story was bounded by no hard-and-fast horizons: she grasped that it is imperative for the writer to expand his range, never contract his method. Perception and language could not be kept too fresh, too alert, too fluid. Each story entailed a beginning right from the start, unknown demands, new risks, unforeseeable developments. Often, she worked by trial-and-error.

So, ever on the move, she has left with us no "typical" Katherine Mansfield story to anatomize. Concentrated afresh, each time, upon expression, she did not envisage "technique" in the abstract. As it reached her, each idea for a story had inherent within it its own shape: there could be for it no other. That shape, it was for her to perceive, then outline—she

thought (we learn from her letters and journal) far more of perception than of construction. The story *is* there, but she has yet to come at it. One has the impression of a water-diviner, pacing, halting, awaiting the twitch of the hazel twig. Also, to judge from her writings about her writing, there were times when Katherine Mansfield believed a story to have a volition of its own—she seems to stand back, watching it take form. Yet this could happen apart from her; the story drew her steadily into itself.

Yet all of her pieces, it seems clear, did not originate in the same order. Not in all cases was there that premonitory stirring of an idea; sometimes the external picture came to her first. She found herself seized upon by a scene, an isolated incident or a face which, something told her, must *have* meaning, though she had yet to divine what the meaning was. Appearances could in themselves touch alight her creative power. It is then that we see her moving into the story, from its visual periphery to its heart, recognizing the "why" as she penetrates. (p. 89)

Katherine Mansfield's masterpiece stories cover their tracks; they have an air of serene inevitability, almost a touch of the miraculous. (p. 90)

Of love for experiment for its own sake, Katherine Mansfield shows not a sign. Conscious artist, she carries none of the marks of the self-consciously "experimental" writer. Nothing in her approach to people or nature is revolutionary; her storytelling is, on its own plane, not much less straightforward than Jane Austen's. She uses no literary shock tactics. The singular beauty of her language consists, partly, in its hardly seeming to *be* language at all, so glass-transparent is it to her meaning. Words had but one appeal for her, that of speakingness. . . . She was to evolve from noun, verb, adjective, a marvelous sensory notation hitherto undreamed of outside poetry; nonetheless, she stayed subject to prose discipline. And her style, when the story-context requires, can be curt, decisive, factual. It is a style generated by subject and tuned to mood—so flexible as to be hardly *a* style at all. One would recognize a passage from Katherine Mansfield not by the manner but by the content. There are no eccentricities.

Katherine Mansfield was not a rebel, she was an innovator. Born into the English traditions of prose narrative, she neither revolted against these nor broke with them—simply, she passed beyond them. And now tradition, extending, has followed her. Had she not written, written as she did, one form of art might be still in infancy. One cannot attribute to Katherine Mansfield the entire growth, in our century, of the short story. . . . We owe to her the prosperity of the "free" story: she untrammeled it from conventions and, still more, gained for it a prestige till then unthought of. How much ground Katherine Mansfield broke for her successors may not be realized. Her imagination kindled unlikely matter; she was to alter for good and all our idea of what goes to make a story. . . . (pp. 90-1)

How good is Katherine Mansfield's character-drawing? I have heard this named as her weak point. I feel one cannot insist enough upon what she instinctively grasped—that the short story, by reason of its aesthetics, is not and is not intended to be the medium either for exploration or long-term development of character. Character cannot be more than *shown*—it is there for use, the use is dramatic. Foreshortening is not only unavoidable, it is right. And with Katherine Mansfield there was another factor—her "stranger" outlook on so much of society. I revert to the restrictedness of her life in England, the eclecticism of her personal circle. She saw few people, saw them sometimes too often. This could account for her tendency to repeat certain types of character. This restless New Zealand woman writing of London deals with what was more than half a synthetic world: its denizens *are* types, and they remain so—to the impoverishment of the London stories. . . . Her sophisticates are cut out sharply, with satire; they are animated, expressive but two-dimensional.

In the South of France stories, characters are subsidiary to their environment; they drift like semi-transparent fish through the brilliantly lighted colours of an aquarium. Here, Katherine Mansfield's lovely crystallization of place and hour steals attention away from men and women. . . . [The] South of France stories are about moods.

Katherine Mansfield, we notice, seldom outlines and never dissects a character: instead, she causes the person to expose himself—and devastating may be the effect. The author's nominal impassivity is telling. I should not in the main call her a kind writer, though so often she is a pitiful one. Wholly benevolent are her comedies: high spirits, good humour no less than exquisite funniness endear to us **"The Daughters of the Late Colonel," "The Doves' Nest," "The Singing Lesson."** Nor is the laugh ever against a daydreamer.

The New Zealand characters are on a quite other, supreme level. They lack no dimension. Their living-and-breathing reality at once astonishes and calms us: they belong to life, not in any book—they existed before stories began. In their company we are no longer in Katherine Mansfield's; we forget her as she forgot herself. The Burnells of **"Prelude," "At the Bay,"** and **"The Doll's House"** are a dynasty. Related, though showing no too striking family likeness, are the conversational Sheridans of **"The Garden Party."** Of Burnell stock, graver and simplified, are elderly Mr. and Mrs. Hammond of **"The Stranger"**—Katherine Mansfield's equivalent of James Joyce's "The Dead." Alike in Burnells, Sheridans, and Hammonds we feel the almost mystic family integration. . . . I do not claim that the New Zealand stories vindicate Katherine Mansfield's character-drawing—the *drawing* is not (to my mind) elsewhere at fault. What she fails at in the European stories is full, adult character-*realization*—or, should one say, materialization? (pp. 91-2)

The New Zealand stories are timeless. Do the rest of the Katherine Mansfield stories "date"? I find there is some impression that they do—an impression not, I think, very closely checked on. To an extent, her work shows the intellectual imprint of her day, many of whose theories, tenets, preoccupations seem now faded. It is the more nearly *mondaine*, the "cleverer" of her stories which wear least well. Her psychology may seem naive and at times shallow—after all, she *was* young; but apart from that much water has flowed under bridges in thirty years. **"Bliss," "Psychology"** and **"Je ne parle pas français"** (technically one of her masterpieces) give out a faintly untrue ring. And one effect of her writing has told against her: it was her fate to set up a fashion in hyper-sensitivity, in vibratingness: it is her work in this vein which has been most heavily imitated, and travesties curdle one's feeling for the original. (pp. 92-3)

She wrote few love stories; those she did today seem distant, dissatisfying. Staking her life on love, she was least happy (I think) with love in fiction. Her passionate faith shows elsewhere. *Finesses,* subtleties, restless analysis, cerebral wary guardedness hallmark the Katherine Mansfield lovers. Was this, perhaps, how it was in London, or is this how Londoners' *amours* struck young New Zealand? She had left at the other side of the world a girlhood not unlike young Aunt Beryl's: beaux, waltzes, muslin, moonlight, murmuring sea. . . .

The stories are more than moments, instants, gleams: she has given them touches of eternity. The dauntless artist accomplished, if less than she hoped, more than she knew. Almost no writer's art has not its perishable fringes: light dust may settle on that margin. But against the core, the integrity, what can time do? Katherine Mansfield's deathless expectations set up a mark for us: no one has yet fulfilled them. Still at work, her genius rekindles faith; she is on our side in every further attempt. The effort she was involved in involves us—how can we feel her other than a contemporary? (p. 93)

Elizabeth Bowen, "Katherine Mansfield," in *Discussions of the Short Story,* edited by Hollis Summers, D. C. Heath and Company, 1963, pp. 89-93.

Aldous Huxley on Mansfield's literary imagination:

Like Conrad, [Miss Mansfield] sees her characters from a distance, as though at another table in a café; she overhears snatches of their conversations—about their aunts in Battersea, their stamp collections, their souls—and she finds them extraordinary, charming beyond all real and knowable people, odd, immensely exciting. She finds that they are Life itself—lovely, fantastic Life. Very rarely does she go beyond this long-range café acquaintanceship with her personages, rarely makes herself at home in their flat, everyday lives. But where Conrad bewilderedly speculates Miss Mansfield uses her imagination. She invents suitable lives for the fabulous creatures glimpsed at the café. And how thrilling those fancied lives always are! Thrilling, but just for that reason not very convincing. . . . Each of Miss Mansfield's stories is a window into a lighted room. The glimpse of the inhabitants sipping their tea and punch is enormously exciting. But one knows nothing, when one has passed, of what they are really like. That is why, however thrilling at a first reading, her stories do not wear. Chekhov's do; but, then, he had lived with his people as well as looked at them through the window. The traveller's-eye view of men and women is not satisfying.

Aldous Huxley, in *The Nation and The Athenaeum,*
16 May 1925.

ANDREW GURR AND CLARE HANSON
(essay date 1981)

[In the following excerpt, Gurr and Hanson survey Mansfield's fiction, commenting on the author's status as a New Zealand expatriate, her use of the modern, plotless short story form, and the influence of Symbolism on her work.]

As a writer Katherine Mansfield produced no single magnum opus. Consequently there is no obvious focus for assessing her achievement or even for identifying her distinctive qualities. Readers who follow Leonard Woolf 's preferences will take *In a German Pension* as her most characteristic achievement, and rank the other stories accordingly. ['Her gifts were those of an intense realist, with a superb sense of ironic humour and fundamental cynicism. She got enmeshed in the sticky sentimentality of Murry and wrote against the grain of her own nature,' Leonard Woolf, in his *Beginning Again:*

An Autobiography of the Years 1911-18, 1964.] The childhood stories will seem stickily sentimental, products of a maudlin escapism. Readers who find her social analysis, particularly of the oppressed position of women, to be her most conspicuously acute and illuminating feature will similarly range the stories according to a preference for which there is a good deal of supporting evidence but which still provides only a limited perspective on the whole achievement. And the view which takes the New Zealand stories, especially **'Prelude'** and the other stories written for the *Karori* collection, as most characteristic will also be limited in so far as it draws attention away from the distinctive qualities of the stories set in Bavaria or London or France. It is difficult to find a central organising principle for assessing her achievement that does not lead to neglect of some aspect of her work. She shines out through too many lantern-faces for any single perspective to give an adequate view. The best we can do is identify the different perspectives, and which face they lead up to. Of them all, probably the broadest is the one relating her exile to the powerful evocation of New Zealand in the major stories of her last years.

The last seven years of her life, the years of her mature achievements from **'Prelude'** onwards, were years of retreat into art isolation made perfect only inside the private circle of the childhood world that she constructed with such meticulous precision. She continued to use Murry and Ida Baker for physical protection, but in her stories she went where neither could hope to follow. She had written work based on her relationship with Murry—**'Je Ne Parle Pas Français', 'The Man without a Temperament', 'Psychology'**—but all of them were in some degree part of the dialogue which they maintained throughout their lives together. As such they perhaps lack the complete detachment and freedom, which writing out of more distant recollections provided.

Rather more than half the stories in her total *oeuvre* are based on or set in New Zealand. Murry's version of her outlook—that she hated the closed-off complacency of bourgeois suburban New Zealand until Leslie's death, when, as she put it, 'quite suddenly her hatred turned to love'—is a thorough oversimplification. She was trying out a narrative by 'Kass' about two little 'Beetham' girls early in 1910 (**'Mary'**, published in the *Idler*, March 1910. 'Kass' also appears in **'The Little Girl'** of 1912). **'A Birthday'**, set amongst the Bavarian stories of *In a German Pension*, has a New Zealand setting. The story which first drew Murry's attention, **'The Woman at the Store'**, written towards the end of 1911, was based on her memory of the camping holiday she underwent (over 240 miles on horseback) in the Ureweras shortly before she finally left New Zealand in 1908. And two stories written in 1915 before she began **'The Aloe'** have distinct affinities with the later New

Zealand material. **'The Apple Tree'**, first published in the *Signature* in October 1915 under the title **'Autumn I'**, is a gently derisive anecdote about her father, told from the viewpoint of his children, girl and boy. **'The Wind Blows'**, published as **'Autumn II'** in the *Signature,* is a more oblique piece about brother and sister, poignant, discontinuous, foreshadowing the symbolist technique which evolved as **'The Aloe'** changed in the following years to **'Prelude'**. Both stories were presumably triggered by the reminiscences of their childhood that she was sharing with Leslie at the time. His death, which took place just before the two stories appeared, changed the tentative, exploratory impulse into a powerful compulsion. From then on she drove towards the ultimate goal of a complete evocation of Karori in a series of minutely detailed epiphanies.

'Prelude' showed her that her New Zealand background was the best quarry for her artistic materials. It contained so much of the experience which, up to that time, she had most deeply lived. Only such experience could be the proper food for her art. This realisation is recorded in a famous journal entry of 1916:

> I feel no longer concerned with the same appearance of things. The people who lived or whom I wished to bring into my stories don't interest me any more. The plots of my stories leave me perfectly cold. Granted that these people exist and all the differences, complexities and resolutions are true to them—why should *I* write about them? They are not near me. All the false threats that bound me to them are cut away quite.

> Now—now I want to write recollections of my own country. Yes, I want to write about my own country till I simply exhaust my store . . .

> Ah, the people—the people we loved there—of them, too, I want to write. Another 'debt of love'. Oh, I want for one moment to make our undiscovered country leap into the eyes of the Old World. It must be mysterious, as though floating. It must take the breath. It must be 'one of those islands . . . '

From this point on, when she began to see her New Zealand background as an artistic positive, something which would both nourish her as an artist and enable her to express something wholly individual, she gained enormously in confidence as a writer.

There is no doubt that she worked at her highest creative level on material that was removed from her in space and time. This is because she was a Symbolist writer, interested not in social contexts and realities, but in the imaginative discovery or recreation of the ideal hidden within the real. With the aid of distance in time and space it is the idealising imagination, or perhaps more precisely what Pater [in 'The Child in the House,' in his *Miscellaneous Studies,* 1910] would call 'the finer sort of memory', which can best discover the ideal

essence of experience, which is obscured in the confusion of immediate impressions and perceptions.

Katherine Mansfield and Rudyard Kipling are among the very few writers in English to establish a reputation entirely on the basis of the short story form. It is no accident that they were writing at approximately the same time. The development of the short story in England lagged behind that in America and Russia chiefly because of differences in opportunities for magazine publication. By the 1890s, however, a huge expansion in the numbers of quarterlies and weeklies created the situation described by H. G. Wells [in his introduction to his *The Country of the Blind, and Other Stories,* 1911]:

> The 'nineties was a good and stimulating period for a short story writer . . . No short story of the slightest distinction went for long unrecognised . . . Short stories broke out everywhere.

Two entirely different types of story flourished together at the close of the nineteenth century. First, there was the story with a definite plot, which was the lineal descendant of the Gothic tale; and second, there was the new, 'plotless' story, concentrating on inner mood and impression rather than on external event. The latter was associated especially with the *Yellow Book,* the famous 'little magazine' of the nineties, and with the circle of writers gathered round its publisher John Lane—George Egerton, Ella D'Arcy, Evelyn Sharp and others. The innovatory quality of many of the stories published by these writers, and the contribution that they made to the development of the short story, is now becoming increasingly evident.

The plotless story seems to arise naturally from the intellectual climate of its time. In a world where, as the German philosopher Nietzsche declared, God was dead, and evolutionary theory had produced a sharp sense of man's insignificance in a changing universe, the only alternative seemed to be the retreat within, to the compensating powers of the imagination. With such a retreat came the stress on the significant moment, which would be called 'vision' or 'epiphany' by later writers such as James Joyce—the moment of insight which is outside space and time, vouch-safed only fleetingly to the imagination, but redeeming man's existence in time.

In fiction a shift in time-scale seems to accompany this emphasis on the moment. Throughout the nineteenth century the unit of fiction had been the year—from *Emma* to *The Ambassadors* we can say that this was so. In the late nineteenth and early twentieth century, the unit of fiction became the day. Elizabeth Bowen has written of this, saying that Katherine Mansfield was the first writer to see in the short story 'the ideal reflector of the day'. It is perhaps significant, however, that many other writers began their careers with short story writing in this period—Forster, for example, with the aptly named *The Eternal Moment,* and also D. H. Lawrence, James Joyce, and Virginia Woolf. It can even be suggested that the novels of these writers—Lawrence excepted—are in a sense simply extended short stories. Virginia Woolf 's *Mrs Dalloway* is an obvious example, but there is also Joyce's *Ulysses,* originally projected as a story for his collection of stories called *Dubliners,* to be titled 'Mr Hunter's Day'. It is as though the short story is the paradigmatic form of the early twentieth century, best able to express its fragmented and fragmentary sensibility.

Katherine Mansfield certainly saw her kind of story as a quintessentially modern form, a point she makes more than once in her reviews of fiction for the *Athenaeum.* She was also very conscious in her use of epiphany as the focal point of her stories. In one of her reviews she discusses the way in which internal crisis has replaced external crisis of plot in modern fiction, at the same time warning against the loss of all sense of crisis or significance which she detected in the work of some modern novelists:

Without [the sense of crisis] how are we to appreciate the importance of one 'spiritual event' rather than another? What is to prevent each being unrelated—complete in itself—if the gradual unfolding in growing, gaining light is not to be followed by one blazing moment?

It is usual in discussing Katherine Mansfield as a story writer to emphasise the influence of Chekhov on her technique. The relationship between her fiction and the plotless story of the nineties, however, is probably more important. She modelled her early stories on those of the *Yellow Book* writers, and it is from them, not Chekhov, that she would have learnt the techniques of stylised interior monologue, flashback and daydream which became so important in her work. By 1909, which was when she probably first read Chekhov, his techniques must have seemed distinctly old-fashioned by comparison with much English fiction.

Chekhov was probably more interesting to her as a type of the artist, especially after she contracted the tuberculosis from which he also suffered, rather than being a specific influence on her work. The two writers differ fundamentally in that Chekhov is a far more re-

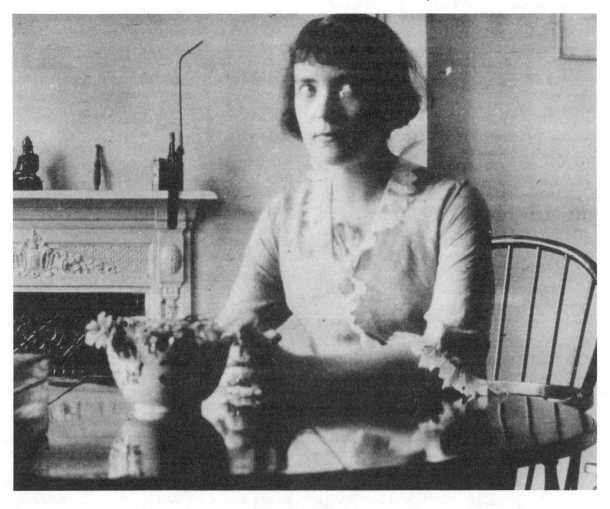

Katherine Mansfield, 1913.

alistic writer than Katherine Mansfield. His characters are always rooted firmly in a social context, and social forces are shown to have a decisive influence on the course of their lives and feelings. The difference is best shown by a comparison of his story 'Sleepy' with Katherine Mansfield's version of it, **'The-Child-Who-Was-Tired'** (1909). Chekhov's story is a restrained, pathological study, in which action is convincingly related to a specific social and psychological context. Katherine Mansfield's story is a symbolic fable, in which certain elements of the original plot are exaggerated and key images repeated in order to express a general, rather than a specific truth: the harshness of woman's lot in life. Although she read and admired Chekhov's stories throughout her career, a limit must be set on any comparison between the two writers. Any easy identification of the two is misleading.

Katherine Mansfield's talents were peculiarly suited to the short story form, as, in a different way, were those of Kipling. She did, however, try on at least three occasions to write a novel. There is the early attempt, *Juliet* (1906); then a novel to be based on the life and experiences of a schoolfriend she had known both in London and New Zealand, *Maata* (written intermittently between 1908 and 1915); finally the novel, *Karori*, which was to be built around the **'Prelude'** and **'At the Bay'** material, and to be based on the Burnell family. She was planning this last novel as late as 1921-22. Speculation about what she might or might not have written is futile, but clearly she continually wanted to experiment with new forms and to widen the boundaries of her talent. Another way of getting out of the critical rut of seeing her solely as a master of the concentrated short story is to recognise the clear development in her later work towards the use of the story cycle form. Two distinct cycles emerge: that centering on the Burnell family (**'Prelude'—'At the Bay'—'The Doll's House'**) and that centering on the Sheridans (**'The Garden Party'—'Her First Ball'—'By Moonlight'—'The Sheridans'**). Although they are all New Zealand stories, the two cycles are quite separate, and are clearly associated in Katherine Mansfield's mind with different themes. Broadly speaking, the Burnell sequence is concerned with the difficulties of the child or young adult coming to terms with the brutal realities of life (the egotism and cruelty of other people, the pressures of sexuality and so on), whereas in the Sheridan sequence there is a much more elegiac note: the theme is, as Katherine once wrote of Hardy's poems,

> that love and regret touched so lightly—that autumn tone, that feeling that 'Beauty passes though rare, rare it be . . . '

The fact that the two sequences were quite distinct is clear from a journal note written as Katherine Mansfield was planning **'The Sheridans':**

> I must begin writing for Clement Shorter today [this refers to a contract she had with the *Sphere*] 12 'spasms' of 2,000 words each. I thought of the Burnells, but no, I don't think so. Much better, the Sheridans, the three girls and the brother and the Father and Mother and so on . . .
>
> And in that playing chapter what I want to stress chiefly is: Which is the real life—that or this?—late afternoon—these thoughts—the garden—the beauty—how all things pass—and how the end seems to come so soon.

The stories in the Sheridan and Burnell cycles are linked together by character, setting and theme, and by repeated images and motifs. A 'dynamic pattern of recurrent development' is established, so that the reader's experience of an individual story is enriched by and enriches his experience of the others in that sequence.

Katherine Mansfield did not herself separate the short story and novel form as absolutely as genre-conscious modern critics have done, and the cycle of related stories may be seen as a kind of bridge for her between the two forms—rather as in William Faulkner's *Go Down Moses*, or, more relevantly, in Joyce's *Dubliners*, a sequence of stories linked together loosely but firmly by a common setting, related characters and related themes. Joyce similarly employs the symbolist technique of imagery repeated throughout the stories.

The relationship between Symbolism and Katherine Mansfield's short story art has been insufficiently recognised. It is accepted that her contemporary, Joyce, was influenced decisively by his early contact with Symbolist literature, but Katherine Mansfield's critics and biographers have failed to register the similar influences at work in her case. They have dismissed her early writing in the Symbolist mode as immature and, by implication, irrelevant, not seeing the intimate connection between this early work and the particular nature and scope of her achievement.

The main influence on her in the period up to 1908 when she left New Zealand for the last time was that of Arthur Symons, who also influenced so many other early twentieth-century writers, notably Yeats and Eliot. Symons's role was as a communicator and purveyor of ideas. It was through his critical books that Katherine Mansfield was introduced to French Symbolist poetry and to other diverse, broadly Symbolist writers like the Belgian Maurice Maeterlinck and the Italian Gabriele D'Annunzio. She also absorbed very thoroughly the condensed version of Symbolist aesthetic theory which Symons presented in his books. Indeed, her early attempts to piece together an aesthetic rely almost entirely on the writings of Symons, and to a lesser extent Wilde. From these two, she took ideas which continually influenced her art. One was the Symbolist belief that in literature an abstract state of mind or feeling should be conveyed not through descriptive analysis but through concrete images or symbols. Such a theme must be evoked, not described, if it is to be successfully conveyed in art. If we read her stories in the light of this ideal—one which she refers to repeatedly in letters and notebooks—it becomes apparent that in a Mansfield story almost every detail has a symbolic as well as a narrative function. The details, or images, are intended to work in concert to create a mood or evoke a theme which is never directly stated. These oblique and indirect stories must thus be read with the same close responsiveness as a Symbolist or Modernist poem, if the full effect is to be realised.

She was also influenced by the Symbolist belief in the organic unity of the perfect work of art. Even in her earliest stories she strove to achieve the 'unity of impression' advocated by Poe, and she wrote many years later that 'If a thing has really come off it seems to me there mustn't be one single word out of place, or one word that could be taken out.' This particular quotation might tend to suggest that she was concerned only with a superficial perfection of style, but her other references to the 'essential form' of the true work of art make it clear that for her such form was truly organic, uniting form and content indissolubly.

Though the work of art could be considered as analogous to natural organic life, it was also, paradoxically, outside organic life, outside reality. She certainly inherited the Symbolist belief in art as an autotelic activity, a fact which should be stressed as a corrective to the impression, frequently given by critics, that she was a writer with a 'mission' or purpose. In fact she was clear in her belief that, though art must be nourished by life, it had its own laws and nature, which were quite distinct from those of reality. The artist must be completely aware of the distinction, and must not confuse the two spheres, nor attempt to impose his vision on life:

> That is to say, reality cannot become the ideal, the dream; and it is not the business of the artist to grind an axe, to try to impose his vision of life upon the existing world. Art is not an attempt of the artist to reconcile existence with his vision; it is an attempt to create his own world *in* this world.

From Symbolist theory and practice came her interest in extending the boundaries of prose expression. Baudelaire and Mallarmé in their prose poem experiments were interested in steering prose away from its innate structural tendency towards abstraction and analysis, towards a more concrete expressiveness. They and other Symbolist writers—including Pater—attempted to convey meaning in prose not only through the use of words as conceptual counters, but also by exploiting the 'physical properties' of language, and 'sound sense'. They repeatedly used the musical analogy for prose, to signify an ideal of nondiscursive

expressiveness, and this is an image which is also used by Katherine Mansfield, for the same reasons, in her frequent discussions of what she was trying to do with her prose medium. For example, she wrote of **'Miss Brill'**:

> After I'd written it I read it aloud—numbers of times—just as one would *play over* a musical composition—trying to get it nearer and nearer to the expression of Miss Brill—until it fitted her.
>
> (pp. 14-23)

Katherine Mansfield's reputation is of a writer with an exquisite and delicate sensibility. Her writing is most often described as though it were a kind of verbal equivalent of an Impressionist painting, and stress is laid on the physical 'surface' of her work—its tone, colour and texture. She is commonly praised for her acuteness of ear, her visual memory, her exquisite rendering of impressions of the natural world. There is a string of verbal nouns—flash, colour, sparkle, glow—by means of which her critics have tried to convey the effect that her work has had on them. But it can more usefully and accurately be compared to Post-Impressionist rather than to Impressionist painting, for we need more emphasis on the solidity of the structure of her stories and on their weight of implication. (p. 24)

Andrew Gurr and Clare Hanson, in their *Katherine Mansfield*, St. Martin's Press, 1981, 146 p.

KATE FULLBROOK
(essay date 1986)

[Fullbrook is an English educator and critic whose *Katherine Mansfield* analyzes Mansfield as an important English Modernist. In the following excerpt from that work, Fullbrook closely examines several of Mansfield's most accomplished short stories from 1921, finding that they recapitulate characteristic concerns of Mansfield's fiction while displaying advances in literary technique over earlier works.]

The early 1920s were the culminating years for literary modernism in English. Pound's *Mauberley* came out in 1920; Lawrence's *Women in Love* and Richardson's *Deadlock* in 1921; Eliot's *Waste Land,* Joyce's *Ulysses,* Yeats's *Later Poems* and Woolf's *Jacob's Room* in 1922. 1921 was the *annus mirabilis* for Katherine Mansfield's later work, during which she produced a crop of brilliant stories that themselves provide a review of all the concerns which had shaped her fiction and which extend her treatment of them through the application of her late technical subtlety.

The overriding interest in the stories of 1921 remains the unpredictability of the self and the impossibility of direct communication between individuals. Katherine Mansfield stressed this point again in 1922, when, in a letter to Murry, she insists on her familiar preoccupation: 'We are all hidden, looking out at each other; I mean even those of us who want not to hide.'

Moments of connection, much less communication, are rare in Katherine Mansfield's work, but in **'At the Bay'** (1921), one of the Burnell stories, she provides accounts of several moments when the barriers between her characters break down. Like **'Prelude'**, **'At the Bay'** is an impressionistic story held together by running motifs of animal images and of varieties of symbolic response to the sea.

'At the Bay' has a pastoral opening, patterned by images that embody the characters, their actions, their deficiencies and the mysterious influences that work upon them. The scene set is primal, an alternative Genesis: the sea is divided from the safety of the land, a flock of sheep and a wise old shepherd with his dog appears, a rebellious cat surveys the controlled, domestic animals with disdain, a huge gum-tree spreads its arms over the whole of the scene. Against the background of these 'timeless' images, the Burnells go into action, locked in roles that are fixed by their historical moment. Stanley plays his usual role of macho buffoon, beginning his day with an officious encounter with his brother-in-law, Jonathan, during his morning dip. It is all that Stanley can do with the possibilities of the unconscious which the sea, in the story, represents. The prose moves from the lyricism of the opening images to the self-important bluster of Stanley's mind, and it stays in this register until the women of the family bundle him into the coach for work. As he leaves, the whole house relaxes, with the narrative catching the change from the women's tension to their harmony in relief at his departure. Even Beryl, still driven by her lack of success in ensnaring a husband, and still en-

gaged in a nervous flirtation with Stanley, is glad to see him go:

> 'Good-bye, Stanley', called Beryl, sweetly and gaily. It was easy enough to say good-bye! And there she stood, idle, shading her eyes with her hand. The worst of it was Stanley had to shout good-bye too, for the sake of appearances. Then he saw her turn, give a little skip and run back to the house. She was glad to be rid of him!

> Yes, she was thankful. Into the living-room she ran and called 'He's gone!' Linda cried from her room: 'Beryl! Has Stanley gone?' Old Mrs. Fairfield appeared, carrying the boy in his little flannel coatee.

> 'Gone?'

> 'Gone!'

> Oh, the relief, the difference it made to have the man out of the house. Their very voices changed as they called to one another; they sounded warm and loving and as if they shared a secret. Beryl went over to the table. 'Have another cup of tea, mother. It's still hot.' She wanted, somehow, to celebrate the fact that they could do what they liked now. There was no man to disturb them; the whole perfect day was theirs.

> 'No, thank you, child,' said old Mrs. Fairfield, but the way at that moment she tossed the boy up and said 'a-goos-a-goos-a-ga!' to him meant that she felt the same. The little girls ran into the paddock like chickens let out of a coop.

> Even Alice, the servant girl, washing up the dishes in the kitchen, caught the infection and used the precious tank water in a perfectly reckless fashion.

> 'Oh, these men!' said she, and she plunged the teapot into the bowl and held it under the water even after it had stopped bubbling, as if it too was a man and drowning was too good for them.

Katherine Mansfield deftly dramatises the relaxation of the women into mutual kindness as they make their various gestures of relief with the departure of Stanley. The women of all ages and social conditions respond more strongly to their moment of liberation than their external behaviour can indicate, but for an instant they are united in the communal expression of freedom grasped with pleasure.

Another writer concerned with portraying the condition of women might have left it at that: with symbolic Alice symbolically drowning all men in her symbolic sink in her symbolic kitchen while the women move in a harmony of rapture through the house. But Katherine Mansfield's moment of shared release is over in an instant. Alice stays at her sink; Beryl's frustration is not eased. The unity is, after all, only temporary; nothing essential has changed. Once the emotional reflex of relief has passed the characters go their separate ways, their female condition of restraint blending with other facets of their personalities to shape them in the series of duet-like encounters that follow. The little girls run off to play with their cousins; Alice visits a jolly widow happy with her independence (' "freedom's best" ', she tells Alice); Kezia confronts the idea of death in a moving conversation with her grandmother; Linda feels a stab of love for her new son, who, up to this point, has left her only hostile or indifferent, and has a moment of connection with Jonathan.

There are only a few instances in all of Katherine Mansfield's fiction where she suggests what a true meeting between the sexes might entail. The most powerful of these occurs in **'At the Bay'** during Linda's conversation with Jonathan. It is important to notice that the fellow feeling in this encounter is only possible because Jonathan falls hopelessly short when measured against standards of orthodox masculine behaviour and success which are typified by Stanley. Linda, as in **'Prelude'**, is unhappy, still enmeshed in the expectations of her class and era. Jonathan, however, interests her.

> Linda thought again how attractive he was. It was strange to think that he was only an ordinary clerk, that Stanley earned twice as much money as he. What was the matter with Jonathan? He had no ambition; she supposed that was it. And yet one felt he was gifted, exceptional. He was passionately fond of music; every spare penny he had went on books. He was always full of new ideas, schemes, plans. But nothing came of it all. The new fire blazed in Jonathan . . . but a moment later it had fallen in and there was nothing but ashes, and Jonathan went around with a look like hunger in his eyes.

Jonathan himself understands what is wrong; he loathes the half of the sexist equation that defines the worth of a man largely by the money he can make, and yet he realises that his own life has been set in its pattern of unease by the very values he rejects.

> 'It seems to me just as imbecile, just as infernal, to have to go to the office on Monday,' said Jonathan, 'as it always has done and always will do. To spend all the best years of one's life sitting on a stool from nine to five, scratching on someone's ledger! It's a queer use to make of one's . . . one and only life, isn't it?'

Jonathan is kept 'in jail' by his marriage and family. ' "I've two boys to provide for," ' he says, but he is wistfully pulled toward a larger life, a world that he sees as a ' "vast dangerous garden, waiting out there, undiscovered, unexplored" '. And it is too late to change. He says, in response to Linda's empathy and sympathy: ' "I'm old—I'm old." ' He bends his head and to Linda's sad surprise shows the grey speckling his hair. Like Kezia with her grandmother in the same story, the characters bow together before knowledge of mortality; age and sexual differences are brushed aside in recognition of the inevitability of death and in wonder at the fixity of personal history.

This single, moving instance of unmasked connection between a woman and a man emphasises the similarities rather than the divergences in the human condition. The moment depends on the fact that Jonathan is capable of wonder and is intellectually alive, and that Linda is in sympathy with these qualities despite her own choice of bourgeois safety. Even if Jonathan is a failed rebel, it is crucial that his disgust with masculine roles is one of the most significant aspects of his character. Sensitivity and rejection of a totally materialist view of the world point to the ways in which the existential bad faith, which Katherine Mansfield sees as generally poisoning life, might be overcome. It is, of course, a traditional spiritual and intellectual solution that is offered, but it is a tradition that Katherine Mansfield herself embraces. Yet even in this rare moment of meeting in her fiction, the direct occasion for abandoning roles is the intimate realisation of mortality. The joy in the characters' easiness together is touched by the corruption of death. Katherine Mansfield sees love and death, pity and fellow feeling, and the realisation of human boundaries and possibilities meeting in a solemn and stoic frame.

If sexual *rapprochment* such as that which takes place between Linda and Jonathan is portrayed as possible to characters able to abandon, even momentarily, the divisive effects of social convention (and one must point out that *both* Linda and Jonathan are failures if judged by the standards of social orthodoxy), and see instead the commonality in the human condition, the experiences of Beryl, in her dealings with the Kembers, illustrate the power that the failure to fulfil conventional sexual expectations has to warp all other relationships. In **'Prelude'** as well as in **'At the Bay'**, Beryl is shown in the process of being driven literally mad by her lack of a husband—a case that balances against Linda's equal distress in her marriage. In Beryl, Katherine Mansfield delineates the process that creates the embittered spinster by providing no option in life but marriage for the respectable woman. Attractive, lively Beryl, able to measure her success as a human being only by the acquisition of a man, enraged by her lack of success as an unmarried aunt, emotionally unfulfilled, financially dependent, is caught in the period between hope of changing and despair at the permanency of her condition. She lives chiefly in her divided imagination; the prose that depicts her consciousness is alternately swooning, romantic and fanciful, and angry, violent and tyrannical. Beryl consistently lashes out at the world which, as far as she can see, allows her only one avenue to happiness which she, by herself, can do nothing to secure. Because she lives so much in her own mind, and is absorbed by its contradictions, she does not even see the disastrous nature of her sister's marriage. Marriage to Beryl seems the answer to every problem, including that of the torment of the internal divisions which assail her. Her hysteria (and she is another of Katherine Mansfield's characters likely to lose herself in moments of panicky breakdown) is rooted in her definition as a woman, and her blind need is punctuated by moments of illumination. In **'Prelude'**, at night, she regards herself in the mirror:

> Oh God, there she was, back again, playing the same old game. False—false as ever . . . False even when she was alone with herself, now. . . .

> 'Oh,' she cried, 'I am so miserable—so frightfully miserable. I know that I'm silly and spiteful and vain; I'm always acting a part. I'm never my real self for a moment.'

Beryl's sense of herself as masked presupposes a different self beneath the mask, waiting for liberation. The narrative, however, does not verify this belief. The mask *is* Beryl, as much as the doubtful and self-critical response to that mask is also a secret part of her identity. But the whole of her discontinuous character has only one function—to save herself from what she sees as her social isolation, her cultural placelessness. In **'At the Bay'**, since no acceptable attachment presents itself, Beryl turns to the unacceptable Kembers.

Escaping from her mother on the beach, Beryl plunges into the sea with 'fast' Mrs Kember, whose disregard for the proprieties goes further than her cigarettes, her 'lack of vanity, her slang, and the way she treated men as though she was one of them, and the fact that she didn't care twopence about her house'. Katherine Mansfield draws a hard line around the relationship between the two women—the external marks of Mrs Kember's 'liberation' say nothing about her moral quality. In fact, she is a sexual predator as much as the men she so closely imitates. Her lesbian predation of Beryl is emphasised in her parody of male seduction, her leering compliments to Beryl about her body, her 'stolen' caressing touches. Like a 'rat', Mrs Kember leaves Beryl, who plays up to her, feeling as if 'she was being poisoned by this cold woman . . . how strange, how horrible!' But Beryl needs to hear the kind of crude seductive comments Mrs Kember makes, and will listen to her in the absence of any man to make them instead. At the end of the story, she does have her chance at a man. Harry Kember, the equally predatory husband of the rat-woman, calls her into the garden at night. Beryl joins him but ends in running away, leaving the silence and 'the sound of the sea . . . a vague murmur, as though it waked out of a dark dream'. What Katherine Mansfield shows Beryl drawing back from is not Mrs Kember's lesbianism nor Harry Kem-

ber's extramarital embrace, but something *both* characters represent. It is the Kember's predation, their being seducers, *victimisers* rather than lovers, that is Katherine Mansfield's concern.

'At the Bay', despite its moments of connection, ends with danger in Beryl's escape from further psychological corrosion. What she flees from is simultaneously her own desire and its fulfilment, and a victimisation that would distortedly enact the marriage she needs for personal validation. The sound of the sea, image of these confusions and possibilities, takes the narrative back to timelessness, and to the chaotic mumblings of dream and desire.

Kezia probably has a less important role in **'At the Bay'** than in any of the Burnell stories, but she is once again at the centre of **'The Doll's House'** (1921). The little girls in this story, like Nora in the play by Ibsen after which it is named, and like the little girl in **'Pearl Button'**, are female rebels in revolt against the sexual and social rules that are meant to divide them into hostile and permanently alienated camps. Kezia is the heroine, and the story concerns her breaking her family's injunction against allowing the 'impossible' Kelvey girls to see the Burnells' new doll's house.

Lil and Else Kelvey are the pariahs of the playground. They are poor children who are used by the school and the parents of the other girls as negative object-lessons of what, for females, is beyond the pale. The Kelveys are 'shunned by everybody'.

> They were the daughters of a spry, hard-working little washerwoman, who went about from house to house by the day. This was awful enough. But where was Mr. Kelvey? Nobody knew for certain. But everybody said he was in prison. So they were the daughters of a washerwoman and a gaolbird. Very nice company for other people's children! And they looked it. Why Mrs. Kelvey made them so conspicuous was hard to understand. The truth was they were dressed in 'bits' given to her by the people for whom she worked.

The narrative mimics the tone of the self-righteous, disapproving, genteel community (and these are women's tones, women's voices defending their class territory). Aside from the fundamental class snobbery in operation here, there is an explicit outline of what conformity to female stereotype must mean. Women must not work, they can only be fully validated on the production of a suitable male from whom they ought to derive their status, their being is closely bound up in their clothes. Self-sufficiency, hard work, and cheerful courage (supposedly valued by the same culture) are unacceptable: Mrs Kelvey and her daughters fail on every sexist point.

On a day that the outcasts have been particularly tormented in the schoolyard, Kezia violates her mother's ban on the girls. Seeing them coming down the road she is torn, in a moment reminiscent of Huck Finn's espousal of the 'nigger' Jim, between the social conscience her culture has been developing and an individual stroke of consciousness.

> Nobody was about; she began to swing on the big white gates of the courtyard. Presently, looking along the road, she saw two little dots. They grew bigger, they were coming towards her. Now she could see that one was in front and one close behind. Now she could see that they were the Kelveys. Kezia stopped swinging. She slipped off the gate as if she was going to run away. Then she hesitated. The Kelveys came nearer, and beside them walked their shadows, very long, stretching right across the road with their heads in the buttercups. Kezia clambered back on the gate; she had made up her mind; she swung out.

As in 'Pearl Button' the gate is a sign of vacillation between being shut into or moving out of convention. And again, the central character swings free. Kezia asks the Kelveys in and they have a chance to see the doll's house before Aunt Beryl shoos them off. The shadows of the girls, 'stretching right across the road with their heads in the buttercups', is what decides Kezia to make her move. The delicacy and beauty of the highly original image contrasts strongly with the clipped, factual language of crude perception that records Kezia's sighting of the girls, and the text reflects the shift from the crudity of dispassionate observation to Kezia's sympathetic recognition of the outlaw children. The shadows that merge the little girls with the beauty of the flowers simply ignore the confining manmade road and its straight lines. Kezia does the same as she obliterates the class lines of her acculturation and recognises the Kelveys as in some sense equals. And in doing so, Kezia denies the values their rejection represents.

The doll's house itself is a complex symbol that precisely suits the story. Given to the Burnell girls by Mrs Hay ('Sweet old Mrs Hay', a woman whose bland, rustic, vegetable name connotes her conformity), the doll's house has to be left outside. As Beryl thinks:

> No harm could come to it; it was summer. And perhaps the smell of paint would have gone by the time it had to be taken in. For, really, the smell of paint coming from that doll's house . . . the smell of paint was quite enough to make anyone seriously ill. . . .

The doll's house is completely furnished, down to 'the father and mother dolls, who . . . were really too big for the doll's house', just as real people are 'too big' for the kind of married life that the doll's house metonymically represents. Even when new, the doll's house smells revolting, like the institution it imitates. And just as the Kelveys are used as a negative lesson

for the Burnell girls, the doll's house is meant for positive female instruction. It is an invitation to sweet domesticity, to boast about possessions; it provides an opportunity for a complete childish parody of the approved method for women to locate their identities in their houses and in the things and people they manage to stuff into them. But the doll's house is also a fabulous toy, a playground for the wayward imagination, and it contains one item that particularly catches Kezia's fancy: a tiny lamp that almost looks as if it could be lit. Katherine Mansfield once more uses the classic association of lamps and knowledge to indicate the rebelliousness of Kezia's reaction to the house. Although the lamp is false, as is the system of values embodied by the house and summed up in the persecution of the Kelveys, it is the *idea* of the lamp that catches Kezia's attention. The linkage of Kezia and the Kelveys earlier in the story is repeated via the mediation of this image. Else nudges Lil at the very end of the story: 'she smiled her rare smile. "I seen the little lamp," she said softly. Then both were silent once more.' The image unites the girl-children, the outcast and the privileged, in their imaginations which refuse the patterns dictated by their culture and create alternative patterns of their own. (pp. 106-17)

['The Garden Party', 'The Daughters of the Late Colonel', and 'Life of Ma Parker'] are stories about mortality, particularly women's consciousness of mortality, and I can think of no other woman writer, with the exception of Emily Dickinson, who gives the subject such close attention. For all that has been made of the connection between Katherine Mansfield's own awareness of impending death at this time, it is necessary to note that her interest in the subject in her writing of 1921 was concentrated on the effect of death on the living, and it adds another dimension to her consistent portraiture of women's isolation and exclusion.

'The Garden Party' is a case in point. As in 'Bliss', Katherine Mansfield sets up a situation in which a woman is suddenly displaced from a frenetic social whirl that supposedly defines the totality of her being. The Sheridans in the story are a variant of the Burnells; the setting is New Zealand and the characters prototypical colonials.

The Sheridan children, all young adults, are giving a party. The excited, happy narrative sees what they see in the terms that they see it—their fine house on a hill, bustling in preparation for the party, full of good things to eat, lovely things to wear, wonderful, expensive flowers to enjoy. The background is crammed with people to order about; the servants 'loved obeying'; friendly workmen swarm in the garden putting up a marquee; deliveries are made from shops; a band has been hired to put the finishing touches on the pleasures of the afternoon. The confident description is soaked in the values of middle-class authority as the genteel bourgeoisie prepares to play and enjoys every minute of the preparation. The pleasures at hand are both material and aesthetic, and even the perfect weather seems to endorse everything the Sheridans stand for. But the narration, insidiously, also undercuts its own exuberance with irony. Here, for example, is one of the daughters, Jose, practising for the display of her musical talents at the party:

> *Pom!* Ta-ta-ta *Tee*-ta! The piano burst out so passionately that Jose's face changed. She clasped her hands. She looked mournfully and enigmatically at her mother and Laura as they came in.
> This Life is *Wee*-ary,
> A Tear-a Sigh.
> A Love that *Chan*-ges,
> This Life is *Wee*-ary,
> A Tear-a Sigh.
> A Love that *Chan*-ges,
> And then . . . Good-bye!

But at the word 'Good-bye,' and although the piano sounded more desperate than ever, her face broke into a brilliant, dreadfully unsympathetic smile.

'Aren't I in good voice, mummy?' she beamed.

Katherine Mansfield mocks Jose's 'female accomplishments' in the same ironic manner and for the same reasons as Jane Austen does in *Pride and Prejudice.* Just as Mary bored the company in 1813, displaying her vanity rather than her love for music, so Jose produces the same eminently false effect in **'The Garden Party'** of 1921. It is something of a shock to recognise the same device working so effectively in this twentieth-century story. Katherine Mansfield's attack on the inadequacy of the education of 'the daughters of educated men' is deepened by the story's account of the suffering taking place in the workmen's cottages just below the Sheridans' privileged hill. The false sentiment of Jose's song echoes the emotional disaster near at hand. The worker's world, which 'mummy' does not fully recognise (though the story emphasises the fact that she and her children live by and through their control of that world), is the scene of a casual tragedy. A workman has been killed in an accident; the news arrives during the preparations for the party. And the question of what is to be done in response to the news arises for only one character.

The character is Laura, a vaguely mutinous Sheridan daughter who, in the course of the story, acts as an intermediary between the two worlds—that of privilege and gaiety, and that of hardship, death and sorrow—and in the process is forced, if only momentarily, into the role of outsider.

We see Laura first in that most typical of middle-class occupations—romantic identification with an idealised working class. Laura, 'who loved having to arrange things', is assigned to direct the workmen who

erect the marquee. Actually she directs nothing; the workmen know their job and choose the best site for the marquee in spite of her alternative suggestions. Laura's class loyalties vie with her sense of adventure; as she deals with the men their ease finally overcomes her slightly wounded dignity when they do not treat her with the deference afforded to a middle-class matron. Looking over the plan the foreman has hastily drawn, Laura dips her toe into rebellion:

> Oh, how extraordinarily nice workmen were, she thought. Why couldn't she have workmen for friends rather than the silly boys she danced with and who came to Sunday night supper . . . It's all the fault, she decided . . . of these absurd class distinctions. Well, for her part, she didn't feel them. Not a bit, not an atom . . . Just to prove how happy she was, just to show the tall fellow how at home she felt, and how she despised stupid conventions, Laura took a big bite out of her bread-and-butter as she stared at the little drawing. She felt just like a work-girl.

This is, of course, transparent affectation, but it is also a potentially significant masquerade, small as the gesture of taking a bite of bread-and-butter might be. What the significance might be is suggested when the news of the death reaches the Sheridans. Laura, still influenced by her thoughts about the workmen, wants to stop the party, but her mother simply cuts her off:

> 'You are being very absurd, Laura,' she said coldly. 'People like that don't expect sacrifices from us. And it's not very sympathetic to spoil everyone's enjoyment as you're doing now.'

'I don't understand,' said Laura, and she walked quickly out of the room into her own bedroom.

Several truths of unequal significance operate in this passage. Death *cannot* be conquered by stopping a party. Pleasure *is* rare enough to deserve protection. The workers do *not* have any expectations. And Laura really does have no idea what she is doing. (That her mother damns herself and her class goes without saying, but at the same time *any* life that paused with every death would soon be unliveable).

Laura's knowledge of the workmen is almost nonexistent. Their lane was forbidden territory in her childhood and since she has 'grown up' she has only walked through it once with her brother (and *alter ego*), Laurie. On the walk she sees the lane as 'disgusting and sordid. They came out with a shudder. But still one must go everywhere; one must see everything.' Laura in no way connects herself with the lane. But this distanced social voyeurism turns into something very immediate with the news of the death, and just for a moment, at the centre of the story, Laura steps outside her class and circumstances into a confrontation with the equality of all humanity in the face of mortality. What

Laura 'sees' at this point is far more important than what she has 'seen' during her educational tour of a working-class habitat. For a moment, the social vocabulary of her tribe fills Laura with disgust.

But only for a moment. What draws Laura back from the isolation of her response to death is another confrontation, this time with her own face framed by a lovely hat that itself is the image of the pleasures of life that only youth and privilege provide. What she sees in a mirror, walking away from her mother, is her identity:

> the first thing she saw was this charming girl in the mirror, in her black hat trimmed with gold daisies and a long black velvet ribbon. Never had she imagined she could look like that. Is mother right? she thought. And now she hoped that her mother was right.

It is an extraordinary moment of conscience callousing over, with the lovely black hat repeating the colour of death. Katherine Mansfield's characteristic attention to detail allows her to conflate conscience and consciousness, beauty and vanity, bodily and mental satisfaction as Laura's politics turn on a glimpse of herself in the mirror. Giving up her chance for a public display of her beauty would be sacrificial; Laura slips easily back into the frivolity of the garden-party. On the next page she is afraid of being 'teased' about even thinking of making her egalitarian gesture.

Since Laura's class complacency is safe and the party is over, Mrs Sheridan gives her daughter a lesson in 'proper' charity. She sends her to the dead man's cottage with scraps from the party. In her stunning hat, her mind filled with the delights of the party, Laura self-consciously walks into the cottage with her basket and into the ceremonies of death. The two social rituals—the celebrations of the rich family, and the solemnity of death for the poor one—stress the discontinuity of experience. The man's wife, huddled like some primitive wounded thing by the fire, looks up at Laura, 'Her face, puffed up, red, with swollen eyes and swollen lips, looked terrible'. Laura, ashamed and embarrassed, blunders into the room with the dead man, and as the corpse is exhibited to her with tender, ritualistic pride, her response remains in the aesthetic mode of the party: 'he was wonderful, beautiful', a 'marvel', much better, in fact, in terms of beauty than her hat for which she now blurts out an excuse. The reader must recall the earlier significance of the hat and all that it has meant for Laura's conscience to understand the meaning of that apology. The story ends with Laura's confusion as she tries to express her feelings to Laurie and the meaning she has drawn from this encounter with death.

'The Garden Party' is radically inconclusive. It is especially interesting in its portrayal of simultaneous but opposing goods, and in its treatment of the confu-

sion of motivations and principles in life as opposed to the clarity of abstract ideas. Katherine Mansfield stressed this aspect of the story in a letter [dated 13 March 1922] to William Gerhardi:

> And yes, that is what I tried to convey in 'The Garden Party.' The diversity of life and how we try to fit in everything, Death included. That is bewildering for a person of Laura's age. She feels things ought to happen differently. First one and then another. But life isn't like that. We haven't the ordering of it.

Katherine Mansfield's writing does, however, impose an order. It rejects the one that Laura accepts when she allows her aesthetic and class assumptions to dominate her at the moment when another kind of response was available to her. Laura only tastes the solitude that is the main diet of the women in many other stories, but the easiness with which a character can be thrust from full membership of a community to absolute exile in an instant, and the way in which such exile depends upon individual consciousness, underscores Katherine Mansfield's insistence on the fragility of identity.

While Katherine Mansfield's portrayal of the relationship between the self and others is always bleak, her late stories, as well as her early ones, are often comic. As Claire Tomalin points out about 'The Daughters of the Late Colonel' [in her introduction to *Katherine Mansfield: Short Stories,* 1983], this very funny story 'offers an almost flawless description of two sisters who have been rendered unfit for life: not entirely a laughing matter.' In turning themselves into perfect objects for their father's will, the two old ladies have denuded themselves of their own. As Tomalin goes on to say of the story, 'it is quite possible to enjoy its jokes about early twentieth-century womanhood and miss the devastating nature of what it is saying.' The querulous, timid narration itself expresses the central experience of the daughters as they try to grope their way out from under their masks after the death of their father.

The title of 'The Daughters of the Late Colonel' gives the circumstances of the story away. The two women, Constantia and Josephine, have indeed been 'constant' to their rumbling old father. These two pathetic creatures have existed only in relation to him, have lived only as 'daughters' and never in their own right. When the Colonel is dead, the world slips its moorings for the women who have been so stripped of the capacity for independent action by their life-long deference that they are scarcely sane.

> 'Oh,' groaned poor Josephine aloud, 'we shouldn't have done it, Con!'

> And Constantia, pale as a lemon in all that blackness, said in a frightened whisper, 'Done what, Jug?'

'Let them bu-bury father like that,' said Josephine, breaking down and crying into her new, queer-smelling mourning handkerchief.

'But what else could we have done?' asked Constantia wonderingly. 'We couldn't have kept him, Jug—we couldn't have kept him unburied. At any rate, not in a flat that size.'

Josephine blew her nose; the cab was dreadfully stuffy.

'I don't know,' she said forlornly, 'It is all so dreadful. I feel we ought to have tried to, just for a time at least. To make perfectly sure. One thing's certain'—and her tears sprang out again—'father will never forgive us for this—never!'

Like frightened birds kept too long in captivity the two sisters cannot even think of flying. At the conclusion of the story, as they try to speak to one another of the future and to tell truths unrelated to their father's rule, they falter.

A pause. Then Constantia said faintly, 'I can't say what I was going to say, Jug, because I've forgotten what it was . . . that I was going to say.'

Josephine was silent for a moment. She stared at a big cloud where the sun had been. The she replied shortly, 'I've forgotten too.'

Like the lives they might have had but which are no longer even memories of possibilities lost, the very words that might mean freedom have lapsed; the two sisters fall into the sun-darkening silence that has been their women's portion all along. Inured in their father's house they will rot with his furniture. Freedom has atrophied with lack of use. The two old women will continue as victims of a father who denied them the right to live.

Katherine Mansfield was angered by accusations of 'cruelty' and 'sneering' in the story. As she explained, again to William Gerhardi, the story was meant 'to lead up to that last paragraph, when my two flowerless ones turned with that timid gesture, to the sun. "Perhaps now . . . " And after that, it seemed to me, they died as surely as Father was dead.'

It is finally, this theme, the 'sunlessness' of women's lives, and perhaps all lives, that is the dominant impression left by Katherine Mansfield's late fiction. It is the fiction of catastrophe, with varieties of deprivation, unhappiness and despair in control of human consciousness which Katherine Mansfield is constantly pushing to the breaking-point. The most important impulses behind the writing are emotions of anger and pity, and in her late work Katherine Mansfield at times abandoned the emotional cynicism of modernism to compose stories which are pure outcry.

'Life of Ma Parker' is the best of these sketches

of despair. As always, Katherine Mansfield provides a social base for her tale in the form of a 'literary gentleman' who is shown priding himself on his 'handling' of Ma Parker, his aged, cheap, exhausted char, whom he overworks and underpays, and then undermines with accusations of petty theft. As the story switches to Ma Parker's consciousness, the way the world looks changes completely. She has a kind heart and merely pities the man for his messes as her mind fingers the memories of her disastrous life. Her husband died young of his baker's trade leaving her with the six of their thirteen children who survived. Her daughters 'went wrong', her boys 'emigrimated', and her last remaining girl was thrown back on her hands after the death of her husband, bringing with her a frail grandson who has been the light of Ma Parker's life and whom she has just buried. The contrast of the extraordinary stoicism of the woman and the tenderness of her love for the fragile child is painfully moving:

'Gran! Gran!' Her little grandson stood on her lap in his button boots. He'd just come in from playing in the street.

'Look what a state you've made your gran's skirt into—you wicked boy!'

But he put his arms round her neck and rubbed his cheek against hers.

'Gran, gi' us a penny!' he coaxed.

'Be off with you; Gran ain't got no pennies.'

'Yes you 'ave. Gi' us one!'

Already she was feeling for the old, squashed black leather purse.

'Well, what'll you give your gran?'

He gave a shy little laugh and pressed closer.

She felt his eyelid quiver against her cheek. 'I ain't got nothing,' he murmured. . . .

This battered old woman, as 'squashed' as the purse that has held so little, has in fact possessed riches, and has lost them all. Katherine Mansfield refuses to mitigate the pathos of memories, and the story turns on the last of the little boy's remembered words. The theme, 'I ain't got nothing', is picked up forcefully when Ma Parker, finally overcome by her grief at her loss, somnambulantly walks out of the flat into the cold street.

There was a wind like ice. People went flitting by, very fast; the men walked like scissors, the women trod like cats. And nobody knew—nobody cared. Even if she broke down, if at last, after all these years, she were to cry, she'd find herself in the lock-up as like as not.

Images of hostility and threat—wind and ice and scissors and cats and prisons—provide the final exclusion, generated by a consciousness that is left with only its own incredible stoicism. There is nowhere even for Ma Parker to cry. The narrative swoops in and out of her vocabulary to a general outcry of desolation and deprivation.

Katherine Mansfield's reputation for most of this century—that of a delicate female stylist with a reassuring line in colonial nostalgia—is rightly being revised. Her stories instead demand to be read as unremittingly critical accounts of social injustice grounded in the pretence of a 'natural' psychological and biological order that is disproved by the experience of con-

sciousness. Image and plot, symbol and idea—all the elements of her fiction function as protests against any ideology of fixture and certainty. Katherine Mansfield's general commentary on her age is couched in her exposition of, her imaging of, contemporary women's consciousness, and in a prose attuned to catch the form of that experience. She implicitly demands the right to see women and their lives as the particulars from which the general historical situation can be deduced. But her fiction goes beyond an attempt to 'reflect' the age in which she lived; it is a body of work that incites to revolt through its critical appraisal of the circumstances Katherine Mansfield sees and records. (pp. 117-28)

Kate Fullbrook, in her *Katherine Mansfield,* The Harvester Press, Sussex, 1986, 146 p.

SOURCES FOR FURTHER STUDY

Berkman, Sylvia. *Katherine Mansfield: A Critical Study.* New Haven: Yale University Press, 1951, 246 p.

Important biographical and critical survey.

Boddy, Gillian. *Katherine Mansfield: The Woman and The Writer.* New York: Penguin, 1988, 325 p.

Examines Mansfield's influences, styles, themes, characterization, and literary techniques.

Gordon, Ian A. Introduction to *Undiscovered Country: The New Zealand Stories of Katherine Mansfield,* by Katherine Mansfield, edited by Ian A. Gordon, pp. ix-xxi. London: Longman Group, 1974.

Surveys the principal themes of Mansfield's fiction with a New Zealand setting and presents the stories in a sequence intended to "reinforce and illuminate the themes and preoccupations that sustain the underlying unity of her work."

Kirkpatrick, B. J. *A Bibliography of Katherine Mansfield.* Oxford: Clarendon Press, 1989, 396 p.

Extensive bibliography listing books and pamphlets; contributions to books, periodicals, and newspapers; books translated by Mansfield; translations of Mansfield's works into foreign languages; large print editions; Braille, embossed, and talking books; extracts from unpublished letters, journals, and other material; stage and film scripts; radio and television productions; ballet, musical, and stage productions; films; and manuscripts.

Meyers, Jeffrey. *Katherine Mansfield: A Biography.* London: Hamish Hamilton, 1978, 306 p.

Revises the idealized portrait of Mansfield created by Murry.

Tomalin, Claire. *Katherine Mansfield: A Secret Life.* London: Viking, 1987, 292 p.

Extensively researched biography that addresses several events in Mansfield's life that have been neglected by previous biographers.

Christopher Marlowe

1564-1593

(Also Kit; also Marlow, Marlo, Merling, Merlin, Marlin, Marley, and Morley) English dramatist and poet. The portrait above is believed to be of Marlowe. No fully authenticated portrait of the author is known to exist.

INTRODUCTION

*T*he author of such renowned plays as *Doctor Faustus* (1593?); *Tamburlaine, Parts I* and *II* (1587-88); *The Jew of Malta* (1590?); and *Edward II* (1592-93), Marlowe was the first English dramatist to reveal the full potential of blank verse poetry. He made significant advances in the genre of English tragedy through keen examinations of Renaissance morality. Although his achievements have been generally overshadowed by his exact contemporary, William Shakespeare, many critics contend that had he not died young, Marlowe's reputation would certainly have rivaled that of the more famous playwright.

Marlowe was born the son of a prosperous shoemaker in Canterbury. He received his early education at the King's School in Canterbury and at the age of seventeen was awarded a scholarship to study for the ministry at Cambridge. He obtained his Bachelor of Arts degree in 1584, but controversy surrounded his attempt to graduate with a Master of Arts degree three years later. Scholars have learned that Cambridge officials attempted to withhold Marlowe's degree based on reports that he had visited a Catholic seminary at Rheims, France, and that he was planning to be ordained a Catholic priest upon graduation. Queen Elizabeth's Privy Council intervened, however, and declared that Marlowe had in fact been sent to Rheims on matters related to national security. Some modern critics interpret this remarkable occurrence as evidence that Marlowe served as a spy for the government on this occasion and perhaps others as well. Ultimately, the Cambridge officials relented and awarded Marlowe his degree, but controversy continued to follow him, this time to London, where he took up residence after graduation. Contemporary accounts indicate that he adopted a bohemian lifestyle and continually abused social norms with boorish and repugnant behavior. During this time Marlowe was implicated in a murder and spent two weeks in jail until he was acquitted as having acted in self-defense. In other clashes with the law, he was accused of atheism and blasphemy and was awaiting a trial verdict on such charges when he was killed in 1593. The circumstances surrounding his death puzzled scholars for centuries until records discovered in the early twentieth century revealed that Marlowe died of a stab wound to his forehead received during a brawl with a dinner companion with whom he had been arguing over the tavern bill. A critical dispute remains, however, over the question of whether Marlowe's death was really inadvertent or if he was assassinated by his companions.

Marlowe wrote during the Elizabethan period, an unsettled age of remarkable change, and one in which the spirit of both the Renaissance and the Protestant Reformation predominated. Society had begun to liberate itself from restrictive medieval institutions and to celebrate the ascendancy of the individual. These revolutionary advances inspired an intellectual and artistic awakening that had not been seen since the Classical Age. Marlowe was a man very much of his time. In his dramas, he often created distinctively Renaissance characters, providing them with such attributes as great strength, wealth, or knowledge. These virtues initially appear to give them unlimited potential, but as events unfold the characters are inevitably consumed by pride and ultimately corrupted. The dangers of excessive ambition and the apparent compulsion to strive for more than one already has forms a major theme in Marlowe's plays. The philosophy of Machiavellianism constitutes another important—and related—theme for Marlowe, for his characters commonly strive to achieve their ambitions with the single-minded, ruthless, and amoral cunning described by Niccolò Machiavelli in his controversial political manifesto *The Prince* (1512-13).

Scholars speculate that Marlowe wrote his first play in 1586, just seven years before his death. In this brief period, he composed *The Tragedy of Dido Queen of Carthage* (1586?); *Tamburlaine the Great: Divided into two Tragicall Discourses; The Famous Tragedy of the Rich Jew of Malta; The Massacre at Paris: with the Death of the Duke of Guise* (1590?); *The Troublesome Raigne and Lamentable Death of Edward the Second, King of England;* and *The Tragicall History of the Life and Death of Doctor Faustus.* In addition, he began the narrative poem *Hero and Leander,* a project not completed at the time of his death. Because Marlowe's literary career was so brief yet prolific, scholars have found the accurate dating of many of his works extremely difficult.

While a critical consensus on the dating of Marlowe's work is lacking, some scholars maintain that *Dido Queen of Carthage* is his first play. Although *Dido* was not published until 1594, these critics assert that it was composed perhaps as early as 1586, when Marlowe was still a student at Cambridge. The title page of the first edition states that the play had already been performed by the company of boy actors known as the "Children of Her Majesties Chapell." The first of Marlowe's plays to appear on the London stage was most likely Part I of *Tamburlaine,* which was probably presented around 1587. It was a great success among Elizabethan theatergoers and in fact was so popular that Marlowe produced a sequel within a year. As the Prologue to Part II states, "The generall welcomes *Tamburlain* receiv'd, / When arrived last upon our stage, / Hath made our Poet pen his second part."

Marlowe wrote *Tamburlaine* as a direct challenge to his audience to rise above the "jigging veins of riming mother wits / And such conceits as clownage keeps in pay" (Prologue, Part I) often found in early Elizabethan drama. Marlowe thus introduces the Scythian shepherd Tamburlaine, a figure of heroic dimensions who epitomizes "Renaissance man" and who single-handedly orchestrates the forging of an empire. According to Gāmini Salgādo, *Tamburlaine* represents "the saga of the self-made man, triumphing through no advantages of birth or inheritance, but entirely through qualities of character." As such, the play reflects transitions in Marlowe's society, in which the dependence of personal advancement upon matters of birthright was gradually giving way to advancement earned through individual achievement. Tamburlaine accomplishes an unbroken series of military and political triumphs by sheer strength—not just physical power as demonstrated by his military prowess, but also by his forceful and eloquent rhetoric. These traits combined with a ruthless will to dominate identify him as a consummate Machiavellian, one who is able to assume and sustain leadership by force of personality. In Part I, Marlowe defies theatergoers' expectations, for Tamburlaine pays no tragic retribution for his overweening pride. The dramatist follows a more classical approach in Part II, however, which is pervaded by a theme of death and decay. With the defeat of all human opposition and his massive consolidation of power, Tamburlaine gradually succumbs to megalomania and attempts to defy Death, his last and most significant adversary. Death slowly erodes Tamburlaine's resolve, first by taking his beloved wife, Zenocrate, and finally by afflicting Tamburlaine himself. Marlowe thus demonstrates that for all the hero's striving and accomplishment, he is nevertheless human; ultimately he must face death, the final limiter of human aspiration.

As already noted, the two parts of *Tamburlaine* were first staged around 1587-88. Their first publication was in a 1590 edition, containing both parts, called "two Tragicall Discourses." Interestingly, although this edition represents the only known printing of any of

Marlowe's plays in his lifetime, his name is nowhere given. His next play may have been *The Jew of Malta,* perhaps performed around 1590, though not published until 1633, long after the dramatist's death. The title page of the first edition of *The Jew of Malta* designates the play a tragedy, but critics have often described it as a black comedy or, in the words of T. S. Eliot, a "savage farce."

As in *Tamburlaine,* Marlowe explores the implications of Machiavellianism in *The Jew of Malta;* but while Barabas, the central figure of the latter drama, shares Tamburlaine's ruthlessness, he manifests none of the earlier character's heroic grandeur. Indeed, nearly all the characters in this bitterly ironic piece are remarkable for their meanness. In *The Jew of Malta,* according to Eric Rothstein, Marlowe creates a world where "all values are inverted by a central diabolism in grotesque form, expressing itself through materialism . . . and a Machiavellian ethic." The inversion of values and the "diabolism" of the play are evident in the confrontation between the wealthy Jew Barabas and his antagonists, the Roman Catholic rulers of Malta. (Significantly, both groups, Jews and Catholics, were objects of fear and distrust to Elizabethan England.) The Governor of Malta, Ferneze, in financial straits, hypocritically denounces Barabas and confiscates his wealth, depriving him not only of his money but also of the love and mercy which Christianity represents. Barabas seeks revenge with unnerving viciousness, and a profusion of brutal murders ensues until Barabas, caught in one of his own traps, dies cursing. Critics maintain that although there is tragedy inherent in Barabas's fall, his overreaching himself in his quest for revenge, the viciousness of his ignoble motives, and his cruel conduct preclude sympathy for him and therefore deprive him of tragic definition.

The Massacre at Paris exhibits similarities of tone and style to *The Jew of Malta* and was perhaps written around the same time. Although it is known to have been performed in 1593, it could not have been composed until after 1589, since it depicts the death of Henry III of France, who died in August of that year. This play survives only in an undated octavo edition that provides what critics commonly regard as a corrupt and unreliable text.

Many scholars consider *Edward II*—probably written during the winter of 1592-93, but not published until 1594—the first great English history play, and possibly Marlowe's most accomplished drama in any genre. George L. Geckle maintains that of Marlowe's major plays, "*Edward II* stands out as the most coherent in terms of structure and as the most complex in terms of the interrelationship between theme and character." Although *Edward II* is not one of Marlowe's best-known plays, critics have identified numerous factors contributing to what they regard as its remarkable

literary success. Marlowe's sensitive construction of the relationships between this play's chief characters marks a significant advance from his earlier work, in which a play's most important motifs are typically centered around one dominant figure. Marlowe's merging of such elements as the selfish, hedonistic relationship between Edward and Gaveston, with its subtle suggestion of homosexuality, and Mortimer's Machiavellian ambition, commentators agree, give *Edward II* unprecedented dimension. Marlowe's eloquent dramatic verse, variously lyrical, comedic, and tragic, additionally draws the play's many elements into a cohesive whole. Commentators have also praised Marlowe's masterful compression of twenty-three years of history into a five-act dramatic structure. It is commonly held that Shakespeare himself was aware of the exceptional literary achievement of *Edward II,* for his *Richard II* (1595) displays marked similarities to Marlowe's drama.

Although it is apparent that *Doctor Faustus* was not widely popular with Elizabethan audiences, today it is generally considered Marlowe's greatest drama. Written in the tradition of medieval morality plays, *Doctor Faustus* explores the implications of one man's pact to sell his soul to the devil for twenty-four years of power and knowledge. Salgādo observes that "built into the very bones of the story is the element of the cautionary tale, with Faustus as the horrible example of what happens when creatures rebel against their lot and aspire to the condition of their Creator." Critics agree that Faustus represents a Renaissance man whose intellectual ambitions cause him to overstep his human bounds. Marlowe masterfully illustrates how Faustus, although he aspires to divinity, is gradually debased throughout the play by the devil Mephistophilis. Succumbing to pride, avarice, and physical gratification, Faustus never realizes he has been duped into trading his soul for a life of triviality, and he refuses to avail himself of numerous chances to repent. The explicitly religious theme of *Doctor Faustus* continues to perplex critics, for many consider it uncharacteristic of Marlowe to treat theological issues in his works. Whether or not *Doctor Faustus* is meant to convey a particular religious message, it nevertheless presents a penetrating philosophical analysis of the consequences of human aspiration.

The dating of *Doctor Faustus* is especially difficult, as two conflicting texts are extant. The earliest recorded performance was in 1594, but it is known that the theatrical manager Philip Henslowe hired two writers to revise the play for this production. Scholars speculate that an edition of 1616 represents *Doctor Faustus* in this form. However, a differing, shorter, version was printed some years earlier, in 1604. This text, researchers postulate, may be the play before it was revised, and may reflect its unfinished state at the time of the dramatist's death.

Marlowe's dramatic works are suffused with the spirit of the Elizabethan age, clearly reflecting the intellectual enlightenment of the Renaissance as well as exhibiting the profound political impact of Machiavellianism. In play after play, Marlowe examines various aspects of these revolutionary changes in an effort to better understand their influence on the human condition. In addition, Marlowe's verse greatly improves upon the crude style of his predecessors and vastly expands the scope and power of dramatic representation. Michael Drayton, the eminent English man of letters, paid tribute to his contemporary's literary genius in the poem entitled "Of Poets and Poesie." He wrote,

"Neat *Marlow* bathed in the *Thespian* springs / Had in him those brave translunary things, / That the first Poets had, his raptures were, / All ayre, and fire, which made his verses cleere, / For that fine madnes still did he retaine, / Which rightly should possesse a Poets braine." Similarly, no less a judge than Ben Jonson hailed the force and beauty of "Marlowe's mighty line." Beyond question, Marlowe, in his brief but brilliant career, helped guide English drama to an unprecedented level of artistic maturity.

(For further information about Marlowe's life and works, see *Dictionary of Literary Biography*, Vol. 62: *Elizabethan Dramatists*; and *Drama Criticism*, Vol. 1.)

CRITICAL COMMENTARY

RICHARD W. VAN FOSSEN
(essay date 1964)

[Van Fossen is an American scholar who has edited plays by Marlowe and Thomas Heywood. In the excerpt below, he provides an introduction to *The Jew of Malta*, commenting on its sources, influences, structure, themes, and language.]

The date when Marlowe wrote *The Jew of Malta*—like the problem of its sources and, indeed, the question of its authorship in its present state remains uncertain. If we assume that the prologue spoken by Machiavelli was written at the same time as the play proper, the death of the third Duke of Guise (referred to in 1.3), December 23, 1588, provides a *terminus a quo*; the first entry in [Henslowe's *Diary*], February 26, 1592, makes a firm *terminus ad quem*. Within the span of time thus defined, critics tend to place the play early or late depending upon their feelings about its stylistic and structural maturity; but the folly of such a procedure is obvious if one thinks of the anomalies in the development of a Tennessee Williams or a William Faulkner. Short of the unlikely eventuality that convincing contemporary documentation turns up, it is surely best to agree with Tucker Brooke that "the year 1590 cannot be far wrong."

For a number of reasons, the prevailing tendency in Marlowe scholarship has been to argue that the play in the form we know it has been heavily revised on one or more occasions, possibly by Thomas Heywood: (1) more than forty years intervened between the writing of the play and the printing of the version that has

come down to us; (2) an old-fashioned play would presumably have had to be "brought up to date" for production at the fashionable court of King Charles I and Queen Henrietta Maria; (3) the text of the 1633 quarto is seriously corrupt; (4) the manner and quality of the play deteriorate badly in the third and fourth acts; (5) Marlowe was incapable of producing the comedy that pervades so many scenes. In recent years, however, it has become more and more common to defend the 1633 text as very probably a faithful version of what Marlowe wrote. (p. xiv)

No source is known for Marlowe's story, but a variety of origins has been suggested for various elements in the play. The historical framework—most unhistorical in Marlowe's handling—is provided by the famous Turkish attack on Malta in 1565. The character of Barabas may have been suggested by the career of either or both of two sixteenth-century Jews, Juan Miques and David Passi. The trick employed by Barabas and Ithamore on Friar Jacomo is derived from a story long popular in many forms; the fact that the subplot of Heywood's *The Captives* is a fuller version of the same anecdote, indeed, has been regarded—without sufficient warrant—as evidence for Heywood's hand in *The Jew of Malta*. Bakeless suggests many other possible specific sources, most of them demanding a considerable reliance on hypothesis. One last source is quite clear: the Bible. In the explanatory notes to the play, attention is called to the many names derived from Old Testament sources, to Barabas' frequent use of Old Testament passages in allusion, paraphrase, and even quotation, and to New Testament doctrines referred to by the Christians and by Barabas—doctrines that the Christians characteristically pervert or, at best, fail to live up to.

Apart from these specific sources, two rather more general influences contribute a great deal to the effect of the play as a whole; these are the conceptions, or misconceptions, of Jewish character and of Machiavellian doctrine that might almost be said to underlie everything else.

First it must be realized that the portrait of Barabas is not—and cannot be—anti-Semitic in the way that a similar portrait would be in the work of a twentieth-century writer. The reason is simply that the typical Elizabethan was unlikely to know very many Jews: the Jews had been expelled from England as long before as 1290, not to be legally readmitted—unless converted to Christianity—until 1656. There were, in fact, a number of Jews, mostly Portuguese and nominally converts, who played a fairly prominent role in commercial affairs. Londoners, certainly, would have had some knowledge of these people, but that there was any considerable amount of real anti-Jewish feeling is improbable. Indeed, in R. W.'s *The Three Ladies of London,* a play published in 1584, there is an extremely favorable portrayal of a Jew. The Jews were blamed for the Crucifixion, and by a long mediaeval tradition were associated with the Devil and the comic Vice character on the stage, but the prevailing attitude toward them was probably one of fascination and wonder. As J. L. Cardozo puts it, "The favourite foreign country [Italy] was also the most important abode of Jews in the 16th century. The bloody-minded, crafty, extortionate Jew was therefore among the few exotic devices available to produce the foreign atmosphere" in the drama. Charles

Knight is close to the truth when he observes in discussing Marlowe's Barabas and Shakespeare's Shylock, "In countries where Jews have abounded and been objects of popular odium, the dramatists who have pandered to prejudice, have uniformly made their Jews mean and ludicrous as well as hateful. Now you may hate Barnabas [*sic*] and Shylock, but you cannot despise them." Perhaps an analogy might be made with the figure of the Indian in Western movies and television plays. Most Americans who watch these productions are not "Indian-haters"; nevertheless, the stereotype—hateful, cruel, inhuman—has been, at least until very recent years, almost universal.

The Machiavelli who introduces *The Jew of Malta* and whose theories Barabas supposedly puts into practice is another such stereotype. Although Niccolò Machiavelli's most influential work, *The Prince,* was not published in English until 1640, translations circulated in manuscript during the later sixteenth century; even earlier, his name had begun to become synonymous with the sort of figure depicted in Marlowe's prologue: an excessively pragmatic, underhanded, treacherous, atheistic, covetous, self-centered, machinating, inhuman monster. . . . This distortion—vestiges of which linger even today in the popular mind—contributes, like the Maltese setting, the Spanish admiral, the Turkish powers, and the Jew-Devil-Vice tradition, to the exotic and villainous atmosphere which pervades the play, heavily colored though it is with low comedy. The expectations of an Elizabethan audience were conditioned by the very presence of these elements for plots and characterizations of the sort that Marlowe provides; the modern reader, who must also attempt to visualize the play as it was performed at the Rose theater, needs to project himself into the Elizabethan mind, insofar as he can, in order to understand and appreciate *The Jew of Malta* properly.

The play so eludes description that readers have never known quite what to do with it. One seventeenth-century bookseller listed it in his catalogue as a history play; another recorded it as a tragedy in 1661, then changed his mind and decided it was a tragicomedy before issuing another booklist ten years later. If a genre must be found, it is best to admit the paradoxical quality of the play by giving it a paradoxical name and calling it a serious farce. It is, moreover, important to insist that the play does *not* break in two: we do not have a serious play for two acts and a farce for three; rather, the serious and comic elements in the play are present together from the beginning of Act I to the end of Act V, admittedly in varying proportions, but still both present, and present throughout. It would be foolish to deny that Barabas has at the beginning of the play a humanity and dignity that he soon loses; in production, however, the impression of humanity and dignity would not dominate so exclusively as it does when the play is read. Although Barabas' physical appearance is not referred to until later (at II.iii.174 Ithamore says to him, "I worship your nose for this," and at III.iii.10 he calls him a "bottle-nos'd knave"), the prominent facial characteristic still regarded as typically Jewish would—enlarged, distorted, and garishly colored—be apparent to an audience from the moment the play began. Quite possibly the actor who played Barabas would have worn a false red wig as well as the false nose, for both props were traditionally associated with the Jew-Devil-Vice figure. As Kirschbaum shows the character is also required to have a beard, presumably red and presumably of comic shape and proportions. The opening soliloquy, impressive though its rhetoric is, would leave a decidedly ambivalent first impression if the actor reciting the lines were pawing through his hoard in exaggerated fashion—as I am sure he was meant to do. This comic side of the character is balanced from the beginning, however, first in the ominous prologue delivered by Machiavelli, second in Barabas' very name, taken from the evil criminal in the Gospels who was released to the Jews in preference to Christ, and third by his "humanness," especially in the earlier part of the play.

Reference has already been made to Barabas' association with the Vice tradition of earlier drama; Bernard Spivack's description makes the relationship clear: "The Vice is at once the allegorical aggressor, the homiletic preacher, and the humorist of the moralities—and of plays which, except for his part in them, belong to the later convention of the literal drama." When, however, Spivack later contends that Barabas splits completely into two halves, "a character," "a man," and "a moral figure" in Act I and part of Act II, converted to the Vice by "a change in theatrical method" for the rest of the play, he does less than justice to the skill of Marlowe's dramaturgy, even though it is true that in the later part of the play Barabas loses "emotional caliber, [which is] replaced by a menial alacrity in word and action that is altogether comic. He is too busy with too many murderous contrivances to be distracted by an adequate sense of provocation for any of them." It is perhaps more useful to recall that Barabas stands alone in the role of comic villain for the opening part of the action but that he is joined, in one way or another, by Ithamore, by the two Friars, and by Bellamira and Pilia-Borza—until Barabas has succeeded in killing them all off. Naturally the texture of the play is somewhat different, then, in Acts III and IV.

But only *somewhat* different, for Marlowe brings a basic unity to the play by a variety of other means. On the level of mere plot, the multiplicity of events—despite a few obvious loose ends here and there, such as the confusion over the events antecedent to the duel between Lodowick and Mathias (III.ii) and Bellamira's reference to the siege (III.i.1)—is marvelously well inte-

grated. The first scene prepares us for the introduction of Martin del Bosco and the political plot (11.94-96) and initiates the theme of the tribute money due the Turks. I.ii states clearly what was suggested in I.i: Barabas has made careful provision for the contingency that has befallen him. The conversion of his house to a nunnery provides a momentary setback, but his fertile mind soon hits on the scheme of using Abigail as an agent of recovery. The true nature of the Friars is hinted at by their exchange at 11.322-323, and the rivalry between Lodowick and Mathias is prepared for. Out of this skillful exposition in the first act everything else emerges: Barabas' recouping his fortune, Malta's decision to defy the Turks under del Bosco's leadership, the purchase of Ithamore, and the series of revenge plots undertaken by Barabas. His determination to get even with Ferneze accounts for the first of these, the death of Lodowick (and, incidentally, Mathias), and each of the later ones emerges inevitably as part of a campaign to protect himself from disaster: hence the poisoning of Abigail (and, incidentally, the other nuns); the murder of the two Friars, who make the mistake of attempting to capitalize on what they have learned from Abigail; the necessary removal of Ithamore (and, not so incidentally, Bellamira and Pilia-Borza); the alliance with the Turks; and the counterplot with Ferneze where Barabas is finally beaten at his own game. Only the Ithamore-Bellamira-Pilia-Borza episodes are introduced relatively late; even they are got under way at the earliest possible moment, the scene immediately following Barabas' purchase of Ithamore. To trace adequately the careful and complex relationships of these several plots requires nothing short of a full-scale plot summary too long to be attempted here.

Just as important as this skillful structure are the thematic concerns that give a unity to the play. We are a long way from having a world where an avaricious Jew lives; we have instead an avaricious world: when Ferneze (disingenuously) asks of Callapine, "What wind drives you thus into Malta road?" Callapine's reply is not for this play a mere hyperbole: "The wind that bloweth all the world besides: / Desire of gold" (III.v.3-4). The Turks, the Jews, the Maltese, the Friars, Ithamore, Bellamira, Pilia-Borza—of all the major characters in the play, only Abigail is exempt from materialistic motives. Of the lesser characters, only Mathias and his mother are exceptions; even Lodowick employs the labored diamond metaphor in his conversations with Barabas about Abigail (see especially II.iii.49-69, 293).

In a similar way, the methods of underhanded double-dealing employed by Barabas are also used by characters on all of the various levels of action. The theme is once again introduced through Barabas, but in so subtle a way as to go unnoticed unless one pays close attention. When we first meet him, Barabas is portrayed as almost a type of the commercial magnate, in touch constantly with an operation that moves on a vast scale. Thus in his opening soliloquy and his conversations with the two merchants we see first the skillful businessman, second the miser who is concerned about the quality as well as the quantity of the wealth he amasses (see especially 11.7-37). A further insight into his true character comes in his comparative reflections on Christians:

> Who hateth me but for my happiness?
> Or who is honor'd now but for his wealth?
> Rather had I, a Jew, be hated thus,
> Than pitied in a Christian poverty;
> For I can see no fruits in all their faith,
> But malice, falsehood, and excessive pride,
> Which methinks fits not their profession.
> Happily some hapless man hath conscience,
> And for his conscience lives in beggary.
> They say we are a scatter'd nation:
> I cannot tell, but we have scambled up
> More wealth by far than those that brag of faith.
> (I.i.110-121)

Thus before receiving the specific motivation of revenge against Ferneze or anyone else, Barabas is revealed to us as one who despises Christianity—when conscientiously practiced because it brings beggary; when, as it usually is, hypocritically practiced because it is so hypocritical. But Barabas' own hypocrisy and egocentric malice appear immediately in his conversation with the three Jews who come to him for his advice. The aside is a device employed to pyrotechnic effect by Marlowe in this play: Barabas, especially, uses it to reveal his true feelings to the audience, as he does in the first aside in the play (I.i.150-151): "Nay, let 'em combat, conquer, and kill all, / So they spare me, my daughter, and my wealth." Having made his friends easier in their minds about the visit of the Turks, Barabas begins to plan for the protection of his own interests, revealing as he does so the extent of his self-centeredness and the hypocrisy which he himself is perfectly willing to practice in order to remain secure:

> Howe'er the world go, I'll make sure for one,
> And seek in time to intercept the worst,
> Warily guarding that which I ha' got.
> *Ego mihimet sum semper proximus.*
> Why, let 'em enter, let 'em take the town.
> (I.i.184-188)

We see, then, that Barabas' scorn and hate are directed not only toward the Christians but toward his three fellow Jews, whose interests Barabas has not the slightest intention of protecting. Only his daughter Abigail does he hold exempt from enmity, and she, as the play soon demonstrates, is only an apparent exception: so long as she is as usable and profitable as a bag of portagues, Barabas has the same affection for her that he has for his wealth. Both are pieces of negotiable

property. When, however, she takes it upon herself to act as a person in her own right, Barabas' love for her is revealed for what it really is: "For she that varies from me in belief / Gives great presumption that she loves me not" (III.iv.10-11).

Barabas' unscrupulousness in personal and commercial relations, like all his other characteristics, is particularly noticeable, of course, because he so dominates the play. In his dealings with the lovers, with the Friars, with Ithamore, with the Turks, with Ferneze, with Bellamira and Pilia-Borza, even with Abigail, Barabas is governed by politic considerations. But the focusing of interest on Barabas must not be allowed to obscure the fact that almost everyone else in the play operates on much the same basis: the Turks have intentionally allowed the tribute to pile up in arrears; Ferneze perpetrates the perfectly fraudulent tax arrangement on the three Jews and, even more unfairly, on Barabas; the Maltese decide to defy the Turks but make no pretense of returning the Jews' money to them; del Bosco is at least partially motivated by his wish to sell slaves; one Friar attempts to outdo the other in cleverness as well as in greed; Bellamira and Pilia-Borza play Ithamore for the fool; Ferneze arranges the grand climax, deceiving the Turks and Barabas together. Except for Ithamore—and Marlowe must surely have been smiling to himself—the Turks show up much better, on the whole, than either the Jews or the Christians. But all (save, once again, the much tried Abigail and a few of the minor characters) operate in terms of *policy,* in its pejorative Elizabethan sense: "In reference to conduct or action generally: Prudent, expedient, or advantageous procedure; prudent or politic course of action; also, as a quality of the agent: sagacity, shrewdness, artfulness; in bad sense, cunning, craftiness, dissimulation" (*OED policy,* I.4.a.). Just as the world of *The Jew of Malta* is a world of avariciousness, so too it is a world of cunning, craftiness, dissimulation—in short, of policy.

To complicate the texture of motives and plots still further, Marlowe employs the device—though it is more than just a device—that was to become the great motif of later Elizabethan and Jacobean tragedy: revenge. We have already seen how Barabas' multiple murders arise out of his need to prevent the discovery of the first two, motivated by revenge. Revenge, moreover, complicates his motives with regard to the Friars and Ithamore; or at least he hauls it in as an excuse. Only in the last scene does he confessedly abandon revenge, having fallen completely in love with policy and the delights that it can bring simply for their own sake:

> Why, is not this
> A kingly kind of trade, to purchase towns
> By treachery, and sell 'em by deceit?
> Now tell me, worldlings, underneath the sun,

If greater falsehood ever has been done?

V.v.46-50)

Earlier in the final act he has at least temporarily forgotten revenge in his obsession with policy and the profit it can bring: "Thus, loving neither, will I live with both, / Making a profit of my policy" (V.ii.111-112). But in almost all his operations, revenge lurks as at least an undercurrent of motive. So too, of course, Ferneze and Katherine seek revenge for the deaths of their sons, who had been seeking revenge on each other; Friar Jacomo thinks he is revenging himself on Friar Barnardine; Ithamore justifies his blackmail in part as a means of revenge for Barabas' mistreatment of him; and Ferneze, in the grand climax of policy, achieves final revenge both on Barabas and on Calymath.

In effect, the play is concerned largely with persons motivated by the basest causes and acting on the basest principles: this world is full of hypocrisy, expedience, greed, and vengeance. As Abigail remarks, "there is no love on earth, / Pity in Jews, nor piety in Turks" (III.iii.47-48). And yet we must return to the curious ambivalence: *The Jew of Malta* is certainly not a tragedy except insofar as a great many people die in it. It does show a world of evil values and culpable behavior, values and behavior which we are not asked to applaud, though whose power we must perforce respect; but throughout, the rhetoric, the costume and makeup, such conventions as the aside, the comedy of the obscene, the ludicrous, and the merely exaggerated—all combine to make us laugh. Howard S. Babb has put the matter astutely in observing, "The main themes gain in body by being dramatized farcically as well as seriously" and, again, "We are asked to respond seriously to caricature."

This same ambivalence appears, finally, in the styles of the play, infinitely various, but each of indisputable brilliance. As in most Elizabethan verse plays, the norm is a fluid, flexible, workmanlike blank verse that almost any of the Elizabethan dramatists could have written (surely they lisped in numbers). It is remarkably more fluid and flexible than the "mighty line" so often regarded as the epitome of Marlowe's achievement: variation in the placement of the caesura and a relatively frequent use of enjambement give the verse a quality quite unlike that of *Tamburlaine*. The striking passages, those that might be culled out for a collection of anthology pieces, show an even greater brilliance. There are first of all the passages of Marlovian rhetoric, where sounds are piled on sounds, images on images, and rising rhythms on rising rhythms, all combining to produce the effects that only Marlowe is capable of:

Give me the merchants of the Indian mines,
That trade in metal of the purest mold;
The wealthy Moor, that in the eastern rocks
Without control can pick his riches up,

And in his house heap pearl like pebble-stones,
Receive them free, and sell them by the weight,
Bags of fiery opals, sapphires, amethysts,
Jacinths, hard topaz, grass-green emeralds,
Beauteous rubies, sparkling diamonds,
And seld-seen costly stones of so great price
As one of them, indifferently rated,
And of a carat of this quantity,
May serve in peril of calamity
To ransom great kings from captivity.

(I.i.19-32)

Such passages, usually appearing in long soliloquies, are counterpointed by the extremely rapid movement of dialogue that the play incorporates so much of, sometimes (as in I.ii.) with stichomythic effect, sometimes as a rapid-fire comic exchange that both reproduces and parodies the rhythms of everyday speech:

FRIAR BARNARDINE. Thy daughter—

FRIAR JACOMO. Ay, thy daughter—

BARABAS. O, speak not of her; then I die with grief.

FRIAR BARNARDINE. Remember that—

FRAIR JACOMO. Ay, remember that—

BARABAS. I must needs say that I have been a great usurer.

FRIAR BARNARDINE. Thou hast committed—

BARABAS. Fornication? but that was in another country: and besides, the wench is dead.

(IV.i.33-41)

Finally, there are passages of prose as adroit in their manipulation of colloquial inflection as anything that had yet been written in English:

I never knew a man take his death so patiently as this friar. He was ready to leap off ere the halter was about his neck; and when the hangman had put on his hempen tippet, he made such haste to his prayers as if he had had another cure to serve. Well, go whither he will, I'll be none of his followers in haste.

(IV.ii.21-26)

This richness of language in passages skillfully alternated combines with the richness of episode and of theme to produce a total effect that is nothing short of dazzling. The play begins slowly, with the long and dignified set speeches of Barabas in Act I, scene i, moves more and more rapidly through the ever-increasing tangles of plot and language in Acts II, III, and IV, and culminates in the intentionally (I would argue) crowded series of climaxes in Act V, where tables turn so rapidly that the sequence of events is hard to follow. It might even be argued that this brilliantly theatrical and entertaining design is Marlowe's greatest achievement in the play, but then one remembers that there is also that horrid world of falsity in political, religious, and personal affairs that is perhaps not so grotesquely a distortion of reality as, for the sake of humanity, one might wish. (pp. xiv-xxv)

Richard W. Van Fossen, in an introduction to *The Jew of Malta* by Christopher Marlowe, edited by Richard W. Van Fossen, University of Nebraska Press, 1964, pp. xii-xxv.

HARRY LEVIN
(essay date 1964)

[Levin is an American educator and critic. In the following essay, written on the occasion of the 400th anniversary of the playwright's birth, Levin addresses major themes in Marlowe's dramatic works.]

On his four-hundredth anniversary, as at all other moments of critical judgment, it is Marlowe's peculiar destiny to be reconsidered in a Shakespearean context. His strongest claim is bound to be the fact that he did so much more than anyone else to bring that context into existence. This was the high point of A. C. Swinburne's eulogy in the *Encyclopaedia Britannica:* "He is the greatest discoverer, the most daring and inspired pioneer, in all our poetic literature." Yet even Swinburne qualified his superlatives: "The place and the value of Christopher Marlowe as a leader among English poets it would be almost impossible for historical criticism to overestimate." The implicit qualification is underlined by our realization that the Victorian poet was far from being a historical critic. Marlowe must abide the question of history, which Shakespeare has all but outflown. Yes, he is for all time, we must agree with Ben Jonson. And Marlowe then, was he primarily for his age? Certainly he caught its intensities, placed its rhythms, and dramatized its dilemmas as no Elizabethan writer had previously done, and as all would be doing thereafter to some extent. Shakespeare, two months younger, could have emerged only by way of Marlovian discipleship. Had he likewise died at twenty-nine, he would have left us no more than Marlowe's seven plays. Most of Shakespeare's comparable sheaf of erotic poems seem likely to have been composed shortly afterward. In 1593 the Shakespearean corpus probably comprised three or four of the cruder histories and two or three of the lighter comedies, plus *Titus Andronicus.*

Neither of these matchless contemporaries, at twenty-nine, was a schoolboy; and it would be presumptuous for us to set them in retroactive competition, awarding Marlowe a special palm for higher achievement to date. Yet it is reciprocally poignant that Shakespeare, who retired early and was not destined to live beyond middle age, had at least twenty years left in which to compose about thirty more plays and thereby to round out the full assertion of his uniqueness. One is almost tempted, on sentimental grounds, by Calvin Hoffman's silly theory [in *The Man Who Was Shakespeare*] that Marlowe was not really killed in a tavern brawl, but was whisked away to a secret retreat wherefrom he proceeded to turn out Shakespeare's plays. As against the other anti-Stratfordian theories [which propose that someone other than the man from Stratford composed the plays of "Shakespeare"], this one has the merit of naming the single alternate who had actually demonstrated a dramaturgic flair. However, such temptations are easily brushed aside, not merely by the documents attesting Marlowe's death and Shakespeare's life, but by the contrasting patterns of their respective careers. Marlowe's was meteoric in its development, and in its expression as well. In that sense his end was not untimely, and it is futile to sentimentalize now over his fragments and unwritten masterworks. Shakespeare needed maturity to express ripeness, although he could never have matured without assuming first the youthful stance that Marlowe has made permanently his own. Insofar as he must seem forever young, we are inclined to feel old as we belatedly reread him. Michael Drayton set the angle for all backward glances at Marlowe, when he described him as having primordial qualities: "those brave translunary things / That the first poets had."

Drayton went on to amplify this description with a famous chemical formula, which implies again as much as it states: "His raptures were / All air and fire . . . " Significantly enough, they are not said to have been compounded of earth or water, which are after all the elements of flesh and blood, and hence are major components for literature. Shakespeare seems to have marked the passing of Marlowe through his own *Richard III,* where he proved himself to be past master of the Marlovian attitudes and tonalities, even while he was ranging on toward richer complexities and subtler nuances of human relationship. To be sure, *Richard II* would be unthinkable without the example of *Edward II,* or *The Merchant of Venice* without *The Jew of Malta.* Speaking more broadly, *Hamlet* owes a certain amount to the precedent of *Doctor Faustus,* and *Coriolanus* to *Tamburlaine.* Yet, in each of these instances, Shakespeare moves on a wholly different plane—and appeals to a wholly different mode—of experience. *Titus Andronicus* itself, perhaps his most derivative work and surely his least effective, already shows a few of his humanely original touches. The ear that has been attuned to Marlowe, of course will catch reverberations throughout the whole repertory. Incongruously Barabas, under a balcony, prepares the ground for Romeo's advances:

> But stay! What star shines yonder in the east?
> The lodestar of my life, if Abigail.
> [*The Jew of Malta,* II.i]

Ophelia's madness would have been less plaintive, had she not been preceded by Zabina:

> Let the soldiers be buried. Hell! Death! Tamburlaine! Hell!
> Make ready my coach, my chair, my jewels! I come, I come, I come.
> [*Tamburlaine,* V.ii]

And Hamlet might not have contemplated the other world so intensively, if it had not been for Mortimer,

> That scorns the world, and, as a traveller
> Goes to discover countries yet unknown.
> [*Edward II,* V.vi]

Nor would Milton's Satan have spanned quite so wide an arc, if Mephistophilis had not declared:

> Hell hath no limits, nor is circumscrib'd
> In one self place, but where we are is hell.
> [*Doctor Faustus,* II.i]

But the very echo sounded increasingly hollow as the theatre gained in depth, and as the histrionic manner of Marlowe's [Edward] Alleyn gave way to the modulated acting of Shakespeare's [Richard] Burbage. Within a decade after the prologue to *Tamburlaine* had so proudly vaunted its forthcoming innovations, they were looked upon as old-fashioned fustian, mouthed by such seedy playgoers as Ancient Pistol [in *2 Henry IV*], and burlesqued by many lesser playwrights. Shakespeare and others paid incidental tribute to the Dead Shepherd; gossip about Kit's wild escapades and shocking opinions continued to spread; and the final stab carried with it an obvious moral to be heavily labored. As for the plays themselves, except for the debasement of *Doctor Faustus* into a puppet show, they went unperformed through the latter seventeenth and eighteenth centuries. They were passionately rediscovered by the Romantics, who saw in Marlowe himself a fellow Romantic, and read him for such purple passages as Charles Lamb extracted in his *Specimens of the English Dramatic Poets.* Signs of growing appreciation included Edmund Kean's revival of *The Jew of Malta,* as well as Alexander Dyce's scholarly edition of the collected works. During the later years of the nineteenth century, Marlowe came into his own—and possibly into something more. His "Best Plays," edited by Havelock Ellis with a general introduction by J. A. Symonds, inaugurated the popular Mermaid Series in 1887. Their artistic novelty, their sensual coloring, their intellectual boldness, along with their underlying legend of genius misunderstood, held an especially powerful appeal for the *fin de siècle* and for the first generation of the twentieth century.

Marlowe was hailed, in Swinburne's panegyric, as "Soul nearest ours of all, that wert most far." We might wonder whether he stands any nearer to, or farther away from, ourselves at his quadricentennial; and we may well ask ourselves what characteristics found so strong an affinity in his admirers of two or three generations ago. The image of the Superman was then in the air, we recall, and it must have seemed more glamorous than it has subsequently become. Symonds and Ellis both talked about *L'amour de l'impossible* as if it embodied an imminent possibility. Ellis was a professional nonconformist, dedicated to sexual reform, French Naturalism, and the iconoclastic side of many other controversial issues of the day. Symonds was the principal English interpreter of the Renaissance, and his interpretations stressed those tendencies which meant most to the advanced thinkers among his contemporaries: neo-pagan aestheticism, hedonistic individualism, secularistic liberalism, naturalistic skepticism. Further reinterpretation, influenced in its turn by some disillusionment over such tendencies, has more recently veered toward the other extreme, stressing the heritage of the Middle Ages and the continuity of its orthodox traditions. Consequently the question, "How modern was Marlowe?" entails the counter-question, "How modern are we?" If we entertain the more conservative view of his period, we can no longer view him as its characteristic spokesman. Douglas Bush would treat him, with some cogency, as a highly idiosyncratic figure. This should not lessen the interest we take in him as a writer, and it should increase his importance as a historic voice, whose dissents from orthodoxy were pioneering affirmations of modernism.

Such may be the most satisfactory placement that we can make for Marlowe's position today, but the anti-modernists would press the argument further. Not content with turning back the clock on the Renaissance itself, they would reinterpret Marlowe's outlook in conformity with the canons of traditional belief. Unlike Rimbaud's apologists, they can tell no tale of deathbed conversion to invest the poet with an aura of posthumous respectability. Marlowe's heresies, for better or worse, are matters of legal record. We may not altogether trust his accusers; and we must distinguish their hostile testimony from the considered purport of Marlowe's writing; yet the cloud of suspicion surrounding the man lends credence to the more radical impression of his work. Paul H. Kocher has traced his thought through his dramaturgy on the justifiable assumption that he was a subjective dramatist. This is something of a contradiction in terms, since we ordinarily assume that the drama is—or should be—an objective medium. But objectivity, in the presentation of ideas, emotions, and characters, is at best an approximation. Shakespeare seems most unique in his "Negative Capability," his capacity for effacing his own personality behind his varied and vivid *dramatis personae*. Marlowe's more insistent and limited gift might be characterized, by inevitable comparison, as positive capability. Where Shakespeare is everybody, Marlowe is always himself. The critical method suggested by David Masson, the detection of "fervors" and "recurrences," proves elusive and hazardous for Shakespeare. But for Marlowe it works, because he keeps obsessively returning to certain themes, rising to particular occasions, and modifying his material in distinctly personal ways.

Consider what Mario Praz has called the Ganymede complex. Whether or not Marlowe was a homosexual can be no concern of ours; it is somewhat more relevant that his conversations, as reported by Thomas Kyd and Richard Baines, consistently exhibit a preoccupation with homosexuality; and it is of real significance, in the history of western literature, that few writers have so candidly dwelt on that theme, between the ancients and the epoch of Proust and Gide and Jean Genet. Both in *Dido, Queen of Carthage,* and in *Hero and Leander,* the conventionally heterosexual plot is augmented by the interpolation of a homosexually motivated episode. It has not passed without remark that Marlowe's one sustained treatment of amorous passion appears in the love of Edward II for Gaveston—a relation adumbrated in Henry II and his minions. One of the ironies of Marlowe's fate, under the circumstances, has been his repute among casual readers as a sort of laureate for young lovers. This may be due in part to his premature demise and to the discredited rumors involving a lovers' duel, but it has mainly resulted from that small handful of quotations from him which have circulated very widely: his much anthologized lyric, "The Passionate Shepherd to his Love"; the rapturous invocation of Doctor Faustus to Helen of Troy, detached from its austere context; and, above all, the quasi-proverbial line about love at first sight that Shakespeare echoed in *As You Like It.* More in the distinctive Marlovian vein is the cynical twist of Barabas' response to the charge of fornication, which T. S. Eliot culled for an epigraph, and which has since provided a title for Ernest Hemingway and latterly James Baldwin:

> . . .But that
> Was in another country; and besides
> The wench is dead.
> *[The Jew of Malta,* IV.i]

Lamb could not, and would not, have gone into concrete details; yet he pointed in the prevailing direction, when he spoke of Marlowe's disposition "to dally with interdicted subjects." His contemporary reputation for "daring God out of Heaven," in Robert Greene's phrase, clearly echoed fervent lines and mirrored recurrent scenes. We need not forget that those

heretical speeches and blasphemous gestures were put into the mouths of protagonists on whose heads they brought down the most exemplary damnations. But if Marlowe is not—what Ellis claimed—his own hero, then his typical heroes tend to be committed heretics, as well as self-made moderns; and *Doctor Faustus,* with a black magic still potent in the curses and conjurations of *Moby Dick* or *Ulysses,* comes perilously close to prefiguring Marlowe's own tragedy: the cut branch, the burnt laurel. The playwright not only takes part in the scholar's blasphemy, but also seems to enjoy his anathema. True, the pagan vision of Helen dissolves before the Gothic grotesquery of the hell-mouth. But it is the perpetual curiosity, rather than the terminal agony, that survives in our minds as the peculiarly Faustian posture. Similarly, we go on thinking of Don Juan as an unrepentant libertine, rather than as a sinner burning in hell. Since the interdiction is duly scheduled to win out over the dalliance, *Doctor Faustus* would have the stark outline of a morality play, if an outline were all that we looked for in it. Neoorthodox moralists would indeed reduce the mighty *Tamburlaine* to the abject level of a cautionary fable, as Roy W. Battenhouse has attempted to do, by emphasizing the dogmatic background at the expense of the dramatic foreground, though the latter expressly flouts the former.

Since every drama is perforce dialectical, there is much that has to be said on both sides; and where opinion was strictly regulated, it would be the right thinkers who had to say the last word; yet though they reaffirm the appropriate taboo, it has been challenged in the process by more fascinating spokesmen. These unbelievers maintain a tense atmosphere of moral ambiguity, made explicit by the theatrical caricature of Machiavelli. The Latin warrant that brings about Edward's murder would make a suggestive paradigm for the reading of Marlowe as a whole. It could convey an innocuous piety: "Kill not the king, 'tis good to fear the worst" [*Edward II,* V.iv]. Or, as repunctuated and retranslated by Mortimer, it could have a subversive and sinister meaning: "Fear not to kill the king, 'tis good he die" (V.iv). So it sounds with Marlowe's ambiguous situations. There is not impiety, from a Christian standpoint, when Tamburlaine burns the Koran; his ensuing death, in any case, might well be regarded as Mohammed's revenge. When the Christian armies break their oath, the Mohammedan leader calls upon Christ, who avenges their just cause against his own adherents. It is in this connection that the infidel Orcanes makes the most elevated of Marlowe's religious pronouncements, affirming the existence of a transcendent God who—like the hell that accompanies Mephistophilis—is not "circumscriptible." This is as far from Marlowe's alleged atheism as it is from any theological dogma; and it does not exclude a thoroughgoing anticlericalism, or a skeptical feeling that few religionists live up to the creeds they profess. As a study in comparative ethics, *The Jew of Malta* is more anti-Christian than anti-Semitic. Here again it is the Christians who do the oath-breaking, and their Governor outdoes the Jew in Machiavellian blackmail and double-dealing.

The gods themselves are pantheistically pluralized by Marlowe, with room among them for both Christ and Mohammed under the ultimate deity of Jove. That classical ruler, who coalesces at times with the Old Testament visage of Jehovah, is likewise seen as the Olympian revolutionary who overthrew the Titans; Tamburlaine cites him as an illustrious forerunner in an eternal conflict; and it is revealing to compare this triumphal account of a perpetually dynamic cosmos, where nature teaches men to have aspiring minds, with the hierarchical conception of order and degree that Ulysses elucidates in *Troilus and Cressida.* The individual movement is upward, with Marlowe; the total framework is more balanced, with Shakespeare. Tamburlaine's be-all and end-all, "The sweet fruition of an earthly crown," becomes, for the Lancastrian kings, the mere beginning of responsibility: "O polish'd perturbation, golden care!" [*2 Henry IV*]. Marlowe's later heroes, though they are no less monomaniacal or megalomaniacal, have more sublimated ambitions—capital, sorcery—than the kingship, which Edward so pathetically loses. Yet even Tamburlaine, in the midst of his amoral drive to power, can pause to speculate on "What is beauty?" Though he remains untouched by his cruel slaughter of the Damascene virgins, he is finally moved by Zenocrate's tears for her father, and he expends the utmost Marlovian eloquence in expressing the problem of poetic inexpressibility. More pointedly, when Faustus apostrophizes Helen, his aesthetic rapture is framed by the ethical situation. And the delights of music and poetry are frankly envisioned as snares to be manipulated by Gaveston, whose introductory monologue concludes by describing an ominous masque, wherein Actaeon will be stricken down for having observed the naked goddess.

Marlowe's chastened and penitential mood, so ambivalently interwoven with his exaltations and exuberances, might be summed up in this distich from a posthumous poem by e. e. cummings:

where climbing was and bright
is darkness and to fall.

These are not the inert and untragic falls of medieval tragedy; for the overriding emphasis is upon the intellectual pride, the extreme *hubris,* the dazzling brightness that went before them and virtually made the price worth paying. Nonetheless it is acknowledged and paid, and herein lies the sharp difference between Marlowe and the Romantics. His psychic pattern is not Titanic, like theirs, but Icarian, since it encompasses both the limitless aspiration and the limiting consequence:

both infinitude and fragmentation. His Faust is much less close to Goethe's hero, who gets out of his diabolic bargain with such Romantic casuistry, than to the guilt-ridden genius of Thomas Mann's *Doktor Faustus.* We cannot read Marlowe as naïvely today as our predecessors could in the nineteenth century; and he might make us happier if we could stick to his bright surfaces; but his stature as a tragic playwright is enhanced by the darker and deeper meanings we may now be finding in his tragedies. The note of triumph that runs through them, Renaissance triumph uncontrolled, rings false already in *Edward II* and takes on an ironic reverberation for us. Among their spectacular properties, which symbolize aspects of the human predicament, Tamburlaine's chariot fascinates us less than Bajazet's cage. Standing—as we do—somewhat closer to Kafka than to Nietzsche, alas, we comprehend the reaching of limits as well as the testing of potentialities. Capitalism seethes in the self-prepared caldron of Barabas. Science itself is tormented by the flames that Faustus has conjured up.

Thus Marlowe still has resonance, albeit in an unexpectedly minor key, for a time which terms itself the Age of Anxiety; and it might not be unduly hopeful to look for a restaging of his drama in the light of what we sometimes term the Theatre of the Absurd. Its antiheroic characters have more in common with the exceptional Edward, standing beardless and bemused in his puddle, than with the more flamboyantly Marlovian figures. It may indeed be no accident that Bertolt Brecht, in his earliest playwriting days, collaborated on a German adaptation of *Edward II.* Marlowe seems to have naturally obtained that effect for which Brecht has been so consciously striving: alienation rather than identification, estrangement and not endearment—and this must be our last and clinching distinction between Marlowe's art and Shakespeare's. Yet we live in a world, and in a universe, where a sense of strangeness may be more pertinent than the illusion of being at home. Every day remote and obscure nations clamor to be heard, vaunts of ever more menacing weapons are thunderously exchanged, while intrepid voyagers are being launched on interplanetary flights. Marlowe, with his insatiable urge to prove cosmography, to confute the geographers, and to transform history into modernity, might have gained more pleasure from such spectacles than many of us may do. To reread him now is to be reminded of the exotic breeds and barbaric hordes that migrate across the poems of St. John Perse, or of those half-forgotten civilizations whose emergences and declines have been so categorically passed in review by Arnold Toynbee. Marlowe is forever the lone explorer. (pp. 22-31)

Harry Levin, "Marlowe Today," in *The Tulane Drama Review,* Vol. 8, No. 4, Summer, 1964, pp. 22-31.

WILBUR SANDERS

(essay date 1970)

[In the following excerpt, Sanders briefly treats Marlowe's use of the devils and angels in *Doctor Faustus*.]

It must be a fairly common experience to come away from a performance (or a reading) of *Doctor Faustus* with very mixed feelings. The scene of Faustus' death is sufficient to convince us that, in Marlowe, we are dealing with a mind of some distinction; but like so many of the play's high points, the soliloquy is followed by a scene of baffling banality, if not naivety:

> Oh, help us, heaven! see, here are Faustus' limbs,
> All torn asunder by the hand of death.
> (Revels Plays edn., xx, 6-7)

The descent from authentic imaginative vision to the perfunctory and the commonplace can occur within the space of a line. The justly famous definition of hell ("Hell hath no limits, nor is circumscrib'd . . . ") is immediately succeeded by

> And, to be short, when all the world dissolves
> And every creature shall be purify'd,
> All places shall be hell that is not heaven.
> (v, 122 ff.)

Although this expands discursively the vision of a hell co-extensive with the consciousness of the damned, the poetic flame has died to an ember—"to be short" is the key to the tone: Marlowe's fitful muse has deserted him again. The same contradiction runs throughout the play, the most obvious and frequently deplored sign of it being the comparative barrenness of the comic scenes (probably written in collaboration with others) that occupy the central section.

Then there are those subtle felicities which are no sooner perceived than you start wondering whether they are not perhaps accidental; there is that curious loose-jointed fragmentariness of Marlowe's writing—a quality consistent with the assumption that the verse was assembled piece by piece from a stock-pile of previously written lines and paragraphs; and there are all the minor inconsistencies of a work insufficiently digested, ideas which have not undergone that inner chemistry of creation which could assimilate them to one complex imaginative organism, but which survive on the surface of the work as excrescences belonging to one historical epoch, not to all time. . . .[The] unity of *Doctor Faustus* is, in many respects, something that we have to create for ourselves, answering questions that were for Marlowe insoluble, pursuing implications further than he was able or prepared to pursue them, making choices between incompatibles that appear side by side in the play as we have it. All of which makes it extremely difficult to find a *point d'appui* from which to tackle the play.

After such a comprehensive vote of no-confidence in an author, it may seem odd to undertake an investigation at all; but what is good in *Faustus* is good in such a uniquely interesting way, that none of these obvious deficiencies has been sufficient to keep the play off our stages or our bookshelves. We continue to be fascinated, though we are at the same time dissatisfied.

The diabolism in which the play deals is, I believe, one of Marlowe's unsolved problems. When he undertook to dramatize that handbook of demonological conservatism, the *English Faust Book*, Marlowe was immediately committed to accepting as a premiss something which was in process of becoming an anachronism—the phenomenon of witchcraft itself (for, though this is not the place to demonstrate it, there was in sixteenth-century England a strong, sceptical, anti-witchmongery party). The complications arising from this commitment were likely to prove troublesome in a play which, on one level at least, concerned itself with the "unsatiable speculation" of a newly emancipated humanism. Yet Marlowe's introduction of devils who are medieval in temper is, I am sure, deliberate—just as the revival of the earlier psychomachia form (the "battle for a soul" of which *Everyman* is the best-known example) is deliberate. Marlowe is studying the collision between the old wisdom of sin, grace and redemption, and the new wisdom of humanist perfectibility; and the archaic flavour of both fable and treatment is a way of giving body to the historical dimension of his theme. It is in order to preserve the integrity of the older view, too, that he refuses to rationalize witchcraft as "natural magic," the exploitation of the occult but natural virtues of things with the assistance of good spirits—though he could have found good precedents for seeing it in this light. But it is axiomatic in the play that witchcraft is damnable: Faustus' incantation includes the direct invocation of Lucifer and a deliberate blasphemy against the Trinity (iii, 16-20).

Nevertheless, in accepting the older diabolism, with its strong sense of the objectivity of the demonic world and its fairly literal view of the methods by which a man could become entangled with that world, Marlowe involved himself in a contradiction which runs deep into the play. For he also has a strong predisposition to see the matter of diabolic liaison in a markedly metaphorical light. Faustus' incantation, Mephostophilis declares, was the cause of his appearance, yet only *per accidens*.

For when we hear one rack the name of God,
Abjure the Scriptures and his saviour Christ,
We fly, in hope to get his glorious soul.

(iii, 49-51)

In place of Faustus' philosophy of manipulation ("Did not my conjuring speeches raise thee? Speak."), rises the vision of a separate and autonomous order of spiritual forces which respond to human action according to laws of their own nature and with which Faustus has unwittingly become embroiled. This more complex relationship between tempter and tempted opens ironic vistas which lie beyond the compass of a mechanical view of the incantation as effective cause. By hinting that Mephostophilis is a metaphysical resultant of events in Faustus' consciousness, the sense of evil that the fiend represents is given increased depth and power. Yet the disturbing thing is that these lines are spoken by an actor who, only a few minutes before, has appeared in all the trappings of the old ranter who used so amiably to distribute fireworks, advice and cracked pates among his auditors in the old days. Furthermore, he's attended by a troop of slapstick clowns of the same kidney and is provided not only with the traditional hell-mouth, but with a specially constructed dragon as well (iii, 21).

The contradiction is woven into the entire dra-

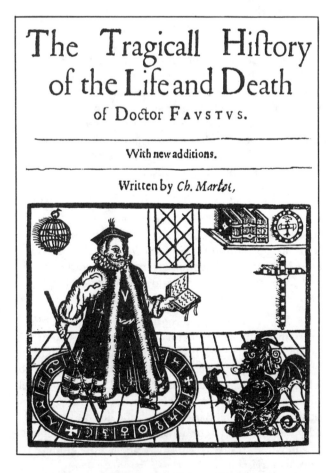

The Tragicall History
of the Life and Death

of Doctor FAVSTVS.

With new additions.

Written by Ch. Marlot,

Title page of the 1628 edition of *Doctor Faustus.*

matic fabric. In part it results from the resurgence of an older, but still powerful, dramatic tradition which, by rendering the demons so irrevocably "other," prevents Marlowe from doing justice to their subjective dimension. But I think it is also a heroic attempt to wed the imaginative efficiency of the old to the psychological profundity of the new. In the case of the demons, we usually get no more than an oscillation, or two alternative accounts of the one event. Thus, the perilous capacity of a man for being his own tempter, so clearly enacted in the first scene, is reduced near the end of the play to a simple matter of demonic violation:

'Twas I that, when thou wert i' the way to heaven,
Damm'd up thy passage; when thou took'st the book
To view the scriptures, then I turn'd the leaves
And led thine eye.

(xix, 93-6)

Or Mephostophilis, requested to describe hell, gives first of all the traditional, localized underworld—

Within the bowels of these elements,
Where we are tortur'd and remain for ever,

(v, 120-1)

but then replaces it with the uncircumscribed state of mental torment to which I have already referred (v, 122-7). The juxtaposition may perhaps be made workable by treating Mephostophilis' first answer as an attempt to fob Faustus off with the "scholarism" he already knows. But the "vast perpetual torture-house" image persists throughout the play, and is physically "discovered" in the penultimate scene:

There are the furies, tossing damned souls
On burning forks; their bodies boil in lead:
There are live quarters broiling on the coals,
That ne'er can die . . .

(xix, 118-21)

I suppose there is a sense in which these lines reflect Faustus' bondage to the medieval horrors of his own consciousness. But the bondage is also Marlowe's, as is the hint of schoolboy sadism in the facilities of the rhythm. In any case, this gross physical hell combines with the "Shaggehayr'd Deuills" and the dismembered corpse of the last scene to superimpose a relatively superficial image of hell upon a dramatic metaphor of great force and range. Hell can never be an anachronism as long as it is used to give shape to the forces which are felt to be ultimately destructive of human significance; but a hell which destroys a man by tearing him limb from limb is an anachronism in the world of *Doctor Faustus.* Its relative superficiality is reflected in the verse which presents it, relying as it does so heavily on the external and the sensational.

Marlowe is, however, more successful in moulding the Angels he inherited from the older drama, into a new artistic instrument. It is true they are abstractions, belonging to no specific time and place, speaking an unmoved, formalized verse from some point clearly outside the area where the play's decisions are taken. Yet the very abstraction keeps them sufficiently un-individualized to be functions of Faustus' conscience, and sufficiently removed from the sphere of dramatic action to symbolize an order outside it.

> BAD ANGEL: Go forward, Faustus, in that famous art.
>
> GOOD ANGEL: Sweet Faustus, leave that execrable art.
>
> FAUSTUS: Contrition, prayer, repentance, what of these?
>
> GOOD ANGEL: O, they are means to bring thee unto heaven.
>
> BAD ANGEL: Rather illusions, fruits of lunacy, That make men foolish that do use them most.
>
> GOOD ANGEL: Sweet Faustus, think of heaven and heavenly things.
>
> BAD ANGEL: No, Faustus, think of honour and of wealth.
>
> [*Exeunt* Angels]
>
> FAUSTUS: Wealth!
>
> (v, 15-23)

Far from being clumsily primitive, this is an immensely dramatic procedure. The first effect of the interruption is to arrest all action on stage, and to focus attention on the protagonist suspended in the act of choice. Not until he speaks do we know to which voice he has been attending. It's the act of choice in slow motion, a dramatization of his strained attention to the faint voices of unconscious judgment. At the same time, his unawareness of their presence has the effect of revealing his blindness to the real issues at stake: what he takes to be a decision between contrition and wealth is really a primal decision between good and evil. And his unconscious echoing of their words is a parable of his inability to evade moral categories. The course of self-gratification on which he's embarked is no more his own than are the angels; yet it is, by the same token, as much his own as they are. He is an involuntary participant in the moral order, yet he shapes that order by his action.

By the device of the Angels, Marlowe breaks down the subjective-objective dualism which dogs other parts of the play, and appeals beyond it to a psychological realism rooted in the individual consciousness of Faustus himself. His dramatic point is not that evil is only the basin-eyed monster of legend and good the angelic visitant—i.e. merely objective; nor that they are only manifestations of states of consciousness—i.e.

merely subjective; but rather that they have the kind of reality which is appropriately represented by an actor in a play. They are real enough to have voices of their own. It is as if the play moved on a plane at right-angles to the one whose axes are "subjective" and "objective"; its co-ordinates are heaven and hell considered as primal symbols, and ranging in their suggested provenance from the purely subjective hallucination to the stonily objective fact.

At times the same break-through is achieved with the demonic order. In Scene iii, Faustus' conjuring is presided over by "Lucifer and four devils above," again embodying the radical moral polarization implicit in all human activity. But, nevertheless, his incantations do have a specific result: Mephostophilis does appear, less "pliant" than Faustus imagines, but a palpable change in the moral landscape which must in some measure be attributed to Faustus' activity. The evil he invokes is both his own and not his own.

The insight shown at times in the handling of the supernatural, yet the disturbing dissonance between metaphorical and literal views, suggest a Marlowe dangerously entangled with the material of his art, still wrestling with unresolved paradoxes which frustrate his grand aim of harmonizing the old and the new wisdoms. (pp. 112-16)

The oscillation between extremes—faith and despair, heaven and hell, God and Lucifer ("Yet will I call on him. O, spare me, Lucifer!")—reveals itself finally as part of the homiletic simplification that so sadly dogs the play, sign of a sensibility too geometrical, too prone to simple oppositions, operating at one remove from the complex flux of sensation and thought.

Yet there remain unmistakable signs of that imaginative grip and utter seriousness for which one returns to *Faustus:* things like the hallucinated vision of a firmament streaming with blood, as the very medium of Faustus' redemption turns to a nightmare of horror and retribution; or the potent imaging of that wrathful deity under whose looming tyranny the individual stands dwarfed and obliterated; or Faustus' agony of prayer with its abject and poignant *non sequitur* ("O God, / If thou wilt not have mercy on my soul, . . . Let Faustus . . . at last be sav'd"). These moments are the more impressive in that they show Marlowe establishing imaginative control over his most appalling fear—the fear of final destitution and rejection.

And at the end he rises superbly to the occasion with an electrically vital rendering of the very moment of dissolution:

> O, it strikes, it strikes! Now, body, turn to air,
> Or Lucifer will bear thee quick to hell!
> O soul, be chang'd into little water drops,
> And fall into the ocean, ne'er be found. (*Enter* Devils)

My God, my God! Look not so fierce on me!
Adders and serpents, let me breathe awhile!
Ugly hell, gape not! Come not, Lucifer;
I'll burn my books!—Ah, Mephostophilis!

(xix, 183-90)

Here there's a physical particularity, an astonishing evocation of sensation (the body turning to air and water, magically weightless and fluid, yet stung into frenzy by adders and serpents of physical agony that will not let it breathe), and a strange compound of terror at, and longing for, extinction. The flat either / or of heaven and hell becomes a fusion in which "My God" may be addressed either to the Deity or to the Devils. That irreducible love-hate that Faustus bears towards both God and Lucifer becomes a cry of erotic self-surrender *and* horrified revulsion as he yields to the embrace of his demon lover—"Ah, Mephostophilis!" Marlowe here masters the central paradox of his theism and makes of it a unique dramatic reality which is genuinely tragic.

There it would be pleasant to leave the final emphasis—if Marlowe would let us. But he adds the Epilogue. And the stringency and shallowness of the "morality" deployed there goes a long way towards explaining the final incoherence of *Doctor Faustus:* any extensive humanization, any development in depth will escape the coarse meshes of this net and assume equivocal control of the play's imaginative energies. Yet Marlowe, by scoring his final bars for such a consort of archaic viols, shows himself sublimely unaware of how revolutionary the drama is that he has just written. (pp. 126-27)

Wilbur Sanders, "Marlowe's 'Doctor Faustus'," in *Shakespeare's Contemporaries: Modern Studies in English Renaissance Drama,* edited by Max Bluestone and Norman Rabkin, second edition, Prentice-Hall, Inc., 1970, pp. 112-27.

J. W. HARPER

(essay date 1971)

[In the following excerpt, Harper describes aspects of *Tamburlaine* that contribute to its dramatic success: style, characterization, construction, and symbology.

The prologues to the two parts of *Tamburlaine* are direct addresses to the audience and exist outside the realm of dramatic illusion. The first promises a new form of drama, elevated in tone and free from the jigs and improvisations of professional actors, and the second proudly points to the great success which that new form had had with the first audiences:

The general welcomes Tamburlaine received,
When he arrived last upon our stage,
Hath made our poet pen his second part . . .

Certainly the two parts of *Tamburlaine* were among the most successful plays of the Elizabethan stage. Although no record of the earliest performances survives, Henslowe's diary records numerous productions in 1594-5 and allusions to the play abound even after the turn of the century. And while, with the notable exceptions of Tyrone Guthrie's productions in 1951 and 1956, modern producers have not attempted to recapture that early success, Marlowe's 'tragical discourses' have enjoyed another sort of vogue in our own day. Since the revival of its author's reputation in the late nineteenth century, *Tamburlaine* has been one of the most widely studied of Elizabethan plays. The scholars' commentaries and interpretations have succeeded to the audiences' applause.

Deprived of the possibility of seeing the play in the theatre, the reader must endeavour to recreate it in imagination; and this involves such difficulties as conceiving of a style of acting, the ponderous declamatory mode of the mighty Edward Alleyn, which disappeared from the stage in the course of Shakespeare's lifetime. *Tamburlaine*, of course, cannot escape from time: a twentieth-century mind brings to it forms of knowledge and varieties of reaction which its author could hardly have anticipated. But any serious critical assessment of the work must include an awareness of its great initial success and an acknowledgement of how well its various elements proved to be adapted to the playwright's purpose.

The most obvious reason for the success of *Tamburlaine* was the surprise and delight with which Marlowe's novel style was received, a style which has often enough been analysed, praised, and parodied. The majestic march of the blank-verse line with its subtle variations in pace and rhythm; the splendour of the language filled with sonorous place-names and words evoking colour, light, and infinite space; the long, intricately arranged sentences which flow through lines abounding in hyperbole and studded with imagery from classical mythology and the new exploration of the world—Marlowe's 'mighty line' was the source from which the rich variety of Elizabethan dramatic blank verse was to flow. But is Marlowe's style in *Tamburlaine,* as has often been claimed, a revelation of the author himself ? Each of the later works reveals significant differences and developments; and though *Tamburlaine* abounds in great lyrical passages, each one is so placed as to achieve a calculated dramatic effect. In its artificiality and in what must be seen, paradoxically, as its severe limitation, the style of *Tamburlaine* exists only as part of a play.

If every character in *Tamburlaine* at every moment of his existence seems to be the victim of a spontaneous overflow of powerful feelings, it is remarkable that the speeches observe the 'rules' of the Renaissance rhetoricians so exactly as to make the play seem an orator's handbook come to life. The characteristic speech, the recurring pattern, in *Tamburlaine* is the 'exhortation', a special type of the 'deliberative oration', and the plot is so arranged as to produce scene after scene in which the characters pursue the rhetorician's primary goal of persuasion, as they urge, exhort, or threaten in an effort to impose their will. *Tamburlaine* is the great drama of primal will, and nearly all of its characters are caught up in the same pattern as the hero, so that nearly all speak alike and the subtlety of characterization to which Shakespeare's drama has accustomed us is scarcely to be found. Though Marlowe can use imagery to differentiate his characters (Bajazeth's speeches, for example, characteristically contain images from the underworld and are full of monsters and darkness, whereas Tamburlaine's images come from the heavens and the classical heroes and soar upward into light), amplification is always the end in view, and the favourite Elizabethan devices of verbal wit—conceits and puns, repetitions, antitheses and parallelisms—are used only sparingly. But this almost monomaniacal constriction is not due to Marlowe's inability to write in a more varied and subtle style, as his later plays show; rather, it is his means of dealing with the problem of making effective drama out of what has to be, in effect, a 'one-man play'. Having chosen as hero an historical personage whose character seemed as single as his unbroken series of victories, Marlowe had to engage our interest completely in this hero's every action if anything like dramatic suspense was to be maintained. This was not to be a play about the complex relationship of one human being with others but an exploration and exhibition of the true nature of the qualities which the historical Timur seemed to illustrate. Thus each of Tamburlaine's own orations and every speech of his admirers or his defeated adversaries have the same ultimate purpose; and whether we respond to the hero with admiration, awe, or horror, 'there can be little doubt that Marlowe wants us to *marvel* at Tamburlaine and his amazing adventures' [Donald Peet in *ELH* XXVI (1959)].

Such a limited style, ill-adapted to complex characterization or to character development, is likely to produce monotony, and monotony was inherent in the very subject which Marlowe chose: an invincible hero who goes from incredible strength to still more incredible strength; 'a hideous moral spoonerism: Giant the Jack-Killer' [C. S. Lewis in *English Literature in the Sixteenth Century*, 1954]. And many critics, even the admiring Swinburne, have found Marlowe a dramatist of monotony, redeemed only by the glories of his poetry. Making exception only for *Edward II*, Havelock Ellis

wrote in one of the first volumes of the original Mermaid series that 'Marlowe's dramas are mostly series of scenes held together by the poetic energy of his own dominating personality. He is his own hero, and the sanguinary Scythian utters the deepest secrets of the author's heart.' If so, the attention of the London audiences in the last two decades of the sixteenth century is hard to explain.

However, analysis of the play's construction suggests that the second reason for *Tamburlaine*'s popular success was its effectiveness as drama. Marlowe displayed considerable ingenuity in moulding inherently undramatic material into an action which contains its own sort of tension and suspense. The first three acts of Part One are a mounting series of victories against greater and greater odds; but this form of interest having been largely exhausted, the crucially important fourth act introduces complications. Tamburlaine's new adversaries, Zenocrate's father and her betrothed, appear with a moral authority which the hero's earlier opponents had lacked. For the first time Tamburlaine is not the underdog in a military sense; and as the Soldan heroically defies the usurper and vows to restore the order which has been violated, we have the first clear indication of the implications of Tamburlaine's heroic 'resolution', his revolting cruelty to his captives and to anyone who opposes his implacable will. Not merely is Zenocrate's plea for her people seemingly brushed aside, but the power-mad despot defies Jove himself; and the ending of the fourth act, with its ridiculous 'course of crowns' and Tamburlaine's assertion of an ambition beyond the bounds of human possibility, leaves the audience with an altogether new sense of Tamburlaine's significance. This man must and will be destroyed, for otherwise there can be no justice in the world.

The fifth act, one of the most complex in Elizabethan drama, begins with the slaughter of the virgins of Damascus. Yet just at the point where Tamburlaine's moral fortunes seem to have reached their nadir, Marlowe inserts the great soliloquy 'What is beauty' (V, ii, 97-127), the play's most brilliant lyrical passage, which suddenly transposes the interest of the drama into a new key and forces us to realize that we have been witnessing not merely a chronicle play about a successful general but a drama of ideas in which the full meaning and implications of heroism, will, and inspiration are being explored. This passage is the idological climax of the play, but it is not the end; for no sooner has the audience shifted its attitude to the hero's character once again than we have the arrival of the enemy army, the suicide of Bajazeth and Zabina, and Zenocrate's portentous lament over their bodies, a traditional *de casibus* speech which prepares for Tamburlaine's seemingly inevitable defeat. But the dilemma of Zenocrate, by now the moral centre of the play, leaves the conclusion still in doubt:

> Now shame and duty, love and fear presents
> A thousand sorrows to my martyred soul:
> Whom should I wish the fatal victory,
> When my poor pleasures are divided thus,
> And racked by duty from my cursed heart?
> My father and my first-betrothed love,
> Must fight against my life and present love:
> Wherein the change I use condemns my faith,
> And makes my deeds infamous through the world.
>
> (V, ii, 319-27)

After this only one conclusion seems possible and right, and it follows with Tamburlaine's lightning victory and his merciful 'league of honour' with the Soldan. But lest the disturbing moral ambivalence which the last two acts' skilful plotting has achieved be swallowed up in general rejoicing, Marlowe concludes the play with a powerful visual symbol: Tamburlaine takes his truce with all the world standing above the dead bodies of Bajazeth and Zabina and the blameless King of Arabia.

Marlowe thus shows considerable skill in manipulating the panoramic structure which his sources naturally imposed; and in the second part of the play, with little historical material left to draw upon, he created a dramatic form of much greater ingenuity. Here the technique of manipulating the audience's expectations for the dramatist's own purposes is clearly present from the beginning. The plot seems to be concerned with the rise of a new and formidable force against Tamburlaine, a force centred in the person of Callapine, who is presented sympathetically in contrast to Tamburlaine's increasing savagery. But parallel to the development of this action is a series of scenes—the death of Zenocrate, Tamburlaine's murder of his effeminate son, the hero's final illness—which reveal the real theme of the play: the inevitable frustration of even the most titanic will by circumstances and mortality. In the action concerning Theridamas' defeat by Olympia Marlowe anticipates the later development of the double plot. Then in the final act comes a surprising reversal, as Tamburlaine effortlessly sweeps aside the just vengeance of his adversaries and at the same time recaptures much of the audience's sympathy, first by proving mortal, and then by a sort of intellectual victory over death. He conquers death by accepting it, by affirming the immortality of his spirit and its continuance on earth in the sons whom he has created. His final defeat proves, unexpectedly, his greatest victory. And yet this part of the play, like its predecessor, ends on an ambivalent note. The speech over the hero's corpse emphasizes his uniqueness, and many of Marlowe's audience must have known as well as the author himself what had come of Tamburlaine's belief in the survival of his spirit in his sons.

As one thus examines the play for the effects which make it good armchair drama, one feels that it must be good theatre too in the form in which Marlowe wrote it; that the 'after-thought' of Part Two is as dramatically effective as the predecessor which called it forth. And yet Granville-Barker disagreed [in *On Dramatic Method,* 1931], feeling that *Tamburlaine's* deficiencies in characterization and Marlowe's willingness to sacrifice drama to poetry make the play a poor risk for the modern producer. It is dangerous to disagree with such a sensitive interpreter of Shakespeare; but perhaps one can clarify the very different way in which Shakespeare's precocious forerunner conceived of drama by some attention to the third obvious explanation of *Tamburlaine's* popular success, the power of the play as spectacle.

For the modern mind the term 'spectacle' is bound up with the spectacular, and certainly *Tamburlaine* seems to contain ample invitations to spectacular display. Its royal personages and exotic locales, its armies and processions and verbal evocations of splendour, might well tempt a modern producer who ignored the simple conditions of the Elizabethan theatre into lavish costumes, massive scenery, elephants, and a great deal of noise. But the word preferred by Marlowe and his contemporaries was 'show', and this word in the Renaissance carried a connotation which it has since lost: a show was a visible means of communicating an intellectual concept. The procession of the Seven Deadly Sins in *Dr Faustus* was a 'goodly show', like Bajazeth in his cage, but its immediate effect upon Faustus is to cause him to ask Mephistophilis to explain its meaning.

Shows, like emblems, were means of communicating moral truth by pictures, and the drama which developed out of the mediaeval mystery cycles and morality plays emphasized the formal emblematic composition of a scene rather than its place in a linear narrative of action. In the evolution of Elizabethan drama Marlowe occupies an earlier place, far closer to mediaeval aims and methods, than Shakespeare, and his plays cannot be approached with the same expectations. Though Marlowe (as has been argued above) can manipulate a linear action for purposes of suspense and tension, and though he shows, in his later plays, some adroitness at psychological analysis, his basic dramatic method is the presentation of a series of emblematic images which, in their suggestion of formal arrangement, communicate their meaning as forcefully to the eye as to the ear. If one objects that the famous slanging match between Zenocrate and Zabina could not possibly have occurred, or that Tamburlaine's speech over his dead wife cannot conceivably represent the actual emotions of such a man in such a situation, or that his turning from his wife's corpse to deliver a lengthy lecture on fortification to his sons does nothing to advance the dramatic action, one is simply refusing to accept

Marlowe's conception of the nature of drama. In the confrontation between Zenocrate and Zabina the two women cease to exist as realistic characters whose actions are in conformity with anything which we have previously seen or can imagine and become visual emblems of the aspiring mind versus pride of place, symbolic of the off-stage battle which Marlowe's theatre cannot adequately display. Tamburlaine's threnody ('Now walk the angles on the walls of heaven . . .') is not a psychological analysis of grief but a formal, patterned ritual designed to evoke the hero's sense of the cosmic significance of his first defeat and the loss of his inspiration. And similarly, Tamburlaine's excursion into the minutiae of military science when he stands before the burning city which represents his grief pres-

ents the essence of his nature in the most revealing dramatic image in the play as, unable to face or to understand the implications of his loss, he finds in the pedantry of his profession the only means to continue action. The passages in *Tamburlaine* which make little sense as narrative sequence exist to make their point as dramatic emblems, each one capable of communicating its intellectual content through appeal to the eye and of occupying its own pageant waggon. *Tamburlaine* is not merely an indulgence in spectacle but a whole series of 'goodly shows'. (pp. x-xvi)

J. W. Harper, in an introduction to *Tamburlaine* by Christopher Marlowe, edited by J. W. Harper, Ernest Benn Limited, 1971, pp. vii-xxviii.

SOURCES FOR FURTHER STUDY

Bloom, Harold, ed. *Christopher Marlowe*. New York: Chelsea House, 1986, 246 p.

Collection of reprinted critical essays by prominent scholars.

Boas, Frederick S. *Christopher Marlowe: A Biographical and Critical Study*. Oxford: Oxford University Press, 1940, 336 p.

Seminal analysis of Marlowe's life and literary career.

Courtney, W. L. "Christopher Marlowe: I and II." *The Fortnightly Review* n.s. LXXVIII, Nos. CCCCLXV and CCCCLXVI (September and October 1905): 467-84, 678-91.

Extensive critical analysis of Marlowe's life and literary career.

Ellis-Fermor, U. M. *Christopher Marlowe*. 1927. Reprint. Hamden, Conn.: Archon Books, 1967, 172 p.

Critical analysis of Marlowe's works by a noted scholar. G. I. Duthie objects to Ellis-Fermor's interpretation of *I* and *II Tamburlaine* as having "no progress, crisis, or solution."

Friedenreich, Kenneth; Gill, Roma; and Kuriyama, Constance B., eds. *"A Poet and a filthy Play-maker": New Essays on Christopher Marlowe*. New York: AMS Press, 1988, 376 p.

Anthology of critical essays on Marlowe's works and literary career by prominent Elizabethan scholars.

Knights, L. C. "The Strange Case of Christopher Marlowe." In his *Further Explorations*, pp. 75-98. Stanford, Calif.: Stanford University Press, 1965.

Comprehensive overview of Marlowe's life and major plays in relation to the political and religious conventions of the Elizabethan period.

Andrew Marvell

1621-1678

English poet and satirist.

INTRODUCTION

*O*ne of the last of the seventeenth-century metaphysical poets, Marvell is noted for his intellectual, allusive poetry that is rich in metaphor and conceit. His work incorporates many of the elements associated with the metaphysical school: the tension of opposing values, metaphorical complexities, logical and linguistic subtleties, and unexpected twists of thought and argument. Although in the past his work has been considered of minor stature next to the artistic genius of John Donne, the most renowned of the metaphysical poets, Marvell has lately come to be viewed as an important poet in his own right. The poems generally thought to be his best, such as "To His Coy Mistress" and "The Garden"—both first published in *Miscellaneous Poems* (1681)—are characterized by complexity and ambiguous morality, which critics believe both define his talent and account for his appeal.

The son of an Anglican clergyman, Marvell was born in Winestead-in-Holderness, Yorkshire. He received his early education at nearby Hull Grammar School, and later attended Trinity College at Cambridge University, where he earned his bachelor's degree in 1638. It is believed that Marvell remained at Cambridge until 1641, though he left without taking a master's degree. During the next four years, Marvell travelled in Europe, evidently employed as a tutor. By the early 1650s he was living at Nunappleton in Yorkshire, where he was tutor to Mary Fairfax, the daughter of Sir Thomas Fairfax, retired commander-in-chief of the Commonwealth Army under Oliver Cromwell; it was during his stay at Nunappleton that Marvell wrote most of the lyric poems which now form the basis of his literary reputation. Marvell next moved to Eton to tutor Cromwell's ward William Dutton, until in 1657 he was appointed Assistant Latin Secretary to the Council of

State through the influence of his friend John Milton, who then held the post of Latin Secretary. Two years later, Marvell was elected Member of Parliament for Hull; from this point on he ceased to write lyric poetry, concentrating instead on political satire and polemics in prose. A dedicated, conscientious statesman, Marvell channeled all his energy and talent into his political career, serving in Parliament until his death. Although it has often been rumored that he was poisoned by his political enemies, it is now generally accepted that Marvell died of an accidental overdose of medicinal opiates.

Much of Marvell's life remains enigmatic. He is not thought to have married, yet shortly after his death a volume of his lyric poetry was published for the first time by a woman claiming to be his widow; that Mary Marvell was truly Marvell's wife has yet to be either disproved or substantiated. More relevant to his poetry is the mystery of Marvell's political convictions, more accurate knowledge of which, scholars believe, would do much to clarify obscurities in his work. Marvell lived during a tumultuous period of British history. Although he did not actively participate in the Civil War, which broke out in 1642 while he was travelling in Europe, Marvell was deeply affected by the bitter fighting between the Royalists and Parliamentarians and later by Charles I's execution and Cromwell's assumption of the Protectorate. Scholars have often attempted to determine where Marvell's sympathies lay, but have been unable to definitively place the poet in either camp. Some suggest that this inconclusiveness mirrors the poet's own indecision. Regardless, critics have emphasized that an understanding of Marvell's life and poetry, particularly "An Horatian Ode on Cromwell's Return from Ireland" and other poems concerning Cromwell, requires some comprehension of this politically volatile time.

The history of critical assessment of Marvell's work is one of shifting focuses and sharp reversals. During his lifetime and for generations after his death, Marvell was known primarily for his political career; he was lauded as an upright, incorruptible statesman, his name becoming synonymous with disinterested patriotism. Consequently, his prose satires and polemics, controversial and often severe attacks on government policy, were highly appreciated. Works such as *The Rehearsall Transpros'd* (1672), a satire against religious intolerance, and *An Account of the Growth of Popery and Arbitrary Government in England* (1677), an attack on the absolute power of monarchy, were valued perhaps less for their literary merit than for the evidence they afforded of Marvell's political dedication and worth. His poetry, when it was considered at all, was judged to be clever and talented, but of secondary importance; throughout the seventeenth and eighteenth centuries Marvell's reputation was that of a major statesman but a minor poet. With the nineteenth century, critical opinion began to shift: critics of Marvell, though few in number, assigned his poetry a greater importance, while his prose works suffered a corresponding decline in popularity. William Hazlitt praised the "elegance and tenderness in his descriptive poems," while decrying Marvell's "forced, far-fetched method of treating his subject" in the political satires. Nineteenth-century commentators emphasized what they deemed his "Romantic" attributes: the theme of the mutability of earthly life in "To His Coy Mistress," the description of nature and solitude in "The Garden," and the sensitive portrayal of human emotion in "The Nymph Complaining for the Death of Her Faun." In the twentieth century, critical appraisal of Marvell's work has undergone a still more radical metamorphosis. Although the satires continue to be generally censured for their heavy-handedness and crudity—considered of some historical interest, perhaps, but of negligible literary importance—the lyric poetry has come to be seen in an entirely new light, largely due to T. S. Eliot's pivotal essay of 1921. Eliot emphasized for the first time Marvell's metaphysical wit, the recognition of which has both enlarged and redefined subsequent critical thought. As Marvell is now seen to be closely allied to the metaphysical school, so also is he viewed as a much more complex and rewarding poet, both thematically and stylistically, than had been previously assumed.

Before Eliot's essay and the major critical reassessment it occasioned, Marvell's poetry had largely been read and examined facilely. As his poetry is easily divisible into four classifications—religious, love, pastoral, and political—his themes were long thought to have been clearly established by the form he chose. Many twentieth-century critics, however, have argued that these distinctions are valid only superficially; though Marvell may have made use of established poetic vehicles, his poetry can by no means be so neatly categorized or explained. Poems once considered simple and straightforward are now believed to be suggestive of deeper themes; an example of this is provided by one of Marvell's most famous poems, "To His Coy Mistress." This poem's narrator importunes a woman to abandon her concerns for her honor and become his lover, arguing that the transience of life and the inevitability of death necessitate their immediate enjoyment of sensual pleasure. For years, "To His Coy Mistress" was assumed to be a fairly representative example of the Cavalier "Carpe diem" (literally "seize the day") love poetry popular among the courtier poets of Charles I and typified by Robert Herrick's "To the Virgins, to Make Much of Time." Recent criticism, however, has revealed complexities and ambiguities within the poem which most critics believe undermine the ostensible message; the suspicion of narrative irony and the curiously inappropriate imagery of the poem cast doubt on its true meaning. The inherent ambiguity of this poem and others is now recognized as the key to understanding much of Marvell's work. Many critics believe that the ambiguities are far more than clever devices and that Marvell's recurring themes exemplify the nature of ambiguity itself. Indeed, such critics claim that underlying all of Marvell's poetry is a unifying and omnipresent concern with a central ambiguity, the tension and duality of opposites, and that this is most often and most successfully expressed through his treatment of the duality of the body and the soul, the temporal and the divine. The dualities of mind and emotion, action and contemplation, and conventionality and nonconformity are secondary, yet related, thematic oppositions that commentators have also observed in Marvell's poetry. All these tensions, critics have noted, place the poems in a fundamentally spiritual or moral context, as each involves opposing human attributes or choices.

Marvell directly addressed the theme of the duality of spirituality and temporality in many of his overtly religious poems, including "A Dialogue between the Resolved Soul and Created Pleasure" and "A Dialogue between the Soul and the Body." As their titles indicate, both these poems are discussions between the body and its pleasures on the one hand and the soul and its spirituality on the other, yet critics have remarked an important distinction between the two works. In "A Dialogue between the Resolved Soul and Created Pleasure," Marvell uncharacteristically and, many commentators believe, unsatisfactorily, resolves the conflict. In this poem, Pleasure tempts the Soul with such delights as music, beauty, wealth, and knowledge, only to be tersely and epigrammatically rebuffed each time. This soul is indeed resolved; the result of the "debate" is a foregone conclusion. This has led many critics to prefer "A Dialogue between the Soul and the Body," in which the tension between the two is greater and the resolution less clear. Not strictly a debate, the poem consists of the lamentations of both body and soul, interdependent yet compelled in different directions by their very natures. Commentators have noted that the body in this poem is not the wily tempter that Created Pleasure is, but rather an essential complement to the soul, and thus their eternal struggle is insoluble.

Marvell's failure to resolve the conflict he presents in "A Dialogue between the Soul and the Body" is but one example of what many critics have seen as deliberate irresolution in his work. This intended ambiguity has frustrated some critics and impressed others with an appreciation of the poet's control over every nuance of meaning and feeling in his poetry; the latter critics have contended that Marvell's ambiguity is indicative not so much of indecision as it is of his rec-

ognition of the potentials and possibilities of both sides of an issue. The tensions found in Marvell's poetry arise not merely from the usual metaphysical attempt to reconcile opposites; as George deForest Lord has stated in his 1968 introduction to *Andrew Marvell: A Collection of Critical Essays:* "Ambiguity for Marvell is not so much a feature of style as it is a way of feeling, thinking, and imagining embedded in his sensibility and in his view of the human condition." Political poems such as "An Horatian Ode Upon Cromwell's Return from Ireland" and "Upon Appleton House" have prompted much critical debate due to their ambiguity. "An Horatian Ode" in particular has invited biographical interpretation as commentators have attempted to clarify Marvell's real attitude toward the political and social upheavals of the Civil War and Cromwell's assumption of the Protectorate. Ostensibly a paean to Cromwell's military and political victories, "An Horatian Ode" includes a moving and sympathetic description of Charles I's execution which commentators have found disconcerting. An additional critical dilemma has been raised by subtle hints in the poem that indicate the poet's belief that Cromwell's base of power, founded as it was on usurpation and bloodshed, may have been inevitable but can hardly be praiseworthy. Ambiguities also abound in "Upon Appleton House," outwardly a poem in praise of the retirement of Marvell's benefactor Fairfax from the political arena. The extent to which this praise may be regarded as sincere has long been a critical stumbling block, as the rest of the poem seems to endorse the course of action and movement.

Marvell dealt again with the tension between retirement and action in "The Garden," which, while generally considered one of Marvell's finest poems, still presents a critical enigma. Garden imagery recurs throughout Marvell's poetry. Critics have agreed that for Marvell the garden represents a tranquil and idyllic retreat, a sanctuary in which he can address his spiritual concerns. In "The Garden," Marvell explores the individual's spiritual journey; however, the validity of the narrator's pastoral retreat as a refuge from earthly cares and passions is compromised by Marvell's sensuous description of the garden itself, which critics have often remarked is couched in undeniably sexual language and imagery. "The Garden" is thus a focal point for critical debate and disagreement, as it so clearly exemplifies Marvell's device of ostensibly endorsing a conclusion only to subtly undermine it. Critics have concurred that the poem is at least in part another example of Marvell's central tension between spirituality and temporality, for the garden echoes the Garden of Eden and is the scene of a quite literal "fall," but the intent of both the religious and sexual imagery remains elusive. Some critics have theorized that Marvell's religious references, while important to note, are not always to be understood either in a strictly literal or a strictly allegorical sense. In a 1960 study, John D. Rosenberg argued that Marvell "appropriates, through metaphor, certain of the great Christian concepts, releasing the fund of emotion attached to them, yet not invoking them directly." Such an explanation has been advanced by some critics with regard to "The Nymph Complaining for the Death of Her Faun," another poem that has occasioned much critical attention and debate. This poem relates the story of a nymph whose pet fawn, given to her by a lover who has since proved unfaithful, has been killed by "wanton troopers." Narrated by the grieving nymph, the poem is unquestionably about loss and suffering, but beyond that there is no critical agreement. Interpretations of "The Nymph Complaining" have been many and varied, ranging from M. C. Bradbrook and M. G. Lloyd Thomas's reading of the poem as a Christian allegory in which the fawn represents Christ, to explications based on the political events of seventeenth-century England, to John J. Teunissen and Evelyn J. Hinz's theory that the nymph laments the death, not of her fawn, but of her unborn child, a circumstance so painful to her that she is aware of the truth only subconsciously. Such divergent and incompatible readings of this single poem exemplify the critical disagreement which exists with regard to much of Marvell's poetry.

Many commentators have attributed Marvell's elusiveness not only to his characteristic thematic irresolution, but also to a deliberate ambiguity of style and language. Twentieth-century scholars have especially emphasized Marvell's adroit use of complex imagery and allegory, as well as his myriad allusive references, all of which augment the difficulties of interpretation that characterize his poetry. This complexity, critics believe, heightens the dramatic tension inherent in his ambiguous use of style, tone, and mood. Often remarked upon are: Marvell's unexpected transitions from playfulness to seriousness, from sincerity to irony, from images of sensuous beauty to an attitude of austere Puritanism; his surprising shifts from one point of view to another, making it difficult to determine which

attitude has authorial backing; his sudden movements from straightforward narrative diction to convoluted metaphor and curious imagery. Also noted as contributing to the general elusiveness of Marvell's meaning is his often cryptic use of language. Although his word choice, in common with metaphysical practice, is usually simple, his poetry abounds with language play—puns, ambiguous syntax, and a complicated and frequently quite unexpected use of imagery, often imbuing a poem with a meaning directly contrary to that explicitly stated. In many works, Marvell's true meaning remains a matter of much critical contention; in the more difficult poems, such as "The Garden" and "An Horatian Ode," much critical energy has been expended to explicate single stanzas, even to unravel the meaning of single lines—coming, in many cases, to no definitive conclusion.

However much critics have argued over Marvell's meaning in the midst of his thematic obscurities and stylistic inconsistencies, most have agreed that it is precisely the elusiveness of his best poems that makes them so intriguing. As John Press has described it: "Marvell's poetry displays and fuses into a harmonious whole a rich Metaphysical subtlety, a moral seriousness and a sensuous lyricism, part of its fascination residing in the ordered interplay of these varied elements." "Balance" is a word commentators have frequently used to describe Marvell's poetry. They allude not only to the tensions and dualities common to metaphysical poetry as a whole, but also to peculiarities of Marvell's own. His poetry has been called both lush and logical, both sensuous and rigidly controlled, the lyrical beauty of his images superimposed on a carefully constructed poetic structure. As Michael H. Markel remarked in his *Classic and Cavalier: Essays on Jonson and the Sons of Ben* (1982), "Marvell is the greatest enigma of all English poets."

(For further information about Marvell's life and works, see *Literature Criticism from 1400 to 1800*, Vol. 4.)

CRITICAL COMMENTARY

ARTHUR CHRISTOPHER BENSON
(essay date 1892)

[Benson was an English educator and author. In the following excerpt from an essay originally published in 1892, he surveys Marvell's career, perceiving a

sharp distinction between the poet's lyrics and his satires.]

At a time like this, when with a sense of sadness we can point to more than one indifferent politician who might have been a capable writer, and so very many indifferent writers who could have been spared to swell the

---

Principal Works

The First Anniversary of the Government under His Highness the Lord Protector (poetry) 1655

The Rehearsall Transpros'd (satire) 1672

The Rehearsall Transpros'd: The Second Part (satire) 1673

An Account of the Growth of Popery and Arbitrary Government in England (satire) 1677

Miscellaneous Poems (poetry) 1681

The Complete Works in Verse and Prose of Andrew Marvell. 4 vols. (poetry and satire) 1872-75

The Poems and Letters of Andrew Marvell. 2 vols. (poetry and letters) 1927

---

ranks of politicians, we may well take the lesson of Andrew Marvell to heart.

The passion for the country which breathes through his earlier poems, the free air which ruffles the page, the summer languors, the formal garden seen through the casements of the cool house, the close scrutiny of woodland sounds, such as the harsh laughter of the woodpecker, the shrill insistence of the grasshopper's dry note, the luscious content of the drowsy, croaking frogs, the musical sweep of the scythe through the falling swathe; all these are the work of no town-bred scholar like Milton, whose country poems are rather visions seen through the eyes of other poets, or written as a man might transcribe the vague and inaccurate emotions of a landscape drawn by some old uncertain hand and dimmed by smoke and time. Of course Milton's *Il Penseroso* and *L'Allegro* have far more value even as country poems than hundreds of more literal transcripts. From a literary point of view indeed the juxtapositions of half a dozen epithets alone would prove the genius of the writer. But there are no sharp outlines; the scholar pauses in his walk to peer across the watered flat, or raises his eyes from his book to see the quiver of leaves upon the sunlit wall; he notes an effect it may be; but his images do not come like treasures lavished from a secret storehouse of memory.

With Andrew Marvell it is different, though we will show by instances that even his observation was sometimes at fault. (pp. 70-1)

[In his] early poems, which are worth all the rest of Marvell's work put together, several strains predominate. In the first place there is a close observation of Nature, even a grotesque transcription, with which we are too often accustomed only to credit later writers. (p. 74)

The aspects of the country on which he dwells with deepest pleasure—and here lies the charm—are not those of Nature in her sublimer or more elated moods, but the gentler and more pastoral elements, that are apt to pass unnoticed at the time by all but the true lovers of the quiet country side, and crowd in upon the mind when surfeited by the wilder glories of peak and precipice, or where tropical luxuriance side by side with tropical aridity blinds and depresses the sense, with the feeling that made Browning cry from Florence,

Oh, to be in England, now that April's there!

Marvell's lines, **"On the Hill and Grove at Billborow,"** are an instance of this; there is a certain fantastic craving after antithesis and strangeness, it is true, but the spirit underlies the lines. (p. 76)

Other poems, such as the **"Ode on the Drop of Dew"** and the **"Nymph Complaining for the Death of her Fawn"** . . . are penetrated with the same essence.

At the same time it must be confessed that Marvell's imagery is sometimes at fault—it would be strange if it were not so; he falls now and then, the wonder is how rarely, to a mere literary conceit. Thus the mower Damon sees himself reflected in his scythe; the fawn feeds on roses till its lip "seems to bleed," not with a possibly lurking thorn, but with the hue of its pasturage. With Hobbinol and Tomalin for the names of swain and nymph unreality is apt to grow. When the garden is compared to a fortress and its scents to a salvo of artillery—

Well shot, ye firemen! O how sweet
And round your equal fires do meet—

and,

Then in some flower's beloved hut
Each bee as sentinel is shut,
And sleeps so, too—but if once stirred,
She runs you through, nor asks the word—

here, in spite of a certain curious felicity, we are in the region of false tradition and rococo expression. The poem of **"Eyes and Tears,"** again (so whimsically admired by Archbishop Trench), is little more than a string of conceits; and when in **"Mourning"** we hear that

She courts herself in amorous rain,
Herself both Danae and the shower;

when we are introduced to Indian divers who plunge in the tears and can find no bottom, we think of Macaulay's "Tears of Sensibility," and Crashaw's fearful lines on the Magdalene's eyes—

Two walking baths, two weeping motions,
Portable and compendious oceans.

Nevertheless Marvell's poems are singularly free as a rule from this strain of affectation. He has none of the morbidity that often passes for refinement. The free air, the woodpaths, the full heat of the summer sun—this is his scenery; we are not brought into contact with the bones beneath the rose-bush, the splintered sundial, and the stagnant pool. His pulses throb with ardent life, and have none of the "inexplicable faintness" of a deathlier school. (pp. 77-9)

The poems contain within themselves the germ of the later growth of satire in the shape of caustic touches of humour, as well as a certain austere philosophy that is apt to peer behind the superficial veil of circumstances, yet without dreary introspection. There is a Dialogue between Soul and Body, which deals with the duality of human nature which has been the despair of all philosophers and the painful axiom of all religious teachers. (p. 79)

Much of Marvell's philosophy however has not the same vitality, born of personal struggle and discomfiture, but is a mere echo of stoical and pagan views of life and its vanities drawn from Horace and Seneca, who seem to have been his favourite authors. Such a sentiment as the following, from **"Appleton House"**—

> But he, superfluously spread,
> Demands more room alive than dead;
> What need of all this marble crust,
> To impart the wanton mole of dust?—

and from **"The Coy Mistress'**—

> The grave's a fine and private place,
> But none, methinks, do there embrace—

are mere pagan commonplaces, however daintily expressed.

But there is a poem, an idyll in the form of a dialogue between Clorinda and Damon, which seems to contain an original philosophical motive. (p. 80)

["Clorinda and Damon"] seems a distinct attempt to make of the sickly furniture of the idyll a vehicle for the teaching of religious truth. Is it fanciful to read in it a poetical rendering of the doctrine of conversion, the change that may come to a careless and sensuous nature by being suddenly brought face to face with the Divine light? It might even refer to some religious experience of Marvell's own: Milton's "mighty Pan," typifying the Redeemer, is in all probability the original.

The work then on which Marvell's fame chiefly subsists—with the exception of one poem which belongs to a different class . . . , the **"Horatian Ode"**— may be said to belong to the regions of nature and feeling, and to have anticipated in a remarkable degree the minute observation of natural phenomena characteristic of a modern school, even to a certain straining after unusual, almost bizarre effects. The writers of that date, indeed, as Green points out, seem to have become suddenly and unaccountably modern, a fact which we are apt to overlook owing to the frigid reaction of the school of Pope. Whatever the faults of Marvell's poems may be, and they are patent to all, they have a strain

of originality. He does not seem to imitate, he does not even follow the lines of other poets; never,—except in a scattered instance or two, where there is a faint echo of Milton,—does he recall or suggest that he has a master.

At the same time the lyrics are so short and slight that any criticism upon them is apt to take the form of a wish that the same hand had written more, and grown old in his art. There is a monotony, for instance, about their subjects, like the song of a bird, recurring again and again to the same phrase; there is an uncertainty, an incompleteness not so much of expression as of arrangement, a tendency to diverge and disgress in an unconcerned and vagabond fashion. There are stanzas, even long passages, which a lover of proportion such as Gray (who excised one of the most beautiful stanzas of the "Elegy" because it made too long a parenthesis) would never have spared. It is the work of a young man trying his wings, and though perhaps not flying quite directly and professionally to his end, revelling in the new-found powers with a delicious ecstasy which excuses what is vague and prolix; especially when over all is shed that subtle, precious quality which makes a sketch from one hand so unutterably more interesting than a finished picture from another,—which will arrest with a few commonplace phrases, lightly touched by certain players, the attention which has wandered throughout a whole sonata.

The strength of Marvell's style lies in its unexpectedness. You are arrested by what has been well called a "predestined" epithet, not a mere otiose addition, but a word which turns a noun into a picture; the "hook-shouldered" hill "to abrupter greatness thrust," "the sugar's uncorrupting oil," "the vigilant patrol of stars," "the squatted thorns," "the oranges like golden lamps in a green night," "the garden's fragrant innocence,"—these are but a few random instances of a tendency that meets you in every poem. Marvell had in fact the qualities of a consummate artist, and only needed to repress his luxuriance and to confine his expansiveness. (pp. 81-3)

Before passing on to discuss the satires I may be allowed to say a few words on a class of poems largely represented in Marvell's works, which may be generally called Panegyric.

Quite alone among these—indeed, it can be classed with no other poem in the language—stands the **"Horatian Ode on Cromwell's return from Ireland."** Mr. Lowell said of it that as a testimony to Cromwell's character it was worth more than all Carlyle's biographies; he might without exaggeration have said as much of its literary qualities. It has force with grace, originality with charm, in almost every stanza. Perhaps the first quality that would strike a reader of it for the first time is its quaintness; but further study creates no reaction against this in the mind—the usual sequel to poems which depend on quaintness for effect. But when Mr. Lowell goes on to say that the poem shows the difference between grief that thinks of its object and grief that thinks of its rhymes (referring to Dryden), he is not so happy. The pre-eminent quality of the poem is its art; and its singular charm is the fact that it succeeds, in spite of being artificial, in moving and touching the springs of feeling in an extraordinary degree. It is a unique piece in the collection, the one instance where Marvell's undoubted genius burned steadily through a whole poem. . . . It is in completeness more than in quality that it is superior to all his other work, but in quality too it has that lurking divinity that cannot be analysed or imitated. (pp. 84-5)

[The] whole Ode is above party, and looks clearly into the heart and motives of man. It moves from end to end with the solemn beat of its singular metre, its majestic cadences, without self-consciousness or sentiment, austere, but not frigid.

Marvell's other panegyrics are but little known, though the awkward and ugly lines on Milton have passed into anthologies, owing to their magnificent exordium, "When I beheld the poet blind yet old." But no one can pretend that such lines as these are anything but prosaic and ridiculous to the last degree—

Thou hast not missed one thought that could be fit,
And all that was improper dost omit;

* * *

At once delight and horror on us seize,
Thou sing'st with so much gravity and ease—

though the unfortunate alteration in the meaning of the word *improper* makes them now seem even more ridiculous than they are. The poems on the **"First Anniversary of the Government of the Lord Protector,"** on the **"Death of the Lord Protector,"** and on **"Richard Cromwell,"** are melancholy reading though they have some sonorous lines.

And as the angel of our Commonweal
Troubling the waters, yearly mak'st them heal,

may pass as an epigram. But that a man of penetrating judgment and independence of opinion should descend to a vein of odious genealogical compliment, and speak of the succeeding of

Rainbow to storm, Richard to Oliver,

and add that

A Cromwell in an hour a prince will grow,

by way of apology for the obvious deficiencies of his new Protector, makes us very melancholy indeed. Flattery is of course a slough in which many poets have wallowed; and a little grovelling was held to be even more commendable in poets in that earlier age; but we see the pinion beginning to droop, and the bright eye

growing sickly and dull. Milton's poisonous advice is already at work.

But we must pass through a more humiliating epoch still. The poet of spicy gardens and sequestered fields seen through the haze of dawn is gone, not like the Scholar Gipsy to the high lonely wood or the deserted lasher, but has stepped down to jostle with the foulest and most venal of mankind. He becomes a satirist, and a satirist of the coarsest kind. His pages are crowded with filthy pictures and revolting images; the leaves cannot be turned over so quickly but some lewd epithet or vile realism prints itself on the eye. . . . It is impossible to treat of vice in the intimate and detailed manner in which Marvell treats of it without having, if no practical acquaintance with your subject, at least a considerable conventional acquaintance with it, and a large literary knowledge of the handling of similar topics; and when one critic goes so far as to call Marvell an essentially pure-minded man, or words to that effect, we think he would find a contradiction on almost every page of the satires. (pp. 85-8)

[Belonging] as they do to the period of melancholy decadence of Marvell's art, we are not inclined to go at any length into the question of the satires. We see genius struggling like Laocoon in the grasp of a power whose virulence he did not measure, and to whom sooner or later the increasing languor must yield. Of course there are notable passages scattered throughout them. In **"Last Instructions to a Painter,"** the passage beginning, "Paint last the king, and a dead shade of night," where Charles II. sees in a vision the shapes of Charles I. and Henry VIII. threatening him with the consequences of unsympathetic despotism and the pursuit of sensual passion, has a tragic horror and dignity of a peculiar kind; and the following specimen from **"The Character of Holland"** gives on the whole a good specimen of the strength and weakness of the author:

Holland, that scarce deserves the name of land,
As but the off-scouring of the British sand,
And so much earth as was contributed
By English pilots when they heaved the lead,
Or what by the Ocean's slow alluvion fell
Of shipwrecked cockle and the mussel-shell,
This undigested vomit of the sea,
Fell to the Dutch by just propriety.

Clever beyond question; every couplet is an undeniable epigram, lucid, well-digested, elaborate; pointed, yet finikin withal,—it is easy to find a string of epithets for it. But to what purpose is this waste? To see this felicity spent on such slight and intemperate work is bitterness itself; such writing has, it must be confessed, every qualification for pleasing except the power to please. (pp. 89-90)

Of his Prose Works it is needful to say but little; they may be characterised as prose satires for the most part, or political pamphlets. *The Rehearsal Transprosed* and *The Divine in Mode* are peculiarly distasteful examples of a kind of controversy then much in vogue. They are answers to publications, and to the ordinary reader contrive to be elaborate without being artistic, personal without being humorous, and digressive without being entertaining; in short, they combine the characteristics of tedium, dulness, and scurrility to a perfectly phenomenal degree. As compared with the poems themselves, the prose works fill many volumes; and any reader of ordinary perseverance has ample opportunities of convincing himself of Andrew Marvell's powers of expression, his high-spirited beginning, the delicate ideals, the sequestered ambitions of his youth, and their lamentable decline. (p. 94)

[We] cannot but grieve when we see a poet over whose feet the stream has flowed, turn back from the brink and make the great denial; whether from the secret consciousness of aridity, the drying of the fount of song, or from the imperious temptations of the busy, ordinary world we cannot say. Somehow we have lost our poet. (p. 95)

Arthur Christopher Benson, "Andrew Marvell," in his *Essays,* E. P. Dutton & Company, 1907, pp. 68-95.

T. S. ELIOT

(essay date 1921)

[Eliot was an American-born British poet and critic whose work strongly affected modern critical thought. In the following excerpt from an essay originally published in 1921, he examines the nature of Marvell's wit. Written on the occasion of the tercentenary of Marvell's birth, Eliot's essay was a pivotal one, sparking a revival of critical interest in Marvell's poetry.]

Wit is not a quality that we are accustomed to associate with "Puritan" literature, with Milton or with Marvell. But if so, we are at fault partly in our conception of wit and partly in our generalizations about the Puritans. . . . [Marvell,] more a man of the century than a Puritan, speaks more clearly and unequivocally with the voice of his literary age than does Milton.

This voice speaks out uncommonly strong in the **"Coy Mistress."** The theme is one of the great traditional commonplaces of European literature. It is the theme of "O mistress mine," of "Gather ye rosebuds," of "Go, lovely rose;" it is in the savage austerity of Lucretius and the intense levity of Catullus. Where the wit of Marvell renews the theme is in the variety and order of the images. In the first of the three paragraphs

Marvell plays with a fancy which begins by pleasing and leads to astonishment. . . . We notice the high speed, the succession of concentrated images, each magnifying the original fancy. When this process has been carried to the end and summed up, the poem turns suddenly with that surprise which has been one of the most important means of poetic effect since Homer:

> But at my back I always hear
> Time's wingèd chariot hurrying near,
> And yonder all before us lie
> Deserts of vast eternity.

> (pp. 253-54)

A modern poet, had he reached the height, would very likely have closed on this moral reflection. But the three strophes of Marvell's poem have something like a syllogistic relation to each other. (p. 254)

It will hardly be denied that this poem contains wit; but it may not be evident that this wit forms the crescendo and diminuendo of a scale of great imaginative power. The wit is not only combined with, but fused into, the imagination. We can easily recognize a witty fancy in the successive images ("my *vegetable* love," "till the conversion of the Jews"), but this fancy is not indulged, as it sometimes is by Cowley or Cleveland, for its own sake. It is structural decoration of a serious idea. In this it is superior to the fancy of "L'Allegro," "Il Penseroso," or the lighter and less successful poems of Keats. In fact, this alliance of levity and seriousness (by which the seriousness is intensified) is a characteristic of the sort of wit we are trying to identify. It is found in . . . Gautier, and in the *dandysme* of Baudelaire and Laforgue. It is in [Catullus and in Ben Jonson] . . . :

> Cannot we deceive the eyes
> Of a few poor household spies?
> 'Tis no sin love's fruits to steal,
> But that sweet sin to reveal,
> To be taken, to be seen,
> These have sins accounted been.

It is in Propertius and Ovid. It is a quality of a sophisticated literature. . . . (p. 255)

The difference between imagination and fancy, in view of this poetry of wit, is a very narrow one. Obviously, an image which is immediately and unintentionally ridiculous is merely a fancy. In the poem **"Upon Appleton House,"** Marvell falls in with one of these undesirable images, describing the attitude of the house toward its master:

> Yet thus the leaden house does sweat,
> And scarce endures the master great;
> But, where he comes, the swelling hall
> Stirs, and the square grows spherical;

which, whatever its intention, is more absurd than it was intended to be. Marvell also falls into the even commoner error of images which are over-developed or distracting; which support nothing but their own misshapen bodies. . . . But the images in the **"Coy Mistress"** are not only witty, but satisfy the elucidation of Imagination given by Coleridge:

> This power . . . reveals itself in the balance or reconcilement of opposite or discordant qualities: of sameness, with difference; of the general, with the concrete; the idea with the image; the individual with the representative; the sense of novelty and freshness with old and familiar objects; a more than usual state of emotion with more than usual order; judgment ever awake and steady self-possession with enthusiasm and feeling profound or vehement. . . .

Coleridge's statement applies also to [**"The Nymph and the Fawn"**]. . . . [The poem] is built upon a very slight foundation, and we can imagine what some of our modern practitioners of slight themes would have made of it. But we need not descend to an invidious contemporaneity to point the difference. Here are six lines from **"The Nymph and the Fawn"**:

> I have a garden of my own,
> But so with roses overgrown
> And lilies, that you would it guess
> To be a little wilderness;
> And all the spring-time of the year
> It only lovèd to be there.

And here are five lines from "The Nymph's Song to Hylas" in the *Life and Death of Jason,* by William Morris:

> I know a little garden close
> Set thick with lily and red rose.
> Where I would wander if I might
> From dewy dawn to dewy night,
> And have one with me wandering.

So far the resemblance is more striking than the difference, although we might just notice the vagueness of allusion in the last line to some indefinite person, form, or phantom, compared with the more explicit reference of emotion to object which we should expect from Marvell. But in the latter part of the poem Morris divaricates widely:

> Yet tottering as I am, and weak,
> Still have I left a little breath
> To seek within the jaws of death
> An entrance to that happy place;
> To seek the unforgotten face
> Once seen, once kissed, once reft from me
> Anigh the murmuring of the sea.

Here the resemblance, if there is any, is to the latter part of **"The Coy Mistress."** As for the difference, it could not be more pronounced. The effect of Morris's charming poem depends upon the mistiness of the feeling and the vagueness of its object; the effect of Marvell's upon its bright, hard precision. And this precision is not due to the fact that Marvell is concerned with cruder or simpler or more carnal emotions. The emotion of Morris is not more refined or more spiritual; it is merely more vague: if any one doubts whether the more refined or spiritual emotion can be precise, he should study the treatment of the varieties of discarnate emotion in the *Paradiso.* A curious result of the comparison of Morris's poem with Marvell's is that the former, though it appears to be more serious, is found to be the slighter; and Marvell's **"Nymph and the Fawn,"** appearing more slight, is the more serious.

> So weeps the wounded balsam; so
> The holy frankincense doth flow;
> The brotherless Heliades
> Melt in such amber tears as these.

These verses have the suggestiveness of true poetry; and the verses of Morris, which are nothing if not an attempt to suggest, really suggest nothing; and we are inclined to infer that the suggestiveness is the aura around a bright clear centre, that you cannot have the aura alone. The day-dreamy feeling of Morris is essentially a slight thing; Marvell takes a slight affair, the feeling of a girl for her pet, and gives it a connexion with that inexhaustible and terrible nebula of emotion which surrounds all our exact and practical passions and mingles with them. . . . [In the verses of Marvell] there is the making the familiar strange, and the strange familiar, which Coleridge attributed to good poetry. (pp. 256-59)

[The] wit which pervades the poetry of Marvell is more Latin, more refined, than anything that succeeded it.

> The Pict no shelter now shall find
> Within his parti-coloured mind,
>   But, from this valour sad,
>   Shrink underneath the plaid:

There is here an equipoise, a balance and proportion of tones, which, while it cannot raise Marvell to the level of Dryden or Milton, extorts an approval which these poets do not receive from us, and bestows a pleasure at least different in kind from any they can often give. It is what makes Marvell a classic; or classic in a sense in which Gray and Collins are not; for the latter, with all their accredited purity, are comparatively poor in shades of feeling to contrast and unite. (pp. 260-61)

The quality which Marvell had, this modest and certainly impersonal virtue—whether we call it wit or reason, or even urbanity—we have patently failed to define. By whatever name we call it, and however we define that name, it is something precious and needed and apparently extinct; it is what should preserve the reputation of Marvell. (p. 263)

T. S. Eliot, "Andrew Marvell," in his *Selected Essays,* Harcourt Brace Jovanovich, Inc., 1950, pp. 251-63.

V. SACKVILLE-WEST
(essay date 1929)

[Sackville-West was an English poet, novelist, and biographer associated with the Bloomsbury group, a circle of English writers, artists, and intellectuals who held informal artistic and philosophical discussions in Bloomsbury, a district of London, from around 1907 to the early 1930s. In the following excerpt from an essay originally published in 1929, she explores the dichotomy between direct inspiration and the influence of other metaphysical poets in Marvell's poetry, concluding with an assessment of Marvell's stature as a poet.]

Temperamentally, Marvell was open to *direct* inspiration, a statement which is not modified by the indisputable fact that the current fashion did frequently trick out his muse with some of her ribbons and furbelows. The source of his direct inspiration was nature; orderly, detailed nature; nature as he saw it in England—though, to be sure, the exotic had a charm for him, for decorative purposes. . . . [Flashes] of personal intimacy and the desire for identification with nature were common to English poets in Marvell's age as in nearly every other. But here is the difference: to Marvell, in the brief years of his poetic creation, the mood was constant. It was no mere occasional flash. Conceits, when they occurred, were an ornament—or shall I say a disfigurement?—rather than an integral part; his real mood, in these nature poems, was the mood of seeing, and feeling; the mysticism which arose as their accompaniment was no conceit, but an inevitable consequence, familiar to everyone who has ever entered into a moment of communion with nature; and, as such, expressed by him in a manner readily distinguishable from the cerebral exertions of his colleagues. There were, in fact, two aspects of Marvell's closeness to nature. The one was the actual gift of observation—an estimable but still a minor gift; the other was that sense of man's eventual harmony with nature, which for want of a better word we must call mysticism in this connection. (pp. 32-4)

[The] principal clue to Marvell's nature-mysticism lies, I think, in the obsession that green had for him. . . . He used it in and out of season, and moreover he supplemented it by constant references to shade and shadow, which were all part of the same line of thought. Marvell was highly sensitive to colour—an argument which could be substantiated by numerous instances;—all variations of light and shade were to him a perpetual delight; but of all colours it was green

that enchanted him most; the world of his mind was a glaucous world, as though he lived in a coppice, stippled with sunlight and alive with moving shadows. . . . Clearly, green was to him . . . the cipher of some significance that he was forever trying to capture. (pp. 35-6)

It was not in vain that Marvell had chased his cipher through poem after poem, not in vain that he had called his love a "vegetable love," if at a given moment he was to throw the net of language so finally over the illusion. With Apollo he had hunted Daphne, and with Pan had sped after Syrinx, that he might at last clasp a tree in his arms. So long as he followed what I have called his direct inspiration, so long as he admitted only the mystical-metaphorical interpretations of that inspiration he was on safe ground. It was when he entered into competition with his colleagues that he went wrong, and in no poem is the difference between his two manners so well exemplified as in **"Appleton House,"** opening as it does with a string of grotesque exaggerations which must be endured before the poem flows out into the simple and splendid verses that rank with Marvell at his best. It is deplorable that the poet who could write verses LXV to LLXIV and LXXVII and LXXXI should also have written, in the same poem, such absurdity as:

Yet thus the laden house does sweat,
And scarce endures the Master great;
But where he comes, the swelling hall
Stirs, and the square grows spherical,
More by his magnitude distrest
Than he is by its straitness prest.

This is in the worst, most inflated style of the metaphysicians, and cannot be excused even by saying that the language of compliment was always notoriously exaggerated. But before considering the Marvell who shared the faults of his day, it is as well to remember also the Marvell of a middle manner; the Marvell who wrote, for instance, **"The Nymph complaining for the death of her fawn."** Here is a poem whose inspiration cannot be said to be personal or wholly direct; it is, moreover, a poem full of conceits; yet the effect is not one of straining or insincerity, but rather of a graceful and deliberate artificiality, underlaid by some genuine compassion—whether for the nymph or for her fawn matters not. . . . This is neither the true country poet nor yet the poet of the true school of wit, but a pastoral poet uniting the rural and the courtly styles. (pp. 39-41)

This aspect of Marvell has been strangely overlooked; he has received his full meed of recognition as a nature poet, and his full meed of disapprobation as the poet who had submitted, all too readily, to the influence of Donne; but this halfway house, this amalgam of the natural and artificial, has never been given sufficient prominence. His very choice of the Mower as the central figure in no less than four poems illustrates his sense of the decorative value of rustic employments. Marvell's Mower simply takes the place of the traditional shepherd. It was Marvell who discovered the scythesman as an ornament to poetry. . . . This discovery is all the more remarkable when we consider that Theocritus makes of his Reapers but a pretext to talk of love, and that Virgil alludes but very briefly to the reaper in the *Eclogues,* and in the *Georgics* mentions him not at all. Moreover, both the Greek and the Roman poet thought of the reaper of corn, whereas Marvell's mower—it is scarcely surprising—is the mower of grass. Another interesting point arises in connection with the Mower poems: Marvell had some appreciation of uncultivated nature, which was not at all proper to the seventeenth century. True, his usual taste was for the mild and orderly aspects of garden-craft, and rugged nature was a thing unknown to him; nevertheless, he gives some indications of an appetite for something a little less sleek, a little less demure. In **"Appleton House"** he had allowed this sentiment to escape him . . . and in **"The Mower against gardens"** he writes a complete poem in condemnation of a pleasant artificiality. . . . Obviously, this is no foreshadowing of the romantic poets; Capability Brown would doubtless have been more to Marvell's taste than Helvellyn; but the hint is worth noting, in conjunction with his constant desire to identify himself with nature in the shape of trees and birds and woods. (pp. 42-3)

It is necessary, however, to turn to that other Marvell—the Marvell who had read too much of Donne, and who exercised his wit either upon ethical questions, or upon love, or even upon religion. It is not to be denied that this Marvell suffered from the faults of his contemporaries. He was capable of writing such preposterous rubbish as the notorious

Upon the rock his Mother drave,
And there she split against the stone
In a Caesarian section;

he took pleasure in the metaphors drawn from cosmography or geometry which were so fruitful a source of disaster, and, like all his fellows, sometimes he managed them successfully and sometimes he came to grief. Sometimes, again, the question of his success or failure is debatable, and must be resolved by personal taste. (p. 44)

If we except **"Appleton House,"** it is, generally speaking, noticeable that Marvell's use of injudicious conceits occurs most frequently in poems which we may presume him to have written round a deliberate thesis—such poems as **"Eyes and Tears," "The Match,"** and **"Upon the Hill and Grove at Billborow."** There are other poems which I am reluctant to include. Is **"On a drop of dew"** to be condemned? or **"The Coronet"**? or **"The Gallery"**? or **"The Fair Singer"**? or the

"Definition of Love," characteristic of the metaphysical school though it is . . . ? Surely not. Conscientiously though one may search through the pages of Marvell's lyrics, the worst offences are not to be found in him. It is impossible to imagine Marvell writing such a set of verses as Cleveland's "Fuscara." Moreover, the true poet bursts out in the most unexpected places. . . . The poet in Marvell died hard, whether he tried to stifle that poet under the weight of fashion or under an absorption in public affairs. (pp. 45-6)

Once at least in his career as a poet Marvell achieved the perfect marriage between conception and expression in a poem which owes nothing to his own particular source of inspiration by nature; nothing to his sense of the pastoral; nothing to stirring events; but, curiously enough, much to the school of Donne. In **"To his Coy Mistress,"** Donne and the school of wit together are superbly justified. **"To his Coy Mistress"** is the supreme example of the metaphysical method of packing image upon image, and of suddenly relating them to the problems of human existence. It combines all the jugglery of "wit," and all the grisly melancholy of Donne. **"To his Coy Mistress"** is unique in Marvell's work. . . . The urgency of passion is its theme, expounded in language which moves from an apparently extravagant frivolity to an intense and menacing seriousness; then swings back to the human plea again, still decoratively presented, but sobered now and dignified by the reflections on mortality which have intervened. It is, in fact, as nicely constructed as a geometrical problem in two propositions and a solution. . . . So many things have seldom been said in so few words; yet the effect is of great luxuriance rather than of economy or compression. The perfection of the phrasing can only be realized if we try to paraphrase the poem and discover the impossibility of substituting other words for Marvell's. The whole poem is as tight and hard as a knot; yet as spilling and voluptuous as a horn of plenty.

Equally repaying are the minor technical details of the poem—which, indeed, as a study is inexhaustible. The octosyllabic line in Marvell's hands became a medium of the utmost elasticity; it was his favourite metre, and he employs it in nearly three-quarters of his total lyrical output. In the **"Coy Mistress"** he makes particularly effective use of enjambment (noticeably absent in both **"Bermudas"** and **"The Garden"**). . . . This, combined with the large proportion of short syllables, explains the effect of rapidity produced by the poem, so admirably adapted to the impatience of the theme. The actual vocabulary plays an important part in the suggestion of subtlety and richness, which might well have been lost in the racing speed that drives the lines along. It is scarcely necessary to pick out the unusual words; they speak for themselves; or to argue such points as the mysterious "lew." . . . Attention may, however, be drawn to the several verbal surprises which supplement the main device of "surprise" occurring half-way through the poem:

> But at my back I always hear
> Time's winged chariot hurrying near. . . .

These verbal surprises are principally based, of course, upon the rich poetic resource of startling but felicitous association: Ganges—rubies; tide—Humber; vegetable—Love and Empire; deserts—Eternity; strength—sweetness. . . . (pp. 51-4)

The use of the consonant V, which occurs no less than seventeen times in the forty-six lines, reinforced by the companion F, is also worth noting. It is not pushing analysis too far to suggest that this use of V is largely responsible for the harmony of

> My vegetable love should grow
> Vaster than empires, and more slow,

and that the alliance of V and F is important in

> The grave's a fine and private place,

which both in euphony and sentiment recalls Cowley's

> After death I nothing crave.
> Let me alive my pleasure have,
> All are Stoicks in the grave.

(pp. 54-5)

What, then, when all has been said, is our eventual estimate of Marvell? . . . [If] we are to remember Marvell by his best, we shall be obliged to place him high, as the author of at least one superlatively excellent poem—**"To his Coy Mistress"**—and as the author of **"The Garden," "Bermudas," "The Horatian Ode,"** part of **"Appleton House," "The Nymph complaining,"** and the translation from Seneca. It is unreasonable to demand more of any minor poet.

The word minor has slipped in, and must be allowed to stand. Marvell seldom strikes the more resonant chord. He strikes it once, and with firm fingers, in the centre panel of the **"Coy Mistress"**; he strikes it again, in . . . the poem on the death of Cromwell; and in his pursuit of the cipher represented by *green* he strikes it repeatedly, or at any rate evokes it; for the rest, we must concede that Marvell, poetically charming, is spiritually somewhat shallow. This comment is not intended to suggest that poetry should be concerned with moral reflections; far from it, Heaven forbid! nevertheless, some implication must be latent, before poetry can aspire to be considered as anything approaching major poetry; and such implication, in Marvell, is frankly lacking. Even to look for it, is attempting to gather grapes off thistles. The **"Coy Mistress"** is largely to blame; she is the cavern which makes the student of Marvell try again and again hopefully for echoes. But where are the echoes to be found? in Marvell's nature-mysticism alone lies some connection. The solitude of the grave and the solitude of the forest are separated by no very great distance, and Marvell, though not often perplexed by the problems of mortality, *was* very constantly preoccupied with the desire for human union with nature—even though that union was to be his own, and the desire never extended itself in any general sense. This is the utmost that we can say. Marvell had his limitations. The vein of his finer inspiration was a genuine one, but we require something further before we can attribute greatness to a poet. The **"Coy Mistress"** alone in Marvell's work deserves the word.

His skill was considerable, and it was to something in his temperament rather than to any default in his art that his comparative failure was due. . . . The very peg upon which he hung his imagination—for it does, when all is said and done, deserve the name of imagination as opposed to the minor dignity of fancy—the very peg upon which he hung his imagination in itself gives proof of a tame, somewhat smug, material outlook. Order, safety, gardens; the simple pleasures and beauties of the cultivated English countryside; the leisure of the cultured mind—for it must always be remembered that Marvell was a man with a classical education behind him—the treat of a sophisticated solitude; such were the ingredients which went to the making of Marvell as a poet. His was no uneasy soul.

Consequently it is probably a mistake even to discuss the possibility of Marvell's admission to the higher plane. We should do better to accept him as the poet of the happy garden-state, the painter of country delights, a miniaturist of the foreground with some suggestion of indistinct, green, and significant background to redeem him from the superficiality of the mere observer and recorder. That coy and tantalizing mistress is again to blame: she, woman or myth, made Marvell strike a note such as he never really hit before or since. She, and not Cromwell, not Hull, not Bishop Parker, is the real enemy of Marvell for posterity. She it is who makes us covetously demand from Marvell more than he was ever temperamentally fitted to give. (pp. 59-63)

V. Sackville-West, in her *Andrew Marvell*, 1929. Reprint by The Folcroft Press, Inc., 1969, 64 p.

CLEANTH BROOKS

(essay date 1946)

[In the following excerpt, Brooks attempts to unravel Marvell's apparently contradictory attitude toward Oliver Cromwell in "An Horatian Ode."]

[What] is "said" in [Marvell's] **"Horatian Ode"**? What

is the speaker's attitude toward Cromwell and toward Charles? (p. 132)

From historical evidence alone we would suppose that the attitude toward Cromwell in this poem would have to be a complex one. And this complexity is reflected in the ambiguity of the compliments paid to him. The ambiguity reveals itself as early as the second word of the poem. It is the "forward" youth whose attention the speaker directs to the example of Cromwell. "Forward" may mean no more than "high-spirited," "ardent," "properly ambitious"; but the *New English Dictionary* sanctions the possibility that there lurks in the word the sense of "presumptuous," "pushing." (pp. 135-36)

The speaker, one observes, does not identify Cromwell himself as the "forward youth," or say directly that Cromwell's career has been motivated by a striving for fame. But the implications of the first two stanzas do carry over to him. There is, for example, the important word "so" to relate Cromwell to these stanzas:

So restless *Cromwel* could not cease. . . .

And "restless" is as ambiguous in its meanings as "forward," and in its darker connotations even more damning. For, though "restless" can mean "scorning indolence," "willing to forego ease," it can also suggest the man with a maggot in the brain. "To cease," used intransitively, is "to take rest, to be or remain at rest," and the *New English Dictionary* gives instances as late as 1701. Cromwell's "courage high" will not allow him to rest "in the inglorious Arts of Peace." And this thirst for glory, merely hinted at here by negatives, is developed further in the ninth stanza:

Could by industrious Valour climbe
To ruine the great Work of Time.

"Climb" certainly connotes a kind of aggressiveness. (p. 136)

But the speaker has been careful to indicate that Cromwell's motivation has to be conceived of as more complex than any mere thirst for glory. He has even pointed this up. The forward youth is referred to as one who "would appear"—that is, as one who wills to leave the shadows of obscurity. But restless Cromwell "could not cease"—for Cromwell it is not a question of will at all, but of a deeper compulsion. Restless Cromwell could not cease, if he would.

Indeed, the lines that follow extend the suggestion that Cromwell is like an elemental force—with as little will as the lightning bolt, and with as little conscience:

And, like the three-fork'd Lightning first
Breaking the Clouds where it was nurst,
　　Did thorough his own Side

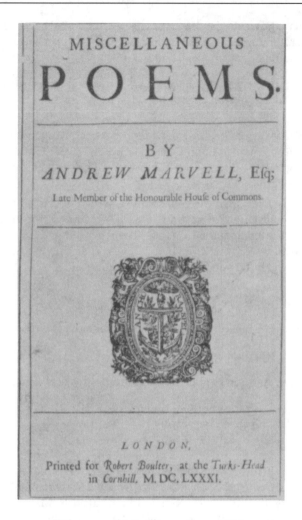

Title page of *Miscellaneous Poems,* 1681.

His fiery way divide.

We are told that the last two lines refer to Cromwell's struggle after Marston Moor with the leaders of the Parliamentary party. Doubtless they do, and the point is important for our knowledge of the poem. But what is more important is that we be fully alive to the force of the metaphor. The clouds have bred the lightning bolt, but the bolt tears its way through the clouds, and goes on to blast the head of Caesar himself. As Margoliouth puts it: "The lightning is conceived as tearing through the side of his own body the cloud." In terms of the metaphor, then, Cromwell has not spared his own body: there is no reason therefore to be surprised that he has not spared the body of Charles.

I do not believe that I overemphasized the speaker's implication that Cromwell is a natural force. A few lines later the point is reinforced with another naturalistic figure, an analogy taken from physics:

Nature that hateth emptiness,
Allows of penetration less:
　　And therefore must make room
　　Where greater Spirits come . . .

The question of right, the imagery insists, is beside the point. If nature will not tolerate a power vacuum, no more will it allow two bodies to occupy the same space. (It is amusing, by the way, that Marvell has boldly introduced into his analogy borrowed from physics the nonphysical term "Spirits"; yet I do not think that the clash destroys the figure.) Since twenty thousand angels can dance on the point of a needle, two spirits, even though one of them is a greater spirit, ought to be able to occupy the same room. But two spirits, as Marvell conceives of spirits here, will jostle one another, and one must give way. True, the greater spirit is immaterial, but he is no pale abstraction—he is all air and fire, the "force of angry Heavens flame." (pp. 137-39)

What are the implications for Charles? Does the poet mean to imply that Charles has angered heaven— that he has merited his destruction? There is no suggestion that Cromwell is a thunderbolt hurled by an angry Jehovah—or even by an angry Jove. The general emphasis on Cromwell as an elemental force is thoroughly relevant here to counter this possible misreading. Certainly, in the lines that follow there is nothing to suggest that Charles has angered heaven, or that the Justice which complains against his fate is anything less than justice.

I began this examination of the imagery with the question, "What is the speaker's attitude toward Cromwell?" We have seen that the speaker more than once hints at his thirst for glory. . . . But we have also seen that the imagery tends to view Cromwell as a natural phenomenon, the bolt bred in the cloud. Is there a contradiction? I think not. Cromwell's is no vulgar ambition. If his valor is an "industrious Valour," it contains plain valor too of a kind perfectly capable of being recognized by any Cavalier:

What Field of all the Civil Wars,
Where his were not the deepest Scars?

If the driving force has been a desire for glory, it is a glory of that kind which allows a man to become dedicated and, in a sense, even selfless in his pursuit of it. Moreover, the desire for such glory can become so much a compulsive force that the man does not appear to act by an exercise of his personal will but seems to become the very will of something else. There is in the poem, it seems to me, at least one specific suggestion of this sort:

But through adventrous War
Urged his active Star. . . .

Cromwell is the marked man, the man of destiny, but he is not merely the man governed by his star. Active though it be, he cannot remain passive, even in relation to it: he is not merely urged by it, but himself urges it on.

Yet, if thus far Cromwell has been treated as naked force, something almost too awesome to be considered as a man, the poet does not forget that after all he is a man too—that "the force of angry Heavens flame" is embodied in a human being:

And, if we would speak true,
Much to the Man is due.

The stanzas that follow proceed to define and praise that manliness—the strength, the industrious valor, the cunning. (You will notice that I reject the interpretation which would paraphrase "Much to the Man is due" as "After all, Cromwell has accomplished much that is good." Such an interpretation could sort well enough with Legouis's picture of Marvell as the cold and detached honest broker between the factions: unfortunately it will not survive a close scrutiny of the grammar and the general context in which the passage is placed.)

One notices that among the virtues comprising Cromwell's manliness, the speaker mentions his possession of the "wiser art":

Where, twining subtile fears with hope,
He wove a Net of such a scope,
    That *Charles* himselfe might chase
    To *Caresbrooks* narrow case.

On this point Cromwell has been cleared by all the modern historians (except perhaps Mr. Hilaire Belloc). Charles's flight to Carisbrooke Castle, as it turned out, aided Cromwell, but Cromwell could have hardly known that it would; and there is no evidence that he cunningly induced the King to flee to Carisbrooke. Royalist pamphleteers, of course, believed that Cromwell did, and used the item in their general bill of damnation against Cromwell. How does the speaker use it here—to damn or to praise? We tend to answer, "To praise." But then it behooves us to notice what is being praised. The things praised are Cromwell's talents as such—the tremendous disciplined powers which Cromwell brought to bear against the King.

For the end served by those powers, the speaker has no praise at all. Rather he has gone out of his way to insist that Cromwell was deaf to the complaint of Justice and its pleading of the "antient Rights." The power achieved by Cromwell is a "forced Pow'r"—a usurped power. On this point the speaker is unequivocal. . . . But the speaker, though he is not a cynic, is a realist. A kingdom cannot be held by mere pleading of the "antient Rights." . . . (pp. 139-42)

In short, the more closely we look at the **"Ode,"** the more clearly apparent it becomes that the speaker has chosen to emphasize Cromwell's virtues as a man, and likewise, those of Charles as a man. The poem does not debate which of the two was right, for that issue is not even in question. In his treatment of Charles, then, the speaker no more than Charles himself attempts to vindicate his "helpless Right." Instead, he emphasizes his dignity, his fortitude, and what has finally to be called his consummate good taste. The portraits of the two men beautifully supplement each other. Cromwell is—to use Aristotle's distinction—the man of character, the man of action, who "does both act and know." Charles, on the other hand, is the man of passion, the man who is acted upon, the man who knows how to suffer. The contrast is pointed up in half a dozen different ways.

Cromwell, acted upon by his star, is not passive but actually urges his star. Charles in "acting"—in chasing away to Carisbrooke—actually is passive—performs the part assigned to him by Cromwell. True, we can read "chase" as an intransitive verb (the *New English Dictionary* sanctions this use for the period): "that Charles himself might hurry to Carisbrooke." But the primary meaning asserts itself in the context: "that Charles might chase himself to Carisbrooke's narrow case." For this hunter, now preparing to lay his dogs in "near / The *Caledonian* Deer," the royal quarry has dutifully chased itself.

Even in the celebrated stanzas on the execution, there is ironic realism as well as admiration. In this fullest presentation of Charles as king, he is the player king, the king acting in a play. He is the "Royal Actor" who knows his assigned part and performs it with dignity. He truly adorned the "Tragick Scaffold"

> While round the armed Bands
> Did clap their bloody hands.

The generally received account is that the soldiers clapped their hands so as to make it impossible for Charles's speech to be heard. But in the context this reference to handclapping supports the stage metaphor. What is being applauded? Cromwell's resolution in bringing the King to a deserved death? Or Charles's resolution on the scaffold as he suffered that death? Marvell was too good a poet to resolve the ambiguity. (pp. 142-44)

Cromwell is now the *de facto* head of the state, and the speaker, as a realist, recognizes that fact. Cromwell is seen henceforth, not primarily in his character as the destroyer of the monarchy, but as the agent of the new state that has been erected upon the dead body of the King. The thunderbolt simile, of the first part of the poem, gives way here to the falcon simile in this second part of the poem. The latter figure revises and qualifies the former: it repeats the suggestion of ruthless energy and power, but Cromwell falls from the sky now, not as the thunderbolt, but as the hunting hawk. The trained falcon is not a wanton destroyer, nor an irresponsible one. It knows its master: it is perfectly disciplined:

> She, having kill'd, no more does search,
> But on the next green Bow to pearch. . . .

The speaker's admiration for Cromwell the man culminates, it seems to me, here. Cromwell might make the Fame his own; he *need* not present kingdoms to the state. He might assume the crown rather than crowning each year. Yet he forbears:

> Nor yet grown stiffer with Command,
> But still in the *Republick's* hand. . . .

Does the emphasis on "still" mean that the speaker is surprised that Cromwell has continued to pay homage to the republic? Does he imply that Cromwell may not always do so? Perhaps not: the emphasis is upon the fact that he need not obey and yet does. Yet the compliment derives its full force from the fact that the homage is not forced, but voluntary and even somewhat unexpected. And a recognition of this point implies the recognition of the possibility that Cromwell will not always so defer to the commonwealth.

And now what of the republic which Cromwell so ruthlessly and efficiently serves? What is the speaker's attitude toward it? To begin with, the speaker recognizes that its foundations rest upon the bleeding head of Charles. The speaker is aware, it is true, of the Roman analogy, and the English state is allowed the benefit of that analogy. But it is well to notice that the speaker does not commit himself to the opinion that the bleeding head is a happy augury. . . . The Roman state was able to take it as a favorable omen, and was justified by the event. With regard to the speaker himself, it seems to me more to the point to notice what prophecy he is willing to commit himself to. He does not prophesy peace. He is willing to predict that England, under Cromwell's leadership, will be powerful in war, and will strike fear into the surrounding states. . . . Specifically, he predicts a smashing victory over the Scots.

But what of the compliments to Cromwell on his ruthlessly effective campaign against the Irish? Does not the speaker succumb, for once, to a bitter and biased patriotism, and does this not constitute a blemish upon the poem? . . . The final appeal in this matter, however, is not to what Marvell the Englishman must have thought, or even to what Marvell the author must have intended, but rather to the full context of the poem itself. In that context, the lines in question can be read ironically, and the earlier stanzas sanction that reading. Cromwell's energy, activity, bravery, resolution—even what may be called his efficiency—are the qualities that have come in for praise, not his gentleness or his mercy. The Irish, indeed, are best able to affirm such praise as has been accorded to Cromwell; and they know from experience "how good he is, how just," for they have been blasted by the force of angry Heaven's flame, even as Charles has been. But I do not mean to turn the passage into sarcasm. The third quality which the speaker couples with goodness and justice is fitness "for highest Trust," and the goodness and justice of Cromwell culminate in this fitness. But the recommendation to trust has reference not to the Irish, but to the English state. The Irish are quite proper authorities on Cromwell's trustworthiness in this regard, for they have come to know him as the completely dedicated instrument of that state whose devotion to the purpose in hand is unrelenting and unswerving.

To say all this is not to suggest that Marvell shed any unnecessary tears over the plight of the Irish, or even to imply that he was not happy, as one assumes most Englishmen were, to have the Irish rebellion crushed promptly and efficiently. It is to say that the passage fits into the poem—a poem which reveals itself to be no panegyric on Cromwell but an unflinching analysis of the Cromwellian character. (pp. 144-48)

Thus far the speaker has been content to view Cromwell from a distance, as it were, against the background of recent history. He has referred to him consistently in the third person. But in the last two stanzas, he addresses Cromwell directly. He salutes him as "the Wars and Fortunes Son." It is a great compliment: Cromwell is the son of the wars in that he is the master of battle, and he seems fortune's own son in the success that has constantly waited upon him. But we do not wrench the lines if we take them to say also that Cromwell is the creature of the wars and the product of fortune. The imagery of the early stanzas which treats Cromwell as a natural phenomenon certainly lends support to this reading. Cromwell can claim no sanction for his power in "ancient Rights." His power has come out of the wars and the troubled times. I call attention to the fact that we do not have to choose between readings: the readings do not mutually exclude each other: they support each other, and this double interpretation has the whole poem behind it.

Cromwell is urged to march "indefatigably on." The advice is good advice; but it is good advice because any other course of action is positively unthinkable. Indeed, to call it advice at all is perhaps to distort it: though addressed to Cromwell, it partakes of quiet commentary as much as of exhortation. After all, it is restless Cromwell who is being addressed. If he could not cease "in the inglorious Arts of Peace" when his "highest plot" was "to plant the Bergamot," one cannot conceive of his ceasing now in the hour of danger.

> And for the last effect
> Still keep thy Sword erect.

Once more the advice (or commentary) is seriously intended, but it carries with it as much of warning as it does of approval. Those who take up the sword shall perish by the sword: those who have achieved their power on contravention of ancient rights by the sword can only expect to maintain their power by the sword. (pp. 148-50)

But, I can imagine someone asking, What is the final attitude toward Cromwell? Is it ultimately one of approval or disapproval? Does admiration overbalance condemnation? Or, is the **"Ode,"** after all, merely a varied Scottish plaid, the reflection of Marvell's own particolored mind—a mind which had not been finally "made up" with regard to Cromwell? I think that enough has been said to make it plain that there is no easy, pat answer to such questions. There is a unified total attitude, it seems to me; but it is so complex that we may oversimplify and distort its complexity by the way in which we put the question. The request for some kind of summing up is a natural one, and I have no wish to try to evade it. For a really full answer, of course, one must refer the questioner to the poem itself; but one can at least try to suggest some aspects of the total attitude.

I would begin by reemphasizing the dramatic character of the poem. It is not a statement—an essay on "Why I cannot support Cromwell" or on "Why I am now ready to support Cromwell." It is a poem essentially dramatic in its presentation, which means that it is diagnostic rather than remedial, and eventuates, not in a course of action, but in contemplation. Perhaps the best way therefore in which to approach it is to conceive of it as, say, one conceives of a Shakespearean tragedy. Cromwell is the usurper who demands and commands admiration. What, for example, is our attitude toward Macbeth? We assume his guilt, but there are qualities which emerge from his guilt which properly excite admiration. I do not mean that the qualities palliate his guilt or that they compensate for his guilt. They actually come into being through his guilt, but they force us to exalt him even as we condemn him. I have chosen an extreme example. I certainly do not mean to imply that in writing the **"Ode"** Marvell had Shakespeare's tragedy in mind. What I am trying to point to is this: that the kind of honesty and insight and whole-mindedness which we associate with tragedy is to be found to some degree in all great poetry and is to be found in this poem.

R. P. Warren once remarked to me that Marvell has constantly behind him in his poetry the achievement of Elizabethan drama with its treatment of the human will as seen in the perspective of history. He had in mind some of the lyrics, but the remark certainly applies fully to the **"Ode."** The poet is thoroughly conscious of the drama, and consciously makes use of dramatic perspective. Charles, as we have seen, becomes the "Royal Actor," playing his part on the "Tragick Scaffold." But the tragedy of Charles is merely glanced at. The poem is Cromwell's—Cromwell's tragedy, the first three acts of it, as it were, which is not a tragedy of failure but of success.

Cromwell is the truly kingly man who is *not* king—whose very virtues conduce to kingly power and almost force kingly power upon him. It is not any fumbling on the poet's part which causes him to call Cromwell "a Caesar" before the poem ends, even though he has earlier appropriated that name to Charles. *Both* men are Caesar, Charles the wearer of the purple, and Cromwell, the invincible general, the inveterate campaigner, the man "that does both act and know." Cromwell is the Caesar who must refuse the crown—whose glory it is that he is willing to refuse the crown—but who cannot enjoy the reward and the security that a crown affords. The tension between the speaker's admiration for the kingliness which has won Cromwell the power and his awareness that the power can be maintained only by a continual exertion of these talents for kingship—this tension is never relaxed. Cromwell is not of royal blood—he boasts a higher and a baser pedigree: he is the "Wars and Fortunes Son." He cannot rest because he is restless Cromwell. He must march indefatigably on, for he cannot afford to become fatigued. These implications enrich and qualify an insight into Cromwell which is as heavily freighted with admiration as it is with a great condemnation. But the admiration and the condemnation do not cancel each other. They define each other; and because there is responsible definition, they reinforce each other.

Was this, then, the attitude of Andrew Marvell . . . ? The honest answer must be: I do not know. I have tried to read the poem, the **"Horatian Ode,"** not Andrew Marvell's mind. (pp. 150-53)

Cleanth Brooks, "Literary Criticism," in *English Institute Essays,* 1946, pp. 127-58.

CLEANTH BROOKS

(essay date 1982)

[In the following excerpt, Brooks imagines that the speaker of "To His Coy Mistress" and that of "The Garden" are one and the same.]

Andrew Marvell's **"The Garden"** and **"To His Coy Mistress"** are, by common consent, two of the finest lyric poems in English. Yet the clash between the world views they involve, though calculated to bring up the ever-thorny question of the poet's sincerity, has been little discussed. (p. 219)

For all their apparent oppositions and contradictions, the two poems have much in common. They share several themes, one of which, I believe, has received in the past less attention than it deserves: the theme of time in relation to eternity.

I suggest that we try to imagine the lover of **"To His Coy Mistress"** to be the same man who steps into **"The Garden"** and savors its cool delights. Let's imagine that he has been unable to persuade his coy mistress to yield. Now, after having run through his "Passion's heat," he has indeed found in this delightful place "Love['s] . . . best retreat." Nature, no coy mistress, offers her innocent pleasures wholeheartedly. Would he, in this situation and this state of mind, find the "lovely green" of nature more "am'rous" than the "white" and "red" of his mistress? An hour before, let us suppose, he has used the phrase "vegetable Love" to dismiss rather contemptuously a love affair that had little to recommend it except the longevity and slow growth characteristic of plant life. But if the "Fair Trees" of the garden are indeed more amorously attractive than any woman, would not their love be also a despised "vegetable Love?" These questions help us see, I think, how much each poem depends on a given dramatic situation, on the mood of the character speaking the poem, and on the tone in which he makes his various utterances.

Let me begin with time and mortality. The lover of the coy mistress never relaxes his concern with the swift rush of time. His account is studded with references to events in the far-off past, such as Noah's flood, or to events that are to occur only in some very remote future, such as the conversion of the Jews.

All this witty hyperbole is meant, of course, to render preposterous so slow-paced a courtship and to prepare for the sudden speed-up of time found in the middle third of the poem—a rush that will soon take the lovers out of life altogether and strand their bodies in "Desarts of vast Eternity." The strategy, of course, is to present with laconic irony a bleak reality that exposes the earlier fantasy of timelessness for the posturing that it is. Having done so, the lover is ready to urge his conclusion: the only course is to beat time at his own game, to live with such breathless speed as to make the sun lag behind them.

Though a reference to speed—that of the lovers' outracing the sun—occupies the final couplet, the dominant image of the closing lines of the poem is one of eating. The lovers are to devour their pleasures greedily. Far from being the love birds of tradition, they are "am'rous birds of prey"—snatching and tearing at the flesh of their kill. Like them, time also is a devourer, but with jaws ponderous and slow as he gradually masticates all that is mortal.

It is not a pretty picture, this scene of ravenous gluttony: the lovers tear their pleasure with "rough strife through The Iron Gates of Life." Nobody seems to know what this refers to. . . . What seems obvious, at any rate, is a sense of creatures savage and violent; and the violence suits the poem, for the poem is realistic and even desperate.

Such images indicate one way in which **"To His Coy Mistress"** differs from most of the carpe diem poems of this period. Another instance of grim insistence on the physical and realistic is the allusion to the rotting corpse and the grave-worm. . . . The note of horror sets up a reverberation that is deeper and more powerful than is to be heard in any other carpe diem poem that I can think of. Compare it with the Anglican Herrick's masterpiece, "Corinna's Going a-Maying." Marvell's poem is not necessarily "better," but it is of another order. (pp. 219-21)

In sum, the lover in **"To His Coy Mistress,"** in spite of his brilliant rhetoric, highflown compliment, urbanity and grace, impresses me, I repeat, as a desperate man, though his desperation is held under firm control.

Time pervades **"The Garden"** as well as **"To His Coy Mistress."** The man whose thoughts constitute the poem is very much conscious of time, even though in this poem he is stepping out of its hurrying blast.

The poem begins on a note of surprise, happy surprise at what the speaker has just discovered when he enters the garden precincts: quiet and innocence. Clearly he has heretofore failed to find them in the "busie Companies of Men" or, as stanzas 3 and 4 indicate, in the society of women and the attendant disappointments in love. His discovery of quiet and innocence is as surprising to him as it is welcome. How else account for the tone of "Fair quiet, have I found thee here, / And innocence thy sister dear!" The note is one of almost shocked relief. (pp. 221-22)

Praise of the beauty of trees and plants to the disparagement of woman's beauty brings up once more the subject of "vegetable Love." (p. 222)

The lover speaking to his coy mistress is properly contemptuous of a love that, like a plant, even a centuries-old yew or redwood, can do little more than keep growing and propagating itself. He asks for a love that has fire and passion.

What, then, does one make of the love for trees, fruit, and flowers professed in **"The Garden?"** How seriously—even setting aside the mocking reference in **"To His Coy Mistress"**—can we accept the assertion?

If we indulge a little further the supposition that the person speaking to his coy mistress is the person now admiring the garden, we may say that after having failed to convince his mistress, he is now venting his pique. In any case, his ironic assessment of the conventional tributes to female beauty plainly does not come from indifference or inexperience. This complainer against women has been very likely one of the "Fond Lovers" at whose folly he now smiles.

Still, there is more to his mood in the garden than mere revulsion from an unrequited love. It springs from genuine joy. To this man Nature is not only delightful in itself but points to delights beyond itself. It hints of a peace and innocence that transcends the mortal world. The lusts of the animal soul, of the "am'rous birds of prey," are here replaced by the contemplations of the rational soul, the bird with "silver wings" that in **"The Garden"** prepares itself "for longer flight."

In **"The Garden"** the speaker's attitude thus shifts from amused reflections on the folly and self-deception of men to happy surprise and glad relief at discovering—almost accidentally?—the true abode of quiet and innocence. Then his delight moves him toward a witty and high-spirited praise of plants and trees and to mockery of the conventional claims for female beauty. With a learned mock-seriousness, he brazens out his case with proofs fabricated by a reinterpretation of two classical myths.

With stanza 5, he gives himself up to the fruits and flowers of the garden's little paradise. He compares his "wondrous Life" to that led by an as yet sinless and solitary Adam during the first hours of his existence in an Eveless Eden. A brave new world, indeed, then made its impact on the first man's unjaded senses. It was a world to be raptly explored, devoid of distraction from anything—even the distraction provided by an Eve. Nature is regarded here as a completely yielding mistress. Her fruits and flowers offer themselves to him without hesitation or reservation. The vines press their grape clusters into his mouth. The melons before his feet seem to wish to make him stumble, and the very flowers ensnare him and pull him down upon the earth. "Stumble," "ensnare," and "fall" are loaded terms in the Christian vocabulary. The words suggest seduction to sensual pleasures and a fall from grace; and indeed, the speaker soon becomes, like Adam, a fallen man. But Nature's embrace is innocent. There are no broken vows, jealousies, or aftermaths of remorse. (In stanza 8 the poet will develop this hint of the Eden story into an explicit reference.)

Yet, though Marvell has deliberately invoked sexual overtones in describing the reception that Nature affords this grateful recipient of its peace, he never relaxes his grasp upon common sense and reality. The man in the garden has given himself up wholly to the garden's cool shade because it offers a blessed respite from the burden and heat of a day within a too-busy life. But we may be sure that he will not try to overstay his hour or so of bliss. The poem is no manifesto for primitivism. The man whose experience it describes has not resolved to live for the rest of his life in solitude as a hermit in some wilderness. He does not even suggest an anticipation of Wordsworth.

The conception of nature implied in **"The Garden"** seems to me thoroughly orthodox. Nature is innocent. In this poem it is not Plato's lower and grosser element on which the divine forms can only imperfectly make their imprint. It is certainly not the

Manichaean's actively evil force at war with good. The natural world has been created good by a good Creator. It has not brought about man's fall. Man has only himself to blame for that. Having in mind the possible influence of his Puritanism on his poetry, we can say that on this particular issue Marvell is as orthodox as that other great Puritan, his friend, the John Milton of *Paradise Lost.* Neither holds nature in contempt. (pp. 223-25)

The best evidence that the speaker of **"The Garden"** regards the pleasures of nature as in themselves innocent is to be found in stanza 6, where the body's delight in nature does not distract the national soul from its higher pleasure. Indeed, it is when the body is appeased and innocently happy that the mind can "[Withdraw] into its happiness" (stanza 6). This pleasure peculiar to the rational soul points toward a transcendence that is fully developed in the final stanzas of the poem. The garden's quiet joys allow the contemplative man to become for a moment a disembodied soul and to gain some sense of what the joyful freedom of pure spirit is.

Yet how carefully Marvell manages the tone. Instead of the high spirits and hyperbole of some of the earlier stanzas or the ironic teasing in others, in stanza 7 he is precise, restrained, careful not to overstate. The Soul, like an uncaged bird, flies only a little way from the body—goes no further than a nearby bough, where "it sits, and sings, / Then Whets, and combs its silver Wings." The image is beautifully apt: it catches the soul's timidity at being outside its familiar habitation, the joy that makes it sing, and its almost childlike pleasure in the discovery that it has silver wings, wings now preened in a sort of innocent vanity.

Stanza 7 provides a nice example of Marvell's classic restraint. Even at this high point of the experience, the metaphor used makes very moderate claims. The soul is allowed no more than a glimpse of its future bliss. It dares not presume on its spiritual powers. The poet is even very practical in justifying its actions in spreading its wings. Now is the time to prepare for the "longer flight" that some day, permanently separated from the body, it must take. When Marvell is thoroughly serious, his assertions are invariably moderate and credible.

The next stanza (8) resumes the banter we have heard earlier. In stanza 6 the speaker has perversely inverted the classic myths of Apollo's pursuit of Daphne and Pan's pursuit of Syrinx; now in stanza 8 he turns upside down the Biblical account of Eve's creation. God gave Eve to Adam not because he needed a suitable helpmeet, but because God thought his delicious solitude entirely too good for a mere mortal to enjoy (as if Marvell were unaware that Adam became mortal only *after* the creation of Eve and the breaking of God's express command, the act that brought death into the world and all our woe). But Marvell is quite cheerful

in his irreverence. He can hardly be trying to delude his readers, saturated as they were in the Scriptures. His case for the delights of solitude is transparently specious.

In the next and final stanza of the poem, however, classic moderation again asserts itself. If he is playful in proposing that "'twas beyond a Mortal's share" to live alone in the earthly paradise, he is very properly serious in implying, as the poem closes, that it is indeed beyond any mortal's share to live continually in the full light of eternity. If one could do that, he would have ceased to be mortal.

Our meditator on the garden's delights has by now clearly reentered the world of time. How do we know this? From, among other things, the reference to the sundial in the final stanza. The numerals of this dial consist of artfully shaped beds of flowers. Such a chronometer is, of course, thoroughly appropriate to the garden. Nevertheless, it is a timepiece, and it reminds us that time has never stopped its motion even during an experience which has seemed a blessed respite from it.

The "industrious" bee, it is claimed, consults the clock for the time of day, and the sun duly moves through his twelve signs ("fragrant Zodiak") of the dial just as he moves through the heavenly zodiac in the course that makes up the year. Thus, the fact of time—winged chariot or no—is acknowledged. Mortal man escapes time only in brief blessed intervals, and even those escapes are finally illusory except as they possibly point to some future state. But to the contemplative man depicted in **"The Garden,"** time is not terrifying, for *his* time does not eventually lose itself in vast deserts of eternity. For him there waits beyond time an eternity in a realm of joy that no earthly garden can do more than suggest.

"To His Coy Mistress" and **"The Garden"** are remarkable poems, but it is not remarkable that one and the same poet could write them. They reflect, to be sure, differing views of time and eternity, but they have much in common in the ideas they touch upon. In any case, they are not declarations of faith but presentations of two differing worldviews. . . . (pp. 226-28)

On the evidence of the two poems we have been comparing, Marvell was not a man who was unable to make up his mind or a waverer between commitments or a trimmer. The poems tell quite another story: they reveal a fair-mindedness, an awareness of alternatives, a sensitivity to the complexity of issues. Marvell's mind is a mind of the late Renaissance at its best. He is learned, thoroughly at home with the earlier literature of the West. He is familiar with classical philosophy as well as Christian theology. He regards both as constituting a valuable inheritance. His aim is to assimilate their lore and to develop, as far as is possible, a synthesis that will take the whole of human experience—animal and rational, active and contemplative, playful and sober, hawk and singing bird—into account. (p. 228)

Cleanth Brooks, "Andrew Marvell: Puritan Austerity with Classical Grace," in *Poetic Traditions of the English Renaissance,* edited by Maynard Mack and George deForest Lord, Yale University Press, 1982, pp. 219-28.

SOURCES FOR FURTHER STUDY

Bagguley, William H., ed. *Andrew Marvell, 1621-1678: Tercentenary Tributes.* London: Oxford University Press, 1922, 131 p.

> Reprints a number of critical essays on Marvell, including studies by J. C. Squire and Edward Wright.

Berthoff, Ann E. *The Resolved Soul: A Study of Marvell's Major Poems.* Princeton: Princeton University Press, 1970, 243 p.

> Critical study of Marvell's poetry. Berthoff organizes her book around two critical objectives: "to define the thematic unity of Marvell's poetry" and "to define the limits by which interpretations of his metaphors should be guided."

Friedenreich, Kenneth, ed. *Tercentenary Essays in Honor of Andrew Marvell.* Hamden, Conn.: Archon Books, 1977, 314 p.

> Collection of fourteen essays covering the critical spectrum from Marvell's lyrics to his political satires.

Lord, George deF., ed. *Andrew Marvell: A Collection of Critical Essays.* Englewood Cliffs, N.J.: Prentice-Hall, 1968, 180 p.

> Essays by Lord, T. S. Eliot, Earl Miner, and seven other critics of Marvell's works.

Patrides, C. A., ed. *Approaches to Marvell: The York Tercentenary Lectures.* London: Routledge & Kegan Paul, 1978, 354 p.

> Collection of fifteen essays covering various aspects of Marvell's work, including Christopher Hill's comparison of Marvell and John Milton and A. J. Smith's study of Marvell's metaphysical wit.

Toliver, Harold E. *Marvell's Ironic Vision.* New Haven: Yale University Press, 1965, 232 p.

> Critical study of Marvell's work. Toliver describes his method: "to explicate particular poems and to look at the times in a perspective sufficiently deep to give some sense of the context of those poems."

W. Somerset Maugham

1874-1965

(Full name William Somerset Maugham) English novelist, short story writer, playwright, critic, and essayist.

INTRODUCTION

Maugham is one of the most prolific and popular authors in world literature. During a career that spanned sixty-five years, he attained great renown, first as a dramatist, then as the author of entertaining and carefully crafted short stories and novels. Maugham's exceptional productivity has sometimes hindered his critical reception, leading commentators to assess him as a merely competent professional writer. A number of his works, however, most notably the novels *Of Human Bondage* (1915) and *Cakes and Ale; or, The Skeleton in the Cupboard* (1930), and the short stories "The Letter" and "Rain," are acclaimed as masterpieces of twentieth-century literature.

Maugham was born to English parents at the British Embassy in Paris, where his father was employed as a lawyer. His mother died in 1882, and when his father died two years later, Maugham was sent to live with a childless aunt and uncle in England. While attending King's School in Canterbury from 1885 to 1889, his inherent shyness, exacerbated by a pronounced stutter, led him to avoid social activities and devote himself to his studies. Although his guardians wanted him to attend Oxford, Maugham persuaded them to allow him to study at the University of Heidelberg in Germany. By the time he returned to England in 1892 Maugham had privately decided to become a writer. Nevertheless, knowing that his guardians would disapprove of a literary career, he began medical training at St. Thomas's Hospital in London. Maugham earned a medical degree in 1897 but never practiced; that same year he published his first novel, *Liza of Lambeth*, set in the milieu he had observed during his training in obstetrics, when he was often called into London's poorest neighborhoods to attend births. This novel manifests some of the elements that characterize Maugham's fiction, including reliance on personal experience and adherence to existing literary traditions. George Gissing and Arthur Morrison, contemporary novelists of the time, had popularized realistic accounts of life in the slums, assuring Maugham of a readership; his depiction of an illicit extramarital relationship aroused sufficient controversy to stimulate further interest in the novel.

The decade following the appearance of *Liza of Lambeth* is often termed the period of Maugham's literary apprenticeship. From 1897 until 1907 he published novels, short stories, a play, and a travel book, receiving increasingly favorable reviews in English literary periodicals. In 1907 his play *Lady Frederick* met with considerable success, and Maugham quickly attained celebrity as a dramatist. In 1908, four of his plays—*Lady Frederick, Jack Straw, Mrs Dot,* and *The Explorer*—ran simultaneously in London theaters. Over the next twenty-six years, twenty-nine of Maugham's plays were produced, many of them among the most well-received of their time. Maugham conscientiously employed contemporary conventions of popular dramatic comedy, portraying sophisticated society with satiric intent. His dramatic plots hinge on secrets, with suspense heightened by the possibility of revelation. Misplaced objects, mistaken identities, and barbed verbal exchanges abound. Climaxes are generally achieved with the reversal of a central character's fortune; the denouement follows quickly as the combined result of the revelations and reversals that have been effected. Maugham's dramas are topical, written to satisfy a contemporary preference for drawing-room comedies patterned after the French well-made-play; rather than alter his characteristic approach to drama he ceased writing plays during the early 1930s as the tastes of the theatergoing public changed.

At the onset of World War I Maugham joined the Red Cross and went to France as an interpreter. There he met Gerald Haxton, and the two became lovers and remained close companions for the next thirty years. During the war the British government recruited Maugham as an intelligence agent and subsequently involved him in covert operations in Switzerland and Russia. Despite the ongoing relationship with Haxton, in 1917 Maugham married Syrie Barnardo Wellcome, with whom he had had a child two years earlier. The marriage was unsuccessful, and they divorced in 1929. During the years between the World Wars, Maugham lived lavishly and wrote prolifically. He bought an expansive villa in southeast France in 1926, which remained his home thereafter, although he traveled widely; his visits to Italy, the United States, the South Seas, and the Caribbean provided the settings for the works that appeared between the World Wars, including the novels *The Moon and Sixpence* (1919) and *Cakes and Ale;* the plays *Our Betters* (1919) and *The Circle* (1921); and the short story collections *The Trem-*

bling of a Leaf: Little Stories of the South Sea Islands (1921), *The Casuarina Tree* (1926), and *Ashenden; or, The British Agent* (1928). Maugham fled France during the Nazi occupation and went to the United States, where he lectured and oversaw the Hollywood production of several motion pictures based on his stories and novels. Haxton, who had accompanied Maugham, died in 1944. In 1948 Maugham returned to France. Although accounts of his later years portray Maugham as somewhat mentally unstable and given to irrational outbursts, he retained a sardonic wit. "Dying is a very dull, dreary affair," he told his nephew, Robin Maugham. "And my advice to you is to have nothing whatever to do with it." He died in 1965 at the age of ninety-one.

Despite his prolificacy, Maugham's renown rests chiefly on only a few works. The most often studied of these is *Of Human Bondage.* Based on an early unpublished manuscript called "The Artistic Temperament of Stephen Carey," Maugham's semiautobiographical coming-of-age novel is commended for its penetrating psychological portrait of its protagonist. Some commentators note that *Of Human Bondage* suffers from excessive length and too-inclusive use of naturalistic detail, but these faults are generally attributed to the novel's basis in a youthful manuscript, and critics have praised the novel as a classic bildungsroman, as well as an acute study of the obsessive love relationship that dominates the protagonist for years and nearly ruins his life. Maugham's most critically esteemed novel is *Cakes and Ale.* In this lively and entertaining story, the second wife of a venerable literary figure attempts to ensure that an official biography will portray her husband and herself auspiciously, while disparaging the man's first wife. *Cakes and Ale* was controversial because it was believed to be based on the life of Thomas Hardy, but commentators subsequently discerned a devastating parody of the novelist and critic Hugh Walpole, on whom Maugham based his characterization of the second-rate litterateur Alroy Kear. *Cakes and Ale* also includes, in Rosie Driffield, Maugham's most sympathetic and fully dimensional female character. *The Moon and Sixpence,* an account of a painter passionately devoted to his art, based on the life of Paul Gauguin, and *The Razor's Edge* (1944), which chronicles a young American's quest for meaning and purpose, are also highly regarded by critics.

Maugham has received greatest recognition for his short fiction. He emerged as a preeminent short story writer in the 1920s, and many commentators maintain that he consistently achieved excellence in this genre, concurring with Anthony Burgess that "the short story was Maugham's true *métier,* and some of the stories he wrote are among the best in the language." Maugham's most successful short stories—which include "Before the Party," "The Book-Bag,"

"Mackintosh," "P. & O.," "The Pool," "Mr. Harrington's Washing," "The Letter," and "Rain"—exploit the oppressive atmosphere of British colonies, featuring petty intrigue, marital infidelity, and sometimes violent death against a background of the rigidly stratified colonial communities in India and the Far East. In "The Letter," for example, the wife of an English plantation owner in Singapore shoots and kills a man whom she claims forced his way into her room. Her lawyer, however, discovers a letter she wrote to the murdered man arranging a tryst on the night of his death. In "Rain" a medical quarantine isolates a number of travelers, including Sadie Thompson, a prostitute; Dr. and Mrs. Macphail; and the Davidsons, a missionary couple, in a remote port of Pago Pago. Davidson becomes obsessed with reforming the flamboyant prostitute, and he bullies her into submission with the threat of a prison term. One night he is found dead, having cut his own throat. Sadie Thompson is angrily defiant, and the words she hurls at Dr. Macphail—"You men! You filthy, dirty pigs! You're all the same, all of you. Pigs! Pigs!"— suggest that what passed between her and the missionary was not entirely spiritual in nature. These two stories are among the most frequently anthologized in world literature; both have undergone several stage and film adaptations. Maugham's Ashenden stories, based on his experiences in the secret service, are credited with originating a style of sophisticated international espionage fiction that has remained popular for decades. His stories resemble his dramas in structure: plots hinge and pivot on a secret; suspense is heightened by the possibility of revelation; and tension builds on strategically timed entrances and exits, lost and found properties, and verbal combat. In fact, Maugham often transformed short stories into plays and rewrote unperformed dramas as novels or short stories, and this ease of adaptation attests to the unity of Maugham's literary construction.

Maugham himself stated that his place in literature was "in the very first row of the second-raters"; many critics concur with this assessment. Maugham's prolificacy, together with the generally even quality of his work, fosters the impression of an adept literary workman turning out competent but unremarkable fiction. While many commentators agree that this is a fair evaluation of much of Maugham's work, some have suggested that it required more than mere competence to sustain Maugham's long and successful career. They cite his consummate achievements in the short story form and suggest that Maugham's many works of fiction include a number of the finest English novels and short stories of the twentieth century.

(For further information about Maugham's life and works, see *Contemporary Authors,* Vols. 5-6, 25-28; *Contemporary Literary Criticism,* Vols. 1, 11, 15, 67; *Dictionary of Literary Biography,* Vols. 10, 36, 77, 100; *Major 20th-Century Writers; Short Story Criticism,* Vol. 8; and *Something about the Author,* Vol. 54.)

CRITICAL COMMENTARY

H. E. BATES

(essay date 1941)

[Bates was an English short story writer, novelist, and critic. In the following excerpt from his *The Modern Short Story: A Critical Survey,* he discusses Maugham's principal influences and pronounces him a proficient but excessively traditional and therefore not influential short story writer.]

Maugham is at once an attractive and a rather disconcerting figure. Beginning as a writer with, as it were, no ear for words, Maugham had very early to choose a stylistic model which his own limitations would permit him to follow without embarrassment. To have chosen a pretentious, poetical, highly coloured writer would have been fatal. Maugham chose Maupassant, and throughout his career has stuck to Maupassant. It is interesting to recall here that Maupassant has been described as "the born popular writer, battered by Flaubert into austerity," and perhaps Maugham is an example of the sort of writer, popular, cosmopolitan, commercial and yet in some way distinguished, that Maupassant might have been if left alone. Maugham is now, at his best, as in *Cakes and Ale,* a master of cultivated acidity. The spare sere detachment of his prose may, with the exception of recurrent lapses into appalling sentimentality, be safely offered as a sound foundation course in commercial-literary craftsmanship.

One other influence, not I believe admitted by Maugham, seems to have shaped his craft. Repeatedly throughout his work, speaking both for himself and through his characters, Maugham reveals an ironic impatience with the stuffiness of literary and moral conventions (see the delicious dissection of the pompous social-climbing novelist in *Cakes and Ale*), and is constantly administering the acid corrective. The parallel

Principal Works

Liza of Lambeth (novel) 1897

The Making of a Saint (novel) 1898

Orientations (short stories) 1899

The Hero (novel) 1901

Mrs Craddock (novel) 1902; revised edition, 1937

A Man of Honour (drama) 1903

The Merry-Go-Round (short stories) 1904

The Land of the Blessed Virgin: Sketches and Impressions in Andalusia (travel book) 1905

Lady Frederick (drama) 1907

The Explorer (drama) 1908

Jack Straw (drama) 1908

The Magician (novel) 1908

Mrs Dot (drama) 1908

Smith (drama) 1909

The Tenth Man (drama) 1910

Loaves and Fishes (drama) 1911

The Land of Promise (drama) 1913

Of Human Bondage (novel) 1915

The Moon and Sixpence (novel) 1919

Our Betters (drama) 1919

The Circle (drama) 1921

The Trembling of a Leaf: Little Stories of the South Sea Islands (short stories) 1921

East of Suez (drama) 1922

The Painted Veil (novel) 1925

The Casuarina Tree (short stories) 1926

The Constant Wife (drama) 1926

The Letter (drama) 1927

Ashenden; or, The British Agent (short stories) 1928

Cakes and Ale; or, The Skeleton in the Cupboard (novel) 1930

The Gentleman in the Parlour (travel book) 1930

Six Stories Written in the First Person Singular (short stories) 1931

For Services Rendered (drama) 1932

The Narrow Corner (novel) 1932

Sheppey (drama) 1933

East and West (short stories) 1934; also published as Altogether, 1934

Don Fernando; or, Variations on Some Spanish Themes (travel book) 1935

Cosmopolitans (short stories) 1936

The Summing Up (autobiographical sketch) 1938

The Mixture as Before (short stories) 1940

Up at the Villa (novel) 1941

The Razor's Edge (novel) 1944

Then and Now (novel) 1946

Great Novelists and Their Novels (criticism) 1948; also published as Ten Novels and Their Authors, rev. ed., 1954

A Writer's Notebooks (journals) 1949

The Vagrant Mood (essays) 1952

Points of View (essays) 1958

Looking Back (autobiographical sketch) 1962

Purely for My Pleasure (essays) 1962

for this side of Maugham's method is not Maupassant, but *The Way of All Flesh,* a book for which Maugham is admirably fitted to write a modern counterpart. Here are two quotations:

Like other rich men at the beginning of this century he ate and drank a good deal more than was enough to keep him in health. Even his excellent constitution was not proof against a prolonged course of overfeeding and what we should now consider overdrinking. His liver would not unfrequently get out of order, and he would come down to breakfast looking yellow about the eyes.

I fancy that life is more amusing now than it was forty years ago and I have a notion that people are more amiable. They may have been worthier then, possessed of more substantial knowledge; I do not know. I know they were more cantankerous; they ate too much, many of them drank too much, and they took too little exercise. Their livers were out of order and their digestions often impaired.

The account of the first paragraph, which is Butler, is pitched in a key identical with that of the second, which is Maugham. The effect in both is gained by a series of apparently matter-of-fact statements, made almost offhand, with a sort of casual formality, qualified by a sort of airy, "Of course I don't really know. Don't go and take my word for it," which in reality injects the note of irony. Maugham and Butler again and again use this trick of creating ironic effect by disclaiming all trustworthy knowledge of what they are talking about, and by pitching their remarks in a negative key. The effect is delicious; butter won't melt in these acid mouths. *The Way of All Flesh* and *Cakes and Ale* will, in fact, repay some pretty close comparative study, and will show, I think, that Maugham found a far more profitable and compatible influence in Butler than in Maupassant.

It is my contention in fact that if Maugham had, as a writer of stories, rejected Maupassant as a model and kept more closely to Butler, we should have been presented with the first full-length English short-story writer worthy of comparison with the best continental figures. Unfortunately Maugham, in spite of an excellent eye, a dispassionate steadiness, a genius for the diagnosis of human frailty, and a cosmopolitan temperament, lacks one very great and supremely important quality. Unlike Tchehov and Maupassant, in whom he professes to see great differences but who were much alike at least in this respect, Maugham lacks compassion. He has no heart, and in place of that heart one has the impression that he uses a piece of clockwork. It is this, I think, that gives Maugham's work the frequent impression of cheapness. This effect is heightened by something else. Maugham, having mastered the art of irony, mistakenly supposed himself to be a cynic. But throughout Maugham's work, and notably in the stories, there exists a pile of evidence to show that Maugham the cynic is in reality a tin-foil wrapping for Maugham the sentimentalist. Maugham's cynicism indeed peels off under too-close examination, thin, extraneous, tinny, revealing underneath a man who is afraid of trusting and finally of revealing his true emotions.

There would be little point, here, in doing more than summarize the quality of Maugham's stories. They are easily available, pleasantly readable; they tell a story—in the sense, that is, that what they have to say can be expressed anecdotally; they deal largely with romantic places, for Maugham, like Kipling and Conrad, loves the East, and to his talent for painting its scenery and people he owes, as they do, much of his popular success. He delights in exposing human frailty, particularly amorous and marital frailty, and the humbug of convention; he is suave and urbane; he has the keenest sense of dramatic situations and delights in leaving the reader, as Maupassant and O. Henry did, with the point of the story neatly sharpened and vinegared in his hands. His natural sense of poetry is nil; his methods are as objective as the newspaper report of a court case, and sometimes as bad; he wisely refrains, except on rare occasions, from the purple passage, yet he has apparently never discovered any conscious and simple method of detecting himself in the act of using a cliché. When he is good, like the little girl, he is very good; and similarly when he is bad he is horrid.

Maugham indeed, though presenting the interesting case of a man who (on his own confession) evolved an attractively individual style without the help of a natural ear for words, has nothing new to offer. He simply perpetuates a tradition of straightforward, objective story-telling, largely derived from French naturalism, that is already well known. Thus Maugham's influence is not, and never has been, wide or important. (pp. 142-46)

H. E. Bates, "Katherine Mansfield and A. E. Coppard," in his *The Modern Short Story: A Critical Survey,* T. Nelson and Sons Ltd., 1941, pp. 122-47.

EDMUND WILSON
(essay date 1950)

[Wilson, considered one of America's foremost men of letters in the twentieth century, wrote widely on cultural, historical, and literary matters. In the following excerpt, first published as a review of *Then and Now* in the *New Yorker* on June 8, 1946, and subsequently revised with a postscript, he offers a negative assessment of Maugham's career.]

It has happened to me from time to time to run into some person of taste who tells me that I ought to take Somerset Maugham seriously, yet I have never been able to convince myself that he was anything but second-rate. His swelling reputation in America, which culminated the other day in his solemn presentation to the Library of Congress of the manuscript of *Of Human Bondage,* seems to me a conspicuous sign of the general decline of our standards. Thirty or thirty-five years ago the English novelists that were read in America were at least men like Wells and Bennett, who, though not quite of top rank, were at least by vocation real writers. Mr. Maugham, I cannot help feeling, is not, in the sense of "having the métier," really a writer at all. There are real writers, like Balzac and Dreiser, who may be said to write badly. Dreiser handles words abominably, but his prose has a compelling rhythm, which is his style and which induces the emotions that give his story its poetic meaning. But Mr. Maugham, whose language is always banal, has not even an interesting rhythm.

Now, unless I am looking for facts, I find it extremely difficult to get through books that are not "written." I can read Compton Mackenzie, for example, of the second rank though he is, because he has a gift of style of a not too common kind. But my experience has always been with Maugham that he disappoints my literary appetite and so discourages me from going on. His new novel, *Then and Now*—which I had sworn to explore to the end, if only in order to be able to say that I had read a book of Maugham's through—opposed to my progress, through all the first half, such thickets of unreadableness, that there were moments when I thought I should never succeed.

Then and Now is an historical novel: it deals with Niccolò Machiavelli and tells the story of his mission, as envoy from Florence, to the headquarters of Caesar Borgia, when the latter, in his campaign of domination, appeared at his most effective and most menacing. The way in which this promising subject is handled suggested, I was shocked to discover, one of the less brilliant contributions to a prep-school magazine. . . .

[The] narrative from time to time is obstructed by the introduction of thick chunks of historical background that sound as if they had been copied out—so compressed and indigestible are they, so untouched by imagination—from some textbook in the history classroom. (pp. 319-21). . . .

The defenders of Somerset Maugham will tell me that he is "old and tired" now, and that historical novels are not his forte—that it is quite unfair to judge him by *Then and Now,* which is one of the least of his books. I know that he has done better stories, but I am not sure that it *is* quite unfair to judge his quality by *Then and Now.* This quality is never, it seems to me, that either of a literary artist or of a first-rate critic of morals; and it may be worth while to say this at a moment when there seems to be a tendency to step up Mr. Maugham's standing to the higher ranks of English fiction, and when Mr. Maugham himself has been using his position of prestige for a nagging disparagement of his betters. Though Mr. Maugham's claims for himself are always carefully and correctly modest, he usually manages to sound invidious when he is speaking of his top-drawer contemporaries. In an anthology which he edited a few years ago, *Introduction to Modern English and American Literature*—a mixture of good writing and tripe that sets the teeth on edge—we find him patronizing, in what seems to me an insufferable way (and with his customary buzz of clichés), such writers as Henry James, James Joyce and W. B. Yeats. "His influence on fiction," he writes of James, "especially in England, has been great, and though I happen to think it has been a bad influence, its enduring power makes him an important figure. . . . He never succeeded in coming to grips with life. . . . This story ("The Beast in the Jungle") reads to me like a lamentable admission of his own failure." Of *Ulysses:* "I have read it twice, so I cannot say that I find it unreadable, but . . . like many of his countrymen, Joyce never discovered that enough is as good as a feast, and his prolixity is exhausting." Of Yeats: "Though he could at times be very good company, he was a pompous vain man; to hear him read his own verses was as excruciating a torture as anyone could be exposed to." Well, it is quite true of Henry James that his experience was incomplete and that he wrote about his own deficiencies, and that Joyce is sometimes too prolix, and it may be true that Yeats was sometimes pompous. It is also true that Mr. Maugham partly sweetens his detraction with praise. Yet, from reading this *Introduction,* you would never be able to discover that all these writers belong to a different plane from that of Michael Arlen and Katharine Brush, whose work is also included—to a plane on which Somerset Maugham does not exist at all. Mr. Maugham would apparently suggest to us that all novelists are entertainers who differ only in being more or less boring (though he grants, with a marked lack of enthusiasm,

that Henry James supplied, "if not an incentive, at least an encouragement to those who came after him . . . to aim consciously at giving fiction the form and significance that may sometimes make it more than the pastime of an idle hour"). We get the impression of a malcontent eye cocked up from the brackish waters of the *Cosmopolitan* magazine, and a peevish and insistent grumbling. There is something going on, on the higher ground, that halfway compels his respect, but he does not quite understand what it is, and in any case he can never get up there.

There are cases in which Mr. Maugham is able to admire more cordially the work that is done on this higher plane, but even here his way of praising betrays his lack of real appreciation and almost always has a sound of impertinence. So, in his speech at the Library of Congress, we find the following remarks about Proust:

Proust, as we know, was enormously influenced by the now largely discredited philosophy of Henri Bergson and great stretches of his work turn upon it. I suppose we all read with a thrill of excitement Proust's volumes as they came out, but now when we reread them in a calmer mood I think what we find to admire in them is his wonderful humor and extraordinarily vivid and interesting characters that he created in profusion. We skip his philosophical disquisitions and we skip them without loss.

Now, it is perfectly obvious here that Mr. Maugham does not know what he is talking about. Some aspects of Bergson's philosophy are still taken very seriously by first-rate philosophers of certain schools; and even if Bergson's whole system were regarded with universal disapproval, that might not affect the validity of the artistic use that Proust has made of one of its features. This feature—the difference between "time" and "duration": how long something takes by the clock and how long it seems while it is going on—is itself only one of the features of Proust's metaphysical picture, which in general has more in common with the implications of relativistic physics than with the Creative Evolution of Bergson. It is this play on the relativistic principle in the social and personal fields that gives Proust his philosophical interest and that makes his book, I suppose, the greatest philosophical novel ever written. In *A la recherche du temps perdu,* the philosophy so pervades the narrative that it is difficult to see how you could skip it: if you jumped over the "disquisitions," you could still not escape from Proust, in a thousand intimations and asides, expounding his relativistic theory; and since the unexpected development of the characters, the astonishing reversals of relationships, all the contrasts and paradoxes that provide the main interest of the story, are dramatizations of this theory, it is difficult to understand how a reader can "admire" the former and yet disregard the latter. The inability of Mr.

Maugham to grasp what there is in Proust helps to explain why he has not been able to make his own work more interesting.

—June 8, 1946

Admirers of Somerset Maugham have protested that this article was unfair to him and have begged me to read his short stories. I have therefore procured *East Is West,* the collected volume of these, and made shift to dine on a dozen. They *are* readable—quite entertaining. The style is much tighter and neater than it is in *Then and Now*—Mr. Maugham writes best when his language is plainest. But when he wants to use a richer idiom, this is the kind of thing you get: "Be this as it may, Ashenden in the last twenty years had felt his heart go pit-a-pat because of one charming person after another. He had had a good deal of fun and had paid for it with a great deal of misery, but even when suffering most acutely from the pangs of unrequited love he had been able to say to himself, albeit with a wry face, after all, it's grist to the mill." These stories are magazine commodities—all but two of them came out in the *Cosmopolitan*—on about the same level as Sherlock Holmes; but Sherlock Holmes has more literary dignity precisely because it is less pretentious. Mr. Maugham makes play with more serious themes, but his work is full of bogus motivations that are needed to turn the monthly trick. He is for our day, I suppose, what Bulwer-Lytton was for Dickens's: a half-trashy novelist, who writes badly, but is patronized by half-serious readers, who do not care much about writing. (pp. 323-26)

Edmund Wilson, "The Apotheosis of Somerset Maugham," in his *Classics and Commercials: A Literary Chronicle of the Forties,* Farrar, Straus and Company, 1950, pp. 319-26.

JOHN POLLOCK

(essay date 1966)

[In the following excerpt, Pollock explores Maugham's principal methods of characterization.]

Somerset Maugham's place in literature will be fixed in years to come. At least a generation must go by before anything like certainty can be achieved about a writer of eminence. Often the favourite of to-day is the outcast of to-morrow, and by no means seldom does the pendulum of critical judgement swing back later from unjust depreciation. There are even now signs that George Meredith is coming again into his own. My view about Somerset Maugham is that he will be set among writers at the top of the first class, both as novelist and as playwright, really great authors being apart

and above. I do not think he can be classed with Fielding, Thackeray, Voltaire, Balzac, Tolstoy, or Gogol; still less with Shakespeare, Goethe, Marlowe, Sophocles, Euripides, Racine, and Molière. As a short-story writer he comes certainly very close to those three masters Kipling, most tremendous of all, Guy de Maupassant, and Henry James, but it may be questioned whether, as a branch of art, the short story permits of development enough to enable true greatness to show itself.

This is by the way. I wish merely to show that Somerset Maugham is worthy to have his methods carefully considered, which might not be the case with an author, however good, of the second class like, say, George Eliot, Joseph Conrad, or Alphonse Daudet. It must always be of interest to see how a first-class writer, Anthony Trollope or Anatole France for instance, works. It is Somerset Maugham's method, or at least one part of his method, that I propose to study here, because it is the part that can best be studied with as little delay as possible after his death.

In the second half of his preface to *First Person Singular* Somerset Maugham deals with the question of how does an author come by his characters, and describes in a few incisive pages how traits from real persons among his acquaintance are used to create imaginary portraits. He refers to the notes of Henri Beyle, the letters of Flaubert, and the journal of Jules Renard as evidence that this is the general practice of authors. 'I think, indeed,' he writes, 'that most novelists, and surely the best, have worked from life. But though they have had in mind a particular person this is not to say that they have copied him nor that the character they have devised is to be taken for a portrait.' And he goes on to assert that to present an exact copy would be to defeat the author's aim, which is verisimilitude. 'Nothing,' he says, 'is so unsafe as to put into a novel a person drawn line by line from life. His values are all wrong and, strangely enough, he does not make the other characters of the book seem false, but himself. He never convinces.' Somerset Maugham's purpose in so discussing a novelist's method was to rebut the charge made against him of 'portraying certain persons so exactly that it was impossible not to know them,' in other words of painting word-portraits of real people. His method, he implies, was the method he has just praised. (pp. 365-66)

Somerset Maugham's own account of the manner in which he built up his characters from observation may be accepted without question. It is borne out by internal evidence. Only, as in Somerset Maugham the power of observation was developed to an unusually acute degree, so do his studies of character in which strokes are drawn from living models tend to resemble those models more than is usually the case with other novelists and more perhaps than Somerset Maugham himself intended or, when challenged, would concede. In one case, he tells us, he did paint a deliberately literal portrait. That is the character of Mortimer Ellis, the 'celebrated' bigamist, in that enchanting story called **"The Round Dozen."** He suggests that we ought all to know who the original was, but I confess that I do not; neither do the few knowledgeable people I have asked. Mortimer Ellis is so vivid and so plausible a character that Somerset Maugham may be supposed, without realizing it, to have added certain features from his imagination, otherwise he would be offering a flat contradiction of his own thesis that 'a person drawn line by line from life . . . never convinces.' In reality his imagination was so keen, if perhaps more keen than wide, that he could hardly have avoided doing so. It is only because his faculty of observation was so uncommonly prominent that he has sometimes been thought deficient in imagination.

Without a powerful imagination, working almost always in the sphere of psychological analysis, Somerset Maugham could never have created the gallery of life-like characters we have from his pen. It is evident that in constructing them he worked as a rule on the lines he described. The method closely resembles that of a painter working from models on an imaginative subject. The degree in which imagination is blended with observation may vary *ad infinitum;* but, however important may be the former in the resultant mixture, it is rare that the model is not recognizable. (pp. 366-67)

Somerset Maugham used two lines of approach to his subjects. In one, he took what may be called the outer psychological values of a real person and wrought them into an imaginary portrait by embodying them in a series of incidents which had no relation, or only a very slight relation, to those of his model's actual life. In the other, he took the fundamental values and put them into fictitious persons who had otherwise no relation at all to his models. This again he would vary by taking real incidents and putting fictitious persons among them, so that his characters took upon themselves a strong colour of being observed from life. An instance of this is his story called **"The Letter,"** which he turned into a still more famous play. Here he took an incident from real life that had, years before, been the subject of a *cause célèbre* in the Far East. It had happened long before Somerset Maugham's visit to the spot, therefore he could not have known any of the persons concerned. But he fitted characters of his imagination to the facts with such skill and force as to create astonishment and no little pain in the minds of those who had been personally acquainted with the protagonists in the real drama. In general, however, he so mixed his variations of method and so embroidered his characters with imaginary touches that readers, unless possessed of special knowledge, might not realize the personages in the story to have been drawn from life.

It is therefore a matter of literary and historical interest to track down some of the models from which Somerset Maugham worked. The list that I can give is doubtless far from complete. Nevertheless it contains some striking figures.

A very good specimen of a canvas containing such an admixture of traits observed in real men and women and of imaginary characters and events is to be found in *Ashenden; or, The British Agent.* Here we are at once confronted with a figure drawn from a living model: that of Ashenden himself, the narrator, who is clearly a self-portrait of the author. In the war of 1914-18, Somerset Maugham was engaged in our Intelligence Service in Switzerland and his note-book served as a basis for the stories. He says so openly. Events are seen through the eyes of the narrator, that is, his own. Apart from the fact that the key is given by Ashenden being a novelist, delicious little touches here and there produce an intimate note that surely reveals a bit of Maugham's own mind. Take this passage: Ashenden is in his bath. He 'sighed, for the water was no longer quite so hot, he could not reach the tap with his hand nor could he turn it with his toes (as every properly regulated tap should turn), and if he got up to add more hot water he might just as well get out altogether.' This is a reflexion so personal that no imagination however vivid could invent it. Ashenden is doubtless not wholly Somerset Maugham, but Somerset Maugham sat as his own model for 'the British Agent.' To clinch the matter, Ashenden reappears later as the narrator and unfashionable novelist in *Cakes and Ale,* with the Christian name of Willie, which was Maugham's own, and gives us therein much interesting insight into Maugham's mind. Later again Maugham explicitly admitted his identity with Ashenden.

The entire book, *Ashenden,* gives the impression of being studded with similar scraps of reality, jotted down here and there from Maugham's actual experiences. (pp. 367-69)

Friendliness to his models was not usual with Somerset Maugham, who doubtless found asperity to give a heightened tone to his portraits. This may have been the main cause of the outburst that greeted *Cakes and Ale,* which contains some of the most remarkable of them. An impulsive American lady even wrote a whole book, so indignant was she at Maugham's treatment of Thomas Hardy in *Cakes and Ale.* The author was thoroughly justified in denying that Edward Driffield was a portrait of Thomas Hardy and Alroy Kear a portrait of Hugh Walpole. They were not portraits in the same sense as Reginald Eves's oil painting is a portrait of Hardy; once more all the facts about the men in the book are invented; and Rosie, who Maugham tells us haunted him for years, is wholly a creature of his imagination. What Somerset Maugham did was to make psychological studies of his models and then let the characters behave as he conceived they must in hypothetical circumstances. (p. 371)

Somerset Maugham's second line of approach to his models, namely by taking their fundamental values and putting them into fictitious persons, is perfectly illustrated by his treatment of himself in *Of Human Bondage.* No one could ever doubt that the hero of his book, Philip, represents Maugham himself; and this is admitted in the preface to the volume in the collected edition of 1937. It is a spiritual autobiography. But the spiritual truth is set in trappings of slender verisimilitude. Philip's experiences at school must be reminiscences of Somerset Maugham's own youth; those at the hospital are evidently drawn from life; but the master thread on which this long chaplet of pearls is strung is not a bit of reporting. This is Philip's club foot. Somerset Maugham was not a cripple. Then how does this dominant motive, absent from the author's life, fit into an autobiographical novel? Very simply. Philip's crippled leg in the book is Somerset Maugham's stammer in real life. The author's infirmity was transmuted by him into a totally different sort of infirmity, graver physically, but morally perhaps not more galling than his. From Philip we know of the dreadful mental pain suffered by Somerset Maugham as the result of his infirmity, just as in Philip's torment in the linen-draper's shop we can read Maugham's detestation of the drudgery entailed by his medical practice in Lambeth. (pp. 373-74)

Another glimpse of Somerset Maugham's soul comes to us, I submit, in that brilliant short story, **"The Human Element."** Here, unless my shot is off the mark, Maugham projected something of his own feelings into the character of Lady Betty Welldon-Burns, daughter of a duke and electric leader of the bright young people in London, who retires to the Isle of Rhodes to live maritally with Albert, formerly 'the second footman at Aunt Louise's.' This drama is kept on the plane of high comedy and we are allowed to feel its deeper repercussions only in the despair of Humphrey Carruthers, the cultured Foreign Office clerk who vainly tries first to win, then to save, Lady Betty. 'What destroys me,' says Carruthers, 'what makes me so frightfully unhappy, is to think of her unspeakable degradation. . . . I admired her courage and her frankness, her intelligence and her love of beauty. She's just a sham and she's never been anything else.' In his rôle as narrator Somerset Maugham makes answer.

> I wonder if that's true. Do you think any of us are all of a piece? Do you know what strikes me? I should have said that Albert was only the instrument, her toll to the solid earth, so to speak, that left her soul at liberty to range the empyrean. Perhaps the mere fact that he was so far below her gave her a sense of freedom in her relations with him that she would have lacked with a man of her own class. The

spirit is very strange, it never soars so high as when the body has wallowed for a period in the gutter.

It is difficult not to see here an apologia for Maugham's own way of life that cut him off for some years and in some degree from regular intercourse with men of his own station and from completely normal society. This partial and self-imposed ostracism, accentuated by Maugham's firm refusal ever to attach himself to a literary clique, seems to be reflected in Lady Betty's withdrawal from the great world, to live with her own thoughts and her own tastes on a far-off Greek island. Maugham was too big a man to fall in with the artifices of London literary snobs. They distrusted and envied his success; they feared his biting pen. His place was achieved by himself alone, against all adventitious aids. But to achieve it he had to withdraw within himself, and his professional aloofness was redoubled not only by his infirmity but by the ordering of his life that was in no way flaunting or tinged with proselytism but, though discreet and purely personal, none the less put him at odds with received British ethical standards. (pp. 374-75)

John Pollock, "Somerset Maugham and His Work," in *The Quarterly Review,* Vol. 304, No. 650, October, 1966, pp. 365-78.

JOSEPH EPSTEIN
(essay date 1985)

[Epstein is an American educator and critic. In the following excerpt, he examines Maugham's career and reputation.]

The critic I am waiting for is the one who will explain why, with all my faults, I have been read for so many years by so many people.

—W. Somerset Maugham

"Four powers govern men: avarice, lust, fear, and snobbishness." Somerset Maugham didn't write that; Hilaire Belloc did. But Somerset Maugham, I think it fair to say, believed it. Avarice, lust, fear, and snobbishness are Maugham's great subjects; they are everywhere in his work, as theme, as motive, as background. Small wonder that they would be, for the same dark quartet—avarice, lust, fear, and snobbishness—were also the four reigning qualities in Somerset Maugham's own triumphant, lengthy, and finally rather sad life.

Cyril Connolly once called Somerset Maugham the "last of the great professional writers." He meant it as an honorific. It has not always been taken that way. One small step down from the professional writer is the hack; one large step up is the artist. A great many more critics have been willing to drop Maugham a step than have been willing to raise him a step. Maugham was always highly conscious of this; and one could string together a quite long necklace composed of the BB's he shot over his lifetime at highbrow critics, small-public writers, intellectual-magazine editors, and others who accorded his work less respect than he thought it deserved. "But you must remember the intelligentsia despise me," Maugham in late life told his nephew Robin Maugham. "Take that magazine that's indoors. What's it called? *Encounter?* Well, all the writers on *Encounter* despise me completely. I read it just to find out what's going on and what people are interested in. But I must confess I find it terribly boring." Not the least interesting item in that snippet of conversation is that, whatever his professed views of *Encounter,* Maugham nevertheless subscribed to and read it. He was a man who didn't miss much. (p. 1)

Somerset Maugham never worked at any other job but that of writer over the course of his ninety-one years. He never descended to journalism, or worked as a publisher's reader, or took on literary or any other kind of odd jobs. He lived on [the £150 income from his small inheritance], not an impressive sum even then. Nor did success come quickly. He published a first novel, *Liza of Lambeth,* at twenty-three, which, though it garnered decent reviews, earned no serious income. He had book-length manuscripts rejected. He wrote plays that were produced but enjoyed only brief runs and others that were not produced at all. At one point he moved to Paris, where he lived, frugally, among English and American expatriate writers and painters, among whom was the businesslike Arnold Bennett, who suggested that Maugham share a mistress with him and a third party. But there was nothing of the bohemian about Maugham, who was an Edwardian under and atop the skin and who, though he took a serious interest in the avant-garde art of his day, wished to avoid the garret style of life that often produced it. It was only in 1907, at the age of thirty-three, that Maugham was able to strike the success gong with a comedy of manners entitled *Lady Frederick,* which ran for 442 performances in London. The music of that gong was something he had longed to hear, for Maugham was a money writer; as he would later aver, "Money was like a sixth sense without which you could not make the most of the other five." Henceforth all that he wrote turned to gold, piles and piles of gold.

Granted that accounting may be no proper part of literary criticism, the amounts of money Somerset Maugham earned by his pen are too impressive to be ignored. As a successful playwright, Ted Morgan asserts [in *Maugham,* 1980], Maugham "bridged the quarter century between Oscar Wilde and Noël Coward," which is chronologically accurate but leaves Shaw out of reckoning. Nonetheless, during these years

Maugham always had a play or two running in London and New York theaters and at one point had four plays running concurrently in London's West End. (He generally took no more than three or four weeks to write a play.) No writer to this day has had more novels, stories, and plays turned into movies. (pp. 3-4)

While widening his social horizons, money broadened his subject matter; it made him worldly in a way that a writer who struggles ceaselessly for a living can never quite hope to be. As the Maughamish character named Ashenden says in the story entitled **"Guilia Lazzari,"** "just as the advantage of culture is that it enables you to talk nonsense with distinction, so the habit of luxury allows you to regard its frills and furbelows with a proper contumely." (p. 4)

Maugham thought of himself, interestingly, as a professional humorist, which in his stories he calls himself more than a few times, and in one of his Ashenden stories, **"The Traitor,"** he speaks of "the pleasant comedy of life." He meant this, I believe, in the sense in which one speaks of the human comedy. He put his case in *The Summing Up,* where he wrote: "A sense of humour leads you to take pleasure in the discrepancies of human nature; it leads you to mistrust great professions and look for the unworthy motive that they conceal; the disparity between appearance and reality diverts you and you are apt when you cannot find it to create it." If the humorist sometimes misses truth, beauty, and goodness, he is nonetheless tolerant, for he has no interest in moralizing but is "content to understand; and it is true that to understand is to pity and forgive."

While there was nothing of the aesthete about Maugham, nor any aesthetic difficulty about his work, few modern writers have been clearer about their own aesthetic program and, with the exceptions of Paul Valéry and Henry James, perhaps none has thought more trenchantly about the aesthetic questions raised by literary creation. Maugham thought, for example, that the artist is not justified in wishing to be judged by his intention; for him the crucial moment in the aesthetic transaction is that of communication—that moment when the work of art addresses the viewer or listener or reader. He thought talent to be made up of a natural aptitude for creation combined with a strong outlook on life shorn of the prejudices of the current day. "Sometimes," he wrote in *Don Fernando,* "there will be found a man who has this facility for writing to an extraordinary degree and to this joins an outlook on life which is not only peculiar to himself, but appeals to all men, and then he will be called a genius." Once, when asked the secrets of his own craft by a Chinese professor, he replied: "I know only two. One is to have common sense and the other is to stick to the point."

Maugham may also have been among the best read of modern writers. He never travelled any distance

Major Media Adaptations: Motion Pictures

The Circle, 1925. MGM [Silent] Director: Frank Borzage. Cast: Elinor Boardman, Creighton Hale, Alec B. Francis.

Sadie Thompson, 1928. [Silent; adaptation of "Rain"] Director: Raoul Walsh. Cast: Gloria Swanson, Lionel Barrymore, Raoul Walsh.

The Letter, 1929. Paramount. Director: Jean de Limur. Cast: Jeanne Eagels, Reginald Owen, Herbert Marshall, Irene Browne.

Strictly Unconventional, 1930. MGM. [Adaptation of *The Circle*] Director: David Burton. Cast: Catherine Dale Owen, Tyrell Davis, Lewis Stone.

Rain, 1932. United Artists. Director: Lewis Milestone. Cast: Joan Crawford, Walter Huston, William Gargan, Guy Kibbee.

Of Human Bondage, 1934. RKO. Director: John Cromwell. Cast: Leslie Howard, Bette Davis, Frances Dee, Reginald Owen, Alan Hale.

The Painted Veil, 1934. MGM. Director: Richard Boleslawski. Cast: Greta Garbo, George Brent, Herbert Marshall, Warner Oland, Jean Hersholt.

The Secret Agent, 1936. Gaumont British. Director: Alfred Hitchcock. Cast: John Gielgud, Peter Lorre, Robert Young, Madeleine Carroll, Lilli Palmer.

The Letter, 1940. Warner. Director: William Wyler. Cast: Bette Davis, James Stephenson, Gale Sondergaard.

The Moon and Sixpence, 1943. United Artists. Director: Albert Lewin. Cast: George Sanders, Herbert Marshall, Elena Verdugo, Florence Bates.

Of Human Bondage, 1946. Warner. Director: Edmund Goulding. Cast: Paul Henreid, Eleanor Parker, Alexis Smith, Edmund Gwenn, Janis Paige.

The Razor's Edge, 1946. Twentieth-Century Fox. Director: Edmund Goulding. Cast: Tyrone Power, Gene Tierney, Clifton Webb, Anne Baxter, Herbert Marshall, John Payne, Elsa Lanchester.

The Unfaithful, 1947. Warner. [Adaptation of "The Letter"] Director: Vincent Sherman. Cast: Ann Sheridan, Zachary Scott, Lew Ayers, Eve Arden.

Miss Sadie Thompson, 1953. Columbia. [Adaptation of "Rain"] Director: Curtis Bernhardt. Cast: Rita Hayworth, Jose Ferrer, Aldo Ray, Charles Bronson.

The Seventh Sin, 1957. MGM. [Adaptation of *The Painted Veil*] Director: Ronald Neame. Cast: Eleanor Parker, George Sanders.

Of Human Bondage, 1964. Warner. Directors: Ken Hughes, Henry Hathaway. Cast: Kim Novak, Laurence Harvey, Siobhan McKenna, Robert Morley.

The Razor's Edge, 1984. Colgems. Director: John Byrum. Cast: Bill Murray, Catherine Hicks, Theresa Russell, Denholm Elliott, James Keach.

---

without a laundry bag filled with books, and he read, as one would imagine, with penetration. He adored the Russian novelists and admired Stendhal. The French called him the English Maupassant, which pleased him greatly. He thought Kipling and Chekhov, along with Maupassant, the ablest of the world's short-story writers. He had mixed feelings about Henry James, on the one hand thinking him amusingly absurd and finding himself unable to believe in the motivations of the characters in his fiction and on the other hand remarking, in his essay **"Some Novelists I Have Known"**: "the fact remains that those last novels of his, notwithstanding their unreality, make all other novels, except the very best, unreadable." But generally he expressed his own personal preference for the straight-forward over the ornate, for among prose writers he preferred Dryden and Hazlitt and Arnold and Cardinal Newman over Dr. Johnson and De Quincey and Carlyle and Pater. Here he joined the majority in preferring those who are most like himself.

One cannot read much in Maugham without recognizing that his own straightforward prose style came into being as a result of conscious artistry. He was a careful student of prose, which he wrote about extremely well in an essay on Edmund Burke as well as in *Don Fernando* and in *The Summing Up.* As a beginning novelist, he wrote under the influence of Pater and Oscar Wilde and other of the late Victorian decorative-prose stylists. He soon enough realized he had no talent in this line and set out to write more plainly, taking Swift as his model. (In later life he claimed he would have done better to have studied Dryden.) His own gifts, he recognized, were not poetical: lyricism was not his cup of tea, nor charming metaphors and cogent similes his sugar and milk. What he did have was clarity, logic, and an appreciation for euphonic language. On the subject of the formation of his own prose style, he wrote; "I knew that I should never write as well as I could wish, but I thought with pains I could arrive at writing as well as my natural defects allowed. On taking thought it seemed to me that I must aim at lucidity, simplicity and euphony."

Maugham's was a strong and a serviceable style. His prose tended to be more elegant when he was writing essays than when he was writing novels and stories. He himself remarked, in his essay on Edmund Burke's prose, that the most settled styles in the history of English prose belonged to essayists, divines, and historians, and that too settled—that is, too polished—a style might even redound to the disadvantage of the writer of fiction, who is primarily a teller of stories and whose prose needs to remain supple enough to capture so many shades of mood and to insinuate itself into the thoughts of various and often vastly different characters. "But perhaps it is enough if the novelist contents himself with avoiding the grosser errors of grammar," Maugham wrote, "for no one can have considered this matter without being struck by the significant and surprising fact that the four greatest novelists the world has seen, Tolstoi, Balzac, Dostoyevsky and Dickens, wrote their respective languages very carelessly. . . ." Here one can add the name Dreiser, the prose in whose powerful novels on occasion didn't even achieve the level of carelessness.

Not that Maugham was ever close to being in the Dreiser class. (Dreiser himself, truth to tell, wasn't that often in the Dreiser class.) I have recently read what must amount to some four thousand pages of Maugham's prose and found myself seldom brought up by infelicities. In his earlier work he occasionally lapses into cliché; more than once he refers to the heart of one of his characters, in the heat of passion, going "pit-a-pat," when, for such a phrase, once is at least ten times too often. In *Of Human Bondage*, Sally Thorpe, the Dickensian sugarpuss heroine whom Philip Carey eventually marries, says to Carey, "You're an old silly, that's what you are," which causes one to blush, not for Carey but for Maugham. In the same book Mildred Rogers, the waitress who has enthralled Carey, is described as "weak as a rat," when rats are not generally thought weak at all but rather sinewy and tenacious. Finally, in *The Razor's Edge* Maugham, who believed that a writer of one nation has little chance of understanding the people of another nation, has his male American characters use the words "gosh" and "gee" more often than Oogie Pringle on the old "A Date with Judy" radio show. Still, for roughly four thousand pages, that isn't bad.

As a stylist what Maugham had was lucidity, fluency, and economy. In a sheer storyteller, which is what he was, these are the paramount qualities. Often his stories seem almost to tell themselves; such ostensible artlessness, of course, can only be conferred through the exercise of high art. Maugham wrote every morning from 9:45 to 12:45, and he wrote quickly and revised little. He received no editing from his publishers, Heinemann's in England and Doubleday in the United States, for he wanted none. As an author he was the equivalent to what in sports is known as a franchise player; with his huge sales, he could make a publishing house single-handedly, and publishers know not to fool with success of the kind such an author brings. In 1935, though, that curious figure Eddie Marsh, who had been a private secretary to Churchill, Asquith, and Joseph Chamberlain, offered to inspect Maugham's manuscripts for lapses in precision and errors in usage, which he did do for fourteen of Maugham's books until his, Marsh's, death in 1953 and for which Maugham felt great gratitude. Maugham learned a good deal from Marsh, as he seemed to learn from everyone and every-

thing, and as he grew older his prose grew more confident and more precise.

As a writer of fiction, Maugham's ambitions were Balzacian. He believed an important writer needed to produce an ample body of work, and from that body deserved to be judged by the best of it. He claimed to have small powers of imagination, which caused him to fall back on industry to make up for it. "I have had one advantage," he wrote, "I have never wanted a subject. I have always had more stories in my head than I ever had time to write." He may not have had large powers of imagination but his powers of observation were of the first order. He plagiarized from life, frequently putting people he knew or had heard about in his stories and novels. (As a result of his writing many stories acquired in his travels in the Malay States, he was said to be considered very much non grata in the British clubs and outposts there.) "I have painted easel pictures," he wrote, "not frescoes." But when he was done he could fill many a gallery.

Why did Maugham write so much? Because, he might have answered, writing is what a writer is supposed to do, and besides, what else was he, who was rather easily bored, to do with his mornings? While at a certain point he no longer needed the money his pen brought in—a pen designed specifically for him, incidentally, with a thick collar that permitted a surer grasp—most assuredly he liked to see it come cascading in. He had, as the small businessmen used to put it, a high nut, with the expenses of maintaining the princely establishment that was Villa Mauresque, paying (always resentfully) alimony to his wife, and travelling in the grand style; doubtless, too, as someone whose young manhood was perforce lived frugally, he had no wish as a middle-aged and older man to dip into interest. But above all he appears to have written as much as he did because he loved to write, to go about with the characters from a story in his head, to work through the technical details of composition, to attempt to bring it all off as nearly perfect as possible. Whatever his motives, working day after day he produced an immense body of writing, although not all of it was of even quality and some of it was pretty poor stuff.

Enter the critics. "This novel, as unmitigated a specimen of fictional drivel as has appeared under respectable authorship within living memory, might be fitly dismissed as the latest triumph of servant-girl's literature were it not for the phenomenal value that still attaches to Maugham's name among modern authors." That explosive sentence is the opening line from a 1941 review by Morton Dauwen Zabel in *The Nation* of Maugham's novel *Up at the Villa*. In its anger this review does not drop off precipitously from this first line. It goes on to attack Maugham for being "hostile to artistic risk," for "his career in the fashionable drawing-rooms and international cocktail sets of Europe," and for his derogations of Henry James; and the review ends by noting that "if the title of 'greatest living English novelist' is to be thrown around any further, it is time it landed in the right quarter. The greatest living English novelist is E. M. Forster." *Up at the Villa,* true enough, is a very poor novel; Maugham himself told Glenway Wescott that he was ashamed of having written it. But the poorness of the novel doesn't quite explain the vehemence of Zabel's review. Whence the anger in that review? Why the personal attack?

Edmund Wilson was even rougher on Maugham, saying that he was "second-rate" and that "his swelling reputation in America"—the year was 1946—showed "a conspicuous sign of the general decline of our standards." The occasion for Wilson's attack was another poor Maugham performance, *Then and Now,* his novel about Machiavelli. The quality of this book, Wilson pronounced, "is never . . . that either of a literary artist or of a first-rate critic of morals; and it may be worthwhile to say this at a moment when there seems to be a tendency to step up Mr. Maugham's standing to the higher ranks of English fiction, and when Mr. Maugham himself has been using his position of prestige for a nagging disparagement of his betters." Who, one may ask, might these betters be? They turn out to be the great modernist writers—Joyce and James and Yeats and Proust—of whom Maugham had, in Wilson's view, a far from adequate appreciation. (pp. 6-9)

Maugham found admirers among men of letters and writers; among his supporters were Cyril Connolly, Virginia Woolf, Desmond MacCarthy, Evelyn Waugh and V. S. Pritchett; and Orwell wrote of him, "I believe the modern writer who has influenced me most is Somerset Maugham, whom I admire immensely for his power of telling a story straightforwardly and without frills." But among what he termed "highbrow critics" Maugham's name has never been an approved one. He knew this, and, though he pretended to be above it, one finds running throughout his work a sputtering volley of shots against "intellectuals," "highbrows," "the intelligentsia," and "critics of the intelligentsia." Maugham is partly to blame for incitement to critical riot against his own work.

Why did they detest Maugham so? Were they jealous of his success, the vast audience and riches his writing earned? Perhaps this entered into it, but more important, I suspect, was that his writing was an affront to them. He was apolitical and he wrote dead against the grain of modernism, with all its difficulty, preferring instead to write as plainly as possible about complex things. Say what one wishes against them, no one can accuse the modernist writers of not keeping critics gainfully employed. In an idle fantasy I sometimes think of these writers—Joyce and Eliot and Yeats and Kafka and the rest—mounted on motorcycles in a parade up the Champs-Élysées, a critic or two sitting

W. Somerset Maugham.

in a small sidecar attached to each cycle, beaming with pleasure at being allowed along for the ride. But Maugham kept no sidecar; each of his books, to switch metaphors rather abruptly, might have carried a small message, à la the Surgeon General's warning on cigarette packages, "No explanation, explication, or exegesis required. Read on without prolegomenon."

But one doesn't have to attack the modernist writers because one admires Somerset Maugham; nor need one think oneself half-serious for admiring him. Maugham remains intensely, immensely readable. Why? One recalls his revealing the secrets of his craft to the Chinese professor: "One is to have common sense and the other is to stick to the point." The point Maugham stuck to throughout his long career was the investigation of that magnificent, comic, admirable, outrageous, depressing, impressive, grim, gracious, grudging, great, and elusive thing called human nature. Human nature was Maugham's enduring subject, and for fiction there is none greater. If you are interested in it, you have to be interested in the writing of Somerset Maugham. As for his common sense, it was pervasive; the test is that he was an artist who knew that there are things in life greater than art. "I think," he wrote in *A Writer's Notebook,* "there is in the heroic courage with which man confronts the irrationality of the world a beauty greater than the beauty of art." Because he was able to insinuate such sentiments, subtly, dramatically, into his work—see, for an example, the story entitled **"Sanatorium"**—Maugham shall always be a writer for readers who care for more than writing alone.

And yet it is difficult to convey a precise impression of the quality of Maugham's work through naming two or three of his best books. He was right about himself in thinking that he was a writer of the kind for whom the body of his work is greater than the parts taken individually. Of his novels, I find only one, *Cakes and Ale,* completely successful. It is, I think, his masterpiece, a rich comedy about the literary life, its exactions and its delights and its fraudulence. It contains a dazzling portrait of the type of the literary widow and an even better account of the young literary hustler in the character of Alroy Kear, modeled, as it turns out, on Hugh Walpole—a man, as Maugham later averred, "easy to like, but difficult to respect." The literary widow, the literary hustler, the utterly self-absorbed artist, these are types that do not disappear, and Maugham was the first to mount them, like so many butterflies, on a narrative of seamless velvet.

Of his own books, Maugham said he liked *Cakes and Ale* best but tended to agree with the common opinion that held *Of Human Bondage* to be his most important work. In this latter, largely autobiographical book Maugham worked on a larger canvas than he ever would again; it is the sort of novel where one can introduce, for the first time, a major character as late as page 421. I first read *Of Human Bondage* when I was twenty and now I have re-read it approaching fifty, and it still seems to me immensely interesting. I tend to think of it as the best nineteenth-century novel written well into the twentieth century. It was publicly promoted at its publication by Theodore Dreiser in a review in *The New Republic* that made its reputation in America. Good as much of the book is, it nonetheless seems badly flawed toward its close by Maugham's need to resolve the action, to put an end to his young hero's troubles in a way that is not only conclusive but happy, and happy in the rather sappiest Dickensian mode.

I shall not run through all of Maugham's books that I have read or re-read, but I do think *The Razor's Edge* is in some ways representative of both Maugham's gifts and deficiencies. This is the novel, it will be recalled, about the quest of a young American named Larry Darrell for the ultimate truths about the meaning of life. In the character Isabel Maturin, Maugham created an extraordinarily vivid and hence persuasive portrait of a grasping American rich girl who wants *merely* everything. In Elliott Templeton, the wealthy expatriate American snob, Maugham has created a character of whom it is not ridiculous to say that, after the Baron de Charlus, he may well be the most interesting snob in modern literature. "I don't in the least mind pigging it at the Ritz," he announces at one point.

Elliott Templeton is one of those characters whom you don't wish ever to leave the page, in the way one wants certain charming character actors never to leave the stage. Almost everything about *The Razor's Edge* is brilliant—except, alas, Larry Darrell's quest. This may be because goodness, which young Darrell is tiresomely meant to represent, is usually less interesting than its reverse; it may be because ultimate truths about the meaning of life are never quite convincing; it may be because Somerset Maugham's powers of idealization had long since withered. But *The Razor's Edge* resembles nothing so much as a ring with a large rhinestone at the center and with smaller but perfect gems all round it.

One is unlikely to encounter Maugham's books in a university curriculum. In my youth his work, because he was an international bestseller, was ubiquitous, and if one was at all bookish one was likely, when young, to have read *The Razor's Edge* and *Of Human Bondage;* or if one thought of oneself as artistic to have found self-justification in reading *The Moon and Sixpence,* his not very good novel modeled on the life of Paul Gauguin. Today I think the best introduction—or re-introduction—to Maugham is through his short stories. So many of these seem so good that it may be unjust to single out a few. But among the four volumes of stories now available in Penguin editions, **"Mr. Harrington's Washing"** is a work of comic genius; **"The Pool"** may be the best story ever written on the subject of going native; **"The Hairless Mexican"** is spy fiction raised to the highest power; and **"Lord Mount drago"** is but one of his many stories that provide a cunning anatomy of snobbery. Maugham's nonfiction also bears looking into. At the top of his form he was a very capable essayist—see the volumes entitled *The Vagrant Mood* and *Points of View*—and *Don Fernando,* the book on Spanish culture, contains many clever and wise things. My sense is that it is best to read Maugham's stories and nonfiction first, and let them lead one back to the novels, where one is likely to discover that Maugham is one of those novelists who can be profitably read when young but who get better as one gets older.

Maugham would probably be best served by a single volume on the order of the "Viking Portable" series, except that, in his case, the volume, to suit his ample talent, would have to be of a thickness beyond portability. Such a volume, if I were its editor, would include all of *Cakes and Ale,* the better part of *The Summing Up,* the portrait of Elliott Templeton from *The Razor's Edge,* the essays on El Greco, Burke's prose, and Kant's aesthetics, and nearly everything he wrote on prose style. What would make the volume bulge, proving a severe test of the binder's art, would be the number of short stories that would have to be included. The short story really was Maugham's best form, and he published more than a hundred of them—among serious writers, perhaps only Chekhov wrote more. Some of his stories are thin, especially those that attempt to point an easy moral or have a trick ending, but the vast majority are very sturdily made. Those set in the Malay States, taken together, conduce to give as complete a picture of the British abroad as do Kipling's stories of India. Maugham's stories about the artistic life—"**The Alien Corn,**" "**The Creative Impulse**" chief among them—are also too good not to be included.

Often Maugham's stories seem akin to reading La Rochefoucauld with illustrations—not drawings of course but illustrations from life. Maugham resembles La Rochefoucauld in taking avarice, lust, fear, and snobbishness for his subjects. Yet unlike La Rochefoucauld, Maugham's dark views about human nature are often stood on their head by evidence of courage, honesty, and integrity, almost always of an unexpected and complicated kind. Maugham is that odd phenomenon: a moralist who is never surprised by immorality. As he puts it in **"The Pool,"** "I held my breath, for to me there is nothing more awe-inspiring than when a man discovers to you the nakedness of his soul. Then you see that no one is so trivial or debased but that in him is a spark of something to excite compassion." (pp. 10-12)

Joseph Epstein, "Is It All Right to Read Somerset Maugham?" in *The New Criterion,* Vol. IV, No. 3, November, 1985, pp. 1-13.

GORE VIDAL

(essay date 1990)

[Vidal is an American novelist, short story writer, dramatist, and essayist. He is particularly noted for his historical novels and iconoclastic essays. In the following excerpt, he offers a lively, acerbic assessment of Maugham's life and career.]

Maugham spent his first twenty-six years in the nineteenth century and for the subsequent sixty-five years he was very much a nineteenth-century novelist and playwright. In many ways he was fortunately placed, though he himself would not have thought so. He was born in Paris where his lawyer father did legal work for the British Embassy, and his mother was a popular figure in Paris society. Maugham's first language was French and although he made himself into the premier English storyteller, his prose has always had a curious flatness to it, as if it wanted to become either Basic English or Esperanto or perhaps go back into French. . . .

Maugham's career as a writer was singularly long and singularly successful. . . . (p.39)

"Few authors," Mr. Calder tells us [in *Willie: The*

Life of W. Somerset Maugham, 1990], "read as widely as Maugham and his works are peppered with references to other literature." So they are—peppered indeed—but not always seasoned. The bilingual Maugham knew best the French writers of the day. He tells us that he modelled his short stories on Maupassant. He also tells us that he was much influenced by Ibsen, but there is no sign of that master in his own school of Wilde comedies. Later, he was awed by Chekhov's stories but, again, he could never "use" that master because something gelled very early in Maugham the writer, and once his own famous tone was set it would remain perfectly pitched to the end.

In his first published novel, *Liza of Lambeth* (1897), Maugham raised the banner of Maupassant and the French realists but the true influence on the book and its method was one Arthur Morrison, who had made a success three years earlier with *Tales of Mean Streets.* Mr. Calder notes that Morrison,

> writing with austerity and frankness, . . . refused to express sympathy on behalf of his readers so that they could then avoid coming to terms with the implications of social and economic inequality. Maugham adopted this point of view in his first novel, and was therefore, like Morrison, accused of a lack of conviction.
>
> (p. 39)

For someone of Maugham's shy, highly self-conscious nature (with a secret, too) the adoption of classic realism, Flaubert with bitters, was inevitable. Certainly, he was lucky to have got the tone absolutely right in his first book, and he was never to stray far from the appearance of plain storytelling. Although he was not much of one for making up things, he could always worry an anecdote or bit of gossip into an agreeable narrative. Later, as the years passed, he put more and more effort—even genius—into his one triumphant creation, W. Somerset Maugham, world-weary world-traveler, whose narrative first person became the best-known and least wearisome in the world. At first he called the narrator "Ashenden" (a name carefully chosen so that the writer would not stammer when saying it, unlike that obstacle course for stammerers, "Maugham"); then he dropped Ashenden for Mr. Maugham himself in *The Razor's Edge* (1944). Then he began to appear, as narrator, in film and television dramatizations of his work. Thus, one of the most-read novelists of our time became widely known to those who do not read.

Shaw and Wells invented public selves for polemical reasons, while Mark Twain and Dickens did so to satisfy a theatrical need, but Maugham contrived a voice and a manner that not only charm and surprise in a way that the others did not, but where they were menacingly larger than life, he is just a bit smaller (5'7"), for which he compensates by sharing with us something that the four histrionic masters would not have dreamed of doing: inside gossip. It is these confidences that made Maugham so agreeable to read: *nothing,* he tells us with a smile, *is what it seems.* That was his one trick, and it seldom failed. Also, before D. H. Lawrence, Dr. Maugham (obstetrician) knew that women, given a fraction of a chance, liked sex as much as men did. When he said so, he was called a misogynist.

In October 1907, at thirty-three, Maugham became famous with the triumphant production of *Lady Frederick* (one of six unproduced plays that he had written). Maugham ravished his audience with the daring trick of having the eponymous lady—middle-aged with ardent unsuitable youthful admirer—save the boy from his infatuation by allowing him to see her unmade-up at her dressing table. So stunned is the lad by the difference between the beauty of the *maquillage* and the crone in the mirror that he is saved by her nobleness, and right before our eyes we see "nothing is what it seems" in spades, raw stuff for the theater of those days.

By 1908 Maugham had achieved the dream of so many novelists: he had four plays running in the West End and he was financially set for life. . . .

In 1915 . . . *Of Human Bondage* was published. Maugham now was seen to be not only a serious but a solemn novelist—in the ponderous American manner. The best that can be said of this masterpiece is that it made a good movie and launched Bette Davis's career. I remember that on all the pre-Second War editions, there was a quotation from Theodore Dreiser to the effect that the book "has rapture, it sings." Mr. Calder does not mention Dreiser but Mr. Frederic Raphael does, in his agreeable picture book with twee twinkly text, *Somerset Maugham and His World.* Mr. Raphael quotes from Dreiser, whom he characterizes as "an earnest thunderer in the cause of naturalism and himself a Zolaesque writer of constipated power." Admittedly, Dreiser was not in a class with Margaret Drabble but—constipated?

The Maugham persona was now perfected in life and work. (p. 40)

Maugham has no reputation at all in North American academe where Mr. Calder is a spear-carrier. The result is a lot of less than half-praise:

His career had been largely a triumph of determination and will, the success in three genres of a man not naturally gifted as a writer.

Only a schoolteacher innocent of how literature is made could have written such a line. Demonstrably, Maugham was very talented at doing what he did. Now, this is for your final grade, *what* did he do? Describe, please. Unfortunately, there aren't many good

describers (critics) in any generation. But I shall give it a try, presently.

At seventy-two, Maugham went to Vevey, Switzerland, where a Dr. Niehans injected aging human organisms with the cells of unborn sheep, and restored youth. All the great and not-so-good came to Niehans, including Pius XII—in a business suit and dark glasses, it was said—an old man in no hurry to meet his Jewish employer. Thanks perhaps to Niehans, Maugham survived for nearly fifteen years in rude bodily health. But body outlived mind and so it was that the senile Maugham proceeded to destroy his own great invention, W. Somerset Maugham, the teller of tales, the man inclined to the good and to right action, and above all, to common sense. By the time that old Maugham had finished with himself, absolutely nothing was what it seemed and the double self-portrait that he had given the world in *The Summing Up* and *A Writer's Notebook* was totally undone by this raging Lear upon the Riviera, who tried to disinherit daughter while adopting [his secretary-companion Alan] Searle as well as producing *Looking Back,* a final set of memoirs not quite as mad as Hemingway's but every bit as malicious. With astonishing ingenuity, the ancient Maugham mined his own monument; and blew it up.

For seven decades Maugham had rigorously controlled his personal and his artistic life. He would write so many plays, and stop; and did. So many novels, and stop; and did. So many short stories. . . . He rounded off everything neatly, and lay back to die, with a quiet world-weary smile on those ancient lizard lips. But then, to his horror, he kept on living, and having sex, and lunching with Churchill and Beaverbrook. Friends thought that Beaverbrook put him up to the final memoir, but I suspect that Maugham had grown very bored with a lifetime of playing it so superbly safe.

•••••

It is very difficult for a writer of my generation, if he is honest, to pretend indifference to the work of Somerset Maugham. He was always so entirely *there.* By seventeen I had read all of Shakespeare; all of Maugham. Perhaps more to the point, he dominated the movies at a time when movies were the lingua franca of the world. Although the French have told us that the movie is the creation of the director, no one in the Twenties, Thirties, Forties paid the slightest attention to who had directed *Of Human Bondage, Rain, The Moon and Sixpence, The Razor's Edge, The Painted Veil, The Letter.* Their true creator was W. Somerset Maugham, and a generation was in thrall to his sensuous, exotic imaginings of a duplicitous world.

Although Maugham received a good deal of dutiful praise in his lifetime, he was never to be taken very seriously in his own country or the United States, as opposed to Japan where he has been for two thirds of a century the most read and admired Western writer. Christopher Isherwood tells us that he met Maugham at a Bloomsbury party where Maugham looked most ill at ease with the likes of Virginia Woolf. Later Isherwood learned from a friend of Maugham's that before the party, in an agony of indecision, as the old cliché master might have put it, he had paced his hotel sitting room, saying, "I'm just as good as they are."

I suspect that he thought he was probably rather better *for what he was,* which was not at all what they were. Bloomsbury disdained action and commitment other than to Art and to Friendship (which meant going to bed with one another's husbands and wives). Maugham liked action. He risked his life in floods, monsoons, the collapse of holy Russia. He was worldly like Hemingway, who also stalked the big game of wild places, looking for stories, self. As for what he thought of himself, Mr. Calder quotes Maugham to the headmaster of his old school: "I think I ought to have the O.M. [Order of Merit]. . . . They gave Hardy the O.M. and I think I am the greatest living writer of English, and they ought to give it to me." When he did get a lesser order, Companion of Honour, he was sardonic: "It means very well done . . . but."

But. There is a definite but. I have just reread for the first time in forty years *The Narrow Corner,* a book I much admired; *The Razor's Edge,* the novel on which the film that I found the ultimate in worldly glamour was based; *A Writer's Notebook,* which I recalled as being very wise; and, yet again, *Cakes and Ale,* Edmund Wilson's famous explosion at the success of Maugham in general and *The Razor's Edge* in particular [see excerpt dated 1950] is not so far off the mark:

> The language is such a tissue of clichés that one's wonder is finally aroused at the writer's ability to assemble so many and at his unfailing inability to put anything in an individual way.

Maugham's reliance on the banal, particularly in dialogue, derived from his long experience in the theater, a popular art form in those days. One could no more represent the people on stage without clichés than one could an episode of *Dynasty:* Maugham's dialogue is a slightly sharpened version of that of his audience.

Both Wilde and Shaw dealt in this same sort of realistic speech but Shaw was a master of the higher polemic (as well as of the baleful clichés of the quaint workingman, rendered phonetically to no one's great delight) while Wilde made high verbal art of clichés so slyly crossed as to yield incongruent wit. But for any playwright of that era (now, too), the *mot juste* was apt to be the well-deployed *mot banal.* Maugham's plays worked very well. But when Maugham transferred the tricks of the theater to novel writing, he was inclined to write not only the same sort of dialogue that the stage required but in his dramatic effects he often set his scene with stage directions, ignoring the possibilities that prose *with* dialogue can yield. This economy won him many readers, but there is no rapture, song. Wilson, finally, puts him in the relation of Bulwer-Lytton to Dickens: "a half-trashy novelist who writes badly, but is patronized by half-serious readers who do not care much about writing." What ever happened to those readers? How can we get them back?

Wilson took the proud modernist view that, with sufficient education, everyone would want to move into Axel's Castle. Alas, the half-serious readers stopped reading novels long ago while the "serious" read literary theory, and the castle's ruins are the domain of literary archaeologists. But Wilson makes a point, inadvertently: If Maugham is half-trashy (and at times his most devoted admirers would probably grant that) what, then, is the other half, that is not trash? Also, why is it that just as one places, with the right hand, the laurel wreath upon his brow, one's left hand starts to defoliate the victor's crown?

A *Writer's Notebook* (kept over fifty years) is filled with descriptions of sunsets and people glimpsed on the run. These descriptions are every bit as bad as Wilson's (in *The Twenties*) and I don't see why either thought that writing down a fancy description of a landscape could—or should—be later glued to the page of a novel in progress. Maugham's descriptions, like Wilson's, are disagreeably purple while the physical descriptions of people are more elaborate than what we now put up with. But Maugham was simply following the custom of nineteenth-century novelists in telling us whether or not eyebrows grow together while noting the exact placement of a wen. Also, Dr. Maugham's checklist is necessary for diagnosis. Yet he does brood on style; attempts to make epigrams. "Anyone can tell the truth, but only very few of us can make epigrams." Thus, young Maugham, to which the old Maugham retorts, "In the nineties, however, we all tried to."

In the preface, Maugham expatiates on Jules Renard's notebooks, one of the great delights of world literature and, as far as I can tell, unknown to Anglo-Americans, like so much else. Renard wrote one small masterpiece, *Poil de Carotte,* about his unhappy childhood—inhuman bondage to an evil mother rather than waitress.

Renard appeals to Maugham, though "I am always suspicious of a novelist's theories, I have never known them to be anything other than a justification of his own shortcomings." Well, that is commonsensical. In any case, Maugham, heartened by Renard's marvelous notebook, decided to publish his own. The tone is world-weary, modest. "I have retired from the hurly-burly and ensconced myself not uncomfortably on the shelf." Thus, he will share his final musings.

There is a good deal about writing. High praise for Jeremy Taylor:

> He seems to use the words that come most naturally to the mouth, and his phrases, however nicely turned, have a colloquial air. . . . The long clauses, tacked on to one another in a string that appears interminable, make you feel that the thing has been written without effort.

Here, at twenty-eight, he is making the case for the plain and the flat and the natural sounding:

> There are a thousand epithets with which you may describe the sea. The only one which, if you fancy yourself a stylist, you will scrupulously avoid is *blue;* yet it is that which most satisfies Jeremy Taylor. . . . He never surprises. His imagination is without violence or daring.

Of Matthew Arnold's style, "so well suited to irony and wit, to exposition . . . It is a method rather than an art, no one more than I can realize what enormous labour it must have needed to acquire that mellifluous cold brilliance. It is a platitude that simplicity is the latest acquired of all qualities. . . ." The interesting giveaway here is Maugham's assumption that Arnold's style must have been the work of great labor. But suppose, like most good writers, the style was absolutely natural to Arnold and without strain? Here one sees the hard worker sternly shaping himself rather than the natural writer easily expressing himself as temperament requires:

> My native gifts are not remarkable, but I have a certain force of character which has enabled me in a measure to supplement my deficiencies. I have common sense. . . . For many years I have been described as a cynic; I told the truth. I wish no one to take me for other than I am, and on the other hand I see no need to accept others' pretenses.

One often encounters the ultimate accolade "common sense" in these musings. Also, the conceit that he is what you see, when, in fact, he is not. For instance, his native gifts for narrative were of a very high order. While, up to a point, he could tell the truth and so be thought cynical, it was always "common sense," a.k.a. careerism, that kept him from ever saying all that he knew. Like most people, he wanted to be taken for what he was not; hence, the great invention W. Somerset Maugham. (pp. 41-2)

Posterity? That oubliette from which no reputation returns. Maugham:

> I think that one or two of my comedies may retain for some time a kind of pale life, for they are written in the tradition of English comedy . . . that began with the Restoration dramatists. . . . I think a few of my best short stories will find their way into anthologies for a good many years to come if only because some of them deal with circumstances and places to which the passage of time and the growth of civilization will give a romantic glamour. This is slender baggage, two or three plays and a dozen short stories. . . .

But then it is no more than Hemingway, say, will be able to place in the overhead rack of the economy section of that chartered flight to nowhere, Twentieth Century Fiction.

I would salvage the short stories and some of the travel pieces, but I'd throw out the now-too-etiolated plays and add to Maugham's luggage *Cakes and Ale,* a small perfect novel, and, sentimentally, *The Narrow Corner.* Finally, Maugham will be remembered not so much for his own work as for his influence on movies and television. There are now hundreds of versions of Maugham's plays, movies, short stories available on cassettes, presumably forever. If he is indeed half-trashy, then one must acknowledge that the other half is of value; that is, *classicus,* "belonging to the highest class of citizens," or indeed of any category: hence, our word "classic"—as in Classics *and* Commercials. Emphasis added. (p. 44)

Gore Vidal, "Maugham's Half & Half," in *The New York Review of Books,* Vol. XXXVII, No. 1, February 1, 1990, pp. 39-44.

SOURCES FOR FURTHER STUDY

Barnes, Ronald E. *The Dramatic Comedy of William Somerset Maugham.* The Hague: Mouton, 1969, 190 p.

    Analysis of Maugham's dramatic comedies, focusing on the relation of technique to content.

Burgess, Anthony. "Somerset Maugham: 1874-1965." *The Listener* LXXIV, No. 1917 (23 December 1965): 1033.

    Obituary tribute in which Burgess declares that "the short story was Maugham's true *métier,* and some of the stories he wrote are among the best in the language."

Calder, Robert. *Willie: The Life of W. Somerset Maugham.* London: Heinemann, 1989, 429 p.

Scholarly biography prepared with the assistance of Maugham's companion-secretary Alan Searle.

Connolly, Cyril. "The Art of Being Good." *The New States-man and Nation* XXVIII, No. 705 (26 August 1944): 140.

Review of *The Razor's Edge* that includes the assessment: "Maugham is the greatest living short-story writer, and so one expects his handling of plot to force one into a breathless, nonstop reading from the first page to the last, and his character-drawing and observation to be in the fine tradition—but one would not expect to be so captivated by the brilliant fluency of the writing. Here at last is a great writer, on the threshold of old age, determined to tell the truth in a form which releases all the possibilities of his art."

Innes, Christopher. "Somerset Maugham: A Test Case for Popular Comedy." *Modern Drama* XXX, No. 4 (December 1987): 549-59.

Considers underlying serious themes and astringent social satire in Maugham's popular comedies.

Morley, Christopher. "Gin and Quinine Tonic." *The New York Times Book Review* (8 October 1950): 3, 24.

Review praising *The Maugham Reader,* comprising novels, short stories, plays, essays, and an autobiographical sketch, as "a generous load of the most continuously readable storyteller of our lifetime."

Guy de Maupassant

1850-1893

(Full name Henri René Albert Guy de Maupassant; also wrote under pseudonyms Joseph Prunier, Guy de Valmont, and Maufrigneuse.) French short story writer, novelist, journalist, poet, dramatist, and travel writer.

INTRODUCTION

*M*aupassant is considered one of the finest short story writers of all time and a champion of the realistic approach to writing. His *contes* and *nouvelles,* noted for their diversity and quality, are characterized by the clarity of their prose and the objective irony of their presentation, as well as their keen evocation of the physical world. To the realist's ideal of scrupulous diction Maupassant added an economy of language and created a narrative style noted for its austere power, simplicity, and vivid sensuousness.

Maupassant was born in Normandy of wealthy parents, and both the setting and character of his childhood are clearly reflected in his fiction. After a bitter and unhappy life together, Maupassant's parents separated when he was eleven years old, and Maupassant was raised by his strong, domineering mother. She became the basis for his characterizations of slighted and overbearing women, who appeared in many of his stories. He attended the Lycée Napoléon in Paris and the Lycée de Rouen and eventually earned a *bachelier ès lettres.* After serving as a soldier in the Franco-Prussian War, Maupassant worked as a clerk in the Naval Office in an attempt to remedy the financial problems facing his family.

Perhaps the greatest influence on Maupassant's life and career was Gustave Flaubert, who had been a childhood friend of his mother and who served as a friend and mentor to the author during his young adulthood. In the company of Flaubert and his circle, which included Ivan Turgenev, Alphonse Daudet, and Émile Zola, Maupassant was truly at the center of European thought, and his work bears its legacy. "Boule de suif," which was his first published story, was part of a collaborative effort, *Les soirées de Medan* (1880), which included the work of several young French Naturalists under the influence and direction of Zola. The work proved a minor success for the young Naturalists, but Maupassant's story was so clearly superior to those of his fellow contributors that it established him immediately as a strong young talent in short fiction. He subsequently broke with the Naturalist school, turning instead to the precepts of realism. These principles, forged by Flaubert, called for a scrupulous concern with form and a dedication to precision of detail and exact description. Maupassant also shared with his mentor a severe pessimism toward life and a disdain for bourgeois values, both of which are reflected throughout his work.

Maupassant spent several years on the staffs of two Parisian newspapers, the *Gil-Blas* and the *Gaulois,* often working under pseudonyms. From 1880 to 1890 he published nearly 300 short stories and six novels, a prodigious literary feat, by constantly reshaping and reworking existing stories and duplicating scenes, descriptions, and vignettes from his newspaper pieces. His creative life was cut short by a degenerate condition stemming from syphilis, which he had contracted as a young man. The disease led to recurrent problems with his eyesight and eventually to a complete physical and emotional collapse. Struggling with bouts of debilitating mental illness, Maupassant attempted suicide in 1892 and was subsequently confined to a sanatorium in Passy, where he died.

Maupassant's critical reception has focused on several major areas, among them his morality, the nature of his realism, the influence of Flaubert on his work, and the autobiographical aspects of his fiction. The inherent sexuality of Maupassant's work was questioned as early as 1880, when his poem "Au bord de l'eau" shocked and offended bourgeois sensibilities, sparking threats of a lawsuit. Henry James, one of Maupassant's most perceptive commentators, called Maupassant a "lion in the path" of moralistic nineteenth-century critics because of the frankly erotic element in his work. A central concern of critics during his own time, Maupassant's sensuality continues to be remarked upon by such modern critics as Martin Turnell, who find his emphasis on sexuality evidence of his limited artistic vision. Maupassant's realism has also provided a focal point for critics. Early commentators were often appalled at what they detected as his lack of compassion for his characters. Later critics have dismissed this contention in favor of commentary on the technical virtuosity of Maupassant's prose, praising the purity of his narrative style, the use of the revelatory detail, and the absence of authorial commentary so much in vogue among novelists of his era.

Discussions of Maupassant's realism often emphasize the influence Flaubert had on his apprentice, prompting a variety of responses. Some critics, including Turnell, see in such works as "Boule de suif " many parallels in structure, theme, and exposition. Edward Sullivan, on the other hand, argues that Maupassant made no effort toward Flaubertian objectivity in his most famous short story, and that his bitterness is rather a clear and subjective response to the Franco-Prussian War and the hypocrisy of the middle class. These arguments have, in turn, led some of Maupassant's critics to focus on what they consider an autobiographical element in his work. Thus, they reassert that his masterpiece, "Boule de suif," is an expression of his disgust for the degradation and folly of war, and stems from Maupassant's days as a soldier. In such stories as "Le Papa de Simon," they claim, Maupassant examined his own childhood and the dilemmas of all rejected women and abandoned children who attempt to establish an identity and a sense of place in a rigid social structure. These commentators similarly find in the short stories that deal with madness—such as "Le horla" and "Lui?"—evidence of Maupassant's mental instability. In this instance, however, this approach is countered by others, who find in these same stories, although written very near the time of Maupassant's physical collapse, a clarity of style and perspective that indicates that he was fully in charge of his faculties, and that it was an artistic and not a confessional motivation that led him to explore madness and the supernatural.

Although Maupassant's poetry collection, dramas, and novels didn't achieve the commercial and artistic success of his short stories, the novels, which include *Une vie* (1883; *A Woman's Life,* 1888), *Bel-Ami* (1885; *Bel-Ami,* 1891), *Pierre et Jean* (1888; *Pierre et Jean; The Two Brothers,* 1889), and *Fort comme la mort* (1889; *Strong as Death,* 1899), have become a center of critical interest in recent years. However, his reputation will continue to be based on his contribution to the development of the short story. For their variety, concision, clarity of prose style, and realistic approach, Maupassant's short stories have earned him a place among the finest exponents of the genre.

(For further information about Maupassant's life and works, see *Nineteenth-Century Literature Criticism,* Vol. 1 and *Short Story Criticism,* Vol. 1.)

CRITICAL COMMENTARY

JULES LEMAÎTRE

(essay date 1885)

[Lemaître was a prominent French critic of the late nineteenth and early twentieth centuries. In the excerpt below, he outlines the bitterness, brutality, and pessimism he finds in Maupassant's short stories, while acknowledging the classic perfection of their form. This essay was originally published in 1885.]

[The] tale, in M. de Maupassant's hands, has become realistic. Glance through its themes. You will see in almost all of them some little fact seized in passing, interesting for some reason or other, as evidence of stupidity, unthinkingness, egoism, sometimes even of human goodness, or pleasing by some unexpected contrast, some irony of things, at all events something that has *happened,* or at least an observation made from life, which little by little has assumed in the writer's mind the living form of a short story. (pp. 164-65)

One consequence of this realism is that these tales are not always gay. Some of them are sad, and some are extremely brutal. This was inevitable. Most of the subjects are taken from classes and 'environments' in which instincts are stronger and blinder. (p. 165)

Add to this that in spite of his natural gaiety, M. de Maupassant, like many writers of his generation, affects a moroseness, a misanthropy that gives an excessively bitter flavour to several of his narratives. It is evident that he likes and searches for the most violent manifestations of love reduced to desire, of egoism, of brutality, of simple ferocity. (p. 166)

M. de Maupassant searches out with no less predilection the most ironical conjunctions of ideas or of facts, the most unexpected and most shocking combinations of feelings, those most likely to wound in us some illusion or some moral delicacy. The comic and the sensual mingling in these almost sacrilegious combinations, not precisely to purify them, but to prevent them from being painful. While others depict for us war and its effects on the fields of battle or in families, M. de Maupassant, hewing out for himself from this common material a portion that is indeed his own, shows us the effects of the invasion in a special world and even in houses which we usually designate by euphemisms. You remember Boule-de-Suif 's astonishing sacrifice, and the unheard-of conduct of those whom she obliged, and, in **"Mademoiselle Fifi,"** Rachel's revolt, the stab, the girl in the steeple who is afterwards

brought back and embraced by the parish priest and at last married by a patriot who has no prejudices. Remark that Rachel and Boule-de-Suif are certainly, along with Miss Harriet, little Simon, and the parish priest in **"Un baptême"** (I think that is all), the most sympathetic characters in the tales. (pp. 167-68)

There is in these stories and in some others a triumphant brutality, a determination to regard men as sad or comical animals, a large contempt for humanity, which becomes indulgent, it is true, immediately when there comes into play *divûmque hominumque voluptas, alma Venus:* all this saved in most cases by the rapidity and frankness of the narrative, by the out-and-out gaiety, by the perfect naturalness, and also (I scarcely dare say it, but it will explain itself) by the very depth of the artist's sensuality, which at least always spares us mere smuttiness. (p. 169)

M. de Maupassant is extraordinarily sensual; he is gladly, feverishly, and enthusiastically sensual; he is as it were haunted by certain images, by the memory of certain sensations. . . . To the initial and crude sensations are added the impressions of surrounding objects, landscape, lines, colours, sounds, perfumes, the hour of the day or night. He enjoys odours thoroughly (see **"Une idylle," "Les soeurs Rondoli,"** etc.), for in fact sensations of this sort are particularly voluptuous and enervating. But, to tell the truth, he enjoys the entire world, and in him feeling for nature and love are invoked and blended. (pp. 172-73)

Thus we see how many new elements are added to the old and eternal foundation of smuttiness—observation of reality, and more readily of dull or violent reality; instead of the old wantonness, a profound sensuality enlarged by the feeling of nature and often blended with sadness and poetry. All these things are not encountered at the same time in all M. de Maupassant's tales. I give the impression left by them taken as a whole. Amidst his robust jollities, he has sometimes, whether natural or acquired, a vision similar to that of Flaubert or of M. Zola; he also is attacked by the most recent malady of writers, I mean pessimism and the strange mania for making out the world to be very ugly and very brutal, for showing it governed by blind instincts, for thus almost eliminating psychology, the good old 'study of the human heart,' and for endeavouring at the same time to represent in detail and with a relief that has not yet been attained this world which is of so little interest in itself and only of interest

Principal Works

Des vers (poetry) 1880

La maison Tellier (short stories) 1881

Mademoiselle Fifi (short stories) 1882

Contes de la bécasse (short stories) 1883

Une vie (novel) 1883
   [A Woman's Life, 1888]

Au soleil (short stories) 1884

Clair de lune (short stories) 1884

Miss Harriet (short stories) 1884

Les soeurs Rondoli (short stories) 1884

Bel-Ami (novel) 1885
   [Bel-Ami; A Novel, 1891]

Contes du jour et de la nuit (short stories) 1885

Contes et nouvelles (short stories and novellas) 1885

Yvette (short stories) 1885

Monsieur Parent (short stories) 1886

La petite roque (short stories) 1886

Toine (short stories) 1886

Le horla (short stories) 1887

Mont-Oriol (novel) 1887
   [Mont-Oriol; A Novel, 1891]

Pierre et Jean (novel) 1888
   [Pierre et Jean; The Two Brothers, 1889]

Le rosier de Mme. Husson (short stories) 1888

Sur l'eau (travel sketches) 1888

Fort comme la mort (novel) 1889
   [Strong as Death; A Novel, 1899]

La main gauche (short stories) 1889

The Odd Number; Thirteen Tales (short stories) 1889

L'inutile beauté (short stories) 1890

New Stories by Guy de Maupassant (short stories) 1890

Notre coeur (novel) 1890
   [Notre coeur (The Human Heart), 1890]

La vie errante (travel sketches) 1890

Musotte (drama) 1891

Madame Tellier's Girls (La maison Tellier); The Inheritance (L'heritage); Butter-ball (Boule de suif) (short stories) 1897

The Life Work of Henri René Guy de Maupassant, Embracing Romance, Travel, Comedy, & Verse, for the First Time Complete in English (short stories, novels, plays, poetry, travel sketches) 1903

Yvette and Other Stories (short stories) 1904

Mademoiselle Fifi and Twelve Other Stories (short stories) 1917

Miss Harriet and Other Stories (short stories) 1923

The Complete Short Stories of Guy de Maupassant (short stories) 1955

---

as material for art; so that the pleasure of the writer and of those who enjoy him and enter fully into his thought consists only of irony, pride, and selfish pleasure. No concern about what used to be called the ideal, no preoccupation with morality, no sympathy for men, but perhaps a contemptuous pity for absurd and miserable humanity; on the other hand, a subtle skill in enjoying the world in so far as it falls within the senses and is of a nature to gratify them; the interest that is refused to things themselves fully granted to the art of reproducing them in as plastic a form as possible; on the whole, the attitude of a misanthropical, scoffing, and lascivious god. (pp. 174-76)

[M. de Maupassant] joins to a vision of the world, to feelings and preferences of which the classics would not have approved, all the external qualities of classic art. Moreover, this has been also one of Flaubert's originalities; but it seems to be more constant and less laborious in M. de Maupassant.

'Classical qualities, classical form,' are easy words to say. What exactly do they mean? They imply an idea of excellence; they imply also clearness, sobriety, the art of composition; they mean, finally, that reason, rather than imagination and sensibility, presides over

the execution of the work, and that the writer dominates his material.

M. de Maupassant dominates his material marvellously, and it is through this that he is a master. (pp. 176-77)

His prose is excellent, so clear, so direct, so unstudied! He has, like everybody to-day, skilful conjunctions of words, lucky hits in expression, but they are always so natural with him, so pat to the subject, and so spontaneous that one only notices this too late. Notice also the fullness, the good disposition of his phrasing, when it happens to stretch out a little, and how it falls back 'squarely' on its feet. (p. 178)

Classic by the naturalness of his prose, by the good standard of his vocabulary, and by the simplicity of the rhythm of his phrases, M. de Maupassant is classical also by the quality of his comedy. . . . In brief, if M. de Maupassant is more than moderately brutal, he is also more than moderately gay. And his comedy comes from the things themselves and from the situations; it does not reside in the narrator's style nor in his wit. M. de Maupassant has never been witty, and perhaps never will be, in the sense in which the word is understood by men about town. But he has the gift by plainly telling stories, without hits, without witticisms, without efforts, without contortions, of exciting un-measured gaieties and bursts of inextinguishable laughter. Read again only **"Boule-de-suif," "La maison Tellier," "La rouille," "Le remplacant," "Décoré," "La patronne,"** the end of **"Les soeurs Rondoli,"** or the episode of Lesable and the handsome Maze in **"L'héritage."** Now, there you have great art employed on little subjects, and, as nothing is more classical than to obtain powerful effects by very simple means, you will find that the epithet of classic is not out of place.

M. de Maupassant displays extreme clearness in his narratives and in the drawing of his characters. He distinguishes and brings into relief, with a great power of simplification and singular sureness of touch, the essential features in the physiognomy of his characters. (pp. 179-81)

M. de Maupassant has yet another merit, which, without being confined to the classics, is more frequently found in them and is becoming rather rare with us. He has in the highest degree the art of composition, the art of subordinating all else to something that is essential, to an idea, to a situation, so that in the first place everything prepares for it, and that afterwards everything contributes to render it more striking and to draw out all its effects. . . . Just as much description or landscape as is needed 'to give the setting' as the phrase runs; and descriptions themselves very well composed, not made up of details of equal value interminably heaped up together, but brief and taking from things only those features that stand out and give an epitome of the whole. . . . Clear, simple, connected, and vigorous, succulent in their deep-seated drollery, such are almost all these little tales; and how rapid is their action!

It is rather curious that, of all the story-tellers and novelists who have a vogue to-day, it should be perhaps the most daring and the most indecent who approaches closest to the sober perfection of the venerable classics; that one is able to observe in **"Boule-de-suif"** the application of the excellent rules inscribed in books of rhetoric, and that **"L'histoire d'une fille de ferme,"** though it may alarm their modesty, is of a sort to satisfy those humanists who are best furnished with precepts and doctrines. And yet this is the case. (pp. 182-84)

Jules Lemaître, "Guy de Maupassant," in his *Literary Impressions,* translated by A. W. Evans, Daniel O'Connor, 1921, pp. 154-86.

HENRY JAMES
(essay date 1888)

[James, an American-born English novelist, short story writer, critic, and essayist, is regarded as one of the greatest novelists of the English language and is admired as an insightful critic. In the excerpt below, he states that Maupassant is an artist of the senses: of smell, sight, and sexuality. Because of this, James concludes, Maupassant is "embarrassing" for a moralist; he is a "lion in the path," a writer who cannot be ignored or dismissed.]

[As] a commentator M. de Maupassant is slightly common, while as an artist he is wonderfully rare. Of course we must, in judging a writer, take one thing with another, and if I could make up my mind that M. de Maupassant is weak in theory, it would almost make me like him better, render him more approachable, give him the touch of softness that he lacks, and show us a human flaw. The most general quality of the author of *La Maison Tellier* and *Bel-Ami,* the impression that remains last, after the others have been accounted for, is an essential hardness—hardness of form, hardness of nature; and it would put us more at ease to find that if the fact with him (the fact of execution) is so extraordinarily definite and adequate, his explanations, after it, were a little vague and sentimental. (p. 245)

[Maupassant's] gifts are remarkably strong and definite, and . . . he writes directly *from* them, as it were: holds the fullest, the most uninterrupted—I scarcely know what to call it—the boldest communication with them. . . . M. de Maupassant neglects nothing that he possesses; he cultivates his garden with admirable energy; and if there is a flower you miss from the rich parterre, you may be sure that it could not possibly have been raised, his mind not containing the soil for it. He is plainly of the opinion that the first duty of the artist, and the thing that makes him most useful to his fellow-men, is to master his instrument, whatever it may happen to be.

His own is that of the senses, and it is through them alone, or almost alone, that life appeals to him; it is almost alone by their help that he describes it, that he produces brilliant works. They render him this great assistance because they are evidently, in his constitution, extraordinarily alive; there is scarcely a page in all his twenty volumes that does not testify to their vivacity. Nothing could be further from his thought than to disavow them and to minimise their importance. He accepts them frankly, gratefully, works them, rejoices in them. . . . M. de Maupassant's productions teach us, for instance, that his sense of smell is exceptionally acute—as acute as that of those animals of the field and forest whose subsistence and security depend upon it. It might be thought that he would, as a student of the human race, have found an abnormal development of this faculty embarrassing, scarcely knowing what to do with it, where to place it. But such an apprehension betrays an imperfect conception of his directness and resolution, as well as of his constant economy of means. Nothing whatever prevents him from representing the relations of men and women as largely governed by the scent of the parties. Human life in his pages (would this not be the most general description he would give of it?) appears for the most part as a sort of concert of odours, and his people are perpetually engaged, or he is engaged on their behalf, in sniffing up and distinguishing them, in some pleasant or painful exercise of the nostril. (pp. 249-51)

Not less powerful is his visual sense, the quick, direct discrimination of his eye, which explains the singularly vivid concision of his descriptions. These are never prolonged nor analytic, have nothing of enumeration, of the quality of the observer, who counts the items to be sure he has made up the sum. His eye *selects* unerringly, unscrupulously, almost impudently—catches the particular thing in which the character of the object or the scene resides, and, by expressing it with the artful brevity of a master, leaves a convincing, original picture. If he is inveterately synthetic, he is never more so than in the way he brings this hard, short, intelligent gaze to bear. His vision of the world is for the most part a vision of ugliness, and even when it is not, there is in his easy power to generalise a certain absence of love, a sort of bird's-eye-view contempt. He has none of the superstitions of observation, none of our English indulgences, our tender and often imaginative superficialities. (pp. 251-52)

As regards the other sense, the sense *par excellence,* the sense which we scarcely mention in English fiction, and which I am not very sure I shall be allowed to mention in an English periodical, M. de Maupassant speaks for that, and of it, with extraordinary distinctness and authority. To say that it occupies the first place in his picture is to say too little; it covers in truth the whole canvas, and his work is little else but a report of its innumerable manifestations. These manifestations are not, for him, so many incidents of life; they are life itself, they represent the standing answer to any question that we may ask about it. He describes them in detail, with a familiarity and a frankness which leave nothing to be added; I should say with singular truth, if I did not consider that in regard to this article he may be taxed with a certain exaggeration. M. de Maupassant would doubtless affirm that where the empire of the sexual sense is concerned, no exaggeration is possible: nevertheless it may be said that whatever depths

may be discovered by those who dig for them, the impression of the human spectacle for him who takes it as it comes has less analogy with that of the monkeys' cage than this admirable writer's account of it. I speak of the human spectacle as we Anglo-Saxons see it—as we Anglo-Saxons pretend we see it, M. de Maupassant would possibly say. (pp. 253-54)

If he is a very interesting case, this makes him also an embarrassing one, embarrassing and mystifying for the moralist. I may as well admit that no writer of the day strikes me as equally so. To find M. de Maupassant a lion in the path—that may seem to some people a singular proof of want of courage; but I think the obstacle will not be made light of by those who have really taken the measure of the animal. We are accustomed to think, we of the English faith, that a cynic is a living advertisement of his errors, especially in proportion as he is a thorough-going one; and M. de Maupassant's cynicism, unrelieved as it is, will not be disposed of offhand by a critic of a competent literary sense. . . . It is easy to exclaim that if he judges life only from the point of view of the senses, many are the noble and exquisite things that he must leave out. What he leaves out has no claim to get itself considered till after we have done justice to what he takes in. It is this positive side of M. de Maupassant that is most remarkable—the fact that his literary character is so complete and edifying. (pp. 254-55)

M. de Maupassant would probably urge that the right thing is to know, or to guess, how events come to pass, but to say as little about it as possible. There are matters in regard to which he feels the importance of being explicit, but that is not one of them. . . . He deprecates reference to motives, but there is one, covering an immense ground in his horizon, as I have already hinted, to which he perpetually refers. If the sexual impulse be not a moral antecedent, it is none the less the wire that moves almost all M. de Maupassant's puppets, and as he has not hidden it, I cannot see that he has eliminated analysis or made a sacrifice to discretion. His pages are studded with that particular analysis; he is constantly peeping behind the curtain, telling us what he discovers there. The truth is that the admirable system of simplification which makes his tales so rapid and so concise (especially his shorter ones, for his novels in some degree, I think, suffer from it), strikes us as not in the least a conscious intellectual effort, a selective, comparative process. He tells us all he knows, all he suspects, and if these things take no account of the moral nature of man, it is because he has no window looking in that direction, and not because artistic scruples have compelled him to close it up. The very compact mansion in which he dwells presents on that side a perfectly dead wall.

This is why, if his axiom that you produce the effect of truth better by painting people from the outside than from the inside has a large utility, his example is convincing in a much higher degree. A writer is fortunate when his theory and his limitations so exactly correspond, when his curiosities may be appeased with such precision and promptitude. . . . M. de Maupassant is remarkably objective and impersonal, but he would go too far if he were to entertain the belief that he has kept himself out of his books. They speak of him eloquently, even if it only be to tell us how easy—how easy, given his talent of course—he has found this impersonality. (pp. 257-59)

He feels oppressively, discouragingly, as many another of his countrymen must have felt—for the French have worked their language as no other people have done—the penalty of coming at the end of three centuries of literature, the difficulty of dealing with an instrument of expression so worn by friction, of drawing new sounds from the old familiar pipe. . . . Everything seems to him to have been done, every effect produced, every combination already made. (p. 261)

If it be a miracle whenever there is a fresh tone, the miracle has been wrought for M. de Maupassant. . . . He has taken his stand on simplicity, on a studied sobriety, being persuaded that the deepest science lies in that direction rather than in the multiplication of new terms. . . . Nothing can exceed the masculine firmness, the quiet force of his own style, in which every phrase is a close sequence, every epithet a paying piece, and the ground is completely cleared of the vague, the ready-made and the second-best. Less than any one to-day does he beat the air; more than any one does he hit out from the shoulder. (pp. 262-63)

He has produced a hundred short tales and only four regular novels; but if the tales deserve the first place in any candid appreciation of his talent it is not simply because they are so much the more numerous: they are also more characteristic; they represent him best in his originality, and their brevity, extreme in some cases, does not prevent them from being a collection of masterpieces. (They are very unequal, and I speak of the best.) (p. 264)

For the last ten years our author has brought forth with regularity these condensed compositions, of which, probably, to an English reader, at a first glance, the most universal sign will be their licentiousness. They really partake of this quality, however, in a very differing degree, and a second glance shows that they may be divided into numerous groups. It is not fair, I think, even to say that what they have most in common is their being extremely *lestes*. What they have most in common is their being extremely strong, and after that their being extremely brutal. A story may be obscene without being brutal, and *vice versâ*, and M. de Maupassant's contempt for those interdictions which are supposed to be made in the interest of good morals is but an incident—a very large one indeed—of his general

contempt. A pessimism so great that its alliance with the love of good work, or even with the calculation of the sort of work that pays best in a country of style, is, as I have intimated, the most puzzling of anomalies (for it would seem in the light of such sentiments that nothing is worth anything), this cynical strain is the sign of such gems of narration as **"La maison Tellier,"** **"L'histoire d'une fille de Ferme," "L'ane," "Le chien," "Mademoiselle Fifi," "Monsieur Parent," "L'héritage," "En famille," "Le baptême," "Le père amable."** The author fixes a hard eye on some small spot of human life, usually some ugly, dreary, shabby, sordid one, takes up the particle, and squeezes it either till it grimaces or till it bleeds. Sometimes the grimace is very droll, sometimes the wound is very horrible; but in either case the whole thing is real, observed, noted, and represented, not an invention or a castle in the air. M. de Maupassant sees human life as a terribly ugly business relieved by the comical, but even the comedy is for the most part the comedy of misery, of avidity, of ignorance, helplessness, and grossness. When his laugh is not for these things, it is for the little *saletés* (to use one of his own favourite words) of luxurious life, which are intended to be prettier, but which can scarcely be said to brighten the picture. I like **"La bête à Maître Belhomme," "La ficelle," "Le petit fût," "Le cas de Madame Luneau," "Tribuneaux rustiques,"** and many others of this category much better than his anecdotes of the mutual confidences of his little *marquises* and *baronnes*.

Not counting his novels for the moment, his tales may be divided into the three groups of those which deal with the Norman peasantry, those which deal with the *petit employé* and small shopkeeper, usually in Paris, and the miscellaneous, in which the upper walks of life are represented, and the fantastic, the whimsical, the weird, and even the supernatural, figure as well as the unexpurgated. These last things range from **"Le horla"** (which is not a specimen of the author's best vein—the only occasion on which he has the weakness of imitation is when he strikes us as emulating Edgar Poe) to **"Miss Harriet,"** and from **"Boule de suif "** (a triumph) to that almost inconceivable little growl of Anglophobia, **"Découverte"**—inconceivable I mean in its irresponsibility and ill-nature on the part of a man of M. de Maupassant's distinction; passing by such little perfections as **"Petit soldat," "L'abandonné," "Le collier"** (the list is too long for complete enumeration), and such gross imperfections (for it once in a while befalls our author to go woefully astray), as **"La femme de Paul," "Châli," "Les soeurs Rondoli."** To these might almost be added as a special category the various forms in which M. de Maupassant relates adventures in railway carriages. Numerous, to his imagination, are the pretexts for enlivening fiction afforded by first, second, and third class compartments; the accidents (which have nothing to do with the conduct of the train) that occur there constitute no inconsiderable part of our earthly transit.

It is surely by his Norman peasant that his tales will live; he knows this worthy as if he had made him, understands him down to the ground, puts him on his feet with a few of the freest, most plastic touches. M. de Maupassant does not admire him, and he is such a master of the subject that it would ill become an outsider to suggest a revision of judgment. He is a part of the contemptible furniture of the world, but on the whole, it would appear, the most grotesque part of it. His caution, his canniness, his natural astuteness, his stinginess, his general grinding sordidness, are as unmistakable as that quaint and brutish dialect in which he expresses himself, and on which our author plays like a virtuoso. . . . If it is most convenient to place **"La maison Tellier"** among the tales of the peasantry, there is no doubt that it stands at the head of the list. . . . Every good story is of course both a picture and an idea, and the more they are interfused the better the problem is solved. In **"La maison Tellier"** they fit each other to perfection; the capacity for sudden innocent delights latent in natures which have lost their innocence is vividly illustrated by the singular scenes to which our acquaintance with Madame and her staff (little as it may be a thing to boast of), successively introduces us. The breadth, the freedom, and brightness of all this give the measure of the author's talent, and of that large, keen way of looking at life which sees the pathetic and the droll, the stuff of which the whole piece is made, in the queerest and humblest patterns. The tone of **"La maison Tellier"** and the few compositions which closely resemble it, expresses M. de Maupassant's nearest approach to geniality. Even here, however, it is the geniality of the showman exhilarated by the success with which he feels that he makes his mannikins (and especially his woman-kins) caper and squeak, and who after the performance tosses them into their box with the irreverence of a practised hand. (pp. 265-69)

M. de Maupassant evidently knows a great deal about the army of clerks who work under government, but it is a terrible tale that he has to tell of them and of the *petit bourgeois* in general. . . . In **"Monsieur Parent,"** **"L'héritage,"** **"En famille,"** **"Une partie de campagne,"** **"Promenade,"** and many other pitiless little pieces, the author opens the window wide to his perception of everything mean, narrow, and sordid. The subject is ever the struggle for existence in hard conditions, lighted up simply by more or less *polissonnerie.* (pp. 271-72)

"L'héritage" is a drama of private life in the little world of the Ministère de la Marine—a world, according to M. de Maupassant, of dreadful little jealousies and ineptitudes. Readers of a robust complexion should

learn how the wretched M. Lesable was handled by his wife and her father on his failing to satisfy their just expectations, and how he comported himself in the singular situation thus prepared for him. The story is a model of narration, but it leaves our poor average humanity dangling like a beaten rag.

Where does M. de Maupassant find the great multitude of his detestable women? or where at least does he find the courage to represent them in such colours? . . . They are a large element in that general disfigurement, that *illusion de l'ignoble, qui attire tant d'êtres,* which makes the perverse or the stupid side of things the one which strikes him first, which leads him, if he glances at a group of nurses and children sunning themselves in a Parisian square, to notice primarily the *yeux de brute* of the nurses; or if he speaks of the longing for a taste of the country which haunts the shopkeeper fenced in behind his counter, to identify it as the *amour bête de la nature.* . . . (pp. 275-76)

[Maupassant has] yet remained, for those who are interested in these matters, a writer with whom it was impossible not to reckon. This is why I called him, to begin with, so many ineffectual names: a rarity, a "case," an embarrassment, a lion in the path. He is still in the path as I conclude these observations, but I think that in making them we have discovered a legitimate way round. If he is a master of his art and it is discouraging to find what low views are compatible with mastery, there is satisfaction, on the other hand in learning on what particular condition he holds his strange success. This condition, it seems to me, is that of having totally omitted one of the items of the problem, an omission which has made the problem so much easier that it may almost be described as a short cut to a solution. The question is whether it be a fair cut. M. de Maupassant has simply skipped the whole reflective part of his men and women—that reflective part which governs conduct and produces character. He may say that he does not see it, does not know it; to which the answer is, "So much the better for you, if you wish to describe life without it. The strings you pull are by so much the less numerous, and you can therefore pull those that remain with greater promptitude, consequently with greater firmness, with a greater air of knowledge." (pp. 284-85)

The erotic element in M. de Maupassant, about which much more might have been said, seems to me to be explained by the same limitation, and explicable in a similar way wherever else its literature occurs in excess. The carnal side of man appears the most characteristic if you look at it a great deal; and you look at it a great deal if you do not look at the other, at the side by which he reacts against his weaknesses, his defeats. . . . Let us not be alarmed at this prodigy (though prodigies are alarming) of M. de Maupassant, who is at once so licentious and so impeccable, but gird ourselves up with the conviction that another point of view will yield another perfection. (pp. 286-87)

Henry James, "Guy de Maupassant," in his *Partial Portraits,* Macmillan and Co., Limited, 1888, pp. 243-87.

GUY DE MAUPASSANT
(essay date 1888)

[In the following excerpt from the preface to *Pierre et Jean*, Maupassant describes the aims of the objective realist.]

[After] a succession of literary schools which have given us deformed, superhuman, poetical, pathetic, charming or magnificent pictures of life, a realistic or naturalistic school has arisen, which asserts that it shows us the truth, the whole truth, and nothing but the truth. (pp. xlvii-xlviii)

The novelist who . . . proposes to give us an accurate picture of life, must carefully eschew any concatenation of events which might seem exceptional. His aim is not to tell a story to amuse us, or to appeal to our feelings, but to compel us to reflect, and to understand the occult and deeper meaning of events. By dint of seeing and meditating he has come to regard the world, facts, men, and things in a way peculiar to himself, which is the outcome of the sum total of his studious observation. It is this personal view of the world which he strives to communicate to us by reproducing it in a book. (pp. xlix-l)

Instead of manipulating an adventure and working it out in such a way as to make it interesting to the last, he will take his actor or actors at a certain period of their lives, and lead them by natural stages to the next. In this way he will show either how men's minds are modified by the influence of their environment, or how their passions and sentiments are evolved; how they love or hate, how they struggle in every sphere of society, and how their interests clash—social interests, pecuniary interests, family interests, political interests. The skill of his plan will not consist in emotional power or charm, in an attractive opening or a stirring catastrophe, but in the happy grouping of small but constant facts from which the final purpose of the work may be discerned. (pp. l-li)

[While] the novelist of yesterday preferred to relate the crises of life, the acute phases of the mind and heart, the novelist of to-day writes the history of the heart, soul, and intellect in their normal condition. To achieve the effect he aims at—that is to say, the sense of simple reality, and to point the artistic lesson he endeavours to draw from it—that is to say, a revelation of what his contemporary man is before his very eyes, he must bring forward no facts that are not irrefragable and invariable. (pp. li-lii)

The realist, if he is an artist, will endeavour not to show us a commonplace photograph of life, but to give us a presentment of it which shall be more complete, more striking, more cogent than reality itself. To tell everything is out of the question; it would require at least a volume for each day to enumerate the endless, insignificant incidents which crowd our existence. A choice must be made—and this is the first blow to the theory of "the whole truth."

Life, moreover, is composed of the most dissimilar things, the most unforeseen, the most contradictory, the most incongruous; it is merciless, without sequence or connection, full of inexplicable, illogical, and contradictory catastrophes, such as can only be classed as miscellaneous facts. This is why the artist, having chosen his subject, can only select such characteristic details as are of use to it, from this life overladen with chances and trifles, and reject everything else, everything by the way. (pp. lii-liii)

Again, in life there is no difference of foreground and distance, and events are sometimes hurried on, sometimes left to linger indefinitely. Art, on the contrary, consists in the employment of foresight, and elaboration in arranging skilful and ingenious transitions, in setting essential events in a strong light, simply by the craft of composition, and giving all else the degree of relief, in proportion to their importance, requisite to produce a convincing sense of the special truth to be conveyed.

"Truth" in such work consists in producing a complete illusion by following the common logic of facts and not by transcribing them pell-mell, as they succeed each other.

Whence I conclude that the higher order of Realists should rather call themselves Illusionists. (pp. liii-liv)

[Each of us] has simply his own illusion of the world—poetical, sentimental, cheerful, melancholy, foul, or gloomy, according to his nature. And the writer has no other mission than faithfully to reproduce this illusion, with all the elaborations of art which he may have learned and have at his command. The illusion of beauty—which is merely a conventional term invented by man! The illusion of ugliness—which is a matter of varying opinion! The illusion of truth—never immutable! (p. liv)

[Instead] of giving long explanations of the state of mind of an actor in the tale, the objective writer tries to discover the action or gesture which that state of mind must inevitably lead to in that personage, under certain given circumstances. And he makes him so demean himself from one end of the volume to the other, that all his actions, all his movements shall be the expression of his inmost nature, of all his thoughts, and all his impulses or hesitancies. Thus they conceal psychology instead of flaunting it; they use it as the skeleton of the work, just as the invisible bony frame-work is the skeleton of the human body. The artist who paints our portrait does not display our bones. (p. lvi)

Everything you want to express must be considered so long, and so attentively, as to enable you to find some aspect of it which no one has yet seen and expressed. There is an unexplored side to everything, because we are wont never to use our eyes but with the memory of what others before us have thought of the things we see. The smallest thing has something unknown in it; we must find it. To describe a blazing fire, a tree in a plain, we must stand face to face with that fire or that tree, till to us they are wholly unlike any other fire or tree. Thus we may become original. (p. lxii)

Whatever the thing we wish to say, there is but one word to express it, but one verb to give it movement, but one adjective to qualify it. We must seek till we find this noun, this verb and this adjective, and never be content with getting very near it, never allow ourselves to play tricks, even happy ones, or have recourse to sleights of language to avoid a difficulty. (p. lxiii)

Give us fewer nouns, verbs, and adjectives, with almost inscrutable shades of meaning, and let us have a greater variety of phrases, more variously constructed, ingeniously divided, full of sonority and learned rhythm. Let us strive to be admirable in style, rather than curious in collecting rare words. (p. lxiv)

It is the nature of the language to be clear, logical, and vigorous. It does not lend itself to weakness, obscurity, or corruption.

Those who describe without duly heeding abstract terms, those who make rain and hail fall on the *cleanliness* of the window-panes, may throw stones at the simplicity of their brothers of the pen. The stones may indeed hit their brothers, who have a body, but will never hurt simplicity—which has none. (p. lxv)

Guy de Maupassant, "Of the Novel," in his *Pierre and Jean,* translated by Edmund Gosse, William Heinemann Ltd., 1923, pp. xliii-lxv.

J. H. MATTHEWS
(essay date 1962)

[In the excerpt below, Matthews argues against Maupassant's objectivity, claiming that in his works Maupassant used narrative structure to project his own attitudes about life and that he deliberately manipulated the reader's point of view to conform with his own.]

We have witnessed for too long a real injustice towards Maupassant short stories. While his novels have gradually earned the respect of the critics—to such a point that commentary upon *Pierre et Jean* has become a minor, but eminently respectable, industry in academic circles—his *contes* have been set aside, though they offer a convenient and enlightening introduction both to the man and his work. It is to give some substance to this claim that this study of theme and structure in Maupassant's short stories has been undertaken.

A very necessary definition of terms must precede any such examination. The term 'narrative structure' is self-explanatory; I refer to the form Maupassant uses, and may reasonably be claimed to have chosen, as best suited to carry the theme he has in mind. But with the word 'theme' we must go more cautiously. In my examination of **"Pierrot,"** I have already suggested that the theme of a Maupassant *conte* is not necessarily the story it tells. The theme, as the term is used here, is the thought, idea, or emotion which underlies the 'story'. That is to say, the theme takes advantage of the story to objectify itself. Seen in this light, the 'story', the narrative structure, is simply an excuse, serving to invite the reader's response. This response will be the result of his perception of the *true* meaning of the *conte*. (p. 136)

It would seem that we can do much to correct the false impression of Maupassant's work which is prevalent, by grouping his *contes* according to another kind of classification, a classification which really is by themes—using the term as it is understood here. For, as I hope to show, it is only by approaching Maupassant's work in this way that we cease to find our attention diverted by suppositions regarding convenience, habit, negligence or cynicism on Maupassant's part. Much that has been readily accepted as valid criticism of his work drops away when we do so. And it is only then that we become aware of recurrent preoccupations, whose reappearance points not to facility but to obsessive compulsion.

Words as strong as these require some support and cannot be fully justified without an exhaustive examination of all Maupassant's short stories. But the validity of the thesis finds considerable confirmation, I believe, if we consider only a few of the major themes which characterize Maupassant's work, and examine how the obsessive themes under discussion are reflected in the very structure of the *conte* in which they find their development and a noteworthy enrichment.

There is, without doubt, an objection which presents itself immediately. To seek to establish a certain complexity in Maupassant's narrative structures seems to point to unnecessary complication of what is, apparently, quite a straightforward issue. After all, is it not true that Maupassant proposed a very simple plan for the writer of realistic fiction? . . . No one would question the fact that the simply rectilinear structure is serviceable enough in, for instance, **"Mon oncle Jules,"** or even in a much better story, like **"Une vendetta."** But we may fairly say that, to perceive the full quality of Maupassant's art, we must keep in mind that he was not always satisfied just to tell a tale. (p. 137)

Even in stories which follow a rectilinear pattern we frequently observe something of what I mean. The only adornment may be the addition of a preliminary section and of a concluding one: the story is 'framed' between an introductory section, designed to evoke a suitable mood or otherwise prepare the reader's emotional or rational response, and a closing section, through which certain crucial conclusions suggest themselves to us. It is these conclusions which embody the story's theme. And so introduction and conclusion are both necessary if Maupassant is to ensure that his readers become sensitive to the import of his theme, which is the *conte*'s justification.

It will be appreciated that it is not here a question of the means which Maupassant borrows so readily, to furnish himself with a neat *entrée en matière*. . . . A more pertinent example is **"La mère sauvage."**

Returning to Virelogne after fifteen years' absence, the narrator sees a burnt-down cottage which provokes from him the remark, "Quoi de plus triste qu'une maison morte, avec son squelette debout, délabré, sinistre?" It is in the passage from which these lines are taken that Maupassant evokes the mood he requires, so as to prepare for the tale of Mère Sauvage. She loves her son. When he is killed at the front, she takes revenge on the Prussian soldiers billeted in her house: she burns it down one night, while they are asleep. Proudly admitting her guilt, she is summarily executed. This is the 'story'. It is when we read the concluding section that we fully appreciate that this narrative is simply a vehicle—not to say an excuse—through which Maupassant seeks to express his theme, which does not become explicit until the very last lines: "Moi, je pensais aux pères des quatre doux garçons brûlés là-dedans; et à l'héroïsme de cette autre mère, fusillée contre ce mur. Et je ramassai une petite pierre, encore noircie par le feu." (p. 138)

The effect provoked by this narrative tone is reinforced by the final image with which Maupassant leaves his readers: all that remains of so much suffering is a blackened pebble in the hand of a stranger, suggesting all the futility and sterility of war. So that it is only now that we fully understand the function of the frame within which Maupassant has placed his narrative. Reported unemotionally by the narrator's friend Serval, the unhappy history of Mère Sauvage stands between the remarks which introduced the necessary mood and the final comment, which changes the focus, setting the

tale in perspective. The effect is to require the reader to view events from a distance, and thus to become aware of the futile waste which is one of the tragic consequences of war (one of the themes Maupassant was to develop fervently in **"Sur l'eau."**) The significant feature of **"La mère sauvage"** is this change of focus, which provokes reflection and leads the reader to the conclusions dictated by this *conte*'s theme. So then it may be said that it is the necessity to make us responsive to his fundamental theme which both leads Maupassant to utilize the narrative structure he uses and is the justification for its use. (pp. 138-39)

[The] effect produced by [several of the] *contes* is increased for any reader who is responsive to the deliberately symbolic value of the circular structure within which the narrative is related. Like **"Pierrot"** with its hole—the marl-pit—these stories are constructed around a central image. In **"A cheval"** and **"En famille"** it is the image of the circle which exemplifies the impossibility of progress, the uselessness of attempting to escape; the endlessly repetitive round of meaningless existence. Indeed, it seems fair to claim that the image of the circle is essential to a writer with an outlook like Maupassant's, working in the medium of the short story. A straight-line development typifies more commonly optimism—the sort of optimism expressed through the energetic progress of Balzac's Rastignac. It indicates—when not used for specifically tragic purposes—an optimism regarding the world (society) and man's place in it. In Maupassant, certainly, the circle is the symbol of defeat, of the impossibility of advancement.

We sense this unmistakably in **"La parure."** It is true that Maupassant does show us, here, people capable of energetic action and dedicated purpose. Placed in a situation which demands effort on their part, they are revealed to be capable of such effort. Madame Loisel devotes ten years to making good the loss of a borrowed necklace. So her example of patient hard work seems to be a salutary one. Indeed, the atmosphere of this *conte*—in in which a deliberately muted tone underplays emotionalism—is in contrast with the stories already mentioned. But this is true only up to a point; a point reached when the owner of the necklace reveals that the original was an imitation. In reality, then, **"La parure,"** although apparently developing in a straight line, so to speak, evokes once more a circular effect as soon as the ironic import of the tale is made plain to us. (p. 141)

[Maupassant's] main concern in his best stories is to involve his readers by any means which present themselves within the framework of the *conte,* and to leave us inescapably with the same conclusions he himself has drawn about life. In this context his frequent recourse to circular structures becomes especially indicative of his outlook and of the view of life he seeks to suggest to us. Similarly, his elaborate use of irony which sometimes, but by no means always, is allied with pity, tends to empty life of real meaning. The irony of our attempts to escape, the repetitious character of human existence marked by cruelty and inexplicable suffering—these are among the recurring themes of Maupassant's stories, just as they were major preoccupations in his own life. . . . (pp. 141-42)

It appears incontestable that many of the stories he wrote, apparently with such effortless ease, were not an end in themselves. They were a means, rather. Maupassant's activity as a writer owes its prompting to something more than the mere instinct for financial reward. He contrives, instead, to project into the world around him his own "sensation de désenchantement", in many typical *contes* which leave with the reader "comme une traînée de tristesse". This is why so frequently, in stories like **"Menuet"** and **"Amour,"** Maupassant concentrates upon the evocation of a mood—profound sadness, or nostalgia for a past gone for ever. (p. 142)

I think it worth remarking that the surprise-ending as it is used by Maupassant is rarely, as it is in O. Henry, just a matter of technical trickery, supporting a wry but shallow comment upon life. **"La parure"** shows that Maupassant aims deeper than this. In his work, the surprise-ending marks the moment of revelation, for the reader, or for the characters, or for both. This is the point at which incidents, attitudes, conduct, are all shown for what they really are. So that, although Maupassant quite often turns the device to comic effect, laughter is far from being the sole motive behind his use of this technique. (p. 143)

[Careful] reading can only strengthen our opinion that the fundamental impetus which resulted in his short stories was of a deeply personal nature, so that the techniques he was led to adopt stem from a genuine *pudeur* rather than from cynical indifference. Yet, though Maupassant succeeded in hiding his feelings, he could never manage to suppress them altogether. They are betrayed as much in his treatment of his material as in its choice. What others may seek to achieve by assertion, Maupassant wishes to infer by example. What others may try to prove, Maupassant is content to illustrate. His stories invite not acquiescence but complicity. Giraudoux's definition of the theatre as designed to convince minds already convinced permits of easy adaptation here. For we do not find ourselves succumbing to proof. Instead we feel ourselves to be recognizing, in the evidence produced with apparent negligence, the confirmation of conclusions we willingly believe to be our own. Pierre Cogny has shown convincingly how much of Maupassant's power comes from his being "l'écrivain de son destin". A detailed analysis of the themes and structures of Maupassant's stories might well lead us to the conclusion that the ap-

peal his *contes* still hold for us today lies in the fact that he is not only the writer of his own destiny but also of ours. (p. 144)

J. H. Matthews, "Theme and Structure in Maupassant's Short Stories," in *Modern Languages*, Vol. XLIII, No. 4, December, 1962, pp. 136-44.

EDWARD D. SULLIVAN
(essay date 1962)

[In the excerpt below, Sullivan provides a thorough analysis of Maupassant's short stories, dividing them into two main categories: the contes, or shorter pieces, and the nouvelles, or more extended short fictions. In addition, the critic explores Maupassant's major themes and techniques.]

The world created by a short-story writer has its own coherence, its own identifying characteristics, its own structure, but when we try to examine it closely we are faced with a set of problems that are quite different from those involved in the analysis of an individual play, a short novel, or even a volume of poetry. Guy de Maupassant wrote over 300 short stories in a period of about ten years, roughly between 1880 and 1890; and, while it would be convenient if we could take one story and show that it embodies the characteristics of all the others, to do so would produce something either highly artificial or hopelessly misleading. Maupassant wrote many different kinds of stories—different in subject, in length, in technique, and in their impact on the reader; his interest changed with the passage of time, as he encountered new experiences, and he rewrote and re-used just about everything that he ever produced. To deal with this large and varied body of work we shall need to examine carefully a number of representative stories and make reference to a good many others if we are to discover the full meaning and value for ourselves of Maupassant's singularly sharp-eyed exploration of the world as he knew it. (p. 7)

Maupassant has been undervalued for some time now, as writers and readers have preferred the Chekov-type story with its greater margin of mystery, its delicate, but enigmatic insights. It is not surprising that an age like ours, which cherishes its own bewilderment and prefers puzzles to solutions, would be rather scornful of a man who felt he could express some clear perception of a truth—however limited. He cultivated a very small garden indeed, but he assumed somewhat arrogantly, and somewhat inconsistently perhaps, that he could speak with authority in his own domain; and although he believed in neither God nor Man—and still less in women—without faith and without illusions, he sought endlessly to expose a truth that his own philosophy told him was not there.

If, in his stories, Maupassant strikes some of us as old-fashioned, it is not only because we have lived for some time nearer to the Chekov end of the spectrum, but because of his old-fashioned arrogance in believing that he could express his own intuition directly. The closer we examine his stories the more we realize that he did not seek to express in his fictions his puzzlement and his problems, but concentrated on communicating to us his insights. . . . His effort was to communicate matters that he knew something about, provide a brief look behind the mask of pretence that people commonly wear. When one reads a large number of his stories one can guess that certain subjects must have obsessed him since they recur so frequently; the question of paternity is one such theme treated with innumerable variations in dozens of stories, yet we learn nothing from the stories and very little from his biography about his own specific relationship to this subject. Similarly, many of his stories are concerned with hallucinations and madness, but they are written in a singularly lucid prose, and if we would learn of his own intimate madness we must rely on his biographers and doctors for our information. (pp. 8-9)

Maupassant's greatest virtue lies in the fact that his narratives sustain the readers' interest and that he develops them with economy and concision, selecting

Caricature of Maupassant.

'unerringly, unscrupulously, almost impudently', as Henry James put it, the precisely pertinent details and excluding all verbal flourishes or elaborate enumeration. But these are exactly the kind of qualities that make him seem all too clear, quite uncomplicated, and possessing none of those particular asperities which offer a handhold to critics and which abound in writers like Flaubert or James. Maupassant was limited, as we all are, but more than most writers he deliberately refused to acknowledge the existence of a moral dimension and denied anyone's capacity to penetrate deeply into the psychological domain. . . . Yet one is sometimes convinced that his limitations result not from a lack of a window but from an overwhelming fear of looking through it into what he guessed must be an unspeakable abyss.

In any case, he gives the appearance of being clear and uncomplicated, yet for all the apparent simplicity—perhaps because of it—he is an exceedingly difficult writer to deal with. We shall need to look clearly and unobstructedly at his work and re-examine the clichés that cling to him as well as the complexities which may be observed, surprisingly, in so simple a writer. (p. 10)

The severe domain of the *conte,* with its strict limitations of length, seems to put intolerable burdens on a writer: a slightly misplaced detail, a single false note can damage the story beyond repair. Here there was no room for the development which enriched his *nouvelles,* yet Maupassant worked easily and gladly within the restrictions of the form. By temperament he was inclined to strip off details rather than to accumulate them, to concentrate on the significant line rather than on the diverting image, to drive directly, relentlessly towards a single effect. (p. 11)

The short form was not an unbearable constraint for Maupassant; it was probably congenial to his vision of the world, which he tended to see in any case as fragmented, disjointed, partial, and lacking in fundamental connections.

Many of Maupassant's stories begin with a preliminary discussion or scene which serves to introduce the main action he wishes to relate. This technical device, called a framework or *cadre,* has been frequently used by tellers of tales in all periods as a way of establishing with some authenticity at the beginning of a story the circumstances under which it is being told. The author may introduce a narrator, either himself (or someone speaking in the first person) or another person, and usually he specifies the kind of audience which hears the tale. This is, of course, an ancient device, reminding us of the oral traditions of story-telling and pretending to simulate them. . . . Maupassant took it over quite naturally and used it for a variety of purposes, although many of his stories get along without any such introduction of a specific narrator. The framework involves also, in most cases, a concluding statement, some kind of conclusion drawn by the narrator or one of his listeners, which brings us out of the world of the tale and back into the society which has been listening to it.

According to one count more than 160 of Maupassant's stories begin by establishing the circumstances of the narration, usually an oral situation, although he had a fondness also for the device of finding a document which reveals its own story. That is to say, more than half his stories have some kind of clearly designated narrator, but it should be borne in mind that there are almost as many which get along without such a scheme. (pp. 11-12)

One can easily attribute altogether too much importance to this question of the framework and its function. As a fictional technique it has now a somewhat old-fashioned air and strikes the modern reader as an outworn convention; when used now it is most frequently handled as a piece of deliberate irony or to evoke a particular atmosphere. It was accepted by Maupassant as a congenial and workable convention which he felt no compulsion to use in every instance. . . .

Oddly enough, in spite of the extensive use of the narrator-device, Maupassant never built up a narrator who could be repeatedly used, and apparently had no desire to create someone like Conrad's Marlow who has a special authority with the reader by virtue of our familiarity with him and his ways. (p. 13)

Maupassant saw the task of the literary artist as something more than putting words together to narrate an action; the artist's great gift—acquired by diligent practice—is immediate perception of the undercurrents of life which pass unnoticed by others. His glance is more penetrating, simple objects are more revealing to him; the single glimpse of his friend in **"Le rosier de Madame Husson"** is enough for the narrator's imagination, '. . . et en une seconde toute la vie de province m'apparut'. An unexpected casual encounter, as in **"Un soir,"** may lay bare an abyss of violent emotions. His fondness for using the framework in so many stories may be nothing more than the desire of a man about to explore the depths who wants to leave a marker on the surface which plots his point of entry and to which he may return. Maupassant, as we shall see when we look into a number of his stories, is fearful of what his explorations might produce and hesitates before the vast uncharted regions of the subconscious or of the irrational lest he be carried away completely. The *cadre* at least ensures that he can climb back out of his own story. (pp. 18-19)

Like **"La parure,"** **"A cheval"** and a great many other stories, [**"Le protecteur"**] relies on plot almost entirely for its effect, the anecdote itself has an interest

and a meaning independently of the way it is told; Maupassant's art in such stories consists in keeping out of the way of the narrative as it plunges forward. This is a line-drawing: he strips off everything that blurs the line, and of character gives us only what is needed to support the tale. . . . (p. 22)

Maupassant wrote many such anecdotes on all sorts of subjects, frequently supporting or justifying them by an introductory *cadre:* **"Ma femme"** is nothing more than an after-dinner story and that is the setting he arranges for it; **"En voyage"** with an elaborate setting on a train is a sentimental anecdote which is kept from disaster by the sense of reality imposed by the *cadre.* In all of them he achieved, usually very skilfully, the line that he sought; the question then arises whether there is more that can be accomplished. Can he also achieve in this limited scope a greater solidity, a greater complexity, some sense of characters who might conceivably exist outside of their function in the tale?

Certain stories of Maupassant take us beyond plot and beyond the process of revelation inherent in plot into a domain where the dimensions are broader, the characters less single-minded, and where curious resonances are audible. In many of these there is a lack of that scorn and irony which marks his attitude towards the *conseiller d'état* and the unhappy horseman or that monumental indifference which polishes the hardness of **"La parure."** The narrator, canons of objectivity to the contrary, allows his sympathetic understanding of his people to be felt, a firmly controlled but evident tenderness and pity for the tricks chance plays and the way they bear their burdens. The counterpart of his disclosure of fakery is his sympathy for unpretentious honesty. **"Miss Harriet"** could so easily have become a satire of the English spinster abroad, but is a deeply moving portrait which, without seeming to do more than describe her actions for a brief period in a Norman inn, conveys the sense of her whole life and a sympathetic and pitying awareness of its meagreness. **"Hautot père et fils,"** is another where the humble people involved are treated with tenderness and dignity in a plot which could easily have been handled cynically or farcically: when the father dies, the son takes over his mistress. (pp. 22-3)

To abandon plot for the creation of atmosphere or mood, to suggest through seemingly purposeless dialogue or random details a world of feeling—this is the domain of Chekov, the kind of story which stands at the opposite pole from Maupassant's brisk anecdote. Maupassant, too, could create atmosphere and evoke feeling from the simplest scenes, and he has done so frequently; but he rarely let the creation of atmosphere carry the whole burden of narration, and we sometimes fail to see it clearly because we are busily following plot. A few examples will suggest ways of exploring an aspect of Maupassant's art that serious students of his stories could pursue with profit.

"**Amour**" is probably the most extreme example, being almost devoid of any anecdotal interest. It is compounded of two elements: the joy of hunting and an awareness of what love can be, as glimpsed in the behaviour of birds: the attachment unto death of the male bird for the female just killed. It is a powerful hunting sketch, a brilliant evocation of the bitter cold, the frozen swamp, the desperate discomfort, and the wild unreasoning joy of the human animal as he plunges back into nature. His ferocity is aroused for he is there to kill—and kill he does even as he observes with sharply contained emotion the affecting behaviour of the birds. It is a story which creates the same kind of direct communication with nature as the huntsman knows it that we find in Turgenev's *A Sportsman's Sketches* or, more highly developed, in William Faulkner's *The Bear*. (pp. 26-7)

The *conte* was originally a fairy tale, an account of something marvellously non-realistic, but this is too narrow a definition to apply to the wide range of stories written in the nineteenth and twentieth centuries and neither useful nor generally accepted as a way of distinguishing *conte* from *nouvelle*. Yet the *conte* never entirely lost its ancient feeling for the fairy story and supernatural occurrences, and such stories now form a recognizable sub-division of the genre. In Maupassant's work the number of stories devoted to the supernatural and the inexplicable reminds us that the *conte* in its original sense survives and that it has great significance for the student of Maupassant's stories.

Maupassant's earliest efforts in the short story, before "**Boule de suif**" was written and while he was still Flaubert's pupil, were more nearly romantic fairy tales than the crisp observation of ordinary life one would expect. "**Le donneur d'eau bénite,**" written about 1877, is full of well-observed details, but tells a traditionally impossible story—a child stolen by gypsies, brought up by a wealthy childless lady, many years later finds his true parents who are old and poor, his father having become a 'donneur d'eau bénite'. Here, too, very early in the game when Maupassant was only twenty-seven, the theme of paternity appears—the child discovering his parents—which was to be the subject of so many of his stories. (p. 28)

There is still another variety of Maupassant story which goes back to an earlier form of the *conte,* and which Maupassant handles with great brilliance. It is not the fairy tale so much as the tale involving folklore and farce, nearer in spirit to the *fabliau* than to Perrault. Many of the stories he wrote about peasants have this genial humour, an exhilarating sense of not being bound to the pretences of life and of dealing with unrestrained primitive folk whose activities are frequently situated on the edge of farce. "**La bête à Maît' Belhom-**

me" is a very funny story of the peasant who had a flea in his ear (literally) and of the efforts of all hands to remove it. The story is made up of wonderful dialogue and keen observation, has the atmosphere of farce and folklore but with a grand ring of sharply observed truth. (p. 30)

More directly related to a continuous tradition are the stories which involve, or seem to involve, the supernatural. Critics have generally been inclined to connect Maupassant's stories of terror, hallucinations and the supernatural more with his biography and his eventual madness, than with the very rich tradition of such tales. Without attempting to solve the biographical problem and without trying to explore the vast literary tradition behind these stories, they can be examined as part of Maupassant's concern for the old problem of appearance and reality, of his persistent effort to remove the outer wrappings, to take off the mask. We depend on our senses, but what if there are phenomena that our senses cannot perceive? His stories are a series of elaborations of such a hypothesis. (pp. 30-1)

Most of Maupassant's stories in this area are not about the supernatural but about the unknown. He was profoundly impressed by the notion that we are strictly limited by the capacity of our senses, that many things must exist which escape our imperfect organs. . . . It is a basic article of faith and leads him to an interest in all efforts to penetrate into the hidden mysteries of life, the whole area of parapsychology involving hypnotism, magnetism, mesmerism and the like. His narrators are usually sceptical men of the world, not inclined to be taken in by charlatans, and they seek a rational explanation for the phenomena they have observed. (p. 31)

His interest in the realm beyond our senses is closely akin to his interest in . . . humble suicides, for his deeply rooted assumption seems to be that the unknown when revealed must be horrible, and this is the source of his diagnosis of fear. It is not the realm of the occult, uniquely, but the sense that reality is even worse than appearance if only we could see it; and even more disturbing is the knowledge that our senses are *constantly* deceiving us. (p. 33)

The very powerful story "**Lui?,**" based on the themes of fear and solitude, carries us one step further into the unknown. This time a man, suffering from a genuine hallucination, sees someone sitting in his room, and this drives him into marriage in order not to be alone. It is not the supernatural as such that bothers him but: 'J'ai peur surtout du trouble horrible de ma pensée, de ma raison qui m'échappe brouillée, dispersée par une mystérieuse et invisible angoisse.' The story is completely credible; it does not depend on any suspension of disbelief, it simply suggests that there may be something more than meets the eye—something disturbing—and furthermore one's eye is not reliable. To say that the man suffers from an optical illusion or an hallucination does not settle the question for him, because what troubles him is that one never knows how much one suffers from such illusions or how radical is the error of the senses. At the bottom of the anxiety and even the madness that Maupassant never ceased to explore is the abominable knowledge that our instruments of perception are hopelessly unreliable. (p. 34)

Nothing that Maupassant wrote before 1880—a few stories, a couple of plays, a great deal of verse, some articles—gives any hint of the precisely engineered perfection of **"Boule de suif."** After years of laborious and tentative efforts under the tutelage of Flaubert, he discovered his real genius with a single stroke, and found at the same time the literary form that was most exactly suited to his particular talents. For **"Boule de suif "** is a *nouvelle*, long enough to allow development without undue haste, yet limited enough to channel our interest in one very specific direction, excluding the exploration of issues, however interesting, which would turn us away from the hard clear line which is relentlessly followed to the end.

That line is the simple line of a journey—a journey by carriage of a small group of people and for no great distance—in the course of which one small drama is played out. The thin line which Maupassant laid out between Rouen and the little town of Tôtes in Normandy becomes a taut string which he plucks with effortless skill to produce surprising overtones and resonances. He is not attempting here the complex counterpoint of the novel, nor is he bound to the simple percussive effect of the *conte*. Here he has a single string and a single theme, but he has time to work out the simple variations and suggest relationships with other themes.

The length of **"Boule de suif "** was determined in part by the fact that it was to appear as one of six stories by six different authors making up a volume to be called *Les Soirées de Médan*. (p. 36)

The theme of *Les Soirées de Médan* was to be antipatriotic, anti-chauvinist and anti-war. The irony and satire contained in **"Boule de suif,"** however, turn out to be directed not at patriotic sentiments as such but at hypocritical professions of patriotism by the cynical and the selfish. Maupassant wrote, as his character Boule de Suif acts, from a deep sense of national feeling and the humiliation of the defeat of the Franco-Prussian War. Reading the first few pages one cannot take seriously the doctrine of objectivity preached by Flaubert and adopted by Maupassant. The author makes no effort to conceal his opinions from the reader, and in fact he makes them forcefully and bitterly clear. (pp. 36-7)

It is a disturbing story because it is not about Boule de Suif 's activities but about the values a society lives by and the terrible gap between the values that society professes and those it uses. Everything is turned upside down, nothing is what it seems to be, and, although Boule de Suif is not that durable literary type, the prostitute with a heart of gold, she has a simple honesty that reveals the sham of the others. Maupassant's rage at the humiliation of military defeat is expressed in the savagery of his delineation of those who accommodate themselves effortlessly and profitably to that defeat. (p. 37)

Maupassant in his first important work sounds clearly the fundamental theme that will be heard in various forms throughout his whole career. He is obsessed by the difference between appearance and reality, between the outer mask and the inner face, and he saw his task as that of a story-teller who catches us by his art and by his narrative skill and reveals to us not life as it appears (as 'realists' are supposed to do) but rather all the aspects of life that are carefully and deliberately concealed from our view by convention, habit, ignorance or timidity. This is pointed up in a dozen ways, by images or brief references that ride smoothly on the surface of his prose; the French officers, for example, we learn from the first pages, although they are dressed in fine military uniforms, are really 'anciens commerçants en drap ou en graines, ex-marchands de suif ou de savon'. The phrase 'marchands de suif ' turns out to be a programme for the rest of the story. We learn, too, again as a thought suggestive for the coming action, that the inhabitants of Rouen find it prudent to be friendly with the German officers billeted with them, but maintain the illusion of aloofness in public. Maupassant hated masks—any kind of mask, even Carnival masks—and whenever he told a story he not only developed a narrative but he lifted a mask. **"Boule de suif "** was a general indictment and he was to spend some ten years in amplifying and illustrating that indictment, looking sometimes with revulsion, sometimes with amusement, frequently with little evidence of any emotion at matters long concealed and which many preferred not to have brought to light.

"La maison Tellier," another of Maupassant's most celebrated *nouvelles*, appeared in May 1881, just about a year after the publication of **"Boule de suif,"** and, although its chief characters are prostitutes and it does give some surprising views of what goes on behind the façade of respectability, the tone is quite different. Maupassant is not indignant at injustice and hypocrisy as he was in **"Boule de suif,"** but amused at working out the possibilities inherent in what is essentially a farcical situation. Again everything hinges on a reversal: prostitutes play the role of *grandes dames*, but it is all carried on in the most light-hearted manner imaginable, far different from the stresses and strains of **"Boule de suif."**

Maupassant, who gives ample evidence of being a sharply critical, even cynical, observer of the foibles of his fellow men, and who found little to admire in what he saw, reserved his sympathy almost exclusively for prostitutes, peasants, and primitives. (pp. 40-1)

"**La maison Tellier**" is a brilliantly conducted story: we are moved unprotesting to accept what the author chooses to put before us. He pulls us from socio-logical observation to what gives every appearance of being a comic narrative, to a zestful comic incident in the train, to a serio-comic masquerade, to a moment of deep feeling, and then a return by easy stages to the *status quo ante* after one last fling. (p. 42)

In a number of instances, some of which we have just seen, Maupassant felt that a given story had been told too quickly and went back to rework it, expand its dimensions, flesh out its bare bones. In most cases he improved his story immeasurably and found himself in the domain of the *nouvelle* where he left some very durable achievements. His ten longest stories are the most frequently remembered and include a remarkable proportion of first-rate tales; only "**Les soeurs Rondoli**" seems out of place and of radically inferior quality, and although "**L'héritage**" is overextended it none the less has a hardness and brilliance that wins our admiration.

Maupassant was a *conteur* as well as a *nouvelliste*, and we have divided his stories on this basis in order to observe the operation of his techniques in both forms. It should be noted that it is in his *contes* that the *cadre* or framework is extensively used; in his ten *nouvelles* he used a *cadre* only once, in "**Les soeurs Rondoli**"; and in several instances when he transformed a *conte* into a *nouvelle* he abandoned the narrative framework and plunged directly into the story without preamble. (p. 56)

The examination we have just made of Maupassant's stories, looking closely at some and gathering others in groups about them, has shown how frequently that author repeats certain subjects and how persistently a few major themes recur. The most strikingly repeated theme is that of *paternity* revealed or discovered, treated in all variations and from all points of view. Somewhere behind there stories, as well as many others, is the general theme of *betrayal*—betrayal in the form of marital infidelity, deceit of any sort in human relations. Closely related is the pervading sense of *hypocrisy*, of the system of pretence that society has established for the conduct of its operations. It is clear from the stories we have studied that the one great premise which underlies his whole art is his belief in the utter disproportion between appearance and reality—everywhere and in all forms. His stories are written out of a need to correct that disproportion, if only fragmentarily, to lift the mask of appearance, to expose hypocrisy, to provide an unobstructed view of a piece of the world as it is, not as it is purported to be.

Such a view of life, when held by an indignant optimist, generally results in high-minded attempts at reform. For Maupassant the result is sadness, and sometimes even fear; the reality that lies behind appearance is no more comforting—probably even less so—than the outer falsity itself. To lift the mask is not lightly to be undertaken by one who believes that the face revealed will be ugly. . . . This perpetual turning over of all manner of stones to see what is under them has even more serious consequences: the obsessive need to see clearly, not to be duped, never to be taken in, leads also to horror at the thought of what one may find. This is what marks deeply the stories which explore the supernatural and the terror that accompanies it and, as we saw when we examined them as a group, revelation can be terrible; anyone who seeks to explore the heart of darkness must, even as in Conrad's terms, be prepared to face 'the horror'.

In such a dark and disillusioned view of life, some relief is indispensable, and Maupassant willingly and frequently sought such relief, but even this is related to his basic vision. Not all of his tales can be attached to the theme of appearance *v.* reality or the lifting of the mask; often he liked to show those areas of human life where the usual masks do not exist, the lives of the simple, the primitive, and, above all, the peasant, who provides comic activity and undisguised passions. (pp. 57-8)

One has the sense that Maupassant is at his most relaxed in the many stories which relate the comical, farcical behaviour of peasants and in the stories, like "**Mouche**" written nostalgically late in his career, of the gay, rowdy life on the Seine, which was like everything else 'pleine de mirage et d'immondices', but a life gloriously uncomplicated. Here he relaxed, but for the most part, in story after story, the insistence on the main theme of the mask is obsessive. (pp. 58-9)

In Maupassant's view there is no way out of the trap: innocence which is ignorance, an uncritical acceptance of appearance, is intolerable; but disillusioned exploration of the realities of existence leads to sadness, bitterness and even to fear. The primitives are not really attractive in themselves, it is just that their violent simplicity is engaging; and the comic peasants whose farces amuse are the same grimly brutal folk who casually let a baby freeze in "**Le Baptême.**" As an artist Maupassant perfects his senses in order to reveal life as it is, but at the same time he believes his senses to be deceptive. He is haunted both by what he may miss and by what he may find, but all he can do is continue his exploration to the end. (p. 59)

Edward D. Sullivan, in his *Maupassant: The Short Stories,* Barron's Educational Series, Inc., 1962, 64 p.

SOURCES FOR FURTHER STUDY

Artinian, Artine. *Maupassant Criticism in France: 1880-1940.* New York: King's Crown Press, 1941, 228 p.

> A historical overview of Maupassant's critical reception in France. This work includes a bibliography of articles on Maupassant from European, English, and American books and periodicals covering the era 1880 to 1940.

Artinian, Robert Willard, and Artinian, Artine. *Maupassant Criticism: A Centennial Bibliography, 1880-1979.* Jefferson, N.C.: McFarland, 1982, 178 p.

> Designed to expand and update the bibliography listed above.

Ignotus, Paul. *The Paradox of Maupassant.* London: University of London Press, 1966, 288 p.

> Biography and critical survey of Maupassant's life and works.

Riddell, Agnes Rutheford. *Flaubert and Maupassant: A Literary Relationship.* Chicago: University of Chicago Press, 1920, 120 p.

> Chronicles the writers' friendship and examines the similarities of their personalities, aesthetic theories, and literary techniques.

Steegmuller, Francis. *Maupassant: A Lion in the Path.* New York: Random House, 1949, 430 p.

> Considered an outstanding account of Maupassant's life and analysis of his work.

Wallace, A. H. *Guy de Maupassant.* New York: Twayne Publishers, 1973, 156 p.

> General biographical and critical study explaining how Maupassant's "achievement was both the result and revelation of his life."

Carson McCullers

1917-1967

(Born Lula Carson Smith) American novelist, short story writer, dramatist, and poet.

INTRODUCTION

*A*long with such contemporaries as Tennessee Williams, Eudora Welty, and Flannery O'Connor, McCullers is considered one of the most enduring authors of the American Southern literary tradition. Although McCullers was originally categorized as a Southern Gothic writer due to her portrayal of social misfits and other unconventional characters, most contemporary scholars agree with Louis D. Rubin, Jr.'s contention that her protagonists function as "exemplars of the wretchedness of the human condition," as symbols of psychological isolation and the failure of communication. McCullers's characters are often androgynous, revealing the inadequacy of physical love to fulfill basic human emotional needs. McCullers explained: "Love, and especially love of a person who is incapable of returning, or receiving it, is at the heart of my selection of grotesque figures to write about—people whose physical incapacity is a symbol of their spiritual incapacity to love or receive love—their spiritual isolation."

Born in Georgia, McCullers exhibited musical talent as a child and in 1935 traveled to New York City to study at the Juilliard School of Music. As a result of financial difficulties, however, McCullers never attended Juilliard; instead, she was forced to work part-time while attending writing classes at Columbia University and New York University. In 1937, she married Reeves McCullers, an aspiring novelist, and in 1940 she published her first novel, *The Heart Is a Lonely Hunter,* which established her reputation and was highly praised for its maturity of vision and bleak but lyrical prose style. This book ostensibly revolves around deaf-mute John Singer, a reluctant confidante of four alienated characters who believe that he can comprehend their dreams and frustrations. Critics generally agree, however, that the novel's protagonist is Mick Kelley, an adolescent tomboy whose dreams of becoming a composer are thwarted by sexual discrimination and financial problems. While many reviewers initially maintained that Mick's decision to abandon her ambitions in order to help support her family represents a realistic and appropriate choice, most contemporary scholars contend that her acceptance of a mundane adult life symbolizes the death of her dreams and individuality. Lawrence Graver described *The Heart Is a Lonely Hunter* as "a parable of the human condition, of human isolation, of the craving to communicate and of the impossibility of communication; and also, perhaps, of the inescapable delusions attendant on the inescapable human need to love."

McCullers's marriage was often unstable, and she and Reeves were divorced in 1940 following their involvement in homosexual affairs. McCullers's second novel, *Reflections in a Golden Eye* (1941), is generally viewed as her reaction to the disintegration of her marriage. Set on an army base, the book depicts archetypal characters whose unfulfilled spiritual and physical needs lead to self-destructive, amoral behavior. Captain Penderton, a sadomasochist and latent homosexual, develops ambivalent feelings for an inarticulate private whose inability to initiate human relationships leads him to engage in bestiality. Fascinated by the feminine beauty of Penderton's wife, the private visits her bedside by night; at the novel's conclusion, Penderton discovers the private leaning over his wife's bed and kills him. Although *Reflections in a Golden Eye* received largely negative reviews due to its unsympathetic characterizations and unorthodox subject matter, several critics maintained that the novel evidences the intensity and candor of McCullers's best writing.

McCullers suffered a series of debilitating cerebral strokes beginning in 1941, but she continued to write and in 1943 published the novella *The Ballad of the Sad Café*. Often considered McCullers's most outstanding achievement, *The Ballad of the Sad Café* was described by Irving Howe as "one of the finest novels ever written by an American" and by Tennessee Williams as "assuredly among the masterpieces of our language." In this work, McCullers's characters serve to reveal how individuals seek out their opposites, people who embody traits they desire but cannot attain. The story revolves around Miss Amelia, a huge woman whose feelings of freakishness lead her to fall in love with Cousin Lymon, a hunchbacked dwarf. Although Cousin Lymon subconsciously despises Amelia, both for her physical size and for the pathetic nature of her love, his attentions transform her into a warm and caring person, and she opens a popular café. When Amelia's handsome ex-husband, a devious criminal, returns following his release from jail, Cousin Lymon falls in love with him, and together the men attack Miss Amelia, destroy her café, and leave town. The novella concludes with Miss Amelia, a physically and spiritually broken woman, closing her business.

The Member of the Wedding (1946), considered McCullers's most accessible and realistic novel, is primarily a coming-of-age story about Frankie Addams, a lonely adolescent who convinces herself that she will discover what she terms "the we of me" by accompanying her brother and his fiancée on their honeymoon and becoming part of their marriage. The novel, which consists largely of conversations between Frankie, her sickly young cousin, and a black housekeeper, encompasses such issues as sexuality, racial prejudice, and death. Frankie's transformation from tomboy to precocious feminine teenager exemplifies society's stifling expectations of what a young woman should be. Spurred by Edmund Wilson's comment that *The Member of the Wedding* contains "no element of drama at all" and encouraged by Tennessee Williams, McCullers adapted the novel for the stage in 1950. Retaining its original emphasis on theme, character, and mood, she created a stylistically innovative play noted for being among the few successful dramatic adaptations of a novelist's own work. *The Member of the Wedding* enjoyed a lengthy Broadway run of 501 performances, winning the New York Drama Critics Circle Award for best play of its season.

In 1945, McCullers remarried Reeves, but their relationship became increasingly hostile. Frightened by his insistence that they carry out a double suicide, McCullers left her husband in 1953. Shortly thereafter, he committed suicide. McCullers used both Reeves's and her mother's death as the basis for the central characters of *The Square Root of Wonderful* (1958), a play which many critics viewed as her attempt to reconcile feelings of loss, guilt, and hostility. Although considered one of McCullers's least successful works, this drama is valued for its insights into her life and techniques. In McCullers's last novel, *Clock without Hands* (1961), a bigot overcomes his racist beliefs after learning that he is dying from leukemia. Although critics generally conceded that the book offers McCullers's most optimistic treatment of existence, most agreed that *Clock without Hands* lacks the cohesion of her earlier fiction. Following another stroke in 1967 McCullers died in Nyack, New York at the age of fifty. Rubin has pointed out that *The Heart Is a Lonely Hunter, Reflections in a Golden Eye, The Ballad of the Sad Cafe,* and *The Member of the Wedding*—all written during her twenties—were McCullers's major works, and "a very impressive body of fiction indeed, adding, however, that "[n]othing that she wrote in the remaining two decades of her life adds much to her achievement." Nevertheless, her vision of human isolation has continued to inspire critical attention. In *Critical Occasions*, Julian Symons has noted: "It is her triumph that from her preoccupation with freaks and with human loneliness she makes fictions which touch and illuminate at many points the world to which all art makes, however obliquely, its final reference: the world of literal reality."

(For further information about McCullers's life and works, see *Concise Dictionary of American Literary Biography, 1941-1968; Contemporary Authors Bib-* *liographical Series*, Vol. 1; *Contemporary Authors* (rev. ed.), Vols. 5-8, 25-28; *Contemporary Authors New Revision Series*, Vol. 18; *Contemporary Literary Criticism*, Vols. 1, 4, 10, 12, 48; *Dictionary of Literary Biography*, Vols. 2, 7; *Something about the Author*, Vol. 27; and *Short Story Criticism*, Vol. 9)

CRITICAL COMMENTARY

IHAB H. HASSAN

(essay date 1959)

[In the following excerpt, Hassan explains the connection between love and pain in McCullers's artistic vision, linking her work with that of other writers of the Southern Renaissance.]

Since the publication of *The Heart Is a Lonely Hunter* in 1940, when its author was only twenty-three years old, Carson McCullers has been recognized as one of the most likely talents in the South. The next decade, which remains the most productive of her career, saw her established as an important writer who brought strange and artful gifts of sensibility to the contemporary novel. The strangeness, however, reminded some readers of Poe's artifices, and it persuaded them to discredit her fiction as simply Gothic. The judgment at best is hasty. It is true that Mrs. McCullers lacks the scope, strength, and fury of Faulkner, lacks his dark apprehension of the Southern past and his profound insight into the American wilderness, symbols both of our guilt and innocence. And it is also true that Mrs. McCullers, hypnotized as she seems to be by the burning point where love and pain secretly meet, foregoes a certain richness of surface which, let us say, Eudora Welty seldom misses. Still, the Gothic element, the personal principle in Mrs. McCullers' work, excludes none of the larger aspects of the Southern tradition to which it belongs. In his recent introduction to *Great Tales of the Deep South*, Malcolm Cowley has summarized well these aspects of the Southern literary mind: a mind preeminently aware of custom and ceremony yet deeply responsive to the elemental nature of existence, a mind anxious to preserve the sense of place and time, of family and community, of folk life and, above all, of oral discourse. Its basic assumption seems to be, as Robert B. Heilman has noted in *Southern Renascence*, that "The concrete evidence of the human being is that he does not change much, that he may actually be harmed by the material phenomena usually implied by *progress*, and that in any case his liability to moral difficulty remains constant." Formal and conservative, oriented at once towards the personal and the mythic, therefore symbolic, the Southern imagination seems determined to capture man in his very essence. Hence its marked antiexistential bias—"in the *ethos* of Jefferson and Yoknapatawpha, the essence of man lies in being, not in having or doing," John Maclachlan has said of Faulkner's country (*Southern Renascence*).

It is precisely within the framework of these assumptions that the Gothic imagination of Carson McCullers operates. Yet being Gothic, which is to say Protestant—for the Gothic may be conceived as a latent reaction to the Catholic hierarchy under God—being both Protestant and Gothic, her imagination derives its peculiar force from a transcendental idea of spiritual loneliness. The relevance of that idea to the work of Carson McCullers has been demonstrated by Oliver Evans in his fine essay in *New World Writing 1*. Our business must remain less specialized; it must encompass the whole spectacle of love and pain which constitutes her fiction, and in which the idea of spiritual isolation comes repeatedly to focus. For so broad a view, some provisional clarifications are necessary.

To say that Mrs. McCullers has a Gothic penchant is but to note, and note superficially, her interest in the grotesque, the freakish, and the incongruous. Such qualities, to be sure, exert a large influence on the contemporary imagination. There is another sense, however, in which the Gothic element may be defined more pertinently. The Gothic insists on spiritualization, the spiritualization of matter itself, and it insists on subjectivism. We have it from Erwin Panofsky that "Late Gothic art broke up into a variety of styles" reflecting the ideological developments of the Middle Ages; these developments were "unified by a subjectivism" which extended from the visual arts to the political sphere (*Gothic Architecture and Scholasticism*). The Gothic impulse is also transcendental: it reaches out in a piercing line to the sky. The distinction Allen Tate has made, in *The Forlorn Demon*, between the symbolic and the angelic imagination is here apposite. The first, like Dante's, is catholic: "It never begins at the top; it carries

Principal Works

The Heart is a Lonely Hunter (novel) 1940

Reflections in a Golden Eye (novel) 1941

The Member of the Wedding (novel) 1946

The Ballad of the Sad Cafe (novella) 1943

The Member of the Wedding (drama) 1950

The Square Root of Wonderful (drama) 1958

Clock without Hands (novel) 1961

Sweet as a Pickle and Clean as a Pig (poetry) 1964

The Mortgaged Heart: The Previously Uncollected Writings of Carson McCullers (essays and short stories) 1971

the bottom along with it, however high it may climb." The second, like Poe's, is both Gothic and Protestant: in a transcendental effort of the will, "it declares itself independent of the human situation in the quest of essential knowledge." It should not be difficult to see how the mysticism of Susó and Eckhart, the idea of prayer in Luther, the experience of spiritual horror without sensible correlative in Poe, and the Gothic nightmare of alienation in the fiction of Carson McCullers fall into a sombre sequence.

Protestant as the fundamentalist tradition of the South may be, and Gothic as its experience of guilt and tragedy is likely to appear, it is the peculiar stamp of subjectivism, wistful and bizarre, that emerges like a watermark on every page Mrs. McCullers has written. Such introversion, we are accustomed to say, is a result of the disjunction between the self and the world which contemporary life has magnified. The point is sharply made by Nathanael West, a past master of the grotesque, through one of the characters in *Miss Lonelyhearts* who says, "The trouble with him, the trouble with all of us, is that we have no outer life, only an inner one, and that by necessity."

The necessity is the wheel, the cross, to which the characters of Carson McCullers are bound, and often bound without hope of remittance. Yet it is only fair to add that her attitude is more complex than I imply. There is, of course, one sense in which Mrs. McCullers can be said to celebrate the lonely and the outcast, the frail children of the earth, those, like Singer in her first novel, who have in their face "something gentle and Jewish, the knowledge of one who belongs to a race that is oppressed." Adolescents and freaks are her rueful heroes because the first are as yet, uninitiated and the latter are forever unacceptable; both do not belong, and in both physical incompleteness is the source of a qualitative, and spiritual difference. And lonely as her characters are, encased as they are in their teeming dreams, most private of human expressions, their ac-

tions usually serve only to intensify their solitude. Their situation is, as Oliver Evans has noted, "not so much a comment on the futility of communication as it is on the undesirability of it." But there is still another sense, deeper and more significant, in which Carson McCullers can be said to underscore the inadequacy of subjectivism. The integrity of her vision depends on her guiding insight into the hopelessness of our predicament, caught as we are between dissipation of the self in a mass society—what Ortega called immersion in the Other—and dissipation of the world leading to madness or her meticism. For the novelist, who is compelled by the exigencies of his form to negotiate continually between the self and the world, the dilemma is an everlasting challenge.

The challenge of form is the measure of insight; the formal tension between the self and the world in the novel corresponds to the thematic juxtaposition of the power of love and the presence of pain in the vision of Carson McCullers. It is in *The Ballad of the Sad Café* that the doctrine of love, implicit in all her fiction, is most clearly enunciated. The passage deserves extensive quotation:

First of all, love is a joint experience between two persons—but the fact that it is a joint experience does not mean that it is a similar experience to the two people involved. There are the lover and the beloved, but these two come from different countries. Often the beloved is only a stimulus for all the stored up love which has lain quiet within the lover for a long time hitherto. And somehow every lover knows this. He feels in his soul that his love is a solitary thing. He comes to know a new strange loneliness and it is this knowledge that makes him suffer. . . . Let it be added that this lover. . . . can be man, woman, child, or indeed any human creature on this earth.

Now, the beloved can also be of any description. The most outlandish people can be the stimulus of love. . . . Therefore, the value and quality of any love is determined solely by the lover himself.

It is for this reason that most of us would rather love than be loved. . . . And the curt truth is that, in a deep secret way, the state of being beloved is intolerable to many. The beloved fears and hates the lover. . . .

Here are some consequences of this remarkable statement: To love is to suffer, to intensify one's loneliness. Love needs no reciprocation; its quality is determined solely by the lover; and its object can be as "outlandish" as the world may offer. Hence the grotesque nature of the objects of love in Carson McCullers' fiction: hunchbacks, deaf mutes, weddings, clouds. Hence also the de-sexualization of love since the love relation, often incongruous, does not admit of sexual communion. "By nature all people are both sexes," Mrs. Mc-

Cullers says. "So that marriage and the bed is not all by any means." Singer, Brannon, Penderton, Amelia, and the men-women freaks who appear in her fiction are all bi-sexual, which is to say a-sexual. Then, too, without reciprocity, love becomes a crazy whirligig, the object of one love becoming the subject of another—witness Macy, Amelia, Lymon, Macy, in *The Ballad of the Sad Café*. Finally, love as a pure attitude of the lover towards *any* object seems to go beyond Protestantism and to arrogate for itself the powers of God. As Tate put it with regard to Poe, man as "angelic delegate of God" is empowered to perform His functions: "not only is every man his own God, every man *is* God."

The Protestant element in disembodied love is as obvious as the Gothic element in the uncouth objects which love must choose. But by far the most startling consequence of Mrs. McCullers' idea of love is its avowal of pain, of *death* itself. It would seem that love, in intensifying the lover's pain, in precluding communion, and in electing outlandish recipients, seeks its own impediments. A revealing parallel is suggested by Denis de Rougemont in his book, *Love in the Western World*. De Rougemont argues that certain types of love which seek continually to defeat their end mask the fearful powers of the death wish. Boundless Eros, or transcendental Love, "despises Venus even when in the throes of sensuality," and whether it manifests itself in Courtly Love or Manichaean mysticism, it "intensifies our desires only to offer them up in sacrifice." Its real end is death. The omnipresence of pain in the work of Carson McCullers, the spectacle of a love forever seeking its own denial, leads us to a similar conclusion. Love, to be sure, redeems, but only provisionally. Pain endures. The single affirmative note is sounded almost accidentally, and it is sounded by those who simply endure: Portia and Brannon in Carson McCullers' first novel, by members of the chain gang in her last story. "Radiance" and "darkness," "ecstasy" and "fright"— these are the words with which the two works end, words that defy resolution. (pp. 311-15)

Ihab H. Hassan, "Carson McCullers: The Alchemy of Love and Aesthetics of Pain," in *Modern Fiction Studies*, Vol. 5, No. 4, Winter, 1959, pp. 311-26.

LOUIS D. RUBIN

(essay date 1977)

[In the following excerpt, Rubin explores the depiction of human isolation in McCullers's fiction, claiming that what the reader is most likely to take away from her works is "the way that it feels to be lonely."]

I think it is not without importance that the all-night restaurant in Carson McCuller's first novel, *The Heart is a Lonely Hunter,* is called The New York Cafe. In the small-sized Southern city in the late 1930's, when the story takes place, there is little doing at night and none of the people involved in the story is either very contented or very hopeful; the New York Cafe is the only place for them to go, and its forlorn hospitality is indicative of what is barren and joyless about the lives of those who go there. From Columbus, Georgia to New York City is a long way.

Biff Blannon's restaurant is presumably called the New York Cafe because of the ironic contrast between what it is and what its name signifies. . . . Set in the backwaters of civilization (as Carson McCullers's imagination saw it, anyway), the pathetic name given the all-night restaurant mocks the romantic dream with its commonplace actuality. . . . [The] inappropriateness of the name New York Cafe is meant by the author to convey a sense of cultural starvation, the provincial dreariness of the kind of city where the sidewalks, as they used to say, are rolled up each night at ten o'clock. As well call it the Café de Paris.

Is that what Columbus, Georgia was like? I suppose it depends upon the viewpoint, and Carson McCullers's viewpoint at the time she was writing *The Heart is a Lonely Hunter* was not exactly that of the Nashville Agrarians, or even of William Faulkner or Eudora Welty. Frankie Addams's view of Columbus and her own, she once remarked, were identical. (pp. 265-66)

In neither McCullers nor [Thomas Wolfe] is the hold of the Southern community upon characters very real. Neither is very much involved in the kind of historical tradition or community identification that writers such as Faulkner and Welty use for the stuff of their fiction.

A major difference between McCullers's South and Wolfe's is that there is no sense of Wolfe himself feeling trapped in it. He is going to leave. Carson McCullers's people are there to stay, and their yearning for something better and finer and more fulfilling has a kind of painful *angst* about it. Their yearning for the metropolis, as has often been said, is like that of Chekhov's provincial Russians for Moscow: for a place of impossible fulfillment that is too far off in time and space to represent anything more than a forlorn hope. (pp. 267-68)

In [*The Heart is a Lonely Hunter, Reflections in a Golden Eye, The Ballad of the Sad Cafe,* and *The Member of the Wedding*], produced over a period of less than a decade and while the author was still in her twenties, we have a very impressive body of fiction indeed.

That was all. Nothing that she wrote in the remaining two decades of her life adds much to her achievement. *Clock Without Hands* was an artistic disaster; only her most devoted admirers could say much for it. Whatever it was she had in the way of a gift, she had lost it. When she died in 1967, I doubt that anyone felt that she was leaving good books unwritten.

We are dealing, therefore, with certain works of fiction written and published during a period of intense and often brilliant creativity, by a young writer, a *wunderkind* as it were, one who did not develop or extend her range afterward. I think it is important to remember that. Whatever the faces and tensions that were central to her life and art, and which ultimately destroyed both, they attained, during this period, an equilibrium that made her fiction possible. (p. 268)

The McCullers fiction, I believe, has at its center a fundamental premise: which is, that solitude—loneliness—is a human constant, and cannot possibly be alleviated for very long at a time. But there is no philosophical acceptance of that condition, and none of the joy in it that one finds in, say, Thomas Wolfe or even Hemingway. The solitude is inevitable, and it is always painful. Thus life is a matter of living in pain, and art is the portraying of anguish. Occasionally, a character of hers knows happiness, but never for very long. (p. 270)

Mrs. McCullers explains it by her remarks on love, which she says involves the lover and the beloved, who come from two different countries. There is no way that such love can be shared, for one of the two must love and the other be loved; no reciprocal relationship, whereby one both loves and is loved in turn, is possible.

Obviously love in this definition involves possession. The lover, she says, "is forever trying to strip bare his beloved. The lover craves every possible relation with the beloved, even if this experience can cause him only pain." For this reason, she points out, it is much more desirable, and most people wish, to be the lover rather than the beloved, since the "beloved fears and hates the lover" who is trying to possess him. . . . Carson McCullers not only declares that it *must* be that way, but that the very nature of being loved, which is to say, wanted and needed by another, is intolerable.

Such of course is the scheme of *The Heart is a Lonely Hunter.* "In the town there were two mutes, and they were always together." Singer is the lover, Antonopoulos the beloved. Antonopoulos accepts Singer because it is convenient and comfortable for him to do so, but then he loses his intelligence and also his need for what Singer can provide, since as a vegetable he requires nothing outside himself. So Singer is left, bereft, loveless. As long as he could retain the illusion that Antonopoulos had a place for him in his affections, he could cope; Antonopoulos's very inchoateness and lack

of awareness were an advantage, since they permitted Singer to believe in the fiction that his love understood and returned.

Singer's self-deception in turn makes possible the self-deception of all the others. . . . So long as Singer will sit and listen to them speak their troubles, they can for a time at least function. Singer understands them only imperfectly; he depends upon lip-reading. The fact that he cannot answer back, cannot carry on a dialogue, is what makes him so satisfactory, for in that way the others are enabled to believe that he understands, sympathizes, and accepts all that they say and feel. In this respect, Singer fills the role of the beloved; he allows himself to be loved, because he is insulated from the demands and the possessiveness of love by virtue of his deafness. If he were not deaf, and thus solitary in a world of talkers, he could never tolerate the others, of course, and this not because he is selfish or mean—he is neither—but because he is a human being. Thus Singer serves the others as the object of their love (which obviously is self-love), while Antonopoulos fills a similar role for him, and the self-deception works—until Antonopoulos dies, whereupon the occasion for Singer's love collapses and he shoots himself, and the others are left stranded. The artistry is in the pain—Mrs. McCullers has never let us participate in the deception; we have witnessed it at all points for the ruse that it is, and when the arrangements collapse we perceive only the inevitable outcome of what we have seen developing all along. Again [as the narrator says in *The Ballad of the Sad Cafe*], you might as well go listen to the chain gang—which is pretty much what as readers we have been engaged in doing. (pp. 271-72)

[What I find most remarkable about *The Heart is a Lonely Hunter*] is that a writer whose imagination is so subjective, whose art is so suffused with emotional coloration and is based upon the capacity to convey the endless sameness of human suffering, could at the same time see and record and catalogue so much, with such clear specificity and concrete objectivity of detail. For one whose view of the human condition is so thoroughly pessimistic to be able to combine that with the kind of knowledge of people and things outside of her that surely stems from a considerable fascination in observing the varieties of experience seems odd, to say the least. (p. 273)

Carson McCullers focuses upon her maimed, misfitting, wounded people not as a commentary upon the complacent "normality" of the community which would term them freakish, but as exemplars of the wretchedness of the human condition. It isn't that freaks are commentaries or criticisms on normality; they *are* normality. Their physical grotesquery merely makes visible and identifiable their isolation and anguish; "normal" people do not confront these on quite such immediate and inescapable terms, perhaps, but they are really no better off, no happier. Everybody that is human is on the chain gang; on some the stripes and chains are merely more readily visible.

The particular vision of Carson McCullers, the capacity for recognizing and portraying and sympathetically identifying with pain and loneliness, could arise only out of a social situation [as in Southern communities] in which the patterns and forms and expectations of conduct and attitude are very firmly and formidably present, so that the inability or failure to function within those patterns seems crucial. If everything is permitted and expected, then there is no need to feel pain or frustration because one's own behavior and inclinations are different from those of others. But if there is a strong set of expectations, and one is unable to fulfill them and yet be oneself, then one searches out for kindred sufferers, in order to feel less lonely through assurance of their pain as well. Thus the portrait gallery of Carson McCullers' "freaks"—i.e., of those who must accept being set apart. And the conviction that this is the way the world goes, and no genuine human sharing is possible.

The appetite of Mrs. McCullers for viewing and identifying the details of human life, and the accuracy with which she was able to create so many sharply delineated people, then, was not exactly a joy in the richness and variety of experience, so much as a hunger for possession. It wasn't enough to see and identify; she had to demonstrate that, despite the varied surfaces and individually realized characterizations, they were really all alike, and what lay at the core of each was suffering and pain deriving from loneliness. One is reminded of a writer that Mrs. McCullers very much admired: Marcel Proust—significantly, a homosexual, as Mrs. McCullers was a lesbian. In that brilliant and profound panorama of men and women who appear in the seven volumes of the *Recherche du Temps Perdu,* each individual struggles to possess and to use others. . . . [At] the core of each one is the unsatisfied desire to possess, to use, to pleasure oneself through or upon (never with) others, and it is all doomed, for life in human time is meaningless, since everything changes and nothing remains. Only the art that derives from personal, involuntary memory can achieve meaning; art is *not* life, but its subjective recreation in the possessive imagination of the artist.

Something like this, I imagine, is what the writing of fiction was for Carson McCullers; art was a way of possessing. It was the creative act of taking what she saw and molding it, transforming it beyond identifiable shape into the form of art, so that it represented her kind of world. And I am tempted to say that, in the tension between the observed authority of the recalcitrant materials she drew upon and the powerful, possessive will to shape them to her desired meaning, the artistic equilibrium came that made her best work possible.

Her first book, *The Heart is a Lonely Hunter,* produced the most convincing and richest of all her characters, Dr. Benedict Maby Copeland, the black physician, and this is because, more so than with any of the others, there was a kind of palpable and inescapable social integrity in the material itself. With the other characters in the novel (and all have their individual integrities), the pain and loneliness were personal, subjective; with Dr. Copeland, there was added a specific and very formidable social deprivation. . . . Dr. Copeland is an educated, talented black man in the segregated society of southwest Georgia; any chagrin, mortification, rage he feels requires no dependence upon personal, subjective sensibility. Thus the kind of sensibility with which Mrs. McCullers invests him—the loneliness and anguish—blends so completely with the social outrage that the one gives body to the other. Each time I reread *The Heart is a Lonely Hunter* I am the more impressed with the characterization of Dr. Copeland. He is masterful, one of the reasons I . . . [feel] that the first novel is the best of all her full-length works.

I say this despite my admiration for so much of *The Member of the Wedding.* Frankie Addams is the most appealing of Mrs. McCullers's people; I like her better than Mick Kelly because she is less strident—less written, I think, to a thesis. She is what Mick Kelly would perhaps have been, had there been room for her to have a whole book of her own. In *The Heart is a Lonely Hunter,* the "Mozart" motif always seemed a bit incongruous and sentimental to me, as if it were somewhat forced upon the characterization. Frankie Addams has the same sensibility without the extraneous element, as I see it, and her struggles with pre-adolescence are entirely convincing and wondrously done—up to a certain point. That point is reached when, two-thirds of the way through, Frankie's sensibility moves beyond that inherent in her situation and becomes something bizarre and genuinely distorted— when the piano tuner goes to work and Frankie and Berenice have some kind of surrealistic, mystic vision of pain and misery. After that point, I cease to believe fully in the meaning Mrs. McCullers is (as it now seems) forcing upon Frankie. That's not Frankie as we have known her, and she never recovers. The novel, in other words, goes beyond the pain of pre-adolescent awkwardness and becomes truly aberrant; it drops off the deep end into distortion for the sake of distortion. The death of John Henry, for example: he seems to be killed off gratuitously, in order to provide more misery. And in the epilogue, when Frankie enters full adolescence, becomes Frances, and is made into a "normal" teenager, it seems too arbitrary, too pat. That isn't Frankie, either. (pp. 275-79)

[Her] two important artist figures, Mick and Frankie, cannot go beyond the point of incipient sexual awakening and yet remain consistent with their characterizations. These young girls, both with masculine names, remain fixed in pre-adolescence; when they have to become women, as they must, they are, as characters, all but destroyed. (p. 279)

Instead of her characters representing aspects of Carson McCullers's sensibility, they seem to have *become* her sensibility. Not only was the gap between life and art erased; the fantasy, and the suffering it embodied, were allowed to become the reality. Whatever anchor to everyday life had existed before, in the form of her childhood identity, her early experience, the necessity of having to fit into and live in a world beyond and outside her emotional needs, ceased to hold. The pain, the suffering, the yearning, no longer a commentary upon experience, were now the experience itself. (p. 281)

She could not draw from the pain and loneliness the truths that, in Proust's words, "take the place of sorrows," since "when the latter are transformed into ideas, they at once lose part of their noxious effect on the heart and from the very first moment the transformation itself radiates joy." For Carson McCullers this never happened. "She was never an intellectual," a onetime friend said of her; "she only felt." If so, she had reached a stage at which the perception of pain was not enough, if she was to go beyond the early fiction. But that was all she knew. There was, for her, no Recapture of Lost Time, but only *Clock Without Hands*.

Like certain other of her contemporaries, Carson McCullers, it seems to me, constructed her art out of the South, but not out of its history, its common myths, its public values and the failure to cherish them. What is Southern in her books are the rhythms, the sense of brooding loneliness in a place saturated with time. Compare *The Heart is a Lonely Hunter* or *The Member of the Wedding* with, say, *Winesburg, Ohio,* and the relationship with the region is obvious. Sherwood Anderson's grotesques are more simple; a few clear, masterful sentences and we get their essential quality. Carson McCullers must show her misfits, whether spiritual or physical, in an extended context; there is plenty of time for everything. The Southern quality is unmistakable, in the unhurried fascination with surfaces, the preoccupation with the setting in which the characterization reveals itself. Character is not for McCullers, any more than for Eudora Welty or William Faulkner or Thomas Wolfe, an idea, but a state of awareness. To repeat, there is plenty of time . . . and when the violence comes, as it so often does, it erupts in a place and a context, and it jars, queerly or terribly or both, the established and accustomed patterns. Before and after, there is lots of waiting, lots of time to think about everything. (pp. 281-82)

Southern literature is filled with depictions of characters who, set for one reason or other on the outside, contemplate the intense coming and going of a community life from a private distance. . . . [This] is an essential element in Southern fiction, and in no other Southern author's work is it more essential than in the fiction of Carson McCullers.

Surely this situation lies at the heart of her relationship with the South, and nowhere is it given more pathetic rendering than by her. This is what one takes away, most of all, from Carson McCullers's people in their time and place: the way that it feels to be lonely.

That is why her people do and say what they do. That is the source of the pain. That is why the New York Cafe keeps open all the time: "the only store on all the street with an open door and lights inside." And that is why her best work may survive. (pp. 282-83)

Louis D. Rubin, Jr., "Carson McCullers: The Aesthetic of Pain," in *The Virginia Quarterly Review,* Vol. 53, No. 2, Spring, 1977, pp. 265-83.

PATRICIA S. BOX

(essay date 1978)

[In the following excerpt, Box studies androgyny in *The Member of the Wedding* and *The Heart is a Lonely Hunter*.]

In *The Heart is a Lonely Hunter* and *The Member of the Wedding,* Carson McCullers examines the problem of spiritual isolation. Both [novels] portray as primary characters young girls who are sexually ambivalent, and *The Heart is a Lonely Hunter* adds a further dimension by including a man who struggles to deny his own sexuality and to become androgynous. These "androgyns," people who embody characteristics and natures of both sexes, uniquely rebel against the loneliness which is the twentieth-century human condition. Significantly, only the androgyns are capable of attempting to escape the isolation of man, whereas distinct sexuality erects a barrier to human interaction and stifles any attempts at unity and understanding between individuals. The androgynous girls of these novels move from adolescent sexual ambivalence to mature womanhood, but as women they fail to experience any hope for escape from isolation. The male androgyn, however, reverses the process: he moves from impotent manhood to an androgyny full of hope.

McCullers' metaphoric medium for expressing the ability to escape from spiritual isolation is music. Only the androgyns are guided by music, and only they are capable of lifting themselves out of the world of superficiality and creating a universe in which people genuinely care about one another. The necessary ingredient for creating this human unity is love, not a sexual love, but a love that denies sex and strives to encompass everyone equally. In these two novels, only the androgyns are capable of giving such love, and consequently any hope for escape from isolation must be hinged on them.

It is no accident that the female protagonists of both novels are given names that are commonly associated with the male sex. Frankie Addams of *The Member of the Wedding* lives up to her name by dressing like a boy and by involving herself in activities which are societally reserved for boys. Although she is sexually confused, she nonetheless recognizes the problem in her existence: she is alone. This perception of the human condition is expressed by Frankie's musing on her exclusion from her peer group: "Yesterday, and all the twelve years of her life, she had only been Frankie. She was an *I* person who had to walk around and do things by herself. All other people had a *we* to claim, all others except her." At this early point in the novel she has not yet seen that all people are actually in the same predicament; she merely knows that she is excluded from the superficial "crowds" and wants desperately to belong to someone or something. She envisions for herself a life with her brother and his bride-to-be, a life that would be rendered complete by the love between the three of them; but that plan has no appeal for characters of a distinct sexual nature. . . . She wants a life of unity and sharing, a life in which all people would care for each other equally, but such a life denies sex and consequently is rejected by the bride and groom. Only an androgyn is capable of giving the kind of love which Frankie gives.

While Frankie is seeking unity and escape from isolation, she is guided by music. McCullers tells us that "forgotten music . . . sprang suddenly into her mind—snatches of orchestra minuets, march tunes and waltzes, and the jazz horn of Honey Brown—so that her feet in the patent-leather shoes stepped always according to a tune." The music further foreshadows the incompleteness of her plans by being itself incomplete at times. . . . (pp. 117-18)

On [one] occasion, when a piano is being tuned, Frankie is stunned by the incompleteness of the scale which the technician plays. She claims that she is saddened and made "jittery" by the abrupt breaking off of the scale; we recognize these feelings as representations of the incompleteness of her dreams of unity. She sees herself in the future drawn into a sexual role which, by the limitation inherent in its definition, precludes the community for which she longs. The sexual nature of men and women prevents them from loving everyone equally; thus when Frankie leaves the world of androgyny, she leaves behind her hopes of escape from isolation. In the third part of the novel, Frankie the androgyn has become Frances the young woman, and the music which pervades the first two parts of the work

is significantly absent. No longer can she plan to extricate herself from the monotonous sphere of common people with common plans; no longer can she dream of a universe in which people give of themselves freely. With womanhood comes a friend, a source of identification for Frankie, but the false sense of inclusion which Frankie derives from that relationship makes her renounce her earlier perception of the human condition and consequently give up her plans for a better life. The conclusion is not optimistic; no androgyns remain to give hope to a world in need of selfless love and community.

Following a similar pattern, Mick Kelly of *The Heart is a Lonely Hunter* is an androgynous adolescent girl who finds herself alone in the world. . . . Although not as distressed by her loneliness as Frankie is, she shares with her fictional counterpart the love of music which serves to partially fill her emptiness. The most revealing passage in the novel explains the function of music as a symbol for the seeking of unification: "But maybe the last part of the symphony was the music she loved the best—glad and like the greatest people in the world running and springing up in a hard, free way. Wonderful music like this was the worst hurt there could be. The whole world was this symphony, and there was not enough of her to listen." The music hurts because Mick recognizes that isolation is the human condition and, moreover, few people seek any escape from that isolation. If more people were able to listen, as Mick is, to the calling of music, a summons to a communal life, then the symphony could be a realistic representation of existence. As it is, the music serves only to remind Mick that people do not seek unification and thus the symphony is a dream fated never to come true. (pp. 119-20)

[In *The Member of the Wedding,* Frankie's housekeeper] Berenice tells Frankie that she recognizes the plight of mankind, but from her limited point of view she sees no alternative. The housekeeper sees the human condition as a trap:

> "We all of us somehow caught. We born this way or that way and we don't know why. But we caught anyhow. I born Berenice. You born Frankie. John Henry born John Henry. And maybe we wants to widen and bust free. But no matter what we do we still caught. Me is me and you is you and he is he. We each one of us somehow caught all by ourself."

The androgynous Frankie, however, is not "caught" as are the other characters; she is perceptive enough to realize that through denial of traditional human values, those which dictate patterns of life by assigning sex roles, and through assertiveness and creativity, she can aspire to a better life. The "savior," then, in McCullers' works, is necessarily an androgyn. . . . (pp. 120-21)

[The androgyny of Biff Brannon in *The Heart is a Lonely Hunter*] has been mentioned by most of the critics who analyze the novel, but many fail to see him as a positive figure. The conclusion of the novel, then, they take as a passive acceptance of the isolation of man, and as such it is hardly optimistic. What is overlooked by that interpretation are the obvious changes which have taken place in Biff and Mick, changes which are signalled by the symbolic music.

Mick's dependence on music is evident throughout most of the novel. The change occurs when she moves from androgyny to womanhood, a shift necessitated by economic circumstances. Significantly, Mick Kelly loses her insights into the human condition at that time; the music in her head disappears and she is resigned to a life of mundane existence and drudgery. (pp. 121-22)

Though this change in Mick signals a pessimistic conclusion, the reader is not left there. McCullers chose to conclude the novel with Biff, for although Mick has lost her perceptivity, Biff is in the process of regaining his. Though he has been an androgyn throughout the novel, he has been forced by his wife to superficially assume the male role. His denial of that role is seen in his refusal to wash below his waist, a symbolic, and practical, method of avoiding sexual contact with Alice. After her death he takes a complete bath, an action which suggests his washing himself of the male role as well as his recognizing that he no longer needs to be physically repugnant. He then becomes even more androgynous, feeling no necessity to hide his sensitivity by conforming to a static sex role.

A character disassociated with music throughout the novel, Biff has been unable to see any hope for change in the human condition. He finds the male role distasteful, but he sees no alternative as long as Alice forces him to provide for them in the traditional manner. He has formerly been a perceptive individual, but marriage has brought loss of his music and his hopes. . . . Biff grows to love the androgynous Mick, as though recognizing in her the possibility for a community between people; but when she deserts the androgynous lifestyle Biff finds that he himself has become the only person with hope. The old song that he whistles near the end of the novel reflects his slowly returning perceptivity, and it is with this cautious ray of hope that McCullers concludes *The Heart is a Lonely Hunter.*

Both *The Member of the Wedding* and *The Heart is a Lonely Hunter* conveys the same message; only androgyns are capable of experiencing the sexless love that can ultimately unite all of mankind and change the condition of humanity from isolation to community. The choice of music as a metaphor for this type of love is particularly appropriate; music connotes harmony, and harmony between people is precisely what a unified life is all about. (pp. 122-23)

Patricia S. Box, "Androgyny and the Musical Vision: A Study of Two Novels by Carson McCullers," in *The Southern Quarterly,* Vol. XVI, No. 2, January, 1978, pp. 117-23.

LOUISE WESTLING
(essay date 1980)

[In the following excerpt, Westling studies crises of identity in *The Heart Is a Lonely Hunter* and *The Member of the Wedding.*]

During the heyday of Carson McCullers's popular reputation, the tomboy heroines of *The Heart Is a Lonely Hunter* and *The Member of the Wedding* established a type of girlish puberty which the American public could take to its sentimental heart. The success of the dramatic and film versions of *The Member of the Wedding* . . . insured a popular acceptance of the wistful boy-girl which never acknowledged the darker implications of sexual ambiguity hovering around Mick Kelly and Frankie Addams in McCullers's fiction. Some scholarly attention has been paid to the motif of sexual ambivalence in the two novels, but no one seems to have seriously considered the possibility of a relation between that ambivalence and the fact that Mick and Frankie are *girls* who share artistic temperaments and serious ambitions. Mick's longing to become a great composer and Frankie's interest in writing plays and becoming a great poet (or the world's greatest expert on radar) set them apart from other girls in their Southern towns, who spend their time reading movie magazines, primping, and having parties with boys. In Mick and Frankie, McCullers dramatizes the crisis of identity which faces ambitious girls as they leave childhood and stumble into an understanding of what the world expects them to become. The images McCullers associates with the crisis are the images of sexual freaks, supported by an ambience of androgynous longings, homosexuality, and transvestitism. Such imagery is of course directly related to the tradition of the tomboy so dear to the hearts of English and American fathers since late Victorian times. In childhood, a lively girl can romp with boys, wear boys' clothes, and cut her hair short. She is free to be impish and tough, a pal for her father, a temporary stand-in for a son. . . . But at puberty she begins to feel strong social pressure to conform to conventional notions of femininity. The girl who persists in her boyishness through adolescence becomes odder and odder, as social indulgence changes to disapproval. Dresses must be worn, manners must be learned, behavior must become restrained and graceful.

Major Media Adaptations: Motion Pictures

The Member of the Wedding, 1952. Columbia. Director: Fred Zinnemann. Cast: Ethel Waters, Julie Harris, Brandon De Wilde, Arthur Franz, Nancy Gates, William Hansen, James Edwards, and Harry Bolden.

The Heart is a Lonely Hunter, 1968. Warner Brothers. Director: Robert Ellis Miller. Cast: Alan Arkin, Laurinda Barrett, Stacy Keach, Jr., Chuck McCann, Biff McGuire, Sondra Locke, Percy Rodriguez, and Cicely Tyson.

Reflections in a Golden Eye, 1967. Warner Brothers. Director: John Huston. Cast: Elizabeth Taylor, Marlon Brando, Brian Keith, Julie Harris, Zorro David, Gordon Mitchell, Irvin Dugan, Fay Sparks, and Robert Forster.

The Ballad of the Sad Café, 1991. Merchant Ivory. Director: Simon Callow. Cast: Keith Carridine, Cork Hubbert, Vanessa Redgrave, and Rod Steiger.

As a girl the tomboy is charming; as an adult she is grotesque.

Ambitions are the psychological equivalents for the physical assertiveness of the tomboy, and again cultural emphasis on submissiveness and graceful restraint operates to discourage pursuit of professional, artistic, or political goals. These pressures exert themselves subtly, woven as they are throughout the texture of adolescent life. But they produce a fear that to be female and to dare to achieve is to venture into dangerous territory, to violate one's gender, to become a kind of freak. The girl who insists on following her ambitions almost inevitably pays the price of shame and guilt as an adult; she must live with a very troubled sense of herself as a woman because she has abandoned the familiar boundaries of her gender. (pp. 339-40)

Understanding these problems of self-definition, we should have no trouble interpreting the psychic paralysis of Sylvia Plath's gifted young writer in *The Bell Jar,* whose talent is rewarded not by serious literary regard but by a summer of luncheons and fashion shows on the staff of *Mademoiselle.* Esther Greenwood's real interests are drowned in a sea of cosmetics, flowers, perfumes, fashionable hats, and piles of flouncy dresses. This conflict between serious ambition and the pressure of conventional femininity is exactly the problem that confronts Mick Kelly and Frankie Addams in Carson McCullers's fiction. McCullers's portrayal of their dilemma is especially valuable because she concentrates on puberty, the time when demands for "femininity" are first clearly recognized, and she allows her protagonists to be more sharply aware of their choices than Plath allows Esther Greenwood to be. Esther is paralyzed because she cannot even look at the contrary impulses within herself. She tries to escape them by blotting herself out, in a sense accepting the verdict implied by *Mademoiselle's* refusal to acknowledge her identity as a serious writer. Mick Kelly and Frankie Addams have the immense advantage of tomboy self-reliance and a habit of scrappy assertiveness. This "boyish" past makes their passage into adult femininity acutely painful, but it allows them to confront their confusion head-on. Through Mick and Frankie, McCullers provides the most coherent fictional presentation of the problem which warps almost every gifted woman's life.

McCullers's first ambitious tomboy was Mick Kelly in *The Heart Is a Lonely Hunter,* the novel with which she made her debut as a published author. From the beginning of *The Heart Is a Lonely Hunter,* Mick Kelly is presented with a deliberate emphasis on her masculine appearance and her unfeminine ambitions. . . . Rejecting her older sisters' obsession with movie stars and continual primping, Mick dreams of becoming famous by the age of seventeen. She imagines herself as a great inventor of tiny radios and portable flying machines, but her most consistent ambitions are focused on music. She tries to build a violin out of an old broken ukelele, practices the piano in the school gym every day, and attempts to compose music in her secret notebook. At night she roams through the rich neighborhoods of town, hiding in the shrubbery outside the windows of houses where the radios are tuned to classical music stations. In her adolescent fantasies, Mick imagines a brilliant future for herself [as a composer]. . . . The images she projects for her future self waver from masculine to feminine, from evening suit to rhinestone-spangled dress, because there is no tradition of female composers upon which she can model her daydreams.

In fact, Mick's sense of romantic heroism is entirely masculine. The key scene tying her musical sensitivity to her troubled emotions is one in which she listens to Beethoven's *Eroica* symphony in the shrubbery outside a wealthy house. Originally written in Napoleon's honor, that symphony is heroically overblown like Mick's emotions. . . . Her response to the music is ecstasy and terrible pain. To alleviate this pain she resorts to a typically female kind of masochism, turning her frustration back upon herself. . . . Her response to the *Eroica* is shockingly violent. "The rocks under the bush were sharp. She grabbed a handful of them and began scraping them up and down on the same spot until her hand was bloody. Then she fell back to the ground and lay looking up at the night. With the fiery hurt in her leg she felt better."

Mick's reaction to the *Eroica* is clearly no voluptuous sublimation or misplaced pleasure but a frantic effort to release intense emotions which she must feel are forbidden. The circumstances of her musical life are fraught with guilt and the corresponding need for secrecy. Her musical pleasure is illicit, stolen in the darkness from wealthy people by a kind of voyeurism. Mick's own world has no time for her impractical addiction to the arts. Thus there is no constructive outlet for the emotion stimulated by the music, an emotion identified with her ambitions and sense of her own importance. So she turns all the energy upon herself, wounding her flesh to blot out her emotions with physical pain. (pp. 341-42)

Despite her independence Mick lives with profound anxiety. Like the young Jane Eyre, she expresses her fears in childish paintings of disasters, the most telling of them called "Sea Gull with Back Broken in Storm." She is haunted early in the novel by a nightmare which opposes her fantasies of success and prefigures her destiny. She dreams she is swimming through enormous crowds of people, pushing and shoving them out of her way. Sometimes she is on the ground, trampled by the crowds until her insides ooze out on the pavement. Mick's sleeping mind, at least, knows that the world will not allow her to succeed in realizing her dreams of independence and art.

McCullers makes us see that the smothering of Mick's ambitions coincides with her acceptance of adult femininity. The novel opens when she is a twelve-year-old tomboy. At thirteen she starts high school and is thrown into the teenage world of cliques and mysterious, clumsy courtship rites which are initiations into adult sexuality. Confused by the social rules, she feels herself an outsider. Boldly she decides to hold a prom party to end her isolation, and her preparations for the party take on the unmistakable significance of a ritual cleansing. For the first time in the novel, she shucks her khaki shorts, tee shirt, and sneakers and takes a long bath to wash the grime and indeed all vestiges of childhood away. She emerges for the party as from a cocoon, metamorphosed into the conventional female in an adult dress, a hairstyle with spit curls, high heels, and make-up. "She didn't feel like herself at all."

The air at Mick's party fairly crackles with sexual tension as boys and girls in unfamiliar plumage try to act their adult roles as dancing partners. When the party is broken up by a crowd of younger neighborhood ragamuffins, all the guests explode outdoors, finding relief in wild games of chase. The crowd erupts in a dash toward a ditch where the city is digging up the street. Jumping into the ditch, Mick learns with a rude shock how she is physically crippled by feminine clothes. The high heel shoes make her slip, and her breath is knocked out as her stomach slams into a pipe. Her evening dress is torn, her rhinestone tiara lost. Back at home, Mick realizes that she is too old to wear shorts: "No more after this night. Not any more." With her renunciation of these clothes, she renounces childhood and its boyish freedom.

Within a year of the symbolic party, Mick is trapped in a narrow adult world which reduces her to little more than a machine. She has a sexual initiation in the spring and soon after leaves adolescence behind, quitting school to take a job. Her first experience with sex occurs on a picnic with Harry Minowitz, the boy next door. . . . She does not like the sensation, and McCullers's imagery suggests why: sex destroys rational control and blots out the self. In a different way, Mick's job at the dime store shuts out her private world of music and stifles her fantasies. The long days of work leave her feeling exhausted, caged, and cheated, but she can find nothing and nobody to blame. At fourteen she is a grown woman whose life seems to have reached a dead end. There McCullers leaves her.

Mick Kelly was only one of five major characters in *The Heart Is a Lonely Hunter,* but *The Member of the Wedding* focuses exclusively on the figure of the ambitious girl. This time the heroine's ambitions are literary rather than musical: Frankie Addams writes plays and dreams of becoming a great poet. Her ambitions are not blighted as Mick's are, but it could be argued that Frankie's attitude toward writing has changed significantly by the end of the novel. However, the focus of McCullers's attention in this book is not on the protagonist's dreams of fame but rather on the psychological trauma she suffers when required to accept her femininity. (pp. 343-44)

In another work written during the years she struggled with *The Member of the Wedding,* McCullers seemed to be examining the consequences of androgynous identity which she had begun to explore in her first book. The folktale atmosphere of *The Ballad of the Sad Cafe* gave her liberty to create her greatest freaks—the hulking man-woman Miss Amelia and her twisted dwarfish lover Cousin Lymon. The story is a nightmare vision of the tomboy grown up, without any concessions to social demands for sexual conformity. This understanding of the grotesque extreme of masculinity in a female must have contributed profoundly to the undercurrent of fear McCullers creates in *The Member of the Wedding* through the image of the freak show which haunts Frankie's mind and indeed the whole novel.

There are several kinds of freaks which Frankie and her little cousin John Henry West visit at the Chattahoochee Exposition. She is afraid of all of them, but Ellen Moers is right to single out the hermaphrodite as the most important, for it is the quint-essential symbol of Frankie's danger. Images of sexual ambivalence are carefully cultivated throughout the novel in the Negro transvestite Lily Mae Jenkins, the Utopias invented by Frankie and John Henry where one could change sex at will or be half male and half female, and John Henry's interest in dolls and dressing in women's clothes. Always such hermaphroditic or androgynous references are placed in a negative frame, for the novel's entire movement is towards Frankie's ultimate submission to the inexorable demand that she accept her sex as female. . . . Children may play at exchanging sex roles, but adults may not, unless they are to be regarded as grotesques fit only for sideshow displays.

This truth begins to force itself upon Frankie Addams in the "green and crazy summer" of her twelfth year. "Frankie had become an unjoined person who hung around in doorways, and she was afraid." McCullers emphasizes the element of fear so rhythmically that the novel's opening pages swim in a fevered, hallucinatory atmosphere. The central setting is the sad and ugly kitchen like the room of a crazy house, its walls covered with John Henry's freakish drawings. Here a vague terror squeezes Frankie's heart. And here she, Berenice, and John Henry constitute a strange family or private world cut off from any other. The real doorway where Frankie lingers in baffled fright is the passage between childhood and the clearly defined sexual world of grown-ups which she must enter, for almost all of the specific sources of her anxiety turn out to be sexual. The older girls who have shut her out of their club are preoccupied with boys and gossip about adult sex which Frankie angrily dismisses as "nasty lies." Yet even she has participated in a secret and unknown sin with a neighborhood boy in his garage, and she is sickened with guilt. (pp. 345-46)

McCullers uses the motif of unfinished music to underline and intensify Frankie's dilemma, suggesting the proper resolution to her confused view of herself. In Part I, Frankie hears a grieving blues tune on "the sad horn of some colored boy" at night. The disembodied sound expresses her own feelings, for she herself is a piece of unfinished music. Just as the tune approaches its conclusion, the horn suddenly stops playing. The music's incompleteness drives Frankie wild, trapping inside her the unbearable emotions it has drawn to a focus. Like Mick Kelly, Frankie tries to find release through masochism, beating her head with her fist, as she will do again several times in the story. When she changes her name to the romantic F. Jasmine in Part Two and waltzes around town in a dress, telling everyone she meets that her brother and his bride will take her away with them on their wedding trip, the unfinished music is resolved in her mind. Her stories about the wedding sound inside her "as the last chord of a guitar murmurs a long time after the strings are struck." Unfortunately her fantasies of the wedding are doomed to disappointment. We know this long before the event because McCullers returns to the motif of unfinished music, this time in the sound made by a piano tuner at work, which embodies F. Jasmine's romantic dream. "Then in a *dreaming way* a chain of chords climbed slowly upward *like a flight of castle stairs:* but just at the end, when the eighth chord should have sounded and the

scale made complete, there was a stop" (My italics). (p. 346)

The meaning of the unfinished music is closely linked to Frankie's spiritual kinship with the blacks of her little Southern town. Both are made clear in the person of Honey Brown, Berenice's young, light-skinned foster brother. Too intelligent and restless to live comfortably in the circumscribed world of Sugarville, the black section of town, he periodically explodes. . . . [The] real cause of Honey's problems is the fact that he, like Frankie, does not fit the categories imposed on him by his Southern town.

Frankie shares a sense of entrapment with Honey and Berenice, but hers is not finally as severe, even though it is more vividly realized in the novel. At first she longs to escape from her hot, stultified town to the cold, snowy peace of Alaska. At the end of Part One, however, she fixes on the wedding in Winter Hill as the means of escape. The old question of who she is and what she will become ceases to torment her when she decides to be a member of the wedding and go out into the world with her brother and his bride. This absurd fantasy is a denial of the adult sexuality which Frankie cannot bear to acknowledge, but her attraction to it is obvious in her infatuation with the engaged couple. McCullers associates the returning motif of unfinished music with the imagery of prison to show that F. Jasmine's romantic dream will not bring escape. (p. 347)

Frankie is caught in a blossoming female body which she must recognize and accept. She must also face the fact that grown men and women make love, and that her body makes her desirable to men. As a younger child she had unwittingly walked in on the lovemaking of a man and his wife who were boarders in her house. Uncomprehending, she thought the man was having a fit. Even at twelve she does not understand the nature of his convulsions, just as she refuses to listen to the "nasty lies" of the older girls and tries not to think of her own wicked experience in the neighbor boy's garage. This innocence makes her dangerously vulnerable when as F. Jasmine she wanders through the town looking older and wiser than her years. The toughness that had served her well as a tomboy betrays her now, so that the soldier she meets in the Blue Moon Cafe assumes she is willing to be seduced. F. Jasmine is paralyzed with horror as the soldier embraces her in his cheap hotel room. She feels she is in the Crazy House at the fair or in the insane asylum at Milledgeville. At the last minute she knocks him out with a pitcher and makes her getaway down the fire escape. Not until late the next night, after the disaster of the wedding, does her mind accept the meaning of this encounter and its relation to her veiled sexual memories and anxieties. By then her brother and his bride have rejected her, and she has suffered the humiliation of being pulled screaming from the steering wheel of their car. Back home, she has made a futile attempt to run away and has been recovered by her father in the Blue Moon Cafe where she had felt she was drowning.

The Member of the Wedding ends in a new world, with Frances reborn as a giddy adolescent. The environment of her childhood has been dismantled completely—John Henry has died horribly of meningitis, Berenice has resigned herself to marriage and quit her job, and Frances is preparing to move to a new house with her father. The final scene takes place in the kitchen, now remodeled so that it is unrecognizable, where Frances is making dainty sandwiches to serve her new soul-mate, an artistic girl two years her senior. No longer a frightened alien, she is united with her friend through a mutual infatuation with poetry and art. (pp. 348-49)

The price for this relief from the tensions of strangeness has been high, perhaps too high. Frances is less attractive at the end of the novel than she was as frightened tomboy Frankie. She has become a silly girl who no longer produces her own juvenile works of art—the shows and plays she used to write—but instead gushes sentimental nonsense about the Great Masters. The hard edge of her mind is gone, and all that is left is froth. The struggle against conformity which had identified her with Honey Brown had been a struggle to assert artistic sensibility and intelligence in a world which refused to accept those qualities in a woman or a black man. Honey had expressed his needs by learning French and playing the trumpet, but his music remained unfinished, and he ended up in prison for trying to "bust free" of the narrow limits around his life. Frances avoids such drastic disappointment by giving up and hiding beneath the protective coloration of giddy young womanhood. But if Frances's intelligence is not destroyed, we might speculate that like Sylvia Plath or Adrienne Rich she will someday feel the old conflict again and awaken to a fearful "sense of drift, of being pulled along on a current which called itself my destiny, but in which I seemed to be losing touch with whoever I had been, with the girl who had experienced her own will and energy almost ecstatically at times. . . ." Without McCullers's two portraits of the artistic twelve-year-old girl and her telling images of sexual freakishness, we could never understand so clearly why "a thinking woman sleeps with monsters" or how those monsters function in the minds of talented girls emerging from childhood. (pp. 349-50)

Louise Westling, "Carson McCullers's Tomboys," in *The Southern Humanities Review,* Vol. XIV, No. 4, Fall, 1980, pp. 339-50.

SAMUEL CHASE COALE
(essay date 1985)

[In the following excerpt, Coale links McCullers's works to those of Nathaniel Hawthorne, noting their similar visions of "the dark labyrinth of the human heart and the brotherhood of all men bound to their separate but equal fates."]

Literary modernism seems tailor-made for the vision and techniques of Hawthorne's romance, thus opening new vistas to that older literary form. The individual self's battle against his/her own consciousness and the primitive world which both surrounds and is embodied within that consciousness rekindles Hawthorne's Manichean vision with a vengeance. Hearts of darkness and haunted minds appear inseparable, just as mythic methods encompass the character's or author's consciousness as the doomed shadow of the past encompassed Hawthorne's. A world of moments produces a literary landscape of scaffold epiphanies, those same episodic tableaux that surface again and again in Hawthorne and Melville, and the poetic spell of language seduces the reader once again into darker "neutral territories" of fevered minds and distraught souls. Isolation and disconnection, those staples of the failed rescues of Hawthorne's romance, thrive in the often imprisoning banks of the stream of consciousness, and the threat of solipsism lurks within every imaginary rush and turn. (pp. 65-6)

"I suppose my central theme is the theme of spiritual isolation," Carson McCullers once said. "I have always felt alone." Her rural South of mill towns and fly-specked cafes, the Columbus, Georgia, of her youth, suggests Hawthorne's Salem in its sense of decay, her vision of alienation and loss more keenly felt, perhaps, in a society which still prized community and tradition. In such a vacuum her characters seem driven inward to a world of private reverie and dream, in her darker fictions into a world of nightmare.

Narcissism plagues McCullers's characters, whether children or adults. An unrelenting solipsism darkens as her people age, the spontaneity of childhood lost in the blind pursuits of adulthood. Sex fuels a gothic world, a place ruled by psychological determinisms, separate selves locked into their fierce habits and obsessions. Her creatures seem possessed by alien forces, the unconscious motivations of lonely, alienated souls, characters fumbling within the primitive mainstream of modernist art. Hence the sense of dread that stalks McCullers's landscape, "that Sense of the Awful" that Tennessee Williams described, "which is the desperate black root of nearly all significant modern art." Individuals are trapped in a gothic Manichean world that knows no exit. At her best McCullers captures that world, unmarred by the adolescent sentimentalities of *The Heart Is a Lonely Hunter* and *The Member of the Wedding,* where child-heroes thrive in an asexual realm still open to the possibilities of a life lived along a sensitive, vague edge.

McCullers referred to art as a "flowering dream," the reflection of her vision of the world around her. Her best books reflect that dreamworld, the territory of romance akin in kind to Hawthorne's and Faulkner's. That dreamworld also reflects the modernist forms of Eliot's *The Waste Land* with its emphasis on cyclical patterns and its individuals trapped in mythic repetitions in a world that has lost any recognition of the possible liberating visions of ancient mythic rebirths and renewals. The psychological determinism of McCullers's fictional world approaches ritual in its ceremonial scenes and intensifies, just as the characters in a romance spill over into the world of allegory, creatures of a metaphoric design that rules their lives and their actions. These often parallel Hawthorne's romantic designs in form if not in style.

McCullers's style for the most part remains objective and concrete in an imagistic manner. The bizarre events and characters in *Reflections in a Golden Eye,* for instance, are reported in an almost clinical manner, as though the writer were viewing her world through a jeweler's eyepiece, with that sharply focused clarity of the imagist poet. Consequently her world ultimately reflects Poe's more than it does Hawthorne's. Any moral sense is replaced by the cold eye dispassionately watching the playing out of events, the setting up of confrontations, the psychic inevitabilities of warring opposites and inner frustrations. The battle between will and instinct rages. The trap of the world is complete in a claustrophobic Manichean manner. And McCullers becomes "a peacock of a sort of ghastly green. With one immense golden eye. And in it these reflections of something tiny and . . . grotesque."

Reflections in a Golden Eye, McCullers's second book, reveals that descent into a nightmare world that Frye describes as the dark romance, in which "life [is] so intolerable that it must end either in tragedy or in a permanent escape." Identities crumble; personal actions become restricted, locked into a world of mirrors and self-reflections; sudden metamorphoses—the Captain's passion for Williams—occur; animals, such as Leonora's horse Firebird, become companions and express a kind of freedom human beings cannot; and the whole is represented by a "symbolic visual emblem," like the scarlet letter or in this case the golden eye of the painted peacock. Imprisonment sets the tone of the entire book, and the inevitable demonic recognition leads to "the realization that only death is certain."

Faulkner's South falls in upon itself, a black hole absorbing all the light within it.

Of the book, McCullers said that once "relieved of the moral and physical strain of *The Heart Is a Lonely Hunter* I wrote *Reflections in a Golden Eye* in the spirit of a somewhat ghostly plane. . . . It's really a fairy story—everything is done very lightly." Nightmare would be more to the point. The withdrawn setting, the territory of romance, appears immediately: "An army post in peace time is a dull place. Things happen, but then they happen over and over again. . . . all is designed according to a certain rigid pattern." Monotony engenders violent and bizarre action; the rigid caste system with its traditions of rank and service, the Old South in microcosm, breeds hostility and envy, the kind of social protest all romances create against the more conservative, realistic world of the novels Hawthorne described. The emphasis on patterns throughout the book primes the reader to discover allegorical designs, just as McCullers's description of her tale like ingredients in a recipe . . . draws attention to the modernist objectivity and external, dramatic "reporting" of her style.

The atmosphere of the book includes intense gloom and explosive light. Captain Penderton's wild ride on Firebird occurs in a dark wood, the same sanctuary from the post where Private Williams suns himself naked. "Green shadowy moonlight" haunts the tale, as well as that "misty lavender glow" after sunset with "a hint of darkness . . . already in the air."

Reflections abound and reverberate. Firebird's name suggests the phoenix, the opposite of Anacleto's golden-eyed peacock. A drugged Penderton feels the presence of "a great dark bird . . . with fierce, golden eyes . . . enfold[ing] him in his dark wings." Penderton glimpses himself as a small grotesque doll, "mean of countenance and grotesque in form," and he resembles a broken doll when he tumbles off Firebird in the forest. Such images reinforce the gothic claustrophobia of the army post, of McCullers's alienated characters, of the world as prison and pit.

But it is the sheer Manichean vision of *Reflections in a Golden Eye* that drives this fictional nightmare. Polarities abound, redouble, repeat, mirror one another. Captain Penderton and Private Williams: a warped aesthetic will and subconscious instinct. Penderton broods on homosexual desires, demands orderliness and rigidity in all his actions, thinks of death and withdrawal. Williams displays the "strange rapt face of a Gauguin primitive" and thrives on naked sojourns in the woods. . . . Penderton's wild ride on Firebird, convincing him that death is near, explodes into "a great mad joy," a mystic delight in physical motion on the edge of extinction. His fall and his subsequent vision of the naked Williams, who can soothe and control the wayward horse in a way Penderton cannot, produces that sudden metamorphosis from smoldering ascetic to passionate lover, and he stalks Williams on the post after their return to it.

If Williams is the Caliban of the fable, Anacleto, Alison Langdon's houseboy, is the Ariel, a "rare bird" who ritualizes everything in his delicate Filipino manner and hates the people he must associate with. If Williams suggests unformed natural impulse tainted with violence and voyeurism, Anacleto represents the other pole of consciousness, the too-refined, artificially artistic will. Each is impotent; each is confined in his own world; each suggests the poles of consciousness between which the Pendertons and the Langdons struggle for self-gratification and fulfillment. And each of these couples reflects the Manichean battle between flesh and spirit, a precarious balance and an ongoing war that is "resolved" only by Leonora Penderton's affair with Morris Langdon. (pp. 79-82)

The mind itself is at war with itself: "The mind is like a richly woven tapestry in which the colors are distilled from the experience of the senses, and the design drawn from the convolutions of the intellect. The mind of Private Williams was imbued with various colors of strange tones, but it was without delineation, void of form." Design battles colors; the intellect battles the senses. And in the end, will murders instinct, Penderton kills Williams: "The Captain had slumped against the wall. In his queer, coarse wrapper he resembled a broken and dissipated monk. Even in death the body of the soldier still had the look of warm, animal comfort." Monk and animal: a final Manichean split. The rigid pattern is complete.

In *The Ballad of the Sad Cafe,* perhaps McCullers's masterpiece, the nightmare realm continues, a place where tradition exists only unconsciously as a series of habits and empty rituals. It is a world trapped in a meaningless and therefore grotesque present, resulting in a labyrinth of dark corridors and Manichean gestures. Strange signs and superstitions permeate this world, as they do in old ballads and folk tales: numbers, events, beliefs, a witch's brew. Narcissism triumphs. Lovers love those who love others in a complete circle of disconnection. The imprisonment of *Reflections* conquers all.

"The Twelve Mortal Men" is McCullers's choral conclusion to her ballad. Here the chain gang is working, and yet from them arises a melody that can be heard, and has been heard constantly throughout [*The Ballad of the Sad Cafe*] in the town. "The voices are dark in the golden glare," and it seems as though "the sound does not come from the twelve men on the gang, but from the earth itself, or the wide sky." It is a transcendent harmony of love and despair, mixed "with ecstasy and fright," the essentials of the human condition. It is a lament sung for the inevitable realities of that condition, a song sung by common men bound to-

gether by their common mortality, a Hawthornesque brotherhood both black and white. They sing not in spite of their chains but because of them. Unlike the participants in the nightmare which has just been completed, they know they must act together in order to survive the mutual degradation that fate has seen fit to thrust upon them. They can see their chains and acknowledge their common bonds. The music sinks down, but it can rise again. In the wake of such a cruel and relentless fate, and not in spite of but because of that fate, McCullers captures a faint glimmer of human endurance and brotherhood, even though she can see "just twelve mortal men who are together."

McCullers's vision of the dark labyrinth of the human heart and the brotherhood of all men bound to their separate but equal fates links her to Hawthorne's "truth" of the human heart, but significant differences exist. In McCullers's world, an abnormal fear of adult sexuality permeates everything. This may be linked to her relationship with Reeves McCullers, the man she married, divorced, and later remarried, who eventually committed suicide. It also may reflect the dark side of her sentimental attachment to childhood and children, acknowledging the fact that the South is "a very emotional experience for me, fraught with all the memories of my childhood." Nostalgia breeds paralysis and claustrophobia and leads to such sentimentalized faith, a kind of bastardized Wordsworthian belief (another primitive undercurrent in modernist art, perhaps), in the "poetry in children. It always strikes me that they are so capable of losing and finding themselves and also losing and finding those things they feel close to. . . . Mrs. Roosevelt says, 'Children are the only people that tell the truth.' I agree with her." Here is no charming, enigmatic, demonic Pearl. Southern sentimentality has fallen in upon itself as it does in other ways in Faulkner's work, but here unrelieved by distance and rhetorical exorcism.

McCullers's world remains as Manichean as her vision, an ultimate trap within or beyond which there is no other, save the murky psychological motives of her characters. A quest for moral significance collapses in such a Poe-esque void. Romance can never be delivered from nightmare, since the descent only ends in death. In the final paragraph of *Reflections in a Golden Eye,* still a strange and powerful fiction, Leonora "stared about her as though witnessing some scene in a play, some tragedy that was gruesome but not necessary to believe." Hawthorne sought belief, however fragmented and scattered in his final romances, or at least sought a vision of the world that suggested a morally significant pattern. McCullers like Poe stages gruesome scenes and pursues them to their inevitable conclusions, a mesmerizing, chilling art but one that harbors no tragedy, since there exists no necessity of belief, no moral significance finally. . . . McCullers recreates a modernist dread, itself perhaps the sentimental side of her childhood simplicities and reveries, and stalks it to its Manichean conclusion. But nightmare leads on only to further nightmare, a dark design of momentary stays against confusion that dissolves into the spiritual paralysis of her gothic art. (pp. 82-4)

Samuel Chase Coale, "Faulkner, McCullers, O'Connor, Styron: The Shadow on the South," in his *In Hawthorne's Shadow: American Romance from Melville to Mailer,* The University Press of Kentucky, 1985, pp. 63-101.

SOURCES FOR FURTHER STUDY

Carr, Virginia Spencer. *The Lonely Hunter: A Biography of Carson McCullers.* Garden City, N.Y.: Doubleday, 1975, 600 p.
    Biography of McCullers which formed the basis for later study of her work.

———. *Understanding Carson McCullers.* Columbia: University of South Carolina Press, 1990, 181 p.
    Study of McCullers and her writings.

Edmonds, Dale Harlan. *Carson McCullers.* Austin, Tex.: Steck-Vaughn, 1969, 43 p.
    Short introduction to McCullers's life and works.

Kiernan, Robert F. *Katherine Anne Porter and Carson McCullers: A Reference Guide.* Boston: G. K. Hall, 1976, 194 p.

Offers a comprehensive guide to criticism of McCullers's works written through 1973.

McDowell, Margaret B. *Carson McCullers.* Boston: Twayne Publishers, 1980, 158 p.
    General discussion of McCullers and her fiction along with analyses of her individual works.

Shapiro, Adrian M.; Bryer, Jackson, R.; and Field, Kathleen, eds. *Carson McCullers: A Descriptive Listing and Annotated Bibliography of Criticism.* New York: Garland Publishers, 1980, 315 p.
    Contains a chronological listing and annotated bibliography of criticism of McCullers's works.

Claude McKay

1889-1948

Born Festus Claudius McKay; also wrote under pseudonym Eli Edwards) Jamaican-born American poet, novelist, short story writer, journalist, essayist, and autobiographer.

INTRODUCTION

McKay was a major writer of the Harlem Renaissance, a period during the 1920s and early
1930s of unprecedented artistic and intellectual
achievement among black Americans. His work includes dialect verse celebrating peasant life in Jamaica, militant poems challenging white authority in the
United States, fictional works depicting black life in
both Jamaica and America, and philosophically ambitious novels about the efforts of blacks to cope in Western society. Perhaps more than any other black writer
of his time, McKay managed to convert anger and social protest into poems of lasting value. The publication
in 1919 of his most popular poem, "If We Must Die,"
was at once a shout of defiance and a proclamation of
the unbreakable spirit and courage of the oppressed
black individual. Today the work is considered a major
impetus behind the Harlem Renaissance and the civil
rights movement in the decade following World War I.
In all his works, McKay searched among the common
folk for a distinctive black identity, hoping to find a way
to preserve the African spirit and creativity in an alienating world.

McKay was born in the hills of Jamaica to peasant
farmers whose sense of racial pride greatly affected
the young McKay. His father was instrumental in reinforcing this pride, telling him folktales about Africa as
well as stories about McKay's African grandfather's enslavement. From accounts of his grandfather's experiences with white men, McKay acquired an early distrust for whites. Under the tutelage of his brother, a
schoolteacher and avowed agnostic, McKay was imbued with freethinking ideas and philosophies. In 1907
he left his rural home to apprentice as a woodworker
in Brown's Town, where he met Walter Jekyll, an English linguist and specialist in Jamaican folklore. Jekyll
helped further McKay's developing interest in English

poetry, introducing him to works by such British masters as John Milton, Alexander Pope, and Percy Bysshe Shelley. He also encouraged McKay to write verse in his native dialect. In 1909 McKay moved to Kingston, Jamaica's capital, where he later served as a constable. His native town, Sunny Ville, was predominantly black, but in substantially white Kingston the caste society, which placed blacks below whites and mulattoes, revealed to McKay alienating and degrading aspects of city life and racism. His exposure to overt racism in Kingston soon led him to identify strongly with the plight of blacks, who, he saw to his alarm, there lived under the near-total control of whites.

In 1912, with Jekyll's assistance, McKay published his first volumes of poetry, *Songs of Jamaica* and *Constab Ballads.* Both works are collections of lyrical verse written in Jamaican vernacular; the former celebrates nature and the peasant's bond to the soil, while the latter decries injustices of city life. In the same year, 1912, McKay traveled to the United States to study agriculture. After attending Tuskegee Institute in Alabama and Kansas State College, he decided to quit his studies in 1914 and move to New York City. By 1917, because of his associations with two prominent men of letters—Frank Harris, editor of *Pearson's Magazine,* in which McKay's militant poem "To The White Fiends" appeared, and Max Eastman, editor of the Communist magazine *The Liberator,* in which the poem "If We Must Die" was first published—McKay established literary and political ties with left-wing thinkers in Greenwich Village. After the publication of "If We Must Die," McKay began two years of travel and work abroad. In London he worked on the socialist periodical *Workers' Dreadnought;* he published his third collection, *Spring in New Hampshire, and Other Poems,* in 1920. McKay returned to the United States in 1921 and took up various social causes. His most highly acclaimed poetry volume, *Harlem Shadows,* appeared the following year. Shortly thereafter, McKay left America for twelve years, traveling first to Moscow to attend the Fourth Congress of the Communist Party.

McKay was extolled in the Soviet Union as a great American poet, but he grew disenchanted with the Communist party when it became apparent he would have to subjugate his art to political propaganda. By 1923 McKay had moved to Paris; later, he journeyed to the south of France, Germany, North Africa, and Spain. From 1923 until his return to the United States in 1934, he concentrated on writing fiction, completing his novels *Home to Harlem* (1928); *Banjo: A Story without a Plot* (1929), and *Banana Bottom* (1933), as well as a collection of short stories, *Gingertown* (1932). All but *Home to Harlem,* which became one of the first bestsellers by a black writer, were almost wholly neglected by critics and the reading public. Once back in Harlem, he wrote his autobiography, *A*

Long Way from Home (1937), in an attempt to bolster his financial and literary status. Following the publication of this work, McKay developed an interest in Roman Catholicism and became active in Harlem's Friendship House, a Catholic community center. His work there led to the writing of *Harlem: Negro Metropolis* (1940), an historical essay collection that sold poorly. By the mid-1940s McKay's health had deteriorated and, after enduring several illnesses, he died of heart failure in Chicago.

McKay reached his zenith as a poet with the publication of *Harlem Shadows* (1922), a collection that "clearly pointed to the incipient Renaissance," according to George E. Kent. Comprised of new works in addition to works previously published in periodicals and in the volume *Spring in New Hampshire, Harlem Shadows* contains poems based on conventional forms, most notably the sonnet. Evident in these poems is the chief conflict McKay faced as an author: he was a black poet writing within a tradition espoused by whites. McKay expressed this conflict when he wrote: "A Negro writer feeling the urge to write faithfully about the people he knows from real experiences and impartial observation is caught in a dilemma . . . between this group and his own artistic conscientiousness." While maintaining a sense of universality that denied judgement of merit based on race, McKay sought a vital identity for the black individual.

Harlem Shadows contains McKay's most militant and race-conscious poems, including his best-known work, "If We Must Die," a sonnet he had excluded from *Spring in New Hampshire* to avoid reference to "color." This piece, composed in response to racial violence that occurred throughout America during the summer of 1919, was interpreted by some commentators as a warlike cry by black radicals. According to Stephen H. Bronz, however, "If We Must Die" was written "to apply to an extreme situation; such desperate fighting need be resorted to only when 'the mad and hungry dogs' are at one's very heels, as McKay felt was the case in 1919." The poem is considered to have a universal message; indeed, British Prime Minister Winston Churchill recited it before the House of Commons in an emotional response to Nazi Germany's threat of invasion during World War II. McKay's militancy has been variously interpreted. Jean Wagner, for example, saw hatred as a significant theme in McKay's poetry and asserted that "among all black poets, [McKay] is *par excellence* the poet of hate." Yet hatred is employed not in the service of destructive aims, but rather as a vehicle of change, as in the sonnet "The White City," which calls upon hatred to vitalize oppressed spirits.

McKay also wrote important novels and short stories, expressing in them the energy and spontaneity of the common folk. His third novel, *Banana Bottom,* is recognized as his greatest achievement in fiction.

Here, as in *Home to Harlem, Banjo,* and several short stories, McKay depicted the black individual in white Western culture. *Banana Bottom* recounts the experiences of a Jamaican peasant girl, Bita Plant, who is rescued by white missionaries after being raped. Bita's new providers try to impose their cultural values on her by introducing her to organized Christianity and the British educational system. Their actions culminate in a bungled attempt to arrange Bita's marriage to an aspiring minister. The prospective groom is exposed as a sexual aberrant, whereupon Bita flees white society, eventually finding happiness and fulfillment among the black peasants. In his previous novels, McKay presented the theme of cultural dualism through two protagonists—one exemplifying the primitive black individual, the other typifying the educated black. Bita, however, embodies both characteristics and merges instinct and intellect. Commenting on the resolution of *Banana Bottom,* Michael B. Stoff noted that "of peasant origin and possessing a cultivated intellect, Bita Plant represents McKay's first successful synthesis of two cultures."

McKay's reputation as an author was never greater than during his period of fame in the 1920s. Despite his apparent decline in later years, his literary accomplishments are acclaimed as pioneering efforts by a black artist, and his influence on later writers is unquestioned. His work not only inspired such Francophone poets as Aimé Césaire and Léopold Senghor—authors whose verse espoused tenets of negritude, a movement begun in the 1930s that sought to reclaim African cultural heritage—but also writers of the Black Arts Movement, which flourished during the 1960s through such acclaimed poets as Amiri Baraka (LeRoi Jones) and Haki R. Madhubuti (Don L. Lee). McKay's poetic forms were once thought by some to be too conventional and limiting for the density of his themes; however, he has recently been praised for the intensity and ardor of his poetry. *Banana Bottom* is recognized as McKay's most skillful delineation of the black individual's predicament in white society. Two other works by McKay, *Harlem: Negro Metropolis* and the essay *The Negroes in America* (1979), have not been closely studied by critics, but most commentators concur that these works show McKay acting in the role of social critic, enhancing his reputation as one who devoted his art and life to social protest.

(For further information about McKay's life and works, see *Black Literature Criticism; Black Writers; Contemporary Authors,* Vol. 104; *Dictionary of Literary Biography,* Vols. 4, 45, 51; *Poetry Criticism,* Vol. 2; and *Twentieth-Century Literary Criticism,* Vols. 7, 41. For related criticism, see the entry on the Harlem Renaissance in *Twentieth-Century Literary Criticism,* Vol. 26.)

CRITICAL COMMENTARY

BURTON RASCOE

(essay date 1928)

[In the following excerpt from a review of McKay's novel *Home to Harlem,* Rascoe lauds the author's tragic portrayal of the "serving class" Harlemite.]

Home to Harlem is a book to invoke pity and terror, which is the function of tragedy, and to that extent—that very great extent—it is beautiful. It is hard to convey to the reader the impression this novel leaves upon the mind, just as it is hard to convey the impression that a blues-song leaves upon the mind. One reads, one hears and the heart is touched.

Out of his individual pain, Claude McKay, the poet, has fashioned his lyrics; and out of his impersonal sorrow he has written a fine novel. *Home to Harlem* is a story involving the lives led by the lost generation of colored folk in the teeming Negro metropolis north of One Hundred and Tenth Street, New York. It is a story not of the successful Negroes who have done well in the trades and professions and have built themselves homes, sent their children to school, and engaged in civil and social pursuits of a sober and respectable nature: it is the story of the serving class—longshoremen and roustabouts, house-maids and Pullman porters, waiters and wash-room attendants, cooks and scullery maids, "dime-snatchers", and all those who compensate for defeat in life in a white man's world by a savage intensity among themselves at night.

Most of the scenes of *Home to Harlem* are in the cabarets and gin-mills where jazz bands stir the blood to lust in an atmosphere as orgiastic as a pagan Saturnalia. But there are scenes, too, on railroads dining-cars where cooks and waiters have scant respect for Pullman porters and feuds are carried on between chef and pantry-man. And there are scenes in buffet flats and in the barrack quarters for railroad employees in Pittsburgh

---

Principal Works

Constab Ballads (poetry) 1912

Songs of Jamaica (poetry) 1912

Spring in New Hampshire, and Other Poems (poetry) 1920

Harlem Shadows (poetry) 1922

Home to Harlem (novel) 1928

Banjo: A Story without a Plot (novel) 1929

Gingertown (short stories) 1932

Banana Bottom (novel) 1933

A Long Way from Home (autobiography) 1937

Harlem: Negro Metropolis (nonfiction) 1940

Selected Poems (poetry) 1953

The Dialect Poetry of Claude McKay (poetry) 1972

The Passion of Claude McKay: Selected Poetry and Prose, 1912-1948 (poetry, fiction, and nonfiction) 1973

Trial by Lynching (short stories) 1977

My Green Hills of Jamaica (essays and short stories) 1979

*The Negroes in America (nonfiction) 1979

*This work was originally published in Russian in 1923.

---

and in the small rooms for which a steep rent is paid in over-congested Harlem.

Home to Harlem is not a novel in the conventional sense. The only conflict in the mind of Jake, the hero, is as to whether he will keep on working at whatever insecure, underpaid drudgery he can find to do on the docks, in the stoke-hole of a steamer and in dining-cars or turn his handsome body and good looks into the shameful asset of a "sweet-man", kept in luxury on the earnings of a woman. The only conflict of wills engaged in by the hero is when he takes a girl away from his former buddy, and anger and hate flare into being, with drawn gun and open razor. When the book closes and he is going away to Chicago with the girl to start life anew, he is the same wondering, indecisive being he was in the beginning, who "preferred the white folks' hatred to their friendly contempt" and found a sinister satisfaction in the fact that the white man is too effete to know the sensual pleasures of the blacks. (p. 183)

The language of *Home to Harlem,* whether Mr. McKay is setting forth dialogue in a perfect transcription of Negro slang and dialect or is telling his story in the Negro idiom, is a constant joy. A big black buck "lazied" down the street; another chap is "sissified"; Aunt Hattie remarks concerning some imported liquor offered her, "Ef youse always so eye-filling drinking it, it might ginger up mah bones some", and a sadistic yellow-brown girl inciting her new lover to attack her for-

mer lover cries "Hit him, Obadiah! Hit him I tell you. Beat his mug up foh him, beat his mug and bleed his mouf ! Bleed his mouf ! Two-faced yaller nigger, you does ebery low-down thing, but you nevah done a lick of work in you lifetime. Show him, Obadiah. Beat his face and bleed his mouf ".

Mr. McKay is not at all solicitous toward his reader. He makes no case, he pleads no cause, he asks no extenuation, and he doesn't explain his idiomatic phrases. There is no glossary at the end of the book as there was to Carl Van Venchten's *Nigger Heaven;* and the unsophisticated happily will read whole pages of this novel depicting the utmost moral degradation without ever knowing what it is about. And this is just as well. (p. 184)

Burton Rascoe, "The Seamy Side," in *The Bookman,* New York, Vol. LXVII, No. 2, April, 1928, pp. 183-85.

W. E. B. DU BOIS
(essay date 1928)

[An American educator and man of letters, Du Bois is an outstanding figure in twentieth-century American history. He was a founder of the NAACP and edited that organization's periodical, *The Crisis*, from 1910 to 1934. Du Bois deplored the movement in black literature toward exploiting sordid aspects of African-American culture, believing instead that black writers should depict exemplary characters who would counterbalance past stereotypes. In the following excerpt from a review of *Home to Harlem*, he vehemently disapproves of McKay's passionate and unrestrained characterizations of black Harlemites.]

[Claude McKay's novel *Home to Harlem*] for the most part nauseates me, and after the dirtier parts of its filth I feel distinctly like taking a bath. This does not mean that the book is wholly bad. McKay is too great a poet to make any complete failure in writing. There are bits of *Home to Harlem,* beautiful and fascinating: the continued changes upon the theme of the beauty of colored skins; the portrayal of the fascination of their new yearnings for each other which Negroes are developing. The chief character, Jake, has something appealing, and the glimpses of the Haitian, Ray, have all the materials of a great piece of fiction.

But it looks as though, despite this, McKay has set out to cater for that prurient demand on the part of white folk for a portrayal in Negroes of that utter licentiousness which conventional civilization holds white folk back from enjoying—if enjoyment it can be called. That which a certain decadent section of the white

American world, centered particularly in New York, longs for with fierce and unrestrained passions, it wants to see written out in black and white, and saddled on black Harlem. This demand, as voiced by a number of New York publishers, McKay has certainly satisfied, and added much for good measure. He has used every art and emphasis to paint drunkenness, fighting, lascivious sexual promiscuity and utter absence of restraint in as bold and as bright colors as he can.

If this had been done in the course of a well-conceived plot or with any artistic unity, it might have been understood if not excused. But *Home to Harlem* is padded. Whole chapters here and there are inserted with no connection to the main plot, except that they are on the same dirty subject. As a picture of Harlem life or of Negro life anywhere, it is, of course, nonsense. Untrue, not so much as on account of its facts, but on account of its emphasis and glaring colors. I am sorry that the author of *Harlem Shadows* stooped to this. I sincerely hope that he will some day rise above it and give us in fiction the strong, well-knit as well as beautiful theme, that it seems to me he might do.

W. E. B. Du Bois, in a review of "Home to Harlem," in *The Crisis,* Vol. 35, No. 6, June, 1928, p. 202.

CLAUDE McKAY

(essay date 1932)

[In the following excerpt from an essay first published in the *New York Herald-Tribune Books* in 1932, McKay responds to black critics who faulted him for his forthright portrayals of lower-class blacks in his fiction.]

When the work of a Negro writer wins recognition it creates two widely separate bodies of opinion, one easily recognizable by the average reader as general and the other limited to Negroes and therefore racial.

Although this racial opinion may seem negligible to the general reader, it is a formidable thing to the Negro writer. He may pretend to ignore it without really succeeding or being able to escape its influence, for very likely he has his social contacts with the class of Negroes who create and express this opinion in their conversation and through the hundreds of weekly Negro newspapers and the monthly magazines.

This peculiar racial opinion constitutes a kind of censorship of what is printed about the Negro. No doubt it had its origin in the laudable efforts of intelligent Negro groups to protect their race from the slander of its detractors after Emancipation, and grew until it crystallized into racial consciousness. The pity is that

these leaders of racial opinion should also be in the position of sole arbiters of intellectual and artistic things within the Negro world. For although they may be excellent persons worthy of all respect and eminently right in their purpose, they often do not distinguish between the task of propaganda and the work of art.

I myself have lived a great deal in the atmosphere of this opinion in America, in sympathy with and in contact with leaders and groups expressing it and am aware of their limitations.

A Negro writer feeling the urge to write faithfully about the people he knows from real experience and impartial observation is caught in a dilemma (unless he possesses a very strong sense of esthetic values) between the opinion of this group and his own artistic conscientiousness. I have read pages upon pages of denunciation of young Negro poets and story-tellers who were trying to grasp and render the significance of the background, the fundamental rhythm of Aframerican life. But not a line of critical encouragement for the artistic exploitation of the homely things—of Maudy's wash tub, Aunt Jemima's white folks, Miss Ann's old clothes for work-and-wages, George's Yessah-boss, dining car and Pullman services, barber and shoe shine shop, chittling and corn-pone joints—all the lowly things that go to the formation of the Aframerican soil in which the best, the most pretentious of Aframerican society still has its roots.

My own experience has been amazing. Before I published *Home to Harlem* I was known to the Negro public as the writer of the hortatory poem **"If We Must Die."** This poem was written during the time of the Chicago race riots. I was then a train waiter in the service of the Pennsylvania Railroad. Our dining car was running between New York, Philadelphia and Pittsburgh, Harrisburg and Washington and I remember we waiters and cooks carried revolvers in secret and always kept together going from our quarters to the railroad yards, as a precaution against sudden attack.

The poem was an outgrowth of the intense emotional experience I was living through (no doubt with thousands of other Negroes) in those days. It appeared in the radical magazine the *Liberator,* and was widely reprinted in the Negro press. Later it was included in my book of poetry *Harlem Shadows.* At the time I was writing a great deal of lyric poetry and none of my colleagues on the *Liberator* considered me a propaganda poet who could reel off revolutionary poetry like an automatic machine cutting fixed patterns. If we were a rebel group because we had faith that human life might be richer, by the same token we believed in the highest standards of creative work.

"If We Must Die" immediately won popularity among Aframericans, but the tone of the Negro critics was apologetic. To them a poem that voiced the deep-rooted instinct of self-preservation seemed merely a daring piece of impertinence. The dean of Negro critics [William S. Braithwaite] denounced me as a "violent and angry propagandist, using his natural poetic gifts to clothe [arrogant] and defiant thoughts." A young disciple characterized me as "rebellious and vitupera-tive."

Thus it seems that respectable Negro opinion and criticism are not ready for artistic or other iconoclasm in Negroes. Between them they would emasculate the colored literary aspirant. Because Aframerican group life is possible only on a neutral and negative level our critics are apparently under the delusion that an Aframerican literature and art may be created out of evasion and insincerity.

They seem afraid of the revelation of bitterness in Negro life. But it may as well be owned, and frankly by those who know the inside and heart of Negro life, that the Negro, and especially the Aframerican, has bitterness in him in spite of his joyous exterior. And the more educated he is in these times the more he is likely to have.

The spirituals and the blues were not created out of sweet deceit. There is as much sublimated bitterness in them as there is humility, pathos and bewilderment. And if the Negro is a little bitter, the white man should be the last person in the world to accuse him of bitterness. For the feeling of bitterness is a natural part of the black man's birthright as the feeling of superiority is of the white man's. It matters not so much that one has had an experience of bitterness, but rather how one has developed out of it. To ask the Negro to render up his bitterness is asking him to part with his soul. For out of his bitterness he has bloomed and created his spirituals and blues and conserved his racial attributes—his humor and ripe laughter and particular rhythm of life.

However, with the publication of *Home to Harlem* the Aframerican elite realized that there was another side to me and changed their tune accordingly. If my poetry had been too daring, my prose was too dirty. The first had alarmed, the second had gassed them. And as soon as they recovered from the last shock, they did not bite their tongues in damning me as a hog rooting in Harlem, a buzzard hovering over the Black Belt scouting for carcasses and altogether a filthy beast.

If my brethren had taken the trouble to look a little into my obscure life they would have discovered that years before I had recaptured the spirit of the Jamaican peasants in verse, rendering their primitive joys, their loves and hates, their work and play, their dialect. And what I did in prose for Harlem was very similar to what I had done for Jamaica in verse. (pp. 132-35)

On the "broader" side (literally at least) my work has been approached by some discriminating critics as if I were a primitive savage and altogether a stranger to civilization. Perhaps I myself unconsciously gave that impression. However, I should not think it was unnatural for a man to have a predilection for a civilization or culture other than that he was born unto. Whatever may be the criticism implied in my writing of Western Civilization I do not regard myself as a stranger but as a child of it, even though I may have become so by the comparatively recent process of grafting. I am as conscious of my new-world birthright as of my African origin, being aware of the one and its significance in my development as much as I feel the other emotionally. (p. 137)

A sincere artist can represent characters only as they seem to him. And he *will* see characters through his predilections and prejudices, unless he sets himself deliberately to present those cinema-type figures that are produced to offend no unit of persons whose protest may involve financial loss. The time when a writer will stick only to the safe old ground of his own class of people is undoubtedly passing. Especially in America, where all the peoples of the world are scrambling side by side and modern machines and the ramifications of international commerce are steadily breaking down the ethnological barriers that separate the peoples of the world. (p. 139)

Claude McKay, "A Negro Writer to His Critics," in his *The Passion of Claude McKay: Selected Poetry and Prose, 1912-1948,* edited by Wayne F. Cooper, Schocken Books, 1973, pp. 132-39.

JEAN WAGNER
(essay date 1962)

[Wagner, a French author and critic, is an authority on American slang and dialects. His *Les poètes nègres des États-Unis* (1962; *Black Poets of the United States*, 1973) is one of the most innovative sources available for the study of African-American poets. In the following excerpt from this work, he presents an extensive overview of McKay's poetry, focusing on stylistic and thematic devices.]

The two collections [of poetry] published in Jamaica in 1912 constitute a diptych of McKay's experience in his native island. The first, *Songs of Jamaica,* is a sort of highly colored epitome of the years of childhood and young manhood spent in the mountains, where he listened to Nature's great voice and shared the life of the black peasantry. Often in direct opposition to these first poems are those of *Constab Ballads,* which reveal the disillusionment and pessimism the poet felt when plunged into the life of the capital. These first two volumes are already marked by a sharpness of vision, an inborn realism, and a freshness which provide a pleasing contrast with the conventionality which, at this same time, prevails among the black poets of the United States.

Not the least original aspect of these seventy-eight poems is the rough but picturesque Jamaican dialect in which most of them are written, and of which they constitute the earliest poetic use. Thus we are far removed from the dialect of the Dunbar school, which was taken over from the whites who had concocted it in order to maintain the stereotype of black inferiority and to limit blacks more surely to the role of buffoons under orders to entertain the master race. An instrument of oppression when handled by white writers, the dialect became an avowal of subservience in its use by Dunbar, most of whose readers were whites. Furthermore, the themes treated in it had also been exploited by the former oppressors before Dunbar's arrival on the scene. None of these afterthoughts need be entertained in the case of McKay's dialect. Here everything is entirely and authentically Negro. It all comes directly from the people and is rooted in the soil, alike the phonology, often flavored with a delightful exoticism, and the rather summary morphology; the typically fantastic placing of the tonic accent and the somewhat rudimentary syntax, seldom in accord with the Queen's English; and, finally, the often unexpectedly roughhewn words and images, which originate in the hard-working folk's immediate contact with a soil reluctant to part with its riches.

As long as he lived, McKay's own speech kept the stamp of this rustic accent, as the recordings that have been preserved bear witness. As for the whimsicalities of the Jamaican tonic accent, they often preclude any certain solution to the problem of scanning many of his lines, whether in dialect or standard English.

Every bit as much as their language, it is the poetic quality of these works that links them genuinely to the people for whom they were written. It was no mere rhetorical flourish when McKay entitled his first collection *Songs of Jamaica.* For six poems, he adds in an appendix melodies which he composed. The songs and ballads he did not set to music are so rhythmical that a musical accompaniment could easily be provided. (pp. 204-05)

How close the bond of sympathy was between McKay and the people is manifested also by the realism with which he characterizes the black Jamaican peasant. Here, too, the contrast with Dunbar is embarrassingly evident. McKay's portraits at once transcend the limits which, in James Weldon Johnson's view, inevitably weighed on American Negro dialect and forced it to sound only the registers of humor and pathos. In any case, there is no humor to be found here, nor will it play any part in the later work. These peasants are not the ignorant, lazy, thieving clowns all too often held up for

ridicule by Dunbar's school, stereotypes designed to amuse the members of a superior race. "Our Negroes were proud though poor," McKay will later declare. "They would not sing clowning songs for white men and allow themselves to be kicked around by them." Unlike the character portraits usually associated with American Negro dialect, these portraits are the actual incarnation of a whole people's racial pride.

All in all, McKay's characterization of the Jamaican peasant is substantially that of the peasant anywhere in the world: deeply attached to his plot of land, over which he labors with an atavistic skill; and unsparing of himself, yet seemingly condemned to unalleviated poverty, since there is always someone to snatch the fruits of his labor. He owes his pride to the sense of work well done, and has no feeling of inferiority vis-à-vis the whites whom, when the occasion arises, he will address in the bluntest terms. (p. 206)

[McKay's critique of society becomes urgent in poems] where the responsibilities of the whites are categorically stated. They have organized the economic life of the island so as to profit from the resources that nature had destined for the blacks. That is the force of the following lines, in which the poet apostrophizes his native island:

> You hab all t'ings fe mek life bles',
> But buccra 'poil de whole
> Wid gove'mint an'all de res'
> Fe worry naygur soul.
>
> (pp. 207-08)

[All of the poems in *Songs of Jamaica*], nevertheless, end on a note of faith in the future. In **"Two-an'-Six,"** Sun's discouragement is dispelled by the loving, consoling words uttered by his wife:

> An' de shadow lef ' him face,
> An' him felt an inward peace
> As he blessed his better part
> For her sweet an' gentle heart.

In **"Hard Times,"** it is faith in Providence that resounds in the last stanza:

> I won't gib up, I won't say die,
>   For all de time is hard;
> Aldough de wul' soon en', I'll try
> My wutless best as time goes by,
>   An' trust on in me Gahd.

All in all, health, vigor, and self-assurance make up the impression left by this portrait of the black Jamaican peasant, whose age-old practical virtues and wisdom have not been sapped by his material poverty. Thus the optimism that McKay discovers in this rural milieu is derived, in the first place, from extant moral values. But there are racial reasons also. For it is highly significant that all these country folks are blacks, excluding the mulattoes whom McKay implicitly rejects as all too eager to see in their white ancestry a justification for disdaining the blacks. Finally, the real values that constitute the superiority of the black peasant reside in his closeness to the soil of Jamaica. One can scarcely overstress the importance of this element in McKay's trinitarian symbolism, which associates the good with the black race and the soil. (pp. 210-11)

[McKay's] roots in the soil of his native island are amazingly deep and lasting. These roots make him one with the soil. Through them he draws in his nourishment; the island's enchanting scenes call forth his earliest verses, and no one will ever rival him in praise for the mildness of its climate, the vividness of its colors, the luxuriance of its vegetation, or the coolness of its streams. (p. 211)

But uniting the black man and the earth is a more intimate, subtle relationship, a secret harmony as it were, and simply to name the familiar scenes is enough to arouse in the poet's sensibilities a physical resonance, to send a tremor through his frame:

Loved Clarendon hills,
Dear Clarendon hills,
Oh! I feel de chills,
Yes, I feel de chills
Coursin' t'rough me frame
When I call your name.

Thus the union of the poet and his land is consummated in a romantic ecstasy. This correspondence between Nature and the poet is indeed "the organic exaltation produced by physical agents" or the recollection of them, "the joy of all the senses in contact with the world" which Cazamian analyzed, many years ago, in the English Romantics. Like them, McKay felt constantly drawn to nature and sensed the need to become totally merged in it. The emotion it aroused in him transcended by far the exclusively aesthetic plane. For Nature is an ever renewed source of strength, and instinctively he returned to commune with it. (pp. 212-13)

McKay, for whom the earth was at the origin of everything, would certainly have signed his name to the exclamation of Shelley's Prometheus: "O, Mother Earth!" The earth is the whole man. He had already proclaimed this before he had turned twenty, and he realized it all the more clearly after he had left it and experienced enormous disillusionment in contact with the city, whose inhabitants he looked on as rootless, in the most concrete sense of the word:

Fool! I hated my precious birthright,
Scorning what had made my father a man.

He attributed to his native soil, the nurturer, all the strength of his character and his poetic vigor. . . . (p. 214)

Between the black man and the earth there is a total identification. When, vexed by the city, he returns to his mountains, he will see in this return not only a reunion with the earth, but with his people also. . . . Thus the racial values he associates with the soil also help to tinge his feeling for nature, and in his mind he conceives nature and the city as mutually exclusive forces. (pp. 214-15)

Hatred of the city is one of the principal motifs in McKay's Jamaican poems, and the American poems will offer variations on the same theme. In Dunbar's work one could already note some aversion toward urban civilization, but this was only sporadic, and the motivation behind it was entirely different. Dunbar was sensitive, above all, to the ravages wrought by industrialization which, as it spread ever wider, made men's lives ugly and polluted the air they breathed. His reaction might even be interpreted, in part, as the tuberculosis victim's struggle for the pure air he knew he needed.

But with McKay the theme is not merely more amply treated; it acquires in the racial context a symbolic importance not found in Dunbar. The city, presented as the antithesis of the land, is consequently the enemy of the black man also. (p. 215)

[In McKay's *Constab Ballads*, the] city symbolizes an evil that is multiple. In part it finds expression in the traditional ways but also, and especially, it adopts other forms that are significant in the racial context.

We will not linger long over the former, which for the most part illustrate the corrupting power of the city, on which McKay superimposes his keen awareness of the corruption rampant among the police. (p. 217)

The police are also reputed to be a tool in the hands of the whites for oppressing the blacks. This is the lament of the apple woman in **"The Apple Woman's Complaint,"** when the police forbid her to sell her wares in the street. If she is not allowed to ply her modest trade honestly, she will have to live by stealing, and in either case she will be at odds with the police, who in any event live at her expense. From this poem we cite only those passages that present the attitude of the police as having originated in hatred of the blacks:

Black nigger wukin' laka cow
An' wipin' sweat-drops from his brow,
Dough him is dyin' sake o' need,
P'lice an' dem headman boun' fe feed.

. . . .

De headman fe de town police
Mind neber know a little peace,
'Cep' when him an' him heartless ban'
Hab sufferin' nigger in dem han'.

. . . .

We hab fe barter out we soul
To lib' t'rough dis ungodly wul';—
O massa Jesus! don't you see
How police is oppressin' we?

The vehemence of this protest against oppression, here placed in the mouth of the apple woman, and the boundless despair of the last stanza, are in violent contrast with the cold objectivity of the social critique voiced in the rural poems of *Songs of Jamaica.* It heralds what will be McKay's stance in his American poems. Of all the Jamaican poems, **"The Apple Woman's Complaint"** is the most bitter, violent, and militant. Thus it serves to make entirely plain the changes that city residence brought about in McKay. (pp. 217-18)

[McKay's] American poems give vent to his racial pride with a forcefulness he had never exhibited before. This outburst is so authentic, and so much in keeping with his own fiery, passionate temperament, that little influence need be attributed to the stimulus he could have found elsewhere in the paeans to race that were being sounded by his compatriot Garvey. Furthermore, as he faced the onslaught of white insolence, his pride grew in militancy without losing any of its nobility:

Your door is shut against my tightened face,
And I am sharp as steel with discontent;
But I possess the courage and the grace
To bear my anger *proudly* and unbent.

His pride is like that of a tree deeply rooted and prepared to withstand the hostile elements:

Like a strong tree that in the virgin earth
Sends far its roots through rock and loam and clay
And *proudly* thrives in rain or time of dearth . . .

As this pride is strengthened and tested by adversity, he raises racial consciousness to the aesthetic plane. One would almost be tempted to affirm that the poet is inaugurating a hedonism of color, when one beholds how with a supremely refined sensuality he savors the heady joy of his blackness, gaining awareness of it amidst a community that tortures him, but to which he feels superior in every fiber of his being. . . . (p. 223)

No one ever expressed with such a wealth of nuances the opposing eddies that swirl in a mind in search of equilibrium amid stupidly hostile surroundings. This attempt at introspective insight clearly demonstrates how racial pride can act as a redemptive force.

Yet it must meet a rude challenge when, gloriously garbed, the poet's sworn enemy, the White City, displays the whole spectrum of her seductive wiles in order to win him over and ruin him. . . . (p. 224)

To no lesser degree than the intoxication of being black, Claude McKay learned in America how intoxi-

cating it is to hate. He vents his joy in **"The White City":**

I will not toy with it nor bend an inch.
Deep in the secret chambers of my heart
I muse my life-long hate, and without flinch
I bear it nobly as I live my part.
My being would be a skeleton, a shell,
If this dark passion that fills my every mood,
And makes my heaven in the white world's hell,
Did not forever feed me vital blood.
I see the mighty city through a mist—
The strident trains that speed the goaded mass,
The poles and spires and towers vapor-kissed,
The fortressed port through which the great ships
  pass,
The tides, the wharves, the dens I contemplate,
Are sweet like wanton loves because I hate.

Hatred has acquired quite a power of transfiguration. It becomes the favored theme of the poet's song, for it alone can make his surroundings bearable.

It was once declared that hatred is not a poetic emotion. If this act of exclusion were to be acquiesced in, it would oblige us to find no poetic merit whatever in Claude McKay's most striking poems since he, among all black poets, is *par excellence* the poet of hate. This, when situated in its racial context, has a very special characteristic. As **"The White City"** so clearly shows, it is the actual prerequisite for his survival, since it transmutes into a paradise the base inferno of the white world. It is a sort of antidote secreted throughout his being and which prevents the White City from emptying him of his substance—were it not for this fostering flood of hatred, which constantly provides him with fresh energies, he would be reduced by the city to the level of a skeleton, of a sea creature's abandoned shell. Hatred is the compensatory factor that assures the equilibrium of his personality, allowing him to adapt himself adequately to his environment. (pp. 225-26)

With the publication of **"If We Must Die,"** the incarnation of the new spirit and the spokesman for a whole people at last resolved to witness no longer, in resignation and submissiveness, the massacre of its own brothers at the hands of the enraged white mob, but to return blow for blow and, if necessary, to die. With the possible exception of James Weldon Johnson's "Negro National Hymn," no poem by any black poet has been so frequently cited and extolled. (p. 229)

The welcome accorded this sonnet is also due, in part, to its being one of those poems in which McKay's poetic gift reaches beyond the circumstances of the day to attain the universal. Along with the will to resistance of black Americans that it expresses, it voices also the will of oppressed peoples of every age who, whatever their race and wherever their region, are fighting with their backs against the wall to win their freedom. . . .

It is important, at this juncture in our examination of McKay's hatred, to try to determine against what, exactly, his hatred was directed. One might, indeed, choose to regard him as a last-ditch defender of Negro culture, filled with a global detestation of America and the Western culture for which, in his eyes, it stood. This interpretation of his cultural attitude has actually found supporters. (p. 230)

McKay appears to have expressed all the complexity of his real feelings about America in the sonnet entitled **"America"'**:

> Although she feeds me bread of bitterness,
> And sinks into my throat her tiger's tooth,
> Stealing my breath of life, I will confess
> I love this cultured hell that tests my youth!
> Her vigor flows like tides into my blood,
> Giving my strength erect against her hate,
> Her bigness sweeps my being like a flood.

What is predominant here, and basic also, is his love for America, whose strength acts on the poet like a stimulant. The other half of the picture, the hatred that America has for blacks, does not obliterate the poet's love for it. McKay's hatred does not mean a rejection of America; it is a reproach directed against the country's inability to reconcile discriminatory practices with egalitarian democratic doctrines. In the last analysis, what he hates is not America, but evil. An unpublished sonnet makes this explicit:

> I stripped down harshly to the naked core
> Of hatred based on the essential wrong.

We know that the essential evil is the division between man and man, the white man's hatred and contempt for his fellow man, and the exploitation of black by white. In the "civilized hell" of America, evil adopts the most varied guises. But a natural defense reaction leads McKay to note those in particular which deny the black man's humanity. The metaphors often depict America as a kind of vampire seeking to deprive the victim of his substance and to leave him a mere shell or skeleton. America becomes, for instance, a tiger, his striped coat representing the stripes of the American flag, who seizes his prey by the throat and nourishes himself on the blood. . . . (pp. 231-32)

In another poem, **"Birds of Prey,"** whites are depicted as birds darkening the sky with their wings, then swooping down on their victims to gorge themselves on the hearts. . . . (p. 232)

Blood and heart quite assuredly have a symbolic value in these poems, which denounce the depersonalization of the black man and his exploitation by society's rulers, who glut themselves on his financial and artistic substance. But this carnage also requires a more literal interpretation, so that the poems may be understood as a condemnation of lynching, like the sonnet **"The Lynching,"** where McKay speaks more openly.

At times, too, McKay succeeds in utilizing a less violent mode to chant the horrors of racial discrimination. **"The Barrier"** is a delightful poem which, in a manner that is partly light and partly serious, considers the interdict prohibiting any love between a black man and a white woman. It is reminiscent of those trials that judged a man's intentions when, in the Deep South, blacks used to be convicted of the "visual rape" of a southern white beauty. . . . (pp. 232-33)

Though McKay may justifiably be called the poet of hatred and rebellion, his real personality would be seriously misrepresented if one were to treat him as an out-and-out rebel. Without meaning to do so, Richard Wright undoubtedly slights McKay in his nobility by asserting of him: "To state that Claude McKay is a rebel is to understate it; his rebellion is a way of life." To adopt this point of view is to overlook the remarkable self-mastery that McKay could summon up, and to neglect the personal purification and, when all is considered, the moral elevation that McKay believed he could derive from his hate.

It is, indeed, admirable that in his case hatred and rebellion did not become, as they might have, a vehicle lurching onward without reins or brakes. Even when he revels in his hate, he does not wallow in it, and in the midst of the hurricane he retains his control:

> Peace, O my rebel heart! . . .

However passionate his rebellious flights of rhetoric, they are always lucid and dominated by an unflagging will to self-transcendence:

> Oh, I must search for wisdom every hour
> Deep in my wrathful bosom sore and raw.

He simply does not look on hatred as an end in itself. It is but a stage on the path that ends in the divine charity, for which its purifying action prepares the way. Understood thus, McKay's hatred is a holy anger the manifestation of which occurs only in entire clarity of mind, as did the divine anger directed against the deleterious hypocrisy of the Pharisees, or against the merchants who had made of the temple a "den of thieves." Ultimately, what sets a limit to hatred is the spiritual. Such is the message of the sonnet **"To the White Fiends,"** in which God compels hatred to stop on the brink of murder, directing it to a higher goal:

> Think you I am not fiend and savage too?
> Think you I could not arm me with a gun
> And shoot down ten of you for every one
> Of my black brothers murdered, burnt by you?
> Be not deceived, for every deed you do
> I could match—out-match: am I not Afric's son,
> Black of that black land where black deeds are

done?
But the Almighty from the darkness drew
My soul and said: Even thou shalt be a light
Awhile to burn on the benighted earth,
Thy dusky face I set among the white
For thee to prove thyself of higher worth;
Before the world is swallowed up in night,
To show thy little lamp: go forth, go forth!

Thus, far from being a "way of life," McKay's hatred undergoes a sublimation that induces it to consume itself. In its place comes a tranquillity that is not indifference, but a deepening and internalization of racial feeling. (pp. 235-36)

In McKay's work, the feeling for nature occupies almost as important a place as racial feeling. . . . Unlike Countee Cullen or Langston Hughes, who never vibrated in unison with nature (which usually remains a mere concept for them), McKay brings to it the understanding and sympathy of a person who grew up in it and whose rare sensitivity brought him to an authentic integration with it. In *Harlem Shadows,* the nature poems make up nearly one-third of the volume. The languorous sweetness of their lyricism is like a cool breeze from the Isles, introducing a note of most welcome tranquillity into the militant fierceness of the poems of rebellion. (p. 236)

It can be seen that McKay's feeling for nature has no autonomous existence. Since it is linked with the racial symbolism of the earth and remains closely subordinated to it, seen from this point of view it most often amounts to the enunciation of a sense of belonging.

Its expressive value, because of this role, falls together with that of the African theme as treated by many poets of the Negro Renaissance. For them, Africa is the land still unpolluted by the inhuman machine outlook of the white man, hungry to enslave his fellow men. But for them—those who are unable to identify with America, the land that treats them inhumanely—Africa is the substitute land where they can seek their roots; Africa is the mother with whom, in the place of stepmotherly America which has rejected them, they try to form an *a posteriori* bond of relationship.

McKay is totally unconcerned with these substitute values. For he comes from a land where blacks are in the majority, where he struck roots both tenacious and extraordinarily deep, a land with which his identification was perfect, if one allows for the extraterritorial status he imposed on the city of Kingston. He has no need to go all the way to Africa to find the palm trees to which he can compare the black girls. Jamaica is his Africa, and its exoticism is a genuine exoticism, not a dream escape to some substitute fatherland the need for which springs from a feeling of frustration.

It is not surprising, therefore, that he keeps the African theme within much more modest limits than the other Renaissance poets, whose feeling of unquali-

fied admiration for Africa he does not share. The whole body of his work contains scarcely more than half a dozen poems devoted to Africa, and not one of them can be considered an apologia. (pp. 238-39)

In **"Outcast,"** it is again the sense of being captive in the white man's empire that occupies the poet's mind, rather than any feeling of solidarity with Africa. Nevertheless, this second factor emerges with greater clarity here than in any other poem by McKay. But he is less intent on affirming his link with Africa than in regretting that the elements forming this link have been lost or forgotten. . . . He must be taken to express his kinship with the blacks of the United States, whose spokesman he has become, and to state the truth, as suggested by the poem's title, that he himself has been rejected by the white American majority. These two ingredients are more obvious than any putative avowal of genuine solidarity with Africa. (p. 242)

Thus if McKay is a forerunner of the Negro Renaissance, this is not due to his vision of Africa. The genuine quality of his Jamaican exoticism had immunized him against the heady African mirage, and his ability to stand resolute against its seductions attests, in the last resort, the cohesiveness and equilibrium of his personality.

McKay has left us only a few poems dealing with Harlem, the "Mecca of the Negro Renaissance." His 1922 volume, though entitled *Harlem Shadows,* has but two poems on the theme, the title poem and **"The Harlem Dancer."** (p. 243)

Yet, though for these reasons he can scarcely be called the poet of Harlem, at least he has the merit of being the first to introduce Harlem into Negro poetry. For in December, 1917, **"The Harlem Dancer"** appeared in *The Seven Arts,* and **"Harlem Shadows"** was included in *Spring in New Hampshire* (1920). Earlier than Langston Hughes, it is Claude McKay who provided the first annotations on the frivolous night life that, until the 1929 crash, would enable Harlem to prosper. These poems might also be said to constitute the first poetic documents on the reactions of the black man borne to the urban centers by the tide of the Great Migration. There is nothing astonishing in the fact that McKay, as a shrewd observer of every aspect of city life, paid particularly close attention to this phenomenon.

"Harlem Shadows" is a poem in a minor key on the prostitutes that urban civilization, with its lack of humanity, had thrown onto the Harlem sidewalks. The poem is reminiscent of those that McKay, in the 1912 volumes, had devoted to the moral debacle of two country girls as a result of their going to live in Kingston. But **"Harlem Shadows"** is an innovation in the sense that McKay attributes a primordial importance to the prostitutes' color (blackening them further by referring to them as shadows) and makes their downfall symbolic of the whole race's. In each case, the blame is implicitly allotted to racial oppression. This biased suggestion deviates significantly from McKay's usually realistic, objective manner, and one would have expected him to treat these prostitutes as victims of the city rather than as slaves of the master race. This deference to racial propaganda spoils the end of the poem, which otherwise would have been very much to the point. . . . (p. 244)

"The Harlem Dancer" plunges us into the atmosphere of one of the countless night spots that sprang up in Harlem after World War I. This sonnet raises the problem of another sort of prostitution, that of Negro art to popular (mainly white) demands. White people appear in the sonnet as drunken spectators who gobble up with their eyes the form of a naked black dancer. Between the young whites, in search of venal pleasures, and the nobility of the black beauty, the comparison is to the advantage of the latter. She appears before us in all the pride of a tall palm tree swaying majestically in the wind, yet she is an uprooted palm tree, torn from a kindlier country where she has left her soul. Her natural grace and beauty contrast with the artificial setting into which she has been transplanted, and her forced smile cannot hide her longing for her native land. Underneath the exoticism of detail, we once again come upon a thesis greatly favored by McKay and the Negro Renaissance, maintaining that the white world, more often than was generally believed, was a setting unfit to receive all that blacks have to offer it. (pp. 244-45)

Poets have often been attracted by the theme of black dancers. Dunbar . . . has left us entertaining portrayals of evenings spent dancing the quadrille with, in his day, the added savor of forbidden fruit. Jazz, in its turn, will soon find its true poet in Langston Hughes. Thus it need not surprise us that McKay also should have chosen to see in the liberation of the dance, as in the spontaneity and the subtle rhythms of the dancers, an especially revealing manifestation of the "immortal spirit" of his race, since here one could note the urge to expand, to express oneself, to free oneself, instincts that in daily life had to be kept in check at every instant.

But whereas Dunbar and Hughes let themselves be swept away by the vortex of the dance, McKay remained the detached observer, though sensing the emotion that radiated from the dancers to him. His view is an external one; a space remains between him and the crowd of dancers and allows him no identification with them. . . . It can be sensed that McKay experiences a measure of despair vis-à-vis the tragedy of this superficial response of a whole race to the oppression and contempt by which it is victimized.

This is, we believe, another manifestation of McKay's reserved attitude when confronted by the

folk temperament, with which he never felt entirely at ease. Other elements that lead us to the same conclusion are the total absence of humor throughout his poetry and his preference for such classical poetic forms as the sonnet. Spirituals, blues, and jazz, whose popular forms were taken over by Langston Hughes, Sterling Brown, and many other poets, have no place in McKay's poetic work. In this connection, it is necessary to correct the mistaken view propounded by Henry Lüdeke (no doubt on the basis of uncertain information) that in *Harlem Shadows* the rhythms were "strongly influenced by popular poetry, above all the spirituals." Quite the contrary, McKay must have had a background awareness that the popular forms and outlook could become, as has in reality often occurred, an excuse for avoiding personal reflection, and so would have been only another sort of escapism for the poet. Thus, while he defends Negro art against the deformations that whites inflicted on it, he defended it no less vigorously against those Negroes who were tempted to ask of it something that it could not provide: a soul. . . . [In] Harlem he could now see to what a degree this culture was emptied of substance the moment it lost contact with the soil, which alone could give it life, and was transported to the city, which in McKay's eyes had ever been a corrupting influence. In a word, he judged Negro popular culture, as he had encountered it in America, to be incapable of fulfilling his need for an authentic spiritual life. (pp. 246-47)

[McKay], with his nonconformist temperament, was repelled by the idea of adhering to traditions that took the place of individual reflection. His religious poetry is the expression of an inner growth, and his discovery of God the result of his individual search for truth. From a more general vantage-point, his poetic opus may be considered as the account of a vast attempt at a synthesis between the antagonistic elements of the black world and the Western world warring within him. There can be no denying that McKay, like every black exiled in a white milieu, was for a long time a divided man, so that it is possible to speak of his cultural dualism. But he never acquiesced in being torn apart by this dichotomy. His whole being urged him to find unity. The critique to which he subjected the antinomies deprived them, little by little, of their contingencies and laid bare their authentic values. In Jamaica, he affirmed the primacy of the soil and contrasted it with the inanity of the dream, cherished by the mulattoes, of a heightened social status. He rejected the mirage of Africa as a source of racial pride, looking on it as merely pathetic. He shunned the nationalism of a Garvey, whom he regarded as a charlatan, and while he defended Negro folklore against whites, who would have denatured it, he nevertheless could not find spiritual sustenance in it. On the other hand, it was his natural instinct to evaluate the possibilities of spiritual advancement offered by Western, Christian culture, but there too he perceived the corroding evil that sowed hatred between men. In his dialogue with the West, conducted through the medium of his hatred, this emotion was slowly filtered of its dross as he came to grasp the necessity of raising himself above it. Unless the individual is engaged in a ceaseless effort to transcend himself, no victory over hatred will ever be possible. Neither rationalism nor Communism could provide the higher principle capable of reconciling the conflicting theses of his cultural eclecticism. At long last he discovered this principle within himself, and at the same time he discovered God. Thus his spiritual itinerary is an account of the internalization of his racial feeling.

"I was always religious-minded as some of my pagan poems attest. But I never had any faith in revealed religion." (pp. 248-49)

[McKay's] skepticism, which was aroused by rationalist influences, signifies an estrangement from the church rather than from God. It would seem equally likely that this estrangement was motivated by certain practices or pastoral attitudes on the part of the Anglican clergy. . . .

Be that as it may, the poet's critique of what we shall call the official faith soon led him to become his own spiritual advisor. This imbues him with a taste for that upward movement of the soul that a victory over his passions represents, and it accustoms him to view progress as a continual upgrading of the individual through self-transcendence, which alone makes existence worthwhile "in an empty world." These are the qualities of soul that McKay brings to the spiritual enrichment of black poetry, as his voice blends in with those of the American black poets. (p. 251)

His fundamental expectation in turning to God, and the object of the prayers he addresses to Him, is the light of truth. . . . That this is the ultimate objective of his spiritual quest is confirmed by the sonnet **"Truth,"** written shortly before he died:

Lord, shall I find it in Thy Holy Church,
Or must I give it up as something dead,
Forever lost, no matter where I search,
Like dinosaurs within their ancient bed?
I found it not in years of Unbelief,
In science stirring life like budding trees,
In Revolution like a dazzling thief—
Oh, shall I find it on my bended knees?
But what is Truth? So Pilate asked Thee, Lord,
So long ago when Thou wert manifest,
As the Eternal and Incarnate Word,
Chosen of God and by Him singly blest;
In this vast world of lies and hate and greed,
Upon my knees, Oh Lord, for Truth I plead.

His prayer will be granted, and divine illumination will bring him to recognize at last that the "essential evil"

he had spent his life hunting down and fighting is not outside, but within him. To track down injustice and oppression by hating America is to fight against shadows. The basic evil is hate itself, and that is what he must hate. It is hate that wrecks unity, setting men one against the other, and the individual against himself. But it is the farthest point to which the pagan doctrines can lead one. God alone can lead a man further on and conquer hate itself:

Around me roar and crash the pagan isms
To which most of my life was consecrate,
Betrayed by evil men and torn by schisms
For they were built on nothing more than hate!
I cannot live my life without the faith
Where new sensations like a fawn will leap,
But old enthusiasms like a wraith
Haunt me awake and haunt me when I sleep.
And so to God I go to make my peace.

(pp. 256-57)

Jean Wagner, "Claude McKay," in his *Black Poets of the United States: From Paul Laurence Dunbar to Langston Hughes,* translated by Kenneth Douglas, University of Illinois Press, 1973, pp. 197-257.

GETA J. LeSEUR
(essay date 1989)

[In the following essay, LeSeur discusses McKay's poetry and comments on aspects of the author's romanticism.]

Jamaica gave to English and American literature a great poet in Claude McKay. As a Negro writer writing at a time when it was popular to use modern forms, he chose to combine the lilting melody and warm human emotion of the earlier romantics in his writing. He wrote poems of exuberance, sorrow, faithful affection, patriotism, and sturdy independence. In such poems as **"The Tropics in New York," "Flame-Heart," "The Spanish Needle," "The Snow Fairy," "Spring in New Hampshire,"** and **"Home-Thoughts,"** these attitudes are poignantly expressed with allegiance to the native and foreign—Jamaica and the United States—the real and the romantic. McKay never saw any of these as being in conflict; they were always two "natures" completely independent of each other. This, however, was a personal and literary philosophy. His poetry is one which says yes to life—rich, free, passionate, and concerned.

McKay has been referred to from time to time as "Jamaica's Bobbie Burns," which in itself is an interesting but valid comparison. Those who knew him personally and those who only know his poetry constantly made this reference. McKay himself made this statement more precise in his autobiography, *A Long Way From Home,* and in the short article **"On Becoming a Catholic"**:

> I had always thought of myself as a pagan. I chose Burns as my model, as he was so strong, sweet and amorous of abundant life, and I was writing in the Jamaican dialect.

The comparison is by no means an accident and seems even more relevant when it is noted that Robert Burns was supposed to visit Jamaica after an unlucky love affair with his Scottish sweetheart. The trip never came to fruition, however. Burns' poetry was only one aspect of British literature that all Jamaicans and British colonials were expected to master. Every school boy and girl was expected to memorize several British lyrics, ballads, and narratives or be whipped for not doing so. It is no accident, therefore, that McKay and his schoolmates knew and admired poets like Burns, Keats, Shelley, and Wordsworth. When McKay says that he used Burns as a model, he is also suggesting a silent rebellion on the part of a West Indian youth. When he wrote poetry in the Jamaican Scottish dialect, he used Burns' Scottish dialect as a model. His first poems published in the dialect were *Songs of Jamaica* (1912) and *Constab Ballads* (1912). This was only the beginning of the sturdy independence and faithful affection he was to exercise throughout his life and writing career.

Allegiances and coalitions were goals visualized by Claude McKay. They are present in his autobiography, as a specific statement of purpose, and in his verse. Although a radical, he was a conservative poet, for his verse forms were traditional. The sonnet was his favorite, and he actually wrote most of his poems on the time-honored subjects of love and nature. Regardless of the fact that the writing tradition adopted by McKay was that of the romantic "movement" from his school days in Jamaica, it was not until he came to the United States in 1912 at age twenty-three that his best poetry-writing began. Max Eastman, his lifelong friend and editor of the *Liberator,* which he coedited, later said this of him:

> It was not until he came to the United States that Claude McKay began to confront the deepest feelings in his heart and realize that a delicate syllabic music could not alone express them. Here his imagination awoke, and the colored imagery that is the language of all deep passion began to appear in his poetry.

And about the poetry written in America, Eastman goes on to say:

> The quality is here in them all—the pure, clear arrow-like transference of his emotion into our breast, without any but the inexitable words—the

quality that reminds us of Burns and Villon and Catullus, and all the poets that we call lyric because we love them so much. It is the quality that Keats sought to cherish when he said that "Poetry should be great and unobtrusive, a thing which enters into the soul, and does not startle or amaze with itself, but with its subject . . . It is the poetry of life and not the poet's chamber. It is the poetry which looks upon a thing and sings."

McKay has said that, of the English models and schools of writing he has been associated with, it is the classicists and romantics that he admires, but he owes "allegiance to no master." He adds that he has used only that which he considered to be the best of the poets of all ages. The language used in his poetry was that derived from the Jamaican dialect, archaic words, and figures of speech, which are then reshaped to suit his specific purposes. The introductory pages ("Author's Word") to *Harlem Shadows* has been cited repeatedly by scholars, critics, and McKay's readers to justify or support theories regarding his poetry. The important information given in that short essay is that McKay thinks the traditional should work best on "lawless and revolutionary passions and words," so as to give the feeling of the "highest degree of spontaneity and freedom." "For me," he says, "there is more quiet delight in 'The golden moon of heaven' than in 'the terra-cotta disc of cloud land'." The last quoted line here is ironically from a poem by one of the best-known Harlem Renaissance poets, Langston Hughes.

It is no accident that Claude McKay felt uncomfortable with the poetry and lifestyle of the New Negro Movement of the 1920s. He was never really a part of that whole milieu. He disagreed with their involvement with "art for art's sake" and with their being self-appointed messiahs to uplift the privileged few. Theirs was a tightly knit circle which excluded many. Because McKay's tendencies were more akin to the European tradition and experience, he was a misfit at a time when blackness was being celebrated. First, McKay's reading was Byron, Shelley, Keats, and the late Victorians. Secondly, his friends, personal and literary, were the whites in New York's suburbs and its downtown Greenwich Village. Thirdly, he was older than most of the Renaissance writers—Hughes, Cullen, Toomer, and others. And fourthly, he lived in Europe during most of the key Renaissance years. Consequently, for these reasons and more, he was, as Frank Harris of *Pearson's Magazine* noted, "an oddity, . . . a noble black poet with romantic intentions."

McKay felt a great tension between black content and traditional white form, and this, for him, was perhaps the hardest problem to solve. He grappled with the two as to where the thrust of his writing should be. He had been praised for producing poems which gave no hint of color. James Weldon Johnson, one of the few close black poet friends he had, advised him to do so; and, from the collection *Spring in New Hampshire,* **"If We Must Die,"** perhaps his best-known poem, was left out to retain the "no color" identity. The poem begins:

> If we must die, let it not be like hogs,
> Hunted and penned in an inglorious spot,
> While round us bark the mad and hungry dogs,
> Making their mock at our accursed lot.

The problem became a personal one of how to keep his allegiance to the British models—whose poetry he truly felt and knew well—and be a black poet emotionally. Writing poetry was not difficult for him, but what was difficult was the personae in conflict, the paradox of self which mars some of the poems.

Consequently, while McKay constantly preferred to keep the West Indian identity and the British training, he was conscious that nothing could change the fact that he was a writer who also happened to be a Negro. When told to mask his identity, and when in his novel *Banana Bottom* (1933) certain words were changed into "Britishisms," he became extremely angry and replied to his publishers and friends in this way:

> Of all the poets I admire, major and minor, Byron, Shelley, Keats, Blake, Burns, Whitman, Heine, Baudelaire, Verlaine and Rimbaud and the rest—it seemed to me that when I read them—in their poetry I could feel their race, their class, their roots in the soil, growing into plants, spreading and forming the background against which they were silhouetted. I could not feel the reality of them without that. So likewise I could not realize myself writing without that conviction.

Again, the problem of allegiance and coalition were surfaced to deal with these constant attempts to subjugate color to content. The natural and the creative became problematic also. McKay, regardless of all the places to which he traveled, realized that the artist's faith had to be in his origins, a patriotism as one might find in Whitman's America and in Yeats' Ireland. Furthermore, McKay's best poetry and prose were about Jamaica; as for him, the artist being inseparable from his roots would be an alien thought.

The title of his autobiography, *A Long Way from Home,* is from a Negro spiritual, the opening line of which is, "Sometimes I feel like a motherless child, a long way from home." The title, however, is not coincidental, and even though McKay never returned to Jamaica but chose American citizenship instead, the title is a misnomer because Jamaican memories permeate his best later writings. The poetry looks romantically to Jamaica and prophetically to blackness. His prophecy for Jamaica as an independent, Third World nation, for example, was fulfilled in the last two decades. *Spring in New Hampshire* (1920) and *The Selected Poems* (1953) have in them mostly nostalgic lyrics about Jamaica and songs celebrating nature, and they reflect those themes found in the nineteenth-century Romantics.

McKay's romanticism exhibits itself in several ways but primarily in his writing and lifestyle. His literary heroes were writers of conventional works, the sonnet his favorite mode of expression, but some of his poems are done in freer style. An example of the combination of Jamaican remembrance and celebration of nature in the less conventional style is **"Flame-Heart."**

> So much I have forgotten in ten years,
> So much in ten brief years! I have forgot
> What time the purple apples come to juice,
> And what month brings the shy forget-me-not.
> I have forgot the special, startling season
> Of the pimento's flowering and fruiting;
> What time of year the ground doves drown the
>   fields
> And fill the noonday with their curious fluting.
> I have forgotten much, but still remember
> The poinsetta's red, blood-red, in warm Decem-
>   ber.

Many critics have lingered over the meaning of the last line, which also closes stanza II, but the intention here is only to show the poems as examples of the different aspects of McKay's romanticism. He has forgotten the cycles of the seasons, but the emotion of the poem is rich in West Indian images.

In **"The Spanish Needle"** McKay uses a more conventional pattern to write about a very common and wild weed in Jamaica by the same name. It is a plant much like a dandelion in America, but the language and tone which he uses in the poem make the Spanish needle become a regal plant; thus the common and everyday in the hands of a romantic like McKay becomes uncommon. The following verses of that poem show the endearment which he feels for the ordinary:

> Lovely dainty Spanish needle
> With your yellow flower and white,
> Dew bedecked and softly sweeping,
> Do you think of me to-night?
>
> Shadowed by the spreading mango,
> Nodding o'er the rippling stream,
> Tell me, dear plant of my childhood,
> Do you of the exile dream?
>
> Do you see me by the brook's side
> Catching crayfish 'neath the stone,
> As you did the day you whispered:
> Leave the harmless dears alone?
> ....
> Lovely dainty Spanish needle,
> Source to me of sweet delight,
> In your far-off sunny southland
> Do you dream of me to-night?

This poem is very much in the romantic tradition of Shelley and Keats and is probably one of the few poems by McKay that every Jamaican schoolchild must recite "by heart." **"Home-Thoughts"** is one of his better poems with the homeland theme:

> Oh something just now must be happening there!
> That suddenly and quiveringly here,
> Amid the city's noises, I must think
> Of mangoes leaning o'er the river's brink,
> And dexterous Davie climbing high above,
> The gold fruits ebon-speckled to remove,
> And toss them quickly in the tangled mass
> Of wis-wis twisted round the guinea grass;
> And Cyril coming through the bramble-track
> A Prize bunch of bananas on his back;
> ....
> This is no daytime dream, there's something in it,
> Oh something's happening there this very minute!

The use of local words like *mango, wis-wis, guinea grass, bramble track, purple apple, ground dove, pimento, pingwing, rose apple, poinsetta,* and *banana* in **"Flame-Heart," "The Spanish Needle,"** and **"Home-Thoughts"** are entire images in themselves, and even without notes to explain their meanings and connotations, the mood, tone and theme of the poems are obvious. These poems all go back to the West Indian scene, and in them are found the similar conflicts and opposing attractions which plagued McKay throughout his lifetime. In them, also, joy and sorrow are accepted with the stoic indifference which was part of the romantic passion.

"The Snow Fairy," "Spring in New Hampshire," and **"After the Winter"** use the same American seasonal landscape as their background. They too are good, have a simplicity of diction and tone, and are full of longing and passion, but they by no means compare with the lilting, spontaneous yet deep emotion of **"Tropics in New York."** In comparing a few lines from **"Spring in New Hampshire"** with **"The Tropics in New York,"** one can see that the differences are very obvious, not only because of the subject, but because of McKay's involvement with the places closest to his heart:

> Too green the springing April grass,
> Too blue the silver-speckled sky,
> For me to linger here, alas,
> While happy winds go laughing by,
> Wasting the golden hours indoors,
> Washing windows and scrubbing floors.

The weariness and tedium of scrubbing floors in spring is felt, while outdoors the enjoyment of nature passes. Rather than being happy in nature, there is sorrow because the speaker is physically removed from it but is mentally aware of its presence. He is a prisoner of circumstance. **"The Tropics in New York"** finds the speaker a prisoner also in a foreign country, but the nostalgia, though sorrowful, is much more lyrical, and he seems closer to this subject, and the poem is richer:

> Bananas ripe and green, and ginger-root,
> Cocoa in pods and alligator pears,
> And tangerines and Mangoes and grape fruit,
> Fit for the highest prize at parish fairs,
>
> Set in the window, bringing memories
> Of fruit-trees laden by low-singing rills,
> And dewy dawns, and mystical blue skies
> In benediction over nun-like hills.
>
> My eyes grew dim, and I could no more gaze;
> A wave of longing through my body swept,
> And, hungry for the old, familiar ways,
> I turned aside and bowed my head and wept.

McKay obviously is the speaker in this poem, although he speaks for the hundreds of West Indians who became exiles away from their homeland primarily because of economic and diplomatic reasons. The poem, therefore, does have a oneness of feeling about it. The alienation felt is one of time and distance, and the consequence and helplessness is clearly felt in the last three lines. The progression is from glorious song to despair. It is one of his most moving poems on this theme, and the experience, as in **"If We Must Die,"** is the universal black experience.

It is not in the poems only that Claude McKay's romantic nature is exhibited, but in his lifestyle and relationship with people and the world. He traveled to Russia, England, Spain, Germany, and Morocco, and he had romances singularly with each of them. The flirting with Communism was short-lived, and in England he was just another West Indian. Both experiences were disappointing because of the romantic notions he held about them. Burns, Keats, Wordsworth, and Shelley were dead, and prejudice was alive. Learning from those two short "romances," he tried to savor the best in all of the other countries which he visited and in which he lived. In Spain it was the romanticism of the bullfight and the world of Hemingway; in Germany and France it was the beautiful art and architecture. The despairing moments were overshadowed by the glorious experiences of the people he met and the new countrysides to sing about. Again, some of McKay's better writings were done in Europe. His best works were not about the New York, Jamaica, or American scenes while he was living in these places but when he was away from them. In Tangiers, Morocco, he felt at home more than at any other time in his life. In a letter to Max Eastman . . . he wrote, "There are things in the life of the natives, their customs and superstitions reminiscent of Jamaica." And in another letter (1 September 1932) he stated, "My attachment to Tangiers is sort of a spiritual looking backwards."

McKay, therefore, seemed to have done his best

work when he maintained a distance between himself and his subject. This in itself was not true of all romantic writers, but it is true of the romantic spirit for nostalgia, mysticism and fascination. About life McKay wrote to Eastman (28 July 1919):

> . . . life fascinates me in its passions. It may survive when everything else is dead and fused into it. I revere all those spirits who in their little (bit?) way are helping the life force to attain its wonderful and beautiful communication.

In the same letter he says, "I love your life more than your poetry, more than your personality. This is my attitude toward all artists."

It is apparent that McKay believes strongly in the nationality, personal identity, and uniqueness that each writer brings to his art. It is that special uniqueness which makes each one different and reinforces the sturdy independence of each human's nature. It was in Europe and elsewhere that he missed America most and in America that he reminisced about Jamaica consistently.

All poetry, McKay thought, should be judged by

Title page of McKays's 1937 autobiography.

its own merits, not by categories of race and nationality. The double standard was something which he opposed, and this too was carried over into his lifestyle. Because he was a "foreign" Negro with white friends, the reality of racial prejudice and the embarrassing moments he experienced from whites and blacks left him torn. He wanted to be accepted, but the pain which nonacceptance brought others plagued him. He was not accepted by the blacks of the Harlem Renaissance group, and his friends were the white literati, not the black "Niggerati," as he called them. It is no wonder, then, that the romantic modes and distances worked best for McKay. Some of the most personal poems are about those experiences such as **"To the White Fiends"** and **"The White House."** The militancy and anger are there and very uncompromising. Regardless of this, it was the realm of "literary truth" with which McKay was most preoccupied. He spoke of and "defined" it in a letter to Eastman:

> I think that if the intellectual idea of literary truth were analyzed, it would prove at bottom to be nothing more than "a wise saying" or a "beautiful phrase" delivered in a unique and startling manner—an addition to the sum of the universal wisdom of mankind. Such a wisdom exists telling of the passions, the folly and the sagacity, success and failure, pain and joy of life. It existed long before modern science and I believe it will continue to exist as vigorous and independent as ever as long as humanity retains the facilities of feeling, thinking—the inexhaustible source of which great and authentic literature springs whether it is cerebral or sentimental, realistic or romantic.

The essence of McKay's romanticism was not only in his poetry, but in the life he lived, the places he visited, and the people and ideas he encountered. His daily vocabulary was very interestingly sprinkled with romantic asides, as was his autobiography, *A Long Way from Home,* and his letters to Max Eastman of *The Liberator.* In *A Long Way from Home,* the Pankhurst secretary is a "romantic middle class woman"; his radical days on *The Liberator* were "rosy with romance"; "The Wondervogel had lost their romantic flavor"; he mentions "D. H. Lawrence's psychic and romantic groping for a way out"; and he comments on the fact that "it was grand and romantic to have a grant to write." It is obvious that McKay was completely immersed in a romantic style of life very similar to that of some of his British models and contemporaries. A vocabulary interspersed with words carrying the romantic notion means that he consciously draws attention to where his allegiances to nature, life, and self lie. All of these coalesced to create poetry which said yes to life by its explicit philosophy.

Claude McKay has been called "Jamaica's Bobbie Burns," although he gave up that citizenship some twenty-eight years later. The land of his birth, Jamaica, about which he wrote his best prose, verse, and lyrics, still claims him as its citizen. The comparison with the Scottish Burns is by no means superficial, however, as there are many similarities in their writing and points-of-view. The romantics—Keats, Shelley, Wordsworth, Whitman, and Yeats—were also his literary heroes, because of the content of their works and the lifestyles which they led. It was, and still is, unusual to have a black man writing in the mode of the romantics, using their themes, subject matter, and meter. The two na-tures of self and art, of allegiance and coalition, were things for which McKay worked throughout his life and career. Regardless of his thoroughly British orientation, emotionally and literarily he never forgot his blackness. For a modern poet, the sonnet was his favorite form, and he wrote most of his poems on the time-honored subjects of love and nature. The universality of his romanticism and poetry surpasses color or time lines. (pp. 296-308)

Geta J. LeSeur, "Claude McKay's Romanticism," in *CLA Journal,* Vol. XXXII, No. 3, March, 1989, pp. 296-308.

SOURCES FOR FURTHER STUDY

Bronz, Stephen H. "Claude McKay." In his *Roots of Negro Consciousness, The 1920's: Three Harlem Renaissance Authors,* pp. 66-89. New York: Libra Publishers, 1964.

> Discusses major events in McKay's life and analyzes their effect on his work. Bronz traces McKay's poetry, fiction, and prose within the context of his life: his Jamaican heritage; his immigration to the United States; his reaction to American racism; his expatriate years in Russia, Europe, and Northern Africa; and his eventual return to America as a forgotten writer.

Collier, Eugenia W. "The Four-Way Dilemma of Claude McKay." *CLA Journal* XV, No. 3 (March 1972): 345-53.

> Analysis of McKay's poetry, suggesting that the author's work was affected by a series of dilemmas peculiar to the black man in white America.

Cooper, Wayne F. *Claude McKay: Rebel Sojourner in the Harlem Renaissance.* Baton Rouge: Louisiana State University Press, 1987, 441 p.

> Comprehensive biography of McKay.

Gloster, Hugh M. "Fiction of the Negro Renascence: The Van Vechten Vogue." In his *Negro Voices in American Fiction,* pp. 157-72. Chapel Hill: The University of North Carolina Press, 1948.

> Examines McKay's three novels, *Home to Harlem, Banjo,* and *Gingertown,* concluding that McKay capitalized on the sex, exaggeration, and libertinism first utilized by Carl Van Vechten in his novel *Nigger Heaven.*

Hansell, William H. "Some Themes in the Jamaican Poetry of Claude McKay." *PHYLON* XL, No. 2 (June 1979): 123-39.

> Analyzes the poems in *Songs of Jamaica* and *Constab Ballads,* discerning four thematic categories that became lifelong concerns in McKay's works: "poems on commonplace settings and activities, love poems, poems portraying the peasant mind, and poems with racial or social themes."

Ramchand, Kenneth. "The Road to *Banana Bottom.*" In his *The West Indian Novel and Its Background,* 2d ed., pp. 239-73. London: Heinemann, 1983.

> Examines McKay's treatment of cultural dualism in the author's three novels.

Herman Melville

1819-1891

American novelist, short story writer, and poet.

INTRODUCTION

M elville, a major American literary figure of the nineteenth century, is best known as the author of *Moby-Dick; or, The Whale* (1851), a complex metaphysical novel involving a quest for a white whale. Virtually unrecognized at the time of his death, Melville is now praised for his rich rhythmical prose and complex symbolism. A master of both realistic and allegorical narrative, Melville was also an incisive social critic and philosopher who strove to understand the ambiguities of life and to define the individual's relation to society and the universe.

Born and raised in New York City, Melville had a relatively comfortable childhood until his father's business failure and early death. Melville ended his formal education at age twelve to help support his family. He worked in the family fur business and as a bank clerk and taught at various schools until, in 1839, he sailed as a cabin boy aboard a merchant ship bound for Liverpool, England. This experience, shocking in its revelation of squalor and human cruelty, inspired his fourth novel, *Redburn: His First Voyage* (1849). Melville's later journey to the South Seas, begun aboard the whaling ship *Acushnet*, provided the background for his greatest works. Finding conditions unbearable aboard the *Acushnet*, Melville deserted the ship in the Marquesas and spent several months in captivity among a tribe of cannibalistic Polynesians. He finally escaped to a passing whaling vessel. Again appalled by the conditions at sea, Melville joined in a mutiny and was briefly imprisoned in Tahiti. He then moved on to Hawaii and later returned to New York aboard a U.S. naval vessel.

Until now, Melville had never contemplated a literary career; however, with no prospects for a career on his return to the U.S., he was encouraged by family and friends to write about his remarkable journeys. His first novels, *Typee: A Peep at Polynesian Life* (1846) and its sequel, *Omoo: A Narrative of Adventures in the South Seas* (1847), are fictionalized versions of his experiences in the Pacific. These novels were immediately successful and made Melville famous as the "man who lived among the cannibals"—a reputation he was never able to overcome and that interfered with the appreciation of his later works. Although they were generally praised for their excitement, romance, and splendid descriptions of the South Seas, *Typee* and *Omoo* infuriated members of the Christian missionary community, who resented Melville's negative portrayal of their motives and labors.

Melville's mature literary voice began to emerge in *Mardi: And a Voyage Thither* (1849). He was growing restless with the adventure narrative and was increasingly drawn to philosophical and metaphysical questions in his novels. Although *Mardi* begins as an adventure story, it quickly becomes a combination of philosophical allegory and satire; as such, it anticipates both *Moby-Dick* and *Pierre; or, The Ambiguities* (1852) in its levels of meaning, concern with metaphysical problems, and use of a questing hero. *Mardi* represents an important step in Melville's artistic development, yet its publication marked the beginning of the decline in his popularity. Discouraged by the novel's poor reception and in need of money, Melville temporarily returned to the travel narrative and produced *Redburn* and *White-Jacket; or, The World in a Man-of-War* (1850).

Like *Mardi*, *Moby-Dick* was initially conceived as a realistic narrative about sea life; but it took on epic proportions as Melville progressed in its composition. In the novel, the narrator, Ishmael, recounts his ill-fated voyage as a hand on board the whaling ship *Pequod*. Outfitted with an eclectic crew including South Sea islanders, North American Indians, blacks, and New England salts, the whaler leaves Nantucket on Christmas Day, bound on a commercial hunt for whales. As the trip progresses, however, Ahab, the ship's captain, exerts his will over the crew and converts the voyage into a quest to destroy his personal nemesis, a celebrated white whale known as Moby Dick. Ahab had lost a leg to the whale in a previous encounter, and his search is further fueled by his monomaniacal conviction that Moby Dick visibly personifies all earthly malignity and evil. The story concludes with a turbulent three-day struggle between the White Whale and the *Pequod*'s crew. The whale has been variously interpreted as God, evil, good, and, perhaps most accurately, a symbol of the ambiguity of nature. Both the influence of William Shakespeare, whose plays Melville was reading as he composed *Moby-Dick*, and his friendship with Nathaniel Hawthorne, to whom he dedicated the novel, had a significant effect on the rhythmic prose and complex levels of meaning found in the work. Although Melville's contemporaries gave it little notice, *Moby-Dick*

has been studied more intensively in the twentieth century than any other American novel and is now considered one of the greatest novels of all time.

Emotionally exhausted following the publication of *Moby-Dick* and desperate for recognition, Melville immediately began work on *Pierre*, a pessimistic novel that is considered the most autobiographical of his works. His popularity, already seriously damaged by the publication of *Moby-Dick*, was nearly destroyed by *Pierre;* the reading public, who preferred the entertainment of *Typee* and *Omoo*, was confused by the novel's metaphysical questionings and offended by its theme of incest. Despite considerable flaws, however, *Pierre* is now noted as a predecessor of the modern psychological novel.

Melville continued writing prose through the 1850s, despite the critical and popular failure of *Pierre* and *Moby-Dick*. He published numerous short stories in periodicals and collected six of his best in *The Piazza Tales* (1856). This volume includes "Benito Cereno," which is generally considered Melville's finest short story. *The Confidence-Man: His Masquerade* (1857), published the following year, is an allegorical satire on mid-nineteenth-century American life; this was the last of Melville's novels to appear during his lifetime. *Billy Budd*, left in manuscript at his death and considered one of his finest novels, was not published until 1924. Focusing on the execution of a young sailor aboard an English warship, the novel has been widely studied in an effort to determine Melville's final views on such issues as justice, morality, and religion. *Billy Budd* is also consistently praised for its philosophical insight, multifaceted narrative technique, and complex use of symbol and allegory.

Melville's poetry has been overshadowed by *Moby-Dick* and his other prose works and has only recently received serious critical attention. He began writing poetry in 1860, although his first collection, *Battle-Pieces and Aspects of the War*, was not published until 1866. That year he also became a customs official in New York, a post he held for twenty years. Two later collections of poetry were issued privately toward the end of his life: *John Marr and Other Sailors* (1888) and *Timoleon* (1891).

At the time of his death, Melville was almost unknown as a writer, and his accomplishments were not properly recognized for over a generation. A tremendous revival of interest in his work began in the 1920s, following the publication of Raymond Weaver's biography, *Herman Melville: Mariner and Mystic*, and constitutes a dramatic reversal nearly unprecedented in American literary history. Melville's works, particularly *Moby-Dick*, have been the subject of innumerable interpretations, and the body of Melville criticism, already immense, continues to grow. Melville is now recognized as one of America's greatest writers, and *Moby-Dick* is widely acclaimed as a work of genius.

(For further information about Melville's life and works, see *Concise Dictionary of American Literary Biography 1640-1865*; *Dictionary of Literary Biography*, Vols. 3, 74; *Nineteenth-Century Literature Criticism*, Vols. 3 12, 29; *Something about the Author*, Vol. 59; and *Short Story Criticism*, Vol. 1.)

CRITICAL COMMENTARY

NATHALIA WRIGHT

(essay date 1949)

[In the following excerpt from a work first published in 1949, Wright comments on Melville's "borrowings" and "conjurings" in his works.]

In all that Melville wrote he was no nearer saying what he had to say at the end than he was at the beginning. His effect, like Shakespeare's, is one of extension rather than of volume. One receives the impression of spaces and distances, of approaches and retreats, of vistas opened but not entered upon. One is always traveling but never arrives. (p. 173)

Above all, one is made to feel that what has been left unsaid is unspeakably vaster than what has been said. The super-abundance of material appals him, and he is driven at last to think of all truth as voiceless and of the question as more final than any answer. "God keep me from ever completing anything," cries Ishmael. "This whole book is a draught—nay, but the draught of a draught."

Had Melville's inspiration been any less inclusive or had his achievement been any more definitive, the irregularities of his thought and his style would be intolerable. As it is, these irregularities are nothing else than the "careful disorderliness" which he declared to be for some enterprises the true method. Not definition is its aim, but suggestion; not keen analysis but bold juxtaposition, contrasts and paradoxes, catalogues and citations, reflections, reminiscences, and reverberations. (pp. 173-74)

To this desire to extend the scope of his work, to this fear of appearing final, all Melville's rhetorical devices and all his voluminous sources are subservient. So indiscriminately are they introduced and associated that they tend at last to lose their separate identities. They are but fragments of a boundless creation, undistinguished otherwise in the hands of its creator. Of them all, however, no single one so far extends the

bounds of what Melville wrote as the Bible. However he alluded to it he was assured of a contrast with his immediate material: between the common and the great, the present and the past, the natural and the supernatural. And though each is a contrast achieved by many other means as well, only this one enabled him to make them all simultaneously, at once magnifying his characters and their affairs, establishing for the briefest moment a background of antiquity, and suggesting the presence of yet another, unseen world beyond the vast scene which meets the eye.

Originally and essentially, of course, all Melville's material is simple and commonplace, becoming transformed through a marvelous imagination. Viewed strictly in the light of fact his characters are of limited powers and lowly station. Yet as their lives unfold in passion and in problem, they seem to be supermen, inhabiting a world one degree larger than life. The effect is deliberate, and it is deliberately more than the general exaggeration of his pen. (pp. 174-75)

This effect of magnitude in Melville's characters is achieved largely by figurative language, since his imagery contains references to so many great personages of history and literature. Side by side with the nameless crews of his ships walk Henry VIII, Charlemagne, Xerxes, Apis, Ammon, Jove, Perseus, Prometheus, Mohammed, Faust, Hamlet, Beelzebub, Abraham. With many of them Melville briefly compared his own characters. . . . The Bible, in fact, provides genealogies to ennoble the meanest of men, for all, it asserts in various accounts, are descendants of the Jehovah-created Adam, of the sons of God who intermarried with the daughters of men, of the patriarch Noah, and spiritually of the New Testament Father. Melville cited them all.

More important than this casual imagery, though, is the deeper relationship which is made to exist between some of these personages and Melville's characters, whereby the patterns of their lives are both clari-

Principal Works

Typee: A Peep at Polynesian Life (novel) 1846

Omoo: A Narrative of Adventures in the South Seas (novel) 1847

Mardi: And a Voyage Thither (novel) 1849

Redburn: His First Voyage (novel) 1849

White-Jacket; or, The World in a Man-of-War (novel) 1850

Moby-Dick; or, The Whale (novel) 1851; also published as The Whale, 1851

Pierre; or, The Ambiguities (novel) 1852

Israel Potter: His Fifty Years in Exile (novel) 1855

The Piazza Tales (short stories) 1856

The Confidence-Man: His Masquerade (novel) 1857

Battle-Pieces and Aspects of the War (poetry) 1866

Clarel: A Poem and Pilgrimage in the Holy Land (poetry) 1876

John Marr and Other Sailors (poetry) 1888

Timoleon (poetry) 1891

The Apple-Tree Table, and Other Sketches (short stories) 1922

Billy Budd and Other Prose Pieces (novel and short stories) 1924

fied and given significance. Some of them are named for the great, and thus the parallel moves with them. (pp. 175-76)

Appropriately are they called. For these same characters . . . wrestle with problems which have preoccupied heroes, sages, prophets, and gods. (p. 176)

The speech of these people, too, is appropriate, containing some of the most magnificent of stylistic echoes from the seventeenth century, the Elizabethans, the Anglo-Saxons, the authors of the Bible. . . . [All] add eloquence to pretentiousness. Like the Teutonic war song of Yoomy and the Shakespearean ranting of Pierre, these words, whether spoken by or about Melville's characters, make each of them seem less and less like a single individual, more and more like Everyman.

It is in just this conception of character, in fact, that the intricate connections between Melville's religious thought, his use of the Bible, and the entire Romantic school to which he belonged are most clearly revealed. Quite likely its belief in the dignity and the possibility of the individual more than all else commended Christianity to him. For this he held to be the great value, the field on which all conflicts were fought, the divinity shaping every end. Man, by the very fact of his being, could be neither common nor insignificant, and often the darkest of skin and the most primi-

tive of mind held closest communion with the heart of the universe.

But it was significantly the Calvinistic and the Lockean elements of this Christian individualism to which he subscribed, not the apostolic or the medieval. It was, in fact, a sublime egotism, at least as much Satanic as theistic, and to no small degree political. Hence all Melville's characters have something in common with the Renaissance and with the Byronic hero. And hence all those in the Bible on whom he depended most to magnify his own were carefully chosen: the ambitious Ahab rather than the repentant David, the rebellious Jonah and the lonely Jeremiah rather than the priestly Isaiah, the aspiring but not the obedient Jesus. For all this is more than magnitude; this is the assault upon the bastions of heaven.

Nor do these characters come alone to Melville's pages. The ancient past to which most of them belong, and which inevitably accompanies them, towers up everywhere, a presence of which he was constantly aware. And again, since none of the scenes of his narratives is older than the eighteenth century, it is largely a figurative method he adopted. (pp. 177-78)

[In] the last analysis Melville considered all recorded history but a fraction of the past, and the cultivated intellect only a part of consciousness. The unexplored regions of the individual and of the racial mind, reaching back into prehistoric mists, beckoned him. Hence he was constantly adding an extra dimension to his scene by suggesting the existence of an invisible world. (p. 182)

In all that he wrote, in fact, the line between the seen and the unseen is almost indistinguishable. So vast is the universe he depicted that its outermost reaches are well nigh beyond perception: the stars which are to Taji worlds on worlds, the mysterious submarine life at which the men of the *Pequod* peer as they sail through the great armada of whales. Reality merges imperceptibly into unreality. Rather significantly, *Typee* and *Omoo* were followed by *Mardi*, which begins like them as a realistic tale of the sea. But once launched in their boats from the *Arcturion*, Jarl and Taji sail gradually but completely out of the natural world into the "world of mind," on which the wanderer gazes, it is added, with more wonder than Balboa in the Aztec glades.

No less casually and utterly do Ahab, Pierre, and Billy Budd move farther and farther from all that is objective until at last the outward circumstances of their lives mean nothing and the inner significance is everything. Vast as the universe is about them, that within themselves is yet vaster and more mysterious. (pp. 182-83)

Dreams and portents, hypersensitive natures, and miraculous events—these outline Melville's invisible world. (p. 183)

[In] his belief in the existence of [a] world beyond the world of sense Melville has often been called, and even called himself, Platonic. Like the Platonists, he did believe truth resided in the unseen world of ideas and conceptions rather than in the world of material manifestations. But in his essentially romantic conception of this invisible sphere he was closer to the Hebrews than to the Greeks. Order, rhetoric, and logic did not represent the primal truth to him as did elemental and undisciplined energy. (p. 184)

[Strangeness and terror are the chief characteristics] of the unseen to Melville. "Though in many of its aspects this visible world seems formed in love," asserts Ishmael, "the invisible spheres were formed in fright." Of the invisible terrors the sea, with the mysterious creatures that pass through it, is the symbol, while the earth is the symbol of the known world. . . .

As the sea and the land thus alternate as symbols in his scenes, so the calm and the storm alternate on Melville's sea. For though calmness is sweet and agreeable, the motionless ship is destined to decay. In the rack of the storm it leaps forward, drawing fire from heaven, approaching its goal according as it courts disaster. At the heart of the storm, in the midst of the Great Mutiny, Melville's seekers of truth find and worship it. (p. 185)

Nothing less than a spirit touching good and evil was adequate to preside over the universe [Melville] envisaged. Even in his earliest voyages he found that the green valley of the Typee was, like the Garden of Eden, but a small plot of the earth. And to the end, side by side in the Maldive sea, swam the pilot fish and the white shark, as long before the white whale swam ahead of Ahab while the beckoning breezes blew softly from the green shore. The law which could hang a criminal could also hang the purest of the pure, and that without shattering the universe, but only dyeing its vast sky a deeper rose. (p. 187)

It is significant that Melville's persistent image for truth . . . is of something hidden. Ultimate reality exists at the core of this complex universe, at the very heart of its vast reaches, indeed well-nigh impossible to attain for the superficies which surround it. . . . Speaking of his own twenty-fifth birthday, Melville wrote to Hawthorne: "Three weeks have scarcely passed, at any time between then and now, that I have not unfolded within myself. But I feel that I am now come to the inmost leaf of the bulb, and that shortly the flower must fall to the mould."

So all Melville's art and all the vast scene it reared are not ends in themselves but means to an end. All his borrowings and all his conjurings are but approximations. They are circumferences of the center, cerements around the mummy, antechambers to the throne room, husks about the kernel. Not truth itself is his culminat-

ing vision, but "cunning glimpses," "occasional flashings-forth," "short, quick probings at the very axis of reality"; symbolic and fragmentary manifestations of the one absolute, which is in the last analysis inviolable. (pp. 187-88)

Nathalia Wright, in her *Melville's Use of the Bible,* Octagon Books, 1969, 209 p.

ALBERT CAMUS
(essay date 1952)

[Camus was an Algerian-born French novelist, essayist, dramatist, and short story writer. In the following excerpt from an essay originally published in 1952, he describes the tone of *Billy Budd* and comments on the artistry and intent of "Benito Cereno."]

[Melville's] unwearying peregrination in the archipelago of dreams and bodies, on an ocean "whose every wave is a soul," this Odyssey beneath an empty sky, makes [him] the Homer of the Pacific. But we must add immediately that his Ulysses never returns to Ithaca. The country in which Melville approaches death, that he immortalizes in *Billy Budd,* is a desert island. In allowing the young sailor, a figure of beauty and innocence whom he dearly loves, to be condemned to death, Captain Vere submits his heart to the law. And at the same time, with his flawless story that can be ranked with certain Greek tragedies, the aging Melville tells us of his acceptance for the first time of the sacrifice of beauty and innocence so that order may be maintained and the ship of men may continue to move forward toward an unknown horizon. Has he truly found the peace and final resting place that earlier he had said could not be found in the Mardi archipelago? Or are we, on the contrary, faced with a final shipwreck that Melville in his despair asked of the gods? "One cannot blaspheme and live," he had cried out. At the height of consent, isn't *Billy Budd* the worst blasphemy? This we can never know, any more than we can know whether Melville did finally accept a terrible order, or whether, in quest of the spirit, he allowed himself to be led, as he had asked, "beyond the reefs, in sunless seas, into night and death." But no one, in any case, measuring the long anguish that runs through his life and work, will fail to acknowledge the greatness, all the more anguished in being the fruit of self-conquest, of his reply.

But this, although it had to be said, should not mislead anyone as to Melville's real genius and the sovereignty of his art. It bursts with health, strength, explosions of humor, and human laughter. It is not he who opened the storehouse of sombre allegories that today hold sad Europe spellbound. As a creator, Melville is, for example, at the furthest possible remove from Kafka, and he makes us aware of this writer's artistic limitations. However irreplaceable it may be, the spiritual experience in Kafka's work exceeds the modes of expression and invention, which remain monotonous. In Melville, spiritual experience is balanced by expression and invention, and constantly finds flesh and blood in them. Like the greatest artists, Melville constructed his symbols out of concrete things, not from the material of dreams. The creator of myths partakes of genius only insofar as he inscribes these myths in the denseness of reality and not in the fleeting clouds of the imagination. In Kafka, the reality that he describes is created by the symbol, the fact stems from the image, whereas in Melville the symbol emerges from reality, the image is born of what is seen. This is why Melville never cut himself off from flesh or nature, which are barely perceptible in Kafka's work. On the contrary, Melville's lyricism, which reminds us of Shakespeare's, makes use of the four elements. He mingles the Bible with the sea, the music of the waves with that of the spheres, the poetry of the days with the grandeur of the Atlantic. He is inexhaustible, like the winds that blow for thousands of miles across empty oceans and that, when they reach the coast, still have strength enough to flatten whole villages. He rages, like Lear's madness, over the wild seas where Moby Dick and the spirit of evil crouch among the waves. When the storm and total destruction have passed, a strange calm rises from the primitive waters, the silent pity that transfigures tragedies. Above the speechless crew, the perfect body of Billy Budd turns gently at the end of its rope in the pink and grey light of the approaching day.

T. E. Lawrence ranked *Moby Dick* alongside *The*

Last page of the manuscript of Melville's "inside narrative," *Billy Budd.*

Possessed or *War and Peace.* Without hesitation, one can add to these *Billy Budd, Mardi,* **"Benito Cereno,"** and a few others. These anguished books in which man is overwhelmed, but in which life is exalted on each page, are inexhaustible sources of strength and pity. We find in them revolt and acceptance, unconquerable and endless love, the passion for beauty, language of the highest order—in short, genius. "To perpetuate one's name," Melville said, "one must carve it on a heavy stone and sink it to the bottom of the sea; depths last longer than heights." Depths do indeed have their painful virtue, as did the unjust silence in which Melville lived and died, and the ancient ocean he unceasingly ploughed. From their endless darkness he brought forth his works, those visages of foam and night, carved by the waters, whose mysterious royalty has scarcely begun to shine upon us, though already they help us to emerge effortlessly from our continent of shadows to go down at last toward the sea, the light, and its secret. (pp. 291-94)

Albert Camus, "Critical Essays: Herman Melville," in his *Lyrical and Critical Essays,* edited by Philip Thody, translated by Ellen Conroy Kennedy, Alfred A. Knopf, 1968, pp. 288-94.

WILLIAM YORK TINDALL
(lecture date 1954-55)

[An American authority on the works of James Joyce, Wallace Stevens, and others, Tindall wrote numerous studies of modern literature. In the following excerpt, originally delivered as a lecture in 1954 or 1955, he describes the form and structure of *Billy Budd* and explores the moral basis of the contrast between good and evil in the story.]

Billy Budd seems to make something almost too tidy out of what remains uncertain in *Moby Dick.* Melville's story of the captain, the villain, and the tar, apparently less a story than a commentary on one, may strike the hasty reader as a product of reason rather than imagination, as something reduced to discourse for ready apprehension by basic Englishmen. What had to be said has been said by Captain Vere or Melville himself. As critics, therefore, we may feel frustrated, as Romantics we may prefer a little teasing mystery around, and as esthetes, confronted with discourse, we are sure that talking about a thing is less admirable than embodying it in image or action. Of Kierkegaard's three categories, the esthetic, the moral, and the divine, Melville seems to have chose the second—to the applause of some and the departure of others, for *Don Giovanni* maybe.

That the matter of *Billy Budd* gratifies what Melville calls "the moral palate" is plain. . . . (p. 73)

The subject is a quandary or what Melville calls "the intricacies involved in the question of moral responsibility." As the captain ponders "the moral phenomenon presented in Billy Budd" and the "elemental evil" of Claggart, he fathoms the "mystery of iniquity." The case of Billy seems, as the captain says, a matter for "psychologic theologians."

Although, as T. S. Eliot observes in *After Strange Gods,* "It is . . . during moments of moral and spiritual struggle . . . that men [in fiction] . . . come nearest being real," Billy and Claggart, who represent almost pure good and pure evil, are too simple and too extreme to satisfy the demands of realism; for character demands admixture. Their all but allegorical blackness and whiteness, however, are functional in the service of Vere's problem, and Vere, goodness knows, is real enough. Claggart is black because, as Philipp G. Frank once observed, a sinner is necessary for the realization of a moral code; and an innocent is almost equally instructive. These abstractions, a sacrifice of verisimilitude to tactical necessity, reveal the "moral quality" of the captain's mind, which becomes a theater for contending opposites and eventual choice. Such dramatic crises are not only the favorite stuff of novelists but of philosophers and poets as well: Kierkegaard wrote *Either/Or* and Yeats "The Choice."

Not only rational, Vere's choice involves his whole sensitive, adult being. Agony shows on his face as he emerges from his interview with Billy, and a final exclamation shows how deeply he is stirred. Involving more than black and white, the captain's choice is between two moral codes, military and natural. The first is evident; the second is either that of the noble savage, in whom Melville was interested, or what Western culture takes for granted. In other words, the captain's conflict is between the balanced claims of justice and equity, order and confusion, law and grace, reason and feeling, or, as Melville puts it, "military duty" and "moral scruple." Vere's eloquent and moving speech to the drumhead court, the climax of such drama as there is, leaves little to add about these issues and his dilemma.

The conflict of military with natural may occupy the stage, but Melville recognizes other codes, that of custom or respectability, for example. Claggart's "natural depravity" appears in respectable guise. Melville also recognizes the cultural, psychological, and absolute bases for morality, and hints in a very modern way at their operation.

"Moral," Melville's favorite word—in this book at least—is one which, though commonly taken for granted, is slippery. . . . As I shall use it and as I think Melville did, morality implies not only action but motive, attitude, and being. It involves a sense of obligation to self, community, and the absolute, which provide a frame by conscience, law, tradition, or revela-

tion. If we demand a single equivalent, Melville's "responsibility" will do.

Vere's action, however sudden and whether we approve of it or not, is plainly responsible. Billy and Claggart act, to be sure: one bears false witness and the other delivers a blow, but neither actor follows reason and each is more important for what he is than what he does. If being as well as action can be moral, however, they are moral figures, too, existing like cherubs or fiends in a moral atmosphere. Good and bad, they occupy the region of good and evil. (pp. 74-5)

[The question we must consider in reading *Billy Budd*] is not how much morality is there but how much is under control, how fully insight and moral intelligence have submitted to esthetic discipline. Our problem, then, is not morality itself but moral art or morally significant form.

Captain Vere's speech to the court adequately embodies the idea of "moral responsibility" in dramatic form; but we must find if Billy's history has found fitting embodiment. At first reading, that history seems a curious and eccentric structure of essays on ethics, digressions or "bypaths," character sketches, and chronicles of the navy, an arrangement that after uncertain progress tails inconclusively off. Such image and action as we find, failing to halt the lamentable decline, seem occasions for an analysis or digression, like biblical texts in a pulpit. Since the crucial interview between Vere and Billy is disappointingly offstage, Melville seems to have avoided the dramatic possibilities of his theme. That the book calls for the dramatization he failed to give it, is proved by attempts at play and opera, which, while affirming excellence of theme, imply that action or image are better ways of presenting it. But something that continues to fascinate us in its present form and calls forth responses beyond the capacity of discourse, suggests art of another kind. Maybe Melville avoided drama in the interests of a less obvious medium. (p. 76)

That Melville was aware of form is clear from passages in *Billy Budd.* When Captain Vere says, "With mankind forms, measured forms, are everything," he probably means usage and custom; but Melville himself, applying Vere's remark to esthetics, says that the symmetry of form desirable in pure fiction cannot be achieved in factual narrative like this. The story is not factual in fact. But Melville, wanting it to seem so, excuses apparent formlessness as a form for giving the illusion of a bare report; for truth, he continues, will always have its ragged edges and matters of fact must lack the finish of an "architectural finial." (pp. 76-7)

What seems at first to be factual is presented, we find, in part by images and allusions that are incompatible with a pretense of factuality. Though unapparent, those images are livelier than we thought. Consider the coloring of the scene between decks before the execution as Billy lies in white amid profound blackness. Catching up the abstract whiteness and blackness of Billy and Claggart, this image of black and white embodies them. At the execution the rosy dawn that seems "the fleece of the Lamb of God seen in mystical vision" promises a kind of renewal while implying much else. Circling birds after the burial at sea offer by the aid of tradition some spiritual import. And that spilt soup, perhaps more action than image, carries suggestions beyond the demands of plot, suggestions so indefinite, what is more, that they confound its rational progress. Even the names of ships, though serving a more comprehensible purpose, are as significant as those in *Moby Dick*. Billy is removed from the *Rights of Man,* for instance, and Vere is mortally wounded by a shot from the *Athéiste.*

The words of *Billy Budd* carry more than denotation. "Sinister dexterity," at once witty and desolating, sounds like something from *Finnegans Wake,* where, indeed, it reappears. Vere's last words, "Billy Budd," are equivocal. Do they imply feeling, regret, self-realization, understanding? Are they a form for something incompletely realized? However "factual" the words of this pseudoreport, they function like the words of poetry.

Not only last words and indeterminate images but a number of hints about Billy's "all but feminine" nature plague our assumptions. Roses and lilies dye his cheeks. He comports himself like a "rustic beauty" at times and like a vestal virgin at others. These qualities and appearances, astonishing in an able seaman, calling forth an "ambiguous smile" from one or another of his shipmates, suggest psychological depths and motives below the level of the plain report. By virtue of such intimations Billy seems at once more and less bottomless than we had supposed, and so do the motives of Claggart, if not those of the captain himself. Among such suggestions, avoidance of the obviously dramatic becomes implicit embodiment that escapes the limits of drama.

What pleases me most, however, is the accompaniment of biblical allusions which, however unobtrusive and irregular, recurs like Wagnerian *leitmotiv.* Time and again Billy is compared to Adam and Jesus. Billy's innocence is as much that of Adam before the Fall as that of the more secular noble savage. As a "peacemaker," a term implying beatitude, Billy seems destined for "crucifixion"; and his hanging, condensing events, be-

Melville's first five books (1846-1850).

comes an ascension. Vere is compared to Abraham about to sacrifice Isaac, obeying God's will with fear and trembling. Becoming a shadow of God, Vere weighs the claims of Adam and Satan. Claggart, whose denunciation is reported in Mosaic terms as "false witness," is compared not only to the Serpent of Eden but to Ananias and to one struck dead by an angel of God, "yet," as the captain says, "the angel must hang!" Man's fall and redemption and all troubles between seem suggested by this large though not fully elaborated analogy, which, bringing to mind the mythical parallels in *Ulysses* and *The Waste Land,* removes Billy a little farther from the abstraction to which, for all his stutter and those rosy cheeks, he seems committed. However incapable of supporting this mythical burden, he becomes by its aid almost as portentous as choosing Vere. The sailors, whose testimony cannot be ignored, are more impressed by Billy than by Vere, reason and all. Not only being and secular victim, Billy becomes saint and martyr and his hanging an omen. Pieces of the spar to which he quietly ascends are venerated like pieces of the true cross, suitable for reliquaries or the holiest of duffle bags. By the aid of myth and military ritual the story of Billy, transformed from an essay on good, evil, and choice, approaches what Yeats called "the ceremony of innocence."

We must conclude that Melville avoided the attractions of the obvious in the interests of indefinite suggestiveness and myth. His work, whatever its air of the factual and the discursive, is symbolist and richer for scarcity of drama and image. Such drama and images as are there function more intensely in their abstract context than profusion could. That the structure as a whole also serves esthetic purpose is likely. As we have seen, the book is a queer arrangement of discourse, action, image, and allusion, with discourse predominating. We have seen how image and action work in this mixture; but we must examine the function of discourse. In such context, discourse, increasing tension, makes allusion and image dramatic or enlarges them, and, working with allusion, image, and action may produce a third something by juxtaposition as in Eliot's *Four Quartets* or Wallace Stevens' *Notes Toward a Supreme Fiction.* Seeming now a structure of conflicts, not only of men and codes but of methods, which become a technical echo of the theme, the book emerges as a structural drama or a drama of structure. An ending that seemed weak afterthought (and was not there in the first version) now unifies all. Vere's exclamation, the saint's legend, and inconclusiveness, working together, comprise a form, which may tail off but tails suggestively off, leaving endless reverberations in our minds. There is more mystery around than we had thought, and we may agree with dying Gertrude Stein that answers are less important than questions. What at a superficial reading had the appearance of exhaus-

tive discourse becomes inexhaustible. The shapeless thing becomes suggestive shape. Neither as loose nor as tight as it once seemed, the strange sequence of precise discourse and indefinite suggestiveness corresponds to our experience of life itself. That the form Melville made fascinates while it eludes and teases is shown no less by popular favor than by the abundance of critical comment.

However different it looks, *Billy Budd* is not altogether different in kind from *Moby Dick,* another structure of digression, discourse, action, and image. The proportions and impact may be different, the images of *Moby Dick* may be more compelling, but both serve symbolic suggestion and both are forms for offering a vision of reality. Not the tidy discourse of our first impression, the work is almost as inexplicable as *Moby Dick.*

What exactly does this form present? It is impossible to answer this question for any symbolist work; for works of this kind escape discursive accounting. We may say that *Billy Budd* is a vision of man in society, vision of man's moral quandary or his responsibility; but its meaning is more general than these, and that is why it haunts us. So haunted, I find the work not an essay on a moral issue but a form for embodying the feeling and idea of thinking about a moral issue, the experience of facing, of choosing, of being uneasy about one's choice, of trying to know. Not a conclusion like a sermon, *Billy Budd* is a vision of confronting what confronts us, of man thinking things out with all the attendant confusions and uncertainties. Disorder is a form for this and the apparently formless book a formal triumph. To do what it does it has to be a fusion of tight-loose, shapeless-shaped, irrelevant-precise, suggestive-discursive—a mixture of myth, fact, and allusion that has values beyond reference. The discursive parts represent our attempts at thinking, while the action, images, and allusions represent what we cannot think but must approximate. Arrangement of these discordant elements forms a picture of a process.

From my guess at meaning it follows that the center of this form is neither Vere nor Billy but rather the teller of the story or Melville himself. Though ghostlier, he is not unlike the Marlow of Conrad's *Lord Jim* and *Heart of Darkness* or the Quentin of Faulkner's *Absalom, Absalom!* Using Vere and Billy as materials, Melville's thought-process, like those of Marlow and Quentin, is the heart of this darkness and its shape the objective correlative, a form for something at once imperfectly understood and demanding understanding. Morality, the substance of this form, becomes an element that limits and directs the feelings and ideas created by the whole. Moral substance, what is more, may be what engages our minds while the form does its work. Value, not from morality alone, issues from the form that includes it and in which it serves. If the form concerned less, I repeat, it would be trivial, but without its formal presentation the morality would remain in Sunday school.

United now, the beautiful and the good create a vision larger than either, a vision transcending the case of Billy Budd or the quandary of Captain Vere. The teller, now any man, presents man's feeling in the face of any great dilemma. Thought and feeling, outdistancing themselves, become objects of contemplation, remote yet immediate. The effect of this form is moral in the sense of enlarging our awareness of human conditions of relationships and of improving our sensitivity. In such a form Kierkegaard's esthetic, moral, and divine become a single thing. (pp. 77-81)

William York Tindall, "The Ceremony of Innocence (Herman Melville: 'Billy Budd')," in *Great Moral Dilemmas in Literature, Past and Present,* edited by R. M. MacIver, The Institute for Religious and Social Studies, 1956, pp. 73-81.

HOWARD C. HORSFORD
(essay date 1962)

[In the following excerpt, Horsford explores structure and symbolism in *Moby-Dick.*]

It is not new to point to Melville's life-long concern with the relation between knowledge and belief, but we need to explore more fully his imaginative rendering of the implications of such a relationship—and its collapse—if we are to understand better our response to his fiction. . . .

Melville grew up with the generations still wracked by the new theory of knowledge developed most fully by David Hume. In the face of the pious complacencies of the "Age of Reason," Hume had argued that nothing can be discovered by reasoning on the subjects with which metaphysics is concerned. Mere custom, only, stands warrant for our ideas of cause and effect; "belief" is not "knowledge" and "is more properly an act of the sensitive, than of the cogitative part of our natures." (p. 234)

[Those] young men of Emerson's and Melville's generations—those who thought about it all—sensed profoundly enough the desperate implications of Hume's skeptical epistemology. "Who is he that can stand up before him," the deeply troubled young Emerson asked his aunt, "& prove the existence of the Universe, & of its founders?"

This is the problem which for Melville so largely shapes the "ontological heroics" (the phrase is his) he passionately argued those years. . . . For Hume, in arguing the purely subjective, the illusory nature of

knowledge, had struck at a rooted habit of thought, one conditioned by milleniums of tradition in the western religious world, one which had almost immemorially asserted the nature and providence of God on the material evidence of His handiwork. (pp. 235-36)

[Suppose] our "knowledge" of this universe, which presumably so manifests its Creator, should be, after all, only subjectively created illusion, delusory? The profound implications in this possibility were what so challenged the imagination of the returned young sailor just discovering the exciting world of the mind. And this is an America where . . . the divinely benign influence of nature on the heroic new men of this new Eden was likely to be proclaimed in any editorial, in any patriotic oration, alike from the orthodox pulpit and the lyceum platform of the self-styled transcendentalists.

Thus, though they by no means define between them all the aspects then dominant in American faiths, Jonathan Edwards and Emerson may speak, the one for American Calvinism in its most intellectually rigorous form, the other for American transcendentalism in its most persuasive idiom. In any event, the impulse to assert symbolic identities between nature and its god was sufficiently universal for a young man to absorb anywhere. At no less a hallowed shrine than his mother's knee, Melville heard the Dutch Reformed Catechism proclaiming man could learn much of God through His created universe—"a most elegant book, wherein all creatures, great and small, are as so many characters leading us to contemplate the invisible things of God." . . .

[Even] the rigorous Edwards went much further in his thought. To him the "images" and "shadows" of the natural world were not merely useful for illustrations of divine truths; they were evidence of Truth itself. . . .

The success of Hume's destruction of the certainty of knowledge, together with all its devastating implications for thought generally, including religious belief, eventually set off what has been called a mania for epistemological investigation. Emerson, like his English and German fellows, was deeply shaken by the Scotch Goliath. But in the end, like them, he was able to reassert a faith, a confidence in the reading of the world as a symbol of God, founded on a depth of *intuitive* conviction beyond—or, at any rate, not susceptible to—rational argumentation or criticism.

At the same time, Emerson went beyond Edwards in denying the tragic possibilities of human error and suffering. It was the easy, cheerful benevolence of transcendentalism in its shallower reaches, as well as the complacent assurance in the myth of the new world paralleling it, which prompted . . . Melville's scorn. Melville, with far more direct experience of the world

WORLD LITERATURE CRITICISM

William T. Porter on the dramatic interest of *Moby-Dick*:

Moby Dick, or the Whale, is all whale. Leviathan is here in full amplitude. Not one of your museum affairs, but the real, living whale, a bona-fide, warm-blooded creature, ransacking the waters from pole to pole. His enormous bulk, his terribly destructive energies, his habits, his food, are all before us. Nay, even his lighter moods are exhibited. We are permitted to see the whale as a lover, a husband, and the head of a family. So to speak, we are made guests at his fire-side; we set our mental legs beneath his mahogany, and become members of his interesting social circle. No book in the world brings together so much whale. We have his history, natural and social, living and dead. But Leviathan's natural history, though undoubtedly valuable to science, is but a part of the book. It is in the personal adventures of his captors, their toils, and, alas! not unfrequently their wounds and martyrdom, that our highest interest is excited. . . .

Moby Dick, or the Whale, is a 'many-sided' book. Mingled with much curious information respecting whales and whaling there is a fine vein of sermonizing, a good deal of keen satire, much humor, and that too of the finest order, and a story of peculiar interest. As a romance its characters are so new and unusual that we doubt not it will excite the ire of critics. It is not tame enough to pass this ordeal safely. Think of a monomaniac whaling captain, who, mutilated on a former voyage by a particular whale, well known for its peculiar bulk, shape, and color—seeks, at the risk of his life and the lives of his crew, to capture and slay this terror of the seas! It is on this idea that the romance hinges. The usual staple of novelists is entirely wanting. We have neither flinty-hearted fathers, designing villains, dark caverns, men in armor, nor anxious lovers. There is not in the book any individual, who, at a certain hour, '*might have been seen*' ascending hills or descending valleys, as is usual. The thing is entirely new, fresh, often startling, and highly dramatic, and with those even, who, oblivious of other fine matters, scattered with profusest hand, read for the sake of the story, must be exceedingly successful. . . .

William T. Porter, in a review of *Moby-Dick; or, The Whale,* in *Spirit of the Times,* 6 December 1851.

---

than Emerson, had found few Edens in the forecastle. (p. 236)

For the increasingly scornful Melville . . . , writers like Emerson or Goethe or Carlyle quickly became that "guild of self-impostors, with a preposterous rabble of Muggletonian Scots and Yankees, whose vile brogue still the more bestreaks the stripedness of their Greek or German Neoplatonical originals." His own "ontological heroics," of which he writes so often to Hawthorne in 1850-1851 while the whale was in his flurry, pursue the same questions of the nature of reality, the nature and existence of God, from a profoundly different vantage.

It would be absurd, of course, to make of *Moby-Dick* a systematic, discursive rebuttal of either Emersonian or more traditional ontological assumptions. Nonetheless, the represented experience of the novel is precisely that of the millennially old tradition viewed in a terrifying new perspective, of sensing faith and conviction disintegrate, so to speak, before one's eyes. We speak often, and with singular aptness, of the novel in metaphors of hunting, of questing, of going out to sea to "see"; what is seen and felt, what is projected here is that experience.

In Edwards and Emerson alike, the verb "see," once noticed, seems everywhere. . . . Yet what Edwards and even more Emerson "saw" they felt as reassurance about God's world. For Emerson, . . . the apparent faults of the world lay not in the reality, but in our own imperfect vision. Life itself is an "angle of vision" and "man is measured by the angle at which he looks at objects." In *Nature* he disposes of evil and ugli-

ness with the facility of a Shaftesbury or Pope: "The ruin or the blank that we see when we look at nature, is in our own eye"; "The Poet" finds that "the evils of the world are such only to the evil eye." But with Melville, . . . such passages provoked exasperated marginal comments. As against the bland pronouncement in "Spiritual Laws," "the good, compared to the evil which he sees, is as his own good to his own evil," Melville noted scathingly, "A perfectly good being, therefore, would see no evil.—But what did Christ see?—He saw what made him weep. . . ."

In the novel much of the hunt, of course, is after fair but much-pursued and slighter game like Biblical literalism, theological hair-splitting and apologetics, or practice versus preaching. The Biblical accounts of Jonah or Job, for example, are old familiar targets, and Melville is neither particularly original nor always at his best in heavy-handed irony and jocularity. Neither is this delighted hatchet-work altogether to the point, dealing as it does only with the engrafted fruit, not the roots of conviction.

The real triumph of the novel, both intellectually and esthetically, lies elsewhere; boldly, Melville adopted a symbolist esthetic—of the kind Emerson proclaimed in *Nature*—to express a vision of experience, with, at the same time, the profoundest questioning of its metaphysical premises. With a fuller sense of the radically symbolic quality of the mind's activity than any artist before him (Coleridge excepted), Melville created a great man tragically destroying himself because he assents fully and dogmatically to a symbolic interpretation of experience. Melville designed the tragedy of Ahab, the art of *Moby-Dick,* from material made to question the very foundation of that art.

It is the triumph of the novel that, as Thoreau would require, every natural fact is so intensely viewed it "flowers in a truth," even as that truth is questioned. Not Emerson himself could ask for a closer attention to the immediate, the familiar, the homely as the novel transmutes the grubby, greasy business of whaling into tragedy. But Emerson, in his determined effort to confront the divinity in the universe, had characteristically laid down the basis for his faith in a celebration of rural, pastoral nature. Melville, when he sent his searchers out to sea, confronted them with a nature vastly different. If, according to the young Thoreau, "Nature will bear the closest inspection"—because, according to Emerson, nature is "the present expositor of the divine mind"—we can suppose Melville sending his seekers out to widen their angle of vision, not by the dimension of a study window in Concord (or Northampton)—but from Ishmael's forecastle. (pp. 237-38)

When Emerson announced that the poet "disposes very easily of the most disagreeable facts," the fatuity of the remark prompted Melville's ironic "So it would seem. In this sense, Mr. E. is a great poet." The *Pequod*'s search, far from disposing of the disagreeable, is exactly the attempt to face those facts, to ponder their significance. The land, with its comfortable securities, is kept only at the price of received opinion, of taking a part for the whole of experience, of seeing with too narrow an angle of vision. As in the familiar apostrophe concluding the abrupt dismissal of Bulkington,

> All deep, earnest thinking is but the intrepid effort of the soul to keep the open independence of her sea; while the wildest winds of heaven and earth conspire to cast her on the treacherous, slavish shore. . . . as in landlessness alone resides the highest truth, shoreless, indefinite as God—so, better is it to perish in that howling infinite, than be ingloriously dashed upon the lee, even if that were safety! . . . (p. 239)

The true whale hunter seeks the living, spouting whale, impatient with the stuffed and dessicated specimens, the inaccurate and misleading pictures offered ashore as representative reality. So it is, too, in the search for illumination, only the whale hunter "burns . . . the purest of oil, in its unmanufactured, and, therefore, unvitiated state . . . He goes and hunts for his oil, so as to be sure of its freshness and genuineness. . . ."

This enforces one of the postulates of the whale hunt—an endless process of hunt, capture, rendering, and hunting again. The other is: "To grope down into the bottom of the sea after them; to have one's hands among the unspeakable foundations, ribs, and very pelvis of the world; this is a fearful thing." . . . But wearying or terrifying, only in the search, in the unremitting, unblinking effort to face the disagreeable facts does manhood realize itself.

To go to sea, to dive more deeply, to enlarge the vision—what is it then that one sees? The Psalmist, St. Paul, the Bishops, Edwards, or Emerson found the revelation of a just divinity. In the novel we approach an immediate tactic (though not the grand strategy) in Queequeg's exclamation of outraged pain when the jaws of a dead shark reflexively snap on his hand. "Queequeg no care what god made him shark . . . wedder Fejee god or Nantucket god; but de god wat made shark must be one dam Ingin." . . . The very first "Extract," with multiple appropriateness from Genesis, reminds us that "God created great whales," and though we are genially warned not to take all "higgledy-piggledy whale statements" for "veritable gospel," we are all the same confronted immediately with the classic logic of the syllogism: The creation, we have the highest assurance, manifests the Creator; but this creation is notorious for its suffering, its indifferent injustice, its ruthless energy and merciless, predatory nature; therefore, such must be its Creator.

Now this outraged conclusion is everywhere forced on our attention in the novel—by Ahab. But properly to assess *Melville's* strategy, we must constantly observe the way he handles the symbolizing mode of perception. The tradition of the symbolic connection between the creation and the creator, in all of its many versions, is also everywhere in question here, but most especially in its transcendental form. The strategic, the fundamental, issue is conveniently though whimsically joined in the mocking of the mast-head dreamer rapt in mystic communion. In an image which could have found an honored place in Emerson's "Oversoul," Ishmael derides such a latter-day Spinoza or Neoplatonist as he risks plunging to his destruction: "lulled into such an opium-like . . . reverie is this absentminded youth by the blending cadence of waves with thoughts, that at last he loses his identity; takes the mystic ocean at his feet for the visible image of that deep, blue, bottomless soul, pervading mankind and nature. . . ." Yet in embodying elusive thoughts in the dimly perceived, beautiful but elusive forms, the dreamer loses his grip; only self-annihilation waits in that mystic ocean.

All the same, it is by the full exploitation of the symbolizing mode of perception that conclusions far other than those entertained in Concord or Northampton are suggested. Persistently images of pastoral or domestic tranquility are juxtaposed against the hidden dreadfulness of the sea. (pp. 239-41)

"The Gilder" chapter describes . . . [a day] when nature gilds the surface with enchantment, and even the wary hunter has a "land-like feeling towards the sea," regarding it as "so much flowery earth," a "rolling prairie" where play-wearied children might sleep in the vales, and men, like colts, might roll in new morning clover. But he who would argue benignity ought in conscience to look beneath the memories of clovered pastures beyond Concord and Walden.

> Consider the subtleness of the sea; how its most dreaded creatures glide under water, unapparent for the most part, and treacherously hidden beneath the loveliest tints of azure. Consider also the devilish brilliance and beauty of many . . . species of sharks. Consider, once more, the universal cannibalism of the sea; all whose creatures prey upon each other, carrying on eternal war since the world began. Consider all this; and then turn to this green, gentle, and most docile earth; consider them both, the sea and the land; and do you not find a strange analogy to something in yourself ? . . .

No longer do we see, with William Cullen Bryant, only "Nature's everlasting smile." All easy symbolizing analogies must undergo a forcible revaluation. We must acknowledge the universal cannibalism in which sharks and men alike participate, and we begin to see, in a wider angle of vision, all that to which custom and convention on land had blindered us. Thoreau had travelled much in Concord, but a whaling ship was Ishmael's Yale College and his Harvard. The vision of remorseless voracity beneath the deceiving surface is the experience of all genuine hunters for the oil of illumination. This is what they have seen that makes *them* weep.

What Emerson would call the veils of Nature are to Ahab, as he calls them in the famous passage, walls, pasteboard masks, deceiving appearance through which he proposes to thrust at the inscrutable malice he sees sinewing it from behind. To this, then, has come for him the effort to confront the image of divinity in the universe. . . . Ahab and Melville unquestionably find a piously interpreted connection between nature and deity no longer tenable; Ishmael and Melville are surely doubtful of any other certainty resulting from a sea-search, but we ignore the progressive thrust of the novel if we fail to recognize that whatever doubts Ahab may entertain at points, by the end he has acceded to a settled and violent conviction terribly but merely the reverse of the traditional. (pp. 241-42)

He, too, insists on the symbolic connection between man and god if only in the malice of destruction. (p. 242)

Ahab, though he has greatly dared beyond his landbound contemporaries in confronting a monstrous vision of the universe, dared greatly in defying the malignant power so conceived, yet not less than his contemporaries ashore does he hold the creation to revolve egocentrically about himself. And in so doing, like them he has only imposed his own solipsistic conception upon that world—a conception which has in no

way any greater warrant for its validity than that of the most egregiously complacent argument from design. Putatively, like Father Mapple, a seeking pilot of a ship's world, he is even more like Father Mapple in being essentially convinced of his truth before he begins; Ahab seeks not to discover what may be truth, but to prove his truth.

What this means in defining Ahab's tragedy, and how we are led to see his position as tragic, can be clarified by reconsidering the effect of Hume's ideas. . . . [Emerson] had at last to accommodate the new epistemology by identifying the creating mind of man with Providential purpose. Even as he discusses the "noble doubt" in *Nature,* Emerson adds, "It is a sufficient account of that Appearance we call the World, that God will teach a human mind . . . Whether nature enjoy a substantial existence without, or is only in the apocalypse of the mind, it is alike useful . . . to me." The assurance in this waiver is founded on the prior conviction, the "relation between the mind and matter is not fancied by some poet, but stands in the will of God . . . " Or as his contemporary journal adds, "The self of self creates the world through you." If by the 1840's, further experience had dampened this "Saturnalia of faith," he was still ready to describe "The Transcendentalist": "His thought—that is the Universe. . . . I—this thought which is called I—is the mould into which the world is poured like melted wax. The mould is invisible, but the world betrays the shape of the mould."

Carlyle's "The Universe is but one vast Symbol of God" or Emerson's equivalent "Nature is the symbol of spirit" assert, in effect, that the object and its significance are one. But for a mind not sharing the conviction of the radical correspondence of mind, matter, and God, such an epistemology must surely open appalling vistas. For if knowledge of the object may be merely illusion, then the avowed significance may be the wildest self-delusion. As Pierre will discover grimly not a year later, "Nature is not so much her own ever-sweet interpreter, as the mere supplier of that cunning alphabet, whereby selecting and combining as he pleases, each man reads his own peculiar lesson according to his own peculiar mind and mood." . . . This, at last, is the "metaphysical terror" contemplated by Ishmael, surpassing even Ahab's conviction in its fatal implications for the religious sensibility.

It is from this point of view, then, that Ahab may be considered as a re-viewed figure of the Emersonian, self-reliant, self-creating, self-destroying man, whose image of the "world, betrays the shape of the mould." (pp. 243-44)

The image which Ahab saw in the world is, finally, only what Narcissus saw—himself.

Modern psychological analysis of religious expression has familiarized us with the sense in which Calvins and Luthers transformed self-hates and guilts in their conceptions of deity. A hundred years ago Melville here creates the meaning of an equivalent insight. As the Calvinist finds wrathful justice in his ideas of the divine, as an Emerson finds his aspirations to benevolent serenity matched in the Concord landscape, so Ahab finds only his own hate and vengeful desire in what he takes to be the malice of the whale. . . .

The assertion of malevolent *intelligence* and *motivation* makes the same enormous leap into pure faith the orthodox and the transcendentalist have made. Ahab's "image" or "picture" of the whale has ultimately no more authenticity than the erroneous pictures found in incompetent books of "whale" lore, literally or metaphorically considered. The mad zealot Gabriel finds the incarnation of the Shaker God with as much or little warrant as Ahab. Ahab is destroyed—to this degree like his Biblical namesake—by establishing false idols of his own making. Ahab, who may long ago have begun by searching for meaning and truth, has finally only succeeded, as Ishmael sees at length, in inverting delusion. (p. 245)

That we see both the magnificence and the peculiarly tragic nature of Ahab's "faith" is due, of course, to the angle of vision which Ishmael supplies. Once Ishmael, like the others, was caught up in the terrible grandeur of Ahab's vision. Once he, too, though with far more dubiety, could assert the "linked analogies"—"some certain significance lurks in all things, else all things are little worth, and the round world itself but an empty cipher. . . . " But the more Ishmael employs the analogical mode of perception, the more aware he becomes of its fatal deceptions.

For if, in a simple inversion of the orthodox view of reality, Ahab has made over the whale into an embodiment of all evil and malevolent purpose in the universe, Moby Dick comes eventually to suggest something quite different to Ishmael. . . . (pp. 246-47)

By a masterly balancing of image against image, Melville defines Ishmael's growing awareness of the desperate possibility of a universe simply meaningless, where all comforting analogies are only self-deceits. Not even malevolent, which would at least be personal, in some ways humanly apprehensible, but simply purposeless. Here is the dubiety in full consciousness—"all things *are* little worth, and the round world itself but an empty cipher," a Newtonian cryptogram without meaning, an empty zero.

We cannot fail to recognize in this chapter Melville's representation of Hume's implications; the dialectic of the material moves inexorably to the probable conclusion: all we can know, finally, of all the baffling phenomena presented by some possibly objective world is sheer illusion, a symbolic construct only of our own minds. From this appalling angle Ishmael must deny the certain validity of any "argument from design," orthodox, transcendental, or Satanic.

To affirm that either Edwards' or Emerson's God was still "the native of these bleak rocks" now seems to Ishmael a Laplandish superstition, as if one were looking at, seeing a very probably colorless world through deifying glasses. In one astonishing passage he sums up the implications of epistemological investigation from Locke to Hume:

> . . . is it, that as in essence whiteness is not so much a color as the visible absence of color, and at the same time the concrete of all colors . . . when we consider that other theory of the natural philosophers, that all other earthly hues—every stately or lovely emblazoning—the sweet tinges of sunset skies and woods; yea, and the gilded velvets of butterflies, and the butterfly cheeks of young girls; all these are but subtle deceits, not actually inherent in substances, but only laid on from without; so that all deified Nature absolutely paints like the harlot, whose allurements cover nothing but the charnel-house within; and when we proceed further, and consider that the mystical cosmetic which produces every one of her hues, the great principle of light, for ever remains white or colorless in itself, and if operating without medium upon matter, would touch all objects, even tulips and roses, with its own blank tinge—pondering all this, the palsied universe lies before us a leper; and like wilful travellers in Lapland, who refuse to wear colored and coloring glasses upon their eyes, so the wretched infidel gazes himself blind at the monumental white shroud that wraps all the prospect around him. And of all these things the Albino whale was the symbol. . . .

Pointedly, the two chapters—"Moby Dick" for Ahab, "The Whiteness of the Whale" for Ishmael—are paired, barely one third of the way through the novel. The remainder of the novel takes all its significance from this differentiation. Now constantly borne in upon our attention, defining and shaping the impact of the novel upon our consciousness, are not only all those many images ambivalently linking pastoral tranquility and horror, but all the many overt statements, all the many images which point to a world neither benevolent nor malevolent, just icily, glacially cold, impersonal, indifferent, purposeless, meaningless. (pp. 247-48)

Beyond the veil, behind the mask, beneath the inscrutable whiteness may be—nothing. This is the terror which Ahab will not, at least for long, contemplate; but this is what the search for the white whale comes to signify for Ishmael. He had begun with the knowledge that to "have one's hands among the unspeakable foundations, ribs, and very pelvis of the world; this is a fearful thing." When he is at last among the ribs and pelvis of the skeleton in the Arsacides, he finds only—death. "I saw no living thing within; naught was there but bones." . . . With an equally grim jocularity, he finds he cannot make out the back parts, still less "how understand his head? much more, how comprehend his face, when face he has none?" . . . (p. 249)

With Ishmael's angle of vision Melville creates an insight transcending . . . Ahab. It is a view uncommitted to any dogmas, neither positively nor negatively theocentric; a view tentative and considerate of alternatives; one that seeks justly to evaluate and arrive at a sanely stable (if constantly provisional) understanding of the "truth of experience." "What plays the mischief with the truth," Melville wrote to Hawthorne late that memorable spring, "is that men will insist upon the universal application of a temporary feeling or opinion."

Without at all displacing Ahab as the dramatic center of the novel—in some sense of that slippery word, as "hero"—Ishmael develops a moral center and defining force, somewhat erratically, doubtless, in Melville's handling, and unsystematically, but nevertheless the indispensable perspective. It is shaped by the recognition at once of the "absurdity" of man's position in a purposeless universe, and yet the sober insistence, since this is all there is, there we must somehow make a life for ourselves. This is the other certainty. (pp. 249-50)

Hume undermined the notion that we can per-

Melville's gravestone, Woodlawn Cemetery, Bronx, New York.

ceive even self as an objective entity, but at least, to be human is, precisely, to be aware of being human. One of the most insistently presented patterns in Ahab's tragic development is his progressive, wilful isolation from humanity and humane values. In defining contrast to this, again, is Ishmael's turning from his defiantly whimsical outcast mood to Queequeg. Between them grows what may inadequately be termed a "communion," undoctrinaire, based on no reference external to itself, transcending all differences of color, race, language, and nominal creed, not as sons of God, but as men. Queequeg's humanity, generosity and selflessness can exist irrespective of any institutionalized ethic, and despite the otherwise all too evident predatory nature of the world.

To be sure, this communion is represented perhaps rather too elaborately in the self-conscious analogy of the monkey-rope, rather too graphically in the symbolic marriage at the Spouter Inn. Yet they together, Ishmael and Queequeg, shielded from the petrifying cold, are the "one warm spark in the heart of an arctic crystal." This is doubtless not an answer to the human predicament, but it is a necessary condition of existence. In one of its aspects it is passional love, just as the mating whales make the still center in the heart of the tornado of the Grand Armada. In its more general aspect it engages that the open independence of the sea and human interdependence, the never-ending self-reliant search and the concomitant responsibility of human love need not and must not be mutually exclusive. Against the weight of this moral center, Ahab is weighed, measured, and found wanting.

The tragic power of Ahab is the power of America's deepest cultural commitment, to the figure of the isolated, self-reliant individual, defining himself against both society and nature. The power of the novel is in the encompassing vision transcending this. What emerges is not a pious orthodoxy of belief and humility, nor yet solely the grandeur of Ahab's defiance, but a dynamic, unresolved tension between an experienced meaninglessness and the stubborn will to find meaning in experience, between the lonely grandeur of the lonely individual soul and the rights of human love. There is no *answer* here, only a vision of the conditions for the never-ending search in which mankind must forever engage—in the new world not less than in the old. Eden is not here, nor anywhere, but must forever be sought, worked for, with all of man's best energies and all his highest hopes, in all humility and in all the meaning of his humanity.

Here Melville has been beyond both piety and despair—not to some new cosmic moral revelation—but to the sobering proposition: If there is to be a moral order at all in this world, man—weak, flawed, fallible as he is—must somehow forge it himself out of his own human experience. (pp. 250-51)

Howard C. Horsford, "The Design of the Argument in 'Moby Dick'," in *Modern Fiction Studies,* Vol. VIII, No. 3, Autumn, 1962, pp. 233-51.

JOYCE CAROL OATES

(essay date 1962)

[Oates is an American novelist, short story writer, and essayist. In the following excerpt from an essay first published in 1962, she explores the theme of nihilism in Melville's works.]

Like Shakespeare, Melville is obsessed with the fragmentary and deceiving nature of "reality"; unlike Shakespeare, he is obsessed as well with the relationship of man to God. Melville's God can take any shape, being magically and evilly empowered—He is a primitive God, related to or actually contained in a beast; He is an intellectual God, existing only in the imagination of man; He is a God of all that is antihuman, perhaps the Devil himself. Melville felt most passionately about the role of the artist, that highest type of man—here is the statement he makes after having read Hawthorne:

> There is the grand truth about Nathaniel Hawthorne. He says No! in thunder; but the Devil himself cannot make him say *yes.*
>
> (pp. 61-2)

[The] naysaying Melville seems impossible to reconcile with the general tone of his last work, *Billy Budd*—that strange, exhausted, flawed tragedy, a work of fiction only partway imagined, in which Melville's powerful rhetoric tries vainly to do the work of his imagination. The problem of *Billy Budd*—its role as a "testament of acceptance" or a pure, dispassionate rejection of the accidental or humanly manipulated injustice of life—is a critical problem that, on the level of an assumed antithesis in its conception, will never be solved. . . . But the problem of the place of *Billy Budd* in Melville's work and the more general, and less obvious, problem of Melville's attitude toward art, life, and nature are not insoluble, at least not unapproachable, if the current critical appeal to Melville—usually as the basis upon which to work out more general phases of American literature—is recognized as not consistent in Melville himself, and, in fact, not borne out by his later major writings.

The "No! in thunder" describes well a youthful climate of mind found in such an early work as *White Jacket*. . . . (pp. 62-3)

The "infinite background" of *White Jacket* is the ocean of a romanticism that is, somehow, always pure in spite of its experience with, and frequent obsession with, the forces of "evil." It must not be considered a romanticism that would eclipse a vision of evil such as Melville has already expressed as early as *Typee,* but rather a romanticism that sees past the existential to the essential, beyond the immediate suffering in man to his capacity for new experience, new roles, an invasion into the universe, perhaps even a masculine victory. The tone of *White Jacket,* for all its social protest, is one of an irrepressible optimism: the optimism that grows out of a faith in one's self and in the solidarity of man as a species, without which the "no" one cries against the devil would be meaningless.

The most famous naysayer of American literature, Captain Ahab, inhabits a world of an "infinite background," which is intolerably hidden from him by the masks of physical reality. Yet it is a temptation to him because he wills it to be so; the nightmare of *Moby Dick* (the annihilation of man by an utterly devastating nature) is not without redemption for us because we are made to understand continually that the quest, whether literal or metaphysical, need not be taken. Man chooses this struggle. The doom that overturns upon the human constituents of the drama is a doom that they, as willful human beings, insist upon: for Ahab does insist upon his doom. (pp. 63-4)

Ahab's monomania does not exclude a recognition of his confusing role in the drama—is he Ahab, or is "Ahab" someone else? What is his identity? Does he exist as an autonomous being or is he merely the acting-out of a decree of another will? His consciousness of his own futility, at times, suggests that he is a tragic hero of a new type—one who knowingly and willingly chooses his "fate," however mistaken this may seem to others. He is a romantic hero, in relation to the white whale as Milton's Satan is to God, an alternately raging, alternating despairing rebel against the supreme order. The human victim within such a tautology is a victim who demands disaster; we feel that if the personified universe did not destroy him he would have to destroy himself. (p. 65)

Pierre is the tale of a quest on land that, like Ahab's on sea, is to lead to a confrontation of "truth" and a definition of the self measured by this truth—ideally; it should lead to a victory and a rejection of the conventional world of social and physical and psychological arrangements. The movement in the novel is away from the appearance of things to the penetration of a supposed reality; it is a concern for the definition of this reality, a qualification of truth by endless ambiguities in the self as well as in the world. Thus the novel seems a psychological fantasy, where the will of the hero creates events in the way in which an author creates. . . . So far as Pierre's rejection of appearance is sincere, and even so far as his gradual awareness of the ambiguity within his own heart is considered in terms of a real dichotomy between good and evil, Pierre belongs to the sphere of the pre-Adamic figure turned Adamic and fallen, in turn changed to the Faustian figure somewhat akin to Ahab—that is, a man involved in a real struggle with appearance and reality, good and evil, God and Satan. (pp. 66-7)

From the ambiguity of his small cloistered world to the ambiguity of the outer world and, finally, to the ambiguity of his own "pure" and unquestioned motives, Pierre is led to the discovery of a world of lies. It is not only a world that tells lies but a world that has been committed—created—in lies. The questioning of Pierre's own motives in protecting Isabel provides one of the most interesting of the novel's ambiguities, for even the motif of incest will not serve as an adequate explanation of sorts for the conflict of the novel. While it can be assumed that the gradual awareness of an incestuous desire for his "sister" comes to Pierre to typify both the ambiguity of the world and his own corrupted purity, the incest-motif might not be the concern or fear of the protagonist at all, but rather its opposite: he is really afraid of a healthy and normal love relationship. (p. 68)

The climate of a swollen, pretentious rhetoric at the beginning of the novel gives way—as nature gives way abruptly to the city—to the statement of nihilism that Pierre offers, partly to rationalize his passion for Isabel, partly as a judgment upon life. He says of Virtue and Vice: "a nothing is the substance, it casts one shadow one way, and another the other way; and these two shadows cast from one nothing; these, seems to me, are Virtue and Vice." . . . Considered in the light of the latter part of the novel, the much-criticized rhetoric of the beginning is justified; it is the "nothing," the sickly, sweet, distorted pastoralism of nature and of human relationships that are to be investigated and found hollow. (p. 69)

[*Pierre*] marks the beginning of the apparent Timonism of *The Confidence-Man,* which is a continuation of the theme of *Pierre;* and it marks also, though the relationships may appear puzzling, the beginning of that climate of mind that can give us, without incongruity, the work *Billy Budd.* (p. 71)

The Confidence-Man is centrally flawed in that its "comedy of action" dissolves backward into a comedy of speculation, to reverse Melville's stated intention. So the work, concerned with philosophical problems, does not always translate itself into art but remains conversation, vaguely dialectical, at its worst accumulative and concentric.

It will help to think of *The Confidence-Man* as a series of tales of a perhaps feigned Manichean dualism, about which the confidence-man dreams a long and complicated dream. The atmosphere of the dream, so much more strident than in *Pierre,* allows the confi-

dence-man a certain omnipotence—the power of assuming and rejecting identity, or the various forms of his central identity; he is, then, in the unique position of an author. If the tales constitute a dream, at their core we find the atmosphere of a fallen world and the peculiar desire on the part of the protagonist to posit faith and test it, perhaps a secret desire for this faith to triumph. . . . When the confidence-man is defeated, Christianity itself is defeated, for it is no longer innocent. The loss of the confidence-man is a token of the hypocrisy of Christianity itself—like the life preserver examined in the concluding pages of the novel, it "looks so perfect—sounds so hollow." The confidence-man is the hero of this world, and the measure of his odd heroism is not his own confidence or cunning but rather the vulnerability of the world that he can easily seduce. (pp. 71-2)

The confidence-man cannot be understood except as the embodiment of an idea. He posits himself as the diabolical agent seeking to lure and betray an unsuspecting "good," and while it is certainly going too far to suggest that the confidence-man really represents Christian value in discord with a secular world, it is assuming too much to see him as an agent of the Devil— or the devil himself—as if this were the extent of the problem Melville sees. . . . Melville surely had some aspects of Milton's Satan in mind, however, in creating his confidence-man: he is equated with the Devil "gulling Eve"; he is associated with snake imagery—he "writhes"; he exercises a hypnotic fascination upon his victims and, in an ironic reversal, he is suggested as the creature who charms man (as opposed to the usual snake-charming human being). But Milton's Satan recognizes a belief—however despised—in the Christian myth that the confidence-man would not be prepared to make. Satan is doomed to defeat within a vast hierarchical tautology, while the confidence-man's problem is more complicated, more resourceful, than the usual struggle between good and evil, between God and the Devil with the earth as the stage; at bottom it is a concern obsessed with the sheer burden of defining this struggle. (pp. 74-5)

The education of the confidence-man progresses in proportion to the degree of complexity and cynicism expressed by the people he meets—though, since the novel does have the persistent atmosphere of a dream, one feels that the confidence-man already possesses whatever knowledge is revealed to him. The "cold prism" of the transcendental intellect is more than a match for the confidence-man's charm. . . . He is educated not to the truth of transcendentalism, or to its finer ethics, but rather to the essential cruelty and inhumanity, even the triteness, of the transcendental ethic when it has been enticed down to the level of the particular.

There is a fault in assuming that, given two apparently antithetical points of view, one must necessarily be right and the other wrong. Melville's intention is to display of hollowness, the inadequacy, of both points of view: the truth that will not be comforted, the "no trust" world, the grave beneath the flowers, the transcendental ethic, the discomforting reality that underlies appearance—and, against this, the world of professed Christianity, the faith in charity, in confidence. The confidence-man's defeat at the hands of the transcendentalist disciple is a token of the ultimate defeat of the surface confidence of the heart by the irrefragable reality that underlies it—the grave beneath. (pp. 77-8)

After his symbolic defeat by the transcendentalist, the confidence-man begins to move away from us. . . . We have at the end not only a confidence-man who does not believe in confidence, but a Christian who does not believe in Christianity—who is, therefore, not a Christian. . . . The final movement is a movement into darkness: it is not the triumph of evil over good but rather the negation of struggle, the disintegration into an underlying nihilism that has resulted, within the novel, from the long series of negations that constitute the confidence-man's experience. . . . It is important to see, though the observation may appear odd, that for the force of evil as well as the force of good the struggle must be sustained, the disintegration into nihilism must be resisted. On the more immediate level, without confidence in man, in society, one falls into despair; and the condition of man is a shuttling movement between the illusory contentment of charity and the confrontation of the truth that will not be comforted—that is, despair. (pp. 79-80)

In *Billy Budd,* the quest theme of Melville has run its course. We have no Adamic-turned-Faustian hero, a superman of sorts like Ahab, Pierre, and the confidence-man; we have instead individuals like Billy and Vere and Claggart, one-dimensional, almost passive role-takers in a triangle of archetypal scope.

The problem of *Billy Budd,* then, stems from the disintegration of the quest and from the acceptance of death as not evil—which leads romantically to the sailor's apotheosis in the folklore of his time, and classically to the acceptance of social necessity, of forms and order. But the intent of the work may well transcend this compatible dichotomy to suggest an acceptance of impending death, of annihilation, in somewhat Nirvanic terms, for the work is "angry," or represents part of a "quarrel" only if death is taken, as it conventionally is, to be at least painful and frightening. The terror of the white whale, infinity pressing back upon its perceiver (or creator), becomes here the transcendental dissolving of considerations of good and evil, of struggle, of life itself. (p. 81)

The experience of Vere is in broad terms that of the father who manipulates the figure of innocence into the transcendent Nirvana of nonexperience and nonidentity that he himself will earn, after a time, but that he has reached only after this experience—which invariably wounds—in the painful world of appearances, of good and evil, of constant struggle, and, most perniciously, of unnatural, repressed lusts. For a writer whose aim is to penetrate into a "basic truth," the sustainment of any two points of view will suggest, in the end, the mockery of assigning to one of two antithetical views a positiveness worthy of one's faith—worthy of one's life. The quest ends, ideally, in the negation and not in the compromise or resolution of tension in Melville's irreconcilable world of opposites; it is at once a transcendence and an annihilation, no longer an image of romantic diffusion as in *White Jacket,* surely not an image of the vicious and self-consuming pessimism of *Pierre.* (p. 82)

Nineteenth-century in his conception of the forms of fiction and of "characterization," Melville is strikingly contemporary in his conception of the internal tensions that comprise a work. In a sense he is not a writer of "fiction" at all, but a writer of ideas who is using the means of fiction; let us speculate that he used fiction because of its essential ambiguity, its "muteness," and because of the possibility of his hiding behind its disguises. Just as he dares to do no more than hint at the homosexual perversion of sailors in *White Jacket* and *Billy Budd,* so, in mid-nineteenth-century America he can do no more than hint at the blankness behind the age-old negotiable forms of virtue and vice, good and evil, God and the Devil. (p. 83)

Joyce Carol Oates, "Melville and the Tragedy of Nihilism," in her *The Edge of Impossibility: Tragic Froms in Literature,* Vanguard Press, 1972, pp. 59-83.

SOURCES FOR FURTHER STUDY

Bryant, John, ed. *A Companion to Melville Studies.* New York: Greenwood Press, 1986, 906 pp.

Twenty-five essays on Melville's work; with eleven devoted to textual studies, fourteen to such topical issues as Melville's relation to religion, aesthetics, modernism, and popular culture.

Mumford, Lewis. *Herman Melville.* New York: Literary Guild of America, 1929, 377 p.

Critical biography.

Sedgwick, William Ellery. *Herman Melville: The Tragedy of Mind.* Cambridge, Mass: Harvard University Press, 1944, 225 p.

Outlines a theory of tragedy informing *Moby-Dick, Mardi,* and other works by Melville.

Stern, Milton R. *The Fine Hammered Steel of Herman Melville.* Urbana: University of Illinois Press, 1968, 225 p.

Complex analysis of Melville's thematic and perceptual development in *Typee, Mardi, Pierre,* and *Billy Budd.*

Thompson, Lawrance. *Melville's Quarrel with God.* Princeton, N.J.: Princeton University Press, 1952, 474 p.

Analyzes religious themes in Melville's works.

Weaver, Raymond M. *Herman Melville: Mariner and Mystic.* New York: George H. Doran Company, 1921, 399 p.

Copiously illustrated critical biography.

Arthur Miller

1915-

American dramatist, essayist, scriptwriter, short story writer, nonfiction writer, novelist, and autobiographer.

INTRODUCTION

Miller's eminence as a dramatist is based primarily on four plays he wrote early in his career: *All My Sons* (1947), *Death of a Salesman* (1949), *The Crucible* (1953), and *A View from the Bridge* (1955). Insisting that "the individual is doomed to frustration when once he gains a consciousness of his own identity," Miller synthesizes elements from social and psychological realism to depict the individual's search for identity within a society that inhibits such endeavors. Although his later works are generally considered inferior to his early masterpieces, Miller remains among the most important and influential dramatists to emerge in the United States since World War II. Critics praise his effective use of vernacular, his moral insight, and his strong sense of social responsibility. June Schlueter commented: "When the twentieth century is history and American drama viewed in perspective, the plays of Arthur Miller will undoubtedly be preserved in the annals of dramatic literature."

Miller was born and raised in New York City, the son of a prosperous businessman who lost his wealth during the Great Depression. A mediocre high school student with little interest in academic pursuits, Miller was rejected upon his initial application to the University of Michigan. He was eventually accepted at the University, however, and there began writing for the stage, showing distict promise as a dramatist and winning several student awards. For a short time after college, he was employed writing scripts for radio plays. While he found the demands of broadcast writing restrictive, this period, together with his college years, served as a valuable apprenticeship for Miller. His first Broadway play, *The Man Who Had All the Luck,* was produced in 1944. Although it lasted only four performances, the play nevertheless won a Theater Guild award and established Miller as an important young playwright.

Throughout his career, Miller has continually addressed several distinct but related issues in both his dramatic and expository writings. In his early plays and in a series of essays published in the 1940s and 50s, Miller first outlined a form of tragedy applicable to modern times and contemporary characters, challenging traditional notions suggesting that only kings, queens, princes, and other members of the nobility can be suitable subjects for tragedy. In "Tragedy and the Common Man," Miller asserts that the "underlying struggle" of all such dramas "is that of the individual attempting to gain his 'rightful' position in society." Consequently, "the tragic feeling is evoked in us when we are in the presence of a character who is ready to lay down his life, if need be, to secure one thing—his sense of personal dignity" within a society that inhibits such endeavors. According to this view, even ordinary people—like Willy Loman, the protagonist of *Death of a Salesman*—can achieve truly tragic stature. It is this issue of the individual's relationship to society, and its representation on stage, that forms the second of Miller's abiding concerns. Throughout his work, Miller has sought to fuse the moral and political messages of "social" plays with the realism and intensity of psychological dramas that focus on the individual. In work after work, from *All My Sons* and *The Crucible* to *Incident at Vichy,* Miller has presented dilemmas in which a character's sense of personal integrity or self-interest conflicts with his or her responsibility to society or its representatives. Finally, Miller has repeatedly returned to the theme of family relations, particularly interactions between fathers and sons. The families depicted in Miller's plays often serve as vehicles for the author's analyses of the broader relations between individuals and society.

These issues are discernable in *All My Sons* and clearly evident in *Death of a Salesman,* widely considered Miller's masterpiece and recognized as a classic of contemporary American theater. In *All My Sons,* set during World War II, the truth about Joe Keller's past is gradually revealed. Keller has sold defective parts to the United States Air Force, resulting in the death of several American pilots. When his sons learn of this, one, a pilot himself, commits suicide by crashing his plane; the other demands that Keller take responsibility for his actions. As the play closes, Keller accepts his obligation to society, recognizing that all the lost pilots were, in effect, his "sons." He then takes his own life to atone for his crime. *All My Sons* was considerably more successful than *The Man Who Had All the Luck,* enjoying a long run and winning the New York Drama Critics Circle Award in 1947.

With the production of *Death of a Salesman* in 1949, Miller firmly established his reputation as an outstanding American dramatist. This play, which represents his most powerful dramatization of the clash between the individual and materialistic American society, chronicles the downfall of Willy Loman, a salesman whose misguided notions of success result in disillusionment and, ultimately, his death. Throughout his life, Willy has not only blindly pursued society's version of success, he has based his own identity and self-worth on social acceptance—on how "well-liked" he is. At the drama's end, he commits suicide, convinced that the settlement on his life insurance policy will provide his son Biff the wealth that had eluded Willy himself; however, Biff's ideals have already been tarnished by the same forces that destroyed his father.

Critics have generally agreed that *Death of a Salesman* is an important dramatic work. Some commentators, however, have taken issue with Miller's insistence that *Death of a Salesman* is a modern tragedy and that Willy is a tragic hero. The noted dramatic critic Eric Bentley argued that the elements of social drama in *Salesman* keep "the 'tragedy' from having genuinely tragic stature." Describing Willy as a "little man," Bentley insisted that such a person is "too little and too passive to play the tragic hero." Bentley and others charged that, according to Miller's own definition, Willy's death is merely "pathetic" rather than tragic. Other critics argued that, to the contrary, the salesman does attain tragic dimensions by virtue of what Miller terms the tragic hero's "total compulsion" to preserve his humanity and dignity. John Mason Brown characterized *Death of a Salesman* as "a tragedy modern and personal, not classic and heroic." Willy Loman is, he observed, "a little man sentenced to discover his smallness rather than a big man undone by his greatness."

Whether or not *Salesman* can be classified as a true tragedy, it has been generally praised for its innovative structure, which merges elements of both realism and expressionism. Reviewers admired the drama's interweaving of the "past" with the "present" and of events inside Willy's mind with those outside. While not "realistic," this technique nevertheless produces a penetrating psychological examination characteristic of dramatic realism. It is appropriate, several critics noted, that Miller's working title for the play was *Inside of His Head. Death of a Salesman* earned Miller a Pulitzer Prize as well as his second New York Drama Critics Circle Award.

Miller followed *Salesman* with an adaptation of Henrik Ibsen's *An Enemy of the People* and, in 1953, *The Crucible.* Although the latter work won the 1953 Tony Award for best play, it received generally lukewarm responses from critics, and the piece had a run that, while respectable, was only one-third the length of *Salesman*'s premier production. Perhaps Miller's most controversial drama, this work is based upon the witch trials held in 1692 in Salem, Massachusetts. Featuring historical characters drawn from this period, *The*

Crucible addresses the complex moral dilemmas of John Proctor, a man wrongly accused of practicing witchcraft. Through his depiction of the mass frenzy of the witch hunt, Miller examines the social and psychological aspects of group pressure and its effect on individual ethics, dignity, and beliefs.

When *The Crucible* was first staged, a number of critics maintained that Miller failed in his characteristic attempt to merge the personal and the social. Many of the figures in the play are poorly developed and merely serve as mouthpieces for Miller's social commentary, they claimed. The play was commonly interpreted as a thinly disguised critique of Joseph McCarthy's Senate investigations of communism in the United States, and it was judged preachy and overly political. Some commentators also questioned the validity of the parallels Miller established between the Salem trials and the congressional investigations. The relationship between the historical events depicted in the play and the events of the 1950s has continued to be the subject of much debate among subsequent critics of *The Crucible.*

Miller was himself called to testify before the House Committee on Un-American Activities in 1957. Although he admitted that he had attended a meeting of communist writers, he refused to identify anyone he had met there and denied ever having been a member of the Communist Party. As a result, he was found guilty of contempt of Congress, a conviction that was later overturned. A year later, after much of the furor over communist activity in the United States had died down, *The Crucible* was revived off-Broadway. This time, freed from much of its association with "current events," the play was warmly received by critics and enjoyed a run of over six hundred performances. It was now seen to have a more lasting and universal significance than had earlier been apparent. As Robert Martin later maintained, *The Crucible* "has endured beyond the immediate events of its own time. If it was originally seen as a political allegory, it is presently seen by contemporary audiences almost entirely as a distinguished American play by an equally distinguished American playwright."

Miller's next offering, produced in 1955, consisted of two one-act plays: *A Memory of Two Mondays*—a semi-autobiographical piece reflecting Miller's own experiences as a young man working in an auto parts warehouse—and *A View from the Bridge,* for which the playwright won his third New York Drama Critics Circle Award. He later expanded this play to two acts. Given Miller's attempts to establish a new, modern form of tragedy, *A View from the Bridge* is significant in that it exhibits many similarities to classical Greek tragedy. Eddie Carbone, the play's central character, unconsciously harbors an incestuous love for his niece, Catherine. Jealous of her attraction to an illegal alien the Carbones are hiding, Eddie exposes the man to immigration authorities and becomes involved in a fatal confrontation with the man's brother. Critics have often noted that, like such Greek dramatic heroes as Oedipus, Eddie brings about his own downfall through his ignorance and inability to see the consequences of his actions.

A nine-year break from playwriting followed *A View from the Bridge,* during which period Miller embarked on his highly publicized marriage to, and subsequent divorce from, Marilyn Monroe. Before they separated, however, Miller adapted one of his short stories into the screenplay *The Misfits* as a vehicle for his wife. He returned to the theater in 1964 with two works, *After the Fall,* and, near the end of the year, *Incident at Vichy. After the Fall* is considered Miller's most experimental and, perhaps, most pessimistic piece. This play takes place, as Miller has stated, "in the mind, thought, and memory of Quentin," a guilt-ridden man who tries to come to terms with his past through conversations with an imaginary listener. In the course of Quentin's examination of the ruins of two failed marriages, the individual, the family, and society are all subjected to harsh criticism. Nearly every character in the play betrays love for the sake of his or her own survival. Reviewers were sharply divided over *After the Fall.* While some considered its structure a brilliant experiment in stagecraft, others faulted Miller for pretentious theorizing and artificial characterizations. In *Incident at Vichy,* Miller continued his exploration of the conflicts between individual and societal responsibility. Set in occupied France during World War II, this play features seven men who, awaiting interrogation by their Nazi captors, discuss their fate and the importance of social commitment to maintaining group freedom. The drama suggests that those who fail to resist oppression are as guilty as the Nazis of crimes against humanity.

In 1968, Miller returned to realistic family drama with *The Price.* In this work two brothers, Victor and Walter Frank, are brought together after many years by the death of their father. Like the characters in *All My Sons* and *Death of a Salesman,* these two men recall the past, trying to come to an understanding of their lives and the choices they have made. *The Price* was Miller's last major Broadway success. His next work, *The Creation of the World and other Business,* a series of comic sketches based on the Biblical Book of Genesis, met with severe critical disapproval when it was first produced on Broadway in 1972, closing after only twenty performances. All of Miller's subsequent works premiered outside of New York. Miller staged the musical *Up from Paradise* (1974), an adaptation of *Creation of the World* (1972), at his alma mater, the University of Michigan. *The Archbishop's Ceiling* was presented in 1977 at the Kennedy Center in Washington, D.C.

In the 1980s, Miller produced a number of short

pieces. *The American Clock* is based on Studs Terkel's oral history of the Great Depression, *Hard Times*, and is structured as a series of vignettes that chronicle the hardship and suffering that occurred during that period. *Elegy for a Lady* and *Some Kind of Love Story* are two one-act plays that were staged together in 1982. Similarly, *Danger, Memory!* (1986) is comprised of the short pieces *I Can't Remember Anything* and *Clara*. Reviewers have generally regarded these later plays as minor works, inferior to Miller's early masterpieces.

Despite the absence of any notable theatrical success since the mid-1960s, Arthur Miller remains an important voice in contemporary American drama. Such early works as *Death of a Salesman* and *The Crucible* are still frequently performed, thereby reaching succeeding generations of playgoers. And though less

compelling, his later works have continued to probe and explore the nature of the individual as an innately social, interactive creature. Much of Miller's work displays his deep and abiding concern with conscience and morality, with one's dual—and often conflicting—responsibilities to oneself and to one's fellow human beings. It is only through relationships with others, Miller's plays suggest, that our humanity truly emerges.

(For further information about Miller's life and works, see *Concise Dictionary of American Literary Biography, 1941-1968; Contemporary Authors*, Vols. 1-4; *Contemporary Authors New Revision Series*, Vol. 2; *Contemporary Literary Criticism*, Vols. 1, 2, 6, 10, 15, 26, 47; and *Dictionary of Literary Biography*, Vol. 7: *Twentieth-Century American Dramatists*.)

CRITICAL COMMENTARY

HAROLD CLURMAN

(essay date 1949)

[A celebrated director and theater critic, Clurman helped found the Group Theatre in 1931. In the review below, he echoes the general critical view that *Death of a Salesman* "marks a high point of significant expression in the American theatre of our time."]

"Attention must be paid to such a man. Attention!" [Requiem] The man his wife refers to is Willy Loman, the central figure of Arthur Miller's *Death of a Salesman*. Perhaps the chief virtue of the play is the attention that Miller makes us pay to the man and his problem, for the man represents the lower middle class, the $50-a-week-plus-commission citizen, whose dream is to live to a ripe old age doing a great volume of business over the telephone. It was not unusual to hear of this person in the thirties, but in the theatre of the forties he has once more become the forgotten man.

The play has tremendous impact because it makes its audience recognize itself. Willy Loman is everybody's father, brother, uncle or friend, his family are our cousins; *Death of a Salesman* is a documented history of our lives. It is not a realistic portrait, it is a demonstration both of the facts and of their import. "We had the wrong dream," says Biff, Willy Loman's son, and what Miller is saying in terms few can miss is that this wrong dream is one the greater part of America still cherishes.

"The only thing you got in this world is what you can sell," the prosperous man next door tells Willy [Act

II]. This is the harsh fact, but Willy, the poor dear fellow, is not satisfied with it. He wants to be *well-liked*. It is natural and healthy to harbor this desire, but the philosophy of Willy's economic situation denatures this desire to the hope of being well-liked or "known" as a way to security, success, salvation. To be a "personality" is to cultivate those traits which make one sufficiently "well-liked" to do a greater volume of business so that one may achieve a brighter place in the sun.

The competition Willy encounters is too tough for his modest talents; the path he has chosen denies his true being at every step. He idolizes the dream beyond the truth of himself, and he thus becomes a "romantic," shadowy nonentity, a liar, a creature whose only happiness lies in looking forward to miracles, since reality mocks his pretensions. His real ability for manual work seems trivial and mean to him. "Even your grandfather was more than a carpenter," he tells Biff [Act I]. From this perpetual self-denial he loses the sense of his own thought; he is a stranger to his own soul; he no longer knows what he thinks either of his sons or his automobile (he boosts and denounces them both in almost the same breath); he cannot tell who are his true friends; he is forever in a state of enthusiastic or depressed bewilderment. "That man never knew who he was" [Requiem], Biff says of him. He never owns anything outright till his death by suicide (committed to give Biff a foundation of $20,000); he has never been free.

His sons suffer the guilt of the father: Biff, the older, with increasing consciousness; Hap, the younger,

Principal Works

The Man Who Had All the Luck (drama) 1944

Situation Normal (nonfiction) 1944

Focus (novel) 1945

All My Sons (drama) 1947

Death of a Salesman: Certain Private Conversations in Two Acts and a Requiem (drama) 1949

An Enemy of the People [adaptation of Henrik Ibsen's play] (drama) 1950

The Crucible (drama) 1953

* A View from the Bridge [one-act version] (drama) 1955

* A Memory of Two Mondays (drama) 1955

A View from the Bridge [two-act version] (drama) 1956

The Misfits (screenplay) 1961

After the Fall (drama) 1964

Incident at Vichy (drama) 1964

I Don't Need You Any More (stories) 1967

The Price (drama) 1968

The Creation of the World and Other Business (drama) 1972

Up from Paradise [musical adaptation of Creation of the World] (drama) 1974

The Archbishop's Ceiling (drama) 1977

The Theater Essays of Arthur Miller (essays) 1978

The American Clock [adaptation of Studs Terkel's Hard Times] (drama) 1980

† Elegy for a Lady (drama) 1982

† Some Kind of Love Story (drama) 1982

Danger, Memory! [two one-act plays, I Can't Remember Anything and Clara] (drama) 1986

Timebends: A Life (autobiography) 1987

*These two works were first performed together in a single production.

†These two works were first performed together in a single production. Elegy for a Lady was published in the United States in 1982; Some Kind of Love Story was issued the following year. They were published together in Great Britain as Two-Way Mirror in 1984.

---

stupidly. Hap seeks satisfaction as a coarse ladies' man. Biff cannot find any satisfaction because, being more trusting and sensitive than his brother, he tries to live according to his father's dream with which he has nothing in common—the boy yearns to live on the land. Only toward the end does Biff discover the spiritual hoax of his father's life, the corruption of heart and mind to which his father's "ideals" are leading him. With his father's death, Biff has possibly achieved sufficient self-awareness to change his course; Hap—like most of us—persists in following the way of his father. He will go on striving "to come out No. 1 man." . . . The point of all this is not that our economic system does not work, but that its ideology distorts man's true nature. Willy's well-adjusted neighbor "never took an interest in anything" [Act II] and has no aspiration beyond the immediately practicable.

Arthur Miller is a moralist. His talent is for a kind of humanistic jurisprudence: he sticks to the facts of the case. For this reason his play is clearer than those of other American playwrights with similar insight whose lyric gifts tend to reflect the more elusive and imponderable aspects of the same situation. There is poetry in *Death of a Salesman*—not the poetry of the senses or of the soul, but of ethical conscience. It might have been graven on stone—like tablets of law. *Death of a Salesman* stirs us by its truth, the ineluctability of its evidence and judgment which permits no soft evasion. Though the play's environment is one we associate with a grubby realism, its style is like a clean ac-

counting on the books of an understanding but severe sage. We cry before it like children being chastised by an occasionally humorous, not unkindly but unswervingly just father. *Death of a Salesman* is rational, dignified and profoundly upright.

Elia Kazan's production conveys these qualities with a swift and masterful thrust—like a perfect blow. He has cast the play admirably, and the entire occasion might be cited as an example of real theatre: meaning and means unified by fine purpose. Lee J. Cobb, who plays Willy Loman, is surely one of the most powerful and juicy actors on our stage today. He displays a tendency in this part to sacrifice characterization to a certain grandiosity. Willy Loman's wife speaks of his exhaustion, and Willy himself refers to his having grown fat and foolish-looking. None of these textual indications is taken into sufficient account, and what is gained in general impressiveness is lost in a want of genuine pathos.

Indeed the tone of histrionic bravura tends to make the others in the cast—for instance, Arthur Kennedy, the beautifully sensitive actor who plays Biff—push a little too hard. The production therefore pays for its virtues by a lack of intimacy, which is the dimension needed to make the event complete. Mildred Dunnock, in her simplicity and delicacy of feeling, is like the symbolic beacon of everything sound in the production. Tom Pedi, as a waiter, is as real and tasty as a garlic salad; Hope Cameron, in the smallest role in the play, suggests a remarkably touching naïveté. Both have a specific reality that I should have liked to see carried through all the longer parts. But virtually everyone in *Death of a Salesman* is better than good; and the whole marks a high point of significant expression in the American theatre of our time. (pp. 26-8)

Harold Clurman, in a review of "Death of a Salesman," in *The New Republic,* Vol. 120, No. 9, February 28, 1949, pp. 26-8.

RICHARD HAYES

(essay date 1953)

[In the following review, Hayes offers guarded praise of *The Crucible.*]

It is altogether possible that Mr. Arthur Miller was prompted to the composition of his latest play by the malign politico-cultural pressures of our society, but whatever the impulse, it has issued in a drama of arresting polemic distinction.

The Crucible, does not, I confess, seem to me a work of such potential tragic force as the playwright's earlier *Death of a Salesman;* it is the product of theatrical dexterity and a young man's moral passion, rather than of a fruitful and reverberating imagination. But it has, in a theatre of the small success and the tidy achievement, power, the passionate line—an urgent boldness which does not shrink from the implications of a large and formidable design.

With the Salem witchcraft trials of 1692 as a moral frame and point of departure, Mr. Miller has gone on to examine the permanent conditions of the climate of hysteria. The New England tragedy was for him, dramatically, a fortuitous choice because it is accessible to us imaginatively; as one of the few severely irrational eruptions American society has witnessed, it retains still its primitive power to compel the attention. And it exhibits, moreover, the several features of the classically hysterical situation: the strange moral alchemy by which the accuser becomes inviolable; the disrepute which overtakes the testimony of simple intelligence; the insistence on public penance; the willingness to absolve if guilt is confessed.

It is *imaginative* terror Mr. Miller is here invoking: not the solid gallows and the rope appall him, but the closed and suffocating world of the fanatic, against which the intellect and will are powerless.

It is a critical commonplace that the commitments of Mr. Miller's plays are ideological rather than personal—that he does not create a world so much in its simple humanity, or its perceptible reality, as in its intel-

lectual alarms and excursions. *The Crucible* reinforces this tradition.

Despite the fact that he is often at his best in the "realist" vein, Mr. Miller, like any good heir of the thirties, is preoccupied with ideology. He has a richer personal sense of it than comparable writers, but the impulse remains unaltered. His characteristic theme is integrity, and its obverse, compromise. In earlier plays, Miller frequently brought to this subject a distressing note of stridency; one often felt that, really, the battle had long since been won, and that this continued obsession with it was an indication not of seriousness, but perhaps of some arrested moral development.

In *The Crucible,* however, he has stated his theme again with a wholly admirable concision and force. His central figure is John Proctor, another spokesman for rational feeling and the disinterested intelligence. Proctor is so patently the enemy of hysteria that his very existence is a challenge to the fanatic temperament, and he is consumed by its malice. What gives the situation a fresh vitality is Miller's really painful grasp of its ambiguities: the dilemma of a man, fallible, subject to pride, but forced to choose between the "negative good" of truth and morality, and the "positive good" of human life under any dispensation. Around this crisis of conscience, Mr. Miller has written an exhaustive, exacerbated scene—one of his most truly distinguished, and one which most hopefully displays the expanding delicacy of his moral imagination.

It is difficult, however, to feel that the political complexities inherent in *The Crucible* have been approached by Mr. Miller with any comparable sensitivity. He has, admittedly, disclaimed intent of contemporary reference in the play, choosing to see in it only the tragedy of another society. But it would be fatuous of Mr. Miller to pretend that our present cultural climate had not always a place in the foreground of his mind. Surely then, he can see that the Salem witch-hunts and our own virulent varieties are parallel only in their effects, not in their causes.

Dramatically, *The Crucible* maintains always that provocative interest and distinction one has come to associate with the work of this playwright. Mr. Miller has, on the whole, handled the Puritan idiom discreetly, despite the somewhat "official" taint of the weak prologue, and several unfortunate lapses into the contemporary. Mr. Miller *will* have his poetry, though; in *Death of a Salesman* he often resorted to a kind of bastard [Walt] Whitman rhetoric, while *The Crucible,* especially in its hysterical imagery, owes an inordinate debt to the King James Bible. But language is handled here generally with considerable skill and sensibility.

Of the production at the Martin Beck, one can have very little criticism. Arthur Kennedy plays Proctor with all his assured style and intense virility, while

Miller on the meaning of tragedy:

There is a misconception of tragedy with which I have been struck in review after review, and in many conversations with writers and readers alike. It is the idea that tragedy is of necessity allied to pessimism. Even the dictionary says nothing more about the word than that it means a story with a sad or unhappy ending. This impression is so firmly fixed that I almost hesitate to claim that in truth tragedy implies more optimism in its author than does comedy, and that its final result ought to be the reinforcement of the onlooker's brightest opinions of the human animal.

For, if it is true to say that in essence the tragic hero is intent upon claiming his whole due as a personality, and if this struggle must be total and without reservation, then it automatically demonstrates the indestructible will of man to achieve his humanity.

The possibility of victory must be there in tragedy. Where pathos rules, where pathos is finally derived, a character has fought a battle he could not possibly have won. The pathetic is achieved when the protagonist is, by virtue of his witlessness, his insensitivity or the very air he gives off, incapable of grappling with a much superior force.

Pathos truly is the mode for the pessimist. But tragedy requires a nicer balance between what is possible and what is impossible. And it is curious, although edifying, that the plays we revere, century after century, are the tragedies. In them, and in them alone, lies the belief—optimistic, if you will, in the perfectibility of man.

Miller, in "Tragedy and the Common Man," *The New York Times*, 27 February 1949.

Walter Hampden, Beatrice Straight and E. G. Marshall lend a grave and sober excellence to other figures in this Salem landscape. Mr. Jed Harris has directed boldly, with no shyness of scenes and curtains operatic in their intensity (and what a splendid opera might be made out of the Salem trials, incidentally). What *The Crucible* enriches and again asserts is the range, the variety and continuing interest of the American polemic tradition.

Richard Hayes, in a review of "The Crucible," in *The Commonweal,* Vol. LVII, No. 20, February 20, 1953, p. 498.

BROOKS ATKINSON
(essay date 1955)

[Atkinson was the drama critic for the *New York Times* from 1926 to 1960. In the following review of *A View from the Bridge*, he praises Miller's vivid, authentic characterizations yet contends that the play does not fulfill its potential as a tragic drama.]

A View from the Bridge has power and substance. It is based on a story that Mr. Miller once heard in the Brooklyn neighborhood where he lives. Eddie, an ordinary longshoreman, is unconsciously in love with his niece—the daughter of his wife's dead sister. Early in the play two of his wife's Italian relatives are smuggled in and start to live furtively in Eddie's apartment. Catherine, the niece, falls in love with the younger Italian brother and proposes to marry him.

Eddie does not understand why he opposes the marriage so violently, nor do any of the other people who are involved. Searching around for a plausible reason, Eddie convinces himself that the young Italian is a homosexual whose only motive in marrying Catherine is a chance to legitimize his citizenship in America. But Eddie's real motive is the undeclared, unrecognized, unappeased hunger he has for her himself. Like the heroes of Greek tragedy, he topples the whole house down on himself in the final catastrophe of a haunted play.

Mr. Miller understands the full tragic significance of this stark drama. Although he scrupulously underwrites the narrative, he introduces a neighborhood lawyer in a pool of light on one side of the stage to serve as chorus and commentator. . . . [The] lawyer analyzes Eddie's malady and puts it into human perspective. He also introduces a poetic strain by relating the Italian immigrants to the heroes of Roman history and the great myths of classical literature. . . .

[The] dimensions of *A View from the Bridge* are those of imaginative drama. Mr. Miller is straining for all the altitudes he can reach, and he is an uncommonly tall man.

The story is vivid. He meets it head-on. His intimate knowledge of the people—their living habits, their principles, their idiom—is solid. What he has to say about life in Italy today makes an illuminating contrast that all the characters like to conjure with. Everything about *A View from the Bridge* rings true.

Yet something inhibits it from expressing the fullness of tragedy that the theme promises. And this is the place where Mr. Miller's principle of underwriting may have been ill-advised. If tragedy is to purge and terrify the audience, in the classical phrase, the characters must have size. Their fate must have spiritual significance. Aristotle limited tragic heroes to kings and queens and people renowned in other respects. If the modern world limited tragedy to such people, we would have very little to write about.

Eddie's deficiency as a tragic character is not a matter of social inferiority. It is simpler than that: Mr. Miller has not told us enough about him. Since the play begins in the middle of a tumultous story, his background is dim and vague. On the basis of what we are told about him, Eddie is not an admirable person. He is mean. He is vicious toward the end, and he gets just about what he deserves. It is difficult to believe that fate has struck a decent human being a staggering blow that enlightens him about himself.

Nor are his wife and niece better portrayed. Their roots are shallow, too. The two Italian immigrants are the only well-defined characters in the central play. When Mr. Miller introduces them in the midst of a story that is already in motion, he is under the necessity of telling us who they are, where they come from and why. They are the only characters whom we can fully understand. . . .

A View from the Bridge needs flesh, not only because the characters are working people, but because Mr. Miller has written his play sparingly. Working in a mood of artistic austerity he has eliminated himself from both of these dramas. Many of us would be very happy to have as much of him as he can give.

Brooks Atkinson, in a review of "A View from the Bridge," in *The New York Times,* Section 2, October 9, 1955, p. 1.

B. S. FIELD, JR.

(essay date 1972)

[In the following essay, Field explores the "sin" or "crime" that justifies Willy Lowman's tragic downfall in *Death of a Salesman*.]

One of the things one looks for in any play, be it comedy, tragedy, or garrago, is the propriety of the catastrophe. How does the final disaster, the embarrassment or the agony of the protagonist, which it is the play's business to recount, stand as an appropriate consequence to the protagonist's sin, his fault, his *hamartia?* A critic's struggle to "explain" a play is often in large measure simply the attempt to verbalize that relationship, to describe the poetic justice of the plays, the propriety of matching that *hamartia* with those consequences.

In Arthur Miller's *Death of a Salesman,* how does Willy's catastrophe stand as a poetically just consequence of his *hamartia?* Many answers to that question have been suggested, and many of them help in some measure to describe why the play succeeds. My thesis is modest enough. It is offered not in any attempt to displace other explanations, but as an addition to the multiple cause-effect relationships in that modern drama: Willy committed a crime for which he is justly punished.

The criticism of *Death of a Salesman* falls into two schools, that which feels it necessary to explain why the play fails, and that which feels it necessary to explain why the play succeeds. Since it seems to me that the play succeeds, and since it seems fruitless to attempt to argue people into liking something that they do not like, let what follows be addressed exclusively to those who agree that the play succeeds.

For it does succeed. In the court that has final provenance in such a case, the stage, the verdict is that *Death of a Salesman* is a success. Most of the adverse criticism of this play, and there is a lot of it, tries to argue that because the play is not unified and coherent in the way a classical tragedy is coherent, it is a failure, not only as a tragedy, but as a work of art of any kind. Alfred Schwarz [in an essay in *Modern Drama* IX, 1966] has pointed out while reviewing the discussions of this issue by Hebbel, Büchner, Luckács, and by Miller himself, that there is not even a theoretical necessity for a modern tragedy to be unified and coherent in the same ways we have learned to expect in a classic tragedy. A modern realistic tragedy, even in theory, is a multiple device. Such tragedy is anchored not in eternal conditions, as man's relation to fate, but in the immediate and ever shifting conditions of men's relations with each other and with their institutions. Thus a modern play, to be successful, even to be effective tragedy, needs not even theoretically to be singular. On the contrary, according to the poetic that Schwarz describes, a modern drama will present manifold causes of a manifold catastrophe illustrating a manifold theme.

It is clear enough from all the criticism that *Death of a Salesman* has a theme that is open to various interpretations. One large group insists that it is, or ought to be, about Willy's isolation from nature. Others point out that Willy suffers from a lack of love, a loss of identity, a worship of the False God of Personality. The causes of Willy's disaster are presented with equal variety: he is defeated by society; he is too weak and immoral for any social conditions; he once made a wrong choice of careers; he married a woman who tried to stifle his sense of adventure; or simply that he got too old. And the condition that constitutes Willy's catastrophe is also variously described: he suffered a miserable and pointless death; he suffered the agony of seeing that he had worthless sons; he suffered the agony of the whole

Lee J. Cobb and Mildred Dunnock as Willy and Linda
Loman in the original production of *Death of a Salesman.*

twenty-four hours of insane self-torture which takes
up the supposed "real" time of the play's performance;
or simply that he had a miserable funeral.

It is pointless to argue that because one of these
can be a correct analysis, the others must be wrong,
even though in Miller's play, in the "Requiem" which
closes it, Charley, Biff, Happy, and perhaps Linda, too,
argue as if their explanations of Willy's catastrophe
were mutually exclusive. They may be all right, even
Linda, who says, "I don't understand," that is, that it
is inexplicable.

Elements of the play that have not received the
attention from critics that they deserve are those scenes
which display Willy training his sons. [Barclay W.]
Bates suggests that one of the roles in which Willy tries
to function is that of the "dutiful patriarchal male intent upon transmitting complex legacies from his forebears to his progeny." The episodes which support that
generalization, however, do not indicate that Willy has
any clear ideas what legacy he has received from his
forebears. He speaks vaguely of his father who was
"better than a carpenter," who made flutes, and in the
scenes with Ben he pleads with his brother to tell him
something that he can transmit.

Please tell about Dad. I want my boys to hear. I want
them to know the kind of stock they spring from.

All I remember is a man with a big beard, and I was
in Mamma's lap, sitting around a fire. . . .

[Act I]

Later he complains to Ben of his fears, that "sometimes
I'm afraid that I'm not teaching them the right kind
of—Ben, what should I teach them?"

Part of this tragedy is that what he has taught
them does not look to him like what he wanted them
to have learned. Miller drops suggestions into the first
part of the play that while Biff is a charismatic young
man, he has also the makings of an amoral punk. In the
bedroom with Happy near the beginning of the play,
Biff speaks of going to see Bill Oliver.

BIFF: I wonder if Oliver still thinks I stole that carton
of basketballs.

HAPPY: Oh, he probably forgot about that long ago.
It's almost ten years. You're too sensitive. Anyway,
he didn't really fire you.

BIFF: Well, he was going to. I think that's why I quit.
I was never sure whether he knew or not.

[Act I]

Biff 's first speech suggests that he feels aggrieved
at being suspected; his second speech suggests that Oliver was right to suspect him. Moments later in the
script Willy brings home a new punching bag. Then
Biff shows off the new football that he has "borrowed"
from the locker room. Willy, laughing, tells him that he
has to return it.

HAPPY: I told you he wouldn't like it!

BIFF: (Angrily) Well, I'm bringing it back!

WILLY: (Stopping the incipient argument, to
HAPPY) Sure, he's gotta practice with a regulation
ball, doesn't he?" (To BIFF) Coach'll probably congratulate you on your initiative.

[Act I]

The boys are not mean boys. Indeed, they are
cheerful and eager. They carry Willy's bags in from the
car. They help Linda carry up the wash. But they steal
things, they cheat. Bernard complains that Biff doesn't
study.

WILLY: Where is he? I'll whip him, I'll whip him!

LINDA: And he'd better give back that football,
Willy, it's not nice.

WILLY: Biff ! Where is he? Why is he taking everything?

[Act I]

Moments later in the script, Willy complains
again:

Loaded with it. Loaded! What is he stealing? He's giving it back, isn't he? Why is he stealing? What did I tell him? I never in my life told him anything but decent things.

[Act I]

Miller underscores these same issues again later on in the same act when Charley suggests that it is a poor idea to steal building materials, and, of course, again in the second half of the play when Biff walks out of Bill Oliver's office with Oliver's pen and then cannot go back and face the man.

BIFF: I took those balls years ago, now I walk in with his fountain pen? That clinches it, don't you see? I can't face him like that!

[Act II]

Among the more famous analyses of *Death of a Salesman* is the one published by a psychiatrist while the original production was still on the Broadway stage. Daniel E. Schneider saw the play as an expression of Willy's aggression against his older brother Ben, as Happy's aggressions against Biff. Schneider speaks of the meeting of the father and his sons in the bar as a "totem feast," the whole play as "an irrational Oedipal bloodbath," of Willy's sudden need to go to the bathroom in that barroom sequence as "castration panic," and points out the possible sexual significance of that stolen pen, those stolen basketballs and footballs. Most commentators on *Death of a Salesman* seem to have found Schneider's analysis of the play of little use. At any rate, few of them mentioned him. And indeed Schneider's attempt to point out a pattern seems perhaps a bit forced, that is, a bit psychoanalytic. But he makes some telling points.

There is a pattern, one I think, that has not been pointed out before. It is worth remembering how often, in scenes involving Willy's training of his sons, that balls, footballs, basketballs, punching bags, appear. If Schneider's suggestion is valid that these balls are images of a concern with castration, the implication follows that Willy is guilty of a crime that can serve as the *hamartia* for which his catastrophe is poetically just.

Willy's crime is that he has tried to mould his sons in his own image, that he has turned them into wind-bags and cry-babies. They are not sexually impotent, no more than Willy is, but they are impotent in a larger sense. Happy complains of the meaninglessness of his life.

Sometimes I sit in my apartment—all alone. And I think of the rent I'm paying. And it's crazy. But then, it's what I always wanted. My own apartment, a car, and plenty of women. And still, goddammit, I'm lonely.

[Act I]

The boys are not impotent sexually, but morally and socially. Willy himself has no basis for making

moral choices. It is not so much that he chooses or has chosen evil, but that he has no idea how to choose at all. Everyone, himself included, is constantly contradicting him. He lives in a morally incoherent universe, an incoherence that is the most striking element of the play which describes his torments. And because he is morally incapacitated, he is socially incapacitated. Everything is against him. The city is killing him. The competition is killing him. He cannot get along with the son he loves most. The very seeds he plants no longer grow. Nothing he does has any consequences. He simply cannot make anything happen.

One may, in describing a person like Willy who has no "character," in the vulgate employed in Miller's dialogue, say of Willy that "he's got no balls." And neither have his sons. Willy's efforts to mould these boys in his own image have not been a failure but a success. They are just like him. They offer two aspects of the same personality, Happy taking more after his mother, perhaps, but both sharing the same defect with their father. They cannot make anything happen. They are morally and socially castrated.

To the other causes of Willy's catastrophe, then, to Willy's weakness, his incompetence to deal with a society too cruel to pay him the attention that he cannot wrest from it with his own strength, to his isolation from nature, to his incapacity to explain his own situation to himself, to his feelings of a loss of identity, of spiritual dryness, of lack of love, to his erroneous worship at the altar of personality, I suggest we may add to all these his crime: he has made moral eunuchs of his own sons. His is a criminality, a *hamartia,* for which the punishment, that miserable life, that miserable death, and that miserable funeral too, are appropriate and decorous consequences. (pp. 19-24)

B. S. Field, "Death of a Salesman," in *Twentieth Century Literature,* Vol. 18, No. 1, January, 1972, pp. 19-24.

ORM ÖVERLAND

(essay date 1975)

[Överland is a Norwegian scholar, critic, and editor specializing in American literature. In the following excerpt, he studies the dramatic form of Miller's best-known plays.]

The process of playwriting is given a peculiar wavelike rhythm in Miller's own story of his efforts to realize his intentions from one play to the other. Troughs of dejection on being exposed to unexpected critical and audience responses to a newly completed play are followed by swells of creativity informed by the dramatist's determination to make himself more clearly understood in the next one. This wavelike rhythm of challenge and response is the underlying structural principle of Miller's "Introduction" to his *Collected Plays.* Behind it one may suspect the workings of a radical distrust of his chosen medium. The present essay will consider some of the effects both of this distrust of the theater as a means of communication and of Miller's theories of dramatic form on his career as a dramatist.

Arthur Miller is not alone in asking what he is trying to say in his plays, nor in being concerned that they may evoke other responses than those the playwright thought he had aimed at. From the early reviews of *Death of a Salesman* critics have observed that a central problem in the evaluation of Miller's work is a conflict of themes, real or apparent, within each play. (p. 1)

Miller himself has often spoken of modern drama in general and his own in particular in terms of a split between the private and the social. (p. 2)

[For Miller synthesis of the private and the social] has largely been a question of dramatic form, and the problem for the playwright has been to create a viable

form that could bridge "the deep split between the private life of man and his social life." In addition to his frustration with audience responses and his desire to make himself more clearly understood, part of the momentum behind Miller's search for new and more satisfactory modes of expression after the realistic *All My Sons* has been the conviction that the realistic mode in drama was an expression of "the family relationship within the play" while "the social relationship within the play" evoked the un-realistic modes. (p. 3)

When Miller is slightly dissatisfied with his first successful play [*All My Sons*], it is because he believes that he had allowed the impact of what he calls one kind of "morality" to "obscure" the other kind "in which the play is primarily interested." . . . These two kinds of "morality" are closely related to the two kinds of "motivation"—psychological and social—that . . . critics have pointed to. The problem may be seen more clearly by observing that the play has two centers of interest. The one, in which Miller claims "the play is primarily interested," is intellectual, the other emotional. The former is mainly expressed through the play's dialogue, the latter is more deeply embedded in the action itself.

Joe Keller gradually emerges as a criminal. He has sold defective cylinder heads to the air force during the war and was thus directly responsible for the deaths of twenty-one pilots. The horror of this deed is further brought home to the audience by the discovery that Keller's elder son was a pilot lost in action. This is what we may call the emotional center of interest, and most of the plot is concerned with this past crime and its consequences for Keller and his family. But it is this emotional center that for Miller obscures the real meaning of the play.

Miller wanted his play to be about "unrelatedness":

Joe Keller's trouble, in a word, is not that he cannot tell right from wrong but that his cast of mind cannot admit that he, personally, has any viable connection with his world, his universe, or his society. . . . In this sense Joe Keller is a threat to society and in this sense the play is a social play. . . . [The] crime is seen as having roots in a certain relationship of the individual to society, and to a certain indoctrination he embodies, which, if dominant, can mean a jungle existence for all of us no matter how high our buildings soar.

This, then, is the intellectual center of the play. Any good drama needs to engage the intellect as well as the emotions of its audience. Miller's problem is that these two spheres in *All My Sons* are not concentric. When a play has two centers of interest at odds with each other, the emotional one will often, as here, have a more immediate impact on the audience because it is more intimately related to the action of the play. Invariably action takes precedence over the sophistication of dialogue or symbols.

Death of a Salesman (1949) may serve as further illustration of the point made about the two centers of interest in *All My Sons.* . . . [The] key scene of the play could be the one in Howard Wagner's office or the one in the hotel room depending on whether the play was "political" or "sexual." There is no doubt, however, as to which scene has the greater impact in the theater. The hotel room scene is carefully prepared for. . . . The point is, however, that it is primarily on the stage that this scene makes such an overwhelming impact that it tends to overshadow the other scenes that together make up the total image of Willy's plight. If the play is read, if one treats it as one would a novel, balance is restored and a good case may be made for a successful synthesis of "psychological" and "social" motivation. . . . (pp. 3-4)

Miller seems to have become increasingly aware of the difficulty of making a harmonious whole of his vehicle and his theme. His story would have sexual infidelity (consider for instance the prominence this factor must have in any brief retelling of the plot of *Death of a Salesman* or *The Crucible*) or another personal moral failure at its center, while the significance the story held for the author had to do with man's relationship to society, to the outside world. The one kind of "morality" continues to obscure the other. When starting out to write *A View from the Bridge* (1955), Miller had almost despaired of making himself understood in the theater: no "reviews, favorable or not," had mentioned what he had considered the main theme of *The Crucible* (1953). Since he, apparently, could not successfully merge his plots and his intended themes, he arrived at a scheme that on the face of it seems preposterous: he would "separate, openly and without concealment, the action of the next play, *A View from the Bridge,* from its generalized significance." . . . (pp. 4-5)

With such an attitude to the relationship between story and theme or "action" and "significance" there is little wonder that Miller was prone to writing plays where critics felt there was a conflict of themes. For while Miller's imagination generates plots along psychoanalytic lines, his intellect leans towards socioeconomic explanations. . . .

[The] historical antecedents and the widespread use of narrators in modern drama should not be lost sight of when considering this aspect of Arthur Miller's plays. Miller's narrators, however, are closely connected with his reluctance to let his plays speak for themselves. They are born from his long and troubled struggle with dramatic form. (p. 5)

[Although Miller has discussed *Death of a Salesman* in terms of a prose narrative, it] succeeds precisely

because Willy's story is shown on the stage, not told. The possible uncertainty as to motivation does not detract from the intense and unified impact of the drama in the theater. The characters reveal themselves through action and dialogue supported by what Miller has called the play's "structural images." . . . All the more striking then, the need Miller evidently felt to have the characters stand forth and give their various interpretations of Willy's life after the drama proper has closed with Willy's death. The chorus-like effect of the "Requiem" is obviously related to Miller's conscious effort to write a tragedy of "the common man," a drama which places man in his full social context, which in his essay **"On Social Plays"** is so clearly associated in Miller's mind with Greek drama. From another point of view the "Requiem" may also be seen as the embryo of the narrator figure who becomes so conspicuous in *A View from the Bridge* and *After the Fall:* after the play is over the characters stand forth and tell the audience what the play is about.

Miller's reluctance to let a play speak for itself became even more evident in his two attempts to add extra material to the original text of *The Crucible* after its first production in 1953. The first of these additions, a second scene in Act Two, helps to explain Abigail's behavior in Act Three, but . . . it is not necessary. . . . [This is] evidence of Miller's sense of not having succeeded in making himself understood in the original version of the play.

More striking is the evidence provided by the series of nondramatic interpolated passages in the first act, where the playwright takes on the roles of historian, novelist and literary critic, often all at once, speaking himself *ex cathedra* rather than through his characters *ex scena.* (p. 6)

In effect the play has a narrator, not realized as a character but present as a voice commenting on the characters and the action and making clear some of the moral implications for the reader/audience. (p. 7)

While [some of the interpolated expository] passages are further instances of Miller's apparent distrust of his medium as a means of communication, other passages speak of an impatience with the limitations of the dramatic form. Miller had researched this play thoroughly, and it is as if on second thought he has regretted that he had not been able to bring as much of his research and his historical insights into the play as he would have liked. But when he in the interpolated passages takes on the roles of historian and biographer he tends to confuse the sharp line that must be drawn between the characters in a play called *The Crucible* and a group of late seventeenth century individuals bearing the same names as these characters. . . . It should further be noted that these interpolated expository passages are often concerned with motivation, and that both psychological, religious and socio-economic explanations of the trials are given. While the information is interesting in itself and throws light on the Salem trials, it cannot add to our understanding of the drama as acted on the stage. Whatever needs to be known about these characters and their motives by the audience must be expressed in action and dialogue. That is, if we do not accept the dichotomy of "action" and "significance," with the latter element presented by a representative of the author, a "Reader" or a narrator.

The assumption of such a dichotomy, according to Miller, lies at the heart of the structure of his next play, *A View from the Bridge*. Here, and in *A Memory of Two Mondays*, the one-act play originally presented on the same play bill, Miller thinks of himself as having followed "the impulse to present rather than to represent an interpretation of reality. Incident and character are set forth with the barest naïveté, and action is stopped abruptly while commentary takes its place." . . . On the face of it, however, it is difficult to see why such commentary should be found necessary, unless the playwright had given up trying to make himself understood through "action" alone or, rather, to let his "action" carry the full weight of the "significance" he saw in it. (pp. 7-8)

As in [*All My Sons*], the emotional center of *A View from the Bridge* is embedded in the action. But in the latter play Miller explains that he deliberately tried not to have the dialogue of the characters involved in the action carry any burden that goes beyond this action. The aspect of the play that dialogue attempted to express in *All My Sons* is now delegated to the narrator. The more explicit splitting apart of "the organic impulse" has been observed in *Death of a Salesman* with its concluding "Requiem." Moreover, Miller has also been seen to depart from the second of his two basic principles of playwriting in introducing narrative and expository passages into *The Crucible*. With *A View from the Bridge* he wrote a play that approaches illustrated narrative. (p. 9)

The story is obviously Alfieri's story. What we see on the stage is Alfieri's memory of Eddie as he ponders on its significance: "This is the end of the story. Good night," he concludes the original one act version of the play. The past tense is the mode of narrative; drama is enacted in the present.

The title *A Memory of Two Mondays* is in itself interesting in this connection as it suggests an implied narrator, someone whose memory is projected on the stage as is Alfieri's. This technique is developed to its furthest extreme in *After the Fall*, where *"the action takes place in the mind, thought, and memory of Quentin."* The play has become illustrated narrative, and is essentially a two act monologue which the narrator and main character Quentin, directs at the audience. Significantly, since the flow of narration is essential to the play and the many dramatizations of situations in the narrative are incidental, Quentin's audience is in Miller's stage directions defined as a *"Listener, who, if he could be seen, would be sitting just beyond the edge of the stage itself."*

The images presented on the stage are illustrations of Quentin's consciously controlled discourse or of the working of his sub-consciousness as he struggles for self-understanding and self-acceptance. In either case, the device of giving characters within *"the mind, thought, and memory of Quentin"* a semi-independent status on the stage and allowing them to speak for themselves, makes possible an objective view of the self-image projected by Quentin in his discourse. Essentially, however, Miller has placed a character on the stage and given him the opportunity of examining his life and motives and explaining himself to a Listener through a monologue that lasts the whole length of a two act play. From point of view of genre the result is a cross between expressionist drama, stream of consciousness novel and dramatic monologue. The result, however, is good theater: it works on the stage. The critical attacks on *After the Fall* have mainly been concerned with Miller's subject matter and theme, not his experiment with dramatic form. (pp. 9-10)

Miller in *After the Fall* made the narrator's attempt to arrive at the significance of his own life and explain himself directly to the audience the center of the play. . . . In his next play, . . . *Incident at Vichy* . . . written immediately after the critical disaster of *After the Fall,* he returned to the form of the straightforward, realistic play. By concentrating on one of the two poorly integrated themes of *After the Fall,* that represented by the concentration camp tower, the later play, moreover, avoids the conflict between two different kinds of "morality" or "motivation" many critics have found in his plays up to and including *After the Fall. Incident at Vichy* may be too much the drama of ideas (and not very new or original ones at that) to be successful in the theater, . . . but at least there is no need for any "Requiem," explanatory footnotes or narrator to express the play's dominantly public theme.

Four years later, Miller returned to the material of *All My Sons, Death of a Salesman* and *After the Fall* in another family drama, *The Price.* The play is also a return to the realistic style and retrospective technique of *All My Sons.* But of course Miller had traveled a long distance since 1947. There is a greater economy of characters and incidents, a more subtle and dramatically integrated use of symbols, no more need for manipulative, mechanistic devices like surprise arrivals or unsuspected letters. Two hours in an attic with old furniture and four people—and the experience in the theater is of something organic, something that comes alive and evolves before us on the stage. The playwright appears relaxed, confident that the "action" expresses its "generalized significance": the characters speak for themselves and the play speaks for Arthur Miller. (p. 10)

Miller's belief, expressed in several essays in the mid-fifties, that it is the unrealistic modes of drama that are capable of expressing man's social relationships, as opposed to the realistic drama which is best suited to present the private life, is seen most clearly at work in *A View from the Bridge* from 1955. The "bridge," however, is rather crudely built: to the side of the realistic action stands the narrator, who in the first version of the play spoke in verse—poetry, according to Miller, being the style most closely related to public themes. In the light of such theories the author's misfired intentions with *After the Fall,* his most "unrealistic" play, may be more easily understood; and the irony of its reception as his most embarrassingly private play more readily appreciated. There is further irony in the successful synthesis of the public and the private spheres in *The Price.* For according to Miller's theory, the realism of this or any other play "could not, with ease and beauty, bridge the widening gap between the private life and the social life." But in his essay on **"The Family in Modern Drama,"** Miller had also wondered: "Why does Realism always seem to be drawing us all back to its arms? We have not yet created in this country a succinct form to take its place." This was written at a time when Miller was trying to break away from realism. This movement, however, had its temporary conclusion in *After the Fall,* the play that more than any other must have lead Miller to despair of communicating his intentions to his audience. (p. 11)

[*The Creation of the World and Other Business*] is his first attempt to express himself through comedy and pure fantasy, and in this his most radical departure from realism his earlier concern with the problems of integrating man's private and social life has given way to teleological speculation. Behind the fanciful cosmological draperies, however, one may discover the playwright's old story of the two sons and familial conflict. Indeed, the new play serves as a reminder that the Cain and Abel story is an archetypal pattern in *All My Sons, Death of a Salesman, After the Fall* and *The Price.*

In a different guise the old question of the two centers of interest is also raised by Miller's attempt at comedy. While God and Lucifer incessantly come together on the stage to discuss the Creator's design, Miller's alleged theme, the audience, who cannot but grow restless after two acts with God, his Angels and a boring couple named Adam and Eve, are finally given the two sons, the responsible and respected Cain and the irresponsible and loved Abel. The rather simplistic psychological presentation of the conflict between them is the kind of dramatic material Miller has successfully handled before, and both because it is welcome relief from the overall tediousness of the rest of the play and

because it has dramatic potential, it will easily lay claim to the attention and the interest of the audience at the expense of the play's concern with the human dilemma. . . . [This] venture thus is not only thematically related to his first one but shows that the playwright has still not been able to solve the problem of dramatic form he then felt had served to obscure his main theme.

The story of Arthur Miller's struggle with dramatic form had its beginning in his realization of the two centers of interest in *All My Sons.* His subsequent theories of social drama and its relationship to the realistic and unrealistic modes of drama should be regarded primarily as rationalizations of his own attempts to express himself clearly, to bridge the gap not so much between the social and the private as between his conscious intentions and the audience and critical responses. This was fully demonstrated in his attempts deliberately to separate the action of a play from its significance. His distrust of the realistic drama as a usable medium was thus properly a distrust of the theater itself as a medium, as evidenced in his use of intermediary commentary and narrators and in his tendency towards illustrated narrative. Realism nevertheless has proved to have a strong hold on Miller, and it is the mode with which, the evidence of his plays suggests, he is most at home. (pp. 11-12)

Orm Överland, "The Action and Its Significance: Arthur Miller's Struggle with Dramatic Form," in *Modern Drama,* Vol. XVIII, No. 1, March, 1975, pp. 1-14.

JEAN-MARIE BONNET
(essay date 1982)

[In the following essay, Bonnet demonstrates how Miller bridges the gap between social drama and drama of the individual in *The Crucible.*]

The Crucible presents us with the picture of a small village falling prey to a collective fear that witchcraft is about, lurking in some of its citizens. A specialist in demonology, the revered Hale, is summoned to seek out the devil and a court of justice is set up to root out the evil by hanging witches. The play constantly shifts between two related poles: the individuals must be purged separately so that the community as a whole may be preserved. We then may wonder whether the play is about an individual's discovery of his true self or about a whole community getting out of hand. As Northrop Frye has pointed out, *The Crucible* has the 'content' of 'social hysteria' but the form of a 'purgatorial or triumphant tragedy'. Arthur Miller himself is of no help for the critic in this matter since he has made two entirely contradictory statements on the subject. In the preface to his *Collected Plays,* he wrote: 'The central impulse for writing at all was not the social but the interior psychological question of the guilt residing in Salem', and, a few years later, in his interview with Richard I. Evans [in Evans's *Psychology and Arthur Miller*] he said that ' . . . the predominant emphasis in writing the play was on the conflict between people rather than the conflict within somebody'.

As Miller's statements clearly show, it is quite difficult to situate the play in a fixed traditional pattern: is it tragic drama involving a hero confronting more than human forces, or drama involving a whole group of people? Miller's play seems in fact to straddle both types and it would be hard to draw a clear line between the two. I shall endeavour here to analyze this fundamental duality in *The Crucible,* and show that the play is highly successful though not easily classified within the traditional categories of drama.

That *The Crucible* is a play about the individual and society is obvious if only by the wide scope of characters presented to the audience: they range from farmers and maids to ministers and court-officials. There are twenty-one characters in all, not to mention the people referred to in the course of the play. A whole town is involved, not simply one family whose drama might be representative of the plight of the community.

The twofold nature of the drama is stressed right from the beginning by Miller himself in his authorial statements accompanying the first act. In a fairly long disquisition sketching out the main features of Salem, Mass., in 1692, Miller is very careful to give his reader a few necessary facts concerning the life of the community. (Miller's statements are available to the reader of the play only; nothing is mentioned of the background when the play is performed on stage). His comments are not those of the 'objective' historian, however, for they serve to prepare the readers for the crisis to come. Miller's commentary is selection of facts chosen primarily for their significance at the time of the crisis, not for their intrinsic importance. Miller first lays stress on the importance of the sense of 'community'. The action takes place in 1692 at a time when people were living in a very closely knit society, based on Puritan principles, and, consequently, prone to a certain amount of intolerance towards any form of opposition or dissent. Discipline and obedience were the primary rules, for society was based on an implicit motto saying that ' . . . in unity lay the best promise of safety' [Act I]. Such an adamantly rigid society of course implies that any form of individuality will be considered subversive and dangerous. Thus, paradoxically, such a society is likely to generate suspicion among its members, to develop, as Miller points out, ' . . . a predilection for minding other people's business' [Act I]. We have therefore an essentially explosive situation where unity

at once ensures and endangers the individual's safety. It is precisely the potentially explosive situation which triggers off the whole drama in *The Crucible,* where the general tragedy can be seen as a magnification of petty, selfish quarrels occasioned because the individual's desires are curbed by the authoritative state. Those squabbles gradually develop into a wider, extensive quarrel that soon gets out of hand both for the individuals and for the society, and becomes impossible to control—the result being, of course, an intensification of the already exaggerated authority. In other words, the play seems to portray some sort of malignant process in which essentially personal grievances are inflated to socially important hatreds.

The main cause of this gangrenous process is a mixture of individual and social forces. It first appears to be Abigail, a girl who has an 'endless capacity for dissembling' [Act I], out of lust for John and out of jealousy for Elizabeth Proctor. Then, this malignancy gradually feeds on the grievances of all the other inhabitants of the community and becomes a social phenomenon: thus we have the Putnams' greed for land, the thirst for revenge aimed at Martha Corey because of a sick pig, the boundary disputes between the Putnams and the Nurses, the argument over lumber between the Proctors, the Coreys and the Putnams, and Mrs. Putnam's cantankerous bitterness at having been able to keep only one of her numerous children alive. All these squabbles seem to be occasions seized upon by individuals in order to assert their rights in a basically oppressive society. A constant lust for power and a pervasive acquisitiveness compensate for their low station. For the women, such as Abigail, witchcraft may be a way of asserting their will and their power in a system centered on and dominated by men.

Thus we see how a society, because of its tight unity, may be subject to ruin as soon as a breach occurs in its defences. This kind of extreme order generates its own undermining germs: the slightest gap in the bulwark is an outlet for all individual and hitherto pent-up passions. Thus jealousy or envy can be seen to fragment friendship and mutual respect, the true cement of unity. Such a rigid state is open to all forms of betrayals and accusations. Every single person can avail himself of the opportunity to wreak his own personal vengeance on his neighbour. At the same time that fallen state of things becomes a social matter, in which even justice is infected by the same process and becomes twisted, warped in its turn.

If one leaves out the first act, which serves as an overture, the three remaining acts all take place— literally or symbolically—in court. At the Proctors', the scene of Act Two, the house is soon equated to a court: in Proctor's own words, it is ' . . . as though he comes into a court when [he comes] into his house'. The same idea is carried on a few moments later in his reiterated

'I confessed, I confessed', which prefigures the future confessions to be exacted from all the victims. The equation with the court is pushed even further when Miller makes Elizabeth describe her husband as having to appear before the tribunal of his own conscience: 'The magistrate sits in your heart that judges you', she tells him; and there we touch the core of the drama, Proctor's case being both an entirely personal drama as well as a social one. This arraignment of Proctor in his own house and in his own conscience helps to convey how closely privates lives are linked with society. Proctor's own problem is inseparable from that of the community: his own personal dilemma transformed into a social crisis, is thereby intensified to a dramatic pitch.

This heightening is clearly demonstrated by situating the fourth act in a prison cell, for it enhances the symmetry of the picture. The fourth act is a pendant to the second act, in that it reverts intensively to Proctor's case. There is a narrowing focus, after the third act, which is placed in an official court with the community at large attending and which culminates in hysteria at the close. The fourth act is not only a static pendant to the second act, but the outcome of what was latent in it, that is, an individual's hesitations between preserving his own integrity at the expense of his life or abandoning it to save his life. It illustrates how conscience, which is the essential being of any man, is manipulated by society. And ending the play in a prison cell is the fitting symbolical way of showing it: for a cell is a limited space and therefore retains some sort of privacy coordinate with matters of private importance; but, at the same time, it is also an official place that can be invaded by the official authorities. Conscience, then, is 'no longer a private matter but one of state administration'. If the play ends with the personal victory of an individual, it also stresses the victory of social authorities over him. Thus the end is double-edged and the two aspects cannot be separated without running the risk of splitting the play in half, forcing a needless dichotomy.

The role of each individual in the development of the hysterical crisis 'walking' Salem can be pointed out by studying Miller's way of depicting his townspeople. As Edward Murray has suggested, most of them appear as static individuals, whereas Proctor and to a lesser extent Elizabeth, are well-rounded characters undergoing a process of evolution. All characters, except Proctor, are presented either as anonymous victims, as people whose pleading for honesty must appear as totally inadequate before a warped court, or as people with rigid unbending attitudes, whether for honest (Rebecca Nurse) or dishonest (Danforth, Abigail) reasons. The static character of individuals is most clearly observed through a study of the language of the play. The whole drama, we could say, is set off, conducted and concluded by the mere force of language.

Language can first be seen as the mainspring of the action. For, the witch hunt does not get its initial impulse from fact; it is based merely on a report: 'the rumour of witchcraft is all about', as Abigail has it [Act I]. A whole community is thus endangered by hearsay which develops into hysteria. Even Danforth perceives it although he fails to rightly understand this basic truth:

> . . . witchcraft is ipso facto, on its face and by its nature, an invisible crime, is it not? Therefore who may possibly be witness to it? The witch and the victim.

[Act III]

There is never any palpable evidence of anything throughout the play, and each individual is required to tell a lie if he wants to save his life. In that sense, language is the demonic force of the play; everything rests on it, and this is true for all characters, on whichever side they stand. Thus Abigail's power over the girls and also over Danforth and the whole community ('Let *you* beware, Mr. Danforth' [Act III]) is essentially verbal. Everyone knows how mobs can easily be mesmerized by the mere power of words, by oratorical gifts which devilishly seduce rational minds. This is precisely the way she acts: at the end of Act One, her hysterical (or rather mock-hysterical) incantatory repetitions of the single phrase 'I saw [so and so] with the Devil', simply degenerate into a cascade of accusations. It is through her perverted use of language that she kindles the fire of hysteria and retains power over the party of deluded girls. She also makes use of language as a way of ensuring her own safety. By pretending she is offended by Danforth's suspicion ('Why this—this—is a base question, sir' [Act III]), she averts his questions and shamefacedly secures her purpose and her life.

Her attitude contrasts with that of Proctor, who is too honest to be artful and delude the judges. Proctor's speech, like those of many other of the accused (like Rebecca's, for instance), is too frank and honest and is no match for the corrupted language of justice. In the court–scenes, language has reached a point when it is of no help to anyone; all means of communication (and understanding) between the individual and society through this medium are blocked. The authorities suggest the answers, or distort and discard all evidence by the mere reply: 'This is contempt of the court.' They thereby cut all answers short, do not allow the accused to express their opinion fully, or lead them into mazes of syllogisms: as Proctor sees it clearly, it is a dead end, 'the accuser is always holy' [Act II].

Hence the necessity of confessing and the misunderstanding over the idea of 'name' between Proctor and the Judges. The word 'name' means at once something entirely personal, but also something social, for it has a value in so far as it distinguishes each individual in society. Besides, it also implies fame, reputation, and, for Proctor, self-integrity. It is in the conjunction of all these aspects that there is a discrepancy between Proctor's view and that of the judges. In other words, when the authorities exact confessions, their preoccupation is with the actual 'saying' of it, even if this means lying on the part of the individual confessing. Confessing a lie is the new institutionalized type of social adjustment as well as a safeguard for life. Those opposing it are inevitably endangering their lives, and Proctor's courage lies precisely in his rejection of a society which institutionalizes falsehood. For him his 'name' does not only mean reputation, but truth to oneself and others. When he refuses to give away other people's names it is because he 'likes not to spoil their names' [Act IV]; and when he refuses to 'sign his name', it is to save his own integrity before God and himself.

This linguistic misunderstanding sums up the conflict between both parties; it is highly ironical since Elizabeth's one lie is tragically believed by the court and, for once, taken as truth.

The play is thus bi-focal, and continually shifting its view from the personal to the public; individuals trying to assert their individuality are strangled by the web of social constraints. The structure seems to point to the personal victory of one character, who has come to a heightened self-awareness and prefers to preserve his own dignity rather than live in a society where falsehood has achieved the status of an institution. We may wonder, however, if this sacrifice will prove beneficial to the community as Hale's doubting words tend to suggest: 'What profit him to bleed. Shall the dust praise him? Shall the worms declare his truth?' [Act IV].

Indeed nobody, even Proctor, is allowed to come out whole at the end of the play, and the 'crucible' seems to be that of society, as well as that of its individuals. (pp. 32-6)

Jean-Marie Bonnet, "Society vs. The Individual in Arthur Miller's 'The Crucible'," in *English Studies,* Netherlands, Vol. 63, No. 1, February, 1982, pp. 32-6.

SOURCES FOR FURTHER STUDY

Bentley, Eric. *What is Theatre? Incorporating the Dramatic Event.* New York: Limelight Editions, 1984, 491 p.

Influential study by the noted critic that features discussions of several of Miller's works, including *Salesman, Crucible, A View from the Bridge,* and *After the Fall.*

Corrigan, Robert W., ed. *Arthur Miller: A Collection of Critical Essays.* Englewood Cliffs, N.J.: Prentice-Hall, 1969, 176 p.

Significant collection of essays about Miller and his works written by a variety of critics up to the mid-1960s.

Hogan, Robert. *Arthur Miller,* University of Minnesota Pamphlets on American Writers, No. 40. Minneapolis: University of Minnesota Press, 1964, 48 p.

Concise overview of Miller's life and works.

Martin, Robert A., ed. *Arthur Miller: New Perspectives.* Englewood Cliffs, N.J.: Prentice-Hall, 1982, 223 p.

Updates Corrigan's collection (see entry above), featuring more recent analyses.

Martine, James J. *Critical Essays on Arthur Miller.* Boston: G. K. Hall & Co., 1979, 217 p.

Anthology that includes reviews of Miller's plays in performance as well critical studies.

Murray, Edward. *Arthur Miller, Dramatist.* New York: Frederick Ungar Publishing Co., 1967, 186 p.

Important study featuring individual chapters on seven of Miller's works, including *All My Sons, Salesman, Crucible, A Memory of Two Mondays, A View From the Bridge, After the Fall,* and *Incident at Vichy.*

Henry Miller

1891-1980

(Full name Henry Valentine Miller) American novelist, critic, short story writer, editor, and nonfiction writer.

INTRODUCTION

*C*onsidered among the most controversial and influential of twentieth-century authors, Miller is best remembered for his first novel, *Tropic of Cancer* (1934). In this and other autobiographical works of fiction, Miller attacked what he perceived to be the repression of the individual in a civilization bedeviled by technology, Victorian mores, and politics. Miller's criticism of Western culture evidenced his affinities with such philosophers as Friedrich Nietzsche and Oswald Spengler. The explicit sexual content of Miller's work and his revolutionary use of scatological humor and obscene language underscored his rebellion and caused his works to be censored in many countries, including the United States and England, until the early 1960s.

Born in Brooklyn, Miller held a variety of jobs and had been married twice when he departed for Paris in 1930. There Miller's talent matured and he wrote the novels which earned him his greatest recognition. In *Tropic of Cancer*, Miller blends naturalism and surrealism in a spontaneous, anecdotal prose style which draws directly from American vernacular. Essentially a fictionalized rendering of Miller's first year in Paris, the book is both a chronicle of Miller's life in the city's impoverished sections and a life-affirming manifesto which revels in the unrepressed expression of bodily functions and sexuality. Miller's aim with this novel was to express his belief in the unconditional acceptance of all aspects of life, good and bad, as equally valid parts of existence. As Miller stated, "One reason why I have stressed so much the immoral, the wicked, the ugly, the cruel in my work is because I want others to know how valuable these are, how equally if not more important than the good things." Although many critics considered the book's bawdy humor, obscene language, and explicit sexual content to be gratuitous or sexist, others claimed that these elements served to exalt the human body in an era which celebrated technological advancement and to shock readers out of complacency.

In his other major works written in Paris, *Black Spring* (1936) and *Tropic of Capricorn* (1939), Miller continues his use of surreal and natural imagery to convey his outrage against Western culture. *Black Spring* contains segments originally intended for inclusion in *Tropic of Cancer* and *Tropic of Capricorn* along with surreal passages culled from Miller's personal "dream book." In other chapters, Miller reminisces about his youth in Brooklyn. Many of the events recounted in *Tropic of Capricorn* predate Miller's experiences in Paris, detailing his life in the United States, his various occupations, and the restrictive atmosphere he viewed as intrinsic to American life.

The novels of Miller's trilogy *The Rosy Crucifixion*—*Sexus* (1949), *Plexus* (1953), and *Nexus* (1960)—were written after he returned to live in the United States. Again based upon personal experience, *The Rosy Crucifixion* chronicles Miller's life in the United States during the 1920s. Focusing primarily on his first two marriages and his literary aspirations, the trilogy has met with less favor than Miller's previous novels because, according to many critics, it fails to resolve the questions it raises regarding love and life. *Quiet Days in Clichy* (1956), a novel intended as a companion piece to *Tropic of Cancer,* is another Paris reminiscence, while *Book of Friends* (1978) concerns Miller's Brooklyn childhood.

Miller also published many works in other genres. *The Colossus of Maroussi* (1941), a travelogue on Greece, is, according to Miller, "less a guidebook than an account of Greece as an experience." In *The Air-Conditioned Nightmare* (1948) and its sequel, *Remember to Remember* (1974), Miller recounts his impressions of consumer America during his travels across the United States. *Big Sur and the Oranges of Hieronymous Bosch* (1957) is a book detailing Miller's life in the 1950s on the California coast. Among Miller's critical works are *Time of the Assassins: A Study of Rimbaud* (1956) and *The World of Lawrence: A Passionate Appreciation* (1980). The latter, detailing the life and career of his literary compatriot, D. H. Lawrence, was begun prior to the publication of *Tropic of Cancer.* *Opus Pistorum* (1984) is a novel reputedly written by Miller in the early 1940s when he was in need of money. Most critics consider the work to be pure pornography, and some question whether Miller is the actual author of the book.

Since Miller's death, critics have reevaluated his influence and contribution to contemporary literature. Several commentators acknowledge that he laid the groundwork for such writers of the Beat movement as Jack Kerouac, Allen Ginsberg, and Lawrence Ferlinghetti by freeing language and subject matter from rigid censorship. While many of Miller's books contain passages of artistry, critics generally agree that *Tropic of Cancer* is his most sustained and successful work.

(For further information about Miller's life and works, see *Concise Dictionary of American Literary Biography, 1929-1941; Contemporary Authors,* Vols. 9-12, 97-100 [obituary]; *Contemporary Authors New Revision Series,* Vol. 33; *Contemporary Literary Criticism,* Vols. 1, 2, 4, 9, 14, 43; *Dictionary of Literary Biography,* Vols. 4, 9; and *Dictionary of Literary Biography Yearbook: 1980.*)

CRITICAL COMMENTARY

PHILIP RAHV
(essay date 1957)

[A Russian-born American critic, Rahv was a prominent and influential member of the Marxist movement in American literary criticism. For thirty-five years he served as coeditor of the prestigious literary journal *Partisan Review.* Rahv's criticism usually focuses on the intellectual, social, and cultural milieu influencing a work of art. In the excerpt below from an essay first published in 1957, Rahv discusses *Tropic of Cancer, Black Spring* and *Tropic of Capricorn,* praising Miller's vivid portrayal of life among the lumpenproletariat.]

[*Tropic of Cancer, Black Spring,* and *Tropic of Capricorn* are autobiographical, and Miller] appears in them in the familiar role of the artist-hero who dominates modern fiction. Where he differs from this ubiquitous type is in the extremity of his destitution and estrangement from society. Reduced to the status of a lumpen proletarian whom the desolation of the big city has finally drained of all illusions and ideals, he is now an utterly declassed and alienated man who lives his life in the open streets of Paris and New York.

Principal Works

Tropic of Cancer (novel) 1934

Black Spring (novel) 1936

Max and the White Phagocytes (essays and stories) 1938

Tropic of Capricorn (novel) 1939

The Cosmological Eye (essays) 1939

The World of Sex (essay) 1940

The Colossus of Maroussi; or, The Spirit of Greece (travelogue) 1941

Sunday after the War (essays) 1944

The Air-Conditioned Nightmare (essays) 1945

*Sexus (novel) 1949

*Plexus (novel) 1953

Quiet Days in Clichy (essay) 1956

The Time of the Assassins: A Study of Rimbaud (criticism) 1956

Big Sur and the Oranges of Hieronymus Bosch (essays) 1957

*Nexus (novel) 1960

The World of Lawrence: A Passionate Appreciation (criticism) 1980

*These works are known together as The Rosy Crucifixion trilogy.

In these novels the narrator's every contact with cultural objects serves merely to exacerbate his anarchic impulses. There no longer exists for him any shelter from the external world. Even the idea of home—a place that the individual can truly call his own because it is furnished not only with his belongings but with his very humanity—has been obliterated. What remains is the fantasy of returning to the womb, a fantasy so obsessive as to give rise to an elaborate intrauterine imagery as well as to any number of puns, jokes, imprecations, and appeals.

It is precisely in his descriptions of his lumpen-proletarian life in the streets that Miller is at his best, that his prose is most resonant and alive—the streets in which a never ending array of decomposed and erratic phenomena gives his wanderings in search of a woman or a meal the metaphysical sheen of dream and legend. In every shopwindow he sees the "sea-nymph squirming in the maniac's arms," and everywhere he smells the odor of love "gushing like sewergas" out of the leading mains: "Love without gender and without lysol, incubational love, such as the wolverines practice above the treeline." In these novels food and sex are thematically treated with such matter-of-fact exactitude, with such a forceful and vindictive awareness of rock-bottom needs, that they cease to mean what they

mean to most of us. Miller invokes food and sex as heroic sentiments and even generalizes them into principles. For the man who is down and out has eyes only for that which he misses most frequently; his condition makes of him a natural anarchist, rendering irrelevant all conventions, moral codes, or any attempt to order the process of experience according to some value-pattern. The problem is simply to keep alive, and to that end all means are permissible. One turns into a desperado, lurking in ambush in hallways, bars, and hotel rooms in the hope that some stroke of luck will enable one "to make a woman or make a touch." He literally takes candy from babies and steals money from prostitutes. As for obtaining regular work, he was always able "to amuse, to nourish, to instruct, but never to be accepted in a genuine way . . . everything conspired to set me off as an *outlaw*."

The fact that the world is in a state of collapse fills him with deep gratification ("I am dazzled by the glorious collapse of the world") because the all-around ruin seems to justify and validate what has happened to him personally. His particular adjustment he accomplishes by accepting the collapse as a kind of apocalyptic show from which the artist who has been rejected by society, and whose role is to revive the primeval, chaotic instincts, might even expect to gain the resurgence of those dreams and myths that the philistines have done their utmost to suppress. It is senseless to interfere, to try to avert the catastrophe; all one can do is to recoil into one's private fate. "The world is what it is and I am what I am," he declares. "I expose myself to the destructive elements that surround me. I let everything wreak its own havoc with me. I bend over to spy on the secret processes to obey rather than to command." And again: "I'm neither for nor against, I'm neutral. . . . If to live is the paramount thing, then I will live even if I become a cannibal." And even in his own proper sphere the artist is no longer free to construct objective forms. He must abandon the "literary gold standard" and devote himself to creating biographical works—human documents rather than "literature"—depicting man in the grip of delirium.

And Miller's practice fits his theory. His novels do in fact dissolve the forms and genres of writing in a stream of exhortation, narrative, world-historical criticism, prose-poetry and spontaneous philosophy, all equally subjected to the strain and grind of self-expression at all costs. So riled is his ego by external reality, so confused and helpless, that he can no longer afford the continual sacrifice of personality that the act of creation requires, he can no longer bear to express himself implicitly by means of the work of art as a whole but must simultaneously permeate and absorb each of its separate parts and details. If everything else has failed me, this author seems to say, at least this book is mine, here everything is fashioned in my own image, here I am God.

This is the meaning, I think, of the "biographical" aesthetic that Miller at once practiced and preached in his early work and which an increasing number of writers, though not cognizant of it as a program, nevertheless practice in the same compulsive manner, not necessarily for reasons as personal as Miller's or with the same results, but because the growing alienation of man in modern society throws them back into narcissistic attitudes, forces them to undertake the shattering task of possessing the world that is now full of abstractions and mystifications through the instrumentality of the self and the self alone. Not "Know Thyself !" but "Be Yourself !" is their motto. Thomas Wolfe was such a writer, and his career was frustrated by the fact that he lacked sufficient consciousness to understand his dilemma. Miller, on the other hand, was well aware of his position when writing his early fictions. Instead of attempting to recover the lost relation to the world, he accepted his alienated status as his inexorable fate, and by so doing he was able to come to some kind of terms with it.

If freedom is the recognition of necessity, then what Miller gained was the freedom to go the whole length in the subversion of values, to expose more fully perhaps than any other contemporary novelist in English the nihilism of the self which has been cut off from all social ties and released not only from any allegiance to the past but also from all commitments to the future. The peculiarly American affirmation voiced by Whitman was thus completely negated in Miller. Total negation instead of total affirmation! No wonder that like Wolfe and Hart Crane and other lost souls he was continually haunted by Whitman as by an apparition. In *Tropic of Cancer* he speaks of him as "the one lone figure which America has produced in the course of her brief life . . . the first and last poet . . . who is almost undecipherable today, a monument covered with rude hieroglyphs for which there is no key." And it is precisely because he had the temerity to go the whole length that Miller is important as a literary character, though his importance, as George Orwell has observed, may be more symptomatic than substantial, in the sense that the extreme of passivity, amoralism, and acceptance of evil that his novels represent tends to demonstrate "the impossibility of any major literature until the world has shaken itself into a new shape."

In all his books Miller apostrophizes the Dadaists, the Surrealists and the seekers and prophets of the "marvelous," wherever they may be found. Perhaps because he discovered the avant-gardists so late in life, he is naive enough to take their system of verbal ferocity at its face value and to adopt their self-inflationary mannerisms and outcries. At the same time he likes to associate himself with D. H. Lawrence, who was not at all an avant-—gardist in the Parisian group sense of the term. He apparently regards himself as Lawrence's successor. But the truth is that they have very little in common, and there is no better way of showing it than by comparing their approaches to the sexual theme.

Miller is above all morally passive in his novels, whereas Lawrence, though he too was overwhelmed by the alienation of modern man, was sustained throughout by his supreme gift for moral activity; and he was sufficiently high-visioned to believe that a change of heart was possible, that he could reverse the current that had so long been running in one direction. Hence his idea of sexual fulfillment as a means of reintegration. Miller, however, in whose narratives sex forms the main subject-matter, presents sexual relations almost without exception in terms of fornication, which are precisely the terms that Lawrence simply loathed. The innumerable seductions, so casual and joyless, that Miller describes with such insistence on reproducing all the ribald and obscene details, are almost entirely on the level of street encounters. He has none of Molly Bloom's earthiness, nor does he ever quake with Lawrence's holy tremors. He treats erotic functions with a kind of scabrous humor, for there is scarcely any feeling in him for the sex-partner as a human being. What he wants is once and for all to expose "the conjugal orgy in the Black Hole of Calcutta." Not that he is open to the charge of pornography; on the contrary, behind his concentration on sexual experience there is a definite literary motive, or rather a double motive: first, the use of this experience to convey a sense of cultural and social disorder, to communicate a nihilist outlook, and second, an insatiable naturalistic curiosity. It is plain that Miller and Lawrence are opposites rather than twins.

Miller's claims as a guide to life and letters or as a prophet of doom can be easily discounted, though one remembers an essay by him on Proust and Joyce, called **"The Universe of Death,"** which is a truly inspired piece of criticism. In his three novels, however, he is remarkable as the biographer of the hobo-intellectual and as the poet of those people at the bottom of society in whom some unforeseen or surreptitious contact with art and literature has aroused a latent antagonism to ordinary living, a resolve to escape the treadmill even at the cost of hunger and degradation. In dealing with this material, Miller has performed a new act of selection. There is in his fiction, also, a Dickensian strain of caricature which comes to the surface again and again, as in the riotously funny monologues of the journalists Carl and Van Norden in *Tropic of Cancer.* The truth is that his bark is worse than his bite. He strikes the attitudes of a wild man, but what he lacks is the murderous logic and purity of his European prototypes. Though he can be as ferocious as Céline, he is never so consistent; and the final impression we have of his novels is that of a naturally genial and garrulous American who has been through hell. But now that he has had a measure of recognition and has settled down at home to receive the homage of his admirers he seems to have entered a new phase, and his work only occasionally reminds us of the role of bohemian desperado which in his expatriate years he assumed with complete authority and conviction. (pp. 79-85)

Philip Rahv, "Sketches in Criticism: Henry Miller," in *Henry Miller and the Critics*, edited by George Wickes, Southern Illinois University Press, 1963, pp. 77-85.

IHAB HASSAN
(essay date 1968)

[An Egyptian-born American educator and critic, Hassan is a highly regarded commentator on post-modern literature. In the following excerpt from his *The Literature of Silence: Henry Miller and Samuel Beckett* (1967), he analyzes *Tropic of Capricorn*, finding the novel to be Miller's most successful in recognizing "his fate as man and artist."]

The obsessive myth of Henry Miller . . . celebrates the periodic deaths and rebirths of his ego and the emergence of his consciousness as an artist. The myth also bitterly laments his birthright, the waste of years in America, that demonic land of his dreams. *Tropic of Capricorn* (1939) gives more scope to this dual aspect of the myth than Miller's earlier books. Shaped again by the free flow of image and association, the work goes even further than *Black Spring* toward denying the ideas of pattern and sequence though it is woven of few winding strands.

The events of the book antecede those of *Tropic of Cancer*. Miller is still in his torture chamber, America, a man without destiny or art. He has just climbed on "The Ovarian Trolley," a grotesque subtitle, that refers us, first, to the diseased ovaries of Hymie's wife and, last, to the womb of all creation. But as in the case of Hymie's insatiable wife, the matrix of the universe we see is a hungry wound trickling pus.

Peter Abelard, noble lover castrated by his own passion, provides the epigraph, *historia calamitatum.* "I too have known some consolation from speech had with one who was a witness thereof . . . ," Abelard confesses, giving to life's outrage the meaning of misfortune shared. Miller follows this ancient example, and his first sentence begins the winding journey of confession, doubling back upon its course many times. He begins by pretending that he has given up the ghost. But there are many more false deaths and rebirths still in store for this narrator—who refers to himself, un-

abashedly, as Henry Miller—and the beginning of the book is also its conclusion. What follows is a sketch of an unregenerate man, passive, frenzied, devoid of piety, a man without aim or task. "There was nothing I wished to do which I would just as well not do," he writes. And as if to prove it, he farts by the coffin of his boyhood friend, Jack Lawson.

Indifference, however, is not Miller's comic flaw. He, who indolently claims to be his own worst enemy, harbors murder in his heart: "I wanted to see America destroyed, razed, from top to bottom. I wanted to see this happen purely out of vengeance . . . ". It is the following episode, relating Miller's experience as personnel manager for the Cosmodemonic Telegraph Company of North America, that transforms this arbitrary feeling into vitriolic comedy. Turned down for a job by a "little runt at the switchboard," Miller goes straight to the vice-president and, by playing on the malice and bigotry of top officials, succeeds in wangling a position, first as spy then as manager, in the company. The company is depicted as a microcosm of American society, a clownish image of brutality and pandemonium. "It was like a page out of the telephone book. Alphabetically, numerically, statistically, it made sense. But when you looked at it up close . . . you saw something so foul and degrading, so low, so miserable, so utterly hopeless and senseless, that it was worse than looking into a volcano." Of course, one seldom sees a volcano in a telephone book; the image lacks cohesive power, which Miller, in his hurry, often sacrifices. Still, the absurdity, hypocrisy, and callousness of the company are real; as a center of communication between human beings, it communicates nothing. Miller reacts to this bizarre farce of efficiency by saying "Yes" to everything his superiors demand. On the sly, however, he hires a ragged crew of tramps and epileptics, Negroes, Chinamen, and Jews, while stealing some quick sex on the table in the back room. He copulates with Valeska, his part-Negro secretary, while his wife is out having an abortion. At his desk, he composes a book of grotesques, a portrait of twelve fierce, crazy, crippled lives, messengers all, who might have stepped out of a picture by Hieronymus Bosch and who will serve, Miller says, to erase once and for all the story of Horatio Alger from the American consciousness. The First World War hardly rumbles in his ears. And when he finally walks out on the company, after five years in a New World inferno, hundreds of employees flock to him in sorrow and love. But Miller feels he must slip away to rejoin an older stream of life, a race of men antecedent to the prairie buffalo, a race that will survive the buffalo. We never actually see Miller join that race.

The foregoing part of the narrative fills roughly one fifth of the book. It is the part, however, to which Miller returns constantly, as one returns to master a compulsion, adding here and there a new reflection, discovering later a buried memory, introducing finally a theme implicit in the whole. The structure is like the music of remembrance, leitmotif and sudden counterpoint. On a trolley ride, Hymie asks Miller about ovaries, and the question bursts open the doors of involuntary recollection. "From the idea of diseased ovaries there germinated in one lightning-like flash a sort of tropical growth. . . . But the associations of Miller are never really free; they are governed, as I have said, by a secret compulsion, which sets a rhythm throughout the book. What is the source of that compulsion, the force behind both rhythm and digression, chance and recurrence? The source, I think, is twofold. It is, first, Miller's fanaticism, his will to believe. "I was born with a crucifixion complex. . . . I was born a fanatic. . . . What is a fanatic? One who believes passionately and acts desperately upon what he believes." Miller's "fanaticism" sustains his errors, and his errors constantly beget new hopes. Therein lies the second source of his compulsion. Miller's life in *Capricorn* is a seesaw of failures and resolutions, frustrations and dreams. He confesses: "it was borne in on me again that I had never done what I wanted and out of not doing what I wanted to do there grew up inside me this creation which was nothing but an obsessional plant, a sort of coral growth . . . ." *Capricorn* is a book shaped by the pent-up spirit of hope and atonement.

The episodes that follow lead nowhere. Miller disports himself with his various cronies: Hymie and Kronsky; Steve Romero, a "prize bull" whom he kept around in case of trouble; O'Rourke, the company detective; Curley, an adolescent psychopath; and his old friend MacGregor, whose devouring interests are sex and venereal disease. At times, Miller rejoices in his "dumb luck" of a goy. At times, he wrings his hands like a maudlin Dostoevski. Conversations pile up high, higher than the Empire State Building from which Miller likes to contemplate the spectacle of modern depravity, then tumble down in a rubble of words. Valeska casually commits suicide; Miller admonishes himself to remain intact. What he needs now is a "frosted chocolate"! Once again, Miller's detachment is more gesture than fact. When his friend Luke dies, he is glad to be rid of a creditor. Yet the same man can describe Broadway, its color and frenzy and corruption, the sheer brilliance of its inhumanity, with a verve that belies his nihilism:

> The great dynamic soul caught in the click of the camera's eyes, in the heat of rut, bloodless as a fish, slippery as mucus, the soul of the people miscegenating on the sea floor, pop-eyed with longing, harrowed with lust. The dance of Saturday night, of cantaloupes rotting in the garbage pail, of fresh green snot and slimy unguents for the tender parts. The dance of the slot machine and the monsters who invent them. The dance of the gat and the slugs who use them. The dance of the blackjack and the pricks

who batter brains to a polypous pulp. The dance of the magneto world, the spark that unsparks. . . .

In sudden juxtaposition with these surreal visions of a diseased or mechanized society are the tender recollections of childhood. It is as if Miller can never find for himself a place in this world, between an Edenic past and a utopian future. (pp. 72-6)

Past the midpoint of the book, the first formal division, entitled "An Interlude," appears. In this section Miller brings into the open the inevitable erotic theme. We had, of course, witnessed many sexual encounters earlier in *Capricorn,* casual, zany, and gross acrobatics of fancy more than of flesh that displayed the powers of imagination of the American male. There was a somber element in this display too, an element of frustration, a spiteful denial of hypocrisy. Sex was a gesture of futility intended to win surcease from futility. But now Miller attempts to give sexuality a larger meaning. He immerses himself in his own hyperboles, embraces his own exaggerations. His aim is to feel, to think with his genitals, to accept the pure, harsh, impersonal reality of desire without reference to heart or mind. He invokes the mythological realm of Dionysos that offers so grave a threat to organized society; then, suddenly changing his tone, he discourses hilariously on the variety of female pudenda or shares with us his irrelevant associations evoked during the act of coitus. Yet the section is really less a hymn than a threnody to Dionysos. A land of brutish sexual intercourse—Miller observes in a rare moment of Laurentian conscience—is a land of cemeteries, a land of death. "Just a couple of quiet maniacs working away in the dark like gravediggers," he writes, describing an old desperation. Beneath the laughter and braggadocio, the rocking rhythm we hear is that of life begetting death and death begetting more death. Pan's flute is still in the streets of New York. "This is the Land of Fuck, in which there are no animals, no trees, no stars, no problems. Here the spermatazoon reigns supreme," Miller says. And having thus reduced all life, he reverses himself unexpectedly:

> Everything is sentient, even at the lowest stage of consciousness.

> Once this fact is grasped there can be no more despair. At the very bottom of the ladder, *chez* the spermatozoa, there is the same condition of bliss as at the top, *chez* God.

This is indeed Miller. Absolute negation becomes merely a pretext for total affirmation. Obscenity clears the way for prophecy. And chaos itself, epitomized for him by a department store like Bloomingdale's, becomes suddenly justified in the sweeping scheme of Bergson's *Creative Evolution.* His next action is to use *Creative Evolution* to seduce a girl he meets on the subway.

There is something disturbing in these antics. We are used to Miller's shifts from frivolity to high seriousness. And his sacramental vision is backed by an ancient, honorable, and sometimes comic, mystic tradition. But Miller's great emphasis in *Capricorn* is on desolation; everything in it cries out against waste and decay. Mystic reconciliation must therefore appear to us like some *deus ex machina,* hurriedly summoned to save a darkling day. We cannot understand how his rage, whatever its cause, can be so suddenly dispelled by an influx of cosmic wonder. Therefore we cannot accept him in the way we accept Blake or Whitman, Boehme or Milarepa.

Yet there are times when the ambivalences of *Capricorn* fuse in archetypal expression. The long ode to Mara is such an instance. It is an extraordinary rhapsody, a romantic outburst of love and hate, fear and awe. Mara, presumably Miller's second wife, had appeared briefly in *Cancer* as Mona. She has something here of Lilith, Circe, and La Belle Dame Sans Merci, something also of the terrible White Goddess and blood-swilling Kali. She may even suggest the shimmering deity of H. Rider Haggard's *She.* In *The Books in My Life,* Miller states: "I dedicated the cornerstone of my autobiography to 'Her'! . . . if 'Her' dealt me death in the Place of Life, was it not also in blind passion, out of fear and jealousy? What was the secret of Her terrible beauty, Her fearful power over others . . . if not the desire to expiate Her crime? . . . that she had robbed me of my identity at the very moment when I was about to recover it." Mara is not only the Dark Lady; she is also the Black Woman, primordial, enigmatic, pervasive, utterly hollow. She is a dead black sun and a great black plunder-bird and a black opening in the sky. . . . The fury of Miller against the woman he loved more than himself, more than God even, fuses the contradictions of his feelings. It is an exaggerated fury, distorted by his own fears into an intuition of ancient evil. But, as we shall see, it gives a focus to the sexual promiscuity of *Capricorn* and a purpose to all its digressions. Mara is the enemy of his personal destiny as man and creator; she stands between him and whatever is in his past, present, or future that may finally give him freedom. Miller rages precisely because she offers the greatest outrage to his being. (pp. 77-80)

The final formal division of *Capricorn,* entitled "Coda," puts its random events in some sort of perspective. We return to Mara; for Miller's theme in this work, as it was in *Cancer,* is self-creation as artist, self-acceptance as man. The "Coda" proves that *Capricorn* is a delayed act of self-discovery; it is written many years after the events it describes and is dedicated to "Her," whom Miller has finally succeeded in exorcising. Standing by the doors of the old dance hall, Miller suddenly realizes that he is at last free of Mara; only the book matters to him now. He then proceeds to describe, for the first time, the circumstances of their meeting. Mara, we discover, is indeed the symbol of Miller's temptation and also the embodiment of his outrage. . . . (pp. 80-1)

Though *Tropic of Capricorn* has less humor and buoyancy than the earlier works, the disorderly progress of its form leads Miller to a fuller recognition of his fate as man and artist. The work ends, as did *Cancer,* on a note of euphoria, a momentary sense of harmony and wholeness. In *Capricorn,* however, that sense takes a specific quality; it is the quality of dualism transcended. (p. 81)

Ihab Hassan, "The Life and Fiction," in his *The Literature of Silence: Henry Miller and Samuel Beckett,* Alfred A. Knopf, 1968, pp. 58-84.

KATE MILLETT

(essay date 1970)

[An American nonfiction writer who is acknowledged as a pioneering figure of the contemporary feminist movement, Millett is best known for *Sexual Politics* (1970), which became a manifesto on the inequality of gender distinctions in Western culture and the sexism in much Western literature. In the excerpt below from that work, Millett castigates Miller for his dehumanizing portrayal of female characters in his writing.]

Certain writers are persistently misunderstood. Henry Miller is surely one of the major figures of American literature living today, yet academic pedantry still dismisses him as beneath scholarly attention. He is likely to be one of the most important influences on our contemporary writing, but official criticism perseveres in its scandalous and systematic neglect of his work. To exacerbate matters, Miller has come to represent the much acclaimed "sexual freedom" of the last few decades. One finds eloquent expression of this point of view in a glowing essay by Karl Shapiro: "Miller's achievement is miraculous: he is screamingly funny without making fun of sex . . . accurate and poetic in the highest degree; there is not a smirk anywhere in his writings." Shapiro is confident that Miller can do more to expunge the "obscenities" of the national scene than a "full-scale social revolution." Lawrence Durrell exclaims over "how nice it is for once to dispense with the puritans and with pagans," since Miller's books, unlike those of his contemporaries, are "not due to puritanical shock." Shapiro assures us that Miller is "the first writer outside the Orient who has succeeded in writing as naturally about sex on a large scale as novelists ordinarily write about the dinner table or the battlefield." Significant analogies. Comparing the *Tropic of Cancer* with Joyce's *Ulysses,* Shapiro gives Miller the advantage, for while Joyce, warped by the constraints of his religious background, is prurient or "aphrodisiac," Miller is "no aphrodisiac at all, because religious or so-called moral tension does not exist for him." Shapiro is convinced that "Joyce actually prevents himself from experiencing the beauty of sex or lust, while Miller is freed at the outset to deal with the overpowering mysteries and glories of love and copulation."

However attractive our current popular image of Henry Miller the liberated man may appear, it is very far from being the truth. Actually, Miller is a compendium of American sexual neuroses, and his value lies not in freeing us from such afflictions, but in having had the honesty to express and dramatize them. There *is* a kind of culturally cathartic release in Miller's writing, but it is really a result of the fact that he first gave voice to the unutterable. This is no easy matter of four-letter words; they had been printed already in a variety of places. What Miller did articulate was the disgust, the contempt, the hostility, the violence, and the sense of filth with which our culture, or more specifically, its masculine sensibility, surrounds sexuality. And women too; for somehow it is women upon whom this onerous burden of sexuality falls. There is plenty of evidence that Miller himself is fleetingly conscious of these things, and his "naive, sexual heroics" would be far better if, as one critic suggests, they had been carried all the way to "self-parody." But the major flaw in his oeuvre—too close an identification with the persona, "Henry Miller"—always operates insidiously against the likelihood of persuading us that Miller the man is any wiser than Miller the character.

And with *this* Miller; though one has every reason

to doubt the strict veracity of those sexual exploits he so laboriously chronicles in the first person, though one has every reason to suspect that much of this "fucking" is sheer fantasy—there is never reason to question the sincerity of the emotion which infuses such accounts; their exploitative character; their air of juvenile egotism. Miller's genuine originality consists in revealing and recording a group of related sexual attitudes which, despite their enormous prevalence and power, had never (or never so explicitly) been given literary expression before. Of course, these attitudes are no more the whole truth than chivalry, or courtly, or romantic love were—but Miller's attitudes do constitute a kind of cultural data heretofore carefully concealed beneath our traditional sanctities. (pp. 294-96)

Miller regards himself as a disciple of Lawrence, a suggestion certain to have outraged the master had he lived to be so affronted. The liturgical pomp with which Lawrence surrounded sexuality bears no resemblance to Miller's determined profanity. The Lawrentian hero sets about his mission with notorious gravity and "makes love" by an elaborate political protocol. . . . But Miller and his confederates—for Miller is a gang—just "fuck" women and discard them, much as one might avail oneself of sanitary facilities—Kleenex or toilet paper, for example. Just "fucking," the Miller hero is merely a huckster and a con man, unimpeded by pretension, with no priestly role to uphold. Lawrence did much to kill off the traditional attitudes of romantic love. At first glance, Miller seems to have start-

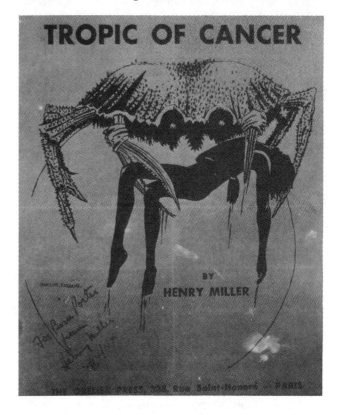

Original cover of *Tropic of Cancer,* first published in 1934.

ed up blissfully ignorant of their existence altogether. Actually, his cold-blooded procedure is intended as sacrilege to the tenderness of romantic love, a tenderness Lawrence was never willing to forgo. In his brusque way, Miller demonstrates the "love fraud" (a species of power play disguised as eroticism) to be a process no more complex than a mugging. The formula is rather simple: you meet her, cheat her into letting you have "a piece of ass," and then take off. Miller's hunt is a primitive find, fuck, and forget. (p. 296)

Lawrence had turned back the feminist claims to human recognition and a fuller social participation by distorting them into a vegetative passivity calling itself fulfillment. His success prepared the way for Miller's escalation to open contempt. Lawrence had still to deal with persons; Miller already feels free to speak of objects. Miller simply converts woman to "cunt"—thing, commodity, matter. There is no personality to recognize or encounter, so there is none to tame or break by the psychological subtleties of Lawrence's Freudian wisdom. (p. 297)

The Victorians, or some of them, revealed themselves in their slang expression for the orgasm—"to spend"—a term freighted with economic insecurity and limited resources, perhaps a reflection of capitalist thrift implying that if semen is money (or time or energy) it should be preciously hoarded. Miller is no such cheapskate, but in his mind, too, sex is linked in a curious way with money. . . . Before exile in Paris granted him reprieve, Miller felt himself the captive of circumstances in a philistine milieu where artistic or intellectual work was despised, and the only approved avenues of masculine achievement were confined to money or sex. Of course, Miller is a maverick and a rebel, but much as he hates the money mentality, it is so ingrained in him that he is capable only of replacing it with sex—a transference of acquisitive impulse. By converting the female to commodity, he too can enjoy the esteem of "success." If he can't make money, he can make women—if need be on borrowed cash, pulling the biggest coup of all by getting something for nothing. And while his better "adjusted" contemporaries swindle in commerce, Miller preserves his "masculinity" by swindling in cunt. By shining in a parallel system of pointless avarice whose real rewards are also tangential to actual needs and likewise surpassed by the greater gains run up for powerful egotism, his manly reputation is still assured with his friends. (p. 298)

The perfect Miller "fuck" is a biological event between organs, its hallmark—its utter impersonality. Of course perfect strangers are best, chance passengers on subways molested without the exchange of word or signal. Paradoxically, this attempt to so isolate sex only loads the act with the most negative connotations. Miller has gone beyond even the empty situations one fre-

quently encounters in professional pornography, blue movies, etc., to freight his incidents with cruelty and contempt. While seeming to remove sexuality from any social or personal context into the gray abstraction of "organ grinding," he carefully includes just enough information on the victim to make her activity humiliating and degrading, and his own an assertion of sadistic will.

Miller boasts, perhaps one should say confesses, that the "best fuck" he "ever had" was with a creature nearly devoid of sense, the "simpleton" who lived upstairs. . . . Throughout the description one not only observes a vulgar opportunistic use of Lawrence's hocus pocus about blanking out in the mind in order to attain "blood consciousness," but one also intuits how both versions of the idea are haunted by a pathological fear of having to deal with another and complete human personality. Happily, Miller's "pecker" is sufficient to "mesmerize" his prey in the dark. . . . One is made very aware here that in the author's scheme the male is represented not only by his telepathic instrument, but by mind, whereas the perfect female is a floating metonymy, pure cunt, completely unsullied by human mentality. (p. 300)

Miller's ideal woman is a whore. Lawrence regarded prostitution as a profanation of the temple, but with Miller the commercialization of sexuality is not only a gratifying convenience for the male (since it is easier to pay than persuade) but the perfection of feminine existence, efficiently confining it to the function of absolute cunt. (p. 301)

Since "whores are whores," Miller is also capable of reviling them as "vultures," "buzzards," "rapacious devils," and "bitches"—his righteous scorn as trite as his sentimentality. He is anxious, however, to elevate their function to an "idea"—the Life Force. As with electrical conductors, to plug into them gives a fellow "that circuit which makes one feel the earth under his legs again." Prostitutes themselves speak of their work as "servicing," and Miller's gratified egotism would not only seek to surround the recharge with mystification, but convert the whore into a curious vessel of intermasculine communication—rhapsodizing: "All the men she's been with and now you . . . the whole damned current of life flowing through you, through her, through all the guys behind you and after you." What is striking here is not only the total abstraction Miller makes of sexuality (what could be less solid, less plastic than electricity?) but also the peculiar (yet hardly uncommon) thought of hunting other men's semen in the vagina of a whore, the random conduit of this brotherly vitality.

There is a men's-house atmosphere in Miller's work. His boyhood chums remain the friends of his youth, his maturity, even his old age. Johnny Paul and the street-gang heroes of the adolescence continue as the idols of adulthood, strange companions for Miller's literary gods: Spengler, Nietzsche, Dostoievski. The six volumes of autobiography, and even the essays, are one endless, frequently self-pitying threnody for the lost paradise of his youth.

As a result, the sexual attitudes of the "undisputed monarch" of the "Land of Fuck," as Miller chooses to call himself, are those of an arrested adolescence where sex is clandestine, difficult to come by, each experience constituting a victory of masculine diligence and wit over females either stupidly compliant or sagely unco-operative. . . . [The] reader is given the impression that sex is no good unless duly observed and applauded by an ubiquitous peer-group jury. And so Miller's prose has always the flavor of speech, the inflection of telling the boys. . . . His strenuous heterosexuality depends, to a considerable degree, on a homosexual sharing. Not without reason, his love story, *The Rosy Crucifixion,* is one long exegesis of the simple admission "I had lost the power to love." All the sentiment of his being, meanly withheld from "cunt," is lavished on the unattractive souls who make up the gang Miller never outgrew or deserted. What we observe in his work is a compulsive heterosexual activity in sharp distinction (but not opposed to) the kind of cultural homosexuality which has ruled that love, friendship, affection—all forms of companionship, emotional or intellectual—are restricted exclusively to males. (pp. 302-03)

Miller is very far from having escaped his Puritan origin: it is in the smut of his pals; in the frenzy of his partners; in the violence and contempt of his "fucking." We are never allowed to forget that this is forbidden and the sweeter for being so; that lust has greater excitements than love; that women degrade themselves by participation in sexuality, and that all but a few "pure" ones are no more than cunt and outrageous if they forget it. "The dirty bitches—they like it," he apprises us; clinical, fastidious, horrified and amused to record how one responded "squealing like a pig"; another "like a crazed animal"; one "gibbered"; another "crouched on all fours like a she-animal, quivering and whinnying." . . . (p. 306)

The very brutality with which he handles the language of sex; the iconographic four-letter words, soiled by centuries of prurience and shame, is an indication of Miller's certainty of how really filthy all this is. His defense against censorship is incontrovertible—"there was no other idiom possible" to express the "obscenity" he wished to convey. His diction is, quite as he claims, a "technical device" depending on the associations of dirt, violence, and scorn, in which a sexually distressed culture has steeped the words which also denominate the sexual organs and the sexual act. . . . Under this sacramental cloak a truly obscene ruthlessness toward other human beings is passed over unnoticed, or even defended. "Obscenity" is analogous to the "uses of the miraculous in the Masters," Miller announces pretentiously. He and the censor have linguistic and sexual attitudes in common: ritual use of the "obscene" is, of course, pointless, unless agreement exists that the sexual is, in fact, obscene. Furthermore, as Miller reminds us again and again, obscenity is a form of violence, a manner of conveying male hostility, both toward the female (who is sex) and toward sexuality itself (which is her fault). Yet, for all his disgust, indeed because of it, Miller must return over and over to the ordure; steel himself again and again by confronting what his own imagination (powerfully assisted by his cultural heritage and experience) has made horrible. The egotism called manhood requires such proof of courage. This is reality, Miller would persuade us: cunt stinks . . . and cunt is sex. (pp. 306-07)

The men's room has schooled Miller in the belief that sex is inescapably dirty. Meditating there upon some graffiti, "the walls crowded with sketches and epithets, all of them jocosely obscene," he speculates on "what an impression it would make on those swell dames . . . I wondered if they would carry their tails so high if they could see what was thought of an ass here." Since his mission is to inform "cunt" just how it's ridiculed and despised in the men's house, women perhaps owe Miller some gratitude for letting them know. (p. 309)

Miller's scheme of sexual polarity relegates the female to "cunt," an exclusively sexual being, crudely biological. Though he shares this lower nature, the male is also capable of culture and intellect. The sexes are two warring camps between whom understanding is impossible since one is human and animal (according to Miller's perception, intellectual and sexual)—the other, simply animal. Together, as mind and matter, male and female, they encompass the breadth of possible experience. The male, part angel, part animal, enjoys yet suffers too from his divided nature. His appetite for "cunt," recurrent and shameful as it is, is, nevertheless, his way of staying in touch with his animal origins. It keeps him "real." Miller staves off the threat of an actual sexual revolution—woman's transcendence of the mindless material capacity he would assign her—through the fiat of declaring her cunt and trafficking with her only in the utopian fantasies of his "fucks." That this is but whistling in the dark is demonstrated by his own defeating experience with Mara, and, even more persuasively by the paralyzing fear which drives him to pretend—so that he may deal with them at all—that women are things. (p. 312)

Miller has given voice to certain sentiments which masculine culture had long experienced but always rather carefully suppressed: the yearning to effect a complete depersonalization of woman into cunt, a game-sexuality of cheap exploitation, a childish fantasy of power untroubled by the reality of persons or the complexity of dealing with fellow human beings and, finally, a crude species of evacuation hardly better than anal in character.

While the release of such inhibited emotion, however poisonous, is beyond question advantageous, the very expression of such lavish contempt and disgust, as Miller has unleashed and made fashionable, can come to be an end in itself, eventually harmful, perhaps even malignant. To provide unlimited scope for masculine aggression, although it may finally bring the situation out into the open, will hardly solve the dilemma of our sexual politics. Miller does have something highly important to tell us; his virulent sexism is beyond question an honest contribution to social and psychological understanding which we can hardly afford to ignore. But to confuse this neurotic hostility, this frank abuse, with sanity, is pitiable. To confuse it with freedom were vicious, were it not so very sad. (p. 313)

Kate Millett, "Henry Miller," in her *Sexual Politics,* Doubleday & Company, Inc., 1970, pp. 294-313.

HAROLD T. McCARTHY

(essay date 1971)

[An American educator and critic, McCarthy is the author of *The Expatriate Perspective: American Novelists and the Idea of America* (1983). In the following excerpt, he assesses Miller's view of the United States and compares it with those of Walt Whitman and Henry David Thoreau.]

When Henry Miller settled down in Paris in 1930, it was with no mere sense of being an expatriate. He believed he had died and been reborn. From this time he dated his birth as a creative artist and the beginning of the "auto-hero," "Henry Miller," whose past and present being he was to examine throughout the whole decade of the Thirties which he spent mainly in Paris. From this time he became a citizen of the universe, occupant of that "enormous womb" which reached to and included the most distant stars. And from this time he began once more to be an American. He felt that he was American in a sense of the term that would have been meaningful to the great transcendentalist writers of America's literary renaissance. In *Democratic Vistas* Walt Whitman had tried to formulate anew what he felt to be the motivating ideals of America, and Miller's work gave expression to similar vistas: a recovered awareness of the roots of democracy in spiritual community; a reorientation in human as distinct from commercial and technological values; the effort to liberate individual identity from conformist pressures and from the "City"; the acceptance of change and of suffering; faith in individual creative power as a force for transforming society; and—here, perhaps, most of all like Whitman—a profound acceptance of love and of death. (p. 221)

As Thoreau moved to Walden Pond, Miller moved to Paris for fear that he would awake one morning and find that he had not lived. He wished to possess himself and to be aware. And like Thoreau's *Walden,* Miller's *Tropic of Cancer* is a mythic birth of personality, a self sculptured into full separateness from the cultural clay that would have leached away the individual nature. Miller saw the threat to individuality as more terrible than mere dissolution in its action: "By simple external pressure, by force of surroundings and example, by the very climate which activity engenders one can become part of a monstrous death machine, such as America, for example." (p. 226)

While Miller frequently raged at America's highly technological society, he believed that the root of its troubles lay in a pseudodemocratic political and social structure, one in which the common man's worst qualities flourished, power and riches were garnered by a few, and there was no foundation of respect "for the sacred human individual who aggregate makes a democracy and in the ultimate will make divinity." (pp. 226-27)

In the process of creating the material out of which he assembled *Tropic of Cancer,* Miller sought with hatred and contempt to cut away from himself those portions of his identity which he conceived as being the cancerous "City," and to bring into recognizable being his separate and unique personality. The narration is autobiographical, but only if one allows for the possibility that dreams, wishes and lies are essential parts of the central consciousness. Although the narrator is in Paris, he is cutting himself free of the disease of civilization which he had absorbed in America; he has reached Cancer, "the extreme point of realization along the wrong path," "the apogee of death in life," and must reverse his course. The novel begins abruptly, and unlike the stream-of-consciousness novels which seek to reproduce an *apparent* discontinuity of thought and an *apparent* dissociation from reality *Cancer,* in form and subject, responds to the narrator's effort to be true only to his nature as animal and as god and thereby to betray his cultural conditioning.

Order, system, pattern, these are aspects of the disease which must be destroyed. All taboos must be challenged because they are taboos; the only authoritative totem is the self. Miller was to describe America as "the schizophrenic Paradise" and as "a far-flung empire of neurosis"; in *Cancer* what is given is the process of analysis through which the author heals himself. Other American characters in the novel, like biblical scapegoats, are heaped with the narrator's afflictions and abandoned to the devils of the American wilderness. A young Hindu, infected with the virus of America, demonstrates that "America is the very incarnation of doom. She will drag the whole world down to the bottomless pit." The auto-hero's temporary job as proofreader of the stock market section of the Paris edition of the *Chicago Tribune* (a job Miller actually held) provides a metaphor of his indifference to the statistical heart of American life.

While Miller hires himself out when it becomes absolutely necessary to earn money, he contrives to make each job serve his purpose of self-creation. The making (of the self, of the book) is always going on. Like Hemingway, he, too, has arrived at a sense of life as play: "Cease laboring altogether and create! For creation is play, and play is divine." Play has its own law, spontaneous and compulsive, operative always at the borderline between exterior and interior life. Early in *Cancer* Miller states his Dadaist determination not to let will, ethical or aesthetic, affect his creation, to make no resistance to his fate, and to pass, as it were, out of the menagerie into the jungle.

He had found himself becoming, in New York, "a city, a world of dead stone, of waste light, of unintelligible motion, of imponderables and incalculables, of the secret perfection of minus," whereas he wished to become "a wild and natural park," where people go to rest and dream. (pp. 228-29)

In his efforts to become a writer, Miller had copied pages of the work of Hamsun, Dostoievski and Céline, fascinated by the way in which these authors could create a protagonist who threaded his holistic way through frenzy like the eye of a hurricane. While Miller shared the destructive need of these authors, he did not as yet possess the deep, upwelling strength—a different kind of strength in each case—which enabled them to hurl their anathemas. With *Cancer* Miller for the first time got off "the gold standard of literature," and instead of creating from what he had drawn from the "City" and "Man" sought to be incorruptibly true to his inner generation. . . .

In creating the disorder of *Cancer,* he created the rebellion of his actual life; he opened the black spring, the "dark, mysterious realm *in the absence of which nothing could happen*"; he made himself into the sublime, absurd rebel who, he believed, was closer to Divinity than was the saint with his revelations in that the rebel was responsive to the sources of human nature. (p. 230)

Miller's concern with change and his contempt for the institutions of western civilization are not necessarily related. He felt that contemporary institutions were particularly destructive of the human spirit, but his concern was almost exclusively with changing the individual—almost exclusively with the creation of that individual, Henry Miller. As an American in Paris he found it possible to stay free of institutions, and to live as though governments, religions, laws, political organizations, social movements and the rest did not exist. (p. 231)

Being concerned with self-fulfillment, Miller felt that the men devoted to social reform were caught in an imaginary wheel rolling clockwise into the future. In their concern with the problems of arranging life to come they failed to solve the problem of living; their action was evidence of individual failure. Miller believed in "spreading" nothing—neither gospel, nor education, nor the wealth, nor brotherhood. To try to do so was to interfere with the sacred privacy of others. He saw "the brotherhood of man" as a permanent delusion common to idealists everywhere in all epochs; it always fails because it reduces men as individuals "to the least common denominator of intelligibility." Individuals and peoples, he believed, can only be helped—and should only be helped—after suffering has played its necessary part in the resurrection of the spirit. (p. 232)

The struggle of the creative artist is not with politics and social reorganization; it is a personal and religious effort to make life a poem. Such an effort, because it is creation, is play, "which just because it has no raison d'être other than itself is the supreme motivating power in life." Instead of trying to impose his ideas of order upon the world, the individual had to learn acceptance, to put himself in order with the world. How? "Through art then, one finally establishes contact with reality: that is the great discovery." (p. 233)

Although the autobiographical material of [*Tropic of Cancer* and *Tropic of Capricorn*] might suggest otherwise, even in the Paris years he was an avid reader and absorbed much of what he read into his creative process. The growth of his theme of the disease of American life found rich nutriment in the prophecies for western culture made by Nietzsche and Spengler. Civic decay, he discovered, had been richly imaged by the French symbolist poets. Joyce, Proust, Lawrence, Céline, all were converted to use in Miller's varied denunciations. A civilization was dying and Miller said bad cess to it in hundreds of pages purportedly dealing with Shakespeare's *Hamlet.* The prospect of the decline and fall of America was to Miller something to be regarded with great joy, for only through its suffering and death could America be reborn. The nation, too, must have its rosy crucifixion. To elaborate this fundamental theme, Miller absorbed Walt Whitman (albeit first through parallels drawn from Balzac novels) into his process of creative realization.

Miller was struck by the similarity between the view of France given in the 1830s by Balzac in *Louis Lambert* and *Seraphita* and the view of America expressed in 1870 by Whitman in *Democratic Vistas.* Even more striking to Miller was the coincidence of Balzac and

Whitman's views with his own view of America in the 1930s. In exploring these related views, especially Whitman's concept of death, Miller arrived at his deepest understanding of the relation of America to his "being." Unlike the successive generations of Americans who have gradually come to a recognition of the virtues of many elements in Whitman's poetry but still cannot truly accept his views of love and death, Miller at once absorbed these views into his own. What America needed, both agreed, was great poems of death.

To Whitman and to Miller it was essential to sing of death in its relation to divinity and to democracy. The civilization dominant in the United States, in the estimation of both men, had lost the sense of death wherein each man, individually, knew his death as passage—a stage in the process of being—a part of divinity being restored to the whole. Out of their separate experiences, both men had arrived at the conception of America as *idea*. America was an idea synonymous with the idea of "Religious Democracy." Like Emerson they believed each individual to be "part or parcel of God," and in this divinity and in this being part of a whole lay the essence of democracy. (pp. 233-34)

The special sense in which, for Miller, Whitman was "America" was expressed in *Cancer* as follows: "Whatever there is of value in America Whitman has expressed, and there is nothing more to be said. The future belongs to the machine, to the robots. He was the Poet of the Body and the Soul, Whitman." When Miller ends *Tropic of Cancer* he is at rest where the Seine leaves Paris and flows on toward the sea. "I feel this river flowing through me—its past, its ancient soil, the changing climate. The hills gently girdle it about: its course is fixed." He is one of Whitman's "identified souls," at one with the flowing river of Man's past, part of nature and part of divinity. In leaving his homeland he was not the man who ran away from something, but "the man who ran *towards* something"—toward those timeless democratic vistas that had the local and temporary name of "America." (p. 235)

Harold T. McCarthy, "Henry Miller's Democratic Vistas," in *American Quarterly*, Vol. XXIII, No. 2, May, 1971, pp. 221-35.

NORMAN MAILER

(essay date 1976)

[An American novelist and essayist, Mailer is one of America's most important and controversial literary figures. His works commonly champion rebelliousness, existentialism, machismo, and sexuality as a means for attaining self-actualization and escaping the restrictions of conventional society. In the excerpt below, he praises Miller as one of literature's great confessional authors who, though he wrote for therapeutic reasons, transformed his life into works of art.]

[Henry Miller] exists in the same relation to legend that anti-matter shows to matter. His life is antipathetic to the idea of legend itself. Where he is complex, he is too complex—we do not feel the resonance of slowly dissolving mystery but the madness of too many knots; where he is simple, he is not attractive—his air is harsh. If he had remained the protagonist by which he first presented himself in *Tropic of Cancer*—the man with iron in his phallus, acid in his mind, and some kind of incomparable relentless freedom in his heart, that paradox of tough misery and keen happiness, that connoisseur of the spectrum of odors between good sewers and bad sewers, that noble rat gnawing on existence and impossible to kill, then he could indeed have been a legend, a species of Parisian Bogart or American Belmondo. Everybody would have wanted to meet this poet-gangster, barbarian-genius. He would have been the American and heterosexual equivalent of Jean Genet.

In fact, he could never have been too near to the character he made of himself in *Tropic of Cancer*. One part never fits. It is obvious he must be more charming than he pretends—how else account for all the free dinners he is invited to, the people he lives on, the whores who love him? There has to be something splendid about him. He may even seem angelic to his friends or, perish the word, vulnerable. . . . (p. 2)

These few details are enough to suggest *Tropic of Cancer* is a fiction more than a fact. Which, of course, is not to take away a particle of its worth. Perhaps it becomes even more valuable. After all, we do not write to recapture an experience, we write to come as close to it as we can. Sometimes we are not very close, and yet, paradoxically, are nearer than if we were. Not nearer necessarily to the reality of what happened, but to the mysterious reality of what can happen on a page. Oil paints do not create clouds but the image of clouds; a page of manuscript can only evoke that special kind of reality which lives on the skin of the writing paper, a rainbow on a soap bubble. Miller is forever accused of caricature by people who knew his characters, and any good reader knows enough about personality to sense how much he must be leaving out of his people. Yet, what a cumulative reality they give us. His characters make up a Paris more real than its paving stones until a reluctant wonder bursts upon us—no French writer no matter how great, not Rabelais, nor Proust, not De Maupassant, Hugo, Huysmans, Zola, or even Balzac, not even Céline, has made Paris more vivid to us. Whenever before has a foreigner described a country better than its native writers? For in *Tropic of Cancer* Miller succeeded in performing one high literary act: he created a tone in prose which caught the tone of a period and a place. If that main character in *Tropic of Cancer* named Henry Miller never existed in life, it hardly matters—he is the voice of a spirit which existed at that time. The spirits of literature may be the nearest we come to historical truth.

For that matter, the great confessions of literature are apart from their authors. Augustine recollecting his sins is not the sinner but the pieties. Julien Sorel is not Stendhal, nor the Seducer a copy of Kierkegaard. *On the Road* is close to Jack Kerouac, yet he gives a happier Kerouac than the one who died too soon. Proust was not his own narrator, even as homosexuality is not like to heterosexuality but another land, and if we take *The Sun Also Rises* as the purest example of a book whose innovation in style became the precise air of a time and a place, then even there we come slowly to the realization that Hemingway at the time he wrote it was not the equal of Jake Barnes—he had created a consciousness wiser, drier, purer, more classic, more sophisticated, and more judicial than his own. He was still naïve in relation to his creation.

The difference between Hemingway and Miller is that Hemingway set out thereafter to grow into Jake Barnes and locked himself for better and worse, for enormous fame and eventual destruction, into that character who embodied the spirit of an age. Whereas Miller, eight years older than Hemingway but arriving at publication eight years later, and so 16 years older in 1934 than Hemingway was in 1926, chose to go in the opposite direction. He proceeded to move away from the first Henry Miller he had created. He was not a character but a soul—he would be various.

He was. Not just a *débrouillard,* but a poet; not just a splenetic vision but a prophet; no mere caricaturist, rather a Daumier of the written line; and finally not just master of one style but the prodigy of a dozen. Miller had only to keep writing *Tropic of Cancer* over and over, and refining his own personality to become less and less separate from his book, and he could have entered the American life of legend. There were obstacles in his way, of course, and the first was that he was not publishable in America—the growth of his legend would have taken longer. But he had something to offer which went beyond Hemingway. (pp. 2-4)

Miller is the other half of literature. He is without fear of his end, a literary athlete at ease in earth, air, or water. I am the river, he is always ready to say, I am the rapids and the placids, I'm the froth and the scum and twigs—what a roar as I go over the falls. Who gives a fart? Let others camp where they may. I am the river and there is nothing I can't join.

Whereas, Hemingway's world was doomed to

collapse so soon as the forces of the century pushed life into a technological tunnel; mood to Hemingway being a royal grace, could not survive grinding gears, surrealist manners, . . . and electric machines which offered static, but Miller took off at the place where Hemingway ended. In *Tropic of Cancer,* he was saying—and it is the force of the book—I am obliged to live in that place where mood is in the meat grinder, so I know more about it. I know all of the spectrum which runs from good mood to bad mood, and can tell you that a stinking mood is better than no mood. Life has also been designed to run in the stink.

Miller bounces in the stink. We read *Tropic of Cancer,* that book of horrors, and feel happy. It is because there is honor in the horror, and metaphor in the hideous. How, we cannot even begin to say. Maybe it is that mood is vastly more various, self-regenerative, hearty, and sly than Hemingway ever guessed. Maybe mood is not a lavender lady, but a barmaid with full visions of heaven in the full corruption of her beer breath, and an old drunk's vomit is a clarion call to some mutants of the cosmos just now squeezing around the bend. It is as if without courage, or militancy, or the serious cultivation of strength, without stoicism or good taste or even a nose for the nicety of good guts under terrible pressure, Miller is still living closer to death than Hemingway, certainly he is closer if the sewer is nearer to our end than the wound.

History proved to be on Miller's side. Twentieth-century life was leaving the world of individual effort, liquor, and tragic wounds for the big-city garbage can

Miller at his watercolor exhibition in Gallery 667 in 1967.

of bruises, migraines, static, mood chemicals, amnesia, absurd relations, and cancer. Down in the sewers of existence where the cancer was being cooked, Miller was cavorting. Look, he was forever saying, you do not have to die of this crud. You can breathe it, eat it, suck it, fuck it, and still bounce up for the next day. There is something inestimable in us if we can stand the smell.

Considering where the world was going—right into the World-Wide Sewer of the Concentration Camps—Miller had a message which gave more life than Hemingway's. (pp. 5-6)

[Miller's] legend, however, was never to develop. With his fingers and his nose and his toenails, he had gotten into the excrements of cancerland—he had to do no more than stay there, a dry sardonic demon, tough as nails, bright as radium. But he had had a life after all before this, tragic, twisted, near to atrophied in some of its vital parts, he was closer to the crud himself than he ever allowed. So he had to write himself out of his own dungeons and did in all the work which would follow *Tropic of Cancer,* and some of the secrets of his unique, mysterious, and absolutely special personality are in his later work—a vital search. We would all know more if we could find him.

Miller is not a writer whose life lends itself to clear and separated aesthetic periods, for it is characteristic of him to write in two directions at once. Even *Tropic of Cancer,* which is able to give the best impression of a single-minded intent, still presents its contrast of styles.

Nonetheless, there is some pattern to his life. Miller has his obsessions, and they are intense enough for him to spend a good part of his aesthetic career working them out. If there is a gauge which separates the artist from everybody else who works at being one, it is that the artist has risen precisely from therapy to art. He is no longer fixed at relieving one or another obsessional pressure on the ego by the act of expressing himself. The artist's ultimate interest is to put something together which is independent of the ego; such work can make you feel that you are traveling through that fine and supple mood we may as well call the truth. *Death in Venice* or *Daisy Miller* has that quality, and *The Red Pony* by Steinbeck. *Breakfast at Tiffany's* by Truman Capote will offer it and Katherine Anne Porter's *Noon Wine.* There are a hundred or rather a thousand such pieces of literature and they are art. It is not to say that they are the greatest achievements of writing itself—nothing of Dostoevsky, for example, could fit such a category of art; indeed it may be said that all of Dostoevsky is therapy, except that he elevated the struggle from his ego to his soul, and so we can all partake of the therapy. Forever beyond art, happily, is genius.

On this herculean scale of measure, if considera-

bly below Dostoevsky, can Miller be found. His life impinges on his work ceaselessly, indeed his relation to the problems of his own life is so unremitting yet so scatterbrained that it is as if life is the only true spouse Henry Miller ever had. A crazy spouse, of course, a confirmed nitwit in her lack of stability. He can never feel calm enough to live in the world of art. In this sense, everything Miller writes is therapy. No American author, not even Thomas Wolfe, emits so intense a message that the man will go mad if he stops writing, that his overcharged brain will simply burst. It is as if Miller was never able to afford the luxury of art—rather he had to drain the throttled heats of the ego each day. Yet his literary act takes on such intensity that we are compelled to awe as we read him. Awe can be a proper accompaniment to great art.

Never pausing to take a breath, it is as if Miller creates art as a species of spin-off from the more fundamental endeavor which is to maintain some kind of relation between his mind and the theater beyond his mind which pretended to call itself reality.

That he was successful is part of his greatness. Most souls who go in for literary self-expression to relieve their suffering end on a treadmill. As they relieve themselves so do they repel readers. Excrement is excrement even when its name is therapy. But Miller brought it off. His product transcended itself and became literary flesh. What he did was therapy in that he had to do it, but it rose above every limitation. Maybe it is because he kept one literary grace—he never justified himself (which is the predictable weakness of all therapy), rather he depended on a rigorous even delighted honesty in portraying his faults, in writing without shit, which is to say writing with the closest examination of each turd. Miller was a true American spirit. He knew that when you have a nation of transplants and weeds the best is always next to the worst, and right after shit comes Shinola. . . . So he dived into the sordid, and portrayed men and women as they had hardly been painted before. (pp. 7-9)

Miller captured something in the sexuality of men as it had never been seen before, precisely that it was man's sense of awe before woman, his dread of her position one step closer to eternity (for in that step were her powers) which made men detest women, revile them, humiliate them, defecate symbolically upon them, do everything to reduce them so that one might dare to enter them and take pleasure of them. . . . [According to Miller, men] look to destroy every quality in a woman which will give her the powers of a male, for she is in their eyes already armed with the power that she brought them forth, and that is a power beyond measure—the earliest etchings of memory go back to that woman between whose legs they were conceived, nurtured, and near strangled in the hours of birth. And if women were also born of woman, that could only compound the awe, for out of that process by which they had come in, so would something of the same come out of them; they were installed in the boxes-within-boxes of the universe, and man was only a box, all detached. So it is not unnatural that men, perhaps a majority of men, go through the years of their sex with women in some contract with lust which will enable them to be as fierce as their female when she is awash in the great ocean of the fuck. As it can appear to the man, great forces beyond his measure are calling to the woman then.

That was what Miller saw, and it is what he brought back to us: that there were mysteries in trying to explain the extraordinary fascination of an act we can abuse, debase, inundate, and drool upon, yet the act repeats an interest. It draws us toward obsession. It is the mirror of how we approach God through our imperfections, *Hot,* full of the shittiest lust. In all of his faceless characterless pullulating broads, . . . in all the indignities of position, the humiliation of situation, and the endless presentations of women as pure artifacts of farce, their asses all up in the air, still he screams his barbaric yawp of utter adoration for the power and the glory and the grandeur of the female in the universe, and it is his genius to show us that this power is ready to survive any context or any abuse. (pp. 17-19)

Norman Mailer, "Henry Miller: Genius and Lust, Narcissism," in *American Review,* No. 24, April, 1976, pp. 1-40.

LAWRENCE J. SHIFREEN
(essay date 1980)

[In the following excerpt, Shifreen summarizes Miller's literary career, claiming that by combining narrative techniques of fiction with reportage, Mailer created a new genre that was a forerunner of the New Journalism movement.]

The one hundred books and pamphlets Miller wrote will certainly provide an important legacy when they are finally understood. For this major author is still considered a pornographer. While the writings are certainly obscene, one must understand that sex is a device that Miller used to satirize American self-righteousness; it was his express purpose to shock the reading public and, thereby, to make them aware of "reality."

Sex became the focus of Miller's work because he hoped that an accurate depiction of American society would help to undermine the country's long standing social, moral, and religious taboos. Once this aim was accomplished, Miller believed, people would gain an increased self-awareness and cultural understanding. To actively promote his position, Miller began writing a series of works—*Tropic of Cancer, Black Spring, Tropic of Capricorn,* and *The Rosy Crucifixion* trilogy.

Therefore, while Miller always claimed that he was apolitical, it is obvious that he was one of the most socially concerned writers of the century. It was his desire to educate people about themselves and about their world. In such essays as **"Glittering Pie," "Mademoiselle Claude," "Money and How It Gets That Way,"** and **"Let Us Be Content with Three Little Newborn Elephants,"** Miller studies various aspects of American society, focusing primarily on the individual-society split and on the subjects of personal freedom and social conformity within American society. In short, Miller is a moralist and a preacher. In fact, his preaching makes many of his essays appear dogmatic and all too literal. This criticism can certainly be levelled at such collections as *Sunday after the War, The Cosmological Eye, Stand Still Like the Hummingbird,* and *The Wisdom of the Heart.*

The best of Miller's works are the early novels. Written in the style of the "storyteller" (a word Miller himself used to describe the writings of such favorite authors as Sherwood Anderson and Isaac B. Singer) [*Tropic of Cancer, Tropic of Capricorn*], and *Black Spring* allow Miller to recapture two decades (the 1920's and the 1930's) in a way that none of his contemporaries was able.

Yet depicting reality undercut Miller's career, since the American public was not ready for the frank depictions of sex found in these works and wished to have "realism" rather than "reality." One readily sees why Singer and Saul Bellow have won Nobel Prizes for Literature while Miller, a man who did more to promote literary freedom throughout the world than any of his contemporaries, remains a literary outcast. For his efforts Miller was persecuted and his books banned throughout the United States and in such other countries as France, England, Germany, and Japan.

Depicting life too realistically shocked Miller's readers; rather than asking what Miller was trying to do in his writing, people dismissed the author. It is too bad that these men and women could not look past the works' sexual explicitness and realize that Miller provides an accurate account and is a historian attempting to recapture his times. These accounts of the 1920's and the 1930's are major contributions to American Literature according to Norman Mailer who suggests that *Tropic of Capricorn* provides one of the best accounts of New York in the Twenties and that *Tropic of Cancer* captures the flavor of Paris in the Thirties.

It is clear from Mailer's statement that Miller's fiction moves beyond the novel and combines fact (history) with fiction. For this reason I consider Miller the first writer of Twentieth Century *Faction*. Miller took the fictional techniques he had learned from reading and combined them with the story of his life and times. The result is a personal and societal history that affords both a study of the individual and of his society in the Twentieth Century.

It is extremely important to realize that the roots of Miller's writing are grounded in American Literature—not in Eastern or European traditions, as some readers argue. In fact, his works have the vision of his Transcendental predecessors—Emerson, Thoreau, and Whitman. They also incorporate the humor traditionally associated with the "Southwest Humorists" like Twain and use satire as a means of dismissing American propriety, much the same device that Benjamin Franklin employs in his *Autobiography*.

Yet, for all of these ties to the American literary tradition, Miller has been called a pornographer because he wrote about a world that none of his contemporaries dared to discuss. Depicting sex and society accurately and graphically allows Miller to explore such conflicts as those between sexual drives and morality and between basic human nature and society. His vision of his world offers a psychoanalytical perspective that demonstrates Miller's ties with Otto Rank. His study explores society's effect on the individual with a clarity and perception that is lacking in Gertrude Stein's language experiments, that is missing from Ernest Hemingway's masculine existentialism, and that cannot be found in F. Scott Fitzgerald's romanticism. Miller is truly the first American writer to depict sex in an open manner and to create a literary revolution in the 1960's.

To retaliate against societal abuse, Miller uses satire to criticize his country's moral standards. In fact, his aim becomes one of "cleansing" his country when he speaks of destroying American cultural taboos. . . . (pp. 2-5)

Hatred for America's lack of creativity led Miller to undermine his country's literature and, indeed, to attempt to destroy the novel as we presently know it. This assassination was first suggested in 1934 in *Tropic of Cancer* which was written as an "anti-novel" (a form that has been wrongly attributed to the 1960's and to such writers as John Barth, Thomas Pynchon, and Donald Barthelme). In fact, *Tropic of Cancer* is the first American anti-novel, a vehicle used to prophesize a new type of historical novel. (p. 5)

The problem Miller saw in American writing was that it lacked the vitality of life, and he determined to capture life in his novels. (p. 6)

[Miller] was realistic in his appraisal of history and human nature. His desire to depict man as he had never been portrayed before shows Miller's attempt to explore the many facets of the human being. To better explore his subject, Miller created a first person narrator whose life, at times, paralleled Miller's own life in Paris and in Brooklyn, and who, at other times, was nothing more than a fictional creation. The persona was used as a device with which to recount Miller's past adventures; by using the persona as if he were a camera, Miller provided accounts of others, as well as himself. In this manner, the character was better able to depict a depraved culture. Therefore, it is no coincidence that *Tropic of Cancer* described Paris as a filthy city (much like T. S. Eliot's *Wasteland*) and that this depiction contradicts Anais Nin's *Diary* which describes Miller's home as spotless. Thus the purpose of Miller's *faction* is to create a new reality which is more accurate in depicting society than is Nin's literal statement.

Miller achieved the distinction of creating a new genre that lacks the pretension of the novel and that looks to real events for its form, content, subject, and meaning. [*Tropic of Cancer*, *Tropic of Capricorn*], and *Black Spring* created a new American novel that is most certainly the basis for the "New Journalism" of the 1960's. It was Miller, not Truman Capote or Norman Mailer, who established the roots of this new genre and who certainly deserves the distinction of standing next to Herman Melville, William Faulkner, Henry James, and Gertrude Stein; for these are the American writers whose experiments helped to change the form and content of the American novel and who provided us with our literary legacy. Like them, Henry Miller was an author who refused to stand pat and copy his predecessors. Moreover, he refused to write *one* type of work and continued to experiment throughout his career. It is Miller's individualism and efforts that have helped to keep the American novel alive. For this, we owe a debt to Henry Miller. (pp. 6-7)

Lawrence J. Shifreen, "Henry Miller's Literary Legacy," in *Under the Sign of Pisces*, Vol. 11, No. 4, Fall, 1980, pp. 2-7.

SOURCES FOR FURTHER STUDY

Brown, J. D. *Henry Miller.* New York: Ungar, 1986, 147 p.

Biography that views Miller as a literary innovator who revitalized the autobiographical form by blending fictional devices, surrealism, and black humor.

Gordon, William A. *The Mind and Art of Henry Miller.* Baton Rouge: Louisiana State University Press, 1967, 232 p.

Places Miller in the Romantic tradition, stressing his concern for the mind and the search for self-knowledge. Also explores his interest in the theories of psychologists Sigmund Freud, C. G. Jung, and Otto Rank.

Martin, Jay. *Always Merry and Bright: The Life of Henry Miller.* Santa Barbara, Calif.: Capra Press, 1978, 560 p.

Widely considered the most complete biography of Miller. Emphasizes Miller's relationships with women to provide insights into his work.

Stuhlmann, Gunther, ed. *A Literate Passion: Letters of Anaïs Nin and Henry Miller.* San Diego, New York & London: Harcourt Brace Jovanovich, 1987, 422 p.

Traces the relationship between the two authors, highlighting their literary interdependence, unsuccessful romance, and subsequent lasting friendship. Offers correspondence written between 1932 and 1953.

Wickes, George, ed. *Henry Miller and the Critics.* Carbondale: Southern Illinois University Press, 1963, 192 p.

Essay collection that focuses on Miller's writings, his life in Paris and the United States, and the censorship of *Tropic of Cancer.* Includes pieces by Edmund Wilson, George Orwell, and Lawrence Durrell.

Widmer, Kingsley. *Henry Miller.* Revised edition. New York: Twayne, 1990, 168 p.

Introductory critical biography.

John Milton

1608-1674

English poet, essayist, dramatist, and historian.

INTRODUCTION

*M*ilton is recognized as one of the greatest writers in the English language and as a thinker of world importance. He is best known for *Paradise Lost* (1667), an epic poem recounting the Biblical story of humanity's fall from grace. This work and its sequel, *Paradise Regained* (1671) are celebrated for their consummate artistry and searching consideration of God's relationship with the human race. Milton also wrote copious prose, some of which is considered among the finest in English. In such essays as *Areopagitica* (1644), *The Doctrine and Discipline of Divorce* (1643), and *The Tenure of Kings and Magistrates* (1649) he questioned prevailing beliefs about human liberty, helping to promote intellectual and social freedom as natural rights. Controversial in his time, during which he was principal propagandist of the Cromwellian Protectorate and frequently characterized as a seditious upstart and self-promoter, Milton also became known as the supreme champion in England of the then-embryonic concept of political self-determination. Today he is considered simply a master of his art and a literary craftsman of the highest order.

Born in Cheapside, London in 1608, the son of a prosperous scrivener and notary, Milton was from an early age immersed in literary and intellectual activity. His father early provided his son with a private tutor, retaining him even after Milton had entered St. Paul's School. Milton was a model student: he excelled in Latin, Greek, and Hebrew; wrote poetry in Latin and English; and studied the classics, modern languages, and music voraciously. (Milton acknowledged that in his youth he rarely quit his books before midnight, and he attributed his later blindness to excessive reading by lamp- and candlelight.) His studies—especially music and the classics—remained lifelong interests for Milton and colored much of his literary work. Milton en-

2394

tered Christ's College, Cambridge in 1625. There, his handsome face, delicate appearance, and lofty but unpretentious bearing earned him the sobriquet "the Lady of Christ's." At first unpopular, Milton eventually made a name for himself as a rhetorician and public speaker. While at Cambridge he probably wrote "L'Allegro," "Il Penseroso," and "On the Morning of Christ's Nativity," three of his earliest great poems in English. Upon leaving the university in 1632 with an A. M. degree, Milton retired to Hammersmith for three years and later to Horton, Buckinghamshire, where he devoted himself to intense study and writing. To this period scholars assign the composition of some of Milton's finest non-epic poems, including "Lycidas," "Arcades," and the sonnet "How Soon Hath Time." While still in Hammersmith, he also wrote his first extended work, *Comus* (1637), a masque, on commission for the Bridgewater family. In May 1638, Milton embarked on an Italian journey which was to last nearly fifteen months. The experience, which he described in *Defensio secunda pro populo anglicano* (*Second Defence of the People of England*, 1654), brought him into contact with the leading men of letters in Florence, Rome, and Naples, including Giovanni Battista Manso, Marquis of Villa, who had been an intimate of the epic poet Torquato Tasso. Scholars view the Italian tour as seminal in Milton's literary development; a new self-confidence emerged in the letters he wrote during his travels, and it was in Italy that Milton first proposed to write a great epic. Upon his return to England, Milton wrote the Italian-inspired *Epitaphium Damonis (Damon,* 1640) a Latin elegy on his longtime friend Charles Diodati. Critics have seen this work as Milton's first heralding of his ambition to be a great poet in the Renaissance vein, the author of classically inspired works on elevated themes.

But with the coming of the English Civil War and Commonwealth, Milton's life changed utterly as his attentions shifted from private to public concerns. Abruptly he left off writing poetry for prose, pouring out pamphlets during the early 1640s in which he opposed what he considered rampant episcopal tyranny. Having, as he related, embarked from a sense of duty upon "a troubled sea of noises and hoarse disputes," he declared his Puritan allegiance in antiprelatical tracts in which he argued the need to purge the Church of England of all vestiges of Roman Catholicism and restore the simplicity of the apostolic church. Around this time Milton also published *The Doctrine and Discipline of Divorce,* in which he maintained that incompatibility is a valid reason for divorce. This work was presumably inspired by his precipitate marriage in 1642 to his first wife, Mary Powell, who left her husband shortly after the wedding (but returned to him three years later; ironically, though Milton was to marry two more times, he was never divorced). In 1644 Milton published *Areo-*

pagitica, a now-classic plea for unlicensed printing in England. During the next few years Milton worked on his *History of Britain* (1670) and *De doctrina christiana* (*A Treatise of Christian Doctrine,* 1825). With the execution of Charles I in 1649, however, Milton entered the political fray with *The Tenure of Kings and Magistrates,* an assertion of the right of a people to depose or execute a ruling tyrant. This view constituted a complete about-face for Milton, who had written as a good monarchist in his early antiprelatical works. Henceforth Milton was permanently of the left. He accepted an invitation to become Cromwell's Latin secretary for foreign affairs and soon issued a number of tracts on church and state issues, including *Pro populo anglicano defensio* (*A Defence of the People of England*) and *Second Defence of the People of England,* two highly laudatory reviews of the achievements of the Commonwealth. The Restoration of Charles II in 1660 left Milton disillusioned and hastened his departure from public life; he lived for a time in peril of his life, but for reasons not entirely clear he was spared harsh punishment.

The remaining fourteen years of Milton's life were spent in relatively peaceful retirement in and around London. Now completely blind—he had been since 1652—Milton increasingly devoted his time to poetry. Amanuenses, assisted sometimes by Milton's two nephews and his daughter Deborah, were employed to take dictation, correct copy, and read aloud, and Milton made rapid progress on projects he had put off many years before. During the making of *Paradise Lost,* Milton spent mornings dictating passages he had composed in his head at night. *Paradise Lost* was published in 1667, followed in 1671 by *Paradise Regained. Samson Agonistes,* a metrical tragedy, appeared in the same volume as *Paradise Regained.* In 1673 Milton embraced controversy once again with *Of True Religion,* a short defense of Protestantism. He died in November 1674, apparently of heart failure. His funeral, wrote John Toland in 1698, was attended by "All his learned and great Friends in *London,* not without a friendly concourse of the Vulgar. . . ."

Milton's works fall neatly into two categories, poetry and prose, and there is very little crossover of theme or purpose from one category to the other; poetry was chiefly an artistic medium for Milton, prose being reserved for exposition only. In his first poetic successes, the twin lyrics "L'Allegro" and "Il Penseroso," Milton contrasted the active and contemplative lives. The imagery, drawn from classical mythology and English folklore, is cultivated and stylized, and both works are tightly argued. Milton's next major poem, *Comus,* is in the Elizabethan court masque tradition. Here, in exchanges between two young brothers, a lady, and the tempter Comus, Milton explored the merits of "moral discipline" and the dangers of sexual license. Critics agree that with "Lycidas," his next major work, Milton came into his own as a poet. In editing his poems in 1645, he called this pastoral a "Monody" in which "the Author bewails a learned Friend, unfortunately drown'd . . . on the *Irish* Seas, 1637. And by occasion foretells the ruin of our corrupted Clergy then in their height." The purpose of the poem was twofold: to honor the late Edward King, a former schoolmate at Christ's College, and to denounce hireling, incompetent clergy—a perennial concern of Milton's. Incidentally, the poem reveals Milton's own philosophical ambitions, later undertaken in *Paradise Lost:* to justify God's ways to men. Many critics consider "Lycidas" the finest short poem in the English language.

Milton's best-known poems are also his longest ones: *Paradise Lost, Paradise Regained,* and *Samson Agonistes.* Of these, *Paradise Lost* is deemed the supreme achievement by far. Milton had long planned an epic which was to be to England what Homer's works were to Greece and the *Aeneid* was to Rome. Originally, he contemplated an Arthurian subject for his national poem, but later adopted a Biblical subject: the Fall of Man as described in the Book of Genesis. As a classicist, Milton was powerfully aware of his antique antecedents; he therefore began the poem *in medias res,* invoking his muse and plunging into the action with a description of Satan in Hell—actually the poem's third crisis, which chronologically follows Satan's revolt in Heaven and descent with his followers through Chaos to Hell. The remainder of the poem treats Satan's deception of Eve in Eden, her deception of Adam, their fall from perfect fellowship with God and with each other, and their banishment from Paradise. Everywhere the poem is strong in its appeal to the ear, the intellect, and the visual imagination. While the iambic pentameter line is the norm, Milton played with the model, contriving syllables and stresses to complement the sense. (Commentators attribute many of Milton's superb metrical effects to his deep knowledge of music and his acutely sensitive ear.) Descriptive passages evoke images at once vague and minute, exposing in precise detail the character (but usually not the exact composition) of Heaven, Pandemonium, Chaos, and the universe. Eden is revealed as a sensuous feast. Milton's high purpose in the poem, to "justify the ways of God to men," is ever in the forefront of the action. Critics agree that this challenging objective, made all the more difficult by the complicated issue of divine foreknowledge of the Fall, is effected chiefly by imbuing Adam with a will as well as a mind of his own, enabling him to disobey God and thus mar an omnipotent Creator's perfect creation. *Paradise Regained*—more a dramatic poem than an epic—completes the action of *Paradise Lost.* Shorter and conceptually much simpler than the earlier work, it depicts Christ in the wilderness overcoming Satan the tempter. By this action, Christ proves his fitness as the Son of God, thereby preparing

himself for his human, substitutionary role in the Crucifixion. *Samson Agonistes* departs from the form and theme of *Paradise Lost* and *Paradise Regained,* but it is clear that Milton recognized affinities among the three works. A retelling of the story of Samson in the Book of Judges, *Samson* is in the tradition of Greek tragedy and is highly ironic, evocative, and ambiguous. Like Christ in *Paradise Regained,* Samson is terribly isolated, "Eyeless in Gaza at the mill with slaves," and undergoes a severe testing of his spiritual strength. He triumphs, gaining renewed faith in God and an improved understanding of his soul.

Milton's prose works are less celebrated than his poetry, but commentators agree that they are excellent examples of English polemic. They are liberally infused with rhetorical devices drawn from classical models; make their points forcefully but with dignity; evidence a marked sensitivity to syntax and sentence length; do not refrain from autobiography when personal notes are thought useful for strengthening the argument; and are resoundingly clear, ordered, and measured—in thought, degree, and execution. In addition to antiprelatical tracts and other topical treatises on religion, Milton wrote on more general theological issues and studies not prompted by strictly political or religious concerns. The short works *A Brief History of Moscovia* and *Accedence Commenc't Grammar* treat Russian history and Latin grammar respectively, and he wrote a number of pamphlets arguing that wedded couples should be allowed release from their marriage commitment if perfect companionship proved impossible. *Of Education,* written in the form of a letter, is the most frequently quoted example of Milton's minor prose. Here, drawing no doubt on his own experience as a student and teacher, Milton petitioned for the creation of an elite class through the careful instruction of boys in small regional academies.

More criticism has been devoted to Milton than to any English author save Shakespeare and perhaps Chaucer. While celebrated as a poet in his lifetime, Milton was scorned by many contemporaries for his anticlerical and anti-moralist stances, although some noted persons, such as Andrew Marvell, rose to his defense. Soon after Milton's death, *Paradise Lost* began to draw increased attention and praise from such critics as John Dryden, who considered Milton an epic poet comparable in stature to Homer and Vergil. With the notable exception of Samuel Johnson, who dismissed "Lycidas" as cold and mechanical and *Paradise Lost* as stylistically flawed, critics throughout the eighteenth and nineteenth centuries upheld Milton's achievement unabated, for various reasons: William Blake and Percy Bysshe Shelley considered *Paradise Lost* a precursor of Romanticism, ennobling Satan as a tragic rebel; William Wordsworth hailed Milton's espousal of libertarian ideals; and Ralph Waldo Emerson praised his infusion of private passion into universal themes. In the 1920s a group of critics, led by T. S. Eliot, began to attack what they perceived as the wooden style and structure of Milton's epics; Eliot, while conceding Milton's talent, lamented his influence on later poets, who, he argued, often created tortuously labored, rhetorical verse in imitation of the earlier poet. But Milton's reputation again waxed in the 1940s as critics discovered his heretofore-neglected prose, which in its emphasis on freedom had particular resonance in the World War II era. Further, because of the influential scholarship of such essayists as Charles Williams and C. S. Lewis, Milton's epic poetry was once again regarded as masterful in its breadth and complexity, and today is considered among the finest in human history.

It would be difficult to overestimate Milton's importance in English letters. In *Paradise Lost* he gave his country its greatest epic, surpassing, most commentators believe, even Spenser in the magnitude of his achievement in this form. And as the author of "Lycidas," "L'Allegro," and "Il Penseroso" he established himself as a master of the shorter poem, too. He also helped fuel Commonwealth reform and argued eloquently for major social amendment. Perhaps most telling of all, he wrote, unlike his nearest English rivals for literary eminence, Chaucer and Shakespeare, in numerous forms on a tremendous range of issues. Of Milton it may therefore be truly said that his scope was wide, his sweep broad, and his capacity for thought deep—the touchstone of intellectual achievement. For, in the words of James Russell Lowell, "If [Milton] is blind, it is with the excess of light, it is a divine partiality, an overshadowing with angels' wings."

(For further information about Milton's life and works, see *Literature Criticism from 1400 to 1800*, Vol. 9.)

CRITICAL COMMENTARY

JOHN MILTON
(essay date 1668)

[In the following statement, inserted into editions of *Paradise Lost* in 1668 "for the satisfaction of many that have desired it," Milton describes the verse form of the poem and supplies "a reason of that which stumbled many . . . [readers], why the Poem Rimes not."]

The measure [of *Paradise Lost*] is *English* Heroic Verse without Rime, as that of *Homer* in *Greek,* and of *Virgil* in *Latin;* Rime being no necessary Adjunct or true Ornament of Poem or good Verse, in longer Works especially, but the Invention of a barbarous Age, to set off wretched matter and lame Meter; grac't indeed since by the use of some famous modern Poets, carried away by Custom, but much to thir own vexation, hindrance, and constraint to express many things otherwise, and for the most part worse than else they would have exprest them. Not without cause therefore some both *Italian* and *Spanish* Poets of prime note have rejected Rime both in longer and shorter Works, as have also long since out best *English* Tragedies, as a thing of itself, to all judicious ears, trivial and of no true musical delight; which consists only in apt Numbers, fit quantity of Syllables, and the sense variously drawn out from one Verse into another, not in the jingling sound of like endings, a fault avoided by the learned Ancients both in Poetry and all good Oratory. This neglect then of Rime so little is to be taken for a defect, though it may seem so perhaps to vulgar Readers, that it rather is to be esteem'd an example set, the first in *English,* of ancient liberty recover'd to Heroic Poem from the troublesome and modern bondage of Riming.

John Milton, "The Verse," in his *Complete Poems and Major Prose,* edited by Merritt Y. Hughes, The Odyssey Press, 1957, p. 210.

SAMUEL TAYLOR COLERIDGE
(lecture date 1818)

[Coleridge is considered an exemplar of the nineteenth-century English Romantic movement, both for his pioneering poetry and for his insightful criticism. In the following excerpt from a lecture delivered in 1818, he probes the structure, subject, and purpose of *Paradise Lost.*]

[In Milton's mind] there were purity and piety absolute; an imagination to which neither the past nor the present were interesting, except as far as they called forth and enlivened the great ideal, in which and for which he lived; a keen love of truth, which, after many weary pursuits, found a harbor in the sublime listening

Principal Works

*A Maske Presented at Ludlow Castle, 1634, on Michaelmas Night, before the Right Honorable John Earle of Bridgewater, Viscount Brackly (drama) 1637

"Lycidas" (poetry) 1638; published in Obsequies to the Memorie of Mr. Edward King, Anno. Dom. 1638

Epitaphium Damonis (poetry) 1640

[Damon, 1900]

"On Hobson the Carrier" (poetry) 1640; published in Witts Recreations, Selected from the Finest Fancies of Moderne Muses

The Reason of Church-Government Urg'd against Prelaty (essay) 1642

The Doctrine and Discipline of Divorce, Restor'd to the Good of Both Sexes from the Bondage of Canon Law (essay) 1643

Areopagitica: A Speech of Mr. John Milton for the Liberty of Unlicenc'd Printing, to the Parlament of England (essay) 1644

The Judgement of Martin Bucer concerning Divorce, Written to Edward the Sixt, in His Second Book of the Kingdom of Christ, and Now Englisht, Wherin a Late Book Restoring the Doctrine and Discipline of Divorce Is Heer Confirm'd and Justify'd By the Authoritie of Martin Bucer (essay) 1644

Of Education: To Master Samuel Hartlib (essay) 1644

†Poems of Mr. John Milton, Both English and Latin, Compos'd at Several Times (poetry) 1645

Tetrachordon: Expositions upon the Foure Chief Places in Scripture Which Treat of Mariage, or Nullities in Mariage (essay) 1645

‡ΕΙΚΟΝΟΚΛΑ'ΣΤΗΣ in Answer to a Book Intitl'd E' ΙΚΩ' Ν ΒΑΣΙΛΙΚΗ, the Portrature of His Sacred Majesty in His Solitudes and Sufferings (essay) 1649

The Tenure of Kings and Magistrates, Proving That It is Lawfull, and Hath Been Held So Through All Ages, for Any Who Have the Power, to Call to Account a Tyrant, or Wicked King (essay) 1649

Pro populo anglicano defensio, contra Claudii Anonymi (essay) 1651

[A Defence of the People of England, 1692]

Defensio secunda pro populo anglicano (essay) 1654

[Second Defence of the People of England, 1816]

The Readie & Easie Way to Establish a Free Commonwealth (essay) 1660

Paradise Lost: A Poem Written in Ten Books (poetry) 1667; also published as Paradise Lost: A Poem in Twelve Books [enlarged edition], 1674

Accedence Commenc't Grammar, Supply'd with Sufficient Rules, For the Use of Such as, Younger or Elder, Are Desirous, without More Trouble Then Needs, to Attain the Latin Tongue (handbook) 1669

The History of Britain, That Part Especially Now Call'd England, from the First Traditional Beginning, Continu'd to the Norman Conquest (history) 1670

Paradise Regain'd: A Poem in IV Books. To Which Is Added Samson Agonistes (poetry) 1671

Of True Religion, Haeresie, Schism, Toleration, and What Best Means May Be Us'd against the Growth of Popery (essay) 1673

The Poetical Works of Mr. John Milton (poetry) 1695

The Works of Mr. John Milton (essays) 1697

A Complete Collection of the Historical, Political, and Miscellaneous Works of John Milton, Both English and Latin, with Some Papers Never Before Publish'd (essays and poetry) 1698

De doctrina christiana libri duo posthumi (essay) 1825

[A Treatise of Christian Doctrine, 1825]

The Sonnets of John Milton (poetry) 1883

The Works of John Milton. 18 vols. (essays, history, and poetry) 1931-38

Complete Prose Works of John Milton. 8 vols. (essays, history, and letters) 1953-

*This work is commonly known as Comus: A Maske.

†This work was revised as Poems upon Several Occasions in 1673 and 1695.

‡This work is commonly known by its transliterated title, Eikonoklastes.

---

to the still voice in his own spirit, and as keen a love of his country, which, after a disappointment still more depressive, expanded and soared into a love of man as a probationer of immortality. These were, these alone could be, the conditions under which such a work as the *Paradise Lost* could be conceived and accomplished. By a life-long study Milton had known—

> What was of use to know,
> What best to say could say, to do had done.
> His actions to his words agreed, his words

> To his large heart gave utterance due, his heart
> Contain'd of good, wise, fair, the perfect shape;

And he left the imperishable total, as a bequest to the ages coming, in the *Paradise Lost*.

Difficult as I shall find it to turn over these leaves without catching some passage, which would tempt me to stop, I propose to consider, 1st, the general plan and arrangement of the work, 2dly, the subject with its difficulties and advantages;—3rdly, the poet's object, the spirit in the letter, the ενθυμιον εν μυθω, the true school-divinity; and lastly, the characteristic excellencies of the poem, in what they consist, and by what means they were produced.

1. As to the plan and ordonnance of the Poem.

Compare it with the Iliad, many of the books of which might change places without any injury to the thread of the story. Indeed, I doubt the original existence of the Iliad as one poem; it seems more probable that it was put together about the time of the Pisistratidae. The Iliad—and, more or less, all epic poems, the subjects of which are taken from history—have no rounded conclusion; they remain, after all, but single chapters from the volume of history, although they are ornamental chapters. Consider the exquisite simplicity of the *Paradise Lost.* It and it alone really possesses a beginning, a middle, and an end; it has the totality of the poem as distinguished from the *ab ovo* birth and parentage, or straight line, of history.

2. As to the subject.

In Homer, the supposed importance of the subject, as the first effort of confederated Greece, is an after-thought of the critics; and the interest, such as it is, derived from the events themselves, as distinguished from the manner of representing them, is very languid to all but Greeks. It is a Greek poem. The superiority of the *Paradise Lost* is obvious in this respect, that the interest transcends the limits of a nation. But we do not generally dwell on this excellence of the *Paradise Lost,* because it seems attributable to Christianity itself;—yet in fact the interest is wider than Christendom, and comprehends the Jewish and Mohammedan worlds;—nay, still further, inasmuch as it represents the origin of evil, and the combat of evil and good, it contains matter of deep interest to all mankind, as forming the basis of all religion, and the true occasion of all philosophy whatsoever.

The FALL of man is the subject; Satan is the cause; man's blissful state the immediate object of his enmity and attack; man is warned by an angel who gives him an account of all that was requisite to be known, to make the warning at once intelligible and awful, then the temptation ensues, and the Fall; then the immediate sensible consequence; then the consolation, wherein an angel presents a vision of the history of man with the ultimate triumph of the Redeemer. Nothing is touched in this vision but what is of general interest in religion; any thing else would have been improper.

The inferiority of Klopstock's Messiah is inexpressible. I admit the prerogative of poetic feeling, and poetic faith; but I can not suspend the judgment even for a moment. A poem may in one sense be a dream, but it must be a waking dream. In Milton you have a religious faith combined with the moral nature; it is an efflux; you go along with it. In Klopstock there is a wilfulness; he makes things so and so. The feigned speech-

es and events in the Messiah shock us like falsehoods; but nothing of that sort is felt in the *Paradise Lost,* in which no particulars, at least very few indeed, are touched which can come into collision or juxtaposition with recorded matter.

But notwithstanding the advantages in Milton's subject, there were concomitant insuperable difficulties, and Milton has exhibited marvellous skill in keeping most of them out of sight. High poetry is the translation of reality into the ideal under the predicament of succession of time only. The poet is an historian, upon condition of moral power being the only force in the universe. The very grandeur of his subject ministered a difficulty to Milton. The statement of a being of high intellect, warring against the supreme Being, seems to contradict the idea of a supreme Being. Milton precludes our feeling this, as much as possible, by keeping the peculiar attributes of divinity less in sight, making them to a certain extent allegorical only. Again poetry implies the language of excitement; yet how to reconcile such language with God! Hence Milton confines the poetic passion in God's speeches to the language in Scripture; and once only allows the *passio vera,* or *quasi humana* to appear, in the passage, where the Father contemplates his own likeness in the Son before the battle:—

> Go then, thou Mightiest, in thy Father's might,
> Ascend my chariot, guide the rapid wheels
> That shake Heaven's basis, bring forth all my war,
> My bow and thunder; my almighty arms
> Gird on, and sword upon thy puissant thigh;
> Pursue these sons of darkness, drive them out
> From all Heaven's bounds into the utter deep:
> There let them learn, as likes them, to despise
> God and Messiah his anointed king.

3. As to Milton's object:

It was to justify the ways of God to man! The controversial spirit observable in many parts of the poem, especially in God's speeches, is immediately attributable to the great controversy of that age, the origination of evil. The Arminians considered it a mere calamity. The Calvinists took away all human will. Milton asserted the will, but declared for the enslavement of the will out of an act of the will itself. There are three powers in us, which distinguish us from the beasts that perish:—1, reason; 2, the power of viewing universal truth; and 3, the power of contracting universal truth into particulars. Religion is the will in the reason, and love in the will.

The character of Satan is pride and sensual indulgence, finding in self the sole motive of action. It is the character so often seen *in little* on the political stage. It exhibits all the restlessness, temerity, and cunning which have marked the mighty hunters of mankind from Nimrod to Napoleon. The common fascination of men is, that these great men, as they are called, must act from some great motive. Milton has carefully marked in his Satan the intense selfishness, the alcohol of egotism, which would rather reign in hell than serve in heaven. To place this lust of self in opposition to denial of self or duty, and to show what exertions it would make, and what pains endure to accomplish its end, is Milton's particular object in the character of Satan. But around this character he has thrown a singularity of daring, a grandeur of sufferance, and a ruined splendor, which constitute the very height of poetic sublimity.

Lastly, as to the execution:—

The language and versification of the *Paradise Lost* are peculiar in being so much more necessarily correspondent to each than those in any other poem or poet. The connection of the sentences and the position of the words are exquisitely artificial; but the position is rather according to the logic of passion or universal logic, than to the logic of grammar. Milton attempted to make the English language obey the logic of passion, as perfectly as the Greek and Latin. Hence the occasional harshness in the construction.

Sublimity is the pre-eminent characteristic of the *Paradise Lost.* It is not an arithmetical sublime like Klopstock's, whose rule always is to treat what we might think large as contemptibly small. Klopstock mistakes bigness for greatness. There is a greatness arising from images of effort and daring, and also from those of moral endurance; in Milton both are united. The fallen angels are human passions, invested with a dramatic reality.

The apostrophe to light at the commencement of the third book is particularly beautiful as an intermediate link between Hell and Heaven; and observe, how the second and third book support the subjective character of the poem. In all modern poetry in Christendom there is an under consciousness of a sinful nature, a fleeting away of external things, the mind or subject greater than the object, the reflective character predominant. In the *Paradise Lost* the sublimest parts are the revelations of Milton's own mind, producing itself and evolving its own greatness; and this is so truly so, that when that which is merely entertaining for its objective beauty is introduced, it at first seems a discord.

In the description of Paradise itself, you have Milton's sunny side as a man; here his descriptive powers are exercised to the utmost, and he draws deep upon his Italian resources. In the description of Eve, and throughout this part of the poem, the poet is predominant over the theologian. Dress is the symbol of the Fall, but the mark of intellect; and the metaphysics of dress are, the hiding what is not symbolic and displaying by discrimination what is. The love of Adam and Eve in Paradise is of the highest merit—not phantoma-

Milton at age 10.

tic, and yet removed from every thing degrading. It is the sentiment of one rational being towards another made tender by a specific difference in that which is essentially the same in both; it is a union of opposites, a giving and receiving mutually of the permanent in either, a completion of each in the other.

Milton is not a picturesque, but a musical, poet; although he has this merit, that the object chosen by him for any particular foreground always remains prominent to the end, enriched, but not encumbered, by the opulence of descriptive details furnished by an exhaustless imagination. I wish the *Paradise Lost* were more carefully read and studied than I can see any ground for believing it is, especially those parts which, from the habit of always looking for a story in poetry, are scarcely read at all,—as for example, Adam's vision of future events in the 11th and 12th books. No one can rise from the perusal of this immortal poem without a deep sense of the grandeur and the purity of Milton's soul, or without feeling how susceptible of domestic enjoyments he really was, notwithstanding the discomforts which actually resulted from an apparently unhappy choice in marriage. He was, as every truly great poet has ever been, a good man; but finding it impossible to realize his own aspirations, either in religion or politics, or society, he gave up his heart to the living spirit and light within him, and avenged himself on the world by enriching it with this record of his own transcendent ideal. (pp. 477-81)

S. T. Coleridge, "Literary Criticism: Milton," in his *Selected Poetry and Prose,* edited by Donald A. Stauffer, The Modern Library, 1951, pp. 475-81.

PERCY BYSSHE SHELLEY

(essay date 1819-20)

[An English poet and the chief literary spokesperson for the Romantic school, Shelley viewed poetry as a resource for the evolution of ideas and the perpetual refinement of human thought. In the following excerpt from an essay believed to have been written in 1819 or 1820, he discusses Milton's portrayal of Satan as a noble rebel.]

[In his account of the origin of Hell] Milton supposes that, on a particular day, God chose to adopt as his son and *heir,* (the reversion of an estate with an immortal incumbent would be worth little) a being unlike the other Spirits, who seems to have been supposed to be a detached portion of himself, and afterwards figured upon the earth in the well-known character of Jesus Christ. The Devil is represented as conceiving high indignation at this preference, and as disputing the affair with arms. I cannot discover Milton's authority for this circumstance; but all agree in the fact of the insurrection, and the defeat, and the casting out into Hell. Nothing can exceed the grandeur and the energy of the character of the Devil, as expressed in *Paradise Lost.* He is a Devil, very different from the popular personification of evil, and it is a mistake to suppose that he was intended for an idealism of evil. Malignity, implacable hate, cunning, and refinement of device to inflict the utmost anguish on an enemy, these, which are venial in a slave, are not to be forgiven in a tyrant; these, which are redeemed by much that ennobles in one subdued, are marked by all that dishonours his conquest in the victor. Milton's Devil, as a moral being, is as far superior to his God, as one who perseveres in a purpose which he has conceived to be excellent, in spite of adversity and torture, is to one who in the cold security of undoubted triumph inflicts the most horrible revenge upon his enemy—not from any mistaken notion of bringing him to repent of a perseverance in enmity, but with the open and alleged design of exasperating him to deserve new torments.

Milton so far violated all that part of the popular creed which is susceptible of being preached and defended in argument, as to the allege no superiority in moral virtue to his God over his Devil. He mingled as it were the elements of human nature as colours upon a single palett, and arranged them into the composition of his great picture, according to the laws of epic truth; that is, according to the laws of that principle by which a series of actions of intelligent and ethical beings, developed in rhythmical tale, are calculated to excite the sympathy and antipathy of succeeding generations of mankind. The writer who would have attributed majesty and beauty to the character of victorious and vindictive omnipotence, must have been contented with the character of a good Christian; he never could have been a great epic poet. It is difficult to determine, in a country where the most enormous sanctions of opinion and law are attached to a direct avowal of certain speculative notions, whether Milton was a Christian or not, at the period of the composition of *Paradise Lost.* Is it possible that Socrates seriously believed that Aesculapius would be propitiated by the offering of a cock? Thus much is certain, that Milton gives the Devil all imaginable advantage; and the arguments with which he exposes the injustice and impotent weakness of his adversary, are such as, had they been printed, distinct from the shelter of any dramatic order, would have been answered by the most conclusive of syllogisms—persecution. As it is, *Paradise Lost* has conferred on the modern mythology a systematic form; and when the immeasurable and unceasing mutability of time shall have added one more superstition to those which have already arisen and decayed upon the earth, commentators and critics will be learnedly employed in elucidating the religion of ancestral Europe, only not utterly forgotten because it will have participated in the eternity of genius. The Devil owes everything to Milton. Dante and Tasso present us with a very gross idea of him. Milton divested him of a sting, hoof, and horns, and clothed him with the sublime grandeur of a graceful but tremendous spirit. (pp. 387-90)

Percy Bysshe Shelley, "On the Devil, and Devils," in his *The Prose Works of Percy Bysshe Shelley,* edited by Harry Buxton Forman, 1876? Reprint by Reeves and Turner, 1880, pp. 382-406.

MATTHEW ARNOLD

(lecture date 1888)

[Arnold was one of the most influential critics of the Victorian era, espousing humanism and classical erudition in the industrial age. In the following excerpt from an 1888 lecture, he praises Milton as the supreme English poet.]

[In] calling up Milton's memory we call up, let me say, a memory upon which, in prospect of the Anglo-Saxon contagion and of its dangers supposed and real, it may be well to lay stress even more than upon Shakespeare's. If to our English race an inadequate sense for perfection of work is a real danger, if the discipline of respect for a high and flawless excellence is peculiarly needed by us, Milton is of all our gifted men the best lesson, the most salutary influence. In the sure and flawless perfection of his rhythm and diction he is as admirable as Virgil or Dante, and in this respect he is unique amongst us. No one else in English literature and art possesses the like distinction.

Thomson, Cowper, Wordsworth, all of them good poets who have studied Milton, followed Milton, adopted his form, fail in their diction and rhythm if we try them by that standard of excellence maintained by Milton constantly. From style really high and pure Milton never departs; their departures from it are frequent.

Shakespeare is divinely strong, rich, and attractive. But sureness of perfect style Shakespeare himself does not possess. I have heard a politician express wonder at the treasures of political wisdom in a certain celebrated scene of *Troilus and Cressida;* for my part I am at least equally moved to wonder at the fantastic and false diction in which Shakespeare has in that scene clothed them. Milton, from one end of *Paradise Lost* to the other, is in his diction and rhythm constantly a great artist in the great style. Whatever may be said as to the subject of his poem, as to the conditions under which he received his subject and treated it, that praise, at any rate, is assured to him.

For the rest, justice is not at present done, in my opinion, to Milton's management of the inevitable matter of a Puritan epic, a matter full of difficulties, for a poet. Justice is not done to the *architectonics,* as Goethe would have called them, of *Paradise Lost;* in these, too, the power of Milton's art is remarkable. But this may be a proposition which requires discussion and development for establishing it, and they are impossible on an occasion like the present.

That Milton, of all our English race, is by his diction and rhythm the one artist of the highest rank in the great style whom we have; this I take as requiring no discussion, this I take as certain.

The mighty power of poetry and art is generally admitted. But where the soul of this power, of this power at its best, chiefly resides, very many of us fail to see. It resides chiefly in the refining and elevation wrought in us by the high and rare excellence of the great style. We may feel the effect without being able to give ourselves clear account of its cause, but the thing is so. Now, no race needs the influences mentioned, the influences of refining and elevation, more than ours; and in poetry and art our grand source for them is Milton.

To what does he owe this supreme distinction? To nature first and foremost, to that bent of nature for inequality which to the worshippers of the average man

is so unacceptable; to a gift, a divine favour. 'The older one grows,' says Goethe, 'the more one prizes natural gifts, because by no possibility can they be procured and stuck on.' Nature formed Milton to be a great poet. But what other poet has shown so sincere a sense of the grandeur of his vocation, and a moral effort so constant and sublime to make and keep himself worthy of it? The Milton of religious and political controversy, and perhaps of domestic life also, is not seldom disfigured by want of amenity, by acerbity. The Milton of poetry, on the other hand, is one of those great men 'who are modest'—to quote a fine remark of Leopardi, that gifted and stricken young Italian, who in his sense for poetic style is worthy to be named with Dante and Milton—'who are modest, because they continually compare themselves, not with other men, but with that idea of the perfect which they have before their mind.' The Milton of poetry is the man, in his own magnificent phrase, of 'devout prayer to that Eternal Spirit that can enrich with all utterance and knowledge, and sends out his Seraphim with the hallowed fire of his altar, to touch and purify the lips of whom he pleases.' And finally, the Milton of poetry is, in his own words again, the man of 'industrious and select reading.' Continually he lived in companionship with high and rare excellence, with the great Hebrew poets and prophets, with the great poets of Greece and Rome. The Hebrew compositions were not in verse, and can be not inadequately represented by the grand, measured prose of our English Bible. The verse of the poets of Greece and Rome no translation can adequately reproduce. Prose cannot have the power of verse; verse-translation may give whatever of charm is in the soul and talent of the translator himself, but never the specific charm of the verse and poet translated. In our race are thousands of readers, presently there will be millions, who know not a word of Greek and Latin, and will never learn those languages. If this host of readers are ever to gain any sense of the power and charm of the great poets of antiquity, their way to gain it is not through translations of the ancients, but through the original poetry of Milton, who has the like power and charm, because he has the like great style.

Through Milton they may gain it, for, in conclusion Milton is English; this master in the great style of the ancients is English. Virgil, whom Milton loved and honoured, has at the end of the *Aeneid* a noble passage where Juno, seeing the defeat of Turnus and the Italians imminent, the victory of the Trojan invaders assured, entreats Jupiter that Italy may nevertheless survive and be herself still, may retain her own mind, manners, and language, and not adopt those of the conqueror.

Sit Latium, sint Albani per secula reges!

Jupiter grants the prayer; he promises perpetuity and the future to Italy—Italy reinforced by whatever virtue the Trojan race has, but Italy, not Troy. This we may take as a sort of parable suiting ourselves. All the Anglo-Saxon contagion, all the flood of Anglo-Saxon commonness, beats vainly against the great style but cannot shake it, and has to accept its triumph. But it triumphs in Milton, in one of our own race, tongue, faith, and morals. Milton has made the great style no longer an exotic here; he has made it an inmate amongst us, a leaven, and a power. Nevertheless he, and his hearers on both sides of the Atlantic, are English, and will remain English—

Sermonem Ausonii patrium moresque tenebunt.

The English race overspreads the world, and at the same time the ideal of an excellence the most high and the most rare abides a possession with it for ever. (pp. 61-8)

Matthew Arnold, "Milton," in his *Essays in Criticism,* second series, 1889. Reprint by The Macmillan Company, 1924, pp. 56-68.

C. S. LEWIS
(lecture date 1941)

[An English novelist and critic, Lewis upheld conservative values in literary criticism, championing a Christian aesthetic and arguing against modern tendencies toward psychological and biographical analysis. In the following excerpt from a 1941 lecture, he examines the Fall of Eve and Adam in *Paradise Lost.*]

Eve fell through Pride. The serpent tells her first that she is very beautiful, and then that all living things are gazing at her and adoring her (IX, 532-541). Next he begins to make her "feel herself impair'd." Her beauty lacks spectators. What is one man? She ought to be ador'd and served by angels: she would be queen of heaven if all had their rights (IX, 542-548). God is trying to keep the human race down: Godhead is their true destiny (703, 711), and Godhead is what she thinks of when she eats (790). The results of her fall begin at once. She thinks that earth is a long way from Heaven and God may not have seen her (811-816); the doom of Nonsense is already at work. Next she decides that she will not tell Adam about the fruit. She will exploit her secret to become his equal—or no, better still, his superior (817-825). The rebel is already aiming at tyranny. But presently she remembers that the fruit may, after all, be deadly. She decides that if she is to die, Adam must die with her; it is intolerable that he should be happy, and happy (who knows?) with another woman when she is gone. I am not sure that critics always notice the precise sin which Eve is now committing, yet there is no mystery about it. Its name in English is Murder. If the fruit is to produce deity Adam shall have none of it: she means to do a corner in divinity. But if it means death, then he must be made to eat it, in order that he may die—for that reason and no other, as her words make perfectly plain (826-830). And hardly has she made this resolve before she is congratulating herself upon it as a singular proof of the tenderness and magnanimity of her love (830-833).

If the precise movement of Eve's mind at this point is not always noticed, that is because Milton's truth to nature is here almost too great, and the reader [of *Paradise Lost*] is involved in the same illusion as Eve herself. The whole thing is so quick, each new element of folly, malice, and corruption enters so unobtrusively, so naturally, that it is hard to realize we have been watching the genesis of murder. We expect something more like Lady Macbeth's "unsex me here." But Lady Macbeth speaks thus after the intention of murder has already been fully formed in her mind. Milton is going closer to the actual moment of decision. Thus, and not otherwise, does the mind turn to embrace evil. No man, perhaps, ever at first described to himself the act he was about to do as Murder, or Adultery, or Fraud, or Treachery, or Perversion; and when he hears it so described by other men he is (in a way) sincerely shocked and surprised. Those others "don't understand." If they knew what it had really been like for him, they would not use those crude 'stock' names. With a wink or a titter, or in a cloud of muddy emotion, the thing has slipped into his will as something not very extraordinary, something of which, rightly understood and in all his highly peculiar circumstances, he may even feel proud. If you or I, reader, ever commit a great crime, be sure we shall feel very much more like Eve than like Iago.

She has still a further descent to make. Before leaving the Tree she does "low Reverence" before it "as to the power that dwelt within," and thus completes the parallel between her fall and Satan's. She who thought it beneath her dignity to bow to Adam or to God, now worships a vegetable. She has at last become 'primitive' in the popular sense.

Adam fell by uxoriousness. We are not shown the formation of his decision as we are shown the formation of Eve's. Before he speaks to her, half-way through his inward monologue (896-916) we find the decision already made—"with thee Certain my resolution is to Die." His sin is, of course, intended to be a less ignoble sin than hers. Its half-nobility is, perhaps, emphasized by the fact that he does not argue about it. He is at that moment when a man's only answer to all that would restrain him is: "I don't care"; that moment when we resolve to treat some lower or partial value as an absolute—loyalty to a party or a family, faith to a lover, the customs of good fellowship, the honour of our profession, or the claims of science. If the reader finds it hard to look upon Adam's action as a sin at all, that is because he is not really granting Milton's premises. If conjugal love were the highest value in Adam's world, then of course his resolve would have been the correct one. But if there are things that have an even higher claim on a man, if the universe is imagined to be such that, when the pinch comes, a man ought to reject wife and mother and his own life also, then the case is altered, and then Adam can do no good to Eve (as, in fact, he does no good) by becoming her accomplice. What would have happened if instead of his "compliance bad" Adam had scolded or even chastised Eve and then interceded with God on her behalf, we are not told. The reason we are not told is that Milton does not know. And I think he knows he does not know: he says cautiously that the situation *"seemd* remediless" (919). This ignorance is not without significance. We see the results of our actions, but we do not know what would have happened if we had abstained. For all Adam knew, God might have had other cards in His hand; but Adam never raised the question, and now nobody will ever know. Rejected goods are invisible. Perhaps God would have killed Eve and left Adam "in those wilde Woods forlorn": perhaps, if the man had preferred honesty to party loyalty or established morals to adultery, a friend would have been ruined or two hearts broken. But then again, perhaps not. You can find out only by trying it. The only thing Adam knows is that he must hold the fort, and he does not hold it. The effects of the Fall on him are quite unlike its effects on the woman. She had rushed at once into false sentiment which made murder itself appear a proof of fine sensibility. Adam, after eating the fruit, goes in the opposite direction. He becomes a man of the world, a punster, an aspirant to fine raillery. He compliments Eve on her palate and says the real weakness of Paradise is that there were too few forbidden trees. The father of all the bright epigrammatic wasters and the mother of all the corrupting female novelists are now both before us. As critics have pointed out, Adam and Eve "become human" at this point. Unfortunately what follows is one of Milton's failures. Of course, they must now lust after each other. And of course this lusting must be something quite different from the innocent desires which Milton attributes to their unfallen intercourse. Wholly new, and perversely delicious, a tang of evil in sex is now to enter their experience. What will reveal itself on waking as the misery of shame now comes to them (they are growing "sapient," "exact of taste") as the delighted discovery that obscenity is possible. But could poetry suffice to draw such a distinction? Certainly not Milton's. His Homeric catalogue of flowers is wide of the mark. Yet something he does. Adam's hedonistic calculus—his cool statement that he has never (except perhaps once) been so ripe for "play" as now—

strikes the right note. He would not have said that before he fell. Perhaps he would not have said "to enjoy thee." Eve is becoming to him a *thing*. And she does not mind: all her dreams of godhead have come to that. (pp. 121-24)

C. S. Lewis, "The Fall," in his *A Preface to Paradise Lost,* revised edition, Oxford University Press, London, 1942, pp. 121-24.

E. M. FORSTER
(broadcast date 1944)

[Forster was an English novelist, essayist, and critic. In the following excerpt from a 1944 broadcast marking the tercentenary of the publication of *Areopagitica*, he explores Milton's arguments for free expression in relation to the contemporary political situation.]

Milton's *Areopagitica* was published exactly three hundred years ago. The Parliament was fighting the King. Milton upheld Parliament, but it had just given him a very unpleasant shock. It had passed a defence regulation for the control of literature, and had placed all printed matter under a censorship. "No book etc. shall from henceforward be printed or exposed for sale unless the same be first approved of and licensed by such persons" as Parliament shall appoint.

There are usually two motives behind any censorship—good, and bad. The good motive is the desire of the authorities to safeguard and strengthen the community, particularly in times of stress. The bad motive is the desire of the authorities to suppress criticism, particularly of themselves. Both these motives existed in 1644, as they do in 1944, and, in Milton's judgment, the bad then predominated over the good. He was profoundly shocked that Parliament, which fought for liberty, should be suppressing it, and he issued his *Areopagitica* as a protest. It is the most famous of his prose works—partly because it is well written, but mainly because it strikes a blow for British freedom. It has been much praised, and sometimes by people who do not realise what they are praising and what they are letting themselves in for. In celebrating its tercentenary let us do so with open eyes.

To begin with one of Milton's smaller points: the inconvenience of a censorship to a creative or scholarly writer. All that he says here is true, though not of prime importance. It is intolerable, he exclaims, that "serious and elaborate writings, as if they were the theme of a grammar lad, must not be uttered without the eyes of a temporising and extemporising licenser." It is being treated like a schoolboy after one is grown up. The censor is probably some overworked and dim little official who knows nothing about literature and is scared of anything new. Yet the writer has to "trudge" to him to get his script passed, and if he makes any alteration afterwards, he must make application again. "I hate a pupil teacher, I endure not an instructor," proud Milton cries, and when he is reminded that the censor does after all represent the State, he hits back fiercely with "The State shall be my governors but not my critics."

All this is very much what a scholar or a creative artist might charge against a censor today: the big mind having to apply for permission to the fidgety small mind, and the small mind being supported by the authority of the State. It is all quite true; though why should not distinguished writers be put to trouble if it is to the general good? Why should they not submit to censorship if the national welfare requires it?

But there is much more to the problem, and the bulk of the *Areopagitica* is occupied with larger questions. Censorship means—uniformity and monotony: and they mean spiritual death. "Where there is much desire to learn, there of necessity will be much arguing, much writing, and many opinions: for opinion in good men is but knowledge in the making." And he apostrophises London at war in words we might gladly use today:

> Behold now this vast City: a city of refuge, the mansion house of liberty; encompassed and surrounded with God's protection; the shop of war hath not there more anvils and hammers working . . . than there be pens and heads there, sitting by their studious lamps, musing, searching, revolving new notions and ideas . . . others at fast reading, trying all things, assenting to the forces of reason and convincement.

All this free writing and reading will pass with the institution of the censorship, and its disappearance means the spiritual impoverishment of us all, whether we write and study or not. Intellectuals, in Milton's opinion, are not and cannot be apart from the community, and are essential to its health.

And then he tackles the problem of bad or harmful books. Might it not be well to prohibit them? The answer, No. It is preferable that bad books should be published rather than that all books should be submitted before publication to a government official. What is bad will be forgotten, and free choice in reading is as important as in action. "Truth is a perpetual progression." Also who is to settle what is bad? Who indeed? I recall in this connection an argument I had with an acquaintance during the first war. He was for prohibiting bad books, and when I asked him which books he answered "Conrad's novels." He did not care for them. He was an able public-spirited fellow, and later on he became an M.P.

If there is no censorship, is the writer or the newspaper editor to be above the law? Not at all. That is not Milton's position. If a book or pamphlet or newspaper is illegal it can, after publication, be prosecuted. The grounds of prosecution in his day were two—blasphemy and libel—and they hold good in our day, prosecutions for blasphemy now being very rare and prosecutions for libel very frequent. Milton did not set writers above the law. He did insist on punishment afterwards rather than censorship beforehand. Let a man say what he likes and then suffer if it is illegal. This seems to me the only course appropriate to a democracy. It is for the courts, and for no one else, to decide whether a book shall be suppressed.

Milton, would'st thou be living at this hour? "Yes and No," Milton would answer. He would certainly be heart and soul with us in our fight against Germany and Japan, for they stand for all that he most detested. And he would note with approval that there is no direct censorship operating on them through the paper control. At the present moment, most of the paper available goes to government departments, the publication of new books gets cut down, and most of our great English classics have gone out of print. Nor would he have approved of any attempt of publishers to combine and decide what books should be published. Would he have liked the wireless? Yes and No. He would have been enthusiastic over the possibilities of broadcasting, and have endorsed much it does, but he would not approve of the "agreed script" from which broadcasters are obliged to read for security reasons. He believed in free expression and in punishment afterwards if the expression turned out to be illegal: but never, never supervision beforehand, and whether the supervision was called censorship or licensing or "agreed script" would have made no difference to him. You can argue that the present supervision of broadcasters is necessary and reasonable, and that a silly or cranky speaker might do endless harm on the air. But if you feel like that, you must modify your approval of the *Areopagitica.* You cannot have it both ways. And do not say "Oh, it's different today—there's a war on." There was equally a war on in 1644. The fact is we are willing enough to praise freedom when she is safely tucked away in the past and cannot be a nuisance. In the present, amidst dangers whose outcome we cannot foresee, we get nervous about her, and admit censorship. Yet the past was once the present, the seventeenth century was once "now," with an unknown future, and Milton, who lived in his "now" as we do in ours, believed in taking risks.

In places, then, the *Areopagitica* is a disturbance to our self-complacency. But in other places it is an encouragement, for Milton exalts our national character in splendid words. He was intensely patriotic—on the grounds that when France was a tyranny and Germany a muddle, we were insisting on freedom of speech and being admired for it by European scholars. He had travelled on the Continent before the civil war, and sat among her learned men, "and," he goes on,

> I bin counted happy to be born in such a place of philosophic freedom as they supposed England was, while they themselves did nothing but bemoan the servile conditions with which learning amongst them was brought. . . . I tooke it as a pledge of future happiness that other nations were so persuaded of her liberty.

And he is proud—and how justly—of the variety of opinion incidental to our democracy of "this flowering crop of knowledge and new light" as opposed to "that dark conjealment of wood and hay and stubble" engendered by the pressure of totalitarianism. Our enemies, he notes, mistake our variety for weakness—exactly the mistakes the Germans were to make about us both in 1914 and in 1939.

> The adversary applauds and waits the hour: "When they have branched themselves out," saith he, "small enough into parties and partitions, then will be our time." Fool! he sees not the firm root of which we all grow, though into branches, nor will beware until he sees our small divided maniples cutting through at every angle of his ill-united and unwieldy brigade.

"Ill-united and unwieldy brigade"—could there be a phrase more prophetic of the Axis? But we must not dwell on the phrase too much, for the subject of the *Areopagitica* is not tyranny abroad but the need, even in wartime, of liberty at home. Not the beam in Dr. Goebbels' eye, but the mote in our own eye. Can we take it out? Is there as much freedom of expression and publication in this country as there might be? That is the question which, on its tercentenary, this explosive little pamphlet propounds. (pp. 51-5)

E. M. Forster, "The Tercentenary of the 'Areopagitica'," in his *Two Cheers for Democracy*, Harcourt Brace Jovanovich, Inc., 1951, pp. 51-5.

NORTHROP FRYE

(essay date 1950)

[A Canadian critic and educator, Frye believed that literary works are structured by myth and symbol, and he adopted a scientific/critical approach aimed at unearthing a work's archetypal resonances. In the following excerpt from the 1950 preface to his edition of *Paradise Lost* and other poems, he dis-

cusses the language, versification, and imagery of Milton's major poetry.]

Some poets—Spenser is a good example—start with experiment and end with conventional forms. Milton, like Shakespeare, begins in convention and becomes increasingly radical as he develops. The **"Nativity Ode"** is written in a tight, intricate stanza: the rhythm is not thereby prevented from bringing out every ripple and curve of the meaning—

> She, crowned with olive green, came softly sliding
> Down through the turning air

—but it is still exactly confined to the pattern of the stanza. It is a miraculous feat of technical skill, but even Milton could not always be performing miracles. He began a complementary poem on the Passion, but abandoned it after eight stanzas, and the stanzaic poem along with it. In the lovely tripping octo-syllabics of **"L'Allegro"** and **"Il Penseroso"** he escaped into a more freely moving and continuous rhythm, and one that he uses for a good part of *Comus*. From that time on he sought mainly for long-range rhythmical units, and consequently moved away from rhyme, with its emphatic recurrence of sound, to the more austere but freer patterns of blank verse. He had a keen appreciation of music, and perhaps the continuity of rhythm in music influenced his poetry: it is noteworthy that in the Preface to *Paradise Lost* he speaks of "musical delight" [see excerpt dated 1668] as consisting among other things in "the sense variously drawn out from one verse [that is, line] into another."

The epic in any case makes heavy demands on the more sustained and cumulative rhythms, and Milton may have found his twenty years of practice in writing prose also of some help. Prose gives the fullest scope for long-range rhythmical construction, and Milton, though he complains about having only the use of his "left hand" in prose, took every advantage of what prose had to give him. His vast periodic sentences that almost never end, his dizzy flights of prayer and peroration, and his labyrinths of subordinate clauses, qualifying epithets, and parenthetical allusions do not always make for what we should now consider ideal prose. But they may well have played some part in developing the motor power that makes *Paradise Lost,* apart from all its other qualities, the most readable epic in English. Milton's long postponement of his epic had its reward in the almost effortless mastery of the final performance. His reference to "Easy my unpremeditated verse" is no idle boast, and from beginning to end it is clear that *Paradise Lost* was not so much written as written out.

As Milton moves from the stanza into the more linear and continuous pentameter forms, a much bigger type of stanza develops, containing a number of pentameter lines in a rhythmic unit for which the most

Title page of the first edition of *Paradise Lost* (1667).

us take a passage from **"L'Allegro"** and compare it with one from **"Il Penseroso"**;

> While the cock with lively din,
> Scatters the rear of darkness thin,
> And to the stack, or the barn-door,
> Stoutly struts his dames before.
> To behold the wandering moon,
> . . . .
> Riding near her highest noon,
> Like one that had been led astray
> Through the heaven's wide pathless way.

We can see how each of these four elements helps to make the contrast between the two poems. The **"L'Allegro"** passage has sharp, light vowels and abrupt, explosive consonants; the **"Il Penseroso"** one has resonant vowels and soft liquids. **"L'Allegro"** has vigorous words like "scatters," "struts," and "din"; **"Il Penseroso,"** quiet and pensive words like "wandering" and "behold." The **"L'Allegro"** rhythm flutters away in the almost unscannable third line and swaggers in the fourth; the **"Il Penseroso"** rhythm, especially in the fourth line, is full of slow and sonorous heavy accents. The first passage describes the clucks and crows of a poultry yard at dawn; the second dwells on the silence of a moonlit night. These points are simple enough, though it takes the highest kind of genius to produce the simplicity, and the principles involved are applicable everywhere in Milton.

Every language has its own body of descriptive sounds, and every poet accepts what his language affords him as a matter of course. *S* is always a hissing letter, suitable for serpents:

> And Dipsas (not so thick swarmed once the soil . . .)

R (which Milton is said to have pronounced very hard) is a martial one:

> Innumerable force of spirits armed;

W is for lonliness and terror:

> Through the world's wilderness long wandered man

and the long *a* and *o* sounds (even more resonant in seventeenth-century pronunciation) herald the approach of the prince of darkness:

> Meanwhile upon the firm opacous globe
> Of this round world, whose first convex divides
> The luminous inferior orbs, enclosed
> From Chaos and th' inroad of darkness old,
> Satan alighted walks.

Milton's poetry is proverbial for its resonance: the sonnet on the massacre in Piedmont, for instance, is a deeply felt and powerfully indignant poem, but this does not prevent it from being also a kind of étude, a technical exercise in sombre vowels. It is natural that

convenient name is "verse paragraph." The opening lines of **"Lycidas,"** down to "without the meed of some melodious tear," constitute an intricately organized verse paragraph, held together by the rhymes to "sere" in the second line and by a varied but consistent pattern of alliteration. The real secret of the unity behind its irregularity, however (the first line, for instance, is unrhymed and the fourth line is not a pentameter), defies all critical analysis. Many of the sonnets, too, are much more verse paragraphs than they are conventional sonnets. This paragraph forms a larger rhythmical unit in *Paradise Lost* too, and its presence enables Milton to handle the pentameter line with such a large number of runon lines and medial pauses. In *Samson Agonistes* the paragraph achieves a much greater independence from the line and forms the basis for those amazing passages of recitativo which are perhaps the "freest" and most radically experimental verse that English poetry has yet reached.

The elements of versification are sound, vocabulary, rhythm, and imagery, and all four demand the closest attention from the reader of major poetry. Let we should find what makes most noise easiest to hear. This is one reason why Satan makes the strongest initial impact on the reader of *Paradise Lost,* for in the great variety of Milton's orchestration Satan gets most of the heavy brass. It is true also that the gloom and terror of hell is not less impressive for being obviously impressive. But it would be a pity to neglect the woodwinds and strings, and fail to hear how the brothers in *Comus* murmur to each other what they have read in praise of chastity; how the flowers are dropped one by one on Lycidas' grave; how the Christ child lies asleep with his legions of angels sitting quietly around him; how the fragrance of Eden is diffused over the earth by lazy breezes. The great hymn of creation in the seventh book of *Paradise Lost,* in which everything seems to dance in the joy of its deliverance from chaos and the release of its form, is a particularly wonderful example of Milton's skill in the subtler and softer harmonies:

> Forth flourished thick the clustering vine, forth crept
> The smelling gourd, up stood the corny reed
> Embattled in her field; and th' humble shrub
> And bush with frizzled hair implicit: last
> Rose, as in dance, the stately trees.

Passing from the sounds to the words, we notice that Milton uses an unusually large proportion of long words of Latin origin. Also that he often uses such words in an original Latin sense different from ours: "frequent" means crowded, "horrid" means bristling, "explode" means to hiss off or drive away, and so on. Many of these Latin words have become dead robot words in our speech, with nothing left in them of the vivid concrete metaphors they once were. But Milton uses them with the whole weight of their etymology behind them, and in reading him we have to wake up this part of our vocabulary. It comes as something of a shock to read in *Paradise Regained* of "elephants endorsed with towers," because we no longer think of *dorsum,* back, in connection with the word. But in Milton "astonished" means not mildly surprised but struck with thunder; "aspect" and "influence" are still partly technical terms in astrology, and "insinuating" has its visual meaning of wriggling as well as its abstract meaning. This principle of traditional weight applies not only to words, but to phrases as well, and the reader should be warned that it is precisely in such lines as "He for God only, she for God in him," where Milton seems to be most typically Miltonic, that he is most likely to be quoting verbatim from the Bible.

Another feature of Milton's vocabulary, the catalogues of proper names, also needs a word of warning. There are two reasons for which these catalogues are never used. They are never used to show off Milton's learning, and they are never used as an easy way of increasing the resonance. When they are lists of strange gods, they suggest the incantation or muttered

spell of the magician who commands them, as in the summoning of Sabrina in *Comus,* and, less obviously, in the roll call of baffled demons in the **"Nativity Ode."** In *Paradise Lost* the rumble and crash of Satan's armies is echoed in the place names of epic and romance; the garden of Eden calls up the luxuriant and fruitful spots of earth, and the storms of advancing chaos sweep from point to point over the wastes of Asia and America. In each case the reader who has to look up several dozen references at once may miss the fact that the vagueness and strangeness of the names is exactly the poet's reason for using them. There are exceptions to this, of course: one should not miss the irony of "Vallombrosa," with its echo of "valley of shadows" in reference to hell, nor of the fateful epithet of Eden, "this Assyrian garden," which links it prophetically with the ferocious children of Nimrod who annihilated the Ten Tribes.

Some of the peculiar features of Milton's rhythm have been mentioned. The prosody of *Paradise Lost* has been exhaustively studied, but the general principle is that Milton can do anything he likes with the pentameter line. One may notice particularly the use of trochaic rhythms to describe falling movement:

> Hurled headlong flaming from th' ethereal sky,
> Exhausted, spiritless, afflicted, fallen;

the placing of two strong accents together in the middle of a line to describe something ominous or foreboding:

> Which tasted works knowledge of good and evil,
> Deep malice to conceal, couched with revenge;

the use of extra syllables to suggest relaxation or lateral movement:

> Luxuriant; meanwhile murmuring waters fall;

and the use of a weak or enjambed ending that pushes the rhythm into the next line to describe the completing of a movement:

> Intelligent of seasons, and set forth
> Their airy caravan high over seas
> Flying.

The long Latin words in Milton's vocabulary also have the rhythmical function of relaxing or increasing the speed. A monosyllable always means a separate accent, however slight, and a series of them produces a slow, emphatic sonority that would soon become intolerable unless relieved:

> Scarce half I seem to live, dead more than half.
> O dark, dark, dark, amid the blaze of noon,
> Irrecoverably dark!

The same principles of variation apply to the other verse forms as well as to the pentameter, and usually the sense will warn us when a change of pace is coming:

> I can fly, or I can run
> Quickly to the green earth's end,
> Where the bowed welkin slow doth bend.

Milton's imagery is more difficult to appreciate than any other aspect of his work. Except perhaps in **"L'Allegro"** and **"Il Penseroso,"** he is not one of the intensely visualizing poets: we are more conscious of degrees of light and shade than of sharply outlined objects. In this Milton is more characteristic of his age than elsewhere: in such painters as Rembrandt and Claude Lorrain, who were Milton's contemporaries, we find the same mysterious shadows and diffused brilliance that we find in Milton's hell and heaven. The relative vagueness of vision in *Paradise Lost* can hardly be due primarily to Milton's blindness, for we find it also in the early poems: in the formless shadows of the old gods retreating from the tiny point of light at the center of the **"Nativity Ode"**; in the dark wood of *Comus* and in the stylized pastoral world of **"Lycidas."** In *Samson Agonistes,* where the hero is blind, the vision is outside the poem: it is focused with unbearable intensity on the hero himself, whose inability to stare back is his greatest torment, an agony of humiliation that makes him, in one of the most dreadful passages in all drama, scream at Delilah that he will tear her to pieces if she touches him. The precision of Milton's poetry is aural rather than visual, musical rather than pictorial. When we read, for instance:

> Immediately the mountains huge appear
> Emergent, and their broad bare backs upheave

the mountains cannot be *seen*: it is the ear that must hear in "emergent" the splash of the water falling from them, and in the long and level monosyllables the clear blue line of the horizon. In every major poem of Milton's there is some reason why the ear predominates over the eye. In the **"Nativity Ode,"** it is because of the pattern of light and shade already mentioned; in *Comus,* it is because of the dark "leafy labyrinth" where one listens intently for rustles and whispers; in **"Lycidas,"** it is because the ritual lament generalizes the imagery; in *Paradise Lost* it is because the three states of existence, heaven, hell, and Paradise, all transcend visualization; in *Samson Agonistes* it is because the Classical form of the tragedy makes it a discussion or reporting of offstage events. The prominence of temptation among Milton's themes is significant too, as temptation is an attempt to persuade one through aural suggestion to seize something that is illusory.

In *Paradise Lost* Milton uses the same Ptolemaic onion-shaped universe that Dante does, with the earth at the center and the *primum mobile* at the circumference. But Dante puts heaven and hell inside this universe;

Milton puts them outside, and the impersonal remoteness of the Copernican universe, with its unthinkable stretches of empty space, thus forms part of his poetic vision. Dante relies on symmetry; Milton on disproportion. Satan is a colossal angel and a toad; Christ is to become a despised son of the Adam he creates; Raphael is a hero of a war that rocks heaven, yet he drops in on Adam and Eve for a cold lunch; all the armies of heaven and hell and the fate of the created universe hang on one apple, and on whether or not a hungry girl will reach for it. What holds this farrago together is nothing that the eye or mind can accept, but the steady flow of the powerful working words that, exactly like the temptations in the poems, persuade us to seize the illusion. Milton, the agent of the Word of God, is trying to awaken with his words a vision in us which is, in his own language, the Word of God in the heart, and in the possession of which we may say with Job, "I have heard thee with the hearing of the ear, but now mine eye seeth thee." If we surrender to his charming and magical spell, and seize his fables of hell and Paradise, they will become realities of earth, and the stories of Adam and Samson our own story. And then, perhaps, we may consider a further question:

> what if Earth
> Be but the shadow of Heaven, and things therein
> Each to other like, more than on Earth is thought?
>
> (pp. xxi-xxx)

Northrop Frye, in an introduction to *"Paradise Lost" and Selected Poetry and Prose* by John Milton, edited by Northrop Frye, Holt, Rinehart and Winston, 1951, pp. v-xxx.

LIONEL TRILLING
(essay date 1967)

[An American critic, essayist, editor, novelist, and short story writer, Trilling stressed in his criticism the symbiotic relationship between art and the wider culture. In the following excerpt from a work originally published in 1967, he considers why Milton employed the pastoral form in *"Lycidas."*]

It is often said by critics and teachers of literature that **"Lycidas"** is the greatest lyric poem in the English language, and very likely it is. But the word "greatest" applied to a work of art is not always serviceable; the superlative judgment can immobilize a reader's response to a work, or arouse his skeptical resistance. It may be that we are given a more enlightening introduction to the poem by a critic who held it in low esteem—so far from thinking that **"Lycidas"** was superlatively great, Samuel Johnson thought it a very bad poem. Without doubt Dr. Johnson was wrong in this judgment and the grounds on which he bases it are quite mistaken. But his erroneous views, stated in his characteristically bold and unequivocal fashion, make plain how the poem ought to be regarded.

The sum of Dr. Johnson's objections is that **"Lycidas"** is insincere. It purports to be a poem of mourning; the poet is expressing grief over the death of a friend [Edward King]. But can we possibly believe in the truth of his emotion? Grief, Dr. Johnson says in effect, inclines to be silent or at least to be simple in its utterance. It does not express itself so elaborately, with as much artifice as Milton uses or with such a refinement of fancy and such a proliferation of reference to ancient legend and lore. "Passion plucks no berries from myrtle or ivy," Dr. Johnson said, "nor calls upon Arethuse and Mincius, nor tells of rough *satyrs* or *fauns with cloven heels.* Where there is leisure for fiction, there is little grief."

Of the poem's elaborateness of artifice, even of artificiality, there can be no question. The poet does not speak in his own person but in the guise of a "shepherd" or "swain." That is to say, he expresses his grief, such as it is, through the literary convention known as the pastoral, so called because all the persons represented in it are shepherds (the Latin word for shepherd is *pastor*). This convention of poetry has a long history. It goes back to the Greek poet Theocritus (c. 310-250 B.C.), who, in certain of his poems, pretended that he and his poet-friends were shepherds of his native Sicily. Far removed from the sophistication and corruption of cities, the fancied shepherds of Theocritus devoted themselves to the care of their flocks and to two innocent pursuits—song and the cultivation of love and friendship. Their only ambition was to be accomplished in song; their only source of unhappiness was a lost love or the death of a friend, the latter being rather more grievous than the former and making the occasion for an *elegy,* a poem of lament. Virgil brought the pastoral convention into Roman literature with his *Eclogues,* and it was largely through his influence that it became enormously popular in the Renaissance. This popularity continued through the eighteenth century, but the mechanical way in which it came to be used in much of the verse of that period justifies Dr. Johnson in speaking of the pastoral mode as "easy, vulgar, and therefore disgusting." In the nineteenth century the convention lost its vogue, but even then it was used for two great elegies, Shelley's "Adonais" and Matthew Arnold's "Thyrsis." For the poets of our time it seems to have no interest.

The fictional nature of the pastoral was never in doubt. Nobody was supposed to believe and nobody did believe that the high-minded poetic herdsmen were real, in charge of actual flocks. Yet the fiction engaged men's imaginations for so long a time because it fulfilled so real a desire of mankind—it speaks of simplicity and innocence, youth and beauty, love and art. And

although the poets were far from claiming actuality for their pastoral fancies, they often used the convention to criticize actual conditions of life, either explicitly as Milton does in the passage on the English clergy (lines 108-131) or by implication.

The traditional and avowedly artificial nature of the pastoral was exactly suited to the occasion which produced **"Lycidas."** Milton could scarcely have felt at Edward King's death the "passion" that Dr. Johnson blames him for not expressing, for King, although a college mate, had not been a close friend. He composed **"Lycidas"** not on spontaneous impulse but at the invitation of a group of Cambridge men who were bringing out a volume of poems to commemorate King. For Milton to have pretended to an acute sense of personal loss would have been truly an insincerity. Yet he could not fail to respond to what we might call the general pathos of a former comrade's dying "ere his prime," and by means of the pastoral elegy he was able to do what was beautifully appropriate to the situation—he associated King's death with a long tradition in which the deaths of young men had been lamented. Ever since the dawn of literature the death of a young man has been felt to have an especial pathos—how often it is evoked in the *Iliad;* and few things in the Bible are more affecting than David's mourning for his young friend Jonathan and his young son Absalom. It is this traditional pathos that Milton evokes from the death of Edward King. Had he tried to achieve a more personal expression of feeling, we should have responded not more but less. What engages us is exactly the universality of the emotion.

The pastoral convention is also appropriate to King's commemoration in two other respects. One is the extent to which the pastoral elegy was known and cultivated by young men in the English universities of Milton's time, if only because in their study of the ancient languages they were assigned the task of composing verses in this genre. Milton's own earliest-known poems are such college exercises, and all the poets who are mentioned or referred to in **"Lycidas"**—Theocritus, Virgil, Ovid—were subjects of university study. And in Milton's age as in ours, the college days of a young man were thought to have something like a pastoral quality—from mature life men look back to that time as being more carefree, and to their relationships then as having been more generous, disinterested, and comradely than now: why else do college alumni return each spring to their old campuses? Our very word *alumnus* expresses what Milton means when he says that he and King were "nurs'd upon the self-same hill," for an *alumnus* is a foster child, a nursling of *alma mater,* the fostering mother.

Dr. Johnson did not make it an item in his charge of insincerity that Milton, mourning a young man dead, is so preoccupied with a young man alive—himself. But we cannot fail to see that this is the case.

Milton begins his poem with an unabashed self-reference, to his feeling about himself as a young poet who has not yet reached the point in his development when he is ready to appear before the public. One reason he gives for overcoming his reluctance and undertaking the poem in memory of King is his hope that this will make it the more likely that someone will write to commemorate him when he dies. When he speaks about the poetic career and about poetic fame in relation to death, it is manifestly his own career and fame and his own death that he has in mind—the thought arouses him to a proud avowal of his sense of his high calling. And as the poem concludes, it is again to himself that he refers. Having discharged his duty of mourning, he turns from death and sorrow back to life and his own purposes:

At last he rose, and twitch'd his mantle blue:
To-morrow to fresh woods, and pastures new.

These passages have led many readers to conclude that **"Lycidas"** is not about Edward King at all but about John Milton. They are quite content that this should be so. They take the view that though the poem may fail in its avowed intention, it succeeds in an intention that it does not avow—they point to the fact that the most memorable and affecting parts of the poem are those in which Milton is his own subject. But in weighing this opinion we might ask whether it is ever possible to grieve for a person to whom we feel akin without grieving for ourselves, and, too, whether the intensity with which we are led to imagine our own inevitable death is not a measure of the kinship we feel with the person who has already died. Certainly nothing in **"Lycidas"** more strongly enforces upon us the pathos of untimely death than that it puts the poet in mind of his own death—for what he says of himself we are bound to feel of ourselves. And how better represent the sadness of death than to put it beside the poet's imagination of the fulness of life?

It must also be observed that Milton speaks of the death of Edward King and of his own imagined death and actual life in a context that does not permit our mere ordinary sense of the personal to prevail. He brings them into conjunction not only with the traditional pathos of young men dead ere their prime but also with the traditional evocations of the death of young gods, and their resurrection. No religious ceremonies of the ancient peoples were more fervently performed than those in which the death of a young male deity—Osiris, Adonis, Atys, Thammuz—was mourned and his resurrection rejoiced in. The myths of these gods and the celebration of their death and rebirth represented the cycles of the vital forces; the dying and reborn god symbolized the sun in its annual course, the processes of vegetation, the sexual and procreative energy, and sometimes, as in the case of Orpheus, poetic

genius. Once we are aware of this, Milton's concern with himself takes on a larger significance. It is not himself-the-person that Milton is meditating upon but himself-the-poet: that is, he is thinking about himself in the service not of his own interests but of the interests of the "divine" power that he bears within him.

In this service Milton is properly associated with Edward King, who was also a poet—it does not matter that King was not distinguished in his art. But there was yet another aspect of the service of divine power in the fact that King was a clergyman, a priest of the Church of England, which licenses the inclusion in the elegy of St. Peter's explosion of wrath against the negligent and corrupt clergy of the time. This famous passage constitutes only a small part of the poem, but the importance that Milton gave it is made plain by his extended reference to it in the "argument." Some readers will find a bitter condemnation of clerical corruption inappropriate to an elegy, and will be jarred and dismayed by the sudden introduction of Christian personages and considerations into a poem that has been, up to this point, consistently pagan. That Milton is himself quite aware that the passage will seem incongruous to the pastoral form is indicated in the lines in which he invokes the "return" of the "Sicilian Muse," who has been scared away by St. Peter's "dread voice." But in Milton's thought ancient pagan literature and mythology and the Judaeo-Christian religion were never really at odds with each other. It is a salient characteristic of his great and enormously learned mind that Milton gave allegiance to both, and used for Christian ideas the literary forms of paganism. In the pastoral convention he found a natural conjunction of the two: we can readily see that the poetic convention has affinity with the feelings attached to the pastoral life by Biblical Judaism and, more elaborately, by Christianity. The peaceable Abel was a shepherd and so was Abraham. So was David, and a poet-shepherd at that, one of whose psalms begins, "The Lord is my Shepherd, I shall not want." It was shepherds who saw the Star of Bethlehem rise; Jesus is both the Lamb of God and the Good Shepherd. *Pastor* is the name for the priest of a parish, the congregation being his flock, and the form of a bishop's crozier is the shepherd's crook.

As the poem moves toward its conclusion the mingling of pagan and Christian elements is taken wholly for granted. This conjunction of the two traditions exemplifies yet another characteristic of the poem, its inclusiveness. **"Lycidas"** gathers up all the world, things the most disparate in space and time and kind, and concentrates them in one place and moment, brings them to bear upon one event, the death of the poet-priest. The poem's action is, as it were, summarized in the lines about "the great Vision" of St. Michael the Angel who, from Land's End, the southernmost tip of England, looks afar to Spain but is adjured to "look homeward." So the poem looks afar to the ancient world and also turns its gaze upon contemporary England. From "the bottom of the monstrous world" it turns to heaven, and from all the waters of the world to all the flowers of all the seasons of the Earth, and from the isolation of Lycidas in death to the "sweet societies" of his resurrection and everlasting life through the agency of Christ. It plays literary games with the most solemn subjects, and juxtaposes the gravest ideas with the smallest blossoms, using their most delicate or homely names (culminating in the daffadillies, which sound like the very essence of irresponsible frivolity). And then, when it has brought all the world together, and life out of death and faith out of despair, it has its "uncouth swain," the shepherd-poet, with the jauntiness of a task fully discharged, announce that the mourning is now at an end. Life calls the poet to other work and he must answer the call. (pp. 194-200)

Lionel Trilling, "John Milton: 'Lycidas'," in his *Prefaces to The Experience of Literature,* Harcourt Brace Jovanovich, 1979, pp. 194-200.

SOURCES FOR FURTHER STUDY

Daiches, David. *Milton.* Rev. ed. London: Hutchinson University Library, 1959, 254 p.
> A general survey of Milton's life and major works.

Darbishire, Helen, ed. *The Early Lives of Milton.* London: Constable & Co., 1932, 353 p.
> Introduces and edits six early biographies of Milton, written between 1681 and 1734.

Empson, William. *Milton's God.* Rev. ed. London: Chatto & Windus, 1965, 320 p.
> Probes Milton's major works for evidence of his views of the nature of God.

Martz, Louis L., ed. *Milton: A Collection of Critical Essays.* Englewood Cliffs, N.J.: Prentice-Hall, 1966, 212 p.
> Anthologizes selected twentieth-century Milton criticism. Essayists include William Empson, Geoffrey Hartman, and Arnold Stein, among others.

Wagenknecht, Edward. *The Personality of Milton.* Norman: University of Oklahoma Press, 1970, 170 p.
> Examines Milton's works for instances of self-revelation.

Webber, John Malory. *Milton and His Epic Tradition.* Seattle: University of Washington Press, 1979, 244 p.
> Attempts to "chart more fully the extent to which Milton's central concerns are compatible with those of earlier epic writers."

Yukio Mishima

1925-1970

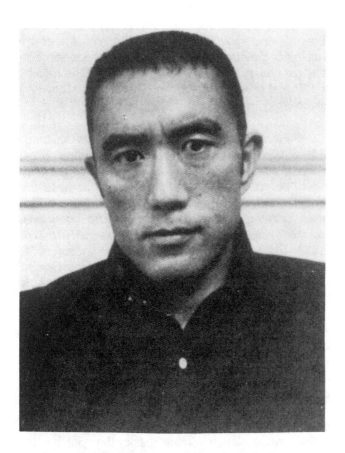

(Pseudonym of Kimitake Hiroaka) Japanese novelist, short story writer, dramatist, film director, essayist, and actor.

INTRODUCTION

*O*ne of the most provocative and versatile modern Japanese writers, Mishima is known for his unorthodox views and eccentric personal life, as well as for his literature. His works often reflect a dedication to the traditional values of imperialist Japan and are characterized by a preoccupation with aggression and violent eroticism. Critics often interpret Mishima's works from a biographical perspective, frequently placing him among the Japanese "I-novelists," who wrote autobiography in the guise of fiction. Although best known in the West for his novels, he achieved great critical success in all genres and was as highly esteemed in Japan for his plays as for his fiction. Mishima received many literary awards in his country and was nominated for the Nobel Prize in 1965.

Mishima was born Kimitake Hiraoka in 1925 in Tokyo, where his father was a senior government official. His paternal grandmother Natsu was obsessively protective of the young Kimitake and would not allow him to live with the rest of the family on the upper level of their home; instead, she kept him with her in her darkened sickroom until he reached the age of twelve. Perhaps because of this extreme isolation, Mishima had difficulty forming social relationships as a youth, and many biographers and critics have attributed the source of his homoerotic and nihilistic tendencies to these formative early years.

A gifted student, Kimitake immersed himself in Japanese and Western classical literature, as well as the works of such European authors as Jean Racine and William Butler Yeats. He began writing stories in middle school and had his first work published while still a high school student. It was upon this occasion in 1941 that Kimitake was given the pen name Yukio Mishima. He later studied law at Tokyo University and subsequently accepted employment in the government's Finance Ministry. Within a year, however, he resigned in order to write full-time. With the great success of his first novel *Kamen no kokuhaku (Confessions of a Mask)* in 1949, he firmly established himself as an important voice in Japanese literature.

Throughout his adult life, Mishima was disturbed by what he felt was Japan's moral vacuum and "effeminate" image as "a nation of flower arrangers." He became increasingly consumed by a desire to revive "the way of the warrior" (*bushidō*), the traditional values and morals of the samurai, and he vehemently opposed the Westernization of his country. A supporter of *Literary Culture (Bungei Bunka)*, the small nationalist magazine that had printed his early short fiction, introduced Mishima to the *Nihon Roman-ha,* a prominent group of Japanese Romanticist intellectuals who stressed the "value of destruction" and called for the preservation of Japanese cultural traditions. The *Nihon Roman-ha* had a profound effect on Mishima, who found reinforcement of his personal ideals in the group's emphasis on death and violence. Thus, Mishima's later works reflect his growing conservative political orientation and his philosophy of "active nihilism," which regards self-sacrifice as essential to achieving spiritual fulfillment.

In 1967 Mishima formed the Shield Society, or *Tate no kai,* a private army dedicated to restoring the prestige of the nation and reestablishing its old imperial glory. The Shield Society consisted of one hundred university students pledged to defend the Emperor—traditionally, the source of all Japanese culture—with their lives. The organization was ridiculed or ignored by the press, and Mishima was accused by some of fascism and cultural elitism. On 25 November 1970, Mishima submitted to his publisher the last installment of *Tennin gosui* (1971; *The Decay of the Angel*), the final section of his novel tetralogy *Hōjō no umi* (1969-71; *The Sea of Fertility*). He and his followers then attacked the commander of the Japanese Self-Defense Forces (*Jietai*). They held the commander hostage, barricading themselves in his office and demanding that Mishima be allowed to address an assembly of defense personnel. After repelling a rescue attempt by *Jietai* officers, Mishima gave a speech exhorting a return to imperial ideals. He advocated overthrowing the American-imposed constitution and restoring the Emperor to his former position of preeminence. Receiving only laughter and jeers in response, Mishima returned to the commander's office humiliated. Aware that his values were not shared by the majority of his countrymen and having failed to incite a coup, Mishima, in affirmation of his personal convictions, committed *seppuku,* a uniquely Japanese form of ritual suicide that involves disembowelment and beheading. (*Seppuku* in the samurai ethos served as a respected form of protest or as a way of preserving personal honor in an otherwise dishonorable situation.)

The passion and violence that characterized Mishima's personal life is conveyed throughout his writing. Indeed, critics often interpret Mishima's writings from a biographical perspective and routinely detect apparent contradictions between and within the man and his literature. An ardent supporter of distinctively Japanese values, he was also steeped in Western aesthetic traditions and lived in a Western-style house. A master of traditional dramatic forms, he yet created some of his country's most notable modern theatrical pieces. A tireless writer, bodybuilder, and swordsman who possessed a vibrant and charismatic personality, Mishima nevertheless displayed in his works a markedly erotic fascination with death. Though he was married and the father of two children, he created some of the most vivid and realistic depictions of homosexuality in literature. *Confessions of a Mask,* an uninhibited account of the protagonist's struggle to come to terms with his homoerotic and aggressive feelings, contains a passage that critics believe unifies many of these oppositions in a single literary aesthetic: since childhood, he recalls, the "heart's yearning was for Death and Night and Blood."

Among Mishima's fiction, the novels *Kinkakuji* (1956; *The Temple of the Golden Pavilion*), *Confessions of a Mask,* and *Gogo no eikō* (1963; *The Sailor Who Fell from Grace with the Sea*) are perhaps the most famous, along with the works in his *Sea of Tranquility* tetralogy: *Haru no yuki* (1969; *Spring Snow*), *Homba* (1969; *Runaway Horses*), *Akatsuki no tera* (1970; *The Temple of Dawn*), and *Tennin gossui* (1971; *The Decay of the Angel*). *The Temple of the Golden Pavilion,* considered one of Mishima's best early books, won the Yomiuri prize in 1957. The novel is based on the true story of a young Buddhist acolyte whose ugliness and stutter have made him grow to hate anything beautiful. He becomes obsessed with the idea that the golden temple where he studies is the ideal of beauty, and in envy he burns the temple to the ground. "But although Mishima has made use of the reported details of the real-life culprit's arrogant and desperate history, culminating in the final willful act of arson," wrote Nancy Wilson Ross in the book's introduction, "he has employed the factual record merely as a scaffolding on which to erect a disturbing and powerful story of a sick young man's obsession with a beauty he cannot attain, and the way in which his private pathology leads him, slowly and fatefully, to self-destruction and a desperate deed of pyromania." Although the simple love story of *Spring Snow* made it the most popular book of the tetralogy, the other volumes were also highly regarded. Many readers were drawn to *Runaway Hero* because the suicide of its protagonist, Isao, foreshadowed in almost exact detail the author's own suicide. *The Temple of Dawn* was acclaimed by Capitanchik, who thought it included "some of Mishima's finest descriptive writing, especially concerning Honda's visit to Benares." Morrow also considered this passage "a small masterpiece." The final volume, *The Decay of the Angel*, "raises more questions than it answers," Susan Heath observed, but she also noted that it "brilliantly epitomizes Mishima's pessimistic outlook." Morrow also praised the book, calling it "a wonderfully frigid dance of death in which Mishima, like a Japanese Prospero, gathers all his artistic belongings together. In its austerity it is among the best of Mishima's novels."

The only collection of his short stories available in English is *Manatsu no shi* (1953; *Death in Midsummer, and Other Stories*). It contains his best-known, and ultimately prophetic, story "Yukoku" ("Patriotism"). In this piece, a young military officer and his wife commit *seppuku* because he feels disgraced by his comrades. The suicide is described in extraordinary, almost sensuous detail. Mishima characterized "Patriotism" as "neither a comedy nor a tragedy, but a tale of bliss." Many critics have found that this story further exemplifies Mishima's tendency to blend death and eroticism.

Mishima's dramatic works often reflect his dedication to the traditional values of imperialist Japan and are further characterized by a preoccupation with aggression and eroticism. Scholars have thus found it unsurprising that he was drawn to the formal, stylized violence of the traditional dramatic forms of Kabuki and Nō (also rendered in English as No or Noh). Mishima's pieces in these genres are, however, also esteemed for their updating of traditional works while preserving the spirit of the originals. Commentators also agree that Mishima's *shingeki* or "new theater" plays successfully combine the finest aspects of Eastern and Western dramatic traditions with the author's own distinctive voice to create some of Japan's most highly acclaimed modern theater pieces. In addition to many Nō, Kabuki, and *shingeki* plays, Mishima also composed other performance works, including a *Bunraku* (puppet theater) piece and a ballet. From 1953 to 1970 he composed one full length play per year while continuing to produce his novels, magazine serials, and short stories. "Plays awaken a different part of my desire," Mishima once said; "that part which is unsatisfied by writing novels. Now, when I write a novel, I want to write a play next. Plays occupy one of the two magnetic poles of my work."

Often overshadowed by his dramatic personal life, Mishima's oeuvre eludes easy critical analysis. His sensational death by *seppuku* has prompted many critics to solicit biographical meanings from his works, while other commentators note a distinct contradiction between Mishima's modern personal lifestyle and his literary aesthetic. Although critics have accused Mishima of self-indulgent prose, he is widely respected for his distinctive style. Translations of his plays have helped introduce the traditional forms of Nō and Kabuki to the world and have provided evidence of the thriving state of the *shingeki* theater in Japan. Even more importantly, Mishima's successful melding of Oriental and Occidental, modern and traditional aesthetics has resulted in a series of timeless dramas that transcend cultural boundaries. A prolific writer, Mishima's mastery of novels, essays, and plays earned him a reputation as the literary genius of Japan's postwar generation as well as a place among the world's finest authors.

(For further information about Mishima's life and works, see *Contemporary Authors*, Vols. 29-32, 97-100; *Contemporary Literary Criticism*, Vols. 2, 4, 6, 9, 27; *Drama Criticism*, Vol. 1; and *Short Story Criticism*, Vol. 4.)

CRITICAL COMMENTARY

HENRY SCOTT-STOKES

(essay date 1974)

[As a Tokyo-based journalist, Scott-Stokes became a friend of Mishima in 1968. In the excerpt below from his full-length biography of the writer, he provides a survey of Mishima's career as a dramatist.]

Once the theater was like a jolly party I enjoyed attending after a hard day's work. There I could find another world—a world of glittering lights and colors, where the characters of my own creation, clad in alluring costumes, stood in front of a handsome set, laughed, screamed, wept, and danced. And to think that I, as a playwright, governed and manipulated all these theatrical worlds from behind the scenes!

Yet such delights gradually turned bitter. The magic of the theater—to give people the illusion of life's noblest moments and the apparition of beauty on earth—began to corrupt my heart. Or was it that I

Principal Works

Kamen no kokuhaku (novel) 1949
  [Confessions of a Mask, 1958]
*Kantan (drama) 1950
*Aya no tsuzumi (drama) 1951
  [The Damask Drum, 1957]
*Sotoba Komachi (drama) 1952
  [translated 1957]
Manatsu no shi (short fiction) 1953
  [Death in Midsummer and Other Stories, 1966]
Yoru no himawari (drama) 1953
  [Twilight Sunflower, 1958]
*Aoi no ue (drama) 1954
  [The Lady Aoi, 1957]
*Hanjo (drama) 1955
  [translated 1957]
Kindai nōgakushū 1956
  [Five Modern Nō Plays, 1957]
Kīnkakuji (novel) 1956
  [The Temple of the Golden Pavilion, 1959]
Dōjōji (drama) 1957
  [translated in Death in Midsummer and Other Stories 1966]
Nettaiju (drama) 1959
  [Tropical Tree; published in Japan Quarterly, 1964]
Gogo no eikō (novel) 1963

  [The Sailor Who Fell from Grace with the Sea, 1965]
Sado kōshaku fujin (drama) 1965
  [Madame de Sade 1967]
Yorobōshi (drama) 1965
  [Yoroboshi: The Blind Young Man; published in Modern Japanese Drama: An Anthology, 1979]
Taiyo to tetsu (essay) 1968
  [Sun and Steel, 1970]
Waga tomo Hittorā (drama) 1968
  [My Friend Hitler; published in St. Andrews Review, 1977]
Hōjō no umi (novel tetralogy) 1969-71
  [The Sea of Fertility: A Cycle of Four Novels, 1972-74]
Haru no yuki 1969
  [Spring Snow, 1972]
Homba 1969
  [Runaway Horses, 1973]
Akatsuki no tera 1970
  [The Temple of Dawn, 1973]
Tennin gosui 1971
  [The Decay of the Angel, 1974]

*These works are included in Kindai nōgakushū and are translated in Five Modern Nō Plays.

grudged being an alienated playwright? Theater, where a false blood runs in the floodlights, can perhaps move and enrich people with much more forceful and profound experiences than anything in real life. As in music and architecture, I find the beauty of the theater in its abstract and theoretical structure, and this particular beauty never ceases to be the very image of what I have always held in the depth of my heart as Ideal in Art.

Yukio Mishima,
Catalogue to the Tobu Exhibition

The modern theater had a slow start in Japan. Whereas Japanese writers were attracted to the Western novel in the decades that followed the Meiji Restoration of 1868, and the first "modern" novels were written in Japan in the late nineteenth century, Western-style theater did not become established until after the Pacific War. Valiant attempts were made by small groups of actors and actresses to create a modern theater long before the war; the beginning of Shingeki is customarily traced to 1906, when a society for the promotion of the arts, the Bungei Kyokai, which specialized in drama, was founded. But the theater suffered

cruelly from official censorship and, after a brief flowering in the 1920's, succumbed to government control. There were always small, politically radical groups ready to brave the authorities' disapproval—but scarcely any permanent achievements were made before the onset of the Pacific War. (An exception is the establishment of the Bungakuza—Literary Theater—in 1938. It survived the war, taking as its slogan "Art for art's sake.") In addition to all this, modern theater had strong competition from both the traditional Japanese theater, the Kabuki, a form established in the seventeenth and eighteenth centuries, and the successful lowbrow theater known as Shinpa, which had none of the intellectual appeal of Shingeki and drew large audiences, catering to a popular taste for Western-style, sentimental drama.

After the war, Shingeki benefited from a relaxation of censorship. The radical character of modern theater in Japan was apparent in the choice of plays made by the leading theatrical groups: works by Ibsen, Gogol, Tolstoy, Chekhov, and a number of Japanese writers who drew on the Russian tradition. The prestige of Western writers was great. Among the most popular Shingeki productions in the 1950's were Tennessee Williams's *A Streetcar Named Desire* and John Osborne's *Look Back in Anger*. The Western classical repertoire was also drawn upon; in 1955 the Bungakuza played *Hamlet* with great success. For the first time, good translations of the plays of Shakespeare were available and Shakespeare was for a time the height of fashion; veteran Kabuki actors vied for the honor of playing Hamlet. Few Japanese writers of the older generation rose to the challenge of the Shingeki in the late 1940's. It was left to the young men—among them Yukio Mishima and Kobo Abé—to respond. Abé did so in a manner consonant with the tradition of Shingeki, in which radical, proletarian protest had played so large a part before the war. In one of his early plays, *Dorei Gari* ("Slave Hunt," 1952), he satirized the business world in Japan—describing a particularly bizarre form of postwar commerce (a trade in the remains of the war dead). Mishima, by contrast, showed no taste for ideology; his forte was style. These two young playwrights, the most successful newcomers to Shingeki after the war, were far apart in politics, which was equally apparent in their novels and in the translations of their works (Abé was taken up by the Soviet literary world; Mishima was translated exclusively in the West). Mishima showed a taste for the Western classical tradition—he was to write plays modeled on works by Racine and Euripides; Abé had a taste for Brecht.

Mishima's first work for the Shingeki was the one-act play *Kataku* ("Fire House," 1949). This was performed by the Haiyuza, one of the two leading Shingeki groups, and he was gratified to hear well-known actors and actresses speaking his lines. His first major success came the following year, in a genre which he made his own, the modern No play. Since its establishment in the fifteenth century as the theatrical form of the feudal aristocracy and the Imperial Court, No has attracted many writers, even in modern times. According to Keene's preface to *Five Modern Nō Plays,* published by Alfred A. Knopf: "Some have fashioned pastiches on the traditional themes, others have tried to fit modern conceptions into the old forms. The hysteria of wartime propaganda even led to the composition of a *Nō* play about life on a submarine. Some modern works have enjoyed temporary popularity, but they were essentially curiosities, having neither the beauty of language and mood of the old plays, nor the complexity of character delineation we expect of a modern work. The first genuinely successful modern *Nō* plays have been those by Yukio Mishima." As an example of Mishima's success, Keene takes *Kantan,* the first of his modern No plays, written in 1950; he compares the classical original with Mishima's work. In the classical No,

a traveler naps on a magic pillow, and during the brief time that it takes his hostess at the inn to cook

a bowl of gruel, he dreams of a glorious life as Emperor of China. He awakens to the realization that life is but a dream. In Mishima's play, instead of a traveler, we have a spoiled young man of today who sleeps on the magic pillow while his old nurse prepares the breakfast. His dreams are not of ancient China but of riches and power as a financial tycoon and a dictator.

Mishima wrote many modern No plays. The second book of his to be translated was a collection of these plays, which had a great success overseas. They were performed in many European countries and in Australia and Mexico as well as in North America, eventually being staged Off-Broadway late in 1960; that production ran for two months and had good notices. It was partly through these short plays—all are one-act dramas—that Mishima first acquired a measure of fame in the West; the dialogue is taut and the playwright retains sufficient of the ghostly quality of the classical No to give his works a unique character. Their appeal was considerable in Japan itself. The plays were produced by Shingeki companies and also appeared on the classical No stage. One play, **The Lady Aoi,** was sung as a Western-style opera. Translations of the classical No plays were long ago done by Arthur Waley, but they can scarcely be performed without the settings of the genuine No—the uniquely shaped stage, the gorgeous costumes and masks, and the musicians and chorus—often compared to classical Greek drama. Mishima's modern No plays gave the West a taste for No some time before it was possible for No companies to travel to foreign cities to perform the superb repertoire of the classical Japanese theater.

Some insight into Mishima's character is afforded by his attitude toward the classical No. While he was in Tokyo he would go "once a month without fail" to see a No play. But his attitude toward the No was peculiar; I do not believe that he really enjoyed No performances—during which he often fell asleep. A month before his suicide, he sent me a copy of an article on the No published in *This Is Japan* for 1971:

There [at the No] one may see in its original form a classical stage art that dates back to the fifteenth century, an art that, complete and perfect in itself, admits of no meddling by contemporary man . . . The No theater is a temple of beauty, the place above all wherein is realized the supreme union of religious solemnity and sensuous beauty. In no other theatrical tradition has such an exquisite refinement been achieved . . . True beauty is something that attacks, overpowers, robs, and finally destroys. It was because he knew this violent quality of beauty that Thomas Mann wrote *Death in Venice* . . . The No cannot begin until after the drama is ended and beauty lies in ruins. One might liken this . . . 'necrophilous' aesthetic of the No to that of works by Edgar Allan Poe, such as *Ligeia* or

Berenice . . . In No lies the only type of beauty that has the power to wrest 'my' time away from the 'exterior' Japan of today . . . and to impose on it another regime . . . And beneath its mask that beauty must conceal death, for some day, just as surely, it will finally lead me away to destruction and to silence.

Mishima also wrote plays for the Kabuki theater in the early 1950's—before he had established himself as a Shingeki playwright. He had a unique advantage over his contemporaries: he alone had mastered classical Japanese and knew sufficient of the difficult language used in Kabuki to write plays in this genre. A photograph taken in 1953 shows him seated with Mantaro Kubota, a grand old man of the Japanese theater with a special affection for Kabuki. Mishima is going over a draft of a play, perspicaciously racing through the script. Kubota looks over one shoulder with a perplexed expression of admiration on his face, while an acolyte of the old man regards the youthful prodigy between them from the other side. Mishima loved the Kabuki; the baroque bloodletting and fierce swordplay appealed to his instincts. So, too, did the theme of many a Kabuki play—that true love may end in a shinju, or double suicide. His attitude toward the No was reverent and a little constricted, even ridiculous; his admiration for Kabuki was unrestrained. Many of the great actors of the day were his friends and he spent long hours backstage conversing with them. . . . Mishima's Kabuki plays are of no great importance; during his life, however, they attracted much attention. In some ways the most successful was his last work for the theater, *Chinsetsu Yumiharizuki* (whose title is untranslatable). He wrote it in 1969 and himself produced it at the National Theater. Mishima was a good mimic and an able Kabuki actor. After this production, he made a record of the play in which he took all forty parts.

Mishima defined his approach to Shingeki, for which he wrote most of his forty plays, in his essay **"The Play and I"** (1951):

The modern play is far, far removed from the chaotic world of the novel, as I see it. It must look like a paper cathedral floating in the sky. No matter how naturalistic a play may be, the theme which makes for dramatic tension is such that it never suits the novel form. Strong emotion bears down upon the details and marches forward, treading the details underfoot.

His first successful long play was *Shiro Ari no Su* (**"The Nest of the White Ant,"** 1955), set on a Brazilian coffee plantation where an aristocratic Japanese couple have taken refuge with two servants—a chauffeur and his wife—after the war. The structure of the play, a tale of adultery and suicide attempts, is excellent, and *Shiro Ari no Su*—the hollow nest of a white-ant colony is the symbol of the empty lives of the Japanese émigrés—established Mishima's reputation as a Shingeki dramatist. Not long after completing this work, for which he won a dramatic award, Mishima declared: "My ideal life would be to write one long novel a year and no short stories at all. Or, if I have to, then nothing longer than twenty pages. Otherwise, I would devote my time to plays." And on the relationship between his novels and his plays he commented: "Plays awaken a different part of my desire, that part which is unsatisfied by writing novels. Now, when I write a novel, I want to write a play next. Plays occupy one of the two magnetic poles of my work."

Mishima never achieved his ideal. He continued to write two or three novels a year, and some of his most striking works—for example, **"Patriotism,"** the tale of hara-kiri—were to be longish short stories. For the remainder of his life, however, with the exception of the last year, he alternated continually between writing plays and novels. In 1956, for instance, he wrote *The Temple of the Golden Pavilion* in the early part of the year and followed it with a play, which he completed in time for the autumn season— *Rokumeikan*. This drama, the most frequently performed of Mishima's plays, is not an interesting play, in my opinion.

Toka no Kiku (**"Tenth-Day Chrysanthemums,"** 1961) was the great triumph of Mishima's career as a dramatist. September 9 is a day of festival in Japan, on which exhibitions of chrysanthemums are staged. Tenth-day flowers would be too late for the show— they would be wasted. The chrysanthemum is a symbol of loyalty in Japan (the Imperial crest is composed of a thirty-two-petaled chrysanthemum). Thus, Mishima's play has as its theme wasted loyalty.

The principal character is a politician, a former Finance Minister named Mori, who had once, before the war, in the 1930's, been the target of an assassination attempt by rightwing terrorists. Mori's attitude toward the incident is brought out during a visit paid him by Kiku, the faithful maidservant who saved his life sixteen years before, who has not seen him since the assassination attempt (described in the play as if it were a minor detail in one of the numerous unsuccessful coups d'état of the 1930's). The old man states that the most honorable day of his life—which he prizes more highly than the day on which he was appointed Finance Minister, his highest office—was the day on which patriotic youths tried to kill him. The most fortunate accident that can befall a statesman, Mori implies, is to be struck down by the hand of an assassin. Death in the service of the nation and the Emperor is to be preferred to life, if that life has no meaning. Mori spends his days pursuing a lonely hobby, the growing of cacti; his activities as a cactus fancier are much dwelt upon in Mishima's play. The old man is depicted as one who, like the cactus, has no blood; his existence is without meaning. The political background to the play is the murderous struggle which took place in the 1930's between those whose prime objective was order—politicians, men of business, and civil servants—and those who put a premium on honor. Mori has belatedly realized that he belongs, at heart, to the latter camp. In Mishima's play, Kiku gives Mori short shrift at their meeting. *Toka no Kiku* may be read as an assault upon sentimental conservatism; the dramatic action favors such an interpretation. The playwright himself, however, had a streak of sympathy for Mori's attitudes; the play was based on the Ni Ni Roku Incident of February 26, 1936, carried out by rebel army officers with whom Mishima later claimed he had much in common.

Not that *Toka no Kiku* is a political play. The dramatic interest lies in the relationship between Kiku and her former master and employer, Mori. The part of Kiku was taken by Haruko Sugimura in the production given by the Bungakuza in November 1961, on the occasion of the twenty-fifth anniversary of the foundation of the theatrical group, and this was one of the most distinguished performances by an actress generally regarded as the finest of Shingeki players. How far the Bungakuza, whose dominant personality was Miss Sugimura, was from regarding *Toka no Kiku* as an ideological drama was made apparent two years later when the group rejected a fairly mild play of Mishima's on ideological grounds, precipitating a furious quarrel between the Bungakuza and Mishima that ended in his resignation from the group with which he had worked, almost exclusively, for nearly a decade. Had *Toka no Kiku* been sympathetic to the right in the eyes of the Bungakuza, it would scarcely have been selected by them for performance at an anniversary.

The play which caused a rupture between Mishima and the Bungakuza was *Yorokobi no Koto* ("**The Harp of Joy,**" 1963), and it is not one of Mishima's important works. It is set in postwar Japan and is based on the Matsukawa Incident—the derailment of a train in 1949 by saboteurs whose identity was never established, although the authorities believed for a time that they were from the left. The principal character is a senior police officer, Matsumura, a veteran who is popular with his subordinates, one of whom, Katagiri, he instructs to investigate the derailment of a train (the Matsukawa Incident is not identified as such in the play). The zealous Katagiri arrests several men and is astonished by their immediate release, when it has been ascertained that they are rightists. There are frequent left-wing demonstrations in the streets, the object of which is to show popular discontent with a government which is trying to pin the blame for the train derailment on the left, without any proof. A strange incident then occurs at the police station where Katagiri

and his men work. A young policeman says he has heard the sound of a koto (a classical musical instrument) while on duty. The others laugh at him—how, in the midst of noisy demonstrations, could he have heard such a thing? Shortly afterward the investigation of the sabotage takes a totally unexpected turn. Matsumura, the man who is carrying out the police inquiry, is himself accused of having organized the sabotage; the police chief is said to have been an undercover Communist agent. The faithful Katagiri is shattered by this. Later the charges against Matsumura are shown to have been fabricated by the right; nonetheless, the younger man loses his faith in his superior. One day, when Katagiri is on duty in the streets, with demonstrators surging about him, he hears the beautiful sound of a koto. A man who had placed his faith in absolute authority, in the immutable system of the law, seeks refuge in fantasy after the collapse of his belief in order.

The turning point in the play comes when Katagiri realizes that Matsumura, his revered leader, has exploited him for his own ends—though these are not political. The Bungakuza, after starting rehearsals of *Yorokobi no Koto* in mid-November 1963, and following the return of Haruko Sugimura from travels in China, suddenly suspended rehearsal and informed Mishima that the production was off. Some of the actors, it was explained to Mishima by a succession of delegations which visited him at his home to give reasons for the suspension of rehearsals, objected to the right-wing lines spoken by the policemen in the play. Mishima was incensed. His angry rebuttal of the Bungakuza was printed as an open letter to the group; it appeared in the *Asahi Shimbun* a few days later, following his resignation from the Bungakuza. It read in part:

> Certainly *Yorokobi no Koto* is quite different from my other works and includes an element of danger. But what have you been thinking about me all this while that you should be astonished by a work such as this? Have you been making a fool of me, saying that Mishima is a playwright . . . who writes harmless dramas which gather large audiences? You set up such safe criteria as 'Art' and conceal within yourselves a vague political inclination [to the left], dropping the phrase 'art for art's sake' from time to time . . . Isn't this just hypocrisy and commercialism? I would like you to understand this: there is always a needle in art; there is also poison; you can't suck honey without the poison too.

The break was complete. Shortly afterward, Mishima joined another theatrical group, the NLT (New Literature Theater). It was a sad moment. Mishima never again found a group as effective to work with as the Bungakuza and the Bungakuza lost their best playwright.

The quarrel is a puzzling one. Within three years

Mishima was to profess political beliefs which would have fully justified the Bungakuza in breaking with him. He was to assert that *Toka no Kiku* was in fact a play about the Ni Ni Roku Incident. He was also to state that he shared the patriotic attitude of the fanatically imperialist young officers who staged the Ni Ni Roku Incident. But his imperialism did not surface clearly in his writing until the summer of 1966, when he wrote *Eirei no Koe* (**"The Voices of the Heroic Dead"**). Nevertheless, there was a surprising violence to the quarrel. Mishima had very few squabbles with people or with organizations during his life. There were disagreements, but Mishima avoided public hostility on almost all occasions. Like many Japanese—and however un-Japanese he may have been in many respects—he abhorred public fracas.

Madame de Sade, the next play, again showed Mishima to be far more interested in problems of structure than in political matters. He wrote it after becoming intrigued with the problem of why the Marquise de Sade, who was absolutely faithful to her husband during his many years in prison, left him the moment he was free. The play was an attempt to provide a solution to the problem; it was "Sade seen through women's eyes." All six characters are women and the action is controlled exclusively through dialogue. Mishima intended that visual appeal would be provided by the rococo costumes of the women; the five characters must form a precise, mathematical system around Madame de Sade. Keene has described the debt owed by Mishima to Racine: "Mishima's classicism . . . is given its most extreme expression in the play *Madame de Sade* . . . Here he adopted most of the conventions of the Racinian stage—a single setting, a reliance on the *tirade* for the relation of events and emotions, a limited number of characters each of whom represents a specific kind of woman, and an absence of overt action on the stage."

Madame de Sade was a considerable success in Tokyo, although the subject matter was a little too recherché. After its translation into English, Mishima hoped that it would be produced on Broadway and pressed his agent in New York, Audrey Wood, to find a theater for it. *Madame de Sade,* however, proved to have no appeal to American actresses; the absence of overt action on the stage was the major problem. Quite possibly, none of Mishima's long plays will ever be performed on the Western stage. Certainly, it is unlikely that Mishima's subsequent major plays, *Suzaku Ke no Metsubo* (**"The Fall of the House of Suzaku,"** 1967)—a play based on Euripides—and *Wagatomo Hitler* [1969, *My Friend Hitler,* 1977], would have great appeal to Western audiences. The latter is set in Germany in 1934; in it Mishima describes the events before and after the Night of the Long Knives. It makes the point that Hitler steered a "neutral" course between the Brownshirts and the conservative forces—the regular army and big business—on that occasion. Mishima neither praises nor criticizes Hitler; nor does he develop the character of the dictator in the play. Mishima treats the Night of the Long Knives as an incident in a struggle for power, a technical operation. The title of the play refers to Roehm, the head of the Brownshirts, one of Hitler's victims on the Night. In the play Roehm believes the Führer is "my friend"—until it is too late. At the première, held in Tokyo on January 19, 1969, Mishima distributed a note to the audience: "The dangerous ideologue, Mishima, dedicates an evil ode to the dangerous hero, Hitler." His intention was to mock the critics and the vaguely leftist neutralism of Japanese intellectuals. Neutralism, the play said, can lead anywhere.

Mishima's last play for the modern theater was *Raio no Terrasu* (**"The Terrace of the Leper King,"** 1969). He invited me to the première and I remember how he looked that evening—he was wearing all-white evening attire and was accompanied by [his wife] Yoko. Tennessee Williams was supposed to put in an appearance and there was an empty seat next to Mishima where he should have been. The performance itself went well enough. *Raio no Terrasu* is an untranslated play about the Khmer king Jayavarman III, the builder of the temple of Bayon at Angkor Wat. The monarch suffered from leprosy; Bayon is his monument. Mishima used the tale to make the point that the material triumphs over the immaterial, the Body over the Spirit—Bayon alone remains. He was especially proud of the last scene, an exchange on the steps of the newly constructed Bayon between the Body—the youthful image of the king—and the Spirit, represented by the voice of the dying, leprous king (a sepulchral, tape-recorded voice in the Teigeki production we saw).

BODY. King, dying king. Can you see me?

SPIRIT. Who is calling me? I remember the voice. That brilliant voice.

B. It's me. Do you see?

S. No. Of course not. I'm blind.

B. Why should the Spirit need eyes? It has been your source of pride that you see things without using your eyes!

S. Such harsh words. Who are you?

B. I'm the king.

S. Absurd! That's me.

B. We share the same name. King, I am your Body.

S. Who am I then?

B. You are my Spirit. The Spirit that resolved to build this Bayon. What is dying is not the Body of the king.

S. My Body was rotten and has vanished. You cannot be my Body, speaking so proudly and boldly.

The actor who played the part of the Body was heavily suntanned and wore a short tunic with straps across his bare chest. As he spoke his lines, he strode about the terrace of the temple, flourishing his arms. Behind him was a giant face made of foot-high blocks of stone, one of many such faces at the temple of Bayon. The actor, Kinya Kiyaoji, was slightly overweight; his voice boomed out cheerfully, while the groaning Spirit endeavored to reply:

B. It's not true. Your Body was never rotten. Your Body is here, shining with youth, full of vigor, like an immortal golden statue. The cursed illness is an illusion of the Spirit. How could such a triumphant king as I be affected by illness?

S. But what could the Body achieve? What imperishable things can he construct? It is not stones that planned and constructed this imperishable Bayon. Stones are nothing but materials. It's the Spirit that made this.

B (*laughing aloud with pride*) The Spirit cannot see Bayon any more, because even the Spirit depended on the Body.

S. No. I don't need to see it. The finished Bayon shines in my spirit.

B. Shining? It's only a small streak of light, which is about to be put out. Think, if it is enough to be shining in the Spirit, why was it necessary to construct Bayon with such an enormous quantity of stones?

S. The Spirit always longs for a shape.

B. That's because you are shapeless. Shape always takes its model from a beautiful body like me. Did you use as a model of this temple the rotten body of a leper?

S. Rubbish! The body of a leper is nothing.

B. Nothing? You suffered for so long.

S. No, nothing. The Spirit is everything.

B. What are they, the rotten, the shapeless, and the blind? They are the shape the Spirit takes. It's not you that suffered from leprosy. Your very existence is leprous. You are a born leper.

S. Sharpness, clarity, and the power to see through to the bottom of this world constructed Bayon. The Body cannot have such power. You are only a slave captured by the Body.

B. You say that you are more free than me? Are you? More free because you cannot run, cannot jump, sing, laugh, or fight?

S. I run through one hundred years. You run only in space.

B. There is light in space. Flowers bloom, bees hum. A beautiful summer afternoon stretches ahead. But what you call time is a damp and dark underground tunnel.

S. Oh, Bayon, my love.

B. Why do you leave it here? Bayon is the present. The forever-shining present. Love? Were you ever so beautiful as to be loved?

S. I'm dying. Each breath is agony. Oh, my Bayon.

B. Die! Perish! . . . You planned and constructed. That was your illness. My breast, like a bow, shines in the sun. Water flows, sparkles, and is still. You didn't follow me. That was your illness.

S. My Bayon . . .

B. The Spirit perishes, as a kingdom perishes.

S. It's the Body that perishes. The Spirit is imperishable.

B. You are dying . . .

S. Bayon . . .

B. You're dying.

S. . . .

B. What has happened?

S. . . .

B. No answer. Are you dead?

S. . . .

B. You are dead.

(*The sound of bird song*)

Look. The Spirit has died. A bright blue sky! Beautiful birds, trees, and Bayon protected by all these! I will reign over this country again. Youth is immortal. The

Body is imperishable. I won. It is I that am Bayon.

Early in 1970, Mishima surprised his friends by announcing that he would write no more plays. The drama had been such an important part of his life for so many years that his decision was incomprehensible: some put it down as a foible; others believed that he was tired by his struggle with *The Sea of Fertility* and had decided to concentrate all his strength on that single novel.

Not long before he killed himself, Mishima arranged a shelf of objects in his upstairs sitting room at home in Magome. These were a Greek vase, a small bronze nude of himself, a collection of translations of his books, and a stage model for the last scene of *Raio no Terrasu*. One evening he showed this display to some friends. "How do you like it?" he asked them in an ironic tone. "This really sums up my life, don't you think?" And he burst into laughter. (pp. 201-16)

Henry Scott-Stokes, in his *The Life and Death of Yukio Mishima,* Farrar, Straus and Giroux, 1974, 344 p.

BARBARA WOLF

(essay date 1975-76)

[In the excerpt below, Wolf discusses the thematic and stylistic scope of *Death in Midsummer, and Other Stories* and comments on the distinction between Mishima's personal life and his art.]

Death in Midsummer is almost a microcosm of Mishima's whole work, representing most of his major styles except for the polemic and the directly confessional. Together, the stories suggest both where he was broad in his concerns and limited by his obsessions.

Death in Midsummer must be surprising to those familiar with Mishima only through headlines. ["Death in Midsummer,"] which opens the collection, is quite unrelated to nationalism, fascism, homosexuality, or seppuku. Rather, it is an elegy on the death of the innocent, and a study of the psychology of mourning. The main character, Tomoko, is the mother of two young children who are drowned in a commonplace incident at a resort. Mishima's method is one with many affinities but no equivalents. The narration is a controlled Tolstoyan analysis, phase by phase, of his character's evolving perceptions, proceeding to an epiphany that is left as ambiguous as a Zen koan or haiku, and that is therefore utterly *un*-Tolstoyan. There is also something rather like Poe or Dostoevsky in the extraordinary lucidity of the descriptions, coupled with the intense hysteria of the passions described. Yet although the passions are hysterical, the person who suffers them is fundamentally sound, and not at all like a character out of Dostoevsky or Poe. Tomoko's irrational state is simply normal for one in her circumstances.

In "Death in Midsummer," the whole process of mourning is described as an unfolding of ironies and contradictions. Tomoko's grief is both hysterical and normal. Her recovery, which she feels is shameful, is perfectly natural. Her quest for meaning is both inevitable and futile. And to enrich the irony, the narrator places her ordeal in cosmic perspective: the children, who mean so much to their mother, mean nothing to Nature; they are swept away by a chance wave and not a sign is left on ocean, beach, or sky. The grief, the shame, the hunger for meaning, all define Tomoko as human; yet all are as irrational and futile as they are unavoidable. Tomoko's personal loss confronts her with something even more terrible: the void itself. Yet despite the void, as despite her grief, she goes on living, protected from destruction by the limitations of her intelligence, limitations not merely specific to her but essential to the species.

For all their outward diversity, the majority of Mishima's sympathetic characters come down to a type much like Tomoko: an individual entranced by inner conflicts, isolated from an exterior world as unconsciously cruel as it is beautiful. Yet it is the diversity that is more immediately obvious. At first sight, few works would seem less alike than "Death in Midsummer," with its bourgeois setting, chaste tone, and unsophisticated protagonist, and so extravagant a period piece as "The Priest of Shiga Temple and His Love." Yet the latter piece too is ultimately reducible to a series of internal perceptions and riddling contradictions.

The story is told in prose of great elaborateness and beauty. An aged monk of famed sanctity falls in love at first sight with a Grand Concubine from the Heian court. Just as his whole life to that point has represented the renunciation of this world for the next, hers has represented the empty enjoyment of the present:

The Great Priest was not young enough . . . to believe that this new feeling was simply a trick that his flesh had played on him. . . . [She] was nothing other than the present world, which until then had been in repose. . . . It was as if he had been standing by the highway . . . with his hands firmly covering his ears, and had watched two great oxcarts rumble past each other. All of a sudden he had removed his hands. . . .

But her response works at cross-purposes to his; as he seeks this world through her, she seeks the next through him. When they finally meet, it is in silence and tears. They feel some enormous event has occurred, but what it is is never made explicit, and no doubt it differs for each character, as it does for each reader. Religion and sensuality are both—and perhaps equally—triumphs of the spirit and follies of the flesh; but above all they are achievements and also deceptions of the imagination. Therefore, Mishima makes the Grand Priest's meeting with his love at once a consummation and an anticlimax, and as solitary an event as his return to his monastic cell.

For in **"The Priest and His Love,"** as in **"Death in Midsummer,"** the great struggles of the characters are not so much internalized as fundamentally internal. The characters live in worlds subjective to the point of isolation. Unable to share either values or feelings, they have nothing to go on but their own impulses and intuitions. Inner states may be set off by something outside the self, like the death of the children or the first glimpse of the Grand Concubine; but from that point on they assume an autonomous life and logic. The *moment* in Mishima tends to have such enormous consequences, because it so often represents a forced awakening from an innocence that is really a kind of unreflecting solipsism. In **"Death in Midsummer,"** Tomoko is literally napping at the moment her children drown; and the Great Priest has figuratively closed his senses to the present world.

Toshiko, heroine of the brief but powerful **"Swaddling Clothes,"** suffers a very similar awakening. When a low-ranking servant in her household unexpectedly gives birth to an illegitimate child, wealthy young Toshiko is shocked into pity and a kind of responsibility. She is aware for the first time of the injustice of the social order, and foresees a time when the despised infant must take revenge against her own pampered baby. This awakening, however, leads to nothing practical. Rather than offering material help, she is impelled toward a masochistic expiation. Deliberately going into the park at night, she invites assault by a young vagrant whom she identifies with the person the newborn outcast must become. Toshiko's sacrifice is both symbolically appropriate and fundamentally hysterical, a psychotic *acting out* rather than a purposeful *act*. Like that of Dostoevsky, and of Tolstoy in his last phase, Mishima's power seems largely a product of his own desperate sincerity, which is of a kind that can find no outlet in the world of action. Such passion creates grand, symbolic gestures, and characters and situations that seem to demand them—in art if not in life. (pp. 848-50)

The incompatibility of emotion and aesthetic beauty is one of the several themes of **"Onnagata."** The drama critic, Masuyama, is fascinated by the art of the Kabuki female impersonator, Mangiku. Mangiku's femininity is greater than any woman's, just as his theatrical roles are more grandly passionate than life. But his only place is on stage, in that bastard world "born of the illicit union between dream and reality." When

Mangiku takes his impersonation out of the theater and into the real world, he immediately disgraces himself and disillusions Masuyama.

With one exception, the rest of the stories in *Death in Midsummer* satirize the contemporary scene. **"The Pearl"** describes a club of housewives with nothing to do but manipulate each other. **"The Three Million Yen"** tells how a young married couple saves for middle-class possessions by giving sex shows for audiences like the housewives in **"The Pearl."** **"The Seven Bridges"** concerns a group of geishas, whose playful approach to a rite of their profession soon exposes their ugly selfishness. **"Thermos Bottles"** follows a smug businessman through his discovery that his perfect egoism has made him expendable to everyone. These modern types have neither beauty nor feeling to recommend them. They recognize nothing capable of transcending or ennobling the self, except possibly money.

How different from these, almost another species, are the Lieutenant and Reiko in **"Patriotism,"** as poetically idealized as their foils are satirically denigrated. **"Patriotism"** is an imaginative reconstruction of an actual double suicide performed by a young married couple trapped in a conflict of loyalties during the insurrection of 1936. The work is, in every sense, "highly wrought," a kind of heroic epic, or even opera, in prose. As charged with splendor and glory, with sensuality and death as *Tristan and Isolde,* it expresses the same striving after transcendence. The young couple's heedless sincerity endows them with the grandeur of figures in legend; or rather, it almost so endows them. But it is one thing to accept heroic gestures from personages at the dawn of history, acting upon archetypal situations, and another to accept them from twentieth-century persons committed to the wrong side of issues. Ironically, **"Patriotism"** succeeds for most readers only to the extent that Mishima's stylistic genius overbalances the theme he is apparently celebrating.

Every story in *Death in Midsummer* is rich in ironies, but perhaps the supreme irony is that the martyred lovers of **"Patriotism"** are the only truly happy characters in the whole volume. They alone are free from both triviality and alienation. They alone are in communion with each other and with the world. Their acceptance of a transcendent principle endows their emotions with beauty and meaning and permits them to live and die both serenely and intensely. Had they martyred themselves to almost any other ideal, it would be easier for liberal readers to sympathize and understand. For what is being celebrated in **"Patriotism"** is not thirties-style militarism per se, but the self-realizing force of idealism and the bliss of martyrdom. The specific principle is less the cause than the occasion.

Mishima's fiction is fiction, not polemics or pro-

Mishima with the Kabuki actor Utaemon in 1958.

paganda. It is true that a good deal of what he wrote conveys an open or implicit criticism of modern society. True, he traced much of the inauthenticity of modern Japanese society to the rejection of tradition that followed defeat in the Pacific war. It is even true that in his last years he became a spokesman for a kind of right-wing reaction, and ultimately martyred himself for that cause. But it is also true that practically nothing in *Death in Midsummer,* except possibly **"Patriotism,"** reasonably lends itself to a right-wing, or even political, interpretation. And only one story in all ten, **"Onnagata,"** is even remotely concerned with homosexuality. Mishima, of course, did write polemics and confessions, but only on a few occasions did he disguise them as fiction.

That Mishima could conceive no better solution for Japan than to revive its past was less a misfortune for him as an artist than as a man. It so happened that the desperate sincerity, disciplined violence, and paradoxical gentleness of the samurai tradition had affinities with fundamental traits of his own nature: his discipline as artist and athlete, his sadomasochism as a sexual being, his despair as a Japanese, his emotionality

as a person. These affinities were destructive to him as a man because they encouraged his tendency to hysteria. But the effect on his work was probably beneficial. Since Mishima universalized his private experience when he wrote, the passions and issues that concerned him personally were rarely allowed to intrude into his fictional universe. Within the limits of his sensibility, he could be an objective and dispassionate artist. Many of his characters do not resemble him at all, but are specimens of types held up for examination. Those in whom he did invest himself are far less likely to share his opinions and habits than his loneliness, his alienation, and his passionate integrity. In other words, the dovetailing of influences that produced hysteria in his life created intensity in his art, just as it did with Tolstoy, Dostoevsky, and Poe.

Mishima died attempting a double impossibility: to inspire Japan to reject the present and return to the past, and to make himself over into a man of the past, a samurai. When so futile a gesture is made in life, it can only appear as madness. But when it occurs in art, as in **"Swaddling Clothes"** or **"The Priest and His Love,"** then it takes on quite another meaning. We seek in art, after all, what we cannot have in a sane life: an unfettered expression of our feelings, wishes, fears, impulses, intentions; a direct confrontation with our human condition in all its madness and cruelty, its contradictions and tragic joys. Mishima declared that he wished to make a poem of his own life. That aspiration is the great romantic quest after the impossible, which in life must always lead to destruction but which is the source of the sublime in art. As an artist, Mishima may have been limited by his own obsessions, but he still gives a great deal of what we go to literature for. Because he kept his own opinions out, his characters and their situations transcend the time and place of their creation. Compared to that accomplishment, the success or failure of the rest of his life must fade into its relative insignificance. (pp. 851-52)

Barbara Wolf, "Mishima in Microcosm," in *The American Scholar,* Vol. 45, No. 1, Winter, 1975-76, pp. 848-52.

HISAAKI YAMANOUCHI
(essay date 1978)

[In the excerpt below, Yamanouchi finds the theme of alienation from life a primary subject of Mishima's novels.]

[Mishima's suicide] was rooted in what may be called his personal and aesthetic motives. No explanation, in either purely political or aesthetic terms, is adequate: the truth may be seen only from a due balance between the two. For Mishima's whole career was one of paradox built on an extraordinary tension between spirit and body, words and action, and artistic creation and commitment to the world. (p. 138)

Mishima's contribution to modern Japanese literature was immense. In embracing both traditional Japanese literary sensibilities and knowledge obtained from European literature he was as masterly as Sōseki and Akutagawa. In Mishima's case, however, the mode of amalgamating the two elements was far more complex than in his predecessors. The philosophy underlying his *seppuku* was definitely Japanese. The last phase of his vindication of Japanese cultural identity was fanatically nationalistic. The literary past and present, or Japanese tradition and Mishima's individual talent, were superbly synthesised in his *Five Modern Noh Plays* (*Kindai Nōgaku Shū* . . .). On the other hand Mishima was well versed in European literature. Raymond Radiguet and François Mauriac, for instance, are among those writers to whom the young Mishima looked for inspiration. Again, one of his plays was adapted from Racine's *Phèdre.* It is easy enough to detect in his work

literary elements of European origin, such as the Greek idealisation of physical beauty, sadism, satanism of Baudelaire's type, and so on. Further, in its logical clarity and rhetorical richness his prose style is by far the most distinguished in modern Japanese literature; he is one of the few Japanese writers whose prose can equal the best of European prose in these qualities. In his achievement, after all, Mishima surpassed many of his Japanese predecessors.

Mishima's place in the history of modern Japanese literature may best be clarified if we compare him with the I-novelists [who wrote autobiography in the guise of fiction] and especially with a typical example of their kind, Dazai Osamu (1909-48). (pp. 138-39)

The almost deliberate morbidity in Dazai's real life was unforgivable to Mishima. And yet Mishima shared with Dazai certain characteristics such as physical frailty, in his youth at least, and a sense of enmity towards the world. Mishima, however, differed from Dazai in that he was a man of extraordinary stoicism who continually transformed his own self into its opposite. Furthermore, Dazai's confusion between life and art led to the failure of the latter. This had a curious result. First, a sensitive and frail young Mishima tried to disguise his real life under a mask of wholesomeness. Secondly, he allowed room in his work for the gloom of his mind's abyss, but made every effort to make the created world of his work independent of his life. It will be my purpose to trace in Mishima's work a hidden morbidity somewhat like Dazai's, and to see at the same time how he succeeded, unlike Dazai, in maintaining the autonomy of his work through his perfect artistic method.

Confessions of a Mask . . . is a short example of a *Bildungsroman,* in which the hero's personal history is traced from his childhood to his adolescence. One of its peculiar features is the author's uninhibited treatment of sexual perversion. What matters, however, is not sexual perversion as such, but its wider implications. (pp. 139-40)

It is worth noticing that the hero's sexual perversion is curiously connected with his attraction to death. . . . The references to death are legion. . . . One may find here the elements that recurrently constitute the trinity in Mishima's novels: death, love (either perverted or not) and eternity.

The hero's obsession with death, furthermore, is placed in a historical setting. He feels his future to be a burden. Accordingly the prospect of death on the battlefield and even in an air-raid is attractive to him. Ironically enough, however, he is dismissed from the army on the very first day of recruitment. This intensifies his desire for death: he looks forward to the time when the American troops will land and devastate his native soil. The defeat in the war therefore deprives him of his hope and brings him back to normal life. Thus for the hero of *Confessions* there are antithetical values: war against peace, abnormality against normality, and inability against necessity to love women. One constitutes reality and the other mere fiction. In other words the hero stands at odds with the society of postwar Japan, which is fictitious only; reality lies in the products of his own phantasy. (pp. 140-41)

In a word the hero is a nihilist who cannot find any meaning in life and in a sense inherits the characteristics of the I-novelists in general and Dazai in particular. What then is the relation between the hero and the author? Is the former a mere reflection of the latter and, if so, would it follow that there is little to choose between Dazai and Mishima and that Mishima's dislike of Dazai is that of one's own counterpart? The question leads us to consider the meaning of the title of the novel: *Confessions of a Mask.*

At first sight the title appears self-contradictory. A confession must be the true voice of feeling, which indeed was the case with the I-novelists, but in Mishima's case it is spoken by a mask. What then is the meaning of the mask? Is it merely a device for the author to disguise himself? If so, the confession would be made by the disguised self of the author. But this author-hero identification does not explain the self-contradiction of the title. There must be something more in the implication of the mask. First, in the context of the novel, the mask could mean the hero who is unable to, and yet pretends to, love a woman. . . . It seems irrelevant to identify the hero with the author and to consider whether or not Mishima himself was homosexual. Certainly homosexuality in itself is an important theme, but it is also the means of presenting a larger theme. The stoicism of the hero who tries unsuccessfully to love a woman becomes a stoicism in putting up with the existing order of the world which he actually does not accept. The second meaning of the mask therefore, is the disguised self of the hero who is at odds and yet must somehow come to terms with the world. It is not the first but the second meaning of the mask that makes possible identification of the hero with the author and hence the third meaning of the mask. So long as Mishima shares with the hero nihilism and stoicism, the hero is the mask of Mishima himself. But the author is so well disguised under the mask of the hero that the confession is not as straightforward as that of the I-novelist. Viewed in this way, the title is not self-contradictory at all, but is a superb artistic device which made it possible for the author of this novel to detach his work from life as the I-novelists had never done before. And yet the fact remains that the nihilism of the hero inevitably reveals the abyss in the mind of the author himself, which made the artistic device all the more necessary. The author's own nihilism and his urgent need to disguise it under the highly ar-

tistic device were to become Mishima's major preoccupations.

Mishima's aim in *The Temple of the Golden Pavilion* . . . was to show the logical consistency of the protagonist's act of setting fire to the Golden Pavilion by enriching his character. On the surface the protagonist looks so defective that one might well call him an anti-hero. Nevertheless he is equipped with some important qualities. The theme of alienation from society is as dominant as in *Confessions.* (pp. 141-42)

From [an] analysis of *Golden Pavilion* there emerge such important features as the protagonist's estrangement from life, his nihilism or inability to find any positive meaning in life, and his obsession with beauty as an absolute value. In fact, these are all relevant to Mishima himself. And yet Mishima's art is so perfect that the created world of *Golden Pavilion* is completely autonomous. The work certainly reveals Mishima's own preoccupations, but there is no confusing the world of art with Mishima's own life. The world of his work in itself is a reality, perhaps even more real than life, and by attaining such a reality Mishima is able to survive his own enmity towards life. In simplified terms phantasy dominates over reality.

Nihilism or the concept of life as fiction still continues in Mishima's work in the 1960s. The precocious boy of thirteen and his companions in *The Sailor Who Fell from Grace with the Sea* . . . despise life as boring, hypocritical, sentimental, fictitious and ultimately meaningless. . . . [The] nihilism of the boys is the obverse of their cult of physical strength. The novel is an autonomous work of art detached from Mishima's own life even more perfectly than *Confessions* and *Golden Pavilion* and yet the curious fact is that worship of physical power is exactly what Mishima had been practising since the mid-1950s in order to transcend his fundamental nihilism.

What is particularly interesting about Mishima is the extraordinary tension between his life and works. In some of his works, such as *Confessions* and *Golden Pavilion,* the major characters, handicapped in various ways, cannot accept the external world except as mere fiction, and their hunger for eternity, coupled with their death-wish, makes them desire the end of the existing order of the world. In others, for example, *The Sound of Waves,* the major characters embody the fullness of life through their ideal physical strength. Here we have in fact the two sides of one coin: the former represents Mishima's own nihilism disguised under the highly artistic device of fiction and the latter Mishima's wish-fulfillment or search for his anti-self. In both cases it is characteristic of Mishima that in contrast to the I-novelists there is no simple confusion between his own life and the artistically created world of his work. Mishima was successful in creating a world of fiction not only as real as life, but even more real. To create such an autonomous world of fiction was the means of compensating for his sense of enmity towards the external world and hence of mastering life. In a word, writing novels as a kind of phantasy-making was for Mishima a means of survival and salvation. There is no doubt that Mishima conceived of *The Sea of Fertility* (*Hōjō no Umi* . . .) as the culmination of his creative work. (pp. 143-45)

The Sea of Fertility is much wider in scope, both thematically and structurally, than *Confessions* and *Golden Pavilion.* But it readily links up with the earlier works. The theme of alienation from life is represented even more dramatically by being reduced to the antithesis between life and death. Such characters as Kiyoaki and Isao, although one is socially immoral and the other a criminal, seem to demonstrate that death is absolute, eternal and pure, whereas life involves absurdity, banality and impurity. Honda, on the other hand, is essentially a rationalist, succeeding as a lawyer and attaining wealth. But he is also under the spell of the irrational: his faith in the idea of reincarnation and interpretation of Kiyoaki's diary and dreams. The ultimate physical decay of Honda and the futility of his life throw into relief the absoluteness of dream and death, which can be even more real than life itself.

The obsession with death and apocalyptic vision of the end of the world are pervasive elements in Mishima's novels. However, if we adopt the view that Mishima's work constitutes an autonomous world, these elements in themselves do not account for his own tragic death. What of the trilogy that deals with the coup d'état of 26 February 1936 [**"Patriotism" "Kiku on the Tenth"** and *The Voices of the Heroic Dead*]. . . . [In these works] we should notice a change in the relation between Mishima's life and art. In his earlier works the apocalyptic wish for the end of the world is conceived by negative characters who are handicapped in various ways and cannot master life. In the army mutineer, however, Mishima represents a character who is no longer handicapped but fulfils his personal integrity through physical strength. Curiously enough, this is exactly what Mishima practised in his own life.

In the last years of his life, martial activities were becoming conspicuous. . . . The remarkable fact was that Mishima's physical training proved useful for his mastery of life as much as the act of writing his novels. Thus Mishima came to find complementary to each other those things which had originally seemed antithetical: the world and words, life and art, body and spirit. As a corollary to this Mishima asserted the Japanese tradition of the union of literary and martial arts and Wang Yang-ming's concept of the unity of knowledge and action. Formerly, the created world of Mishima's art was a compensation for his disenchantment with his unmanageable life. Now Mishima was the master of both spheres of art and life, and, paradoxically enough, the two spheres came to encroach upon each other in a way they did not with the I-novelists. Now the muscular and masculine Mishima could realise his desire for an apocalypse in the sphere of action, and did so in his final attempt at a coup d'état and his own suicide. (pp. 148-50)

Mishima's death . . . was no mere passive defeat since he had the will to control his own life. The situation was one of paradox. If Mishima had remained the type of writer who, as in his earlier years, felt handicapped in life but compensated for it by creating his work, he would have kept on living in that mode. Now he had acquired physical strength, by means of which he could extinguish his own body so that his soul could live. It seems likely that for all his success as a great literary figure the external world remained alien to him and that the content of his life, even including his last attempt at a coup, was a product of his phantasy. He lived all along in a phantasy world, which could never be authentic except through serving the ultimate purpose of being transformed into an art form. (p. 152)

Hisaaki Yamanouchi, "A Phantasy World: Mishima Yukio," in his *The Search for Authenticity in Modern Japanese Literature,* Cambridge University Press, 1978, pp. 137-52.

NORIKO MIZUTA LIPPIT
(essay date 1980)

[Lippit has published numerous works on comparative literature, modern Japanese literature, and feminist issues. In the following excerpt, she examines the imagery and aesthetics of *Confessions of a Mask* (1949), describing it as the "story of the birth of an artist, that of Mishima himself."]

Kamen no kokuhaku (*Confessions of a Mask*), Mishima Yukio's second full-length novel, appeared in 1949, the fourth year of Japan's postwar literary activities, and established the literary reputation of the twenty-four-year-old Mishima instantly and unshakably. Although the novel shocked some critics and puzzled others, all of them recognized Mishima's undeniable and "unusual" talent, and agreed that he was a "unique," "new" writer whose writings were a marked departure from Japan's literary tradition. The novel was considered shocking and puzzling not only because its protagonist's confession of his homosexuality was unprecedented as a literary subject, but also because the protagonist's attitude toward the war and his experiences in it was diametrically opposed to the humanistic criticism of the war which characterized the postwar literary mainstream. The publication of the novel, therefore, was a significant event not only for Mishima, whose literary efforts had hitherto met a varied response, but also for postwar literary history. Soon after the novel appeared, Hanada Kiyoteru wrote that after a delay of half a century, Japan's twentieth century had started with the appearance of this novel.

Mishima himself considered the work to be "the logical conclusion" to his temperament, a temperament which infused the world of his early works. Yet *Confessions of a Mask* is a new starting point for his novels as well as the conclusion to his early works, for the "logical conclusion" meant not only the metaphysical or aesthetic clarification of his perception and temperament, but also the rationalization of his methodology, a way to fictionalize his temperament and thereby to create the world of his metaphysics and aesthetics.

Mishima, who considered himself a poet by nature, depended heavily upon his "temperament" in his early fiction. If *Confessions of a Mask* marks a new start in his literature, it is because the work is a "novel" while his early works are "poems," open expressions of his temperament; yet this "novel," like all of his others, is poetry in disguise.

Mishima stated that he had come to understand that the true substance of poetry is realization, and that he had decided to part from his "sensuous talent" and from his "sensuous perception" itself. He tried to do so by writing *Confessions of a Mask,* "forcibly, through the form of the novel." As Hanada said, the novel is filled with "logical lyricism" and is basically a poem in the form of a novel. Mishima created his own type of "novel" in his attempt to provide the "logical conclusion" to his temperament. Therefore, when Mishima stated that he had "somehow conquered his inner monster" by writing *Confessions of a Mask,* it did not mean merely that he had finally confronted his homosexual temperament, but also that he had found the way to deal with his desire to express his temperament in literature, the way to fictionalize his temperament.

Besides being a confessional novel, *Confessions of a Mask* is a novel about Mishima's method for the novel; indeed, it is as significant to Mishima's novel as *The Counterfeiters* is to Gide's. If the temperament and "sensuous perception" underlying his metaphysical and aesthetic world are poetry, this novel is the logical architecture of that world and the means to give it logical form (by fictionalizing it). For Mishima, the novel meant the method, and the question of the novel and the question of methodology were inseparable. Indeed, for Mishima, who preferred masks to real faces, structure to lyricism, and artificial effects to real facts, "fiction" was the key term.

When it first appeared, however, *Confessions of a Mask* was considered solely as an openly autobiographical work, an I-novel in which a bold confession of the author's homosexuality takes place. In fact, the protagonist of the novel is meticulously presented as identical to the author insofar as his biographical data are concerned. If the novel is a confessional I-novel, then the identification of the protagonist with the author is not in doubt, and the confession of the protagonist is the confession of the author. The novel must be understood accordingly as the removal of the protagonist-author's social mask, an exposé of the real face hitherto hidden behind the mask.

It is true that the protagonist constantly wears a mask and that he "gestures" in order to carry on his everyday life; he engages in "the masked theater to show it to myself," and the plot of the novel is the protagonist's realization of his "abnormality" and his analysis of his "life of gestures." There is no doubt that Mishima meant the protagonist to be taken as the author himself, as his meticulous effort to make the protagonist identical to him indicates, and it is also evident that Mishima intended to make his homosexuality public by writing this novel. Indeed, confession exists at the core of modern fiction, and the modern novel is a means for "confession." As can be seen in Flaubert's statement that Emma is himself, the fictional confession provides the basic metaphysics of the modern novel. If characters are masks through which the authors "confess," then the homosexual protagonist of Mishima's novel is the author's mask which enabled him to confess. *Confessions of a Mask,* then, must be understood as Mishima's self-revelation "in terms of " the protagonist. As Hanada pointed out, Mishima wore a mask in order to confess. The mask was Mishima's means of fictionalizing his inner drama.

What did Mishima intend to do by letting his protagonist confess, and what did he want to reveal by wearing the mask of the homosexual protagonist? Mishima was not like Shimazaki Tōson and Tayama Katai, writers who were urged on in their art by a desire for self-revelation for ethical or artistic reasons; nor was he like Shiga Naoya, a writer for whom the search for self provided the structure and the materials for his novels. Yet in creating his prototypal, ideal heroes, Mishima was almost exclusively involved in creating heroes who reflected various aspects of his own personality. Whether Mishima was an egomaniac seeking to express himself in terms of his heroes or merely tried fastidiously to identify himself with the heroes he created, there is no doubt that the protagonists' worlds were what inspired Mishima's dream and passion as his own inner world.

Mishima's well-known dislike of Dazai Osamu certainly reflects on the surface his criticism of those I-novelists who use openly their own weakness and desperation as subjects of literary pursuit. Yet one cannot but feel that Mishima's dislike of Dazai is due to his disgust at seeing in Dazai his own egotistical inclination exposed so defenselessly. Mishima's attack on confessional I-novels and their authors—brooding, self-destructive intellectuals who could be interested only in their own inner agonies—and his criticism of the tendency among Japanese writers to identify life and art, can best be understood as paradoxical rhetoric used to hide his egotistical involvement in himself.

Mishima was consistent, however, in insisting on his creative theory—that is, that art belongs to a logically constructed fictional world dimensionally different from that of life. Mishima stated that he started his writing by searching for a method to hide rather than to reveal himself. With Japanese writers who confused art and life in mind, Mishima declared, quite deliberately that for him art and life belong to different dimensions, just as intellect and flesh belong to different dimensions. At the same time, Mishima always revealed the central themes and essential qualities of his protagonists at the start of his novels. Whether they are criminals, perverts or madmen is made clear to the reader from the beginning, and Mishima's art is a kind of magic—his analysis of the mechanism of the human spirit—which draws the reader into the depths of the protagonist's world. Mishima's "logical" analytical eyes were always open, particularly when he described the protagonists who were masks for himself, and he was never "drunk" in writing the drama of his alter ego. Although there is no doubt that *Confessions of a Mask* is about himself, what is revealed by the confession is not the real face of Mishima; the novel is another "masked play," enabling him to survive not as a man who lives in daily social life, but to survive as a writer.

Prior to writing *Confessions of a Mask,* Mishima wrote several nihilistic aesthetic works which appeared anachronistic in the postwar literary atmosphere. He had already discovered his central theme, the life whose beauty and brilliance are supported by its impending annihilation. His "sense of ending" had already found the metaphors of summer and sea, metaphors which were to occupy an increasingly important place in his later works. Mishima started as a writer with his "aesthetics of annihilation (ending)" serving as the raison d'être for both his life and his art. Just as Mizoguchi in *Kinkakuji* (*The Temple of the Golden Pavilion,* 1956) felt threatened when he learned that the temple had escaped, now that the war was over and destruction no longer seemed inevitable, Mishima felt threatened by having to face the postwar era of peace in which a long life seemed assured to him, thus depriving his art of its basic metaphysics. The tragic stance which Mishima and his protagonists could assume when confronted by predicaments in which their death seemed assured would no longer be possible for them, and Mishima had to create new predicaments which would enable them to be tragic heroes, heroes in the world of his "aesthetics of the ending."

In this sense, *Confessions of a Mask* is his successful attempt to create a new "fate" for his hero, a fate that would condemn him to inevitable "destruction." In the novel, his destruction or death is only a social one, taking the form of absolute alienation in a spiritual sense from peaceful, "everyday life." The novel is a deliberate declaration of the identity of the author and his hero as masochistic homosexuals. The declaration is a challenge to society, but not a challenge to accept the protagonist-author as a homosexual. Rather, establishing his "abnormality" was an attempt to separate himself absolutely from the world of daily life and to force society, therefore, to condemn him.

The novel is, therefore, a rational articulation of his relation to the world and to the age. It is a novel in which Mishima made a statement about his "being in the world," to use Sartre's phrase, attempting thereby to retain the possibility of being identified as a tragic hero and thus to maintain his aesthetics of death. If Mishima "confessed" in the novel, he confessed his deep-seated fear of living in the peaceful postwar world where his raison d'être as a man and as a writer no longer existed. The tragic sentiment in the novel is that created by accepting the protagonist-author's fated destruction as the condition for his life's fulfillment. Mishima's hero is one who maintains a heroic stance in exchange for his own death. When there was no war to demand the sacrifice of young lives for the sake of the emperor, what fate could a man accept to die gloriously?

Mishima's homosexuality was a "fate" which he deliberately chose, a fate which separated him (and his protagonist) from ordinary life. For the protagonist, to whom the tragic is the only salvation of life, leading a daily life in which tragic fate is absent is "gesturing." Life is, after all, a masked play. Mishima's aspiration for the tragic was obviously conceived in terms of Nietzsche's Dionysus, whose aspiration for the tragic is an aspiration to transcend himself. The truly tragic hero, for Mishima, had to possess a beautiful body whose principle was being and action. The writer, engaged in words, could create a tragedy but could not participate in it. Likewise, the homosexual protagonist suffers from his initial awareness of the "nonexistence of the self," and yearns for a beautiful body—for a tragic hero. His homosexuality, therefore, is not only what separates him from daily life, but also what enables him to participate in tragedy by aspiring to be one with, that is, to love, a tragic hero. Fulfilling his aspiration for the beautiful flesh he lacks and for the heroic tragic death which he is not qualified to obtain requires a sacrifice of blood and death. The protagonist's love for St. Sebastian and Omi reveals this clearly.

In order to make his homosexuality "fate," it was necessary for both society and Mishima himself to condemn his trait or temperament. Mishima indicated that he regarded this temperament, a temperament without which his very identity would have been destroyed, as his enemy. Although his homosexuality or temperament was the fate he chose by his own will, it had to remain a negative element against which he had to fight. To desire not to be oneself was essential. By choosing the identity of a homosexual, he was able to stand alone against a hostile world, one composed of the totality of hostile others. Yet in order to maintain his temperament as negative, he had to remain immersed in the image of himself reflected in heterosexuals and thus exist in the consciousness of others constantly. The protagonist's masochism is a method of existing solely in the consciousness of others and thus gaining a sense of himself and of life.

In *Confessions of a Mask,* Mishima's protagonist finds that although he is unable to desire women, he can still love them. He feels that although he wears the mask of an ordinary man in his association with Sonoko, his love, when he is not in fact an ordinary man, love can exist between them. The world of love he shares with Sonoko is a world of spiritual eros, a world of harmony in which an aggressive life of the flesh is lacking. The earnestness with which he questions whether he can love a woman without desire makes it appear almost as though he is undertaking a religious quest to overcome the impossible, human limitation, and his agony appears to be that of the religious chosen. The mask almost becomes a metaphor for the human condition, and the novel impresses the reader as a tragic poem in disguise; yet life makes itself felt with a surge that threatens to overwhelm his body.

> Life-force—it was the sheer extravagant abundance of life-force that overpowered the boys. They were overwhelmed by the feeling he gave of having too much life, by the feeling of purposeless violence that can be explained only as life existing for its own sake, by his type of ill-humored, unconcerned exuberance. Without his being aware of it, some force had stolen into Omi's flesh and was scheming to take possession of him, to crash through him, to spill out of him, to outshine him. In this respect, the power resembled a malady. . . . As for me, I felt the same as the other boys—with important differences. In my case—it was enough to make me blush with shame—I had had an erection, from the first moment in which I had glimpsed that abundance of his.

It is when the protagonist meets an aggressive challenge of life that he is provoked to the eros of the flesh. The first man who sexually provoked him was a night-soil gatherer. His very fear of the crazed mobs at festivals or of revolutionaries driven into an ecstatic state by the aggressive force of life creates his ambivalent attachment to them.

> Through it all there was only one vividly clear thing, a thing that both horrified and lacerated me, filling

my heart with unaccountable agony. This was the expression on the faces of the young men carrying the shrine—an expression of the most obscene and undisguised drunkenness in the world. . . .

In his fantasies, he is constantly a victim attacked by animalistic mobs in action, pure flesh which is the embodiment of the aggressiveness of life itself. His fear, hostility and attachment to the pure flesh and his desire to identify himself with the aggressor he fears create his masochistic world of eros. Thus his relation to the world becomes his relation to himself. The protagonist's masochistic desire to identify himself with the aggressive force of life and Mishima's later fetishism of the well-built body both stem from Mishima's initial recognition of his lack of flesh and fear of flesh.

Defining oneself as an outsider, a "pagan" who cannot occupy a place in a normal, humane life, is one of the singular means artists have used for self-definition in modern industrial society, a utilitarian society hostile to art. Tonio Kröger's dichotomy definitely underlies Mishima's isolation from the "normalcy" of life.

In modern Japanese literature, such I-novelists as Katai and Toson converted their failure in everyday life into privileges of the novelist which would enable them to concern themselves exclusively with their isolation and to write about it. Dazai Osamu also deliberately acted out the role which others forcibly imposed on him. In Mishima's case, homosexuality presented a stronger rationale for the protagonist's isolation and uniqueness, for the isolation is physically real rather than just mental. As for Mishima himself, in like fashion precisely, his "abnormality" was the license for his art, his license for writing.

Mishima's hero, having lost the "blessing" of a tragic fate with which the war provided him, had to choose his own fate by his own will, a fate that would assure his destruction. In most of Mishima's works, the sense of life, the experience of eros, is inseparably connected with death, the death the protagonist envisions for himself. Yet in *Confessions of a Mask,* although blood and death provoke the protagonist to a sense of life and eros, he does not envision his own glorious death. Through his masochism, he attains a kind of heroism, but unlike the protagonist in **"Yūkoku" ("Patriotism"),** he does not actively seek his own death. This is because he is attracted by the erotic sweetness which the idea of death provokes rather than by death itself. Moreover, as in the case of Mizoguchi in *The Temple of the Golden Pavilion,* his fulfillment in homosexuality is his attempt to live. Mishima wrote that when he finished the novel, he felt clearly that he wanted to survive.

> After writing a novel like *Confessions of a Mask,* through which I conquered my inner monster in any

event, two opposing aspirations appeared clearly in the mind of the then twenty-four-year-old me. One was the feeling that I must live under any circumstance. The other was a leaning toward classicism that is precise, intellectual and clear.

Confessions of a Mask is the story of the birth of an artist, that of Mishima himself. The homosexual protagonist who at once fears and aspires for pure flesh is a metaphor for the writer who, belonging to the world of intellect, writes because he aspires for the tragic intensity of life. In this sense the novel is about himself, about the search for the author. The self-search of the protagonist is identified with the self-search of the author, his ontological quest for what he is; it is the self-search of "a creature, non-human and somehow strangely pathetic." In this sense the novel can be called truly confessional.

The novel is, however, a fictional work and not a real account of Mishima's life. In his notes for *Confessions of a Mask,* Mishima wrote that true confession is impossible ("the true essence of confession is its impossibility"), for only a mask with flesh can confess, and that he intended to write a perfect fictional work of confession. In order to pursue the ontological quest of the mask, a mask must deliberately be worn. If Mishima's mask were forcibly taken away, we might discover that there is neither a face nor any naked facts at all behind it; there would be nothing, or at best abstract passion, which was for him the substance of life. (pp. 181-90)

Noriko Mizuta Lippit, "Confessions of a Mask: The Art of Self-Exposure in Mishima Yukio," in her *Reality and Fiction in Modern Japanese Literature,* M. E. Sharpe, Inc., 1980, pp. 181-90.

SOURCES FOR FURTHER STUDY

Keene, Donald. "Mishima." *The New York Times Book Review* (3 January 1971): 4, 24-5.

> Memorial tribute to Mishima in which Keene reflects on their friendship and comments on the artist's suicide.

——. "Mishima and the Modern Scene." *The Times Literary Supplement* (20 August 1971): 989-90.

> Discusses Mishima's personal philosophy, reputation, and suicide. Keene notes contradictions between Mishima's lifestyle and his professed ideals.

Nathan, John. *Mishima: A Biography.* Boston: Little, Brown and Company, 1974, 300 p.

> Portrait by a translator and one-time friend of Mishima. Nathan had the cooperation of Mishima's family, and much of the description of the artist's early life is based on a biographical reading of *Confessions of a Mask.*

Petersen, Gwen Boardman. "Mishima Yukio." In her *The Moon in the Water: Understanding Tanizaki, Kawabata, and Mishima,* pp. 201-336. Honolulu: University Press of Hawaii, 1979.

> Introduces the major themes in Mishima's works and comments on the stylistic elements of his fiction within the context of Japanese literature.

Scott-Stokes, Henry. *The Life and Death of Yukio Mishima.* New York: Farrar, Straus and Giroux, 1974, 344 p.

> Account by a friend that attempts to explain Mishima's suicide in terms of the complex contradictions present in his life and evidenced in his works.

Wolfe, Peter. *Yukio Mishima.* New York: Continuum, 1989, 200 p.

> Biographical and critical study that exposes many of the unresolved conflicts of Mishima's life and works. Wolfe concentrates on Mishima's novels but also considers his dramatic works, which, Wolfe observes, encompass some of the author's more controversial ideas.

Molière

1622-1673

(Pseudonym of Jean Baptiste Poquelin) French dramatist.

INTRODUCTION

Molière is widely recognized as the greatest comic writer of seventeenth-century France and one of the foremost dramatists in world literature. In such masterpieces as *Le Tartuffe* (1664; *Tartuffe*), *Dom Juan* (1665; *Don Juan*), and *Le misanthrope* (1666; *The Misanthrope*) he set precedents that completely altered the focus and purpose of comedy, introducing realism to the French stage and elevating comic drama from farcical buffoonery to an important forum for social and religious criticism. Molière thus profoundly influenced the development of modern comedy and established comic drama as a legitimate literary medium, equal to tragedy in its ability to portray aspects of human nature.

Born in Paris, Jean Baptiste Poquelin was the eldest of six children of a well-to-do bourgeois who held a prestigious royal appointment as *valet de chambre* and *tapissier,* or upholsterer, to Louis XIII. Jean Baptiste was apprenticed in his father's trade but showed little inclination for the family business. The boy's interest in acting was sparked by his grandfather, who had a passion for the theater and occasionally took his grandson to see productions at the famous Hôtel de Bourgogne. Jean Baptiste attended one of the finest secondary schools in Paris and studied law briefly before inheriting his father's position at court. In 1642 he met and became romantically involved with Madeleine Béjart, a young actress. She and her family strongly influenced Jean Baptiste: in 1643 he formally renounced his royal appointment, sacrificing a highly respectable living to pursue a theatrical career. Within one year he adopted the stage name of Molière (possibly out of respect for his father's desire to avoid being associated with the theater, which was then deemed disreputable) and together with the Béjarts established the troupe l'Illustre Théâtre (The Illustrious Theater), in which he

2432

acted and of which he eventually became director and stage manager. But numerous expenses, the troupe's general inexperience, and Molière's particularly bad tragic acting led to the company's collapse in July 1645. Despite being sued for bankruptcy and temporarily imprisoned for the theater's debts, Molière continued to actively pursue his theatrical career, touring the provinces with the Béjarts as strolling players. During this crucial thirteen-year apprenticeship Molière wrote his first plays—*La jalousie de Barbouillé* (1645?; *The Jealousy of Le Barbouillé*), *Le médecin volant* (1645?; *The Flying Doctor*), and *L'étourdi* (1653; *The Blunderer*)—all short adaptations of Italian farces in the tradition of the commedia dell'arte.

Upon returning to Paris in 1658, Molière's troupe staged his farce *Le dépit amoureux* (*The Amorous Quarrel*); the play was greeted with overwhelming enthusiasm, and the production earned them both the favor of Louis XIV and the privilege of sharing a theater with the famous Italian performers of Scaramouche. In 1659 Molière gained lasting recognition with *Les précieuses ridicules* (*The Affected Ladies*), a one-act comedy of manners satirizing two foolish provincial ladies who imitate the artificial social graces and overrefined manners of the Parisian upper class. Molière's portrayal of pretentiousness in high society was so accurate that it outraged numerous aristocrats who believed themselves the targets of the dramatist's parody. Molière thus earned the first of many influential enemies; thereafter, his life and plays were almost always at the center of controversy.

In 1661 Molière wrote *Dom Garcie de Navarre* (*Don Garcia of Navarre*), a heroic tragedy that failed dismally, convincing him to relinquish his ambition of writing tragedy. The following year he married Armande Béjart, a twenty-year-old woman (thought to be either the sister or daughter of Molière's former mistress, Madeleine Béjart) ill suited to the reputedly serious nature of her forty-year-old husband; the union was unhappy and was marked by periodic separations. The extent to which Molière's marital difficulties affected his dramas is still debated, but the problems of marriage, especially between older men and much younger women, became the subject of many of his plays. Armande's uncertain parentage and rumored infidelities provided fodder for Molière's enemies, who, in the controversy following the production of his next play, *L'école des femmes* (1662; *The School for Wives*), accused him of incest and labeled him a cuckold. Written within a few months of his marriage, *The School for Wives* concerns the schemes of a middle-aged man to create a wife incapable of cuckolding him by raising her from girlhood in complete ignorance and innocence. Although it was Molière's greatest commercial success, the play was severely criticized as immoral and sacrilegious and its author was castigated for failing to

conform to formal dramatic rules. Molière responded in 1663 with two one-act plays, *La critique de "L'école des femmes"* (*The "School for Wives" Criticised*) and *L'impromptu de Versailles* (*The Impromptu of Versailles*) in which he defended his dramatic technique and satirized his enemies.

The charges of impiety against Molière peaked in 1664 with the production of his most renowned work, *Tartuffe*. The play reveals the intrigues of Tartuffe, a hypocritical spiritual advisor who attempts to gain control over an entire household by manipulating one man. Molière's daring exposure of the vices of false *dévots* and the hypocrisy of certain practices condoned by the Catholic church sparked perhaps the most important censorship battle of seventeenth-century France. *Tartuffe* was condemned as sacrilegious by people of almost every religious persuasion including the Jesuits and Jansenists—dominant rival factions of the Catholic church—as well as the influential underground society, Compagnie du Saint Sacrement, which boasted such powerful and prestigious members as Molière's former patron, Armand de Bourbon, Prince de Conti. These disparate sects all believed themselves the targets of Molière's satire—persuasive evidence of the misunderstandings the play fostered. Although *Tartuffe* was extremely popular with audiences and was acclaimed by Louis XIV, the Archbishop of Paris issued a decree threatening to excommunicate anyone who performed, attended, or even read the play. In the midst of the controversy, Molière produced *Dom Juan*, a cynical recasting of the legend of the irreligious libertine who embraces hypocrisy and commits unpardonable sins. *Dom Juan*'s sensitive subject matter invited further censorship from outraged church officials, who had the play suppressed after only fifteen performances. In an appeal to Louis XIV, Molière expressed his conviction that comedy could have a legitimate social and critical value: "I believe that I can do nothing better than attack the vices of my time with ridiculous likenesses; . . . hypocrisy is, without doubt, one of the most common, the most disagreeable, and the most dangerous of these." Although Louis was reluctant to oppose powerful religious interests, his personal support of Molière was unfailing, and it is possible that without his royal favor and protection, the dramatist might well have been executed for heresy. It was not until 1669—after the bulk of political and religious power had shifted away from his most adamant opponents—that Molière was permitted to perform publicly the final version of the play. Following the controversy surrounding *Tartuffe*, Molière reverted on several occasions to writing less consequential farces. Plagued with recurrent illnesses due primarily to exhaustion from overworking, the dramatist was diagnosed a hypochondriac by angry doctors whose profession he had parodied. Ironically, Molière died of a lung disorder in 1673 following the fourth performance of his final comedy, *Le malade imaginaire* (*The Imaginary Invalid*), in which he played the role of the hypochondriac. Molière's conflicts with the Church continued even in death. Denied both the ministrations of a priest and interment in consecrated ground because of his profession, he was granted but a serviceless funeral and that only after Louis XIV intervened on his behalf.

Commentators agree that Molière's strength as a dramatist lies in his diverse, insightful characterization rather than in his plots, a number of which have been deemed unoriginal, contrived, and awkward. Portraying recognizable characters in ordinary circumstances and using a simpler, more natural language than had been previously utilized by writers of farce or tragedy, Molière exposed artificiality and vice in society. His plays frequently depict a specific character flaw in its extreme—for example, the obsessive avarice of Harpagon in *L'avare* (1668; *The Miser*)—or pillory a social institution, as in the merciless ridiculing of members of the medical profession in *The Imaginary Invalid*. Juxtaposed with such monomaniacs as Alceste in *The Misanthrope* are such *honnêtes hommes* and *raisonneurs* as Alceste's rational counterpart, Philinte, who add balance and serve to restore social harmony at the play's conclusion. Though often extremely critical, even caustic, Molière's comedies are considered good-natured, and commentators note that they are surprisingly free of bitterness. Indeed, critics generally agree that rather than wishing to destroy existing social structures, Molière intended to point out specific, willful vices in hopes that society might eventually correct itself. This goal, along with Molière's desire to make audiences laugh, resulted in a legacy of dramas of human nature considered humorous yet profound.

In addition to the religious and moral criticism which he received during his career, Molière was attacked during his lifetime by critics who scorned his perceived crudity and his departures from such honored dramatic traditions as the five-act play and alexandrine verse. Nonetheless, Molière's innovations soon became the norm on the French stage as his rivals adopted his popularly successful style, and a number of playwrights of the English Restoration period adapted, translated, or borrowed freely from his comedies. Molière retained his stature abroad through the eighteenth century, but in his own country, his reputation again fell to that of a vulgar writer of tawdry farces which lacked the depth of serious theater. During the early nineteenth century, Molière returned to high esteem, championed by Romantic writers who saw his career as the great struggle of an iconoclastic individual against rigid classicism, as well as by social and political reformers who embraced his satire of institutions. Some scholars also contend his cause was bolstered by critical and nationalistic reaction against the German critic August Wilhelm von Schlegel, who savaged Molière's *oeuvre* in a series of lectures delivered between 1809 and 1811, dismissing his work as unoriginal, irrelevant, and "altogether obsolete." By the end of the century, Molière's admirers in France and abroad were so numerous and fervent as to secure him a preeminent place in the history of the stage. As early as 1835, critic C. A. Sainte-Beuve wrote: "In poesy, in literature, there is a class of men beyond comparison, even among the very first; not numerous, five or six in all, perhaps since the beginning, whose characteristic is universality, eternal humanity, intimately mingled with the painting of manners and morals and the passions of an epoch. . . . Molière is one of these illustrious witnesses."

During the twentieth century, scholars have probed virtually every literary, scientific, and historical aspect of Molière's work. Several valuable critical biographies by noted scholars, including Gustave Michaut, Brander Matthews, and John Palmer, appeared in the early part of the century. More recent studies have explored and analyzed the psychology of such renowned characters as Tartuffe, Don Juan, and Alceste. While scholars still seek philosophical, ethical, and religious messages in Molière's comedies, critical interest has, in many instances, shifted away from assessments of Molière's didactic intent toward purely aesthetic examinations of his comic technique, as exemplified by Will G. Moore's pioneering work, *Molière: A New Criticism* (1949). Variously considered a blasphemer, a moralist, a stinging social satirist, and a writer of pure comedy, Molière has, as Alvin Eustis notes, "borne a different message for each successive generation since his own." Heralded by critics of every century as the father of modern comic drama, Molière is esteemed for the universality of his comic portraits. As Matthews concludes, "Molière is in many ways . . . the embodiment of certain dominant characteristics of the French people. . . . But he is more than French, for his genius transcends the boundaries of race; it has the solid elements of the universal and the permanent."

(For further information about Molière's life and works, see *Literary Criticism from 1400 to 1800,* Vol. 10.)

CRITICAL COMMENTARY

PIERRE ROULLÉ

(essay date 1664)

[In the following excerpt from his *Le roi glorieux du monde* (1664), Roullé, one of Molière's most fervent critics in the controversy surrounding *Tartuffe*, condemns the morality of Molière and his work.]

A man, or rather a demon in flesh and habited as a man, the most notably impious creature and libertine who ever lived throughout the centuries, has had the impiety and abomination to bring forth from his devilish mind a play [*Tartuffe*] ready to be rendered public, and has had this play performed on the stage, to the derision of the whole church. . . . He deserves for this sacrilegious and impious act the severest exemplary and public punishment; he should be burned at the stake as a foretaste of the fires of hell in expiation of a crime which is a treason against heaven and calculated to ruin the Catholic religion by censuring and counterfeiting its most religious and holy practice, which is the conduct and direction of souls and families by means of wise guides and pious conductors. His Majesty, having severely reproached him, though moved by a strong indignation, has, in the exercise of his ordinary clemency, in which he imitates the essential gentleness of God . . . pardoned the devilish hardihood of this creature in order to give him time to devote the rest of his life to a public and solemn penitence; but, to keep this licentious and wicked composition from public sight and view, His Majesty has ordered the author, on pain of death, to suppress, tear up, stifle and burn all that he has set down, and to do nothing in the future so infamous and so unworthy, or to produce anything to the light of day so insulting to God and so outrageous to the church, religion, and the holy sacraments.

Pierre Roullé, in an extract from "Le Roi Glorieux du Monde," in *Molière* by John Palmer, 1930. Reprint by Benjamin Blom, Inc., 1970, p. 335.

FRANÇOIS MARIE AROUET DE VOLTAIRE

(poem date 1733)

[A French philosopher and one of the principal literary figures of the Enlightenment, Voltaire consistently championed individual liberties in his writing. In the following excerpt from his poem *Le temple du goût*, he imagines a meeting with Molière.]

I saw the inimitable Molière, and I made bold to accost him in these terms:

> Terence the sage, and the polite,
> Could well translate, but could not write;
> His elegance is cold and faint,
> He could not Roman manners paint:
> You the great painter of our nation,
> Have drawn each character and station;
> Our cits with maggots in their brain,
> Our marquises as pert as vain,
> Our formal gentry of the law,
> All by your art their likeness saw;
> And you would have reformed each fault,
> If sense and virtue could be taught.

(pp. 67-8)

François Marie Arouet de Voltaire, "The Temple of Taste," in *The Works of Voltaire: A Contemporary Version, Vol. X*, edited by Tobias Smollett, translated by William F. Fleming, revised edition, E. R. Du Mont, 1901, pp. 40-69.

HENRI VAN LAUN

(essay date 1875)

[In the following excerpt from a preface to his translation of Molière's works, Van Laun explores Molière's skill as a satirist through an examination of his characters.]

I think it will be generally admitted that Molière is the greatest comic poet France has produced, and that he is equal, if not superior, to any writer of character-

Principal Works

La jalousie de Barbouillé (drama) 1645?
  [The Jealousy of Le Barbouillé, 1876]
Le médecin volant (drama) 1645?
  [The Flying Doctor, 1876]
L'éstourdy; ou, Le contre-temps (drama) 1653; also published as L'étourdi, 1888
  [Sir Martin Mar-All, 1714; also published as The Blunderer; or, The Counter-plots, 1732]
Le dépit amoureux (drama) 1656
  [The Amorous Quarrel, 1714]
Les précieuses ridicules (drama) 1659
  [The Affected Ladies, 1714]
Sganarelle; ou, Le cocu imaginaire (drama) 1660
  [The Imaginary Cuckold, 1714]
Dom Garcie de Navarre; ou, Le prince jaloux (drama) 1661
  [Don Garcia of Navarre; or, The Jealous Prince, 1714]
L'école des maris (drama) 1661
  [A School for Husbands, 1714]
L'école des femmes (drama) 1662
  [A School for Women, 1714; also published as The School for Wives, 1732]
La critique de "L'école des femmes" (drama) 1663
  ["The School for Women" Criticised, 1714; also published as "The School for Wives" Criticised, 1875]
L'impromptu de Versailles (drama) 1663
  [The Impromptu of Versailles, 1714]
Le mariage forcé (drama) 1664
  [The Forced Marriage, 1714]
Le Tartuffe (drama) 1664; also performed as L'imposteur, 1667 and Le Tartuffe; ou, L'imposteur, 1669 [revised versions]
  [Tartuffe: or, The Hypocrite, 1714; also published as Tartuffe: or, The Imposter, 1732]

Dom Juan; ou, Le festin de pierre (drama) 1665
  [Don John; or, The Libertine, 1714; also translated as Don Juan; or, The Feast with the Statue, 1875]
Le médecin malgré lui (drama) 1666
  [The Forced Physician, 1714; also published as The Doctor in Spite of Himself, 1915]
†Le misantrope (drama) 1666; also published as Le misanthrope, 1851
  [The Misantrope; or, Man-Hater, 1714; also published as The Misanthrope, 1819]
L'avare (drama) 1668
  [The Miser, 1714]
George Dandin; ou, Le mary confondu (drama) 1668
  [George Dandin; or, The Wanton Wife, 1714]
Le bourgeois gentilhomme (drama) 1670
  [The Gentleman Cit, 1714; also published as The Bourgeois Gentleman, 1972]
Les femmes savantes (drama) 1672
  [The Learned Ladies, 1714]
Le malade imaginaire (drama) 1673
  [The Hypocondriack, 1714; also published as The Imaginary Invalid, 1876]
The Works of Mr. de Molière. 6 vols. (drama) 1714
The Dramatic Works of Molière. 6 vols. (drama) 1875-76
The Plays of Molière in French with an English Translation. 8 vols. (dramas) 1902-07

*Most of the English translations of Molière's plays were first published in the 1714 collection The Works of Mr. de Molière. A few first appeared in The Dramatic Works of Molière (1875-76).
†The English translation of this work was originally published in the journal Monthly Amusement in 1709.

comedies on the ancient or modern stage. His plays may be divided into six classes or groups:—*First,* the small dramatic poems or pastorals, such as *Psyché, les Amants magnifiques, la Princesse d'Élide, les Fâcheux, Mélicerte, la Pastorale comique,* and *Amphitryon,* which he wrote for court festivals, by order of Louis XIV.; *Second,* his farces, written to suit the taste of the less refined, such as *les Fourberies de Scapin, le Bourgeois-gentilhomme, la Comtesse d'Escarbagnas, Monsieur de Pourceaugnac, le Médecin mal-gré lui, George Dandin, le Sicilien, l'Amour Médecin, le Mariage forcé, Sganarelle,* and *les Précieuses Ridicules,*—and yet, notwithstanding their absurdity, attracting the higher classes by their witty descriptions of grotesque characters; *Third,* his comedies—*l'Etourdi, l'École des Maris, l'École des femmes, l'Avare, Don Garcie de Na-*varre, *le Dépit amoureux,* and *le Malade imaginaire*— in each of which the principal object seems to have been to bring into prominence one particular vice or folly, with all its necessary consequences; *Fourth,* those splendidly conceived plays, *Don Juan, les Femmes savantes, Tartuffe,* and *le Misanthrope,* which pourtray humanity in all its aspects; *Fifth,* those critical short pieces, *la Critique de l'École des femmes* and *l'Impromftu de Versailles,* in which, with masterly acumen, he defends his own plays and attacks his adversaries; and *Sixth,* those early attempts of his comic muse, *le Médecin volant* and *la Jalousie du Barbouillé,* which gave ample promise of what he afterwards became.

It is always difficult to state when a playwright has taken from any other author, for the saying, *"Je pre-*

nds mon bien partout où je le trouve'' has covered, and still covers, a multitude of literary sins. Moreover, Molière possessed a power of absorption and assimilation which enabled him so to vivify the materials he borrowed that they became new creations of incomparable value. In this sense, to take an idea or a mere thought from another author can hardly be called an imitation; and though Molière, in his first two or three plays, translated several scenes from Italian authors, he has scarcely ever done so in his latter pieces. To mention which of his comedies I consider, or rather which are generally thought, the best, would be difficult, where everything is so eminent; for in all his plays characters will be found which demonstrate his thorough knowledge of nature, and display his genius. To discover these little peculiarities in which the specific difference of character consists; to distinguish between what men do from custom or fashion, and what they perform through their own natural idiosyncracy; to select, unite, and draw these peculiarities to a dramatic point, demands real genius, and that of the highest order.

Generally Molière's satire is directed against hypocrites, against quacks, against the affectation of learning amongst ladies, and against snobbishness. If I were to enumerate, however, all the characters our author has created, I should arrive at the sum total of all human passions, all human feelings, all human vices, and at every type of the different classes of society. In *l'Avare* sordid avarice is represented by *Harpagon*, and want of order and lavish prodigality by his son *Cléante;* in *le Festin de Pierre* the type of shameless vice is *Don Juan, Donna Elvira* displays resignation amidst love disgracefully betrayed, *Mathurine* primitive and uncultivated coquetry, and *Mons. Dimanche* the greed of a tradesman who wishes to make money. *Tartuffe,* in the comedy of that name, represents hypocrisy and downright wickedness. *M. Jourdain,* a tradesman who has made money and who imitates a nobleman, is, in *le Bourgeois-gentilhomme,* no bad specimen of self-sufficient vanity, folly, and ignorance; whilst *Dorante,* in the same play, is a well-copied example of the fashionable swindler of that period. In *le Misanthrope, Alceste* pourtrays great susceptibility of tenderness and honour, *Célimène,* wit without any feeling, and *Philinte,* quiet common sense, amiability, intelligence, instruction, knowledge of the world, and a spirit of refined criticism. This is also displayed by *Chrysalde* in *l'École des Femmes,* by *Béralde* in *le Malade imaginaire,* and by *Ariste* in *l'École des Maris;* whilst *Sganarelle* in the latter play is an example of foolish and coarse jealousy. *George Dandin,* in the comedy of that name, is a model of weakness of character and irresolution, *Angélique,* an impudent and heartless woman, and her father, *Monsieur de Sotenville,* the coarse, proud, country squire of that age. *Argan,* in *le Malade imaginaire,* represents egotism and pusillanimity; *Vadius* and *Trissotin,* in *les Femmes sa-*

vantes, pedantic foolishness and self-conceit; *Agnès,* in *l'École des Femmes,* cunning as well as ingenuity; and *Aglaure,* in *Psyché,* feminine jealousy. Finally, *Nicole, Dorine, Martine, Marotte, Toinette,* and *Lisette* personify the homely servant-girls, who, possessing plain, downright common-sense, point out the affectation and ridiculous pretensions of their companions and superiors; whilst *Claudine,* in **George Dandin,** Nérine, in **Mons. de Pourceaugnac,** and *Frosine,* in the *Avare,* represent the intriguant in petticoats,—a female *Mascarille.* (pp. i-iii)

Another not less remarkable faculty of Molière is that the language his personages employ is precisely suited to them. It varies according to their age, character, rank, and profession, whilst the very sentence becomes long or short, stilted or tripping, pedantic or elastic, finical or natural, coarse or over-refined, according as an old or young man, a marquis or a citizen, a scholar or a dunce, has to speak. It can be said of Molière, more than of any other author we know, that he always employs the right word in the right place. . . . Even his peasants speak correctly the dialect of the province or county Molière gives them as the land of their birth; all his creations bear proofs of his genius in an incisiveness of expression and clearness of thought which no other writer has equalled.

Molière has written some of his comedies in prose, others in verse,—and in verse that has none of the stiffness of the ordinary French rhyme, but which becomes in his hands a delightful medium for sparkling sallies, bitter sarcasms, well sustained and sprightly conversations. He has also managed blank verse with wonderful precision,—a rare gift among French authors. The whole of *le Sicilien,* the love scenes of the *Avare,* the monologues of *Georges Dandin,* and certain scenes of *le Festin de Pierre,* are written in this metre.

Molière's plays have been translated into every language of Europe, and some of them even into the classical tongues; they have found admirers wherever intellectual beings are congregated; they have been carefully conned and studied by literary men of every age and clime; and Goethe himself read some of these comedies every year. (pp. iv-v)

Molière wrote his plays to be represented on the stage, and not to be read in the study only; that therefore we must recall, on reading him, the change of voice, the step, the smile, the gesture, the twinkle of the eye or movement of the head in the actor. Thus we are never tired of perusing him; he never cloys; we can remember all his good sayings, quote them, study him again and again, and every time discover fresh beauties.

A remarkable characteristic of Molière is that he does not exaggerate; his fools are never over-witty, his buffoons too grotesque, his men of wit too anxious to display their smartness, and his fine gentlemen too fond of immodest and ribald talk. His satire is always kept within bounds, his repartees are never out of place, his plots are but seldom intricate, and the moral of his plays is not obtruded, but follows as a natural consequence of the whole. He rarely rises to those lofty realms of poetry where Shakespeare so often soars, for he wrote, not idealistic but character-comedies; which is, perhaps, the reason that some of his would-be admirers consider him rather commonplace. His claim to distinction is based only on strong common sense, good manners, sound morality, real wit, true humour, a great, facile, and accurate command of language, and a photographic delineation of nature. It cannot be denied that there is little action in his plays, but there is a great deal of natural conversation; his personages show that he was a most attentive observer of men, even at court, where a certain varnish of over-refinement conceals nearly all individual features. He always makes vice appear in its most ridiculous aspect, in order to let his audience laugh at and despise it; his aim is to correct the follies of the age by exposing them to ridicule. (pp. vi-vii)

Henri Van Laun, in a preface to *The Dramatic Works of Molière, Vol. I,* translated by Henri Van Laun, William Paterson, 1875, pp. i-xviii.

W. P. KER
(essay date 1922)

[In the following excerpt from a 1922 essay, Ker focuses on *The Misanthrope* in an evaluation of Molière's skill at comic drama.]

To begin with, let the Devil's Advocate have his say. Molière's enemies provide him with arguments; Molière's best friend among the poets, Boileau, admits some of their charges, particularly that of clowning and buffoonery. . . . It is not a charge that can be lightly evaded, and it is not farfetched or hypercritical. It is there all the time, and the English reader need not be primed with Meredith's *Essay on Comedy* in order to see the difference between Scapin and the Misanthrope. Is it worth while, when Don Juan is on the scene, to get a laugh out of the blow which is meant for Pierrot and lands on Sganarelle? Not even the *Misanthrope* is safe: the scene with Alceste's stupid servant at the end of the fourth act is noted by the corrector as rather too elementary for the finest of all comedies in the world.

The finest? Yes; and so fascinating that true believers, who of course are true lovers, will swear, as they follow it, that it is the only play in the world—here at last the quintessence, the eternal Idea, not in abstraction, but full of the life and movement of pure comedy, nothing omitted, nothing lost, nothing left over for other comic poets to attempt. This frame of mind, which is worship, may of course be misunderstood; it is going too far, says the sober critic. After all, there are other plays in the world, and Congreve's Millamant is not discountenanced in comparison with Molière's Célimène. But to the true believers this is irrelevant: they have found in the *Misanthrope* the end of their quest for the very essence of comedy; here they are at home, triumphant. And here, naturally, the noise of the adversary is silenced—his censures and complaints not refuted, simply ignored. (pp. 350-51)

Molière in his critical remarks on his challengers says many things very quietly and shortly that sum up and dispose of long, large, and tedious controversies. Thus on the dramatic unities (in the *Critique de l'Ecole des Femmes):* "These are easy notes made by good sense to secure the pleasant effect of the play, and good sense is capable of the same at any time without recourse to Horace or Aristotle. *Je voudrois bien savoir si la grande règle de toutes les règles n'est pas de plaire"* ["I should much like to know whether the grand rule of all rules is not the art to please"]. The result of this on the Abbé d'Aubignac and other patrons of the unities is like the simple speech in *The Emperor's New Clothes:* "The Emperor has nothing on." Hear what the innocent child says! (pp. 351-52)

Matthew Arnold, it is true, in his essay on the French Play in London (when the Comédie-Française came here in 1879), thinks that Molière ought to have been a tragic poet, and that he was put off by the weakness of French tragic verse. The critic, with his favourite device of quotation, has no difficulty in contrasting the effect of the French tragic Alexandrine with that of Shakespeare's blank verse, or in proving that the rhythms and rhymes of *Hernani* leave him cold. It may be admitted that Molière's verse in heroic drama—that is, in *Don Garcie de Navarre*—makes little attempt to do better than the ordinary conventional style, and does not scruple to repeat "vos divins appas" ["your divine Charms"] and similar customary phrases, which make one think of the notary's eloquence in a later most admirable French comedy: "Daignez, Mademoiselle, corroborer mes espoirs!" ["Deign, Mademoiselle, to corroborate my hopes!"]. But Matthew Arnold's objection to French verse leads him too far when he finds *Tartuffe* and the *Misanthrope* actually suffering from their burden of rhyme. "The freshness and power of Molière are best felt when he uses prose, in pieces such as the *Avare* or the *Fourberies de Scapin* or *George Dandin."* The freshness and power of Molière's prose who would deny? But it is going too far to find his genius better expressed in *L'Avare* or in *George Dandin* than in the two great rhyming comedies; to find in the verse of Alceste and Célimène constraint and artifice. M. Rigal is surely more plausible when he detects in

LE TARTVFFE

Engraved handbill for an early production of *Tartuffe*.

Racine the pupil of Molière, using for tragedy the natural easy mode of dialogue which is the poetry of Molière. There is no need, for the present, to say more on this point: what is really important is that Molière did not think less highly of his dramas because they were not tragical; that he saw and appraised truly the right task of the comic poet. . . . It is not that the lovers of comedy are hard to please: contrariwise, they find true comedy everywhere—in fragments and patches and medleys. What they do not find, or hardly, is the perfect work, where the Muse herself conducts the orchestra, and nothing is flat, superfluous, or grating. The *Misanthrope*—some would add *Tartuffe,* and some *Les Femmes Savantes,* but the *Misanthrope* surely—has this place. Here is what is meant by comedy.

The persons are few, but no one notices this as a defect or a lowering of vitality. There are enough for the whole world of good society to be represented there. It is the comedy of good manners, like not so very many: not like *Tartuffe,* or *L'Ecole des Femmes,* or *L'Avare.* One other play of Molière's, *Les Femmes Savantes,* keeps to the true world: without are *bourgeois* and peasants. But *Les Femmes Savantes* is the play of

good manners in a different sense from the *Misanthrope:* it is narrower in scope, being more definitely satirical and depending on "humours" more occasional and transitory than the eternal contradiction, the immortal harmony of Alceste and Célimène. The scene of Trissotin and Vadius is all very well in its way, but it is rather mechanical and caricatural: it is not out of place in *Les Femmes Savantes,* though that play, in the main, is more subtle than this scene: but there is no room in the *Misanthrope* for any such exhibition. In the *Misanthrope,* it is true, the sonnet of Oronte belongs to the world of *Les Précieuses* and of *Les Femmes Savantes,* but it is not introduced to show up the faults of fashionable taste: that is a secondary thing: its real purpose is to bring out Alceste's uncompromising sincerity. We are gainers by the way in hearing the lovely old verse of Alceste's ballad. . . . But the theatrical value of this lies in Alceste's refusal to be conventionally polite, and in his disgust at Philinte's conventional compliments.

The characters in the *Misanthrope,* as usual in comedy (and not infrequently in real life also), fall into contrasting pairs—Alceste and Célimène, Alceste and Philinte, Célimène and Arsinoé. Philinte, the good-natured, easy-going man of the world, has to argue with his friend's stubborn principles to prove that truth is not always convenient. Arsinoé, a very valuable person, a prude in the old as well as the later sense of the word, well deserving her place in the comedy, puts out her cold malignity against the more lively and brighter mischief of the spirit of Célimène. Part of the play, indeed most of it, is in the old fashion of debates and contentions—the mode from which, as Mr. Neil showed us in his edition of the *Knights,* all comedy is descended. Now contrasts and debates on the stage are dangerous; they may look too much like got up things, not imaginative, but merely calculated contrasts. The way to cure this is to use imagination to fill up the abstract outlines. And there is another way, well understood by Molière and nowhere more excellently employed than here, and that is to let the surrounding world, the fashion of life common to all the characters, have its right proportion in the story. Atmosphere counts for as much in the *Misanthrope* as in the "Meniñas" of Velasquez: the people on the stage are not, as many of the Elizabethan *dramatis personae* are, hard-shelled individual atoms of humanity, moving in worlds unrealised, without any visible means of subsistence. The fashion of the age is one of the antagonists of Alceste, but it is much more than an object to be railed at for complacent and undiscriminating flattery. It is much more than that, and more than Alceste recognises. If he himself were not in that world, living as part of it along with Célimène, Philinte, Oronte, Arsinoé, and a few marquises, his proud soul would be nothing to us; and it is Molière's great success that he has kept this world alive, along with and through his characters.

Are the friends of Molière to be judged according as they judge Célimène? It is a very delicate question, and indeed it must not be pressed. The facts of the case are considerably against the lady; she is, if not perfidious, at any rate not scrupulously sincere, and she speaks with a cruel tongue. Are we to accept the obvious judgment, and congratulate Alceste on being well rid of her? Possibly not.

The historians of Molière tell us that the comedy of Alceste and Célimène followed the heroic comedy of *Don Garcie de Navarre,* and used over again some of the drama of jealousy that had failed to impress the public in its original shape. *Don Garcie* undoubtedly was a failure, and as a failure it is often allowed to remain unnoticed. But there are some strong scenes in it, and they have their bearing on the *Misanthrope.* Don Garcie is not Alceste; he is simply the humour of jealousy dressed up for an heroic Spanish play; with just enough human life to serve for a contrast to the noble lady Done Elvire. Elvire in the heroic comedy is not a counterpart of Célimène, except that she has a half reasonable man to deal with: Elvire is much less amusing than Célimène, being no more than true heart and good sense. But in her treatment of Don Garcie, since the problem is not unlike what Célimène has to face, we can to some extent make out what Molière had at the back of his mind. He does not tell us everything about Célimène, and the partisans of that lady may be justified in believing that she is worth fighting for. And it may be said here that generally those who refuse to take the ordinary view of Beatrix Esmond will be found, with as much wisdom or the want of it, on the side of Célimène. Done Elvire gives them some encouragement. She has to talk to a man, Don Garcie, who is jealous perpetually and on all sorts of occasions: she explains to him that it will not do, most admirably; and, contrary to the usual practice of elegant females in drama, she does not take the first opportunity of misunderstanding her lover, nor even the last occasion, when she might have broken with him for ever and incurred no blame. What would she have said if Don Garcie had been of the same mind as Alceste? Clearly she would have told him a truth or two, plainly but with no bitterness; she would not have let him go; neither would she have accepted his lodge in a wilderness as a feasible scheme of a happy life. She would have seen the vanity of the creature, have felt that his emulation of the noble savage was really selfish, a touch of the egoist; and since Alceste, though suffering from "the distempered devil of self," is a right sort of man, he would have come round. Molière, it is proved, had not forgotten Don Garcie when he wrote the *Misanthrope;* if Célimène at the end does not talk like Done Elvire, it is not that Molière thinks she has no case to

defend. What Alceste exacts from his wife to be is more than Done Elvire would have yielded, we are sure of; and that being so, we refuse to think the worse of Célimène on account of Alceste's indignation.

The English ("tardy, apish nation" though they may be) need not be altogether discontented when they review their transactions with Molière. . . . John Dennis was one of the first Englishmen to see the Alps "with a delightful Horrour, a terrible Joy," and one of the first to praise Molière:

> For *Molière's* Characters in his *Tartuffe* are Masterpieces, mark'd, distinguish'd, glowing, bold, touch'd with a fine yet daring Hand . . . ['Tis] by this Comedy and by the *Misanthrope* that Molière perhaps has born away the prize of Comedy from all Persons in all Ages, except Ben Jonson alone.

"Ben Jonson alone" we may find unnecessary, but this is proof of Dennis's good faith. His strong language is not careless or indiscriminate, nor is his regard for Ben Jonson merely literary or antiquarian. . . . Happily there is no compulsion laid on us to compare Molière with Ben Jonson, nor with Shakespeare either. (pp. 352-59)

Shakespeare seems to have been left free to choose his subjects and vary his methods as he thought fit. Molière has very little freedom: he is hindered in *Tartuffe,* an invention of his own; he is hindered in *Don Juan,* which was anyone's subject, as hackneyed as Punch and Judy. He is dependent on the Court, and is called on for *comédies-ballets;* he has to please the parterre, and he gives them (not all grudging) the thumpings of Sganarelle and the mockery of Medicine. Terence is translated to Tabarin (the zany of a mountebank), as Boileau complained; the *Phormio* of Terence to the *Fourberies de Scapin.* And this near the end, close upon *Les Femmes Savantes.* To the last of his days, and he died in the *Malade Imaginaire,* he kept the old talent for all the fun of the fair, and with all his irritability and nervous ill-temper he never seems to have found anything wrong in it, anything degrading in a change from high to low comedy. He had his great disappointments; not to speak of the *tracasseries* ["bickering"] about *Tartuffe* and the *Festin de Pierre,* he must have been hurt at the failure of *Don Garcie de Navarre,* at the poor success of the *Misanthrope.* But does he ever complain of anything that is required of him for the King's entertainment? Never, except incidentally when he has not enough time to invent, compose, rehearse, and stage what is wanted. Nor is there want of spirit in the compulsory pieces. *Les Fâcheux* is not a play; it is a hurried set of odd characters, satire rather than comedy. Nothing in Molière is livelier, though you may hesitate whether the greatest and therefore the most amusing bore is the hunting man or the gentleman who insists on your hearing his hand at piquet, all of it, to the end. . . . The French stage in the House of Molière has never discouraged the more obvious sort of comedy, and it is really part of the spirit of Molière that he should have agreed with the groundlings in their easy laughter, as well as with the quality in their finer shades.

> "Courage, Molière! violà la bonne comédie!"
> ["Courage, Molière! This is a good comedy!"]

That was the voice of the people, they say, after *Les Précieuses Ridicules.* It was a good opinion, though the cry of "Courage!" was not needed for one of the bravest spirits that ever lived. This essay is written to salute his memory on his birthday, with a grateful sense that "la bonne comédie" finds inexhaustible variety of meaning in his works, and, further, that when all is said, the people of this island, which gave shelter to Saint-Evremond in his exile and a hearty welcome to the Comédie Française at a later date, may fairly ask leave to praise the author in whom they see more clearly than in any other the spirit and soul of France. (pp. 360-62)

W. P. Ker, "Molière," in his *Collected Essays of W. P. Ker, Vol. I,* edited by Charles Whibley, Macmillan and Co., Limited, 1925, pp. 350-62.

ALLARDYCE NICOLL
(essay date 1949)

[Nicoll's writings on the history of drama have been praised for their thorough research and their inestimable value to scholars and students of the theater. In the following excerpt, Nicoll evaluates and provides an overview of Molière's career.]

All the comic authors of the second half of the seventeenth century . . . fade into insignificance when we turn to Jean-Baptiste Poquelin, who, under the name of Molière, stood forward in this time as one of the greatest masters in the art of comedy that the world has known. (P. 318)

Before *L'étourdi* it is possible, even likely, that Molière had written one or two short farces; if so, we have a suggestion of their style in two pieces, *La jalousie du Barbouillé (The Jealousy of Le Barbouillé)* and *Le Médecin volant (The Flying Doctor),* first published in 1819 from an early manuscript. Clearly based on the style of the *commedia dell' arte,* yet displaying affinities with medieval farce, they well illustrate the manner in which their author may have served his apprenticeship, drawing strength and assurance from the popular French tradition, and enlivening that with material

taken from Italian sources. The former play introduces to us a jealous fool, Le Barbouillé, married to Angélique. At a loss to know what to do, he consults a doctor, who, refusing to listen to him, gives him a long discourse on his own merits. In the end, thinking to trap his wife as she returns home late from a party, he is himself locked out of his house and severely chided by Angélique's father. Equally slight is the plot of *Le médecin volant.* Here also a doctor appears, but in this case a pretended one. Gorgibus, father of Lucile, does not wish his daughter to marry Valère, whereupon the young man's servant, Sganarelle (played by Molière himself), takes upon him to dress as a doctor, and, despite his ridiculous patter, completely dupes Gorgibus and is thus enabled to effect the union of the lovers. . . . The title of the farce comes from the fact that in the course of his intricate deception Sganarelle is forced to impersonate not only the doctor, but also his own supposed twin brother—all of which necessitates his flying on and off the stage in disguise and out.

For the longer and more pretentious comedy of *L'étourdi* Molière passed from the *commedia dell' arte* to the *commedia erudita,* choosing for inspiration *L'inavvertito (The Indiscreet Man),* by Nicolò Barbieri, already used by Quinault for his *L'amant indiscret.* The plot is little more than a series of episodes. Lélie is in love with Célie, and in order to win her agrees that his servant, Mascarille, should indulge in a series of stratagems. To the disgust of this witty and ingenious rogue, however, Lélie destroys plot after plot by his blunderings. Sometimes he wrecks his servant's plans through ignorance of what is being arranged, sometimes through excessive honesty, sometimes through his own love obsession. There is an undoubted advance here upon the style of the short farces, but dramatic intricacy is lacking, the characters are as yet only surface-drawn, and there is no sign of that comedy of social criticism which later was to prove Molière's greatness.

After the series of episodes in this play we move to a mass of complication in *Le dépit amoureux (Lovers' Spite;* acted first at Béziers in 1656), another work based on an Italian comedy—*L'interesse (Self-interest),* by Niccolò Secchi. Although it can hardly be esteemed to show an advance upon *L'étourdi,* individual scenes exhibit a widening of the author's dramatic skill. Such episodes, for example, are the lovers' quarrels, which are the core of the play, and the scene in which Albert tries in vain to get the attention of the pedant Métaphrase. . . . (pp. 318-20)

Towards the end of the year 1658 Molière brought his company to Court and won royal favour with a repertoire of farces, his own and others'. To those he added, in 1659, *Les précieuses ridicules (The Affected Ladies)*—also a farce, but a farce with a mighty difference. Here for the first time the individual style of the author becomes apparent, for *Les précieuses ridi-*

cules is in essence a social comedy. The externals of the plot are not unlike those of many earlier plays—the disguising of a witty servant—but in this case the servant's masquerading has a different dramatic purpose. When Mascarille parades as a marquis it is not in order to cheat an old man and win a lady for his master, but to expose the absurd affectations of the ladies themselves. In the cult of preciosity, fed by the interminable romances of the time, Molière saw an object well worthy of the laughter of social comedy; he sought to entertain, and to reform through entertainment. The Marquis has himself carried directly into the house, and the girls at once are infatuated with his elegant hauteur and languid grace. "My dear," says Cathos, "we should call for chairs"; "Almanzor," replies Madelon to her page, "convey me hit her at once the appliances of conversation." To cover her mistake in thus vulgarly alluding to chairs, Cathos turns to the Marquis: "For pity's sake," she begs,

> do not be inexorable to that armchair which for the last quarter of an hour has stretched out its arms to you; satisfy the desire it has of embracing you.

The attack on what was then a fashionable diversion of Parisian Society soon had various ladies of the Court protesting violently, and, although Molière assured them that he was but aiming his shafts at absurd provincials, he found that the hornets' nest he had aroused suggested the taking of more cautious steps for at least the immediate future. In *Sganarelle, ou le cocu imaginaire (Sganarelle; or, The Cuckold in his own Imagination)* he accordingly produced an innocuous, and a highly successful, farce in which the citizen Sganarelle thinks his wife unfaithful and yet cannot rouse up courage enough to seek vengeance on her supposed lover. He considers the claims of honour, lets prudence calm his rage, and then, with anger once more rising, comes to his final conclusion. He will address himself to some manly action:

> Yes, my blood is up, I will revenge myself on the scoundrel, I will be no coward! And to begin with, in the heat of my passion, I am going to tell every one everywhere that he is living with my wife.

After a somewhat unfortunate excursion into the field of tragi-comedy *(Don Garcie de Navarre)* the actor-dramatist once more swung back to social comedy in *L'école des maris (The School for Husbands)*, the first truly great comedy from his pen, and one destined for a lengthy career. Although lacking the ease and organic structure of some of his later works, this comedy, based on Terence's *Adelphi* and on Lope de Vega's *Discreta enamorada*, exhibits clearly the qualities that give him his real title to fame—the development of a social comedy in which excesses are ridiculed wittily, good sense is enthroned, and the golden mean is made the

prize of man's endeavour. Externally this comedy is, like Ben Jonson's, classically realistic; like the English dramatist, Molière endeavours to present in imaginative terms deeds and language such as men do use; yet there is an essential difference between the two. Jonson bent all his energies to the creation of satire, and the things he satirized were those follies that touched him nearly; for Molière the task was to shed comic laughter on follies he deemed inimical to the social structure. Jonson was ego-centred; Molière's orientation was towards the society to which he belonged.

The School for Husbands is somewhat mechanically planned, but Molière's typical approach is well exemplified in its scenes. The two main characters are set before us at the very beginning—Ariste, who argues that one should bow to the ways of society, and Sganarelle, his brother, who churlishly insists on the expression of his own individuality. "We should always fall in with the majority," says Ariste, "and never cause ourselves to become conspicuous. All excesses are offensive, and every truly wise man ought not to display affectation either in his dress or his language, but willingly follow the changing customs of his time." These two men are revealed in relation to their wards, Isabelle in the charge of Sganarelle and Léonore in the charge of Ariste. Where the socially amenable Ariste allows Léonore her freedom, the puritanically individualistic Sganarelle insists on imposing his will upon Isabelle. The greater part of the play is devoted to showing how this girl, irked by the restrictions imposed upon her, eventually tricks her guardian and marries Valère, while at the end Léonore expresses her willingness to marry Ariste, whose kindness has won her heart. Poor Sganarelle, the misanthropist, is left alone cursing the female sex and the more strongly confirmed in his misanthropy.

Following *The School for Husbands* came the rather slight sketch entitled *Les fâcheux (The Bores)*, which formed a *comédie-ballet* presented before the King in 1661. *L'école des femmes (The School for Wives)* soon followed, and in this Molière made a notable advance in his comic art. The serious element is overpronounced in *The School for Husbands:* brilliant as are many of the scenes, the play is written to a thesis. Far greater freedom and more liveliness in the character delineation animate its successor. The difference between the two comedies may be realized when we contrast the Ariste and Sganarelle of the one with the other's Chrysalde and Arnolphe. Basically they represent the same types, but here the types are made richer and more delicately humanized. Arnolphe is also a surly individualist, but instead of having a philosophy on which his actions are dependent, he is presented as an ambitious, self-confident egotist. Similarly, Chrysalde appears not as a mouthpiece for a particular view of life, but as a good-humoured, cynical man of the world. (pp. 320-23)

The play immediately made a stir, and there were not wanting moralists and literary critics who attacked its contents and its style, whereupon Molière made dramatic history and added to his stock of comic scenes by penning the first play upon a play—*La critique de l'école des femmes (The School for Wives criticized)* Climène, a *précieuse*, feels faint with disgust after seeing it; Uranie protects it against her strictures; Élise satirically agrees with Climène; a marquis thinks it must be altogether silly because it has proved so popular; the poet Lysidas feigns to praise, but easily allows himself to reveal his belief that such pieces are not true comedies. Into the mouth of Dorante Molière has put his own defence. He argues that the general applause given to the drama is a testimony to its value and to good sense, that the "rules of art" cannot be taken as definitive laws. "I should like to know," he remarks, "whether the greatest rule of all rules is not to please, and whether a piece which has gained that end has not followed the right road."

The controversy continued. Edmè Boursault gave to the Hôtel de Bourgogne his *Le portrait du peintre, ou la contre-critique de l'école des femmes,* whereupon Molière replied with *L'impromptu de Versailles (The Impromptu at Versailles),* in which his actors are gathered together for a rehearsal. Here, again, Molière seems to have been making dramatic history: the play within the play was a well-known device, but this seems to be the first "rehearsal" piece on record. Ironically he hits out at the style of acting at the Hôtel de Bourgogne. Once more a single individual, Brécourt, is introduced to put forward the claims of common sense. The comic author does not present satirical portraits, he argues: "The business of comedy is to represent in a general way all the defects of men, and particularly those of our own age"—and consequently he ought to remain free from the strictures of those petty individuals who fail to see that in his work is to be found a corrective for society.

Immediately after these plays came a couple of slight *comédies-ballets—Le mariage forcé (The Forced Marriage)* and *La Princesse d'Élide (The Princess of Elis)* both acted in 1664, the one at the Louvre and the other at Versailles. Neither deserves much attention, although the former—which shows Sganarelle anxious to marry, and then, having seen his future wife's flirtatious propensities, at the end aghast at the thought of the wedding—is written with verve and gaiety.

A third time Molière was asked during this year to contribute in the diversion of the Court, but instead of these two flimsy shows his chief offering to the gorgeous spectacle at Versailles, entitled the *Plaisirs de l'île enchantée,* was the first version of his deepest and his bitterest comedy, *Tartuffe, ou l'imposteur (Tartuffe: or, The Impostor).* We cannot tell precisely, of course, what relationship this bears to the drama we now possess, but the fact that, after its Court performance, it was not again given until 1667, and then was forbidden public representation until 1669, suggests that basically it contained the same material as that with which we are now familiar.

Here was the most complete fusion of comedy and purpose. From the portraits of folly Molière now turns to vice. Tartuffe is a sensual, self-seeking hypocrite who trades on credulity. Fastening upon the dull-witted Orgon, he insinuates himself into his household and threatens to bring it to complete disaster. Only his own lust and his over-confidence, brought to betrayal by the innate honesty of Orgon's wife, result in his unmasking, discomfiture, and punishment. Technically the comedy is a true work of genius. For two entire acts Tartuffe himself does not appear before us, yet a powerful impression of his personality is built up through the references to him on the part of the other characters: thus the looming character of his personality comes upon us with the greater force, while his eventual entry is made the more impressive. In the first scene the bigoted Madame Pernelle, mother of Orgon, gives him praise, while his true nature is hinted at in the words of Damis, her grandson, and the maid, Dorine. The whole family is set before us in inimitably etched lines, so that we are thoroughly acquainted with their personalities before ever the main figure appears—and his appearance is effectively contrived. Dorine, the maid, is on the stage when he enters. Catching sight of her, he immediately turns to his servant:

> TARTUFFE. Laurent, lock up my hair-shirt and my scourge, and pray Heaven ever to enlighten you with grace. If anybody comes to see me, say that I am gone to the prisons to distribute my alms. . . . (*Turning to* DORINE) What is it you want?
>
> DORINE. To tell you—
>
> TARTUFFE. (*taking a handkerchief out of his pocket*) Ah! Heaven! before you speak to me, take this handkerchief, pray.
>
> DORINE. What's the matter?
>
> TARTUFFE. Cover this bosom, of which I cannot bear the sight. Such objects hurt the soul, and are conducive to sinful thoughts.

Almost at once we see him making love to Élmire, Orgon's wife; Damis, her son, tells his father, and Tartuffe shows his genius by refusing to deny the specific accusation; instead, he piously declares that he is "a wicked, guilty, miserable sinner," and, when Orgon angrily turns on his son, magnanimously chides his patron:

Ah! let him speak; you blame him wrong-
fully, and you would do better to believe
what he tells you. Why should you be so
favourable to me in this instance? Do you
know, after all, what I am capable of doing?
Do you, brother, trust to the outward man;
and do you think me good, because of what
you see? No, no, you are deceived by appearances, and I am, alas! no better than
they think. . . .

His unmasking comes only when Orgon is persuaded to listen while he makes further love to Élmire
and seeks speciously to argue that she may without sin
lie with him because of "the purity of the intention."
Even then he is not defeated and almost succeeds in ruining Orgon, who is saved only by direct intervention
of the King.

There is an atmosphere here closely akin to that
of Jonson's *Volpone,* but, whereas in the English play
there is hardly a worthy character among all the *dramatis
personae,* and whereas all these *dramatis personae* are exaggerated caricatures, Molière's domestic interior, although treated idealistically, is true to life, and good
shines among the bad. Madame Pernelle is the typical
old bigot, Orgon the besotted fool, Élmire the wife who
would rather suffer inconveniences than have trouble
in the house, Dorine the keen-eyed little maid, Damis
the honest youth who has not tact enough to make his
honesty known. In reading *Volpone* we are not concerned with the interests of society; in *Tartuffe* Molière
seeks to arouse laughter that he may warn his fellows
of an insidious danger.

Tartuffe was a hypocrite: in *Don Juan, ou le festin
de pierre (Don Juan; or, The Banquet of Stone)* Molière
delineated the atheist for whom no conventional morality has any meaning, the brave soul whose daring
leads him to disaster. There is a mood of continual dissatisfaction about his hero; like Faust, although in another way, he seeks for the unattainable. . . . Accompanied by the timorous Sganarelle, he is revealed in diverse aspects, in the end—like Tartuffe—donning the
garb of the hypocrite in order to effect his purposes,
and after this final evil being consumed in hell-fire,
while Sganarelle, true to the spirit of comedy, can think
only of the money owed him and now lost to him for
ever:

Oh! my wages! my wages! His death is a
reparation to all. Heaven offended, laws violated, families dishonoured, girls ruined,
wives led astray, husbands driven to despair, everybody is satisfied. I am the only
one to suffer. My wages, my wages, my
wages!

An apparently more joyous play followed—
L'amour médecin (Love is the Best Doctor), acted in

1665 as part of an elaborate *comédie-ballet*—but the bitter
tone apparent in the two dramas immediately preceding cannot quite be concealed by its gaiety. The plot is
a simple one. Lucinde, daughter of Sganarelle, pretends
illness in order to further her love-affair with Clitandre.
Four pompous doctors are called in to attend her, and
spend most of their time in boring talk about the social
aspects of their profession. Eventually Clitandre dresses as a physician, declares that Lucinde's trouble is
mental, and persuades Sganarelle that she must be hu-
moured:

CLITANDRE. However, as one must flatter the
imagination of patients, and as I see in your
daughter signs of distress of mind that
would be dangerous if prompt remedies
were not administered, I have made use of
her own fancies and have told her that I was
here to ask her of you in marriage. Then her
face changed in a moment, her complexion
cleared up, and her eyes brightened. If you
keep up that delusion in her for a few days,
you will see that we shall save her. (pp.
324-28)

L'amour médecin was followed by what many
critics regard as Molière's greatest play, *Le misanthrope,* in which his comic view of life becomes darker
and his consideration of man more philosophic. Basically this is a study in the opposition in the human
being between his own individuality and his needs as
a social animal. The central figure is Alceste, a character
akin to the individualist of *L'école des maris,* but more
intimately and effectively delineated. The empty po-
litenesses that accompany social life arouse his anger
and annoyance; why, he asks, should he praise a
wretched sonnet on which his opinion is requested or
bow and smile to a man whom he has no intention of
seeing again? To his own disgust he finds himself emotionally attracted by the young widow Célimène, a gay,
flirtatious coquette, and the greater part of the comedy
is occupied with tracing his repulsion to her follies and
his paradoxical desire to possess her. Contrasted with
him is the good-humoured, complacent Philinte, who,
while recognizing the absurdities of the world, is prepared to accept its manners and to comply with its conventions. The two sides of the picture are presented
with scrupulous balance. Alceste is undoubtedly a figure that stirs in us both admiration and sympathy;
compared with Célimène, he possesses an honesty and
integrity wholly worthy. Yet the individualist is an
ever-potent menace to his companions; the only logical
course for him and for the society to which he belongs
is to have him sent out in loneliness to a desert. This,
indeed, is the end of Alceste. Célimène's frivolity has
been amply demonstrated, but even a realization of her
pettinesses cannot kill the love for her he has in his
heart: he consents to forgive her, on condition that she

will follow him into the solitude where he has vowed to live. "What!" cries Célimène, "renounce the world before I grow old, go and bury myself in the wilderness?" Alceste argues with her:

> But if your love answers to mine, what can be to you all the rest of the world; are not all your desires centred in me?

> CELIMENE. Solitude at twenty years of age frightens me. I do not find in my heart greatness and self-denial enough to yield to such a fate; if the gift of my hand can satisfy your wishes, I am willing; and marriage—

This offer Alceste indignantly rejects, and the play ends with his departure, while Philinte and Éliante prepare for their common-sense wedding, and Célimène retires, no doubt to capture other hearts. These characters are sensible, yet to the very conclusion the balance is preserved: there is a moving quality in the hero's final words:

> As to myself, betrayed on all sides and crushed with injustice, I will escape from a gulf where vice triumphs, and look in all the earth for a desert place where one may be free to be a man of honour.

Laughter, gay and uninhibited, comes again in *Le médecin malgré lui (The Doctor in spite of Himself)*, in which a woodcutter, Sganarelle, is mistakenly forced to act as a physician. . . . (pp. 329-30)

Many plays were still to follow, although some, such as *Le Sicilien, ou l'amour peintre (The Sicilian; or, Love the Painter)*—an anticipation of the *opera-comique*—may be disregarded. *Amphitryon*, except for the vivacious part of Sosie (written for himself), does not add much to the body of his work, and *Georges Dandin, ou le mari confondu (George Dandin; or, The Baffled Husband)*, although replete with verve, is little more than an elaboration of *La jalousie du Barbouillé*, with development of character and the provision of a firmer social background.

In *L'avare (The Miser)*, as in *Amphitryon*, Molière sought his theme among the plays of Plautus, selecting for this purpose the *Aulularia*. Although this play is superior to [*Amphitryon* and *George Dandin*], it betrays a falling off from the brilliance of *Tartuffe* and *Le misanthrope*. The miser, Harpagon, is rather farcically conceived, and the plot tends to be confused. One has the double impression that Molière, unlike Ben Jonson, is not at his happiest in dealing with miserliness and that his skill of hand is declining. What is of interest, however, is the manner in which the French dramatist has departed from his original by associating the old man with a large household instead of leaving him an isolated recluse. Within that household, too, there is one per-

son, Maître Jacques, who is a masterpiece of comic portraiture. He is both cook and coachman, and keeps two coats ready for his assumption of either of his two duties. A somewhat stupid but good-willed fellow, he provides much of the laughter of the play.

A *comédie-ballet* entitled *Monsieur de Pourceaugnac* followed in 1669—a merry record of the painful adventures suffered by a provincial lawyer among the professional sharks of Paris. In this piece Molière experimented upon, and considerably improved, the comic-opera style already tried in *L'amour médecin*. The mediocre *Les amants magnifiques (The Magnificent Lovers)* was of the same character, as was also the joyous *Le bourgeois gentilhomme (The Bourgeois Gentleman)*, produced during the same year. The picture painted of M. Jourdain is superb. A middle-class shopkeeper who has amassed a small fortune, he determines to figure in the world of Society. He enters in dressing-gown and nightcap, having been told that in this wise aristocrats hold their morning levees; amid the dancing- and music-masters whom he has summoned to instruct him he meanders along in simple-minded delight. Soon the professional teachers are at each others' throats, each claiming the superiority of his own subject, until the exponent of philosophy, flying at his companions, remains lord of the stage. *"Nam sine doctrina vita est quasi mortis imago,"* declares the philosopher. "You understand this, and you have no doubt a knowledge of Latin?" "Yes," replies M. Jourdain; "but act as if I had none. Explain to me the meaning of it." "The meaning of it is that 'without science life is an image of death'." "That Latin is quite right," says M. Jourdain. A ludicrous lesson follows, and rises to a culmination in Jourdain's famous discovery that he has been speaking prose all his life without knowing it. Into this world of the fantastically real the Turkish episode at the end fits with perfect harmony: M. Jourdain is made a Mamamouchi by a group of men disguised to hoodwink him, and the play ends with the simple, foolish, and rather pathetic little shopkeeper thoroughly pleased with himself and entirely ignorant of the figure of fun he has become.

In *Les fourberies de Scapin (The Tricks of Scapin)* a return is made to that admixture of *commedia dell' arte* and native farce with which Molière began his work, with Scapin keeping the scenes in constant movement by his skilful impostures. Provincial pretensions are satirized in the rather slight *La Comtesse d'Escarbagnas*, and then, somewhat surprisingly after these efforts, comes the magnificent *Les femmes savantes (The Learned Ladies)*. Here the theme is that of education for women. Central in the picture is the pedantic Philaminte, the middle-aged wife of the honest bourgeois Chrysale, who neglects her home for the sake of philosophy. She has two daughters, Armande, a prudish *précieuse*, and the common-sense Henriette. Clitandre is the lover, once the wooer of Armande, but, disgusted by her affectations, now the avowed adorer of her sister. Philaminte deems him too unlearned to marry one of her daughters, preferring the wit Trissotin. On this basis the comedy proceeds. Armande professes repugnance at the thought that Henriette can even dream of marriage—although secretly and almost unknown to herself she is consumed with jealousy. Poor Chrysale tries from time to time to put in a word, but the masterful Philaminte ever bears him down. One hilarious occasion occurs when the maid Martine is being dismissed. Chrysale tentatively inquires the cause, but is soon forced to berate the girl without knowing why: he eventually discovers that she has been guilty of using a word disapproved of by a famous grammarian. Towards the very conclusion of the drama, when Philaminte seems certain to compel Henriette to marry Trissotin, a *deus ex machina* appears in the person of Chrysale's brother, Ariste, who falsely announces that the family has lost all its money: Trissotin immediately backs out of his pretensions to Henriette, while Clitandre nobly offers the household all he possesses. Anticipating many a later sentimental heroine, Henriette now refuses to wed Clitandre, because she would not burden him with their poverty, when Ariste reveals the fact that his news was merely a device to expose Trissotin. The last words are spoken by Chrysale, anxious at last to assert his authority: turning to the notary, he bids him, "Execute my orders and draw up the contract in accordance with what I said."

The brilliance of this comedy cannot be denied, and yet that last sentimental note is troublesome: it is an indication that a new world is approaching. Molière's own career, however, was now near its end. Suffering from a disease he knew would soon bring his end, he ironically penned his last comedy, *Le malade imaginaire (The Imaginary Invalid)*, at the fourth performance of which he collapsed and died. Argan here is a hopeless hypochondriac who surrounds himself with doctors and apothecaries, and it is his person who dominates in the play. Opposed to him is the gay maid Toinette, whose frank enjoyment of life and refusal to think of the morrow provides a vivid contrast to his dark thoughts. A further foil is established in Argan's brother, Béralde, who, mocking the hypochondriac's fancies, counsels a visit to the theatre to see some of Molière's plays. It is in this scene that Béralde quotes the author himself as saying that he will have nothing to do with the doctors:

> He is certain that only strong and robust constitutions can bear their remedies in addition to the illness, and he has only just strength enough to endure his sickness.

Thus closed Molière's career. During its course he had succeeded in creating a comic world which places him among the greatest of comic playwrights. Building

from the individual, yet concerned with the presentation of types, he wrote plays in which an inimitable gallery of memorable portraits is placed before us. His fundamental attitude is one of common sense; frankly he accepts the world, and strives to show that excesses of all kinds are fatal to the even tenor of social life. Although his plays include many farces, and even his darkest comedy contains much of hilarity, his greatest power lies in his skill in arousing what has been called "thoughtful laughter," where a smile takes the place of the guffaw and in the mind is left a dominant concept. Logical proportion, avoidance of extremes, honest acceptance of the facts of life, the application of reason to social affairs—these were the messages which Molière constantly preached to his fellows even as he contributed richly to their entertainment. (pp. 331-34)

Allardyce Nicoll, "Molière and the Comedy of Manners," in his *World Drama: From Aeschylus to Anouilh,* George G. Harrap & Company Ltd., 1949, pp. 316-34.

JAMES F. GAINES
(essay date 1984)

[In the following essay, Gaines examines *The Miser* in relation to the rise of the bourgeoisie in seventeenth-century France.]

All social groups must come to grips with problems and tensions within their own boundaries as well as with intergroup confrontations. The survival of the bourgeoisie in seventeenth-century France, torn by bouts of internal strife, depended on a deceptively delicate balance of social engagements and reciprocal gifts, exchanges of children and wealth that were institutionalized in the form of marriages and dowries. . . . We of the twentieth century, who are accustomed to viewing the emerging bourgeoisie through a glass darkened by merchant villains like Dickens's Ebenezer Scrooge and Uriah Heep, Balzac's Baron Nucingen and his accomplice Du Tillet, or Flaubert's Monsieur Lheureux, may too easily forget how essential compromise and reciprocity were to the bourgeois clans during the insecure era before the appearance of organized capitalism and the self-made man. Fernand Braudel's theories about the *ancien régime's* overriding concern with "material life" and "capital before capitalism" help to put in a proper perspective the force of mutual dependency in the thought of Molière's fellow citizens.

The divine and secular approbation of social relations evoked by Domat found its most perfect expression in the rite of marriage, which provided for a contractual blending of family fortunes in the form of dower and dowry, as well as for the continuation of the lineage through another generation. (pp. 169-70)

[It] would be unreasonable to expect universal observation of even a mutually beneficial standard such as the code of bourgeois reciprocity; the system of exchange contained, and may even have encouraged, a certain number of disruptors—individuals who attempted to destroy the balance of familial alliance for egotistical ends. The phenomenon of imbalance appears to some degree in many of Molière's plays, often in combination with other structural failures. For example, the *précieuses ridicules,* Cathos and Magdalon, refuse to accept bourgeois reciprocity. So do Sganarelle of *L'Ecole des maris* and Arnolphe of *L'Ecole des femmes.* Yet, it was not until 1668 that a five-act play, *L'Avare,* was devoted particularly to the struggle between reciprocity and imbalance.

The words spoken by *L'Avare's* protagonist, Harpagon, at the end of a desperate soliloquy on the theft of his buried gold, are most revealing: "Je veux faire pendre tout le monde; et si je ne retrouve mon argent, je me pendrai moi même après" ["I will hang the whole world; and if I do not find my money, I will then hang myself "]. These utterances express the miser's lonely struggle against a society he can neither understand nor control. They guarantee Harpagon a prominent place in the pantheon of greed, along with such other literary creations as Shakespeare's Shylock, and Le Sage's Turcaret. Yet, Molière takes care to show that, unlike Shylock who extends credit to Venetian merchants, or Turcaret, who farms the king's taxes, Harpagon is not a professional usurer and has no institutional justification for his avarice. Rather than serving the monarch or the business community, he preys upon gullible heirs and seeks to gobble up their patrimonies. Compared to the nonprofessional miser on whom he is based, Euclion in Plautus's *Aulularia,* Harpagon is far more active and dangerous; for Euclion accidentally discovered his gold in a fireplace and passively continued to hide it, but Harpagon seeks to enlarge his treasure by illicit means. From Boisrobert's *La Belle Plaideuse* Molière derived the striking scene of a father arranging to lend at usurious rates to his own child. When angered, Shylock is content to pursue his creditor Antonio in the courts, and Turcaret quells his rage by smashing china; but Harpagon nearly leaps into the audience in his frenzied persecution of those who took his treasure. Molière thus invites the reader to inquire whether his miser's pattern of behavior can be of any benefit to household, family, or state, or whether it threatens, on the other hand, to destabilize the bourgeois world reflected in the play.

Among the numerous status indicators in *L'Avare,* the key to establishing Harpagon's condition as a distinguished burgher is the large sum of money he has hidden in his garden, 10,000 écus, or about 30,000 livres tournois—enough money to buy a political office in the sovereign courts, to establish an attractive dowry, or to pay about one hundred servants' salaries for a year. A messenger who arrives in the third act with further business propositions leads one to suspect that the 30,000 livres may represent only a fraction of Harpagon's cash reserves, which in turn make up, according to Pierre Goubert's research, less than ten percent of most bourgeois fortunes.

As befits his standing, Harpagon has a house, a carriage and team, and numerous servants, including his son's valet La Flèche, Maître Jacques the cook-coachman, the maid Dame Claude, two lackeys named La Merluche and Brindavoine, and most important of all his *intendant* Valère. The services of the latter were required only in a large estate with diverse business interests and farmland, for his duties included dealing with the tenant farmers and signing sharecropping leases, as well as auditing the accounts of the *maître d'hôtel.* The existence of a nearby farm is suggested by the arrival of a *cochon de lait* ["suckling-pig"] in act five, an event that the bloodthirsty Harpagon misinterprets, for he believes at first that it is the robber who is to be split open, grilled, broiled, and hung. It was common bourgeois practice to invest heavily in property in the nearby countryside and to stipulate that part of the rent be paid in kind in order to furnish the larder.

These social indicators tend to depict Harpagon as a member of the middle bourgeois stratum, which produced many magistrates and other public officers. . . . *Officier* or not, Harpagon is identified with the upwardly mobile segment of the bourgeoisie that yearned for nobility. He has clearly risen above the precarious level of the struggling artisan. Even those for whom immediate *anoblissement* was impossible would attempt to "live nobly" from the interest on conventional investments, to avoid any dishonorable activity, and to hope that, with the passage of time, their descendants might, through the accumulation of offices and marriage alliances, elevate themselves to the *état* ["state"] of nobility.

Molière's audience would expect a man in Harpagon's position to be absorbed with the concerns of his lineage. The son had to be provided with a legal or financial office or with a commission in the army, as well as with a dower for marriage. Even more crucial was the daughter's dowry money, which might well claim the major share of the patrimony. Not only would this sum be the bride's only sure resource in case of need, but the quality of son-in-law it attracted, and his chain of alliances, might also have a decisive effect upon the rise of the family. (pp. 170-73)

Having determined as nearly as possible from the status indicators in *L'Avare* the social identity of Harpagon and the normative concerns that Molière's contemporaries would have associated with this level, one must return to the text to appreciate the nature of the miser's transgressions. According to the master plan explained in the first act, Harpagon's son, Cléante, is betrothed to an old widow, his daughter, Elise, to the ancient Anselme, and the miser himself is to wed the young Mariane. The obvious danger in this design is that none of the couples is very likely to produce off-spring, thus threatening the survival of the lineage in an age when, as most demographers would agree, nature was given free rein to produce all the births biologically possible. Harpagon has no doubt arranged these sterile unions to protect his hoarded gold from the claims of potential heirs. (pp. 173-74)

Relying on what he supposes to be absolute parental authority, Harpagon intends to compel Cléante and Elise to follow his plans, although marriage required the consent of *both* parents and children, and unilateral compulsion was denied legality by jurists. . . . The miser cannot envision the possibility that two families may both gain through the reciprocal gift of their children and their fortunes, the exchange of their genetic and economic identities. Any provision for the welfare of the youngsters must, in his view, subtract from his personal wealth, if not from his very identity. Thus, he must live by the outlandish credo of refusal, "sans dot" ["without dowry"], which sounds like a death knell for the future of his family.

Engraved handbill for an early production of *The School for Wives.*

It is not surprising that the miser is just as inadequate in the role of suitor as in the role of father. He shows none of the lighthearted generosity that his son demonstrates, and instead of an elegant contract feast, he orders disgusting, inedible dishes. . . . Whereas most men would seek to regale their lady, he orders the servants to pour the wine sparingly. Rather than to escort her to some gallant entertainment, such as the theater, he offers to take her as far as the fair, which is free. In his overwhelming fear of giving anything away, Harpagon ironically chooses in Mariane a partner who will bring him nothing in return, except an imaginary 12,000 livres annually in spared expenses. . . . (pp. 174-75)

Harpagon's relationship with his servants shows that his obsession with hoarding money has discredited him beyond the boundaries of the family unit. Master-servant associations depended to a great extent on decorum and esteem, but as La Flèche says of Harpagon, "Il aime l'argent, plus que réputation, qu'honneur et que vertu" ["he loves money more than reputation, honour and virtue"]. The valet mocks the miser, who, he says, will not even give a person good-day, but only lend it. When the servants show him the holes in their threadbare clothes, he advises them, "Rangez cela adroitement du côté de la muraille, et présentez toujours le devant au monde" ["Always manage to keep that side of you to the wall, and show people your front only"]. It is true that he scarcely takes better care of his own physical appearance, judging by the obsolete ruff and quaint hat he wears. This fear of the movement of money surpasses thrift and constitutes a wasteful neglect, for Harpagon would rather see his people deteriorate like his decaying carriage and unshod horses than to restore them to a state congruent with his *condition*. The dowries, apprenticeships, and other rewards that many masters bestowed on their servants are unknown to the miser. Instead he subjects the staff to constant humiliations, such as the insults he hurls at La Flèche, "maître juré filou, vrai gibier de potence" ["you arrant thief, you cursed gallow bird"], and the hilarious close inspection of the valet's pants. Sarcastic Maître Jacques speaks for all the servants when, disappointed that Harpagon pulls a handkerchief from his pocket instead of a reward, he sneers, "Je vous baise les mains" ["I thank you kindly"]. As with his children, Harpagon shirks paternalistic responsibilities toward his servants and crassly exploits them.

Harpagon's patterns of irresponsible misbehavior seem impervious to any lessons of reform; he is certainly one of Molière's most "unreconstructed" characters, to use Robert J. Nelson's terminology. Without some extraordinary measures for survival, his lineage seems doomed to wither and die, for he is in a position to deny his approbation for any normal bourgeois marriage. It is in this light that one must judge the antiauthoritarian reactions of La Flèche, Valère, and Cléante. La Flèche explains that he robs Harpagon not for personal gain, nor to recoup the servants' rightful wages, but as a moral example to combat the miser's perversions. . . . Valère's deception of his master through the disguise that permits him to woo Elise clandestinely is counter-balanced by the suitor's deserving actions. He has earned Elise's love by giving her the precious gift of life when he saved her from drowning. His generosity and her gratitude developed into "cet ardent amour que ni le temps ni les difficultés n'ont rebuté" ["ardent love which neither time nor difficulties discouraged"].

The force of natural reciprocity that draws the young people together is thus identified as a sort of bourgeois "cri du sang" ["call of the blood"]. Cléante's motives in helping Mariane are typical of this spirit of good will: "Figurezvous, ma soeur, quelle joie ce peut être que de relever la fortune d'une personne que l'on aime; que de donner adroitement quelques petits secours aux modestes nécessités d'une vertueuse famille" ["Just think how good it would be to increase the comfort of those we love, to give a worthy family some slight aid"]. Contrast these sentiments with those of Harpagon, who says of the girl: " . . . je suis résolu de l'épouser, *pourvu que j'y trouve quelque bien*" ["I have resolved to marry her, provided I find she has some means"] (emphasis added). The miser is quick to reproach his son for indulging in un-bourgeois luxury. . . . Yet, it is the son who is the true guardian of the family's social identity. When Harpagon is exposed engaging in usury in act two, Cléante reminds him that such conduct constitutes derogation for anyone claiming to live nobly. . . . This ban rested on the fact that since 1560 *roturiers* ["plebeians"] holding offices exempt from the *taille* were treated like nobles in matters of derogation and were forbidden even from engaging in commerce; furthermore, all lenders were expressly forbidden to loan to "fils de famille" ["young men of good family"]. Indeed, it seems that Harpagon's activities extend far beyond this one incident of derogation, for La Flèche declares that he doesn't recognize any of the furniture mentioned in the promissory note and that it must come from a secret warehouse associated with other loans.

In the third act, Clèante's generosity once again confronts Harpagon's avarice, as both seek to woo Mariane. It would seem that Harpagon should have the upper hand, since he enjoys the advantages of money and authority, but he ruins his opportunity to impress the young lady by scrimping on the entertainment and by failing to conceal his coarseness. Speaking of his daughter, he cannot resist the urge to use rustic proverbs: "Vous voyez qu'elle est grande; mais mauvaise herbe croît toujours" ["You see how tall she is; but rank grass grows apace"]. Cléante, on the other hand, quickly demonstrates a command of refined conversation

when he upstages his father and compliments Mariane. . . . Cléante further emphasizes his own virility and Harpagon's decrepitude by putting the old man's diamond ring on Mariane's finger. In a gesture that demonstrates his willingness to share and his sophistication as a lover, he makes her keep it, insisting, "Il est en de trop belles mains" ["It is in hands too beautiful"].

On witnessing this, Harpagon erupts in a series of curses. The son, wise and worldly, has stolen the center of attention, proving his mastery of the social ritual of courtship. The more the old man rages, the more Cléante urges Mariane that she must keep the ring. Molière underscores Harpagon's impotence by stressing his inability to share with his betrothed or even to articulate a reasonable response to his son's gallant rivalry. The only recourse he has at the end of the scene is to send his valet to collect the leftovers of the feast, of *cadeau,* that Cléante had secretly arranged for Mariane. (pp. 175-78)

The miser and his fellow characters differ noticeably in the degree of trust they have in society. Although the young people rebel against Harpagon to the extent that they secretly meet with their lovers, they retain enough confidence in social conventions that they never attack the principle of paternalism or seek to wed without fatherly permission. Both Cléante and Valère admit to their passions when the truth becomes necessary. . . . It is significant that Harpagon misunderstands this openness, assuming that Valère is a thief, since gold is the only thing the miser considers worthy of devotion. For this sociopath, "de tous les humains l'humain le moins humain" ["of all the human beings the least human"], all life becomes the occasion for fear and larceny; he thus fails to appreciate the return of his strongbox by his son. . . . Harpagon is alienated from both the generous and the needy and lacks faith in all segments of the social network.

The dénouement of *L'Avare* resolves all questions of social disparity by reorganizing a new clan around old Anselme . . . He withdraws all plans of marriage in favor of his son's future role as family leader. After all, the recovery of his long lost heir removes from his shoulders any responsibility for beginning another family and obviates his motives for marrying Elise. At the same time, his riches replenish Mariane's dowry and eliminate the need for her to choose a husband on the basis of support. For the sake of bourgeois reciprocity, he is obliged to make several petty concessions to Harpagon's avarice, including paying the legal officers and purchasing a wedding suit for the miser, but this is a small price to pay for removing the only obstacle to the double marriage. Valère, his status and fortune restored, may now totally discard his *intendant* disguise and marry Elise. Mariane, freed from poverty, can accept the proposal of Cléante rather than that of his disagreeable father. In a fitting twist of reciprocal irony,

Harpagon's children, who seemed at the beginning of the play to be too well placed in the hierarchy for their loved ones, are finally in a position to benefit greatly from their alliance.

Critics since the eighteenth century have followed the example of Riccoboni in arguing that the ending of *L'Avare* is immoral because it fails to punish adequately either Harpagon or his antagonists, a charge based mainly on the financial crimes of usury and burglary and on the children's disobedience. However, even La Flèche realized that Harpagon's gold was not the central issue of the play when he exclaimed, "Que nous importe que vous en ayez ou que vous n'en ayez pas, si c'est pour nous la même chose!" ["What does it matter to us whether you have any or you have not? It is all the same to us!"] The morality of fleecing a Shy-lock or a Turcaret in the name of comic example is at best debatable; the chastisement of Harpagon is never an issue, for sums of wealth are overshadowed by the forms of social solidarity that they are meant to represent. The *scène de reconnaissance* and the advent of Anselme mark the triumph of conscious mutual responsibility over the monomaniacal money interests of the protagonist. Having removed his opposition to the marriages, he can do no further harm and is free of others as others are free of him. As Anselme's new clan leaves the stage to sign the contracts that will solemnly bind them together, Harpagon heads for a lonely rendez-vous with his *chère cassette* ["dear money-box"]. (pp. 178-80)

James F. Gaines, in his *Social Structures in Molière's Theater,* Ohio State University Press, 1984, 283 p.

SOURCES FOR FURTHER STUDY

Chatfield-Taylor, H. C. *Molière: A Biography.* New York: Duffield & Company, 1906, 466 p.

> Critical biography concerned mainly with those comedies (including *The School for Wives, Tartuffe,* and *Don Juan*) whose public reception and response directly affected Molière's personal and professional life.

Guicharnaud, Jacques, ed. *Molière: A Collection of Critical Essays.* Englewood Cliffs, N. J.: Prentice-Hall, 1964, 186 p.

> Essays by several twentieth-century Molière scholars, including Gustav Lanson, Will G. Moore, Ramon Fernandez, Lional Gosman, and H. Gaston Hall.

Howarth, W. D., and Thomas, Merlin, eds. *Molière: Stage and Study.* Oxford: Oxford University Press, Clarendon Press, 1973, 293 p.

> Collection of French and English essays by such authorities on Molière as Jacques Guicharnaud, J. D. Hubert, and H. Gaston Hall.

Johnson, Roger, Jr.; Neumann, Editha S.; and Trail, Guy T., eds. *Molière and the Commonwealth of Letters: Patrimony and Posterity.* Jackson: University Press of Mississippi, 1975, 873 p.

> Includes examinations of Molière's influence on later literature, critical analysis of his works, and discussions of the staging of his plays. Also continues Paul Saintonge's *Fifty Years of Molière Studies: A Bibliography* (see citation below).

Lewis, D. B. Wyndham. *Molière: The Comic Mask.* London: Eyre & Spottiswoode, 1959, 214 p.

> Critical biography.

Saintonge, Paul. *Fifty Years of Molière Studies: A Bibliography, 1892-1941.* Baltimore: The Johns Hopkins Press, 1942, 313 p.

> Bibliography of critical writings on Molière. Continued by Roger Johnson, Jr. and others in *Molière and the Commonwealth of Letters: Patrimony and Posterity* (see citation above).

Michel de Montaigne

1533-1592

(Full name Michel Eyquem de Montaigne) French essayist, diarist, and translator.

INTRODUCTION

*T*he inventor of the essay form as a literary genre, Montaigne raised introspection to the level of art in his monumental work *Les essais* (1580; *The Essays*). The French "essai" means an experiment, test, or attempt, and such was Montaigne's intention in his series of essays: to attempt to understand himself and, by extension, the human condition in a series of introspective "experiments." In so doing, Montaigne extended his questioning to the very limits of human knowledge, for throughout *The Essays* runs the thread of thoughtful skepticism that is the trademark of its author, who took for his motto the words "Que sçay-je?" ("What do I know?").

Montaigne was born Michel Eyquem in the district of Périgord in the Gascony region of France. Although his forebears had long been bourgeois traders, in 1477 his great-grandfather had purchased the château of Montaigne along with the right to add the noble title "de Montaigne" to the family name. (Michel was the first to do so.) Little is known of Montaigne's Protestant mother, who is given only cursory mention in *The Essays*. It is his staunchly Catholic father, Pierre Eyquem, who figures prominently in the work and who exerted the greatest influence on the author's early childhood. Pierre Eyquem's innovative child-rearing techniques included sending his son to spend his infancy with peasant godparents so that he might develop a sense of attachment to the lower classes, and insuring that Michel's native language was Latin rather than French by requiring that the entire Eyquem household speak only Latin to the boy until he reached the age of six. At this time Montaigne was sent to the Collège de Guyenne in Bordeaux, where he spent seven years. The particulars of his activities after he left the school are unclear, but it is thought that he studied law, probably in Toulouse. In 1557 Montaigne became a councillor in the parliament of Bordeaux, acquitting his duties competently though unenthusiastically. Here he met and befriended fellow councillor Étienne de La Boétie, the subject of one of Montaigne's most famous and moving essays, "De l'amitié" ("Of Friendship"). La Boétie's death in 1563 was a great shock and a deep sorrow to his friend. A few years later Montaigne married Françoise de La Chassaigne; their marriage (apparently an arranged match) was amicable if not passionate.

Until his middle years, Montaigne was only slightly involved in the literary world: he had arranged the publication of some of La Boétie's writings and his translation (1569) of Raimond Sebond's *Theologia naturalis.* Only in 1571 did his literary career begin in earnest. Leaving his law career and retiring to the Montaigne estate (of which he was now lord, his father having died a few years earlier), Montaigne began the task that occupied him for the remainder of his life: writing *The Essays.* Following the work's first publication in 1580, Montaigne, an enthusiastic traveler, embarked on an extensive journey through France, Italy, Switzerland, and Germany, recording his observations and experiences in his *Journal de voyage* (1774; *The Journal of Montaigne's Travels*), which, unlike *The Essays,* was not written for publication. While still traveling, Montaigne was elected mayor of Bordeaux, a position he accepted for two two-year terms. In the last years of his life Montaigne contracted another important friendship, this one with Marie de Jars de Gournay, whom he met on a trip to Paris in 1588 and whom he called his "fille d'alliance" ("adopted daughter"); it was she who edited and published the posthumous edition of *The Essays.* Suffering from quinsy, Montaigne died at his château at the age of fifty-nine.

The length and complexity of *The Essays* have baffled critical attempts to categorize the work satisfactorily, for in it form and content, subject and style, are so closely interwoven and interdependent that it is difficult to focus on any single aspect of *The Essays* apart from the whole. Hence, a knowledge of the formal arrangement and composition of *The Essays* is essential to an understanding of the work in its entirety. *The Essays* consists of three books of 107 chapters (Montaigne's use of the term "essay" referred to his method and intent, not to his individual chapters), which range in length from a few paragraphs to over a hundred pages, and which treat myriad subjects from the trivial to the profound—Montaigne's attitude toward radishes as well as his feelings about God. Montaigne never considered his essays "finished." Books I and II, first published in 1580, were revised for republication two years later and again for the 1588 edition, which included a third book. The process of revision continued, and the posthumous edition of the three books incorporates Montaigne's further annotations and marginalia.

Attempts to assign some sort of structural, the-matic, or stylistic unity to *The Essays,* both within individual essays and among them, have usually proved difficult. The mercurial nature of *The Essays* resists generalities; the only observation that may be made with any certainty is that, despite some exceptions, the essays tend to become longer, less imitative, and more personal as the work progresses. A random selection of essay titles—"Des coches" ("Of Coaches"), "Sur des vers de Virgile" ("On Some Verses of Virgil"), "De la cruauté" ("Of Cruelty")—reveals the remarkable diversity within *The Essays.* The issue of unity is further clouded by the frequent disparity between essay title and essay content: Montaigne's ostensible subject may be completely overshadowed by another topic, either related or unrelated; or the stated subject may serve as but a springboard for Montaigne's real concern; or Montaigne's stated intention may have no discernable relation to the actual essay content at all. While recurring themes and preoccupations have been noted—among them, the dichotomies of mutability and stability and of the public and private realms; the limits of human reason and knowledge—such recurrences fall short of providing a logical structure to *The Essays.* Even a chronological unity is sometimes invalid or suspect, as Montaigne published some of the essays in a different order from that in which he wrote them. Yet for all the lack of surface cohesion in *The Essays,* the work is united philosophically by its unwavering emphasis on introspection and self-discovery. As Montaigne himself wrote: "Je suis moy-mesmes la matière de mon livre" ("I am myself the subject of my book"). Commentators therefore find no fault with *The Essays'* lack of formal coherence, agreeing that the author's communication of the evolving essence of himself, if it be honest and natural, must preclude the usual strictures of art. As Edward Dowden expressed it: "When Montaigne wanders from his professed theme, why should we quarrel with him? He never wanders from himself, and from humanity which is his true theme."

Commentators assert that beyond Montaigne's egoism lies a higher purpose; believing as he did that he, as one man, manifested within himself the quintessential humanity common to all people, Montaigne held that in seeking to understand his individual self, he was examining the universal traits of humanity. In a much-quoted passage, Montaigne declared: "I am a man, and nothing human is alien to me." As the spontaneous and random record of a man's beliefs and impressions as they occur and as they develop, *The Essays* has been described as an experiment in becoming rather than being. This evolutionary aspect of the work is both reflected in and augmented by the style Montaigne employed. His approach is informal and meandering; he moved from one subject to another, following a train of thought or chasing an association of ideas. This relaxed style, spiced with the idiom and dialect of his native Gascony, is conducive to the general atmosphere of *The Essays,* which scholars call one of friendly intimacy. Approximating as they do a genial conversational style—one which is, in J. B. Priestley's words, "as easy and flexible and racy as good talk"—the essays have been applauded for their simplicity of speech and directness of sentiment. Though often circuitous in route, they are forthcoming in honesty; indeed, Montaigne's experiment as an introspective essayist required sincerity, and critics believe he achieved it. Wrote Montaigne in his preface, "C'est un livre de bonne foy" ("This is a sincere book"), and with this assessment commentators concur. Montaigne's rambling, intimate style and unpretentious manner foster a sense of camaraderie between writer and reader that largely accounts for the work's success.

Neither Montaigne's position as spokesman for ordinary humanity nor his disarming homeliness precludes intellectualism in *The Essays.* On the contrary, as Montaigne's exploration of self embraced an exploration of the human condition, so *The Essays* is replete with its author's philosophical, political, and social concerns. A few critics have disagreed on this point, denying Montaigne status as a serious thinker, notably seventeenth-century French philosopher Blaise Pascal, who decried *The Essays* as impious and vain, as well as intellectually specious in their meandering technique. However, most commentators concur that Montaigne's philosophical speculations, while not amounting to a doctrine of systematic thought, nevertheless exist and are important. Attempts have been made to categorize Montaigne's philosophical thought as it evolved throughout the essays. In his *Les sources et l'evolution des Essais de Montaigne* (1908), Pierre Viley argued that Montaigne's philosophy evolved from stoicism in the first book, to skepticism in the second, to a reliance on nature and an increasing epicureanism in the third book. While Villey's categories are still considered useful indicators of the main thrust of thought in *The Essays,* recent critics have argued that though these elements of philosophical thought are decidedly present, their pattern is not so easily determined. It appears that Montaigne tested and explored philosophy as he tested and explored himself. Classical and contemporary quotations are liberally sprinkled throughout *The Essays,* testifying to Montaigne's wide range of knowledge, and scholars have traced in his work the influence of a wide array of thinkers, including Socrates, Seneca, Aristotle, Plutarch, and the Stoics. But by far the most consistent and omnipresent element of Montaigne's thought is his Pyronnism, or radical skepti-

cism, expressed in his motto, "Que sçay-je?" As Francis Thompson described it: "He proves—*i.e.,* tests—all things. His criticism is a dissolving acid. But when it comes to deciding what is finally true, he prefers to play with a number of possibilities, and leave the reader to decide."

Because of Montaigne's omnipresent skepticism, critics frequently debate the nature of the principles he actually embraced, particularly concerning politics and religion, for these were important subjects in his time: sixteenth-century France was wracked by religious wars between the government-sanctioned Catholics and the Protestant reformers known as Huguenots. Critics have characterized Montaigne as a political conservative for his desire to preserve the status quo, even where repressive, and as a liberal for his tolerance and open-mindedness. He has been considered a devoutly orthodox Catholic, a humanist, or even, according to Charles Augustin Sainte-Beuve, one who evidences "consistent paganism." This confusion is exemplified by the fact that although in Montaigne's lifetime *The Essays* was virtually untouched by the rigid papal censorship that then prevailed, in the early eighteenth century the work was listed in the Papal Index of Prohibited Books. Perhaps there can be no definitive conclusions concerning such questions, for in a real sense, the very exercise of writing *The Essays* constitutes Montaigne's attempt to discover what he could know and how he could know it.

Ultimately, many conclude, it is not Montaigne's answers that matter, but his questions; not his precise philosophy, but his method of exploring it; not the conclusions he drew but the self-examination he essayed. "These essays," wrote Virginia Woolf, "are an attempt to communicate a soul." That attempt has attracted and retained appreciative readers from the sixteenth century to the twentieth. Traces of Montaigne's influence have been cited in countless thinkers and writers—among them, René Descartes, Friedrich Nietzsche, and William Shakespeare. The enduring appeal of Montaigne's *Essays* lies in its questioning introspection and the intimacy created between author and reader, an intimacy which Ralph Waldo Emerson felt in reading the book and described thus: "It seemed to me as if I had myself written the book, in some former life, so sincerely it spoke to my thought and experience."

(For further information about Montaigne's life and works, see *Literature Criticism from 1400 to 1800,* Vol. 8.)

CRITICAL COMMENTARY

BLAISE PASCAL
(essay date 1662?)

[A French theologian and mathematician, Pascal is best known for his writings on moral philosophy. In the following excerpt from his *Pensées*, a work that remained unfinished at the time of his death in 1662, he assails the morality and style of Montaigne's work.]

To speak of those who have dealt with self-knowledge; of Charron's divisions which depress and bore; of Montaigne's confusion; how he was aware of his want of method, which he tried to avoid by skipping from topic to topic; how he sought to be in the fashion.

The folly of trying to paint his own portrait! And that not by the way, and against his own principles— we all make mistakes—but on principle, and of set and primary purpose. For to talk nonsense by chance and out of weakness is a common failing, but to do so deliberately is intolerable. . . . (p. 17)

Montaigne's faults are grievous. Wanton expressions; this is all wrong, whatever Mademoiselle Gournay may say. Credulous, men without eyes. Ignorant, squaring the circle, another great world. His sentiments on suicide. On death. He induces indifference to salvation, without fear and without repentance. His book was not written to teach piety, so he was not bound to attempt that; but one is always bound not to turn men away from piety. One may excuse his rather loose and voluptuous sentiments on certain occasions . . . , but one cannot excuse his wholly heathen sentiments concerning death; for we must say goodbye to piety if we have no desire for at least a Christian death. Now throughout his book he thinks only of a soft and easy death.

The good in Montaigne is difficult to acquire. The bad—apart from immorality—could have been quickly cured if he had been informed that he told too many tales and talked too much about himself. (p. 365)

Blaise Pascal, in his *Pensées,* translated by H. F. Stewart, Pantheon Books, 1950, 543 p.

FRANÇOIS MARIE AROUET DE VOLTAIRE
(essay date 1733)

[A French philosopher and one of the principal literary figures of the Enlightenment, Voltaire consistently championed individual liberty and the primacy of reason over faith and authority. In the following excerpt, he rebuts Pascal's criticism of Montaigne in the *Pensées* (see excerpt dated 1662?).]

I am sending you the critical remarks I have been making for some time on the *Pensées* of M. Pascal. Don't compare me in this matter with Hezekiah, who wanted to burn all the books of Solomon. I respect the genius and the eloquence of Pascal, but the more I respect them the more I am persuaded that he would himself have corrected many of these *Pensées,* which he had jotted down on paper for further examination later. It is while admiring his genius that I challenge some of his ideas. . . .

I have chosen with care some thoughts of Pascal and put the rejoinders after them. It is for you to judge whether I am right or wrong. (p. 120)

Montaigne's defects are great. He is full of lewd and improper words. This is thoroughly bad. His sentiments about suicide and death are horrible.

Montaigne is speaking as a philosopher, not as a Christian, and he is stating the pros and cons of suicide. Philosophically speaking, what harm does a man do society by leaving it when he is of no further use to it? An old man who suffers unbearable agonies with the stone is told: "If you don't have it cut out you will die, if you do you may dodder on, dribble and drag about for another year, a burden to yourself and everybody else." I presume that the old man decides to cease being a burden to anybody: that is roughly the case Montaigne sets out. (pp. 135-36)

What a foolish project of Montaigne to portray himself ! And to do so not by the way and against his own principles, for all of us fall short sometimes, but acting according to his principles and with a prime and main design. For saying silly things by chance

Principal Works

*Theologia naturalis [translator] (essay) 1569

Les essais de Messire Michel Seigneur de Montaigne (essays) 1580; revised editions 1582, 1588, 1595

[The Essayes; or, Morall, Politike, and Millitaries Discourses of Lo: Michaell de Montaigne, 1603; also published as The Essays of Michael Seigneur de Montaigne, 1685-86]

Journal de voyage de Michel de Montaigne en Italie par la Suisse et l'Allemagne en 1580 et 1581 (travel journal) 1774

[The Journal of Montaigne's Travels, 1903]

The Complete Works of Montaigne (essays, travel journal, and letters) 1957

*Translation of a work by Raimond Sebond.

or weakness is an ordinary complaint, but to say them deliberately cannot be tolerated, and especially such things as those.

What a delightful design Montaigne had to portray himself without artifice as he did! For he has portrayed human nature itself. And what a paltry project of Nicole, Malebranche and Pascal, to belittle Montaigne! (p. 139)

Voltaire, "On the 'Pensées' of Pascal," in his *Letters on England,* translated by Leonard Tancock, Penguin Books, 1980, pp. 120-45.

CHARLES AUGUSTIN SAINTE-BEAUVE

(essay date 1842)

[A widely respected French literary critic of the nineteenth century, Sainte-Beauve focused his critical writings on the individual mindsets and social milieux of authors, presaging the psychological approach of many twentieth-century critics. In the following excerpt from an 1842 essay, he favorably assesses the philosophy and style of *The Essays,* focusing largely on "An Apology of Raymond Sebond."]

Over the past two centuries a great deal has been written about Montaigne. Authors as important and brilliant as Pascal have spoken their minds [see excerpt dated 1662?], and yet there is one point that, in my opinion, has not been stressed enough. Namely, that Montaigne does not give us a philosophical system, is not primarily the Pyrrhonian skeptic—Montaigne is the very embodiment of nature.

He is nature in all her purity, yet civilized; nature in her broadest, most typical expressions as well as in her most individual moods, not excluding her aberrations. All of nature untouched by grace. (p. 13)

The more I reflect about Montaigne, the more I am convinced that he was the natural man par excellence.

Let me dwell on this point, if I may. The phrase is so often and so vaguely used, I should like to analyze it more carefully and to develop its fuller implications.

There is something of Montaigne in every one of us. Every one of our inclinations, moods, and passions—every one of our diversions, amusements, and flights of fancy upon which Christianity has made no mark—all such states of mind deserve to be called "Montaigne" states of mind. To accept the "naturalness" of our lives, for all the operations of what is called "divine grace"—a sort of unreflective nakedness into which we relapse when following our natural inclinations, as though the soul had never been redeemed—to accept this "Tahiti" of the soul is also to accept Montaigne's empire, the realm in which he lived and wrote. We ought not to be surprised that Pascal had such difficulty disposing of Montaigne. The problem Montaigne poses is not one of philosophy but that of nature itself, of the individual self: he poses a philosophical problem only in the sense that he represents nature in all its purity.

Pascal inveighed against Montaigne, studying him closely so as to condemn him more sternly—and with a vehemence such as only the true believer may permit himself (and then only on the condition that the end justifies such means). And yet, in order to gain full understanding of Montaigne and of the "indulgence of so many intelligent persons" who "have failed to realize how dangerous he is" (as Arnauld complains in his *Art de penser*), we must consider Montaigne's thought in its original, informal, loose expression. The tidiness of Pascal's indictment is a barrier to grasping Montaigne as a whole. The fact is, all things considered, three-quarters of Montaigne does not essentially differ from what we find in a number of other writers: but those others do not arouse criticism, because they speak without malicious intent. Had M. de Saci read Montaigne before talking to Pascal about him—M. de Saci who made it his rule to follow the will of God at every moment . . .—he would have said something like this to Pascal:

"This author to whom you ascribe so much intelligence and whose ideas you erect into a system, does not rely upon arguments to all that extent. What appeals to the reader is present in most men, including those who call themselves Christians, but who live as if the Cross had never been. When I am walking in the countryside—when, perhaps, I have retired there in my old age, taking my ease, free of responsibility, with no-body to think of but myself—where then is my Christianity? When I look at a lovely flower, admire a shaft of sunlight, or lie down on a patch of greensward to take a little nap, there to dream of who knows what fantastic things, wholly caught up in concerns of this world, forgetting all else—where then is my Christianity? When I read, as I like to do, of unusual manners and customs in books of travel, and meet the Devil in a hundred guises, now as a naked cannibal, now as an Italian fop, not caring so much that he is the Devil but only whether he is interesting—where then is my Christianity? And when I sit down to Montaigne in moments of leisure, with nothing more in my mind than reading Montaigne—where then is my Christianity?

That is enough about what I call "three-quarters of Montaigne." Now we must address ourselves to the rest, his attitude toward religion, which Pascal and the recluses of Port-Royal condemned so harshly. They did not misrepresent him. Montaigne is, indeed, naïve, and we do not underestimate the naïve, casual, easygoing aspect of his thought. However, there is also in him a background of conscious intention, which gives a special sense to the whole. The hostility and fear which Montaigne has aroused in religious men comes from their realization that his portrayal of nature conceals a consistent paganism. He almost always treats religion as a thing apart, as something much too respectable to be discussed—but this does not prevent him from discussing it constantly. He is against translating and reading the Scriptures—a point on which, as on many others, he prefers the Catholic Church to the Reformers. Politically, such an attitude was not unwise, but there is more to it. He also says that the use of the "sacred and divine songs" (i.e., the Psalms) ought to be restricted to the priesthood. Being himself but a layman, a mere writer of imagination, he would not presume so far as to recite the Psalms. For him, a simple Lord's Prayer is quite enough, he tells us. Such is his way of inspiring respect for religion! Where Voltaire said, "These things are sacred, *because* no one will touch them"—he was speaking of canticles by Lefranc de Pompignan—Montaigne in effect says, "These things are sacred, *therefore* no one should touch them." The higher the portals of the Temple, the less risk we run of knocking our heads against them as we go in or out. He knows very well that so extreme a point of view was out of date in his own day. That he would have been perfectly happy in certain countries where, apart from the obligatory observances, one does as one likes, where you can be a cardinal and a man of the world at the same time—this is clear from the general tenor of his book. I know that he made a proper Christian death—Gassendi and La Rochefoucauld also received the sacraments. It is not for me to judge his sincerity at

such an awesome moment, but his book is there for all to read, and my judgment is of it.

Many a chapter—that on Prayers and Orisons, and that on Repenting, for example—would be as revelatory, on close analysis, as the **"Apology of Raymond Sebond."** In such chapters, we find sentences that are moderate and unobjectionable from the religious point of view, but they are not enough to modify the general tone. In fact, we never know quite where we are with men of this ilk—with Bayle any more than with Montaigne. We might say of them what Pascal said of Opinion, that it is the more fraudulent for not being consistently so.

Pascal also said: "One saying of David, or of Moses, for instance that 'God will circumcise the heart,' enables us to judge of their spirit. If all their other expression were ambiguous, and left us in doubt whether they were philosophers or Christians, one saying of this kind would in fact determine all the rest. From that point on, ambiguity no longer exists." The very opposite is true of Montaigne: if some passages state his thought, others conceal it. He is betrayed by random remarks that are like flashes of lightning illuminating a whole landscape. Montaigne's "dirty" passages are especially revealing, when he addresses himself to the most intimate aspects of human life. He really enjoys tearing away the poor rags with which we cover our baser nature—and it is then that we glimpse him as he truly is under the high spirits, the eloquence, and the gentility. He sets out to humiliate us in such passages (try listening to them read aloud). Unlike Pascal's, his tone is never one of grief at our natural condition, but one of malicious delight: he fairly rubs his hands with self-satisfaction.

Montaigne's longest, most vigorous, and most important chapter is the one titled **"An Apology of Raymond Sebond."** This is the heart of the *Essais;* everything about it is purposeful, and the calculated tortuous sentences which say the opposite of what the author really thinks nonetheless convey it. Studying it closely, we find that his so-called Pyrrhonism rings hollow: for all his restless rambling Montaigne knows where he is going. Out of this **"Apology"** I can imagine assembling a chapter that might be headed "Montaigne's Dogmatism." Where Spinoza's form is geometrical, Montaigne's is skeptical, but the essence of his doctrine seems to me unmistakable. (pp. 15-19)

To humor his father (who was more of an enthusiast for the new learning than himself learned) the youthful Montaigne had translated a Latin book by the fifteenth-century Spanish author, Raymond de Sebond. Titled *Theologia naturalis,* it demonstrated the existence of God and the truth of the Christian religion on the basis of rational arguments, drawn as far as possible from observation of nature. (pp. 19-20)

Montaigne's French version of *Theologia naturalis* was published in 1569, in compliance with a wish expressed by his father on his deathbed—the older Montaigne had been charmed and consoled by this book. It was criticized on two counts. Some (the Catholic party) said that the attempt to give revelation and faith a foundation in reason was opening a door that should remain closed. Others maintained that Sebond's arguments were weak and failed to make their point. It was ostensibly to answer both types of objection that Montaigne wrote this chapter of the *Essais.*

He addresses himself first to his religious critics, treating them with conspicuous respect. He says that he cannot blame those who, because of their "zeal of piety," are afraid to let reason be used in support of religion. But while he is well aware that the knowledge of God can be attained only by extraordinary supernatural means, he "fears" that we could not "enjoy" it unless we had access to it "not only by discourse, but also by humane means." For, he says, if we could grasp Godhead "through the interposition of a lively faith," surely we would not find so many contradictions and inconsistencies between Christian words and Christian deeds. Citing one instance after another, he goes on maliciously to demonstrate the inadequacy of precisely these "humane means," that is, without the intervention of divine grace. What is he driving at? It is obvious that from this point on he is no longer concerned with Raymond de Sebond. He had translated the latter's book to please his father; now, on the pretext of defending that author, he is pursuing another aim altogether. If he is not actually refuting Sebond, he is using him as a pretext for carrying on a very broad and "probing" discussion of religion. His tone of respect for all who would place faith above reason makes him seem to be on their side. With the greatest humility he confines his defense of Sebond to the observation that the latter's method, though very crude and limited, might have a certain practical value for bringing certain persons back to the faith. And he cites one such instance: he knew a man who had actually been influenced by Sebond's arguments. As he puts it, "Faith, giving as it were a tincture and lustre unto Sebond's arguments makes them the more firme and solid."

However, when he addresses himself to those of his critics who were not inspired by "zeal of piety" and who found Sebond's arguments weak and inconclusive, his tone changes. Now he is as outspoken as one could wish. "Such fellowes must somewhat more roughly be handled," he says, "for they are more dangerous and more malicious than the first." In fact, it is he who becomes more dangerous and more malicious at this point. For what does he do? To refute the second type of objectors, he proceeds to outdo them at their own game on a tone of high indignation. What he says, in effect, is: Of course, I am well aware that poor Se-

bond's arguments are weak and don't prove much. Yet, madmen that you are, proud wretches (he is taking up the cudgels in defense of the Godhead they would defame)—tell me, how can there be any arguments capable of proving anything in such matters? Cannot every one of them be countered with an argument equally—that is to say, just as little—convincing? Thereupon, as though carried away by his own self-righteousness, he embarks on a long discussion, in the course of which he enumerates ad infinitum every possible cause of errors and ineffectuality to which the human reason is prone when unsupported by religious beliefs. Once this chapter has been properly understood, we realize that Montaigne is from beginning to end playing a part. Only a reader determined to be deceived could be taken in by it. For Montaigne, Sebond serves the same function the Manichaeans were to serve for Bayle.

To begin with, Montaigne tries to show that man "alone without other help," without the grace and knowledge of God, is but a miserable and wretched creature. "Who hath perswaded him that this admirable moving of heavens vaults; that the eternal light of these lamps so fiercely rowling over his head; that the horror-moving and continuall motion of this infinite vaste Ocean, were established, and continue for so many ages for his commodite and service?" In such connections, Montaigne does not seem to notice that he is actually refuting the same Raymond de Sebond whose apology he claims to be undertaking. The latter had argued in favor of final causes, and had defended the idea that the universe is made for man. To chastise such human presumptuousness, he studies each animal in turn—the swallow, the dog, the falcon, the elephant, the ox, the magpie, the spider—each of whom has his own instincts, his own language, his own way of life, his own talents, his own reasoning power, his own capacity of loyalty, even his own (in the case of the elephant) kind of religious worship. Consequently, they are all our "fellow bretheren and compeers." This is the opposite pole from Descartes, who viewed animals as automatons, and whose ideas on that score influenced Pascal and Port-Royal. Pascal, the inventor of the adding machine, had no difficulty thinking of animals as pure automatons. In this connection, there is a much-quoted passage: "Touching strength, there is no Creature in the world open to so many wrongs and injuries as a man: He need not a Whale, an Elephant, nor a Crocodile, nor any such other wilde beast, of which one alone is of power to defeat a great number of men: seely lice are able to make Sulla give over his Dictatorship: The heart and life of a mighty and triumphant Emperor, is but the breakfast of a seely little worme."

Pascal imitated and rediscovered Montaigne's words when he attributed the death of Cromwell, the modern Sulla, to "one little grain of sand." He was also indebted to Montaigne when he said: "Man is but a reed, the most feeble thing in nature; but he is a think-ing reed. The entire universe need not arm itself to crush him. A vapor, a drop of water suffices to kill him. But if the universe were to crush him, man would still be more noble than that which killed him, because he knows that he dies and the advantage which the uni-verse has over him; the universe knows nothing of this."

It has been said that Montaigne's thought has been incorporated and completed in Pascal. When the latter employs coarse language calling attention to man's baser nature, we feel that he speaks in all sinceri-ty, and that his purpose is to lift man above the mire in which he finds himself; when he speaks of the mis-eries of the human condition, we are sure that he really wants to put an end to them. Montaigne, for his part, seems always to be gloating. Nonetheless, there are several passages in the **"Apology"** where Montaigne rises to real heights of sincerity and eloquence: "This manyheaded, divers-armed, and furiously raging mon-ster [an army] is man; wretched weake and miserable man: whom if you consider well, what is he, but a crawling, and ever-moving Ants-neast? . . . A gust of contrarie winds, the croking of a flight of Ravens, the false pase of a Horse, the casual flight of an Eagle, a dreame, a sodaine voyce, a false signe, a mornings mist, an evening fogge, are enough to overthrow, sufficient to overwhelme and able to pull him to the ground. Let the Sunne but shine hot on his face, he faints and swel-ters with heat: Cast but a little dust in his eyes, as do the Bees mentioned by our Poet, all our ensignes, all our legions, yea great Pompey himselfe in the forefront of them is overthrown and put to rout."

When Pascal treated this subject, he could at best equal, not surpass, such passages.

After this humbling comparison between man-kind and the animals, Montaigne addresses himself to each of the philosophical schools in turn, beginning with Thales. Making the most of their disagreements, he puts himself to great trouble, summoning up every resource of learning, to pit the arguments of each school against those of the other schools, so as to con-fute them all. Having accomplished this, he is at pains not to be misunderstood, and he warns Queen Margue-rite and his other readers that the tactic he has em-ployed, rejecting reason so as to deprive his adversary of its aid, is a "desperate" tactic, and one to be resorted to but rarely.

At the very moment he utters his warning, how-ever, and we might think he will not go on in this vein, he abandons the philosophers' changing systems and attacks all human faculties in so far as they might be supposed to be means of getting at the truth. Having doubted of reason, now he doubts of the senses, and we read: "It is not onely fevers, drinkes and great acci-dents, that overwhelme our judgement: The least thing

in the world will turne it topsieturvie." This and the passage that follows directly anticipate Pascal's saying: "The mind of this sovereign judge of the world is not so independent that it is not liable to be disturbed by the first din about it."

As we trace the development of Montaigne's thought in this part of the *Essais,* we are continually reminded of Pascal. The latter's *Pensées* could be de-scribed as a profounder version or revision of the apol-ogy of Sebond. Pascal repeats many of Montaigne's sayings on the vanity, weakness, and contradictoriness of mankind. In doing so, however, he makes the sign of the Cross over Montaigne's words, and what is more striking than their obvious similarities (which Pascal would certainly have acknowledged in publication) is their difference in tone. Where Montaigne was simply employing a novel intellectual tactic, Pascal has a seri-ous purpose. Where the former abandons himself to every passing current, the latter knows where he is going and works hard with the oars. The one is distract-ed, even entranced with his own shipwreck, while the other clings to the bit of driftwood with whose help he still can, by indomitable effort, reach the distant shore, his homeland in eternity. The feebleness, the wretch-edness, the nullity of human life: this is their common refrain. But while Montaigne finds amusement in the spectacle, and sneers at man's kinship with the animals, Pascal counsels courage and prayer. To him, man, how-ever wretched, is an exiled monarch, of the noblest lin-eage, and it behooves him to regain his rightful place.

We have said enough about this Apology, which is very long, and which concludes with a pompous quotation from Plutarch. God alone *IS,* we are suddenly told, and aside from God, who is eternal, necessary, and immutable, all things are transitory and in flux. Mon-taigne's intention in quoting this religious-passage from Plutarch is highly suspicious. If we scrutinize it carefully, taking into account where Montaigne inserts it, and in the light of the chapter as a whole, we must conclude that the ideas it expresses are Spinozist and pantheistic. By elevating God above created things, in-cluding mankind, Montaigne denies the notion of a provident and personal God. We are now in possession of a key that enables us to pass from conjecture to cer-tainty, to assess Montaigne's intentions both stated and unstated.

His playfulness and casualness are purely superfi-cial. Montaigne, in the **"Apology"** as well as through-out the *Essais,* is a kind of sorcerer, an evil genius who takes us by the hand, and who, guiding us through the labyrinth of opinion, tells us at every step, just when we think we know where we stand, "All this is false or at least dubious; don't give your trust so readily; don't pay too much attention to this or that in the hope it can serve as a landmark. All you can trust is the light I go by; nothing else matters. This light is enough." And after he had led you far afield, got you thoroughly disoriented and exhausted from being led down so many garden paths—just then he blows out the light and leaves you utterly in the dark. You may hear a little snicker from your guide.

To what conclusion does Montaigne lead? Universal doubt? But if so—if this is his final conclusion, what a vastly significant conclusion it is! When we stand there, finally having lost our way in utter darkness, it is Spinoza whom we are to call upon. The world is to be grasped as a great, gloomy, endless universe moving silent and unknown under skies perpetually gray. A bit of life appears now and again for a brief span, only to flicker out and die like an insect in a swamp. Such is the supreme answer a number of men have given, sometimes in the form of mathematical demonstration, sometimes in the form of Pyrrhonian argument. Montaigne's charm and good humor serve merely to screen off the spectacle of the abyss or, as he would put it, to prettify the tomb.

One of the great reasons for Montaigne's popularity—indeed, the one and only explanation for it—is his magical style. Style, in the exalted degree to which Montaigne possessed it, suffices to absolve any writer in the eyes of posterity. The disorderliness of his argument, his inconsistencies, licentiousness, and lapses of taste—all are covered over most attractively, plausibly, and pleasantly. We can never admire him enough. Style is the golden scepter which, in the last analysis, holds sway over the kingdom of this world.

Perhaps more than any other man, Montaigne had the gift of pleasing expression; his style is one continuous metaphor, sustained and renewed at every step. He always presents ideas in the form of images, varying them and yet keeping them clear and striking. Only the slightest interval separates one from another—the reader is given but a moment to prepare for the transition. Any one of his pages is a luxuriant, untamed field bursting with rustling plants and fragrant flowers, buzzing insects, and gurgling brooks. His is no integral conception, no ordered large-scale structure. He did not put himself to so much trouble. To him, inventiveness in detail and unflagging brilliance of expression sufficed. He understood this very well: "I have no other Sergeant of band to marshall my rapsodies, than fortune."

In Montaigne, idea and image are one and the same thing. . . . There is no real link between image and image; one merely succeeds the other: like a surefooted Basque, he jumps from rock to rock. (pp. 20-6)

In respect of style, Montaigne is like Ovid and Ariosto. The rhapsodic felicity of the successive images, however varied, is an unbroken stream. The thread of his thought is never lost amid the continual metamorphoses.

Shakespeare and Molière, geniuses with the gift of creating unified wholes, could with ease endow characters with life. Montaigne's imagination, on the other hand, operates within individual sentences and in the articulations of the ideas. The result is just as alive, and, viewed closely, just as marvelously poetic. Every detail, every stage in the development of the thought, takes shape and wakes to life as though of itself, and is sufficient unto itself. The result is a whole new world most agreeable to dwell in. This very personal style—I shall not weary of repeating—is an important characteristic of Montaigne. Pascal, who takes little joy in his own style and keeps firm control of it, did not make enough of this characteristic of Montaigne's. Montaigne uses the expression *"avoir le boutehors aisé,"* meaning to have what we would call "the gift of the gab"; actually, with him language is the *boute-en-train*—the life and soul of the party. (p. 27)

Charles Augustin Sainte-Beuve, "Montaigne," in his *Selected Essays,* edited by Francis Steegmuller, translated by Norbert Guterman, Doubleday & Company, Inc., 1963, pp. 13-28.

VIRGINIA WOOLF

(essay date 1924)

[A preeminent British novelist and literary critic, Woolf greatly influenced the development of Modernist literature through her stylistically innovative fiction, her numerous critical essays in the *Times Literary Supplement*, and her establishment of the literary circle known as the "Bloomsbury Group." In the following excerpt from a 1924 essay, she attempts to capture the essence of Montaigne's style and sensibility.]

Once at Bar-le-Duc Montaigne saw a portrait which René, King of Sicily, had painted of himself, and asked, "Why is it not, in like manner, lawful for everyone to draw himself with a pen, as he did with a crayon?" Off-hand one might reply, Not only is it lawful, but nothing could be easier. Other people may evade us, but our own features are almost too familiar. Let us begin. And then, when we attempt the task, the pen falls from our fingers; it is a matter of profound, mysterious, and overwhelming difficulty.

After all, in the whole of literature, how many people have succeeded in drawing themselves with a pen? Only Montaigne and Pepys and Rousseau perhaps. The *Religio Medici* is a coloured glass through which darkly one sees racing stars and a strange and turbulent soul. A bright polished mirror reflects the face of Boswell peeping between other people's shoulders in the famous biography. But this talking of oneself, following one's own vagaries, giving the whole map, weight, colour, and circumference of the soul in its confusion, its variety, its imperfection—this art belonged to one man only: to Montaigne. As the centuries go by, there is always a crowd before that picture, gazing into its depths, seeing their own faces reflected in it, seeing more the longer they look, never being able to say quite what it is that they see. (p. 18)

To tell the truth about oneself, to discover oneself near at hand, is not easy. . . . There is, in the first place, the difficulty of expression. We all indulge in the strange, pleasant process called thinking, but when it comes to saying, even to someone opposite, what we think, then how little we are able to convey! The phantom is through the mind and out of the window before we can lay salt on its tail, or slowly sinking and returning to the profound darkness which it has lit up momentarily with a wandering light. Face, voice, and accent eke out our words and impress their feebleness with character in speech. But the pen is a rigid instrument; it can say very little; it has all kinds of habits and ceremonies of its own. It is dictatorial too: it is always making ordinary men into prophets, and changing the natural stumbling trip of human speech into the solemn and stately march of pens. It is for this reason that Montaigne stands out from the legions of the dead with such irrepressible vivacity. We can never doubt for an instant that his book was himself. He refused to teach; he refused to preach; he kept on saying that he was just like other people. All his effort was to write himself down, to communicate, to tell the truth, and that is a "rugged road, more so than it seems."

For beyond the difficulty of communicating oneself, there is the supreme difficulty of being oneself. This soul, or life within us, by no means agrees with the life outside us. If one has the courage to ask her what she thinks, she is always saying the very opposite to what other people say. (pp. 18-19)

Really she is the strangest creature in the world, far from heroic, variable as a weathercock, "bashful, insolent; chaste, lustful; prating, silent; laborious, delicate; ingenious, heavy; melancholic, pleasant; lying, true; knowing, ignorant; liberal, covetous, and prodigal"—in short, so complex, so indefinite, corresponding so little to the version which does duty for her in public, that a man might spend his life merely in trying to run her to earth. The pleasure of the pursuit more than rewards one for any damage that it may inflict upon one's worldly prospects. The man who is aware of himself is henceforward independent; and he is never bored, and life is only too short, and he is steeped through and through with a profound yet temperate happiness. He alone lives, while other people, slaves of ceremony, let life slip past them in a kind of dream. Once conform, once do what other people do because they do it, and a lethargy steals over all the finer nerves

and faculties of the soul. She becomes all outer show and inward emptiness; dull, callous, and indifferent.

Surely then, if we ask this great master of the art of life to tell us his secret, he will advise us to withdraw to the inner room of our tower and there turn the pages of books, pursue fancy after fancy as they chase each other up the chimney, and leave the government of the world to others. Retirement and contemplation—these must be the main elements of his prescription. But no; Montaigne is by no means explicit. It is impossible to extract a plain answer from that subtle, half-smiling, half-melancholy man, with the heavy-lidded eyes and the dreamy, quizzical expression. . . . He had always mixed with clever men, and his father had a positive veneration for them, but he had observed that, though they have their fine moments, their rhapsodies, their visions, the cleverest tremble on the verge of folly. Observe yourself: one moment you are exalted; the next a broken glass puts your nerves on edge. All extremes are dangerous. It is best to keep in the middle of the road, in the common ruts, however muddy. In writing choose the common words; avoid rhapsody and eloquence—yet, it is true, poetry is delicious; the best prose is that which is most full of poetry.

It appears, then, that we are to aim at a democratic simplicity. We may enjoy our room in the tower, with the painted walls and the commodious bookcases, but down in the garden there is a man digging who buried his father this morning, and it is he and his like who live the real life and speak the real language. There is certainly an element of truth in that. Things are said very finely at the lower end of the table. There are perhaps more of the qualities that matter among the ignorant than among the learned. But again, what a vile thing the rabble is! "the mother of ignorance, injustice, and inconstancy. Is it reasonable that the life of a wise man should depend upon the judgment of fools?" Their minds are weak, soft and without power of resistance. They must be told what it is expedient for them to know. It is not for them to face facts as they are. The truth can only be known by the well-born soul—"l'âme bien née." Who, then, are these well-born souls, whom we would imitate if only Montaigne would enlighten us more precisely?

But no. "Je n'enseigne poinct; je raconte" ["I do not instruct; I relate"]. After all, how could he explain other people's souls when he could say nothing "entirely simply and solidly, without confusion or mixture, in one word," about his own, when indeed it became daily more and more in the dark to him? One quality or principle there is perhaps—that one must not lay down rules. The souls whom one would wish to resemble, like Étienne de La Boétie, for example, are always the supplest. "C'est estre, mais ce n'est pas vivre, que de se tenir attaché et obligé par nécessité a un seul train" ["It is to be, but not to live, to hold oneself bound and obliged of necessity to only one course"]. The laws are mere conventions, utterly unable to keep touch with the vast variety and turmoil of human impulses; habits and customs are a convenience devised for the support of timid natures who dare not allow their souls free play. But we, who have a private life and hold it infinitely the dearest of our possessions, suspect nothing so much as an attitude. Directly we begin to protest, to attitudinize, to lay down laws, we perish. We are living for others, not for ourselves. We must respect those who sacrifice themselves in the public service, load them with honours, and pity them for allowing, as they must, the inevitable compromise; but for ourselves let us fly fame, honour, and all offices that put us under an obligation to others. Let us simmer over our incalculable cauldron, our enthralling confusion, our hotchpotch of impulses, our perpetual miracle—for the soul throws up wonders every second. Movement and change are the essence of our being; rigidity is death; conformity is death: let us say what comes into our heads, repeat ourselves, contradict ourselves, fling out the wildest nonsense, and follow the most fantastic fancies without caring what the world does or thinks or says. For nothing matters except life; and, of course, order.

This freedom, then, which is the essence of our being, has to be controlled. But it is difficult to see what power we are to invoke to help us, since every restraint of private opinion or public law has been derided, and Montaigne never ceases to pour scorn upon the misery, the weakness, the vanity of human nature. Perhaps, then, it will be well to turn to religion to guide us? "Perhaps" is one of his favourite expressions: "Perhaps" and "I think" and all those words which qualify the rash assumptions of human ignorance. Such words help one to muffle up opinions which it would be highly impolitic to speak outright. For one does not say everything; there are some things which at present it is advisable only to hint. One writes for a very few people, who understand. Certainly, seek the Divine guidance by all means, but meanwhile there is, for those who live a private life, another monitor, an invisible censor within . . . , whose blame is much more to be dreaded than any other because he knows the truth; nor is there anything sweeter than the chime of his approval. This is the judge to whom we must submit; this is the censor who will help us to achieve that order which is the grace of a well-born soul. . . . But he will act by his own light; by some internal balance will achieve that precarious and everchanging poise which, while it controls, in no way impedes the soul's freedom to explore and experiment. Without other guide, and without precedent, undoubtedly it is far more difficult to live well the private life than the public. It is an art which each must learn separately, though there are, perhaps, two or three men, like Homer, Alexander the

Great, and Epaminondas among the ancients, and Etienne de La Boétie among the moderns, whose example may help us. But it is an art; and the very material in which it works is variable and complex and infinitely mysterious—human nature. To human nature we must keep close. " . . . il faut vivre entre les vivants" ["We must live among the living"]. We must dread any eccentricity or refinement which cuts us off from our fellow-beings. Blessed are those who chat easily with their neighbours about their sport or their buildings or their quarrels, and honestly enjoy the talk of carpenters and gardeners. To communicate is our chief business; society and friendship our chief delights; and reading, not to acquire knowledge, not to earn a living, but to extend our intercourse beyond our own time and province. Such wonders there are in the world; halcyons and undiscovered lands, men with dogs' heads and eyes in their chests, and laws and customs, it may well be, far superior to our own. Possibly we are asleep in this world; possibly there is some other which is apparent to beings with a sense which we now lack.

Here then, in spite of all contradictions and all qualifications, is something definite. These essays are an attempt to communicate a soul. On this point at least he is explicit. It is not fame that he wants; it is not that men shall quote him in years to come; he is setting up no statue in the market-place; he wishes only to communicate his soul. Communication is health; communication is truth; communication is happiness. To share is our duty; to go down boldly and bring to light those hidden thoughts which are the most diseased; to conceal nothing; to pretend nothing; if we are ignorant to say so; if we love our friends to let them know it. (pp. 20-4)

There are people who, when they travel, wrap themselves up, "se défendans de la contagion d'un air incogneu" ["defending themselves from the contagion of an unfamiliar air"] in silence and suspicion. When they dine, they must have the same food they get at home. Every sight and custom is bad unless it resembles those of their own village. They travel only to return. That is entirely the wrong way to set about it. We should start without any fixed idea where we are going to spend the night, or when we propose to come back; the journey is everything. Most necessary of all, but rarest good fortune, we should try to find before we start some man of our own sort who will go with us and to whom we can say the first thing that comes into our heads. For pleasure has no relish unless we share it. As for the risks—that we may catch cold or get a headache—it is always worth while to risk a little illness for the sake of pleasure. "Le plaisir est des principales espèces du profit" ["Pleasure is one of the chief kinds of profit"]. Besides if we do what we like, we always do what is good for us. Doctors and wise men may object, but let us leave doctors and wise men to their own dismal philosophy. For ourselves, who are ordinary men and women, let us return thanks to Nature for her bounty by using every one of the senses she has given us; vary our state as much as possible; turn now this side, now that, to the warmth, and relish to the full before the sun goes down the kisses of youth and the echoes of a beautiful voice singing Catullus. Every season is likeable, and wet days and fine, red wine and white, company and solitude. Even sleep, that deplorable curtailment of the joy of life, can be full of dreams; and the most common actions—a walk, a talk, solitude in one's own orchard—can be enhanced and lit up by the association of the mind. Beauty is everywhere, and beauty is only two fingers' breadth from goodness. So, in the name of health and sanity, let us not dwell on the end of the journey. Let death come upon us planting our cabbages, or on horseback, or let us steal away to some cottage and there let strangers close our eyes, for a servant sobbing or the touch of a hand would break us down. Best of all, let death find us at our usual occupations, among girls and good fellows who make no protests, no lamentations; let him find us "parmy les jeux, les festins, faceties, entretiens communs et populaires, et la musique, et des vers amoureux" ["among games, feasts, jests, general and popular conversation, music, and love poetry"]. But enough of death; it is life that matters.

It is life that emerges more and more clearly as these essays reach not their end, but their suspension in full career. It is life that becomes more and more absorbing as death draws near, one's self, one's soul, every fact of existence: that one wears silk stockings summer and winter; puts water in one's wine; has one's hair cut after dinner; must have glass to drink from; has never worn spectacles; has a loud voice; carries a switch in one's hand; bites one's tongue; fidgets with one's feet; is apt to scratch one's ears; likes meat to be high; rubs one's teeth with a napkin (thank God, they are good!); must have curtains to one's bed; and, what is rather curious, began by liking radishes, then disliked them, and now likes them again. No fact is too little to let it slip through one's fingers, and besides the interest of facts themselves there is the strange power we have of changing facts by the force of the imagination. Observe how the soul is always casting her own lights and shadows; makes the substantial hollow and the frail substantial; fills broad daylight with dreams; is as much excited by phantoms as by reality; and in the moment of death sports with a trifle. Observe, too, her duplicity, her complexity. She hears of a friend's loss and sympathizes, and yet has a bitter-sweet malicious pleasure in the sorrows of others. She believes; at the same time she does not believe. Observe her extraordinary susceptibility to impressions, especially in youth. A rich man steals because his father kept him short of money as a boy. This wall one builds not for oneself, but be-

cause one's father loved building. In short, the soul is all laced about with nerves and sympathies which affect her every action, and yet, even now in 1580, no one has any clear knowledge—such cowards we are, such lovers of the smooth conventional ways—how she works or what she is except that of all things she is the most mysterious, and one's self the greatest monster and miracle in the world. ". . . plus je me hante et connois, plus ma difformité m'estonne, moins je m'entens en moy" ["the more I associate with and know myself, the more my hideousness astonishes me, the less I understand myself"]. Observe, observe perpetually, and, so long as ink and paper exist . . . , Montaigne will write.

But there remains one final question which, if we could make him look up from his enthralling occupation, we should like to put to this great master of the art of life. In these extraordinary volumes of short and broken, long and learned, logical and contradictory statements, we have heard the very pulse and rhythm of the soul, beating day after day, year after year, through a veil which, as time goes on, fines itself almost to transparency. Here is someone who succeeded in the hazardous enterprise of living; who served his country and lived retired; was landlord, husband, father; entertained kings, loved women, and mused for hours alone over old books. By means of perpetual experiment and observation of the subtlest he achieved at last a miraculous adjustment of all these wayward parts that constitute the human soul. He laid hold of the beauty of the world with all his fingers. He achieved happiness. If he had had to live again, he said, he would have lived the same life over. But, as we watch with absorbed interest the enthralling spectacle of a soul living openly beneath our eyes, the question frames itself, Is pleasure the end of all? Whence this overwhelming interest in the nature of the soul? Why this overmastering desire to communicate with others? Is the beauty of this world enough, or is there, elsewhere, some explanation of the mystery? To this what answer can there be? There is none. There is only one more question: "Que scais-je?" (pp. 24-6)

Virginia Woolf, "Montaigne," in her *Collected Essays, Vol. III,* Harcourt Brace Jovanovich, 1967, pp. 18-26.

JOHN MIDDLETON MURRY
(essay date 1938)

[An English critic and editor, Murry lent early support to such authors as James Joyce, D. H. Lawrence, and Marcel Proust. In the following excerpt, he discusses the introspective and autobiographical nature of *The Essays.*]

No other equally great writer in the world's history makes so slight an initial demand upon us when he seeks our complicity in re-entering existence, as Montaigne. He is like a gift of nature: a sunshiny day. We have nothing to do but to bask in it and him. There is nothing to pay, nothing to wrestle with, nothing to be endured. The path to enjoyment, and to the essential Montaigne, seems to lie open on every page. "The bees plunder the flowers," he says, "here a little, and there a little; but afterward they make honey of them which is all their own: it is not thyme, or marjoram, any more." That is the perfect figure for the kind and quality of delight which Montaigne distilled. His honey is neither thyme nor marjoram any more, it is honey. But it is honey which always faintly reminds us of where it was gathered, and has so many subtle tones of flavor that we can never forget how widely ranging was the creature who made it. And not in books alone.

That easy approach, that natural familiarity, that sense of belonging to the family which Montaigne bestows upon his reader, is not fortuitous. When gradually it has begun to dawn upon us that Montaigne is not merely a friendly man but a great one, indeed a Colossus, we begin to realize at the same moment that he has grown into a giant almost by accident—or rather by that necessity of nature which always wears the appearance of accident. He starts, so to speak, where everybody started; he is compiling another enormous commonplace book; he is gathering the truth, as so many had gathered it before him. Slowly we become conscious that the emphasis has shifted; he is doing something different, or rather—such is the massive and impersonal force of his accumulation—something different is being done through him. The Man is not exploring the Truth, but the Truth is exploring Man. In creating a book, he had created himself. He knew it. "I have not made my book any more than my book has made me." And in responding to his book, we have been witnesses, accomplices, collaborators almost, in the work of a demiurge—the creation of the first conscious individual man.

Not the least mark of Montaigne's peculiar greatness is that nothing he tells us directly about himself cannot be corroborated, and given amplitude and richness from the body of his work. . . .

I have not studied at all in order to make a book, but I have studied to some extent because I had made one, if it be any kind of studying to skim over and catch, by the head or the feet, now one author and now another, with a view not to form my opinions but to assist those long since formed, to second them, and to be of service to them.

A thousand subtle gradations, differences, dis-

tinctions in his experience had thus been recognized, and by being thus recognized had been in some sense created. The quotations were not merely his own, they were himself. And this again in no perfunctory or vaguely metaphorical meaning. The Montaigne of whom these quotations were part was a man who grew, and who never ceased to grow; and the quotations were part of that growth. (pp. 49-50)

[By Montaigne's] effort to know himself entirely, he had lifted himself above the flux of circumstance. He was under no illusion that he did know himself entirely: that was impossible. Like Socrates, he was as ignorant as other men save in his knowledge of his own ignorance: but, being Montaigne, he gives the famous saying a turn of his own. "Je me tiens de la commune sorte, sauf en ce que je m'en tiens"; "I am an ordinary man, except that I know it." The lingering trace of Socratic intellectualism departs. Montaigne, to himself, is simply a man, who knows it.

But the process and achievement of that knowing—how great it was! And he makes it so easy for us to forget that it was great. The Montaigne we meet is already mature. The storm and stress are over. He has already learned the secret; he is a man, who knows it. The manner of his coming to a knowledge so simple and so rare has been all his own. It seems familiar enough. "Moi, qui m'espie de plus prez, qui ay les yeulx incessament tendus sur moy" ["I, who see myself the closest, who have my eyes incessantly turned on myself "]. An Amiel, surely, might claim to be as perfect in the art of self-examination? So it seems; but only seems. For Montaigne's method has been to find himself in the men of old time. He has been guarded by a prophylactic against egoism. From the beginning his discovery had been, not how much and how strange there was in him, but how much of what was in him had been in other men. He was looking for the truth, searching out all that in the experience of the ancients had been ratified by his own, establishing how completely he had been anticipated—in all, except the occupation. And the exception is the essence of Montaigne. To the extraordinary essay in which he describes the sensations of his nearly fatal accident, he subsequently added pages which perhaps more directly than any others convey the sensation of this conquistador of the human personality—"silent, upon a peak in Darien."

We hear but of two or three ancients who have traveled this road, and yet we cannot say it was at all in this manner, since we know nothing of them except their names. No one since has rushed into their path. It is a thorny undertaking, and more so than it seems, to follow a movement so wayward as that of the mind, to penetrate the opaque depths of its innermost folds, to pick out and arrest so many of its little breathlike stirrings. It is a new and extraordinary occupation, that withdraws us from the ordinary employments of the world, ay, from those most in repute.

But this was, as it were, the unexpected and residual quintessence in Montaigne's alembic after a process of self-discovery through self-cancellation. So little of himself was indeed his own, he found, that there was nothing left but "the corner in his soul" where he could rest in the recognition that he belonged to the common sort. In his own inimitable way, following his own natural bent, having for his native bias that passion for the total truth which he regarded as the one basic human virtue, Montaigne had undergone an arduous spiritual discipline before the composition of the *Essais* began. He was already capable of looking upon himself dispassionately as an object. He had had a glimpse of Montaigne *sub specie aeternitatis;* irresistibly he followed the gleam, and organized it into a vision.

He had discovered a profound philosophy, and in his book we watch him taking complete possession of it, or it of him. As his book grows so does he. Degree by degree, trait by trait, he comes under the lucid scrutiny of his own increasing awareness. What is happening he knows well, far better than most of those who have sought to expound his philosophy. The philosophy of a man, who understands by the word "philosophy" the seeking of wisdom, is always elusive to those for whom the word means a systematic doctrine. They look down upon Montaigne as an amateur; they do not notice that he is smiling at them as professionals. . . . He must be taking the name of philosopher in vain.

But not at all. He is serious while he smiles; he is serious because he smiles. He is establishing, *à bon escient* ["wittingly"], a solid and unsuspected claim to have climbed to the very pinnacle of philosophy, to have become a man so imbued and pervaded with awareness that he can put reason in its own subordinate place without having to invoke the aid of faith, if by faith is meant something different in nature from experience. He is become a man, who knows he is only a man, and is content; because the knowledge is of such a kind that it fills him with happiness. And that, for Montaigne, is the end of all philosophy, if philosophy would but know it. . . . Philosophy for him is the pursuit of perfect consciousness, which when achieved returns, by virtue of its own perfection, to be the finer life of the body. Then there is no division any more. The total man is, as it were, redeemed and purified by the imaginative spirit, so that he is made whole and made one, not with an enforced but with a natural unity. And this unity of the man, being a natural unity, is not a uniformity; it is compact of variety and animated by conflict.

Such discourses are, in my opinion, infinitely true, and reasonable: but we are, I know not how, double

in our selves, so that what we believe, we disbelieve, and cannot rid ourselves of what we condemn.

Once more, it is not the utterance of an easy skepticism; it is the self-knowledge of a great man who knows that "without contraries there is no progression," and that here can be no finality in the growth of a man indeed. Those who seek finality can have it at a price: they must eradicate some part of their humanity. To Montaigne that was sacrilege. To let die an appetite was one thing, to mortify it quite another; and to him they were as different as life and death. Not to conceal oneself from oneself, not to hide one's secret shames by violence, but to look serenely upon them, was the way of life. It was also the way of truth.

The doctrine is not an easy one, nor is it easy to be a Montaigne. Many have found that to their cost, who, charmed by his transparency, have sought to emulate him. They have proved to be as wide of the mark on one side as have been on the other those austere interpreters who have believed that Montaigne taught men "to follow nature," which seems to them an easy and dangerous doctrine. Perhaps it is; but Montaigne did not teach it. His doctrine is not dangerous, and is very difficult. It is that, if you have a nature like Montaigne's, you were best to follow it, because you will not be able to do otherwise. The essential requisite, for a nature to be like Montaigne's, is that it should possess, and be possessed by, a fundamental generosity of soul. With that to start with, you will meet Montaigne somewhere; because from that beginning the conclusion is inevitable. Finally, one is a man and knows it, and that is to have become a man.

A generous heart must not disown its own thoughts; it desires that its inward parts be seen; everything in it is good, or at least, everything is human.

Nothing more simple, nothing more difficult. In that transparent dictum is unambitiously expressed what philosophers have meant by passing beyond good and evil, what mystics have meant by passing beyond creatures, what Blake meant by declaring that "Art could not exist except by naked beauty display'd." Montaigne's *Essais* are, precisely, art in this high sense. "If I had lived among those nations which are reported still to live under the sweet liberty of the original laws of nature, I assure you that I would very willingly have painted myself entire and naked," *tout entier et tout nu.*

Montaigne is the standing confutation of all that is excessive and inhuman in Pascal. By his mere being he dissolves the menace of the judgment: "le *moi* est toujours haïssable"; "the *Self* is always hateful." Not that Montaigne would deny it, exactly: but he has something more to tell us than that, something wiser and therefore less distinctly formulable. It is that the Self is lovable, if a man can bring himself to love it.

What the Self becomes depends on how we behave toward it. It can be lovable, because it can be loved; but it can be loved only by the not-Self. In his early manhood Montaigne knew the secret of love. Self-obliteration came to him naturally in his friendship with Étienne de la Boétie. "If I should be pressed to say why I loved him, I feel that that cannot be expressed." And afterward he added the immortal phrase: "Except by saying, because it was he, because it was I." The very pulse of human love beats in those words. To have felt it is to have known that life is blessed: for love is the vision of the incomparable, the nonpareil, and the vision is seen only in self-forgetfulness.

To have turned his power of self-forgetfulness upon himself—this was Montaigne's triumph. He looked upon the Self with the eyes of the not-Self. And the history of that singular achievement is written at large in his book; indeed, the *Essais* are the embodied process of that achievement. Montaigne knew that also better than posterity has known it. His book is one long and infinitely various act of self-discovery, self-objectification, made possible only by self-forgetfulness. (pp. 54-8)

[Compare him] with the later masters of self-revelation, with Rousseau of the *Confessions,* with Châteaubriand of the *Memoires d'Outretombe.* The difference is not of degree, but of kind. In Rousseau and Châteaubriand we are interested; we read avidly all that they have to say; nevertheless, at the end, with Pascal at our elbow sternly demanding our final judgment, we are forced to confess that "the Self is always hateful." But with Montaigne it is quite different. Where Rousseau and Châteaubriand blench before the sentence of Port Royal, Montaigne stands secure and invulnerable, as though he had been refined in the fire, and all the dross purged away. Because he defends nothing, conceals nothing, he has nothing to defend or conceal. He is proof against all the acids of modern analysis; he had applied a radical skepticism, not to others, but to himself.

As the features of such a man—head and shoulders above his great age, with only Shakespeare for his peer—began to define themselves to Montaigne's consciousness, it was impossible that he should not see the significance of his instinctive enterprise. His book stood then before him as a work to be completed "with all his faith and all his force." He dedicated himself to it, and his sense of the spiritual significance of his "attempts" is conveyed in his suggestion that his book is a new and more veracious form of the practice of Christian confession, as though it were a solitary and unprecedented effort to bring religion into the stream of life. "I hold that it requires wisdom to make an estimate of oneself, whether it be high or low, impartially, and conscientiousness to publish it." Yet such was the unerring natural genius of the man that not even the strong determination which speaks in such phrases could corrupt his own spontaneity. Returning home to his work after a year and a half of travel, he said:

Meanwhile, I do not correct my first imaginations by second ones; yes, it happens that I correct a word, but to vary it, not to take it away. I wish to represent the progress of my humors, and desire each piece to be seen as it was born. I should like to have begun earlier, and be able to recognize the process of my mutations.

Beneath the apparent carelessness is the scruple of the new completely conscious man. Montaigne, who knows what he is doing, knows also the dangers of such knowledge. He must be faithful to his own growth. He must not prune, he must not trim, above all he must not suppress what he had written. It had come from him spontaneously, "naturally, as the leaves to a tree"; therefore it had its place in the final pattern. The scruple did not prevent him from making his language more vivid and nervous, and saying more exactly what he had meant to say. That would have been a fanaticism. As artist, and as man, Montaigne knew when not to be bound by his own rules. Since his style had always been one in which "les choses surmontent," in which things "showed their back above the element they lived in," it was his duty to let them rise still sharper and clearer if he could. But in the essential substance there must be no change. He felt not merely that right and proper reverence for his own past which is the privilege of men who know their own integrity, but also the peculiar obligation of his own great work.

Indeed, the *Essais* are wonderful—a book of destiny, that had to be. "A man's life of any worth," said Keats, "is a continual allegory"; and the obvious and exoteric side of the allegory of Montaigne may be found in the history of the word which his book launched into European currency—the word "essays." How startling and mysterious is the contrast between the sense of the urge and heave of creation which the word awakens as the title of Montaigne's book, and its meager and finical connotation today! . . . The *Essais* and the plays of Shakespeare complement one another. They are personal obverse and impersonal reverse of a single medal that imperishably commemorates the inward spirit of the high Renaissance in Europe. It is, in my eyes, far from an accident that in *The Tempest* Shakespeare turns to Montaigne for help in his great and final argument for forgiveness. In that halcyon moment it was as though in Montaigne and Shakespeare, nature had come to her own in man once more, and inspired him, as she must in her perfection, with a new kind of reverence for man.

Nativity, once in the main of light,
Crawls to maturity, wherewith being crowned,
Crooked eclipses 'gainst his glory fight,

And Time that gave doth now the gift confound.

But the conscious Individual who emerges in Montaigne's *Essais* was saved from eclipse by his own spiritual humility. That is the fragrance which preserved this great man from corruption. Beside him we feel that even Pascal was proud, and for very lack of humility was driven desperately to redress the balance by humiliating himself and man. But, alas, in this man of a second nature, who takes shape as concrete individual in Montaigne, and as imaginative creation in the works of Shakespeare, the religious impulse takes forms which are too generous for the age in which they live. They, like Hamlet, are beyond revenge; they cannot be fanatical. They are too aware of the individual for that.

They saw too far and too wide. Conscience makes cowards of them; they could not be men of action. Yet the man of action is necessary if the crust of custom is to be upheaved. Yet what conceivable action could express the universal tolerance which blossoms out of their recognition and realization of the Individual? Tolerance, it seems, can only suffer; its activity is passivity.

Hamlet's question is real. It is the one real question for humanity, henceforward.

> Whether 'tis nobler in the mind to suffer
> The slings and arrows of outrageous fortune,
> Or to take arms against a sea of troubles,
> And by opposing, end them?

Cromwell will have no doubt about taking arms; and he will be able to take arms for tolerance and for the individual, because he does not see too much or too far. He believes in a God of Vengeance still. Shakespeare and Montaigne cannot. Yet Cromwell's God of Vengeance is divided against himself; he calls for vengeance only on those who will not abandon vengeance. He is the authentic God of the Bible, revered as a work of total inspiration. What comes after the Bible? The gospel of Christ? Or the gospel of Man? But these are the same gospel—the gospel of the Divine Humanity. In another three hundred years it will be not a dream of the individual, but a necessity of the world, if it is to escape catastrophe.

Of that universal church of Christ, Montaigne is a forerunner. He liberates the individual that the individual may know his limitations; he makes man free in order that man may surrender his freedom, knowing that he must. He rediscovers—in a new world of freedom and responsibility—"the misery and grandeur of man." (pp. 59-62)

John Middleton Murry, "The Birth of the Individual," in his *Heroes of Thought,* Julian Messner, Inc., 1938, pp. 49-62.

FRIEDA S. BROWN
(essay date 1963)

[In the following excerpt, Brown attempts to explain the seemingly contradictory strains of liberalism and conservatism in Montaigne's philosophy.]

The religious and political conservatism of Montaigne must be understood in the context of the turbulent situation that prevailed in sixteenth-century France. . . . (p. 94)

Montaigne was temperamentally and intellectually opposed to "nouvelletés" ["novelties, changes"]. The civil wars had demonstrated conclusively, in his opinion, that the desire for inordinate reform was productive only of violence and cruelty, which he had detested ever since childhood, and that it had brought inordinate harm to France. From an intellectual point of view, his awareness of the weaknesses of human reason and his knowledge of the myriad religious and political opinions professed throughout the world made him a vigorous opponent of Protestant exegetical presumption. He could not rationally conceive of the intrinsic superiority of any one philosophy.

On the other hand, he did not attack the religious beliefs of the Huguenots. Religion to him was a matter of conscience, and obedience to conscience was the principle on which Montaigne's entire life, both public and private, was based. His constant appeals to the *réformés* ["reformers"] to return to the fold were rooted not in theological but in civic reasons. An attack on the Catholic Church constituted for him an attack on the monarchy, for he viewed the State as an organic structure which would surely be overturned if any of its important members were destroyed. In his eyes, the only possibility for peace and harmony lay in the indissoluble unity of Church and State. Given the tragic experiences of sixteenth-century France and his conviction that reason was impotent to cope either with the matter of faith or the complexities of social organization, he had concluded that the most rational course was obedience to established laws and customs.

The *Essais* attest repeatedly to the fact that their author was not primarily concerned with religious belief but with human betterment and moral improvement. Since he may not have reached the ultimate conviction that Christianity had found the solution to these problems, he established a rule of conduct divorced from religion and religious constraints and depended rather on rational principles and self-knowledge. This, however, does not preclude his profound faith in Catholicism, which is explicit throughout his writings. The Catholic religion was the only thing he never doubted, for he had placed it outside the realm of reason, and as a permanent result of his radical skepticism with regard to the efficacy of reason in religious matters, his faith remained permanently secure.

Montaigne's ultimate position was the resultant of irresistible forces, social and intellectual, that determined his political and religious attitudes throughout his life. He believed that the Christian religion and the laws of conscience commanded obedience to authority, and this belief was profoundly corroborated not only by the strain of skepticism that in certain respects never entirely abandoned him, but perhaps even more by what he had personally witnessed of the unspeakable disorders resulting from the politico-religious wars. He therefore adhered and urged adherence to the institutions and traditions of France. If many of its laws were unjust and even barbaric, it was not the right of the citizen to revolt against them. Revolution, as had amply been demonstrated, bred destruction, not progress. Human reason was too weak to guarantee that a proposed reform would necessarily be better in practice than its predecessor.

Social change, however, was neither undesirable nor impossible to Montaigne, and there is good evidence to support the belief that during a long public career, while never deviating from the conservative path which his conscience had marked out, he attempted to implement many of the liberal ideas so often and earnestly expressed in the *Essais.* For this reason and to the extent that the *Essais* are frequently a plea for religious tolerance, humanity and respect for the rights of the individual, we cannot agree with the position taken by numerous scholars to the effect that Montaigne was liberal only in thought and conservative in action.

To place his liberalism and conservatism in irreconcilable opposition is an oversimplification of the seeming paradox between the two positions as they apply to Montaigne. Far from being in contradiction with each other, Montaigne's conservatism and liberalism were necessarily complementary attitudes growing from the single Socratic principle of the self-realization of the individual in his political, religious and ethical relationships. For him, peace and order in society, in so far as they could be attained without the sacrifices of personal autonomy and integrity, created the indispensable conditions for the achievement of the self-realization of the individual, and with it, of human dignity and liberty. (pp. 94-6)

Frieda S. Brown, in her *Religious and Political Conservatism in the "Essais" of Montaigne,* Librairie Droz, 1963, 109 p.

MARK HALL
(essay date 1984)

[In the following excerpt, Hall examines *The Journal of Montaigne's Travels* as a chronicle of Montaigne's personal hardships and sixteenth-century society.]

[Michel de Montaigne's *Travel Journal*] was not written to edify the fireside reader, inspire the adventurous, or educate the provincials back home. It is in fact not an intentionally written work; rather, it is a splendid accident of literary history.

The *Journal* . . . was written by two men. The chronicle begins in the hand of Montaigne's unnamed secretary, who . . . is under the direction of his employer. For more than half the book we are treated to his anonymous and clever observations of M. Montaigne's journey. This abruptly changes when Montaigne's first person informs us: "Having dismissed one of my men who was doing this fine job, and seeing it so far advanced, whatever trouble it may be to me, I must continue it myself." He does so in Italian, then later he changes to French, his native language.

This complexity gives the work both its distinctive and appealing qualities, as well as its disconcerting and tiresome moments. There are delightful anecdotes, abundant in the secretary's portion, and asphyxiating details of the costs of everything, interesting only to those of us with an intimate understanding of the economics of the Reformation era. There are sections of great intellectual force and others of rambling, useless moaning.

While reading the latter part of the work in Montaigne's words, we are given nauseating and tedious details of the poor man's discomfort. His unrelenting pain spills onto the pages with the frenzy of a man possessed. It is this same suffering, however, that brings him to his rational Stoicism, his insightful perspective on the human condition. "And in the meantime," he writes, "it will be wise to accept joyously the good that it pleases God to send us. There is no other medicine, no other rule of science, for avoiding the ills, whatever they may be and however great, that beseige men from all sides and at every hour, than to make up our minds to suffer them humanly, or to end them courageously and promptly."

Montaigne is the true thinker. His literate secretary cannot match the quality of his master. Still, this unknown writer offers us more insight into the compulsiveness of his boss and the compellingness of the countryside.

We know from the secretary that Montaigne endured extreme conditions in his urinary and bowel functions. In fact, the trip is being taken in large part to allow Montaigne to take a "cure" through the baths and waters of France, Switzerland, Germany, and Italy. We also witness the abandon at which the great essayist throws himself into the cure. If one bath calls for drinking "seven pounds of water" every morning, so be it. If another demands that a man sit in sulphur-smelling water for eight hours, Montaigne would comply. To relieve his agony, Montaigne would go to the greatest of lengths.

The secretary is at his best, however, when he relates the stories told to him by the local population. From him we learn of the sexual ambiguity of some 16th-century peasant girls. Having just entered Vitry-le-Francois early on in the journey, the travellers have just missed the execution of a girl who "was hanged for using illicit devices to supply her defect in sex." We can infer, then, that pretending to be a man in Montaigne's sexist society was a capital offense. Compounding this "crime" was the fact that "for four or five months" the girl had been married to another young woman from

Vitry "to her satisfaction, so they say." Had the girl renounced her behavior, the locals would have probably spared her life. But she refused and so died by the hangman's rope.

Neither Montaigne nor his ghost writer are prudes. The story is related without any moral condemnation for the girl or the people who put her to death. To these travellers, sex seems to be a normal and pleasurable part of man's meagre lot in life. Montaigne says, "the greatest pleasure is derived . . . to see the ladies at the windows . . . who show themselves how they tantalize our eyes as they do," as he recalls his walks through the Italian cities. Sex, like his health, was a part of life. It existed in all manner and form. It was a subject as fascinating as any other, no more, no less.

The book, lively and anecdotal as it is, was not intended for publication and suffers from lack of focus. There are passages that serve no purpose other than as a release for Montaigne's continual and horrible pain. *Travel Journal* is a rare and raw portrait of a great man in his most human form. (pp. 23, 26)

Mark Hall, "The Unintentional Book: Michel de Montaigne's 'Travel Journal'," in *San Francisco Review of Books,* Spring, 1984, pp. 23, 26.

SOURCES FOR FURTHER STUDY

Boase, Alan M. *The Fortunes of Montaigne: A History of the "Essays" in France, 1580-1669.* London: Metheun & Co., 1935, 462 p.

> Exhaustively examines the influence of *The Essays* on "the development of Humanism as opposed to orthodox Christianity" in the years preceding the Enlightenment.

Chambers, Frank M. "Pascal's Montaigne." *PMLA* LXV, No. 5 (September 1950): 790-804.

> Attempts to explain the ambivalence toward Montaigne on the part of French theologian Blaise Pascal, who excoriated Montaigne for his perceived self-absorption and immorality but drew on his writings for philosophical inspiration.

Frame, Donald M. *Montaigne: A Biography.* San Francisco: North Point Press, 1984, 408 p.

> Reprint of Frame's definitive 1965 biography of Montaigne.

Insdorf, Cecile. *Montaigne and Feminism.* Chapel Hill: North Carolina Studies in the Romance Languages and Literatures, 1977, 102 p.

> Examines Montaigne's attitudes toward women in his writing and in his life.

Norton, Glyn P. *Montaigne and the Introspective Mind.* The Hague: Mouton, 1975, 219 p.

> Comprehensive study of introspection in Montaigne's literature.

Taylor, George Coffin. *Shakespeare's Debt to Montaigne.* New York: Phaeton Press, 1968, 66 p.

> Exhaustive study of Montaigne's influence on William Shakespeare in which Taylor juxtaposes passages from Shakespeare's dramas and *The Essays* in order to demonstrate similarities of content, style, and thought.

Toni Morrison

1931-

(Born Chloe Anthony Wofford) American novelist, dramatist, and editor.

INTRODUCTION

Morrison's critically acclaimed novels chronicle black American life, employing "an artistic vision that encompasses both a private and a national heritage," according to Angel Wigan. In such works as *The Bluest Eye* (1969), *Song of Solomon* (1977), and *Beloved* (1987), she portrays troubled characters who struggle to gain individual and cultural identity in a society that warps or impedes such discovery. Critics have often observed themes of initiation and a quest for love in her works, emphasizing her technique of magic realism. According to Charles Larson, each of Morrison's novels "is as original as anything that has appeared in our literature in the last 20 years. The contemporaneity that unites them—the troubling persistence of racism in America—is infused with an urgency that only a black writer can have about our society." Morrison herself has stated that she willingly accepts critical classification as a "black woman writer" because the label does not limit her writing. She maintained: "I really think the range of emotions and perceptions I have had access to as a black person and a female person are greater than those of people who are neither. . . . My world did not shrink because I was a black female writer. It just got bigger."

Morrison was born in Lorain, Ohio, to Ramah Willis Wofford and George Wofford, a shipyard welder. As an adolescent, she read classic Russian novels, Gustave Flaubert's *Madame Bovary*, and the works of Jane Austen. Morrison later commented: "These books were not written for a little black girl in Lorain, Ohio, but they were so magnificently done that I got them anyway—they spoke directly to me out of their own specificity. I wasn't thinking of writing then . . . but when I wrote my first novel years later, I wanted to capture that same specificity about the nature and feeling of the culture *I* grew up in." Morrison attended Howard

University, and in 1955 she received a master's degree from Cornell University. In 1957 she returned to Howard to teach English, and there met Harold Morrison, a Jamaican architect; she married Morrison and had two sons. After their divorce in 1964, she worked as an editor for a textbook subsidiary of Random House, where she is currently a senior editor. During this time she wrote her first novel, *The Bluest Eye,* which was published in 1969.

Often considered a novel of initiation, *The Bluest Eye* focuses on a young black girl named Pecola Breedlove. Pecola perceives herself as ugly and is obsessed with her desire for blue eyes, thinking that they will make her beautiful. Viewing Shirley Temple as the epitome of female beauty, she often drinks several quarts of milk from a Shirley Temple mug, gazing into young Temple's blue eyes. Pecola's fixation turns to insanity, however, following several traumatic events; she is raped by her father, and conceives a child who dies. Withdrawing into a world of fantasy, she comes to believe that she has the bluest eyes of anyone. The conflict between black identity and white cultural values depicted in *The Bluest Eye* is reflected by the work's opening in which Morrison presents three versions of the same "Dick and Jane" primer. The first version describes a happy family, a nice house, friends, and pets, representing an idealized white family. The second version closely resembles the first but is written without standard capitalization or punctuation, reflecting a struggling yet happy black family. In the third version, words are obfuscated; they run together without distinction or spaces. This "distorted run-on," according to Phyllis R. Klotman, is the Breedlove family, and Pecola "lives in a misshapen world which finally destroys her." Praising Morrison's first novel as an excellent depiction of black girlhood, Ruby Dee wrote that Morrison "digs up for viewing secret thoughts, terrible yearnings and little-understood frustrations common to many of us. She says these are the gnawings we keep pushed back into the subconscious, unadmitted, but they must be worked on, ferreted up and out so we can breathe deeply, say loud and truly believe 'Black is beautiful.' "

Nominated for a National Book Award in 1974, Morrison's next work, *Sula* (1973), focuses on the unusual friendship between a submissive woman named Nel, and Sula, a rebellious woman who becomes the pariah of her town. Some critics interpreted the relationship between the two characters as mirroring an intrinsic conflict experienced by black women—the conflict between the desire to rebel and the urge to conform. Perceived as evil by her community, Sula acts out violent impulses; in the course of the story she drops a young boy to his death, watches with interest as her own mother dies by fire, and seduces Jude, her best friend's husband. However, she is also considered an inspiring symbol of freedom in her community. Critics were impressed by the bizarre characters in *Sula*—among theme Eva Peace, Sula's despotic, crippled grandmother, and Shadrack, a World War I veteran and the founder of National Suicide Day. Yet some commentators found the novel's violent deaths and apparent amorality disturbing. For example, Jerry H. Bryant perceived "something ominous" in "the chilling detachment" with which Morrison drew her characters.

Song of Solomon, Morrison's third novel, won the National Book Critics Circle Award the year of its publication, 1977. The work chronicles the story of Milkman Dead, focusing on his quest for identity and his search to discover his ancestry. Milkman acquires his first name when his mother is discovered breast-feeding him when he is four years old. His surname, however, is the result of a mistake: a drunken Yankee soldier incorrectly registered his grandfather with the Freedmen's Bureau. When Milkman's grandfather told the soldier that his father was dead and that he was born in Macon, his name became "Macon Dead." In a review of *Song of Solomon,* Anne Tyler commented: "I would call the book poetry, but that would seem to be denying its considerable power as a story. Whatever name you give it, it's full of magnificent people, each of them complex and multilayered, even the narrowest of them narrow in extravagant ways." Morrison followed *Song of Solomon* with *Tar Baby* (1981), a novel critics generally found less impressive than Morrison's earlier works. Jadine Childs, a black Sorbonne-educated model, is the "tar baby" who entraps the "rabbit" represented by William Green, called Son. This "novel of ideas" has been called an allegory of colonization. For example, the "white imperialist" candy-maker Valerian Street, who paid for Jadine's schooling and employs her aunt and uncle as domestics, "colonizes" an isolated French West Indian island, Isle des Chevaliers, by building an estate there. Morrison explained that she used this setting for the novel because she wanted the characters to have "no access to any of the escape routes that people have in a large city." Although *Tar Baby* was praised for its provocative themes and beautiful language, some critics found the work obscure and claimed that its characters lack motivation for their behavior. With the publication of this novel, however, Darwin T. Turner called Morrison a major American novelist and "an artful creator of grotesques destined to live in worlds where seeds of love seldom blossom."

Morrison published her next novel, *Beloved,* in 1987. A central incident in the work involves a fugitive slave who murders her infant daughter to spare her a life in bondage. Morrison based this scenario on an article she read in a nineteenth-century magazine while editing *The Black Book* (1974), an unconventional history of blacks in America, for Random House. Like

Sethe, the protagonist of *Beloved*, Margaret Garner was a runaway slave who was tracked by her owner to Cincinnati, where she sought refuge with her freed mother-in-law. Faced with imminent capture, Garner attempted to murder her four children, succeeding in killing one. "I just imagined the life of a dead girl which was the girl that Margaret Garner killed," Morrison explained. "And I call her Beloved so that I can filter all these confrontations and questions that she has . . . and then to extend her life . . . her search, her quest." In *Beloved*, Sethe's daughter returns from the grave after twenty years, seeking revenge for her death.

This highly acclaimed novel became a source of controversy several months after publication. When *Beloved* failed to win the 1987 National Book Award or the National Book Critics Circle Award, forty-eight prominent black writers and critics signed a tribute to Morrison's career and published it in the January 24, 1988, edition of the *New York Times Book Review.* The document suggested that despite the international acclaim Morrison has garnered for her works, she has yet to receive sufficient national recognition. The writers' statement prompted heated debate within the New York literary community, and some critics charged Morrison's supporters with racist manipulation. When *Beloved* was awarded the 1988 Pulitzer Prize for fiction, Robert Christopher, the secretary of the Pulitzer board, stated: "[It] would be unfortunate if anyone diluted the value of Toni Morrison's achievement by suggesting that her prize rested on anything but merit."

Morrison is recognized as an important and highly original writer, and her depiction and understanding of her black American heritage have drawn a wide readership. Morrison, who is presently teaching at Princeton University and at work on another novel, strives to make her works distinctly African-American and thereby locate a common element in black literature. In the essay "Rootedness: The Ancestor as Foundation," she wrote: "I don't regard Black literature as simply books written *by* Black people, or simply as literature written *about* Black people, or simply as literature that uses a certain mode of language in which you just sort of drop *g*'s. There is something very special and very identifiable about it and it is my struggle to *find* that elusive but identifiable style in the books."

(For further information about Morrison's life and works, see *Authors and Artists for Young Adults,* Vol. 1; *Black Literature Criticism; Black Writers; Concise Dictionary of American Literary Biography, 1968-1987; Contemporary Authors,* Vols. 29-32; *Contemporary Authors New Revision Series,* Vol. 27; *Contemporary Literary Criticism,* Vols. 4, 10, 22, 55; *Dictionary of Literary Biography,* Vols. 6, 33; *Dictionary of Literary Biography Yearbook: 1981;* and *Something About the Author,* Vol. 57.)

CRITICAL COMMENTARY

PHYLLIS R. KLOTMAN

(essay date 1979)

[In the following excerpt, Klotman focuses on Morrison's *The Bluest Eye*, emphasizing its depiction of the dichotomy between black identity and white cultural values.]

Toni Morrison's novel *The Bluest Eye* (1970) is a female *Bildungsroman*, a novel of growing up, of growing up young and black and female in America. The story centers around the lives of two black families, the McTeers and the Breedloves, migrants from the South, living in Lorain, Ohio. But its emphasis is on the children, Claudia and Frieda McTeer and Pecola Breedlove—their happy and painful experiences in growing up, their formal and informal education. In fact, education by the school and society is the dominant theme of *The Bluest Eye*.

The novel opens with three versions of the "Dick and Jane" reader so prevalent in the public schools at the time (the 1940s) of the novel. Morrison uses this technique to juxtapose the fictions of the white educational process with the realities of life for many black children. The ironic duality of the school/home experience is illuminated through the ingenious structure of the novel. The "Dick and Jane" referent effectively introduces the fictional milieu of Morrison's characters; it is one with which we are all familiar. . . . It is the world of the first-grade basic reader—middle-class, secure, suburban and white, replete with dog, cat, nonworking mother and leisure-time father. . . . This first version of the simulated-reader quotation is clear, straight, rendered in "Standard English"—correct and white. The second, while it repeats the message exactly, assumes a different visual appearance on the page which is less clear yet still comprehensible although written without proper capitals or punctuation. . . . The third, the wording of which is likewise unaltered, is completely run together, one long collection of consonants and vowels seeming to signify nothing. . . .

Principal Works

The Bluest Eye (novel) 1969

Sula (novel) 1973

The Black Book [editor] (history) 1974

Song of Solomon (novel) 1977

Tar Baby (novel) 1981

Dreaming Emmett (drama) 1986

Beloved (novel) 1987

Jazz (novel) 1992

Playing in the Dark: Whiteness and the Literary Imagination (lectures) 1992

These three versions are symbolic of the lifestyles that the author explores in the novel either directly or by implication. The first is clearly that of the alien white world (represented by the Fisher family) which impinges upon the lives of the black children and their families while at the same time excluding them. The second is the lifestyle of the two black McTeer children, Claudia and Frieda, shaped by poor but loving parents trying desperately to survive the poverty, the Northern cold and Northern style of racism they encounter in Ohio. The Breedloves' lives, however, are like the third—the distorted run-on—version of "Dick and Jane," and their child Pecola lives in a misshapen world which finally destroys her. The simulated "here is the house" quotation, with its variants, serves several purposes: as a synopsis of the tale that is to follow, and as a subtly ironic comment on a society which educates—and unconscionably socializes—its young with callous disregard for the cultural richness and diversity of its people. (p. 123)

The epitome of the good, the true, and the beautiful is, of course, Shirley Temple. Morrison uses the contrast between Shirley Temple and Pecola, like the contrasting versions of "Dick and Jane," to underscore the irony of black experience. Whether one learns acceptability from the formal educational experience or from cultural symbols, the effect is the same: self-hatred. Pecola's actual experience cannot be found in "Dick and Jane," for in the school primer, society denied her existence. In yearning to be Shirley Temple, she denies her own: "A little black girl yearns for the blue eyes of a little white girl, and the horror at the heart of her yearning is exceeded only by the evil of fulfillment." . . .

Very early in the novel, Pecola's terribly pathetic desire to be Shirley Temple is demonstrated by her fascination with Frieda's blue-and-white Shirley Temple mug. She would inundate herself with milk (three quarts worth) just to hold the cup with "the silhouette of Shirley Temple's dimpled face," . . . and gaze fond-

ly into the blue eyes. It is in fact the blue eyes for which Pecola prays nightly; they are the answer to all things. . . .

Pecola does not have joy and love to balance the pain and ugliness of her "normal" everyday experiences. Growing gradually into puberty is a luxury denied her. So she retreats into madness, a madness that includes the blue eyes she has prayed for, bestowed upon her by a "magic man," Soaphead Church, a strange outcast of a man suffering from his own delusions. (p. 124)

Pecola takes on some of the scapegoat characteristics that Trueblood has in Ellison's *Invisible Man,* at least for those in the black community. While Trueblood is rejected by the Blacks, he is supported by the white community and "displayed" as a kind of atavistic throwback, a comforting reminder of the dark, libidinous forces truly civilized man has repressed. The white community in the world of Morrison's novel has little or nothing to do with Pecola: She is rejected out of hand. But Claudia, struggling toward maturity and understanding, finally perceives the depth of her involvement in Pecola's descent into madness: "All of us—all who knew her—felt so wholesome after we cleaned ourselves on her. We were so beautiful when we stood astride her ugliness. . . ."

Nature serves as the unifying element in the novel. Each of the major sections is designated by season from autumn to summer. Time moves back and forth for the characters, whose lives unfold against the natural but inexorable progression of the seasons. The novel sets up its own tensions between the natural and unnatural, between the aberrations of nature and those of man. What makes the earth unyielding? What aborts life and stunts the growth of nature's offspring? These are the questions explored by the novelist through the marigold imagery and through the pattern of relationships intricately worked out around an act of violence against a child.

Although the Dick-and-Jane and Shirley Temple techniques set up a dichotomy between black experience and white culture, the issue of growth and development set into the framework of the *Bildungsroman* points to the commonality of human experience. All stages of life from birth to death are engaged. The rite of passage, initiating the young into womanhood at first tenuous and uncertain, is sensitively depicted. We also learn about the beauty and ugliness of the lives of women at the other end of the continuum—old women whose lives "were synthesized in their eyes—a purée of tragedy and humor, wickedness and serenity, truth and fantasy." . . . *The Bluest Eye* is an extraordinarily passionate yet gentle work, the language lyrical yet precise—it is a novel for all seasons. (p. 125)

Phyllis R. Klotman, "Dick-and-Jane and the Shirley Temple

Sensibility in 'The Bluest Eye'," in *Black American Literature Forum,* Vol. 13, No. 4, Winter, 1979, pp. 123-25.

ANNE Z. MICKELSON
(essay date 1979)

[In the essay excerpted below, Mickelson discusses the theme of rebellion in Morrison's novels.]

In her first novel, *The Bluest Eye* (1970), Toni Morrison deals with children and that element of belief by many black people, as she sees it, that an ultimate glory is possible. Pecola Breedlove yearns for blue eyes as the next best thing to being white. Blue eyes become for her a symbol of pride and dignity. She seeks the glory of blue eyes through prayer . . . and eventually through madness when, believing that blue eyes have finally been granted her, she walks about flapping her arms like wings, convinced that she can fly. Secure in her madness, she has no knowledge that she has become the town pariah.

The author's second novel, *Sula* (1974), expands the theme of pariah by charting her heroine's odyssey from childhood to adulthood. . . . Toni Morrison develops the theme by focusing on two women and their friendship: an extraordinary friendship in which one is a rebel who becomes the town's scandal, and the other a conformist who does all the proper things expected of her. Analyzing their different households at the age of twelve, Morrison brings together the components of their lives with a fine sympathy for a friendship which, though broken, ultimately assumes a dramatic meaning for the story and the women. Though it is Nel, the conformist woman, who voices the idea that Sula had been her glory, the book ends with each woman's thoughts centered on the other, despite the fact that no reconciliation has taken place. (pp. 124-25)

Toni Morrison combines the psychological, the symbolic, and the philosophical in her portraits of Nel and Sula in order to demonstrate that each complements the other. There is a hint of Dostoevsky's *The Double* and the Dostoevskyan idea that in every person there lurks a double. Morrison's fictional method is character counterpoint, rather than the Dostoevskyan technique of encompassing the timid and the masterful in one figure. (pp. 125-26)

A radically fresh approach to the theme of rebellion is that the author works with symbols and the psychological to establish Nel and Sula as projections of different aspects of the same character. In appeearance one is light, the other dark. Nel's skin is described as the color of wet sand, while Sula's is a heavy brown color and she has a birthmark over one eye. . . .

The symbolic use of names is important. Nel (knell) connotes the pealing note of doom on which Nel's life ends not once but three times, with each separation from Sula. The first time is when Nel marries and Sula goes away for ten years. The second time is the break with Sula over Jude, Nel's husband, with whom Sula sleeps briefly. The third and most poignant is Nel's realization that in Sula's grave is buried the passion, the life, the fun, and the healthy womanhood which Sula represented. On the other hand, Sula's name suggests an abbreviation of Suleiman, The Magnificent. . . .

In terms of psychological analysis, the actions of Sula and Nel are "figure splitting"—the separation and projection of character into component parts. Nel is calm, passive, or frightened in a crisis. Sula's emotions erupt in some action that is strong or even violent. (p. 128)

Each significant part of the two women's characterizations, both as children and as women, then, comes from the author's repeated insistence that they are one person split into two; as Sula's grandmother says, "never was no difference." . . .

In the author's structuring of Sula and Nel, then, they are less persons in their own right than representations of rebel and conformist, which the author views as the black woman's intrinsic conflict. Particularly with Sula, the writer seems to be going beyond such representation, addressing herself to the idea of the great rebel—the one who exceeds boundaries, creates excitement, tries to break free of encroachments of external cultural forces and challenges destiny. What, for example, does she have Sula do? Believing that an unpatterned, unconditioned life is possible, Sula tries to avoid uniformity by creating her own kind of life. (p. 129)

The author, however, is not just working with the idea of the importance of experience. There are times in the book when one gets the impression that in dealing with the theme of a woman's right to an experimental life, the writer is pushing the reader to consider something much more unconventional. This is that the impulse to murder and violence in the human psyche is endemic not only to men; women, too, are capable of violence, Morrison seems to be saying. (p. 130)

In [*Sula*] the moral initiative which underlies Sula's experimental life is rooted in her capacity to initiate violence, as is illustrated in two childhood scenes. The author hits us with the idea that Nel and Sula as women recall the different scenes of violence with the same emotion—pleasure, or more accurately "satisfaction." Whether or not the author is exploring repressed drives or even pathological complexes, the following two scenes are presented boldly. As a twelve-year-old,

Sula drowns Chicken Little when she swings the child around so vigorously that he slips from her hands and lands in the nearby river. . . .

The author follows this immediately with another scene which underscores D. H. Lawrence's idea that no act of murder is "accidental." Sula's mother catches on fire while tending a fire in the yard, and Sula watches her mother's burning not with horror, as would be expected, but with an "interested" expression. . . . (p. 131)

Without question, the description of the two scenes and the emotions of Sula/Nel has sexual overtones. As Mailer dramatizes with Rojack in *An American Dream,* the act of murder can be as orgasmic as the act of sexual love. There is more than an implication of this idea in Morrison's novel; disguised as a psychological novel, it is really a novel of ideas prodding us to think on the experimental life for woman. . . . (p. 132)

Yet the author does not seem at ease with her characterization of Sula, violence, and the experimental life. She steps in with an armload of explanations distributed over several pages. Sula had inherited her grandmother's arrogance and her mother's self-indulgence; she had never felt any obligation to please someone unless their pleasure pleased her; she was as willing to receive pain as to give it; she had never been the same since she overheard her mother Hannah explain that she loved Sula but did not like her; the boy's drowning had closed something off in her; and so forth.

The author soon drops this line of reasoning and turns with relief to a defense of Sula summed up as: Sula was not afraid of "the free fall." . . . (It's a phrase which has a possible echo of Milton's Lucifer.) The conventional women of the Bottom were. These women had allowed their husbands to dry up their dreams, and those without men looked like "sour-tipped needles featuring one constant empty eye." . . . Sooner or later, all died with their aprons on. The writer makes it clear that Sula's one lapse into conventionality, when she falls in love with Ajax and begins to dream of a commitment from him, results in sorrow and the common fate reserved for the black woman—desertion.

Unfortunately, the literary destiny of most rebel women—death—does not spare Sula. . . . She dies at thirty, but not without stating that her rebellion has been the natural outcome of her dialectic. On her death bed, she sustains her position philosophically by weighing the pros and cons of what is good and bad, renounces the accepted definition of goodness, and reiterates her belief that it is only life that matters. Life is important, life must be lived and duty and suffering on this earth are too high a price to pay for heavenly immortality. (pp. 132-33)

The novel bears the same incompleteness as

Sula's search for freedom. . . . Sula makes of life a defiant gesture which liberates her to an extent, and keeps her from self-pity. She is sustained by her pride in the fact that she walks through life with no blinders on. Yet, there is no happy ending. Sula collapses in the loneliness of the search for freedom, and proves what? That love is necessary? That the human heart cannot entertain equal proportions of good and evil? That everything is not relative? These and other unanswered questions are given more scope in [Morrison's next novel], *Song of Solomon.* (p. 134)

In this novel, she deals not only with the woman who breaks away from the established society to create an individualistic life for herself, but with the black man who yearns to fly—to break out of the confining life into the realm of possibility—and who embarks on a series of dramatic adventures. . . . But whether or not the hero, Milkman, as he is nicknamed, will continue to ride the air or die at the hands of his former black friend is unresolved. However, this question, posed at the end for the reader, throws in sharper focus the themes which the writer carries over from her previous books: flight, the journey, family, friendship, violence, the paradox of good and evil, the world of black society: its code, superstitions, plus fable, song, and myth.

The achievement of this novel is its willingness and ability not only to explore these areas in further detail, but to use black folklore, the ready acceptance of the supernatural, and magic as part of black culture. (p. 135)

Many of Morrison's characters in [*Song of Solomon*] believe in the capacity of the mind to see through the chinks of the cavern—even the money-hungry and materialistic Macon Dead. But it is Macon's sister Pilate who emerges as the most powerful figure in the book with her calm acceptance of this world, as well as of another reality other than the fixed one of the world. She is thoroughly at home with herself, and has the kind of sensibility which is not disturbed by anything she experiences or witnesses. There is something splendidly pagan and primitive about her, and she is represented at the time we first meet her as having the power to evoke from others various reflections of her own kindliness and understanding. Implicitly, the author establishes Pilate's capacity for placing herself in harmony with the laws of the earth and nature. Within the orbit of Morrison's moral vision, these laws have to do with the truths of the human heart. They are the necessity to demonstrate courage, endurance, sympathy, and desire to help others, while surviving with dignity. (p. 136)

The story of Pilate is part of a black family history which spans almost a century of American history. It is given special enrichment through the tracing of many lives. More notably, it forms a fascinating parallel with the odyssey of her nephew Milkman, who is the other chief character in the story. The fullness of the book even incorporates within it an ironic twist on the Faulknerian theme: the collapse of a proud, white Southern family, and the faithful black retainer who continues to serve with humility and devotion. Braided in with the lives of the black people is also a brief story of the decline of a white family whose men killed Pilate's father. . . . The dominant motif in the book, however, is not revenge, but the proud realization by a black family of who and what they are. Morrison's fiction is the opposite of Richard Wright's in this respect. Where Wright finds no sustaining values in the past of black people, Morrison celebrates the past. Pilate, Macon, and Milkman, whose last name is Dead, did not just drop from nowhere. They go back to a long line of succession. There was a beginning. A source. It is this knowledge which gives them a sense of renewal; even Macon experiences renewal in a small way. (p. 138)

The design of the book is sprawling and the narrative texture depends on a great many cumulative effects. Together with the author's allusions and indirect use of archetypal patterns about Pilate, she never lets us lose sight of the fact that Pilate is a woman grounded firmly in the social reality of black society. Pilate's twenty-year odyssey, and her subsequent life in the small town in which she finally settles not far from her brother (to his rage, embarrassment and shame over her unconventional life), enables the author to move further than in the previous novel in her discussion of black society and women—married and unmarried.

The young Pilate, alone and completely dependent on her own resources, cannot find acceptance. . . . [Her] life takes on a habitual pattern. She is either asked to leave the community, or she is deserted by these people who simply disappear during the night, since they are migrant workers. Pilate, however, resists any sense of permanent personal displacement. (p. 141)

The writer is careful not to make Pilate into a romantic Pantheist. Hence, we see Pilate appraising her situation, the social scene, and debating the means of personal salvation available to her. She does this with no semblance of self-pity, sentiment, and brooding introspection. . . . Like Sula, she decides to take "the free fall," but in a different way.

She rejects the traditional image of woman by cutting off her hair, binding it into a turban and wearing clothes functional to her way of life. With two people now to support (daughter and granddaughter), she looks around the social scene, and realizing that throats are thirsty as long as there is prohibition, she becomes a bootlegger, making and selling wine and whiskey. The author stresses that Pilate never loses her humanity, nor debases herself and other women by allowing traffic in women flesh. She only *sells* wine and whiskey

(author's italics). There is no consumption on the premises. Thus Pilate soon enjoys that status so difficult for black women (and white women) to acquire—economic independence. As an economically-independent woman, she is able to function outside of patriarchal values and rise successfully above the social forces which are a constant threat to the black woman. (pp. 141-42)

Interestingly enough, while Morrison presents women who eventually free themselves somehow from an unnatural life, Pilate's daughter and granddaughter are portrayed differently. Although leading a natural life in some respects, they are essentially weak women. (p. 145)

Ironically, Pilate, who is able to break out of the enclosures of conventional thinking and make a brave and happy life for herself, cannot inspire either woman in her house to follow her example. The author tries to get around it by hinting that Reba is somewhat simple-minded, and that Hagar is one of those pretty, spoiled black women who either want to kill or die for love. Perhaps the more plausible answer is that Pilate exercises individual will, whereas the others simply do not.

The explorations of the lives of these women reveal a growth in the author's feminist consciousness not present in the previous novel. Alternatives are possible, says the author, and in the character of Pilate she creates a woman who finds life worth living and lives it. Perhaps, Toni Morrison would not care to be discussed in terms of feminist consciousness, but the fact remains that her depiction of Pilate stresses that Pilate's pattern of living does not follow the achievement pattern associated with successful men. Pilate is always the humanist. . . .

The order of things is questioned and judged not only from social and moral viewpoints, but also from the metaphysical. If Pilate is not accepted by kin and society, she is very much at home with her dead father, who appears before her periodically with advice. One piece of advice is to go back to the cave and collect the bones of the dead man, which she does. It makes for the extraordinary ending to the book: for the bones are really those of her father. Their proper burial adds a note of the classic to the details of family history. (p. 146)

Life and death, then, hold no terrors for Pilate, whose sense of contact with this and other worlds is a natural one. She is able to survive in a society which denies her "partnership in marriage, confessional friendship, and communal religion." . . . The author concludes her tribute to Pilate by commenting that Pilate makes a life for herself in which for sixty-eight years she has shed no tears since the day Circe offered her white bread and storebought jam. In return for rudeness, she extends politeness, and her concern for troubled people ripens with the years. Yet for some reason, as in *Sula,* the woman who dares to live by her own rules must die. True, Pilate doesn't disappear from life at the early age that Sula does, but she is rendered with such loving detail that her death from the shot of a black killer comes as a shock to the reader. . . .

Needless to say, in Pilate Morrison finds a powerful voice that fulfills the promise of a personality who has resolved the seminal conflict between the claims of nature and the claims of culture. However, *Song of Solomon,* unlike the writer's previous novels, gives men a more prominent place, and specifically Milkman, son of Macon Dead and nephew of Pilate. The book is fairly equally divided between the respective journeys of Pilate and Milkman. Both take the standard path of the formula observed in mythology: separation, initiation, and return. The connection with mythology is elusive. (p. 147)

Certainly, one hears overtones of the Jason myth and his quest for the Golden Fleece in Milkman's search for gold and his desertion of Hagar, whose name means to forsake. But, since Morrison is working with a reality of her own which is not primarily connected with logic, science, and related fields, her language is often symbolical, and particularly her use of names. . . .

What we have in *Song of Solomon,* with Milkman's story, is that constant in American literature—the undertaking of the journey to free oneself. Pilate's efforts to liberate herself from cramped conditions of living are a result of society's rejection of her. Milkman's energies are concentrated on liberating himself from the confining and bitter atmosphere of his father's home, from the role thrust upon him—being his father's flunky—and from the provincial town in which he lives. (p. 148)

Milkman's journey arrests his selfish egotism and puts him on a whole new path of thinking about himself and the world. He learns about isolation, terror, suffering, survival, joy, triumph, and coming together. Though the ending is deliberately ambiguous, because Guitar is waiting for him with a gun, we get a strong feeling that Milkman will live. Pilate has instilled in him the life-affirming principle, and Milkman will be able to return with his newfound knowledge and help others. (p. 149)

Morrison's tracing of Milkman's journey through Pennsylvania and Virginia can be regarded, in many places, as in the tradition of the picaresque, in which each episode brings the protagonist into contact with some aspect of black society. But, in fact, it can more profitably be examined as a journey in which each place becomes a test of character and soul, with the results that the hero grows in understanding as he learns bits of family history and starts piecing it together. His-

tory becomes a choral symphony to Milkman, in which each individual voice has a chance to speak and contribute to his growing sense of well-being.

The pattern is something like this. In Reverend Cooper's parsonage, Milkman hears that it was right in this room that Pilate's snuff box was soldered. The information makes him feel "real." . . . He also learns more details about his grandfather's murder, as well as the fact that the killers were never brought to justice. It forces him to think about justice and injustice, something that as the son of a prosperous black man he has not had much occasion to do. (pp. 150-51)

His next step is to survey the acres which his grandfather cleared single-handed, and which are now as overgrown as his grandfather found them. The sight arouses his admiration and pride in his ancestor and he feels diminished because of the life he has led personally. Later, attacked by black men, he realizes that the flaunting of his prosperity (well-cut suit, expensive luggage, good Scotch) is an affront to those less fortunate than he. Finally, faced with the unknown when he goes on a hunting expedition with older black men, he proves his manhood and achieves harmony with nature and man in the forest.

None of these episodes is fully realized, but they form a chain. Together with Milkman's increasing excited realization that he is no longer on the scent of gold, but looking for his origins, we discover the change from callous, selfish, uncaring man to caring man. In the end, the revelation that the town in which his great grandfather lived had just about everything named after him, and that there is even a legend about his ancester, brings him exultation.

It is this legend surrounded in the romantic myth of man flying which raises some problems for me. The story holds that Milkman's ancestor lifted his arms one day and soared into space toward Africa, leaving wife and twenty children behind. . . . The effect of the story on Milkman is electrifying: "Oh, man! He didn't need no airplane. He just took off; got fed up. *All the way up!* (author's italics). . . . No more bales! . . . Nor more shit! . . . Lifted his beautiful black ass up in the sky and flew on home . . . and the whole damn town is named after him." . . .

All of the events of the journey, then, coalesce in a single vision—flying. The black man must fly, thinks Milkman. The book's structure reinforces the idea. It begins with the unsuccessful attempt of a black man to fly on the day Milkman is born, and ends with the story of the successful flight of Milkman's ancestor. A question is inevitable: flight from what, one asks? Poverty? Home? Wife? Children? Yes. It is the traditional poor man's divorce, common in life and in fiction. . . . It is interesting that Toni Morrison, whose attitude on desertion of family in *Sula* is uncompromising, should have softened her thinking. (pp. 151-52)

Anne Z. Mickelson, "Winging Upward, Black Women: Sarah E. Wright, Toni Morrison, Alice Walker," in her *Reaching Out: Sensitivity and Order in Recent American Fiction by Women,* The Scarecrow Press, Inc., 1979, pp. 112-74.

JANE S. BAKERMAN
(essay date 1981)

[Below, Bakerman asserts that failed initiation is the pervasive experience of Morrison's female characters.]

[Toni Morrison] has achieved major stature through the publication of only three novels. *The Bluest Eye* (1970) and *Sula* (1973) are brief, poetic works which explore the initiation experiences of their black, female, adolescent protagonists. *Song of Solomon* (1977) is a much longer but still lyrical story relating Macon (Milkman) Dead's search for familiar roots and personal identity. Milkman's development is framed and illuminated by the maturation stories of three women important in his life, and the presence of these subplots in the tale of a male protagonist is a good indication of the importance of female initiation in Morrison's thought.

For Toni Morrison, the central theme of all her work is [love]. . . . Certainly, this theme is evident in *The Bluest Eye, Sula,* and *Song of Solomon,* their female characters searching for love, for valid sexual encounters, and, above all, for a sense that they are worthy. (p. 541)

In Toni Morrison's novels, she joins her basic theme with the initiation motif, and the initiation experiences, trying and painful as they are, fail. Pilate invents her own standards and lives almost outside society, a choice which eventually brings tragedy upon her family. Sula rebels and is rejected. Nel marries; Corinthians takes a lover, and both are diminished. Hagar and Pecola attempt to transform themselves; Hagar dies, and Pecola goes mad. All live lives of profound isolation in a society which does not want them. (pp. 542-43)

[*The Bluest Eye*] is effective because of the importance of its theme and the skill with which the inevitability of the failed initiation is developed through the compelling foreshadowing encounters. This device keeps the story convincing even while distancing Pecola from the reader, perhaps the final dramatization of her hopelessness and her eventual ostracism from a society which would rather destroy than accept her.

Though the initiations of Sula Peace and Nel Wright also fail, *Sula* differs from *The Bluest Eye* in both complexity and the assignment of responsibility. Here, while it is still made clear that Sula and Nel are undervalued and that their families legislate toward the initiation failure, both girls make specific decisions and choices which also contribute. Pecola struggles with the fate assigned to her; Sula and Nel help to choose their fates.

Like *The Bluest Eye, Sula* is highly episodic, and flashbacks dramatize the damage done to adult family members who influence and shape Sula and Nel. In *Sula,* as in *The Bluest Eye,* the protagonists undergo a series of experiences, each incorporating racial and sexual overtones, but here the encounters fall into two categories: those undergone individually and those suffered together. The division is important, for the experiences within the families have made the girls what they are as individuals; the experiences outside the families, all shared, indicate one of Morrison's most important points in the novel—the personalities of Sula and of Nel, could they have been merged, would have amounted to one whole person.

Just as their friendship is essential to their well-being as children, so would their learning from one another's faults have made them adult women capable of well-being. The real tragedy in *Sula* is that Nel and Sula are unable to learn that lesson; their friendship ruptures and they live isolated, frustrated lives. The interrelationship of the girls' personalities, symbolized by their friendship, and the recurring sexual and racial themes provide unity; the results are powerful and effective. (pp. 548-49)

Separated by Nel's resolution to settle for respectable calm, both women live lives of desperate isolation; Sula becomes the scapegoat for the town's ills; Nel lives a cold, severely respectable life as a put-upon woman. Symbolically, neither ever achieves a truly sustaining sexual union. When, finally, they do meet again, for Nel, meeting with the dying Sula is merely a part of her "respectable" role; they converse, but they do not come together, and it takes still longer for Nel to realize that the *great* loss she has suffered is really the destruction of their friendship, the one chance they had to learn to be full, complete women.

Sula, a more multifaceted book than *The Bluest Eye,* uses the maturation story of Sula and Nel as the core of a host of other stories, but it is the chief unification device for the novel and achieves its own unity, again, through the clever manipulation of the themes of sex, race, and love. Morrison has undertaken a more difficult task in *Sula.* Unquestionably, she has succeeded.

Song of Solomon is a somewhat more hopeful book than *The Bluest Eye* or *Sula;* Milkman's quest is ironically successful, and this note of modified hope is echoed in the female initiation patterns in that one of them leads to happiness—at least temporary happiness—for the initiated, First Corinthians Dead. Morrison reveals her admirable tendency to adapt rather than to adopt traditional patterns in these initiation stories by delaying the initiations of both Corinthians and her cousin, Hagar Dead, until the women are well beyond their teens; Corinthians is in her forties; Hagar is in her thirties. The device is successful, indicating the extreme difficulty of the black woman's search for self-determination, and certainly the results of these initiations underscore that point.

The initiation of Pilate Dead, however, takes place during her adolescence, as is traditional. During the main action of *Song of Solomon,* Pilate, aunt of the protagonist, Milkman, has no real identity at all, and in a long flashback, Morrison reveals the reasons for this lack as she recounts Pilate's initiation experiences. Pilate has never known her mother's name, and her father's, that of the first Macon Dead (Milkman's grandfather), was invented by a careless, belittling white official. (pp. 553-54)

[Pilate] painfully learns that she is not welcome in any community. . . . Twice, she joins bands of pickers and gets on well with them until she takes lovers who report that she has no navel. Taking the lack to be a sign that she is unnatural, the groups expel her. When she finds a haven on an isolated island off the coast of Virginia, she contrives to conceal her belly from her lover, and after their baby is born, refuses to marry him, reasoning that she cannot hide her lack of a navel from a husband forever. She is cut off from permanent sexual commitment, a symbol in Morrison's work for fruitful maturity. . . .

Pilate's initiation is complete; she has learned the lessons of the world. She knows the danger of the white world because it blew her father off the fence; she has learned that the black world cannot or will not truly accept her. Being strong, she undertakes, then to build a world of her own. . . .

But Pilate's place within those boundaries is marginal: she is the black district's bootlegger, and people come to her house for goods, not for companionship. Her world is both huge and small. . . . It is small in that it includes almost no people except her daughter, Reba; her granddaughter, Hagar—and her father's ghost; " 'I seen him since he was shot. . . . It's a good feelin to know he's around. I tell you he's a person I can rely on. I tell you something else. He's the *only* one'." . . . Her father's spirit becomes the source of the wisdom around which she constructs her life. (pp. 555-56)

Pilate does not really understand her father's messages at all; she cannot because she does not know

her family history. The self-definition she builds, the world view she constructs based upon his advice keeps her sane and active, but it further isolates her, cuts her off from her community. Pilate's initiation has failed because her family have not been able to equip her for success, and the resulting singularity also colors and controls the lives of her daughter and granddaughter. The failure of Pilate's way of life foreshadows Hagar's tragedy. (p. 556)

It is significant that Hagar's single act of rebellion takes place during Milkman's first visit to her home, for he is responsible for her long delayed initiation. The cousins become lovers and remain lovers for years. For Hagar, the commitment is absolute . . . ; Milkman represents something of her own, and he also represents a regulated life quite different, potentially, from the careless, disorganized life of her family. But Milkman never considers Hagar seriously as a mate, and he finally breaks off the affair.

With nothing on earth to cling to but her concept of herself as Milkman's lover, Hagar fails her initiation test. She sees herself only as she imagines he sees her and comes to doubt her own very great beauty. In her view, that is the one means she has to hold Milkman, and holding Milkman is the only thing worth doing. When she comes to believe that he prefers another kind of beauty, she has nothing, and she determines to kill him. (pp. 557-58)

All her life Hagar has known (as all of Southside knows) that the white community has no use for her; all her life she has known that she is only marginally tolerated by the black community. For a time, she has believed that her beauty, passion, and desirability were the keys to a life structured around Milkman. When he rejects her, when it is time for her to initiate herself into a life of her own, she cannot, and when even violence fails her (her attempts to murder Milkman abort), she decides to transform herself. She intends to sacrifice her one great asset, her beauty, to change herself into the kind of woman Milkman will love and value forever. Even this attempt, impassioned, chaotic, and pitiful as it is, fails, and in the process, Hagar becomes fatally ill. She cannot possibly succeed because nothing in her life has prepared her to define herself; she cannot succeed even in imitating Milkman's "real" girl friends because nothing in her background arouses in him a sense of her true value. There remains nothing else for her to do but to die.

At first glance, the story of Milkman's sister, First Corinthians Dead, seems to be a sharp contrast to the tragic story of Hagar, her cousin, though like Hagar's initiation, Corinthians' is delayed until late in her life, and also like Hagar's, it centers around her willingness to meet the needs of a man. But unlike Hagar, Corinthians manages the accommodation. (pp. 559-60)

Morrison on the origin of the idea for
Beloved:

I was amazed by this story I came across about a
woman called Margaret Garner who had escaped from
Kentucky, I think, into Cincinnati with four children. . . . And she was a kind of cause célèbre among
abolitionists in 1855 or '56 because she tried to kill the
children when she was caught. She killed one of them,
just as in the novel. I found an article in a magazine of
the period, and there was this young woman in her
20's, being interviewed—oh, a lot of people interviewed her, mostly preachers and journalists, and she
was very calm, she was very serene. They kept remarking on the fact that she was not frothing at the mouth,
she was not a madwoman, and she kept saying, "No,
they're not going to live like that. They will not live the
way I have lived."

Morrison, in Mervyn Rothstein's 1987 *New York
Times* article "Toni Morrison, in Her New Novel,
Defends Women."

Her most important test comes when she meets
and falls in love with Henry Porter, who does yard
work for a living. The pair date like teenagers, but Porter never meets the Deads; Corinthians dreads her father's reaction. . . . Eventually, Porter forces the issue,
telling Corinthians that she must defy her father or give
up her lover. When Corinthians makes her choice, she
does so by subjugating and humiliating herself
completely. . . . (p. 561)

Once her choice is made, Corinthians is happy
with it; she suppresses the hatred born of shame. . . .
She even summons the courage to move away from the
Deads' home and into a place she and Porter share. The
sexual phase of her initiation, like the economic phase,
seems to be acceptable to her, given the fact that she
can make the necessary accommodations. And there is
one further factor here. In a very real way, Corinthians
has rejected her father's false values, values assumed
and copied from whites, by embracing Porter, for Porter also has a secret life. He is one of the Seven Days,
a band of black men who avenge their race every time
the white community murders a black. (p. 562)

Song of Solomon, then, offers three portraits of
women whose initiation experiences fail because their
families have not prepared them for the transition into
fruitful maturity. Each of the three defines herself only
according to the standards and desires of a beloved
man: Pilate lives her entire life under her misapprehen-
sion of her father's messages; Hagar dies because she
cannot be the kind of woman Milkman desires; and
Corinthians abandons the self-image she has cherished
for a lifetime to find menial work in a white-controlled
world and to find sexual release with a man who de-

mands that she submit completely. Of the three, only
Corinthians has any chance for even modified happiness. Corinthians' slim chance makes *Song of Solomon*
Morrison's least despairing portrait of the black
woman's condition. At best, this note of hope is muted.

In her fiction, then, Morrison has united her
theme, the explorations of love, and a traditional device, the initiation motif, along with a series of brilliantly dramatized foreshadowing events, skillfully
made frames, and splendid characterizations. The resulting novels are compelling statements of the failure
of human values. The inversion of a traditional motif—
that is, the treatment of failed initiations—is successful, its effect devastating. The achievement is remarkable, making it clear that Toni Morrison is, indeed, a
major American novelist. (p. 563)

Jane S. Bakerman, "Failures of Love: Female Initiation in the
Novels of Toni Morrison," in *American Literature,* Vol. 52, No.
4, January, 1981, pp. 541-63.

WEBSTER SCHOTT

(essay date 1981)

[In the following excerpt, Schott highlights the major
themes of *Tar Baby*.]

Because Toni Morrison is black, female, and the author
of *Song of Solomon . . . ,* one expects from her a fiction of ideas as well as characters.

Tar Baby has both. And it's so sophisticated a
novel that *Tar Baby* might well be tarred and feathered
as bigoted, racist, and a product of male chauvinism
were it the work of a white male—say, John Updike,
whom Morrison brings to mind.

One of fiction's pleasures is to have your mind
scratched and your intellectual habits challenged.
While *Tar Baby* has short-comings, lack of provocation
isn't one of them. Morrison owns a powerful intelligence. It's run by courage. She calls to account conventional wisdom and accepted attitude at nearly every
turn of her story. She wonders about the sacrifice of
love, the effects of racial integration, the intention of
charity. Continually she questions both the logic and
morality of seeking happiness or what Freud said passes for it, freedom from pain, by living in social accommodation. Although Morrison tells a love story—
indeed, she tells two or three stories about love—her
narrative lines run to complexities far beyond those of
physical or emotional bonding. . . .

Tar Baby opens as a black American merchant
sailor jumps his Swedish ship and swims toward Isle
des Chevaliers, a Haitian island owned by a handful of

U.S. millionaires. . . . He tells Valerian Street, the 75-year-old imperious Philadelphia candy king, whose retirement retreat he invades, that his name is William Green. But he calls himself Son.

Son fascinates Morrison. He personifies freedom. She says he comes from that "great underclass of undocumented men . . . day laborers and musclemen, gamblers, sidewalk merchants, migrants . . . part-time mercenaries, full-time gigolos, or curb-side musicians," all distinguished by "their refusal to equate work with life and an inability to stay anywhere for long."

Part of Morrison's attraction to Son is literary fantasy. She sees him as kin to Huck Finn or Nigger Jim, Caliban or John Henry, and other mythic wayfarers. But mostly, I think, Morrison sees Son as the official heroic black male. Son doesn't jive or wear gold chains. He is proud of his farmer father. He jumps ship because he is homesick for Eloe, Florida. His yearnings are toward his sources, not a future of assimilation.

Son also thinks black woman, not white, and finds her at Valerian Street's estate. He gets her—for a while, anyway—after turning the established order upside down. (p. 1)

While it's not clear why the family fight drives Jadine into Son's arms, Morrison wills it. Perhaps it's because Jadine sees "savannas in his eyes." The pair flee to New York. Jadine tries to remake Son into an upwardly mobile black male. He takes her to his beginnings in Eloe, where rooms have no windows, unmarried couples don't sleep in the same bed, and Son takes orders from his father, "Old Man." The bond breaks. Jadine heads for Paris by way of Isle des Chevaliers. Son comes back too late, bounding through the beach trees like a god, "Lickety-lickety-lickety split."

There is so much that is good, sometimes dazzling, about *Tar Baby*—poetic language (despite pathetic fallacies), arresting images, fierce intelligence—that after climbing past the stereotyped marriage of Valerian and Margaret Street, one becomes entranced by Toni Morrison's story. The settings are so vivid the characters must be alive. The emotions they feel are so intense they must be real people.

The ideas Morrison suggests—that blacks seek ways to hate whites, that black people cannot be fully human on white values, that integration is another way of control, that physical prowess is embedded in black masculinity are arguable enough to keep you awake at night.

But something is missing in *Tar Baby*. It's a credible set of motives. Would a penniless, homesick Son jump ship in the Caribbean to get back to Florida and then head first to New York? Would Jadine drop 25 years of rearing, education, and conscience for a semiliterate she knew two weeks and slept with, perhaps, twice? Would a manipulator and observer as shrewd as

Valerian Street miss the signs that his only child was verging on psychosis, and do nothing? Margaret's explanation for torturing her child is no explanation; she had a maid to soften the impact of child-rearing. Logic takes flight in *Tar Baby*.

To believe Toni Morrison's characters isn't to believe their dramatic behavior. They are real people—in a story. The reason we can't credit their behavior is because, except for the most minor of figures, their actions are determined by Morrison's convictions, not their histories. Such is the curse of novels of ideas. (pp. 1-2)

Webster Schott, "Toni Morrison: Tearing the Social Fabric," in *Book World—The Washington Post,* March 22, 1981, pp. 1-2.

MARGARET ATWOOD
(essay date 1987)

[Atwood is a Canadian novelist, poet, critic, and short story writer. In the essay excerpted below, she examines the ramifications of slavery as depicted in *Beloved*.]

Beloved is Toni Morrison's fifth novel, and another triumph. Indeed, Ms. Morrison's versatility and technical and emotional range appear to know no bounds. If there were any doubts about her stature as a preeminent American novelist, of her own or any other generation, *Beloved* will put them to rest. In three words or less, it's a hair-raiser. (p. 1)

The supernatural element is treated, not in an *Amityville Horror,* watch-me-make-your-flesh-creep mode, but with magnificent practicality, like the ghost of Catherine Earnshaw in *Wuthering Heights*. All the main characters in the book believe in ghosts, so it's merely natural for this one to be there. As Baby Suggs says, "Not a house in the country ain't packed to its rafters with some dead Negro's grief. We lucky this ghost is a baby. My husband's spirit was to come back in here? or yours? Don't talk to me. You lucky." In fact, Sethe would rather have the ghost there than not there. It is, after all, her adored child, and any sign of it is better, for her, than nothing. (p. 49)

Through the different voices and memories of the book, including that of Sethe's mother, a survivor of the infamous slave-ship crossing, we experience American slavery as it was lived by those who were its objects of exchange, both at its best—which wasn't very good—and at its worst, which was as bad as can be imagined. Above all, it is seen as one of the most viciously antifamily institutions human beings have ever devised. The slaves are motherless, fatherless, deprived of their mates, their children, their kin. It is a world in which people suddenly vanish and are never seen again, not through accident or covert operation or terrorism, but as a matter of everyday legal policy.

Slavery is also presented to us as a paradigm of how most people behave when they are given absolute power over other people. The first effect, of course, is that they start believing in their own superiority and justifying their actions by it. The second effect is that they make a cult of the inferiority of those they subjugate. It's no coincidence that the first of the deadly sins, from which all the others were supposed to stem, is Pride, a sin of which Sethe is, incidentally, also accused.

In a novel that abounds in black bodies—headless, hanging from trees, frying to a crisp, locked in woodsheds for purposes of rape, or floating downstream drowned—it isn't surprising that the "whitepeople," especially the men, don't come off too well. Horrified black children see whites as men "without skin." Sethe thinks of them as having "mossy teeth" and is ready, if necessary, to bite off their faces, and worse, to avoid further mossy-toothed outrages. There are a few whites who behave with something approaching decency. There's Amy, the young runaway indentured servant who helps Sethe in childbirth during her flight to freedom, and incidentally reminds the reader that the 19th century, with its child labor, wage slavery and widespread and accepted domestic violence, wasn't tough only for blacks, but for all but the most privileged whites as well. There are also the abolitionists who help Baby Suggs find a house and a job after she is freed. But even the decency of these "good" whitepeople has a grudging side to it, and even they have trouble seeing the people they are helping as full-fledged people, though to show them as totally free of their xenophobia and sense of superiority might well have been anachronistic.

Toni Morrison is careful not to make all the whites awful and all the blacks wonderful. Sethe's black neighbors, for instance, have their own envy and scapegoating tendencies to answer for, and Paul D., though much kinder than, for instance, the woman-bashers of Alice Walker's novel *The Color Purple,* has his own limitations and flaws. But then, considering what he's been through, it's a wonder he isn't a mass murderer. If anything, he's a little too huggable, under the circumstances.

Back in the present tense, in chapter one, Paul D. and Sethe make an attempt to establish a "real" family, whereupon the baby ghost, feeling excluded, goes berserk, but is driven out by Paul D's stronger will. So it appears. But then, along comes a strange, beautiful, real flesh-and-blood young woman, about 20 years old, who can't seem to remember where she comes from, who talks like a young child, who has an odd, raspy voice and no lines on her hands, who takes an intense, devouring interest in Sethe, and who says her name is Beloved.

Students of the supernatural will admire the way this twist is handled. Ms. Morrison blends a knowledge of folklore—for instance, in many traditions, the dead cannot return from the grave unless called, and it's the passions of the living that keep them alive—with a highly original treatment. The reader is kept guessing; there's a lot more to Beloved than any one character can see, and she manages to be many things to several people. She is a catalyst for revelations as well as self-revelations; through her we come to know not only how, but why, the original child Beloved was killed. And through her also Sethe achieves, finally, her own form of self-exorcism, her own self-accepting peace.

Beloved is written in an antiminimalist prose that is by turns rich, graceful, eccentric, rough, lyrical, sinuous, colloquial and very much to the point. Here, for instance, is Sethe remembering Sweet Home:

> . . . suddenly there was Sweet Home rolling, rolling, rolling out before her eyes, and although there was not a leaf on that farm that did not want to make her scream, it rolled itself out before her in shameless beauty. It never looked as terrible as it was and it made her wonder if hell was a pretty place too. Fire and brimstone all right, but hidden in lacy groves. Boys hanging from the most beautiful sycamores in the world. It shamed her—remembering the wonderful soughing trees rather than the boys. Try as she might to make it otherwise, the sycamores beat out the children every time and she could not forgive her memory for that.

In this book, the other world exists and magic works, and the prose is up to it. If you can believe page one—and Ms. Morrison's verbal authority compels belief—you're hooked on the rest of the book.

The epigraph to *Beloved* is from the Bible, Romans 9:25: "I will call them my people, which were not my people; and her beloved, which was not beloved." Taken by itself, this might seem to favor doubt about, for instance, the extent to which Beloved was really loved, or the extent to which Sethe herself was rejected by her own community. But there is more to it than that. The passage is from a chapter in which the Apostle Paul ponders, Job-like, the ways of God toward humanity, in particular the evils and inequities visible everywhere on the earth. Paul goes on to talk about the fact that the Gentiles, hitherto despised and outcast, have now been redefined as acceptable. The passage proclaims, not rejection, but reconciliation and hope. It continues: "And it shall come to pass, that in the place where it was said unto them, Ye are not my people; there shall they be called the children of the living God."

Toni Morrison is too smart, and too much of a

writer, not to have intended this context. Here, if anywhere, is her own comment on the goings-on in her novel, her final response to the measuring and dividing and excluding "schoolteachers" of this world. An epigraph to a book is like a key signature in music, and *Beloved* is written in major. (pp. 49-50)

Margaret Atwood, "Haunted by Their Nightmares," in *The New York Times Book Review,* September 13, 1987, pp. 49-50.

SOURCES FOR FURTHER STUDY

Alexander, Harriet S. "Toni Morrison: An Annotated Bibliography of Critical Articles and Essays, 1975-1984." *CLA Journal* XXXIII, No. 1 (September 1989): 81-93.

> Bibliography of essays about Morrison's novels and of interviews with the author.

Fabre, Genevieve. "Genealogical Archaeology or the Quest for Legacy in Toni Morrison's *Song of Solomon.*" In *Critical Essays on Toni Morrison,* edited by Nellie Y. McKay, pp. 105-14. Boston: Hall, 1988.

> Discusses the African-American legacy upheld by *Song of Solomon.*

Horvitz, Deborah. "Nameless Ghosts: Possession and Dispossession in *Beloved.*" *Studies in American Fiction* 17, No. 2 (Autumn, 1989): 157-67.

> Examines the ghost Beloved as a symbol of "generations of mothers and daughters—hunted down and stolen from Africa. . . . "

McKay, Nellie. "An Interview with Toni Morrison." *Contemporary Literature* 24, No. 4 (Winter 1983): 413-29.

> Morrison discusses the characters in her first four novels and the influence of black women on her writing.

Morrison, Toni. "Unspeakable Things Unspoken: The Afro-American Presence in American Literature." *Michigan Quarterly Review* XXVIII, No 1 (Winter 1989): 1-34.

> Morrison analyzes the first sentences of her five novels, emphasizing the qualities that make them distinctly African-American.

Traylor, Eleanor W. "The Fabulous World of Toni Morrison: *Tar Baby.*" In *Critical Essays on Toni Morrison,* edited by Nellie Y. McKay, G. K. Hall & Co, pp. 135-49. New York: Quill, 1983.

> Analyzes Morrison's portrayal of African-American culture in *Tar Baby.*

Vladimir Nabokov

1899-1977

(Full name Vladimir Vladimirovich Nabokov; also wrote under pseudonym V. Sirin) Russian-born American novelist, poet, short story writer, essayist, playwright, critic, translator, biographer, autobiographer, and scriptwriter.

INTRODUCTION

Nabokov is widely recognized as one of the outstanding literary stylists of the twentieth century. His intricate, self-conscious fiction often investigates the illusory nature of reality and the artist's relationship to his craft. Nabokov maintained that "art at its greatest is fantastically deceitful and complex"; by emphasizing stylistic considerations above notions of moral or social significance, he championed the primacy of the imagination, through which he believed a more meaningful reality might be perceived. Viewing words as significant objects in themselves as well as vehicles for meaning, Nabokov made use of intellectual games involving wordplay, acrostics, anagrams, and multilingual puns to create complex, labyrinthine narratives. Although some critics fault Nabokov for his refusal to address social and political issues, many maintain that beneath his passion for "composing riddles with elegant solutions," as he himself stated, his fiction conveys a poignant regard for human feelings and morality. Arthur Mizener, his colleague from Cornell University, described Nabokov's writing as "a joke within a joke within a joke, an enormously complicated and subtle joke which is deadly serious."

Nabokov was born into an aristocratic family in St. Petersburg, Russia. His father, one of the founders of the Constitutional Democratic Party, instilled in the Nabokov children the importance of education and liberal thinking. Numerous critics express astonishment at Nabokov's adroit mastery of English, but he actually learned the language before Russian. The Nabokovs fled the country during the Bolshevik Revolution, ultimately settling in London. Nabokov began studying Russian and French literature at Cambridge University on a scholarship awarded him for "political tribulation." After graduating in 1922, Nabokov moved to Berlin to work on a Russian refugee newspaper that his father, who had recently been assassinated at a political rally, had helped to found. He remained there for several years, marrying in 1925 and writing poetry, fiction, and translations to earn a living. His wife's Jewish ancestry necessitated their relocation to France in 1937 and to the United States three years later to escape Nazi persecution. Nabokov became an American citizen in 1945 and accepted a post at Cornell University as a professor of Russian literature, a position he held from 1948 to 1958. During his tenure there, he wrote *Lolita* (1955), the work that brought him notoriety and popular success as a novelist. Nabokov settled in Switzerland in 1960, concentrating solely on his writing until his death in 1977.

Nabokov's first novel, *Mashenka* (translated as *Mary*), appeared in 1926. The original Russian version of the book received little attention, but after Nabokov's reputation burgeoned and the work was translated into English, *Mary* received closer scrutiny. A nostalgic tale of a young emigre's longing for the love he left behind in Russia, it details what life was like for the residents of a Berlin pension in the early 1920s.

In addition to their contributions to his thematic development, Nabokov's early fictions also shaped his literary technique. "It was in his Russian novels . . . that he developed his art of incorporating literary allusion and reference as an inherent device of fictional narration," writes Simon Karlinsky. Nabokov's second novel, *Korol', dama, valet* (1928; translated as *King, Queen, Knave*), marks the first appearance of this device. "It is . . . the first of his novels to have a plot and character serve as vehicles for the real subject, which is form, style and the strategies of total creation," writes Eliot Fremont-Smith in the *New York Times*. In this story, merely one of several Nabokovian variations on the eternal love triangle, a vain and selfish woman named Martha diabolically plots with her bumbling young lover, Franz, to kill her unsuspecting husband and Franz's uncle, Dreyer. The force controlling Martha's fate is, of course, the author, and Nabokov uses this power to manipulate the narrative in unexpected ways. Although he is patterning his tale on a situation readers will certainly have encountered in many other novels, "nothing ends as it's supposed to," according to *Washington Post* reviewer Geoffrey Wolff, who thinks the novel "abounds in comic incongruities: Martha is cold, selfish, aloof and beautiful, yet Nabokov has her slip into passionate love with a bumbling, graceless post-adolescent hayseed. Their rendezvous are made in a grubby comic-opera parody of a clerk's garret as it might be imagined in a nineteenth-century Russian novel."

In the late 1930s, Nabokov began to experiment with English, translating his Russian novel *Otchayanie* (1934) into the English *Despair* in 1937. Initially hesitant about his command of the language, Nabokov re-

quested the assistance of a professional to proofread his work. H. G. Wells was recommended, but never materialized; a second candidate bowed out, declaring himself unsuited to the work. Finally, an English woman agreed to make corrections, but when her list of recommendations was completed, Nabokov found it spurious. "All of this stuff is completely insignificant, for any Russian reader can find just as many birthmarks on any page of any of my Russian novels, and any good English writer commits just as many grammatical imprecisions," he wrote in a letter to his wife, Vera. The book was published exactly as he wrote it. Indeed, his very next book, *The Real Life of Sebastian Knight* (1941), was written in English and marks the demise of the pseudonymous V. Sirin and the emergence of Vladimir Nabokov, an American writer. Filled with autobiographical tidbits and typically Nabokovian allusions to chess, *The Real Life of Sebastian Knight* chronicles the narrator's search for the "essence" of his half-brother, the titular Sebastian Knight—a Russian emigre writer who died an early death in relative obscurity. The brothers had been out of touch for years, but V. (as the narrator is called) remains convinced of Sebastian's genius and sets out to write a biography that will insure his brother's critical stature and refute a second-rate biography that Sebastian's former secretary has published. Rather than clarifying the details of Sebastian's life, however, V.'s search only raises more questions. The book draws to a close with V. retrospectively visiting Sebastian on his death bed and wondering if perhaps he himself is Sebastian Knight or if he might be a third person unknown to them both.

Nabokov did not gain widespread popularity until the publication of *Lolita*. The story of a middle-aged man's obsessive and disastrous lust for a twelve-year-old schoolgirl, *Lolita* is widely considered one of the most controversial novels of the twentieth century. Rejected by four American publishers because of its pedophiliac subject matter, the book was finally published by Olympia Press, a Parisian firm that specialized in pornography and erotica. *Lolita* attracted a wide underground readership, and tourists began transporting copies of the work abroad. While United States Customs permitted this action, the British government pressured the French legislature to confiscate the remaining copies of the book and forbid further sales. However, the English author Graham Greene located a copy and, in a pivotal *London Times* article, focused on the novel's language rather than its content, designating *Lolita* one of the ten best books of 1955. Public curiosity and controversy merely fueled the book's popularity, and in 1958 it was published in the United States. Within five weeks, *Lolita* was the most celebrated novel in the nation, and remained on the *New York Times* best-seller list for over a year. Initial reviews were varied; while several critics expressed shock and distaste, the majority believed the "pornography" charges to be erroneous. Praising Nabokov's lively style, dry wit, and deft characterizations, many reviewers concurred with Granville Hicks, who called the novel "a brilliant *tour de force.*" Beat novelist Jack Kerouac described *Lolita* as "a classic old love story," and Charles Rolo commented, "*Lolita* seems to me an assertion of the power of the comic spirit to wrest delight and truth from the most outlandish materials. It is one of the funniest serious novels I have ever read; and the vision of its abominable hero, who never deludes or excuses himself, brings into grotesque relief the cant, the vulgarity, and the hypocritical conventions that pervade the human comedy."

The plot of *Lolita* revolves around the sexual desire of Humbert Humbert, a brilliant, middle-aged European professor and aesthete, for Dolores Haze, a promiscuous twelve-year-old schoolgirl whom he pursues to compensate for the loss of a love during his adolescence. Some critics feel that Dolores, whom Humbert idealizes as "Lolita," is representative of the superficiality of American culture viewed from a sophisticated European perspective. While other literary scholars don't deny this interpretation, they perceive an examination of the effects of the artist's asocial impulses in addition to *Lolita*'s satirical vision of American morals and values. Several commentators maintained that the accusations of pornography stemmed from Nabokov's lack of authorial judgment regarding Humbert's actions, while some argued that the true crime of the novel is not the murder Humbert commits but his curtailment of Lolita's childhood. Critics feel that Lolita is not entirely blameless, however, for at twelve she is already sexually experienced, and, despite Humbert's extravagant designs, it is *she* who first seduces him. As Lolita begins to realize her power over Humbert, she gradually becomes manipulative. Lolita's portrait, as well as other characterizations in the novel, have won Nabokov consistent, unified praise for his ability to evoke both repugnance and sympathy in the reader. For example, it is generally agreed that Lolita has a highly unattractive personality, yet her unhappy life inspires compassion. Humbert is a pedophile and murderer but wins the reader's admiration for his humor and brutal honesty, while Charlotte is depicted as both a piranha and a pawn.

Throughout *Lolita*, Nabokov engages the reader in a battle of wits. The novel's foreword, written by "John Ray, Jr., Ph.D.," a bogus Freudian psychiatrist, introduces Humbert's confession through obtuse psychological jargon, which Nabokov deplored. Unwary readers believe the foreword is sincere, especially because of *Lolita*'s controversial subject matter. Nabokov's myriad uses of anagrams, acrostics, and puns provide clues and red herrings concerning Lolita's mysterious lover; Humbert learns of Quilty's existence

late in the novel, but notes that astute readers should have realized this sooner. Nabokov also parodies numerous styles of literature in *Lolita;* it is variously viewed as a satire of the confessional novel, the detective novel, the romance novel, and, most frequently, as an allegory of the artistic process.

One of Nabokov's first projects following *Lolita* was to resume work on a novel (originally entitled *Solus Rex*) he had begun years earlier. Entitled *Pale Fire* (1962), this difficult work demonstrates the increased emphasis on form and structure that dominates Nabokov's later fiction.

Pale Fire consists of a 999-line poem in four cantos, composed by the late John Shade, an American poet recently assassinated by a madman's bullet, and a foreword, commentary, and index, contributed by Dr. Charles Kinbote, an emigre scholar of dubious sanity. Since Kinbote's footnotes are keyed to various lines in the poem, the reader cannot simply read the book from cover to cover, but must continually flip back and forth from the commentary to the verse. "This is not the drudgery it may sound, for every vibration of the pages carries the reader to a fresh illumination, a further delight," writes Donald Malcolm in the *New Yorker*. "But on the other hand, it is not reading in the ordinary sense. It more nearly resembles the manipulation of a pencil along a course of numbered dots until the hidden picture stands forth, compact, single, and astonishing." For some critics, this elaborate mechanism tends to overshadow the story. "Indeed the structure is so witty, and so obtrusive, that it threatens constantly to become its own end; and we are made to attend so closely to it that the novel itself seems wholly subordinate to its mode of enclosure," *Nation* contributor Saul Madoff concludes.

In his seventieth year, Nabokov produced his last major work, *Ada or Ardor: A Family Chronicle* (1969), a sexually explicit tale of incest, twice as long as any other novel he had written and, according to the *New York Times*'s John Leonard, "fourteen times as complicated." An immediate best-seller, *Ada* evoked a wide array of critical response, ranging from strong objections to the highest praise. While the value of the novel was debated, *Ada* was universally acknowledged as a work of enormous ambition that represented the culmination of all that Nabokov had attempted to accomplish in his writing over the years. On the surface, Ada chronicles the incestuous love affair between Van Veen and his cousin (soon revealed to be his sister) Ada, who fall in love as adolescents, embark upon a blissful sexual odyssey, are pulled apart by social taboo and circumstance, only to be reunited in late middle age, at which time they prosper together until both are in their nineties. Van's memoir of his love affair with Ada, ostensibly "Van's book," is actually an anagram for "Nabokov's," and "once the creator's name has been uttered, *Ada*'s profoundest purpose comes into view. . . . Ada is the supreme fictional embodiment of Nabokov's lifelong, bittersweet preoccupation with time and memory," a *Time* reviewer concludes.

Nabokov continued writing well into the 1970s, though his last books are considered minor additions to his oeuvre. Upon his death at seventy-eight, *New York Times* contributor Alden Whitman concluded his obituary with these words: "Anyone so bold as to venture explanations might attempt to show how Mr. Nabokov's fiction was the refinement through memory and art of his own experience as a man who lost both father and fatherland to violent revolution, who adopted another culture, who mastered its language as few of its own have mastered it and who never forgot his origins. But one hesitates to undertake such explorations. Mr. Nabokov always forbade intrusions into his privacy; he hated psychologists; and he would scoff at such extraesthetic adventures. . . . But as long as Western civilization survives, his reputation is safe. Indeed, he will probably emerge as one of the greatest artists our century has produced."

(For further information about Nabokov's life and works, see *Concise Dictionary of American Literary Biography*, 1941-1968; *Contemporary Authors*, Vols. 69-72; *Contemporary Authors* (revised edition), Vols. 5-8; *Contemporary Authors New Revision Series*, Vol. 20; *Contemporary Literary Criticism*, Vols. 1-3, 6, 8, 11, 15, 23, 44, 46, 64; *Dictionary of Literary Biography*, Vol. 2: *American Novelists Since World War II*; *Dictionary of Literary Biography Documentary Series*, Vol. 3; and *Dictionary of Literary Biography Yearbook: 1980*.)

CRITICAL COMMENTARY

MATHEW WINSTON

(essay date 1975)

[In the following excerpt, Winston offers a close reading of *Lolita*.]

In *Lolita* Vladimir Nabokov plays a very serious game with the relations between a work of art, the experiences that underlie it, and the effects it may have upon its readers. The book's protagonist, narrator, and supposed author, Humbert Humbert, continually forces us to maintain a double perspective by calling on us to pass moral and legal judgment upon him as a man and aesthetic judgment upon him as an artist. "You can always count on a murderer for a fancy prose style," Humbert informs us in the book's third paragraph, and from that point on the murderer, madman, and pedophile is balanced against the artistic creator, stylist, lover of language, and master of literary allusion. Although Humbert sometimes tries to separate his Jekyll and Hyde aspects, as when he assures us that "the gentle and dreamy regions through which I crept were the patrimonies of poets—*not* crime's prowling ground," his own book proves that the same habits of mind guide both writer and criminal.

Humbert tells us that he thought at one time of using his notes for his defense in the forthcoming trial. But the main impulses of his imaginative recreation are artistic and celebratory. The artist wants "to fix once for all the perilous magic of nymphets." The lover wants to write a history which will glorify his beloved for future generations (it is to be published only after both of them are dead). In his final words, "this is the only immortality you and I may share, my Lolita," Humbert appears as Renaissance sonneteer, boasting that he will make his love immortal in his writing, while ruefully admitting that such permanence is no adequate substitute for possessing the lady, or, as Humbert expresses it, "Oh, my Lolita, I have only words to play with!"

Humbert's desire for the literary immortality of his book reflects his need to stop the passage of time in his life or at least to pretend it does not exist. His actions, as we shall see, are designed toward this end, and his language is consistent with his actions. Twice in a single paragraph he mentions that his interrupted sexual liaison with Lolita's predecessor took place on an "immortal day." He says that his ultimate quest is for "the eternal Lolita." Even when he is on the verge of his final separation from Lolita, Humbert still pleadingly holds out the hope that "we shall live happily ever after."

Lolita, then, is Humbert's bid for the immortal future of which he and his nymphet are personally incapable. But the book is also a memorial of the past, a "souvenir" of Humbert's travels, a record of events that have already happened. Humbert is preoccupied with memory, that dead thing which was once living experience, now resurrected and transmuted by the imagination. He is "a murderer with a sensational but incomplete and unorthodox memory," the author of essays

Principal Works

The Empyrean Path (poetry) 1923

Mashenka (novel) 1926
  [Mary, 1970]

Korol', dama, valet (novel) 1928
  [King, Queen, Knave, 1968]

Soglyadatay (novel) 1930
  [The Eye, 1965]

Vozurashchenie chorba (short stories) 1930

Zashchita luzhina (novel) 1930
  [The Defense, 1964]

Kamera obskura (novel) 1932
  [Laughter in the Dark, 1938]

Podvig (novel) 1932
  [Glory, 1971]

Otchayanie (novel) 1934
  [Despair, 1937]

Dar (novel) 1938
  [The Gift, 1963]

Izobretenie val'sa (drama) 1938
  [The Waltz Invention, 1966]

Priglashenie na kazn' (novel) 1938
  [Invitation to a Beheading, 1959]

Soglydatay (short stories) 1938

Volshebnik (novel) 1939

[The Enchanter, 1986]

The Real Life of Sebastian Knight (novel) 1941

Nikolai Gogol (criticism) 1944

Bend Sinister (novel) 1947

Nine Stories (short stories) 1947

Conclusive Evidence (autobiography) 1951

Poems: 1929-1951 (poetry) 1952

Lolita (novel) 1955

Vesna v Fialte i drugie rasskazy (short stories) 1956

Pnin (novel) 1957

Nabokov's Dozen (short stories) 1958

Poems (poetry) 1959

Pale Fire (novel) 1962

Nabokov's Quartet (short stories) 1966

Speak Memory: An Autobiography Revisited (autobiography) 1966

Ada or Ardor: A Family Chronicle (novel) 1969

Transparent Things (novel) 1972

Strong Opinions (essays) 1973

Lolita: A Screenplay (screenplay) 1974

Look at the Harlequins! (novel) 1974

A Russian Beauty (short stories) 1975

Tyrants Destroyed and Other Stories (short stories) 1975

---

on "Mimir and Memory" and "The Proustian theme in a letter from Keats to Benjamin Bailey," and the possessor of a powerful nostalgia for his Mediterranean past. He is obsessed by his memory of Annabel Leigh to the point that his entire life becomes an attempt to make his "immortal" moment with her in the past eternally present, to possess her forever. He fails to perpetuate Annabel through Lolita, who effaces her, and he cannot make his liaison with Lolita permanent, but he does succeed by writing his "memoir." (pp. 421-22)

The experiences of a lifetime undergo the selective distortions of memory and of artistic shaping and become a book. So far so good. But the process does not stop there, for a work of art affects its readers or spectators in turn. As Humbert knows, any art form consists of a set of conventions and so it tends to develop conventional expectations in its participants. Dolores Haze is partially molded by the promises of advertisements and the advice of movie magazines. Charlotte Haze has her perceptions and her "mode of expression" shaped by "soap operas, psychoanalysis and cheap novelettes." Humbert is familiar with the patterned experiences and clichéd phraseology of these forms and is able to use his knowledge to deceive Charlotte. He is similarly aware of "the rules of the movies" and tellingly describes the stereotyped plots of "musicals, underworlders, westerners." As a writer, Humbert shows his mastery of such literary forms as the detective novel, the confessional autobiography, and the Gothic romance; he parodies them at will. (pp. 422-23)

Yet Humbert is curiously trapped by his own predilection for seeing his life through a veil of literature. To begin with, he tends to view himself as a character in a work of fiction. He first perceives Lolita in the context of a fairy tale and in the same framework later enters Pavor Manor to murder Quilty. He elaborately stages his opportunity to masturbate against Lolita ("Main character: Humbert the Hummer. Time: Sunday morning in June. Place: sunlit living room. Props: . . . "), and he plots his subsequent seduction of her, part of which he compares to "a cinematographic scene," with equal care. He "rehearses" the death of Richard Schiller when he thinks that unfortunate man is Lolita's abductor. He executes Clare Quilty in a singularly literal version of "poetical justice" and then comments to himself, "This . . . was the end of the ingenious play staged for me by Quilty." When Charlotte discovers his diary, Humbert thinks to excuse himself by claiming that its entries are "fragments of a novel," which, in a manner of speaking, they are indeed. Later, he invents a film on which he is supposed to work as an excuse to withdraw Lolita from Beardsley School.

While writing *Lolita* and living through the experiences it relates, Humbert repeatedly imagines literary parallels to whatever situation he finds himself in. His references, allusions, and quotations reveal that Lolita suggests to him Petrarch's Laura at one moment, Proust's Albertine at another, and Mérimée's Carmen at regular intervals. One of the most important equations he makes is between his childhood love, Annabel Leigh, and the heroine of Edgar Allan Poe's poem "Annabel Lee." The name and early death of the former seem to suggest the parallel to Humbert, although it is probable that Annabel Leigh's name, like Humbert's own, is his creation. In any case, once he has made the association, Humbert continues to see himself as a version of Poe in many other circumstances as well. Such a fusion of life and art may be merely the harmless game of a literary mind, but it is an exercise which must necessarily distort the narrator's memory of events as they happened and which, insofar as it shapes his perceptions and understanding, influences his actions as well.

The most serious danger of subjugating life to literature in this way is that one may begin to regard the people one knows as literary characters and to treat them accordingly. Humbert reflects on this process in a passing comment about John Farlow:

> I have often noticed that we are inclined to endow our friends with the stability of type that literary characters acquire in the reader's mind. No matter how many times we reopen *King Lear,* never shall we find the good king banging his tankard in high revelry, all woes forgotten, at a jolly reunion with all three daughters and their lapdogs. . . . Whatever evolution this or that popular character has gone through between the book covers, his fate is fixed in our minds, and, similarly, we expect our friends to follow this or that logical and conventional pattern we have fixed for them. Thus . . . Y will never commit murder. Under no circumstances can Z ever betray us. We have it all arranged in our minds, and the less often we see a particular person the more satisfying it is to check how obediently he conforms to our notion of him every time we hear of him. Any deviation in the fates we have ordained would strike us as not only anomalous but unethical.

Humbert's casual remark about what *we* are inclined to do accurately describes a limitation of his own perceptions and a consequent tendency of his actions. He sees his first wife, Valeria, as a "comedy wife" and so treats her as a "brainless *baba*"; he is overwhelmed when she acts "quite out of keeping with the stock character she was supposed to impersonate" by breaking out of her assigned role and deserting him for a taxi driver. Since Humbert needs to impose upon his life the fixity of a literary work, he later attempts to force Lolita into the invariable pattern of a literary character, and therein lies his crime and his sin.

Who is Lolita? "She was Lo, plain Lo, in the morning, standing four feet ten in one sock. She was Lola in slacks. She was Dolly at school. She was Dolores on the dotted line. But in my arms she was always Lolita." Humbert wishes to negate Lo, Lola, Dolly, and Dolores and, just as he wants her always in his arms, he wants her to be always and only Lolita. "*My* Lolita," he keeps insisting, "my own creation." Humbert's solipsistic imagination refuses to acknowledge the individuality of the girls he loves or to allow them freedom to shape their own lives. First, his unorthodox memory converts his childhood love into a Poe-etic Annabel Lee. Then, he tell us, "I broke her spell by incarnating her in another." He reincarnates Annabel in Dolores Haze, whom he makes into a creation he names Lolita. "It was the same child," he claims, "Annabel Haze, alias Dolores Lee, alias Loleeta."

Humbert recreates Annabel Leigh only in his memory and imagination, but he directly interferes with the life of Dolores Haze when he imposes on her the stability of type of a literary character called Lolita, a creature "not human, but nymphic." He wants to turn his life with Lolita into a revision of "Annabel Lee" with a happy ending in which she will be immutably young and forever his and they will live happily ever after. Humbert desperately and pitiably attempts to stop the movement of time, which presents to him the threat of his enchanting nymphet metamorphosing into an ordinary woman. Of course he cannot succeed, for people stubbornly persist in changing and even, as John Ray's foreword reminds us, in dying. "The past was the past" insists Lolita after she has managed to escape from Humbert and to redefine herself as Clare Quilty's mistress and then as Mrs. Richard F. Schiller. But Humbert must ignore the passage of time as best he can: "I could have filmed her! I would have had her now with me." He needs the stability of type that equates Lolita with Annabel Leigh and through time in his imagination to an eventual Lolita the Third who will merrily cavort with Grandfather Humbert.

Eventually Humbert begins to acknowledge the evil and the futility of the web of multiple entrapment he has spun about Lolita and the cruelty of keeping her from a life in which, as she puts it in Nabokov's screenplay of the novel, "everything was so—oh, I don't know—normal." He gradually learns that he knew nothing about her thoughts or feelings and, in fact, carefully avoided any recognition of her personality which might interfere with the satisfaction of his own physical and psychological needs. He is able to feel for the first time the full pathos of "her sobs in the night—

every night, every night." He discovers, in short, that Dolores Haze is a person and not a character.

Separated from Lolita, alone in a psychopathic ward and then in prison, afflicted by his heart in more ways than one, Humbert turns to "the melancholy and very local palliative of articulate art. To quote an old poet: 'The moral sense in mortals is the duty / We have to pay on mortal sense of beauty'." In his supposed quotation Humbert plays moral values against aesthetic ones. Humbert has been a monster, as he himself confesses. He has tried to "fix" Dolores Haze within the unchanging boundaries of a literary character he has created. Repentant and remorseful, he glorifies her and compensates himself by writing a book about his love for her. The corollary of this process, of course, is that both of them are converted into the literary characters we encounter in *Lolita,* a book which, as we have seen, endeavors "to fix once for all the perilous magic of nymphets." Humbert's greatness as a writer lies in his success at "fixing" Lolita within the pages of a book, but the identical process in his life constitutes his greatest crime as a human being.

The novel *Lolita* makes its readers question the possibility of valid judgment and the ambiguity of value. Our questioning begins with John Ray's condescending foreword, which treats the book as a case history, as a work of art, and as an ethical treatise. It is continued by Humbert's frequent attacks against and defenses of himself. Humbert sees and presents himself in different lights—as a degenerate, as a faunlet trapped in an aging body, as a father and a lover, as a poet and a madman. Sometimes he claims he is innocent, or at least "as naïve as only a pervert can be." He begins with good intentions and is initially determined to preserve what he thinks is Lolita's purity, although it turns out that she seduces him. (Ironically, his admirable intent may only prove that he is no longer a faunlet, since he made no such attempt to keep Annabel chaste.) At other times, and increasingly as the book progresses, he condemns himself as guilty. It is possible to take either perspective, as is shown in Humbert's climactic encounter with Quilty:

> "Concentrate," I said, "on the thought of Dolly Haze whom you kidnapped—"
>
> "I did not!" he cried. "You're all wet. I saved her from a beastly pervert."

Who is the protective guardian and who the selfish sex fiend? Handy-dandy, which is the justice, which is the thief?

The ultimate judgment on Humbert is up to us. In order to help us arrive at it (or perhaps to further hinder us), we are presented with various kinds of evidence: numbered exhibits one and two, a reconstructed diary, a few letters, a class list, a diagram of an automobile accident, some poems. We are also given examples of famous writers who loved young girls and statistics about the sexual maturation of females in different parts of the world. Comparative sexual customs and the varying attitudes and laws at different times, in several countries, and even in separate states of the United States emphasize the point that there is no single standard of judgment and no trustworthy norm either for Humbert or for us to be guided by. Is Humbert innocent or guilty? And of what? Can we determine whether he is sane or mad? Is he the creator of a splendid character or the despoiler of a young girl's life?

We are made into Humbert's judge and jury and are accordingly addressed as "your honor" and as "ladies and gentlemen of the jury," for Humbert presents his legal and moral case to us. Beyond that, we are also "the astute reader" who is called upon to appreciate Humbert's artistry. Although Humbert asks his "learned readers" to view his history with "impartial sympathy," he also wants us to recognize how much we have in common with him: "Reader! *Bruder!*" Our dilemma is that we simultaneously have to evaluate a man's life and criticize his artistic creation. Our identities as judges and as readers come together when Humbert implores us, "Human beings, attend!"

A further complication in the reader's situation emerges when Humbert invokes our aid: "please, reader," he begs, "imagine me; I shall not exist if you do not imagine me." By reading the book we bring Humbert and Lolita back to life. We transform the past incidents of Humbert's life into the present as they take place anew for us. We also help to provide Humbert the literary immortality he hopes for from the future. As past and future merge within the reader's consciousness, we enable the lovers to transcend time and achieve the timeless present which Humbert so ardently desires. But we do so at the cost of trapping them eternally within an unchangeable pattern. Each time we read the book we participate in the seduction at The Enchanted Hunters, in Lolita's desertion of Humbert, and in Humbert's grotesque murder of Clare Quilty by reenacting these events in our minds. Just as King Lear will never be merrily reunited with all his daughters, so Humbert and Lolita will never live together happily ever after.

If we do not read the book, then Humbert and Lolita are "dead" and forgotten, even nonexistent. But if we do, we compel them to repeat the identical events, and so we fix them as literary characters. The reader relives the experience of Humbert as writer, which in turn recapitulates the manner in which Humbert has led his life. And far off in time and space, Vladimir Nabokov grins, assumes his alias of Aubrey McFate, and makes it all happen. (pp. 423-27)

Mathew Winston, " 'Lolita' and the Dangers of Fiction," in *Twentieth Century Literature,* Vol. 21, No. 4, December, 1975, pp. 421-27.

RONALD WALLACE
(essay date 1979)

[In the following excerpt, Wallace studies theme and characterization in *Lolita*.]

Two basic questions . . . confront us in *Lolita*. First, is Humbert Humbert "really" a lover and an artist or a pervert and a fool, or is he some curious combination of opposites? Second, what is the thematic focus of the novel as a whole? Critics who attempt to answer such questions, of course, risk provoking Nabokov's wrath. In his afterword to the novel, Nabokov sarcastically dismisses "Teachers of Literature [who] are apt to think up such problems as 'What is the author's purpose?' or still worse 'What is the guy trying to say?' " Nabokov insists that his only purpose in writing a novel is "to get rid of " it. . . . Nevertheless, the risk seems worth taking, since disagreement about Humbert and the novel's theme has resulted in critical confusion. (p. 67)

[The] best generic description of the novel is, perhaps, a parody of comic form. In parodying the form of both Shakespearean romantic comedy and Meredithian satiric comedy, Nabokov complicates the character of Humbert Humbert and defines the thematic focus of the book. A description of the "parodic-comic" intrinsic genre of the novel should help clarify some of the perplexing critical questions.

Nabokov's parody of romantic comedy is most obvious, and critics have generally acknowledged it. . . . [In] typical romantic comedy two lovers are opposed by a blocking figure, usually societal or paternal, who disrupts the lovers' union. Usually, the lovers manage to escape or convert the blocking figure and celebrate the integration of society through their own symbolic marriage. In *Lolita*, Humbert Humbert and Lolita are one such pair of lovers opposed by a humorous society. In some ways, Humbert resembles the typical hero of romance, "an exceptionally handsome male; slow-moving, tall with soft dark hair and a gloomy but all the more seductive cast of demeanor." . . . Lolita, with the gray eyes and blond hair typical of romance heroines, is his paramour. In the course of the action, the lovers manage to overcome one blocking figure, Charlotte, through her death, and another blocking figure, the reader, by converting him to their cause. Although the humorous society continues to oppose their union, the lovers manage to escape it, at least temporarily, by leaving on a continental tour.

Like a good romantic comedy hero, Humbert

Humbert idealizes his love, anxiously protecting her "purity" and defending her "chastity." (pp. 67-8)

Humbert's "protection" of Lolita's "chastity" is absurd, however, since it usually takes the form of an attack on her chastity. Humbert characteristically protects Lolita from everyone but himself, though he is the worst threat of all. While his language is always delicate and pure, his actions are ugly, and the discrepancy between his description of his acts and the acts themselves is ludicrously comic. One of the best examples of Humbert's comic protection of his lover is the masturbation scene early in the novel. Alone with Lolita in the living room of the Haze house, Humbert perceives a chance for bliss. Tussling with his nymphet over an Eden-red apple, Humbert manages to use the friction generated by Lolita's legs across his lap to accomplish a private climax. . . . Comically exaggerating masturbation into "the longest ecstasy man or monster had ever known," . . . Humbert continues to insist that since Lolita was "safely solipsized," . . . he has not in any way compromised her tender purity. The ludicrous scene undercuts Humbert's claims of idealism and his concern over Lolita's innocence. (pp. 68-9)

Humbert, then, is an ugly parody of the typical romance hero. His "protection" of Lolita is really just a method of imprisoning her in his lust, and his "love" quickly degenerates into "a quick connection before dinner." . . . The discrepancy between the two Humberts—the romance hero and the ugly pervert—provides the incongruity necessary for comedy.

Similarly, the discrepancy between the two Lolitas in the book is comic. Humbert's romantic vision of her constantly clashes with the gum-chewing, obnoxious little girl she prefers to be. Nabokov often exposes this discrepancy through linguistic incongruity. In the very first paragraph, for example, Humbert's lovely lyrical description of his paramour is undercut by a single vernacular phrase. "Lolita, light of my life, fire of my loins. My sin, my soul. Lo-lee-ta . . . standing four feet ten in one sock." . . . Lolita's vernacular, juxtaposed with Humbert's sophisticated vocabulary, constantly exposes the distance between the vision and the actuality. Further, Nabokov keeps us constantly aware that the sensuous female form described by Humbert is actually that of a "seventh-grader." . . . Throughout the novel, then, the discrepancy between Humbert's vision of Lolita's charms and her actual childishness is comic.

By the end of the novel it becomes clear that Humbert . . . is less the hero of romance than he is the traditional blocking figure, the paternal force preventing his daughter from forming any kind of personal relationship. When Humbert does finally allow Lolita to see other males, he comically lurks in the car, looking on protectively. Lolita, however, like the typical romance-comedy heroine, does escape Humbert with her lover, Quilty. . . . Although she doesn't marry him, she does marry Richard Schiller. Thus the novel could be viewed as a parodic romantic comedy, told not from the point of view of the lovers, as is usual, but from the point of view of the blocking figure, Humbert Humbert. At the end, as in traditional romantic comedy, the blocking figure is expelled, and the lovers escape his influence.

But *Lolita* is more than a parody of romantic comedy. If that were an adequate description, the novel would be fairly simple and straightforward. It is, however, more complicated because Humbert himself perceives that he is a fool, that he has been his own deceiver. It is Humbert who writes this parody of romantic comedy, consciously exposing himself. The fact that Humbert is the self-conscious author of his own exposure complicates the form.

Aware of his own foolishness, Humbert knows that he is in danger of losing reader sympathy and support. In order to regain that support, Humbert adopts a rather sophisticated narrative strategy, a strategy that has fooled a number of critics. His strategy is to write a Meredithian comic novel in which he is both an *alazon* (a boastful impostor and fool) and an *eiron* (a witty self-deprecator and artist). By satirically exposing himself

as well as his society and by posing as a poet, Humbert hopes to persuade the reader-juror that he is really a good fellow underneath. In his role as artist and comic spirit, he ridicules his former self in hopes that this ridicule will reflect the reformation that is the function of the comic spirit, according to Meredith.

To understand Humbert's strategy more clearly, we might compare his narrative technique with Pip's in *Great Expectations*. Both *Great Expectations* and *Lolita* are narrated by a character looking back on the foolishness of his earlier life. Pip exposes his foolish love for his dream girl, Estella, and Humbert exposes his foolish love for his dream girl, Lolita. Surveying their past experience, both characters have attained a detachment that enables them to see themselves in a comic perspective. In *Great Expectations,* the reader laughs at the young Pip while admiring the older Pip for his ability to criticize his own folly. By adopting a similar narrative strategy, Humbert hopes to persuade the reader that, like Pip, he has gained a mature perspective on his folly and has been reformed through love. If he can convince the reader that he is really two characters, Humbert the wise narrator and Humbert the foolish actor in a comedy, he can perhaps claim the kind of sympathy we give to Pip. By consciously casting himself in the role of *alazon,* boastful impostor and pervert, Humbert hopes to elevate himself to the role of *eiron,* witty self-deprecator and artist.

Like Pip, Humbert starts by giving himself a comic name. . . . In the course of the novel Humbert distorts his name comically into Humbug, Humbird, Homburg, and Hamburger, among others, suggesting his comic perception of himself. (pp. 69-71)

But Humbert isn't content merely to expose himself in this droll way. He also mercilessly berates himself throughout the book. He calls himself "pathetic," . . . a "brute," . . . a "humble hunchback abusing myself in the dark." . . . Humbert seems prepared to criticize himself more viciously than any reader possibly could. He criticizes not only his actions, but the very style in which he articulates his criticism. After evoking a lyrical picture of Lolita in the first paragraph, he consciously undercuts himself: "You can always count on a murderer for a fancy prose style." . . . (pp. 71-2)

All of these comic devices of self-deprecation are evident in Humbert's most masterfully realized comic scene, the "climax" of the book, *"le grand moment."* . . . From the outset Humbert seems to take a comic view of his first night with Lolita in the Enchanted Hunters Hotel. . . .

When Humbert finally approaches his sleeping beauty . . . , the scene remains comically mundane and trivial. The noisy toilets seem to conspire against him, he has heartburn, and to top it all, Lolita has cruel-

LOLITA

VLADIMIR NABOKOV

A NOVEL

BY THE AUTHOR OF PNIN

Complete and unabridged

Dust jacket of Nabokov's best-known work.

ly appropriated both pillows, forcing him to sneak one back when she asks for a drink of water. As Humbert leans over the half-awake Lolita, she confuses him with Barbara, the girl with whom she had shared Charlie's manhood at camp. Humbert comically sees himself in the third person as Barbara, adding a further element of farce to the already farcical situation. . . . (p. 72)

Then, for the biggest joke on himself of all, Humbert turns to the jury and confesses, "it was she who seduced me." . . . "Sensitive gentlewomen of the jury, I was not even her first lover." . . . By laughing at himself, undercutting his own earlier foolishness, Humbert seeks to gain reader sympathy. By making his lust risible, he hopes to neutralize any moral objections that might be raised. (pp. 72-3)

If Humbert marshals reader sympathy by exposing his own foolishness, he increases that sympathy by showing how much worse is his humorous society. Although Nabokov claims that he himself has "neither the intent nor the temperament of a moral or social satirist," his character Humbert has a keen satirical eye for American manners and morals. In the course of the novel he satirizes American songs, ads, movies, magazines, products, tourist attractions, small towns, camps, schools, hotels, and motels, among other things. By satirically exposing the society around him, Humbert . . . reveals his perceptive wit, thus effectively qualifying his own absurdity.

Humbert's first satiric target is Charlotte Haze, the representative middle-class American clubwoman and moralist. From the first, Charlotte is a neurotic woman who rarely deviates into sense and never fails to miss her own comicality. . . . Charlotte has no ideas of her own but relies instead on "the wisdom of her church and book club," the comic juxtaposition of the two organizations suggesting their equal importance in her mind. . . . Humbert observes that Charlotte "did not notice the falsity of all the everyday conventions and rules of behavior, and foods, and books, and people she doted upon." . . . Humbert, of course, is one of the people she dotes upon, and she manages to remain oblivious of his true feelings toward her for some time. Charlotte's banality and self-deception thus make her a proper victim of Humbert's satiric exposure. We cannot feel too critical of Humbert for duping her, since she practically asks to be duped. (p. 73)

Like Charlotte, Lolita embodies material for satire. Humbert realizes that his nymphet is partially an extension of her mother, and that, as Mrs. Dolly Schiller, she will slip easily into her mother's role. Lolita's potential vulgarity provokes Humbert to satirically expose its causes, and his prime target is the American educational system. Referring to Lolita's incongruous seduction of him in the Enchanted Hunters Hotel, Humbert insists that "modern co-education, juvenile mores,

the campfire racket and so forth had utterly and hopelessly depraved" her. . . . (p. 74)

Humbert, however, saves his most pointed satire for Beardsley School. Headmistress Pratt, one of the more obvious caricatures in the novel, describes Beardsley's educational philosophy in terms so absurd that no undercutting comment from Humbert is required. . . . Although Humbert is disturbed by all the meaningless jargon and cant, "two intelligent ladies" assure him that "the girls did quite a bit of sound reading and that the 'communication' line was more or less ballyhoo aimed at giving old-fashioned Beardsley School a financially remunerative modern touch." . . . In other words, this American school has to pretend to be appallingly bad in order to remain funded.

School, camp, and family life are dedicated to integrating the child into American society, and as Humbert points out, Lolita is ideally suited to consumerism. . . . To keep his little concubine in tow, Humbert concludes that all he has to do is reward her with "things." After *le grand moment*, for example, he buys her a veritable catalogue of consumer items. . . . The satiric thrust of the catalogue is brutally intensified by its juxtaposition with the announcement of Lolita's mother's death. (pp. 74-5)

It is easy to identify with Humbert as a comic hero who criticizes himself while undercutting the pretensions of stuffy ladies and pompous dentists. . . . [In] laughing at himself and his society, Humbert reveals his comic perspective. In a world gone wrong, a cheap, tawdry world filled with hot fudge sundaes, comic books, shoddy motels, neon, and cement, we have to value the kind of intelligence and perspicacity Humbert seems to embody.

If Humbert thus boasts a comic perspective, he also boasts a potential artistry, continually insisting that he is more of a poet than a pervert. "The artist in me has been given the upper hand over the gentleman," he confesses. . . . Referring to *le grand moment*, Humbert presents his strongest argument for reader sympathy: "If I dwell at some length on the tremors and gropings of that distant night, it is because I insist upon proving that I am not, and never was, and never could have been, a brutal scoundrel. The gentle and dreamy regions through which I crept were the patrimony of poets—*not* crime's prowling ground." . . . As an artist, Humbert is concerned with something much more significant and beautiful than mere sex. . . . In the course of the novel, he does manage to create an ideal romantic creature out of a rather common little girl. (pp. 76-7)

As the artist creating a world around himself, Humbert is squarely in a recognizable comic tradition. From Aristophanes' Dicaeopolis, who creates a world of peace around himself; through Shakespeare's Prospero, who conjures up a magical island; to Barth's Todd

Andrews, who recreates his own history; and Hawkes's Skipper, who imagines a pastoral paradise, artistic creation has been a central theme of comic art. If the artist-hero cannot integrate himself into an existent society, he manages to create a new society around himself that is much more beautiful than the existent humorous one. (p. 77)

The ending of Humbert's novel seems to reinforce this comic affirmation, reflecting elements of both an exposure comedy, like *Great Expectations,* and a romance comedy, like those of Shakespeare. In an exposure comedy, the deluded protagonist is usually reformed through ridicule. In *Great Expectations,* for example, Pip escapes his dark self. . . . Humbert's novel ends similarly, as he defeats his bad self, Quilty, criticizes his earlier folly, and confesses real love for Lolita, though she marries her Dick.

Humbert's ending also parallels that of a typical romance comedy. In romance comedy, the lovers escape the paternal blocking figure and celebrate their union. In *Lolita,* the heroine escapes Humbert, marries Richard Schiller, and prepares to live happily ever after with Humbert's money, her unborn child reflecting the promise of social continuity present at the ends of most comedies. The foolish character is converted; the lovers celebrate their union. (pp. 77-8)

But Humbert's comic novel is not Nabokov's. In fact, Humbert's self-criticism and artistry is, in some ways, but another and subtler pose, a pose that Nabokov undercuts through parody. If Humbert casts himself in the role of comic hero, Nabokov parodies that role. As I suggested earlier, Humbert's narrative strategy is similar to Pip's in *Great Expectations.* Both characters look back on their prior folly, exposing themselves from their new comic perspective. But the difference between *Lolita* and *Great Expectations* helps to define more accurately Nabokov's method. In *Great Expectations,* the older Pip never fools himself or the reader, and Dickens never criticizes him. Humbert Humbert, however, continually fools both himself and the reader, and Nabokov constantly undercuts him through parody. (p. 78)

Throughout the book Nabokov has his character expose himself in ways Humbert doesn't realize.

Humbert's self-criticism, for example, is rather selective. While consciously emphasizing some of his less attractive attributes, he fails to notice others. He never undercuts his boastful vanity, a typical characteristic of the comic *alazon.* Describing himself as a romance hero, he observes, "I was, and still am, . . . an exceptionally handsome male; slow-moving, tall, with soft dark hair and a gloomy but all the more seductive cast of demeanor." . . . By itself this remark does not seem unduly boastful. But repeated dozens of times, it becomes comic. . . . Although Humbert thus claims

that he is irresistible to women, the action of the novel shows how resistible he really is. His first wife, Valeria, runs off with a taxi driver, and his nymphet, Lolita, runs off with a playwright, having never loved Humbert at all.

Humbert not only boasts about his physical charms, but also insists that he is spiritually and emotionally superior to everyone else. Early in the novel he poses as Christ. . . . Later he insists that he is capable of a depth and intensity of bliss unavailable to ordinary human beings. . . . Humbert is special. No one, not even a writer of genius, could so much as imagine the heights Humbert has reached. Although he can enjoy normal sexual relationships as well as the next man, his special sensitivities elevate him to an almost religious realm where masturbation must be sanctified with an amen. . . . Egotistically isolating himself from the human community, Humbert resembles the comic humors that people the plays of Molière.

Humbert exposes himself unconsciously, but he also consciously lies to the reader, trying to trick him into sympathy. It is important to remember that the purpose of Humbert's novel is self-defense. He imagines that the reader is a jury, sometimes a human jury, sometimes a heavenly court of "winged gentlemen," and that he is arguing for his soul. To save himself, Humbert will use whatever rhetorical strategy seems to work, and his rhetoric shifts to suit his needs. When he wants to show the superiority of his artistic passion, he claims to be a unique individual. . . . When he wants to show the generality of his folly, he claims to be merely a poor pervert, one of many sad and harmless similar cases of "innocuous, inadequate, passive, timid strangers who merely ask the community to allow them to pursue their practically harmless, so-called aberrant behavior, their little hot wet private acts of sexual deviation without the police and society cracking down upon them. We are not sex fiends! . . . Emphatically, no killers are we. Poets never kill." . . . Similarly, when it strengthens his case to argue that he is an artist more interested in creation than intercourse, he claims to be a poet, . . . but when he wants the reader-juror to believe that he is merely presenting the facts of the case, he underplays his imaginative embroideries on the real situation. "I am no poet," he explains. "I am only a very conscientious recorder." . . . (pp. 79-81)

Thus, for all of Humbert's self-criticism, he remains unaware of much of his egotism and ignorance. Similarly, his conscious social satire often reflects on him comically. Although he successfully ridicules Charlotte, for example, as a representative middle-class American buffoon, he fails to see that her very inadequacies expose him as well. In some ways Charlotte is very much like Humbert. Charlotte's hopeless passion for Humbert, for example, parallels Humbert's for Lolita. Despite Humbert's ridicule, Charlotte's romantic feelings are not so different from his, belying his claims that his ecstasies are special. (pp. 81-2)

[Although] Humbert seems to be shaping his own novel, it is evident that another hand is guiding his. While Humbert seems to have control over character and style, "McFate" (Nabokov) controls the plot. Nabokov's most effective method of exposing Humbert's imposture is the use of extensive comic structural doublings. Two kinds of doubling are typical of comedy. One device is the inclusion of one or more parody characters grouped around the major character to focus his exposure by embodying more clearly his various absurd aspects. . . . Another comic device is the doubling of scenes in the plot in order to expose their comedy. (p. 83)

The sexual affairs that Humbert catalogues early in the novel, for example, function to expose the central situation of Humbert's "love" for Lolita. Humbert traces this emotion to his early love for another nymphet, Annabel Leigh, but Annabel is just the first in a long line of females, young and old, with whom Humbert has had relations. He enumerates the eighty prostitutes and other women in his life. . . . The repetition and exaggeration of girls, women, lovers, wives, and nymphets renders Humbert's obsession comic. Even after he meets Lolita and confesses his great love for her, he can't resist dreaming about other nymphets who are, in some ways, preferable even to Lolita. The comedy of Humbert's early sex life establishes the context for his later life with Lolita.

Humbert's marriage to Valeria early in the book is the most obvious comic doubling of the central situation, parodically paralleling Humbert's later progress with Lolita. When Humbert marries Valeria she seems like a little girl, and Humbert assumes she is a virgin. But, like Lolita, she ages rapidly, and Humbert soon discovers that he was no more her first lover than he will be Lolita's. . . . Like Lolita, Valeria finds the "irresistible" Humbert eminently resistible and leaves him for another man. Her subsequent marriage to Taxovitch is a grotesque parody of Lolita's grotesque marriage to the hard-of-hearing Dick Schiller. Humbert's first impulse upon discovering that the driver of their taxi is Valeria's lover is to shoot them both; later he actually does kill Quilty. Although Humbert is prevented from stomping on Valeria with his boots as he wants to, he is later able to hit Lolita in the mouth. . . . Finally, like Lolita, Mrs. Maximovitch dies in childbed. Thus Humbert's marriage to Valeria is a parodic doubling of his later relationship with Lolita, ridiculing the basis of the central situation and exposing Humbert's later protests of true love and compassion.

If Humbert's relationship with Lolita is comically doubled by his relations with other females, Humbert himself is doubled by several caricatures. (pp. 83-4)

Both Charlotte Haze and John Ray comically double Humbert, but his most significant comic double is Clare Quilty. Most critics have accepted Humbert's treatment of Quilty as a dark alter ego, Humbert's bad self, his psychological *Doppelgänger*. If that is true, then Humbert's killing of Quilty is an heroic act, symbolizing Humbert's triumph over his past, allowing the good artist and lover to shine through. But Humbert misunderstands Quilty's function. . . . Quilty is not a psychological double, but a comic caricature who reflects in simplified form the foolishness of the protagonist.

Nabokov emphasizes the comic parallels. Early in the novel, for example, Humbert reads a biography of the playwright and discovers that Quilty wrote *The Little Nymph* and *Fatherly Love* and that "his many plays for children are notable." . . . Like Quilty, Humbert has a little nymph, practices fatherly love of a sort, and makes "many plays for children." The two characters even resemble each other. . . .

Quilty comically exposes Humbert by doubling two of his central characteristics, his sexual perversion and his effort to turn his life into comic art. If Humbert manages to blur his perversion, Quilty is obviously a pervert. Like Humbert, Quilty is attracted to little girls, and after freeing Lolita from Humbert he tries to imprison her in his own fantasies. (pp. 84-5)

Since Quilty comically reflects Humbert's perversions, it is no wonder that the narrator would like to kill him. But killing Quilty proves more difficult than Humbert had anticipated because, in addition to reflecting Humbert's perversion, Quilty reflects Humbert's strategy of combatting his enemies with laughter. Humbert thinks that by smiling at his own actions and by persuading the reader to smile, he will be able to overcome any objections to his behavior. . . . Quilty's genre is comedy, and he uses Humbert's techniques in an effort to defeat him. Instead of taking Humbert's murder threat seriously, Quilty tries to turn it into a joke or an esthetic experience. When Humbert hands Quilty an Eliotic poem explaining his motives for killing him, Quilty absurdly turns it into an exercise in literary criticism. . . . Undercut by the comedy, Humbert is unable to shoot; the gun goes limp in his hands. If Quilty can't turn the whole scene into a joke, he can perhaps turn it into a play, using art, as Humbert would, to save himself, Quilty is, after all, the real artist, having written numerous plays, while Humbert is merely an impostor. . . . When Humbert does manage to shoot the playwright, Quilty combines his efforts, turning the scene into a comic play, parodying Shakespeare. (pp. 85-6)

Quilty's comic doubling of Humbert reflects Humbert's perversion and his efforts to turn his experience into comedy or art; the structural doubling exposes Humbert's obsessions and pretensions in ways he doesn't perceive. A final example of Nabokov's parody is evident in the ending of the novel. While Humbert's novel ends with the marriage and promise of continuity typical of romance comedy, and with the expulsion and conversion of the blocking figure typical of satiric comedy, Nabokov's novel ends rather differently. In Nabokov's parody of the comic ending, Humbert dies of a coronary thrombosis, and Lolita and her daughter die in childbed. The deaths have been overlooked by some readers because they are announced at the beginning rather than the end of the novel. Other readers have argued that the deaths make the novel tragic. But the novel is not tragic; it is parodic. If Lolita, her child, and Humbert die in a parody of the comic ending, society, as represented by John Ray, Jr., and the reader, goes on. The fact that it is a humorous society merely reinforces the parody. (p. 86)

The reader presumably begins *Lolita* with a moral scheme that rejects a disgusting pervert like Humbert Humbert. Then Humbert, with the help of John Ray, convinces the reader to shift his moral perspective and accept Humbert, perhaps even to admire him for his artistry and love. By the end of the novel, however, the reader who has inverted his moral scheme has himself become the butt of the joke. Having held two antithetical attitudes toward Humbert, total rejection and complete admiration, the reader perceives the fragility and tenuousness of moral schemes in general. The result is a more complex moral scheme, which can balance opposites and increase one's capacity for compassion. In this way parody becomes for Nabokov what it was for Sebastian Knight: "a kind of springboard for leaping into the highest region of serious emotion."

Further, in parodying comic form, Nabokov is also mocking the assumptions inherent in that form. One basic assumption of comedy is that by ridiculing and reforming folly, represented by the aberrant individual, society can renew itself and celebrate its continuity. Through parody, Nabokov ridicules such an easy solution. For one thing, it is absurd to hope to improve society by excluding or converting the aberrant individual because, as Humbert demonstrates, everyone is an aberrant individual. Thus, in parodying comedy, Nabokov is parodying the didactic Meredithian theory of improvement through ridicule. (pp. 87-8)

It is too late in the game, Nabokov seems to be saying, to rely on such simplistic notions of the power of love.

But the virtue of parody is that it can ridicule a form or an idea while at the same time *using* that form or idea. With parody you can have it both ways. A parody of romance comedy uses the conventions of romance; a parody of satiric comedy uses the methods of satire; a parody of love and art uses the concepts of love and art. Parody has the unique capability of simultaneously ridiculing and celebrating the form and assumptions of its original. The effect is one of infinite

Nabokov at age seven, with his brother, Sergey, six. Sergey later became the model for Sebastian in *The Real Life of Sebastian Knight.*

complication. Humbert's claims of artistry and love are comically balanced by Nabokov's exposure of perversion and lust.

It is impossible, finally, to choose one view over the other. Revising and expanding our conventional notions of morality and art, Nabokov's parody forces the reader to hold all the contradictory impulses in mind at the same time. That is some trick indeed. (p. 88)

Ronald Wallace, "No Harm in Smiling: Vladimir Nabokov's 'Lolita'," in his *The Last Laugh: Form and Affirmation in the Contemporary American Comic Novel,* University of Missouri Press, 1979, pp. 65-89.

PHILLIP F. O'CONNOR
(essay date 1980)

[In the following excerpt, O'Connor relates *Lolita* to other works by Nabokov.]

Lolita stays like a deep tattoo. Critics tumble over one another racing to publish articles on its twists, myths and artifices. Paperback houses have reprinted it again and again. It is the second most often cited title in *Book Week*'s Poll of Distinguished Fiction, 1945-65. It has been made into a movie, a successful one at that. Sales and critical attention have opened the way for the appearance of many of Nabokov's other novels, particularly his early or Russian novels. Without *Lolita,* Nabokov's rise to literary sainthood might have been delayed beyond his natural years. Indeed, it might never have occurred.

Nabokov's twelfth novel was brought out in 1955 by Maurice Girodias' Olympia Press in Paris when the author was fifty-six years old. It had been rejected by four American publishers on a variety of grounds, all, according to Andrew Field, stemming from "a compound of fright and incomprehension" (*Nabokov, His Life in Art*). Though Girodias had now and then published the works of distinguished writers such as Durrell, Beckett and Genet, he was known mainly for an output of "dirty books." He saw in *Lolita,* some of whose literary values he recognized, mainly a weapon in the fight against moral censorship. Nabokov was soon forced to insist that he would be hurt if his work became a *succes de scandale.* The author needn't have worried; during the year following its publication, *Lolita* was given not a single review and soon became just another book on the Olympia list, not even sufficiently pornographic to compete with some of Girodias' other titles, such as *White Thighs* and *The Sex Life of Robinson Crusoe.*

An early sign of the lastingness of *Lolita* seems to be the unanimity of contempt it aroused in snobs and slobs alike after it did find a public of sorts. Orville Prescott in the daily *New York Times* (August 18, 1958) declared:

> *Lolita,* then, is undeniably news in the world of books. Unfortunately it is bad news. There are two equally serious reasons why it isn't worthy any adult reader's attention. The first is that it is dull, dull, dull in a pretentious, florid and archly fatuous fashion. The second is that it is repulsive.

Prescott shared contempt with "Stockade Clyde" Carr, a barracks-mate of Nabokov's former student and, later, editor, Alfred Appel, Jr. Appel found and purchased the Olympia edition in Paris in 1955 and brought it back to his Army post, where Clyde, recognizing the publisher said, "Hey, lemme read your dirty book, man!" Urged to read it aloud himself, Clyde stumbled through the opening paragraph: "Lo . . . lita, light . . . of my life. Fire of my . . . loins. My sin, my soul. Lo . . . lee . . . ta" then tossed down the book and complained, "It's goddam littachure!" . . . Nabokov seems to have anticipated some of the fads, fash-

ions and contempts of both schools. In the foreword to the novel, Nabokov's alter-ego, or mask, the scholar John Ray, Jr., says " . . . those very scenes one might ineptly accuse of a sensuous existence of their own, are the most strictly functional ones in the development of a tragic tale, tending unswervingly to nothing less than moral apotheosis." Nabokov's works are full of such clues and warnings, but only sensitive readers pick them up. In fact, *Lolita* remained an underground novel until 1956 when Graham Greene in *The London Times* placed it on his list of the ten best novels published during the previous year. As Field points out:

> Greene's pronouncement aroused great controversy, but also stimulated the interest of many important and respected critics and writers, who, with few exceptions, were quick to recognize the enormous importance and nonpornographic nature of the novel.

By 1959 many literary people had taken and followed Greene's signal (I might say, "*Not until* 1959 . . . "). V. S. Pritchett in *The New Statesman* appreciated the novel and addressed the problem of the so-called pornographic content, no doubt aware that the U.S. Customs Bureau had for a time confiscated copies of *Lolita:*

> I can imagine no book less likely to incite the corruptible reader; the already corrupted would surely be devastated by the author's power of projecting himself into their fantasy-addled minds. As for minors, the nymphets and schoolboys, one hardly sees them toiling through a book written in a difficult style, filled on every page with literary allusions, linguistic experiment and fits of idiosyncrasy.

Such praise seems mild, given what we now know of the general richness of the novel. To one degree or another, for example, critics have demonstrated that *Lolita* is a full-blown psychological novel with roots deep in nineteenth century models; a detective novel with conventions that date back to Poe, perhaps beyond; a confessional novel; a Doppelganger Tale; an extended allegory for the artistic process; a sexual myth more complicated and mysterious than comparable Freudian stereotypes; even a fable with correspondences to the Little Red Riding Hood story. And of course it to some degree parodies these types.

In his final confrontation with Quilty, "the kidnapper," Humbert, "the detective," comically plays his role to the extreme. Then, as if to remind us that popular genres often share both conventions and cliches, Nabokov mixes matters; that is, for moments at least, a scene from a detective novel becomes, as well, a scene from a Western, "detective" becoming "cowboy," etc. Quilty has just knocked Humbert's pistol ("Chum") under a chest of drawers:

Fussily, busibodily, cunningly, he had risen again while he talked. I groped under the chest trying at the same time to keep an eye on him. All of a sudden I noticed that he had noticed that I did not seem to have noticed Chum protruding from beneath the other corner of the chest. We fell to wrestling again. We rolled all over the floor, in each other's arms, like two huge helpless children. He was naked and goatish under his robe, and I felt suffocated as he rolled over me. I rolled over him. We rolled over me. They rolled over him. We rolled over us.

The final sentences signal exhaustion, not only in the narrator and his opponent but, as importantly, in the author who lurks behind them and the reader who waits ahead.

Yet Nabokov still isn't satisfied; as parodist he has recognized and used the possibilities for exhaustion in the detective/Western, pushing the scene to its sterile limits; now he provides the rewarding twist, presented in Humbert's comment:

> In its published form, this book is being read, I assume in the first years of 2000 A.D. (1935 plus eighty or ninety, live long, my love); and elderly readers will surely recall at this point the obligatory scene in the Westerns of their childhood. Our tussle, however, lacked the ox-stunning fisticuffs, the flying furniture. . . . It was a silent, soft, formless tussle on the part of two literati, one of whom was utterly disorganized by a drug while the other was handicapped by a heart condition with too much gin. When at last I had possessed myself of my precious weapon,—both of us were panting as the cowman and the sheepman never do after their battles.

Heretofore in the scene we've been presented with a mocking of roles and literary genres; but now we find connections between poor detective writing and poor Western film making, specifically in the fight-scene cliche. Not only do genres share cliches; so do modes (fiction and film).

Here, as in many of Nabokov's novels, parody is close to essence. Literature is not the only object of Nabokov's playful pen. Material as unrelated as the author himself (anagramatically called Vivian Darkbloom) and artifacts of the American culture, such as motels, come under the writer's amused eye. That Nabokov's work and its parts are at the same time themselves and imitations of themselves is no surprise to readers of *The Real Life of Sebastian Knight, Laughter in the Dark,* and other of the author's subversive fictions. (pp. 139-41)

Characters imitate literary or historical figures outside the work (Humbert Humbert as Edgar Allan Poe), they imitate characters within the work (Humbert as Claire Quilty) and they imitate themselves (Humbert, the lecherous father and Humbert, the dutiful father). They constantly confront mirrors, adopt disguises or masks, and become, at least in terms of *motif* butterflies, hunters and chess pieces. Word-games abound, particularly those that involve repetitions (Humbert Humbert or John Ray, Jr. J—RJ—R) and connotative resonances (like the surname Haze). Punning and similar games which allow a kind of verbal playback appear frequently. Clues, false clues, symbols and allusions are bounced against each other like the white dot in an electronic tennis game, though the author's hand remains steadily, constantly on the controls. And beneath all the trickery and games, as if in concession to realists like Flaubert and Saul Bellow, there lies a more or less traditional, a tragic, love story.

Humbert's comment on the fight, quoted above, also reveals a quality that readers attending Nabokov's parodic vision may easily overlook: a depth of characterization. There are dimensions to Lolita, Quilty, Charlotte and others in the novel. Humbert is extraordinarily complicated: a lover, criminal, detective, cowboy, mocker, serious in each endeavor, even the most foolish. After noting "this mixture in my Lolita of tender dreamy childishness and a kind of eerie vulgarity," Humbert shares the depths of his feelings for her, saying:

> . . . all this gets mixed up with the exquisite stainless tenderness seeping through the musk and the mud, through the dirt and the death, Oh God, oh God. And what is most singular is that she, *this* Lolita, *my* Lolita, has individualized the writer's ancient lust, so that above and over everything there is—Lolita.

The subject here, however, is the novel and its readers: what happened and what might have happened. Consider. Because Lolita survived, as literature, as a popular novel, it prepared the way for subsequent Nabokov works, especially *Pale Fire* and *Ada,* which might otherwise have found no audience of notable size, might not even have been published by a commercial press. In sustaining a reasonably healthy life for itself, *Lolita* also made possible the translation and publication of Nabokov's important early novels, including *Mary, King, Queen, Knave, The Defense* and *The Eye.* Further, it brought invitations for Nabokov's short stories from editors of good-paying magazines who previously had ignored his work. . . . Finally, it provided for the author that glowing credential of a writer's popular success, a movie, which came about largely because of solid paperback sales. A work, then, which at the beginning was completely ignored, then existed as a controversial under-the-counter pornographic novel was finally published by a respectable house (The first Putnam edition appeared in August, 1958, and there were seventeen printings in the following thirteen months.) seemed to catapult its author into daylight. Yet this was decades after he had begun writing. How strange, especially when one recalls that *Lolita* was not discovered by an informed critic making a studied response *or* by an enterprising editor at a commercial publishing house but as the result of the bare mention of it made by another practitioner of Nabokov's lonely craft, a mention that itself might have gone unnoticed had the novel lacked the power to stir and sustain controversy. The oddness of it all might appeal to no one more than to Nabokov himself.

And so it did.

In **"An Afterword to Lolita"** he recalls his experiences with the four American publishers who's rejected his novel before he sent it to Girodias: He found some of the reactions "very amusing." One reader thought the book would be all right if Lolita were turned into a twelve-year-boy and he was seduced by Humbert, "a farmer, in a barn, amidst gaunt and arid surroundings, all this set forth in short, strong, 'realistic' sentences." Nabokov insists that everybody knows that he detests symbols and allegories,

> . . . an otherwise intelligent reader who flipped through the first part described *Lolita* as "Old Europe debauching young America," while another flipper saw in it "Young American debauching old Europe." Publisher X, whose advisers got so bored with Humbert that they never got beyond page 188, had the naivete to write me that Part Two was too long. Publisher Y, on the other hand, regretted that there were no good people in the book. Publisher Z said if he printed *Lolita*, he and I would go to jail.

The author, after years of absurd neglect, had developed a shell of protection; any response now would amuse him. In jail or an asylum he would surely have laughed, perhaps scribbled out the folly of his fate on the walls of his cell.

I've intended my remarks to be informative and stimulating, not conclusive, and therefore I must warn myself away from the temptation to make something definite of all of this. The best closing is to be found in some of the words Nabokov himself wrote about *Lolita*. They seem to be a gentle phosphorescent light by which trailing fish—critics, teachers, writers, students, publishers and the like—might be guided. When he thinks of the novel, he says:

> . . . I seem always to pick out for special delectation such images as Mr. Taxovich, or that class list of Ramsdale School, or Charlotte saying "waterproof," or Lolita in slow motion advancing toward Humbert's gifts, or the pictures decorating the stylized garret of Gaston Godin, or the Kasbeam barber (who cost me a lot of work), or Lolita playing tennis, or the hospital at Elphinstone, or pale, pregnant, beloved, irretrievable Dolly Schiller dying in the Gray Star (the capital town of the book), or the tinkling sounds of the valley town coming up the mountain trail (on which I caught the first known female of *Lycaeides sublivens* Nabokov).

These parts he calls "the nerves of the novel." They are the "secret points, the subliminal co-ordinates by means of which the book is plotted."

And surely, I dare add, some of the reasons the novel has survived even its own audiences. (pp. 141-43)

Phillip F. O'Connor, " 'Lolita': A Modern Classic in Spite of Its Readers," in *A Question of Quality: Seasoned "Authors" for a New Season*, Vol. 2, edited by Louis Filler, Bowling Green University Popular Press, 1980, pp. 139-43.

ERICA JONG
(essay date 1988)

[Jong is an American novelist, poet, and critic. In the following excerpt, she examines *Lolita* thirty years after its first appearance in the United States.]

"Lolita is famous, not I," Nabokov said to one of the many interviewers who came to interrogate him after the *succès de scandale* of *Lolita*. And like so many Nabokovian utterances, it was both true and the mirror image of true. Lolita's fame made her creator both a "brand-name" author—to use that distressing contemporary locution—and an adjective.

Vladimir Vladimirovich Nabokov, alias V. Sirin (Volodya to his friends), born on Shakespeare's birthday, 1899, became famous in 1958-59, at the fairly ripe age of 60, through the notoriety of his fictive daughter Lolita, Dolly, Lo, Dolores Haze, of the soft brown puppybody and equivalently gamy aroma.

Like most famous literary books, *Lolita* seduced the world for the wrong reasons. It was thought to be dirty. It has this in common with *Ulysses, Miller's Tropics, Lady Chatterley's Lover*: it won its first passionate proponents by being banned. When it came to wide public consciousness, it was reputed to be a scandalous book about a scandalous subject: the passion of an aging roué for a 12-year-old girl.

As one whose literary debut was also steeped in scandal, I know intimately the ambivalent feelings of an author who gains wide fame and commercial acceptance through a misunderstanding of motives. Much as one wants the acceptance conferred by best-sellerdom, it is bittersweet to win this by being thought a pervert. This alone explains Nabokov's half-mocking reference to *Lolita*'s fame. Nabokov knew that he had been toiling in the vineyards of the muse since adolescence. The public did not. Nabokov knew that he had translated *Alice in Wonderland* into Russian, the public did not. With 11 extraordinary novels, a study of Gogol, an autobiography, numerous short stories, poems and translations behind him, the author of *Lolita* was hardly a literary novice. His identity as a novelist, poet and literary scholar had been honed and polished in three languages since he privately printed his poems in St. Petersburg at the age of 15, and he had endured more traumas than sudden fame. The generous, amused, self-mocking way he reacted to *Lolita*'s stardom contains within it all the paradoxes of a career rich in paradoxes, a career that seems to have the very symmetry, balance and irony of his novels themselves.

It is almost superfluous to introduce *Lolita*—even on her 30th birthday—because Nabokov, who thought an author should control the world in his book with godlike authority, anticipated all the possible front (and rear) matter any reader could wish.

We have the mock-introduction by "John Ray, Jr., Ph.D.," a spoof on scholarly psychobabble and tendentious moralizing, two things Nabokov detested as much as he detested Freudian symbol-mongering in literary criticism. . . .

His impersonation of "John Ray" in the foreword to *Lolita* is one of the most delicious of literary parodies, and his own afterword **"On a Book Entitled Lolita"** is, I believe, the last word on the subject of the sensual versus the pornographic. I always wonder why it is not quoted more often in those endless, predictable and anesthetizing debates that go on about the nature of pornography and eroticism (and to which I am inevitably invited).

Here is Nabokov on that dreary subject:

While it is true that in ancient Europe, and well into the eighteenth century . . . deliberate lewdness was not inconsistent with flashes of comedy, or vigorous satire, or even the verve of a fine poet in a wanton mood, it is also true that in modern times the term 'pornography' connotes mediocrity, commercialism, and certain strict rules of narration. Obscenity must be mated with banality because every kind of aesthetic enjoyment has to be entirely replaced by simple sexual stimulation which demands the traditional word for direct action upon the patient. Old rigid rules must be followed by the pornographer in order to have his patient feel the same security of satisfaction as, for example, fans of detective stories feel—stories where, if you do not watch out, the real murderer may turn out to be artistic originality. . . . Thus, in pornographic novels, action has to be limited to the copulation of cliches. Style, structure, imagery should never distract the reader from his tepid lust.

People who cannot tell the difference between that sort of masturbatory stimulation and imaginative literature deserve, in fact, the garbage they get. . . .

Nabokov thought of *Lolita* as his best novel in English and he had been trying to write it at least since his Berlin days. (Perhaps the literary artist is born like a woman with all her eggs present in their follicles; they have only to ripen and burst forth—and ripeness is all. But sometimes it takes half a lifetime for them to ripen.) Nabokov began what was to become *Lolita* as a novella in Russian called *The Enchanter* (*Volshebnik*), which he composed in the fall of 1939. . . .

In *The Enchanter* all the elements of *Lolita* are present: the Central European lover, the nymphet, the marrying-her-mother theme, but in *The Enchanter* it is the nymphet's unnamed lover (who later becomes Humbert) who is killed by a truck, not the nymphet's mother. Nabokov claimed he destroyed *The Enchanter* soon after moving to America; but his memory apparently lied to him, for the novella turned up in his files and was published in 1986.

One of the many glories of *Lolita* is the evocation of the American landscape, American slang, American teenagers of the 50's—all seen with the freshness only a twice-exiled European would bring. The difference between *The Enchanter* and *Lolita* is the difference between a postcard of Venice and a Turner painting of the same scene—all the difference in the world—and it inheres in the details, the divine details. Even before *The Enchanter* the idea for *Lolita* was present in Nabokov's imagination. In *The Gift* (*Dar*), Nabokov's autobiographical Russian novel (published serially in Berlin in 1937-38, and in its entirety in 1952 in New York), there exists this amazing premonition of *Lolita*:

Ah, if only I had a tick or two, what a novel I'd whip off! From real life. Imagine this kind of thing: and old dog—but still in his prime, fiery, thirsting for happiness—gets to know a widow, and she has a daughter, still quite a little girl—you know what I mean—when nothing is formed yet, but already she has a way of walking that drives you out of your mind—A slip of a girl, very fair, pale, with blue under the eyes—and of course she doesn't even look at the old goat. What to do? Well, not long thinking, he ups and marries the widow. Okay. They settle down the three of them. Here you can go on indefinitely—the temptation, the eternal torment, the itch, the mad hopes. And the upshot—a miscalculation. Time flies, he gets older, she blossoms out—and not a sausage. Just walks by and scorches you with a look of contempt. Eh? D'you feel here a kind of Dostoevskian tragedy? That story, you see, happened to a great friend of mine, once upon a time in fairyland when Old King Cole was a merry old soul.

The language of *Lolita* is as amazing in its way as the language of *Ulysses* or *A Clockwork Orange*. Nabokov has the same lexicographical itch. *Lolita* teems with loving lexicography, crystalline coinages, lavish list-making—all the symptoms of rapture of the word. "Nymphet" was a coinage of this novel, as were the more obscure "libidream," "pederosis," "nymphage" and "puppybodies." (French critics pointed out that

Ronsard had used the word "nymphette" to mean little nymph—a fact Nabokov knew—but he used his English term in a different sense.)

Lolita is a novel about obsession. The subject was hardly a new one for Nabokov, though the form the obsession takes is new in this novel: nymphage. Luzhin in *The Defense* is obsessed with chess; Sebastian Knight in *The Real Life of Sebastian Knight* with literary immortality; Kinbote in the later novel *Pale Fire* with regaining his Zemblan kingship; Hermann in *Despair* with killing his double; Fyodor in *The Gift* with transcending time through literary creation. (p. 3)

Humbert Humbert is in love with something which by definition cannot last. That prepubescent state he calls nymphage lasts from 9 to 13 at best, a fleeting four years, often less. The honey-hued shoulders, the budbreasts, the brownish fragrance of the bobby-soxed nymphet all are destined to be abolished by the advent of womanhood, which Humbert despises every bit as much as he worships nymphage. Humbert's dilemma puts the dilemma of all obsessional lovers in high relief. What he loves he is doomed never to possess. It cannot be possessed because time rips it away from him even as he possesses it.

The villain here is time. And the dilemma is the dilemma of the mortal human being who foresees his own death. It is not a coincidence that so many of Nabokov's heroes are doomed and so many of his novels are cast in the form of posthumous autobiographies. His subjects are nothing less than mutability and time, Eros and Death, the twin subjects of all muse-poetry.

Humbert Humbert is, like so many Nabokovian narrators, a man obsessed with an irretrievable past. When he rediscovers his nymphet in Ramsdale (even the place names in *Lolita* are full of sexual innuendo and irony), he recognizes at once that he has discovered the reincarnated essence of his Riviera puppy love, who perished of typhus decades earlier:

> It was the same child—the same frail, honey-hued shoulders, the same silky supple bare back, the same chestnut head of hair. A polka-dotted black kerchief tied around her chest hid from my aging ape eyes, but not from the gaze of young memory, the juvenile breasts I had fondled one immortal day. And, as if I were the fairy-tale nurse of some little princess (lost, kidnapped, discovered in gypsy rags through which her nakedness smiled at the king and his hounds), I recognized the tiny dark-brown mole on her side. With awe and delight (the king crying for joy, the trumpets blaring, the nurse drunk) I saw again her lovely indrawn abdomen where my southbound mouth had briefly paused; and those puerile hips on which I had kissed the crenulated imprint left by the band of her shorts—that last mad immortal day behind the 'Roches roses.' The twenty-five years I had lived since then, tapered to a palpitating point, and vanished.

Time is what he seeks to abolish. Time is the enemy of all lovers. Obsession has a life of its own: the object, however irreplaceable and particular it seems, can change, though it is in the nature of obsession not to recognize that.

The obsession of Humbert with Lolita has been compared to many things: the obsession of the artist with the creative process, the butterfly collector with his specimen, the exile with retrieving a lost homeland (a characteristic Nabokovian theme). It is all these things, and more. And yet the book works, above all, because it is so clearly the story of a man maddened by an impossible love, the impossible love for an impossible object: a banal little girl who calls him "kiddo." Are not all impossible, obsessional loves inexplicable to other people? Do our friends *ever* understand what we see in them? Isn't that inexplicability the wonder and the terror of obsessional loves?

The publishing history of *Lolita* is almost as Nabokovian as any of Vladimir Nabokov's creations: it seems almost a case of life imitating art. . . .

It is not surprising that the typescript of *Lolita* was rejected by four major New York publishers (Viking, Simon & Schuster, New Directions and Farrar, Straus & Giroux). Although it contained not one "mural word," *Lolita* was a genuinely new creation and genuinely new creations do not usually fare well with mainstream publishers in any age. It was not only that *Lolita* dealt with forbidden obsessions; *Lolita* was, above all, literary. American puritanism is more comfortable with sex when it stays in the gutter than when it rises to the level of art.

What is even more amazing than the response of the publishers was the early response of Nabokov's friends Edmund and Elena Wilson and Mary McCarthy to this masterpiece, which Nabokov thought "by far my best English work." We are amazed to read in the Nabokov-Wilson letters that Edmund Wilson wrote to Nabokov of *Lolita*, "I like it less than anything of yours I have read," and that Mary McCarthy, who did not finish the manuscript, called the writing "terribly sloppy all through." (p. 46)

Had Edmund Wilson not dubbed the book "repulsive," "unreal" and "too unpleasant to be funny," had he not conveyed these sentiments to his own publisher, the publishing history of *Lolita* might have been different. As it was, fate—which is such an important character in *Lolita*—arranged that *Lolita* would have her first publication in English, in France, in 1955 under the auspices of Maurice Girodias's Olympia Press. . . . The printing was small, perhaps only 5,000 copies, but big enough so that Graham Greene found a copy and pronounced *Lolita* one of the three best novels of 1955 in *The Times* of London. (pp. 46-7)

Graham Greene saw literature and language

where others had seen only perversion and pornography. *Lolita*'s eventual triumph can be traced ultimately to his intervention. . . .

It was widely assumed that *Lolita* would provoke legal action in England and the United States (the Olympia Press edition had even been banned at one point in Paris at the request of British authorities) and the novel was debated in the British Cabinet, but the publication proceeded without legal impediment. (A New Zealand ban came later.) United States publication took place on July 21, 1958 (Putnam), and the book hit No. 1 on the New York Times best-seller list in January 1959, where it was eventually nudged out of place by another child of Russia, *Dr. Zhivago* by Boris Pasternak.

Most of *Lolita*'s reviews paid more attention to "l'Affaire Lolita" than to the book. One exception was Elizabeth Janeway, writing in *The New York Times Book Review*, who understood that the tragi-comedy was Shakespearean in nature:

Humbert's fate seems to be classically tragic, a most perfectly realized expression of the moral truth that Shakespeare summed up in the sonnet that begins, 'The expense of spirit in a waste of shame / Is lust in action': right down to the detailed working out of Shakespeare's adjectives, 'perjur'd, murderous, bloody, full of blame.' Humbert is the hero with the tragic flaw. Humbert is every man who is driven by desire, wanting his Lolita so badly that it never occurs to him to consider her as a human being, or as anything but a dream-figment made flesh—which is the eternal and universal nature of passion.

The great thing about masterpieces is that they seem always to have existed, unopposed. Outrageous, inevitable, infinitely rereadable, *Lolita* at 30 is as young as she was as a glimmer in her author's eye. She has, in fact, defeated time—her enemy, her inspiration. (p. 47)

Erica Jong, "Time Has Been Kind to the Nymphet: 'Lolita' 30 Years Later," in *The New York Times Book Review,* June 5, 1988, pp. 3, 46-7.

SOURCES FOR FURTHER STUDY

Bloom, Harold, ed. *Vladimir Nabokov: Modern Critical Views.* New York: Chelsea House Publishers, 1987, 312 p.

Comprises essays on Nabokov and his works by several well-known contemporary critics.

Clancy, Laurie. *The Novels of Vladimir Nabokov.* London: The Macmillan Press, 1984, 180 p.

Detailed treatment of the novels.

Page, Norman, ed. *Nabokov: The Critical Heritage.* London: Routledge & Kegan Paul, 1982, 400 p.

Critical essays on Nabokov's works, arranged chronologically to present a history of reaction to his writings.

Rampton, David. *Vladimir Nabokov: A Critical Study of the Novels.* Cambridge: Cambridge University Press, 1984, 220 p.

Reaffirms the new directions of Nabokov criticism by reconsidering the old criticism. Claims that *Lolita* is the Nabokov work with "the best chance of becoming a classic" in that its greatness depends on the human situation it portrays.

Roth, Phyllis A., ed. *Critical Essays on Vladimir Nabokov.* Boston: G. K. Hall & Co., 1984, 242 p.

Collection of critical studies on various aspects of Nabokov's works.

Trilling, Lionel. "The Last Lover." *Encounter* XI, No. 10 (October 1958): 9-19.

Influential early essay examining many of the themes on which later critics would focus, including Nabokov's use of ambiguity and irony, and his portraits of Humbert and the United States.

Pablo Neruda

1904-1973

(Born Ricardo Eliezer Neftalí Reyes y Basoalto; adopted pseudonym Pablo Neruda in 1919, legally changing his name in 1946 to Pablo Neruda) Chilean poet, essayist, short story writer, editor, memoirist, and dramatist.

INTRODUCTION

Widely regarded as one of the most important Latin American poets of the twentieth century, Neruda was noted for his innovative techniques and influential contributions to major developments in modern poetry, both in his native Chile and abroad. Geoffrey Barraclough called Neruda "a one-man Renaissance . . . who has modified the outlook of three generations of Latin Americans. His roots are firmly planted in Chile . . . ; his appeal is to the whole continent." Although translations of his works have existed since the 1940s, Neruda remained relatively unknown to English-speaking readers prior to the translation of several of his works in the early 1960s.

Born in the agricultural region of Parral, Neruda moved with his family at a young age to Temuco, a rainy region of Chile that later figured in his poetry. Neruda commented: "Nature there went to my head like strong whiskey. I was barely ten at the time, but already a poet." He started publishing poetry at the age of fifteen under the pseudonym Pablo Neruda and at the age of sixteen entered Chile's Instituto Pedagógico, where he majored in French. At the age of twenty, Neruda began studying poetry in Santiago at the University of Chile; the same year he established a promising reputation with *Veinte poemas de amor y una canción desesperada* (1924; *Twenty Love Poems and a Song of Despair*). In honor of his ensuing achievements, Neruda was appointed to the Chilean diplomatic service in 1927 and traveled to Burma as the Chilean consul in Rangoon, later serving in Ceylon and the Dutch East Indies. Neruda returned to Chile from the Far East in 1933 and was reassigned to Buenos Aires, where he became friends with Spanish poet Federico García Lorca and other poets of the Generation of 1927. While serving as secretary to the Chilean embassy in Mexico City from 1939 to 1941, and as a consul from 1941 to 1943, he became increasingly involved in leftist causes. *Nuevo canto de amor a Stalingrado* (1943), a poem in which he praises the defenders of Stalingrad in Russia, led to his dismissal from his diplomatic post in 1943. Although he was recalled to his country following his dismissal, Neruda instead traveled to France in 1943 to arrange for the passage of refugees of the Spanish Civil War to Chile. Neruda returned to Chile in 1944 and was elected to the Chilean Senate in 1946. There he denounced the prevailing anti-communist stance of his government and in 1947, published letters in the Mexican and Venezuelan press charging Chile's president, Gabriel González Videla, with violating his country's constitution by betraying the national interest in collusion with the United States government. Indicted for treason, Neruda fled Chile in political exile in 1949. During the early 1950s, Neruda received the Stalin Prize for literature as well as the Lenin Peace Prize. He was permitted to return to Chile in 1953. A member of the Chilean Communist Party since 1945, Neruda became a nominee for the presidency of Chile in 1970, but his name was withdrawn from consideration when the five parties that made up Chile's political left decided to endorse Salvador Allende. Under Allende's government Neruda served as Ambassador to France prior to his death in 1973. Neruda received the Nobel Prize for literature in 1971.

La canción de la fiesta (1921), Neruda's first volume of verse, reflects the influence of the Symbolists and of Walt Whitman and Rubén Darío in its quiet, confessional tone. The poems in this collection address such themes as love and death in a traditional style. A similar blend of Romantic and Symbolist influences characterizes his second volume, *Crepúsculario* (1923), which Neruda later dismissed as unsophisticated but which is often considered a classic of Chilean poetry. Neruda's next major volume, *Twenty Love Poems and a Song of Despair,* is considered to mark his transition from Symbolist to Surrealist poetry. A best-seller, this volume is apparently chaotic and arbitrary in its enumeration of material objects and complex evocation of thought and sensation. The book features poems that convey personal emotion in mystical natural terms. Although these verses initially shocked critics with their everyday language and lyrical yet explicit treatment of the joys and failures of love and sex, Neruda later asserted in his famous essay "Sobre una poesía sin pureza" ("On a Poetry without Purity") that poetry should be "corroded as if by an acid, by the toil of the hand, impregnated with sweat and smoke, smelling of urine and lilies." Since its initial appearance, Neruda's love poems have been variously faulted and commended for their dualistic celebration of woman as both the seductress of man and his vital link to mother earth and nature. However, *Twenty Love Poems and*

a Song of Despair is widely regarded as a masterpiece of erotic poetry.

Neruda broke further with poetic convention in *Tentativa del hombre infinito* (1925), an experimental work that marks his first use of interior monologue and abandonment of traditional structure, rhyme, syntax, and punctuation. Scholars concur that critical misinterpretation of the surrealistic images in this volume resulted in critical neglect, and the collection is now regarded as one of Neruda's major achievements. During the mid 1920s, Neruda further experimented with new constructions in *El habitante y su esperenza* (1925), a volume of short fiction. While serving as Chilean diplomat in Burma and the Dutch East Indies, Neruda began writing the poems in *Residencia en la tierra* (1933; *Residence on Earth, and Other Poems*), the first volume in a continuing cycle that established him as a leading figure in Spanish-language literature. Complex in structure and meaning, this work makes use of dense, hermetic language and introspective interior monologue to express a vision of existence as a continuous process of decay and despair.

The second volume of *Residencia en la tierra* (1935), written after Neruda's appointment as Chilean consul in Barcelona in 1934, features a lighter, declamatory style and a more direct approach to communication with his reader than his previous works. In this cycle, Neruda reveals a more pragmatic view of world problems and expresses less anguish over his inability to resolve human contradictions. *Tercera residencia, 1935-1945* (1947), a third installment in the *Residencia* cycle written over ten years later, is less highly regarded than its predecessors due to its didactic espousal of ideological concerns. Following the onset of the Spanish Civil War in 1936, Neruda's life and poetry took an abrupt political turn. In *España en el corazón* (1937; *Spain in My Heart*), an impassioned tribute in verse dedicated to the cause of the Spanish Loyalists, Neruda's poetry became less personal and began to depict political concerns from a socialist perspective. In "Las furias y las penas," a later poem that was revised and incorporated into *Tercera residencia* following its original publication as a single work in 1939, Neruda stated that his poetry had changed to reflect the transformation of his life and the world following two decades of global conflict and economic depression.

In 1943 Neruda published his acclaimed poem *Alturas de Macchu Picchu* (*The Heights of Macchu Picchu*), a work inspired by a visit to the Incan ruins of the title. This piece was later integrated into his epic work *Canto general de Chile,* a collection extensively revised between its original appearance in 1943 and its final revision in 1950 that features 340 poems on Chile's natural, cultural, and political history. With this volume, Neruda renounced his work written prior to

1937 and proclaimed himself a populist poet. Writing in a direct, documentary style, Neruda treats each canto as an individual chapter, skirting the boundaries between political reportage, propaganda, and art to enlist reader support for his socialist cause. While most critics have agreed that his Marxist view of Chile's history of poverty and tyranny results in a work of uneven quality, *Canto general* is often regarded as one of Neruda's major achievements.

After being accused of treason in 1949 and driven into exile by his country's leader, González Videla, Neruda traveled extensively, finished his revised *Canto general,* and completed an expose of Chile's president, *González Videla, el Lavel de la América Latina* (1949). In such works of political verse as *Poesía política* (1953) and *Las uvas y el viento* (1954), Neruda employs a new, simpler style to communicate more directly with the common people, a goal that had eluded him despite the popular and political thrust of his earlier poetry. His next major work, *Odas elementales* (1954; *Elementary Odes*), is a cycle of poems free of political intent that humorously exalts banal objects and the mundane occurrences of everyday life. These short-lined poems, written in free verse and displaying such titles

as "Ode to the Tomato" and "The Dance of the Artichoke," elevate fruits and vegetables to poetic stature while mocking the traditional ode. Fernando Alegría called Neruda's *Elementary Odes* "a song to matter, to its dynamism and to the life and death cycles which perpetuate it." Neruda later completed several additional volumes of odes.

Most critics agree that *Estravagario* (1958; *Extravagaria*) signals the last major development in Neruda's poetry. Like the *Odas elementales,* the poems in this volume are characterized by a flippant, self-indulgent tone and lucid style. Returning to the egocentrism of his earliest verse, Neruda employs self-parody to gently satirize his previous works and persona, particularly mocking his early stance of the poet as hero. His later poetry includes didactic political poetry, light, frivolous verse, and serious, prophetic works, often combining elements from all three styles.

(For further information about Neruda's life and works, see *Contemporary Authors,* Vols. 17-20, 45-48 [obituary]; *Contemporary Authors Permanent Series,* Vol. 2; and *Contemporary Literary Criticism,* Vols. 1, 2, 5, 7, 9, 28.)

CRITICAL COMMENTARY

ROBERT PRING-MILL
(essay date 1966)

[Pring-Mill is an English scholar and educator at Oxford University. In the following excerpt from his preface to Nathaniel Tarn's translation of Neruda's *The Heights of Macchu Picchu,* he provides a biographical and critical introduction to what he considers Neruda's "finest poem."]

Neruda is one of the greatest poets writing in Spanish today, and *The Heights of Macchu Picchu* is his finest poem. He made his name over forty years ago, with his second book, *Veinte poemas de amor y una canción desesperada* (1924), which has sold over one and a quarter million copies in the Spanish text alone—and goes on selling. Born in 1904 in Parral, in the south of Chile (son of a crew foreman on the Chilean railways), he spent most of his childhood in the small provincial town of Temuco. (p. vii)

Like other Latin American countries, Chile sometimes honors her poets by giving them a diplomatic post, and in 1927 Neruda was sent as consul to Rangoon. He spent the next five years in various consulates in Southeast Asia, and during this time a sense of isola-

tion which had already marked the earlier love poetry grew into a desolate bleakness, under the pressure of two alien cultures: that of the indigenous Asiatic peoples, with whom he could make little intellectual contact, and that of the European merchants and colonial administrators with whom he had to deal. His poetry turned tortuously in upon itself, displaying resentment and disgust at every form of city life, whose routine emptiness oppressed him as much in Asia as it had done in Santiago. The inherited world-picture went to pieces around him, and Neruda mirrored its collapse in a meticulous disintegration of traditional poetic forms. His poems became series of seemingly random metaphorical approximations to clear statement, organized into a studied semblance of "chaos" around a central core of emotion. Some of this poetry (collected in the two volumes of *Residencia en la tierra,* 1933 and 1935) is extremely obscure, largely due to his use of private symbols under the influence of the Surrealists, and it reflects the consciousness of spiritual sterility one finds in so many poets between 1918 and 1936.

He was transferred to Barcelona in 1934, and to Madrid the following February. The outbreak of the Spanish civil war in July 1936, together with García

Principal Works

La canción de la fiesta (poetry) 1921

Crepúscular io (poetry) 1923

Veinte poemas de amor y una canción desesperada (poetry) 1924; definitive ed., 1932

   [Twenty Love Poems and a Song of Despair, 1969; also translated as Twenty Love Poems: A Disdaining Song, 1970; later tr., 1973]

El habitante y su esperanza (short stories) 1925

Tentativa de hombre infinito (poetry) 1925

*Residencia en la tierra, Vol. 1, 1925-1931 (poetry and prose) 1933

Homenaje a Pablo Neruda de los poetas espanoles: tres cantos materiales (poetry) 1935

   [Tres cantos materiales: Three Material Songs, 1948]

*Residencia en la tierra, Vol. 2, 1931-1935 (poetry and prose) 1935

† España en el corazón: himno a las glorias del pueblo en la guerra (1936-1937) (poetry) 1937

Las furias y las penas (poetry) 1939

Selected Poems (poetry) 1941

Canto general de Chile (poetry) 1943; definitive ed., 1950

Nuevo canto de amor a Stalingrado (poetry) 1943

Selected Poems by Pablo Neruda (poetry) 1944

Nocturnal Collection (poetry) 1946

Tercera residencia, 1935-1945 (poetry and prose) 1947

   [Residence on Earth, Vol. 3, 1973]

Alturas de Macchu Picchu (poetry) 1948; definitive edition, 1954

   [The Heights of Macchu Picchu, 1966]

González videla, el Lavel de la América Latina (nonfiction) 1949

Let the Rail Splitter Awake and Other Poems (poetry) 1951

Poesía política: discursos politicos. 2 vols. (poetry) 1953

Odas elementales (poetry) 1954

   [Elementary Odes, 1961]

Las uvas y el viento (poetry) 1954

Nuevas odas elementales (poetry) 1955

Oda a la tipografía (poetry) 1956

   [Ode to Typography, 1964]

Estravagario (poetry) 1958

   [Extravagaria, 1972]

Selected Poems (poetry) 1961

Plenos poderes Buenos Aires (poetry) 1962

   [Fully Empowered, 1975]

‡ Memorial de Isla Negra (poetry) 1964

   [Isla Negra: A Notebook, 1981]

Bestiary/Bestiario (poetry) 1965

Twenty Poems (poetry) 1967

A New Decade (Poems, 1958-1967) (poetry) 1969

Selected Poems (poetry) 1970

La rosa separada: obra póstuma (poetry) 1973

   [The Separate Rose, 1985]

Confieso que he vivido: memorias 1974

   [Memoirs, 1977]

Defectos escogidos: 2000 (poetry) 1974

Elegía (poetry) 1974

   [Elegy, 1983]

Five Decades, A Selection (Poems, 1925-1970) (poetry) 1974

Passions and Impressions (poems, essays, and lectures) 1983

*These works were published in one volume as Residencia en la tierra (1925-1935) in 1944, and in English with other poems in one volume as Residence on Earth, and Other Poems, 1946; later tr. as Residence on Earth, 1962; later tr., 1973.

†This work, translated as Spain in the Heart, appears in Residence on Earth, and Other Poems.

‡This work was originally published in five volumes: Donde nace la lluvia (Vol. 1); La luna en el laberinto (Vol. 2); El fuego cruel (Vol. 3); El cazador de raices (Vol. 4); and Sonata critica, (Vol. 5).

Lorca's murder, shattered the mood of introspection which had produced the poems of *Residencia en la tierra.* Hitherto a somewhat romantic anarchist, he became a Communist supporter (although he did not join the party until nine years later). His first volume of "committed" poetry (*España en el corazón,* 1937) had a stark directness and a strident note absent from everything he had previously written. He spent the civil-war years helping the Republican cause—in Spain, France, and Chile—later going back to Europe to organize the emigration of Spanish Republican refugees to Latin America. In August 1940, he was appointed Chilean consul-general in Mexico.

Neruda held this post for just over three years, during which his reputation steadily grew. His return to Chile in October 1943 was a triumphal journey, on which he found himself acclaimed in capital after capital by huge crowds for whom his poetry seemed to voice the sufferings and aspirations of all the Latin American peoples. It was during this journey that Neruda made the trip to Macchu Picchu which inspired the poem he wrote almost two years later, in September 1945. Its central symbol is the ascent to the ruins of this lost Inca city high up in the Peruvian Andes, whose very existence was unknown till 1911, though it is barely eighty miles from Cuzco.

Cuzco had been the Inca capital, center of an empire stretching three thousand miles from north to south, with a very highly developed civilization and a complex social structure. A few miles northeast of Cuzco stands Pisac, a fortress city on a massive pinnacle of rock, guarding the upper Urubamba. From Pisac, the river surges on through the craggy gorges of a winding V-shaped valley toward the distant basin of the Amazon, with a whole system of fortress sanctuaries—once linked by a stone-built road—set on the heights from fifteen hundred to two thousand feet above the Urubamba, and about ten miles apart: Ollantaytambo (still under construction when the Spaniards came in 1536), Huamanmarca, Patallacta, Winay-whayna, Botamarca, and Loyamarca. There, as far as anybody knew for centuries, the series ended. Farther downstream, however, stood the most spectacular of all these cities: set high between two peaks, to overlook the place where the Urubamba goes cascading into humid jungles and to protect the highway to the capital from their untamed tribes.

The peaks are Macchu Picchu and Huayna Picchu—Old and New Picchu—and the former gave its name to the citadel which stands in the saddle between them, when Hiram Bingham found it at a time when Neruda was a boy of seven, down south in Temuco. A "tall city of stepped stone," Macchu Picchu stands in a grandiose setting, clinging to its geometrically terraced slope above the swirling river, among enormous mountains—their lower reaches and the lesser peaks all densely forested. Except for the absence of its straw-thatched roofs, the unpeopled city is intact: intricately patterned, with terraces, watercourses, squares, temples, and the high-gabled walls of empty houses interlocking to form a single architectural complex—planned as a unit, and built by collective labor. It is an abstract composition: a pattern of right angles and perpendiculars and horizontals, with slanting stairs and gable ends and the typical Inca trapezoidal doors and gates and niches, without a curve save where walls bend. The structure has an almost crystalline appearance, its rectilinear symmetries giving an impression of immutability—polished by the winds, but otherwise unchanged since its inhabitants abandoned it for no known reason and at an unknown date.

In the poem which Neruda wrote about the ruins, this citadel becomes the center of a tangled skein of associations with disparate and intertwining strands. It is by no means a clear-cut symbol, because its meaning shifts as the strong current of emotion winds between past and present, but Neruda's journey gradually takes on the nature of a highly personal "venture to the interior" in which he explores both his own inner world and the past of Latin American man. There is no explicit mention of the city till the sixth of the twelve poems which form the sequence, its earlier sections dealing not with Neruda's physical journey but with a kind of pilgrimage through human life in search of meaningful truth. When Neruda does reach Macchu Picchu, its heights turn out to be the place from which all else makes sense, including his own continent.

In *The Heights of Macchu Picchu,* Neruda's earlier work falls into place. Its first five poems are almost a recapitulatory survey of the different moods and settings of his previous poetry, whose various strands he weaves into a single complex fabric. In this, he makes repeated use of the whole range of heightened meanings with which he had endowed his major themes and images: earth and sea, the air; the fecund cycle of the seasons and the renewal of nature; the tree as an image of mankind and man; grain and bread, sexual love; irresistible Death, and the humiliating petty deaths and diminutions of humdrum urban life; the transience of the individual seen against the expanse of time; life as a rushing torrent; the experience of chaos and the hunger to discern some principle of order; the pointless surface of existence and the search for meaning; isolation among one's fellows, and the longing to "communicate" and thus discover some significant identity defined by a reciprocal relationship. These images are profoundly disturbing, whether or not one understands the details of Neruda's personal cosmology or shares his views on man, and the poem takes on a special meaning for each reader in terms of his response to his own experience.

This is in one sense true of any poem, yet the range of one's freedom of response is far more rigidly controlled by poems with an explicit line of argument. Neruda works with ambiguities, not stating but suggesting, and usually suggesting a number of different lines of thought and feeling at any given time. It is this feature of his approach which makes his poetry so extraordinarily hard to translate, and he exploits the full range of ambiguity by means of numerous technical devices. Thus, no sooner has the sequence opened than it moves into a web of two-way syntax that creates conflicting patterns of association around the imagery. Ambiguous syntax is one of the most fascinating aspects of Neruda's manner of proceeding in all his complex poems, yet it is a feature which is peculiarly tantalizing to translators. They can rarely hope to establish a corresponding ambiguity, and therefore have either to opt between layers of meaning, or else to give the grammatical sense of a single layer while trying to suggest the others by words which carry heightened and conflicting associations, as Tarn does. Sometimes, too, a word will have to be intensified because of a degree of abstraction which seems nebulous in English, requiring some kind of concrete rendering to achieve an equivalent impact: this is particularly true of some very frequent terms like *vacío,* or *manantiales,* or *diseminado,* and Neruda's thinking is not necessarily imprecise because such terms seem vague. He has very often taken a fairly neutral word and loaded it with his own associations by using it in numerous previous contexts, whose cumulative effect has been to extend and clarify its field of meaning: such terms cannot always be translated here by a single intensified equivalent, since different shades of meaning have to be brought out in different contexts. A further difficulty lies in the fact that Neruda's poetry has a natural setting whose grandeur obliges a translator to work close to the brink of what might seem hyperbole—a danger Tarn tries to avoid by using taut-phrased, sharp-edged images wherever possible.

The first poem of the sequence opens with the image of an empty net, "dredging through streets and ambient atmosphere," sifting experience but gathering nothing. This opening section shows us Neruda drained by the surface of existence, seeking inwards and downwards for a hidden "vein of gold"; then sinking lower still, through the waves of a symbolic sea, in a blind search to rediscover "the jasmine of our exhausted human spring"—an erotic symbol, tinged by its contextual imagery with the associations of a vanished paradise, and leading us like Eliot's "Burnt Norton" back "through the first gate" and "into our first world."

The second poem contrasts the enduring values of self-perpetuating nature, as rich and fecund in the rocks as in the seed, with man grinding things down until he finds his own soul left impoverished. It shows us the poet longing for time to stand and stare and thus to find his way back to the kind of truth he had "fingered once in stone," or experienced in the lightning flash released by love (the source of such urgent beauty in the *Veinte poemas*). This kind of truth endures in grain, as well as in the "ghost of home in the translucent water": water, perpetually flowing from the Andes down to the Pacific, is a constant feature of Neruda's Chilean background, taking on symbolic overtones in his poetry that go far beyond the traditional Spanish equation between men's lives and rivers which flow steadily toward the sea of death. Such truth cannot be found, however, in the cluster of men's empty faces: in city life—all shops and stores and factory whistles, mankind reduced to robotlike automata—there seems to be no trace of the undying "quality of life" in which Neruda still believes. Where then can it be found? That question stays unanswered for three further poems, devoted to considering the nature of two facets of death: one great and noble, and (like the "quality of life") not to be found in cities; the other a gradual and humiliating process.

The latter is the subject of the third poem, which looks directly at modern man's existence: seeing it husked off the cob like maize and settling into the granary of mean events, as each individual is whittled away by routine living—not proudly scythed at a single stroke. Urban men wilt slowly away: Neruda regards their kind of life as a wasting death in a black cup, filled with hardship, illness, toil, and loneliness. This image of the black cup, trembling—because they tremble—as they tip it back, prepares the way for the contrasting image of Macchu Picchu as a "permanence of stone . . . raised like a chalice." The religious overtones of such an image seem quite deliberate, and I think that Neruda often uses Christian imagery (part of the general Catholic heritage of South America) to heighten a vital point much as Renaissance poets used the pagan myths, bringing the textured associations of an extended frame of reference into play without implying the literal truth of its conceptual framework.

The fourth poem takes us a stage further, not only showing Neruda wooed by the greater Death (using sea imagery to hint at its attraction) but also introducing the theme of love for the poet's fellow men. This remains unrealizable, however, as long as all he sees of them is just their daily death: his own experience in the urban context progressively closes him off from them, driving him street by street to the last degrading hovel where he has to face his own small death, in an empty mood which recalls the desolation of *Residencia en la tierra.* The short fifth poem defines this kind of death even more closely in a series of seemingly surrealistic images, leaving a final vision of modern life with nothing in its wounds "save wind in gusts," to chill one's "cold interstices of soul." At that point, the tide is at the ebb: this is the lowest, coldest stage of the whole sequence.

Then, quite suddenly, the poem begins to rise (in the sixth section) as Neruda climbs upward in space toward the heights of Macchu Picchu and backward in time toward the moment when that geometrically perfect city was created: a moment in time which is a point where all lines come together, things click abruptly into place, and the pattern of past and present suddenly makes sense—a sense which will later turn out to contain built-in lessons for the future (but these are not immediately made clear, perhaps not even seen yet by the poet). Here, "two lineages that had run parallel" meet and fuse: the line behind small men and petty deaths and the line of permanence behind the recurring fertility of nature have been produced into the past, as it were, until they paradoxically met at one still point which *"was* the habitation . . . *is* the site"—resembling the "still point of the turning world" where "past and future are gathered," in "Burnt Norton."

Macchu Picchu is the place where "maize grew high" and where men carded the vicuña's fleece to weave royal robes and both funereal and festive garments. What endures is the collective permanence those men created: all that was transitory has disappeared, leaving the stone city to the lustration of the air. Section VII picks up this contrast between what endures and what has vanished, and sees "the true, the most consuming death" (which Neruda could not find in modern streets) as having slain those long-past men—their death being nobler because it was a collective experience (they are the "shades of one ravine" who "plummeted like an autumn into a single death"). What they left behind them was their citadel—"raised like a chalice in all those hands"—which Neruda sees as "the everlasting rose, our home" (*la rosa permanente, la morada*). This "rose" is one of Neruda's favorite symbols, taken up in the **"Oda al edificio"** (*Odas elementales,* 1954) in a way which seems to me to illuminate its meaning here: in the later poem, men have to overcome all petty prides so as to build a dome—a deft balancing of calculated forces—thereby bringing order out of the various materials which they have taken from nature, in the erection of "the collective rose" which is "the edifice of all mankind," structured on reason and steel in the pursuit of happiness. The implications of the "everlasting rose" in *Macchu Picchu* are not yet as clear-cut, but it points in this direction.

Neruda feels that he can "identify" with the absolute Death he finds on the heights, but his search for this true death has been a search for a more positive kind of identity as well, and also for identification through nature with his fellow men. The journey backward in time and upward in space was an exploration in which the poet learned—more by means of feeling than by means of thought—to see new facets of the truth, both about himself and about the nature of existence. The journey does not end, however, at this still point, with the discovery of the city living its enduring "life of stone." There is already a hint of the final outcome in "life of stone *after so many lives,*" but the buoyancy of his discovery lasts through the next two poems: VIII, with its vivid evocation of surging nature and pre-Columbian man linked in their common dawn, and fused together by a warm instinctive love which the poet summons up from the past to transfuse the present and embrace the future (anticipating the more personal summons to his past "brothers" in XI); and IX, a solemn and incantatory chant made up of units based on interlocking metaphors, with the phrase *de piedra* ("of stone") recurring like the "Ora pro nobis" of a litany, building up to a final pair of lines which brings us starkly back both to the great mass of men who raised the citadel and to the one-way thrust of man-slaying time.

The poem's last major turning point comes with the question opening its tenth section: "Stone within stone, and man, where was he?" Neruda begins to wonder whether the men who built up stone on stone, in long-past time, may not perhaps have been like urban man today, and whether the geometrical precision of the citadel might not in fact have been erected on a base of human suffering: "stone above stone on a groundwork of rags." If built by slaves, in what conditions did these live? Was Ancient America—that not only "bore the rose in mind" but could translate it "into the radiant weave of matter"—based on starvation, hoarding "the eagle hunger" in its depths?

In the eleventh section, Neruda strives to get beyond the weave of matter until he can hold "the old and unremembered human heart" in his hand (feeling it pulse like a captive bird), seeing behind the "transcendental span" of Macchu Picchu to the invisible "hypotenuse of hairshirt and salt blood" implied by each right angle in those ruins. Man is what matters because "man is wider than all the sea," and Neruda wants to get through to all the men who died building this city, so that they may rise again to birth—with him and through him—as his "brothers." It would be easy to smile at this in the light of other prejudices, seeing it as a kind of futile retroactive "Workers of the world, unite!" But the moral it draws from the past thrusts forward in the same direction as devouring time, and the Neruda who summons the vanished craftsmen of Macchu Picchu in the final poem, asking them to show him the places of their agony (evoked in language linking their sufferings to the stations of the Cross), is a noble and imposing figure, who finds his ultimate fulfillment in becoming the valid spokesman of the dead—of his South American dead in particular, but in the last resort, of all mankind.

What really matters to Neruda now is that which his own experience has in common with the experience of other men, plus the urgency of his need to show men to themselves in such a way that they can feel the identity behind their separate lives, and share his insight. Yet on its way toward this "public" ending, the sequence has explored numerous more private interpenetrating layers of human existence, and the force of its discoveries at these different levels lingers on despite the public nature of the resolution. (pp. vii–xix)

Robert Pring-Mill, in a preface to *The Heights of Macchu Picchu* by Pablo Neruda, translated by Nathaniel Tarn, 1966. Reprint by Farrar, Straus & Giroux, 1967, pp. vii–xix.

ROBERT BLY

(essay date 1968)

[A prominent and influential American poet, Bly is regarded as one of the most accurate and faithful translators of Neruda's poetry. The following essay was originally published in slightly different form in 1967. Here, Bly provides an introduction to Neruda's major works, including *Residencia en la tierra*, *Canto general*, and *Odas elementales*.]

Poets like St John of the Cross and Juan Ramon Jiménez describe the single light shining at the centre of all things. Neruda does not describe that light, and perhaps he does not see it. He describes instead the dense planets orbiting around it. As we open a Neruda book, we suddenly see going around us, in circles, like herds of mad buffaloes or distracted horses, all sorts of created things: balconies, glacial rocks, lost address books, pipe organs, fingernails, notaries public, pumas, tongues of horses, shoes of dead people. His book, *Residencia en la Tierra* (*Living on Earth*—the Spanish title suggests being at home on the earth), contains an astounding variety of earthly things that swim in a sort of murky water. The fifty-six poems in *Residencia I* and *II* were written over a period of ten years—roughly from the time Neruda was 21 until he was 31, and they are the greatest surrealist poems yet written in a Western language. French surrealist poems appear drab and squeaky beside them. The French poets drove themselves by force into the unconscious because they hated establishment academicism and the rationalistic European culture. But Neruda has a gift, comparable to the fortune-teller's gift for living momentarily in the future, for living briefly in what we might call the unconscious present. Aragon and Breton are poets of reason, who occasionally throw themselves backward into the unconscious, but Neruda, like a deep-sea crab, all claws and shell, is able to breathe in the heavy substances that lie beneath the daylight consciousness. He stays on the bottom for hours, and moves around calmly and without hysteria.

The surrealist images in the *Residencia* poems arrange themselves so as to embody curious and cunning ideas. In **"La Calle Destruida"**, for example, he calls up injustice, architecture exploding, massive buildings weighing us down, exhausted religions, horses of pointless European armies—all of these things, he says, are acting so as to eat life for us, to destroy it, to disgust us so we will throw life away like old clothes. The poems give a sense of the ferocity and density of modern life.

Neruda's poetic master in the *Residencia* poems is not a European poet but the American, Walt Whitman. He looked deeply into Whitman.

Neruda writes:

I look at ships,
I look at trees of bone marrow
bristling like mad cats,
I look at blood, daggers and women's stockings,
And men's hair,

I look at beds, I look at corridors where a virgin is
 sobbing,
I look at blankets and organs and hotels.

I look at secretive dreams,
I let the straggling days come in,
and the beginning also, and memories also,
like an eyelid held open hideously
I am watching.

And then this sound comes:
a red noise of bones,
sticking together of flesh
and legs yellow as wheatheads meeting.
I am listening among the explosion of the kisses,
I am listening, shaken among breathings and sobs.
I am here, watching, listening,
with half of my soul at sea and half of my soul on
 land,
and with both halves of my soul I watch the world.

And even if I close my eyes and cover my heart over
 entirely
I see the monotonous water falling
in big monotonous drops.
It is like a hurricane of gelatin,
like waterfall of sperm and sea anemones.
I see a clouded rainbow hurrying.
I see its water moving over my bones.

He shows what it is like, not to be a poet but to be alive. The *Residencia* poems, however, differ from *Song of Myself* in one fundamental way. The *Residencia* poems are weighed down by harshness, despair, loneliness, death, constant anxiety, loss. Whitman also wrote magnificently of the black emotions, but when Neruda in *Residencia* looks at the suicides, the drowning seamen, the blood-stained hair of the murdered girl, the scenes are not lightened by any sense of brotherhood. On the contrary, the animals and people on all sides isolate him still further, pull him down into his own body, where he struggles as though drowning in the stomach and the intestines.

It so happens I am sick of being a man . . .

I don't want to go on being a root in the dark,
Full of fears, getting larger, shivering in my sleep,
going on down, into the moist guts of the earth,
taking in and thinking, eating every day. . . .
I don't want so much misery.
I don't want to go on as a root and a tomb,
alone under the ground, a warehouse full of
corpses. . . .

Pablo Neruda was born on July 12, 1904, in a small frontier town in southern Chile, the son of a railroad worker. The father was killed in a fall from his train while Neruda was still a boy. He said: 'My father is buried in one of the rainiest cemeteries in the world.' He described his childhood in Temuco in an essay called **"Childhood and Poetry"**, printed as a preface to his *Collected Poems.* His given name was Nefthali Beltran, and his pseudonym was taken very young, out of admiration of a nineteenth-century Czech writer.

In 1920, when he was 16, Neruda was sent off to Santiago for high school. His poem **"Friends on the Road"** is written about those days. He was already composing poems, a poetry of high animal spirits and enthusiasm. At 19, he published a book called *Twenty Poems of Love and One Ode of Desperation,* which is still loved all over South America.

> I remember you as you were in that ultimate autumn.
> You were a grey beret and the whole being at peace.
> In your eyes the fires of the evening dusk were battling,
> And the leaves were falling in the waters of your soul.

He said later that 'love poems were spouting out all over my body'.

> Body of a woman, white slopes and white thighs,
> You resemble the world in your attitude of surrender.

Federico García Lorca and Neruda prior to the advent of the Spanish Civil War in 1936 and Lorca's assassination by Fascists.

My body, savage and peasant, undermines you
And makes a son leap in the bottom of the earth.

In the preface to a short novel he wrote at this time, he said: 'In my day-to-day life, I am a tranquil man, the enemy of laws, leaders, and established institutions. I find the middle class odious, and I like the lives of people who are restless and unsatisfied, whether they are artists or criminals.'

The governments of South America have a tradition of encouraging young poets by offering them consular posts. When Neruda was 23, he was recognized as a poet, and the Chilean Government gave him a post in the consular service in the Far East. During the next five years, he lived in turn in Burma, Siam, China, Japan and India. Neruda has said that those years were years of great isolation and loneliness. Many of the poems that appear in the first two books of *Residencia en la Tierra* were written during those years.

Neruda came back to South America in 1932, when he was 28 years old. For a while he was consul in Buenos Aires; he met Lorca there, when Lorca came to Argentina on a lecture tour. *Residencia I* was published in 1933. In 1934 he was assigned to Spain.

The Spanish poets had already known his wild poems for several years, and greeted him with admiration and enthusiasm. The house in Madrid where Neruda and his wife Delia lived soon overflowed with poets—Lorca and Miguel Hernandez especially loved to come. *Residencia II* was published in Spain in 1935. Lorca, Hernandez and many others published their surrealist poems in Neruda's magazine *Caballo Verde por la Poesia* (*Green Horse for Poetry*). Spain had been for fifteen years in a great period of poetry, the most fertile for Spanish poetry since the 1500s. This period was brought to an end by the Civil War.

On July 19, 1936, Franco invaded from North Africa. Neruda, overstepping his power as consul, immediately declared Chile on the side of the Spanish Republic. After being retired as consul, he went to Paris, where he raised money for Spanish refugees, helped by Breton and other French poets, and by Vallejo. Neruda's poetry now became seriously political for the first time. Neruda had come to love Spain, living there, and he shared the shock of the Spanish poets, which was essentially the loss of their country to the right wing. The growth of political energy in his poetry was probably inevitable in any case. In *Residencia I* and *II,* the outer world is seen with such clarity, and with such a sense of its suffering, that the later development of political poetry does not come as a surprise. He returned to America in 1940, and served as Chilean consul to Mexico during 1941 and 1942. The poems he had written about the Spanish Civil War were also incorporated into *Residencia,* under the title of *Residencia III.*

In 1944, the workers from Antofogasta, the nitrate mining section of Chile, asked Neruda to run for Senator from their district. He did, and was elected. He now found himself in his country's Senate as Yeats had. He took a keen interest in Chilean politics. Several years later he described in a long poem written to the Venezuelan poet, Miguel Otero Silva, how happy the Senators would have been if he had remained a love poet:

> When I was writing my love poems, which sprouted
>   out from me
> everywhere, and I was dying from depression,
> nomadic, abandoned, gnawing the alphabet,
> they said to me: 'What a great man you are, Theocri-
>   tus!'
> I am not Theocritus: I took hold of life,
> and faced her, and kissed her until I subdued her,
> and then I went through the tunnels of the mines
> to see how other men live.
> And when I came out, my hands stained with de-
>   pression and garbage,
> I held up my hands, and showed them to the gener-
>   als,
> and said, 'I do not take responsibility for this crime.'
> They started to cough, became disgusted, left off
>   saying hello,
> gave up calling me Theocritus, and ended by insult-
>   ing me
> and assigning the entire police force to arrest me,
> because I did not continue to be occupied exclusive-
>   ly with
>   metaphysical subjects.

Neruda's experience as a Senator ended, as he mentions, with his pursuit by the secret police. It came about in this way: In 1948, Gonzalez Videla, a right-wing strong man supported by United States interests, took over as dictator. Six months later Neruda, as Senator, attacked him for violations of the Chilean constitution. Videla responded by charging Neruda with treason. Neruda did not go into voluntary exile, as expected, but attacked Videla once more, and Videla ordered him arrested. Most people assumed he would have been killed if he had been arrested. Neruda went underground; miners and working people, to save his life, passed him from one house to another at night, first in Chile, later in other South American countries. He remained in hiding for some months. Finally he crossed the Andes on horseback, and made it to Mexico; from there he flew out of the continent to Paris. All this time he was working on his new book, which he called *Canto General;* it was finished in February of 1949.

The title suggests a poetry that refuses to confine itself to a specific subject matter or kind of poem. Neruda worked on the book for fourteen years. It is the greatest long poem written on the American continent since *Leaves of Grass.* It is a geological, biological and political history of South America. The book contains 340 poems arranged in fifteen sections. The fertility of

imagination is astounding. Not all of the poems, of course, are of equal quality. In some, especially those written while Neruda was being hunted by the Chilean secret police, the anger breaks through the container of the poem.

The book as a whole gives a depressing picture of the relations between the US State Department and South American governments. Neruda's *Canto General* is not a great favourite of US cultural organs dealing with Pan-American relations. North Americans, both in universities and in the USIS, who know Neruda's work often say quite soberly that since Neruda became interested in politics, he has not written a poem of any value.

Neruda went from Paris to Russia for the 150th anniversary celebration of Pushkin's birth, and then back to Mexico, where the first edition of *Canto General* was published in 1950.

When Gonzalez Videla's government fell, Neruda returned to Chile. Since 1953 he has lived on Isla Negra, a small island off the coast near Santiago; in recent years he also has spent part of his time in Valparaiso.

There was a considerable change in style from the inward, surrealist poems of *Residencia I* and *II* to the narrative, historical poems of *Canto General.* However, the style of his poetry has changed several more times since then. Both the *Residencia* and *Canto General* poems used, for the most part, the long loping line into which he could put so much power. In the middle 1950s he began writing odes using willowy lines only two or three words long. They were *Odas Elementales,* or *Odes to Simple Things.* He wrote an ode to a wrist watch, which Jerome Rothenberg has translated very well, an ode to air, to his socks, to fire, to a watermelon, to painting, to salt. Book after book of these odes came out until he had published 100 or so odes in three or four years. More recently he has embarked on a book of autobiographical poems called *Memorial to Isla Negra.*

At the moment, Neruda entirely dominates South American poetry. I heard a young South American poet complain of Neruda's abundance. He said that whenever a new idea appears in the air, and some younger poet manages to finish a poem on it, Neruda suddenly publishes three volumes! But, he said, 'how can we be mad at Pablo? The poems continue to be good—that's the worst part of it!'

In **"Childhood and Poetry"**, Neruda speculates on the origin of his poetry.

> One time, investigating in the backyard of our house
> in Temuco the tiny objects and minuscule beings of
> my world, I came upon a hole in one of the boards
> of the fence. I looked through the hole and saw a
> landscape like that behind our house, uncared for,
> and wild. I moved back a few steps, because I sensed

vaguely that something was about to happen. All of a sudden a hand appeared—a tiny hand of a boy about my own age. By the time I came close again, the hand was gone, and in its place there was a marvellous white toy sheep.

The sheep's wool was faded. The wheels had escaped. All of this only made it more authentic. I had never seen such a wonderful sheep. I looked back through the hole but the boy had disappeared. I went into the house and brought out a treasure of my own: a pine cone, opened, full of odor and resin, which I adored. I set it down in the same spot and went off with the sheep.

I never saw either the hand or the boy again. And I have never again seen a sheep like that either. The toy I lost finally in a fire. But even now, in 1954, almost fifty years old, whenever I pass a toyshop, I look furtively into the window, but it's no use. They don't make sheep like that any more.

I have been a lucky man. To feel the intimacy of brothers is a marvellous thing in life. To feel the love of people who we love is a fire that feeds our life. But to feel the affection that comes from those whom we do not know, from those unknown to us, who are watching over our dream and solitude, over our dangers and our weaknesses—that is something still greater and more beautiful because it widens out the boundaries of our being, and unites all living things.

That exchange brought home to me for the first time a precious idea: that all of humanity is somehow together. That experience came to me again much later; this time it stood out strikingly against a background of trouble and persecution.

It won't surprise you then that I attempted to give something resiny, earth-like, and fragrant in exchange for human brotherhood. Just as I once left the pine cone by the fence, I have since left my words on the door of so many people who were unknown to me, people in prison, or hunted, or alone.

That is the great lesson I learned in my childhood, in the backyard of a lonely house. Maybe it was nothing but a game two boys played who didn't know each other and wanted to pass to the other some good things of life. Yet this small and mysterious exchange of gifts has perhaps remained inside me, like a sedimentary deposit, bringing my poems to life.

This curious and beautiful story, which Neruda carefully links to the origins of his own poetry, is a conscious rejection of the connection between poetry and sickness, so often insisted on by Europeans. What is most startling about Neruda, I think, when we compare him to Eliot or Dylan Thomas or Pound, is the great affection that accompanies his imagination. Neruda read his poetry for the first time in the United States in June of '66 at the Poetry Center in New York, and it was clear from that reading that his poetry is intended as a gift. When Eliot gave a reading, one had the feeling that the reading was a cultural experience, and that Eliot doubted very much if you were worth the trouble, but he'd try anyway. When Dylan Thomas read, one had the sense that he was about to perform some magical and fantastic act, perhaps painting a Virgin while riding on three white horses, and maybe you would benefit from this act, and maybe you wouldn't. Pound used to scold the audience for not understanding what he did. When Neruda reads, the mood in the room is one of affection between the audience and himself.

We tend to associate the modern imagination with the jerky imagination, which starts forward, stops, turns around, switches from subject to subject. In Neruda's poems, the imagination drives forward, joining the entire poem in a rising flow of imaginative energy. In the underworld of the consciousness, in the thickets where Freud, standing a short distance off, pointed out incest bushes, murder trees, half-buried primitive altars and unburied bodies, Neruda's imagination moves with utter assurance, sweeping from one spot to another almost magically. The starved emotional lives of notaries public he links to the whiteness of flour, sexual desire to the shape of shoes, death to the barking sound where there is no dog. His imagination sees the hidden connections between conscious and unconscious substances with such assurance that he hardly bothers with metaphors—he links them by tying their hidden tails. He is a new kind of creature moving about under the surface of everything. Moving under the earth, he knows everything from the bottom up (which is the right way to learn the nature of a thing) and therefore is never at a loss for its name. Compared to him, most American poets resemble blind men moving gingerly along the ground from tree to tree, from house to house, feeling each thing for a long time, and then calling out 'House!' when we already know it is a house.

Neruda has confidence in what is hidden. The establishment respects only what the light has fallen on, but Neruda likes the unlit just as well. He writes of small typists without scorn, and of the souls of huge, sleeping snakes.

He violates the rules for behaviour set up by the wise. The conventionally wise assure us that to a surrealist the outer world has no reality—only his inner flow of images is real. Neruda's work demolishes this banality. Neruda's poetry is deeply surrealist, and yet entities of the outer world like the United Fruit Company have greater force in his poems than in those of any strictly 'outward' poet alive. Once a poet takes a political stand, the wise assure us that he will cease writing good poetry. Neruda became a Communist in the middle of his life and has remained one: at least half of his greatest work, one must admit, was written after that time. He has written great poetry at all times of his life.

Finally, many critics in the United States insist that the poem must be hard-bitten, impersonal and rational, lest it lack sophistication. Neruda is wildly romantic, and more sophisticated than Hulme or Pound could dream of being. He has few literary theories. Like Vallejo, Neruda wishes to help humanity, and tells the truth for that reason. (pp. 24-35)

Robert Bly, "On Pablo Neruda," in *London Magazine,* n.s. Vol. 8, No. 4, July, 1968, pp. 24-35.

JAIME ALAZRAKI
(essay date 1972)

[An Argentine-born American educator and critic, Alazraki is the author of many books on Latin American literature, including *Poetica y poesia de Pablo Neruda* (1965). In the essay excerpted below, he offers a biographical and critical overview of Neruda's career up to 1972, the year Neruda won the Nobel Prize for literature.]

For those familiar with Pablo Neruda's work and his literary career the recent award of the Nobel Prize for literature comes as no surprise. For nearly twenty years his name has been among the candidates considered by the Swedish Academy for the coveted prize. Any student of Latin American literature knows that if one were to choose a poet who best echoed the hopes and struggles of a whole continent, this poet would undoubtedly be Pablo Neruda. What is not so self-evident, however, is the fact that Neruda's work has been a sort of seismograph through which one could learn what was happening not only in the poetry of Latin America but also in contemporary poetry at large.

If with Rubén Darío and the modernist poets Latin America shapes a poetic language of its own, with Neruda and the poets of his generation that poetic language reaches adulthood. Neruda himself has said, referring to Darío: "Without him we would not speak our own tongue, that is, without him we would still be talking a hardened, pasteboard, tasteless language" (*Viajes*). It is not surprising, therefore, to find in Neruda's first published book—*Crepusculario* (*Twilight Book,* 1923)—clear imprints of Darío's dazzling brilliance "which so radically modified the Spanish language."

With the publication of *Veinte poemas de amor y una canción desesperada* (*Twenty Love Poems and One Song of Despair*) one year later, Neruda gave expression to a new poetic mood. Love is no longer approached as in modernism by way of mythological gods and godesses, nymphs and satyrs, Sirens and Tritons. In a much more straightforward fashion, Neruda takes the reader to the scene where love is being made and describes, uninhibitedly, a true feast of the senses, at times splashed with suggestive birds, wild flowers, woods, cherries, and chestnuts reminiscent of Tagore's poem which the young poet was then reading. With this brief collection Neruda won an early popularity that he has enjoyed ever since and his name became a myth among youngsters and lovers.

From this openly romantic tone, he moved to a totally different form. At approximately the same time the first Surrealist Manifesto appeared, Neruda wrote a long poem—*Tentativa del hombre infinito (Venture of Infinite Man)*—published in 1925, which bears all the traits of surrealist theory. The paradox can be explained if one remembers that Neruda was then reading the French romantic and symbolist poets who were later to become the major sources of many surrealist innovations and techniques. The little book was ignored (even today it has remained as one of his least studied works), but for Neruda it paved the road to the poetry of *Residencia en la tierra* (*Residence on Earth*), one of his finest achievements.

The two volumes of *Residencia* contain poems written between 1925 and 1935. Unlike most surrealist poets of that period Neruda did not attempt to prove any theory or illustrate any manifesto. He sought more effective means to express his ferocious loneliness and an altogether bitter and absurd view of life; he found some of those means in surrealism. He did not have any commitment to surrealism or any other literary school. His only commitment was to his world of experience and feeling and he put it in blunt words the year he published *Tentativa:* "Yo tengo un concepto dramático de la vida, y romántico; no me corresponde lo que no llega profundamente a mi sensibilidad." The result was a poetry in which form and experience fully integrate, bringing forth a poetic equilibrium one misses in much of the deliberate surrealist poetry. Neruda was not then, and has never been, interested in experimenting with form for its own sake. Form was to him, as it has always been to poets in all ages, the flesh through which experience is born in the lines of a text. It was this approach to literature which, perhaps, preserved the poetry of *Residencia* from a sterile drabness one often finds in surrealist poetry. It is also his response to human sensibilities, no matter how gloomy they may be in the poems of *Residencia,* that presumably moved one critic to state that they are "the greatest surrealist poems yet written in a western language." One may agree with such a verdict, but the fact remains that while a great deal of surrealist poetry has aged and become merely objects of literary curiosity, the poems of

Residencia have kept an urgency which is the hallmark of poetry at its best. Miguel Hernández—a Spanish poet of Neruda's generation—wrote after his reading of *Residencia:* "I must communicate the enthusiasm that stirs me since I have read *Residencia en la tierra.* I feel like throwing handfuls of sand in my eyes, like getting my fingers caught in the doors, like climbing to the top of the toughest and tallest pine. . . ."

A great deal of poetry included in *Residencia* was written while Neruda lived isolated from his people and his language in countries such as Burma, Java, Singapore, and Ceylon as the consul of Chile from 1927 to 1932. In 1934 he was appointed to the same consular post in Barcelona, and the year after in Madrid. It was during those years in Spain, and particularly after the Civil war broke out, that the so-called "poetic conversion" of Neruda took place. With *España en el corazón* (*Spain in the Heart,* 1937) the seemingly hermetic texture of his poetry yielded to a quasi-conversational language with which the poet explained the motives of his "conversion." In a poem titled **"Explico algunas cosas"** (**"Explaining a Few Things"**), Neruda wrote that in an agonizing Spain flooded by gunpowder and blood, burned and murdered, sacked and broken there was no place for exquisite poetry. . . . The truth is that Neruda's poetry was never exquisite. In fact he himself has coined the concept of "impure poetry" (as opposed to the French idea of "pure poetry"), which best defines his own poetic credo. Before and after the "conversion" Neruda's poetry was and remained open to human experience. Before, it aired much of his own solitude and anguish, but at the same time it revealed what was throbbing deep in the heart of modern man. Afterward, his poetry moved from the emotions of the inner ego to the emotions of the outer world. Neruda could no longer see himself detached from the conflicts and problems of his time. When he took sides with the Loyalists, he did so shocked by the bloody violence of the war rather than coldly convinced by political arguments. What happened to him happened to a great number of well established poets and writers from many parts of the world. In Neruda it produced a drastic turn in the themes of his poetry and the turn itself became a favorite motif. He treated it again and again in order to present and justify his new poetic faith. In 1942, while he was in Mexico as the consul of Chile, he wrote a poem of solidarity with the defense of Stalingrad. When the poetic value of the poem was questioned, Neruda answered by writing a new poem—*Nuevo canto de amor a Stalingrado* as well as his own "committed" poetry: "Yo escribí sobre el tiempo y sobre el agua / describí el luto y su metal morado, / yo escribí sobre el cielo y la manzana, / ahora escribo sobre Stalingrado." The long poem is a sort of "mea culpa" for his past individualistic and introverted poetry, but at the same time it is an apology for his new poetic

creed. Neruda chose the same meter (hendecasyllable) and the same rhyme (*abab*) chosen by his master Rubén Darío in 1905 to explain a similar poetic turn in the poem "Yo soy aquel que ayer no más decía. . . ." The two poems came to represent a watershed in the work of both poets.

After returning to Chile in October of 1937, Neruda actively engaged in the political life of his country and in 1945 he was elected senator for Tarapacá and Antofagasta. Between 1940 and 1950, alternating with his diplomatic and political activities, he completed his most ambitious work—*Canto general.* Somebody has called the book "the Bible of the Americas" because it traces a poetic account of the continent's history since its origins, through pre-Columbian times and the Spanish conquest up to the most recent events. One feels tempted to call it an epic poem, but it is not. The very difficulty in categorizing the book indicates that Neruda has achieved in it a form without counterpart in Western poetry. It is comprised of fifteen sections which depict a gigantic poetic mural of the Americas. The first edition, in fact, published in Mexico in 1950, includes two plates of mini-murals specially designed for the book by the Mexican muralists Diego Rivera and Alfaro Siqueiros. The first section is the story of the continent's genesis: its vegetation, its birds and beasts, its rivers and minerals, its people. The second is devoted to Macchu Picchu as the grandest monument in all pre-Columbian America, as the most majestic witness of an untold past. Yet in these two, as in other sections, Neruda is not merely chronicling historical events. The poet is always present throughout the book not only because he describes those events, interpreting them according to a definite outlook on history, but also because the epic of the continent intertwines with his own epic. Thus he presents Macchu Picchu as the place where the continent on one hand, and the poet on the other, become fully aware of their plight. In parts III, IV and V of *Alturas de Macchu Picchu,* for example, Neruda tells the story of his constant intercourse with death. In parts VI and VII he recounts his climbing to Macchu Picchu—which truly occurred in October of 1943 where he discovers that the "alto arrecife de la aurora humana" is also inhabited by death. After exalting the city's magnificence by means of a string of eighty-six splendid metaphors in poem IX, X is dedicated to indict those who built the city at the expense of the people: "Macchu Picchu, pusiste / piedra en la piedra, y en la base, harapo? / Carbón sobre carbón, y en el fondo la lágrima? / Fuego en el oro, y en él, temblando el rojo / goterón de la sangre? / Devuélveme el esclavo que enterraste!" Here, as in the rest of the poem, the destiny of Macchu Picchu can be understood as the destiny of the entire continent. The last poem of this section is an appeal for hope and an exhortation to be reborn from those same ashes of tatters, tears, and blood in which primeval America was buried. Neruda has managed to coalesce his own personal search ("y, como un ciego, regresé al jazmín de la gastada primavera humana") with the expectations of a whole continent: "Piedra en la piedra, el hombre, dónde estuvo? / Aire en el aire, el hombre, dónde estuvo? / Tiempo en el tiempo, el hombre, dónde estuvo?" He further manages to do the same with the book as a whole. Paralleling the history of the continent described throughout the entire book, the last section of *Canto general* is devoted to the story of the poet's life. By bringing together his own odyssey and the drama of the continent, Neruda has simultaneously given to *Canto general* the quality of a lyric and an epic poem. The lives of conquistadores, martyrs, heroes, and just plain people recover a refreshing actuality because they become part of the poet's fate and, conversely, the life of the poet gains a new depth because in his search one recognizes the continent's struggles. *Canto general* is, thus, the song of a continent as much as it is Neruda's own song.

Since Neruda joined the Communist party in 1945, much of his poetry has become heavily politicized. Neruda himself calls it "poesía política" and in 1953 he published a two-volume anthology (*Poesía política*) of this type of poetry. He believes that with this poetry he fulfills one of his "deberes de poeta" (duties of a militant poet). The trouble is that today's politics changes so fast all over the world that the man who is today glorified as a hero could tomorrow become an execrable tyrant. These changes have often been an embarrassment to Neruda's "poesía política." In *Las uvas y el viento* (*The Grapes and the Wind,* 1954), for example, Stalin is portrayed as a beacon of peace sending doves to the most distant peoples on earth (**"En su muerte"**); fifteen years later, in *Fin de mundo* (1969), Stalin's lamblike mustache turned into a jaguar's threatening whiskers (**"El culto, II"**). Mao Tse-tung goes through a similar transmutation.

In spite of his "deberes de poeta" Neruda continued to write good poetry. The same year that he published *Las uvas y el viento,* his first volume of *Odas elementales* (*Elemental Odes*) appeared. Here he inaugurated a new poetic form with which he celebrated (or, at times, execrated) things and beings of the elemental world: a pair of socks, a tomato, the dictionary, a lizard, laziness, a bicycle, an orange, a rooster, a saw, numbers, fire, the skull, etc. Neruda rediscovered in these objects and creatures from daily life an essential beauty that use and routine seemed to have worn out. If poetry is a form of rediscovering or rather reinventing reality, these odes epitomize that understanding of poetry. Neruda turns here to forgotten things and in their material substance he finds a hidden soul poets have always sought. He also finds a transparent language which may have been motivated by his efforts to make

poetry "utilitaria y útil, como metal o harina, / dispuesta a ser arado, / herramienta, / pan y vino, . . . " (**"Oda a la poesía"**)—hence the frequent moralizing and didactic overtones of the odes—, but which could only have been achieved by the consummate and ripe poet Neruda was when he wrote them. The lyric clarity he reached in the "elemental odes" is a point of arrival in his poetic development. Neruda produced four full volumes of these odes before he realized that the svelte and agile odes were growing fat and showing signs of exhaustion.

While Neruda was still writing "elemental odes," he published *Estravagario* (*Book of Vagaries,* 1958), a new form of poetry in which the militant poet gives way to a poet perplexed and amused by the bizarre paradoxes of his own personal life. The tone is sardonic. . . . Combining irony and jest, Neruda has a good laugh at people and events that, earlier, would have awakened rage and triggered deprecation. There are no facile answers to the oddities of life and Neruda acknowledges this: "Nadie lo sabe ni lo ignora." In spite of his commitment to clarity in his early "elemental odes" (see, for example, **"Oda a la claridad"**), Neruda confesses to himself towards the end of *Estravagario* that "toda claridad es oscura" (**"Testamento de otoño"**). Approaching the autumn of his life, he has come to terms with a notion that poets seemed to have accepted since Baudelaire, merely the idea that the "essential *obscurity* of poetry is due to the fact that it is the history of a soul and that it seeks to comply with the mystery of that soul; but this obscurity is luminous . . . ," in Jean Royère's words. Without deserting his "deberes de poeta" Neruda vindicates that "essential obscurity" with which poetry attempts to touch light. In the last poem of *Plenos poderes* (*Full Powers,* 1962) Neruda closes the book with this lapidary verse: "A plena luz camino por la sombra."

But Neruda is an unpredictable poet. He can write a book of sonnets (*Cien sonetos de amor,* 1959), a book on the stones of Chile (*Las piedras de Chile,* 1960), a five-volume autobiography in verse (*Memorial de Isla Negra,* 1964), a fable which reenacts the eternal history of love (*La espada encendida,* 1970), and, at the same time, poems which dig deep into "the mysteries of the human soul," poems on the birds, trees, and rivers of Chile, poems on Cuba and Vietnam, poems on sex and bombs, poems on roses and silences. This exuberance is reminiscent of Walt Whitman's, and Neruda himself has provided a suitable explanation: "Poetry in South America is a different matter altogether. You see, there are in our countries rivers which have no names, trees which nobody knows, and birds which nobody has described. . . . Our duty, then, as we understand it, is to express what is unheard of. Everything has been painted in Europe, everything has been sung in Europe. But not in America. In that sense, Whitman was a great teacher. Because what is Whitman? He was not only intensely conscious, but he was open-eyed! *He had tremendous eyes to see everything*—he taught us to see things. He was our poet." Traces of Whitman's influence on the work of Neruda are not hard to find. In the section "I Wish the Wood-cutter Would Wake Up" of *Canto general* he significantly invokes Walt Whitman's voice: "Dame tu voz y el peso de tu pecho enterrado / Walt Whitman, y las graves / raíces de tu rostro / para cantar estas reconstrucciones." But what is even more significant is the fact that Neruda has defined Whitman in the same terms he now defines himself. In a poem from *La barcarola* (1967) he wrote: "Pablo Neruda, el cronista de todas las cosas" (Pablo Neruda, the chronicler of all things). (pp. 49-54)

Jaime Alazraki, "Pablo Neruda, the Chronicler of All Things," in *Books Abroad,* Vol. 46, No. 1, Winter, 1972, pp. 49-54.

ANDREW P. DEBICKI
(essay date 1972)

[A Polish-born educator and critic residing in the United States, Debicki has written many essays on Latin American literature. In the excerpt below, he assesses Neruda's influence and literary stature following his acceptance of the Nobel Prize for literature.]

The award of the Nobel Prize for Literature to Chile's Pablo Neruda gives well-deserved recognition to one of America's greatest poets. Author of many books of verse which use many styles and offer various perspectives on reality, Neruda always manages to transform his subject matter into a new vision, thus creating unique experiences for his reader.

Born Ricardo Eliecer Neftalí Reyes in 1904, Neruda adopted his present name as a pseudonym (in 1946 he made it his legal name as well). He started writing poetry very early; his first works recall those of the preceding *modernistas*. But *Veinte poemas de amor,* published in 1924, already shows Neruda's talent and originality. Centered on the theme of love, the book embodies its speaker's melancholic and alienated vision in intense sensorial images. It employs "visionary images" and structural devices which take poetry away from an anecdotal presentation of reality, and objectify the emotive meanings created.

Residencia en la tierra, consisting of three books written between 1925 and 1945, is one of Neruda's most important works. It is centered on an anguished view of modern reality: its speaker keeps focusing on the chaos, the meaninglessness, and the lack of communication which surround him. But the value of *Residencia* resides in its ability to objectify these feelings and to make us partake in them. Neruda uses images, the seemingly random enumeration of objects, careful manipulation of tone, and a variety of structural devices to convey his speaker's perspective. Often his images do not make logical "sense," but catch perfectly a mood:

> Monday burns like gasoline
> when it sees me coming with my jail-like face
> and it howls like a wounded wheel
> and moves along, like warm blood,
> on toward night.

The poems of *Residencia* have been called "surrealistic"; they do indeed move away from objective presentations, and portray reality as distorted by the mood of its speaker. But at the same time they reveal a very conscious and careful use of language to communicate their emotive meanings with great precision. In the poem *Barcarola,* for example, a single grammatical construction (a conditional sentence) is developed and varied to catch the speaker's constantly diminishing hope. In the latter part of the second *Residencia,* Neruda seeks to discover in material things some basic principles of reality, to find in our concrete surroundings higher values of life.

Beginning with the third *Residencia* and continuing in *Canto general* and *Las uvas del viento,* Neruda started writing about social themes. He combined attacks on dictatorships, on Franco's Spain, and on American "imperialism" with a defense of Spanish America, of an idealized communism and of the importance of solidarity among humble people. Much of the poetry of these books was inspired by the circumstances of Neruda's life; he was present during the Spanish Civil War, and joined the Communist Party. The style of these works is quite direct. Much of the poetry is very conceptual, and offers a simplistic defense of dogmatic beliefs. But Neruda keeps on using images with great success in some poems; the *Canto general* captures, via grandiose metaphors, a picture of America's greatness. (Sublime visions of America replace the more personal feelings of *Residencia.*) Thematically, the new vision of social problems which appears in these books suggests Neruda's efforts to overcome the horrors of the modern world. Poetically, it leads to a rather uneven set of works.

This attempt on Neruda's part to find a meaningful and positive perspective on reality leads to more successful poetry in a different series of books, composed after World War II. The *Odas elementales* (1954), the *Nuevas odas elementales,* and the *Tercer libro de odas* all focus on a variety of common objects. They modify these objects through imagery, present them from unusual perspectives, and often adopt a playful tone. In this fashion, they discover and convey unexpected possibilities in everyday reality, and produce a great sense of excitement in the reader, in the face of objects he would normally take completely for granted. The language of this poetry seems very direct, but is handled so as to produce maximum sensorial effects. We can see all of this in **"Ode to an artichoke"**:

> under the soil
> slept the red-whiskered carrot
> ....
> the cabbage
> strove
> to try on skirts,
> the marjoram
> to perfume the world
> and the sweet
> artichoke
> over there, in its garden
> got dressed in armor
> burnished
> like a grenade

Although far removed from the anguish and the tortured complexity of the *Residencias,* the poetry of the *Odas* picks up Neruda's earlier interest in focusing on concrete reality and in finding within this reality personal meanings, hidden to a purely utilitarian outlook. It signals a renewed desire to find durable values in our fleeting surroundings.

In *Versos del capitán* and *Cien sonetos de amor* Neruda deals with love; but again he stresses the essential nature and the permanent value of certain human experiences. All in all, his post-war poetry combines simple language with striking imagery and a careful use of tone to offer us a fresh look at our surroundings. This is perhaps most apparent in *Estravagario* (1958), in which tone and imagery combine to elevate the everyday to the poetic, and to make us feel the presence of the most important themes of life—time, love, death, beauty—amidst seemingly trivial happenings. A whimsical tone often serves to widen our perspective, as in these lines from **"To a foot, from its child"**:

> this foot worked with its shoe
> it barely had time
> to be naked in love or in dreams
> it walked, they walked
> until the whole man stopped.
> And then it came down into the earth
> and knew nothing
> because everything was dark there.
> It did not know that it had stopped being a foot,
> and whether it had been buried so that he could fly
> or so that it could become
> an apple.

For all its variety, Neruda's poetry marks a constant effort to find wider meanings in common sur-

roundings, and to capture the emotions—the sense of excitement, of horror, of wonder—which reality can evoke in the sensitive human being. By means of imagery, of tone, and of a wealth of linguistic techniques, Neruda creates unique experiences.

Neruda's poetry has had great resonance, in Spain as well as in Spanish America. The imagery and the anguished outlook of the *Residencias* marks the emergence of non-rational perspectives and of emotive meanings in Hispanic poetry; the everyday language and the poetization of colloquial idiom in Neruda's later poetry opens the way to the poetry of the 1950's and 1960's. Neruda's presence and attitude have also had a profound effect on other writers; his stay in Spain in the 1930's (he was the Chilean consul) gave great impetus to writers like Emilio Prados and Miguel Hernández, who were beginning to write a poetry oriented to basic human problems. And in the United States, Neruda has become for many young poets an example of a writer deeply concerned with the human condition as well as the need to express it effectively in well-crafted poetry. (pp. 380-82)

Andrew P. Debicki, "The Poetry of Pablo Neruda," in *Hispania,* Vol. 55, No. 2, May, 1972, pp. 380-82.

MICHAEL WOOD
(essay date 1974)

[In the essay excerpted below, Wood comments on Neruda's major works through *Extravagaria.*]

Pablo Neruda was born Neftalí Reyes in 1904 and died in September, 1973, twelve days after Allende. There was a cruel symbolic suitability in such timing. Neruda, a communist since the Spanish Civil War (although he joined the Party later), a Chilean senator for much of his life, a candidate for the Chilean presidency in 1970, who stood down in favor of Allende, had lived to see his country come closer to his hopes for it than it had ever been. He fell ill at the end of 1972 and returned to Chile from his post as Allende's ambassador to France. He had an operation for cancer of the prostate. Then the coup came and Neruda died of heart collapse, his country slithering off into a dictatorship of a kind that had already hounded Neruda into exile in the late Forties. Neruda's death, like his life, kept pace with the fortunes of Chile.

In this perspective, even Neruda's greatest poetry is merely part of a larger picture, just an element in a pattern of life and writing which embodies and pleads for a whole set of Latin American possibilities: the poet in politics, the politician who is a great poet; the public man with the incomparable common touch; the popular poet, even the oral poet, since people who can't read still know and love and recite and sing poems by Neruda, who receives international critical acclaim. It is a vision of a vast but integrated personal life, and beyond that a vision of a multifarious but coherent community, summarized in one exemplary individual. It is an attractive prospect, although it may be something of an illusion—if you have to be Pablo Neruda to bring it off, the example is eccentric rather than prophetic or symptomatic—and many younger Latin American writers would say such a prospect was crippling, damaging to all kinds of talents who live less comfortably in the public eye than Neruda did. In any case, when it comes to literature, history has a way of turning out to be a New Critic rather than a student of culture and society. It remembers texts and forgets the rest, and we can turn to Neruda's literary career without feeling unnecessarily trivial—as trivial as Neruda himself would have thought us were he still alive.

The Heights of Macchu-Picchu, written in 1945, is a sequence of twelve poems, a section of the *Canto General* and a major work in its own right. It is perhaps the best of all introductions to Neruda, since his gifts receive their full expression there and since it is also a form of spiritual autobiography, a description of a moral and aesthetic journey out of baffled solitude into a sense of poetic mission. It points backward toward *Residence on Earth,* Neruda's early masterpiece, most of which was written before 1935, and forward to the *Canto General* (1950), into which it was incorporated. It parodies earlier manners and scouts for later ones. Above all it balances perfectly two insistent, enduring strains in Neruda's work: the desire to clear up confusions and the desire to hang on to them.

"I am sure / of the unmoving stone," Neruda writes in a later poem, "but I know the wind." He loves the stillness and ideal geometry of Macchu-Picchu, the spectacular Andean ruin of an ancient Inca city, but he finds a battery of questions and uncertainties there, change and extinction among that rocky permanence: "Stone upon stone, but where was man?" Was Macchu-Picchu a city erected, like so many others, on misery and hunger and death, and who will speak now for the vanished laborers who built it and supplied it with meat and grain? They themselves can't return from subterranean time, as Neruda puts it, but perhaps the poet's concern for them will lend their voices to his poem. In effect Neruda is asking for their blessing on the whole of the *Canto General,* a colossal, unequal monument, a long celebration of the American continent, an angry, at times sentimental, at times very compelling plea for the wretched of the American earth.

It is hard to see where a poet could go after such a book—Whitman, in similar circumstances, just kept adding poems to his. Neruda's life's work was done by the time he was forty-five, and there is a sense in which he simply managed to outlive himself elegantly for twenty years, remaining as prolific as ever without really finding a subject that mattered enough. Many people admire the four books of elementary (or elemental, or both) odes published in 1954, 1956, 1957, and 1959, but for me they have, along with *Extravagaria* (1958), too much the tone of the great man showing us how humble and playful he can be.

The odes are poems of very short lines addressed to pianos, elephants, socks, artichokes, books, tomatoes, laziness, Guatemala, winter, Leningrad, rain, wine, summer, sadness, life, and much else. Many of them are appealing, but generally their simplicity seems strained, and the reverse of the authentic simplicity of Neruda's best work. There is a poem about Vallejo in *Extravagaria* which is an insult to the reader and to Vallejo's memory. We were just two poor carpenters, the argument runs, and now that he is dead, there is nobody big enough to understand me. Vallejo's reputation and a disagreeable fake naïveté on Neruda's part both serve as the instruments of a piece of self-congratulation.

On the other hand, there is the remarkable verse autobiography, *Memorial de Isla Negra* (1964), which is really casual and relaxed in the way that *Extravagaria* merely tries to be. Without pretensions of either humility or grandeur, the poet remembers patches of his life: his father, his family's friends, his loves; places, thoughts, moods, moments. I should say also that early and late in his career (and in between) Neruda wrote incomparable love poems, and that he seems never to have written a bad poem about the sea.

But *Residence on Earth* remains, in my view, the greatest of all Neruda's books. Neruda himself came to regard it very harshly. It helped people to die rather than to live, he said, and if he had the proper authority to do so he would ban it, and make sure it was never reprinted. No doubt there was an element of pose in that pronouncement since, as Rodriguez Monegal remarks, Neruda never took any steps to keep the baleful book out of his collected works, and continued to regard it as one of his best volumes. Still, Neruda told Rita Guibert that a boy had committed suicide with the book beside him, so it certainly helped at least one person to die.

It is a painful, brilliant, despairing work, full of surprising turns of phrase and marvelously simple, inventive imagery. "I understand the harmony of the world," Paul Claudel once wrote, "when shall I come across the melody?" *Residence on Earth* in its earlier parts—the last section is devoted to the Spain of the Civil War—presents a man who understands neither the harmony nor the melody, who sees only chaos and multiplicity, a busy or bored, frantic or lethargic alien world in which he has no place or purpose. Neruda wrote much of the book in India, when he was intensely lonely, and the whole of the exotic East parades across the text like a broken-down circus, an array of odd, cruel customs which add up only to nightmare. As late as in *Memorial de Isla Negra* we hear Neruda saying, "And if I saw anything in my life it was one evening / in India, on the edge of a river: a woman of flesh and bones being burned."

Yet there is a curious quality to all this unmistakable anguish, and I quoted Claudel for this reason: not just because one can hear actual echoes of Claudel in some of Neruda's longer lines, or because both men were much-traveled diplomats, professional exiles for large portions of their lives, but because both appear to have had exceptional propensities for despair, which they simply smothered in orthodoxy—Neruda's communism seems to have served much the same purpose as Claudel's Catholicism—and conjured away in expansive displays of ingenuousness and optimism. More important—and this is the point of the comparison here—the despair which speaks in the early works of both men is not the spleen and self-doubt of Vallejo or Kafka or Proust or any other of those heirs of Baudelaire whom we think of as paradigmatically modern men, but a sense of separation, a sense of uselessness, of a life of pure contingency in a profuse, pointless universe, which is accompanied by a seemingly entire and undiminished self-confidence.

"An unchanging angel lives in my sword," Neruda writes at the end of a dark poem. He begins another,

"I have defeated the angel of the dream." Again: "I like the tenacity that lives on in my eyes." Neruda's very impermeability to the attractions of the East is a form of strength, the sign of a substantial, unshaken identity. Like Claudel, Neruda rarely doubts himself but constantly frets about his lack of connection with others; and it is this connection with others that Neruda finally encounters in Spain—in poets and companions first of all, in Lorca and Rafael Alberti, and then in a whole attacked nation. From Spain, Neruda can return to Chile by way of Macchu-Picchu, and feel at one with the dead and the living of his continent. He found in Spain what Claudel found in a stormy, adulterous relationship: a path to the blurred world outside the certain, even the arrogant, self, a way of making that world come clear, a release for the self from its proud, bewildered gloom.

The loneliness of *Residence on Earth* takes on a special, metaphysical edge because it is *not* the loneliness of a generally tormented, unhappy man. "Perhaps I was condemned to happiness," Neruda says in a later poem; but then the sentence was in many ways severe, for until his Spanish experience Neruda seems to have failed to find in the world any answer to his own energy and generosity and abundance. Perhaps health has its neuroses, Nietzsche wrote. *Residence on Earth* reflects the hovering dementia of the insufficiently demented, the echoing solitude of an undivided self. (pp. 10-12)

Michael Wood, "The Poetry of Neruda," in *The New York Review of Books,* Vol. XXI, No. 15, October 3, 1974, pp. 8, 10, 12.

SOURCES FOR FURTHER STUDY

Costa, René de. *The Poetry of Pablo Neruda.* Cambridge: Harvard University Press, 1979, 213 p.

> Reassessment of Neruda's career. Attempts to lay grounds for critical consensus regarding the significance of his major works.

Durán, Manuel, and Safir, Margery. *Earth Tones: The Poetry of Pablo Neruda.* Bloomington: Indiana University Press, 1981, 200 p.

> General biographical and critical study focusing on such topics as Neruda's love and nature poetry and his posthumously published works.

Gallagher, D. P. "Pablo Neruda." In his *Modern Latin American Literature,* pp. 39-66. London: Oxford University Press, 1973.

> One of the best scholarly overviews of Neruda's major works, including *Residencia en la tierra, Canto general, Odas elementales,* and *Estravagario.*

Holzinger, Walter. "Poetic Subject and Form in the *Odas elementales.*" *Revista Hispánica Moderna* XXXVI (1970-1971): 41-9.

> Frequently cited study of structure and poetic technique in Neruda's *Odas elementales.*

Santí, Enrico-Mario. *Pablo Neruda: The Poetics of Prophecy.* Ithaca: Cornell University Press, 1982, 255 p.

> Study of rhetoric in Neruda's major works in which Santí aims "to probe Neruda's sense of prophecy as the significant metaphor for modern poetry."

Woodridge, Hensley C., and Zubatsky, David S. *Pablo Neruda: An Annotated Bibliography of Biographical and Critical Studies.* New York: Garland Publishing, Inc., 1988, 629 p.

> Comprehensive bibliography of biographical and critical studies on Neruda in Spanish and English.

Joyce Carol Oates

1938-

(Has also written under pseudonym Rosamond Smith)
American novelist, short story writer, poet, dramatist,
essayist, critic, and editor.

INTRODUCTION

*O*ne of the United States's most prolific and versatile contemporary writers, Oates has published
nearly twenty novels, sixteen volumes of short
stories, nine collections of verse, several plays, and numerous nonfiction works since her first book appeared
in 1963. In her fiction, Oates focuses upon the spiritual,
sexual, and intellectual decline of modern American
society. Employing a dense, elliptical prose style, she
depicts such cruel and macabre actions as rape, incest, murder, mutilation, child abuse, and suicide to delineate the forces of evil with which individuals must
contend. Oates's protagonists often suffer at the hands
of others as a result of emotional deficiencies or socio-
economic conditions. Greg Johnson commented:
"[Oates's] particular genius is her ability to convey psychological states with unerring fidelity, and to relate the
intense private experiences of her characters to the
larger realities of American life."

Oates was born into a working-class Catholic
family outside Lockport, New York, and was raised
amid a rural setting on her maternal grandparents'
farm. She attended a one-room schoolhouse in Erie
County, a parallel community to her fictitious Eden
County where many of her works are set, and displayed
an early interest in storytelling by drawing picture-tales
before she could write. Oates has said that her childhood "was dull, ordinary, nothing people would be interested in," but has admitted that "a great deal frightened me." In 1953 at age fifteen, Oates wrote her first
novel, though it was rejected by publishers who found
its subject matter, which concerned the rehabilitation
of a drug dealer, exceedingly depressing for adolescent audiences.

Oates began her academic career at Syracuse
University and graduated from there as class valedicto-
rian in 1960. In 1961 she received a Master of Arts de-

gree in English from the University of Wisconsin, where she met and married Raymond Joseph Smith, an English educator. The following year, after beginning work on her doctorate in English, Oates inadvertently encountered one of her own stories in Margaret Foley's anthology *Best American Short Stories*. This discovery prompted Oates to write professionally, and in 1963 she published her first volume of short stories, *By the North Gate* (1963). Oates taught at the University of Detroit between 1961 and 1967. In 1967 she and her husband moved to Canada to teach at the University of Windsor, where together they founded the *Ontario Review*. Since leaving the University of Windsor in 1977, Oates has been writer-in-residence at Princeton University in New Jersey.

Oates's first novel, *With Shuddering Fall* (1964), foreshadows her preoccupation with evil and violence in the story of a destructive romance between a teenage girl and a thirty-year-old stock car driver that ends with his death in an accident. Oates's best-known and critically acclaimed early novels form a trilogy exploring three distinct segments of American society. Critics attribute the naturalistic ambience of these works to the influence of such twentieth-century authors as William Faulkner, Theodore Dreiser, and James T. Farrell. Oates's first installment, *A Garden of Earthly Delights* (1967), is set in rural Eden County and chronicles the life of the daughter of a migrant worker who marries a wealthy farmer in order to provide for her illegitimate son. The woman's idyllic existence is destroyed, however, when the boy murders his stepfather and kills himself. In *Expensive People* (1967), the second work in the series, Oates exposes the superficial world of suburbanites whose preoccupation with material comforts reveals their spiritual poverty. The final volume in the trilogy, *them* (1969), which won the National Book Award for fiction, depicts the violence and degradation endured by three generations of an inner-city Detroit family. Critics acknowledge that Oates's experiences as a teacher in Detroit during the early 1960s contributed to her accurate rendering of the city and its social problems. Betty DeRamus stated: "Her days in Detroit did more for Joyce Carol Oates than bring her together with new people—it gave her a tradition to write from, the so-called American Gothic tradition of exaggerated horror and gloom and mysterious and violent incidents."

Oates's novels of the 1970s explore characters involved with various American professional and cultural institutions while interweaving elements of human malevolence and tragedy. *Wonderland* (1971), for example, depicts a brilliant surgeon who is unable to build a satisfying home life, resulting in estrangement from his wife, children, and society. *Do with Me What You Will* (1973) focuses upon a young attorney who is lauded by his peers for his devotion to liberal causes. *The*

Assassins: A Book of Hours (1975) is a psychological tale which dramatizes the effects of the murder of a conservative politician on his wife and two brothers. *Son of the Morning* (1978) documents the rise and fall from grace of Nathan Vickery, an evangelist whose spirituality is alternately challenged and affirmed by various events in his life. *Unholy Loves* (1979) revolves around the lives of several faculty members of a small New York college. Considered the least emotionally disturbing of Oates's novels, *Unholy Loves* was praised for its indirect humor and gentle satire.

During the early 1980s, Oates published several novels that parody works by such nineteenth-century authors as Louisa May Alcott, Charles Dickens, Edgar Allan Poe, and Charlotte and Emily Brontë. *Bellefleur* (1980) follows the prescribed formula for a Gothic multigenerational saga, utilizing supernatural occurrences while tracing the lineage of an exploitative American family. Oates included explicit violence in this work; for example, a man deliberately crashes his plane into the Bellefleur mansion, killing himself and his family. *A Bloodsmoor Romance* (1982) displays such elements of Gothic romance as mysterious kidnappings and psychic phenomena in the story of five maiden sisters living in rural Pennsylvania in the late 1800s. In *Mysteries of Winterthurn* (1984), Oates borrowed heavily from the works of Poe as she explored the conventions of the nineteenth-century mystery novel. The protagonist of this work is a brilliant young detective who models his career after the exploits of Sir Arthur Conan Doyle's fictional sleuth, Sherlock Holmes. While some critics viewed these works as whimsical, others, citing Oates's accomplished depiction of evil, maintained that they are significant literary achievements.

Oates's recent novels explore the nature and ramifications of obsession. *Solstice* (1985) revolves around a relationship between a young divorcée and an older woman that evolves into an emotional power struggle. In *Marya: A Life* (1986), a successful writer and academician attempts to locate her alcoholic mother, who had abused and later abandoned her as a child. *Lives of the Twins* (1987), which Oates wrote under the pseudonym of Rosamond Smith, presents a tale of love and erotic infatuation involving a woman, her lover, and her lover's twin brother. With *You Must Remember This* (1987), Oates returned to a naturalistic portrait of families under emotional and moral distress. Suicide attempts, violent beatings, disfiguring accidents, and incest figure prominently in this novel, which centers on an intense love affair between a former boxer and his adolescent niece. Set in Eden County and containing references to such historical events as Senator Joseph McCarthy's anti-Communist campaign, the executions of Julius and Ethel Rosenberg for conspiracy to commit espionage, and the Korean War, *You Must Remember This* earned high praise for its evocation of American life during the early 1950s. John Updike stated that this work "rallies all [of Oates's] strengths and is exceedingly fine—a storm of experience whose reality we cannot doubt, a fusion of fact and feeling, vision and circumstance which holds together, and holds us to it, through our terror and dismay."

Oates's works in other genres also address darker aspects of the human condition. Most critics contend that Oates's short fiction, for which she has twice received the O. Henry Special Award for Continuing Achievement, is best suited for evoking the urgency and emotional power of her principal themes. Such collections as *By the North Gate; Where Are You Going, Where Have You Been?: Stories of Young America* (1974); *The Lamb of Abyssalia* (1980); and *Raven's Wing* (1986) contain pieces that focus upon violent and abusive relationships between the sexes. One widely anthologized story, "Where Are You Going, Where Have You Been?," a tale of female adolescence and sexual awakening, is considered a classic of modern short fiction and was adapted for film. Oates has also composed several dramas that were produced off-Broadway in New York and has published numerous volumes of poetry. In addition, she is a respected essayist and literary critic whose nonfiction works are praised for the logic and sensibility with which she examines a variety of subjects.

(For further information about Oates's life and works, see *Authors in the News*, Vol. 1; *Concise Dictionary of American Literary Biography, 1968-1987; Contemporary Authors*, Vols. 5-8; *Contemporary Authors New Revision Series*, Vol. 25; *Contemporary Literary Criticism*, Vols. 1, 2, 3, 6, 9, 11, 15, 19, 33, 52; *Dictionary of Literary Biography*, Vols. 2, 5; *Dictionary of Literary Biography Yearbook: 1981;* and *Short Story Criticism*, Vol 6.)

CRITICAL COMMENTARY

ALFRED KAZIN
(essay date 1971)

[A highly respected American literary critic, Kazin is best known for his essay collections *The Inmost Leaf* (1955), *Contemporaries* (1962), and *On Native Grounds* (1942). In the following excerpt from a 1971 essay, he discusses the theme of social violence in Oates's novels.]

A "sense of fright, of something deeply wrong." In Joyce Carol Oates's most notable novel, *them,* this seemed to express itself as a particular sensitivity to individual lives helplessly flying off the wheel of American gigantism. While writing *them* (a novel which ends with the 1967 eruption of Detroit's Blacks) she said that Detroit was "all melodrama." There a man can get shot by the brother of the woman he is lying next to in bed, and the body will be disposed of by a friendly policeman. The brother himself pops up later in the sister's life not as a "murderer," but as a genially obtuse and merely wistful fellow. Nothing of this is satirized or moralized as once it would have been. It is what happens every day now; there are too many people for murders to count. There are too many murderers about for the murderer to take murder that seriously.

Joyce Carol Oates seemed, more than most women writers, entirely open to *social* turmoil, to the frighteningly undirected and misapplied force of the American powerhouse. She plainly had an instinct for the social menace packed up in Detroit, waiting to explode, that at the end of the nineteenth century Dreiser felt about Chicago and Stephen Crane about New York. The sheer rich chaos of American life, to say nothing of its staggering armies of poor, outraged, by no means peaceful people, pressed upon her. It is rare to find a woman writer so externally unconcerned with form. After teaching at the University of Detroit from 1962 to 1967, she remarked that Detroit is a city "so transparent, you can hear it ticking." What one woman critic, in a general attack on Oates, called "Violence in the Head," could also be taken as her inability to blink social violence as the language in which a great many "lower-class" Americans naturally deal with each other.

Joyce Carol Oates is however, a "social novelist" of a peculiar kind. She is concerned not with demonstrating power relationships, but with the struggle of people nowadays to express their fate in terms that are cruelly changeable. Reading her, one sees the real tragedy of so many Americans today, unable to find a language for what is happening to them. The drama of society was once seen by American social novelists as the shifting line between the individual and the mass into which he was helplessly falling. It has now become the freefloating mythology about "them" which each person carries around with him, an idea of causation unconnected to cause. There is no longer a fixed point within people's thinking. In the American social novels

Principal Works

By the North Gate (short stories) 1963

With Shuddering Fall (novel) 1964

Upon the Sweeping Flood, and Other Stories (short stories) 1966

A Garden of Earthly Delights (novel) 1967

Expensive People (novel) 1968

Women in Love, and Other Poems (poetry) 1968

them (novel) 1969

Love and Its Derangements: Poems (poetry) 1970; also published as Love and Its Derangements, and Other Poems [expanded edition], 1974

The Wheel of Love, and Other Stories (short stories) 1970

Wonderland (novel) 1971

Marriages and Infidelities (short stories) 1972

Do with Me What You Will (novel) 1973

The Goddess, and Other Women (short stories) 1974

The Hungry Ghosts: Seven Allusive Comedies (short stories) 1974

Where Are You Going, Where Have You Been?: Stories of Young America (short stories) 1974

The Assassins: A Book of Hours (novel) 1975

The Poisoned Kiss, and Other Stories from the Portuguese (short stories) 1975

The Seduction, and Other Stories (short stories) 1975

Childwold (novel) 1976

Crossing the Border: Fifteen Tales (short stories) 1976

Night Side: Eighteen Tales (short stories) 1976

Triumph of the Spider Monkey: The First Person Confes-

sion of the Maniac Bobby Gotteson as Told to Joyce Carol Oates (novella) 1976

All the Good People I've Left Behind (short stories) 1978

Son of the Morning (novel) 1978

Cybele (novel) 1979

Unholy Loves (novel) 1979

Bellefleur (novel) 1980

The Lamb of Abyssalia (short stories) 1980

Angel of Light (novel) 1981

A Sentimental Education: Stories (short stories) 1981

A Bloodsmoor Romance (novel) 1982

Invisible Woman: New and Selected Poems, 1970-1972 (poetry) 1982

Mysteries of Winterthurn (novel) 1984

Last Days: Stories (short stories) 1984

Solstice (novel) 1985

Marya: A Life (novel) 1986

Raven's Wing: Stories (short stories) 1986

On Boxing (nonfiction) 1987

You Must Remember This (novel) 1987

Lives of the Twins [as Rosamond Smith] (novel) 1988

(Woman) Writer: Occasions and Opportunities (essays) 1988

American Appetites (novel) 1989

SOUL/MATE [as Rosamond Smith] (novel) 1989

Because It Is Bitter, and Because It Is My Heart (novel) 1990

---

earlier in the century, the novelist was a pathfinder and the characters were betrayed as blind helpless victims of their fate, like Hurstwood in *Sister Carrie* or virtually everybody in Dos Passos's *U. S. A.* Joyce Carol Oates is not particularly ahead of the people she writes about. Since her prime concern is to see people in the terms they present to themselves, she is able to present consciousness as a person, a crazily unaccountable thing. The human mind, as she says in the title of a recent novel, is simply "wonderland." And the significance of that "wonderland" to the social melodrama that is America today is that they collide but do not connect.

Praising Harriette Arnow's strong, little-known novel about Southern mountain folk, *The Dollmaker,* Joyce Oates said:

It seems to me that the greatest works of literature deal with the human soul caught in the stampede of time, unable to gauge the profundity of what passes over it, like the characters of Yeats who live through terrifying events but who cannot understand them; in this way history passes over most of us. Society

is caught in a convulsion, whether of growth or of death, and ordinary people are destroyed. They do not, however, understand that they are "destroyed."

This view of literature as silent tragedy is a central description of what interests Joyce Oates in the writing of fiction. Her own characters move through a world that seems to be wholly physical and even full of global eruption, yet the violence, as Elizabeth Dalton said is in their own heads—and is no less real for that. They touch us by frightening us, like disembodied souls calling to us from the other world. They live through terrifying events but cannot understand them. This is what makes Oates a new element in our fiction, involuntarily disturbing.

She does not understand why she is disturbing. She takes the convulsion of society for granted, and so a writer born in 1938 regularly "returns" to the 1930s in her work. *A Garden of Earthly Delights* begins with the birth on the highway of a migrant worker's child after the truck transporting the workers has been in a collision. Obviously she is unlike many women writers in her feeling for the pressure, mass, density of violence in American experience not always shared by the professional middle class. "The greatest realities," she has said, "are physical and economic; all the subtleties of life come afterward." Yet the central thing in her work is the teeming private consciousness, a "wonderland" that to her is reality in action—but without definition and without boundary.

Joyce Oates is peculiarly and painfully open to other minds, so possessed by them that in an author's note to *them* she says of the student who became the "Maureen Wendall" of the novel, "Her various problems and complexities overwhelmed me. . . . My initial feeling about her life was, 'This must be fiction, this can't be real!' My more permanent feeling was, 'This is the only kind of fiction that is real.' " Her ability to get occupied by another consciousness makes even *them,* her best novel to date, a sometimes impenetrably voluminous history of emotions, emotions, emotions. You feel that you are turning thousands of pages, that her world is as harshly overpopulated as a sleepless mind, that you cannot make out the individual features of anyone within this clamor of everyone's existence.

This is obviously related to the ease with which Joyce Oates transfers the many situations in her head straight onto paper. I sense an extraordinary and tumultuous amount of purely mental existence locked up behind her schoolgirl's face. She once told an interviewer that she is always writing about "love . . . and it takes many different forms, many different social levels. . . . I think I write about love in an unconscious way. I look back upon the novels I've written, and I say, yes, this was my subject. But at the time I'm writing I'm not really conscious of that. I'm writing about a certain person who does this and that and comes to a certain end." She herself is the most unyielding lover in her books, as witness the force with which she follows so many people through every trace of their feeling, thinking, moving. She is obsessive in her patience with the sheer factuality of contemporary existence. This evident love for the scene we Americans make, for the incredible profusion of life in America, also troubles Joyce Carol Oates. Every writer knows himself to be a little crazy, but her feeling of her own absurdity is probably intensified by the dreamlike ease with which her works are produced. It must indeed trouble her that this looks like glibness, when in point of fact her dogged feeling that she writes out of love is based on the fact that she is utterly hypnotized, positively drugged, by other people's experiences. The social violence so marked in her work is like the sheer density of detail—this and this and this is what is happening to people. She is attached to life by well-founded apprehension that nothing lasts, nothing is safe, nothing is all around us. In *them* Maureen Wendall thinks:

Maybe the book with her money in it, and the money so greedily saved, and the idea of the money, maybe these things weren't real either. What would happen if everything broke into pieces? It was queer how you felt, instinctively, that a certain space of time was real and not a dream, and you gave your life to it, all your energy and faith, believing it to be real. But how could you tell what would last and what wouldn't? Marriages ended. Love ended. Money could be stolen, found out and taken . . . or it might disappear by itself, like that secretary's notebook. Objects disappeared, slipped through cracks, devoured, kicked aside, knocked under the bed or into the trash, lost. Her clearest memory of the men she'd been with was their moving away from her. They were all body then, completed.

The details in Oates's fiction follow each other with a humble truthfulness that make you wonder where she is taking you, that is sometimes disorienting, for she is all attention to the unconscious reactions of her characters. She needs a lot of space, which is why her short stories tend to read like scenarios for novels. The amount of *listening* this involves is certainly singular. My deepest feeling about her is that her mind is unbelievably crowded with psychic existences, with such a mass of stories that she lives by being wholly submissive to "them." She is too attentive to their mysterious clamor to *want* to be an artist, to make the right and well-fitting structure. Much of her fiction seems written to relieve her mind of the people who haunt it, not to create something that will live.

So many inroads on the suddenly frightening American situation is indeed a problem in our fiction just now; the age of high and proud art has yielded to the climate of crisis. Joyce Oates's many stories resemble a card index of situations; they are not the deeply plotted stories that we return to as perfect little dramas; her novels, though they involve the reader through the author's intense connection with her material, tend as incident to fade out of our minds. Too much happens. Indeed, hers are altogether strange books, haunting rather than "successful," because the mind behind them is primarily concerned with a kind of Darwinian struggle for existence between minds, with the truth of some limitless human struggle. We miss the perfectly suggestive shapes that modern art and fiction have taught us to venerate. Oates is another Cassandra bewitched by her private oracle. But it is not disaster that is most on her mind; it is the recognition of each person as the center of the coming disturbance. And this disturbance, as Pascal said of his God, has its center everywhere and its circumference nowhere.

So her characters are opaque, ungiving, uncharming; they have the taciturn qualities that come with the kind of people they are—heavy, hallucinated, outside the chatty middle class. Society speaks in them, but *they* are not articulate. They do not yet feel themselves to be emancipated persons. They are caught up in the social convulsion and move unheedingly, compulsively, blindly, through the paces assigned to them by the power god.

That is exactly what Oates's work expresses just now: a sense that American life is taking some of us by the throat. "Too much" is happening; many will disappear. Above all, and most ominously, hers is a world in which our own people, and not just peasants in Vietnam, get "wasted." There is a constant sense of drift, deterioration, the end of things, that contrasts violently with the era of "high art" and the once-fond belief in immortality through art. Oates is someone plainly caught up in this "avalanche" of time. (pp. 157-60)

Alfred Kazin, "On Joyce Carol Oates," in *Critical Essays on Joyce Carol Oates,* edited by Linda W. Wagner, G. K. Hall & Co., 1979, pp. 157-60.

CONSTANCE AYERS DENNE
(essay date 1974)

[In the following excerpt, Denne praises the vision of the feminine psyche in Oates's fiction.]

Joyce Carol Oates's special achievement is her ability to reduce contemporary American social reality to liberating fictions. Her resources are courage and a knowledge of self and the literary past. Open and receptive to what is, Oates sees the present as a variation of what has already been, and by reducing "now" to familiar fictions, she tames, civilizes and, through the catharsis provided by her art, educates.

Oates believes strongly in the authority of the individual's experience of reality. Not one to confuse behavior, or what one does, with identity, or who one is, she defines experience as a process in which external reality impinges significantly not only upon the conscious life of the individual but upon the unconscious as well. Life is a series of encounters, each of which has the potential to make the unconscious more accessible. The truly human life requires continual growth, which in turn depends upon the individual's ability to integrate a new experience into the total personality. (More often than not, however, in an effort to maintain equilibrium, one simply denies or resists the healthful disintegrating effects of new experiences, and such reactions lead either to stagnation or to "madness.") Each state of integrity, albeit temporary, reveals more, but one can never fully understand the self, for the learning process is unending.

Oates's fictions, products of her own descent into the abyss, are designed, like all generous art, to human-

ize and make whole. Although Oates has been regarded with suspicion because of the violence of her subject matter, the writer is psychologically healthy, and her art remarkably sane. She informs and makes meaningful the facts that assault us daily in the newspapers. For example, *them* (1969), a naturalistic novel of life in a Detroit slum, shocks only because it is perceived as fiction, and this, of course, is its value. This constitutes its ability to liberate. As a news story or case history, it would be absorbed easily enough by sensibilities inured to misery, and catharsis would be impossible.

The fearless commitment to go wherever she must go emotionally, demonstrated in *them,* characterizes all of her half-dozen novels and seventy or more short stories. . . .

Having absorbed the shaping myths of the Greek and Judeo-Christian traditions, of Western literature and of the American experience, Oates both resurrects and domesticates them in her fiction, providing a link between the past and present, between the collective unconscious and modern life. Putting us in touch with the collective unconscious, she reveals the primitive meaning and, therefore, the humanity of contemporary life, for the vital source of all action is the unconscious life of the race itself. But she is not simply writing "clever art," that is, "art based upon cultural knowledge of earlier art." Her art is "deadly serious and wants to absolutely re-create and reinterpret the world." Her notion of bringing back to life is closely allied with the artist's special mission of bringing *to* life. At the end of the tradition, she is creating a new beginning, which is very intimately related to her consciousness as a woman and as an artist. (p. 597)

Elena, the central character of *Do With Me What You Will,* unlike so many fictional women whose quest for selfhood ends in suicide, madness or marriage, breaks through to a higher level of awareness and, newly integrated, affirms not only what she wants but also how she will get it. Her newfound freedom and its direction are of course historically conditioned, a solution that does not make the novel popular with more radical feminists. Oates, however, is neither an idealist nor an ideologist, yet it is not surprising that having chosen to make liberation her subject, she sought to dramatize it in a woman. Women are at the present time more interesting to her than men. She believes that "men have a far more difficult time . . . existing, trying to measure up to the absurd standards of 'masculinity' in our culture and in nature," and that women are more likely consciously to feel the need for self-emancipation. Less locked into roles, women are more open to the energies of the unconscious and, therefore, the prehistoric sources of identity are more accessible to them than to men. This view of women, however, has always been a strong structuring tenet in Oates's work—this and the very real historical obstacles that limit women in time. One can see Oates discovering the subject as one goes through her work. Thus, Elena represents the logical culmination of an artistic interest in the lives and consciousness of women that Oates has been exploring with increasing concentration in her fiction for more than a decade. (pp. 597-98)

Oates's women have never been any less free than her male characters; all have inhabited a world that they are powerless to change. However, in *Do With Me What You Will* which, incidentally, synthesizes Oates's theory of art, her method, and her interest in women, she sees a way out, not through the law or any other of our present institutions but through awakened human consciousness. Where but in a character forced by experience to journey into the self in order to find both authenticity and authority would this new consciousness appear? Oates suggests that it would be born of woman. *Do With Me What You Will* is—to use terms with which Oates herself is so comfortable—a myth of creation; it is about the divinity in women. Galvanized by an orgiastic experience, which puts her, mystically, in direct contact with an ultimate reality, the source of her energy, Elena, the Queen of Sleep, awakens, harnesses the animal energy of the universe, and discovers the courage to "clear a passageway through the world" for herself. Like the symbolic act of Adam and Eve in the Christian myth, this too is a criminal act, an act of self-assertion which shatters the old paternalistic structures. Mysticism, however, has always been regarded with suspicion, and it is Oates's prophecy that salvation or liberation will not be possible in our time for anyone until her image of woman becomes both paradigm and prologue of a new heresy. (pp. 598-99)

Constance Ayers Denne, "Joyce Carol Oates's Women," in *The Nation*, New York, Vol. 219, No. 19, December 7, 1974, pp. 597-99.

CHARLOTTE GOODMAN

(essay date (1977)

[In the following excerpt, Goodman discusses the portrayal of women and sexual relationships in Oates's works.]

The Gothic world which Joyce Carol Oates has projected in her novels and short stories is one that is shaped by irrationality, extreme emotions, and violence. Oates's female characters, in particular, are born into a hostile world that fails to nurture them. Rejecting the lives of their unhappy mothers, they long to forge a more meaningful existence for themselves. However,

few life options seem available to Oates's women. Most seek fulfillment through sexual relationships, or marriage and motherhood; but sexual relationships in Oates's fiction usually end disastrously, and wives and mothers fail to be affirmed by the traditional female roles they have chosen. Like the women whose lives Phyllis Chesler has documented in *Women and Madness,* Oates's female characters often experience acute psychological malaise because of their powerlessness, and many ultimately become suicidal or psychotic. (p. 17)

The life choices made by Oates's female protagonists reflect both a desire on their part to live a more satisfying life than that of their mothers, and an inability to create alternate, more meaningful roles for themselves. Oates's prototypical young female protagonist sets forth from her family home in quest of a new life. Like Natasha in *Expensive People,* she runs away from her home, seeking a "rebirth and rebaptizing." . . . (pp. 17-18)

Poverty is one of the factors that contributes to the unhappiness of [some of her female characters]. However, a similar determination to avoid the fate of their mothers is expressed by Oates's more affluent female protagonists: Nadine, a major character in *them,* is as eager to escape from her family's richly carpeted Grosse Pointe mansion as is Maureen Wendall from her shabby apartment in the slums of Detroit, and in *Wonderland,* Shelley Vogel, daughter of a famous neurosurgeon, runs away repeatedly from her elegant home. (p. 18)

The means of escape usually chosen by Oates's young female protagonist is that of a sexual liaison. "A woman does not matter to another woman," says one of Oates's characters (**"Inventions,"** *Marriages and Infidelities* . . .). What does "matter" to Oates's women are the attentions of men who will, they hope, validate their existence. (p. 19)

[Even] Oates's affluent young women seek relationships with men as a means of adding excitement or fulfillment to their lives. Often these women seem to be searching for a father-substitute, a man who will provide them with the attention and security that they are denied by their own fathers. . . . It is ironic that the fathers who have abandoned them arouse the love and admiration of their daughters, while the mothers who have also been abandoned only arouse their daughters' contempt.

Though the mothers in Oates's fiction have suffered as a result of their own sexual and marital relationships, it is they who encourage their daughters, above all else, to seek the attentions of a man. Phyllis Chesler's explanation for such behavior is pertinent here: mothers, she says, "must be harsh in training their daughters to be 'feminine' in order that they learn how to serve in order to survive." To train their daughters how to be "feminine" in Oates's world is to teach them how to exploit their sexual attractiveness. (pp. 19-20)

The search of Oates's female characters to better their status or find happiness and fulfillment through relationships with men, marriage, and motherhood usually ends in failure. Sexual relationships in Oates's fiction do not provide women with the sense of completion that they long for and often trigger off violence either directly or indirectly. Losing autonomy over their lives as they obsessively follow their lovers, the women who fall in love frequently become psychologically unbalanced. Marriage is destructive to Oates's women, who are frequently treated brutally, or ignored, betrayed, or abandoned by their husbands. The children who are the products of these unhappy marriages also fail to bring happiness to the mothers in Oates's fiction, and in several of her stories, in fact, mothers have death wishes for their offspring.

The reason that sexual relationships prove to be so destructive to Oates's female characters is that such relationships have an obsessive quality to them and that they ultimately fail to confirm the woman's sense of self. Oates, who called one of her short stories **"What Is The Connection Between Men and Women?"** and entitled a volume of poems *Love and Its Derangements,* seems to view the love/sex "connection" between men and women as a bewildering kind of disease, a fever in the blood which often succeeds in unbalancing both partners. . . . Despite the fact that the women in Oates's fiction actively seek sexual partners, they are usually reluctant participants in sexual relations, and are often depicted as frigid or as passive recipients, rather than equal partners in the lovemaking process. Pejorative terms and words which suggest acts of a pathological nature are often used by Oates to describe sexual intercourse. In one passage [from *Do With Me What You Will*], For example, the following words appear: "terrible," "spasm," "brutal," "scream," "wildly," "viciously," "agony," "crazy," "murderous," and "mad." . . . (pp. 21-2)

It is not surprising that Oates, who has such a negative and even idiosyncratic view of sexual relations, shows those characters who seek completion through the sexual act as doomed to failure. Oates's women are driven to find sexual partners—and are in despair once the relationship has been consummated. . . . Since in Oates's fiction sadomasochism is such a major component of sexual relations, it is not surprising that she portrays physical relationships as certainly disappointing and even destructive.

Oates's fiction suggests that one of the major problems that women face in sexual relationships is that men place unreal expectations on them and fail to see them as they really are—not as lowly sex objects or lofty fertility goddesses, but as human beings with virtues and shortcomings like their own. (pp. 22-3)

Another reason given by Oates for the disappointment women experience in sexual relationships is that rather than trying to establish a mutually affirming bond with their partners, men seek instead from their lovers a narcissistic confirmation of their own powers. . . . The woman in such a relationship cannot help but feel diminished or negated.

In Oates's fiction, marriage and motherhood are also shown to be damaging to the female ego. Her lower class women are often physically assaulted by their husbands or abandoned by them, and the wives of successful men are frequently treated as menials. The work by Oates which perhaps best illustrates the way women can be damaged psychologically by marital relationships is *Wonderland,* a novel whose two main female characters are the wives of successful physicians. Women like these, with their big houses and expensive clothes, would be the envy of a poor girl like Maureen Wendall in *them;* yet both Mrs. Pedersen and Helene Vogel are shown to be desperately unhappy. (pp. 23-4)

Helene Vogel is typical of many of Oates's women who are devastated when motherhood fails to be as positive an experience as it is touted to be. Despite her sense of disappointment, Helene tries to be a good mother; several mothers in Oates's fiction, however, actually turn against their children. In two stories mothers have subconscious death wishes for their children, and they experience breakdowns when the children accidentally die. (p. 25)

The psychological disturbances that can be seen in Oates's female characters include anxiety, depression, and psychosis, and among her characters are alcoholics, drug addicts, catatonics, and those who are suicidal. What a good many of her characters commonly experience are feelings of depersonalization and disembodiment. In *The Divided Self,* R. D. Laing speaks of these feelings as being characteristic of individuals who fear that their own identity is in constant danger of being obliterated. Such individuals tend to see themselves and others as objects rather than people. Laing uses the term "petrification" to describe the process of depersonalization: "To turn oneself into stone becomes a way of not being turned into a stone by someone else," Laing writes, and then he goes on to say that turning others into objects serves to rob them of their power. Many of Oates's characters see themselves and/or others as objects. (p. 26)

Perhaps the best example in Oates's fiction of a "petrified" character is Elena in *Do With Me What You Will.* As the title of the novel suggests, Elena is a person completely lacking a will of her own, a mechanical doll who can be manipulated by others. At the beginning of the novel we see how she is traumatized in early childhood. . . . In response to this experience Elena develops an impassivity which insulates her from others. . . . Her behavior perfectly illustrates what Laing means by "petrification."

Phyllis Chesler has observed that depression, rather than aggression, is the characteristic female response to disappointment or loss. Depression is commonly found in many of Oates's female characters. Though a rare female character commits a violent or aggressive act, it is usually Oates's male characters who react violently, and her female characters who are the victims of their violence. (pp. 26-7)

"What does it mean to be a woman?" the catatonic Maureen Wendall thinks in *them*. . . . This question is explored in work after work by Joyce Carol Oates as she examines the roles of women and their relationships. Oates's view of women's lives is certainly a bleak one, and she does not give easy answers to the question of how women should live their lives so as to avoid the anxiety and despair that often leads to madness. Her fiction, however, does provide valuable insights about the powerlessness of women and the causes of their desperation. Unable to gain autonomy over their lives, and threatened by a brutal world where violence against them may break out at any moment, Oates's female characters often become anxious or depressed, and sometimes retreat into madness, which confers upon them the blessings of safety and peace. (p. 28)

Charlotte Goodman, "Women and Madness in the Fiction of Joyce Carol Oates," in *Women & Literature,* Vol. 5, No. 2, Fall, 1977, pp. 17-28.

G. F. WALLER
(essay date 1979)

[In the following excerpt, Waller compares Oates with the English novelist D. H. Lawrence, noting similarities between their artistic objectives and thematic concerns.]

The almost obligatory topic with which to introduce Oates is, in fact, the amount she has published. A survey of her work may suggest a compulsive writer and maybe even a lack of self-criticism. Her poems . . . are often jagged and metrically uncertain, and sometimes over-packed with superfluous words; but frequently they can crystallize with electrifying clarity inexplicable moments of experience on the edge of fear, despair, terror, or joy. Many read, in fact, like passionate footnotes to her stories or novels. . . . As well as overlapping with her fiction, her criticism, it should be noted, is often extraordinarily suggestive, especially in the way it opens up, by analogy or brooding meditation, startling psychological and philosophical perspectives.

It is in the short stories perhaps that Oates's best work is to be found. . . . Many of the stories are certainly repetitive or trivial. But some—**"Where Are You Going, Where Have You Been," "Unmailed, Unwritten Letters," "Accomplished Desires"** from *The Wheel of Love,* **"The Sacred Marriage"** from *Marriages and Infidelities,* to mention a few of the best—are so bewilderingly evocative that they must rate along with the masterpieces of the genre. . . . [But] it is with her novels that her reputation and importance must rest. It is there that her prophetic urgency, the obsessive desire to "dream America," emerges at its most tantalizing, frustrating, and evocative. The early novels, although technically more cautious, nevertheless share the same obsessions as the mature works of the seventies, where Oates attempts to dramatize the mystery of the human spirit struggling amongst our personal and shared nightmares. (pp. 2-4)

Alongside most of her contemporaries, Oates does stand out as a curiously chameleon figure. "America outdoes all its writers," observes Richard, the narrator of *Expensive People,* and Oates takes her role seriously as searching for ways of surviving within the flux of modern America. At times . . . she moves vigorously towards postcontemporary fictionists like Robert Coover or Donald Barthelme, but even in such stories, "the social and moral conditions of my generation" are kept consistently in view. Rather waspishly, she criticizes "new fictionists" and "black humorists" for their refusal to "deal with the utterly uncontrollable emotions that determine our lives." (p. 6)

Biographical trivia aside, there is a real sense in which, in Oates's words, "all art is autobiographical." It is initially the record of an artist's psychic experience, an attempt to explain something to himself. Just as in her novels and stories the "real" Detroit becomes "transparent" in her imaginative X ray of the felt experience of living there, so her everyday life as woman, writer, wife, professor, or housewife, provides only a superstructure of a literary personality: quiet, passive, yet fiercely creative, crystallizing not (or not only) her own but her era's deepest, most tangled, obsessions. . . . We can see that there is an explorative unity in Oates's work; despite its surface variety, like D. H. Lawrence's, the diversity of her writing is already forming itself into what we might term an emotional autobiography, although one that is hardly a mirror of the surfaces of her own life. Looking at obvious affinities, we can set her early writing in a realist tradition, then note the frequent flirtation with the antirealists or fabulators in the late sixties, and see her, in the seventies, taking up a cautiously experimental but hardly avant-garde place in the contemporary city of words. (pp. 8-9)

But a more interesting means of defining the importance and power of her fiction can be achieved by a less academically predictable route. Oates's fictional mode, more than most novelists', has developed as a distinctive state of feeling thrust at her reader. Some of the most compelling writing in contemporary fiction, her stories force upon readers an often frightening sense of our own fears, obsessions, and drives. Indeed, her work operates in terms best described by that increasingly fashionable motif in contemporary fictional theory, the notion of the "implied reader." . . .

[In] Oates's fiction we have a vivid example of how a writer must rely heavily on the emotional cooperation of the reader. Her geographical landscapes evoke our own emotional or moral dilemmas and allegiances and in reading her we attend not so much to the shifts of plot or scene but to our own changing emotional reactions. (p. 9)

In order for her novels, to use D. H. Lawrence's phrase, to "inform and lead into new places the flow of our sympathetic consciousness," Oates's fiction plunges us into a distinctively felt atmosphere. All the novels are similarly structured, often as triptychs (with an occasional summary addendum, as in *Do With Me What You Will*), usually concentrating on three phases of a central character's growth to self-awareness. The underlying pattern of discovery in the novels is evoked by the charisma of emotional extremism: actions seem inevitably violent, speech is ejaculative and hostile, underlying fears constantly burst through the surface of the action. Oates's typical imagery reinforces this extremism: imprisonment, shattering glass, bursting and breaking, explosions dominate the emotional field of the action. . . . As Phyllis Grosskurth points out, *crazy* is a favorite word in the novels, and all of Oates's important characters live just on the boundaries of sanity as they clutch and claw at the possibility of momentary order in the flux of their lives. Her intention is partly to achieve a shock of emotional extremism which will involve both attention and recognition in the reader's experience. . . . The form, or formlessness, of her work, then, is deliberately perspectival as we, her readers, are driven to create the form, or formlessness, of our own lives and our own private fictions. . . . (p. 11)

[There] is also in Oates's fictional world something of what she perceives in Lawrence's poetry, where one finds "literally everything: beauty, waste, 'flocculent ash,' the ego in a state of rapture and in a state of nausea, a diverse streaming of chaos and cunning." . . . In Oates's novels such chaos is invariably situated in the emotions, in the convulsive eruption of obsessive feeling, in the pain, anguish, distraught embarrassment, and violence of the personality. . . . Our understanding of Oates's fiction depends on our sensing how the "meaning" . . . is as much in the voice as in the words: the reader is asked to respond to an unusual extent to mood, timbre, and modulation of voice. We may, of course, be nauseated, appalled,

fearful, and hostile. But once seized by that voice, we cannot choose but listen, and to submit to Oates's world is to enter a realm of psychic violence potentially disturbing to any sensitive reader. Oates has an unusual ability to bring out the reader's own hidden fears and psychic nightmares. . . . The real "events" by which Oates's characters are motivated lie deep within the protean chaos of the personality, and her readers are directed back into the depths of their own inner worlds, perhaps to encounter chaos there. (pp. 11-12)

Oates's fiction can be tellingly approached through a Lawrentian perspective. Her brilliant account of Lawrence's poetry—surely, despite its brevity, one of the most suggestive pieces of Lawrence criticism in recent decades—speaks of him in terms that strangely reverberate upon her own approach to the artist's role. . . . Fascination with flux, with art as prophecy, with the therapeutic exposure of the self—these central Lawrentian motifs are fused and re-created in Oates's work. (pp. 12-13)

It is because of the seriousness with which Oates takes the novelist's role as prophet that we might judge her by Lawrence's understanding of "morality" rather than by purely aesthetic criteria, or within the conventional formal terms of fiction. . . . His argument was that only the novel could express its reader's deep awareness of the age's perspectival relativism. . . . Only the novel, the bright book of life, could reflect and direct the dynamism of the age. (pp. 14-15)

[It] is above all the novelist's responsibility to "recreate and reinterpret the world," to provide, even though forced to employ the slipperiness of words, the impetus towards what Lawrence called "the *Deed* of life." Paradoxically, even tragically, the writer "is committed to re-creating the world through language. . . . The use of language is all we have to put against death and silence." The destiny of the novelist is therefore to simultaneously subject himself to and evoke for us the chaos within, exorcising and exhorting at once, providing the reader, one would hope, with the challenge of a profound waking dream. Our dreams offer to show us the deepest roots of our creativity: we hunger for significance and art satisfies that hunger. So the novelist's role, today, becomes that of "dreaming America," an attempt to master in fiction the "chaos outside and inside ourselves," occasionally "winning small victories," then facing the inevitability of "being swept along by some cataclysmic event of our own making." The novelist, [Oates] writes, encounters Lawrence's "madness for the unknown," his "diverse streaming of chaos and cunning" and attempts to render a stasis in his own fiction and, through our receptivity, in the fictions we ourselves constantly create, revise, and re-create. (pp. 15-16)

But it is [the] emphasis on the apocalypse beyond and through corruption, or in Oates's own terms, the transcendence achieved through obsession, that she shares fundamentally with Lawrence. Oates apparently came to Lawrence relatively late, but she must have sensed immediately a genius whose characteristic stance uncannily challenged her own obsessions, leading her to assert that ultimately only someone spiritually attuned to Lawrence could comprehend his work.

The most obvious connection between Lawrence and Oates is their fascination with sexuality. . . . Like Lawrence, Oates is fascinated with the power and the dynamic of sex. She focuses repeatedly on the numinous aura of sexuality, on how sexuality contributes to, or so often mocks, our attempts to order our lives. . . . [While] Oates's view of sexuality acknowledges its embodiment of our hunger for purpose, she also notes that love must be acknowledged as a violent and unstoppable force, not simply an instinctive urge to achieve rest of transcendence. Again, an interesting comparison is with Lawrence. In both writers sexual relations are relations of possibility and power. They may be like the destructive preying of Gudrun upon Gerald, the fierce battle for equilibrium between Birkin and Ursula, or in Oates's work, what she terms "the totally irrational, possessive, ego-destroying love, which can't be controlled and is, perhaps, a pathological condition of the soul," such as the relationship between the lovers in *Do With Me What You Will* or the tragically unfulfilled desires brought out in stories like **"Scenes of Passion and Desire"** or **"I Must Have You."** The most painful and evocative scenes in Oates's work focus on the power of sexual attraction and repulsion and it is in her concentration on sexual desire as an unpredictable and awesome force for change in the personality that her closest thematic connection with Lawrence is found. In love, all we have fixed and made "permanent" . . . may be suddenly and fearfully shattered. Life becomes fragmentary and unpredictable; where once we had lived by rationality and comfort, in love we become defined primarily by fear and fragility. As in Lawrence's fiction, with Oates's best work we are involved in the affective dimension of the writing. Its rhythmic surges and melodramatic intensification make us face, in ourselves, that same fear and fragility.

As readers we are forced by Oates's concentration upon our feelings to focus on the intense state in which her characters make discoveries about themselves. The typical Oates character, usually a woman, is continually bombarded by sensation—fear, insecurity, a sense of formlessness from within, pursuit from without. (pp. 17-18)

Like [Lawrence's] Ursula desperately climbing the tree to escape the horses to tumble "in a heap on the other side of the hedge" and realizing that she is "trammelled and entangled" and "must break out . . . like a nut from its shell," so Oates's women characters must

make some radical act of the whole integral personality to discover their true inner direction.

It is perhaps the very totality of both writers' obsession for the importance of sexual connections that makes them reach for what Lawrence saw as a dimension of experience found through and yet somehow beyond sex. Both writers link human sexuality with the Nietzschean vision of the self struggling to overcome itself. . . . [Pain,] memory, and fear are transformed as sexuality becomes, in its mystery, terror and joy, part of the neutral rhythm of the circumambient universe, the life of sensation and emotions by which men and women transcend time, place, and limitation. From such connections, not only do all life-affirming human commitments grow, but humanity is challenged to reach beyond itself. Lawrence's thought here, Oates has argued, "is really revolutionary; it is a total rejection of that dogma of the West that declares *Man is the measure of all things."* . . .

Lawrence's vision of sexual transcendence often strikes readers as paradoxical in a writer so obsessed with sexual attraction and repulsion; but at its strongest, sexual connection was for Lawrence a means of finding a nourishing relationship with nature and the universe: perhaps, he wrote, the human race is dying, but there is "a flame or a Life Everlasting wreathing through the cosmos for ever and giving us our renewal, one we can get in touch with." Fifty years later, less ideologically explicit, but with equivalent passion and evocation, Oates's prophetic vision attempts to define the tragedy of our age, in which individuals yearn towards a new consciousness, sensed through and yet ultimately transcending sexuality, by exploring similarly the way passion and its necessary violence "redeem and may perhaps make a kind of eternity." . . . (pp. 19-21)

In *Lady Chatterley's Lover* the mechanism of industrialization is a symbol of the repetitive, mechanical forces of human reason and repressed emotion. With the woods increasingly shrinking back from the encroaching mines and factories, for Lawrence it was increasingly urgent to seek the dark flame of human spontaneity, and the deed rather than the word of life. Similarly, from Oates's work we sense just how crucial it is to move beyond the limitations of our isolated self-concentration. We must ultimately open ourselves to the obliteration of the ego and our fixation with its uniqueness. Just as Lawrence saw the fulfillment of the individual consisting in going beyond the individual, to a relationship of star-equilibrium, so Oates looks beyond the guilt-obsessed individuality of our era. (p. 23)

Lyrical prophecy is usually irritatingly unanalyzable; it is exhortatory not descriptive, demanding the assent of faith not logic. But in these two writers there is an accompanying grasp of sensual reality that roots their vision in the world. Lawrence's apocalyptic mysticism was based on a vision of a transformed individuality; Oates speaks of "the potential of normality" and of the growing contemporary realization "(so clear in imaginative literature, so muddled elsewhere) that it is here, in the soul, inside the fantastically complex phenomenon of man, that the salvation of the world will take place." (p. 25)

Both Lawrence and Oates . . . are only superficially novelists of place and landscape. "Landscape," wrote Lawrence, is "*meant* as a background to an intenser vision of life." So Oates's Detroit . . . , like her Eden County or her California, like Lawrence's Derbyshire or Swiss Alps, exist not as settings in their own right but are created through the leaps of lyrical, passionate feeling with which they are experienced by the characters and the reader. Throughout Oates's fiction, details of setting are habitually chosen for their associations of feeling. In **"Ruth,"** from *The Goddess and Other Women,* the incipient violence within a decaying marriage is evoked by the deceptively realistic opening description. . . . The concentration of natural surroundings—the original wood, the swamp, the dying trees mysteriously connected with the highway—not only set a mood, they provide the reader with an initial emblem, a moral focus for developments later in the story. Similarly, although evoked tactilely, at times almost photographically, Oates's Detroit in *them* particularly possesses the vivid significance of an X ray rather than the gaudy realism of a Kodakchrome print. In a not dissimilar way, Lawrence's Derbyshire in *The Rainbow* or his Australia in *Kangaroo* are imbued with the spirit, not the pictorial details of place. (p. 75)

Oates's vision of places like Detroit similarly arises from her concern with the city as symbol. She is obsessed not merely by the social profusion of America, but by the ways eddying, brooding currents of feeling tie our society together, and her fiction evokes the city as a revelation of psychological rather than social realism. . . . The sense of victimization, the rootless bewilderment and paucity of relationships are all rooted in the psyche, and they emerge in our involuntary movements, or cryptic, frustrated ejaculations of command or insult. Likewise, the autonomy of transcendence that may liberate us in the city is possible only from within ourselves. Detroit is everywhere. We cannot escape its pressure upon us, but we may transcend it through the resources we discover within our inner lives. (pp. 75-6)

As with setting, so with character. Lawrence's famous letter to Edward Garnett outlines a view of character which has been strikingly influential in subsequent fiction and psychology, and it is, I suggest, as helpful a key to many of Oates's characters as the American romance-gothic tradition into which she more obviously fits. "You mustn't," he wrote, "look in my novel for the old stable *ego* of the character. There

is another *ego,* according to whose action the individual is unrecognizable, and passes through, as it were, allotropic states which it needs a deeper sense than any we've been used to exercise to discover are states of the same single radically unchanged elements." We respond to his characters, in their violent, rhythmical lyricism, as states of feeling, as vivid, personified intuitions of human potential, attracting or repulsing other centers of feeling (including the reader's). The very concept of a fixed self was for Lawrence a disastrously over-conscious conception of being, not only in fiction but in life, a solidification of experience that ignores the risk and chaos in the personality. . . . In a similar way, and despite her careful attention to surface detail, to the social trivia of the farm, city, hospital, or university, Oates concentrates on the moving, shifting surges of the personality that not only respond to but create their surroundings. Her most significant characters curiously combine, in the way romance characters do, heightened cliché and symbolic vividness that resound back upon their surrounding world—and then out to the reader's own world. The horrendous Dr. Pedersen in *Wonderland,* the dead Andrew Petrie in *The Assassins,* the ambitious Clara in *A Garden of Earthly Delights* are all evoked as centers of passionate consciousness, not depicted in the clear objectivity of the "stable ego" of personality. We fix on insignificant objects or incidents and project our inner urges upon them. Thus, minor details of setting, incident, or surroundings are heightened by and are reflections of the personality's obsessive subjectivity. . . . Tiny details of life suddenly, terrifyingly seize upon us and become obsessions. (pp. 78-9)

Her characters are seized upon by obscurely motivated, inexplicable urges which frequently erupt obsessively, turning apparently solid reality into something else, forcing us tragically to confront our limits and battle unsuccessfully to transcend them. (p. 80)

Because Oates's characters tend to exist as the foci of such obsessions, not as case histories of social or political development, they are frequently depicted in stereotypical form. (p. 81)

Even though Oates's work in the seventies shows more experimentation, her choice of form continues to be determined by the material of the story; she is not interested, it seems, in simply playing with fictional forms. She once criticized Donald Barthelme for his reliance on fragments, quoting a remark in one of his stories, that "fragments are the only forms I trust." It is therefore ironic, and perhaps heartening, to see the skill with which she too can employ fragmentary, openended fictions even if she uses fragments without the playful panache of Barthelme or Sukenick. Her . . . two novels, *The Assassins* and *Childwold,* show just how she has developed in her longer fictions. *Childwold,* in particular, presents us with a polyphony of

Joyce Carol Oates.

dislocated epiphanies—scraps of dialogue, isolated memories, written and unwritten fantasies, long naturalistic scenes, few (and sometimes no) transitions, ritual chants, diary entries, quotations from philosophers, snatches of action, long Faulknerian sentences, blocks of space, disjointed paragraphs. Paradoxically, behind the randomness of the novel's surface story is not only an impressive intensification of conflict and self-discovery but a deeply pessimistic story of moral consequence and fearful accident. Rather than producing an atmosphere of cosmic randomness, the formal incertitude of the novel reinforces Oates's grimly coherent vision. The spaces, dislocations, and frayed ends of her fiction invariably point to the apocalyptic state of contemporary America. There are inevitably echoes of her earlier novels . . . but her technical control and experimentation . . . are startling. Probably never before has Oates handled such a difficult fictional form so effectively, especially the transition she achieves at the novel's end, as an apparent, if complex, order dissolves into chaos and randomness. (p. 84)

Oates has searched, often repetitively and restlessly, for forms which will be appropriate vehicles of her vision. The world around us appears material and trustworthy, rational and comprehendable—and she sees our salvation as lying in the gaps between the material things and the rational thoughts of our world. Dislocation, fragments, and evocative incoherence may be the way her vision is articulated, but in a sense, her vision chooses her. . . . Whereas we cannot see Oates in the forefront of the explorers of the postmodernist

terrain, her recent work especially shows her capable of leading bivouacs over the most difficult areas of that terrain. (p. 85)

G. F. Waller, in his *Dreaming America: Obsession and Transcendence in the Fiction of Joyce Carol Oates,* Louisiana State University Press, 1979, 224 p.

CHRISTINA MARSDEN GILLIS
(essay date 1981)

[In the following excerpt, Gillis examines themes of lost innocence and transgression in "Where Are You Going, Where Have You Been?"]

Joyce Carol Oates' **"Where Are You Going, Where Have You Been?"** is a story about beginnings and passage points; and it is a story about endings: the end of childhood, the end of innocence. The account of fifteen-year-old Connie's encounter with a mysterious stranger named Arnold Friend, a man who leads his victim not to a promising new world, but, rather, to a violent sexual assault, is a tale of initiation depicted in grotesque relief.

But **"Where Are You Going"** is also a story where spatial limitations are of crucial concern, and to this degree it provides a commentary on stories and storytelling. As Oates transforms elements of fairy tale and dream into a chilling description of temptation, seduction, and probable rape, we are forced to consider the distinctions between fairy tale and seduction narrative, to note particularly that in **"Where Are You Going"** seduction involves the invasion of personal, interior space: " . . . his words, replete with guile,/Into her heart too easy entrance won," Milton says of Satan's meeting with Eve. Women are vulnerable to seduction, and of course rape, Susan Brownmiller has reminded us, for what at first may be seen as purely physiological reasons; and there is little doubt of physical violence when Arnold Friend croons to Connie, "I'll come inside you where it's all secret"; but the seduction motif functions so successfully in **"Where Are You Going"** because the delineation of interior space figured in the female body analogizes invasion at several levels: the domestic space, the state of childhood associated with the home, and, of course, the individual consciousness. (p. 65)

At the outset we may identify **"Where Are You Going"** as an American "coming of age" tale, the main character Connie joining that cast of characters which includes Huckleberry Finn, Isabel Archer, and Jay Gatsby. But while the poles of Oates' story are innocence and experience, the focus of attention is the process of seduction, or the threshold between the two states. The lines are clear, the threshold visually realized. Connie belongs to a tradition of domesticated Eves; for them, Satan's entrance into the garden is replaced by the invasion of a rake like Lovelace (in Richardson's *Clarissa*) into one's private chamber—or ultimately, in the twentieth century, by the approach of the cowboy-booted Arnold Friend to the kitchen door of an asbestos-covered ranch house. The physical world shrinks in this fiction; unlike Eden, the perimeter of a private room, or body, lends itself to specific accounting. Within a described locus, space itself is at issue, the fiction setting up a tension whereby the private is open to both attack and transformation.

Spatial limits are increasingly important in **"Where Are You Going."** If the threshold of the kitchen door ultimately receives the burden of tension in the tale, Oates carefully prepares us for the climactic scene by setting up, at the outset, contrasting *loci.* The very title of the story calls attention to duality: a future (where you are going) and a past (where you have been). The tale catches its main character at a passage point where, it is implied, the future may depend precipitously on the past. More specifically, the two major locations of the tale are the home and family unit it signifies, and the outside world represented first in the drive-in hamburger joint, later in Arnold Friend himself. Connie herself lives in two worlds, even dressing appropriately for each: she "wore a pull over jersey blouse that looked one way when she was at home and another way when she was away from home. Everything about her had two sides to it, one for home and one for anywhere that was not home." Home is the daylight world, a known, established order where so-called parental wisdom would seem to negate the dreams and desires of youth. Connie is, then, constantly at odds with her family, ever looking forward to her excursions to the drive-in, the nighttime world, the "bright-lit, fly-infested restaurant" which she and her friend approach, "their faces pleased and expectant as if they were entering a sacred building that loomed up out of the night to give them what haven and blessing they yearned for." A mood of expectation pervades Connie's night-time world. Like the light on Daisy Buchanan's pier that promised romance to Jay Gatsby, the bright-lit hamburger joint also holds out new worlds within its "sacred" precincts: cars, music, boys, experience.

Even when the initial meeting with a boy named Eddie—the experience "down the alley a mile or so away"—is over, when the clock has struck eleven and the Cinderella land fades back into the night, a "big empty parking lot [with] signs that were faded and ghostly," even then, the mood of expectation is only temporarily broken. There will be other nights in this midsummer dream-time. Eddie and his like, all the boys, Oates tells us, "fell back and dissolved into a single face that was not even a face but an idea, a feeling, mixed up with the urgent insistent pounding of the music and humid air of July." No wonder that Connie resists being "dragged back to the daylight" by her mother's too-insistent voice. The mother who had once been pretty ("but now her looks were gone and that was why she was always after Connie") sees in Connie a dim outline of her own former self; but the dream perception seems long faded, and Connie's sister June, the only other female family member, is a plain, stalwart sort who has clearly never had much to do with dreams.

But mother and sister are not the villains here, of course, Connie no Cinderella for whom a night-time dream becomes daylight reality. Rather, dream becomes nightmare when Connie first meets at the drive-in Arnold Friend, no Prince Charming, but a man with metallic, cold eyes, driving a bright gold jalopy. And Arnold Friend only pretends to be young. Later, with the discovery of Arnold's true age, Connie will feel her heart pound faster; the bizarre realization that Friend's companion has the face of a "forty year old baby" will cause the teenager to experience a "wave of dizziness." And we are shocked too: there is no fairy tale world here, no romance after all. Friend's first muttered threat, "Gonna get you, baby," is to be played out not in a dream, but in the daylight hours and within a domestic space.

Even before Arnold Friend's entrance into the driveway of Connie's home, reality and dream are beginning to clash dangerously. Connie sits in the sun "dreaming and dazed with the warmth about her as if this were a kind of love, the caresses of love;" but when she opens her eyes she sees only a "back yard that ran off into weeds" and a house that looked small. Arnold's appearance in Connie's driveway on the Sunday morning when her family have gone off to a barbecue only underlines the confused merging of two worlds Connie has always kept apart. She approaches the kitchen door slowly, hangs out the screen door, "her bare toes curling down off the step." Connie is not yet ready to make the step outside.

With Arnold's arrival the significance of separate locations in **"Where Are You Going"** acquires new intensity, and the delineation of space becomes a matter of crucial concern. Connie's refusal to move down off the step bespeaks her clinging to a notion that walls and exact locations offer the protection of the familial order. Now, with Friend's initial invitation to join him and his friend in the car, and with his assertion that he has placed his "sign" upon her, Connie moves further back into the kitchen: she "let the screen door close and stood perfectly still inside it." From the familiar kitchen space, she attempts to make sense of her experience. But the mirror sunglasses make it impossible for the girl to see what Friend is looking at; the enigmatic smile tells nothing; and even as she attempts to amass assorted physical data on her visitor, she finds that "all these things did not come together."

Then the familiar and the private begin to give way to the unexpected visitor. Having realized the true age of the two intruders and being told that they will not leave until she agrees to go along with them, Connie has the sense that Friend "had driven up the driveway all right but had come from nowhere before and belonged nowhere . . . everything that was so familiar to her was only half real." The drawing of the magical sign, a sign of ownership over her, suggests control over her own private consciousness. Connie wonders how Friend knows her name; but later, much more troubling, is his knowledge that her father is not coming back soon, that the family is at the picnic. Connie finds herself sharing a perhaps imaginary, perhaps real, view of the barbecue. Friend refers to a "fat woman" at the barbecue:

> "What fat woman?" Connie cried.
> "How do I know what fat woman. I don't know every goddamn fat woman in the world!" Arnold Friend laughed.
> "Oh, that's Mrs. Hornsby. . . . Who invited her?" Connie said. She felt a little lightheaded. Her breath was coming quickly.

And penetration of consciousness is only the preamble to penetration in a sexual sense: "And I'll come inside you where it's all secret and you'll give in to me and you'll love me—" says Friend. The disorder implied in Friend's knowing too much, more than can be rationally explained, is now to be played out in trespassing upon the body itself. A limit has been passed. Connie does not want to hear these words; she "backed away from the door. She put her hand up against her ears as if she'd heard something terrible."

Connie retreats further within the kitchen, but the space of the room also loses familiarity as interior worlds break down. Just as earlier in the morning the adolescent has begun to see her own home as small, now the kitchen looked "like a place she had never seen before, some room she had run inside but that wasn't good enough, wasn't going to help her." Doors too become meaningless. "But why lock [the door]?" Friend taunts; "it's just a screen door, It's just nothing." Friend is still articulating spatial limits—"[I] promise not to come in unless you touch the phone"—but such limits no longer have meaning. The statement, "I want you," the words of the teenager's love song, now connote a world where the limits around self are not viable. The breaking of a limitation and the opening of a door . . . destroy both individual innocence and the order of the innocent's world. "It's all over for you here," Friend tells Connie. Crying out for the mother that will not come, Connie feels not the protective parental embrace,

but rather a feeling in her lungs as if Friend "was stabbing her . . . with no tenderness." And then the horrible statement muttered in a stage voice, the statement which spells the end of a world: "The place where you came from ain't there any more, and where you had in mind to go is cancelled out. This place you are now—inside your daddy's house—is nothing but a cardboard box I can knock down any time."

Obliteration through violent assault is multidimensional in **"Where Are You Going."** The domestic space, a house as the nurturing place of childhood, yields to attack from outside no less than the body, consciousness, even "heart" of the girl is forced to give way. Observing that the house looks solid, Friend tells Connie, "Now, put your hand on your heart, honey. . . . That feels solid too but we know better." And when Connie feels her own pounding heart, "she thought for the first time in her life that it was nothing that was hers, that belonged to her." If **"Where Are You Going"** is the story of the end of childhood, the end of romance, the invasion and probable destruction of private and self-contained space provide one important definition of the end of innocence. Friend's taking over the "heart" of the young girl so that "it was nothing that was hers" spells a conquest of both space and will: his intimation that he will wait for and then kill the family if Connie does not go with him is the more terrible because of Connie's own ambivalent feelings about her family, the breaking in the child's trust in her parents. Finally, the satanic visitor's incantation, "We'll go out to a nice field, out in the country where it smells so nice and it's sunny," represents not only a chilling perversion of pastoral—for the words of Satan can lead not toward, but only away from, Eden—but a ritualized statement that all of the walls defining an individual self have been destroyed. Connie's pushing open the screen door to go off with Arnold Friend, the ultimate yielding, signifies that indeed the place she came from "ain't there any more." (pp. 66-70)

Christina Marsden Gillis, " 'Where Are You Going, Where Have You Been?': Seduction, Space, and a Fictional Mode," in *Studies in Short Fiction,* Vol. 18, No. 1, Winter, 1981, pp. 65-70.

GREG JOHNSON

(essay date 1987)

[In the following excerpt from his *Understanding Joyce Carol Oates,* Johnson favorably assesses Oates's literary career.]

In the 1980s Oates remains a major force in contemporary American writing. Aside from her fiction and her teaching, she is a prolific poet, critic, and book reviewer; several of her plays have been produced in New York; and she is an extremely popular, engaging speaker on college campuses across the country. She also serves as coeditor of *The Ontario Review,* a literary magazine which she and her husband inaugurated in 1974 in Windsor, and continue to operate from their home in Princeton. Her achievement is all the more extraordinary when one considers that she is still in her forties and may now be viewed as entering the middle stage of her illustrious career.

Joyce Carol Oates's versatility as a fiction writer relates directly to her overwhelming fascination with the phenomenon of contemporary America: its colliding social and economic forces, its philosophical contradictions, its wayward, often violent energies. Taken as a whole, Oates's fiction portrays America as a seething, vibrant "wonderland" in which individual lives are frequently subject to disorder, dislocation, and extreme psychological turmoil. Her protagonists range from inner-city dwellers and migrant workers to intellectuals and affluent suburbanites; but all her characters, regardless of background, suffer intensely the conflicts and contradictions at the heart of our culture—a suffering Oates conveys with both scrupulous accuracy and great compassion.

Her particular genius is her ability to convey psychological states with unerring fidelity, and to relate the intense private experiences of her characters to the larger realities of American life. "I think I have a vulnerability to a vibrating field of other people's experiences," she told an interviewer in 1972. "I lived through the '60s in the United States, I was aware of hatreds and powerful feelings all around me." Her frequently remarked tendency to focus upon psychological terror and imbalance thus relates directly to her vision of America, what Alfred Kazin has called "her sweetly brutal sense of what American experience is really like." Though she has been accused of using gratuitous or obsessive violence in her work, Oates has insisted that her violent materials accurately mirror the psychological and social convulsions of our time. In an acerbic essay titled **"Why Is Your Writing So Violent?,"** she points out that "serious writers, as distinct from entertainers or propagandists, take for their natural subjects the complexity of the world, its evils as well as its goods. . . . The serious writer, after all, bears witness."

In responding to the "vibrating field of other people's experiences," Oates's imagination has created hundreds and possibly thousands of fictional characters: people coping with the phantasmagoric wonderland of American life and suffering various degrees of psychological and spiritual isolation. Her typical protagonist is tragically blinded to the possibility of the "communal consciousness" that Oates sees as a likely salvation for our culture. . . . Positing the hopeful idea that the violent conflicts in American culture represent not an "apocalyptic close" but a "transformation of being," Oates suggests that we are experiencing "a simple evolution into a higher humanism, perhaps a kind of intelligent pantheism, in which all substance in the universe (including the substance fortunate enough to perceive it) is there by equal right."

Because this epoch of cultural transcendence has not yet arrived, Oates has conceived her primary role as an artist who must dramatize the nightmarish conditions of the present, with all its anxiety, paranoia, dislocation, and explosive conflict. Her fiction has often focused particularly on the moment when a combined psychological and cultural malaise erupts into violence; and despite the notable variety of her character portrayals, there are several representative "types" that recur frequently and present distinctive facets of the turbulent American experience.

There are the confused adolescents, for instance, like Connie in **"Where Are You Going, Where Have You Been?"** and Jules in *them,* essentially innocent, romantic souls whose fantasies and ideals collide with the environment and with the imperatives of their own maturity. There are the young women seeking fulfillment in adulterous love, like the heroines of **"Unmailed, Unwritten Letters"** and **"The Lady with the Pet Dog,"** and like Elena of *Do With Me What You Will,* all of whom seek redemption outside marriages originally based upon the expectations of others. There are the tough, earthy women like Clara in *A Garden of Earthly Delights,* Loretta in *them,* and Arlene in *Childwold,* each rising from an impoverished childhood, developing considerable resilience and cunning, and dealing shrewdly with a male-dominated society. There are the brilliant but emotionally needy intellectuals like Hugh in *The Assassins* (1975), Kasch in *Childwold,* Brigit in *Unholy Loves* (1979), and Marya in *Marya: A Life,* whose lives dramatize Oates's ironic view of a culture that values "masculine" intellect at the expense of "feminine" intuitive knowledge and that inhibits, on the individual level, a healthy integration of reason and emotion. There are the middle-aged men who control society, like the businessman Curt Revere in *A Garden of Earthly Delights,* the megalomaniac Dr. Pedersen in *Wonderland,* and the lawyer Marvin Howe in *Do With Me What You Will.* And there are the doomed, literally "mad" characters, like Allen Weinstein in **"In the Region of Ice,"** Richard Everett in *Expensive People,* and T. W. Monk in *Wonderland,* young people whose inner conflicts drive them to the point of madness or suicide.

This bare-bones summary of the most frequently recurring character types in Oates's fiction scarcely does justice to the subtlety of individual characterization she lavishes on each, but it does suggest Oates's major fictional concerns and the distinct ways in which her work focuses upon the intense conflict between the individual and his social environment. While some aspects of her work—especially the increasingly hopeful resolutions of her more recent novels—may hint at "transcendence," she remains notable as an industrious chronicler of America's personal and collective nightmares.

Understanding the violent and frequently ironic terms of the American experience, Oates has employed a notable variety of aesthetic approaches in her attempt to convey such an immense, kaleidoscopic, and frequently grotesque reality. In a much-quoted remark Philip Roth has said that "the American writer in the middle of the 20th century has his hands full in trying to describe, and then to make credible, much of the American reality. It stupefies, it sickens, it infuriates, and finally it is even a kind of embarrassment to one's own meager imagination. The actuality is continually outdoing our talents."

Yet Joyce Carol Oates has met this challenge with increasingly bold and resourceful experiments in fiction, sharing not the postmodernist concerns of John Barth or William Gass solely with language and its aesthetic possibilities, but rather the Victorian faith of Dickens or George Eliot in the efficacy of the novel in dealing with profound social and philosophical themes. Oates has thus adhered throughout her career to the novel of ideas and to the mode of psychological realism, while at the same time producing highly experimental works of fiction that both complement her more traditional work and allow her to present the daunting American reality in terms of myth, antirealism, and other forms of literary intrigue. As John Barth noted in a seminal essay dealing with the traditional versus the experimental in fiction, "Joyce Carol Oates writes all over the aesthetical map." (pp. 7-13)

Some of Oates's best-known short stories published during this same period showed similar concerns, dealing with such "representative" characters as the adolescent girl from an affluent home who has a compulsion to shoplift and eventually serves as the sardonic narrator for **"How I Contemplated the World from the Detroit House of Correction and Began My Life Over Again";** the reserved Catholic nun of **"In the Region of Ice,"** suffering a crisis of faith and conscience in her dealings with an unstable Jewish student; the well-to-do businessman in **"Stray Children,"** drawn unwillingly into a relationship with a dependent, drug-saturated girl who claims to be his daughter; and the married woman conducting a doomed love affair in **"The Lady with the Pet Dog,"** Oates's "re-imagining" of the famous Chekhov story. These stories along with dozens of others published in *The Wheel of Love, Marriages and Infidelities* and other collections have in common both a riveting psychological intensity and an authoritative, all-inclusive vision of "what American experience is really like" for people who suffer various

kinds of emotional turmoil and who, like the title characters in *them,* become emblematic of America as a whole.

Oates's attempts to dramatize this turmoil, and often to convey psychological states at the very border of sanity, have often led her into the fictional mode loosely described as "gothicism." Her work combines such traditionally gothic elements as extreme personal isolation, violent physical and psychological conflict, settings and symbolic action used to convey painfully heightened psychological states, and a prose style of passionate, often melodramatic intensity. The combination of rural settings and psychological malaise in her earlier fiction, for instance, prompted some reviewers to align Oates with the gothic tradition of Southern literature, suggesting that she had been influenced by William Faulkner, Flannery O'Connor, and Carson McCullers. Certainly her bewildered, inarticulate characters, fighting their losing battles against a backdrop of brooding fatalism, do bear a spiritual kinship to the Southern isolates of Faulkner and McCullers in particular. Oates has often stated her admiration for Southern fiction, but the dynamic, hallucinatory power of her best work recalls not only Southern gothicism but also the psychological explorations of Dostoevsky, the nightmare visions of Franz Kafka, and even the fantastic world of Lewis Carroll. . . . (pp. 15-17)

To describe much of Oates's fiction as gothic in nature is not to resort to a convenient label or to suggest any limitations of theme or subject matter. The tenor of Oates's prose, however—her distinctive "voice"—often conveys the kind of extreme psychological intensity, and occasionally the outright horror, traditionally associated with gothic fiction. As Oates commented in 1980, "gothic with a small-letter 'g' " suggests "a work in which extremes of emotion are unleashed"—a description which could be applied to virtually all her novels. Whether rich or poor, cultured or uneducated, the majority of her characters live within a psychological pressure-cooker, responding to intense personal and societal conflicts which lead almost inevitably to violence. The critic G. F. Waller has discussed at length this "obsessive vision" at the heart of Oates's rendering of the American reality. As Oates herself has observed, "Gothicism, whatever it is, is not a literary tradition so much as a fairly realistic assessment of modern life.

Oates has also used the gothic tradition explicitly in short stories dealing with the paranormal, collected in *Night-Side* (1979), and in her cycle of genre novels begun in 1980, novels appropriately described by Oates as Gothic "with a capital-letter G." In *Bellefleur* (1980), *A Bloodsmoor Romance* (1982) and *Mysteries of Winterthurn* (1984), Oates combines her usual psychological realism with a free-wheeling, explicit use of fantasy, fairy tales, horror stories, and other Gothic elements; the central settings of all three novels, for instance, include a huge, forbidding mansion and such assorted horrors as a female vampire (*Bellefleur*) and a painting which comes to life and murders a couple on their honeymoon (*Mysteries of Winterthurn*). . . . [Of *Bellefleur,* Oates said] "I set out originally to create an elaborate, baroque, barbarous metaphor for the unfathomable mysteries of the human imagination, but soon became involved in very literal events."

Her handling of these "literal events" shows a characteristic inclusiveness in her desire to present a sweeping social and philosophical vision of American history. Oates has described her specific attraction to the Gothic mode in these novels:

> To 'see' the world in terms of heredity and family destiny and the vicissitudes of Time (for all five novels are secretly fables of the American family); to explore historically authentic crimes against women, children, and the poor; to create, and to identify with, heroes and heroines whose existence would be problematic in the clinical, unkind, and one might almost say, fluorescent-lit atmosphere of present-day fiction—these factors proved irresistible.
>
> (pp. 17-20)

It should be clear that despite the sheer abundance and inclusiveness of Oates's fiction, her work does not represent an aesthetic surrender to the chaos of "real life" or the failure of a driven, highly productive artist to organize her materials; yet such well-known critics as Alfred Kazin and Walter Sullivan, accustomed to the more typical modern writer who might manage a single book every five or even ten years, leveled exactly these charges against her work in the 1970s and helped create the impression of Oates as a careless, haphazard writer, working in a trancelike state and continually pouring forth novels and stories without adequate concern for their literary integrity or coherence. (pp. 20-1)

Critics in the 1980s occasionally repeat these charges, but one suspects that they cannot have read Oates's work very extensively or thoughtfully. As the late John Gardner remarked in an appreciative review of *Bellefleur,* "for pseudo-intellectuals there are always too many books," and over the years Oates has patiently responded to the charges of excessive productivity. (pp. 21-2)

Late twentieth-century criticism, nourished on modernist and postmodernist works, has frequently devalued or simply lost sight of the artist as a committed, energetic craftsman, producing the kinds of ambitious, socially relevant novels that had virtually defined the genre in the Victorian era. Such esteemed nineteenth-century writers as Dickens, Balzac, Trollope and Henry James all wrote steadily, daily, and produced many volumes, unharassed by critical suggestions that they slow down or stop altogether. The modernist conception of the creative process as infinitely slow and tortuous, resulting in a single exquisite work after long years of painstaking labor, combined with the particularly American view of the writer as a hero of experience, like Ernest Hemingway or F. Scott Fitzgerald, someone who must travel the world, live as colorfully as possible, and preferably drink to excess, has perhaps influenced critical attacks on Oates, who not only writes voluminously but leads a quiet, disciplined life that she once called "a study in conventionality." And much of the criticism clearly stems, as Oates herself has noted, from simple envy.

Any reader making his way through such a skillfully paced family chronicle as *them,* or the complicated series of interlocking tales that comprise *Bellefleur,* or an intricately constructed political novel like *Angel of Light* (1981), can have little doubt that Oates is an extremely careful and deliberate craftsman. . . . Occasionally her patience in the face of critical attacks has worn thin. In 1979 she emphasized her dedication to craftsmanship, reacting angrily to one critic's speculation that she wrote in a trancelike state, "a fever of possession": "I revise extensively. I am passionate about the craftsmanship of writing. I am perfectly conscious when I write, and at other selected times. . . . Will I never escape such literary-journalism drivel? Year after year, the same old cliches."

Oates will probably never escape the "drivel" of those critics who prefer attacking her to considering thoughtfully her voluminous, carefully written works. What matters to Oates is the work itself, not its critical reception or her own notoriety. Despite her occasional remarks hinting at exhaustion, her passionate engagement with her craft continues. . . . Despite the occasional criticism, her reputation continues to grow not only in the United States but worldwide: she is a member of the American Academy and Institute of Arts and Letters, and has been nominated several times for the Nobel Prize for literature. Although it is pointless to speculate about which of her works future generations will consider her masterpiece—quite possibly, she has not yet written the book that will be viewed as representing the full range of her talents—it is clear that Joyce Carol Oates has already earned her place alongside the major American writers of the twentieth century. (pp. 22-5)

Greg Johnson, in his *Understanding Joyce Carol Oates,* University of South Carolina Press, 1987, 224 p.

SOURCES FOR FURTHER STUDY

Bastian, Katherine. *Joyce Carol Oates's Short Stories: Between Tradition and Innovation.* Frankfurt am Main: Verlag Peter Lang, 1983, 173 p.

> Study focusing on Oates's short stories. Bastian examines Oates's reworking of classic short stories, her experimentation with traditional short story genres, and her creation of short story cycles.

Bender, Eileen Teper. *Joyce Carol Oates, Artist in Residence.* Bloomington and Indianapolis: Indiana University Press, 1987, 207 p.

> Critical study of Oates's novels. Bender writes: "It is the intention of this study to consider Joyce Carol Oates as a writer who is always in some sense a critic, and to define her intentions and achievements as part of a larger statement about contemporary American life and letters."

Creighton, Joanne V. *Joyce Carol Oates.* Twayne's United States Authors Series, edited by Warren French, no. 321. Boston: Twayne Publishers, 1979, 173 p.

> Biographical and critical study, focusing on Oates's short stories and novels published from 1963 to 1976.

Grant, Mary Kathryn. *The Tragic Vision of Joyce Carol Oates.* Durham, N.C.: Duke University Press, 1978, 167 p.

> Discusses Oates's focus on violence and the tragic aspects of modern life throughout her fiction.

Oates, Joyce Carol. "The Nature of Short Fiction; or, The Nature of My Short Fiction." Preface to *Handbook of Short Story Writing,* edited by Frank A. Dickson and Sandra Smythe, pp. xi-xviii. Cincinnatti: Writer's Digest, 1973.

> Autobiographical statement examining the personal motivations behind her fiction.

Wagner, Linda W., ed. *Critical Essays on Joyce Carol Oates.* Critical Essays on American Literature, edited by James Nagel. Boston: G. K. Hall & Co., 1979, 180 p.

> Collection of reviews and critical essays, with a preface by Oates.

Flannery O'Connor

1925-1964

(Full name Mary Flannery O'Connor) American short story writer, novelist, and essayist.

INTRODUCTION

O'Connor is considered one of the foremost short story writers in American literature. She was an anomaly among post-World War II authors—a Roman Catholic from the Bible-belt South whose stated purpose was to reveal the mystery of God's grace in everyday life. Aware that not all readers shared her faith, O'Connor chose to depict salvation through shocking, often violent action upon characters who are spiritually or physically grotesque. Commenting on this tendency toward bizarre action and caricature, she explained: "To the hard of hearing you shout and for the almost blind you draw large and startling figures." While O'Connor used exaggeration to express her ideas, her prose is considered compressed and brilliantly polished. Moreover, her penchant for employing ironic detachment and mordant humor prompted some critics to classify O'Connor as an existentialist or nihilist. She also infused her fiction with the local color and rich comic detail of her southern milieu, particularly through her skillful presentation of regional dialect. A complex system of symbolism and allegory adds further resonance to O'Connor's writing.

O'Connor was the only child of devout Roman Catholics from prominent Georgia families. She attended parochial schools in Savannah and public high school in Milledgeville, where the family moved after her father developed disseminated lupus, the degenerative disease that O'Connor later inherited. Soon after her father's death when she was nearly sixteen, O'Connor entered the nearby Georgia State College for Women, where she majored in social sciences. In her spare time she edited and wrote for school publications to which she also contributed linoleum block and woodcut cartoons. O'Connor then enrolled in the graduate writing program at Iowa State University, where she earned her Master's degree in 1947 with six stories, including "The Geranium," which had appeared the previous year in the periodical *Accent.* Throughout her career, O'Connor's stories were readily published, occasionally by popular magazines such as *Mademoiselle,* but more often by prestigious literary journals including *Sewanee Review, Shenandoah,* and *Kenyon Review.*

O'Connor began her first novel, *Wise Blood,* while living at Yaddo writers' colony in upstate New York in 1947-48. She continued working on the novel while living in New York City and then in Connecticut, where she boarded with her friends Sally and Robert Fitzgerald, a young married couple who shared O'Connor's Catholic faith and literary interests. However, O'Connor's independent lifestyle ended abruptly at age twenty-five when she suffered her first attack of lupus. From that point onward, O'Connor lived with her mother at Andalusia, a small dairy farm outside Milledgeville. She maintained a steady writing pace, publishing *Wise Blood* in 1952, followed by the story collection *A Good Man Is Hard to Find* in 1955, and a second novel, *The Violent Bear It Away,* in 1960. Each volume attracted significant critical attention, and she was awarded three O. Henry prizes for her short stories in addition to several grants and two honorary degrees. As her reputation grew, she traveled when her health permitted to give readings and lectures. O'Connor also enjoyed such pastimes as oil-painting and raising exotic fowl—peacocks, her particular favorites, bear significant symbolic weight in some of her stories. Even during her final illness, which was triggered by abdominal surgery, O'Connor wrote devotedly, and she finished her final story, "Parker's Back," several weeks before she died.

In her fiction O'Connor frequently criticizes the materialism and spiritual apathy of contemporary society, faulting modern rationalism for its negation of the need for religious faith and redemption. Employing scenes and characters from her native southern environment, she depicts the violent and often bizarre religiosity of Protestant fundamentalists as a manifestation of spiritual life struggling to exist in a nonspiritual world. The protagonists of both of her novels—Hazel Motes in *Wise Blood* and Francis Marion Tarwater in *The Violent Bear It Away*—experience intense spiritual conflict. Often considered "Christ-haunted" characters, they are tormented by visions of God and the devil and by the temptation to deny the reality of their revelations. Critics have described O'Connor's protagonists as grotesque in personality, inclined to violence, and isolated and frustrated by their spiritual struggle.

Reflecting the religious themes of her novels, a recurrent motif in O'Connor's thirty-one short stories is that of divine grace descending in an often bizarre or violent manner upon a spiritually deficient main character. She often depicts a rural domestic situation sud-

denly invaded by a criminal or perverse outsider—a distorted Christ figure who redeems a protagonist afflicted with pride, intellectualism, or materialism. In one of O'Connor's best-known stories, "A Good Man Is Hard to Find," for example, a smugly self-complacent grandmother is shocked into spiritual awareness by a murderer who kills first her family and then her. The story reflects O'Connor's comment regarding her work: "The look of this fiction is going to be wild . . . it is almost of necessity going to be violent and comic, because of the discrepancies it seeks to combine." Critics have noted that O'Connor's tales, while expressing intense action, are related in concise, almost epigrammatic prose. They have also praised her use of richly complex imagery and symbols, observing that spiritual meaning is often conveyed through vivid descriptions of nature in her works.

O'Connor's artistic style and vision were shaped by a variety of influences. Critics have noted that her stark imagery, caustic satire, and use of the grotesque reflects the black humor tradition exemplified by Nathanael West, whose novel *Miss Lonelyhearts* was among the twentieth-century works O'Connor most admired. While some commentators were eager to align O'Connor with her southern contemporaries, such as Eudora Welty, Carson McCullers, and Erskine Caldwell, she resisted being confined to regional status, and critics now generally recognize that her aims were wholly different from those of her contemporaries. Nevertheless, many critics note the influence of William Faulkner's fiction on her vision of the southern gothic and her masterful prose rhythms and cadences. Most crucial, however, and underlying all O'Connor's fiction, is her deep grounding in biblical tradition and Catholic theology, which she nurtured all her life with intense reading in not only early Catholic literature, but also works by twentieth-century Catholic apologists. Particularly significant among modern influences were the French Catholic authors Georges Bernanos, François Mauriac, and Pierre Teilhard de Chardin, whose philosophical writings inspired the title of O'Connor's posthumous short story collection, *Everything That Rises Must Converge* (1965).

The predominant feature of O'Connor criticism is its abundance. From her first collection, O'Connor garnered serious and widespread critical attention, and since her death the outpouring has been remarkable, including hundreds of essays and numerous full-length studies. While her work has occasioned some hostile reviews, including those which labeled her an atheist or accused her of using the grotesque gratuitously, she is almost universally admired, if not fully understood. In addition to wide-ranging studies of her style, structure, symbolism, tone, themes, and influences, critical discussion often centers on theological aspects of O'Connor's work. In inquiries into the depth of her religious intent, critics usually find O'Connor to be the orthodox Christian that she adamantly declared herself, although some trace the violence and sense of evil in her work to what John Hawkes termed an "essential diabolicism."

(For further information about O'Connor's life and works, see *Contemporary Authors First Revision*, Vol.

1; *Contemporary Authors New Revision Series*, Vol. 3; *Contemporary Literary Criticism*, Vols. 1, 2, 3, 6, 10, 13, 15, 21; *Dictionary of Literary Biography*, Vol. 2: *American Novelists Since World War II*; *Dictionary of Literary Biography Yearbook: 1980*; and *Short Story Criticism*, Vol. 1.)

CRITICAL COMMENTARY

MICHAEL D. TRUE

(essay date 1969)

[In the following excerpt, True discusses themes of Christian redemption in O'Connor's fiction.]

[Flannery O'Connor] brought a vision as accurate and piercing as any Old Testament prophet; and her work, like the prophets', was aimed at quickening the conscience and calling an estranged people to the tragic glory of God's chosen. . . . In the fiction of Flannery O'Connor one finds a . . . preoccupation with the woes and evils of a decaying civilization—a civilization in which the law and fervor and even fanaticism of the backwoods prophets test the metal of the prophets of the secular city, the mouth-wash liberals and Northern do-gooders, and warns them, in the words of Isaiah . . . : "Woe to you that are wise in your own eyes, and prudent in your own conceits . . . for they have cast away the law of the Lord of hosts, and have blasphemed the world of the Holy One of Israel" (5:24). A dominant theme in her fiction strongly resembles the lament of the Prophet: "The city of thy sanctuary is become a desert, Sion is made a desert, Jerusalem is desolate. The house of our holiness, and of our glory, where our fathers praised thee, is burnt with fire, and all our lovely things are turned into ruins" (64:10-11).

Unlike many of the writers of the past century who confronted essentially religious questions, sometimes even consciously exploiting traditional Christian symbolism (T. S. Eliot and Graham Greene, for example), Flannery O'Connor spoke openly—never defensively—about her religious mission as a fiction writer. Like any great writer, she understood extraordinarily well her own limitations and assumed the responsibilities of her craft within these limits. She knew that she spoke to an audience that did not share her preoccupations, her feeling that "the meaning of life is centered in our Redemption by Christ . . . and that what I see in the world I see in its relation to that." So she had to find a way of conveying the fact of Redemption to an audience, readers of fiction in the 1950's, who dis-

missed any Christian principle or, worse, did not care enough even to deny Salvation. The not caring about Redemption was to her a distortion—a more serious distortion than the physical disabilities or the mental deficiencies of her characters, both heroes and villains. Asked once why her people were so grotesque, she answered that she would be willing to argue whether her characters were really more grotesque than the man in the gray flannel suit; whether a man was truly grotesque or not depended upon your angle of vision and the strength of your perception. In order to "make these appear as distortions to an audience which is used to seeing them as 'natural,' " she had to make her vision apparent "by shock—to the hard of hearing you shout, and for the almost blind you draw large and startling figures."

Whether or not Flannery O'Connor conveyed this vision will depend upon the reader to some extent, I suppose; obviously, in some of her stories this vision is not conveyed as effectively as it is in others. The meaning, "the integrity of the completed form" (in Northrop Frye's phrase), is less clear; the vision is delivered in an injured state, without unity; occasionally the story is a mixed bag of humorous episodes, peculiar characters, and violent events. But even in these failures she manages to escape the doom, once described by Chad Walsh as the unlucky fate of the Christian writer who manages to be only "an esoteric, coterie figure, speaking only to those who share his pair of eyes."

She manages to escape this trap by the use of comic irony which, in her work, helps the reader see the world consistently and see it whole, aware—but never self-consciously aware—of the intelligent narrator who takes him through the Inferno, never passing up a chance to remind him that he is, after all, in hell. Some of the characters are evil . . . , some ripe for redemption (Obadiah Elihue Parker in **"Parker's Back,"** Mrs. McIntyre in **"The Displaced Person"**); and others merely gross and shiftless, like Mrs. May's hired man in **"Greenleaf."** . . . But all the types inhabit the same universe, and often one is as likely as the other to be

Principal Works

Wise Blood (novel) 1952

A Good Man Is Hard to Find (short stories) 1955

The Violent Bear It Away (novel) 1960

Everything That Rises Must Converge (short stories) 1965

Mystery and Manners: Occasional Prose (nonfiction) 1969

The Habit of Being: Letters of Flannery O'Connor 1979

Flannery O'Connor: Collected Works 1988

the recipient of God's grace. In this chaotic world, the just and the unjust await redemption, and like stupid Mr. Greenleaf, they may become the instrument of salvation, that "strange discovery" Mrs. May makes through Mr. Greenleaf just as she dies.

Now this irony would not be so powerful if, as in the work of other modern writers (Katherine Anne Porter, Eudora Welty, and sometimes Faulkner), there was not such a strong basis for the standard of behavior applied here. In the best stories, in **"Revelation"** or *Wise Blood,* for example, the irony is never detached; it is not merely the play of a sensibility about surfaces. In a brief preface to the second edition of *Wise Blood,* Miss O'Connor called the book "a comic novel . . . and as such, very serious, for all comic novels that are any good must be about matters of life and death." The statement reminds one of the tradition within which she writes, and it explains also why, like many comic writers, from Aristophanes to Evelyn Waugh, she combines a radically conservative religious position with a great distrust of detached intellectualism and shuns such "easy" terms as compassion and tolerance. If she often, in her fiction, defends the indefensible, a woman prejudiced toward Negroes or a man who is a religious fanatic, it is because she insists upon recognizing the strengths of these people—their family loyalty and bumbling generosity—and particularly their capacity for grace and redemption. If her stories indicate an anguish, she once said (she satirized in her fiction and at times in conversation the popularized *Time*-magazine-style existential *angst*), it is that the South "is not alienated enough," that the region is being forced out "not only of our many sins but of our few virtues. This may be unholy anguish but it is anguish nevertheless." For her, the Southern narrative tradition and the Christhaunted environment were virtues not to be lost to "them cold interleckchuls" up North. (pp. 212-15)

I mention the region here because, in defining and understanding the nature of her heroes, the backwoods prophets, one must understand the importance of region in the formation of the religious temperament. She never pretends that the region (the backwoods) is all good, just as she never claims that the South is necessarily Christ-centered. . . . But, for the religious vision of both those who preach the Church *With* Christ . . . or those who preach the Church *Without* Christ . . . , the backwoods origin is a source of their strength. Jesus lives in the woodland country; and those who lose Him temporarily in the city (such as little Bevel in **"The River,"** and the idiot child in *The Violent Bear It Away*) find "the Kingdom of Christ in the river" or in the primitive surroundings of a Southern revival. (pp. 215-16)

In the city, the Christian message degenerates into a social, life-adjustment message; the blood of the lamb becomes the milk of human kindness; the salt loses its savor. Miss O'Connor is never confident that, without an iron faith and a kind of fanatic zeal, the Christian message will survive in the midst of the corrupting, "civilized" urban intelligence that threatens to reason us out of our reason. She is careful, however, not to make her indictment against the modern city too generalized, and she seems often at pains not to confuse and to mistake secularization and dechristianization, while at the same time insisting upon the necessary distinction between the secular and the sacred. As with all prophets, however, she never doubts that there is a difference. Her suspicions are those of the traditionalist that "all who seek to interpret revelation by reason alone inevitably reduce it to a secular truth and eliminate mystery." (pp. 216-17)

Her stories explore again and again that area of man's experience which "remains sacred and never becomes secular," where God is present to men and faith is never "mastered by human intelligence." As a writer of fiction, however, Miss O'Connor could not enjoy the luxury of merely figurative language. Like the prophets, she might have tried to "convey by analogie a remote idea of the reality of which they speak." But unlike the prophets, she had to convey the idea in flesh and blood fact, as well. As readers we participate in her narrative, her ritual, through our response to rhythm and pattern. For the modern reader, the word must be made flesh first, before it can move beyond immediate reality to total significance and symbolic meaning. In the stories . . . , the Word becomes flesh particularly and paradoxically through the demonic characters. The reader experiences it viscerally, as she intended, shocked into the recognition that for these anti-Christs, the matters they are concerned with *count.*

The peculiar nature of her demonic "heroes," the backwoods anti-prophets, is best illustrated by characters in three stories, the Misfit in **"A Good Man Is Hard To Find,"** Rufus Johnson in **"The Lame Shall Enter First,"** and Manley Pointer, the Bible salesman in **"Good Country People."** . . . In these prophetic tales, the "villain" is often treated very sympathetically; he becomes, in these thinly disguised romances (Good and Evil jousting for the highest stakes), a hero of a religious quest. (pp. 217-18)

The paradox of keeping Christ alive by making heroes of His most formidable antagonists lies in the center of Miss O'Connor's fiction, best illustrated by a remarkable story in the post-humously published volume called **"The Lame Shall Enter First."** The central character, a fourteen-year-old boy named Rufus Johnson, brings the message of Christ, salvation, and agonizing love to a man named Sheppard and his son, by taking the devil's part. Rufus recognizes that Sheppard, for all his condescending tolerance, is an atheist; having failed to continue the religious education of his son after the death of his wife, Sheppard prides himself on his intelligence and his no-nonsense, anti-Biblical humanism. He has destroyed any remnants of his son's religious faith, and he tries his pseudopsychology on Rufus, in an effort to "save" him from his ridiculous beliefs in the resurrection and the prophets. But Sheppard is completely unsuccessful with his scheme; in fact, Rufus wins Sheppard's son, Norton, to his side by telling the boy stories from the Bible. Eventually, Norton, in an effort to "rejoin" his mother in the sky, commits suicide.

Rufus is the son of a backwoods prophet, a descendant of a man with the terrible vision of the religious fanatic. When Norton asks Rufus once where his father has gone, Rufus tells him, "He's gone with a remnant of the hills . . . Him and some others. They're going to bury some Bibles in a cave and take two of different kinds of animals and all like that. Like Noah. Only this time it's going to be fire, not flood." The glory of Rufus is that he believes in it, too; that is the reason he chooses the devil's part, submitting to Satan's power, as he says, with a kind of joy. . . . For Rufus, Satan's friend, there is only one Jesus Christ. For him, as for Flannery O'Connor, one of the major sins is for anyone else to behave as if he were Christ, without the proper respect for His Book, and for His enemy, the devil.

The trouble with Sheppard is that, with all his education, his dogooder philosophy, he never knows evil when he sees it and, consequently, is easily victimized by a really evil person like Rufus Johnson. His stupidity is shared by many of the educated people in Flannery O'Connor's fiction: by Rayber, the nephew of a backwoods prophet in *The Violent Bear It Away,* . . . by Asbury, the maudlin undergraduate who comes home to die in **"The Enduring Chill"** . . . by Mary Grace, the fat, ugly Wellesley girl (her face "blue with acne") who sits and scowls over a book entitled *Human Development,* in **"Revelation."**

But the stupidity of all these characters is outdone by the central character in another of the early stories, **"Good Country People."** Hulga (née Joy) Hopewell is

a woman with a Ph.D. in philosophy, an artificial leg, and no common sense. Hulga feels superior to her mother and her friends because of her formal education—she's read the existentialists and the logical positivists (or at least has picked up a few clichés about them) and decided, like any other "thinking modern," that the world is blind chaos. One day an itinerant Bible salesman named Pointer, describing himself as a simple country boy making a living by spreading the word of God, comes to her house and wins her mother's affection by exchanging clichés, much in the manner of the Grandmother and Sammy Butts in **"A Good Man is Hard to Find."** He indicates an interest in Hulga. . . . When the Bible salesman makes advances, she agrees to meet him in the barn loft. As it turns out, however, he is more interested in seeing how her artificial leg hooks on and off than in making love to her, especially since she's "too intelligent" to say she loves him with much feeling. (pp. 219-21)

The Bible salesman, like the Misfit and Rufus, are obviously heroes for Miss O'Connor. If the secularist pseudo-Christians (the social workers, psychologists, sociologists, existentialist philosophers) find no antagonists in the true believer among the faithful, they should find a real antagonist in the devil, in the Satanic characters who give witness to Christ by wilfully defying Him. In the stories described here, the weak in spirit, the vulgar in speech, the superficial and even insipid in moral and religious values, the demonic characters often stand out clearly as the ones to be preferred. Better the honesty and directness of the latter than the vapid, pseudoethic of the ubiquitous, condescending mouth-wash liberal, Miss O'Connor seems to say; in a chaotic world, plagued by casual violence and meaningless pursuits, she finds much to admire in those valiant foes who take the devil's part knowingly and enthusiastically, bent on the annihilation of a world without meaning. . . .

In **"A Good Man Is Hard to Find," "The Lame Shall Enter First,"** and **"Good Country People,"** the myth of the triumph of the powers of darkness is recounted with great vividness; and at the end of each story the personification of evil, having banished the pretenders to reason and good sense, triumphs. Evil, one discovers, has through the creative power of language, been given a kind of magnificent, if destructive form. Whether the world harbors forces of light sufficiently strong to triumph over the powers of darkness is not entirely clear in the body of Flannery O'Connor's fiction. (p. 222)

What Flannery O'Connor does in her fiction is to confront the crisis of divinity in the modern world without hesitancy and at times without hope. As in the Biblical prophets, whenever she found God, He brought not peace, but a sword. Divinity lived for her, not as for the woman in [Wallace] Stevens' "Sunday

Morning," "within herself," but in the fiery furnace of violent death or severe judgment.

She finds God in the backwoods prophet, in the misfit, in sin, in deformity, in guilt, in perversion—as if it were necessary "to traffic with insanity," as Michael Harrington said of Thomas Mann, in order to make sense out of a mad world. God lives more surely, she seems to say, among those who boldly deny Him or cannot find Him; He seems most absent from those who pretend to call His name. In her stories, however joyful the sweet music of salvation, the prophet's news that God is not dead, after all, strikes man's untrained ears with the harshness of a sonic boom. He receives the prophecy of his redemption, "with the look of a person whose sight has been suddenly restored but who finds the light unbearable."

Maybe, to conclude on a somewhat more positive note, through a character like the young Francis Marion Tarwater, in *The Violent Bear It Away*, the work of the Redemption will be continued. At the end of the novel, the young inventor of the Law succeeds in fulfilling the mission imposed upon him by his uncle. He baptizes Rayber's idiot child (though drowning him in the process), and receives the prophet's command, heralded by a red-gold tree of fire: "He knew that this was the fire that had encircled Daniel, that had raised Elijah from the earth, that had spoken to Moses and would in the instant speak to him. He threw himself to the ground and with his face against the dirt of the grave, he heard the command, GO WARN THE CHILDREN OF GOD OF THE TERRIBLE SPEED OF MERCY." The vessel of honor, like the power of darkness, brings a rather terrifying fate. Although the difference between the Misfit, the antiprophet, and young Tarwater, the true prophet, is obvious on one level, on another level, it is rather slight. Tarwater moves into "the dark city," "where the children of God lay sleeping," with much the same fierceness as the Misfit does, doing meanness: "His singed eyes, black in their deep sockets, seemed already to envision the fate that awaited him." Both are children of the backwoods with a mission in the modern city—one to destroy and another to warn. But as religious heroes, reminiscent in their awful strength of the paradoxical relationship between the great sinner and the great saint, they both move with "a terrible speed" and with a singlemindedness that the reader is forced to admire. (pp. 222-23)

Michael D. True, "Flannery O'Connor: Backwoods Prophet in the Secular City," in *Papers on Language & Literature*, Vol. V, No. 1, Winter, 1969, pp. 209-23.

JOSEPHINE HENDIN
(essay date 1970)

[In the essay excerpted below, Hendin focuses on the isolation and brutality experienced by O'Connor's protagonists.]

The fiction O'Connor lived had its roots in that Southern need to do pretty regardless of what you feel, and in her own remarkable ability to divorce behavior from feeling and even to conceal feelings from herself. Much as she hated the Mrs. Hopewells, Mrs. Mays, and Mrs. Turpins she wrote about, she was, in many ways, like them. . . . She seems to have gone through the motions of conventional behavior without becoming deeply involved in the conventional world around her and without expecting any deep human contact. She . . . seems to have been oddly out of touch with those more essential feelings that explode in her work. And it is through her very ability to detach herself from those feelings that she came closest to being what she had never admired: a Southern Lady. (p. 13)

The great strength of O'Connor's fiction seems to me to spring from the silent and remote rage that erupts from the quiet surface of her stories and that so unexpectedly explodes. It appears, for example, when the Misfit with great politeness has the family exterminated, or when he answers the grandmother's "niceness" with a gunshot and thereby suggests that neither Christian charity nor Southern politeness can contain all the darker human impulses. It appears again in the punishment of the vain, self-satisfied Mrs. Turpin, who gets a book thrown at her. Perhaps it has a quieter voice in those sweetly nasty comments Mrs. Turpin's Negroes make as they talk among themselves to comfort her: "You the sweetest lady I know." "She pretty too." "And stout." And perhaps it is there in the impulses of all those resentful sons and daughters in the pages of Flannery O'Connor's fiction who are frozen in an extended, rebellious adolescence where, in a perpetual dependency because of illness or fear, the price they ought to pay for being cared for is silence, acquiescence to an effective, controlling, exasperatingly polite, and very removed mother. (pp. 14-15)

To assume [as some critics do] that her work is merely a monologue on redemption is to see it only in part, to ignore much of its meaning, and to lose sight of the believer behind the belief. My own feeling is that O'Connor never merely wrote about Redemption, but that the very act of writing was itself a redemptive process for her. It may have been the only, and perhaps unconscious, way she could express all the contradictions within her. . . . I do not think O'Connor's fiction can be explained by her Catholicism alone. (p. 17)

Flannery O'Connor . . . created an art that is, in many instances, as emotionally flat as Robbe-Grillet's, an art where object and gesture simply *are.* In Flannery O'Connor's most powerful fiction, to paraphrase William Carlos Williams, there are no ideas about things, there are only the things themselves. (p. 23)

O'Connor's characters are, in general, so estranged from their emotional life that they feel their emotions do not even belong to them. They seem to belong to someone else, a stranger who is, nevertheless oddly familiar; a double who, in some way, recapitulates their own experience. Her heroes are so emotionally dead that they can perform the most outrageous acts without any conscious awareness of feelings of elation or despair. It is not surprising that the Misfit corrects his comment that there's "no pleasure but meanness," with "It's no real pleasure in life."

Believing that the only relation possible between men and between men and things is "strangeness," Robbe-Grillet claims to record the distance between objects and reified men without an emotional sense of loss. While O'Connor sometimes achieves a similar detachment in isolated scenes, she usually displays a certain joy in human isolation, a perverse relish for it. She may resemble Robbe-Grillet in style, create characters as emotionally flat as his, and stress the mechanical quality of life, but she never merely reproduces a neutral universe or records the distance between men. O'Connor does not reflect the real world; she reduces it.

Many of O'Connor's stories move by a process of constriction in which abstract, spiritual, or expansive longings shrink into a concrete act, an act that is with remarkable frequency akin to murder or suicide. Since she never treats interiors of thought or feeling, these acts are forced to bear the entire meaning of the story. As I have suggested, they are usually effected quietly and without apparent emotion. Yet, . . . action erupts from an emotional void so frequently in O'Connor's work that you are forced to see the peculiar combination as one of her preoccupations. (pp. 24-5)

O'Connor's heroes rarely want to feel compassion because they fear human contact more than they fear emotional death. . . . O'Connor's heroes can never connect with themselves or with others. They come closest in momentary acts of violence in which they murder or commit suicide. For the duration of the destructive act, for the moment in which they annihilate some human tie, they are able to come most powerfully alive, to transcend the otherwise engulfing emotional "ice." Yet O'Connor reduces and diminishes the significance of their acts by a variety of stylistic devices. As

I have said, she not only simplifies and objectifies her hero's psychological state at the moment of his most "passionate" act, she places that act near the end of her story, where it expresses the final step in the progressive reduction of symbolic meanings. Her reductive impulse is embedded in the structure of her stories, which, in general, move from the symbolic toward the objective. (p. 27)

O'Connor will often begin with an abstraction or metaphor that becomes more and more concrete as she continues. This is a way of destroying the significance of symbols, of making them specific and concrete or, in other words, of making the spiritual physical or the abstract literal. . . . (pp. 27-8)

O'Connor not only destroys all transcendent qualities by burying them in the body, she regards the body itself as repulsive. In her love for the material, her obsession with animal reality—perhaps best shown by the ubiquitous hogs that fill her world—she resembles the creators of what has been called the literature of disgust, best known from the work of William Burroughs and Hubert Selby, Jr. Considering the absence of visceral prose in O'Connor's work, such a comparison may seem unlikely at first. Yet her work has a similar impulse and direction. Burroughs' image of ultimate reality—the junkie naked in the sunlight—is not unlike Mrs. Turpin's final vision of her pigs luminous at sunset. . . . Burroughs, Selby, and O'Connor write about people trapped within their own bodies, figuratively drowning in their own juices. O'Connor describes visually what they describe tactilely and, substituting an obsession for violence and religion for their concern with sex and drugs, makes a similar statement in a less "sensuous" way. Like so many American writers of the last century, O'Connor substitutes a concern for deformity, murder, and religion for violent sexuality. In this she is traditional, but the affectless, mechanical quality of violence in her world, and the lack of profound human involvement, give her work a peculiar modernity. While the primary themes of her fiction are traditional . . . , O'Connor's development of what could be called the affectless grotesque makes her work remarkably new. (pp. 28-30)

[Conflict], most generally stated as one between the present and the past, appears in all O'Connor's work in different forms: psychological, social, religious. Its recurrence contributes to a body of work of remarkable uniformity and persistent design. O'Connor consistently expresses her themes as conflicts or embodies them in images of opposites. Whether she exalts her alienated hero (as she does in **"A Temple of the Holy Ghost"**) or burlesques him (as she does Motes in *Wise Blood*), all her heroes alternate between the same peculiar, almost contradictory forces: emotional death and violence, confusion and certainty, detachment from human contact and domination by it. (p. 30)

[Strife] finds a social and religious expression as a conflict between a secular, relativistic sense of life in which man is perfectible through reason and technology, and a religious belief in absolutes in which human evil and human suffering are unredeemable. The conflict between a secular and a religious sense of life appears in nearly all O'Connor's fiction, but it is expressed most powerfully when it is added to a social conflict between rural and urban life. . . .

Through O'Connor's cities stalk those *bêtes noires* she loves to thwart, the social worker and the teacher who advocate the examined life, human commitments, and the bonds of human compassion. (p. 31)

O'Connor's heroes, the saints and martyrs of her fictive world . . . are generally murderers, psychic cripples, sometimes freaks, always brutal men who have a sense of sin and think about God, sometimes. The Misfit's despair, murder of his "father," and imprisonment suggest one of O'Connor's pervasive metaphors for life: a prison in which man suffers for a crime he cannot remember. From a theological point of view, the crime may be original sin. But from a human standpoint, it is "ice in the blood." O'Connor's heroes have lost all sense of human kinship. . . . Having taken the right to act as inexplicably as God, O'Connor's hero finds himself in godlike isolation, alien to human suffering and joy. He can kill without pleasure or remorse. (pp. 35-6)

If violence in the social realist novels in the Thirties reflected the horror of life in Marxist terms, violence in O'Connor's work reflects a more modern brutality. O'Connor's most violent men have been so crushed by life that they suffer with remarkable passivity the alarming pity or open contempt of a society that does not value the "sanctity" of hermaphrodites or psychic freaks. They can never fully shout out their rage at any of the Authorities who shut them up in asylums, jails, or on isolated farms; who demand they analyze themselves, and whose pity or compassion render them still more impotent. It is only in acts of violence that they give voice to their mute fury.

Even in their violence O'Connor's heroes are estranged from their inmost rage. O'Connor always gives their fury a detached, oblique quality. (p. 36)

Images of burial or entrapment define every kind of human relation in O'Connor's incredibly hostile universe. It is not only social institutions, social workers, other people in general, and controlling parents in particular who can trap you; the very fact of growing up can do it. Images of entrapment often define adult life to a child. . . . [The] most prevalent relationship between people of all ages in O'Connor's fiction [is] oppressors and oppressed, murderers and victims. (p. 39)

I think O'Connor describes man's piggish qualities while ignoring his spiritual ones. That Holy Spirit dwelling within the hermaphrodite does not allow him to transcend his deformity, it conforms to its shape much as Joy-Hulga's identity took the shape of her artificial leg. Making her see her soul in terms of her body, and not her body in terms of her soul, it welds her further to her flesh. Like her description of the convent, O'Connor's treatment of the Holy Spirit seems to be ironic, undercutting, as it does, its power as a traditional symbol of transcendence. All the outward signs of invisible grace shown by her characters are signs of multilation, marks of deformity they cannot transcend. It may be that God can only be found in O'Connor's world in connection with finite, unredeemable human ugliness. Yet this seems unlikely to me.

What explodes from these stories is the sense that the Misfits, Shiftlets, Manley Pointers, and hermaphrodites are O'Connor's God. Their godliness resides precisely in their ability to escape from the chain of human involvements that binds Mrs. Crater to her daughter, Mrs. Hopewell to Hulga, and the child to her cousins. O'Connor's brutal heroes detach themselves from human problems by detaching themselves from life in human, familial terms.

O'Connor's heroes are gods because they have won freedom from the nexus of human needs and longings that always, for O'Connor's characters, ends in overpowering frustration and rage. They are beyond sexual desire, love, or compassion. As the stories in *Everything That Rises Must Converge* . . . explicitly show, the enduring crucifixion, the endless agony is close human contact. God, like the Misfit, is a force that can obliterate anguish, that can destroy all the "grandmothers" of the world—all the forces of tradition and family that bind people to each other. (pp. 94-6)

When her work is compared to such Southern contemporaries as William Faulkner, William Styron, and Truman Capote, its distinctive qualities become clear.

Those habitués of Southern fiction, the one-horse farmer, the outlaw, the peddler, the itinerant workman, and the black appear in the work of all four writers. Like other Southerners, they write about fundamentalist religion, display that distrust of intellect and abstraction claimed for the South by Robert Penn Warren, and show a world with violent contrasts filled with men doing violence to each other and to the land. Those animals, pecans, chicken coops, and trees that have become the furniture of postbellum Southern fiction can be found in the work of all four authors. Here the resemblances end.

Faulkner and Styron build their work on a different scale from O'Connor and Capote. Writing about man mythologizing himself, Faulkner and Styron give the least of his acts the greatest magnitude. The humblest of Faulkner's creations, that idiot Isaac Snopes in

The Hamlet who falls so passionately in love with his cow, achieves a depth of feeling no one in O'Connor's work ever reaches. Popeye and Temple Drake, whose closest analogue in O'Connor's work is the wooden Sarah Ham of **"The Comforts of Home,"** pursue their sexual violence with such pleasure and devotion that their sordidness achieves a cosmic stature, far exceeding the capacity of O'Connor's heroes, who find "it's no real pleasure in life." Styron's Nat Turner, like so many of the violent heroes of Southern fiction, from William Gilmore Simms's Guy Rivers through Bayard Sartoris, is a romantic transcending himself in his acts, mythologizing them even as he performs them. Like Joe Christmas of *Light in August,* Turner is an American Manfred, a Byronic hero of the Southern backwoods. Both Faulkner and Styron write poems about violence in which action disappears into lyricism, into the legend it creates.

Both O'Connor and the mature Capote write about a world without myths. Even ultimate acts have no power to suggest that feeling of meaning, that sense of overpowering significance that legends are made of. While Styron and Faulkner expand the dimensions of reality, O'Connor and Capote reduce or reflect them. (pp. 131-32)

O'Connor's fiction lacks that sense of the interpenetration of the past and present that such a traditionalist as Allen Tate considers essential to the writer with a sense of his homeland. The present and the past do not merge in her work but confront each other like monoliths. Where Faulkner could say, "The past is never dead. It is not even past," O'Connor's characters emerge almost historyless from the backwoods with no sense of the historical past and little of their own. (p. 133)

O'Connor's heroes are neither human, nor symbolic, nor heroic in any traditional sense. On one level, they are projections of O'Connor's fantasies of revolt; on another they are heroes of our time. O'Connor made fiction out of their emptiness, tragedies out of the ice in their blood. She cut so deep into that ice that she reached the general American tragedy of living in cold blood. This is the tragedy of being totally incapable of tragedy, of pervasive emotional death, of minimal human involvement. In committing herself creatively to characters who have neither soul nor depth, O'Connor made poetry out of the surface of reality. (pp. 153-54)

O'Connor's world has lost its symbols. It is filled with objects and acts which become signs of what things might mean, if they had significance, or what men might feel, if they felt at all. Her reductive, leveling impulse may be part of the demythologizing process in American fiction, a process usually associated with Northerners like William Carlos Williams or the more urbane Wallace Stevens. The career of

O'Connor's fellow Southerner, Capote, from his neo-gothic *Other Voices, Other Rooms* through *In Cold Blood* may indicate a similar process in Southern fiction. That both an avowed Catholic and a purveyor of rococo fantasies should be fascinated by the meaningless violence of men flat as the Kansas prairies may show that Southern literature is becoming as "Americanized" as the economy of Atlanta. But it is impossible to say for sure whether O'Connor's work anticipated or foretold the sensibility that would create *In Cold Blood,* or whether it suggests the direction Southern fiction will take in the future. (p. 156)

Josephine Hendin, in her *The World of Flannery O'Connor,* Indiana University Press, 1970, 177 p.

JANE CARTER KELLER
(essay date 1972)

[Below, Keller examines the satirical elements of O'Connor's fiction.]

Flannery O'Connor was a passionate critic of her age. As an orthodox and ardent Roman Catholic, she viewed the essentially godless condition of modern times as anathema and the secular society as doomed to depravity by its own wrongheaded refusal to recognize the truth of God and to follow God's commandments. She was particularly critical of the secular notion that men can define moral absolutes for themselves. Man's reliance upon reason to define such absolutes as goodness and compassion leads only to Auschwitz, she believed, for reason in men is by definition corrupt and can only be depended upon to lead to self-deception. Secular humanism, for all its professed unselfish idealism, leads not to the love that it posits as its goal but to the suicide of a whole civilization. Some of Miss O'Connor's best writing blazes with the force of her desire to make society look at the reality that it tries to ignore and to destroy men's illusions and pretenses about themselves and their times by exposing the naked truth. Such a confrontation with truth is all that can save the world in Flannery O'Connor's view, and to this end she wished to persuade her readers to share her critical attitude.

Miss O'Connor's stance in these matters is that of the satirist, and it is not surprising that she makes extensive use of satire in her fiction. Keenly aware of the indifference of her audience to Christian truth, she consciously and deliberately set out to enlarge, exaggerate, and distort, after what Leonard Feinberg calls the traditional manner of the satirist, and her purpose was to shock the willfully blind into seeing. In her stories and novels she plays with the reader's response and makes him think that the wild prophets and mad saints in her fiction are the objects of her satire; it is not these people, however, but rather the apparently saner men and women of the secular world whom she so devastatingly criticizes. Finally, it should be noted that the strength of this satiric attack against the people who represent the secular mode of thought reflects the power of the Christian belief from which she proceeds.

There are two types of men who are most often the targets of Flannery O'Connor's satire, and both are secular men who do not believe in God. One is the empiricist, who, like Hazel Motes at the beginning of *Wise Blood,* believes that only what one can empirically prove is true. . . . The second type of man she satirizes is the rationalist, like George Rayber in *The Violent Bear It Away,* who believes with Hegel that the real is rational and the rational real, that the universe has order which man by himself is capable of comprehending and of controlling, and that in the animal life of a man there is both dignity and worth. Men of both types believe that truth is objective and that subjectivity is not and cannot be truth. Both types are the products of the secularity that Miss O'Connor hated, and their fates point the lesson: cutting oneself adrift from God leads to despair, to spiritual death and damnation. Only those characters who can make a Kierkegaardian leap of faith are, in her opinion, saved from the spiritual abyss. (pp. 263-64)

The intent of Miss O'Connor's satiric treatment of the two types, the empiricists and the rationalists, is as clear and direct as the intent of Swift in *A Modest Proposal.* The reader's laughter at these people is meant to spur him into an examination of his own state of being. Unlike Hazel Motes, who was stunned by the nonbelievers of Taulkinham, Miss O'Connor knew altogether too well the spiritual state of the audience to which she spoke. In her view, secular men are fools to think they can deny God; they are fools to think they can define morality; they are fools to think they can play God. Not only is their foolishness ridiculous, it is disastrous for many of them. Because they regard themselves as the source of knowledge and wisdom, they can comprehend only things that are small enough to be dealt with in terms of a rational system. (p. 273)

Jane Carter Keller, "The Figures of the Empiricist and the Rationalist in the Fiction of Flannery O'Connor," in *Arizona Quarterly,* Vol. 28, No. 3, Autumn, 1972, pp. 263-73.

ANDRÉ BLEIKASTEN
(essay date 1978)

[In the following excerpt, Bleikasten discusses the major themes of O'Connor's fiction, emphasizing such religious elements as the juxtaposition of good and evil and the influence of grace.]

[No] reader can fail to discern the permanence and seriousness of [O'Connor's] religious concerns. Fall and redemption, nature and grace, sin and innocence—every one of her stories and novels revolves around these traditional Christian themes. It is hardly surprising that O'Connor should have acknowledged close affinities with Hawthorne. Her fiction is of a coarser fabric than his, less delicately shaded in its artistry and far less muted in its effects, but it belongs without any doubt to the same tradition of American romance: characters and plots matter less than "the power of darkness" one senses behind them; symbol, allegory, and parable are never far away, and with O'Connor as with Hawthorne, the accumulated mass of allusions and connotations derives in a very large measure from the rich mythology of Christian culture. The temptation is therefore great to decipher works like theirs through the cultural and hermeneutic codes which the Christian tradition provides, and in O'Connor's case it is all the more irresistible since we have the author's blessing. (pp. 53-4)

O'Connor's public pronouncements on her art—on which most of her commentators have pounced so eagerly—are by no means the best guide to her fiction. As an interpreter, she was just as fallible as anybody else, and in point of fact there is much of what she has said or written about her work that is highly questionable. The relationship between what an author thinks, or thinks he thinks, and what he writes, is certainly worth consideration. For the critic, however, what matters most is not the extent to which O'Connor's tales and novels reflect or express her Christian faith, but rather the problematical relation between her professed ideological stance and the textual evidence of her fiction.

Ideologically O'Connor was an eccentric. Her commitments were definitely off-center: antisecular, antiliberal, antiindividualistic, and she had as little patience with the cozy assumptions of conventional humanism as with the bland pieties and anemic virtues of its fashionable Christian variants. What counted for O'Connor was not so much man as his soul, and perhaps not so much his soul as the uncanny forces that prey on it. Hers is a world haunted by the sacred—a sacred with two faces now distinct and opposed, now enigmatically confused: the divine and the demonic. Hence, we find in most of her characters the double postulation noted by Baudelaire: one toward God, the other toward Satan.

In accordance with this dual vision, the human scene becomes in her fables the battleground where these two antagonistic powers confront each other and fight for possession of each man's soul. To judge from O'Connor's hellish chronicle, however, the chances hardly seem to be equal. To all appearances, Evil wins the day. Or rather: Satan triumphs. For in her world Evil is not just an ethical concept; it is an active force, and it has a name, personal, individual. In the middle of the twentieth century O'Connor, like Bernanos, was rash enough to believe not only in God but also in the Devil. And, like the French novelist, she had the nerve to incorporate him into her fiction. In *The Violent Bear It Away* we first hear his voice—the voice of the friendly "stranger" who accompanies young Tarwater during his tribulations; then we see him in the guise of a homesexual sporting a black suit, a lavender shirt, and a broad-rimmed panama hat. (pp. 54-5)

But the Devil does not have to strut about the stage to persuade us of his existence and power. Reflected in the implacable mirror O'Connor holds up to it, the whole world becomes transfixed in a fiendish grimace: mankind has apparently nothing to offer but the grotesque spectacle of its cruel antics. At first glance, it almost looks as if all souls had already been harvested by the Demon. For, despite O'Connor's firm belief in the existence of immortal souls, her world strikes us most often as utterly soulless. There is indeed little to suggest the "depths" and "secrets" of inner life which are the usual fare of religious fiction. The ordinary condition of most of her heroes is one of extreme emotional exhaustion and spiritual numbness, and from that catatonic torpor they only emerge to succumb to the destructive forces of violence or insanity. Moreover, in their deathlike apathy as well as in their sudden convulsions, O'Connor's characters are ruthlessly stripped of any pretense to dignity. People, in her fiction, suffer and die, but pettily, just as they are pettily evil. Wrenching from the Devil the dark, handsome mask afforded him by romantic satanism, O'Connor exposes his essential banality and restores him to his favorite hunting ground: the everyday world. The color of evil, in her work, is gray rather than black—a grim grayness set off by lurid splashes of red. Its face is difficult to distinguish from that of mediocrity, and its most characteristic expression is meanness. The banality of evil is what brings it within range of mockery: insofar as it thrives on human folly and wretchedness, it becomes laughable.

Yet with O'Connor laughter is never harmless, and her savage humor seldom provides comic release.

It is not an elegant way of defusing horror. Far from dissolving evil in farce, it emphasizes its demonic character, and calls attention to its terrifying power of perversion and distortion. Woven into the fabric of everydayness, evil becomes trivial, but at the same time the world of common experience is defamiliarized and made disquieting through its contagion by evil. Under Satan's sun the earth spawns monsters. O'Connor's tales drag us into a teratological nightmare, a ludicrous Inferno partaking at once of a hospital ward, a lunatic asylum, a menagerie, and a medieval *Cour des Miracles.* Like a Brueghel painting or a Buñuel film, the stories of *A Good Man Is Hard to Find* invite us to a sinister procession of freaks and invalids. . . . (p. 55)

O'Connor's penchant for freaks, idiots, and cripples, her fascination with the morbid, macabre, and monstrous, are traits she shares with many southern writers. The same gothic vein can be found to varying degrees in Erskine Caldwell, Eudora Welty, Carson McCullers, William Goyen, and Truman Capote, as well as in William Faulkner. Like them, she belongs to the manifold progeny of Poe. Yet the primal function assumed in her art by the grotesque cannot be explained away by fashion or tradition. Nor can one ascribe it merely to the gratuitous play of a perverse imagination. O'Connor used the grotesque very deliberately, and if it became one of her privileged modes, it was because she thought it fittest to express her vision of reality. As she herself stated, its meaning in her fiction is closely linked to her religious concerns; in her eyes, the grotesque can no more be dissociated from the supernatural than evil can be separated from the mysteries of faith. The grotesque has the power of revelation; it manifests the irruption of the demonic in man and brings to light the terrifying face of a world literally *dis-figured* by evil. The derangement of minds and deformity of bodies point to a deeper sickness, invisible but more irremediably tragic, the sickness of the soul. Gracelessness in all its forms indicates the absence of grace in the theological sense of the term.

This, at least, is how O'Connor vindicated her heavy reliance on grotesque effects and how she expected her readers to respond to them. Yet her vigorous denunciation of spiritual sickness is not devoid of ambiguity, and its ambiguity partly proceeds from the very rage with which she fustigates man's sins and follies. . . . Between her and her characters (with a few notable exceptions) lies all the distance of contempt, disgust, and derision, and it is the very harshness of the satire that arouses suspicion. . . . With methodic thoroughness and almost sadistic glee, O'Connor exploits all the resources of her talent to reduce the human to the nonhuman, and all her similes and metaphors have seemingly no other purpose than to degrade it to the inanimate, the bestial, or the mechanical. Like Gogol and Dickens, she possesses a weird gift for deadening people into things while quickening things into objects with a life of their own (Hazel's rat-colored Essex in *Wise Blood,* the giant steam shovel in **"A View of the Woods"**).

Hence a world both frozen and frantic, both ludicrous and threatening. O'Connor's landscapes—her fierce, fiery suns, her blank or blood-drenched skies, her ominous woods—are landscapes of nightmare. . . . Yet, even though O'Connor defended her use of the grotesque as a necessary strategy of her art, one is left with the impression that in her work it eventually became the means of a savage revilement of the whole of creation.

Questions then arise on the orthodoxy of her Catholicism. For Barbey d'Aurevilly, Catholicism was, in his own phrase, an old wrought-iron balcony ideally suited for spitting upon the crowd. It would be unfair, certainly, to suggest that O'Connor used it for similar purposes. Yet one may wonder whether her Catholicism was not, to some extent, an alibi for misanthropy. And one may also wonder whether so much black derision is compatible with Christian faith, and ask what distinguishes the extreme bleakness of her vision from plain nihilism. (pp. 56-7)

If we are to believe the Christian moralists, one of the Devil's supreme wiles is to leave us with the shattering discovery of our nothingness and so to tempt us into the capital sin of despair. From what one knows of O'Connor's life, it seems safe to assume that this was the temptation she found most difficult to resist, and it might be argued that her writing was in many ways a rite of exorcism, a way of keeping despair at a distance by projecting it into fiction. Small wonder then that in her work the demon of literary creation, as John Hawkes so judiciously noted, is inseparable from the Demon himself. When, as in *The Violent Bear It Away,* O'Connor makes the Devil speak, his sarcastic voice sounds startlingly like the author's. (p. 57)

Yet it is not enough to say that O'Connor was of the Devil's party. Many ironies and paradoxies interact in her work, and exegetes of Christian persuasion would probably contend that in its very abjection O'Connor's world testifies to the presense of the divine, the fall from grace being the proof *a contrario* of man's supernatural destination. O'Connor's heroes live mostly in extreme isolation, yet they are never truly alone. However entrenched in their smugness or embattled in their revolt, they find no safe shelter in their puny egos, and sooner or later, by degrees or—more often—abruptly, some invisible force breaks into their lives to hurl them far beyond themselves. They are *called*—called by whom? By what? How can anyone tell if the calling voice is God's or the Devil's?

A major theme in O'Connor's fiction, the enigma of *vocation,* is nowhere more fully explored than in her two novels. As most critics have pointed out, *Wise Blood* and *The Violent Bear It Away* offer very similar narrative and thematic patterns. Their heroes, Hazel Motes and Francis Marion Tarwater, are likewise obsessed by their vocation as preachers and prophets, and in both of them the obsession is significantly embodied in the figure of a despotic old man, the more formidable since he is dead: a fanatical grandfather, "with Jesus hidden in his head like a stinger" . . . for Hazel; a great-uncle no less single-minded and intolerant for young Tarwater. . . .

Prophets or false prophets? The question is not easy to answer. Many of O'Connor's backwoods preachers are simply frauds, and for a sincere Christian there is perhaps nothing more scandalous than religious imposture. . . . Satirizing southern evangelism, however, was obviously not O'Connor's main concern. Her preachers and prophets are by no means all vulgar charlatans. Nor are we supposed to regard them as lunatics. The reader is of course free to dismiss characters such as Hazel Motes or the two Tarwaters as insane, and to interpret their extravagant stories as cases of religious mania, but it is clear that this is not how the author intended them to be read. As a Roman Catholic, O'Connor must have had her reservations about the fanatic intolerance and apocalyptic theology of primitive fundamentalism. Yet, as she herself admitted on several occasions, its integrity and fervor appealed to her, for she found them congenial to the burning intransigence of her own faith. Her fascination with the southern evangelist—whom she came to envision as a crypto-Catholic—is not unlike the attraction Bernanos and Graham Greene felt for the priest figure. (p. 58)

In O'Connor violence rules man's relation to the sacred, just as it rules his relation to other men. Nothing here that suggests "spirituality": the word is too smooth, too polished, too blandly civilized to apply to the compulsions and convulsions of these savage souls. For Motes and Tarwater as well as for the "Misfit" of **"A Good Man Is Hard to Find,"** God is above all an idée fixe, and the divine is primarily experienced as an intolerable invasion of privacy, a dispossession—or possession—of the self. What torments O'Connor's heroes, at least at first glance, is not their being deprived of God, but rather the fact that their obsession with Him cannot be escaped. Religious experience, as it is rendered dramatically in her fiction, comes pretty close to Freud's definition: a variant of obsessional neurosis.

God is the Intruder. Therefore the first move of O'Connor's "prophet freaks" . . . is to resist or to flee. (p. 59)

Rebellious children, O'Connor's heroes assert themselves only by willful transgression of the divine order, as if only the certainty of flouting God's will and of doing evil could give them an identity of their own. Their revolt springs essentially from a refusal to submit, to alienate their freedom and have their fate coerced into some preestablished pattern. In their stubborn striving for autonomy, they commit what Christian tradition has always considered to be the satanic sin par excellence: the sin of pride.

Yet pride is not the only obstacle to the fulfillment of their spiritual destinies. Soiled from birth by the sin of their origins, how could these fallen souls hoist themselves up to God's light? They do not know God; they experience only his burning absence. For the theologian and the philosopher God is a matter of speculation; for the mystic he may become the living object of inner experience. For O'Connor's Christomaniacs he becomes "the bleeding stinking mad shadow of Jesus." . . . Their God is above all a haunting specter, a power felt and feared in its uncanny emptiness, and this ominous power they can only apprehend anthropomorphically through the incongruous phantasmagoria of their guilt-ridden imaginations. There is apprehension, but no comprehension. Their notion of the godly is not exempted from the distortions of the corrupt world in which they live, and therefore the divine gets so often confused with the demonic. In its extreme form, this rampant perversion comes to manifest itself as radical inversion. Everything, then, is turned upside down, and the religious impulse is subverted into its very opposite: desire for God is transformed into God-hatred, prayer into blasphemy, and the quest for salvation turns into a mystique of perdition.

Nothing exemplifies this inversion better than the *imitatio Christi* in reverse which O'Connor presents us in *Wise Blood*. After turning himself into the prophet of the Church Without Christ (the negative of the Church of God, the very image of the "body of sin" referred to by St. Paul), Hazel Motes ironically becomes a Christ without a church, an anonymous, solitary pseudo-Christ or anti-Christ. His disciples are morons and mountebanks, his preaching meets only with indifference, and his calvary at the close of the novel ends in a seemingly pointless death. Worn out by self-inflicted pain and privation, he is clubbed to death by two fat policemen. Motes dies like a dog, and his atrocious end reminds one strongly of the last pages of *The Trial*, when two men appear and lead Joseph K. to the outskirts of the town to kill him. The life and death of O'Connor's hero appear likewise as an absurd Passion. (pp. 59-60)

Christian references and Christian parallels abound in O'Connor's fiction, and more often than not they strike us as ironic. In *Wise Blood*, especially, parodic overtones are so frequent that the whole novel might almost be read as sheer burlesque. A "new jesus" appears in the guise of a shrunken museum mummy; a slop-jar cabinet becomes the tabernacle to receive him, and Sabbath Lily Hawks, a perverse little slut, cradles the mummy in her arms as if she were the Madonna. O'Connor's penchant for travesty is likewise re-flected in the eccentric ritualism of many of her characters: baptismal drownings (in **"The River"** and *The Violent Bear It Away*), rites of exorcism (Tarwater setting fire to his great-uncle's house), purification rites (Tarwater firing the bushes where the rape occurred), initiation rites (Enoch Emery's shedding of clothes in *Wise Blood* and Tarwater's in *The Violent Bear It Away*), sacrificial rites (Motes's self-blinding), etc. In their appalling extravagance, these ritual actions are likely to shock any reader, whether Christian or not. But here again, if we are prepared to accept the premises of the author, we shall avoid mistaking them for mere fits of madness, for to her, in a desacralized world like ours, these savage and sacrilegious rites paradoxically assert the presence of the sacred through the very excess of its distortion or denial. (pp. 60-1)

O'Connor's satiric stance, her penchant for parody, her reliance on the grotesque, and her massive use of violence—the features of her art we have examined so far all contribute to the subtle interplay of tensions and ambiguities through which it comes alive, and they resist alike reduction to a single interpretative pattern. The same irreducible ambiguity also attaches to another significant trait of her fictional world: the enormous amount of suffering and humiliation which is inflicted on most of her characters, and the inevitability of their defeat and/or death. Hazel Motes's destiny probably offers the most telling example of this process: after an active career in sin and crime, all his aggressiveness is eventually turned against himself, driving him to a positive frenzy of masochism and self-destruction. He blinds himself with quicklime, exposes himself to cold and illness, walks in shoes "lined with gravel and broken glass and pieces of small stone," . . . wraps three strands of barbed wire round his chest, and when his baffled landlady protests at so much self-torture, Motes replies imperturbably: "I'm not clean," or again "I'm paying." . . . (p. 61)

According to the prototypal Christian pattern, the hero's journey leads in both novels from sinful rebellion to the recognition of sin and to penance. O'Connor would have us believe that her protagonists are responsible for their fates, that they possess freedom of choice, and are at liberty to refuse or accept their vocation. . . . But her readers, even those who sympathize with her Christian assumptions and are willing to make allowances for the mysterious working of grace, will hesitate to take her at her word. For in the text of the novel there is indeed little to indicate that Motes or Tarwater could have made a differnt choice and that events might have followed another course. Her heroes are not allowed to shape their destinies; they only *recognize* fate when it pounces upon them. . . . O'Connor's heroes are . . . like sleepers: they traverse life in a driven dreamlike state, and with the sense of impotence and anxiety one experiences in nightmares. They go through the motions of revolt, but their violent gestures toward independence are all doomed to dissolve into unreality. They are nothing more than the starts and bounds of a hooked fish. Tarwater and Motes both act out scenarios written beforehand by someone else. (p. 62)

On the face of it, [the novels] develop in accordance with the three major phases of the *rite de passage:* separation, transition, and reincorporation, but they give no sense of moving forward in time and no evidence of psychological development. Instead of inner growth, there is a backward circling which takes O'Connor's heroes inexorably back to where they started. *Wise Blood* and *The Violent Bear It Away* both follow the same circular and regressive pattern, made conspicuous by the close similarities between opening and final scenes. In *Wise Blood* Mrs. Hitchcock's fascination with Hazel's eyes in the initial train scene anticipates Mrs. Flood's perplexed watching of his burnt-out eye sockets at the close of the novel. In much the same way the punishment he inflicts upon himself at ten—walking through the woods, his shoes filled with pebbles—prefigures the penitential rites preceding his near-suicidal death. In *The Violent Bear It Away,* on the other hand, the parallelism is emphasized by the use of the same setting: the novel starts with Tarwater's departure from Powderhead and closes with his return to it. "I guess you're going home," . . . Mrs. Hitchcock says to Hazel Motes on the train; in symbolic terms, his journey is indeed a journey home, and Tarwater's is quite literally a homecoming. These repetitions, to be true, are repetitions with a difference, and one could say that the movement is spiral-like rather than circular: there are intimations that through his harrowing ordeals Motes has moved toward a state of saintliness, and his physical blindness may be taken for an index to the spiritual insight he has at last achieved. It is obvious too that in *The Violent Bear It Away* the fire symbolism of the closing scenes reverses the meaning it was given in the first chapter. And it might be argued finally that recurring situations, settings, and imagery are part of the author's elaborate technique of foreshadowing.

But this is perhaps precisely where the shoe pinches: O'Connor's foreshadowing is so dense as to become constrictive; the signs and signals of destiny clutter so thickly around the protagonists of her novels that no breathing space is left to them. The author plays God to her creatures, and foreshadowing becomes the fictional equivalent of predestination. Everything propels her heroes toward submission to their predetermined fates and, at the same time, pushes them back to their childhood allegiances. Not only does their rebellion fail, it also ends each time in unconditional surrender to the parental powers from which they had attempted to escape.

In *Wise Blood* the prophetic mission is anticipated in the haunting figure of the grandfather, but Hazel's backward journey is essentially a return to the mother. The return motif is already adumbrated in the remembered episode of his visit to Eastrod after his release from the army. The only familiar object Hazel then found in his parents' deserted house was his mother's walnut chifforobe, and before leaving he put warning notes in every drawer: "This shiffer-robe belongs to Hazel Motes. Do not steal it or you will be hunted down and killed." . . . In the claustrophobic dream touched off by this reminiscence, the chifforobe is metamorphosed into his mother's coffin, while the coffin itself is fused with the berth in the train where Hazel is sleeping. What is more, Hazel, in his dream, identifies with his dead mother. . . . This dream is significantly related to another one, in which Motes dreams that he is buried alive and exposed through an oval window to the curiosity of various onlookers, one of whom is a woman who would apparently like to "climb in and keep him company for a while." . . . Furthermore, these two coffin dreams relate back to the traumatic childhood scene of Motes's initiation into evil: the disturbing sight of a nude blonde in a black casket, exhibited in the carnival tent where the ten-year-old boy had secretly followed his father. At his return from the country fair, his mother (whose image he superimposed mentally on that of the woman in the casket) knows, after one look at him, that he has sinned, and it is her accusing look that induces his first penitential rite. In the visual symbolism of the novel, the urge to see and the fear of being seen are recurrent motifs, and in this scene as in several others they both point to sin and guilt. What also appears through the interrelated imagery of these oneiric and actual scenes is the close conjunction of sex and death. But the most remarkable feature is that the themes of sin and guilt, sex and death, all coalesce around the mother figure and its surrogates. Motes's mother, while being deviously linked to his sordid sexual experiences, is at the same time a haunting reminder of the demands of religion: when he goes into the army, the only things he takes with him are "a black Bible and a pair of silver-trimmed spectacles that had belonged to his mother." . . . (pp. 62-4)

In *Wise Blood* Motes is finally reabsorbed into his mother. In *The Violent Bear It Away* Tarwater is likewise reabsorbed into his great-uncle. Raising the orphan boy to be a prophet like himself, the tyrannical old man has molded him in his own image and conditioned him for a destiny similar to his. When he dies, young Tarwater does his utmost to assert his own separate self through repeated acts of defiance, but what the novel seems to demonstrate is that there can be no escape from the self-ordained prophet's posthumous grip. In the concluding scene the repentant boy submits to what he so fiercely rejected, and his act of submission reminds one of the etymological origin of "humility" (humus = soil): prostrate on old Tarwater's grave, smearing his forehead with earth from his burial place, he acknowledges at last the absolute power of the past over the present, of the dead over the living or, to put it in terms of kinship, of the father over the son. The story comes full circle: otherness is resolved into sameness, difference into repetition. Having forever renounced his desire for autonomous selfhood, young Tarwater is now willing to become a faithful replica of old Tarwater, and in all likelihood his ulterior fate will be nothing more than a reenactment of the dead prophet's.

For neither protagonist of O'Connor's novels, then, is true separateness possible. Nor can they ever achieve true relatedness. Theirs is a demented mirror world of doubles, where the self is always experienced as other, and the other apprehended as a reflection of self. The schizophrenic dilemma they are both confronted with is either the madness of extreme isolation or the deadness of total engulfment. In both cases, the failure to define a viable identity leads ultimately to complete self-cancellation; in both cases, the inability to grow up provokes helpless surrender to an omnipotent and all-devouring parent figure. (pp. 64-5)

For almost all of O'Connor's characters there is a time for denial and a time for submission, a time for sin and a time for atonement. The passage from one to the other is what she has attempted to describe in her two novels, but as we have seen, she shows relatively little interest in the continuities and intricacies of inner growth. Her heroes do not change gradually; they progress—or regress—in fits and starts, through a series of switches and turnabouts rather than through a slow process of maturation. What engages most deeply O'Connor's imagination—and this, incidentally, may account for her feeling more at home in the short story than in the novel—is not so much time as the sudden encounter of time with the timeless: the decisive moments in a man's existence she would have called moments of grace. . . . Grace plays indeed a major part in her novels as in most of her stories, especially the later ones, and as a religious concept it forms the very core of her implicit theology. Left to his own devices, man, as he appears in her fiction, is totally incapable of ensuring his salvation. Whether it degrades itself in grotesque parody or exhausts itself in mad convulsions, his quest for the holy is doomed to derision and failure from the very start. Grace alone saves, and even that is perhaps going too far: reading O'Connor's tales, one rather feels that grace simply makes salvation possible. (p. 65)

The impact of grace, as evoked by O'Connor, is that of a painful dazzle; it does not flood the soul with joy; her characters experience it as an instantaneous deflagration, a rending and bursting of the whole fabric of their being. For the revelation it brings is first and foremost self-revelation, the terrified recognition of one's nothingness and guilt. As each character is brutally stripped of his delusions, he sees and knows himself at last for what he is: "Asbury blanched and the last film of illusion was torn as if by a whirlwind from his eyes." . . . Not until the soul has reached that ultimate point of searching self-knowledge does salvation become a possibility. (p. 66)

In O'Connor, grace is not effusion but aggression. It is God's violence responding to Satan's violence, divine counterterror fighting the mutiny of evil. The operations of the divine and of the demonic are so disturbingly alike that the concept of God suggested by her work is in the last resort hardly more reassuring than her Devil. In fairness, one should no doubt allow for the distortions of satire, and be careful to distinguish the God of O'Connor's faith from the God-image of her characters. Her handling of point of view, however, implies no effacement on the part of the narrator, and her dramatic rendering of spiritual issues as well as the imagery she uses to evoke the actions of grace, provide enough clues to what God meant in her imaginative experience.

O'Connor's imagination is preeminently visual and visionary. Like Conrad's, her art attempts in its own way "to render the highest kind of justice to the visible universe," and far from clouding her perception, her sense of mystery rather adds to its startling clarity and sharpness. It is worth noting too how much of the action of her stories and novels is reflected in the continuous interplay of peeping or peering, prying or spying eyes, and how much importance is accorded throughout to the sheer act of seeing—or not seeing. *Wise Blood* is a prime example: a great deal of its symbolism springs from the dialectic of vision and blindness, and a similar dialectic is also at work in *The Violent Bear It Away* and in many of her stories. For O'Connor seeing is a measure of being: while the sinner gropes in utter darkness, the prophet—in O'Connor's phrase, "a realist of distances"—is above all a seer. In God the faculty of vision is carried to an infinite power of penetration: God is the All-seeing, the absolute Eye, encompassing the whole universe in its eternal gaze.

The cosmic metaphor for the divine eye is the sun. Through one of those reversals of the imagination the sun, in O'Connor's fiction, is not simply the primal source of light that makes all things visible, it is itself capable of vision, it is an eye. In *The Violent Bear It Away* there are few scenes to which the sun is not a benevolent or, more often, malevolent witness. After the old man's death, while Tarwater is reluctantly digging his grave, the sun moves slowly across the sky "circled by a haze of yellow," . . . then becomes "a furious white blister" . . . as he starts listening to the seductive voice of the "stranger." (pp. 66-7)

O'Connor's sun is both cosmic eye and heavenly fire. It thus condenses two of her most pregnant symbol patterns in a single image. For fire imagery is indeed as essential in her symbolic language as eye and sight imagery: incandescent suns, flaming skies, burning houses, woods, trees, and bushes—hers is an apocalyptic world forever ablaze. Fire is the visible manifestation of the principle of violence governing the universe, and the ordeal by fire is the *rite de passage* all of O'Connor's heroes are subjected to. A symbol of destruction and death, and a reminder of hell, it is also the favorite instrument of divine wrath and, as the old prophet taught young Tarwater, "even the mercy of the Lord burns.". . . Associated with purification and regeneration as well as evil, fire is the ambiguous sign of the elect and the damned, and its voracity is God's as much as Satan's.

That eye, sun, and fire are all emblems of the sacred is confirmed by another symbolic figure which both unites and multiplies them in animal form: the peacock. In **"The Displaced Person,"** instead of being associated with human pride and ostentatiousness, the peacock becomes a symbol of the Second Coming, evoking the unearthly splendor of Christ at the Last Judgment. His tail, in O'Connor's description, expands into a cosmic wonder: " . . . his tail hung in front of her, full of fierce planets with *eyes* that were each ringed in green and set against a *sun* that was gold in one second's light and salmon-colored in the next." . . . (p. 68)

Immensity, brilliance, splendor, a dizzying profusion of eyes and suns, such are the features O'Connor chooses to celebrate God's power and glory. And one can hardly refrain from the suspicion that power and glory are in her imagination if not in her belief the essential attributes of divinity. In cosmic terms, her God is sun and fire. . . . Small wonder then that the spiritual errancy of O'Connor's heroes turns into a paranoid nightmare: aware of being watched and scrutinized by the relentless eye of the almighty Judge, they are unable ever to see their remote and silent persecutor. Not until grace descends to seize and possess their tormented souls is the infinite distance separating them abolished. Now the celestial Watcher, now a God of prey; first hovering, motionless, above his victim, then swooping with terrible speed to devour it.

One might have expected so fervent a Catholic as O'Connor to focus her fiction on the figure of Christ. In a sense, to be true, she does: whether in prayer or profanity, his name is obsessively referred to, and the question of whether Jesus suffered and died for our sins is indeed of vital concern to many of her characters. Yet her work is not so much Christ-centered as Christ-haunted. Unlike T. S. Eliot's later poetry, it is by no means a reaffirmation of the Christian mystery of the Incarnation. O'Connor's divisive vision perpetuates the idealistic cleavage between spirit and body, eternity and time, God and man, and Christ is likewise split into two irreconcilable halves. His image in her work constantly oscillates between the extremes of radical humanity and radical divinity. Now he is the mythical paradigm of human suffering, as Christ crucified and recrucified, now he appears in the plenitude of his majesty as Christ the King, most startlingly represented in the image of the Byzantine Pantocrator tattooed on Parker's back. Or, to put it otherwise, he is alternately the impotent victimized Son and the omnipotent Father. These are images quite common in Christian literature and iconography. The point is that in O'Connor they never meet and merge in the dual unity of Christ, the God become man, the Word become flesh. The mediating function associated with Jesus by the Christian and particularly the Catholic tradition is hardly acknowledged, and what characterizes O'Connor's fictional world is precisely the absence of all mediation, of all intercession. On the one hand, there is the utter darkness of evil, on the other, the white radiance of divine transcendence. Between the two: man, battered and blinded, the victim of Satan or the prey of God, doomed to be defeated and dispossessed whatever the outcome of the dubious battle fought over his wretched soul. (pp. 68-9)

O'Connor envisioned the writer's relation to his work on the same pattern as God's relation to his creation, as if art were simply the fulfillment of preexisting intentions, the embodiment of a fixed vision prior to the writing process. In defining herself as a writer, she failed to acknowledge the insight so admirably dramatized in her fiction: that the self is not even master in its own house. For the writing self is certainly not exempted from the common lot: its imaginative constructs escape its mastery both in their deeper motivations and in their ultimate effects.

The truth of O'Connor's work is the truth of her art, not that of her church. Her fiction does refer to an implicit theology, but if we rely, as we should, on its testimony rather than on the author's comments, we shall have to admit that the Catholic orthodoxy of her work is at least debatable. O'Connor is definitely on the darker fringe of Christianity, and to find antecedents one has to go back to the paradoxical theology of early church fathers like Tertullian, or to the negative theology of stern mystics like St. John of the Cross. Pitting the supernatural against the natural in fierce antagonism, her theology holds nothing but scorn for everything human, and it is significant that in her work satanic evildoers (the "Misfit," Rufus Johnson) are far less harshly dealt with than humanistic do-gooders (Rayber, Sheppard). What is more, of the two mysteries—or myths—which are central to Christianity, the Fall and the Redemption, only the first seems to have engaged her imagination as a creative writer. Gnawed by old Calvinistic ferments and at the same time corroded by a very modern sense of the absurd, O'Connor's version of Christianity is emphatically and exclusively her own. Her fallen world, it is true, is visited by grace, but is grace, as she evokes it in her last stories, anything other than the vertigo of the *nada* and the encounter with death? And who is this God whose very mercy is terror?

It may be argued of course that these are the paradoxes of faith, or that O'Connor's rhetoric of violence was the shock therapy which her benumbed audience needed. There is little doubt that there will be many further exercises in exegetical ingenuity to establish her orthodoxy. Yet her work is not content with illustrating Christian paradoxes. It stretches them to breaking point, leaving us with Christian truths gone mad, the still incandescent fragments of a shattered system of belief.

Flannery O'Connor was a Catholic. She was not a Catholic novelist. She was a writer, and as a writer she belongs to no other parish than literature. (pp. 69-70)

André Bleikasten, "The Heresy of Flannery O'Connor," in *Les Américanistes: New French Criticism on Modern American Fiction,* edited by Ira D. Johnson and Christiane Johnson, Kennikat Press, 1978, pp. 53-70.

SOURCES FOR FURTHER STUDY

Driskell, Leon V., and Brittain, Joan T. *The Eternal Crossroads: The Art of Flannery O'Connor.* Lexington: University Press of Kentucky, 1971, 175 p.

Focuses on literary and theological influences in O'Connor's work.

Eggenschwiler, David. *The Christian Humanism of Flannery O'Connor.* Detroit: Wayne State University Press, 1976, 148 p.

Approaches O'Connor as a Christian humanist and places her within a modern intellectual tradition.

Flannery O'Connor Bulletin. (1972-   )

Quarterly bulletin devoted to biographical, bibliographical, and critical works on O'Connor.

McFarland, Dorothy Tuck. *Flannery O'Connor.* New York: Frederick Ungar, 1976, 132 p.

Introduction to key aspects of O'Connor's fiction.

Montgomery, Marion. *Why Flannery O'Connor Stayed Home.* La Salle, Ill.: Sherwood Sugden, 1981, 476 p.

Includes chapters ranging from general topics to detailed analyses of O'Connor's fiction, emphasizing the significance of Roman Catholicism and the South in her works.

Walters, Dorothy. *Flannery O'Connor.* Boston: Twayne, 1973, 172 p.

Biographical and critical study.

Eugene O'Neill

1888-1953

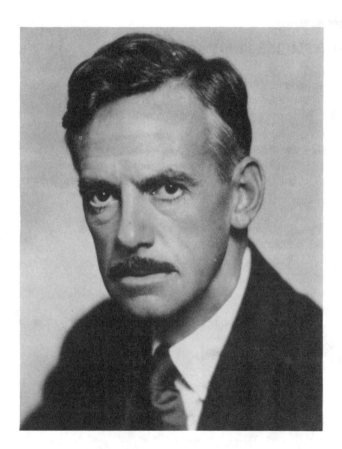

(Born Eugene Gladstone O'Neill) American dramatist and poet.

INTRODUCTION

O'Neill is generally considered America's foremost dramatist. His plays consistently examine the implacability of an indifferent universe, the materialistic greed of humanity, and the problems of discovering one's true identity. Considered the first American playwright to replace the musicals and mediocre melodramas and farces of the American stage with a theater of serious ideas, O'Neill's tragic vision of life led him to write dramas aspiring to the power of ancient Greek tragedy. Such works as *Desire Under the Elms* (1924) and *Mourning Becomes Electra* (1931) gained him a respected reputation in the American theater by 1934. But O'Neill fell from popular appeal around the same time and did not produce another original play until *The Iceman Cometh* (1946), a work positing illusion and death as the only hope for humankind, and *Long Day's Journey into Night* (1956), an autobiographical tragedy dramatizing the loss of hope in the modern age; both works are considered masterpieces of modern drama. O'Neill was awarded the Nobel Prize for literature in 1936, the only American playwright so honored.

The son of a professional actor, O'Neill was brought up on the road and acquired a precocious knowledge of the theater. His early years were profoundly affected by the pressures of his mother's recurring mental illness and drug addiction, his tempestuous relationship with his father, and his elder brother's alcoholism, a discordant family situation that he later drew upon when writing *Long Day's Journey into Night*. He spent his childhood on theatrical tours with his family and received his education in various New England boarding schools. After expulsion from Princeton University in 1907 for a student prank, and a brief, unsuccessful marriage, O'Neill embarked on a life at sea. For two years he lived alternately as a seaman and as a panhandling drifter in several South American ports, experiences that provided material for many of his early plays. During this period he attempted suicide by taking an overdose of barbiturates.

A turning point in his life came in 1912, when he suffered a mild attack of tuberculosis. While recovering in a sanatorium, O'Neill began reading works by August Strindberg. His pessimistic dramas powerfully affected O'Neill, and he left the sanatorium vowing to become a playwright. He attended Harvard in 1914 to study playwrighting under George Pierce Baker, but left after one year and moved to Greenwich Village where he joined an avant-garde group of artists and writers. Known as the Provincetown Players, the group performed experimental works in Provincetown, Massachusetts. In 1916, O'Neill's first appearance as a playwright came when the troupe produced his one-act sea play *Bound East for Cardiff.* In four years, they performed all of his one-act plays and gained for him a small but favorable reputation. These initial works were rather modest and contained melodramatic events at sea and seedy characters previously ignored in American drama. In 1920, seven years after he began writing, O'Neill produced his first full-length drama, *Beyond the Horizon,* for which he received the Pulitzer Prize. Over the next twenty years he slowly developed into one of America's finest playwrights, earning three more Pulitzer Prizes for *Anna Christie* (1921), *Strange Interlude* (1928), and *Long Day's Journey into Night.* In these and other works O'Neill focused on life's seamy aspects: alcoholism, poverty, and madness. His penchant for the depressing culminated in *Mourning Becomes Electra* (1931), a mythologically derived work which presented women in three archetypical roles—daughter, mother, and mistress.

O'Neill retreated from public life abruptly in 1934 and for twelve years worked on a cycle of one-act plays (of which *Hughie* (1959) is a small masterpiece) and a cycle of full-length plays. His work was frustrated by disease and repeated suffering from alcoholism and family neuroses. The last and finest stage of his career began with the triumph of *The Iceman Cometh.* This heavily symbolic drama of lost illusions and death revived interest in O'Neill's work. In his last years, numerous ailments continued to plague the playwright. Unable to work, he isolated himself in a Boston hotel room, where he died in 1953.

O'Neill's career can be divided into five somewhat distinct periods that include, after a term of dramatic apprenticeship, a second period during which he wrote primarily one-act plays about the sea. According to some critics, O'Neill's first performed play, *Bound East for Cardiff,* marks the initial departure in America from nineteenth-century melodrama and the beginning of serious American theater. During a third phase of his career, which lasted from 1920 through 1924, O'Neill

began writing longer plays. Foremost among these is *Desire under the Elms,* one of his few conventional tragedies and one of his most critically acclaimed dramas. Throughout this period O'Neill utilized many experimental theatrical techniques. *The Emperor Jones* (1920), for example, is considered one of the principal dramatic works of the time executed in a symbolistic style, and *The Hairy Ape* (1922) is regarded as a prominent example of Expressionism in the American theater. O'Neill's fourth, sometimes called his "cosmic," period extends from 1924 to 1935. The plays of this period are often much longer than traditional productions, and demonstrate O'Neill's continuing experimentation with theatrical technique. The most important among these plays, the trilogy *Mourning Becomes Electra,* retells the Oedipus and Electra myths, with Freudian psychosexual drives replacing fate as the motivating factor in the characters' lives. Despite his award of the Nobel Prize in literature in 1936, O'Neill's reputation declined steadily after 1935. It was not until after his death that the plays of his last period gained critical and popular recognition of a high order. These plays—*The Iceman Cometh, Long Day's Journey into Night, A Moon for the Misbegotten* (1947), *A Touch of the Poet* (1958), and *Hughie*—employ most directly the realistic dramatic styles of Henrik Ibsen and August Strindberg, whom O'Neill had always cited as primary influences. These last plays received little attention until after the initial performance of *Long Day's Journey into Night* in 1956, but once "rediscovered," they led many critics to call for a reevaluation of O'Neill's entire career.

It is generally agreed that O'Neill wrote some of the most important modern dramas. In his plays he experimented with almost every dramatic innovation of the early twentieth century, including the interior monologue, stream-of-consciousness dialogue, the aside, symbolic masks, the chorus, thematic repetition, and mythological motifs. Unfortunately, experimentation with theatrical effects sometimes became an end in itself, and technique could not enhance such puerile, poorly conceived works as *The Great God Brown* (1926), and *Lazarus Laughed* (1928). For this reason O'Neill's most realistic plays are considered his best. Similarly, while O'Neill was a master at sketching character, he also wrote melodramatic, needlessly verbose dialogue. It is such seeming contradictions that make O'Neill's work fascinating to contemporary critics; they often attack several elements of his plays while applauding the ultimate effects. O'Neill is universally acknowledged as an important tragedian who is credited with creating the traditions of twentieth-century American drama and is as integral to modern world literature as Bertolt Brecht and August Strindberg.

(For further information about O'Neill's life and works, see *Concise Dictionary of American Literary Biography, 1929-1941; Contemporary Authors,* Vol. 110;

Dictionary of Literary Biography, Vol. 7: *Twentieth-Century American Dramatists;* and *Twentieth-Century Literary Criticism*, Vols. 1, 6, 27.)

CRITICAL COMMENTARY

EDMOND M. GAGEY
(essay date 1947)

[In the following excerpt, Gagey outlines the diversity of O'Neill's dramas from his first plays in the early 1900s to *The Iceman Cometh*, concluding that the author will be remembered as a realist who introduced some imaginative elements into his work.]

In the many critical works about him Eugene O'Neill has been called variously realist, poet, mystic, seer, and plain writer of highbrow melodrama. These designations all fit to a certain degree, for, regardless of his eventual reputation, O'Neill remains a many-sided figure. . . . Furthermore, his plays were experimental—in style, in treatment, in the use of ingenious devices—and thus lent themselves readily to imaginative production.

O'Neill was twenty-six when his first work, *Thirst and Other One-Act Plays,* was published. . . . (p. 39)

The journeyman work of famous dramatists, while usually mediocre, is always revealing. O'Neill himself . . . selected *Bound East for Cardiff* . . . as most important in including the germ of his later work. Equally significant, however, are the five plays of the *Thirst* volume, despite their lack of merit. All are melodramatic and unhappy in ending. The title play, for instance, presents three persons—a girl in dancing costume, a gentleman, and a West Indian Negro—tortured by thirst on a raft in tropical seas until they become raving mad and die or kill off one another. Here we find already romantic setting and characters, exploitation of the sea, and a sense of malevolent destiny. (pp. 40-1)

[In] the collection as a whole, to summarize, are already discoverable many of the ingredients of his great successes: novelty of characters, realism of scene and language, romantic and unusual settings, interest in experimentation, use of melodramatic situations. Also we find O'Neill's identification of himself with the dreamer and the poet, tired of the world but looking with scorn upon the American business man, the pre-Sinclair-Lewis Babbitt. Finally, while fate appears as a tricky and ironic jade, O'Neill did not rule out in life the possibilities of mysticism and the religious spirit. (p. 42)

Taken as a whole, the one-act plays of [the] period from 1916 to 1920 are interesting and theatrically effective. They continue, with greater skill and power, the blend of romance and realism characteristic of his first published work. They are melodramatic, with violent and unhappy endings, dramatic irony, and occasional sentimentality. While most are about the sea, others deal with New England and several with Negro life. Four of the best-known sea plays are set on the same British tramp steamer and, as a matter of fact, were presented together . . . under the general title *S.S. Glencairn.* . . . [*Bound East for Cardiff*], which O'Neill found so significant in relation to his later work, deals with the affecting death at sea of Yank. . . . The play shows O'Neill's latent if unorthodox concern with life after death and with religion, his fine conception of friendship, and his common theme of "not belonging." . . . [*In the Zone*], the most popular of the one-acters both in America and abroad, dramatizes the sudden hysterical belief in the fo'c's'le that Smitty is a German spy. What the men later find in a black box which aroused their suspicion is merely a package of love letters revealing Smitty's unhappy love affair. The piece is sentimental but does not ring so false when we consider the time of its writing, when spy scares were commonplace and sentimentality more in vogue. *The Long Voyage Home* . . . tells the tragic and ironic story of a sailor who decides to give up the sea and return to his native Sweden, only to be drugged in a London dive and shanghaied on a windjammer going round the Horn. *The Moon of the Caribbees* . . . , probably the most interesting of the group, is a study in mood and setting. (pp. 42-3)

Of the other one-act plays special mention must be made of *Ile* . . . , a dramatic study of a whaling captain who chooses to let his wife go insane rather than bear the disgrace of returning to port without a full quota of oil. In melodramatic force this must be held one of O'Neill's best. (p. 44)

[O'Neill's first full-length play, *Beyond the Horizon,*] was a grim, modern tragedy of New England, intensely realistic yet not without poetic beauty, a play of frustration and irony that ended in wholesale disaster. Two brothers on a New England farm near the sea are of diametrically opposite character: Robert Mayo is

Principal Works

*Thirst, and Other One Act Plays (dramas) 1914

Before Breakfast (drama) 1916

Bound East for Cardiff (drama) 1916

Ile (drama) 1917

In the Zone (drama) 1917

The Long Voyage Home (drama) 1917

The Moon of the Caribbees (drama) 1918

The Rope (drama) 1918

Where the Cross Is Made (drama) 1918

The Dreamy Kid (drama) 1919

Beyond the Horizon (drama) 1920

Diff 'rent (drama) 1920

The Emperor Jones (drama) 1920

Anna Christie (drama) 1921

Gold (drama) 1921

The Straw (drama) 1921

The First Man (drama) 1922

The Hairy Ape (drama) 1922

All God's Chillun Got Wings (drama) 1924

Desire under the Elms (drama) 1924

Welded (drama) 1924

The Fountain (drama) 1925

The Great God Brown (drama) 1926

Lazarus Laughed (drama) 1928

Marco Millions (drama) 1928

Strange Interlude (drama) 1928

Dynamo (drama) 1929

Mourning Becomes Electra (drama) 1931

Ah, Wilderness! (drama) 1933

Days without End (drama) 1934

The Iceman Cometh (drama) 1946

*Lost Plays (dramas) 1950

Long Day's Journey into Night (drama) 1956

A Moon for the Misbegotten (drama) 1957

A Touch of the Poet (drama) 1958

*Hughie (drama) 1959

Poems, 1912-1924 (poetry) 1980

*These are dates of first publication rather than first performance.

---

poetic, restless, curious about what lies beyond the horizon; Andrew is matter-of-fact, practical, unimaginative, perfectly content with his lot as farmer. Fate intervenes with a typical O'Neill trick. As Robert is about to realize his life-long ambition to travel the seven seas on a sailing vessel, he discovers and reveals his romantic love for Ruth, Andrew's sweetheart. She accepts him and he immediately forsakes his dream, with the result that it is Andrew who goes to sea and Robert who stays at home to tend the farm. The inevitable outcome is frustration and tragedy for the three principals, who discover that they have made an irrevocable mistake. The tragic impetus of the play proves truly affecting, though one must admit that the cards are stacked pretty heavily against the characters. . . . The play has faults of construction and characterization, but in opposition to the escapist pabulum of Broadway it won an enthusiastic hearing and a significant victory for the art theatre as well when it was awarded the Pulitzer Prize. (pp. 45-6)

O'Neill develops in [*The Emperor Jones*] the colorful and dramatic career of Jones, former Pullman porter, now self-styled emperor of an island, who claims he is invulnerable to any but a silver bullet. Fully prepared for an uprising of the people he has tyrannized, he escapes to the tropical forest as the sound of tom-toms in the distance indicates that the revolt is gathering strength. But night has come sooner than he expected and he loses his way in the forest, where in a series

of terrifying visions he recapitulates not only the main events of his life but also the primitive history of his race. He ends by killing himself with his own last silver bullet after finding that he has traveled a wide circle during the night, while the beat of the drums becomes faster and more menacing. With his racy dialogue and superb strutting Jones possesses epic grandeur, so that we can only regret his downfall. . . . (pp. 46-7)

[The story of *Anna Christie*] is a realistic one about old Christ Christopherson, captain of a barge, who sentimentalizes over a daughter he has not seen for fifteen years; Anna, the daughter, who becomes regenerated from a career of prostitution as a result of her new life on the barge; and Mat, a loquacious Irishman, who falls in love with Anna and is tortured to drink and madness when he learns of her past life. From such a set of characters only tragic irony and suffering can result, and we find Anna voicing the theme of this as well as other early plays by O'Neill: "Don't bawl about it. There ain't nothing to forgive, anyway. It ain't your fault, and it ain't mine, and it ain't his neither. We're all poor nuts, and things happen, and we just get mixed in wrong, that's all." (p. 48)

[*The Hairy Ape*] was immediately termed expressionistic, although O'Neill denied any direct influence from the expressionism of German writers. . . . Expressionism may be defined in simple terms as an attempt to portray inner reality in nonrealistic terms by the use of abstraction, symbolism, and distortion. . . .

[*The Hairy Ape*] relates in a series of short scenes the story of a man who . . . loses his old harmony with nature. Yank, a stoker on a transatlantic liner, has always gloried in his work and in his brute strength until he is startled and infuriated when Mildred Douglas, spoiled daughter of a millionaire, visits the stokehold. Driven to thought and unable to rationalize his place in the scheme of things, Yank is obsessed by the idea that he "doesn't belong." He is clapped into jail for starting a riot on Fifth Avenue, and he is even thrown out of the I.W.W. as an unwelcome intruder. Finally he attempts to shake hands with a gorilla at the zoo but is crushed to death by the animal—O'Neill's symbolism for his inability to get back to a lower order of existence. The play, obviously, is concerned not so much with Yank as with Man and his struggle to find himself, and to bring out the symbolism O'Neill has departed from naturalism, as in the famous Fifth Avenue scene where the passers-by are represented as mere walking automatons. Reality is still present and recognizable, however, especially in the salty speech of the stokehold, and the play might very well be called another example of imaginative realism. (pp. 49-50)

[*All God's Chillun Got Wings*] represents the author's first extensive invasion of Freudian territory. *All God's Chillun* is a clinical study of miscegenation and racial hatred, handled with restraint and yet with dramatic power. (p. 51)

[*Desire under the Elms*] is a starkly realistic portrayal of a New England farm tragedy. Old Ephraim Cabot, seventy-five years old, stern and Bible quoting, has just taken to himself a third wife, Abbie. Partly because she wants an heir to insure her possession of the farm, she seduces Eben, Ephraim's son by an earlier marriage. From this illicit relationship a child is born which old Ephraim proudly believes to be his own. Eben and Abbie, however, have found themselves caught in a passion stronger than they. In a desperate attempt to prove her love Abbie smothers the infant and reveals its true paternity to old Cabot. Eben, who in his first horror has rushed to call the sheriff, realizes the depth of his love for Abbie, and the two lovers face the uncertain future with a sense of exaltation. It is this closing note that keeps *Desire under the Elms* from being merely sordid and endows it, according to various critics, with something akin to the catharsis of Greek tragedy. (p. 52)

[In *The Great God Brown* O'Neill] plunged boldly into symbolism, employing the ancient device of masks, which the players took off or put on or even exchanged to indicate changes in personality. The play, which almost defies analysis, deals with the fortunes of William Brown . . . and Dion Anthony . . . , both in love with the same girl at the time of their graduation from high school. It is the artistic and erratic Dion, however, and not Billy Brown, that Margaret prefers

and later marries. After college Brown becomes successful as builder and architect but finds that he needs the aid of Dion's artistic genius. Dion, however is maladjusted and unhappy, in spite of his love for the faithful Margaret, who has borne him three sons. He is driven to drink and gambling, and finds his main solace with the town prostitute, Cybel. Eventually Dion dies in the house of Brown, who takes his mask (hence his personality) and poses sometimes as Dion, sometimes as himself, until his death in the arms of the sympathetic Cybel. This unusual plot becomes more intelligible when O'Neill explains that Dion Anthony represents a combination of Dionysus and St. Anthony, "the creative pagan acceptance of life, fighting eternal war with the masochistic, life-denying spirit of Christianity as represented by St. Anthony"; that Brown stands for the demigod of the materialistic American myth of success, "building his life of exterior things, inwardly empty and resourceless"; that Margaret is the eternal girl-woman, modern descendant of Marguerite in Goethe's *Faust;* and finally that Cybel personifies Cybele, the Earth Mother of Greek mythology. In his note to the Wilderness edition of his plays O'Neill states further that the play "attempts to foreshadow the mystical patterns created by the duality of human character and the search for what lies hidden behind and beyond words and actions of men and women. More by the use of overtones than by explicit speech, I sought to convey the dramatic conflicts in the lives and within the souls of the characters."

Confusing as are the theme and symbolism, as well as the use and exchange of masks, *The Great God Brown* remains an artistic success. Nowhere else is O'Neill's dialogue more charged with emotion and lyrical beauty. Even where we are uncertain about the meaning of the words, they offer at times sudden glimpses of the ineffable mystery of human life—something he never succeeds in doing in his more "philosophical" plays, such as *Lazarus Laughed.* Whereas most of O'Neill's prostitutes are unconvincing and juvenile, Cybel becomes much more than the personified abstraction she was meant to be. The other characters are equally well realized. It is only when Brown seizes the mask from the dead Anthony and starts putting it on and removing it at frequent intervals that the audience, not to mention Margaret, is lost in bewilderment. The play bogs down at this point, but perhaps a more conventional treatment would have meant a loss of vividness and dramatic power. (pp. 53-5)

[In *Marco Millions* O'Neill turned] to fantasy with a pseudo-historical background, adding only the new element of satire. In an ironical foreword he states his intention of whitewashing the soul of Marco Polo, which he proceeds to do by revealing him as a glorified traveling salesman, a true Babbitt—shrewd, aggressive, materialistic, uxorious, entirely devoid of sensibility. (p. 55)

[With *Strange Interlude* O'Neill revived] the ancient aside and soliloquy to express the inner thoughts of the characters. So completely were these last two devices used that one might almost say that O'Neill employed the regular dialogue to supplement the asides, rather than vice versa. This was an attempt, of course, to adapt in drama the stream of consciousness method of contemporary fiction, and except for slowing up the action it proved fairly successful. The nine acts of *Strange Interlude* represent the intimate relations of Nina Leeds, daughter of a college professor, to several men who affected her life, especially to three. Emotionally upset because of the death in France of her fiancé, Nina hates her father, whom she considers responsible for preventing their marriage. She leaves home to become a nurse and returns only at her father's death. She is then prevailed upon to marry Sam Evans, diffident and good-natured, and feels almost happy at the discovery of her pregnancy until she learns of a strain of insanity in Sam's family. She resorts to abortion, but unhappy and maladjusted once more, she takes as her lover Dr. Darrell, who lives up to his bargain of supplying her with another child. As little Gordon grows up, he feels instinctive hatred for his real father but, ironically enough, loves Sam, his ostensible one. Later Nina goes through the maternal torture of losing Gordon, now grown up, to the girl he loves, and after the death of Sam Evans she decides to marry Charlie Marsden, a spinsterish childhood admirer, whom she has come to associate psychologically with her father. This fragmentary synopsis may suffice to indicate O'Neill's invasion of the novelistic medium and his dependence on Freudian psychology—the Oedipus complex and the father-daughter fixation, for example—in such manner that the soliloquies and asides become almost imperative to indicate inner motives, loves, hates, and by-plays. (pp. 56-7)

[What most critics consider O'Neill's masterpiece, *Mourning Becomes Electra*,] is described as a trilogy; the three parts, with a total of thirteen acts, were entitled respectively *Homecoming, The Hunted,* and *The Haunted.* . . . In the new play O'Neill attempts to reinterpret the old story of Agamemnon, Clytemnestra, Orestes, and Elektra in terms of modern psychology. The result is a New England tragedy, not particularly Greek, but remarkably effective and moving. The main incidents of the classic plot have been preserved. (p. 59)

Giving force and direction to this tragic plot, the Freudian concepts of the subconscious are employed freely to suggest a twentieth-century version of fate. Christine, having felt nothing but revulsion on her wedding night, hates both Mannon and her eldest child, Lavinia. The latter, on the other hand, starved for affection in childhood, is jealous of her mother and in

love with her father. Her secret passion for Captain Brant, her mother's lover, who resembles her father, adds to this jealousy—her hatred being rationalized into a sense of duty to avenge her father's murder. After Christine's death Vinnie temporarily blossoms out and, interestingly enough, begins to affect her mother's dress and manner. But [her brother] Orin, victim of an Oedipus complex, transfers his incestuous love to Vinnie and becomes insanely jealous of her attentions to other men. "Can't you see," he exclaims, "I'm now in Father's place and you're Mother? That's the evil destiny out of the past I haven't dared predict! I'm the Mannon you're chained to!" Orin's rantings in the third part of the trilogy become a little tedious but nevertheless the underlying psychological motivation works out extremely well. (p. 60)

Up to this point a dominant note in O'Neill's plays . . . had been a sense of futility at the tragedy of human life, finding expression in dramatic irony or in the unhappy ending. At least, no one would have accused the playwright of philosophical optimism. Man might have an essential nobility of character, but Fate or God or his own self was always getting him "balled up." Lazarus expresses positive affirmation in the goodness of life, but in spite of his optimism his wife was poisoned and he himself burned at the stake. It came, therefore, as a distinct shock to find the author suddenly turned kindly, wistful, reflective, and reminiscent in his first comedy, *Ah, Wilderness!* . . . *Ah, Wilderness!* is a homely, bourgeois comedy of "the American large small-town at the turn of the century." . . . The protagonist here is really the entire family, typical American and upper middle-class, with the kindly father, the adolescent child, the maiden aunt, the family drunkard, and so on. All are depicted graphically with the faithfulness of portraits in a family album. (pp. 61-2)

[*The Iceman Cometh* shows O'Neill] concerned philosophically with the mystery of human illusion. Employing the bare yet leisurely simplicity of *Days without End*—in contrast to the more luxuriant and melodramatic style of his earlier work—he exhibits in *The Iceman Cometh* a group of down-and-outers that frequent Harry Hope's West Side saloon in 1912. The place is described sardonically by one of the characters as the No Chance Saloon, Bedrock Bar, the End of the Line Café, the Bottom of the Sea Rathskeller. And yet its habitués are far from unhappy; they manage somehow to remain drunk and they delude themselves "with a few harmless pipe dreams about their yesterdays and tomorrows." (p. 65)

As the play opens, the entire group of derelicts is waiting for the arrival of Hickey, a hardware salesman, who never fails to appear with plenty of money and jovial talk to celebrate Hope's birthday party. In the past Hickey has enlivened the occasion with comic gags, the favorite one being that he has just left his wife in the hay with the iceman. This time, however, he is no longer the life of the party—he even refuses to drink with the gang. As he tells them, he no longer needs alcohol; he has faced the truth about himself and now, being at last without illusions, he is completely at peace. This peace he insists on bestowing on his comrades by the process of destroying their pipe dreams of yesterday and tomorrow. The task of thus saving them is both difficult and painful, resulting in quarrels and burning hatred. . . . By next day Hickey has driven most of his companions out of the saloon in an effort to bring their pipe dreams to the test of actual realization. They all rush back in panic, as he knew they would, but he believes that the shattering of their final illusions will bring them the peace that he has himself attained. But to Hickey's surprise they are completely licked; even when they drink they find the whiskey has lost its kick. In spirit and appearance they are dead. To convert them by his own example Hickey then tells them the sordid story of his marriage to Evelyn. In spite of his many moral lapses she always forgave him, deluding herself into thinking that this was the last time and that he would reform. The only way to free Evelyn from this pipe dream of reformation, to give her the peace she always wanted, Hickey tells the startled group, was for him to kill her. He insists he committed the murder with love, not hate, in his heart. But suddenly, in the course of his recital, Hickey comes to the unexpected realization that he too has been deluding himself, that he really killed Evelyn because he hated her. The revelation is too much for Hickey to face, and he says he must have been insane. Pouncing avidly upon this straw of Hickey's insanity, which would nullify the cogency of his persuasive arguments, Hope and most of his cronies regain their composure and their illusions, ending the play in a good old drunken brawl. (pp. 66-7)

It is evident that *The Iceman Cometh* presents an O'Neill sobered by experience, a step further in philosophical disillusionment, concerned for the moment not with the inhumanity of God but with the mystery of man's own soul. Is it possible for mankind to live without pipe dreams, illusions? The answer seems to be no. In the course of the play Larry identifies the Iceman with Death, and Hickey's attempt to strip life of all rationalizations results in death—for his wife, for the young radical, for Larry perhaps, for the others temporarily; Hickey deceives himself that he has found peace, but it is the peace of insanity or maybe of the electric chair. . . . As in earlier plays, O'Neill writes much about tortured marital and filial relationships, but though Freud looms in the background, the language and the technique are no longer the professional psychologist's. In fact, *The Iceman Cometh* gives rather the impression of being a modern morality play with its symbolism disguised in grimly realistic terms. As in the past the author makes no concessions to popular ap-

peal, the play's theme, its characters, its length all militating against its acceptance. In deliberately avoiding the dramatic cohesion and sweep of his earlier work, O'Neill often makes his action seem slow and repetitious. Yet, if *The Iceman Cometh* falls short of his highest dramatic achievement, no one can deny on the other hand that it has a depth and power rarely found on the Broadway stage.

An accurate estimate of Eugene O'Neill's place in American drama cannot with justice be given until his work is complete. . . . His main contributions to American drama, very considerable ones as we have seen, belong mainly to his first ten years on Broadway. They may be summarized briefly as (1) revival of tragedy and the unhappy ending; (2) romantic novelty of scene; (3) realism of situation and character in the depiction of sailors, prostitutes, farmers, Negroes, and others of humble station; (4) use of profanity and realistic diction on the stage; (5) experimentation in form, including the use of multiple scenes and acts; (6) interest in symbolism, leading to unnaturalistic scenery, revival of masks, and other devices; (7) adoption of Freudian psychology with ingenious revival of the soliloquy and aside to represent the stream of consciousness; (8) development of historical fantasy, tending toward the masque form in such plays as *Marco Millions* . . . ; (9) passionate absorption in the problem of man's rapport with himself and with God, leading at various times to frustration, to dramatic irony, or to conversion. The enumeration may be incomplete but it will at least indicate the variety of O'Neill's interests and experiments. He was of particular significance as a pioneer, even when his innovations were considerably modified by subsequent writers. . . . He had, in short, the genius to select timely themes and techniques, and if some of his plays appear dated, the reason is partly that his innovations were so widely adopted that we no longer recall how revolutionary they once were. O'Neill's experimental boldness helped to establish his position as the first great dramatist of the art theatre and as a poet, but from the start he was also a realist and will probably best be remembered for those plays that show an ideal fusion of realism and imagination. (pp. 67-70)

Edmond M. Gagey, "Eugene O'Neill," in his *Revolution in American Drama*, Columbia University Press, 1947, pp. 39-70.

ROBERT BRUSTEIN

(essay date 1964)

[In the following excerpt, Brustein claims that O'Neill will be remembered primarily for the plays of his later career, specifically those written after *Ah, Wilderness!*]

As some of the dust begins to settle over the controversial reputation of Eugene O'Neill, and our interest shifts from the man to art, it becomes increasingly clear that O'Neill will be primarily remembered for his last plays. The earlier ones are not all without value, though none is thoroughly satisfying. Some contain powerful scenes; some have interesting themes; and some are sustained by the sheer force of the author's will. Still, the bulk of O'Neill dramatic writings before *Ah Wilderness!* are like the groping preparatory sketches of one who had to write badly in order to write well; and in comparison with the late O'Neill even intermittently effective dramas like *The Hairy Ape, All God's Chillun Got Wings,* and *Desire Under the Elms* are riddled with fakery, incoherence, and clumsy experimental devices. No major dramatist, with the possible exception of Shaw, has written so many second-rate plays. (p. 321)

O'Neill came to prominence in the second and third decades of the century, when America was just beginning to relinquish its philistinism in order to genuflect before the shrine of Culture. The American culture craze was largely directed towards the outsides of the literature, which is to say towards the personality of the artist rather than the content of his art; and the novelists and poets inducted into this hollow ritual found themselves engaged in an activity more priestly than creative. O'Neill's role was especially hieratic, however, since he had the misfortune to be the first dramatist with serious aspirations to appear on the national scene. . . . But to a large body of hungry critics and cultural consumers, who were indifferent to the quality of the product so long as it was Big, O'Neill was a homegrown dramatic champion to be enlisted not only against Ibsen, Strindberg, and Shaw, but against Aeschylus, Euripides, and Shakespeare as well. (pp. 321-22)

Afflicted with the American disease of gigantism, O'Neill developed ambitions which were not only large, they were monstrous; he was determined to be nothing if not a world-historical figure of fantastic proportion. Trying to compress within his own career the whole development of dramatic literature since the Greeks, he set himself to imitate the most ambitious writers who ever lived—and the more epic their scope, the more they stimulated his competitive instinct. The scope of his own intentions is suggested by the growing length of his plays and the presumptousness of his public utterances. *Mourning Becomes Electra,* which took three days to perform, he called "an idea and a dramatic conception that has the possibilities of being the biggest thing modern drama has attempted—by far the biggest!" And his unfinished eleven-play "Big Grand Opus," as he called it, was designed to have "greater scope than any novel I know of . . . something in the style of *War and Peace.*" At this point in his career, O'Neill, like his public, is attracted to the outsides of literature, and he wrestles with the reputation of another writer in order to boost his own. But to O'Neill's public, ambitions were almost indistinguishable from achievements; and the playwright was ranked with the world's greatest dramatists before he had an opportunity to master his craft or sophisticate his art. (pp. 322-23)

Subjected to closer scrutiny, the very qualities which had inspired so much enthusiasm in O'Neill's partisans now seemed the marks of a pretentious writer and a second-rate mind. Pushed about by this critical storm, the winds of literary fashion shifted, and O'Neill's reputation was blown out to sea. Although the playwright was awarded the Nobel prize in 1936, obscurity had already settled in upon him, and it deepened more and more until his death in 1953. During these dark years, ironically, O'Neill's real development began. Before, he had prided himself on having "the guts to shoot at something big and risk failure"; now, he had the guts not to bother himself about questions of success and failure at all. Maturing in silence, stimulated only by an obsessive urge to write and a profound artistic honesty, he commenced to create plays which were genuine masterpieces of the modern theatre. Most of these were not published or produced until after his death, some by the playwright's order. In proscribing *A Long Day's Journey into Night,* O'Neill was trying to hide his family's secrets from the public eye; but O'Neill's desire to keep his works off the stage was undoubtedly influenced, too, by the hostile reception accorded to *The Iceman Cometh* and *A Moon for the Misbegotten,* the first of which failed on Broadway, the second, before even reaching New York. The public and the reviewers, having found new idols to worship (the Critic's prize the year of *The Iceman Cometh* went to a conventional social protest play by Arthur Miller called *All My Sons*), began to treat O'Neill with condescension—when they thought of him at all. And he was not to be seriously reconsidered until 1956, when a successful revival of *The Iceman Cometh* and the first Broadway production of *A Long Day's Journey* brought him so much posthumous recognition that his inferior work was soon dragged out of storage for some more unthinking praise. (pp. 323-24)

Aside from the one-act sea plays, which are modest in scope and relatively conventional in form, O'Neill's early drama tends to be Expressionist in its symbolic structure and messianic in its artistic stance. Both O'Neill's Expressionism and messianism, I hasten to add, are borrowed, illfitting robes. By the time O'Neill begins to write, the theatre of revolt is an established movement in every country except America, where the theatre has produced nothing more exhilarating than the fabricated fantasies of Fitch, Boucicault, and Belasco. Thus, the drama of the continent constitutes an untapped mine of material, and O'Neill, recognizing its potentialities, becomes the first dramatist to exploit it; with the aid of the Provincetown Players, he does for the American awareness of European drama what Shaw and the Independent Theatre did for the English.

Although O'Neill is originally considered a wild, untutored genius, therefore, his early work is clearly the offshoot of a very intellectualistic mind, attuned more to literature than to life. Aligning himself with the more radical of the rebel dramatists, he is soon impersonating their postures, imitating their doctrines, and copying their techniques. One can detect the influence of Ibsen, Toller, Shaw, Gorky, Pirandello, Wedekind, Synge, Andreyev, and others in the early plays of O'Neill, but chief among his dramatic models in this period is August Strindberg, whom O'Neill, in his Nobel prize acceptance speech, called "the greatest of all modern dramatists." . . . O'Neill's relation to his plays . . . is very Strindbergian: he is almost always the hero of his work, trying to work out his personal difficulties through the medium of his art. (pp. 324-26)

As an experimental dramatist, O'Neill would naturally be attracted to the greatest innovator in the modern theatre; and O'Neill's Expressionism is certainly indebted to Strindberg's dream techniques. The difference is that Strindberg's formal experiments grow out of his material, while O'Neill's seem grafted onto his, and thus give the impression of being gratuitous and excessive. . . . Thus, O'Neill uses Expressionistic devices to communicate ideas which he is either too inarticulate or too undisciplined to express through speech and action. And his masks, asides, soliloquies, choruses, split characters and the like are really substitutes for dramatic writing (most of these conventions are borrowed from the novel), provoked not by a new vision but rather by a need to disguise the banality of the original material. Thus, instead of opening up uncharted territory, O'Neill's devices invariably fog up already familiar ground, as for example the interminable soliloquizing of *Strange Interlude* which, instead of going deeper into the unconscious mind, merely compounds the verbalized trivialities of the characters with their trivial unspoken thoughts. Moving from mono-dramas to miracle plays to historical dramas to mob plays to

Greek tragedies, O'Neill appears to experiment largely for the sake of novelty without ever staying with a form long enough to perfect it. (pp. 327-28)

O'Neill exposes the philosophical incertitude of the Strindbergian rebel—the pain, the doubts, the confusion. But although there are undoubtedly genuine feelings beneath all this, O'Neill's spiritual crises seem very literary, and his expression of them comes to him secondhand. Furthermore, one is never convinced that O'Neill has read very deeply in those philosophies that he affirms and rejects; his works display the intellectual attitudinizing of the self-conscious autodidact. It is this aspect of the early O'Neill, in fact, which most arouses the spleen of the second generation of his critics. "Mr. O'Neill is not a thinker," asserts Francis Fergusson, while Eric Bentley adds, "He is so little a thinker, it is dangerous for him to think." Both critics go on to demonstrate how O'Neill's superficial treatment of fashionable ideas was his main appeal to a superficial and fashionable audience; and both have shown how emotion and thought fail to cohere in his drama. . . . O'Neill's failure, I would suggest, is not a failure of mind so much as a failure of feeling. It is not that he is incapable of thought but rather that he is incapable of *thinking like a dramatist*, communicating his ideas through significant action. And this may be because all of his ideas, in this period, are borrowed rather than experienced. Thus, we find notions of Tragedy out of Nietzsche, of the Puritan Booboisie out of Mencken and Nathan, of the Racial Unconscious out of Jung, of the Oedipus Complex out of Freud, and of Hereditary Guilt out of Aeschylus and Ibsen—all grafted onto plots which are largely unconvincing, irrelevant, or inconsequential.

In fact, the major components of his plots, in this particular phase, are romantic love and swashbuckling adventure, both treated in a manner more appropriate to the melodramatic stage of his father, James O'Neill, than to the theatre of revolt. Ironically, O'Neill always thinks he is defining himself *against* this kind of theatre. . . . (p. 333)

O'Neill's attempt to introduce large themes into his work is a sign of his rebellion against the mindless nineteenth-century stage, but he has assimilated more of "the old, ranting, artificial romantic stuff" than he knows. . . . In O'Neill, everything seems to render down to romance or sex, despite the fact that the author has an extremely naive conception of sexuality. One has only to note his puerile sentimentalization of whores, his Romantic idealization of chaste women— or still worse, his laughable ideas about extramarital affairs, exposed in that fantastic *Strange Interlude* scene where Darrell and Nina cold-bloodedly decide to mate only to produce a child, and discuss the liaison in the third person for the sake of scientific impartiality.

Allied to O'Neill's treatment of sex is his treat-

Major Media Adaptations: Motion Pictures

Anna Christie, 1923. Associated First National Pictures (Thomas H. Ince). [Silent] Director: John Griffith Wray. Cast: Blanche Sweet, George F. Marion, William Russell, Eugene Besserer, Ralph Yearsley.

Anna Christie, 1930. MGM. Director: Clarence Brown. Cast: Greta Garbo, Charles Bickford, Marie Dressler, James T. Mack, Lee Phelps.

Strange Interlude, 1932. MGM (Irving Thalberg). Director: Robert Z. Leonard. Cast: Norma Shearer, Clark Gable, Robert Young, Maureen O'Sullivan.

The Emperor Jones, 1933. UA. Director: Dudley Murphy. Cast: Paul Robeson, Dudley Digges, Frank Wilson.

Ah, Wilderness!, 1935. MGM (Hunt Stromberg). Director: Clarence Brown. Cast: Wallace Beery, Lionel Barrymore, Mickey Rooney, Frank Albertson.

The Long Voyage Home, 1940. Walter Wagner. Director: John Ford. Cast: John Wayne, Thomas Mitchell, Ian Hunter, Ward Bond, Wilfred Lawson.

The Hairy Ape, 1944. Jules Levy. Director: Alfred Santell.

Cast: William Bendix, Susan Hayward, John Loder, Dorothy Comingore, Roman Bohnen.

Mourning Becomes Electra, 1947. RKO/Theatre Guild (Dudley Nichols). Director: Dudley Nichols. Cast: Michael Redgrave, Rosalind Russell, Kirk Douglas, Nancy Coleman.

Summer Holiday, 1948. MGM. [Musical adaptation of *Ah, Wilderness!*] Director: Rouben Mamoulian. Cast: Mickey Rooney, Gloria DeHaven, Walter Huston, Frank Morgan, Agnes Moorehead.

Desire under the Elms, 1958. Paramount (Don Hartman). Director: Delbert Mann. Cast: Sophia Loren, Burl Ives, Anthony Perkins, Frank Overton, Pernell Roberts.

Long Day's Journey into Night, 1961. Ely Landau. Director: Sidney Lumet. Cast: Ralph Richardson, Katherine Hepburn, Jason Robards, Dean Stockwell.

The Iceman Cometh, 1973. American Film Theatre. Director: John Frankenheimer. Cast: Lee Marvin, Fredric March, Robert Ryan, Jeff Bridges.

---

ment of incest, which is also romanticized in the pulsing accents of *True Confessions* magazine. In *Mourning Becomes Electra,* for example incest becomes as common as weeds, and equally inevitable. . . . "Fierce, bruising kisses" are called for in almost every one of O'Neill's earlier plays—the more fierce and bruising when they are incestuously motivated—accompanied by bathetic odes to Beauty and jerky apostrophes to Nature. But sex in O'Neill remains without complexity, darkness, or genuine passion, the mentalized fantasy of an adolescent temperament, and totally incompatible with the portentous philosophical attitudes it is meant to support. (pp. 334-36)

[*The Iceman Cometh*] is a chronicle of O'Neill's own spiritual metamorphosis from a messianic into an existential rebel, the shallow yea-saying salvationist of the earlier plays having been transformed into a penetrating analyst of human motive rejecting even the pose of disillusionment. O'Neill's "denial of any other experience of faith in my plays" has left him alone, at last, with existence itself; and he has looked at it with a courage which only the greatest tragic dramatists have been able to muster. *The Iceman Cometh,* despite its prosaic language, recreates that existential groan which is heard in Shakespeare's tragedies and in the third choral poem of Sophocles's *Oedipus at Colonus,* as O'Neill makes reality bearable through the metaphysical consolations of art. O'Neill has rejected Hickey's brand of salvation as a way to human happiness, but truth has, nevertheless, become the cornerstone of his drama, truth combined with . . . compassionate understanding. . . . Expunging everything false and literary from

his work, O'Neill has finally reconciled himself to being the man he really is.

This kind of reconciliation could only have come about through penetrating self-analysis; and it is inevitable, therefore, that the process of self-analysis itself should form the material of one of his plays: *A Long Day's Journey into Night*. . . . Here, combining the retrospective techniques of Ibsen with the exorcistic attack of Strindberg, O'Neill compresses the psychological history of his family into the events of a single day, and the economy of the work, for all its length, is magnificent. Within this Classical structure, where O'Neill even observes the unities, the play begins to approach a kind of formal perfection. Like most Classical works, *A Long Day's Journey into Night* is set in the past. . . . And like most Classical works, its impact derives less from physical action (the play has hardly any plot, and only the first act has any suspense) than from psychological revelation, as the characters dredge up their painful memories and half-considered thoughts. (pp. 348-49)

O'Neill . . . is not only the author of the play but also a character in it; like Strindberg, he has written "a poem of desperation," composed in rhythms of pain. . . . The play, written as he tells us "in tears and blood," was composed in a cold sweat, sometimes fifteen hours at a stretch: O'Neill, like all his characters, is confronting his most harrowing memories, and putting his ghosts to rest in a memorial reenactment of their mutual suffering and responsibility.

Because his purpose is partially therapeutic, O'Neill has hardly fictionalized this autobiography at all. (p. 349)

In view of this fidelity to fact, it is a wonder that O'Neill was able to write the play at all, but he is in astonishing control of his material—the work is a masterpiece. While *The Iceman Cometh* has fewer arid stretches and deeper implications, *A Long Day's Journey* contains the finest writing O'Neill ever did—and the fourth act is among the most powerful scenes in all dramatic literature. O'Neill has created a personal play which bears on the condition of all mankind; a bourgeois family drama with universal implications. *A Long Day's Journey* is a study of hereditary guilt which does not even make recourse to arbitrary metaphors, like Ibsen's use of disease in *Ghosts.* (p. 350)

In the plays that follow, O'Neill continues to work the vein he had mined in *The Iceman Cometh* and *A Long Day's Journey:* examining, through the medium of a faithful realism, the people of the fog and their illusionary lives. And in writing these plays, he stammers no more. In the lilting speech of predominantly Irish-Catholic characters, O'Neill finally discovers a language congenial to him, and he even begins to create a music very much like Synge's, while his humor bubbles more and more to the surface. Despite effective comic passages, however, O'Neill's plays remain dark. (p. 358)

[*A Touch of the Poet* and *A Moon for the Misbegotten*] are minor masterpieces; *The Iceman Cometh* and *A Long Day's Journey* major ones. And in all four plays, O'Neill concentrates a fierce, bullish power into fables of illusion and reality, shot through with flashes of humor, but pervaded by a sense of melancholy over the condition of being human. Like Strindberg, therefore, O'Neill develops from messianic rebellion into existential rebellion, thus demonstrating that beneath his Nietzschean yea-saying and affirmation of life was a profound discontent with the very nature of existence. O'Neill's experiments with form, his flirtations with various philosophies and religions, his attitudinizing and fake poeticizing represent the means by which he tried to smother this perception; but it would not be smothered, and when he finally found the courage to face it through realistic probes of his own past experience, he discovered the only artistic role that really fit him. In power and insight, O'Neill remains unsurpassed among American dramatists, and, of course, it is doubtful if, without him, there would have been an American drama at all. But it is for his last plays that he will be remembered—those extraordinary dramas of revolt which he pulled out of himself in pain and suffering, a sick and tired man in a shuttered room unable to bear much light. (p. 359)

Robert Brustein, "Eugene O'Neill," in his *The Theatre of Revolt: An Approach to the Modern Drama,* Little, Brown and Company, 1964, pp. 329-59.

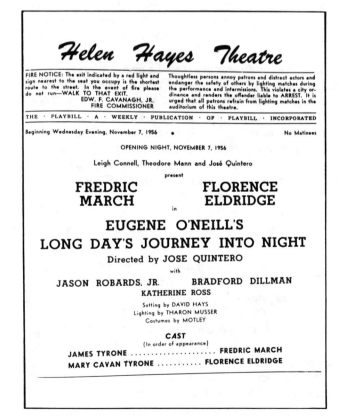

Playbill from the American premier of *Long Day's Journey into Night.*

JACKSON R. BRYER
(essay date 1970)

[In the following excerpt, Bryer describes *Long Day's Journey into Night* as one of the very few tragedies in modern American theater.]

One of the many ironies in the career of Eugene O'Neill is that, in 1931, when he deliberately tried to write a modern play which would approximate the Greek ideal of tragic drama, he produced *Mourning Becomes Electra.* This thirteen-act monstrosity is one of the great white elephants of our theater history. Not only does it lack the great dialogue of tragedy but it also fails because of its over-simplified view of characters entirely motivated by Freudian complexes which O'Neill substituted for the Greek idea of Fate. A decade later, however, when he simply sat down and wrote out the story which had been torturing him for years—that of his own family—O'Neill produced, in *Long Day's Journey Into Night,* one of the very few modern plays which we can see as tragic.

To talk about any modern play as a tragedy is immediately to enter what are at best muddy waters. For decades critics have quarreled over what constitutes a "modern" tragedy. A few distinctions are clear, however. One is that the structures which Aristotle supplied in classical times no longer apply. The assumption of the Greeks that theirs was a universe controlled by the gods has never been less warranted than today, when the very existence of any deity is questioned. And there is little or no agreement as to the nature and omnipotence of a God even when His existence is acknowledged. But to remove Fate as the major cause in tragedy is not to suggest that, in the modern theater, we have been unwilling to substitute other forces for this Greek idea. Not surprisingly, we seem to have supplied causes which result from universally held notions of our day, as the idea of Fate deriving from the gods was held by the Greeks. Because we live in a highly scientific age—and because the beginnings of modern drama parallel the dawn of that age—our causes, principally heredity and environment, are major determinants in the lives of individuals and, hence, we accept them as irreversible and uncontrollable forces in the lives of dramatic characters. Thus, Ibsen in *Ghosts* and Chekhov in *The Cherry Orchard* represent the two germinal strands of the modern theater, each writing plays of tragic proportions based primarily on heredity and environment, respectively.

But I would carry this one step further and suggest that for a modern play to be truly tragic we must have more than these uncontrollable forces operating on an individual. His demise must also be partially his own fault before a true ambivalence can exist. Again, the reason can be found in the assumptions of our society as opposed to the Greeks. We live in an essentially humanistic age. Because of this, while we accept the influence of heredity and environment, we do not see them as totally determining our lives. The Greeks, on the other hand, did see the gods in this way. We have a more sophisticated and complicated view of the causes for our actions and for the directions our lives take. To be convincingly tragic a modern play must reflect this more complex perspective. There are relatively few examples of American drama that meet this challenge; but where it is met we can see the attributes noted above. In Tennessee Williams' two great classics, *The Glass Menagerie* and *A Streetcar Named Desire,* and in Arthur Miller's *Death of a Salesman* and *The Crucible,* we see characters who are victims both of their backgrounds and environments and of characteristics within themselves.

Finally, it is possible to make some further observations about the nature of these characteristics which are partially responsible for the figurative or literal downfall of the tragic protagonist. In many cases, the character's flaw—to borrow from Aristotle—is often the quality which in another sense makes him exceptional. Laura's flaw in *The Glass Menagerie* is, at least to

some extent, that she cannot exist in the real world (this is, in fact, the flaw of all three Wingfields); but is it not also her strength, the basis of her uniqueness? Similarly, in *The Crucible,* it is John Proctor's integrity and honesty which set him apart; but it is these very qualities which make him choose death instead of a false confession. Even in *Oedipus Rex,* if we discount for a moment the overall causative factor of Fate, Oedipus' outstanding quality is his inquiring mind which has enabled him to solve the riddle of the Sphinx; but it is the same spirit of inquiry which makes him continue to question Tiresias and thus bring about his tragedy. This, then, seems to be one of the paradoxes inherent in tragedy—that a man's weakness is also his strength and that this very quality which sets him apart from other men may cause his destruction—or at least be responsible for his unhappiness.

Long Day's Journey Into Night exhibits most of these characteristics of modern tragedy; and it goes beyond other plays of the modern American theater in two major respects: first, it involves four tragic characters whose lives are inextricably bound but who are nonetheless decided individuals, complexly and completely depicted and explored; and second, rather than offering only heredity and environment as the partial—and uncontrollable—elements in the destinies of these figures, O'Neill offers a far more profound and abstract additional factor—love. Love binds together the four Tyrones; but love is also at the basis of their tragedy. Were there not love between the members of the family, Jamie and Edmund could leave, James could detach himself from his wife's illness and his sons' problems, and Mary could, in a sense, return to the safety of her girlhood. But, as in Sartre's *No Exit,* hell for the Tyrones is other people, each other.

All of them in the course of the play express, either explicitly or implicitly or both, a yearning for an isolated existence. The most overt examples of this are Edmund's speeches at the beginning of Act IV in which he admits that all he wants is "to be alone with myself in another world where truth is untrue and life can hide from itself." For him, the sea is the epitome of this condition and in his long reminiscence about his experiences at sea he expresses total satisfaction with an existence in which he was alone with nature, with "none of the crew in sight," a time when he belonged "to a fulfillment beyond men's lousy, pitiful, greedy fears and hopes and dreams."

Jamie's continual state of drunkenness is an expression of *his* longing for isolation; just as Mary's drug addiction implies the same sort of desire to escape the real world and envelop herself in a protective fog. James' escapes are more subtle. In one respect, his refuge is *The Count of Monte Cristo,* the "big money-maker" on which he has squandered his talents. It has enabled him to stop living creatively. His pose as a patrician land-owner also provides him with an escape from his true heritage as a shanty Irishman and makes it possible for him often to dissociate himself from his contemporaries.

But at the same time that the Tyrones seek escape, they see that it is impossible; they realize that they are hopelessly tied to one another for life. This realization, combined with the desire to escape, produces what is perhaps the major tension in the play, a tension which is expressed primarily in a continual series of expressions of love and hatred on the part of each character. Throughout the play, each Tyrone says and does many things deliberately to hurt another. They strike out at each other like the caged animals that they are; but, in virtually the next breath, they profess deep and genuine affection. This ambivalence provides *Long Day's Journey* with one of its most complex elements.

In Act IV, Jamie drunkenly admits to Edmund that he deliberately introduced him to the dissolute existence that he, Jamie, relishes because he "never wanted you to succeed and look even worse by comparison." He then blames Edmund's birth for Mary's dope addiction and, while he admits that it is not Edmund's fault, he declares, "God damn you, I can't help hating your guts—!" But, almost immediately, he adds, "But don't get the wrong idea, Kid. I love you more than I hate you." Similarly, in Act I, when all three Tyrones are concerned about the possible return of Mary's habit, it is Jamie, whose love for his mother is the cause of his hatred of Edmund, who deliberately lets slip the fact that Edmund's illness is more than a cold, a disclosure which he knows is likely to help drive her back to morphine. Later in the same act, Edmund, who is even closer to Mary than Jamie is, unnecessarily tells her that he heard her go into the spare room the night before, a sure indication that she is back on the drug.

Mary and James accuse one another continually, Mary blaming her husband for not providing a home for his family and for being a miser, James bitterly blaming her for ruining their happiness. Yet, at the end of their most heated exchange, early in Act II, Scene 2, Mary exclaims, "James! We've loved each other! We always will!" And, in Act II, Mary reminds Jamie that he should have more respect for his father: "You ought to be proud you're his son!" Both Mary and James also reminisce often about how happy they were with one another once; and they do so in terms that make it very clear that they still love each other a great deal.

Both sons lash out at their father throughout the play. Mary even at one point tells Edmund, "I never knew what rheumatism was before you were born!" Yet, despite all this rancor, there is abundant evidence of abiding affection. This is ironically and appropriately symbolized at the very end of the play when Mary, completely under the influence of morphine, drifts in dragging her wedding gown and wanders about the room reminiscing about her girlhood. The reverie concludes with her memory of senior year when she decided to be a nun; but then, she recalls, "in the spring something happened to me. . . . I fell in love with James Tyrone and was so happy for a time." This brief passage sums up all of one aspect of the tragedy. Mary's love for James, and all the Tyrones' love for each other, is both their great strength and the cause of their torture. If they did not love each other so much, they could not strike out so cruelly, they could not hate. Edmund's remark about Mary—"It's as if, in spite of loving us, she hated us!"—might well be changed to read because she loves us, she hates us, and then applied equally to all the relationships in this family. And, finally, each character's desire to escape the others, to find an isolation away from the complications of other people, is really no more nor less than a wish to evade one of the major responsibilities of the human condition, contact with other human beings and all the conflicting emotions and attitudes that these contacts produce. As Edmund says in Act IV—and as many an O'Neill protagonist could and does echo—"It was a great mistake, my being born a man. I would have been much more successful as a sea gull or a fish."

But there are other tragic aspects to *Long Day's Journey*. An important one is suggested by my earlier remarks about the forces operating on an individual in modern tragic drama. In O'Neill's play, each of the Tyrones is both responsible and not responsible for the part he is playing. The best example of this is James. The three members of his family accuse him of being miserly and there is ample confirmation of this charge, most especially in his efforts to send Edmund to an inexpensive sanitorium. But, in Act IV, James admits to Edmund that perhaps he is a "stinking old miser" and goes on to explain this trait by describing his childhood when he "learned the value of a dollar" working twelve hours a day in a machine shop, a "dirty barn of a place where rain dripped through the roof," for fifty cents a week. With this disclosure it becomes clear that James is not entirely to blame for his penurious ways. It is not his fault that he was brought up in a penniless and fatherless family. This background understandably has made him overly sensitive to the evils of the poorhouse. And yet we cannot totally excuse this quality in James because we feel that, once he became financially successful, he should have developed more generous instincts in accordance with normal familial devotion. Clearly, however, the responsibility for James' weakness is divided between forces in his background over which he had no control and present factors which he should be able to alter.

The same sort of divided responsibility can be seen in the three other characters. Jamie's drunken and dissolute ways are certainly his own fault to an extent, but they can also be traced to the family situation. His father introduced him to drink and brought him up in an atmosphere where he could meet the cheap tarts and low types with whom he now associates. Jamie's failures in life can also be linked partially to his father's refusal to allow him to be a success. This is perhaps because James realizes that he has sold his own talents for a sure financial return and he must therefore keep his son from being any more successful than he is. Jamie's problems are also further compounded by his relationships with his mother and his brother. He feels, with considerable justification, that Mary dotes on Edmund and ignores him. He also is, as he admits to Edmund in Act IV, extremely jealous of his brother and of the possibility that he will succeed and make him look worse by comparison.

Mary also is both victim and causative factor. She is guilty of forcing her family into an almost death-like inaction by her drug addiction; but when we look at her background and the cause of her illness, we find ample extenuating circumstances. She is, in many ways, still the shy convent girl who, as O'Neill stresses in his long stage direction introducing her, "has never lost" her "innate unworldly innocence." Because of this she is totally unable to cope with the cruel realities of the world around her. In this she shares more than a literal kinship with Edmund, who also cannot face the world because of a sensitive poetic nature. Both Mary and Edmund feel a tremendous lack of belonging, a loneliness. It is difficult to decide whether Mary's addiction, like Laura's limp in *The Glass Menagerie,* causes her isolation or whether the addiction is merely an overt manifestation of the isolation which is already there. Mary has not been at peace since she left her father's house to marry James. While it is true that James has never given her the house she so desperately wants, she would undoubtedly have been unable to cope with one had she been asked to do so. Mary's retreat into the past through drugs is her way of going back to what was for her an ideal world, an escape from a real world which she cannot handle. Her addiction is probably no more than a means towards an end which she would have reached—or tried to reach—through another method had morphine not been available. Thus, we cannot totally blame her problems on James and the "cheap quack doctor" who attended her at Edmund's birth. Nor can we blame Edmund's present illness for her reversion to dope. Mary's difficulties are far more deep-seated than this. Her protected childhood has made her constitutionally and emotionally unable to deal with life. On the other hand, Mary *is* guilty of refusing to face her problem. Unlike James, she will not admit either to herself or to her family that she cannot exist in the real world and hence she is torturing her husband and her sons. James can look objectively at his background and see it as a major influence upon his present personality; but Mary, while she can realize that the

"past is the present" and "the future too," cannot act on that understanding.

As I've already said, Edmund is much like his mother—and this probably accounts for the fact that he understands her more fully than anyone else. He is the typical O'Neill protagonist who, he himself realizes, "never feels at home, who does not really want and is not really wanted, who can never belong, who must always be a little in love with death." Unlike his mother and like his father, Edmund does try to face up to his inadequacies and attempts to understand why he does not belong. Mary totally rejects life because she cannot understand it and does not want to try; Edmund accepts life, understanding that he can never really be a part of it. In his long soliloquy midway through Act IV, after he describes the ecstasy of life at sea, he tells how, after that moment, "the hand lets the veil fall and you are alone, lost in the fog again, and you stumble on toward nowhere, for no good reason." But Edmund too is both the victim and the originator of his troubles. His sensitive nature makes him unable to deal with most of the world around him, just as so many O'Neill characters from the Mayo brothers in *Beyond the Horizon* and Yank in *The Hairy Ape* down to the denizens of Harry Hope's bar in *The Iceman Cometh* cannot belong in the real world with which they are faced. But he is also a victim of that world which is so insensitive to him and to his special needs. He is a poet in a world which rejects its poets. And his understanding of this fact is revealed in Act IV, just as Jamie's and James' awareness are disclosed during this final explosive section of the play.

In fact, this last act serves to complicate our responses to these characters enormously in that their capacity to understand and articulate their own weaknesses makes them fit objects of our respect as well as our pity. Up to this point, we are quite ready to accept James as a miser who has repressed his family disastrously, Jamie as a wastrel who has been the major disappointment of his father's life, and Edmund as a foolish dreamer; for these are the pictures we get of them from the three other characters. But when, in Act IV, we hear their side of the story, we can no longer be content simply to dismiss them this easily. What we end up with is the sense of divided responsibility which I defined at the beginning of this essay. It is expressed overtly in *Long Day's Journey* through two brief passages. The first, appropriately enough spoken by Mary, expresses the forces over which she and her family have no control: "None of us can help the things life has done to us. They're done before you realize it, and once they're done they make you do other things until at last everything comes between you and what you'd like to be, and you've lost your true self forever." The second occurs when Edmund remarks to his father that life is "so damned crazy" and James corrects him:

"There's nothing wrong with life. It's we who—*He quotes*. 'The fault, dear Brutus, is not in our stars, but in ourselves that we are underlings.' "

The consequence of this divided responsibility is that, as in any tragic play of the modern era, it is impossible to assign blame. Both controllable and uncontrollable forces operate on the lives of the Tyrones, with the added complication that the very family situation they live in is both a contributor to and a result of the tragic situation. Not only could each of these characters by himself be the subject of a tragic drama—as he could—but also a major share of the tragic element is attributable to their interrelationships. Unlike the Greeks who tended to center their tragedies on one flawed protagonist, O'Neill in *Long Day's Journey* (and, to a certain extent, other modern playwrights like Chekhov, Ibsen, and Williams), seem to see groups of individuals—most often families—caught in webs partially of their own devising but woven by outside forces as well.

The degree of struggle possible within these webs varies from play to play. In *Long Day's Journey* there seems to be very little. In the terms of the passage from *Antigone* quoted as the epigram to this essay, there is definitely a "tranquility" here, a "fellow-feeling" among the four Tyrones, who are, in numerous ways, one character. They are certainly all subject to many of the same tensions and ambivalences. There is, as I've stressed, no easily assigned guilt or innocence; we certainly can find no villain or hero in this play. While there may be some hope for Edmund, it is primarily medically-based or founded quite irrelevantly on the assumption that he is Eugene O'Neill who, after all, did become a successful playwright. Far more germane is the obvious fact that Edmund will never "belong" in

the real world any more than his mother will; he will always be "the stranger" that he realizes he is now. Without hope, as Anouilh notes, a tragic play like *Long Day's Journey* is "restful." The characters are "trapped," as the single set for the play and the fog continually rolling in explicitly indicate. There is a good deal of shouting in the play, but most of it is the ultimately ineffectual beating at the bars of four caged animals who have no other means of voicing their frustrations.

Just as in a later American play with which it shares many common elements, *Who's Afraid of Virginia Woolf ?*, nothing really happens in *Long Day's Journey*. There is very little action, in the conventional dramatic sense of the term; and none of the characters change at all. The reason for this is simple: nothing can happen to four figures in this situation. All we can do is contemplate them in their web and endeavor to understand them with the assistance of the skill of the playwright who unfolds their lives to us. Because no American playwright has depicted more complex and complete characters with more compassion and sheer dramatic power than Eugene O'Neill in *Long Day's Journey*, it deserves a place among the great plays written in any age in any language. It is a further measure of its magnitude that it is also one of the few American plays which meet most of the measures of modern tragedy. That it does so within the framework of a generally conventional realistic four-character domestic drama, rather than through a consciously super-imposed classical mold, merely makes O'Neill's achievement that much more remarkable. (pp. 261-70)

Jackson R. Bryer, " 'Hell Is Other People': 'Long Day's Journey into Night'," in *The Fifties: Fiction, Poetry, Drama*, edited by Warren French, Everett/Edwards, Inc., 1970, pp. 261-70.

SOURCES FOR FURTHER STUDY

Floyd, Virginia. *The Plays of Eugene O'Neill: A New Assessment*. New York: Frederick Ungar, 1985, 605 p.

Collection of critical essays on O'Neill's works.

Frenz, Horst, and Tuck, Susan, eds. *Eugene O'Neill's Critics: Voices from Abroad*. Carbondale: Southern Illinois University Press, 1984, 225 p.

Collection of European, Asian, and South American critical essays about O'Neill's dramas.

Miller, Jordan Y. *Eugene O'Neill and the American Critic*. Rev. ed. Hamden, Conn.: Archon Books, 1973, 553 p.

Most complete annotated bibliography of American criticism on O'Neill.

Ranald, Margaret Loftus. *The Eugene O'Neill Companion*. Westport, Conn.: Greenwood Press, 1984, 827 p.

Valuable study guide, listing all of O'Neill's plays and characters with plot summaries and descriptive commentary. Three appendices offer a chronology of plays, a listing of adaptions of O'Neill's works in other genres, and an essay discussing his theory and practice of the theater.

Sheaffer, Louis. *O'Neill: Son and Playwright*. Boston: Little, Brown, 1968, 543 p.

Major biography. This first of two volumes covers O'Neill's life to 1920.

―――. *O'Neill: Son and Artist.* Boston: Little, Brown, 1973, 750 p.

    The second volume of Sheaffer's biography, covering O'Neill's life from 1920 until his death.

George Orwell

1903-1950

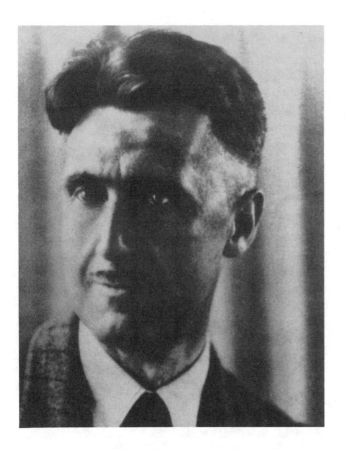

(Pseudonym of Eric Arthur Blair) English novelist, essayist, critic, and journalist.

INTRODUCTION

*O*rwell is significant for his unwavering commitment, both as an individual and as an artist, to personal freedom and social justice. While he wrote a variety of works, his novels *Animal Farm* (1945) and *Nineteen Eighty-Four* (1949) are best known and most widely read. *Animal Farm,* a deceptively simple animal fable about a barnyard revolt, satirizes the consequences of the Russian Revolution, while also suggesting reasons for the universal failure of most revolutionary ideals. Orwell's skill in creating a narrative that functions on several levels is almost unanimously applauded, and the novel is generally regarded as a masterpiece of English prose. *Nineteen Eighty-Four* attacks totalitarianism, warning that absolute power in the hands of any government can deprive a people of all basic freedoms. Although the novel is based in part on the Soviet example, it is set in England to underscore Orwell's conviction that unchecked power even in the hands of a Western democracy could result in a repressive regime. Orwell's ability to perceive the social effects of political theories inspired Irving Howe to call him "the greatest moral force in English letters during the past several decades."

Orwell was born into a lower-middle-class family that struggled to provide him with an education. His mother managed to find him a place, at reduced rates, in a preparatory school where, despite his intellectual accomplishments, he felt demeaned because of his low social standing. In his essay "Such, Such Were the Joys" Orwell explained the guilt and shame he felt throughout his school years and how those experiences fostered his extreme sensitivity to social victimization. After attending Eton College on scholarship, Orwell enlisted in the Indian Imperial Police. Stationed in Burma, he encountered the harsh realities of colonial rule: his reactions are vividly evoked in the essays

"Shooting an Elephant" and "A Hanging," and in the novel *Burmese Days* (1934). Although *Burmese Days* has often been criticized for its awkward attempts at descriptive writing, it has also been called an excellent study of the guilt, hypocrisy, and loneliness that infects the rulers of a subject population.

Disgusted with colonial life, Orwell left the police after five years, determined to become a writer. His first novel, *Down and Out in Paris and London* (1933), which was based on a year he spent in self-imposed poverty, sympathetically examines the life of the poor. While writing this book Orwell discovered that the lower classes of society are exploited much like colonial subjects. His indignation over this fact is reflected throughout his subsequent work. Orwell's other novels written during the thirties deal with victimization: his protagonists are confused individuals, preyed upon by society and their own weaknesses, who attempt to rebel against their lot and fail. During this period Orwell also wrote two books of autobiography and social criticism. In *The Road to Wigan Pier* (1937), commissioned by the socialist Left Book Club, Orwell described the life of English coal miners, but he enraged his sponsors by examining at length the failure of socialists to address the needs of England's poor. In December 1936 Orwell's commitment to justice and freedom led him to travel to Barcelona to investigate and write about the causes and progress of the Spanish Civil War. He joined a militia unit and fought with the Republicans. After being wounded, Orwell returned to England and wrote *Homage to Catalonia* (1938), an account that depicts the absurdities of warfare, the duplicity of every political ideology, and the essential decency of ordinary people caught up in events beyond their control.

Orwell's first major critical and popular success as an author came with the publication of *Animal Farm* in 1945. In his 1946 essay "Why I Write," he stated that "every line of serious work that I have written since 1936 has been written, directly or indirectly, *against* totalitarianism and *for* democratic Socialism, as I understand it." He went on to say that "*Animal Farm* was the first book in which I tried, with full consciousness of what I was doing, to fuse political purpose and artistic purpose into one whole." His income from the book's sales, though not great, enabled him in the spring of 1947 to rent a house on the Scottish island of Jura, where he began work on a new novel. In December of 1947 Orwell was hospitalized for treatment of the tuberculosis from which he had suffered since his midthirties. He spent the first half of 1948 in Hairmyres Hospital in Glasgow, and on his release returned to Jura to complete the novel, tentatively entitled *The Last Man in Europe* but ultimately called *Nineteen Eighty-Four*. Although very ill and under a doctor's orders to work no more than an hour each day, Orwell was unable to find a typist willing to come to the isolat-

ed island, so he prepared the final manuscript of *Nineteen Eighty-Four* himself. He collapsed almost immediately upon completing the task, and was bedridden for the remaining two years of his life. Many critics contend that the overwhelming pessimism of *Nineteen Eighty-Four* is directly related to Orwell's fatal illness, a position supported by Orwell's remark that the novel "wouldn't have been so gloomy if I hadn't been so ill." Friends and acquaintances of Orwell, however, have emphatically maintained that *Nineteen Eighty-Four* was not meant to be Orwell's last book, or his last word as an assessment of the future. Orwell was a prolific writer who had lived by his pen for years, and often spoke of plans for essays and for another novel he hoped to write upon his recovery. He also remarried just three months before his death, telling his friend T. R. Fyvel that the marriage would give him another reason to live.

Nothing in Orwell's career indicated that his desire to write politically committed literature that was "also an aesthetic experience" would find expression in a skillfully executed animal fable. *Animal Farm* has been described by J. R. Hammond, for example, as "totally different in style and conception from anything Orwell had previously written," and by Laurence Brander as "a sport, out of [Orwell's] usual way; and yet more effective in the crusade to which he was dedicated than anything else he wrote." *Animal Farm* does represent a radical departure from the documentaries, essays, and novels that Orwell wrote in the 1930s; however, many commentators have noted that Orwell was undoubtedly aware that the genre of the beast fable was uniquely suited to his own purposes of social and political satire. Traditionally in such fables, each animal represents not only itself—and in the finest examples of the genre the animal characters are always recognizable as animals—but also a single aspect of human nature which the author has fixed upon for comment, thus avoiding the psychological complications inherent in presenting fully developed human characters. As George Woodcock has noted, "A fable drives home its satiric intent by presenting a simplification of complex happenings of life." The conventions of the animal fable enabled Orwell to examine simply and directly the multifarious moral decisions made within a political system. According to Rama Rani Lall: "Animal allegory prescribes two levels of perception which interact to purvey the irony in comparison and contrast. In *Animal Farm* the animals are consistently animals and Orwell keeps the reader conscious simultaneously of the human traits satirized and of the animals as animals. He has successfully played upon the two levels of perception, making us feel that his animals are really animals and are yet as human as ourselves. Though he has couched his criticism in the simplest of terms, it is convincing because of the realistic pictures of animal life."

Although Orwell intended *Animal Farm* to depict the inevitable course of all revolutions, the Soviet Union was the primary target of the novel's pointed allegory. Critics have demonstrated many parallels between Orwell's narrative and the history of the USSR from the time of the Revolution through World War II. Commentators hostile to Orwell's political position have endeavored to demonstrate that the novel is an inadequate treatment of extremely complicated issues, or that *Animal Farm* does not contain exact parallels to the historical events being satirized and is therefore invalid. Others maintain that Orwell's negative opinions about human nature and the development of political revolutions rendered *Animal Farm* primarily an expression of his own pessimism and thus without relevance to social or political reality. Nevertheless, most critics concur that the basic plot of the novel closely parallels events in the Soviet Union. Snowball and Napoleon, the pigs who formulate the animals' revolutionary principles and who govern the farm following the overthrow of the human masters, represent Leon Trotsky and Josef Stalin, even to Snowball's eventual ouster by Napoleon, who subsequently rewrites the history of the revolution to make Snowball appear to be a villain collaborating with the humans who are constantly scheming to retake the farm. The pig Squealer represents the official Soviet news agency *Pravda;* his persuasive oratory convinces the animals that with pigs in charge conditions are better than ever, when in fact they are worse. The simple and hardworking cart-horses and the anonymous sheep stand for whole classes of people whose uncomprehending complicity aids the tyrants who pervert revolutionary ideals of equality to establish themselves as the new ruling elite.

The most common critical approach to *Animal Farm* acknowledges that, while Orwell's specific political purpose was to show that the Soviet Union was not fulfilling the promise of socialism, the novel was also intended as an illustration of the inherent dangers of all totalitarian systems. One of the novel's primary themes is the inevitable failure of the egalitarian ideals that first encourage revolt against an established order. According to Orwell, the violence necessary to overthrow one system and establish another carries over into the new regime and leads to abuses of power on the part of the new leaders, who seek to retain their hold. Cyril Connolly writes that "the commandments of the Animal Revolution, such as 'no animal shall kill another animal' or 'all animals are equal' can perhaps never be achieved by a revolutionary seizure of power, but only by the spiritual operation of reason or moral philosophy in the animal heart." Many critics maintain that long after historical awareness of the Russian Revolution as the main target of Orwell's satire fades, the novel will

retain its powerful appeal because of its universally applicable message about the dangers of totalitarian rule.

Nineteen Eighty-Four was identified by Geoffrey Stokes as the first major twentieth-century dystopian novel, which is a modern variation of the traditional utopian novel. The utopian novel has been an established genre since the appearance of Sir Thomas More's *Utopia* in 1516. Until the early twentieth century, works of this sort commonly expressed a belief in humanity's potential for individual and social perfectibility. These ideal societies were usually depicted as lying not in the future but in some remote geographical area. Following World War I, anti-utopian, or dystopian, novels began to appear. These works frequently projected contemporary social, political, and economic trends into a foreseeable future. Probably the two best-known dystopias before *Nineteen Eighty-Four* are Yevgeny Zamyatin's *We* (1924) and Aldous Huxley's *Brave New World* (1932), with which *Nineteen Eighty-Four* is often compared. However, Orwell's novel differed from Zamyatin's and Huxley's in that he did not posit any technological advances—often a staple of futuristic fiction—but only adapted existing technology in the creation of such devices as the telescreens and speakwrites.

Nineteen Eighty-Four vividly portrays life in Oceania, a totalitarian state controlled by a mysterious Inner Party that exacts blind devotion to the Party and to its leader, Big Brother, by means including constantly rewritten history (which retrospectively proves the Party infallible) and two-way telescreens monitored by Thought Police. The world is divided into three superstates—Oceania, Eastasia, and Eurasia—that are continually realigning and continually at war. The constant warfare cripples the productive capabilities of each superpower so that the population of each exists in poverty and ignorance, kept in a state of patriotic frenzy aided by reports of glorious victories on the battlefields, parades of captured enemy soldiers, and frequent public executions of spies and traitors to the State. The novel recounts the brief revolt of one man, Winston Smith, against the control of the Party, and his eventual, inevitable defeat. In one of the novel's most often quoted passages, Smith writes in his diary that he understands "how" but not "why" the Inner Party maintains its absolute control over the past and over the minds of the inhabitants of Oceania. The "why" is not revealed until near the end of the novel in a dialogue between Smith and his betrayer O'Brien, an Inner Party official who has pretended to belong to an underground movement dedicated to overthrowing the Party and Big Brother. In this scene, Orwell employs the fictional device of an extended dialogue between an adherent of the old order and a proponent of the new, a device which enables the author to present to the reader a closely reasoned explication of the inner logic of the society under discussion. O'Brien tells Smith that the

Party seeks power for its own sake, thus differing from totalitarian states of the past, such as those that existed in Stalinist Russia or Nazi Germany, which at least employed the pretense of serving the people whom they subjugated. The Inner Party in *Nineteen Eighty-Four* offers no moral justification for its actions.

Beginning with the earliest reviews of *Nineteen Eighty-Four*, critics have tended to interpret the novel in one of three ways: as a satire of the contemporary social and political scene; as an attack on a specific political party or system (most often thought to be Stalinist Communism); or as a general warning about the dangers of totalitarianism, which could result if any government assumed absolute power. The last interpretation was Orwell's own, and he issued a statement to this effect through his publisher, Fredric Warburg, after noting that many early reviews of the book—particularly in the United States—assumed that the novel was meant as a pointed attack on a particular government. Despite Orwell's disclaimer, which included the remark that the novel was set in Britain "in order to emphasize . . . that totalitarianism, if not fought against, could triumph anywhere," some critics have applied a narrower interpretation to *Nineteen Eight-Four*. Mark Schorer, for example, early interpreted the novel as an attack upon aspects of British socialism, and a *Life* magazine review of the novel in 1949 indicated that the novel warned against the rise of "left-wing totalitarianism." As recently as 1980 Isaac Asimov wrote that *Nineteen Eighty-Four* "was clearly an anti-Soviet polemic," a picture "of Stalinism, and Stalinism only." V. S. Pritchett was one of the earliest reviewers

of the novel to theorize that despite the futuristic setting, *Nineteen Eighty-Four* actually satirized Orwell's own milieu—post-World War II England. Many of the details of life in Oceania correspond to situations in Orwell's essays and letters describing life in England during the 1930s and 1940s—in particular the drab living conditions, inadequate food, bombed-out buildings, and the shortage, at one time or another, of nearly every commonplace household item.

Many ideas from Orwell's fiction have become a part of the modern imagination. The seventh commandment of Animalism and its final perversion in *Animal Farm*—"All animals are equal, but some animals are more equal than others"—is widely familiar. Various terms used in *Nineteen Eighty-Four*, such as "Newspeak" and "double-think," have become part of the mass consciousness of the late twentieth century, while "Big Brother," perhaps the work's most famous coinage, has become synonymous with oppressive government. Now any overly intrusive government program or policy is likely to elicit the adjective "Orwellian." Richard I. Smyer has concluded that "Orwell belongs to that small group of twentieth-century writers whose fictional works have influenced the thinking of readers who are only slightly interested in imaginative literature."

(For further information about Orwell's life and works, see *Contemporary Authors*, Vol. 104; *Dictionary of Literary Biography*, Vol. 15: *British Novelists, 1930-1959; Something about the Author*, Vol. 29; and *Twentieth-Century Literary Criticism*, Vols. 2, 6, 15, 31.)

CRITICAL COMMENTARY

GEORGE WOODCOCK

(essay date 1966)

[Woodcock is a Canadian educator, editor, and critic best known for his biographies of George Orwell and Thomas Merton. In the following excerpt, he contends that *Animal Farm* was the first work of Orwell's political and artistic maturity.]

For more than six years, from the end of 1938 to early 1945, Orwell published neither fiction nor any important autobiographical writing, and even in terms of actual work there was a gap of more than four years between the termination of *Coming Up for Air* early in 1939 and the commencement of *Animal Farm* some time in 1943. Yet these were not wasted years for him, even as a writer. Nearly half the pieces in his *Collected*

Essays were first published between 1939 and 1943, and almost all the others in this rather massive volume appeared between 1944 and 1947. To these eight busy years, in other words, belongs virtually all the critical writing Orwell considered important enough to preserve, plus a great many political essays and three polemical pamphlets (*The Lion and the Unicorn* in 1941, *James Burnham and the Managerial Revolution* in 1946, and *The English People* in 1947), plus the scores of uncollected articles and reviews which appeared in the *Tribune, Partisan Review, Observer, Manchester Evening News* (for which he did a weekly book column for two or three years) and a dozen small journals and little magazines. All this he did, it must be remembered, while he was still working either at the BBC or editorially at the *Tribune* and while he was allowing at least

Principal Works

Down and Out in Paris and London (novel) 1933

Burmese Days (novel) 1934

A Clergyman's Daughter (novel) 1935

Keep the Aspidistra Flying (novel) 1936

The Road to Wigan Pier (autobiography and social criticism) 1937

Homage to Catalonia (autobiography and social criticism) 1938

Coming Up for Air (novel) 1939

Inside the Whale, and Other Essays (essays) 1940

Animal Farm (novel) 1945

Dickens, Dali, & Others: Studies in Popular Culture (criticism) 1946; published in England as Critical Essays, 1946

The English People (essays) 1947

Nineteen Eighty-Four (novel) 1949

Shooting an Elephant, and Other Essays (essays) 1950

Such, Such Were the Joys (essays) 1953

The Collected Essays, Journalism and Letters of George Orwell. 4 vols. (essays, letters, and diaries) 1968

part of his spare time to be consumed by a series of "causes" from the Home Guard to the Freedom Defense Committee. His life was also expanding in other ways, for it was during this period that he ceased to be a real solitary, and though he never became a truly gregarious man, at least he now felt himself accepted on his own terms and built up that extraordinary variety of friendships which mellowed his final years. All these forms of action seemed to stimulate each other, and doubtless they were all stimulated by the atmosphere of the time, for the war years and the period immediately after peace, up to about the time when Orwell left for the Hebrides, were much more lively from a literary and a political point of view than the period from 1948 or 1949 down to the present.

In the case of Orwell it was not merely that he worked with immense energy and produced a great quantity of writings of various kinds. There was an extraordinary change in quality, which had been foreshadowed by *Homage to Catalonia,* also the product of a period of life in a peculiarly stimulating atmosphere. Orwell's expository writing became steadily clearer and more flexible, and his critical powers, first demonstrated impressively in the long 1939 essay on Charles Dickens, were inspired and informed by an awareness which he would call political, but which—seen in the perspective of the years—seems rather to have been moral in essence. Orwell was always a moralist, even

at Eton if one is to accept Cyril Connolly's account of him in *Enemies of Promise,* and when he acquired political opinions they merely channeled his moralism, but by no means tamed it. The test always came when political expediency or party interests clashed with his ideas of what might be true or decent; most often—and always in his later years—it was party interest that he let go in favor of decency.

The influence of this moral-political awareness can be seen not merely in an increased sensitivity to the social and ethical dimensions of a book or a situation he might be discussing, but also in the directness of writing it began to foster, even when he turned back again near the end of the war from essays to fiction. He tried to write, as he put it, "less picturesquely and more exactly." And he gave a more definitely political character than before to the theme of caste and alienation which re-emerges, in varying forms, in all his late works, beginning with *Animal Farm.*

"*Animal Farm,*" said Orwell in 1947, "was the first book in which I tried, with full consciousness of what I was doing, to fuse political purpose and artistic purpose in one whole." He succeeded admirably, and produced a book so clear in intent and writing that the critic is usually rather nonplussed as to what he should say about it; all is so magnificently there, and the only thing that really needs to be done is to place this crystalline little book into its proper setting.

Conciseness of form and simplicity of language are the qualities which immediately strike one on opening *Animal Farm* after having read Orwell's earlier works of fiction. The fable is about a third the length of *Keep the Aspidistra Flying,* though the events of which it tells are much more complicated, and it is written in a bare English, uncluttered by metaphor, which contrasts strongly with both the elaborately literary diction of *Burmese Days* and the racy but sometimes over-rich narrative style of *Coming Up for Air.*

> Mr. Jones, of the Manor Farm, had locked the hen-houses for the night, but was too drunk to remember to shut the popholes. With the ring of light from his lantern dancing from side to side, he lurched across the yard, kicked off his boots at the back door, drew himself a last glass of beer from the barrel in the scullery, and made his way up to bed, where Mrs. Jones was already snoring.

So it begins, and so it continues to the end, direct, exact and sharply concrete, letting events make their own impacts and stimulating the creation of mental pictures, so that one remembers the book as a series of lively visual images held together by a membrane of almost transparent prose.

There was no doubt in Orwell's mind about his intention in writing *Animal Farm.* He felt that the English in 1943 were allowing their admiration for the military heroism of the Russians to blind them to the faults of the Communist regime, and he also believed that the Communists were using their position as unofficial representatives of Russia in England to prevent the truth from being known, as they had done in Spain. *Animal Farm* was meant to set his compatriots thinking again.

At that time Orwell was fascinated by the craft of pamphleteering, which had something of a wartime vogue among British writers, so that not only likely people, such as Orwell, Read and Spender, produced pamphlets, but even unlikely people such as Forster, Eliot and Henry Miller. Besides the three unimpressive and not very successful pamphlets which he himself wrote in the 1940's, Orwell edited with Reginald Reynolds an anthology of classic pamphlets from the past, entitled *British Pamphleteers;* he believed that a revival of pamphleteering was possible and desirable. In a pamphlet one could state a case simply and concisely, and it would stand on its own feet as no article in a periodical could ever do. But pamphleteering in fact never took on that new lease of life in the postwar years which Orwell had anticipated; this was due partly to lack of interest among the booksellers and partly to the devitalization of British politics after 1945.

Yet *Animal Farm,* which was really a pamphlet in fictional form, did succeed, because it created within the dimension of a fable a perfect and self-consistent microcosm. There was nothing very original about the basic idea of a community of animals acting like men, which had been used about fifteen hundred years before by the anonymous Indian author of that extraordinary collection of political fables, the *Panchatantra.* But, like the author of the *Panchatantra,* Orwell gave his work freshness by inducing that peculiar blend of humor, incongruity and apparent candor which creates in the reader a willingness to suspend disbelief and to transfer himself in mind into the changed dimensions of a world where the pursuits of men can be seen dispassionately because it is animals which are following them.

Orwell liked animals, though he detested the sentimental British animal cult. In his world picture animals, children, oppressed people stood on one side, and the oppressors, whether they were farmers, schoolteachers, sahibs or party bosses, on the other. In *Burmese Days* . . . the relationship of Asians to animals is quite clear, and later on in *Nineteen Eighty-Four* there were to be several identifications of proles with animals. "Proles and animals are free," runs one of the Party slogans, and O'Brien, Winston Smith's tormentor, voices the dogma of the Inner Party when he says that "the proletarians . . . are helpless, like the animals. Humanity is the Party. The others are outside—irrelevant." On the other hand, for Winston in his rebellion, an inestimable power seems to lie in "the animal instinct . . . that was the force that would tear the Party to pieces."

In *Animal Farm* it is the outsiders, the helpless ones, who rise in rebellion and destroy the power of the oppressors, personified in the drunken Mr. Jones. The idea of class division which in earlier books comes very near to the conception of two nations, rich and poor, is here modified to suggest two kinds—men and animals. "All men are enemies. All animals are comrades," says the prophetic old boar Major in his great oration shortly before the uprising.

The original division between man and animal corresponds to the old social division between hereditary upper and lower castes or classes which Orwell represented in his earlier works. But his experiences in Spain had led him to delve into the history of the development of power structures during revolutions, and on this subject he was now as knowledgeable as anyone outside the ranks of specialist historians. He had learned that social caste could be replaced by political caste, and *Animal Farm* is a study in fable form of this process at work in a minuscule world which we can observe as closely as a community of ants under the glass lid of a formicarium.

The history of the revolution betrayed in the animal world is based, therefore, partly on what Orwell had seen of the Communist usurpation of power in Spain and partly on what he had read of the Russian Revolution and its abortion by the Bolsheviks. But his anticommunism does not mean that he is on the side of the traditional ruling class, represented by men. On the contrary, when the animals originally rise in revolt against the tyrannical Farmer Jones, he wins our sympathies for them, and we remain on their side throughout their subsequent struggles with humanity, accepting the fact that no matter what the pigs may do, no animal wants to be ruled again by Farmer Jones or his kind.

Yet from the very first day of insurrection it is evident that a new elite is replacing the vanished human rulers—the elite of the pigs, who are the equivalent of the Party. Immediately they arrogate privileges to themselves—first a monopoly of milk, then of apples. They become supervisors, while the other animals, with the sole exception of that arch anticollectivist, the cat, do the work. The pigs, it should be noted, are united when it is a question of defending their rights as an elite against the other animals. Orwell had no intention of making *Animal Farm* an apology for Trotskyism, as he make quite clear in a conversation which Julian Symons recorded:

And just in case I had any illusions about his attitude, he pointed out that Trotsky-Snowball was potentially as big a villain as Stalin-Napoleon, although he was Napoleon's victim. The first note of corruption was struck, he said, when the pigs secretly had the cows' milk added to their own mash, and Snowball consented to this first act of inequality.

The struggle between Snowball and Napoleon is in fact a struggle within the party elite whose final result, whichever had won, would have been the increased consolidation and centralization of power in the hands of the pigs. This is what happens when Napoleon outmaneuvers Snowball and immediately after his expulsion initiates the career of purges, atrocities and deepening tyranny that reproduces in minuscule the history of the Russian Revolution from 1917 to the 1940's.

At no point in *Animal Farm* does Orwell shift his side. Though it is a third-person story, as all fables are, the point of view of the reader is always nearest to that of the unprivileged animals, and perhaps nearest of all to that of Benjamin, the sad and cynical old donkey who sides with no factions and always says that "life would go on as it had always gone on—that is, badly." Yet despite his exposure of the mounting iniquities committed by the pig elite, Orwell never falls into the error of suggesting that the farmers are any better. On the contrary, there is really nothing to choose, and the book ends in that fantastic scene in which the pigs entertain the neighboring farmers in a social gathering, and the other animals, looking in, see a quarrel break out over cheating at cards.

> Twelve voices were shouting in anger, and they were all alike. No question, now, what had happened to the faces of the pigs. The creatures outside looked from pig to man, and from man to pig, and from pig to man again; but already it was impossible to say which was which.

In other words, old and new tyrannies belong to the same family; authoritarian governments, whether they are based on the codes of old social castes or on the rules of new political elites, are basically similar and present similar dangers to human welfare and to liberty. For the interests of oppressors are identical; as Mr. Pilkington jests at a more peaceful stage in the banquet, "If you have your lower animals to contend with, we have our lower classes!"

By transferring the problems of caste division outside a human setting, Orwell was able in *Animal Farm* to avoid the psychological complications inevitable in a novel, and thus to present his theme as a clear and simple political truth. In the process he left out one element which occurs in all his other works of fiction, the individual rebel caught in the machinery of the caste system. Not until he wrote *Nineteen Eighty-Four* did he elaborate the rebel's role in an *Animal Farm* carried to its monstrously logical conclusion. (pp. 190-98)

George Woodcock, in his *The Crystal Spirit: A Study of George Orwell,* Little, Brown and Company, 1966, 366 p.

FREDERICK R. KARL
(essay date 1972)

[In the following essay, Karl evaluates the strengths and weaknesses of Orwell's literary artistry.]

The novel was for [Orwell] a way to discuss the issues of his day while providing a maximum of instruction for a large audience. (p. 148)

Orwell does frequently fail us, however, in not clearly indicating what belongs to literature and what is proper to history. History demands, among other things, blinding clarity, while literature can be impressionistic, frenzied, symbolic, romantic. Between the two, as Aristotle remarked in his *Poetics,* there is bound to be a clash, for the intention of one differs crucially from that of the other. Thus, we often feel that Orwell as a topical writer has not integrated the two elements sufficiently, so that one frequently gains at the expense of the other. There is no "conscious sacrifice" on Orwell's part, but there is an evident lack of imagination, the synthetic process capable of wedding dissimilars. Having accepted Naturalism as *the* mode for his type of novel, Orwell forsakes those techniques that might have projected his political ideas into deeply felt literary experiences. Lacking Zola's tremendous intensity, he cannot compensate for what he loses through unadventurous methods.

Nevertheless, because Orwell so cherishes middle-class comforts—although he can forgo them and survive—he conveys, within his limitations, the pathos and terror involved in a man caught between what he wants for himself and what the political system has to offer him. The prison life of *1984* merges with the enclosed life of the private school he attended as a young boy, both visions of what life offers. If the reader recognizes that for Orwell, as for Kafka, the nightmare is an inner one, then he can see the political matter as secondary to the personal content. This is not to relegate Orwell's politics to a less important position, but to retain perspective on the man's talents. Less able than Kafka to project a fully rounded inner vision, Orwell nevertheless sees much that is internal even while seeming to be a reporter.

He is a great reporter simply because he reports impressionistically and does not attempt false objectivity. At his best, he merges history with literature. He reports as he sees, but he recognizes that what he sees is tinged by what he is and by what he chooses to look at. Yet despite the subjectivity of much of Orwell's reporting, we are struck by the compelling clarity of his vision and the sharpness of his images. (pp. 149-50)

[The quality of an Orwell "hero"] is measured by his ability to strike through cant: his own and society's. Orwell is not particularly troubled by what his protagonist is or what he tries to do; he is, however, much concerned with what society prevents him from doing. As in the naturalistic novels of the nineteenth century in which the "hero" is caught in a trap of cause and effect, so here, the "hero" is caught by forces which reduce his desires and needs to those of an animal. He is brought to subsistence level, and few elements of civilization can do him good, for to have enough to eat is the sole luxury in which he can indulge. (pp. 150-51)

[The] quality of an Orwell protagonist is his ability to perceive the hypocrisy of the world and to react to it so that his own aims become clouded. An Orwell "hero" rarely has any hope for the future—except perhaps for his next meal. He has few ambitions, and his chief emotion, when not hungry, is the sexual itch. Thus, in *Burmese Days* . . . , Flory pursues Elizabeth, the sole available white woman in the area, despite the fact that he and she have nothing in common. Flory fails to see her as she is, and this lack of clarity on his part is a measure of his agony. Everything Flory believes in is vitiated by his feeling for Elizabeth, but nevertheless because of his own weakness he becomes a fool of love.

Consequently, when hypocrisy does appear, it results from a character's need for something that scorns his true feelings. Were Orwell a comic writer, this grim irony would be a subject for social comedy in the manner of Evelyn Waugh, or for playful banter in the style of Henry Green. Flory's ordeal—one that he cannot possibly sustain—is to discover the depth of his self-deception and to lose Elizabeth in the bargain. An honest man is unable to survive self-deceived, and Flory commits suicide. Like one of Conrad's solitaries, Flory cannot exist outside the community of men, although to exist inside would be self-corrupting, for the community itself is rotten. (pp. 152-53)

As a social novelist, Orwell is less interested in man than he is in the society that has infected him. He has shifted emphasis from *the* man to the social group. Like a good naturalist, Orwell "gets" at people through the accumulation of social detail and external phenomena. This method defines both his success and failure. As a way of realizing a particular milieu, such a method has proven successful; as a way of developing people, the method leaves much to chance.

Unfortunately, Orwell's chief characters frequently exist only as social animals. They are indicated in terms of status, race, caste, tradition; and their place in this scheme is more important than what they are. (p. 153)

Orwell was caught in the difficult position of standing strongly behind the individual and yet trying to create through his novels a mold in which individuality is frustrated. He never clearly resolves the conflict between his point of view—individualistic and atomistic—and the naturalistic bent of his technique. . . . [Orwell] starts with the premise that the system traps the individual, and although he may want the individual to succeed, the latter . . . is cursed from birth. This type of frustration has of course been the stuff of great literature, from Cain on, but only when the author has been able to project and intensify his material imaginatively. Otherwise, the novel becomes merely another demonstration of society's attempt to crush its dissenters.

Even Orwell's ability to evoke disgusting sights and smells suggests his need to root everything in definite time and space. And yet this man whose novels seem based so solidly in modern rot is nostalgic for an irrecoverable Eden. . . . [He] tries to recapture the idylls of the past, a golden age that he is too realistic to believe ever really existed. (pp. 157-58)

[Orwell] presents the paradox of a heroic figure who tries to face every major moral decision that the age offers, and yet remains a man with a wistful nostalgia for the days when life was better, or less obviously bad. Even in *Homage to Catalonia,* that cataloguing of deceit and treachery during the Spanish Civil War, Orwell glances back at the time when alliances were just that, and a man at least knew whom he was fighting for before he died. Now, although men continue to fight for what they believe in, they find that their heroics are hopeless and that they are being undermined at the very moment they are dying for what they think is a worthy cause. In *Homage,* Orwell might have had the tragic theme which eluded him in his other works. But here, where he had perhaps the strongest material of any of his books, he turned to journalism, albeit of a superior kind, which precluded characterization and drama. The human drama of the Civil War was partially lost in the urgency of the experience and the necessity to transmit a political message. (pp. 158-59)

In Orwell's earlier work, all society was a prison, whether the prison of Flory's Burma, the prison of London and Paris, the prison of living on a pound a week in *Keep the Aspidistra Flying,* the prison of working in the coal mines in *The Road to Wigan Pier. . . . 1984* seems a logical outgrowth of these books, the work of a man more interested in analyzing crushed human beings than in placing the individual in conflict with other people. Orwell's characters are generally in struggle against a system, sometimes against themselves, but rarely against other people. One thinks of Orwell's having thrown his characters into a circular machine and then noting their struggle against the machine, their attempts to escape it or compromise themselves with it.

The loss in mature contact is great. Perhaps the thinness apparent in all of Orwell's fiction is the author's failure to provide dramatic confrontation for his chief characters, so that the latter would seem to move in a world of people as well as of events. Since Orwell makes events predominate, people always appear less than what they actually are. The result suggests the same faults contained in the naturalistic novel—the system catches and drains the individual so that his own actions become ultimately meaningless. (pp. 160-61)

Orwell's vision has always been connected to the humanistic and romantic tradition. His books suggest a kind of civilized pastoral in which man fulfills himself through work and sex without regard for money, competition, and self-seeking. Like William Morris's Utopia, Orwell's socialistic state is tinged with this nostalgia for a past that the latter is surely too astute to believe ever existed outside of man's imagination. Orwell argues what seems a tough brand of socialism, but ac-

tually his socialism, once the economic machine is controlled, insists on the possibilities of man's goodness. . . . Orwell's Utopia, tinged by its author's optimism, is too permissive to seem possible, too idyllic to make sense in an industrialized society. (pp. 164-65)

[Orwell wished that the world could be] a private place where a man can realize his own aims with decency and propriety.

This ideal is what the reader comes away with after going through Orwell's writing. No single work predominates, no single idea is clearly remembered, no theory has been set up for future expansion or discussion. What cannot be doubted is the sense of decency of this man who was often wrong, often unjustifiably opinionated, but who in his anger tried to become the moral conscience of his generation. Orwell lived through one of the most chaotic periods in history, and he saw radical changes occurring in the world, unprecedented ones, but he chose to retain hard-gained truths and human dignity. Perhaps more than any of his contemporaries, Orwell has to be read as a whole, or else the keenness of a mind which saw through the falsity of his day will ultimately be forgotten, or at best remembered by overpraised works like *Animal Farm* and *1984*. Possibly, he was better as a man than as a novelist. (pp. 165-66)

Frederick R. Karl, "George Orwell: The White Man's Burden," in his *A Reader's Guide to the Contemporary English Novel*, revised edition, Farrar, Straus and Giroux, 1972, pp. 148-66.

Orwell with his adopted son, Richard, in 1946.

BERNARD CRICK

(essay date 1980)

[Crick was the first biographer to be granted unrestricted access to the private papers held by Sonia Orwell, Orwell's second wife. In the following excerpt, he discusses the political nature of Orwell's writings and places the author among the three most important political writers in English history.]

I saw and still see Orwell as someone who fully succeeded, despite his tragically early death, in the task he set himself in mid-career. He succeeded in such a way that he moved, even in his lifetime, from being a minor English writer to being a world figure, a name to set argument going wherever books are read. In 1946 he wrote in **"Why I Write"**: "What I have most wanted to do throughout the past ten years is to make political writing into an art," adding that "looking back through my work, I see that it is invariably where I lacked a *political* purpose that I wrote lifeless books and was betrayed into purple passages, sentences without meaning, decorative adjectives and humbug generally."

Orwell came to see himself as a "political writer", and both words were of equal weight. He did not claim to be a political philosopher, nor simply a political polemicist: he was a writer, a general writer, author of novels, descriptive works that I will call "documentaries", essays, poems and innumerable book reviews and newspaper columns. But if his best work was not always directly political in the subject matter, it always exhibited political consciousness. In that sense, he is the finest political writer in English since Swift, satirist, stylist, moralist and stirrer, who influenced him so much. (pp. xiii-xiv)

Orwell's reputation and influence have increased since his death and show no sign of diminishing. The actual life of such a writer is, alas, only half the story. His greatest influence has been posthumous and has been for liberty and tolerance, but not as passive things to be enjoyed, rather as republican virtues to be exercised: the duty of speaking out boldly ("the secret of liberty," said Pericles, "is courage") and of tolerating rival opinions not out of indifference, but out of principle and because of their seriousness. And plain speaking always meant to him clear writing: communality, common sense, courage and a common style. He saw his literary and his political values as perfectly complementary to each other, he could not conceive of them being in contradiction—even if plain style sometimes limited the kind of literature he could enjoy as well as the development of his own more theoretical ideas. His own style became a cutting edge which, with much trial and error, by fits and starts, he slowly forged into a weapon of legendary strength. He made common words sharp, made them come to life again until under his spell one thinks twice before one uses any polysyllables, still less neologisms.

So in the term "political writer" the second word is as important as the first. Obscure, pretentious or trendy language was to Orwell always a sign of indecision or of deceit, as much when used by private men as by party hacks. (p. xiv)

He became a Socialist (somewhat later than people think) and denied fiercely, whether in reviewing a book by Professor Hayek or in the story of *Animal Farm,* that equality necessarily negates liberty. On the contrary, he stood in that lineage of English socialists who, through Morris, Blatchford, Tawney, Cole, Laski and Bevan, have argued that only in a more egalitarian and fraternal society can liberties flourish and abound for the common people. It was a tradition that stressed the importance of freely held values, to which the structural arguments of Marxism were, at best, only marginal. Yet his influence has been to reprove backsliding socialists, to sustain democratic Socialists (he always capitalised it thus) and to win back Communist

fellow-travellers rather than to convert non-socialists. Many liberals seem unimpressed by Orwell's socialist values, taking what they want from him, admiring him rather abstractly as a *political* writer, but not wanting to come to terms with the content of his politics, with his actual views about the needs of humanity (always humanity, and not just Europeans) and the constraints of a capitalist, acquisitive society. Some either ignore his socialism or espouse a legend that by 1948 and in *Nineteen Eighty-Four* he had abandoned it. . . . Part of his anger against the Communists was not only that they had become despots who squandered human life and despised liberty, but that they were also discrediting democratic Socialism. There is really no mystery about the general character of his politics. From 1936 onwards he was first a follower of the Independent Labour Party and then a *Tribune* socialist; that is, he took his stand among those who were to the Left or on the Left of the Labour Party: fiercely egalitarian, libertarian and democratic, but by Continental comparisons, surprisingly untheoretical, a congregation of secular evangelicals.

What was remarkable in Orwell was not his political position, which was common enough, but that he demanded publicly that his own side should live up to their principles, both in their lives and in their policies, should respect the liberty of others and tell the truth. Socialism could not come by seizure of power or by Act of Parliament, but only by convincing people in fair and open debate and by example. He would take no excuses and he mocked pretentious talk of "ideological necessity". Truth to tell, he made rather a name as a journalist by his skill in rubbing the fur of his own cat backwards. At times he was like those loyal and vociferous football supporters who are at their best when hurling complaint, sarcasm and abuse at their own long-suffering side. Sometimes, of course, it is deserved; and it may always be said to keep them on their toes. Small wonder that some of Orwell's fellow socialists have at times been tempted, like Raymond Williams . . . , or like Isaac Deutscher in his polemic against *Nineteen Eighty-Four,* to doubt whether he should be on their terraces at all. But he chose to and he was, whether they like it or not or would prefer quieter spectators. At most times there was a touch of the true Jacobin about him rather than the John Stuart Millite.

Certainly to call Orwell a supreme political writer, both for what he said and how he said it, is to point only to his major talent and influence. There were other good things as well. He began as a novelist and was planning a new novel when he died. Later he repudiated his early novels, except *Burmese Days* and *Coming Up For Air.* (pp. xiv-xv)

He developed as an essayist. Much critical opinion now locates his genius in his essays. There is much to be said for this view, especially if *Down and Out in*

Paris and London, The Road to Wigan Pier, and *Homage to Catalonia* can be treated as long essays, since they are all as unusual a mixture of description and speculation as one of them is of fact and fiction. His best essays are by no means all political, though those on politics and literature, language and censorship have become classics of English prose, anthologised and translated throughout the world, even where they are not supposed to be read. A small history could be written of *samizdat* and illegal translations of such essays and of *Animal Farm* and *Nineteen Eighty-Four* (read behind the Iron Curtain as angry satire rather than a pessimistic prophecy). (pp. xv-xvi)

While angry at injustice and intolerance, he never seemed to ask too much of ordinary people: his anger centred on the intellectuals, precisely because they hold or influence power and should know better. His politics were Left-wing, but many of his prejudices were conservative. And he wrote about many positive values that have nothing directly to do with politics, love of nature above all: he did not wish to live in a world in which everything could be manipulated, even for the public good. (p. xvi)

His patriotism is important. He was almost alone among Left-wing intellectuals in stressing the naturalness and positive virtues of loving, not exclusively but none the less intensely and unashamedly, one's native land. He held this view because of his rather old-fashioned radicalism that links his "Tory anarchist" or individualist phase to his final socialist period. . . . He was, indeed, a "revolutionary patriot". For he saw our heritage and the land itself as belonging to the common people, not to the gentry and the upper middle classes. . . . He held this view before the War, even in his anti-militarist, quasi-pacifist mood: it was neither an overreaction to accepting the necessity of war in September 1939 nor a lapse back to Edwardian jingoism. . . . But part of his anger was reserved for those intellectuals who had yielded the native field without a fight, departing for a shallow cosmopolitanism or, worse, staying at home to mock. He was intellectually but never socially intolerant of pacifists on this score. He detested their policies but defended their principles and liked their company. (pp. xvii-xviii)

Orwell was careful, amid all his diatribes, to distinguish between *patriotism,* as love of one's own native land (so that anyone who grows into that love can be a patriot), and *nationalism,* as a claim to natural superiority over others (so that States must naturally consist of one nation and seek to exclude others). It is typical that he makes this distinction, which is of extraordinary importance, briefly and almost in passing, neither elaborating it theoretically nor exploring its implications. But it is clear, deliberate, and it is there in his essay **"Notes on Nationalism"** of 1945.

Certainly there was a gentler patriotism in Orwell

which preceded his socialism and stemmed from his love of English literature, customs and countryside. In many ways he remained socially conservative, or as his friend Cyril Connolly put it in a famous aphorism, "a revolutionary who was in love with the 1900s". Orwell said of himself in **"Why I Write"** of 1946, the same essay that declared himself to be a political writer: "I am not able, and do not want, completely to abandon the world-view that I acquired in childhood. So long as I remain alive and well I shall continue to feel strongly about prose style, to love the surface of the earth and to take pleasure in solid objects and scraps of useless information." (p. xviii)

He is a specifically English writer and a specifically English character, both in his seeming amateurism— sometimes truly amateurish—and in his eccentricities. He lived and dressed as simply as he came to write, and in some ways as oddly. But he was never insular. He was steeped in French and also in Russian literature through translation, though hardly at all in German. He knew more about European and colonial politics in the 1930s and 1940s than most of his literary contemporaries, or politicians for that matter. He followed contemporary American writing closely but knew little about American history and politics—had he known more he might have avoided misunderstandings when *Animal Farm* and *Nineteen Eighty-Four* were published in America. His other best works also came to be reprinted and translated well and widely. He had things to say which are still of universal significance, more so than those of some far more systematic philosophical and academic thinkers. And something of his characteristic style, discursiveness and colloquial ease, the buttonholing directness, the zeal to write for a broad, rather than a purely intellectual public, must come across even in translation, for his style has influenced a generation of young writers in Germany, Japan and Italy, for instance, who do not all read him in the original. Throughout the world "Orwellian" means this English essayist's manner as well as the quite different connotation that "Orwellian" has gained from *Nineteen Eighty-Four.*

He is also, perhaps in the very security of his Englishness (it is Englishness, not Britishness, incidentally), a writer of historical stature on English national character. (pp. xviii-xix)

Some literary friends in Orwell's last years of fame never understood his politics nor accepted the importance he attached to politics in general. Cyril Connolly, for instance, often urged Orwell to get away from his political journalism and back to the writing of real novels. Such English intellectuals themselves represented that divorce of political and literary sensibility which Orwell's life contradicted and which so many of his essays railed against. (p. xix)

[As] well as a political writer, Orwell was a political thinker of genuine stature. *Nineteen Eighty-Four* can be seen as a "development model", of a kind familiar to economic historians and social scientists, and every bit as tightly organised, logical and internally consistent as Thomas Hobbes' *Leviathan*, the masterpiece of English political philosophy. The governing regime is a wickedly clever and plausible synthesis of Stalinism and Nazism. *Nineteen Eighty-Four* is to the disorders of the twentieth century what *Leviathan* was to those of the seventeenth. Orwell chose to write in the form of a novel, not in the form of a philosophical tractatus. He would, indeed, have been incapable of writing a contemporary philosophical monograph, scarcely of understanding one. . . . To theorise about political developments in the form of a novel rather than as a treatise has advantages in reaching a wider public and for intuitive understanding, but disadvantages in credibility and explanatory precision.

Hobbes believed that a breakdown in good government would cause a return to a hypothetical state of nature, a condition of violent anarchy where "the life of man is solitary, nasty, brutish and short". Orwell believed that a breakdown in good government (by which he meant a breakdown in liberty, tolerance and welfare) could cause a leap forward into a hypothetical world order of one-party total power, a kind of State that the world had never seen before. He thought it would be novel in that the last vestiges of genuine ideology, whether Communist or Fascist, would have withered away and yet merged in a single hierarchy of oppression and propaganda motivated by a desire for power for its own sake: "If you want a picture of the future of humanity imagine a boot stamping on a human face—forever."

Orwell had first formulated the concept of totalitarianism shortly after his escape from Spain. He argued that common factors were emerging in Stalinism and in Nazism concerned with the retention and extension of power by the inner party elite. These lead the State to mobilise all society as if for perpetual and total war, a common process more important than the vestigial and nominally antagonistic ideologies. (p. xx)

If one takes the term "political writer" in its broadest sense to include philosophers, statesmen, publicists and pamphleteers who might claim to be secure in the canon of English literature, three names seem indisputably preeminent: Thomas Hobbes, Jonathan Swift, and George Orwell. The intellectual historian might make some claims for Edmund Burke, J. S. Mill or William Morris, but Burke and Mill, while fine writers indeed, seem too narrow in their range, sonorous but pedestrian compared to the nominated three; and to read Morris after Swift and Orwell is to condemn him as being too consciously literary by far, however original and influential were many of his ideas. Hobbes was a philosopher, grinding and ground-

ing every point, but also indulging in a vast polemical irony that makes *Leviathan* a masterpiece of baroque prose. Swift was a pamphleteer and the supreme satirist, able to satirise knowledgeably philosophy and theology as well as party politics, but not himself philosophical; and his style was a forceful blend of classical form and of colloquial diction, so that *Gulliver* is a masterpiece of Augustan prose. Orwell in one work approached the importance and the scale of Hobbes, but he had none of his philosophical knowledge or disposition; and in many others of his works he learned consciously from Swift how colloquiality and formality can be mingled both for comic and polemic effect, and in so doing evolved his own flexible plain style which, while not the most beautiful modern English prose, is certainly the best model of English writing for a hundred and one different purposes. Orwell's common style rested on the questionable assumption that all knowledge can be reduced to common sense. But if he did not have the philosophical sophistication of Hobbes, yet his common sense saved him from Swift's bitter pessimism, at times hatred of humanity. For the thing about common sense is that one believes that other people, quite ordinary people, have it too.

The achievement is more important than the man. The main theme of a biography might therefore simply be how he came to hold the original and heterodox views of *Homage to Catalonia, Animal Farm* and *Nineteen Eighty-Four*. But that would be too narrow, excluding not only a picture of the life he led but also the achievement of the writer. Many of the best essays would get lost. And the essays raise at once the peculiarly Orwellian problem of the image of the writer and the character of the man. The very image he came to exhibit or established is complex, for such a simple man (so it is said). To hold Orwellian views and to write in an Orwellian manner mean different things. How could the essayist Orwell, revelling in natural variety, produce the Orwellian vision of a totally machined society? The common-sense answer is that being a writer of great ability, he adopted another style and mode of writing when he wanted to warn against the *possibility* of something happening. But if one reads *Nineteen Eighty-Four* before any other book of Orwell's or is told that it was his last testament, then one may well believe that it is a prophecy or forecast of the future, not simply an awful warning. Then there is, indeed, a contradiction between the two images of Orwell, and so people have presumed a change of character and of values in his last years. I examined this view very carefully, since it was commonly held and important, but I am bound to say that I found no evidence for it.

Some people still underestimate him as a writer. Why identify the final and utter pessimism and defeat of Winston Smith with the milder pessimism of the author? Why identify the shallow and imperceptive nostalgia of George Bowling in *Coming Up For Air* with George Orwell's loving, but knowing and measured, even half-ironic nostalgia? Mere names mislead. With what other novelist would so many readers and critics so confidently identify characters with author? Is the man so simple or does his art lull or gull some of his readers into simplicity? Perhaps the trouble arises from the nature of the essayist who appears to talk about himself so much, about *his* experiences and *his* prejudices. How closely related is that "George Orwell" to Eric Blair who became known as George Orwell? The art of the colloquial essayist, himself constantly and amusingly breaking the normal divide between fact and fiction, between the real person and the persona, this is well enough understood; but it can make things difficult when the same man is also a novelist; it can actually encourage critics and readers to think of Winston Smith as what Orwell thought he himself might become. Suppose there was, however, an Orwell mask that got stuck upon the private and modest person, Eric Blair? Does that diminish the performance?

"Orwell" sets many traps both for himself and for his readers. The question is only important, of course, if one is primarily concerned with the man. Some have said that the man is more important than his writings, meaning the example of the life he led. I do not share this view. A biographer should not, in any case, accept such absolute disjunctions between "character", "circumstances" and "works". Also the view diminishes his works. I suspect that when his old friend, Sir Richard Rees (in his *George Orwell: Fugitive from the Camp of Victory . . .*), called him "almost saintly", it was because he was never as happy with the content of Orwell's writing as he hoped to be.

Some have found an easier solution to this problem of the literary Orwell and a real Orwell. But I have found no evidence that a man called Eric Blair changed character when he came to call himself for the publication of his first book, "George Orwell". I have observed, however, a more subtle and gradual process, that Julian Symons first noted, by which Blair came to adopt the Orwell part of himself as an ideal image to be lived up to: an image of integrity, honesty, simplicity, egalitarian conviction, plain living, plain writing and plain speaking, in all a man with an almost reckless commitment to speaking out unwelcome truths: "liberty is what people do not want to hear." But a public image of Orwell grew up even in his lifetime which was like a vulgarised version of this somewhat ideal image. It presented Orwell as the corporal of the awkward squad, that perennial difficult fellow who speaks unwanted home truths out of order, asks embarrassing questions, pricks the bubbles of his own side's occasional pomposity, who goes too far in all this, making the whole Labour movement sound like a swarm of pacificist, naturist, fruit-juice-drinking cranks, and loses

his own sense of humour when he cannot appreciate that a pack of lies is ideological necessity, or that an election address is necessarily humbug. (pp. xx-xxii)

Bernard Crick, in his *George Orwell: A Life,* Little, Brown and Company, 1980, 473 p.

ALFRED KAZIN
(essay date 1984)

[A highly respected literary critic, Kazin is best known for his essay collections *The Inmost Leaf* (1955), *Contemporaries* (1962), and *On Native Grounds* (1942). In the following excerpt, he examines the political aspects of Orwell's works, focusing in particular on *Nineteen Eighty-Four.*]

In Orwell's novel [**1984**] thirty rocket bombs a week are falling on the capital; nothing more is said of them. Like the "atom bomb" that explodes over Oceania's "Airstrip I"—England—and by destroying a church provides a hiding place in the belfry for the lovers in an "almost deserted stretch of country," all these bombs are abstractions in a book that, except for the hardships of daily living borrowed from the 1940s, is meant to be an abstract of a wholly political future. Orwell was an efficient novelist not particularly interested in fiction; he used it for making a point. Bombs in *1984* symbolize Orwell's pent-up rage about everything in the political world from the mass unemployment of the 1930s (which continued well into the war period) to the ignorance of the left intelligentsia justifying Stalinism because the Russian people were pouring out their blood. By 1948, when Orwell was finishing the novel he had conceived in 1943, he was also maddened by the postwar division of the world, the atom bombs on Japan, and England's dependency on America. The ex-radical neo-conservative proponents of America-as-ideology now trying to claim Orwell overlook the fact that England's currency in *1984* is American. England is Oceania Airstrip I. We know whose airstrip it is.

Winston Smith and his fellows in the Ministry of Truth spend their days rewriting the past: "Most of the material you were dealing with had no connection with anything in the real world, not even the kind of connection that is contained in a direct lie." Not Orwell's novel is fiction but the world itself. Fiction as deliberate abstraction from life is what this terror society lives on. By political fiction Orwell means a society that has no meaning. A collectivized insanity is what a wholly tendentious politics has reduced us to. *We* have become the vacuum. Appearance has replaced reality, and appearance is just propaganda. In this future emptiness any two of the three great powers dividing the world

(Orwell was grimly sure there would soon be two) may be officially but only symbolically at war. This is a war without end, because it is probably being waged in the "Ministry of Peace." Or if it is really going on, like the present war between Iran and Iraq, the belligerents may not recall why they went to war. Truckloads of enemy prisoners are regularly shown to London, but they may not be prisoners or even enemies. Bombs do occasionally fall on the city, but like Somoza [of Nicaragua], or Assad [of Syria], the rulers of this society probably bomb their own people to keep them cowed. (p. 13)

The thirty bombs falling each week in *1984* are symbols of the routine terror that Orwell imagined for the end of the century. Politics for him had become the future as complete domination. Pervasive injustice had certainly become his vision of things. In *1984* only the utter disregard of the masses by the Party (a theme fundamental to the book but not demonstrated as fully as the devastation of language and the elimination of the past) shows Orwell's compassion struggling against his shuddering vision of the future. "Work and bed," I used to hear English factory workers complain. "Might as well be dead." The deadly fatigue of 1939-1945 is captured in one line about Winston Smith's neighbor Mrs. Parsons. "One had the impression that there was dust in the creases of her face."

What Orwell would not transfer from 1945 to 1984 was the positive and liberating aspects of wartime controls. England was in many respects more fully mobilized for war than Nazi Germany. A general improvement in national health and social services convinced many people that such efficiency called for widespread nationalization. An impatient drive for a better life increasingly filled the atmosphere as Germany finally went down to defeat. To the amazement of many people in the "movement," this brought the Labour party to power with the greatest majority in the history of British socialism. Orwell's writings of the period reflect little of this. It is true that he was ailing with the lung disease that was to kill him in 1950, that his wife Eileen had died in March 1945 when he was in Germany as a correspondent, that he was still writing for the left-wing *Tribune*. It is also true that the author of the wickedly brilliant satire on Stalinism, *Animal Farm*, continued to proclaim himself a supporter of the Labour party and a libertarian Socialist.

Nevertheless, the bread-and-butter issues that brought Labour to power did not get into the novel that made Orwell's name a symbol for the fear of socialism. The tyranny in this book is called "Ingsoc," English Socialism. Like so many Americans on the left, Orwell was more concerned with what Russia portended for socialism than with the actual struggles of the working class. "Socialism" in America is just a rumpus between nostalgic and former radicals. In England it was a national movement, a government in power, an aroused consciousness. What was more on Orwell's mind, despite his undiminished sympathy for Labour, was the issue of domination which he knew so well from his upper-class background, though he derived, he said, from the lower part of it. Or as Lenin put it, Who Whom?—who's going to run the show and drive the rest of us?

Socialism to George Orwell, as to the utopian reformers and idealists of the nineteenth century, was not an economic question but a moral one. The welfare state little interested Orwell. He was naive, or perhaps just literary, when he wrote in *The Road to Wigan Pier*, his documentary of British poverty in the Thirties, "economic injustice will stop the moment we want it to stop, and no sooner, and if we genuinely want it to stop the method adopted hardly matters." To the twenty-six-year-old Karl Marx writing in the *Economic and Philosophical Manuscripts* (1844), the purpose of socialism was to end, for once in human history, the economic struggle for existence that has always kept man from "reappropriating" his essence. Exactly a century later Orwell wrote in a book review, "The real problem of our time is to restore the sense of absolute right and wrong when the belief that it used to rest on—that is, the belief in personal immortality—has been destroyed. This demands faith, which is a different thing from credulity."

Just at the moment when twentieth-century technology had shown itself capable of feeding the hungry, when everything in sight justified Marx's testimony in *The Communist Manifesto* to the power of new productive forces and Whitehead's praise of "the century of hope" for "inventing invention," socialism in its original meaning—the end of tribal nationalism, of man's alienation from his own essence, of wealth determining all values in society—yielded to the nightmare of coercion. What drove Orwell into an opposition all his own, what made for the ominousness of *1984*, for a deadliness of spirit that fills the book and helped to kill him at forty-six, was his inability to overlook the source of the nightmare. Lenin had seized the state in the name of the long-suffering working class. Thomas Hobbes in 1651 had called Leviathan "the mortal God." He ascribed its power over men to their fear of violent death at each other's hands in the brute state of nature. Fear causes men to create a state by contracting to surrender their natural rights and to submit to the absolute authority of a sovereign. By the social contract men had surrendered their natural liberties in order to enjoy the order and safety of the organized state. But under the total domination of the socialist state men could be just as afraid of violent death at each other's hands as they had been in the state of nature.

"Socialism" was not a fetish to Orwell. . . . With his dislike of absolutist intellectuals, he would not have been astonished to see the ease with which so many former radicals have managed to overcome their disillusionment in the arms of the Pentagon, the CIA, the National Security Administration, and other current examples of how to get "the State off our backs." No great admirer of the United States, which he never cared to visit, Orwell would have made note of the fact that last year the average American household watched television for seven hours and two minutes each day, that households with cable now watch fifty-eight hours a week, and that in this year of 1984 readers of a liberal weekly could read the following:

> Is Big Brother watching? If you are tired of Gov't . . . tired of Big Business . . . tired of everybody telling you who you are and what you should be . . . then now is the time to speak out. . . . Display disgust and declare your independence. Wear a Big Brother Is Watching Shirt today, Tee shirt $10/ . . . Canadians remit $US. Big Brother is Watching LTD, Neenah WI . . .

Orwell thought the problem of domination by class or caste or race or political machine more atrocious than ever. It demands solution. Because he *was* from the upper middle class and knew from his own prejudices just how unreal the lower classes can be to upper-class radicals, a central theme in all his work is the separateness and loneliness of the upper-class observer, like his beloved Swift among the oppressed Irish. Everyone knows by now that he was born in India, that he was brought up to the gentility, snobbery, and race-pride of the British upper classes, especially in the more anxious forms of class consciousness dictated by genteel poverty. He was put through the scholarship mill for Eton and revolted against the system by not going on to Oxford or Cambridge, choosing instead to become a policeman in Burma.

After five years of this, furiously rejecting British imperialism, he threw himself into the life of the *Lumpenproletariat* in Paris and London, the "people of the abyss" as his admired Jack London put it. In England he lived the life of a tramp for months at a time in spite of his weak lungs, and after publishing his first book, *Down and Out in Paris and London* (1933), he went out to the mining districts of the North to do his extraordinary firsthand investigation of working-class life and poverty, *The Road to Wigan Pier* (1937).

Hostile critics of *1984* have eagerly picked on the fact that despite his attempt to immerse himself in workingclass life, Orwell did not commit himself to socialism until he returned to England in 1937, after being wounded in the Spanish Civil War and hunted by Loyalist police for having fought with the proscribed anti-Stalinist POUM. It was the wonderful fraternalism of the anarchists and other obstinate idealists on the left that gave Orwell his one image of socialism as a transformation of human relationships. In Catalonia, for a

brief season after Franco's revolt in 1936, the word "comrade" really meant something. In *Homage to Catalonia* Orwell recited with wonder the disappearance of the usual servility and money worship. What a glorious period that was—until the nominally socialist government in Madrid, instigated by the communists, frustrated every possibility of social revolution from within. Even before Franco conquered in 1939, the old way of life had been restored in Catalonia.

Orwell never forgot what he had seen in Catalonia. This was more than "socialism with a human face," it was socialism as true and passionate equality. Socialism, he wrote near the end of his life, can mean nothing but justice and liberty. For Orwell socialism was the only possible terminus—where? when?—to the ceaseless deprivations suffered by most human beings on earth. But since he equally abominated the despotisms still justified by many English and American left intellectuals, he made a point in *1984* of locating the evil in the thinking of the leading Thought Policeman, O'Brien.

Political intellectuals on the left, the ex-left, the would-be left, the ideological right, can be poison. By the time he summed up all his frustration and rage in *1984,* Orwell had gone beyond his usual contempt for what he called "the boiled rabbits of the left." He was obsessed by the kind of rationale created by modern intellectuals for tyranny by the state. O'Brien's speeches to the broken Winston Smith in the Thought Police's torture chamber represent for Orwell the core of our century's political hideousness. Although O'Brien says that power seeks power and needs no ideological excuse, he does in fact explain to his victim what this power is.

The power exerted and sought by political intellectuals is that they must always be right. O'Brien is frightening because of the way he thinks, not because of the cynicism he advances. Dostoevsky in *The Possessed* said of one of his revolutionist "devils"—"When he was excited he preferred to risk anything rather than to remain in uncertainty." O'Brien tells his victim: "You are a flaw in the pattern, Winston. You are a stain that must be wiped out. . . . It is intolerable to us that an erroneous thought should exist anywhere in the world, however secret and powerless it may be."

Every despotism justifies itself by claiming the power of salvation. Before salvation by the perfect society, there was salvation by the perfect God. One faction after another in history claims to represent perfection, to the immediate peril of those who do not. My salvation cannot tolerate your disbelief, for that is a threat to my salvation.

O'Brien tortures Winston Smith because of O'Brien's necessary belief that the mind controls all things. There is in fact no external reality. The world is nothing but man and man nothing but mind. Winston, not yet electro-shocked into agreeing to this, protests from his rack: "The world itself is only a speck of dust. And man is tiny—helpless! How long has he been in existence? For millions of years the earth was uninhabited." O'Brien: "Nonsense. The earth is as old as we are, no older. How could it be older? Nothing exists except through human consciousness. . . . Before man, there was nothing. After man, if he could come to an end, there would be nothing. Outside man there is nothing."

That is the enemy in *1984,* and against it the exhausted and dying English radical, in the great tradition of English commonsense empiricism, is putting forth his protest that the world is being intellectualized by tyrants who are cultural despots. They are attempting to replace the world by ideas. They are in fact deconstructing it, emptying it of everything that does not lend itself to authority which conceives itself monolithically, nothing but consciousness.

George Orwell's explicitly old-fashioned view is that reality does start outside of us; it is in fact political. Because we are never really alone, whatever introspection tells us, power is always exerted in the name of what we have in common. Life is lived, little as some of us recognize it, as manufactured and coercive loyalties, unmistakable threats and terrible punishments, violent separations from the body politic. The sources of social control and domination are swallowed up in our anxiety, which in an age of psychology deludes itself as being wholly personal, and are embedded in a consumer society professing the elimination of all wants and having no other goal but satisfaction. Actually, we are creatures of society, which is why the tyrant state arises in answer to some mass deprivation. Then the tyranny that afflicts us in our name attempts to reconstitute us by forces so implacable that we internalize them. This is the aim of the Party in *1984.*

Nineteen Eighty-Four is in one respect an exception to the methodical social documentation that was Orwell's usual method. The most powerful details in the book relate to our identification with compulsion. The book is a prophecy, or, as Orwell said, a warning about a future terrible because it rests on a fiction and so cannot be substantiated. It would never occur to Orwell's unwearied enemy on the British left, Raymond Williams, that every pious mouthful he still utters about "Socialism" is the merest abstraction couched in the in-house vocabulary of a religious sect. Orwell's attack on O'Brien as the Grand Inquisitor of an enforced solipsism has not been widely understood. Unlike nineteenth-century individualists, who still had some perspective on the society that was forming around them, we no longer recognize the full extent of the social controls *for* which we more and more live. Orwell would have enjoyed the irony. Our media culture confirms Einstein's belief that the history of an epoch is represented by its instruments. Yet nothing in the sensationalist discussion of Orwell's novel has been so mindless as television's pointing with alarm at the telescreen in *1984* peeking into our bedrooms. You would think that the telescreen had invented itself.

Orwell had the peculiar ability to show that social coercion affects us unconsciously. It becomes personal affliction. In *Down and Out in Paris and London* and in *The Road to Wigan Pier* he showed poverty not just as destitution but as the crippling of the spirit. In *Homage to Catalonia* and in *1984* he demonstrated the extent to which a state at war must hold its own people hostage. (pp. 13-14, 16)

Orwell's passion for the social detail—politics is how we live, how we are forced to live—was of the kind that only resistant solitary minds are capable of. "Not one of us," indeed. The social coercion that most people are no longer aware of became his fated subject because he took coercion as his personal pattern. The clue to his blunt style, with its mastery of the single sentence meant to deliver a shock, is its constant aggression on the reader. Orwell is always telling the reader how innocent everyone is about the reality of society. Orwell's speciality is his awareness of limits in all things, not least the limits of his own talent and interest. "Truth" is his writer's ace in the hole, not imagination. Only Orwell, shot through the throat, would have made a point of saying in *Homage to Catalonia,* "I ought to say in passing that all the time I was in Spain I saw very little fighting."

He clearly made up his mind very early that his ability as a writer was his ability to absorb truth in the form of pain and to give it back. In **"Why I Write,"** a 1946 statement at the head of his *Collected Essays, Journalism and Letters,* he said that even as a boy "I knew that I had a facility with words and a power of facing unpleasant facts, and I felt that this created a sort of private world in which I could get my own back for my failure in everyday life." Writing he imagined as a "continuous" story about himself, "a sort of diary existing only in the mind." When he began writing actively, it consisted for him as "a descriptive effort almost against my will, under a kind of compulsion from the outside, . . . [it] always had the same meticulous descriptive quality."

Orwell remains the best commentator on his own work because he could never modify the sense of fatality behind it. Without grandiosity and without apology, he knew himself to be, vis-à-vis the unending storm of political compulsion and terror, in an exceptionally vulnerable position. "His subject matter will be determined by the age he lives in—at least this is true in tumultuous, revolutionary ages like our own—but before he even begins to write he will have acquired an emotional attitude from which he will never completely escape." But this sense of fate made him perhaps one of the few lasting writers produced by the 1930s. Unlike Silone, Malraux, or Koestler, Orwell was never a true believer and so had nothing to repent of.

Like the stronger and more drastic Solzhenitsyn, Orwell knew why literature in the face of totalitarianism will be documentary. He knew how to face a reality entirely political. In a way, he knew nothing else. But unlike the communist writers formed by the 1930s, Orwell also knew that good writing must be entirely consistent, that the merest touch of eclecticism or a message is fatal. Literature in an age of political atrocity, as the exiles and dissidents from Eastern Europe are showing us, may take the form of fable, but the fable is designed to embarrass, to impart a sense of infliction. Orwell's sense of literature always focused on the unbearable detail. In life as in his books, he delighted in extreme gestures. In the bitter post-war winter of 1946, when fuel was scarce, Orwell actually chopped up his son's toys. But anyone who thinks that the extreme gesture in our day is found more in private life than in our relation to the state has not been aware of the Holocaust, the Gulag, and the latest from the war between Iran and Iraq. This Orwell foretold in *1984,* just as brooding on Stalin as Big Brother he also imagined Khomeini. In Brazil I heard a government minister say, "We have a hundred million people in this country, most of whom we do not need." More and more leaders of the third world talk that way. In private many of us dream that *for* the billions of the third world.

Orwell admitted that he was too ill when writing *1984* to round it all out. But of course it succeeds, it threatens, it terrorizes, because it represents a wholly oppositionist point of view that calls for the downright and repeated emphases of the great pamphleteer rather than the subtly developing action within a novel. Orwell's marked tendency to directness, flatness, laying down the law, along with his powerful anticipation of fact, belongs to a radical and adversary tradition of English pamphleteering not practiced by American writers—the tradition of Swift, Tom Paine, Hazlitt, Blake, Cobbett, Chesterton, Shaw, founded on some enduring sense of injustice, on the need to break through those English class prejudices that Orwell called "a curse that confronts you like a wall of stone." Edmund Wilson used to say that the English Revolution took place in America. In Britain literature has been the revolution. Orwell represents this for the first half of our century as none of his countrymen do. As always, the revolution stays in just one head at a time.

Nevertheless, the great pamphleteers are the great issue raisers. Issues became Orwell's writing life, which is why even when he was near death he could never resist accepting still another book for review. His "I Write as I Please" column for the *Tribune* makes up the central section of his work; the four volumes of his collected essays, letters, journalism are more interesting to me than his novels. *Nineteen Eighty-Four,* novel or not, could have been conceived only by a pamphleteer who in his migratory life insisted on keeping his extensive collection of English pamphlets. His way of writing is always more or less an argument. His writes to change your mind. Socialism, which had meant justice and liberty, in its regression now forced him to choose liberty in *1984* as the response of "the last man in Europe" (the original title for the book) to the State's organized atrocities against a man alone.

But that is not the whole story behind *1984,* as Orwell bitterly insisted, just before he died, against all those attempting to turn him into a defender of the system he described in *The Road to Wigan Pier.* "We are living in a world in which nobody is free, in which hardly anybody is secure, in which it is almost impossible to be honest and to remain alive. . . . And this is merely a preliminary stage, in a country still rich with the loot of a hundred years. Presently there may be coming God knows what horrors—horrors of which, in this sheltered island, we have not even a traditional knowledge." Rosa Luxemburg, the critic on the left most trenchant on Lenin's despotism, warned before she was murdered in 1919 that true victory lay "not at the beginning but at the end of revolution." The true radicals are those who conceive the beginning but cannot bear the end. Ignazio Silone as an exile in Switzerland used to lament: "We are the anti-fascists, always anti! anti!" Orwell's problem was no doubt that, like so many of us, he knew best what he was against. All the more reason to take him seriously at a time when it has become unfashionable and even dangerous to be "against." (pp. 16, 18)

Alfred Kazin, " 'Not One of Us'," in *The New York Review of Books,* Vol. XXI, No. 10, June 14, 1984, pp. 13-14, 16, 18.

SOURCES FOR FURTHER STUDY

College Literature XI, No. 1 (1984): 1-113.

Issue devoted to studies of *Nineteen Eighty-Four,* including essays by Gorman Beauchamp on "*1984:* Oceania as an Ideal State," Joan Weatherly on "The Death of Big Sister: Orwell's Tragic Message," and Paul Schlueter on "Trends in Orwell Criticism, 1968-1983."

Howe, Irving, ed. *1984 Revisited: Totalitarianism in Our Century.* New York: Harper & Row, 1983, 276 p.

Collection of original essays about Orwell and the major themes and ideas of *Nineteen Eighty-Four.* Included are essays by Mark Crispin Miller on "The Fate of *1984,*" Bernard Avishai on "Orwell and the English Language," and Robert Nisbet on "*1984* and the Conservative Imagination."

Hunter, Lynette. *George Orwell: The Search for a Voice.* Stony Stratford, England: Open University Press, 1984, 242 p.

Examines Orwell's narrative voice in his major works.

Jensen, Ejner J., ed. *The Future of Nineteen Eighty-Four.* Ann Arbor: University of Michigan Press, 1984, 209 p.

Collection of essays originally delivered at a 1983 University of Michigan conference designed to examine the significance of *Nineteen Eighty-Four* as the year of the title approached. Included are essays by Bernard Crick on *"Nineteen Eighty-Four: Satire or Prophecy?",* Richard W. Bailey on "George Orwell and the English Language," Alex Zwerdling on "Orwell's Psychopolitics," and Joseph Addison on "The Self and Memory in *Nineteen Eighty-Four.*

Lee, Robert A. *Orwell's Fiction.* Notre Dame, Ind.: University of Notre Dame Press, 1968, 188 p.

Important examination of Orwell's novels as works of fiction, not as fictionalized autobiographies or social criticism.

Stansky, Peter, and Abrahams, William. *The Unknown Orwell.* New York: Alfred A. Knopf, 1972, 316 p.

Biography of Orwell's first thirty years. This is the first volume of a proposed three-volume biography.

——. *Orwell: The Transformation.* New York: Alfred A. Knopf, 1980, 302 p.

Biography of Orwell from the publication of his first novel to his involvement in the Spanish civil war. This is the second volume of a proposed three-volume biography.

John Osborne

1929-

(Full name John James Osborne) English dramatist, scriptwriter, and autobiographer.

INTRODUCTION

Osborne's landmark play, *Look Back in Anger* (1956), established him as a leading English dramatist and helped initiate a new era in British theater emphasizing aggressive social criticism, authentic portrayals of working-class life, and anti-heroic characters. Osborne is often associated with a loosely categorized group of English writers called the "Angry Young Men," whose literature contributed to the heightened social and political awareness developing in England during the 1950s and 1960s. Osborne's plays are often dominated by strong, articulate protagonists who express disgust with bourgeois complacency and materialistic social values through outbursts of abusive language. The rebellious attitudes of his characters contributed to the popularity of his early dramas among postwar British youth.

Look Back in Anger, Osborne's first major work, focuses on Jimmy Porter, a twenty-five-year-old university-educated sweetshop owner who shares a cramped attic apartment with his wife, Alison, and his co-worker and friend, Cliff. Embittered and alienated by his inability to advance socially and angered by the apathy he encounters in others, Jimmy strikes back at the world with explosive intensity. His diatribes, which range in subject from the failings of his marriage to the inequalities of English society, are often directed toward Alison, whose upper middle-class background Jimmy resents. Many critics considered *Look Back in Anger* an insightful commentary on England's social and political situation during the 1950s. Subsequent interpretations of the play have emphasized the personal nature of Jimmy's vituperation. James Gindin observed: "Jimmy Porter does rant against bishops and 'posh' Sunday papers, against any form of aristocratic gentility or pretense, but his invective is part of a plea for human honesty and vitality, for people to live emotionally as fully and deeply as they can." *Look Back in Anger* won the New York Drama Critics Circle Award for best foreign play. Osborne's next work, *The Entertainer* (1957), focuses on Archie Rice, an irascible vaudeville comedian whose emotional instability is reflected by the deterioration of the music-hall tradition. The failing state of the music hall has been interpreted as a metaphor for England's decline in world power and loss of national identity following World War II. Critics praised Osborne's inventive adaptation of vaudeville techniques; he uses short sketches, or "turns," as structural devices, and his characters directly address the audience.

Often considered to be Osborne's angriest and most uncompromising work, *The World of Paul Slickey* is a biting musical satire of the London press and an attack on individuals who allow themselves to be influenced and manipulated by the mass media. The play received predominantly negative reviews, although critics acknowledged Osborne's attempts to expand the scope of musical drama and to challenge the conventions of British theater. In contrast, *Luther* (1961), a critical and popular success, is a historical and psychological portrait of the leader of the Protestant Reformation chronicling his years as an Augustinian monk, his confrontations with royal and papal authority, and his later role as husband and father. Osborne focuses on Luther's private life, emphasizing his troubled relationship with his father. Many critics attributed Osborne's use of a narrator to supply background information and his reliance upon epic costumes, set designs, and other theatrical devices to the influence of Bertolt Brecht. *Luther* won both a New York Drama Critics Circle Award and an Antoinette Perry (Tony) Award. Osborne's next major work, *Inadmissible Evidence,* is regarded by many critics as a culmination of the themes developed in his earlier plays and his finest dramatic achievement. The play concentrates on Bill Maitland, an unscrupulous London lawyer who is haunted by feelings of guilt and self-doubt that eventually lead to his disengagement from society and his nervous breakdown.

Although some critics have asserted that Osborne's subsequent plays contain some of his best writing, they have been less popular than his earlier works. In *A Patriot for Me* (1965), a historical drama set against the decline and fall of the Hapsburg empire in Austro-Hungary during the early twentieth century, Osborne examines the tragic military career of Captain Alfred Redl, a double spy who is blackmailed because of his homosexuality. The play's production was impeded by British theater censors, who demanded large deletions due to Osborne's treatment of unconventional sexuality. *The Hotel in Amsterdam* (1968) is an ensemble play—an uncharacteristic form for Osborne—in which three English couples escape the unwelcome presence of their boss for a weekend of rest and revealing conversation. Several central characters are also featured in *West of Suez* (1971), in which Osborne examines the decline of England's colonial tradition through the political upheaval experienced by an expatriate family living on a former British colony in the Caribbean. Emotional crisis is the central theme of *Watch It Come Down* (1976), in which a film director and his wife attempt to reconcile their marital problems.

Osborne's literary career has also included several plays for British television, collaboration on the scripts for the film adaptations of his stage dramas, and an autobiography entitled *A Better Class of Person* (1981), which relates his life story through the age of twenty-six. The work caught the attention of critics for its caustic, even bitter, descriptions of Osborne's home life, especially his relationship with his parents. Ray Sawhill observed: "[Osborne] has an explosive gift for denunciation and invective, and what he's written is—deliberately, nakedly—a tantrum. . . . He can blow meanness and pettiness up so large that they acquire a looming sensuality, like a slow-motion movie scene. His savage relish can be so palpable that you share his enjoyment of the dynamics of rage."

(For further information about Osborne's life and works, see *Contemporary Authors,* Vols. 13-16; *Contemporary Authors New Revision Series,* Vol. 21; *Contemporary Literary Criticism,* Vols. 1, 2, 5, 11, 45; and *Dictionary of Literary Biography,* Vol. 13: *British Dramatists Since World War II.*)

CRITICAL COMMENTARY

CHARLES MAROWITZ

(essay date 1962)

[In the following excerpt from an essay that first appeared in *The Drama Review* in 1962, Marowitz discusses Osborne's *Luther*, especially its structure, language, and religious motif.]

If one looks closely at the crotchety, constipated, hypercritical figure of Martin Luther in John Osborne's [*Luther*], one is forcibly reminded of that fuming British malcontent, Jimmy Porter [protagonist of *Look Back in Anger*]; a protestant who bitched against the Welfare State as vehemently as the theologian wrangled with the Pope. The similarities do not end there.

Despite the jump in time, the clerical context and the change of venue, the play is not (as has been charged . . .) a *departure* for Osborne. There is a clear link-up between Luther's sixteenth-century Germany and our time. In both, the sense of cosmic imminence is very strong. "The Last Judgement isn't to come. It's here and now," says Luther, and the doomsday-mountain-squatters and the nuclear-psychotics echo his words. The church-sale of indulgences is put forward as if it were a commercial advertisement, and the suggestion here is that the Catholic Church at its lowest moral ebb is an appropriate symbol for modern ad-mass culture. And who is the cleric Tetzel but a kind of bloated Arthur Godfrey pushing piety with the same unctuousness used to boost Lipton's Tea?

The Osborne of *Look Back in Anger* and *The Entertainer* gave us the *temperature* of social protest. And it was blisteringly hot. In *The World of Paul Slickey*, no longer content with the charged implication and the social inference, Osborne issued indictments. One of these was made out for the church. There was something compulsive in the way that Osborne humiliated his churchmen in *Slickey*. I have a stark image of an obscenely capering clergyman shedding all the moral restraints one usually associates with the cloth. Osborne seemed to be taking it out on the church because of some fundamental failing, and it was tinged with a personal bitterness—as if Osborne himself had been let down.

The religious disturbance is implicit in all the earlier plays. In his first play, *Epitaph for George Dillon*, there is an arbitrary scene whose only purpose is to deflate the condescending, sold-on-God visitor to the Elliot home. And if we ask ourselves (as so many have) what was bugging Jimmy Porter and George Dillon, the answer would seem to be: loss of faith. (pp. 117-18)

It is almost as if Osborne, tracing skepticism down to its roots, had to move from George Dillon to Jimmy Porter to Archie Rice to Martin Luther—almost as if they were all part of the same family. (p. 118)

Structurally, [*Luther*] is a series of taut interviews interspersed with sermons and smeared thick with cathedral atmosphere. Formalistically, Osborne (like practically every other modern playwright) appears to be under the sway of Bertolt Brecht. Like Brecht, he has strung together a series of short, stark tableaux. Like Brecht, he has backed them with evocative hangings (flags, banners, tapestries, crucifixes). Like Brecht, he employs a narrator to fill in background and make comment. Like Brecht, he has balanced the man and the social structure so that every moment of one produces a gesture from the other. But unlike Brecht, he has not endowed his play with that added intellectual dimension around which the drama may cohere. He has not, in this tart dramatization of history, furnished an underlying concept with which to interpret events.

Spectacle and rhetoric propel the play's first two acts, but by Act Three it comes to a dead stop because language which has already posited the argument, no longer has a job to perform. The only promising dramatic situation in the play concerns Luther's encouragement and subsequent betrayal of the peasants in their revolt against the lords. This is merely reported after the event in a beautifully written narrative speech which doesn't make up for the lack of action. This is the Brechtian influence at its most destructive. The dramatic climaxes are siphoned dry; characters are involved with the intellectual implications of their behavior rather than with the blood and bone of their situations. A narrative, imagistic language is giving us the "point" of the Luther story in a series of historical passages annotated with theological footnotes. The strongest character in the second half is a Knight who helped put down the peasants' rebellion, and what gives him such presence is the fact that he has just waged war and arrives at least with the residue of an involvement. The real battle has been in Luther's conscience and we have felt only its mildest repercussions. No one has come forward to oppose our protagonist. His anti-clerical father has raged only against losing a son to the monastery. The Pope has threatened but backed down. The beaten peasants have shied off with

Principal Works

The Devil inside Him [with Stella Linden] (drama) 1950

Personal Enemy [with Anthony Creighton] (drama) 1955

Look Back in Anger (drama) 1956

Epitaph for George Dillon [with Anthony Creighton] (drama) 1957

The Entertainer (drama) 1957

The World of Paul Slickey (drama) 1957

A Matter of Scandal and Concern (television drama) 1960

Luther (drama) 1961

Plays for England: The Blood of the Bambergs [and] Under Plain Cover (drama) 1963

Inadmissible Evidence (drama) 1964

Tome Jones (screenplay) 1964

A Patriot for Me (drama) 1965

A Bond Honoured (drama) 1966

The Hotel in Amsterdam (drama) 1968

Time Present (drama) 1968

The Right Prospectus: A Play of Television (television drama) 1970

Very Like a Whale (television drama) 1970

West of Suez (drama) 1971

The Gifts of Friendship (television drama) 1972

Hedda Gabler (drama) 1972

A Sense of Detachment (drama) 1972

The End of Me Old Cigar (drama) 1975

The Picture of Dorian Gray: A Moral Entertainment (drama) 1975

Watch It Come Down (drama) 1976

You're Not Watching Me, Mummy [and] Try a Little Tenderness: Two Plays for Television (television dramas) 1978

A Better Class of Person: An Autobiography, 1929-1956 1981

their tails between their legs. From scene to scene we find ourselves being cheated by authenticity.

The play's final moments emphasize the dearth of development. . . . In place of the last-act solidification of ideas (not a desirable way to write a play, but obviously the kind of play Osborne *was* writing), we get the scene of pregnant ambiguity which invites us to moor the play in whichever dock we like, as the writer wasn't going anywhere in particular anyway. (pp. 118-20)

If the play proves nothing about Luther it proves a great deal about John Osborne. It proves that he has the ability to grasp dramatic ideas and the language to convey them on a hard, bright poetical level. Also, he can don period costumes and still hold a twentieth century stance, and in a theatre where an historical milieu automatically produces turgid posturing, this is a real asset. His structural and intellectual shortcomings do not diminish these gifts.

Osborne, I would guess, is fishing round for a new theme—or rather a new objective correlative in which to express his old theme: personal idealism in collision with institutional dogmas. He has gravitated from anger to contemplation, and that is a healthy progress. (p. 120)

At the start of what promises to be the swinging sixties [that is, at the time of this essay], Osborne remains the most ornery dramatist in England. He still smarts, seethes and occasionally rages. He refuses to conform to other people's idea of his nonconformity. He rejects the cosy club chair and the gutless protest that crackles in the lounge and smolders on the street. He still winces at the stench in his country and refuses

to pretend it is only someone burning leaves in the back yard.

He is the closest thing England has to a Norman Mailer. . . . He produces in me a warm sense of security, for I always feel that he is one of the few (small "c") committed playwrights who really writes out of a conviction—that it is a social and humanist conviction and not an allegiance to maintain the fashion of the irate, verbose radical—and that unlike the (capital "C") Committed writers, he is not partial to anything except his art. (pp. 120-21)

Charles Marowitz, "The Ascension of John Osborne," in *Modern British Dramatists: A Collection of Critical Essays,* edited by John Russell Brown, Prentice-Hall, 1968, pp. 117-21.

GEORGE WELLWARTH

(essay date 1964)

[In the following excerpt, Wellwarth studies themes of anger and social criticism in Osborne's plays.]

Look Back in Anger was a rallying point. It came to represent the dissatisfaction with society reflected in the novels of such young writers as John Wain, Kingsley Amis, and John Braine. Jimmy Porter, its rancorous protagonist, was thought to symbolize the fury of the young postwar generation that felt itself betrayed, sold out, and irrevocably ruined by its elders. The older generation had made a thorough mess of things, and there was nothing the new generation could do except withdraw. (p. 223)

John Osborne must have been the most surprised man in England when he suddenly found himself placed at the head of the angry-young-man movement. He had written a carefully and intelligently worked out dramatic study of a psychotic marriage relationship and was hailed instead as the creator of a revolutionary literary movement. Certainly Jimmy Porter makes a good many cutting remarks about contemporary society, but he only makes them as a result of his own peculiar personality problems. There is absolutely no indication in the play that Osborne ever intended Jimmy's remarks to be taken as a general condemnation of society. (p. 224)

Look Back in Anger was strenuously fiddled up into an epoch-making play by the London critics. It is nothing of the sort; but, on the other hand, it is by no means a worthless play either. Osborne has created an excellent, minutely accurate dissection of a perverse marriage in the style of Strindberg. *Look Back in Anger* irresistibly recalls the Swedish author's *Dance of Death.* (p. 225)

By the time *Look Back in Anger* and *The Entertainer* were produced, Osborne had been hailed as the angry young man so much that he had actually become one. If there is a prototype of the angry-young-man play, *The World of Paul Slickey* is it. Written as a musical, it failed when first produced. And no wonder. There is so much direct criticism of society (castigation would perhaps be a better word) in it that just about everyone must have been made uncomfortable. When criticizing social institutions on the stage it is advisable to use the gentle touch if one wishes to have a successful show. People will accept the offhand slaps of a witty mind because if they can laugh at the object of the satire they can feel superior to it: nobody consciously identifies himself with ridiculousness. But even if they will allow themselves to be slapped under the illusion that someone else is being slapped, they will not allow themselves to be openly and directly attacked. . . . *The World of Paul Slickey* is pure spit and vomit thrown directly into the teeth of the audience. Commercially it has been Osborne's least successful play; artistically it is his best. Inability to compromise may be disastrous from a diplomatic viewpoint, but art is not diplomacy: it is truth. (pp. 227-28)

In *A Subject of Scandal and Concern* (1960) and *Luther* (1961), Osborne continues to be the angry young man, but he seems to have absorbed the lesson of *The World of Paul Slickey*. In these two plays Osborne attacks the establishment indirectly instead of leaving his glove in its face. Both plays concern historical characters, and Osborne leaves the implication very clear for us that "it could happen again." (p. 229)

It is doubtful that anything significant can be expected from John Osborne after *Plays for England*. He has become a victim of his own critical success. Left alone, he might have developed into a modestly talented writer of competently constructed, slightly acidulous hack plays. The strong streak of trite sentimentality which marred *Look Back in Anger* would undoubtedly have taken over had Osborne not been promoted into the figurehead of a new "movement," and he would have peacefully joined the ranks of the television and provincial repertory company playwrights. Osborne is now committed to being angry; but he got all his anger off his chest in *The World of Paul Slickey*. In *Luther* he tackled a subject far beyond his intellectual powers. The result was ludicrous rather than enlightening. In *Plays for England* he is preaching—and making no more sense than if he were fulminating from a real pulpit. (pp. 233-34)

George Wellwarth, "John Osborne: 'Angry Young Man'?" in his *The Theater of Protest and Paradox: Developments in the Avant-Garde Drama*, New York University Press, 1964, pp. 222-34.

JOHN RUSSELL BROWN
(essay date 1968)

[In the following excerpt, Brown focuses on the structure and style of Osborne's major works.]

Osborne's first plays were structurally conventional: *Look Back in Anger* and *Epitaph for George Dillon* are three-act plays set within realistic walls like most of their immediate predecessors. Exposition, development, and conclusion, clear character presentation and progressive building of conflict and tension are all duly there. What was new was the kind of life these plays mirrored in detail: Osborne's own world—young, uneasily married and loving—and its thwarted idealistic pretensions. All the conventional discretion, polish, and good manners of the English drama had gone; and there was no condescension—indeed there was a great show of sympathy—towards what his predecessors would have called "low" characters. Also, the central character in each was a misplaced artist, reduced to anger, double-talk and, temporarily, compliance. From this center, Osborne's later plays were to develop: the best of them are largely monologues, while the others use plot and situation to present an occasion for understanding and revaluation. (p. 9)

[In *Inadmissible Evidence*] Osborne is no longer angry and defiant; he is asking for compassion and understanding and, more surprisingly to judge from his early work, has found a way of recreating in physically realizable language, the inner, half-conscious pressures within his hero. The nightmare of a defeated idealist is not easily admissible in the theatre; even more rarely is it presented in palpable and challenging form, rather than in soliloquy. (This is the technique of *Lear* over against that of *Hamlet,* or a means of fusing the comic and serious plots of *The Changeling* or *'Tis Pity She's a Whore.*)

In other plays—*A Patriot For Me, Plays For England,* and *A Bond Honoured*—Osborne creates groups around his central characters that display their situation in society and, with the last play (developed from one by Lope de Vega), in the tradition of Christian thought and feeling. From his first play onwards Osborne has been moving with difficulty and energy towards a wider and truer relationship with the world around him. The plays have been fantastic and accurately realistic; large and small; historical and contemporary; monologue and babel. This variety is bred of responsibility and growing knowledge, not of ease or mere success. (p. 10)

John Russell Brown, in an introduction to *Modern British Dramatists: A Collection of Critical Essays,* edited by John Russell Brown, Prentice-Hall, 1968, pp. 1-14.

ANDREW K. KENNEDY

(essay date 1975)

[In the excerpt below, Kennedy focuses on the relationship between personal and social elements in Osborne's dialogue.]

There appears to be something improvised, even haphazard, in the way Osborne moves from one play-style to another. There are no long-deliberated changes from one mode of language to another (as in Eliot), nor does there seem to be a compelling inner movement (as in the gradual compression of language in Beckett and Pinter). Yet one can see in Osborne's zig-zagging line of development two main play-forms—the room-based and the open-stage play—and two distinct stage languages—histrionic self-expression and the dialogue of characters intended to be socially, or historically, representative. The tension between these two modes of language keeps recurring in both types of play. Sometimes Osborne attempts to create an interplay between the two modes of language within a double or shifting structure: in *The Entertainer* through connecting Archie Rice's domestic talk with his music hall 'turns', in *Luther* through the shift from the private interior of Act I to the 'epic' propensities of the other two acts. The histrionic monologuist keeps re-entering the

large-scale 'open' plays; and the dialogue of more or less monologue-centred plays keeps expanding (or thinning out) to catch, in almost gratuitous sketch-like scenes, the *language,* the up-to-date idiom, of this or that *contemporary* cartoon type. . . . In all this we find versatile inventiveness at the cost of imperfect artistic control. And we recognise Osborne's at once generous and anxious urge to embody *both* the inner and the outer world; to express troubled psychic states and to represent all kinds of 'interest'—voices, social movements, scenes. In brief, the urge towards wholeness.

Yet it is precisely in his language that Osborne has been least able to develop, to match his ideal conception of a drama that is at once personal and social or communal. There is a recurrent loss of 'felt life' in his dialogue of relationship, group, and large-scale public events, both in the contemporary and the historical or quasi-historical plays. (In the latter Osborne has found it particularly difficult to give life to 'the potentially fascinating dialectic' between an ideology or an institution and the principal character—the potential Brechtian direction.) By contrast, he has given a new voice to the isolated or wounded character, the play seen through a temperament, the line from Strindberg. (pp. 194-95)

In a witty simplification, Mary McCarthy wrote that Osborne 'like a coloratura or countertenor, finds that he is limited to parts of experience, as it were, already written for his voice's strange timbre'. In other words, Osborne cannot extend the range of his dramatic language—though he keeps straining to do so—through a personal creative limitation. Yet, is it not possible that such a limitation is intensified by the difficulty, in our time, of creating a language that has dramatic life *both* on the personal and on the communal plane? (p. 196)

Osborne's drama, which keeps striving towards some balance of the personal and social in the dialogue itself, repeatedly makes one conscious of an acute imbalance. Frequently, the imbalance is exactly what is being dramatised. In the early and contemporary plays the hyperarticulate character (George Dillon, Jimmy Porter) defines himself by rejecting, with ribald contempt, the language as much as the values of a group (the clichés of the Elliot family, the genteelisms of Alison and her sort). In a later play like *Inadmissible Evidence* Osborne goes much further—towards a curiously externalised form of solipsism: the self-alienated monologue of Bill Maitland absorbs solid clusters of vocabulary from the social world—technology, legal jargon and so on—only to spit them out again as alien stuff. (p. 198)

There is much in Osborne's dramatic language that seems to connect with the desire to 'hear the words out loud', in order to reach some certainty (if only the reassurance of 'I talk, therefore I am'—as Mary McCarthy suggests). Histrionic rhetoric in particular is inseparable from the *feeling* that words are self-authenticating. Further, Osborne is essentially a verbal dramatist. . . . Perhaps it is no accident that the term 'old-fashioned'—also used by Osborne about the form of his first play—is now applied to his 'allegiance to words', in a context that makes it clear that Osborne is aware of the shrinking area of meaning through words. The power of language is asserted against its felt decline. The texture of Osborne's rhetoric itself embodies this tension—the attempt to gain new theatrical vitality for what is, after all, an 'old-fashioned' language. (p. 204)

[There] is considerable stylistic variation in feeling in Osborne's rhetoric of self-dramatisation, both in particular speeches and from one play to another. It may not be what Eliot called 'an improvement in language', but it does amount to a revitalisation of rhetoric.

The limitations of Osborne's rhetoric seem to be these: it is an over-externalised rhetoric, which cannot accommodate 'thinking aloud' or genuine inwardness: it has 'no time for' pauses and silences, reflection and implicit self-seeing. . . . It is a rhetoric which amplifies a mediocre speaker, or intensifies a naturalistically based idiom; it does not create a new dramatic language capable of expressing unexpected states of mind and experience—though that might be too much to expect. At the same time the energies of this rhetoric seem to be too much at the mercy of moments of empathy releasing the right kind of verbal paroxysm—with the risk of sheer exhaustion. By now Osborne himself seems to have got tired of rhetoric. *Inadmissible Evidence* was the last play where rhetoric was consistently expressive; the later plays either avoid, or (as in *Time Present*) look back on that style fitfully.

It is probable that Osborne would be more at home in a theatre which still had a central rhetorical convention—somewhere between Elizabethan drama and Victorian melodrama. As it is, his persistent naturalism has tended to inhibit; and his 'restless search for a style' has only rarely—in *The Entertainer* and in *Inadmissible Evidence*—led to a roughly satisfying fusion between the structure of the play and texture of the dialogue—releasing and controlling a 'full-blooded' theatrical language. (pp. 211-12)

Andrew K. Kennedy, "Osborne," in his *Six Dramatists in Search of a Language: Studies in Dramatic Language*, Cambridge University Press, 1975, pp. 192-212.

JOHN ELSOM
(essay date 1976)

[In the excerpt below, Elsom discusses Osborne's contributions to the theater, emphasizing his unconventional approach to dialogue and characterization and the theme of rebellion in his plays.]

In many respects . . . , *Look Back in Anger* is just a conventional, wordy and rather clumsy play, and twenty years after, we might well wonder what was so significant about it. It has been both over- and under-estimated. 1956 was a year of theatrical changes, as well as of political disillusion. *Waiting for Godot* transferred to the West End, the Berliner Ensemble visited London for the first time, and while regional theatres were closing around the country in the face of commercial television, there were . . . hopeful signs for the theatrical future. (p. 74)

In a year of changes, *Look Back in Anger* came to symbolise the urgent demand for change, and if we require a useful illustration as to what we were changing from, the leading H. M. Tennent production of the year was Enid Bagnold's *The Chalk Garden* . . . , which concerned a widow living with an old retainer in a country house on the South Downs. It was a comedy with sinister undertones whose dialogue (according to Kenneth Tynan) provided speech of 'exquisite candour, building ornamental bridges of metaphor, tiptoeing across frail causeways of simile, and vaulting over gorges impassable to the rational soul'. The key word, indeed, was exquisite.

The Chalk Garden was the high point in a West End season dominated (as before) by middle-brow, middle-class, middle-aged tastes. Terence Rattigan's invention, 'Aunt Edna', represented the audiences for whom he was supposed to write; genteel, tea-sipping matinée fodder. She would have hated *Look Back in Anger,* just as the young audiences who supposedly liked Osborne's play would have hated to be associated with Aunt Edna. Kenneth Tynan wrote in the *Observer:* 'I agree that *Look Back in Anger* is a minority taste. What matters, however, is the size of the minority. I estimate it at roughly 6,733,000, which is the number of people in this country between twenty and thirty.' Did *Look Back in Anger* represent a class and age rebellion? Was that its true significance?

Perhaps so, but on this level it is easy to exaggerate its claims. Class may have been a barrier to widespread appreciation of the theatre, particularly in the West End, but *Look Back in Anger* was scarcely the chief battering ram against it. Jimmy is snobbish in his tastes, more of an Aunt Edna than Alison. The only character who emerges with his solid good sense intact is Alison's father, the Colonel. Nor was Jimmy a typical proletarian example: he was a minor spiv. Nor could Osborne claim to be a 'working-class writer', like Arnold Wesker or Bernard Kops. *Look Back in Anger* expressed, above all, middle-class discontent, and its class significance (if we want to consider the play in such terms) was not that it was a proletarian play but that it presented such a gloomy picture of a dispossessed ex-graduate that the truly working-class plays at the Theatre Workshop seemed cheerful by comparison.

Was it then a play of Oedipal rebellion? Osborne quickly became associated with a group of writers, including Colin Wilson and John Braine, who were known as angry young men. Osborne, through Jimmy Porter, was voicing the natural uncertainties of the young, their frustrations at being denied power, their eventual expectations of power and their fears of abusing it, either in running a country or a family. The familiar features of Oedipalism are there, staring through Jimmy's malignant-innocent eyes, his desire to shock, his loquaciousness, his sexual longings and his dread of responsibility, his curious ambivalence towards the Colonel, who is both noble and an *éminence grise*. Did this play acquire its prestige because it was staged in an 'old' country, with firm traditions, relentlessly upheld? Was Jimmy a youth knocking at the door of a stately country mansion, threatening to knock it down if it is not opened. In a sense, it is opened to him, through his marriage to Alison. He has one foot in the mansion's hall, and this is what confuses him. He has wandered into a world which looks more impressive from without than within. He has lost his main enemy, but not the habit of fighting. (pp. 75-6)

But the Oedipal argument also has its flaws, for the effect of *Look Back in Anger* was not to glorify the young rebel, but rather the reverse. Although there were many films and plays in the late 1950s which presented the angry young man as a hero, uncertain or otherwise, they came from different territories, from the United States (with James Dean and Marlon Brando) and from British universities, with their satirical revues. Jimmy was neither an *East of Eden* rebel, nor a *Beyond the Fringe* one. Osborne made no attempt to glamorise the anger. Jimmy was not just the critic of his society, he was also the object for criticism. He was the chief example of the social malaise which he was attacking. Through Jimmy Porter, Osborne had opened up a much wider subject than rebelliousness or youthful anger, that of social alienation, the feeling of being trapped in a world of meaningless codes and customs. Osborne's ambivalence towards Jimmy is apparent even from his descriptions of him in the script: Jimmy is 'a disconcerting mixture of sincerity and cheerful

malice, of tenderness and freebooting cruelty'. The significance of these divided feelings was that it represented as well the tension between the longing for security and the desire for change: alienation, in short, in action, where we feel dissatisfied whatever we do. (p. 77)

In his subsequent plays, Osborne also developed two themes expressed in *Look Back in Anger,* the rottenness of the State (usually, but not invariably, Britain) and the problems of being an alienated man. This is not to suggest that his plays do not have a wide range of historical situations and techniques, but rather that, at some point and particularly in his early plays, this variety combs and folds around these central preoccupations.

These themes also suggest the limits of his work, for at worst Osborne can become a confused and predictable writer. He can hit out clumsily at easy targets, as in his satire on royal weddings in *The Blood of the Bambergs* (1963), and diffuse his 'State of the Nation' attacks until they include everyone and everything, as in *A Sense of Detachment* (1972). He botched up an adaptation of a difficult play, *A Bond Honoured* (from Lope de Vega's *La Fianza Satisfecha*), by not appreciating the difference between an existentialist rebel, living in a world where 'good and evil are men's opinions of themselves', with the God-defying hero of de Vega's play, whose sacrilege is the reverse side of his god-centredness and who experiences a miraculous conversion.

At best, however, Osborne managed to combine these themes within precise and direct statements. His capacity to write strong central characters and vivid, passionate dialogue fired the imagination of other writers, who without his rhetorical gifts caught something of his inner urgency. In *The Entertainer* (1957), Osborne considered the decline of Britain through the dead eyes of a stand-up comic, Archie Rice, who works within the tatty variety shows (with nudes), the remaining fragments of a once-great music-hall tradition. . . . The loss of ordinary dignity, in private and in public life, leads to a personal despair. In *Luther* (1961), Osborne was concerned with a man who is frightened of his own rebelliousness. It is partly a historical account of Martin Luther's life, although the second act, which condenses history, is less successful than the first, where Luther grapples with the conflicts caused by his intellectual belief in the justice of his cause, his doubts that his rebelliousness may derive from more personal, less honourable reasons and where he finally forces himself to defy the Papacy at the Diet of Worms: 'Here I stand. God help me, I can do no more.'

With such characters as Jimmy Porter, Archie Rice and Martin Luther, Osborne proved his capacity to write magnificent single roles, a talent which no actor or manager could ignore. . . . [*Inadmissible Evi-*

dence] was a play about a guilty, middle-aged solicitor, Maitland, whose sexual fantasies merged into (and derived from) the realities of his daily life, his different relationships with his wife, mistresses and daughter. In *Inadmissible Evidence,* Osborne extended his attacks on society to include the way in which social codes can deform the sexual instinct, a theme which was also part of *Under Plain Cover* (1963) and *A Patriot for Me* (1966). In *Under Plain Cover,* a quiet young couple, brother and sister, play sexual games together, mainly sado-masochistic, until their secrets are exposed to the world of a meddling reporter; while in *A Patriot for Me,* based on the career of the master spy Redl in the Austro-Hungarian Empire before the First World War, he showed how a prevailing social atmosphere, encouraging homosexuality, might still not prevent, may indeed assist, the blackmail of a homosexual—with international, as well as personal, repercussions.

The year 1966 appears to have been a turning point in Osborne's career. He had formed a particularly close association with the Royal Court Theatre whose artistic director, George Devine, discovered *Look Back in Anger* and appeared briefly in *A Patriot for Me.* Devine had the insight to encourage Osborne and the authority to give him advice: but in 1966, he died, which was a great personal loss to Osborne. The impact of this loss can perhaps be seen in *A Bond Honoured,* written at Kenneth Tynan's instigation for the National Theatre: the conversion episodes at the end of this play give the impression of being absentmindedly written, very clumsy and brief. But after 1966, there was also a change in direction in Osborne's plays: they were no longer so heavily dependent on strong central characters. In the quiet *Hotel in Amsterdam* (1968) . . . , the main character is off-stage, the domineering father-figure of a film crew for whose instructions the others wait. *Hotel in Amsterdam,* like *West of Suez* (1971) and *A Sense of Detachment* (1972), is an 'ensemble' play. *Time Present* (1968) was a return to the theme expressed in *The Entertainer* in that a dead Edwardian actor-manager is remembered as having belonged to a golden age of Britain (and the theatre): the nostalgia attached to the music hall in *The Entertainer* now spreads to the whole Edwardian period, and it was this mixture of nostalgia and self-loathing which characterised *West of Suez,* about the decaying colonial heritage of Britain. Osborne's later plays, however, lack that telling ambivalence towards the alienated man, so notable a feature of his early plays. The attacks against society are all-out slaughter; the nostalgia becomes sentimental. Sometimes both emotions are present, cheek by jowl, in the same play. (pp. 77-80)

Osborne's contribution to the theatre cannot be seen simply in terms of his plays. His influence particularly during the late 1950s and early 1960s was pervasive, but largely indirect. Few dramatists tried to mimic the Osborne style in the way in which Pinter was imitated. The success of *Look Back in Anger,* however, destroyed several inhibiting myths about plays: that the theatre had to be genteel, that heroes were stoical and lofty creatures, that audiences needed nice people with whom to identify. Even the recognised clumsiness of Osborne's plays were indirectly encouraging to other dramatists, for it seemed to prove that passion and dramatic substance mattered more than obedience to the rules. Other writers of the time were not likely to be so overawed by the complexity of writing plays, nor, with the example of Osborne's success, were they so likely to be deterred by the hopeless impracticability of finding managements to produce their works. Osborne also demonstrated that it was possible to write vivid and powerful speeches without making them sound verbally narcissistic. His background as an actor gave him an instinctive knowledge as to what lines would work in the theatre and which would not. He had also given the first telling expression in modern British theatre to the theme of social alienation. (pp. 80-1)

John Elsom, "Breaking Out: The Angry Plays," in his *Post-War British Theatre,* Routledge & Kegan Paul, 1976, pp. 72-87.

JOHN LAHR
(essay date 1981)

[In the following excerpt, Lahr examines the formative life events depicted in Osborne's autobiography.]

A Better Class of Person, Osborne's superb account of his early, unfamous years, is haunted by [Noel] Coward. As a dissection of English life and the origins of his own volatile temperament, the book surpasses Coward's *Present Indicative* as the most vivid chronicle of the making of an English playwright. "That voice that cries out in the wilderness doesn't have to be a weakling's does it?" says Jimmy Porter, the hectoring hero of *Look Back in Anger.* Jimmy Porter's disgust isolates him from the world he wants to purify with his rage. Osborne, like his hero, was hell on a short fuse. His loathing of mediocrity and his loneliness were the byproducts of a lifetime of lower-middle-class making do. He reacted to the lace-curtain gentility on both sides of his family with a hatred of quiet resignation, of routine, priggishness and the ambitions of the herd. To Osborne, peace was something for the dead; and the suburbs were a cemetery for the living: "women pushing prams along the clean pavements with their grass verges, fresh as last week's graves." He grew up boxed in by class inferiority, a terror built into the pretensions of language as well as personality. (pp. 1, 30)

Although Osborne claims "no adult ever addressed a question to me," he remembers the adults with photographic clarity. "Disappointment was oxygen to them," he writes of the bitter, quarreling family whose Christmas rows were the only action in their fixed lives. They had no hope, no dream, no energy. And Osborne saw no courage in their winded lives. "The grudge that was their birthright they pursued with passionate despondency to the grave."

Osborne's fierce determination to live intensely came from an early immersion in death. His sister died at 2 of tuberculosis; and Osborne's father, absent for long convalescent periods throughout his childhood, finally succumbed to the same disease when Osborne was 11. Osborne himself was a sickly child, often kept home from school so his mother would have company and later because of rheumatic fever. Relentlessly scrubbed and cleaned by his mother, Osborne's home was a joyless place, barren of ornaments or books, with "hardly any evidence of life lived or being lived."

Osborne's mother, to whom "hospitality was as unknown as friendship," is wickedly referred to throughout the memoir as Nellie Beatrice, a name which captures both her commonness and her pretension. Describing wartime treat luncheons with his mother at the Trocodero, a restaurant in Kensington whose French menu confounded them and where they invariably settled for fish and chips, Osborne writes; "Her technique with waiters, as in life, was to either bully or fawn upon them. 'Oh, you really are very kind,' 'Oh, yes, we *did* enjoy that.' If this ladylike charm got no response from the waiter she would resort to her usual bad temper, giving both the waiter and myself Black Looks." Osborne's depiction of her blackmailing Black Looks, her "flare-ups," her constant moving from house to house and her mania for a germ-free home, with the vacuum cleaner "bellowing and bullying a filthy uncomprehending world," is brilliant. (p. 30)

Expelled from his minor public school for punching the headmaster, who'd slapped him, Osborne fell into theater as an escape from the drudgery of daily routine and the responsibilities of being both son and, at 18, fiancé. The theater became at once his family and the repository for his vague, untested passion for excellence. Osborne's account of his lackluster career as a bungling stage manager, leching actor, gouging company manager and occasional playwright is wonderful.

Few famous names grace the regional backwaters and town halls where Osborne got his training. The desperation and delight of those days are stylishly recreated. "We committed our lines," he writes of being imprisoned in yet another dreary, dispirited rep company, "as if we were sewing mailbags." Already the young Osborne, who as a student had formed a secret society of spleen called "The Viper Gang" with his only high-school chum, was exhibiting the arrogance and talent for invective of the playwright-to-be. In his outspoken hatred of toadies, timeservers, prigs, form-serving bullies of postwar Britain, he was frequently fired from jobs. "The sack," he writes, "was becoming my only foreseeable work satisfaction."

Osborne's initiation into sex and writing plays came at the hands of a 30-year-old rep leading lady, Stella Linden, with a pelvic arch like the skull of an ox. Stella, whose husband was a small-fry impresario, schooled Osborne in the plays of Pinero and in all the boulevard folderol that Osborne would turn upside down in 1956. Osborne in love is as swaggering and exhilarating as Osborne in anger. His account of his passion for Stella and for his first wife, the actress Pamela Lane (the model for Alison in *Look Back in Anger*), is full of bittersweet nostalgia. Of his separation from Pamela he writes, "I was absorbed in loss, unmistakable loss, inescapable loss, unacceptable to all but gamblers."

A Better Class of Person is the best piece of writing Osborne has done since *Inadmissible Evidence* (1965). After that, his verbal barrages became grapeshot instead of sharpshooting. He neither revised his scripts nor moderated his cranky outbursts. His plays, like his pronouncements about an England he could no longer fathom, became second-rate and self-indulgent. But *A Better Class of Person* takes its energy from looking backward to the source of his pain before fame softened him. In this first installment of his autobiography, Osborne rediscovers the daring and cheek which distinguished his early, good work. With *A Better Class of Person* John Osborne once again is making a gorgeous fuss. (pp. 30, 32)

John Lahr, in a review of "A Better Class of Person," in *The New York Times Book Review,* November 8, 1981, pp. 1, 30, 32.

BENEDICT NIGHTINGALE
(essay date 1982)

[Below, Nightingale considers the relationship between Osborne's personality and the style and themes of his plays.]

John Arden has said that *Look Back in Anger* supplied the theatre with "passion and contemporary relevance" at a time when their absence was no longer even noticed; and Tom Stoppard has doubted whether he would have become a playwright at all, had it not been for the excitement Osborne's play generated, the feeling it created that the drama was "the place to be at." It did much to resuscitate a comatose British theatre, increasing the sweep of its subject-matter and, hence, of its audience appeal; and, in spite of ups and downs, the patient's heart, brain and lungs have been firing more or less satisfactorily ever since. Yet what has happened to the man responsible for that feat? . . . Off the stage, and to a large extent on it, the battling dramatist has transformed himself into a puny blimp—and the obvious question is, why? Have his brains been turned by the strain of living up to his own legend? Or is there something more deeply lacking in his character? Perhaps the first episode of his autobiography [*A Better Class of Person*] may have a clue or two to offer.

Since it comes to an end immediately before George Devine accepted *Anger* for performance at the Royal Court, the book does not contain a great deal of obvious and overt interest to the dramatic historian. (p. 64)

The real interest of Osborne's autobiography is what it tells us about his formative years, or, rather, what it tells us he felt about them. (p. 66)

[The] picture we're given is of a young man of strong likes and (and more often) dislikes, capable of passion but also, as he himself wryly recognises, of a disconcerting pettiness; a dedicated rebel, though mainly in the sense of not hesitating to make himself objectionable to the dull, drab or conventional. Interestingly, he seems to be without social or political convictions.

It is always presumptuous to put a writer on the psychiatrist's couch on the basis of his work, even if that work includes an autobiography; but, in so far as it is possible in Osborne's case, we may, I think, conclude that his family, and especially his mother, did much to define him both positively and negatively. His upbringing presumably helps explain his work's insistence on the primacy of emotion, the idea that we must keep caring, keep responding, or die. He once said that his aim as a writer was to give "lessons in feeling", meaning in love, friendship, outrage, hate and, perhaps, despair; and from the time of Jimmy Porter, who incessantly makes it plain that a sentient war is to be preferred to a moribund peace, to that of Ben and Sally Prosser, the acrimonious yet loving couple at the heart of *Watch It Come Down,* he has attempted to do precisely that. And, at least in the early days, the public enthusiasm for his work suggests he substantially succeeded, too.

But from the start, or at least from the time of his first failure, *The World of Paul Slickey,* it was apparent that his strength was also his limitation; and the passing years have made his weaknesses the clearer. Bluntly, he lacks mind, meaning both the organising and the appraising intellect. He has always tended to allow a single character, one in conflict with apathy, triviality, stupidity, cupidity, or some other manifestation of an uncaring society, to dominate the proceedings and shape what, for want of a better word, we'll call the plot. In recent years, however, both character and plot have become thinly camouflaged excuses for Osborne to propagate his feelings about and to the world.

This might not matter if those feelings were arresting in themselves, or were at least the result of sharp observation and analysis. But even those who were his warmest admirers of yore find it difficult to make any such claim. . . . Increasingly, his "drama" has consisted of using thinly realised characters to offer unsubstantiated opinions about the state of Britain from a stance that one can call nostalgic, reactionary or blimpish, depending on one's own convictions and charity.

Take Pamela, the actress-heroine of *Time Present.* She admittedly has a generosity that counteracts what would otherwise be unrelieved bitchiness, and gives her some solidity as a character; but her identity is mainly rhetorical, her function to be a blend of sentimental obituary and searing editorial. For her father, a thespian of the old school dying offstage, she has the respect Osborne's people all seem to share when they look back towards the Edwardian era; for those around her, little but distaste. Her verbal hit-list becomes positively encyclopaedic: hippies, drugs, boutiques, trendy clothes, swinging London, underground papers and bookshops, Viet Nam protesters, women novelists and biographers, women politicians, the Labour Party, the nation's technological pretensions, committed actresses, "faggots" and "pooves", Americans, American drama, modern poetry, and, of course, the critics, with their "frigid little minds."

This list is expanded by subsequent plays, perhaps most contentiously by *A Sense of Detachment,* at once a desultory satire on avant-garde theatre and an exploitation of its techniques. What, after all, is proved by juxtaposing snippets from Shakespeare, Yeats and other poets with extracts from modern pornography? That our generation uniquely lacks the capacity to love? This idea comes to the surface when a character goes on to denounce technological innovation, industrial progress and economic union: "People don't fall in love: that idea is no longer effective in the context of modern techniques." The interesting questions, of course, are why people need porn and whether the Common Market will alter the British way of life for the better or worse; but Osborne's puppets are not there to explore and argue, rather to buttonhole and pronounce on his behalf.

What makes this still more maddening is his fondness for dividing the world into Us, who for all our faults safeguard honest feeling and decent values, and Them, the enemies of such things. This is so in *West of Suez,* at the end of which an eminent writer, centre of a group of expatriate English, is first harangued by an American yippie who conveniently incarnates much that Osborne finds mindless in the young, and is then killed by rampaging blacks. "They've shot the fox", incants someone over his body, implying, with scant justification, that all that is cultivated and honourable has been desecrated. The tendency is still more marked in *Watch It Come Down,* at whose end a commune of writers and artists is assailed by country "yobbos." "We all, *the few of us,* need one another", wails Sally Prosser over the dying Ben. The italics are Osborne's; but nothing he has shown, as opposed to declared, proves that this is a cultural élite worth conserving or that those outside are as malevolently philistine as we're meant to believe.

This was in 1976, and Osborne has written no play since, which may be just as well. His most recent work represents the victory of vague feeling over hard thought, impression over observation, notion over idea, prejudice over conviction, paranoia over anger, clutter over art, and, just conceivably, his mother over himself. He has, one feels, reacted violently and often usefully against her. Yet something of her temperament continues to fester inside him, as he himself seems ruefully to recognise. At any rate, his autobiography contains suggestive extracts from his writer's notebooks, including this: "I am ashamed of her as part of myself that can't be cast out, my own conflict, the disease which I suffer and have inherited, what I *am* and never could be whole. My disease, an invitation to my sick room."

Something of that "disease" is surely there in his quick contempts, his instinctive and sometimes barely rational distastes, and the mean-mindedness with which he is capable of expressing them. . . . Indeed, there are many times in the biography when one's natural empathy with the author disappears, and one is left wondering who is the real villain, the "costive slug" (or whomever) he has just been gleefully evoking, or Osborne himself.

And so, of course, it is with many of the hate-objects in the plays themselves. Who wrote much of *Time Present, A Sense of Detachment* and *West of Suez*? Was it the Osborne we once knew, the crusader (so it seemed) for a society at once more caring and more responsive to the oppressed individual? Or was it his dear old mum, casting Black Looks from above her knitting, and peevishly animadverting on the inexplicable failure of a bad world to accord her her infinite due? Both, no doubt. Both were probably there from the beginning. The trouble is that the second seems substantially to have taken control of the house.

When I say that both were there from the beginning, I have in mind not only *Look Back in Anger,* whose main character had his share of peevishness, self-pity, lack of charity and prejudice, but *Inadmissible Evidence,* whose main character suffered from all that and more. The difference is that in those days Osborne seemed to know it. Those traits were coolly per-

ceived aspects of a variegated personality, and not items in a critique, attack or sermon we were supposed to applaud. This was particularly so in the case of *Inadmissible Evidence,* probably Osborne's masterpiece, and certainly the last play in which he turned his limitations into a positive advantage.

One character dominates the stage throughout. The supporting characters barely exist, and then only in relation to the solicitor, Bill Maitland. Indeed, the plot consists mainly of their mass exodus from his life. He has betrayed his wife, offended his friends, seduced the office girls and dropped them, insulted his daughter, bent his mistress's ear with a torrent of self-doubt, and given every indication to both his subordinates and clients that he's losing control of himself and his business; and consequently one after another rejects him, leaving him alone at the end in his empty office, awaiting the arrival of a representative of the Law Society, which has been investigating his dubious professional ethics.

Again, he spends long monologues railing, complaining or simply introspecting. The opening scene is actually one of his nightmares. He appears in a court accused of having published an obscenity, namely his life, and proceeds emotionally to expose himself in lurid detail. We gather he's a heavy drinker, a hypochondriac, forever dosing himself with pills; a self-made man, envious of those with more pukka backgrounds than his; self-disgusted, to the extent that he feels "irredeemably mediocre" and suspects he has never made a decision that wasn't shoddy or wrong; fearful of the rejection that, as we've seen, his behavior tends to court; friendless, and, though not loveless, inclined to think he's inflicted more pain than pleasure in love. And the litany of self-accusation rises to an anguished climax: "I can't escape it, I can't forget it, and I can't begin again."

It could all add up to self-pity and acrimony. Yet we don't feel, as we do so often with the later plays, that Maitland is just a cracked trumpet through which the baleful playwright is woozily blazoning his own manifold beefs. On the contrary, Maitland is a character he sees with complete clarity, in the round, from outside as well as inside. Indeed, *Inadmissible Evidence* may be seen as a scrupulously chronicled journey into the head of a man on the brink of mental, emotional and spiritual breakdown, an arena that naturally limits the reality of the supporting cast. It is an objective picture of a subjective experience, and, by the end, an archetypal—no, *the* archetypal—study of middle-aged ennui, despair and disintegration. Ronald Bryden did not vastly exaggerate when he called the play a modern tragedy—"Osborne has gathered our English terrors in Maitland's image, and purged them pitiably and terribly."

That was in 1964, an achievement worth recalling

and celebrating when one has been goaded and exasperated by his later work to dismiss Osborne from serious consideration. If one can't in all honesty see him writing with the same scathing detachment in the future, one must surely remember that he produced one play of historical importance in *Look Back in Anger,* one of undoubted excellence in *Inadmissible Evidence,*

and, in *The Entertainer* and *A Patriot for Me,* two plays that future generations may well think worth reviving. Very few modern playwrights may have made such abject fools of themselves as Osborne; but very few can claim as much as that. (pp. 66, 68-70)

Benedict Nightingale, "The Fatality of Hatred," in *Encounter,* Vol. LVIII, No. 5, May, 1982, pp. 63-4, 66, 68-70.

SOURCES FOR FURTHER STUDY

Bierhaus, E. G., Jr. "No World of Its Own: *Look Back in Anger* Twenty Years Later." *Modern Drama* (March 1976): 47-55.

> Asserts that *Look Back in Anger* fails to generate the level of audience enthusiasm evoked upon its initial production as a result of the play's structural and technical faults.

Carter, Alan. *John Osborne.* Edinburgh: Oliver & Boyd, 1969, 194 p.

> Biographical and critical study of Osborne.

Corrigan, Robert W. "Anger and After: A Decade of the British Theatre." In his *The Theatre in Search of a Fix.* New York: Delacorte Press, 1973, pp. 301-15.

Critical discussion focusing on the main character of Osborne's *Inadmissible Evidence.*

Ferrar, Harold. *John Osborne.* New York: Columbia University Press, 1973, 48 p.
> Critical study of Osborne.

Hare, David. "Opportunities for Blasting Off." *New Statesman* 102, No. 2639 (16 October 1981):23-4.
> Positive review of *Look Back in Anger.*

Trussler, Simon. *The Plays of John Osborne: An Assessment.* London: Victor Gollancz Ltd., 1969, 252 p.
> Examines the development of Osborne's playwriting technique, focusing on strengths and weaknesses of his works.

Wilfred Owen

1893-1918

(Full name Wilfred Edward Salter Owen) English poet.

INTRODUCTION

*O*ne of the leading English poets of the First World War, Owen is primarily remembered for realistic protest poems inspired by his experiences at the Western Front in 1916 and 1917. Regarding the true subject of his poems as "the pity of war," he sought to present the grim realities of warfare and its effects on the human spirit. His unique voice—he is considered less idealistically patriotic than Rupert Brooke though more compassionate than Siegfried Sassoon—is complemented by his unusual and experimental technical style. Owen is recognized as the first English poet to fully utilize para-rhyme, that is, rhyme achieved by matching the initial and final consonants of words while altering the vowel sounds. This distinctive technique and the prominent note of social protest in his works influenced the poets of the 1920s and 1930s, most notably W. H. Auden, C. Day Lewis, and Stephen Spender.

Owen was born in Oswestry, Shropshire, the eldest son of a minor railroad official. Described by his brother as a "grave, healthy little boy," Owen was a serious student, profoundly influenced by his Calvinist mother. A thoughtful, imaginative youth, he developed an interest in poets and poetry, especially in John Keats, whose influence can be seen in many of Owen's poems. After attending schools in Birkenhead and Shrewsbury, Owen hoped to enter a university in 1911; however, he failed to win a scholarship and instead became a lay assistant to the Vicar of Dunsden in Oxfordshire. He tried unsuccessfully for a scholarship again in 1913 and subsequently accepted a position teaching English at the Berlitz School in Bordeaux. In France he was befriended by the Symbolist poet and pacifist Laurent Tailhade, whose encouragement affirmed Owen's dedication to poetry. Leaving the language school to tutor privately, Owen remained in France until September 1915, more than a year after the First World War began. Shortly after his return to England, he enlisted in the Artist's Rifles and, while training in London, frequently visited Harold Monro's Poetry Bookshop, becoming acquainted with Monro and regularly attending public poetry readings. At the end of his training, he was commissioned as a lieutenant in the Manchester Regiment; in late 1916 he was posted to the Western Front where he participated in the Battle of the Somme.

Suffering shell-shock after several months of service at the front, Owen was declared "unfit to command troops." He was invalided out of action in May 1917, and in June he was admitted to Craiglockhart War Hospital in Edinburgh. One of the most important events of his poetic career occurred there when he met fellow-patient Siegfried Sassoon, an outspoken critic of the war who encouraged him to use his battle experiences as subjects for poetry. The poets quickly became friends and spent many evenings together discussing their latest works. Critics often emphasize that the realistic presentation of war and the use of colloquial phrasing in Sassoon's poems greatly influenced Owen's works at the time, and Sassoon's respect and encouragement confirmed for Owen his ability as a poet. He wrote most of his critically acclaimed poems after this meeting in the fifteen months prior to his death. After being discharged from the hospital, Owen rejoined his regiment in Scarborough. He returned to the front in early September 1918 and shortly afterwards was awarded the Military Cross for gallantry. He was killed in action at the Sambre Canal in northeast France on November 4, 1918—one week before the Armistice. He is buried at Ors, France.

At the time of his death only a handful of Owen's poems had been published, and his early works are generally considered derivative and undistinguished, though they do indicate his developing interest in various rhyme techniques. Even his first war verses are regarded as conventional, patriotic songs of valor. Critics generally date Owen's mature period from his encounter with Sassoon at Craiglockhart Hospital, for under Sassoon's guidance Owen first adapted his poetic techniques to nontraditional war subjects. He added compassion to the pronounced anger of Sassoon's satiric verses, and, according to Jon Silkin, Owen's more complex emotional response "permitted a more flexible understanding of war." He based new works solely on his personal experiences, making the expression of the truth of war the aim of his poetry. Shortly before his death Owen began preparing a collection of his works for publication, and the preface he drafted is considered the chief statement of his aesthetic principles. In the preface Owen wrote "This book is not about heroes. My subject is War, and the pity of war. I am not concerned with Poetry. The Poetry is in the Pity. Yet

these elegies are to this generation in no sense consolatory. They may be to the next. All a poet can do today is to warn."

Many critics view that statement as a key to understanding the motive behind Owen's poetry. He viewed his literary role as the voice of infantrymen who were unable to effectively articulate their own experiences and emotions. Many of Owen's works assail poets in England who continued to write conventional verses espousing the traditional values of wartime heroism and the appropriateness of dying in battle on behalf of one's country.

Among his best known poems are *"Dulce et Decorum Est,"* "Anthem for Doomed Youth," and "Strange Meeting," an uncompleted poem which is considered by many critics the finest of the First World War. An elegy, "Strange Meeting" presents Owen's historical, humanistic, and mystical themes, while considering the conflict between ego and conscience in war. In a dreamlike vision the narrator of the poem encounters a soldier whom he has killed, and the ensuing dialogue renders Owen's protests of the futility of war. By not identifying the nationalities of the two soldiers in the poem, Owen achieved an ambiguity that allows the verses to be viewed as commentary on World War I or on the universal nature of war. "Strange Meeting" also suggests analogies between the soldier and Christ and between the enemy and oneself. In this and other poems, the Christian ethical principle of "greater love," based on the New Testament teaching "Greater love hath no man than this, that a man lay down his life for his friends" (John 15:13), is considered highly significant. Many critics have noted that while Owen rebelled against the strict institutional religion of his mother, he retained a deep love of Christ, with whom he often identified the young men sacrificed on the battlefields.

Owen's reputation as a poet was firmly established in the years immediately after the war by the publication in 1920 of *Poems,* a volume edited by Sassoon. He subsequently gained a wide audience through collections edited by Edmund Blunden and C. Day Lewis as well as the inclusion of his poems in numerous anthologies. For several decades after his death, however, Owen scholars were limited in their analyses by a lack of biographical information, and the tentative research that followed resulted in confusion and invalid claims over the dates of the various poems and the progress of Owen's development as a poet. With the publication of several biographical studies, including Harold Owen's three-volume memoir of his family, more definitive critical studies have been made possible.

Generally critics have agreed that Owen's verses represent a unique, emotional response to war and a masterful technical achievement. This consensus was challenged by W. B. Yeats, who omitted Owen's poetry from his anthology *The Oxford Book of Modern Verse* (1937), commenting that "passive suffering is not a theme for poetry"; however, the exclusion of Owen's verses was protested by numerous commentators, who questioned Yeats's selection criteria. Perhaps the greatest indicator of Owen's importance lies in the influence he had on poets of the next generation: W. H. Auden has named Owen one of the poets who most affected him and his fellow-writers of the 1930s—Day Lewis, Christopher Isherwood, Louis MacNeice, and Stephen Spender. The younger poets were especially impressed by Owen's versatile rhyme techniques and compassionate protests against suffering and war. According to John H. Johnston: "[Owen's] youth, his small but eloquent body of verse, his intense dedication to the truth, his untimely and unnecessary death— all of these factors combined to make him an irresistible figure to the succeeding generation, whose 'stable background' of traditional forms and values had, like

Owen's been destroyed by the war." Modern scholars tend to judge Owen's work as the limited but nonetheless real achievement of a poet who made rapid progress over the course of his brief and unsettled career. In the words of Richard Hoffpauir: "Rather than bemoan what might have been, we should perhaps marvel that the few successful but minor poems (those of vivid description and honest feeling) were written at all at such a disruptive time. But we should also not overvalue the achievement . . . for then we do a disservice to all poetry and especially to those few poems that do meet the poetic demand of the difficult and extraordinary conditions of war."

(For further information about Owen's life and works, see *Contemporary Authors*, Vol. 104; *Dictionary of Literary Biography*, Vol. 20: *British Poets, 1920-1945*; and *Twentieth-Century Literary Criticism*, Vols. 5, 27.)

CRITICAL COMMENTARY

DYLAN THOMAS

(essay date 1946)

[Thomas was a prominent Welsh poet and critic. In the following excerpt from a work originally published in 1946, he discusses Owen's war poems.]

[In a volume of his poems, Wilfred Owen] was to show, to England, and the intolerant world, the foolishness, unnaturalness, horror, inhumanity, and insupportability of War, and to expose, so that all could suffer and see, the heroic lies, the willingness of the old to sacrifice the young, indifference, grief, the Souls of Soldiers.

The volume, as Wilfred Owen visualised it in trench and shell hole and hospital, in the lunatic centre of battle, in the collapsed and apprehensive calm of sick-leave, never appeared. But many of the poems that were to have been included in the volume remain, their anguish unabated, their beauty for ever, their truth manifest, their warning unheeded. (pp. 117-18)

[He] was the greatest poet of the first Great War. Perhaps, in the future, if there are men, then, still to read—by which I mean, if there are men at all—he may be regarded as one of the great poets of all wars. But only War itself can resolve the problem of the ultimate truth of his, or of anyone else's poetry: War, or its cessation. (p. 118)

[The] voice of the poetry of Wilfred Owen speaks to us, down the revolving stages of thirty years, with

terrible new significance and strength. We had not forgotten his poetry, but perhaps we had allowed ourselves to think of it as the voice of one particular time, one place, one war. Now, at the beginning of what, in the future, may never be known to historians as the "atomic age"—for obvious reasons: there may be no historians—we can see, rereading Owen, that he is a poet of all times, all places, and all wars. There is only one War: that of men against men.

Owen left to us less than sixty poems, many of them complete works of art, some of them fragments, some of them in several versions of revision, the last poem of them all dying away in the middle of a line: "Let us sleep now . . . " I shall not try to follow his short life, from the first imitations of his beloved Keats to the last prodigious whisper of "sleep" down the profound and echoing tunnels of **"Strange Meeting."** Mr. Edmund Blunden, in the introduction to his probably definitive edition of the poems [*The Poems of Wilfred Owen*], has done that with skill and love. His collected poems make a little, huge book, working—and always he worked on his poems like fury, or a poet—from a lush ornamentation of language, brilliantly, borrowed melody, and ingenuous sentiment, to dark, grave, assonant rhythms, vocabulary purged and sinewed, wrathful pity and prophetic utterance. (pp. 118-19)

Who wrote [**"Exposure"**]? A boy of twenty-three or four, comfortably born and educated, serious, "literary," shy, never "exposed" before to anything harsher

Principal Works

Poems (poetry) 1920

The Poems of Wilfred Owen (poetry) 1931

Thirteen Poems (poetry) 1956

The Collected Poems of Wilfred Owen (poetry) 1963

Collected Letters (letters) 1967

Wilfred Owen: War Poems and Others (poetry) 1973

The Complete Poems and Fragments (poetry) 1983

than a Channel crossing, fond of *Endymion* and the open air, fresh from a tutor's job. Earlier, in letters to his mother, he had written from the Somme, in 1917, in that infernal winter: "There is a fine heroic feeling about being in France, and I am in perfect spirits . . . " Or again, he talked of his companions: "The roughest set of knaves I have ever been herded with." When he heard the guns for the first time, he said: "It was a sound not without a certain sublimity."

It was *this* young man, at first reacting so conventionally to his preconceived ideas of the "glory of battle"—and such ideas he was to slash and scorify a very short time afterwards—who wrote the poem? It was this young man, steel-helmeted, buff-jerkined, gauntleted, rubber-waded, in the freezing rain of the flooded trenches, in the mud that was not mud but an octopus of sucking clay, who wrote ["**Anthem for Doomed Youth.**"] . . . (p. 122)

There is no contradiction here. The studious, healthy young man with a love of poetry, as we see him set against the safe background of school, university, and tutordom, is precisely the same as the sombre but radiant, selfless, decrying and exalting, infinitely tender, humble, harrowed seer and stater of the "**Anthem for Doomed Youth**" and for himself. There is no difference. Only, the world has happened to him. And everything, as Yeats once said, happens in a blaze of light.

The world had happened to him. All its suffering moved about and within him. And his intense pity for all human fear, pain, and grief was given trumpet-tongue. He knew, as surely as though the words had been spoken to him aloud, as indeed they had been though they were the words of wounds, the shape of the dead, the colour of blood, he knew he stood alone among men to *plead* for them in their agony, to blast the walls of ignorance, pride, pulpit, and state. He stood like Everyman, in No Man's Land. . . . And out of this, he wrote the poem called ["**Greater Love.**"] . . . (pp. 123-24)

It was impossible for him to avoid the sharing of suffering. He could not record a wound that was not his own. He had so very many deaths to die, and so very

short a life within which to endure them all. It's no use trying to imagine what would have happened to Owen had he lived on. Owen, at twenty-six or so, exposed to the hysteria and exploded values of false peace. Owen alive now, at the age of fifty-three, and half the world starving. You cannot generalize about age and poetry. A man's poems, if they are good poems, are always older than himself; and sometimes they are ageless. We know that the shape and the texture of his poems would always be restlessly changing, though the purpose behind them would surely remain unalterable; he would always be experimenting technically, deeper and deeper driving towards the final intensity of language: the words behind words. . . . Owen, had he lived, would never have ceased experiment; and so powerful was the impetus behind his work, and so intricately strange his always growing mastery of words, he would never have ceased to influence the work of his contemporaries. Had he lived, English poetry would not be the same. The course of poetry is dictated by accidents. Even so, he is one of the four most profound influences upon the poets who came after him; the other three being Gerard Manley Hopkins, the later W. B. Yeats, and T. S. Eliot.

But we must go back, from our guesses and generalisations and abstractions, to Owen's poetry itself; to the brief, brave life and the enduring words. In hospital, labelled as a "neurasthenic case," he observed, and experienced, the torments of the living dead, and he has expressed their "philosophy" in the dreadful poem "**A Terre**" . . . . (pp. 125-26)

To see him in his flame-lit perspective, against the background now of the poxed and cratered warscape, shivering in the snow under the slitting wind, marooned on a frozen desert, or crying, in a little oven of mud, that his "senses are charred," is to see a man consigned to articulate immolation. He buries his smashed head with his own singed hands, and is himself the intoning priest over the ceremony, the suicide, the sunset. He is the common touch. He is the bell of the church of the broken body. He writes love letters home for the illiterate dead. Ignorant, uncaring, hapless as the rest of the bloody troops, he is their arguer shell-shocked into diction, though none may understand. He is content to be the unhonoured prophet in death's country: for fame, as he said, was the last infirmity he desired. (pp. 129-30)

There are many aspects of Owen's life and work upon which I haven't touched at all. I have laboured, in these notes . . . , only one argument, and that inherent in the poems themselves. Owen's words have shown, for me, and I hope (and know) for you, the position-in-calamity which, without intellectual choice, he chose to take. But remember, he was not a "wise man" in the sense that he had achieved, for himself, a true way of believing. He believed there was no one true way because all ways are by-tracked and rutted and pitfalled with ignorance and injustice and indifference. He was himself diffident and self-distrustful. He had to be wrong, clumsy, affected often, ambiguous, bewildered. Like every man at last, he had to fight the whole war by himself. He lost, and he won. In a letter written towards the end of his life and many deaths, he quoted from Rabindranath Tagore: "When I go hence, let this be my parting word, that what I have seen is unsurpassable." (pp. 130-31)

Dylan Thomas, "Wilfred Owen (1946)," in his *Quite Early One Morning,* New Directions, 1954, pp. 117-33.

C. DAY LEWIS

(essay date 1963)

[Day Lewis was a British poet, essayist, novelist, and critic strongly influenced by Owen's works. In the excerpt below, he discusses the strength of Owen's mature poetry.]

Wilfred Owen must remain, in one respect at least, an enigma. His war poems . . . seem to me certainly the finest written by any English poet of the First War and probably the greatest poems about war in our literature. His fame was posthumous—he had only four poems published in his lifetime. The bulk of his best work was written or finished during a period of intense creative activity . . .—a period comparable with the *annus mirabilis* of his admired Keats. The originality and force of their language, the passionate nature of the indignation and pity they express, their blending of harsh realism with a sensuousness unatrophied by the horrors from which they flowered, all these make me feel that Owen's war poems are mature poetry, and that in the best of them—as in a few which he wrote on other subjects—he showed himself a major poet.

The enigma lies in this maturity. Reading through what survives of the unpublished poetry Owen wrote before 1917, I found myself more and more amazed at the suddenness of his development from a very minor poet to something altogether larger. It was as if, during the weeks of his first tour of duty in the trenches, he came of age emotionally and spiritually. His earlier work, though an occasional line or phrase gives us a pre-echo of the run of words or tone of thought in his mature poetry, is for the most part no more promising than any other aspiring adolescent's of that period would have been. It is vague, vaporous, subjective, highly 'poetic' in a pseudo-Keatsian way, with Tennysonian and Ninety-ish echoes here and there: the verse

of a youth in love with the *idea* of poetry—and in love with Love.

And then, under conditions so hideous that they might have been expected to maim a poet rather than make him, Owen came into his own. No gradual development brought his work to maturity. It was a forced growth, a revolution in his mind which, blasting its way through all the poetic bric-à-brac, enabled him to see his subject clear—'War, and the pity of War'. The subject made the poet: the poet made poems which radically changed our attitude towards war. The front-line poets who were Owen's contemporaries—[Siegfried Sassoon, Isaac Rosenberg, Robert Graves, Edmund Blunden, Osbert Sitwell]—played a most honorable part, too, in showing us what modern war was really like; but it is Owen, I believe, whose poetry came home deepest to my own generation, so that we could never again think of war as anything but a vile, if necessary, evil. (pp. 11-12)

What Wilfred Owen's future as a poet would have been, had he survived the war, it is impossible to say. War is the subject of nearly all his best poems, and a reference point in others, such as **"Miners"**. It is true that he wrote a few poems of great merit on other subjects. But when, during the great productive period, he sought to write or finish such poems, we often notice in them a regression to his immature manner. It is interesting to speculate upon what subject might have fired his imagination and possessed his whole mind, as did the war experience. Would the vein of savage indignation prove exhausted, or might Owen have found it renewed in the struggle against social injustice which animated some of his poetic successors? It seems possible; but his honesty, fervour and sensuousness might have been directed elsewhere to produce a Catullan kind of love-poetry. My own conviction is that, whatever poetry he turned to, he would have proved himself in it a poet of a high order. His dedication was complete: he passionately wanted to survive the war, so that he might continue to write poetry.

Certainly, in the writings of his last two years, he showed himself both a serious poet and an increasingly self-critical one. If we follow the successive drafts of the poems over which he worked longest—**"Anthem for Doomed Youth"**, for instance—we can see how admirably he kept sharpening the language, focusing ever more clearly his theme. Clumsiness there sometimes is, in these later poems; but nothing facile, and no shallow amateurism. Even his juvenilia, undistinguished though for the most part they are, present one promising feature—a gift for sustaining, in the sonnet form particularly, what musicians call *legato;* for keeping the movement of the verse running unbroken through an elaborate syntactical structure.

The language and rhythms of Owen's mature poetry are unmistakably his own: earlier influences have been absorbed, and we recognize in the style an achieved poetic personality. But it was achieved not solely through the impact of war. . . . (pp. 23-4)

Although his later work was largely cleared of derivativeness and false poeticism, Owen was not a technical innovator except in one respect—his consistent use of consonantal end-rhymes (grained/ground; tall/toil). . . . Consonantal rhyme, and other forms of assonance, are common in Welsh poetry and had been used previously in English by Vaughan, Emily Dickinson and Hopkins. There is no evidence that Owen had read any of the three last; nor could he read Welsh—his parents were both English and he was born in England. The first surviving poem in which he experiments with consonantal rhyme is **"From My Diary, July 1914"**, while **"Has your soul sipped?"** . . . may be another early experiment. (p. 25)

Again, it has been noticed how Owen tends to have a lower-pitched vowel following a higher one as its rhyme; and this has been explained as a method of stressing the nightmare quality or the disillusionment of the experience about which he was writing. It may be so. But, lacking a theoretical statement by Owen about his rhyme, we should be cautious in attributing its workings to any *methodical* practice. Poets, when they have such urgent things to say as Owen had, seldom attend so consciously to musical detail; the harmonies of the poem, and its discords, are prompted by the meaning rather than imposed upon it. (p. 26)

By temperament and force of circumstances, Owen had led a solitary life, cut off from any close fraternity with other men, out of touch with the cultural movements of pre-war England. Shy and diffident as he was, this previous isolation must have heightened the sense of comradeship he felt when, in the army, he found himself accepted by his fellows and able to contribute to the life of a working unit. The old solitude was fertilized by the new fraternity, to enlarge his emotional and imaginative scope. Laurent Tailhade's eloquently uttered pacifist beliefs had, no doubt, impressed themselves upon the young Owen; but I can find no evidence that Owen was influenced by his poetry. At the Craiglockhart War Hospital, Owen met a man whose poetry and pacifism appealed to him alike. Siegfried Sassoon brought out, in a way almost embarrassing to him, all the younger poet's capacity for hero-worship: he had been a most gallant Company commander; he had written poems and a prose manifesto condemning the war in an uncompromising manner. No wonder Owen felt at first like a disciple towards him.

It was a sign of Owen's integrity and growing independence as a poet that his work was not radically affected by his admiration for this new friend. In a few satirical or colloquial poems, such as **"The Letter"**, **"The Chances"**, or **"The Dead Beat"**, we may perceive

Sassoon's influence; but Owen must have known that Sassoon's ironic and robust satire was not for him, and he continued in the tragic-elegiac vein which he had started working before he met the other poet. What Sassoon gave him was technical criticism, encouragement, and above all the sense of being recognized as an equal by one whose work he respected: it meant the end of his isolation as an artist. (pp. 26-7)

Wilfred Owen described himself as "a conscientious objector with a very seared conscience". He had come to see the war as absolutely evil in the agonies and senseless waste it caused: on the other hand, only as a combatant could he conscientiously and effectively speak for the men who were suffering from it. This conflict within himself . . . , was a basic motive of the war poems. It is a conflict every honest poet must face under the conditions of modern total war; for, if he refuse to take any part in it, he is opting out of the human condition and thus, while obeying his moral conscience, may well be diminishing himself as a poet. This conflict is seldom overt in Owen's war poetry, which, although it makes use of his personal experiences, is remarkably objective: his 'seared conscience' and his inward responses to that experience provided a motive power, not a subject, of the poetry.

Looking once again at this poetry, thirty-five years after I first read it, I realize how much it has become part of my life and my thinking—so much so that I could hardly attempt dispassionate criticism of it. Now, as then, I find Owen's war poetry most remarkable for its range of feeling and for the striking-power of individual lines. "He's lost his colour very far from here" would stand out even in a play by Shakespeare or Webster: "Was it for this the clay grew tall?" has a Sophoclean magnificence and simplicity. Ranging from the visionary heights of **"Strange Meeting"** or **"The Show"** to the brutal, close-up realism of **"Mental Cases"** or **"The Dead Beat"**, from the acrid indignation of such poems as **"Dulce Et Decorum Est"** to the unsentimental pity of **"Futility"** or **"Conscious"**, and from the lyricism of **"The Send-Off "** to the nervous dramatic energy we find in **"Spring Offensive"**, the war poems reveal Owen as a poet superbly equipped in technique and temperament alike. He was not afraid to be eloquent; and because he was speaking urgently for others, not for self-aggrandisement, his eloquence never ballooned into rhetoric. The war experience purged him of self-pity and poetic nostalgia. During his great productive year, the pressure of his imaginative sympathy was high and constant, creating poems that will remain momentous long after the circumstances that prompted them have become just another war in the history books. They, and the best of his poems not directly concerned with war, are in language and character all of a piece. (pp. 27-8)

C. Day Lewis, in an introduction to *The Collected Poems of Wilfred*

Owen, edited by C. Day Lewis, Chatto & Windus, 1963, pp. 11-29.

JOHN H. JOHNSTON

(essay date 1964)

[An American educator and critic, Johnston is the author of *English Poetry of the First World War*. In the following excerpt from that work, he surveys Owen's later war poetry and discusses his concept of "greater love."]

Most World War I poets dealt only with material that was subjectively or experientially important, since their purposes ranged from that of simple self-dramatization to that of shocking the British public out of its ignorance and apathy. Owen, however, seemed to realize the limitations of a narrowly subjective or experiential approach; the numerous revisions in the British Museum manuscripts, according to D. S. R. Welland, reveal a "progressive movement toward impersonality in the gradual elimination of pronouns in the first and second person in favor of less personal constructions." By controlling the subjective element in his verse, Owen sought a greater freedom in exploring the larger moral and spiritual aspects of the conflict. His rapid poetic growth during the Scarborough period [a period of light duty at a military hotel in Scarborough where he was stationed from November 1917 to Spring 1918] is also visible in his gradual mastery of an individualized lyric technique that embodied the discords of modern warfare and in his rejection of the rather narrow experiential bias implicit in **"Apologia pro Poemate Meo."** Instead of insisting upon the exclusive nature of the soldier's experience, Owen was henceforth to dwell upon its universality.

Although Owen's **"Greater Love"** is undated, its relationship to other poems indicates that it was composed in the spring or summer of 1918. The theme of pity touched upon in **"Apologia pro Poemate Meo"** (November 1917) and fully developed in **"Miners"** (January 1918) is here combined with Owen's most eloquent statement of the "greater love" ideal. In **"Miners"** the poet associates himself with the pathos of a sacrifice forgotten by future generations; the centuries "will not dream of us poor lads / Lost in the ground." In **"Greater Love,"** however, he has abandoned his earlier self-concern and assumed the responsibility of "pleader" for those too dedicated or too inarticulate to plead for themselves. At first an observer, Owen becomes a deeply involved participant, then advances to the more demanding and more disciplined role of intermediary. Thus the emotional force of an experienced

truth submits to the control of a maturely conceived poetic purpose in **"Greater Love."**

The structure of the poem involves a point-by-point contrast between sensuous love and the "greater love"; the poet evokes the familiar imagery of the one in order to bring fresh meaning to the other. The contrast, therefore, is more than a revelation of pathetic discrepancies; it is the re-definition of a spiritual concept in terms of its lesser physical counterpart. Sensuous love is aroused by the beauty of lips, eyes, and limbs, and it is expressed through the voice, the heart (the emotions), and the hands. Owen uses each of these images to draw out the contrasting implications of sacrificial love. . . . The consuming intensity of the "greater love" is described in terms of an explicit sexual analogy. Just as the sexual act represents the fruition of sensuous love, so the agonies of the dying represent the fulfillment of the "greater love." The analogy, of course, evokes a whole range of opposed associations that are too profound for irony:

> Your slender attitude
>   Trembles not exquisite like limbs knife-skewed,
> Rolling and rolling there
> Where God seems not to care;
> Till the fierce Love they bear
>   Cramps them in death's extreme decrepitude.

The fourth line touches another, less obvious contrast that embodies the spiritual doubts which had troubled Owen since his first exposure to the sufferings of war. Since God—in whom man finds the perfection of love—is apparently indifferent to the fate of the dying, man himself becomes the real exemplar of the "greater love." Thus the deeper levels of the poem reveal an irony that turns upon man's capacity for a love greater than sensuous love and greater, apparently, than the love that God bears for man. (pp. 191-93)

Life, of course, is the corollary of sensuous love; death is the corollary of the "greater love," the purity and intensity of which shame the ordinary expressions of love between man and woman. If, as the poet believes, "God seems not to care," Christ himself—the original exemplar of the "greater love"—voiced the same sense of dereliction that is implicit in Owen's attitude: "My God, my God, why hast thou forsaken me?" Thus the poem advances on two closely related levels of meaning. The first level involves a complex pattern of contrasts between sensuous and spiritual love; the second level suggests an analogy between two manifestations of the "greater love": Christ and the modern infantryman. Owen's basic purpose, of course, is definition. Only when we comprehend the nature of the "greater love" can we begin to understand the terrible demands that are made upon those whom that love destroys.

"Greater Love" is a key utterance because it

marks a stage in the development of Owen's ability to give his inner conflicts an explicit and compelling poetic form. Another key utterance is **"Strange Meeting."** . . . Here the major concept is not the "greater love" but the truth upon which the "true Poets" must base their appeal to posterity. In the absence or inadequacy of other standards, the "greater love" may be the only positive guide for man in modern warfare; the self-sacrifice implicit in the "greater love" may never be necessary, however, if future generations heed the warnings of the "true Poets."

Although it takes the form of a possibly unfinished colloquy, **"Strange Meeting"** opens with a dramatic incident which was almost certainly inspired by Sassoon's "The Rear-Guard." Sassoon's brief narrative, it may be recalled, deals with the experience of a solitary soldier lost in the darkness of a tunnel below the Hindenburg Line; when he attempts to arouse a recumbent figure, he is confronted with the agonized face of a dead German soldier. . . . Sassoon emphasizes only the physical and psychological shock of his experience in the Hindenburg tunnel; he retreats with the "sweat of horror in his hair," "unloading hell behind him step by step." Owen, however, goes far beyond the experiential effects developed by Sassoon; he remains in hell and confronts the truth behind the horror. In **"Mental Cases"** (written in May 1918), Owen had employed Dante's rhetorical and dramatic technique. In **"Strange Meeting"** he utilizes Sassoon's experience as a background for a colloquy that is again appropriately Dantesque in method and effect. In the profound silence of the tunnel ("no guns thumped, or down the flues made moan") he isolates himself from the tumult and distractions of battle ("no blood reached there from the upper ground") in order to assess the personal, artistic, and historical implications of the conflict. (pp. 194-96)

[In **"Strange Meeting"**] Owen forecasts the social and economic crises of the postwar years as well as the rise of the totalitarian state. More remarkable than the prophecy, however, is his conception of the role of the poet amid the evils of chaos and regimentation. Had he lived, the apparition would have had the insight and the skill to voice his protest, to tell the "truth untold" about war, to assert his faith in the values that men relinquish for the "vain citadels" of political absolutism and militarism. It is in this re-definition of the poet's role that **"Strange Meeting"** reveals a dramatic transition between the general attitudes of nineteenth-century poetry and those of the poetry written in the twenties and thirties. When men "boil bloody," the poet may no longer hunt "the wildest beauty in the world"; his function is broadly social rather than personal or aesthetic. . . . When "none will break ranks" from the march that leads inevitably to war, the poet emerges as seer and spokesman; he has access to a truth that immunizes him against the passions of national-

ism. Thus he may no longer endorse imperialism, as did Kipling; it is not his duty to fight as a soldier or, as a poet, to deal with the external phenomena of war. This completely independent attitude is a measure of the poet's sensitivity rather than of his objectivity: "Foreheads of men have bled where no wounds were." Yet it is only through the exercise of his objectifying power (his courage and wisdom) that the poet has been able to renounce traditional claims upon his art as well as the more recent claims advanced by the stunning physical realities of modern warfare. Those physical realities must be "distilled" rather than crudely transmitted as experiential effects; the metaphor carries over to the "sweet wells" of truth, which represent a distillation of the poetic experience.

"Strange Meeting" concludes with a poignant revelation that makes pity and the "greater love" a part of the "truth untold" which must perish with the poet:

I am the enemy you killed, my friend.
I knew you in this dark; for so you frowned
Yesterday through me as you jabbed and killed.
I parried; but my hands were loath and cold.
Let us sleep now. . . .

Although we assume that the two soldiers are British and German, they are not identified as such; it is the bond of humanity that must now be stressed and not the opposition of rival nationalities. Sorley described the tragic blindness of such an opposition in his 1914 sonnet "To Germany"; that blindness is now lifted, ironically, in the darkness of the "profound dull tunnel" where the truth of war lies buried with those who yearn to tell it. The lack of national identification also permits an alternative or additional interpretation of the poem; the "enemy" is the poet himself, seen as the slayer and the slain and sharing the guilt of murder as well as the innocence of the "greater love." . . . This interpretation, however, alters neither the basic meaning of the poem nor its external literary significance. With **"Strange Meeting"** Owen joins the small company of English poets who have been privileged to speak for their art in a time of crisis and change. He was the only war poet who seemed to be conscious of the implications of "war poetry" for poetry in general. The change in his own conceptions anticipates a radically altered conception of poetic purpose and method, itself a product of inadequacies which the war—and the poetry of the war—clearly revealed. The summary of nineteenth-century traditions which the Georgians represented could not cope with the moral and physical complexities of the twentieth century; poetry, if it would live, must change. Owen had time only to mark the transition, to lament the "undone years," to prophesy—as did Matthew Arnold in "Dover Beach"—the effects of absolutism and anarchy. (pp. 197-99)

Owen's arrival in France in September 1918 coincided with preparations for the last great offensive of the war, the effort that was to result in the breaking of the Hindenburg Line. Just prior to or during his participation in the September attacks, the poet produced **"Spring Offensive," "The Sentry,"** [and **"Smile, Smile, Smile"**]. . . . (pp. 199-200)

"Smile, Smile, Smile" records, after the colloquial manner of Sassoon, the secret derision of the wounded as they read distorted newspaper accounts of the war, which is still being managed as if a "victory" were possible. Sassoon's *Counter-Attack* had appeared only two months before this poem was completed, so possibly Owen felt justified in renewing his own "counter-attack" on the misconceptions encouraged by the daily press. In **"Spring Offensive"** and **"The Sentry,"** however, Owen seems to be experimenting with the possibilities of the brief narrative form. **"The Sentry"** is related in the first person by a participating observer; the fluent colloquial style is Sassoon's, as well as the range of blunt physical notation. . . . (p. 200)

In **"Spring Offensive,"** on the other hand, the story is told in the third person with the poet as an omniscient but remote narrator. The style is formal, elevated, and controlled. Apparently Owen had some misgivings about the contrasting effects of **"The Sentry"** and **"Spring Offensive,"** for he feared that the latter poem, because of its deliberately "poetic" technique, would evoke a *"No Compris!"* from the ordinary soldier. (p. 201)

In **"Spring Offensive"** Owen attempts to encompass the objective as well as the subjective reality of war. In so doing he seems to have been developing a technique that would represent the significant aspects of both external and internal realities. "I do not doubt that, had he lived longer," writes Sassoon, "he would have produced poems of sustained grandeur and ample design." Certainly the narrative technique employed in **"Spring Offensive"** would have been equal to the conceptions involved in any such poems.

Both **"At a Calvary near the Ancre"** and **"Le Christianisme"** are explicit in their indictments of formal Christianity. In poems such as **"Anthem for Doomed Youth"** and **"Greater Love,"** Owen had explored the implications of his disillusionment with Christianity as an external symbol, but in these two late lyrics he writes with the casual bitterness of a man whose doubts have settled into convictions. (pp. 202-03)

"The End" may also be read as a rejection of orthodox Christianity. . . . The mood of **"The End"** is clearly pessimistic, but its personifications and rhetorical tenor represent an abstract treatment of the subject rather than a spontaneous confession of disbelief:

> After the blast of lightning from the East,
> The flourish of loud clouds, the Chariot Throne;

> After the drums of Time have rolled and ceased,
> And by the bronze west long retreat is blown,

> Shall life renew these bodies? Of a truth
> All death will He annul, all tears assuage?—
> Fill the void veins of Life again with youth,
> And wash, with an immortal water, Age?

> When I do ask white Age he saith not so:
> "My head hangs weighed with snow."
> And when I hearken to the Earth, she saith:
> "My fiery heart shrinks, aching. It is death.
> Mine ancient scars shall not be glorified,
> Nor my titanic tears, the sea, be dried."

Aside from its formal excellence as a sonnet, **"The End"** is interesting because the poet's mother chose lines 5-6 for his tombstone at Ors. In the epitaph, however, the second question mark is omitted, thus reversing the pessimism of the sestet:

> Shall life renew these bodies? Of a truth
> All death will He annul, all tears assuage.

Thus a final ambiguity rounds off what has proved to be (aside from textual problems) the most perplexing aspect of Owen's poetry. Disputes about his orthodoxy are likely to continue until a full biography and an edition of his letters are available. It is obvious, however, that his finest work was inspired not by cynicism or despair but by a doctrine close to the heart of Christianity. This fact itself is responsible for the complexities and ambiguities that trouble so many of his readers. Owen's grasp of the implications of "pure Christianity" inevitably led to his rejection of an "impure" Christianity buried under "its rubbish and its rubble"; he held to the concept of the "greater love" as the only spiritual and poetic truth which could illuminate and possibly redeem the sufferings of the modern soldier. We may sometimes feel, however, that in doing this Owen has drawn the virtue of the "greater love" so far out of its Christian context of faith and hope that it stands in his poetry only as a source of ironic reproach or anguished appeal.

Despite Owen's extraordinary sensitivity and his efforts to reconcile that sensitivity to the demands of formal poetic art, his achievement does not measure up to the vast tragic potentialities of his material. His sense of personal involvement in the war resembled Rupert Brooke's in that it was a motive for as well as a source of poetry. Although he moves far beyond the Georgian attitude with his vision of pity, that vision was not enough. His compassion and his concept of the "greater love" grew out of his perhaps too exclusive concern with the aspects of suffering and sacrifice; these aspects do not assume their place or proportion in the total reality. Unlike Blunden, whose poetic interests range less intensely but more widely over the field of war, Owen cannot shift his eyes from particulars that represent merely a part of an enormous complex of opposed human energies comprehensible only on the historic or tragic scale. Although he attempts to give these particulars a universal significance, his vision of pity frequently obscures rather than illuminates the whole; we are likely to lose sight of the historical reality as well as the underlying tragic values that inspire the pity. In Owen's case the pity produces the poetry; only in a partial and sporadic fashion does the poetry produce pity as an effect of tragic events. Furthermore, if it is true that an enlightened compassion was apparently the only poetically fruitful point of view permitted by the nature of modern warfare, is it not also true, as Stephen Spender suggests in his essay on Owen ["Poetry and Pity"], that "poetry inspired by pity is dependent on that repeated stimulus for its inspiration"? The best of Owen's lyrics are necessarily developed in terms of a single emotion—an emotion that cannot be maintained or repeated without psychological strain or aesthetic loss. How many successful poems can be written in the tenor of **"Disabled"**? The very intensity of the author's compassion tends to exhaust both the emotion and the force of its stimulus. Unless pity is generated and objectified within a large tragic context, it cannot of itself support a tragic vision; as a motive for lyric poetry, it tends to become sentimental or obsessive regardless of the eloquence with which it is developed. When the compassionate attitude is apparently the only attitude with which war can be truthfully described, the possibilities of poetry are severely restricted: only passive suffering and death can provide its materials.

William Butler Yeats excluded Owen's poetry from his *Oxford Book of Modern Verse* on the basis of his judgment that "passive suffering is not a theme for poetry." A "pleader" for the sufferings of others necessarily makes those sufferings his own; "withdrawn into the quicksilver at the back of the mirror," he loses his objectivity and his sense of proportion: "no great event becomes luminous in his mind." The function of the epic narrative, of course, was to communicate that luminous effect; the epic poet, dealing with and illuminating great events, interpreted his tale in the light of heroic values. These values affected the form as well as the materials of the narrative; the epic vision determined the attitude and technique of the poet as well as the motivations and actions of his characters. In Owen's poetry we have the physical background of war, the sense of hazard and duress, the pathos of suffering, and even a perception of tragic extremity. But these, at best, are but fragmentary aspects of the whole. They appear not as products of a unified and comprehensive poetic vision but as effects of a lyric sensibility vainly attempting to find order and significance on a level of experience where these values could not exist—where, in fact, they had been destroyed. Owen and his

contemporaries inherited a sensibility deprived of vision and value; their experiences—so alien to anything dealt with by the romantic tradition—required an intellectual and imaginative discipline far beyond that provided by the vision of pity, which was itself a product of tortured sensibility. Unlike Sassoon, Owen recovered from an early experiential bias; this bias, he discovered, was as poetically unproductive as the Georgian "retrenchment" from which it was an abrupt and sensational reaction. His ironic use of romantic terms and concepts indicates the conflict between a sensibility long devoted to "Poetry" and experiences that demanded the truth. Lacking a positive and comprehensive lyric vision, Owen drew his poetry from this inner conflict while attempting to find his bearings in a period of rapid historical and artistic transition. **"Strange Meeting"** is his final word on the social responsibilities of the "true Poet"; but even in this statement, where the "truth untold" is seen as the pity—"the pity war distilled," Owen can present no further justification of the poet's new role than his sensitivity to suffering. (pp. 204-07)

Owen's influence on the postwar poets has been summarized by C. Day Lewis [in *A Hope for Poetry* (1934)], who nominates Hopkins, Owen, and Eliot as the "immediate ancestors" of the Auden group. Owen's contribution, however, was less technical than inspirational. Auden, Day Lewis, and Louis MacNeice employed Owen's most notable innovation—half-rhyme—for a variety of effects, but with the exception of Day Lewis they did not seriously explore the musical possibilities of this device, which does not lend itself to every poetic purpose. It is rather as a prophet that Owen earns Day Lewis' designation as "a true revolutionary poet." Owen's protest against the evils of war has been rather unwarrantably extended to the social and economic evils of modern life; he "commends himself to post-war poets largely because they feel themselves to be in the same predicament; they feel the same lack of a stable background against which the dance of words may stand out plainly, the same distrust and horror of the unnatural forms into which life for the majority of people is being forced." Owen is actually a symbol rather than a prophet; his youth, his small but eloquent body of verse, his intense dedication to the truth, his untimely and unnecessary death—all of these factors combined to make him an irresistible figure to the succeeding generation, whose "stable background" of traditional forms and values had, like Owen's, been destroyed by the war. He is a "revolutionary poet" not in the sense that he deliberately undertook any radical reformation of his art but in the sense that his work embodies, more dramatically than that of any other poet, the changing values of the time. (pp. 208-09)

John H. Johnston, "Poetry and Pity: Wilfred Owen," in his *English Poetry of the First World War: A Study in the Evolution of Lyric and Narrative Form,* Princeton University Press, 1964, pp. 155-209.

TIMOTHY O'KEEFFE

(essay date 1972)

[In the following excerpt, O'Keeffe discusses ironic allusions to literature and the Bible in Owen's poetry.]

Faced with the incredible horror of warfare in the trenches, Wilfred Owen sought to find some yardstick with which to measure its carnage. He had been nurtured on the aestheticism of the Georgians, of Tennyson, and particularly of Keats, but the irrelevance of poetry of excessive self-pity and beauty to Owen's life on the Western Front became distressingly clear. (p. 72)

Although Owen often echoes the poets he had read in a straight-forward manner, many of his more effective poems depend upon ironic allusions not only to past British poets but also to at least two Roman authors and to the Bible. The irony of these allusions consists in the enormous distance between the sense of values of the writers of the past and their naive conception of war and Owen's immediate knowledge of its mindless obscenity. Byron, among the English poets of the past century, had anticipated Owen with his description of the siege of Ismail in *Don Juan.*

Owen also criticizes the religious establishment through references to the Bible which project the disparity between the gentle teachings and example of Christ and the English Church's support of the war. The irony is telling because of the unquestionable authority of the soldier-poet in speaking of life and death on the battlefield. In a letter from a hospital on the Somme, he indicated the distinction he made between Christianity and Christ:

And am I not myself a conscientious objector with a very seared conscience? . . . Christ is literally in "no man's land." There men often hear His voice: Greater Love hath no man than this, that a man lay down his life for a friend. Is it spoken in English only and French? I do not believe so. Thus you see how pure Christianity will not fit in with pure patriotism.

For Owen the past could not comprehend the present.

Two patriotic poems of Classical literature provide ironic parallels to poems by Owen. **"Arms and the Boy"** clearly parodies the opening of the *Aeneid,* Virgil's claim, "Arma virumque cano," and his flattery of Augustus's apparent descent from a line of gallant Trojan warriors. In Owen's poem the innocence of the boy is caustically contrasted with the Classical allusions to harpies and (possibly) to Actaeon, who had violated with his eyes the chastity of Diana:

For his teeth seem for laughing round an apple.
There lurk no claws behind his fingers supple;
And God will grow no talons at his heels,
Nor antlers through the thickness of his curls.

The young soldier's innocence is despoiled by his need to embrace bayonets and bullets. Owen is as aware as Shaw in *Arms and the Man* of the specious glow surrounding military glory.

The well known **"Dulce et Decorum Est"** was written to Jessie Pope, a contemporary British poetess who had extolled the pleasure of dying for one's country, but Owen chose a more formidable poet to oppose in Horace, who had written the prototypical poem on the subject. Owen's tactic is simple: to portray the death of a soldier from chlorine gas in the most graphic terms and then bitterly end the poem with the admonition that if anyone had seen the sight of this horrible death,

My friend, you would not tell with such high zest
To children ardent for some desperate glory,
The old Lie: Dulce et decorum est
Pro patria mori.

At this early stage of Owen's career, he allows the ironic contrast to remain relatively undeveloped, or at least to develop only one side of the parallel. In later poems he juxtaposes correspondences in scrupulous detail.

Most of Owen's ironic references to the poetry of the past are to the works of the Romantics, who had influenced him deeply, particularly Keats. These allusions indicate the poet's disillusionment with the ideals of the Romantics, which sounded rapturous and inspiring in peacetime but which, to Owen, echoed hollow and fatuous in war. Just as Owen's preface emphasized the distinction between the literature of beauty and of war, an earlier poem, **"On My Songs,"** although written in sonnet form, manifests the poet's growing disenchantment with the poetry of his predecessors:

Yet are there days when all these hoards of thought
Hold nothing for me. Not one verse that throbs
Throbs with my head, or as my brain is fraught.

This effort was composed long before Owen had been involved in the stark realities of war.

Several war poems exhibit an ironic incongruity of allusion to poems of the past. The eerie **"Strange Meeting"** describes the man the narrator has killed (just as Hardy had done in "The Man He Killed") as the slain soldier speaks in the role of a *Doppelgänger,* reminding the narrator of all the profitable things left undone because of his death:

Then, when much blood had clogged their chariot-
wheels,
I would go up and wash them from sweet wells,
Even with truths that lie too deep for taint.

The last line here parodies the last line in Wordsworth's "Intimations Ode," "Thoughts that do often lie
too deep for tears," in that the speaker in Wordsworth's
poem depicts the therapy that nature offers to the soul
that has lost some of its original grandeur. In **"Strange
Meeting,"** on the other hand, the speaker would attempt a cleansing therapy in the world above which
would make it see the futility of war, but death has incapacitated him, preventing him from remedying the
conditions which caused both his death and the deaths
of others to follow.

"Apologia pro Poemate Meo" defines beauty in
a context far different from that of Keats's Odes which
appear as an ironic background to Owen's portrayal of
the ugliness which achieves a strange beauty in war because of human courage. Truth may be beauty, according to Owen, but not because the subject in the poem
is aesthetically attractive like an urn, but because a
beauty is born to the human spirit amidst the ugliness
of war. The poem pictures

. . . Joy, whose ribbon slips—
But wound with war's hard wire whose stakes are
strong;
Bound with the bandage of the arm that drips;
Knit in the webbing of the rifle-thong.

The echo here of **"Ode on Melancholy"** is most
apropos in a grimly ironic sense; Keats's "And Joy,
whose hand is ever at his lips" even contains the same
rhyme (*lips—drips*) as Owen's portrait of Joy. Keats is
saddened by the vanishing of pleasure in its act of consummation, but Owen sees a sturdier beauty in unde-
sired human suffering.

"A Terre" and its sub-title, ("Being the Philosophy of Many Soldiers"), laconically provide a grimly
witty joke at the expense of Shelley, who continually
desired some kind of annihilation because life was too
arduous. Owen had little patience with such self-pity
and explains how the British soldier under bombardment agreed with Shelley's desire for union with the
earth:

"I shall be one with nature, herb, and stone,"
Shelley would tell me. Shelley would be stunned:
The dullest Tommy hugs that fancy now.
"Pushing up daisies" is their creed, you know.
To grain, then, go my fat, to buds my sap,
For all the usefulness there is in soap.

In trench warfare it was difficult to distinguish
who was alive, who dead, who above, and who below
the earth. D. S. R. Welland remarked about this poem
that

obliged to live in close proximity to them. Many
who were buried suffered an untimely and grisly
resurrection through a bursting shell, a land subsistence or a digging party, and many became visibly
assimilated into the squelching mud. There was no
escaping the sight or smell of this putrescence.

"Inspection" recalls Lady Macbeth's pathological
need to remove the spot of blood on her hands, which
was symbolic of her guilt. In Owen's poem the spot is
also symbolic of the guilt of those who send soldiers to
be killed. The dramatic irony in the poem depends
upon the obtuseness of the sergeant-speaker, concerned only with the ritual of cleanliness and not with
the meaning of the bloodstains he finds on the soldier's
uniform during an inspection. He relates his own insensitivity without comprehending its myopia:

Some days "confined to camp" he got,
For being "dirty on parade."
He told me, afterwards, the damnéd spot
Was blood, his own. "Well, blood is dirt," I said.

[Note how the acute mark in *damnéd* emphasizes
the allusion.]

Like Pilate, who insisted upon immaculate hands,
the sergeant is interested in cleanliness because it is a
proper virtue. The meaningless theatricality of army
inspections is exposed here, but more subtly the poem
suggests the metamorphosis of blood into clay, an
image without irony since the trenches were continually stained with blood.

An allusion more difficult to ascertain appears in
"Soldier's Dream," in which a soldier dreams that all
the weapons of war have become fouled or jammed and
the war can no longer continue. Owen may have had
Book Six of *Paradise Lost* in mind when at the end of the
poem God sees to it that the war can continue:

But God was vexed, and gave all power to Michael;
And when I woke he'd seen to our repairs.

The pun on "our repairs" indicates that the soldiers will be fixed as well, so that they can no longer
function as whole human beings. It is significant that
Michael becomes the symbol of divine military power
and not Christ, for in *Paradise Lost* Christ is the supreme
military conqueror in Heaven. Either Owen was not
thinking of Milton at all but instead working from tradition, or else he had the epic specifically in mind and
wanted to reserve Christ for a gentler symbolic role as
the sacrificial soldier, to be discussed under the category of Biblical allusions.

The final literary reference with ironic overtones
is to Gray's *Elegy*: "The paths of glory lead but to the
grave." The line was commonplace enough, and in
Owen's **"Fragment: Not One Corner . . ."** the allusion, although agreeing in spirit and concept with
Gray's elegy (The title of the fragment was to be "An

Imperial Elegy" or "Libretto for Marche Funèbre"), ironically contrasts the concept of a glorious path with a vision of Europe as a vast soldier's cemetery:

I looked and saw.
An appearance of a titan's grave,
At the length thereof a thousand miles.
It crossed all Europe like a mystic road,
Or as the Spirits' Pathway lieth on the night.
And I heard a voice crying,
This is the Path of Glory.

Humphrey Cobb's novel, *Paths of Glory*, also exploited the irony of Gray's phrase, but it is also possible that Owen is ridiculing the traditional *Via Mystica* in the phrase, "mystic road," since the Christian mystics attempted to reach God through this process while the soldier reaches God with the speed of a bullet or shrapnel fragment. The soldier, however, dies not a mystical but a literal death.

Owen grew more and more to reject traditional, or perhaps the better word nowadays is "establishment," Christianity because it was enthusiastically supporting the war, at least in its early stages, as a Crusade. Eventually he distinguished Christ from Christianity and identified Christ with the soldiers in the trenches through their shared suffering. In a letter written on 4 July 1918, he recounts his training the troops:

For 14 hours yesterday I was at work—teaching Christ to lift his cross by numbers, and how to adjust his crown; and not to imagine his thirst till after the last halt. I attended his Supper to see that there were not complaints; and inspected his feet that they should be worthy of the nails. I see to it that he is dumb, and stands at attention before his accusers. With a piece of silver I buy him every day, and with maps I make him familiar with the topography of Golgotha.

D. S. R. Welland points out [in his *Wilfred Owen*] how in **"Strange Meeting"** the soldier bleeds without a wound:

I would have poured my spirit without stint
But not through wounds; not on the cess of war.
Foreheads of men have bled where no wounds were

Welland explains, "The implied reference to Christ's 'agony and bloody sweat' is inescapable, illuminating, and wholly successful." The common experience of Christ and the soldier is sacrifice (as Owen's letter quoted above, indicated), not the militancy of "Onward Christian Soldiers." (pp. 72-8)

["**At a Calvary near the Ancre**"] clearly exploits the Gospel accounts of the Crucifixion as a foil to the horrors of war. The first stanza depicts the ironic situation of the image of Christ "wounded in action":

One ever hangs where shelled roads part.
In this war He too lost a limb,

But His disciples hide apart;
And now the Soldiers bear with Him.

The civilian Christians are nowhere to be seen, just as many, including Peter, denied Christ when danger was imminent, and even more ironically, the modern soldiers bear a load just as Christ bore his cross. In the second stanza the priests who have been seduced by the sins of pride and of the flesh are "flesh-marked by the Beast," the Anti-Christ, who opposes the suffering Saviour. In the final stanza the poem expands to condemn the noisy war propagandists in contradistinction to the quiet soldiers who offer their lives in love, like Christ:

The scribes on all the people shove,
And brawl allegiance to the state,
But they who love the greater love
Lay down their life; they do not hate.

The scribes and pharisees correspond perfectly to the war propagandists because both groups protest too much about their fervor.

The last poem illustrating ironic allusion to the Bible, **"The Parable of the Old Man and the Young"** (in some MSS "Old Men"), has been too often superficially examined because of the obviousness of the reference to the twenty-second chapter of Genesis, the story of Abraham and Isaac. Just as in other poems suggesting the sacrifice of Christ, **"The Parable"** utilizes the intended sacrifice of Abraham. The irony of this allegory, however, emanates from the contrast between the relieved humanity of Abraham and the wilful homicide of the leaders of Europe. The contrast is sharpened by a rather close ironic correspondence between the Biblical text and the poem; that is, the subtle differences between the two indicate that Owen probably had the text of Genesis close by when he wrote the poem and that he intensified the irony scrupulously. Thus, in Genesis Isaac remarks on the preparations of "fire and wood," but in the poem he observes the "fire and iron" of the battlefield; in Genesis Abraham simply "bound Isaac" but in the poem:

Then Abram bound the youth with belts and straps,
And builded parapets and trenches there.

Further, in the original Abraham sees the ram caught in a thicket as a possible sacrifice, but in the poem Abram is too blind to see, and an angel, representing a good spiritual impulse, tells Abram to "Offer the Ram of Pride instead of him." The ending of the poem then offers an obvious contrast in the slaying of "half the seed of Europe, one by one" with Abraham's saving of his son. Genesis xii. 17 deepens the irony in the blessing given by God to Abraham's seed as opposed to the sterility and destruction effected by the old man of Europe: "That in blessing I will bless thee, and in multiplying I will multiply thy seed as the stars of the heaven, and as the sand which is upon the sea shore; and thy seed shall possess the gate of his ene-mies." Clearly the opposite, Owen prophesies, will be the result of the sacrifice in **"The Parable."**

Owen also took advantage of what is now called folk culture, as in his picture of the maimed and wounded reading the optimistic propaganda from home in **"Smile, Smile, Smile."** Every soldier knew the lines from the marching song,

Pack up your troubles in your old kit bag
And smile, smile, smile.
. . . . .
Smile, boys, that's the style.

But the smile of the casualties in the face of the glorious programmes for the youth of England depends upon the realization that the future of England was really in France:

That England one by one had fled to France,
Not many elsewhere now, save under France.

For the poet this was the true "Lost Generation."

Wilfred Owen in his poetry found ironic allu-sions to literature and the Bible effective in driving home to his readers the horror of war and the inability of the values and morality of Western Christian civili-zation to comprehend the nature of World War I. Orig-inally seeking the traditions of his past and its literature to support his poetry and writing an often too deriva-tive verse, the poet discovered that the traditional sup-port he was seeking simply wasn't extant, and so he paradoxically found sustenance in those traditions by displaying their impotence in explaining the cataclysm of modern warfare. (pp. 79-81)

Timothy O'Keeffe, "Ironic Allusion in the Poetry of Wilfred Owen," in *Ariel: A Review of International English Literature,* Vol. 3, No. 4, October, 1972, pp. 72-81.

DOMINIC HIBBERD

(essay date 1975)

[In the following excerpt, Hibberd asserts that Owen was an original poet who went beyond the influ-ences of his Victorian predecessors.]

The criticism is sometimes made of Owen that he was always too much under the domination of the Victori-ans. It is true that his facility for imitation and his habit of venerating great writers made him an easy prey to the captivating music of Tennyson and Swinburne, but at his best he was able to get the upper hand. Although the influence of other poets is frequently evident in his work, his style in unmistakable and unique; often the trace of another poet in his lines adds to the poem's

meaning and is meant to do so, as in the echoes of Keats's *Hyperion* and Shelley's *The Revolt of Islam* in **'Strange Meeting'.** The red roses in **'The Kind Ghosts'** are more terrible than anything Swinburne ever man-aged in his numerous images of blood and flowers, while **'Futility'** shows what Owen could do with the Tennysonian tradition. . . . This is, in the opinion of many, Owen's most nearly flawless poem. . . . It is far from a damaging criticism in this case to suggest that **'Futility'** is in direct descent from the great stanzas in *In Memoriam.* . . . (pp. 31-2)

Nature in many of Owen's poems is a hostile force, as in the deathly snow of **'Exposure'** or the 'winds' scimitars' in **'Asleep',** but this hostility is a re-sponse to war. In **'Spring Offensive,'** where his under-standing of this problem is most fully set out, nature tries to prevent men from going into an attack, launches a violent onslaught against them when they ignore the appeal and becomes peaceful again as soon as the attack is over. His early poems show repeatedly that he be-lieved nature to be a source of blessing to those in har-mony with the natural order, and the reader of his let-ters soon becomes accustomed to his odd elaborations of this belief ('we ate the Vernal Eucharist of Hawthorn leaf-buds'). His poems are consistent with the Roman-tic tradition in this and other ways; they are not the ironic denial of it that some critics have understood them to be.

Owen is not an easy poet, yet from the details of his technique to the largest statements of his elegies there runs a consistent pattern. A line such as 'Rucked too thick for these men's extrication' (**'Mental Cases'**) shows his characteristic rhyming ('Ruck-/thick/-tric-') and an equally characteristic use of an unexpected but simple word ('Rucked') leading to the more elaborate 'extrication'. This kind of combination can be seen again in, for example, **'Strange Meeting',** where a sin-gle line contains the colloquial 'thumped' and the ar-chaic 'made moan'; or in **'Futility',** where the startlingly simple familiarity of 'kind of sun' precedes a complex image of clay that is developed from biblical and older origins. Similarly, the tunnel in **'Strange Meeting'** is at once a dug-out and the Underworld, the men in **'Men-tal Cases'** are inhabitants of a mental hospital and of the Inferno, and the infantry in **'Spring Offensive'** charge both an unseen human enemy and the Romantic landscape itself. Parallel to these ambivalences, which are wholly deliberate, are Owen's frequent allusions to earlier poets, particularly Shelley, Keats and Dante; these, too, are deliberate and they bind his poetry into literary tradition. The echo of Keats's odes in the de-scription of the landscape in **'Spring Offensive'** sug-gests the strange possibility that the landscape *is* that of the odes, a suggestion which, if we follow it, adds much to the significance of the poem; yet it is easy to dismiss the echo as being unintentional, proof only of

Owen's inability to get away from nineteenth-century diction. The old view of his poems as products of the war, forced out of an immature and ill-informed mind under the pressure of intense experience, is slow in dying but does not deserve to live; the major poems are the result of long years of training and preparation, finding fruit not in some hasty scribble done on the back of an envelope in the trenches but in the meticulous, protracted labour which went on at Ripon in the spring of 1918.

If memories of the Great War ever fade, much of the verse we associate with it will also be forgotten. Owen's poetry seems more likely to endure than most; it is uneven, incomplete and sometimes of poor quality, but at his best he belongs to English literature and not just to an historical event. (pp. 33-4)

Dominic Hibberd, in his *Wilfred Owen*, edited by Ian Scott-Kilvert, British Council, 1975, 44 p.

DENNIS WELLAND
(essay date 1978)

[In the following excerpt, Welland addresses Owen's concept of Christianity.]

In all Owen's writing no phrase is more revelatory than his description of himself as 'a conscientious objector with a very seared conscience', which occurs in the important letter where he records poignantly his realisation that 'pure Christianity will not fit in with pure patriotism'. Already in his earliest poetry we have seen an uneasiness over religious belief finding expression in a somewhat derivative idiom that detracts from its spontaneity, but of the intensity of the spiritual crisis into which his participation on the war plunged him there can be no doubt. . . . The significance of that elaborate metaphor [in a letter to Osbert Sitwell Owen portrays himself as preparing the Christ-soldier for his suffering and death] lies in the role the writer assigns to himself: he is in every instance betraying the Christ-soldier and thus alienating himself from the mercy of Christ.

Such popularly-accepted phrases as 'the supreme sacrifice' illustrate how readily the soldier came to be thought of in a role similar to that of the crucified Saviour. . . . The basis of this identification is, of course, the scriptural text which Owen quotes in the following form in the letter speaking of his seared conscience, and again at the end of 'At a Calvary' (it also gave him the title for one of his most deeply-felt poems): 'Greater love hath no man than this, that a man lay down his life for a friend'; but the same letter contains the realisation that the soldier who makes this sacrifice may in the course of so doing disobey 'one of Christ's essential commands . . . do not kill'. . . . [The] greatness of 'Strange Meeting' lies, in part, in the success with which it (like 'The Show') develops the *doppelgänger* theme as a perfect symbol of this dichotomy. Since this religious problem underlies so much of Owen's poetry it is not extravagant to see a possible reference to Christ in the sun 'whose bounty these have spurned' in 'Spring Offensive': ignoring the 'essential commandment' is tantamount to spurning the salvation Christianity offers.

This is not to attribute to Owen in these poems a wholly orthodox Christian view. In 'At a Calvary near the Ancre' he is as much at odds with the 'pulpit professionals' as in the letter on pacifism, but in both cases his accusation is that Christ has been betrayed by His Church. . . . In this sentiment Owen was by no means alone. The religious assurance of earlier war poets was dying out by 1917: Christ in Flanders was too much of a paradox to be easily accepted any longer. (pp. 85-6)

Yet it would be unjust to dismiss [the later war poets] as irreverent, godless, and blasphemous. Their agnosticism is the product of their circumstances and often conceals . . . a very real desire to believe. The frequent invocation of Christ . . . suggests something deeper than army blasphemy, and the tendency to draw on Biblical stories for satires is surely an indication of how prominent their old faith was in their minds, even if they found temporary difficulty in reconciling it with their circumstances. Thus the sacrifice of Isaac by Abraham provided both Osbert Sitwell and Owen with a theme, while Sassoon draws on the story of Cain and Abel. That these are Old Testament stories is not unconnected with the fact that whereas the 'bardic' poets had usually invoked God in their patriotic poetry, it is to Christ that the later poets more frequently appeal. (p. 87)

God, that is, has been identified with Jahveh, the Old Testament God of battles and of wrath, whose interest in the perpetuation of the war is sharply contrasted with the compassion of Christ who, as Divinity incarnate, can sympathise with the human suffering war involves. In the face of this prolongation of suffering neither victory nor death has any great significance. The war that Jahveh wishes for is death, the death of the spirit, whereas the compassion represented by Christ is life-giving and kind, like the sun in 'Futility' and in 'Spring Offensive' where the antithesis between the sun, 'the friend with whom their love is done', and the 'stark, blank sky' full of incipient menace and hostility may be a reflection of this antithesis between Christ and God.

Questionable as its theology may be, Owen's position here is one to which many must, in varying degrees, have been attracted . . . , and it is one for which the Church was itself partly to blame because of the ardent and uncritical support it appeared to give to the continuance of the war. . . . It is hardly surprising that Owen's poetry should contain such statements as 'God seems not to care' and 'love of God seems dying', though his refusal to word either of them more dogmatically indicated the strength of the religion in which he had been brought up.

Owen's pacifism, however, although usually expressed in Christian terms, is not entirely the outcome of the conflict between his military experience and his religious upbringing. There is another influence behind it, more powerful than is sometimes recognised. During his stay in Bordeaux he had made the acquaintance of the French poet Laurent Tailhade. . . . [Despite] the discrepancy between their ages, a real friendship seems to have developed between them. . . . [But] it is not as a poet that Tailhade most significantly influenced his young English friend. Originally intended for the Church, Tailhade had early in life revolted against Christianity but was none the less a confirmed pacifist who had been in considerable trouble with the authorities for his *Lettre aux Conscrits*. . . . This and his address *Pour la Paix*. . . . anticipate Owen so markedly in sentiment and even on occasion in turns of expression that it is impossible that Owen should not have known them. The definition of poetry in *Pour la Paix* is very close indeed to the conception of it that underlies Owen's draft preface. . . . (pp. 87-9)

The only call to which Owen answers is not that of the church but of human suffering. It is human sympathy rather than abstract morality that determines his ethical position. . . . (p. 90)

The lonely independence . . . becomes increasingly dominant in Owen's poetry in direct proportion to the increase in his dedication to the task of speaking for 'these boys . . . as well as a pleader can'. His sense of comradeship and solidarity leads to no sentimentally Whitmanesque merging of identity with them, but at the same time his awareness of isolation is more firmly grounded and poetically more valuable than the uneasy Romantic pose of the juvenilia to which it is directly related. The ten-stanza poem, of which **'This is the Track'** originally formed the three last (and only revised) verses, develops an image used in a letter to Sassoon in November 1917 ('I was always a mad comet; but you have fixed me'); in the poem he aspires to be a solitary meteor awakening in men premonitions and intimations of eternity, the published stanzas illustrate a similarly purposeful self-sufficiency coupled with an almost messianic belief in the poet's responsibility, the exercise of which may even 'turn aside the very sun', but another and rather better poem of probably similar date puts the other side.

'Six o'clock in Princes St' is just as Tennysonian in origin as is the contemporaneous **'Hospital Barge'**

sonnet which he described as "due to a Saturday night revel in **'The Passing of Arthur',"** but it is more critical of that revel than is **'Hospital Barge'**. A half-envious watching of the home-going crowds creates dissatisfaction with his own loneliness. . . . Certainly the mood is antithetical to that of **'The Fates'**, written less than six months earlier, with its Georgian confidence in beauty and art as an escape from 'the march of lifetime'; and the choice of the verb 'dared' in the last line shows an honesty of self-knowledge anticipatory of those letters of the following summer in which he told at least two of his friends how glad he was to have been recommended for the Military Cross 'for the confidence it will give me in dealing with civilians'. (pp. 93-4)

There is a richness and complexity about **'Miners'** that is quite absent from, for example, so slight a piece as **'The Promisers'** and even from **'Winter Song'**. The burning coal becomes a symbol for, in turn, the remote past, the miners who dug it, and, by a well-managed and apparently easy but none the less effective transition, the war dead. The atmosphere of the opening stanzas with their leaves, frond-forests, ferns, and birds is reminiscent of **'From My Diary'** and the **'Sonnet: to a Child'**, but where **'From My Diary'** contents itself with the creation of that atmosphere and the sonnet associates it pleasantly but conventionally with the ideas of anamnesis and growing old, **'Miners'** contrasts it with the 'sourness' of the sacrificed lives (to use Owen's own word for the poem's quality). Out of the oxymoron of this fusion comes a new strength, while the end of the poem gains in emotive force by the unexpected identification of the poet with the suffering of the lost which he has hitherto described detachedly. (It is of course the same device that he uses so effectively in **'The Show'**, **'Mental Cases'**, and **'Strange Meeting'**. (pp. 95-6)

Though not specifically war-poems, these, like **'The Kind Ghosts'**, illustrate Owen's range and may offer some indication of how his poetry might have developed had he lived, but they are important also as examples of the positive though indirect influence on his poetry of the compassion and the sense of isolation induced by his 'very seared conscience'. (p. 98)

[There are] two types of poems with which Owen experiments: his poems of dramatic description (such as **'The Chances'**) and the more subjective lyrics of personal response (such as **'Greater Love'** or **'Apologia'**). Both have their advantages and their limitations, but what Owen needed for the full attaining of his purpose was a poetry where the more objective detachment of the one could be harnessed with the emotional intensity of the other. He often achieved this in his poems of imaginative description such as **'Spring Offensive'** but he also accomplished it in what I would call poems of visionary description; of these **'The**

Show' is a good example, but **'Strange Meeting'**, the poem that Sassoon once called Owen's passport to immortality, and his elegy to the unknown warriors of all nations', is the best, especially for the way in which it brings together so many strands of his work already discussed. Essentially a poem of trench warfare, realistically based on the First World War, it is a fine statement of Owen's moral idealism as well, but it is also a poem that shows his true relationship to the Romantic tradition as something much more positive and creative than his earlier aestheticism suggests. (pp. 98-9)

From his echoing of it in an unpublished poem, we may be certain that he knew Wilde's line 'Yet each man kills the thing he loves' and this too lies at the back of **'Strange Meeting'.** The point is well made by the enemy's identification of himself with his killer in lines that are in effect Owen's own elegy, the final comment on his spiritual progress from the artificial aestheticism of the early years to the altruistic, splendid pity of these last poems. . . . The enemy Owen has killed is, he suggests, his poetic self, and 'the undone years, The hopelessness' of which the enemy speaks are in one sense very personal to Owen, while in another sense they are tragically universal. Other poets had mourned the cutting-off of youth before its prime, but usually in terms of the loss to the individuals themselves or to their friends; if they envisaged the world becoming poorer they did not envisage it becoming actually worse, because tacitly or explicitly they assumed that the progress which the war had interrupted could be resumed by the survivors when it ended. Owen's vision is more penetrating and less comfortable. The war has not merely interrupted the march of mankind; it has changed its whole direction and done incalculable and irreparable damage. It is this terrible prophetic vision of a dying world embodied in this and other poems that gives Owen's work abiding relevance, but what he mourns is not merely the men themselves. Not only

'the old Happiness' but the potentialities offered by the past are unreturning, and there is truly no sadness sadder than the hope of the poet here foreseeing the disintegration of values, the retrogression of humanity, involved in this second Fall. . . . Only the men who fought in that war had, in Owen's belief, been vouchsafed an insight into the Truth, but it was too late to put that knowledge to any constructive use. If only they could have held themselves apart from the process of disintegration, had they only had the opportunity . . . they might, in the fullness of time, have been empowered to arrest that march and to restore the truth. . . . Here perhaps is the last flourish of that messianic impulse which Christianity and Romanticism had combined to implant in Owen in the dedicated ideal of service to humanity. . . . But the opportunity for such service is gone, and characteristically in one of his simplest but most effective phrases Owen indicts himself as much as anyone else for the destruction of that opportunity: 'I am the enemy you killed, my friend'.

Despite the technical maturity with which this rich complex of ideas is developed, despite the creative genius that evolved so superb a myth for its poetic purpose, it is more than the loss of a poet that one laments after reading **'Strange Meeting'.** The sleep to which the dead enemy invites him is certainly

> less tremulous, less cold,
> Than we who must awake, and waking, say Alas!

for **'Strange Meeting'** carries its own conviction of the irreparable loss to humanity of 'us poor lads / Lost in the ground'—irreparable not for what they were but for what they would have been, not for what they gave but for what they would have given. (pp. 100-03)

Dennis Welland, in his *Wilfred Owen: A Critical Study,* revised edition, Chatto & Windus, 1978, 192 p.

SOURCES FOR FURTHER STUDY

Lane, Arthur E. *An Adequate Response: The War Poetry of Wilfred Owen and Sigfried Sassoon.* Detroit: Wayne State University Press, 1972. 190 p.

Examines the artistic milieu in which Owen and Sassoon worked, their poetic responses to the experience of war, and their relationship to other poets.

McIlroy, James F. *Wilfred Owen's Poetry: A Study Guide.* London: Heinemann Educational Books, 1974, 124 p.

Handbook containing an introductory sketch, analyses, survey of critical opinion, and bibliography.

Orrmont, Arthur. *Requiem for War: The Life of Wilfred Owen.* New York: Four Winds Press, 1972, 192 p.

Appreciative, noncritical biography.

Owen, Harold. *Journey from Obscurity: Wilfred Owen, 1893-1918: Memoirs of the Owen Family.* 3 vols. London: Oxford University Press, 1963-65.

Complete biography of Owen and his siblings, by his brother.

Sitwell, Osbert. "Wilfred Owen." In his *Noble Essences: A Book of Characters,* pp. 101-24. Boston: Little, Brown and Co., 1950.

Biographical and critical discussion of Owen, with references to specific poems.

White, Gertrude M. *Wilfred Owen.* New York: Twayne Publishers, 1969. 156 p.

Studies Owen and his poetry, particularly his poetic craftsmanship and the growth of his posthumous success.

Boris Pasternak

1890-1960

(Full name Boris Leonidovich Pasternak) Russian poet, novelist, short story writer, essayist, memoirist, and non-fiction writer.

INTRODUCTION

Awarded the 1958 Nobel Prize in literature, which he declined under political pressure, Pasternak is regarded in Russia as among the foremost poets of the twentieth century. He garnered international acclaim, however, as the author of the novel *Doktor Zivago* (1957; *Doctor Zhivago*). An epic portrayal of the Russian Revolution and its consequences, *Doctor Zhivago* ignited a political and artistic controversy that continues to overshadow Pasternak's achievements in other genres. While his complex, ethereal works often defy translation, Western critics laud his synthesis of unconventional imagery and formalistic style as well as his vision of the individual's relationship to nature and history. C. M. Bowra asserted: "In a revolutionary age Pasternak [saw] beyond the disturbed surface of things to the powers behind it and found there an explanation of what really matters in the world. Through his unerring sense of poetry he has reached to wide issues and shown that the creative calling, with its efforts and its frustrations and its unanticipated triumphs, is, after all, something profoundly natural and closely related to the sources of life."

The son of an acclaimed artist and a concert pianist, both of Jewish descent, Pasternak benefited from a highly creative household that counted novelist Leo Tolstoy, composer Alexander Scriabin, and poet Rainer Maria Rilke among its visitors. Encouraged by Scriabin, Pasternak began studying music as a fourteen-year-old, but abandoned this pursuit six years later over what he perceived as a lack of technical skill. He then turned to philosophy, eventually enrolling in Germany's prestigious Marburg University where he studied Neo-Kantianism. In 1912, however, Pasternak abruptly left Marburg when his childhood friend, Ida Vysotskaia, rejected his marriage proposal, compelling Pasternak to reevaluate his professional as well as personal choices. Deciding to commit himself exclusively to poetry, he eventually joined Centrifuge, a moderate group of literary innovators associated with the Futurist movement. Rejecting the poetic language of such nine-teenth-century authors as Alexander Pushkin and Leo Tolstoy, the Futurists advocated greater poetic free-dom and attention to the actualities of modern life. Pas-ternak's first two poetry collections, *Blitzhetz tuchakh* (1914) and *Poverkh barerov* (1917), largely reflect these precepts as well as the influence of Vladimir Mayakovsky, Pasternak's close friend and among the most revered of the Futurist poets.

Partially lamed by a childhood riding accident, Pasternak was declared unfit for military service and spent the first years of World War I in the Ural Moun-tains as a clerical worker. When news of political tur-moil reached Pasternak in 1917, he returned to Mos-cow, but the capital's chaotic atmosphere forced him to leave for his family's summer home in the outlying countryside. There he composed *Sestra moia zhizn: leto 1917 goda* (1923; *My Sister, Life: Summer 1917*). Considered Pasternak's greatest poetic achievement, this volume celebrates nature as a creative force that permeates every aspect of human experience and im-pels all historical and personal change. Often uniting expansive, startling imagery with formal rhyme schemes, *My Sister, Life: Summer 1917* is lauded as an accomplished and innovative synthesis of the prin-cipal poetic movements of early twentieth-century Rus-sia, including the Futurists, the Acmeists, and the Imag-ists. Pasternak's next poetry collection, *Temi i variatsi* (1923), solidified his standing as a major modern poet in the Soviet Union. He also received critical acclaim as a prose writer with *Rasskazy* (1925), his first collec-tion of short stories, which includes the previously pub-lished pieces "Apellesova cherta" ("Apelles' Mark"), "Pisma iz Tuly" ("Letter to Tula"), "Vozdudhnye puti" ("Aerial Ways"), and "Detstvo Liuvers" ("The Child-hood of Luvers").

In 1923, enthusiastic about the possible artistic benefits of the Revolution, Pasternak joined Mayakovsky's Left Front of Art (LEF), an alliance be-tween Futurist writers and the Communist party that used the avant-garde movement's literary innovations to glorify the new social order. His work from this peri-od, *Vysockaya bolezn* (1924), *Deviatsot piatyi god* (1926), and *Leitenant Schmidt* (1927), are epic poems that favorably portray events leading up to and sur-rounding the uprisings of 1917. However, socialist crit-ics faulted the distinctly meditative, personal tone of the poems as bourgeois, a charge also leveled against *Povest* (1934; *The Last Summer*), a novella, and *Okh-rannaya gramota* (1931), an autobiographical work. In this volume, Pasternak recalls the men who shaped his artistic sensibility, including Mayakovsky, Scriabin, and Rilke, while further outlining his concept of nature and

its mystical role in the creative process. During the late 1920s, Pasternak grew disillusioned with the govern-ment's increasing social and artistic restrictions as well as with Communism's collective ideal that, in his opin-ion, directly opposed the individualistic nature of hu-manity. He then broke with the LEF, a decision finalized by Mayakovsky's suicide in 1930.

The following year, Pasternak divorced his first wife, Evgeniya Lurie, as a result of his affair with Zinaida Neigauz, whom he later married. Critics often cite this new relationship and the couple's friendships with sev-eral Georgian writers as the source of the revitalized poetry found in *Vtoroye rozhdenie* (1932). A collection of love lyrics and impressions of the Georgian country-side, *Vtoroye rozhdenie* presented Pasternak's newly simplified style and chronicled his attempt to reconcile his artistic and social responsibilities in a time of politi-cal upheaval. Pasternak's newfound optimism, howev-er, was subdued following the inception of the Soviet Writer's Union, a government institution that abolished independent literary groups and promoted conformity to the precepts of socialist realism. Recognized as a major poet by the Communist regime, Pasternak partic-ipated in several official literary functions, including the First Congress of Writers in 1934. He gradually with-drew from public life, however, as Joseph Stalin's re-pressive policies intensified, and he began translating the works of others rather than composing his own, possibly incendiary, prose and poetry. His many trans-lations include Johann Wolfgang von Goethe's *Faust* as well as the major tragedies of Shakespeare, which remain the standard texts for staging the plays in Rus-sian.

Following the publication of *Vtoroye rozhdenie,* Pasternak reissued several of his earlier poetry vol-umes under the titles *Stikhotvoreniia v odnom tome* (1933), *Poemy* (1933), and *Stikhotvoreniia* (1936). His new collections of verse, however, did not appear until World War II. *Na rannikh poezdakh* (1943) and *Zemnoy proster* (1945) reflect the renewed patriotic spirit and creative freedom fostered by the conflict while eschew-ing conventional political rhetoric. Suppression of the arts resumed following the war, and many of Paster-nak's friends and colleagues were imprisoned or exe-cuted. Historians and critics disagree as to why Paster-nak, who had publicly condemned the actions of the government, escaped Stalin's purges of the intelligen-tsia. While some credit his translation and promotion of writers from Stalin's native Georgia, others report that the dictator, while glancing over Pasternak's dossier, wrote "Do not touch this cloud-dweller."

In 1948, Pasternak began secretly composing his novel *Doctor Zhivago,* which he completed in 1956. Drawn from his personal experiences and beliefs, the novel utilizes complex symbols, imagery, and narrative techniques to depict Yury Zhivago, a poet and doctor who is caught up in and eventually destroyed by the

Communist revolution of 1917. When Pasternak submitted *Doctor Zhivago* to Soviet publishers in 1956, they rejected the novel for what the editorial board of *Novy mir* termed its "spirit . . . of nonacceptance of the socialist revolution." Pasternak then smuggled the manuscript to the West, where reviewers hailed the novel as an incisive and moving condemnation of Communism. In 1959, the Swedish Academy selected Pasternak for the Nobel Prize in literature, citing his achievements as both a poet and novelist. Nevertheless, the implication that the award had been given solely for *Doctor Zhivago* launched a bitter Soviet campaign against Pasternak that ultimately forced him to decline the prize. Despite his decision, the Soviet Writer's Union expelled Pasternak from its ranks, and one Communist party member characterized the author as a "literary whore" in the employ of Western authorities. In memoirs he kept during the mid-1960s, however, Nikita Khrushchev, the Soviet premier who suppressed the novel in 1956, concluded: "I regret that I had a hand in banning the book. We should have given readers an opportunity to reach their own verdict. By banning *Doctor Zhivago* we caused much harm to the Soviet Union."

Evaluations of *Doctor Zhivago* in the years following "The Pasternak Affair" often disagree as to the novel's importance. Several critics regarded its many coincidences and Pasternak's distortion of historical chronology and character development as technically flawed. Other commentators compared Pasternak's thorough portrayal of a vast and turbulent period to that of nineteenth-century Russian novelists, particularly Leo Tolstoy. Additionally, the major themes of the novel, often distilled in the poems attributed to the title character, have been the subject of extensive analysis.

Through Zhivago, critics maintain, Pasternak realized his vision of the artist as a Christ-like figure who bears witness to the tragedy of his age even as it destroys him. This idea is often linked to Pasternak's contention that individual experience is capable of transcending the destructive forces of history. It is this concept, commentators assert, that gives *Doctor Zhivago* its enduring power. Marc Slonim observed: "In *Doctor Zhivago* man is shown in his individual essence, and his life is interpreted not as an illustration of historical events, but as a unique, wonderful adventure in its organic reality of sensations, thoughts, drives, instincts and strivings. This makes the book . . . a basically anti-political work, in so far as it treats politics as fleeting, unimportant, and extols the unchangeable fundamentals of human mind, emotion and creativity."

Pasternak published two more works outside the Soviet Union, *Kogda razgulyayetsya* (1959; *When Skies Clear*), a volume of reflective verse, and *Autobiogratichesey ocherk* (1959; *I Remember*), an autobiographical sketch, before his death in 1960. At his funeral, Pasternak was not accorded the official ceremonies normally provided for the death of a member of the Soviet Writer's Union. However, thousands accompanied his family to the grave site, which remains a place of pilgrimage in Russia. In 1987, under the auspices of Communist leader Mikail Gorbachev's policy of social reform, or *glasnost,* the Writer's Union formally reinstated Pasternak, and in 1988, *Doctor Zhivago* was published in the Soviet Union for the first time.

(For further information about Pasternak's life and works, see *Contemporary Authors,* Vols. 116 [obituary], 127; and *Contemporary Literary Criticism,* Vols. 7, 10, 18, 63.)

CRITICAL COMMENTARY

THE TIMES, LONDON

(essay date 1958)

[In the following excerpt from a review of *Doctor Zhivago,* the critic compares the novel to Tolstoy's *War and Peace* and praises Pasternak's rendering of the detrimental impact of the communist revolution on the individual.]

Is it another *War and Peace?* This question is immediately raised by the scope, the grandeur, the compassion and the beauty of Boris Pasternak's epic, [*Doctor Zhivago*]. Like Tolstoy, he searches deep into the meaning of life by tracing the loves, hopes, anguish and deaths of about a score of men and women during years of titanic struggle and upheaval in Russia. The superficial likenesses between the two books are many. As Tolstoy chose Pierre Bezukhov, the earnest and bewildered bystander and philosophiser, to be one of the pivots and interpreters of his story, so Pasternak has chosen Yury Zhivago, the poet, almost the quietist, who shrinks more and more from the October revolution and the civil war until he falls, worn out, into physical and moral decay.

Yet it would be wrong to pursue the parallels too far. Pasternak does not try to enter directly into the

Principal Works

Biltzhetz tuchakh (poetry) 1914

Poverkh barerov (poetry) 1917

*Detstvo Luvors (short story) 1919

[Childhood, 1941; also published as The Adolescence of Zhenya Luvers, 1961]

Sestra moia zhizn (poetry) 1923

[Sister, My Life: Summer 1917, 1967; also published in My Sister, Life; and Other Poems, 1976]

Temy i variatsi (poetry) 1923

Vysockaya bolezn (poetry) 1924

*Rasskazy (short stories) 1925

†Deviatsot piatyi god (poetry) 1926

†Leitenant Shmidt (poetry) 1927

*Okhrannaya gramota (autobiographical nonfiction) 1931

Vtoroye rozhdenie (poetry) 1932

Poemy (poetry) 1933

Stikhotvoreniia v odnom tome (poetry) 1933

Povest (autobiographical nonfiction) 1934

[The Last Summer, 1959]

Stikhotvoreniia (poetry) 1936

Na rannikh poezdakh (poetry) 1943

Zemnoy proster (poetry) 1945

Doktor Zhivago (novel)

[first published as Il dottor Zivago in Italian, 1957; published as Doctor Zhivago in English, 1959; published in Russian, 1988]

I Remember: Sketch for an Autobiography (memoirs; from the Russian manuscript "Autobiogratichesey ocherk.") 1959

Kogda razgulyayetsya (poetry) 1959

[Poems, 1955-1959, 1960]

Sochineniya (collected works) 1961

Lettere agli amici georgiani (letters; from the Russian manuscript "Pis'ma k gurinskim druz' iam") 1967

[Letters to Georgian Friends, 1968]

Slepaia krasavista (play) 1969

[The Blind Beauty, 1969]

Boris Pasternak: Perepiska s Ol'goi Freidenberg (letters) 1981

[The Correspondence of Boris Pasternak and Olga Friedenberg, 1910-1954, 1982]

Letters, Summer 1926 (letters) 1985

*Translated and published in The Collected Prose Works of Boris Pasternak, 1977.

†Published together as Deviastsot piatyi god in 1927.

---

minds of the dynasts—the Kaiser or Hitler, or Lenin, Trotsky or Stalin—as Tolstoy spoke through the minds of Napoleon and Kutuzov. Indeed, one of the reasons why his book—already published in Italian and French, and now in English—has not yet been allowed in Russia is that he does not deal in any detail with the motives of the revolutionary leaders after 1917 or their material achievements. To that extent the book is truncated. The tragedy works itself out at a lower level of history than Tolstoy's. But that is because of Pasternak's own view of life. He denies that essential human life can be reshaped, and his chief concern is with the price that is paid in human misery when the attempt is made.

He is appalled (speaking through Zhivago and other characters) by the sequel to the revolution which they all had originally welcomed; appalled by the "spirit of narrowness" that set truth aside and demanded to be worshipped as holy itself; contemptuous of the limitations and self-centredness of Marxism; and horrified by mass direction. "The great misfortune, the root of all the evil to come, was the loss of faith in the value of personal opinions." Against it all he sets the Galilean message of love and compassion. "From that moment there were neither gods nor peoples, but only man." And at another place, "communion between mortals is immortal." The religious message burns with a clear flame in the twenty-five poems at the end. He asserts the duty of the intellectual, the poet, the believer, to pass judgment on the actions of men.

How misleading, though, to think of the book as a kind of fictionalized political treatise. It is a protest and a challenge certainly, but it springs from life itself, presented in the stories of quite ordinary men and women, Zhivago, Lara, Tonya, Strelnikov, and the rest. The developing theme through all the turmoil is awe-inspiring, a passionate and vibrant work of art that has the force, and the emotional power, of a symphony. . . .

Above all, there is the end of Lara. In this most Russian of novels Pasternak—perhaps to reinforce his message that life is concerned "not with peoples, but with persons"—has made his chief heroine the Russian-born daughter of a Belgian father and a Russianized French-woman. She lights up the whole story in every word and action. "One day Lara went out and did not come back. She must have been arrested in the street, as so often happened in those days, and she died or vanished somewhere, forgotten as a nameless number on a list which later was mislaid, in one of the innumerable mixed or women's concentration camps in the north."

An English reader may find the many Russian first names, patronymics and surnames a little perplexing. . . . He may also find something far-fetched in the coincidences which bring so many of the characters together after so many long journeys, spread over years. But these are small tribulations along the road. Pasternak has written one of the great books, courageous, tender, tragic, humble.

"A Modern Russian Novel on the Grand Scale," in *The Times*, London, September 4, 1958, p. 13.

MARC SLONIM

(essay date 1958)

[Slonim was a Russian-born American critic who wrote extensively on Russian literature. In the excerpt below, he presents the major themes of *Doctor Zhivago*.]

At last we have the English version of *Doctor Zhivago*, the great novel from Russia that suddenly sprang into prominence last year in Europe and became the subject of passionate discussion among critics and readers. It is easy to predict that Boris Pasternak's book, one of the most significant of our time and a literary event of the first order, will have a brilliant future. It also has had an extraordinary past. (p. 1)

In the solitude of his bungalow in the neighborhood of Moscow, Pasternak wrote between 1948 and 1953 a long work in prose. "I always dreamt of a novel," he said, "in which, as in an explosion, I would erupt with all the wonderful things I saw and understood in this world." This novel, *Doctor Zhivago*, was accepted after Stalin's death by the State Publishing House; but following a closer examination of the manuscript (and instructions from higher party echelons), the work was barred. In the meantime Pasternak had sold the foreign rights to Feltrinelli, a Milan publisher. Moscow, seeking to prevent the publication of *Doctor Zhivago* abroad, compelled Pasternak to wire Feltrinelli, asking him not to publish the Italian translation of the novel and begging him to return the manuscript "for revisions." Feltrinelli's refusal brought about all sorts of pressure, including intervention by the Soviet Embassy. Nevertheless, the Italian version of *Doctor Zhivago* came out in November, 1957, and immediately provoked a great stir (seven reprints in less than a year). Translations into most European languages followed and made the name of Pasternak universally known. The novel is still not available, however, in its original Russian text.

The central figure in the novel is Yurii Zhivago,

son of a rich Siberian industrialist and orphan at the age of 10. He is brought up in the house of Moscow intellectuals and patrons of the arts and becomes a typical product of upper class, pre-revolutionary Russian culture. Yet as an individual, Zhivago cannot be so easily classified. An excellent physician, he studies philosophy and literature, and has decidedly personal views on many matters. He writes poems, and twenty-four of them form the ending of the novel. His main aim is to preserve his own spiritual independence. In a way he is an outsider, and does not become completely involved in current events.

Zhivago's refusal to become "engaged," however, is of an entirely different nature from the aloofness of a Camus "stranger": Zhivago loves life and lives intensely, but he does not want to be limited in his freedom. He welcomes the revolution, enjoying its stormy sweep, its dream of universal justice and its tragic beauty. Yet when the Communists begin to tell him how to live and how to think, he rebels. He leaves Moscow with his family and takes refuge in a forlorn hamlet beyond the Urals. To reach this haven he crosses the whole of Russia, going through burning cities and villages in uproar, through districts hit by famine and regions ravaged by civil war.

In the Urals he enjoys calm, but only for a short time. Soon his whole existence is upset by his passion for the fascinating Lara, whom he had met earlier, and by his wanderings in Siberia with the Red partisans, to whom he is forcibly attached as a physician. At the end of the civil strife he finds himself all alone; his family has been banned from Russia by the Soviet Government; his mistress has had to flee to Manchuria. Zhivago returns to Moscow, a broken man, to die in the street of a heart attack.

This vast epic of about 200,000 words has varied layers of narrative. Chronologically it encompasses three generations and gives a vivid picture of Russian life during the first quarter of our century, between 1903 and 1929 (its epilogue takes place at the end of World War II). It is primarily a chronicle of Russian intellectuals, but it contains some sixty characters from all walks of society. All form part of a complex and often symbolic plot, and the interdependence of individual destinies constitutes one of the main themes of the novel. Pasternak's heroes and heroines are shown not as puppets in a historical show, but as human beings obeying the laws of attraction and hatred, in an open universe of change and coincidence. This is particularly true of the love affair between Zhivago and Lara—a highly romantic and beautifully written story of chance, choice, joy and death.

Presented as a succession of scenes, dialogues, descriptions or reflections, *Doctor Zhivago* deliberately avoids any psychological analysis. Allusive and symbolic, fragmentary and impressionistic, the novel breaks away from the tradition of a well-structured "flowing narrative." It creates its own highly subjective form, with a peculiar mixture of dramatic and lyrical elements, with a combination of verbal simplicity, emotional complexity and philosophical depth. It has a strange, illuminating quality: a light shines in those beautiful pages (unfortunately dulled in an honest but uninspiring translation) in which realistic precision alternates with romantic, yet perfectly controlled, passion.

To those who are familiar with Soviet novels of the last twenty-five years, Pasternak's book comes as a surprise. The delight of this literary discovery is mixed with a sense of wonder: that Pasternak, who spent all his life in the Soviet environment, could resist all the external pressures and strictures and could conceive and execute a work of utter independence, of broad feeling and of an unusual imaginative power, amounts almost to a miracle. The Communist fiction of today always depicts man as a "political animal," whose acts and feelings are being determined by social and economic conditions.

In *Doctor Zhivago* man is shown in his individual essence, and his life is interpreted not as an illustration of historical events, but as a unique, wonderful adventure in its organic reality of sensations, thoughts, drives, instincts and strivings. This makes the book, despite all its topical hints and political statements, a basically anti-political work, in so far as it treats politics as fleeting, unimportant, and extols the unchangeable fundamentals of human mind, emotion and creativity. The main efforts of Zhivago, his family and his beloved Lara are bent toward protecting their privacy and defending their personal values against the distorting and destroying impact of events. They are victims and not agents of history, which is what makes their world so distinct and so contrary to that of revolutionary leaders. They are not reactionaries. Yurii Zhivago does not want to turn the clock back; he accepts social and economic changes brought about by the revolution.

His quarrel with the epoch is not political but philosophical and moral. He believes in human virtues formulated by the Christian dream, and he asserts the value of life, of beauty, of love and of nature. He rejects violence, especially when justified by abstract formulas and sectarian rhetoric. Only through goodness do we reach the supreme good, says Zhivago: if the beast in man could be overcome through fear and violence, our ideal would be a circus tamer with a whip and not Jesus Christ. Life cannot be forced into an artificial pattern by death sentences and prison camps, and it cannot be made better by legislation.

Zhivago laughs at the Partisan chief Liberius for whom "the interests of the revolution and the existence of the solar system are of the same importance." "Revolutionaries who take the law into their own hands are horrifying not because they are criminals but because they are like machines that have got out of control, like runaway trains," says Zhivago. And when a Communist speaks to him of Marxism as a science, he replies: "Marxism is too uncertain of its grounds to be a science. I do not know a movement more self-centered and further removed from the facts than Marxism. . . . Men in power are so anxious to establish the myth of their own infallibility that they do the utmost to ignore the truth. Politics do not appeal to me. I don't like people who don't care about truth."

Of course it would be wrong to attribute to Pasternak all the statements made by his protagonists and to identify the author completely with Doctor Zhivago. But there is no doubt that the basic attitudes of Pasternak's chief hero do reflect the poet's intimate convictions. He believes that "every man is born a Faust, with a longing to grasp and experience and express everything in the world." And he sees history as only part of a larger order.

Every reader of *Doctor Zhivago* will be struck and enchanted by its beautiful descriptions of landscapes and seasons. Where time and space are the great protagonists of Tolstoy's *War and Peace,* nature is at the center of Pasternak's work. Before his death Zhivago "reflected again that he conceived of history, of what he called the course of history, not in the accepted way but by analogy with the vegetable kingdom." Leaves and trees change during the cycle of seasons in a forest, but the forest itself remains the same—and so does history with its basic immobility beneath all external changes. And so does life, which can be understood and felt and lived only within the framework of nature.

This organic, I would say cosmic, feeling gives a particular dimension to Pasternak's writing. Despite all the trials and horrors and death it depicts, despite the defeat of its heroes, his novel leaves the impression of strength and faith. It is a book of hope and vitality. And it is a book of great revelation. Even if we admit that communism represents a part of Russian life, mentality and history, it does not encompass all the Russian people and all the country's traditions and aspirations. A whole world of passion, yearnings, ideals and creativity exists next to or underneath the Communist mechanism. It lives, it stirs, it grows. Pasternak's novel is the genuine voice of this other Russia. (pp. 1, 42)

Marc Slonim, "But Man's Free Spirit Still Abides," in *The New York Times Book Review,* September 7, 1958, pp. 1, 42.

RENATO POGGIOLI

(essay date 1960)

[Poggioli was an Italian-born American educator and critic. In the following excerpt from his *The Poets of Russia: 1890-1930*, he surveys Pasternak's career.]

[Pasternak] was born in Moscow in 1890. His mother was a gifted pianist, his father a well-known painter, who illustrated Tolstoj's novel *Resurrection,* and taught at the local Academy of Fine Arts. The young Pasternak devoted himself to the arts cultivated by his parents, especially music, which he studied under no less a master than the famous composer Skrjabin. He also studied philosophy at the Universities of Moscow and Marburg. . . . He began his poetic career at a precocious age, in that feverish advance-guard atmosphere which marked the first prewar era. He was one of a special group of Moscow Futurists who were connected with Khlebnikov, but who also went back to other models, as recent as Ivan Konevskoj or as remote as Jazykov. That group took its name from the almanac *Centrifuga,* published in 1913, to which Pasternak contributed his earliest poems. The young poet was destined to keep a loose association with the Futurist movement, and later contributed to the *LEF* of Majakovskij. In 1914, he published his first volume of verse, *The Twin in the Clouds,* which remained unnoticed. His second book, *Above the Barriers,* appeared in 1917, and was already the work of an expert craftsman, although it did not bear the imprint of his more mature genius.

It was to be Pasternak's two succeeding volumes that would reveal the rarity and novelty of his gift. In 1922, when the poems collected under the title *My Sister, Life,* which had been written in 1917 and circulated for years in manuscript, finally appeared in book form, they marked the emergence of a major talent. In 1923, Pasternak published his second important collection, *Themes and Variations,* in which his style became at once more sober and more extreme. The best work from these two volumes, which exercised a perceptible influence not only on younger poets but also on the more established writers, was afterwards collected in *Two Books* (1927). After a long interval, Pasternak returned to lyric poetry with *Second Birth* (1933), which was followed in the same year by *Poems,* the first full collection of his verse.

It was in that period of time that the poet's ordeal began. He remained steadfastly loyal to his calling within a social order admitting no other loyalty than to itself. He had to fight singlehandedly a sustained rear-guard action in order to avoid surrendering unconditionally to the political pressure of the regime, augmented by the vicious attacks of sycophantic critics, by the whispering campaigns and the outright calumnies of enemies and rivals. The main accusations leveled against him were that he had committed the unspeakable crimes of individualism and formalism, and that he had shown indifference, and even hostility, to Marxist ideology. His stubborn refusal to obey the party's "general line," and to change his poetry into an instrument of propaganda, was branded as a betrayal. The literary press treated him as an outlaw; the writers' association, as an outcast.

Yet, in a spirit not of compromise but of humility, Pasternak tried to give poetical expression to his desire to connect himself with the will of the Russian people. He did so by trying to understand the Russian present through the perspective of history, and in 1926 he published his poem *Spektorskij,* in which, following similar experiments by Belyj and Blok, he used the protagonist's character, whose name gives its title to this work, as an autobiographical mirror, reflecting not only the poet's personality, but also the society and the age out of which he had come. In the same years Pasternak wrote and published (1927) a cycle of lyrical fragments, re-evoking, under the title *The Year 1905,* the political turmoil of that year. That rhapsody was followed by a long, simple episode, *Lieutenant Shmidt,* more epic in tone and content, retelling the story of the mutiny of the battleship *Potemkin* in the Black Sea, with a naked power reminiscent of Ejzenshtejn's film.

It was in the same period that Pasternak composed his prose tales, which he collected twice, under the titles *Stories* and *Airways,* in 1925 and 1933. The most important of them is the opening piece, **"The Childhood of Ljuvers,"** written originally in 1918, in a tone and style that Western critics have compared to Proust's, although it is more reminiscent of *Malte Laurids Brigge* by Rainer Maria Rilke. (The Austrian poet had remained a lifelong friend of the Pasternak family from the time of his journeys to Russia, when the elder Pasternak had painted his portrait.) The theme of this story is feminine puberty, the foreshadowings of womanhood in the body and soul of a young girl, which the writer evokes with psychological subtlety and poetic insight. In 1931 Pasternak published his literary and intellectual autobiography, which he entitled, with enigmatic irony, *The Safe-Conduct.* The narrative is written in the first person, yet the ego of the narrator never intrudes and often retires into the background, giving way to a detached representation of persons and places, of ideas and things. The last part of the book is dominated by the figure of Majakovskij, acting like a mask or a ghost. In the finale, which recalls the official funeral of that poet, the palpable, almost bodily presence of that monstrous abstraction, "our Russian state," haunts the scene. Quite understandably, the authorities never permitted a reprint or a new edition of *The Safe-Conduct.*

In the following years, Pasternak managed to evade the required lauding of the regime and still function as a writer by devoting almost all his energies to translating. In his youth he had translated many foreign writers, especially German, from the Romantics to the Expressionists, but later he was attracted to more exotic models, and in 1935 published a rich anthology of poets from that Caucasian region which is called Gruzija in Russia, and Georgia in the West. More recently he tried his hand at the tragedies of Shakespeare, producing splendid versions of such plays as *Hamlet, Macbeth, King Lear, Othello, Romeo and Juliet,* and *Antony and Cleopatra.* Yet even then he never gave up his own writing, although very little of his appeared in print after the publication of his *Collected Poems* in 1932 and 1936. A decade later he took advantage of the short-lived calm after the Second World War to publish two slim collections (the second is but an expansion of the first), entitled *On Early Trains* (1943) and *The Vast Earth* (1946). They were followed by a long, silent spell which the poet broke by issuing his translation of Goethe's *Faust* and later by publishing a few new poems in literary periodicals, during the brief thaw following Stalin's death.

Despite its native originality and independent growth, Pasternak's poetry still seems to preserve the traces of its early connection with Futurism. What ties his poetry to the Futuristic experiment, and especially to the manner of Khlebnikov, is his conception and treatment of the word. While the typical Decadent or Symbolist poet seems to control the music of language by yielding to it, Pasternak masters his medium by doing violence to the very nature of poetic speech. His idiom is like a mosaic made of broken pieces. The fragments are shapeless, and if they finally fit within the pattern of a line, or within the design of a poem, it is only because of the poet's will. The cement holding them together is either syntax or rhythm; more frequently, both. From his early beginnings, Pasternak tightened the syntax of Russian poetic speech as no modern poet had ever done. At the same time, in reaction against both the vagueness of late Symbolistic verse . . . , he chose to use, with strictness and rigor, duly regular and even closed metrical forms. In doing so he succeeded in reconciling within his poetry the demands of both the old and the new. Like all the most successful figures of the advance guard, Pasternak (who is its only surviving representative in Russia today) was thus able to prove that tradition also must play a role in the revolutions of art.

There is an obvious parallel between this historical function and the internal structure of the poetry of Pasternak. With terms taken from the vocabulary of our "new critics," one could say that his verse constantly aims at tension and paradox. His poems are equally ruled by passion and intelligence, or rather, by a reciprocal interplay of emotion and wit. This is why Prince Mirskij compared him to John Donne, by which that critic probably meant that Pasternak's poetry is "metaphysical" not in the original, but in the modern and revived, sense of that term. Yet his work is better understood if placed within the immediate and local tradition from which it sprang. If we do so, we may find that the concept of "transmental poetry" is the frame of reference we need. We know already that in their attempt to create a poetry purely verbal in essence, some of the so-called Cubo-Futurists wrote poems in what they named "transmental tongue," or in newly coined words without meaning, and with no other semantic value than that of their sound effects. The experiment was bound to fail; poetry can never become, at least in the sense that painting or sculpture can, an abstract art. Poetry cannot but be either expressionistic or ideational, and Pasternak made poetry nonrepresentational, so to speak, by forcing it to be both things at once. One could say that he succeeded where the Cubo-Futurists had failed, by using, instead of nonsense language, a highly complex linguistic mosaic, made of an interplay of denotative and connotative values: or, more simply, by employing a diction ruled at once by mental balance and emotional stress. It is only in such a context that one might define his style as a modern Baroque, reducing to sense and order a verbal matter apparently incongruous and absurd.

Pasternak's poetry, to quote a line from his favorite foreign master and friend, Rainer Maria Rilke, seems thus to lead *zum Arsenal den unbedingten Dinge.* Yet in the process it changes all the nondescript objects cluttering the world of experience not into abstract symbols, but into living, suffering, humanlike creatures. The anthropomorphic pathos of Pasternak's imagination brings him closer to the Romantics than any other of his immediate predecessors with the exclusion of Blok. The poet must have been aware of this since, unlike his great and distant contemporary, Khodasevich, who found a master in Pushkin, he sought a model in Lermontov, the Russian poet who felt and understood better than any other the tears of things, and who would perhaps have approved of Pasternak's claim that "one composes verses with sobs." It is equally significant that in recent times Pasternak has shown some interest in Shelley, whose vision he finds akin to that of Blok. Yet Pasternak's neoromanticism is strange and novel: so strange and novel that it can be compared only to some of the most novel works of modern art. (pp. 321-26)

The artistic game of Pasternak consists in a sort of balancing act: or in the attempt to fix in a precarious, and yet firm, equilibrium, a congeries of heterogeneous objects, of vibrant and labile things. His poetry seems to pass, almost at the same time, through two different and even opposite phases. The first is a moment of eruption and irruption, of frenzy and paroxysm; and second, which often overlaps the first, is the moment when matter seems to harden and freeze. Burning rivers of lava congeal at a nod. The sound and fury of lightning suddenly become, as in the poem so named, "a thunder eternally instantaneous." Fires are extinguished at a breath. Showers and thunderstorms abruptly stop; floods suddenly dry up. Often the same poem seems to be written now in hot, now in cold, blood. This dualism may perhaps be traced in, or symbolized by, the early education of the poet, which was both philosophical and musical. Yet, while his music ends in dissonance, and his logic leads to dissent, such a double discordance resolves itself into a harmony of its own.

The raw material of Pasternak's poetry is introspection. Yet Pasternak treats the self as object rather than as subject. . . . Sometimes he seems to treat the psyche as a neutral and an alien being, to be seldom, and if possible only indirectly, approached. Hence the negative hyperbole by which he claims, in one of his poems, to have appealed in prayer to his soul only twice in a hundred years, while other men do so at every instant. Pasternak, with the firm hand of a hunter or tamer, always holds his own spirit in his power, like a fluttering, wounded bird, and often encloses it in the solid cage of a stanza, from which the winged prisoner vainly tries to escape through the broken mesh of a rhyme.

Many critics have remarked that Pasternak looks at the world with the eyes of one newly born. It would be better to say that he looks at it with *reborn* eyes. As suggested by the title of one of his books, poetry is for him a "second birth," through which man sees again the familiar as strange, and the strange as familiar. Yet, whether strange or familiar, every object is unique. To give the effect of this uniqueness, the poet paints every single thing as if it were a monad, unwilling or unable to escape from the rigid frame of its own contours. Such an effect is primarily achieved through the harshness and hardness of his imagery, through the frequent ellipses of his speech, through the staccato quality of his meter. Rhythmically, he prefers a line heavily hammered, where no stress is blurred, and every beat is pounded as in a heel dance. He fails, however, to extend this rapid, metallic quality to rhyme. . . . (pp. 326-27)

Though some of his poems are romantically set against the lofty mountains of the Caucasian landscape, Pasternak usually prefers a restricted, bourgeois, and prosaic scenery, such as a city park, a country orchard, a home garden, or a villa in the suburbs. Yet even "back-yards, ponds, palings" are not mere backdrops,

but, as the poet says, "categories of passions, hoarded in the human heart." His poetry thus leans toward a highly personal version of the pathetic fallacy, involving in his case not only nonhuman creatures, such as animals and plants, but also inanimate things, or manmade objects. For many of his poems Pasternak chooses, like Mallarmé in his *poèmes d'intérieur,* indoor settings. Yet, unlike the French poet, the Russian introduces within the four walls of a room cosmic powers and elemental forces. This is especially true in the cycle "Themes and Variations," which is part of the book by the same title. In the third piece of this cycle Pasternak describes the now empty study where Pushkin has just finished writing his famous poem "The Prophet." Great geographical and historical landmarks, from the arctic city of Archangel to the river Ganges, from the Sahara to the Egyptian Sphinx, seem to witness in silence, along with the molten wax dropping from a burning candle, the drying of the ink on the manuscript.

In this, as in other poems, Pasternak surprises not only by a violent association of disparate elements, but by the even more violent dissociation of each one of them from the frame of reference to which it naturally belongs. The ripe pear which one of his poems describes while falling to the ground along with its leafy stem and torn branch can be taken as an emblem of his art. Hence the frequency in his verse of such words and ideas as "fracture" or "breach." At the end of the closing poem of the cycle **"Rupture"** (meaning here a lovers' quarrel, or their break), even the opening of a window is equated with the opening of a vein. In the same piece the poet transfers the trauma of life to an uncreated thing: for instance, to the piano, which "licks its foam," as if it were a human being in an epileptic fit. Yet even in metaphors like these the poet transcends both pathos and bathos, reshaping the disorder of experience into a vision of his own. If he succeeds in doing so, it is because in his poetry (as he said in *The Safe-Conduct*) the author remains silent and lets the image speak. In this ability to infuse words with passion, rather than passion with words, Pasternak has no rival among his contemporaries, and, among the poets of the previous generation, he yields only to Aleksandr Blok. (pp. 327-28)

Pasternak's [verse] is dramatic and pathetic, aiming at conveying the poet's vital experience in psychic terms. His metaphors tend to express the shock and wonder of being in abridged and concentrated form. In his recent *Notes on Translating Shakespearean Tragedies* (1954), the poet bases his theory of metaphor on the truth which the old saying *ars longa vita brevis* seems to have stated once for all; "hence metaphors and poetry," says Pasternak, and concludes: "imagery is but the shorthand of the spirit." As hinted in these words, Pasternak views metaphor not as an emblem or symbol, which suggests and conceals, but as a graphic scheme or a sketchy outline of the experienced thing. This may well be the reason why this artist has never indulged, like so many modern poets, in the false mystique of his own calling and craft. Poetry is for him not the revelation of a higher harmony, but simply the direct expression of "the dissonance of this word."

A poetry so understood gives the immediate sense of a reality endowed with no other glamor than that of being reality itself; poetry, as Pasternak says, is "a suburb, not a refrain." The dreams of such a poet are made of the stuff life is made of. One could then say that this artist has always unconsciously followed the principle which he has recently uttered through the fictional protagonist of his last book: "Art never seemed to me an object or aspect of form, but rather a mysterious and hidden component of content." Such a statement indicates the importance of that book, which is worth discussing at length, even though the medium in which the poet chose to write it is not lyric verse, but narrative prose.

It was in April 1945 that Pasternak announced in the Leningrad literary journal *The Banner* the imminent completion of a work in progress, entitled *Doctor*

Pasternak as a young man.

Zhivago. The author defined it as "a novel in prose," an obvious play on the subtitle "novel in verse" of Pushkin's *Evgenij Onegin.* The announcement was followed by a series of poems, supposedly written by the novel's protagonist. . . . Although the poet declared that the series was destined to close the novel as a fictitious appendix of posthumous papers or documents, through which the reader would understand better the personage to whom the writer attributed their authorship, everybody read those pieces as if their real author had written them in an autobiographical vein rather than in a fictional key. Later on, when the "thaw" which followed Stalin's death was already over, Pasternak submitted the complete draft to the Moscow literary monthly *New World,* but its editors (including such well-known writers as Konstantin Fedin and Konstantin Simonov) rejected the novel with a letter which convinced Pasternak that his book could never appear in Soviet Russia without changes so radical as to disfigure it. Shortly afterward the author handed the manuscript to a scout of Giangiacomo Feltrinelli, an Italian publisher with left-wing leanings. Notwithstanding his political sympathies, and despite official Soviet protests, Signor Feltrinelli managed to issue in 1957 an Italian translation of the original text. This was followed a year later by versions in French, English, and other languages, many of which became best sellers shortly after they appeared, making of the book a world-wide success. (pp. 328-30)

Doctor Zhivago, this new and challenging product of Pasternak's talent, is huge in size and broad in scope. The narrative rehearses the life and fate of its hero from his childhood to his premature death on the eve of the great Stalinist purge. Raised in the idealism of the early part of the century, Zhivago trains himself to become both a doctor and a poet, thus following the double call of charity and grace. He marries, but the Revolution forces him to settle in the Urals, where he is forever separated from his family and is made to serve as a medical officer in a Red guerrilla unit during the Civil War. His only consolation is his love for Lara, an old Moscow acquaintance, who represents in the novel the intuitive wisdom of life. When the crisis is over, he returns to Moscow, and in 1929 he dies there of a heart attack.

The narrative of Dr. Zhivago's existence merges with that of other, numberless characters, originally connected as neighbors, relatives, or friends, and who, in the course of the story, meet again in the most surprising circumstances. Although traditional in structure, the novel lacks a well-made plot: coincidence works beyond the limits of verisimilitude, taxing the credulity of the reader, and failing to raise the whims of chance or the writer's fancy to the level of either destiny or providence. Deprived of an epic or tragic design, the narrative unfolds as a rhapsody: and this explains why all its beauties are but fragmentary ones. There are many memorable episodes, but the novel's high point is the section describing the hibernation of the Red partisans in the wilderness of the far North, and the attempt by some of their wives to reach them by cutting a path through the snow and ice of a primeval forest.

The protagonist survives many physical trials, besides that of winter; yet he dies still young, worn out by an inner ordeal, wasted by the fever of life. Up to the end he faces each test with both the passive compliance of his will and the active resistance of his conscience. He acts at once like a witness and a victim, never like an avenger or judge. His mind often says "yea" to the reality to which his heart says "nay." Ivan Karamazov accepted God while rejecting the world He had created; Doctor Zhivago similarly accepts the postulate of the Revolution while rejecting many of its corollaries. From this viewpoint there is no doubt that the protagonist represents the author's outlook. The writer refuses, however, to intervene directly in the narrative, he thinks only with the thoughts of his characters, and speaks with no other words than theirs. Yet we hear his unique voice in the descriptive passages, and especially in those vivid images by which he constantly suggests to the reader that man, as well as time, is out of joint.

Perhaps the only characters who speak solely for themselves are those representing the younger generation in the novel's epilogue. The latter projects Russian life as seen now, twenty years after the death of the protagonist, in the immediate aftermath of the Second World War. There we meet again also some of the novel's main characters. The regime has recalled them before their term from deportation and exile; and they have rehabilitated themselves politically by defending the fatherland against the German invaders. It is difficult to say whether Pasternak considers these men and their sons as the children of the old bondage or the harbingers of a freer covenant. In a sense they seem to turn more toward the past than toward the future: perhaps they are also, as the author says of many others, naïve and innocent slaves who cannot help idealizing the slavery which is still their lot. Survivors of one upheaval, they may well disappear in the next one.

Despite all appearances to the contrary, it is this perplexing epilogue, more than any other parallel, which reveals that Pasternak wrote Doctor Zhivago— as other readers have already remarked—on the pattern of War and Peace. . . . Yet, despite its strong ties with Tolstoj's masterpiece, Doctor Zhivago is not a historical novel in the sense of War and Peace, since it deals with the contemporary age, an epoch not yet closed. Hence its epilogue is problematic rather than prophetic. Yet this difference is not important; whether or not it is a historical novel, Doctor Zhivago, like War and Peace, is written against history. What really matters is that Pasternak's protest rests on other grounds, and may well

contain a message just the opposite of Tolstoj's. In War and Peace all the violence and cunning of history ultimately yield to the law of nature, to the universal principles of life and death, to the wars and peaces of being, which reduce strategy and diplomacy to senseless games, vainly attempting to shape the destiny of the human race. In Tolstoj's view mankind survives the ordeal of history in the wholeness and singleness of the species. The immortal cell of human life is the family, which triumphs, always and everywhere, over the destructive force of that monster which men call "reason of state." In Tolstoj's novel the issue is simplified, since the "reason of state" is symbolized by the aggressive imperialism of a foreign power; hence patriotism coincides with the moral and practical interests of that patriarchal household which for Tolstoj represents an ideal way of life.

Pasternak, however, sees the perfection of human existence in the person, in the inviolate integrity of its inner conscience. Such a form of being implies the refusal of all constraints, including the ties of blood and the bonds of the heart. This is why his hero must go his way even though against his own will, never to rejoin his wife and offspring; and perhaps his almost fleshless love for Lara should be seen as the sign of a personal destiny which must unfold itself in a cold and distant solitude, far away from the comforting warmth of the fireplace, from the charmed circle of the family nest. Doctor Zhivago differs from War and Peace in its view of the human condition; it differs, also, in its interpretation of the function of history. In Pasternak's novel history manifests itself as civil war and domestic strife, in a "permanent revolution" which is at once material and spiritual warfare, a total struggle without quarter or truce. Through technology, ideology, and social planning, history is now able to submit to its will the nation, the class, and the family—perhaps the world itself. But its weakest victim may be also its most elusive enemy, and that victim and enemy is the single person, the individual soul. Hence the voice protesting here is the one that says not "we," but "I." Here it is not Mother Russia, but one of her orphan children, who, like a fairy-tale Kutuzov, defends the homeland of the soul, the little realm of personal dignity and private life, first by trading time for space rather than space for time, and then by withdrawing into other dimensions than those. Such a stubborn retreat of the spirit, or, if we wish, the passive resistance of an inflexible soul which repels the temptation as well as the threat of all violence, is Doctor Zhivago's main motif, perhaps its only one; and it is the exceptional nobility of this theme that turns Pasternak's novel, if not into a masterpiece, at least into a spiritual document of great significance, which brings to us a very different message from that of War and Peace. Nothing conveys better the sense of this difference than the two plants symbolizing the "tree of life" in each novel. In one we have the old oak which Prince Andrej suddenly sees rejuvenated by the sap of spring, with its once bare trunk and despoiled limbs covered by a crown of new leaves; in the other we have that evergreen thicket, almost buried by ice and snow, holding high a branch full of berries in the heart of the Siberian winter. Pasternak's "golden bough," unlike Tolstoj's, is thus a burning bramble that shines and consumes itself mystically and ecstatically in the desert of the self, in the cold land of the spirit.

Despite the urgency and immediacy of its message, *Doctor Zhivago* must be viewed as an old-fashioned novel even if looked at from a less superficial perspective than that of its conventional structure. Its spiritual quality may be conveyed by saying that [*Doctor Zhivago* fulfills] Goethe's definition of the novel form as a "subjective epos." . . . [Yet this] "subjective epos" fails to grow and ripen into a *Bildungsroman*. The reason for this is that its main character, who acts as if he were both accepting and refusing the lesson of history, seems already to know all too well the lessons of life. The novel treats all events or experiences as if they were not dreams or crises, but tests or ordeals, which the protagonist undergoes more like a martyr than like a hero, and which he overcomes with the help of a grace which is not of this world. This, as well as the fact that all its figures are not painted in the round but drawn like abstract, allegorical outlines, turns *Doctor Zhivago* into a kind of morality play. It is this quality of the novel's vision that fully justifies Pasternak's use of religious imagery and Christian symbolism. Such imagery and symbolism need not be explained as polemical devices, or as the signs of the author's conversion to another creed. Like many a poet raised in another faith, or who lost his religious beliefs, Pasternak seems to have found no better language than the one which the Christian imagination shaped forever to convey the sacraments and the redemptions of the soul.

In an article published in *Partisan Review* immediately after the Italian edition of the novel, Nicola Chiaromonte described *Doctor Zhivago* as "a meditation on history, that is, on the infinite distance which separates the human conscience from the violence of history, and permits a man to remain a man. . . . " This is true, and well said, and it is no less true that the extension and depth of such a meditation represents something new in Pasternak's work. There is no doubt that in such poems as *The Year 1905* and *Lieutenant Schmidt* the poet had tried to come to terms with historical reality, rather than to face it as a critic and a judge. Only once did he express his sense of alienation from Soviet society: in that page of his long autobiographical essay *The Safe-Conduct* where he described Majakovskij's funeral, haunted by the weird presence of that state power which the dead poet had served only to be crushed by it. As for Pasternak's lyrical poems, they

had often expressed in passing (and not without a sense of guilt) the poet's attempt to shun or to transcend the historical experience of his nation and time. Nothing exemplifies better such an attempt than an early piece dealing with the secluded workings of the poetic imagination, where the poet's voice suddenly bursts out with the question: "Children, what century is it, outside in our courtyard?" That question, both sophisticated and naïve, hints that the poet was then convinced that the artistic mind is innately indifferent to the dimension of time, to the category of history. Later, however, Pasternak seemed to realize that such an indifference is impossible, and that the self was bound to merge, whether willingly or unwillingly, with the historical process. He once conveyed the sense of this awareness in a famous line where he significantly spoke in the first person plural, although that plural refers to a few, rather than to the many: "We were people: we are epochs now." But it is true that in another poem he claimed that the poet could at least evade contemporary history by projecting himself into the future, or, as he said, by escaping like steam, through the chinks of fate, from the burning peat of dead time.

Many similar statements could be quoted from Pasternak's earlier and later verse: yet, taken together, all of them sound like apologies which the poet addressed not so much to the regime as to public opinion, or rather, to an elite able to understand equally the reason of poetry and the reason of state. Yet the poet seemed to know, at least in the depth of his heart, that any reconciliation between art and politics was fundamentally impossible. Hence that sense of both pride and shame in all of Pasternak's statements on the subject: the pride of his unconquerable loneliness, and the shame of being unable to pay the Revolution the tribute which all pay, and which may well be justly due it.

Pasternak continued to grapple with these questions during the long years of a silence which was at least in part self-imposed; and at the end of that period he reached the conclusion that lyrical poetry had become too limited and subjective a vehicle to allow him to express what was no longer a purely private attitude toward the problematics of revolution and the dialectics of history. After presenting his poet's case in verse, he felt that now he should present the case of man in prose. The writer was still in an apologetic mood, but the apology he now wanted to make was a far more universal one; and he wished to address it, beyond official Russia, to the Russian people, and even to his Western brethren. He felt that the proper vehicle for such an apology, which was also to be a protest, could be only fictional and narrative prose, the traditional tool of the Russian literary genius, which has found the master road of its ethos and art in that "classical" and "critical" realism of which Socialist Realism was but a monstrous caricature. If Pushkin's "poetry" had never denied "truth," so the "truth" of the "classical" and "critical" realists had never denied "poetry"; and this may help us to understand why, the first time Pasternak spoke in public of the novel he was then writing, he called *Doctor Zhivago,* with a formula which was not a mere pleonasm, a "novel in prose."

The poet himself recently explained this new aesthetic and moral view in a reply to a series of questions submitted to him by a South American magazine: "Fragmentary, personal poems are hardly suited to meditations on such obscure, new, and solemn events. Only prose and philosophy can attempt to deal with them. . . . " Here Pasternak seems to re-echo, unknowingly, Sartre's statement that prose, unlike poetry, should always be *engagée;* nor does it matter that *engagement* for Pasternak involves different, and even opposite values: not social obligations but moral ones. Pasternak seems to feel that such an *engagement* was impossible while he was only a lyrical poet; and this is why the author of *Doctor Zhivago* spoke disdainfully of his poetic work in his reply to that questionnaire. By doing so he merely underscored something at which he had hinted in the novel itself. Nothing in *Doctor Zhivago* has a more autobiographical ring than the comment on the literary career of the protagonist. According to his creator, Doctor Zhivago "had been dreaming of writing a book on life, in which to express the most wonderful things he had seen and understood in the world. Yet for such a book he was too young, and meanwhile he went on writing poems, like a painter who all his life draws studies for a painting still in his mind."

Yet if these words apply to the author himself, as the latter undoubtedly meant them to do, then what dictates the truth they may contain is not insight, but hindsight. It would be unfair to Pasternak both as man and writer to accept his retrospective claim that his poetic production was but a gradual preparation for *Doctor Zhivago,* which is a moral act and a psychological document of great value, but not the single culmination of his work. His poems are more than simple preludes to the novel; and though *Doctor Zhivago* towers over all Soviet fiction, this is due not only to Pasternak's stature as a novelist but also to the mediocrity of his rivals. What I prefer to emphasize is that this "novel in prose" proves more passionately and eloquently, yet in a less spirited and witty way than his poems, the same truth: that even in Communist Russia there are moral "corners" or spiritual "pockets" permitting the cultivation of the most bourgeois of all psychological activities, which could be defined in literary terms as the "sentimental education" of the soul.

In his poetry and his earlier prose, no less than in this novel, Pasternak had asserted and defended the private rights of the spirit in a forthright manner, without a wrong idealization, or a false mystique. . . . He has always known, as he says in one of his poems, that when in contact with reality human passion cannot heed the warning which reads "Fresh paint: do not touch." In short, Pasternak has never longed after a purity which is not of this world. He is one of those who feel that the soul is too rooted in life to be disinfected, as if it were merely a wounded limb. We may "purge" the soul, rather than "cleanse" it, and this is the catharsis which *Doctor Zhivago* in the end finally achieves. Perhaps after such an act of purgation, the author might feel free to publish poetry again. Like a Jonas delivered from the whale, he may now walk again on the mainland of his art. If we must hope that he will do so, it is because Pasternak's poems are more vital and exciting than this novel, which lacks the inner tension of his previous works in verse or prose, so challenging in their inborn advance-guardism. (pp. 330-38)

In view of this, it is perhaps worth remarking that when the Swedish Academy decided, in October 1958, to crown Boris Pasternak with the second of the two Nobel Prizes ever granted to Russian writers, it chose to honor him as poet as well as novelist. That, after having gratefully accepted that deserved honor, Pasternak was forced by the vilifications of the Soviet press, and by such official acts as his expulsion from the writers' association, first to reject the greatest of all international literary awards, and then to address a pathetic and nobel petition to Krushchev, lest the regime deprive him of his birthright, of the privilege to live, work, and die on his native soil, is another story. There is no doubt that it was this scandal, even more than the circumstances that had led the writer to publish his novel abroad, that stirred in the West the heated controversy now going under the name of Pasternak's case. Sad as it is, the tale cannot be forgotten, and should be retold again and again, not only in admiration, to bless the gift of the poet, but also in anger, to curse that party or state power which, like another Moloch, demands every day a new holocaust. Not content with the thousands of nameless victims on which it has built its jails, its fortresses, and its factories, the Soviet regime seems to require the public sacrifice of their life, liberty, or happiness even by those artists, who, like Majakovskij and Esenin, or like Akhmatova and Pasternak, either remained the loyal friends of the Revolution, or refused to become its active enemies. (pp. 338-39)

Renato Poggioli, "Poets of Today," in his *The Poets of Russia: 1890-1930,* Cambridge, Mass.: Harvard University Press, 1960, pp. 316-42.

OLGA R. HUGHES

(essay date 1974)

[In the excerpt below, Hughes discusses Pasternak's poetics.]

Next to nature and love, art itself is one of the permanent themes in Pasternak's work. (p. 3)

There is an overwhelming and ever-present tendency in Pasternak's work to penetrate to the essential reality of life, whether it is in art, in human relations, or in history. His approach—which consciously avoids everything formal and scholastic—can be termed "existential" in the broadest sense of the term, as a concern with the fundamental problems of existence rather than with systems or ideologies. In his rejection of rigid categories and classifications, Pasternak is very consistent. Not only formal aesthetics is denied existence for losing touch with the reality of life; the protagonists of *Doctor Zhivago* consider formal philosophy as something superfluous and assign to it the role of a "seasoning" in art and life. (p. 5)

For Pasternak the nature of art is best revealed at the time of its first appearance in the life of a creative artist—hence the recurrence in his work of the theme of "the birth of a poet."

In the experience of the poet, the origin of art is most closely connected with love and nature. Actually it is love—which is identified with the energy of life—that brings about the birth of the poet, who at this point suddenly perceives the inherent ties between himself and nature.

The essence of life appears to the poet as a dynamic principle. Change is one of life's basic characteristics. It is experienced directly, but can be depicted by the means accessible only to art. (p. 7)

For Pasternak, the intensity of emotions and the direct and spontaneous expression of them are essential elements of artistic creativity. . . . Passion is what art attempts to depict; it is the subject of art. The figurative language of art, according to Pasternak, is the direct language of passion. The highest achievement that art can hope to attain is to overhear the true voice of love. (pp. 17, 20)

Despite [the] apparent equality of man and nature in Pasternak's poetic scheme, it is, undoubtedly, man who occupies the central position: his individuality is never dissolved in his surroundings. Nature actually lives man's emotions. When a bog is feverish, a forest depressed, a meadow nauseated, a room trembling, or a city—dusty and exhausted from travel—is falling into bed, there is little doubt that those sensations, responses, and actions are the poet's. Nature's sharing man's emotions emphasizes his predominance. This anthropocentric attitude is especially noticeable in *Doctor Zhivago*. (p. 23)

The poetic trope that Pasternak employs to convey the interrelation of things is metonymy. In **"Wassermann Test,"** attempting a description of what in his opinion is basic to the "metaphorical vision of the world," Pasternak, without naming it, describes metonymy and explains his predilection for metonymic expression. This trope, according to him, is comparable to an intricate lock, the key to which is in the poet's possession. The reader can only peek through the keyhole at that which is concealed within. A poet who resorts to similarity as the basis for constructing his tropes tosses the keys into the hands of "the amateurs from the crowd." Contiguity rather than similarity should, in Pasternak's opinion, be at the basis of metaphorical association, for it is contiguity that possesses the quality of necessity and the dramatic quality mandatory for metaphorical expression. For him it is the "morbid necessity" of bringing together dissimilar but proximate objects that gives life to an image. . . . This "metonymic vision of the world" is largely responsible for the originality of Pasternak's verse. (pp. 25-6)

The extraordinary means needed to keep up with life's pace are provided by art, which concerns itself with the presence of energy in life, with the dynamics of life; it depicts life "traversed by a ray of energy." Art succeeds in not falling behind the present by being ahead of it, by looking into the future. Likewise, by not being preoccupied with man's actual individual achievements and by speaking of his potentialities, it is capable of revealing the truth about man. As Pasternak puts it, in art a man's individual voice is silenced, and the image of man takes over.

Energy is the only "aspect of consciousness' that needs some tangible proof of its existence, because it is evident only at the moment of its appearance. Art is the only means capable of depicting energy. . . . In terms of individual consciousness, energy is emotion. Human spirit cannot be confined to the material world; it transcends it. (pp. 36-7)

The material world, inert and static, calls for an active, creative interference, and this is art's sphere of action. . . . When Pasternak writes that his experience of the city did not correspond to the place where he lived, he is opposing the life in the realm of the spirit to the material world, the vivid exterior of which is a complete expression of its essence. Pasternak describes himself at the time when he was turning from music to poetry as being physically affected by this heavy world, which is untouched by the transforming spirit. These "attacks of chronic impatience" were his response to the all-pervasive rule of necessity. Human activity that implied an active application of an individual's will and energy to the fabric of life did not cause this sensation in the young poet. By investing his surroundings with his emotion, the poet endows the spiritually static material world with the dynamics of his own spiritual condition. Pasternak's dynamism is a dynamism of spirit. Physical storms and violent movement in his poetry are there to speak of this spiritual quality of life, the depiction of which is the poet's aim. (p. 37-8)

His reiteration of the apparently self-evident truth that a work of art has as its starting point the experience of reality suggests that the realization of this, indeed, must have been one of the most intense and enduring impressions of Pasternak the poet: he undertook several times to show how a work of art is born. [One detailed account is given in *A Tale* (1929)]. (p. 42)

In his poetic practice Pasternak achieves a synthesis of the futurist attempt to counteract the automatization of poetic language and the symbolist view that poetic language represents the essence of the world perceived intuitively by the poet. In Pasternak's work these two aspects become inseparable. [Hughes notes elsewhere that although Pasternak's connections with Russian futurism have been questioned, Vladimir Markov, in his *Russian Futurism*, clearly demonstrated the connection and elaborated the dispute.] (p. 46)

According to his own assertion, Pasternak did not share the futurists' dream of creating a new language; in his opinion, the overabundance of *what* an artist wants to say should leave him no time for seeking new means of expression. . . .

Among the features that separate Pasternak from the futurists—apart from his fundamentally different view of language as an indissoluble unity of sound and meaning and, on an entirely different level, his inability to go along with their behavior—is his very pronounced and conscious affinity with cultural tradition. (p. 55)

What underlies Pasternak's anti-aestheticism and is the most important element of his affinity with futurism is the struggle against the automatization of poetic speech. (p. 56)

It is hardly necessary to argue that the realism that Pasternak talks about [in the 1950's] and considers a foundation of his own art is neither the traditional nineteenth-century realism nor the twentieth-century domestic variety known as socialist realism. For Pasternak, to be realistic art has to be truthful to life; this does not imply, however, that art has to follow the methods of the realist school.

One area where Pasternak's definition of realism is very close to the traditional definition of realism is that of language. The simple and unadorned style of late Pasternak tries to reproduce the natural word order of contemporary spoken Russian, and magnificently succeeds in the effort. (p. 68)

Not unexpectedly, the principal form that history assumes in Pasternak's work is that of the Revolution. The relationship of poetry and history—referring mainly to contemporary social and political events—occupies a prominent place in Pasternak's work beginning with the 1920's. In **"Lofty Malady"** (1923, 1928) the role of poetry is assessed against the epic proportions of the Revolution. In the poems of the early 1930's Pasternak repeatedly returns to the poet's paradoxical position in a socialist state. He attempts to accept the existing regime and searches for its justification. . . .

What underlies the problem of the poet's relationship to society, as reflected in Pasternak's work, is essentially the conflict between the eternal and the temporal. (p. 78)

In *Doctor Zhivago* the ultimate purpose of history is spoken of as the overcoming of death: and it is not surprising that the "dead history" of the Soviet state—which subordinates reality to an idea—is rejected as a betrayal of life. It is in the name of life—which for Pasternak by definition is immortal—that he comes to reject temporal ideologies and systems. (p. 79)

[In a 1916 article **"Black Goblet"**] Pasternak wrote that life is gravitating toward two opposing poles: poetry and history. Equal value was assigned to each, but the poet insisted on not crossing the border from one to the other. Pasternak's long poems of the twenties can be viewed as an attempt to bring together poetry and history, to cross the boundary between the two. The conclusions to which Pasternak came in *Doctor Zhivago* show that in the end he did not follow the path suggested by the critics and traveled by many of his contemporaries.

In the opening stanzas of **"Lofty Malady,"** the value of history and poetry no longer appears equal. The magnitude of the events of the Revolution dwarfs poetry. It becomes merely the "lofty malady" of the title. Under the catastrophic circumstances poetry cannot be accepted as a normal condition; it is an abnormality. The poet is even ashamed of his gift of song. (pp. 81-2)

The picture of the Revolution in **"Lofty Malady"** is contradictory: it is perceived both as an approaching spring and as a threat of future privations. (p. 83)

What was contradictory in **"Lofty Malady"** became clearly polarized in *Doctor Zhivago*. The unconditional and joyful acceptance of the Revolution in 1917 remained. Zhivago thinks of the Revolution on a cosmic scale and senses greatness in its directness and its disregard for everything that stands in its way. Later, having attained a certain perspective, he clearly distinguishes between the Revolution itself and the regime that issued from it. . . . Finally, Zhivago comes to a conclusion that the fate of revolutions is invariably self-defeat. They are short-lived, and what remains when they pass is a fanatical devotion to the narrow-mindedness of their leaders. (p. 85)

It has to be emphasized, however, that Zhivago accepts the social and economic changes brought about by the Revolution. (p. 86)

A very perceptive analysis of the reasons why Pasternak's open break with the official line in Soviet literature came only at the end of his life with the publication of *Doctor Zhivago* is made by Nadezhda Mandelstam in her *Reminiscences.* She observes that Pasternak's conscious efforts to find common ground with contemporary Soviet literature were facilitated by his having some points of contact with traditional literature and, above all, by being a Muscovite and therefore, in a sense, "belonging" to Soviet literature. . . .

Pasternak's rejection of the regime is essentially of an existential nature. It is a free human personality that he defends against an ideology. His revolt is in the name of life itself. Zhivago at one point explains the change in his attitude toward the Revolution in vaguely Tolstoyan terms: "I used to be very revolutionary, but now I think that nothing can be gained by brute force. People must be drawn to good by goodness." (p. 94)

According to Zhivago, the failure of the regime originates in its attempts to change and to reform life by means of an ideology that has nothing to do with real life. Zhivago stresses that he objects to a generally utopian approach of "building life anew," because for him life is an ever-rejuvenating and dynamic principle rather than an inert material that can be shaped and molded to fit some abstract scheme. (p. 98)

For Pasternak, the freedom of every individual is of primary importance, and therefore the right of leaders to deprive individuals of their freedom is questioned and eventually condemned. (p. 104)

By virtue of his poetic gift, the poet is only a visitor, not a permanent inhabitant of this world. Under all social orders and economic systems the poet is someone who does not belong. . . . The artist is kept hostage by time although by nature he belongs to eternity. . . . The poet belongs to the two worlds: the eternal and the temporal; in his work the timeless beauty of life acquires flesh that unmistakably belongs to the time when the poet lives and writes. . . . An artist's original perception of the world becomes a part of this world that remains after his death. (pp. 113-15)

The idea of a poet's becoming a part of life and nature upon his death Pasternak shares with Rainer Maria Rilke, whose influence he acknowledged as one of the most significant and lasting in his life. (p. 116)

It has been repeatedly and convincingly suggested that Pasternak has an affinity with romanticism. Specific links between his poetry and certain features of the poetry of the Russian romantics—Lermontov, Tyutchev, and Fet—have been pointed out. On the other hand, it has been asserted—on the basis of other specific peculiarities of his poetry—that Pasternak is not a romantic. One has to admit that both views are essentially true. (pp. 168-69)

Pasternak shared the basic tenets of romantic aesthetics: for him art was a means of cognition of the world; the organic unity of the cosmos and man's part in it were a tangible reality for the poet. Art, in Pasternak's view, was not engaged in imitating nature but rather in continuing its creative work.

Among Russian symbolists, Blok and Skryabin were most influential for Pasternak's formative period. The elements of Skryabin's world view—his influence was the earliest and perhaps the strongest—that had the greatest impact on the young Pasternak were the belief in the transforming powers of art and in the exceptional role assigned to the creative artist.

But it has to be remembered that one of the fundamental characteristics of Pasternak's personality was the extreme selectivity of approach. Romantic hero worship Pasternak rejected as a very young man. Despite the importance he continued to attach to the role of the creative artist, he was invariably suspicious of those views which conceivably might have led to a dramatization of the poet's life. The romantic view of the significance of an individual took a Christian turn in his world view. Pasternak went further than just asserting the value of every individual: his poet cannot exist without other people. Pasternak's aversion to "organizations" and "societies" reflects his strong antiutopian convictions. His mistrust of collective actions, which, as he was to remark, without exception are tinged with hysteria, only strengthened his faith in the individual. (pp. 169-70)

The belief in the transforming powers of art remained one of the cornerstones of Pasternak's poetics. His view differed from that of the symbolists, however, in that for Pasternak it was not a potential that would be realized in the art of the future, nor, as the forerunner of Russian symbolists, Vladimir Soloviev, believed, at the end of history; this power is realized here and now, in every true work of art. . . .

Romantic hero worship was not the only feature of romanticism that had no place in Pasternak's poetics. The realm of the fantastic held no appeal for the poet, for he was able to perceive the exceptional in the most ordinary and in the everyday. (p. 170)

Pasternak's poetics can be described as aesthetic realism. He rejected both aestheticism and the utilitarian approach to art. Art for him was an objective reality;

he shared the modern outlook that poetry has a purpose of its own, which it achieves by its own means. Pasternak's concept of realism presupposes a never-ending fascination with everyday existence, but it does not eliminate spiritual values from his conception of life and art and therefore, in essence, is not related to nineteenth-century positivism and its perpetuation in our time.

In his nontraditional usage of the term "realism," Pasternak follows Blok, who in 1919 spoke of true realism as not imitating but transforming nature, and thus being a legitimate heir to romanticism, which is not a rejection of life but a new vision and a more intense experience of life, the "sixth sense" of mankind. Pasternak's realism fits what has been described as the "imaginative realism" of post-symbolist poetry, with its desire to enter into all spheres of existence and to be minutely precise in its depiction of the poet's complex experiences and impressions. (pp. 172-73)

Olga R. Hughes, in her *The Poetic World of Boris Pasternak,* Princeton University Press, 1974, 192 p.

RUFUS W. MATHEWSON, JR.

(essay date 1975)

[Mathewson was an American critic and professor of Russian and comparative literature. In the following excerpt from his *The Positive Hero in Russian Literature,* he contends that Zhivago's personal struggles represent a larger conflict between the destructive impulse of Revolution and the affirming force of Life.]

When Pasternak sent the manuscript [of *Doctor Zhivago*] abroad for publication he invoked an important tradition in Russian writing, that of the "smuggled" text, published abroad. Mere place of publication may seem remote from serious critical concerns, and the charge of heresy which propelled *Doctor Zhivago* and the principal works of Solzhenitsyn and Sinyavsky across their native boundaries threatens to limit criticism of the texts to political analysis. And yet, heresy—generated out of the novel's moral critique of the political system—is central to any reading of these works which would illuminate their design as well as their meaning. Read, as I propose, with close attention to the local meanings of heresy, read as we can guess Pasternak meant his contemporaries to read it, *Doctor Zhivago* nevertheless remains available for more timeless readings, as arcane religious utterance—as a gloss on the Book of Revelations, perhaps—or as a forest of coded symbols or a parable of the eternal situation of the artist. My eye-level reading discloses a structural completeness and a related complexity of statement, which may be enriched by other readings but deserves full demonstration, I think, on intentional, expository, and didactic writer-to-reader grounds. I have taken my text from Pasternak's remark in an interview: "It seemed to me that it was my duty to make a statement about my epoch." The elucidation of this statement, it seems to me, should precede other kinds of analysis.

Two vast constellations of ideas, attitudes, and values—intellectual, moral, and aesthetic—come into mortal conflict. One may be called the ethos of Revolution, the other the continuum of Life. At first these bodies of thought, or ways of taking experience, coexist more or less harmoniously in Zhivago's mind. As war and revolution progress, they become disengaged when Zhivago pursues a lonely personal existence, beyond the reach of historical events. In the novel's denouement they become re-engaged when the revolution, an anonymous menacing force, pursues and crushes Zhivago, who in his own eccentric person has come to represent the forces of life. Pasternak then attempts a counter-enveloping movement in the complex epilogue, in the rhapsodic words Lara utters over Zhivago's corpse, in the eventual coming to maturity—and to an understanding of what Zhivago stood for—of Zhivago's two lifelong friends. . . . By refusing publication, the Soviet government attempted a final extra-literary countermovement, which failed when the novel was published abroad and then filtered back into the USSR illegally. (pp. 259-61)

[Zhivago's] vision of the good life, derived from Christian mythology, is presented early in the novel. It recedes under the flood of historical and personal experiences in the novel's center, and then reappears, restated and amplified in the concluding chapters. (p. 261)

Art . . . touches the essence of man's involvement in the world; the beauty it discovers everywhere—even in the mutilated corpses Zhivago encounters in his medical work—answers the deepest human needs.

A doctrine which denies beauty, corrupts language, disfigures art and disconnects it from its roots is anti-human. Pasternak is close to his classical predecessors in setting a view of human nature resting on feeling and imagination against a schematic materialist ideology, or in this case, against the acting out of the ideology's inner potential in revolution and civil war.

Zhivago comes to this understanding in the course of the novel—the process of learning defines its central movement—as he is battered by public and private calamities. (p. 262)

Zhivago's existential resistance seems to promise a correction of error, the beginning, at least, of a process in which coercive, blueprinted change will give way to the flow of genuine history, hospitable to art, morality, and human individuality, a final vindication of Zhivago's values. He has survived in the thoughts and feelings of his friends—Pasternak's own definition of immortality—and the doomed end of his mortal life has been eclipsed by his survival in literature.

The full chordal effect of the novel's ending includes a further vindication from beyond the grave: Zhivago's twenty-five poems constituting a second epilogue. They are the record of his most intense engagement with life. The experience reported in the poem or the moment of its composition can sometimes be fixed in the text of the novel, sometimes not. Zhivago's poems repeat themes which are central to Pasternak's own poetic vision: the human is merged with the natural, particularly in the cycle of seasons; night, winter, and death are set against dawn, spring, and rebirth; lovers separate and reunite. Important moments in the life of Christ—the Nativity, the night in Gethsemane, the Crucifixion and Resurrection—are less familiar in Pasternak's work but are securely rooted in the novel's pattern of ideas and motifs. Mary Magdalene, whose relationship to Jesus symbolizes the origins of genuine human history in the novel, is the subject of the penultimate poem.

Taken as a whole, these poems express Zhivago's chief assertion of his identity, of his rooted being. Their appearance at the end of the novel "corrects" for his personal defeat and presents him to us as a tragic but finally redeemed figure. (p. 276)

Rufus W. Mathewson, Jr., "Pasternak: 'An Inward Music'," in his *The Positive Hero in Russian Literature,* second edition, Stanford University Press, 1975, pp. 259-78.

ALFRED CORN

(essay date 1976)

[Corn is an American poet and critic. In the excerpt below, he comments on the prominence of music, philosophy, religion, and nature in the poetry of Pasternak.]

For Pasternak, . . . poetry may be seen as lying within the pentagram described by music, philosophy, love, physical nature and Renaissance religious humanism in painting.

Pasternak's concern with musical analogies in verbal composition isn't unique to him, of course. In the 20th century all the arts have aspired to the condition of music, with the frequent exception of music itself. The title poem of Pasternak's collection *Themes and Variations* (1923) goes farthest in the direction of musical form, still keeping, however, a modicum of paraphrasable content. Also, critics with an eye or an ear for it have described his collection of short stories as a classical four-movement symphony, the first story in sonata allegro form, the second, a scherzo, and so forth.

Philosophy is present in Pasternak's writings— too much so in the novel, probably. . . . Many of his formulations revolve around one central insight: when we perceive and feel the world intensely, we are the world, and we truly *exist,* in some sense eternally. This is a fertile point of departure for an artist, one found mainly among great poets and bad ones. In Pasternak, the theme finds beautiful, powerful expression. When, on the other hand, he ventures into historical or religious philosophy (mostly through the intermediary of characters in *Doctor Zhivago*), his footing is less sure; still, his statements are always interesting.

In Pasternak, the theme of love and verbal pictorialism intertwine. . . . In love, we see truly, we receive a vision of the beloved in a "climate," a world; and this world proves to be interior, a heartland. As in Italian painting, the writer discovers poses and attitudes where the real and ideal coincide in one figure, a figure in an environment of radiant details. (p. 635)

[The] period of Pasternak's most explicit concern with society and history . . . takes part of its character from Pasternak's repudiation of his earlier, elaborate style (described . . . as "Soviet rococo"), in favor of plainer, more direct statement. He wrote *Doctor Zhivago* during this period and fewer poems; nevertheless, these are among his best, and especially the "poems of Yurii Zhivago," which conclude the novel. The novel itself, the work of one of the century's great modernists, paradoxically takes its place in the Russian tradition that moves from the 19th century and Tolstoy through Pasternak to the present and Solzhenitsyn. In that tradition, the Russian novelist is a kind of prophet, and his prophecies take the form of large historical frescoes that make palpable the dialectic of time and eternity. In *Doctor Zhivago,* a very concrete referent for that dialectic is the counterpointed juxtaposition of prose and poetry in the novel's structure. Though the poems by placement have the last word, Pasternak shouldn't be viewed finally as either the Poet or the Prose Writer. He is, paradoxically, the relationship between the two. (p. 636)

Alfred Corn, "World of the Interior," in *The Nation,* New York, Vol. 222, No. 20, May 22, 1976, pp. 635-36.

SOURCES FOR FURTHER STUDY

Cornwell, Neil. *Pasternak's Novel: Perspectives on "Doctor Zhivago."* Keele, England: Essays in Poetics Publications, 1986, 165 p.

> Close textual and thematic analysis of *Doctor Zhivago.*

de Mallac, Guy. *Boris Pasternak: His Life and Art.* Norman: University of Oklahoma Press, 1981, 450 p.

> Biography of Pasternak that includes an extensive discussion of his works.

Fleishman, Lazar. *Boris Pasternak: The Poet and His Politics.* Cambridge, Mass.: Harvard University Press, 1990, 359 p.

> Links Pasternak's artistic and ideological development to the literary and political events that occurred during his lifetime.

Levi, Peter. *Boris Pasternak.* London: Hutchinson, 1990, 310 p.

> Discusses Pasternak's life in relationship to his work.

Livingstone, Angela. *Boris Pasternak: Dr. Zhivago.* Cambridge: Cambridge University Press, 1989, 118 p.

> Provides a close reading of the novel, an account of its historical, cultural, and intellectual background, and a discussion of its influence on Western literature.

Pasternak, Evgeny. *Boris Pasternak: The Tragic Years 1930-60.* Translated by Michael Duncan. London: Collins Harvill, 1990, 278 p.

> Surveys Pasternak's life from the publication of his autobiography *Safe Conduct* through the political conflict surrounding *Doctor Zhivago* to his death.

Alan Paton

1903-1988

(Full name Alan Stewart Paton) South African novelist, autobiographer, essayist, short story writer, biographer, poet, and dramatist.

INTRODUCTION

*O*ne of the earliest proponents of racial equality in his native South Africa, Paton is best known for his novels *Cry, the Beloved Country* (1948) and *Too Late the Phalarope* (1953). In these and other works, he confronted the horrors of South Africa's racist system of apartheid. Paton's works have been praised in particular for their perceptive and sympathetic examination of the exploitation of nonwhites by the elite ruling class and the effect this has not only on the exploited, but also on the whole of South African society.

Paton was born in 1903 in Pietermaritzburg, Natal, a former British colony which is now part of the Republic of South Africa. In 1919 he entered Natal University College to prepare for a career in teaching, and while there he began writing dramas and poetry. After graduating in 1922, Paton worked as a high school teacher and served as the principal of the Diepkloof Reformatory school from 1935 to 1948. He began writing *Cry, the Beloved Country* in 1947 while touring European and American prisons and reformatories. In the early 1950s, Paton participated in the creation of the Liberal party of South Africa and increased his opposition to his country's racist policies. Paton's passport was confiscated in 1960 after he returned from a trip to New York to accept a Freedom House Award honoring his opposition to racism. In 1968 the Liberal party dissolved, preferring this course to purging its nonwhite members, as the government demanded; three years later, however, Paton's request for the return of his passport was granted. In his later years Paton was criticized by many antiapartheid activists because he opposed their efforts to pressure the government by discouraging foreign investment in South Africa. Such sanctions, Paton argued, would unduly punish South Africa's poorest blacks, and he decried even Nobel

Prize–winning clergyman Desmond Tutu for supporting such a strategy. Though controversial, Paton saw his actions as consistent with a lifelong belief in progress through moderation and mutual understanding. As he wrote in *Journey Continued* (1988): "By liberalism I don't mean the creed of any party or any century. I mean a generosity of spirit, a tolerance of others, an attempt to comprehend otherness, a commitment to the rule of law, a high ideal of the worth and dignity of man, a repugnance for authoritarianism and a love of freedom." Paton died of throat cancer in 1988 shortly after completing this work.

Cry, the Beloved Country concerns the fate of Absalom Kumalo, a young black South African who, while committing a robbery, murders Arthur Jarvis, a white social activist. The novel is divided into three sections. The first section follows the journey of Kumalo's father, a rural Anglican pastor, to the city of Johannesburg to search for his missing son and ends with his discovery that Absalom has confessed to the murder. In the second section, Jarvis's father reads the papers and speeches left behind by his son, ultimately acquiring an understanding of the hostility and squalid living conditions facing most of South Africa's nonwhites and the harmful impact of destroying indigenous tribal cultures. After the execution of Absalom in the third section, the two fathers meet and gain a comprehension of the loss that each has suffered. Though some critics found *Cry, the Beloved Country* pretentious and occasionally awkward, the book proved enormously successful, and Paton was soon perceived as an important figure in South Africa's antiapartheid movement.

Too Late the Phalarope focuses on Pieter van Vlaanderen, an Afrikaner police lieutenant who violates the South African Immorality Act of 1927 by engaging in sexual intercourse with a black woman. Convicted of this "offense against the race," Pieter is imprisoned and subsequently shunned by his family. While some critics note elements of propaganda in this work, most praise its compelling condemnation of the injustices inflicted by the Immorality Act. As Harold C. Gardiner observed: "*Too Late the Phalarope* is one of those rare books which make a reader face in terms of suffering and agony and ideals a situation which he may know

only theoretically. We have all read, I suppose, of the racial discriminations still prevalent in South Africa. But how remote and impersonal they seem to us in news stories. Here they are driven home to us in terms of persons whom we get to know very well indeed as the tale progresses."

A blend of historical and fictional characters and events, Paton's last novel, *Ah, But Your Land Is Beautiful* (1981), was planned as the first part of a trilogy of novels about South African race relations. The story opens with an act of quiet rebellion. An Indian teenager named Prem enters the Durban Library in Natal and sits down to read. Since she is not white, she is barred from using the facility. However, Prem defies the authorities, and her struggle ignites the embryonic antiapartheid campaigns of the 1950s. The work goes on to trace the history of such organizations as the Liberal party.

Paton's autobiographies *Towards the Mountain* (1980) and *Journey Continued* describe his early years as an educator and his later involvement with the Liberal party. Paton's other works include biographies of apartheid opponents Jan Hofmeyr and Geoffrey Clayton, as well as the short story collection *Tales from a Troubled Land* (1961), which was inspired by his experiences as the principal of the Diepkloof Reformatory. Paton's works have been recognized as a valuable commentary on the social injustices inflicted by the racial discrimination and segregation. Edmund Fuller observed: "The measure of [Paton's] books is that while distilling the essence of South Africa, they speak to many aspects of the condition of the whole world. He has struck universal notes, and the world outside his own land honors him for his art, his humanity, and his integrity."

(For further information about Paton's life and works, see *Contemporary Authors*, Vols. 15-16, 125; *Contemporary Authors New Revision Series*, Vol. 22; *Contemporary Authors Permanent Series*, Vol. 1; *Contemporary Literary Criticism*, Vols. 4, 10, 25, 55; *Major 20th-Century Writers*; and *Something about the Author*, Vols. 11, 56.)

CRITICAL COMMENTARY

HAROLD C. GARDINER, S.J.
(essay date 1948)

[In the following excerpt from a 1948 review, Gardiner offers a highly favorable appraisal of *Cry, the Beloved Country.*]

I have just finished a magnificent story. Its subject matter is as explosive as any that can be handled in today's fiction—the tensions between Negroes and whites—and yet there is not the faintest whisper of shrill propaganda; it deals plainly with the lusts of the flesh, and yet there is not the slightest suggestiveness; it plumbs deep into human suffering and punishment without a hint of moralizing or of maudlin sentimentality. It is a fine, indeed a great book.

It is *Cry, the Beloved Country,* by Alan Paton. The scene is South Africa, the main character a magnificently conceived native Anglican minister, the theme a twofold one: the struggle of the natives, attracted from the land and their tribes to the huge mining towns like Johannesburg, for tolerable living and working conditions; and the decline of tribal life and customs, fostered by the white man who had nothing to give the natives in return. All this is superbly told in a rather stately style, which is presumably a fairly literal transcription of the Zulu idiom and which gives the poignant tale a somewhat Biblically patriarchal tone.

Kumalo, the hero, is summoned from his little church among his tribe to go down to the frightening big city to help his sister, who has fallen on evil ways, and to find his son, from whom his parents have not heard since he left to work in the mines. The boy runs away from a reform school and becomes involved in a killing, the victim being the son of the white farmer whose lands lie near Kumalo's church; the son himself had sacrificed a career of great promise to work for the betterment of the natives. The pastor's sister agrees to return home with him but runs off at the last minute, leaving the crushed and, he thinks, disgraced man to go back to his tribe with his sister's child and the pregnant young wife of his condemned son. Drought and poor farming are threatening the life of his tribe when no one else steps in to assist them but the father of the murdered son, who does it in remembrance of his own son's devotion to the natives.

But the story is pre-eminently one of individuals. There are no sweeping and grandiose statements about "the race problem." Jarvis, the white father, and Ku-malo, the black one, are two men sorrowing for their sons, and the reader soon realizes that it matters not a tinker's dam what the color of their respective skins is. It is the human (and divine) values by which the two men live, the human dignity both portray, the sublimation of human suffering they achieve, which puts the black man and the white man shoulder to shoulder in the book and suggests by implication that the black and the white populations of South Africa and indeed of all the world can work shoulder to shoulder as well, if only every person will stop looking at the "race question" and start looking at the individual soul. This thought the book presents superbly. Though its very theme is race tension, in the inner workings and motivation of the characters the book shows utter unconsciousness of "race."

I wish there were space to quote many of the deeply moving passages of this most truly compassionate book. There is the scene in which Kumalo tells Jarvis that it was his son who had killed the white man's, or the scene in which Kumalo says farewell to his son, awaiting execution, or that which depicts the old pastor, back with his parish, leading prayers for his condemned son. But as I want to draw the comparison suggested at the start of this discussion, I must leave you to read these for yourself. I must remark, in passing from this truly noble novel, that there is one defect in it. It is marred by a page or so of some very shallow remarks on what law is and whence it derives its authority. (pp. 109-10)

The loud and startling things are not always the significant things in life; they are rarely the important things in a novel. *Cry, the Beloved Country* is an Everest in the flat wastes of modern fiction precisely because it is not shrill about the riots, the broken heads, the sullen hatreds of race tensions, but rather delves deeply into the serenity of love, compassion, consideration, and devotion that can alone solve race tensions. (p. 112)

Harold C. Gardiner, S.J., "Chapter Three: On Saying 'Boo!' to Geese," in his *In All Conscience: Reflections on Books and Culture,* Hanover House, 1959, pp. 108-12.

Principal Works

Cry, the Beloved Country (novel) 1948

Too Late the Phalarope (novel) 1953

The Land and People of South Africa (essay) 1955; revised edition, 1974; also published as South Africa and Her People, 1957

Tales from a Troubled Land (short stories) 1961; also published as Debbie Go Home, 1961

Hofmeyr (biography) 1964; also published as South African Tragedy: The Life and Times of Jan Hofmeyr [abridged edition], 1965

Sponono [with Krishna Shah] (drama) 1964

The Long View (essays and speech) 1968

For You Departed (memoir) 1969; also published as Kontakion for You Departed, 1969

Apartheid and the Archbishop: The Life and Times of Geoffrey Clayton, Archbishop of Cape Town (biography) 1973

Towards the Mountain (autobiography) 1980

Ah, But Your Land Is Beautiful (novel) 1981

Journey Continued (autobiography) 1988

HAROLD C. GARDINER, S.J.

(essay date 1953)

[In the following excerpt from a 1953 review, Gardiner praises *Too Late the Phalarope*.]

One of the tiny triumphs in which I take some small if immodest pride is the fact that *America* was well in the vanguard of those who recognized the quality of Alan Paton's *Cry, the Beloved Country*. The book was originally published in February 1948. In the March 13, 1948 issue of *America* it was given an article-length review under the somewhat misleading title of "On Saying 'Boo!' to Geese." There we summed up our impressions of the book by saying, "It is a fine, indeed a great book."

Several more months were to pass before the general reading public began to realize what a fine book it really was. It then appeared on the best-seller lists and attracted the praise of critics in general. Since then it has been reprinted several times and has attained the stature of at least a minor classic, since it is now included in the Modern Standard Author Series (Scribner's).

It seems, however, that we won't be quite so vanguardish in recognizing the quality of Mr. Paton's sec-

ond novel, *Too Late the Phalarope*. This book has already been hailed in publicity releases and preview encomia from critics as being even more impressive than *Cry, the Beloved Country*.

I believe the critics and the admen are right. First, it is a much more tautly drawn tale. Mr. Paton has tightened up his narrative technique and though his first novel was by no means sprawling, this one has some of the spare muscularity about it that characterizes Graham Greene's technique. Second, *Too Late the Phalarope* is simply plunged into an atmosphere of what the critics generally call compassion. Let this not be understood as meaning that the book is drippy with humanitarian sentiment. It is not. The compassion is strong and manly and manifests (as does Mr. Paton's current political activities against the racists in South Africa) a deeply felt realization of the moral plight, of the agony of soul of others, which is not content merely to sermonize but which strives to burst forth into action.

At first reading one would be inclined to think that here is just another version of the plot of Graham Greene's *The End of the Affair*. The story itself is simple. Pieter van Vlaanderen is a young police lieutenant in South Africa. He is a decorated veteran of the war, a famous Rugby player, respected and admired by white and colored alike in the community. In addition, he is happily married, with two children. On a certain night while making his rounds he surprises a young white boy who is in pursuit of an attractive mulatto girl. He is able to prevent anything untoward happening and asks the young man to come to him the next evening for a talk.

There, speaking as a friend, he lays before him the sordidness and danger of the whole situation. When the young man leaves, repentant and straightened out, the young lieutenant drops upon his knees and prays, "God have mercy upon him." But then he goes on—and here is the first hint of tragedy in the story—to pray, "God have mercy upon me."

The tragedy quickly and almost inevitably develops. Despite his happy marriage, something has been missing in it. The deep love he feels for his wife has not been fully and completely reciprocated, and as he broods more and more upon the situation, he finds himself with a great loathing and strange fascination drawn toward the Negro girl whom the young man had been pursuing. During the period when his wife and children are off on a short vacation he meets the young Negro girl clandestinely and has an affair with her.

The upshot of the whole matter is that the liaison is discovered; the young lieutenant is ruined and his family almost literally destroyed.

This is all told through the reminiscences of a maiden aunt who has loved Pieter as her own son and who had realized early in the tragic coil the agony he was going through. It is told in admirable style which catches with real skill the loneliness, the simplicity, the God-fearing reverence of one whose great cross in life was that she had never had a love of her own.

This may sound as though the story is a simple account of passion. It may even sound as though it is simply a sordid tale. Let me hasten to say, first of all, that there is a delicacy and chasteness of expression which immediately lifts the book above any suspicion of sensationalism. Let me add that there is a religious tone running through every step of the account which makes it a truly Christian approach to the problem of sin and sinner.

But the book is infinitely more than this. It is infinitely more than a mere tale of misguided passion. The great passion that emerges in the pages is the passion of Mr. Paton's own hatred of racial discrimination—which must be the passion of everyone who reads the book, even had he not entertained it before. Mr. Paton's whole thesis is that the criminal law in South Africa has succeeded for generations in making the Negro no more than an animal. It is, he says, "the iron law that no white man may touch a black woman nor may any white woman be touched by a black man. And to go against this law of a people of rock and stone, in a land of rock and stone, was to be broken and destroyed." This terrible philosophy, we are informed in the book, is enshrined in the South African Immorality Act of 1927.

If Pieter had had an affair with a white woman, he would, so far as the law is concerned, have been untouched by the horrible penalty which was inflicted upon him. But the mere fact that his offense had been with a Negro woman was enough to hurl him outside the pale of civilized life. It was enough to separate him from wife and children. It was enough to kill his stern, unbending father. All this means that under the law in South Africa the Negroes are looked upon simply as animals. Pieter was not punished for adultery. He was punished because he had overstepped racial boundaries, simply because he had "defiled" the sacred Afrikaans blood, sacred because (as they almost blasphemously thought and think) "as God had chosen them for a people, so did they choose Him for their God, cherishing their separateness that was now His Will."

This is admirably summed up in the response of the police captain whose duty it had been to break the lieutenant and to inform his family. When the captain had told the story to Pieter's father, the fierce old man struck the arm of his chair and said:

—I would shoot him like a dog. Then because no one spoke he said to the captain, wouldn't you?
And the captain said—No
—But he has offended against the race.

Then the captain said, trembling
—Meneer, as a policeman, I know an offense against the law and as a Christian I know an offense against God, but I do not know an offense against the race.

Too Late the Phalarope is one of those rare books which make a reader face in terms of suffering and agony and ideals a situation which he may know only theoretically. We have all read, I suppose, of the racial discriminations still prevalent in South Africa. But how remote and impersonal they seem to us in the news stories. Here they are driven home to us in terms of persons whom we get to know very well indeed as the tale progresses.

The book may in one sense be called propaganda but it is propaganda that is strong with deep and valid emotion. It is propaganda which does not merely uphold a thesis but which portrays human persons being crushed by a thesis. Mr. Paton deserves the gratitude of everyone who would make real to himself the injustice, the dehumanization, which is implicit in every act of racial discrimination, however slight it may be. (pp. 112-16)

Harold C. Gardiner, S.J. "Chapter Three: Alan Paton's Second Masterpiece," in his *In All Conscience: Reflections on Books and Culture,* Hanover House, 1959, pp. 112-16.

HORTON DAVIES

(essay date 1959)

[In the following excerpt, Davies discusses clerical characters in *Cry, the Beloved Country*.]

[The] so-called 'foreign missionary' may become a diminishing figure in a world in which the West and its religion are increasingly rejected by the East and in which missionaries themselves speak, not of 'Mission-Fields' but of 'The Younger Churches'; but the problems of racial tensions are more rather than less acute in the twentieth century. One might even risk the generalization that the great problem of the latter nineteenth century was the conflict between Christian ethical norms and the economic order, while in the twentieth century the chief problem is the antagonism between Christian principles and race hatreds and prejudices. It is therefore of the utmost relevance that an important novelist, out of the heart of the interracial complexities of South Africa with its many bitter racialists and its few intrepid Christian and humanist anti-segregationists, should have chosen this theme in his moving novel, *Cry, the Beloved Country* (1948).

While the hero is a social reformer who, ironically, is killed by a member of the people he is trying to uplift, he is moved by Christian impulses and convictions. More important for our purpose, however, is that the author, Alan Paton, gives a sympathetic portrayal of two priests, the Rev. Stephen Kumalo, an African rural priest of the Church of the Province of South Africa (the Anglican or Episcopalian Church) and an English missionary priest of the same Communion, Father Vincent. The understanding and compassionate English priest is a portrayal of Father Trevor Huddleston, a great friend of Paton's, who was a notable priest of the Anglican Community of the Resurrection in Johannesburg. Paton thus seems to be saying that while educational, political, and social amelioration is essential, (and he was himself a teacher and for many years the principal of the Reformatory School for African offenders in Johannesburg), the ultimate reconciliation of racial tensions is to be found in Christian humility, forgiveness, and compassion, which are the gift of Christ, the Reconciler of men with God and with themselves. The constructive meaning of suffering with Christ is 'The Comfort in Desolation,' which is the subtitle of the novel.

Reduced to a fleshless skeleton, the story is that of an old African minister's search for his prodigal son, which causes him to leave his little valley church in Natal for the Babylon of Johannesburg, where industrialization, de-tribalization, and a shoddy imitation of the material aspects of civilization are turning so many of the Africans into prodigals. In the end, after a search that takes him through many aspects of the lives of the city Africans, he finds his son in jail, where he is to be charged with the murder of Jarvis, the social reformer—the two other equally, if not more, guilty accomplices having escaped from justice. The minister also discovers that his own sister has become a prostitute in Johannesburg, the city of Gold, where the African gold miners are not permitted to bring their wives to share their quarters. His brother has become a rabble rouser and critic of the Church in Johannesburg. In Johannesburg old Kumalo is greatly helped by the white priest, with whom he stays (hotels for whites are forbidden to Africans) and who interprets the meaning of suffering constructively. In the end he returns home, saddened but unbroken in faith to find that his great helper is the local white farmer, previously prejudiced in racial matters, whose son Jarvis had been killed by Kumalo's son. Only a profound and mutual and, as Paton believes, supernaturally originating forgiveness could have made this relationship possible. It is in such possibilities of creatively overcoming race tensions that the greatest hope in South Africa lies. It is a novel that avoids the usual dangers of a bitter realism (though it spares nothing in its description of the common decay of European and African moral life) and of a facile sentimentalism (though it shows that Christian love is deeply sacrificial and forgiving in its compassion).

The Rev. Stephen Kumalo is a simple and poorly educated man. His church is no more than a wood-and-iron construction; there are no temptations to wealth here. There might be temptations to prestige and bullying his people. But this humble man is always God's servant, sometimes his bewildered servant, never the master of his flock. He is, of course, in his search for his lost son, the type of God. In the same way Jarvis, sacrificed though a reconciler, is a shadowy type of God's eternal Son, Christ. When Kumalo sets out on the search he and his wife have ten pounds in the savings bank and a little more than twelve pounds that they have set aside for their son's education. This money, earned with the sweat of their brows and saved by much skimping, is immediately used for the great search, for in their estimation human values always predominate over money values—and yet to whom does money mean more than to the honest poor? Yet these savings have to be spent on a journey which—for a simple countryman—is into the anxious frontiers of sophistication and civilization. As the train takes him farther away from the green valleys he loves to the unfamiliar industrial metropolis, his fear mounts. In Paton's own words:

> And now the fear back again, the fear of the unknown, the fear of the great city where boys were killed crossing the street, the fear of Gertrude's sickness. Deep down the fear for his son. Deep down the fear of a man who lives in a world not made for him, whose own world is slipping away, dying, being destroyed, beyond any recall.

For reassurance he turned to the pastoral world of the Bible, which alone was real for him. And even there, in his later agony and perturbation, he was to lose his way until the Anglican missionary priest helped him stumblingly to find it again.

The old priest's simplicity means that he trusts everyone and is as easily gulled as his eighteenth-century prototype, Goldsmith's *Vicar of Wakefield*. In his case it is not green spectacles or a sorry nag that is his undoing, but a fellow African who absconds with his pound note after pretending to buy a bus ticket from the depot. His disillusionment deepens when he learns that his sister, who went to seek her husband, has become a prostitute, and that his brother is no longer a business man but a rabble-rousing politician, symptom and channel of African resentment, who says:

> What God has not done for South Africa, man must do.

The diagnosis of the racial problem is given in several parts of the novel. A younger African priest, Msimangu, who befriended old Kumalo, gives his view first:

'My friend, I am a Christian. It is not in my heart to hate a white man. It was a white man who brought my father out of darkness. But you will pardon me if I talk frankly to you. The tragedy is not that things are broken. The tragedy is that they are not mended again. The white man has broken the tribe. And it is my belief—and again I ask you pardon—that it cannot be mended again. But the house that is broken, and the man that falls apart when the house is broken, these are tragic things. That is why children break the law, and old white people are robbed and beaten.' Msimangu continues: 'It suited the white man to break the tribe . . . But it has not suited him to build something in the place of what is broken . . . They are not all so. There are some white men who give their lives to build up what is broken.—But they are not enough . . . They are afraid, that is the truth. It is fear that rules this land.'

The same deep African priest develops his diagnosis more subtly later:

. . . there is only one thing that has power completely, and that is love. Because when a man loves, he seeks no power, and therefore has power. I see only one hope for our country, and that is when white men and black men, desiring neither power nor money, but desiring only the good of their country, come together to work for it.

Msimangu was grave and silent and then he said somberly,

I have one great fear in my heart, that one day when they are turned to loving, they will find we are turned to hating.

The liberal and intelligent white man, young Jarvis, had been penning his own diagnosis when death struck him. This was even more subtle, as well as profound, in its exploration of the dilemmas in South Africa and the utter contradictions. Its final words are worth pondering, because almost universal in their scope:

The truth is that our civilization is not Christian; it is a tragic compound of great ideal and fearful practice, of high assurance and desperate anxiety, of loving charity and fearful clutching of possessions.

Meanwhile, as time runs out, Paton hopes that Christians will be able to implement their moral imperatives and by a mutual forgiveness increase the healing of the antagonisms.

Father Vincent's role is deserving of consideration—especially when it is realized that behind this fictional character stands Father Trevor Huddleston. As Paton portrays Father Vincent, four characteristics predominate. Like all confessors he is an excellent listener, and never a perfunctory one. He knows when a man has become so numb with grief that no words can com-

fort him. So profound in his capacity for communication that he can speak as the African pastor wishes him to speak, in parables. This conversation is typical of his method:

—My friend, your anxiety turned to fear, and your fear turned to sorrow. But sorrow is better than fear. For fear impoverishes always, while sorrow may enrich. Kumalo looked at him, with an intensity of gaze that was strange in so humble a man, and hard to encounter.
—I do not know that I am enriched, he said.
—Sorrow is better than fear, said Father Vincent doggedly. Fear is a journey, a terrible journey, but sorrow is an arriving.
—And where have I arrived? asked Kumalo.
—When the storm threatens, a man is afraid for his house, said Father Vincent in that symbolic language that is like the Zulu tongue. But when the house is destroyed, there is something to do. About a storm he can do nothing, but he can rebuild a house.

Father Vincent is also a surgeon of the soul and he now speaks severely, certain that this will best help Kumalo and recall him to his vocation as a priest:

—We spoke of amendment of life, said the white priest. Of the amendment of your son's life. And because you are a priest, this must matter to you more than all else, more even than your suffering and your wife's suffering.
—That is true. Yet I cannot see how such a life can be amended.
—You cannot doubt that. You are a Christian. There was a thief upon the cross.

Finally, Father Vincent is a practical man and knows that hope arises when a man is reminded of his many tasks and duties and of the dependence of others upon him. He is counseled to pray in a severely practical and concrete way which will also be, though this is not mentioned, a way of healing and forgiveness:

Do not pray and think about these things now, there will be other times. Pray for Gertrude, and for her child, and for the girl that is to be your son's wife, and for the child that will be your grandchild. Pray for your wife and for all at Ndotsheni. Pray for the woman and the children that are bereaved. Pray for the soul of him who was killed. Pray for us at the Mission House, and for those at Ezenzelini, who try to rebuild in a place of destruction. Pray for your own rebuilding. Pray for all white people, those who do justice, and those who would do justice if they were not afraid. And do not fear to pray for your son, and his amendment . . . And give thanks where you can give thanks.

When Kumalo would have thanked the rosy-cheeked priest from England, Father Vincent replied,

We do what is in us, and why it is in us, that is also a secret. It is Christ in us, crying that men may be succoured and forgiven, even when He Himself is forsaken.

In the novel Father Vincent is merely a profile, taking up only a chapter, but his outline is so firmly etched that the essential priest is here, and, though of a different Christian Communion, he challenges comparison with Mauriac's Abbé Calou, with due allowance for the much briefer treatment.

Much could be written of the poetic quality of the novel and its Biblical simplicity and profundity of speech, of the deliberate inversion of the order of the words to suggest in English the dignity of the Zulu language, of the contrasts between the village and primitive and the city and sophisticated environments, were our concern with the technique of the novel rather than the meaning. Its ultimate meaning is the necessity for reconciliation between the races, which are necessary to each other for the establishment of a harmonious society that will reflect the variety of the gifts of God to men—the example, incentive, and power for compassion and forgiveness that Christ the Reconciler shows and gives. It is only a superficial though obvious and easy judgment that would imply that the white man has all the giving to do and the black man all the receiving. But civilization is not merely European and Western, though its latest phase has been so. The Africans themselves have, as Paton's novel shows us, their own important human gifts to provide. They are a marvelously patient people, whose contentment should shame the neurotic greed characteristic of so many in the West. They have a profound concern for the young and the old, and will share their food and shelter with the widows and fatherless in their affliction, however little of this world's goods of their own they have. Here again their social solidarity and generosity should make Western individualists uncomfortable in their isolation and atomism. They have a rich capacity for joy, as shown in their singing and dancing. They have a very gracious courtesy, grave and tender. Their eye for color is exotic, as may be seen in their tribal decoration and on the lintel posts of their beehive huts in their kraals. And while only the antiquarian anthropologist (of whom there are few left) and the sentimental segregationist want them to live in their reserves and their poor city 'locations,' Paton has shown that detribalization has gone too far. They must be integrated in a new Western society in which their human qualities will be needed even more than at present along with the skills that they have proved they can learn when the white man gives them their opportunity.

It is not the least of Paton's distinctions that he has provided a moving sociological document, which is a human document and at the same time a theological document, a Christian interpretation of racial tensions and of the spirit by which they can be overcome. In the same volume he has also supplied an account of a simple yet dignified Zulu pastor and of a clever but humble English missionary priest, which helps to wipe out the sneers of Somerset Maugham. It was altogether typical of Paton that his next novel, *Too Late the Phalarope,* should attempt to deal sympathetically and understandingly with the problem of the Afrikaner, the other and larger part of the white minority in South Africa which is exacerbating the racial problem, apart from certain distinguished exceptions. He seems to have made it his concern to apply the Biblical adage to tell the truth in love. (pp. 128-36)

Horton Davies, "Pilgrims, Not Strangers," in his *A Mirror of the Ministry in Modern Novels,* Oxford University Press, Inc., 1959, pp. 113-38.

F. CHARLES ROONEY
(essay date 1961)

[In the following excerpt, Rooney discusses the relationship between the moral content and literary qualities of Paton's works.]

It is interesting, yet not altogether surprising, that one of the most skilled and sensitive writers of recent years, Alan Paton, has been suspected of moralizing. Everything about him seems to lend basis to this suspicion. He is an ardent and inspired advocate of racial justice in the most professedly segregationist nation in the world, the Union of South Africa. He is a former reformatory warden and has pioneered for institutional reform in a land not reputed to be especially progressive. And finally (worst of all!) he has written three books, each of which is built upon the foundations of his personal experience. His first two, *Cry, the Beloved Country* and *Too Late the Phalarope* unhesitatingly grapple with striking, race-conflict themes.

The third, *Tales from a Troubled Land,* a book of short stories published this spring focuses predominantly on situations in a boys' reformatory. With such an obvious parallel between his life and writing, Paton's readers almost automatically assume that he has a message to put across in his books. And how, one asks, can such a message be anything but propaganda?

With so many counts against him, a writer would have to be especially talented and restrained to keep himself sufficiently out of his stories—to keep his aesthetic distance. Only a highly disciplined writer could keep from haranguing. Yet Paton's readers know that he accomplished exactly that. He tells two taut absorbing stories with characters unmatched in contemporary fiction for their spontaneity and inherent drama for being themselves.

Thus the onlooker is hard put to account for the charge against Paton of propagandizing (except to a limited extent for *Tales from a Troubled Land,* as we will point out below), unless he attributes to the critic either an indiscriminating biocritical method or insufficient objectivity. To bring an author's personal life into the evaluation of his work is fraught with the danger of unjustified assumption. This peril is nowhere more evident than in the criticism of Paton's two novels. A more accurate index of his accomplishment is the warm acceptance of his tender, yet powerful, stories by thousands of perceptive readers. However, the publisher's eulogies of Paton as a humanitarian only bolster suspicions of "preaching."

The most severe effect of this prejudice about his "purpose" is that it puts a shadow on his stature as a writer. Alan Paton is no mere craftsman though his diction and rhythm are stirring. He is a mature artist telling a story of power, insight and significance. He searches the dilemma of man's fear and disregard of his fellows with all the compassion and force of Steinbeck

in *Grapes of Wrath.* Yet he has what Steinbeck never had, a vision of the life of the spirit. He has all Steinbeck's heart, plus *soul.*

For Paton love, supernatural forgiving love, is the imperative of life; without it life is destroyed. It is the vacuum created by fear and hate that is the cause of all conflict in his novels; his insight into this void has set Paton's novels not only beyond but on a different plane from the bulk of modern fiction.

Cry, the Beloved Country is a great novel, but not because it speaks out against racial intolerance and its bitter effects. Rather the haunting milieu of a civilization choking out its own vitality is evoked naturally and summons our compassion. There are no brutal invectives, no blatant injustices to sear the reader's conscience, no vicious hatred, no righteously unleashed passion. It is a great compliment to Paton's genius that he communicates both a story and a lasting impression without bristling, bitter anger.

Restraining himself and the reader within the bonds of probability, he etches the portrait of the family of Stephen Kumalo, a humble colored Anglican parson. The family is separated and destroyed by the ad-

Scene from the 1952 film adaptation of *Cry, the Beloved Country.*

vent of an industrial culture in South Africa. Kumalo's son, Absalom, and Arthur Jarvis, the white man whom the son has accidentally killed, are both destroyed by the fear and distrust that have accompanied technological "progress."

But this is a silent destruction, one for which the blame is not pinned down; the directions of real life are not so apparent. The reader's impression of the milieu Paton describes is rather of *corrosion*. Paton's protest to injustice consists in pointing out, not accusing. The South Africa we find in his books is a manifestation of Christian heart that has forgotten what it should be. It has seen itself and has found no love that might embrace all. Therefore it proceeds to exclude, to segregate, to separate, to fear. Self-enclosed, the soul of a nation quickly begins to distort everything it sees until finally it finds that life itself has been squeezed of every value that makes it worthwhile and noble. Indeed the total impression one gets from Paton's work is of a nation frightened by its own shadow. This is the tragedy that elicits our compassion.

Cry, the beloved country, for the unborn child that is the inheritor of our fear. Let him not love the earth too deeply. Let him not laugh too gladly when the water runs through his fingers, nor stand too silent when the setting sun makes red the veld with fire. Let him not be too moved when the birds of his land are singing, nor give too much of his heart to a mountain or a valley. For fear will rob him of all if he gives too much.

These are words of a people, forcing themselves up from the wellsprings of the human spirit. They are the warning cries of a lover fearing for the beloved. Here, as throughout the novel, there is no maudlin commentary from the author. Rather the innermost emotions of a whole nation are expressed in various ways, in many passages scattered throughout the book to emphasize their independence of any particular figure in the story.

A seeming interpolation by the author (as narrator) in chapter twenty-eight provides an excellent example of Paton's technique. The passage is a stinging rebuke to the gold fever of the rich white men who own the mines and unmercifully exploit native labor. It concludes with a mention of the plan of Sir Ernest Oppenheimer, a farsighted white leader, to permit native mine workers to live in villages with their families instead of in compounds:

They want to hear your voice again, Sir Ernest Oppenheimer. Some of them applaud you, and some of them thank God for you in their hearts, even at their bedsides. For mines are for men, not for money. And money is not something to go mad about, and throw your hat into the air for. Money is for food and clothes and comfort, and a visit to the pictures. Money is to make happy the lives of children. Money is for security, and for dreams, and for

hopes, and for purposes. Money is for buying the fruits of the earth, of the land where you were born. . . . No second Johannesburg is needed upon the earth. One is enough.

It is not hard to imagine a socially conscious writer stepping beyond the legitimate limits of the novel form to express such sentiments. But Paton does not do this. Chapter twenty-eight is a natural and integral part of his story, a sequel to the brilliant ninth chapter which describes the overnight rise of a shanty village. To deny the kind of judgment expressed in the above passage a legitimate place in literature is surely to take such an exclusive and rarified view of the writing art that it no longer touches life.

Another startling reflection on the inner corruption of South Africa might seem, at first, open to criticism as extraneous to the story, put in simply to make a point.

In the deserted harbour there is yet water that laps against the quays. In the dark and silent forest there is a leaf that falls. Behind the polished panelling the white ant eats away the wood. Nothing is ever quiet, except for fools.

Yet here too we are eventually forced to admit Paton's genius to express his nation's pulse and his people's conscience. Here we see not a lone angry commentator but a compassionate sufferer witnessing the decline of that which he loves. We do not hear the clear voice of the author telling us what to think; these "asides" always spring from the story: In fact we might wonder at the reticence if they were unsaid, for the very rocks cry out.

Again in *Too Late the Phalarope* there are innumerable sequences in which we may detect the influence of the author's convictions. However, the narrator of the story, Tante Sophie, becomes such a real person to the reader that there is never a question of sermonizing. In her Paton has created his only really well-defined woman; this portrait is a work of technical mastery and avoids a potential sore spot. Furthermore, *Too Late the Phalarope* is not a story of racial injustice, at least not in any usual sense of that phrase. It is more a witness to the consequences of fear and the loss of love.

In the plight of Pieter van Vlaanderen, Paton has caught the tragedy of racism at its weakest link. A prominent, loved and respected white family is crushed through a single infidelity to the white man's law. Paton traces the cause of this catastrophe, from fear to smoldering distrust to fatally harsh laws to destruction. The justice of man grinds exceeding small, all the more unrelenting because it lacks God's mercy. The tragedy of this unforgiving venegeance is not lost to all white men. Pieter's police superior says, "An offender must be punished. . . . I don't argue about that. But to punish and not to restore, that is the greatest of all offences."

Soon afterward the captain says to Pieter's father-in-law, who epitomizes the force behind the laws which punish unmercifully every offense "against the race": "*Meneer,* as a policeman I know an offence against the law, and as a Christian I know an offence against God; but I do not know an offence against the race." And he continues, "If a man takes unto himself God's right to punish, then he must also take upon himself God's promise to restore." Here is the central conflict and theme of Paton's writing: the insufficiency of man's love and the terrible repercussions of its absence. Yet nowhere in this story does the reader sit back and think, "Such a clever writer, to be convincing me of his belief through this novel instead of through an essay." If the bulk of his intelligent readers were to say this, there would be serious doubt about Paton's standing as an artist. In reality his work supports no such assertions.

We may point out three significant criteria for judging whether a writer has shared a vision of reality with us or has only told us something. The first is whether the story conforms to the demands of reality or the plot is labored and the characters stereotyped. Paton satisfies this requirement admirably. His Christianity and talent have conspired to produce a just picture of the relationship of the races. In both novels real guilt is punished (Absalom for murder, Pieter van Vlaanderen for having intercourse with a colored woman); it is the *spirit* and *degree* of punishment—not its injustice—that Paton upbraids.

He admits virtue and good will among those who, almost inculpably, demand such unchristian laws, although his equity does not prevent him from being slightly cynical at times about that virtue. In neither novel do we find a Simon Legree; these are men who have lost their identity in the faceless group, like the lynching party in *To Kill a Mockingbird.* If the fickleness of human justice is reproved, still no barbs are hurled. It is difficult to envisage a more fair and dispassionate characterization of the conflict he presents. And because of the writer's fidelity to fact the story rings true.

The second rule of judgment is that the writer must not be expressing merely personal prejudices or his favorite "cause." Every sentiment must be not his own private feeling but the expression of a widely felt or universal feeling or conviction. Both novels present plots that command our assent by the inner cogency of their appeal to the reader's sense of justice and his compassion. There is nothing petty, nothing that the reader feels is being imposed upon him.

The third standard, closely related to the second, is that every reflection upon moral or ethical issues should find expression naturally within the framework of the story. This criterion is more a technical problem than the other two, but it can only be satisfied by a valid artistic intuition. That is, the writer cannot choose to expound some didactic instruction, and then decide who will say it. What is said must grow out of a fully developed, real character who can lay claim to our acceptance as a genuine person who *should* say this. As has been pointed out in several characteristic instances, Paton has not succumbed to the temptation of simply saying something. In his novels the story is the thing, and whatever is said must grow out of the story.

With his latest book of short stories, *Tales from a Troubled Land,* Paton has fallen into the snare he hitherto had avoided so successfully, of speaking outside the story, or just as bad, using the story as a foil for his message. In **"Sponono,"** and to a more pronounced degree in **"Ha'penny,"** the author's reflections become almost too private. After relating the extremely brief but precisely told story of this twelve-year-old orphan (nick-named "Ha'penny") who can find no one to love him until it is too late, the narrator (a reformatory warden) says: "And I was left too, with the resolve to be more prodigal in the task that the State, though not in so many words, has enjoined on me."

In **"The Waste Land,"** a tense four-page story that climaxes in the junk-yard death of a gang member who turns out to be the son of the man the gang was attacking, the father turns away from the dead body and cries out to the world which has destroyed even filial love. "He buried his face in his arms and said to himself in the idiom of his own language, 'People, arise! The world is dead.' Then he arose himself, and went heavily out of the waste land." Although the story is extremely dramatic, these words in the mouth of the stricken father are clearly out of character.

"Death of a Tsotsi" tells of a young colored lad who, to assert his independence, associates himself with a band of hooligans (tsotsis); after he leaves the reformatory he attempts to break away from them and they stab him to death. The story is filled with the same feeling of doom that marks *Too Late the Phalarope.* It ends unfortunately:

DeVilliers and I went to the funeral and spoke of sympathy to Spike's mother and wife and sister. But the words fell like dead things to the ground, for something deeper than sorrow was there. We were all of us, white and black, rich and poor, learned and untutored, bowed down by a knowledge that we lived in the shadow of a great danger, and were powerless against it. It was no place for a white person to pose in any mantel of power or authority; for this death gave the lie to both of them.

And this death would go on too, for nothing less than the reform of a society would bring it to an end.

It was the menace of the socially frustrated, strangers to mercy, striking like adders for the dark reasons of ancient minds, at any who crossed their paths.

And in the book's last tale, **"A Drink in the Passage,"** a colored artist says to the narrator, a white man: " 'Do you think we'll ever touch each other? Your people and mine? Or is it too late?' But I didn't give him any answer. For though I may hope, and though I may fear, I don't really know."

In each instance Paton has unfortunately abandoned his story to profess his heart. Though the words come through a character more real than the narrator of *Cry, the Beloved Country,* they do not have conviction or a natural flavor; they are superfluous, extrinsic. Perhaps these flaws would not be noted if Paton were less of a writer. But since he is an outstanding craftsman, writing about a living tragedy with an intensity and vision beyond nearly all his contemporaries, he cannot afford such lapses. If he will only remain faithful to the restrictions of the novel, Alan Paton will surely be remembered as the most sensitive writer of an epoch. (pp. 93-8)

F. Charles Rooney, "The 'Message' of Alan Paton," in *The Catholic World,* Vol. 194, No. 1160, November, 1961, pp. 92-8.

EDMUND FULLER

(essay date 1962)

[In the following excerpt, Fuller discusses the nature of tragedy in Paton's fiction.]

Much has been published recently about the decline of tragedy, and the question has been asked whether tragedy can be written in this age. Offstage, during the discussion, Alan Paton went ahead and did it—in terms of the novel—in *Too Late the Phalarope.* It was the book that followed his much-acclaimed first novel, *Cry, the Beloved Country.* It offered him, therefore, all the notorious "second book" challenges, as well as the problems of tragedy. The two books are an interesting study in the tragic—and an element beyond. For the purposes of this discussion, I will reverse the order in which they were written.

The core of *Too Late the Phalarope* is classically simple: Pieter van Vlanderen, a police lieutenant, honored in the community, breaks the iron law of the South African Immorality Act. Thereby he is destroyed and his family with him. A secret flaw has brought about the fall of a man of stature. He comprehends what has happened, and recognizes his own responsibility in it. Nevertheless, the story contains forces that become cumulative inevitabilities, helping to thrust

him on an inexorable path. As in *Cry, the Beloved Country,* we are given a balanced picture of environmental influences coexistent with personal responsibility.

Four major factors—two of which are social and two, personal—produce the tragedy. The first of these is the psychotic rigidity of the Afrikaner community in South Africa. An illicit sexual encounter might cause varying degrees of trouble in marriage, family, and community anywhere. But it is not sex that destroys Pieter—it is race. Even in his puritanical environment, the shock of a misstep with a white woman could have been absorbed. But by sexual contact with a black woman, Pieter has violated taboo, far more formidable than statutory law, though in this case a law gives formal expression to the taboo. An irrational horror, a sense of ritual uncleanness, attaches to the offense. Within that community, he can never be cleansed. His name is destroyed irreparably and all who bear his name are consumed in the shame of it.

The second social element is puritanism, in the community and in Pieter's father, Jacob van Vlanderen. The puritanism of the community, of course, has theological and historical roots that predate the race psychosis. But there has been a natural, inevitable absorption of the one strain into the other, so that they have become indissoluble and mutually reinforcing. Thus a deep emotional disturbance has been given the sanction of morality and the prejudice of man translated into the law of God.

It is such men as Jacob van Vlanderen who make up the Afrikaner community, and it is partly the community that has formed Jacob van Vlanderen, putting its own stamp upon those elements of character that are uniquely his. He is a good man in the letter of the law and of puritan moral codes, but praise of him, if such it be, must stop there. He is as hard and merciless a judge of men as any who ever walked in the line of Calvin and Knox in colonial America or puritan England.

The unyielding will and emotional insensitivity of Jacob are the root of the first of the personal disorders that prepare the long way for Pieter's fall: a deep hostility between father and son. In the boy's childhood, the father had honored only the hard, masculine side of a more complex nature. He had trodden roughly on the sensitive or intellectual elements of his son—the qualities derived from his mother and responsive to her gentleness. Indeed, the mother has largely been compelled, through her husband's hardness, to cede the boy to the hungry maternal love (and ambiguously more) of Jacob's sister, Tante Sophie, the hare-lipped spinster who is the elegiac narrator of the tale.

Tante Sophie, who frankly calls herself a "watcher," tells the tale in a generally direct way, though the limits of knowledge in first-person narration are occasionally strained, in spite of the device of a secret journal of Pieter's, from which she quotes in retrospect. In recurring passages of high rhapsodic tone—definitely conventionalized—she functions as chorus. It is both effective and slightly overdone. In the classic tragic manner, she reiterates the already accomplished doom, so that the suspense, which is great, is not the suspense of "whether" but the greater one of "how."

The tensions between father and son flared up over the Second World War, when Pieter enlisted for what Jacob called an "English war." The two are opposed on every major question in life, including attitude toward the race question and the notion of what religion should be. The father never gives up trying to assert over Pieter the utter dominance he wields over the rest of the family. Yet he and Pieter grope vainly for some bond between them.

The fourth of the major destructive factors is the tension between Pieter and his wife, Nella. She is of a gentle and timorous nature, loving her husband but un-

able to venture into the depths of his mind and spirit where his dangerous conflicts rage. Also there is an inhibition upon their sexual life. Puritanism has conditioned Nella to believe in a sharp division between the bodily passions and the other elements of love, which in her eyes are essentially "higher." She gives herself and then withdraws. Pieter longs for a sustained sexual harmony with her, based on an acceptance of the unity of all aspects of love. Failure to achieve this does contribute to Pieter's *swartgalligheid,* the deadly black mood, but we shall examine whether this whole factor is as crucial as he believes it to be—or in the way he thinks it is.

I have not cited Tante Sophie as a factor in the disaster, though she regards herself as one. She is not causative, but may have failed to be preventive. Whether or not if she had "cried out not ceasing" she could have averted the catastrophe is unprovable. It belongs among all the other *ifs* that tantalize hindsight.

I put aside also the active malice of Sergeant Steyn, Pieter's subordinate who betrays him, for it is a by-product of Pieter's tensions and is a circumstantial factor. Pieter was courting exposure unconsciously—if not by one, then by another.

The obsessive drive that carries Pieter to the secretly-smiling black girl, Stephanie, takes its rise from a constellation of factors which I would not presume to analyze clinically. Paton has captured the agony of obsession powerfully. But sex surely is more the operational means than the aim of it. A game of symbol-hunting might be played with the image of the bird and the name of the bird that is the occasion of a fleeting communication between this father and son. On the face of it, however, Paton, by his emphasis, has given this relationship the crucial place. He suggests that if some bond of emotion and interest had really united these two, in Pieter's boyhood, the tragedy would not have happened. The search for the phalerope, with its flash of grace, comes too late; ironically, it is after Pieter is already fatally entangled.

A bitter, buried core of hostility is the explosive charge in Pieter. It takes its shattering force from the thick, hard casing of the social environment which provides the containing pressure that makes all great explosions. The immediate fuse is the sexual strain with Nella.

But Pieter is confused in his sense of this. He pleads obliquely to Nella about the "safety" in her love.

. . . if you could love me more often, I'd be safe, I said. . . .
—Safe? Against what, Pieter?
—Against anything, my love. Against fear and danger. And the black moods.

I wanted to say against temptation, I wanted to say against the thing that tempts me, the thing I hate; I wanted to tell her every word, to strip myself naked before her, so that she could see the nature of the man she loved, with all his fears and torments, and be filled by it with such compassion as would heal and hold him for ever.

Tante Sophie is mistaken on this point, too. She remarks:

For have I not seen a score of times with my eyes, when men and women are denied, how they go seeking? Like a man who is robbed of a jewel, and goes seeking it amongst the dross and filth, and all men look on him with pity and contempt, not knowing of his distress.

The observation has truth in it, but is not as applicable to Pieter as he and she believe.

If it were simply consuming sexual hunger driving Pieter he could and would have found means to appease it, secretly and safely, within his own race. But "the thing that he hates," this "something that could bring no joy," is not only sexual, with the piquancy of a primitive, raw lust, it is also destruction and revenge. This is the one sure and deadly blow against his father, against Nella and his children, against Tante Sophie, and against the Afrikaner community. To this should be added—and against himself. These are his hates. He does not comprehend them; his real motivation is well below the level of his consciousness. He does not understand that he loves and hates at the same time.

Tante Sophie, interpreting him partly from his own journal, has him tormenting himself with the question, "What kind of man would destroy what he had created, and hurt what he had loved?" But this is the symbolic enigma of Euripides' *The Madness of Herakles*. It is the tortured refrain of Oscar Wilde, in "The Ballad of Reading Gaol":

For each man kills the thing he loves. . . .

In Wilde, the generalization is romantically, indulgently exaggerated and facile—but there is a seed of truth, and that seed is what sprouts in the heart of Pieter van Vlanderen.

His ambivalence toward Nella (and their children are, in this context, an extension of her) springs from frustration and confinement. Her gentleness exists within the communal harshness and is conditioned by it. At the beginning of the book, Pieter lets off with a warning the boy, Dick, who was pursuing that same Stephanie with whom Pieter is to become entangled. He warns the boy that conviction may be a year, two years—"But outside it's a sentence for life."

When Pieter confides the episode to Nella she says first,

. . . to think he was in this house.

Then:

. . . you forgave him.
—Yes.
—I'll not forgive him.

Pieter cannot reach her in complete unity, sexually, because of her deep-grained puritan conditioning, though she loves him and tries. But that is not a total impasse and is not enough to drive him to the black girl. The basic trouble is, he cannot communicate his whole nature to Nella as he desperately needs to do. For expressing and exploring his rebellion against the communal code, her softness is as impermeable as his father's hardness. Ironically, only to the cloying, smothering, self-tormenting Tante Sophie, whose love for him has more of a buried sexual tinge than she can bear to face, could Pieter have communicated his whole heart and mind. For while she is a disquieting and faintly repellent woman, she is nonetheless a remarkable one. There is one scene of cruel laceration between herself and Pieter when he lashes savagely at her smothering possessiveness, the quality that hopelessly nullifies the possibility of a saving communication between them. "In God's name, have you no pride?" She recoils into her shame "that a man should think me a woman to whom such words could be spoken."

Pieter is driven by rebellious resentment against a total community that confines him everywhere, and crowns the injury by idolizing him as an athlete. He is forced to be what they will have him be. Jacob is the archetypal figure of the community; in him, Pieter can focus both the communal and the filial resentments. In loving them all and hating them all, the one sure, irrevocable blow he can strike against them and his hated self, is the breaking of the racial-sexual taboo.

He is not sophisticated in matters of deep psychic cleavages. As the darkness and light struggle in him, he thinks only vaguely and remotely—and that too late—of going to Johannesburg, to "see one of those psychiatrists, who might tell him some secret of salvation. . . . " There is no priest who can help him, in this puritan church. So he looks among his learned books [Paton is disappointingly vague about *what* books]

that told all the sins and weaknesses of men, hoping to find himself . . . he read there of the misery of other men's lives, and the dark crimes and sins that they committed, and he did not know if they were sinning, or asking, and knocking at strange and terrible doors. And he found himself in a sad tormented company, and had pity for all twisted souls, and most for himself that found himself with them.

Inevitably, comparisons with *The Scarlet Letter* and *Crime and Punishment* arise. Once Pieter has committed his act, there is no possible release for him but total exposure—a dilemma he shares in part with Arthur Dimmesdale and Raskolnikov. Paton gives us a long sequence of superb suspense, arising out of guilty misunderstandings of innocent natural coincidences. But just as the death wish is commonly unconscious, so Pieter suffers an agonized dread of discovery, unconscious of the fact that it is that exposure and its consequences that have motivated him from the start.

This, it seems to me, is what Paton has wrought intuitively. It is not made wholly clear to any of the persons in the book and it is not possible to say how far it was present in Paton's conscious intention, but it is at least intuitively unerring in all the elements as presented.

Paton remains unswervingly honest in his resolutions. Jacob's implacable striking out of Pieter's name from the very book of life, and his embittered death, are the inevitable course of his nature. The savage lines of the 9th Psalm, that the old man reads in a ritual of casting off, are ambiguous, for in them he indicts the son, and we indict the father.

Tante Sophie goes keening down the wind. No easy claim is made for Nella's and Pieter's future. The sentence was for life, in the sense in which he had warned Dick. We know that Pieter and Nella could go away from that rigid country to start again, after he leaves prison, but we do not know that they will. We know that Nella could be changed by Pieter's secret journal, but we do not know if she will.

What we know concretely are a number of responses to the facts. Sergeant Steyn disappears, a necessary Judas somehow trapped in this role as his great prototype had been. The young policeman, Vorster, to whom Pieter had shown much kindness and who had hero-worshipped him, turns to rend him. Pieter's mother, as always, is mutely wounded, though loving. His sister withdraws from her betrothal in an access of shame. Kappie, the Jew, remains perceptively loyal, grieving that he could not have averted his friend's disaster. Nella's father is only a slightly less overpowering equivalent of Jacob.

The great responses, which bring the book to its final dimensions, are those of the English police captain and Tante Sophie. It is the captain who says to Sophie, in lines that touch the person, in Jacob, and also the community and the state:

> . . . an offender must be punished, *mejuffrou,* I don't argue about that. But to punish and not to restore, that is the greatest of all offenses.
> —Is that the sin against the Holy Ghost? I said.
> —I don't know, he said, but I hope not, for I once committed it.
> And I dared to say to him, was that your son?

—Yes, he said. Yes, it was my son. But I am resolved never again to commit it.

When Nella's father says fiercely that he would shoot Pieter like a dog, because "he has offended against the race," the captain replies:

> . . . as a policeman I know an offense against the law, and as a Christian I know an offense against God; but I do not know an offense against the race.

The tragedy is complete, with its full purgation through pity and terror. If something arises after it, for Pieter and Nella, that will be another story, as Dostoyevsky remarks of Raskolnikov's future at the end of *Crime and Punishment.*

Cry, the Beloved Country is tragic, but is not a tragedy in the formal literary sense, and it carries the clear affirmation of an element transcending the tragic view of life. This element is Christian, but it is not only in Christianity that such transcendence of tragedy is possible. That most tightly implacable of the Greek tragedies, *Oedipus Tyrannus,* is followed by the mystical transcendence of *Oedipus at Colonnus.* Again in a Christian frame, there are transcendent elements at the close of *The Brothers Karamazov* which would have come to flower in the projected further novel about Alyosha which Dostoyevsky did not live to write.

In *Cry, the Beloved Country* the primary story is pathetic, in that the suffering characters are more bewildered victims than prime movers in their difficulties. The tragic elements are social, and as always, complexly interlocked in cause and effect. The destruction of the soil, the breaking of the tribal system and the home, the tight segregation of South African society producing ghetto slums, the compound system in the mines, the provocative juxtaposition of the haves and the have-nots: these are the specific and local social factors working upon the general and universal human nature. The story is fiction, but Paton says in an Author's Note, "as a social record it is the plain and simple truth."

The shock effects of a cultural frontier are not unique to Africa. Interesting parallel elements can be seen in Oliver LaFarge's *Laughing Boy,* in terms of the American Indians. When any tribal system is shattered by the white man, but the tribal people are not taken into the white man's culture, deterioration and tragedy are inevitable. The African priest Msimangu, in Johannesburg, one of the compelling figures of the book, says,

> The tragedy is not that things are broken. The tragedy is that they are not mended again. The white man has broken the tribe. And it is my belief . . . that it cannot be mended again.

Cry, the Beloved Country is a splendid piece of craftsmanship, extraordinary as a first book by a man in middle life, whose work had been in education and penology. The most jaded reviewers were won by the fresh, individual lyricism of its style and the passion of its conviction and its thirst for justice. Paton's use of idioms and rhythms from Zulu, Bantu, Xosa and Afrikaans speech contributed greatly to the fresh effect. Now that his work is well known, and now that other writers have used these language patterns, Paton's style still has its personal stamp, and we must not let familiarity dull our recollection of its first invigorating impact.

The book is skillfully constructed in parallels. The simple African Anglican priest, Stephen Kumalo, loses his son, Absalom. The African-English farmer, James Jarvis, loses his son, Arthur. It is Absalom who kills Arthur, for which the state kills Absalom.

By the keenest of the ironies in which the book is rich, Arthur Jarvis was among the greatest friends of the black man, in the forefront of the struggle for justice. The senseless tragedy that links the two sons ultimately links the two fathers. There is no finer scene in a consistently moving book than that in which Stephen Kumalo and James Jarvis first come face to face, by chance, after the shooting, and realize one another's identities.

The ramifications of the story are comprehensive, showing the life of the tribal country and of the city. Through Stephen's journey to Johannesburg to search for his sister and his son, we see how that city, with its mine compounds and shantytown slums, swallows up people and breeds criminals. The quest involves a vivid tour of the native districts, and of the reformatory of which Paton himself had been superintendent. In interpolated meditations on the courts, and upon a new gold field, he deepens the social texture. Most adroit touch of all: the papers and speeches and books of the dead Arthur Jarvis are made the medium of direct polemical statement, and also of growth in the character of James Jarvis.

The father had not approved or understood his son's position on the race question. One could have imagined an implacable hardening on the issue after the tragedy, as would have been found in a temperament like Jacob van Vlanderen's: "I always told him he was a fool—and now one of the so-and-so's has shot him!" Instead, the grace that gradually works in James Jarvis is that of love, for he had loved the young man, even without comprehending him. When he is exposed to his son's papers, in the solitude of grief, he finds him for the first time and perceives that to repudiate his son's principles now will be truly to lose him utterly. By honoring and carrying forward his son's actions, something is retained that cannot be lost even in death. It is a measure both of the man, and of the remedial power of love. The new James Jarvis is "a man who put

his feet upon a road, and . . . no man would turn him from it."

Among the central threads of the book is the question of Stephen Kumalo's response to his son's guilt, as contrasted to the attitude of his politician-brother, John Kumalo, toward his own son's involvement as an accessory in the shooting.

John Kumalo, whose experience of the city has led him to cast off the faith, is solely concerned with evading punishment for his son and trouble for himself. He is aware that the boy was present, but is successful in obtaining his acquittal through perjury. In John's terms, he has been successful, but we expect that the last state will be worse than the first. The prospects are not bright for his son.

Stephen, on the other hand, faces a profound discovery. Once his son's guilt is established, it is impossible for him, as a Christian, to seek to evade punishment. His most urgent concern is for his son's repentance. He sees that Absalom, whose name, "his father's peace," is as ironic for Kumalo as it had been for King David, is more unhappy that he has been caught than for what he has done. To lead the boy to repentance becomes his first aim. For the Christian, ultimate welfare is not a question of the life or death of the body, but the life or death of the soul.

Repentance is validated by the acceptance of punishment. After the confessed guilt, after the accepted punishment, then mercy (in men's terms) may or may not be forthcoming. But mercy is not to be given on sentimental impulse. Mercy follows judgment; it does not precede it.

John Kumalo would save his son's life and does not believe in his soul. Stephen would be grateful for his son's life, but would not wish it bartered for his soul. At the end, there is hope for Absalom's repentance—though only God can judge of it.

Gertrude, Stephen's sister, whose degraded state had been the direct cause of Stephen's summons to Johannesburg, is lost. She has gone beyond her personal point of return. The effort of self-examination and rehabilitation is more than she can sustain. She slips away, just before the return of the little party of family survivors to the home village of Ndotsheni.

Yet there is salvage from the loss and pain. It is this that leads Paton beyond tragedy and that prompts the subtitle of the book: "A Story of Comfort in Desolation." If Absalom has repented, he has not lost both life and soul, as he had been in the way to do. Carried back to Ndotsheni (the account of their arrival is a magnificent lyrical passage), from the certainty of loss in Johannesburg to the possibility of new life, are Gertrude's son, Absalom's wife, and her unborn child. Stephen Kumalo and James Jarvis are enlarged in spirit, and from the spirit come works that promise the renewal of the land around Ndotsheni.

No voice out of South Africa has been so eloquent, so passionately just, with a social morality so deeply grounded in a religious premise. Granted Paton's fine gifts, his work also demonstrates the opportunity offered the writer in a place and time of acute moral and social crisis.

His books have flowed from humane indignation, anxiety, and the desire for reform. They are a patriot's books, for South Africa, in which he is so much a minority voice, is indeed, to him, the beloved country. What further work we may expect from him, who has given us so much in the two novels, depends partly on events in South Africa. Both novels were written outside the country, for he has found the internal pressure and involvement too great for sustained work there. Yet these were the fruit of separate and relatively short absences, for he steadfastly refuses to become an expatriate.

At this present writing, his passport has been taken from him, following his brief visit to the United States in the fall of 1960, to accept an award from Freedom House. Until it is restored, he cannot leave the country without incurring exile. The volume of stories and sketches published in 1960 as *Tales from a Troubled Land* (in England, *Debbie Go Home*), reflects his problem of working in the midst of his direct political involvements, such as his post as president of the Liberal Party of South Africa.

These tales are interesting, sometimes moving. The best group is those which directly relate events during his administration of Diepkloof Reformatory. They show the appalling problems in the path of the native in Johannesburg. They would be worth reworking, with additional material, into a complete book about this extraordinary experience, whether presented as fiction or memoir. The most powerful and terrifying of the other stories, in which some of the force and cadence of the novels appears, is **"Life for a Life,"** which describes the events after the killing of an Afrikaner farmer. In sum, the stories have an importance because Alan Paton wrote them. They would not have made Alan Paton important as the novels did.

Thus one of the most intensely individual literary talents of our day stands perhaps temporarily silenced, in the strife-torn land that gave him his great themes. From his experience in the beloved country there may yet come other major works. There could always come personal tragedy. The measure of his books is that while distilling the essence of South Africa, they speak to many aspects of the condition of the whole world. He has struck universal notes, and the world outside his own land honors him for his art, his humanity, and his integrity. (pp. 83-101)

Edmund Fuller, "Alan Paton: Tragedy and Beyond," in his *Books with Men Behind Them*, Random House, 1962, pp. 83-101.

SOURCES FOR FURTHER STUDY

Breit, Harvey. "Alan Paton." In his *The Writer Observed*, pp. 89-93. New York: World Publishing Co., 1956.

Reprint of a 1949 interview with Paton.

Callan, Edward. *Alan Paton*. Rev. ed. Twayne's World Author Series, edited by Bernth Lindfors, no. 40. Boston: Twayne Publishers, 1982, 143.

Critical and biographical study.

———. *Cry, the Beloved Country: A Novel of South Africa.* Twayne's Masterwork Studies, no. 69. Boston: Twayne Publishers, 1991, 127 p.

Critical study focusing on Paton's most famous novel.

Matlaw, Myron. "Alan Paton's *Cry, the Beloved Country* and Maxwell Anderson's/Kurt Weill's *Lost in the Stars:* A Consideration of Genres." *Arcadia* 10, No. 3 (1975): 260-72.

Discusses the adaptation of Paton's novel into the theatrical production *Lost in the Stars*.

Prescott, Orville. "Four Great Novels." In his *In My Opinion*, pp. 235-48. New York: Bobbs-Merrill Co., 1952.

Identifies *Cry, the Beloved Country* as one of four great recent novels.

Tucker, Martin. *Africa in Modern Literature: A Survey of Contemporary Writing in English*, pp. 223ff. New York: Frederick Ungar Publishing Co., 1967.

Briefly discusses suffering and forgiveness in *Cry, the Beloved Country* and *Too Late the Phalarope*.

Octavio Paz

1914-

Mexican poet, essayist, critic, nonfiction writer, dramatist, editor, journalist, and translator.

INTRODUCTION

*P*az has earned international acclaim for poetry and essays in which he seeks to reconcile divisive and opposing forces in life. Paz's writings accommodate such antithetical elements as culture and nature, the meditative and the sensuous, and the linear and the circular nature of time, stressing that language and love can provide means for attaining unity and wholeness. His works reflect his knowledge of the history, myths, and landscape of Mexico as well as his interest in surrealism, existentialism, romanticism, Eastern thought, and diverse political ideologies. In his verse, Paz experiments with form and strives for clarity and directness as well as vitality and vivacity. He stated: "Wouldn't it be better to turn life into poetry rather than to make poetry from life? And cannot poetry have as its primary objective, rather than the creation of poems, the creation of poetic moments?" Paz's essays are praised for their lyrical prose, witty epigrams, and insightful explorations of art, literature, culture, language, and political philosophies. The first Mexican to receive the Nobel Prize in Literature, Paz was commended by the Swedish Academy in 1990 "for impassioned writing with wide horizons, characterized by sensuous intelligence and humanistic integrity."

Paz was born in Mexico City. His mother's family had emigrated to Mexico from Spain and his father's ancestors traced their heritage to early Mexican settlers and indigenous peoples. Paz's paternal grandfather was a journalist and political activist and his father was an attorney who joined Emiliano Zapata's agrarian revolution in the early 1900s. During the Mexican Civil War, Paz's family lost their home and relocated to a nearby suburb of Mexico City where they lived under financially unstable conditions. Nonetheless, Paz received his secondary education at a French school administered by Marist priests and later attended the National University of Mexico. While in his late teens, he founded *Barrandal,* an avant-garde journal, and published his first volume of poems, *Luna silvestre* (1933). In 1937, he traveled to Spain and participated in several antifascist movements before moving on to France. In Paris, he became interested in Surrealism, a highly influential literary and artistic movement dedicated to examining the irrational, paranormal, and subconscious aspects of the human mind. After returning to Mexico in 1938, Paz founded and edited several literary and political periodicals and wrote newspaper columns on international affairs. In 1944, he traveled extensively in the United States, where he became influenced by the formal experiments of such modernist poets as William Carlos Williams and Wallace Stevens.

Paz joined the Mexican diplomatic service in 1955 and was assigned to the Mexican embassy in Paris. While in France, he became reacquainted with the aesthetics of Surrealism and the philosophy of existentialism, eventually favoring what he termed "the vital attitude" of Surrealism. During the 1950s, Paz's reputation as a major literary figure was secured with the publication of the nonfiction work *El laberinto de la soledad* (1950; *The Labyrinth of Solitude*) and *Piedra de sol* (1957; *Sun Stone*), a long poem generally considered his finest achievement in verse. Paz was named ambassador to India in 1962 and served in this position until 1968, when he resigned in protest following the killings of student demonstrators in Mexico City by government forces. Since relinquishing his ambassadorship, Paz has traveled extensively while continuing his literary career.

In his early verse, Paz experimented with such diverse forms as the sonnet and free verse, reflecting his desire to renew and clarify Spanish language by lyrically evoking images and impressions. In many of these poems, Paz employs the surrealist technique of developing a series of related or unrelated images to emphasize sudden moments of perception, a particular emotional state, or a fusion of such polarities as dream and reality, life and death. According to Paz, Surrealism is a "negation of the contemporary world and at the same time an attempt to substitute other values for those of democratic bourgeois society: eroticism, poetry, imagination, liberty, spiritual adventure, vision." Topics of Paz's formative verse include political and social issues, the brutality of war, and eroticism and love. *Aguila o sol?* (1951; *Eagle or Sun?*), one of his most important early volumes, is a sequence of visionary prose poems concerning the past, present, and future of Mexico. *Selected Poems,* published in 1963, and *Early Poems: 1935-1955* (1973) contain representative compositions in Spanish and in English translation.

Critics frequently note that *Sun Stone,* which adheres to the arrangement of the Aztec calendar, initiates a more radical phase of experimentation in Paz's

career. Comprising 584 eleven-syllable lines that form a circular sentence, this poem blends myth, cosmology, social commentary, and personal and historical references in a phantasmagoric presentation of images and allusions to project the psychological processes by which an individual attempts to make sense of existence. Sven Birkerts noted: "*Sun Stone* is, like so many of Paz's longer poems, a lyrically discursive exploration of time and memory, of erotic love, of art and writing, of myth and mysticism." The variety of forms and topics in Paz's later poems mirror his diverse interests. *Blanco* (1967), widely considered his most complex work, consists of three columns of verse arranged in a chapbook format that folds out into a long single page. Each column develops four main themes relating to language, nature, and the means by which an individual analyzes and orders life. In *Ladera este: 1962-1968* (1968), Paz blends simple diction and complicated syntax to create poems that investigate Oriental philosophy, religion, and art. In his long poem *Pasado en claro* (1975; *A Draft of Shadows*), Paz examines selfhood and memory by focusing on poignant personal moments in the manner of William Wordsworth's autobiographical poem *The Prelude. Vuelta* (1975) collects topical verse that Paz wrote after resigning from his ambassadorship and *The Collected Poems of Octavio Paz, 1957-1987* (1988) reprints poems in Spanish and in English translation from the latter phase of his career. A recent volume, *Arbol adentro* (1988), includes a sequence of highly descriptive poems devoted to such Surrealist painters as Marcel Duchamp and Joan Miró.

Paz's numerous essays on culture, art, politics, and language are collected in several volumes. *The Labyrinth of Solitude,* in which Paz explores Mexican history, mythology, and social behavior, is his most famous prose work. According to Paz, modern Mexico and its people suffer a collective identity crisis resulting from their mixed Indian and Spanish heritage, marginal association with Western cultural traditions, the influence of the United States, and a recurring cycle of war and isolation. While critics debated Paz's contention that this description also symbolizes the modern human condition, *The Labyrinth of Solitude* received widespread praise. Irving Howe commented: "This book roams through the phases of Mexican past and present seeking to define the outrages, violation and defeats that have left the Mexican personality fixed into a social mask of passive hauteur. . . . At once brilliant and sad, *The Labyrinth of Solitude* constitutes an elegy for a people martyred, perhaps destroyed by history. It is a central text of our time." Several of Paz's other nonfiction works concern linguistics, literary theory, and literary history, including *Corriente alterna* (1967; *Alternating Current*), *El mono gramático* (1972; *The Monkey Grammarian*), and *Los hijos del limo: Del ro-*

manticismo a la vanguardia (1974; *Children of the Mire: Modern Poetry from Romanticism to the Avant-Garde.*)

(For further information about Paz's life and works, see *Contemporary Authors*, Vols. 73-76; *Contemporary Literary Criticism*, Vols. 3, 4, 6, 10, 19, 51; and *Poetry Criticism*, Vol. 1.)

CRITICAL COMMENTARY

J. M. COHEN
(essay date 1966)

[In the following excerpt, Cohen surveys Paz's early verse.]

The first poet to draw together the Spanish and the Náhuatl strands of Mexican poetry has been Octavio Paz who has come to his task by way of a persistent questioning of all reality. 'Paz seems to have set out in search of the most desperate experience in order to emerge from it with at least a grain of hope', wrote the critic Ramón Xirau. Certainly Paz's early poetry is of violence and disbelief. Technically the influences upon him were both social and surrealist; he witnessed the defeat of the Spanish Republic, and shared with Aleixandre and Neruda the emotional rediscovery of man's physical kinship with nature. But unlike them he came through to no positive values. Paz's early poetry is so negative that it questions both the poet's own existence and the validity of the poetic act. But the solitude that he finds at the heart of every activity rouses in him a glimmer of expectation. Paz's search is in essence religious. In one of his few purely social poems, his **"Elegy for a friend killed in the civil war"**, he states that we stand at the opening of a new epoch in the world:

> You died, comrade,
> at the burning dawn of the world.
> You died when your world
> and ours was scarcely dawning.

This is partially a political statement; Paz has always supposed that a new political organisation was a necessary prelude to the spiritual change that has been the true subject of his poetry. Like Neruda, he was, in his early writing, necessarily on the side of death, but all the time in search of some power with which to counterbalance it. He moved towards participation, but was driven back into solitude by lack of belief in his own existence. . . . (pp. 228-29)

Against this despair only one force could be set, the moment of experience outside time, which is the subject of Eliot's *Four Quartets*. But Paz's escape from his

Waste Land was far from complete. Theoretically he had accepted a religious attitude: expectation began to outweigh despair. Yet the experience itself never took clear shape; or rather many experiences masqueraded as the true one; vision and hallucination remained indistinguishable, and Freud, the Marquis de Sade, Rimbaud, André Breton and the Masters of Zen Buddhism were all accepted on a par as prophets of the new certainty that could be born out of utter negation. In the poem **"La poesía" ("Poetry")** the dilemma is stated:

> Opposing images cloud my eyes,
> and other images
> from a greater depth deny these,
> like a burning babble,
> waters that a more secret and heavier water drowns.

The poet is describing the processes prior to the composition of his poem. This is a situation in which he finds himself unreal; only the poem, rising from a depth at which

> Tranquillity and movement are the same. . . .

triumphs over all contradictions and by its existence proves to the poet that he too exists. . . . (p. 229)

Yet in the next verse, the poem too is described as a dream, a dream in which there is both violence and movement. Paz is in fact most in love with the world at the moment when it seems about to slip away into abstraction. The moment of creation is for him a moment of intense living. The parallel is with the harsh imagery of Aleixandre's early poetry. But where Aleixandre moves in a direct line from solitude to participation, Paz, in three most important poems, sets out to reconcile the two opposites, solitude and utterance. The first is the principal piece in the book *Libertad bajo palabra* (*Liberty behind the Words*), a vision set in 1948, and entitled **"Himno entre ruinas" ("Hymn among the ruins")**. Here there is an alternation between stanzas of vision and stanzas of comment. The vision is at first abstract, of colour, sea and stone, but it is succeeded by an evocation of contemporary Mexico. Boys are smoking marihuana on top of an Aztec

Principal Works

Luna silvestre (poetry) 1933

Raiz del hombre (poetry) 1937

Bajo tu clara sombra (poetry) 1941

A la orilla del mundo y Primer dia: Bajo tu clara sombra, Raiz del hombre, Noche de resurrecciones (poetry) 1942

Libertad abjo palabra (poetry) 1949

El laberinto de la soledad (nonfiction) 1950

   [The Labyrinth of Solitude, 1961]

Aguila o sol? (poetry) 1951

   [Aquila o sol? Eagle or Sun?, 1970]

Semillas para un himno (poetry) 1954

El arco y la lire: El poema, la revelación, poetica, poesia, e historia (criticism) 1956

   [The Bow and the Lyre: The Poem, the Poetic Revelation, Poetry, and History, 1973]

Piedra del sol (poetry) 1957

   [Sun Stone, 1963]

La estacion violenta (poetry) 1958

Agua y viento (poetry) 1959

Salamandra, 1958-1961 (poetry) 1962

Selected Poems (poetry) 1963

Blanco (poetry) 1967

Corriente alterna (essays) 1967

   [Alternating Current, 1973]

Ladera este: 1962-1968 (poetry) 1968

La centana: Poemas, 1935-1968 (poetry) 1969

Conjunciones y disjunciones (nonfiction) 1969

[Conjunctions and Disjunctions, 1973]

Posdata (nonfiction) 1970

   [The Other Mexico: Critique of the Pyramid, 1972]

Configurations (poetry) 1971

Renga: Un Poema (poetry) 1972

Le singe grammairien (nonfiction) 1972

   [published in Mexico as El mono grámatico, 1974; The Monkey Grammarian, 1981]

Early Poems: 1935-1955 (poetry) 1973

Los hijos del limo: Del romanticismo a la vanguardia (criticism) 1974

   [Children of the Mire: Modern Poetry from Romanticism to Avant-Garde, 1974]

Pasado en claro (poetry) 1975

Vuelta (poetry) 1975

Poemas, 1935-1975 (poetry) 1979

Selected Poems (poetry) 1984

Tiempo nublado (essays) 1984

   [One Earth, Four or Five Worlds: Reflections on Contemporary History, 1985]

On Poets and Others (essays) 1986

Convergences: Essays on Art and Literature (essays) 1987

Arbol adentro (poetry) 1988

The Collected Poems of Octavio Paz, 1957-1987 (poetry) 1988

---

pyramid. Then in the third verse, the vision becomes more sensual; eyes and hands confirm and expand the message of the inner eye. But actuality again breaks in with a 'waste land' picture of Europe in ruins, and the rich consuming the poor. (p. 230)

The poet's thoughts divide, start again and lose motion. 'Must everything end in a spatter of stagnant water?' he asks. But the last stanza triumphantly proclaims that the poem begins where thinking stops; the solitary broodings of the early work are transcended; the minute becomes rich as the commenting mind sinks into peace:

Intellect finally incarnates in forms,
the two hostile halves are reconcile,
and the conscience-mirror liquifies,
becomes once more a fountain, a source of stories:
man a tree of images,
words that are flowers, that are fruit, that are deeds.

The title poem of a small collection of lyrics *Semillas para un himno* (*Seeds for a hymn*) which he pub-

lished five years later, returns to the theme of the moment overflowing with all time in a manner somewhat reminiscent of Eliot. . . . (p. 231)

"Piedra de sol" ("Sunstone"), the outstanding poem in his next volume, *La estación violenta* (*The season of violence*) of 1958, is the most sustained piece that Paz has so far attempted. It is a hymn to the planet Venus in her two aspects as morning and evening star and, by Náhuatl symbolism, as sun and water. It is at the same time a hymn to sexual love as the supreme form of communion between creatures who are otherwise no more than shadows with no true experience of their own lives. . . . (pp. 231-32)

With the exception of T. S. Eliot, Octavio Paz is the only contemporary poet capable of feeling his metaphysics, and calling them to life. **"Piedra de sol"** is a closely organised poem, composed of precisely one line for each of the 584 days of the revolution of Venus. It is woven of two strands, that of memory and that of vision. For Paz calls up scenes of the past in which love has made life real—in particular a moment during the siege of Madrid in which two lovers embrace to 'defend their portion of eternity, their ration of time and paradise' in face of the Fascist bombardment. The conclusion of the poem, though philosophically more completely worked out, is similar in feeling to the conclusion of **"Himno entre ruinas",** an affirmation of birth and light in contrast to the perpetual presence of death and shadow. In time all is dark, out of time lies the moment of communion, the sudden striking of the sun's light on the waters, Eliot's 'still point of the turning world'. One is carried back to the primal imagery of the first chapter of *Genesis.*

> open your hand
> lady of seeds that are days,
> the day is immortal, it ascends, grows,
> ends by being born and never ends,
> each day is a birth, a birth
> is every dawn and I am rising,
> we all rise,
> the sun rises with its sun face, John rises
> with his John face, with his everyone's face.
> Gateway to being, awake me, dawn,
> and let me see the countenance of this day.

The male principle celebrates the female principle, night hymns day, and the poet performs his magical act in calling up shapes from the inchoate, light out of darkness. This poem of 1957, one of the last important poems to be published in the western world, marks a culminating stage in Paz's development. His next collection, *Salamandra* (1962), continues to explore metaphysical problems of time and reality, but in a more lyrical and traditional manner. Some of the love-poems are as simple as Eluard's; an occasional landscape resolves into the essential lines of a Chinese painting on silk. Yet in his last poem, *Viento entero (Intact wind)* of 1965, he once more considers the 'eternal present" of a land—Afghanistan in which he was travelling—and of human history. (pp. 232-33)

J. M. Cohen, "Virgin Soil," in his *Poetry of This Age: 1908-1965,* revised edition, Hutchinson University Library, 1966, pp. 205-34.

OCTAVIO PAZ WITH ROBERTO GONZÁLEZ ECHEVARRÍA AND EMIR RODRÍGUEZ MONEGAL

(interview date 1972)

[In the following interview, Paz discusses his theory of modern poetry.]

[Roberto González Echevarría]: *Could we begin by talking about your* **Piedra de sol** *and* The Waste Land?

[Octavio Paz]: I don't see any relationship between them. The form is different, the vocabulary is different, the images, the vision of the world, the structure—everything is different. *Piedra de sol* is a linear poem that ceaselessly turns back upon itself, it is a circle or rather a spiral. *The Waste Land* is much more complex. It has been said that it is a *collage,* but I would say that it is an *assemblage de pièces détachées.* An extraordinary verbal machine that sends forth poetic significations by means of the rotation and the friction of one part against another and of the whole with the reader. No, I prefer *The Waste Land* to *Piedra de sol,* frankly. If one wants to compare something of mine with *The Waste Land*—but I see neither the reason nor the necessity for the comparison—it seems to me that one would have to think of **"Homenaje y profanaciones," "Salamandra," "Viento entero"** or *Blanco.* At the same time, all those poems say something very different from what Eliot's poems say. . . .

[Emir Rodríguez Monegal]: *Why don't you tell us how you came to know Eliot?*

His poetry. I never knew the man. Eliot's poetry became known very early, relatively speaking, in Mexico. Until the thirties he was a poet almost entirely unknown in Spanish. Juan Ramón Jiménez had published, at the beginning of the thirties, some translations of Eliot's short poems, such as "Marine." They were all in prose, if I remember correctly. The first translation of *The Waste Land* was done by a Mexican poet, Enrique Munjía, and it was published in the magazine *Contemporáneos* in 1931 or 1932. . . . He also did some translations of Valéry. Shortly afterward, Angel Flores' translation came out, one which is very superior to Munjía's, don't you think? At the end of that decade and in the first years of the forties, Eliot was a great influence in Mexico and several translations of his poems were published.

[RGE]: *In Cuba, translations also appeared in the magazine* Orígenes, *where you also published some poems.*

They came later. Let me sketch some history. The Mexican poets of the generation preceding mine, like the majority of Latin Americans, were immersed in French poetry. Nevertheless, around 1920 an interest in North American poetry sprang up in Mexico. . . . Salvador Novo published an *Anthology of Young North-American Poetry* in those years. In the following decade, beginning with the Flores translation of *The Waste Land,* Eliot came into vogue in the Spanish-speaking world. In Mexico the poet Ortiz de Montellano translated—and very well—several poems of the intermediate period, such as "Ash-Wednesday." Octavio Barreda also did some excellent translations. And there is a very good one by Rodolfo Usigli of "The Love Song of J. Alfred Prufrock." It's a memorable translation, the product of an affinity. Not because Usigli resembled Eliot but rather Prufrock. All these Mexican translations are a bit earlier than those of *Orígenes.* (p. 35)

[ERM]: *I would like to go back to* **Piedra de sol.** *How do you see it, since you say it bears no relationship to* The Waste Land?

No, it has nothing to do with Eliot. It is another world, another vision of the world. The word *pleasure* is one of the axes of *Piedra de sol.* A word that doesn't exist in Eliot's poetry. Even the word *death* has a meaning, a *flavor,* which is very different. And the word *rebellion.*

[RGE]: *I hesitate to bring up this topic, but in that very negative review which Bly wrote about* **Configurations,** *he seemed to have in mind a connection between you and Eliot the academic poet.*

I have very little to say about Bly, and even that is negative, so I prefer to say nothing. It is not a problem of intellectual, political, or literary differences, or even one of sensitivity—it is an *affaire* of hygiene. After pronouncing certain names it is necessary to wash out one's mouth. Apart from this reason of an *olfactory* order, as Duchamp would say, it seems to me that Bly does not have the authority to speak about Latin American poetry. And I suspect that he is likewise unqualified to talk about poetry in his own language.

[ERM]: *Bly's note was so absurd because it ignored an entire form of poetry, let's say, from Mallarmé, Pound and Eliot onward.*

Yes, he had previously attacked Pound, Wallace Stevens, Eliot, and how many others . . . Bly's name leads me to touch on another more important topic. Bly speaks of a "Spanish Surrealism," and he thus repeats a widespread error. Stefant Baciu put things in their proper place in the essay which he published some years ago in *Cahiers Dada.* It is necessary to begin by saying that there is only *one* surrealist movement, so that it is absurd to talk about various Surrealisms, be they Spanish, French, Chilean, or Egyptian. Surrealism was an international movement that extended over almost the entire world. Breton always emphasized the international character of Surrealism. It is true that in the field of literature—the case of painting is different— the manifestations of Surrealism were particularly important in the French language, although there were also Surrealist poets in other languages and other countries. . . . All those poets and artists *belonged—in effect— to the Surrealist movement;* they established relations with other Surrealist groups, especially with the French, and carried out a Surrealist program, in the true sense of the word. There was, in addition, a different phenomenon: the existence, in many places and many languages, of poets *influenced* by Surrealism. In our language, Surrealism influenced and branded perhaps the best period of the poetry of García Lorca, Cernuda, Aleixandre, Neruda, and Alberti. But none of them can rightfully claim

to be a Surrealist poet. They do not appear in any anthology of the Surrealists and it is possible that they themselves would not be pleased to be so called.

[RGE]: *And so?*

And so it is nonsense to speak of two Surrealisms: one, the French, which would be intellectual, florid, speculative, decadent, literary; and another, the Hispanic, that would be terrestrial—mundane, telluric, virile, sexual. . . . This is comical. It is a literary "machismo"—which, like all machismos, is hardly virile. It is certain that there were poets of the Spanish language who were influenced by the French Surrealists, but the inverse is not true. This does not imply a negation of the contribution of Spaniards or Hispanoamericans to Surrealism. Their contribution was great, and André Breton frequently acknowledged it. . . . Among the Hispano-americans, one would have to cite the painters Matta, Lam y Gerzo, and several poets: the Peruvians César Moro and Adolfo Westphalen; the Chileans Braulio Arenas, Gómez-Correa, and Cáceres; the Argentinians Enrique Molina and Aldo Pellegrini; and one Mexican. . . .

[RGE]: *Octavio Paz?*

Precisely.

[RGE]: *Then you consider yourself a Surrealist?*

I was a Surrealist at a certain moment in my life, as were Buñuel, Moro, Lam and so many others of our language. I try not to be unfaithful to that moment. In the *Anthology of Surrealist Poetry* of Jean Louis Bedouin— which is, one might say, the "official" anthology of Surrealism—several Hispanic figures appear: Picasso, Picabia, Dali, César Moro, Arrabal and myself. In fact, Bedouin has written a history of the Surrealist movement *after* 1939 that completes Maurice Nadeau's book. Bedouin's book takes apart another critical prejudice, which insists on bringing Surrealism to its conclusion in 1939, with the beginning of the Second World War. That's absurd, isn't it? During the war, and in the Forties, Breton wrote two of his best works: "Arcane 17" and the *Ode à Fourier.* Shortly afterward Benjamin Péret wrote his greatest poem: "Air mexicain." After the war, a great poet entered the surrealist group: Aimé Césaire. Julien Gracq, André Pieyre de Mandiargues, and a poet of Lebanese origin whom Breton admired and whom Saint-John Perse considered to be one of the best contemporary French poets, Georges Schehadé, also joined the movement.

[RGE]: *But wasn't the period of the post-war dominated by existentialism?*

Yes, it is true that the post-war was dominated by existentialism, but that ideological movement was of an extraordinary artistic and poetic indigence. Who today can read the novels or the theater of Sartre? The *littérature engagée* tried to be historical but it grew old before history itself. . . . What remains is Beckett,

Genet, some texts of Camus, and especially the work of several poets closely linked with Surrealism: Michaux, Char, Ponge. No, it is not true that Surrealism was dead in 1939. In Latin America it had a great influence after the war. (pp. 36-7)

[RGE]: *I would like to discuss "Homenaje y profanaciones," that poem in* **Salamandra** *which is a kind of gloss of the celebrated sonnet of Quevedo, "Amor constante más allá de la muerte." Which of the Baroque poets have influenced you most?*

I think there are three: Góngora, Quevedo, and Sor Juana. When I wrote that poem I was a true believer in the poetry of Quevedo. Now I like him less.

[RGE]: *And that sonnet in particular?*

It is admirable as a perfect rhetorical machine. Although its theme is love, it is not an impassioned poem, but rather a poem whose theme is passion. It is the baroque culmination of Petrarchism, with its affirmation of the eternity of love: love is eternal because the soul is eternal. But bodies aren't eternal. Modern passion is not an eternity in time, but rather in *this* time. It is not *ex*tensive, but *in*tensive. It is corporeal. For that reason, my poem is an homage and a profanation—a mockery in the same vein in which Picasso repainted *Las meninas*—a mockery and a veneration. My poem is a sonnet of sonnets. It is divided into three parts. The first sonnet represents the first quartet, the second, the second quartet, and the third, divided into two parts, represents the tercets. There is in each part, in addition, another sonnet. Just like the image of a mirror in a mirror: sonnets of sonnets of sonnets. But free sonnets and, finally, hardly sonnet-like. Praise and profanation. The whole composition is governed by a numerical proportion that would be very tedious to explain. Suffice it to say that it is the projection of a sonnet and its parts.

[RGE]: **Piedra de sol** *is also based on a numerical structure, isn't it?*

The number of verses of *Piedra de sol* is exactly the number of days in the revolution of the planet Venus. The conjunction of Venus and the sun is realized after a circular course of 584 days, and that of the poem with itself, after 584 verses. Venus is a double planet: Vesper and Lucifer. In pre-Columbian Mexico there was Quetzalcoatl: celestial body, bird, and serpent at the same time. The text unfolds within this mythical-astronomical framework. That is to say, the unique history of one man, who belongs to a generation, a country and an epoch, is inserted into the circular time of the myth.

[RGE]: *Unique?*

Time perhaps is cyclical and thus immortal. Such, at least, is the time of myths and poems: it turns back over upon itself, it repeats itself. But man is finite and is not repeated. That which indeed repeats itself is the experience of finiteness: all men know that they are going to die. They know it, they feel it, they dream it,

and they die. The same thing happens with the other basic human experiences: love, desire, work. These experiences *are* historical: they happen to us, and they pass. At the same time, they are *not* historical: they are repeated. For that reason, poems can be written about these experiences. Poems are machines that produce time and that continually return to their origin: they are anti-historical mechanisms. On the other hand, poems cannot be made from ideas, opinions and other purely historical experiences of man. That was the error of *engagée* literature several years ago, in its existentialist and Communist branches. That is the paradox of our condition: our fundamental experiences are almost always instantaneous, but they are not historical. Our experiences are not historical, but we are. Each one of us is unique but the experiences of death or love are universal and are repeated. Poetry is born of this contradiction. In fact, it is made out of this contradiction.

[RGE]: *Isn't that the central theme of* **Blanco?**

That is the theme of all poems and all poets.

[RGE]: *Would you care to tell us, in conclusion, something more specific about* **Blanco?**

Well, it's terrible (and also tempting) to speak about what one has written. But I will allow you that pleasure, as bittersweet as it may be to me. In *Blanco* the combinations are not temporal but rather spatial. The poem is constructed from diverse parts, like a crossword puzzle. The reader can associate or dissociate the parts; there are more than twenty possibilities. Each part is in itself a poem and each association or dissociation yields a text. Thus, unlike a crossword puzzle which has only one solution and one figure, *Blanco* has more than twenty figures, more than twenty texts. Each text is different and they all say the same thing. The extreme flexibility of *Blanco* is resolved in rigidity. Quite the contrary of *Piedra de sol,* which is a linear poem that flows continuously. *Blanco* tends to crystallize, that is, to convert itself into a mere verbal transparency, and then, to dissolve. That's why it's called *Blanco.* It is the negation of *Piedra de sol* since, in a certain way, it negates time; only the present exists. That present is its presence: the feminine body seen, touched, smelled, and felt like a landscape; and both, the earth and the woman, gathered up and read like a text, heard and pronounced like a poem. *Blanco* is a verbal body; a body that reveals itself and, upon doing so, passes out of sight. That, at least, is what I wanted it to be. (pp. 39-40)

Octavio Paz with Roberto González Echevarría and Emir Rodríguez Monegal, in an interview translated by Rolena Adorno, in *Diacritics*, Vol. II, No. 3, Fall, 1972, pp. 35-40.

CLAUDE ESTEBAN

(essay date 1980)

[The essay excerpted below is from a translation of "De la poésie comme insurrection," Esteban's introduction to the French edition of Paz's *Ladera este*.]

On the verge of each poem by Octavio Paz, in the first breath which gives birth to it, there is less the desire for an affirmation than the sudden awakening, as in the morning—the individual, mind and body, in an almost uncontrollable flight towards what is undefined, outside; towards what has neither place nor form nor figure; and will gain all this from a man and from his glance. What claims our attention, even beyond the magnificence of a word—from the first lines of *Luna silvestre* to the feverish overture of **"Petrificada petrificante,"** written some forty years later—is this refusal of the inevitable, this rebellion incited without end against the certainties already gained—yesterday's knowledge—and facing that knowledge, the dark wall, as if unbroached, of the world.

> I open my eyes
>   I am
> Still alive
>   At the center
> Of a wound still fresh

Others—and so near us—have invested the poetic enterprise with the value only of "restricted action," abandoning the world of the senses to its enigmas, to its wanderings, in order to save in the end, the joy of a few words set side by side. Octavio Paz has not heard these invitations—or, fervent reader of Mallarmé, he has not believed that the destiny of modern poetry should be wholly identified with the dark descent towards the tomb of Midnight in which Igitur's will was buried, and with his will the ambition of a word which could sustain Being. Isn't it still the poet's task to fight off the menacing hegemony of Signs, to keep the distance from growing too great between the vocables that summon reality and the little reality which remains to us? . . . It is true that the gods have left; that our symbols have grown old; that things have lost their native force, their substance; and those who question them, with their gestures, their words, have lost the power to restore their weight, their place, their presence at the heart of a universe which slips through their hands and where they themselves are at a loss for a footing. This ontological failure, pushed at times to the edge of the intolerable, is the only foundation on which Octavio

Paz will build those "wandering republics of sound and meaning" which constitute his poems. (pp. 83-4)

The word of poetry is made in the image of this earth, of this history which we live: sparse, ruined with emptiness, incomplete. If in so many poems by Octavio Paz we confront landscapes of flint and ash, shouldn't we hesitate to identify these landscapes with memories of a life and its travels? These high plateaus of broken stone, these deserts from the Orient or Mexico, represent in their cruel evidence something like the crystallization, at once metaphorical and tangible, of another abandonment that grips us at the edge of a world in so many ways *deserted*—a dead world, as we would say of a dead language, and one which offers our mental vision only "the signs of an alphabet in ruins." This is the birthplace of a poetry which knew itself from the beginning to be the approach, perhaps the sad apprehension of absence.

But that is also the end, for Octavio Paz, of what I will call the fascination with Mallarmé, if not of the discomfort which this fascination provokes. For the apprehension—even lucid—of a "default" in the world's being, the discovery of a metaphysical solitude lends itself to a nostalgia anchored in the deep memory, which we must relinquish each morning. (p. 84)

We know the significance which his meeting with that "important passerby" of our century, André Breton, held for Octavio Paz. Paz himself has confirmed all that his own questioning, his poetic and even his political choices, owed during those years to the healthy mutiny of the word rising against the artifices and conventions of the concept. I do not mean to minimize the importance of this rebellion; but I think it necessary to define the ways in which Paz's attitude differs from a poetics with which he sympathized, but which he did not embrace. Where surrealism finds a second certainty— the discursive capacity of the unconscious—and builds on this certainty a system of perception and representation of the psychic universe, Octavio Paz sees an ambiguous return to rationality, a new law of the relations between consciousness and appearance, in short a reassuring logic which he cannot fully accept. To define the *surreal* and to set its limits, to find a touchstone within oneself—wasn't this, for Western thought, yet another return to the old mandate of the *logos*, wasn't this to push farther from us what fails and fades before speech? Surrealism did not question the authenticity of the deep self, still less its seemingly innocent epiphany in the word. Descending step by step, venturing in the dark of himself, Octavio Paz did not find this kind, ceaseless murmur, but only more darkness, more silence and more danger than in the space of the visible. "There is nothing in me but a great wound." A wound through which the sap escapes, the substance of the world and of the self—and which it would be futile to disguise, resorting to some turning in on oneself. The *space within* has not yielded all its monsters. . . . And not everyone can force them up from the depths and, like Henri Michaux, seize and conjure them.

If the poetry of our time, as Paz has said, cannot on its own escape its isolation, poets owe it to themselves to fight, with all their strength, against a condition of moral isolation which compromises their desire for communication, which diminishes them, and which walls them into their own monologue. Throughout his great meditation on the poetic act, *El arco y la lira*, Octavio Paz reaffirms that "To be oneself, is to condemn oneself to mutilation, for humankind is the perpetual desire to be other." And still more explicitly in these phrases which question a certain egomania of contemporary poetry: "I aspire to Being, to the Being which changes, not to the salvation of the self." How far from this or that concern for individual salvation, the salvation which orients so many experiments today—intellectual, poetic, pictorial—experiments guided by an extravagant love of self. . . . And what a horizon stretches before the poem, what progress is promised to one who is no longer afraid to lose himself! I spoke earlier of the first impulse in Octavio Paz's writing, consubstantial with the poem's ascent, and which continues to set its direction. I will not distort the meaning of this impulse if I say that it represents a purgation—in the ascetic sense—of the passions, the subjective drives; the writer placing himself outside himself for the sake of what will be written through him. Octavio Paz has said again and again that poets are the ones who work "outside themselves." It is not that he exalts a delirium, or yields to the famous "derangement" (*dérèglement*) more or less concerted of all the senses which certain fragile disciples of Rimbaud have practiced, not to deliver themselves from this unhappy self, but to amplify it beyond measure and to better possess it. To wish himself "outside himself" is for Octavio Paz to refuse the limits which consciousness imposes, and more, to abandon all the refuges which our subjectivity, jealous of its quiet, does not cease to propose. It is finally and above all to respond to this vocation of *otherness* inherent in humankind, the prestige of its power which our fear disguises. (pp. 85-6)

Poetry—Octavio Paz tells us—is a movement *towards*, never a preestablished itinerary which could award itself the reassuring perspective of an *as far as*. And if the unappeased *I* of the poet aspires to become that *other* which Rimbaud dreamt, he cannot attain his dream except by that abandon of self and by the loss even of the memory of loss. Poetry is a bow aimed towards the improbable, but if it is not now for us to reach the target, still the arrow is new in our hands.

It is the presence of death which we find at the threshold of this journey undertaken by the thought and poetry of Octavio Paz. Moving and unmoving, solemn and furtive, death enters—as, always alive, it enters the flesh—the heart of the words which refuse it. Octavio Paz does not believe in the god who came with the ships from Europe, who claims to redeem, and complete what's left undone, save Being from its wound or from its blasphemy. But Paz reverses a dark force which rules us and which we must not oppose, but accept with open eyes. "The dead do not exist, only Death, our mother." We can feel sure that it is not a taste for the archaeological restoration of a culture, its religious imagery and its rituals which has led Paz to give the Aztecs' cosmology and their anthropological vision a privileged place in his thought and, from early in his career, in his poems. Christianity could not vanquish the old mysteries in Mexico any more than it could in Asia; unable to convert them, it could only give a name to the great terror of things. Octavio Paz has rejected the too simple assurances of Christianity in order to hear the lessons of the sacred Serpent. Quetzalcóatl does not fear death or despise it; death is not a place of despair or the physical sign of a punishment. He passes through death—in order to join the two aspects of being and to fuse them. He gives himself to secret liturgies of the sun; he offers life, in the guise of death. Octavio Paz has long contemplated this demiurge of astral and terrestrial revolutions: *Piedra de sol*, among other poems, bears the sign of the crowned and rampant god. Paz has done more than adhere to this highest figure among Mexican deities, figure which has in fact nourished his experience and his writing. I will leave it to the commentators to verify certain correspondences which seem obvious to me and which, moreover, Paz has discussed. I believe his return to the great drama of pre-Columbian consciousness has confirmed and comforted a feeling in him, an intimate experience of death, experience which has escaped the imperatives of a Christian ethic—as it has abandoned the form and the spirit of those Hispanic models which influenced the poet for a time. (pp. 87-8)

The poetry of Octavio Paz does not forsake the sensible world; nor does Paz take refuge in an imaginary or unreal world, evasions which so often represent the last subterfuge of a poetics chafing at its limits. It is the "creatures" nearest us, in the universe which surrounds us—a tree, an instant of rain, this insect crying in the underbrush—that claim Paz's attention and a keenness of perception more speculative than visual. For Paz, to see and to retain these few images is already to raise them beyond a purely spatial and temporal vision, to discern their tangible presence and at the same time to feel that they may change. "Things are the same, and other."

We can certainly hear an echo of Buddhist doctrine and something of the great teaching of the Tao. But what is in Oriental thought an ascent beyond the body, silence and plentitude beyond gestures and words, regains an active dimension in Paz's writing, which seems to generate energy—a dimension which the Orient has nearly always refused. Not that I wish to minimize their enterprise or claim that it is easy to attain the transcendence of contradictions which alone permits one, according to the Upanishads, to experience the beatific state of *ananda,* delight of the spirit in the breast of the One. But I think it as much of an adventure, for a consciousness which operates in the ambiguous space of language—and our Latin idioms more than others, with their play of mental mirrors . . . —yes, I judge that the adventure is at least as perilous for a Western poet to escape the dualist idea of the world and to reunite in words what remains separated in things. For me, this is Paz's essential ambition, and the surprisingly modern grandeur of his poetry. The critique of writing to which he has devoted himself does not lead, as so often in our poetry, to an ethics of suspicion, to the decor of signs which seek only to be persuaded of their futility and to deconstruct. Octavio Paz orients his search towards a less desolate horizon. If he distrusts the certainties of language, it is in order to reassert another power of which language has let itself be stripped—not to represent but to express the live flesh of things, to be of one substance with things, to rediscover itself, as in the first sun-filled morning, both word and presence. "Names seek a body." Words will no longer stay behind the glittering bars of abstractions. A world waits for them—only a mortal world, our world, but where a heart will beat again, where "We feel our lost unity beyond the invisible walls, the rotten masks which separate us from each other." Names seek a body—and the body, in its turn, seeks a name which will free it from the old fears of the self, from its silence.

It is love which allows us this glimpse of our lost unity—and which may restore it to us, if we consent. Not the love which sanctifies itself in its difference, but that which is incarnate in the embrace of two bodies. The poetry of Octavio Paz seeks to become a passionate celebration, a fervor and even at times a furor of Eros. Since the eclipse of the natural myths, we have too often confused erotic poetry with a licentious confession, with a verbal exaltation whose only motivation seemed the private satisfaction of a sensuality. Octavio Paz has returned to eroticism some of its panicked seriousness, the signs of its truth. For him, love is more than the desire which carries individuals outside themselves—and withdraws them briefly from their solitude; it is a rebirth of the other, and through the intermediary of these bodies joining, the hope of a fusion with the protean substance of the world. Paz's most beautiful erotic poems, **"Maithuna,"** *Blanco,* are also those in which the cosmic reality is revealed in all its transparence. As if by embracing a bare body, marrying its landscape, quenching its thirst, the reality of the world would become more tangible, its firmament fill

with light above us, the conjunction of male and female stars endure in a single flash of light. The distance which subsisted between the self and the other, between things and words, will now be effaced in the act of love—mingling and fusion of You and Me in We who are created indivisible. . . .

> The world is visible now in your body,
> Transparent in your transparence

In the new mythology generated by the poet, Eros is no longer the futile god of the legends, blind and blinding. He is once more the dazzled walker, the pilgrim hungering for the absolute—and in his steps, as once for Orpheus, the dark fails and the dead stones come alive. The world has found its center again—not determined by a despotic consciousness but by a will rising in each of us and which transcends us, "an unnamed pronoun" which is Eros' force becoming a poem. (pp. 90-2)

For Octavio Paz, the image is the unquestionable manifestation, at the climax of writing, of that eroticism which sets the entire universe in motion, which carries it off—live matter, heart and spirit—in a whirlwind of metamorphosis. What intrigues Paz's reader from the start, what will always fascinate us, is an explosion, a fertile exchange among forms and figures which seem to give birth to one another, to separate, rejoin, burst into a thousand suns of signs, into constellations of metaphors, into a stardust of metonymies. . . . But the image, as it is practiced here does not depend on an arbitrary proceeding of the intellect, any more than it leads to the caprices of an imaginary world. (p. 93)

Through images, the poetry of Octavio Paz approaches a *reconciliation*—the hope of all unitive philosophies—and not a problematic conciliation of opposites. He escapes in this way, and even at the level of language, the intolerance which has been the pride of Western thought, in which each conscious subject is confined within its domain, and perceives others only in the belligerent relations of supremacy or submission. By affirming that "things are the same and other," Octavio Paz not only blurs the categories we hold to—that was surrealism's objective—he captures the naturant energy of the universe in "cages of light where identity is annulled among likenesses, difference in contradictions." For Octavio Paz, the poem is an insurrection of the word against the conventions and the precarious equilibriums of the concept. More, it is the insurrection of sense against the repressive system of particular meanings. Faced with a rhetoric of reification, with ideologies of the beautiful totality, the poem rediscovers itself as *uprising,* at once rebellion and rebirth. Uprising of the sensible world, towards a transparence which is more than an intelligibility promised to the mind. Uprising of Being towards a *truth,* the truth of which Rimbaud spoke, present at last *in one body and soul.*

Poetry must now free itself, as much as possible, from its fascination with the figure of destruction in whom Mallarmé recognized a guardian angel, his Beatrice. . . . If poets have come to distrust, and not without reason, the capacity of language to recover a real and not a simulated presence, they must also fear that the conscience and conduct of negativity, taken to extremes, may be lost in mutism, or, more perniciously, may end in verbal terrorism, in a didactics of overabundance or of emptiness. Octavio Paz affirms that if poetry is first of all the cruel ordeal of separation, it must transcend this negative stage of the "Deus absconditus" and force itself, once more, to gather the sparse words of the real in a single phrase—always threatened, always to be born—of certainty. The poet refuses the dispersion of sensible phenomena which others have made a fatality. As Eros reunites the You and the Me in a single pronoun—a single presence—so the poem is a moment of fervor, an act of faith which will carry the poet "to the other side of night where I am you, where we are others." For words are that much more our own if, in the exchange with others, in their recognition, they can once more belong to everyone. The language of poetry cannot be reduced to an idiolect, to a system of signs which is indecipherable for those who do not hold the key. Poetry is, in the real sense of the term, the creation of a "common place," the affirmation of a shared word, the reassertion of an unbroken history. (pp. 94-5)

Claude Esteban, "Poetry as Insurrection," translated by Susanna Lang, in *Octavio Paz: Homage to the Poet,* edited by Kosrof Chantikian, Kosmos, 1980, pp. 83-95.

MANUEL DURÁN

(essay date 1982)

[Durán is a Spanish-born American critic who has written extensively on Mexican and Spanish literature. In the following excerpt, he discusses how Paz's concerns about language and identity are evident throughout his poetry and prose.]

The poet Derek Walcott remarked recently, "The greatest writers have been at heart parochial, provincial in their rootedness. . . . Shakespeare remains a War- wickshire country boy; Joyce a minor bourgeois from Dublin, Dante's love of Florence was very intense. Hardy's place, of course, was rural Essex: 'I can understand / Borges's blind love for Buenos Aires, / How a man feels the veins of his city swell in his head'." There are many books and poems by Paz that proclaim his rootedness, his intimacy with Mexican traditions, landscapes, people. Books like *The Labyrinth of Solitude,*

for instance, or *Posdata* could not have been written by anyone outside the mainstream of Mexican culture. No foreign observer could have given such books the impact and urgency they possess. Paz is not content with describing some of the deepest and most relevant aspects of Mexican psychology; he involves the reader in the system of values he describes because he is himself involved in it for better or for worse, inescapably. It is ancient Mexican culture with its circular patterns that molds a long poem such as *Sun Stone;* it is the experience of being an adolescent in and around Mexico City that imparts distinctive flavor to Paz's **"Nocturno de San Ildefonso."**

Yet very often at the conclusion of Paz's sustained efforts to explore his roots and the origins of his culture a change of mood and of ideas begins to emerge. From the poet's direct and intimate experience he leads us toward a deeper knowledge of what it is to be a Mexican living and working in the present century, within a culture as tragic and fragmented as it is rich and complex. But the poet's experience allows him to express also much that belongs to our experience. His exploration of Mexican existential values permits him to open a door to an understanding of other countries and other cultures. What began as a slow, almost microscopic examination of self and of a single cultural tradition widens unexpectedly, becoming universal without sacrificing its unique characteristic.

This is a special gift, a gift few poets possess. The inescapable conclusion is that Paz belongs to a select group of poets who can expand the limits of poetry until they invade the realm of philosophy. Paz is a poet-philosopher, a philosophical poet. Such a gift has never been widespread. Among the classics, for instance, Lucretius would qualify, but not Catullus. Dante was a philosophical poet, and so were Shakespeare and Milton, Donne and Eliot. In each of these instances we find a persistent exploration of nature, of the place of human beings in nature. What is our place in the cosmos? Are we, as we often think in our pride, the masters of nature, the almost perfect creation of a protecting and loving God? Are we intruders barely tolerated? Are we, as Shakespeare claims in a somber moment, no more to the gods than flies are to wanton children, flies which they kill as a pasttime? Or are we enveloped by the very same love which, as Dante explains, is the force that moves the Sun and the other stars? Philosophical poets may differ widely with respect to the answers they give to the riddles of life. What they have in common, however, is a mixture of curiosity and awe, and this is much more important than what separates them.

The philosopher-poet is always ready to travel with his mind and his body, through time and through space. Octavio Paz has traveled as widely as he has written, and as Anna Balakian has said, he "belongs to that new breed of humans, more numerous each day, who are freeing themselves of ethnic myopia and walking the earth as inhabitants of the planet, regardless of national origin or political preferences."

It is entirely possible that all human beings are born poets, born philosophers, born scientists, but that circumstances and a poor education shrink or atrophy the imagination and the curiosity that would sustain such activities. Fortunately for us, Paz was a poet and a curious observer since childhood and has managed to retain a child's heart and vision. A sense of being open to the world was among his childhood's more precious gifts. Paz has said about himself:

> As a boy I lived in a place called Mixcoac, near the capital. We lived in a large house with a garden. Our family had been impoverished by the revolution and the civil war. Our house, full of antique furniture, books, and other objects, was gradually crumbling to bits. As rooms collapsed we moved the furniture into another. I remember that for a long time I lived in a spacious room with part of one of the walls missing. Some magnificent screens protected me inadequately from wind and rain. A creeper invaded my room. . . . A premonition of that surrealist exhibition where there was a bed lying in a swamp.

I see in this room invaded by rain, wind and plants a symbol of the poet's career, always open to the wind coming from every direction of the compass, always exposed to the outside world and the forces of nature—a room quite the opposite of a fortress or an ivory tower. From this exposed vantage point the poet ventures forth. His goal is not only to see infinity in a grain of sand, as William Blake proposed, but at the same time to describe the texture and color of the grain of sand, to see its reflection in his eye—and ours.

Paz knows that human beings have many roots, not a single taproot, fibrous roots that connect them with many cultures, many pasts. The themes, meanings, images by which poetic imagination seeks to penetrate to the heart of reality—the permanence and mystery of human suffering, human hope, joy and wonder—reach the poet from many sources. The poet sees existence with the double vision of tragedy, the good and the evil forever mixed. He is constantly under strain, admitting dire realities and conscious of bleak possibilities. Yet he is aware that love, knowledge, art, poetry allow us to experience the unity and final identity of being.

Ultimately Paz as a poet is a master of language, yet one who recognizes that language is also our shaper and ruler. If the German philosopher Ernst Cassirer defined man as the animal who can create language and myths, we can also state that it is language, myths, poetry that have created man, that have made man into

Paz receiving the Cervantes Prize from King Juan Carlos of Spain, 1982.

a speaking, mythmaking, poetry-writing animal. It is through language that Paz faces the world, sees the world as a unity, confronts the diversities of culture and explains their apparent oppositions and contradictions, their conjunctions and disjunctions, as different responses to the same identical questions. To understand is to see correspondences and patterns, structures of symmetry and dissymmetry, constellations of signs in space and time—yet anything can be expressed and related through words. In Paz's many-splendored vision the poet is capable of flying through space and time, because like the magical monkey of Hindu legend, Hanumān, he has invented grammar and language.

From above, in his vertical flight, drunk with light and with love, the poet contemplates the fusion of opposites, the marriage of Heaven and Hell, the radiance of the void, the dark luminosity where life and death meet. The movements of planets, the patterns of seasons and nature, are circular, yet the circle becomes a spiral pointing toward vaster spaces where everything becomes possible, where I become the Other, where the labyrinth of mirrors fuses into a single blinding light. We learn to say "no" and "yes" at the same time, because through poetry we reach the certain knowledge that Becoming and Being are two facets of the same reality. As Paz describes it, "The spirit / Is an invention of the body / The body / An invention of the world / The world / An invention of the spirit" (*Blanco*). Within this is language, poetic language, the language of myths and of passion that has made us what we are. Language is a huge shuttle going back and forth, weaving our world, and the poet is at the center of this operation. "By passion the world is bound, by passion too it is released," reads the epigraph from Buddhist tradition (*The Hevajra Tantra*) that frames what is perhaps Paz's most famous poem, *Blanco*. As a poet, Paz is the master of words. Words of passion, words of wisdom. They can create our ultimate vision; they can also erase it.

An English poet-philosopher, John Donne, wisely warns us that when we hear the bell toll for someone's death we should realize that it tolls for us, that someone else's death in a subtle but certain way diminishes us, partially kills us, for we are part and parcel of the fabric which this death unravels. I would like to point out a reverse situation: when a poet's work is heard, understood, applauded, it is a triumph for life, a celebration of Being, and therefore it is *our* victory, *our* glory, that is heard in the joyous pealing of the bell.

This celebration of Being is instinctively clear to the philosophical poet because he or she is often conscious of speaking, feeling, writing not only for himself or herself, but for all of us. Sympathy unites the philosophical poet to other human beings that he or she may not know and with whom he or she may superficially have little in common. A capacity for generalized feel-

ings, visions, ideas is another feature of the philosophical poet that makes his or her voice different from the voices of other poets. The philosophical poet sees and describes a specific flower, a yellow rose or a purple iris, and at the same time there is a space in his mind, in his imagination, in his soul, where the rose and the iris come closer and closer to a perfect flower, the Platonic flower described by Mallarmé as "l'absente de tout bouquet"—the flower that is the essence of all flowers and therefore absent from any real bouquet.

Unless the description given above sounds too precious, we should agree on a few basic points. Aristotle stated that there can be no scientific description, no scientific knowledge, until and unless it is generalized description, knowledge, statement. The efforts of the pre-Socratic Greek philosophers were already moving in the same direction. Poetry is a personal statement, the most individualistic and intimate statement if we mean by *poetry* what most readers accept as its basic definition: that is to say, lyric poetry. How can any writer bridge the gap between the individual vision and the generalized overview of our world?

Octavio Paz gives us the answer in almost every one of his books. An analysis of his techniques as related to both his style and his ideas would become lengthy if applied to all his texts. It is reasonable to choose two individual texts, one old and one relatively new, one a prose book and the other a poem. The first is perhaps Paz's most celebrated and widely read book, his obvious best seller, *The Labyrinth of Solitude*, whereas the second, chosen in order to show how Paz is a consistently philosophical poet, is *Blanco*, a philosophical poem which both rivals and complements—perhaps *contradicts* would be a better word—T. S. Eliot's *The Waste Land*.

In *The Labyrinth of Solitude* Paz approaches a difficult problem: how to define and explain the feelings of identity and lack of identity of today's Mexicans, especially of those Mexicans who are conscious of living, thinking and feeling according to a Mexican system of values. He uses the vocabulary and the stylistic resources of poetry: images, metaphors, oxymorons, conceits, all the figures of speech. Images and symbols, however, cluster around certain basic observations, which are often derived from a comparison with other sensitivities, other systems of values, whether American, West European or from the Orient. Early enough in the book Paz avows that most of what he has to say about being Mexican came to his mind during the two years he resided in the United States. In order to define what is Mexican, he had to understand and define several other cultural traditions and value systems: only then, profiled by the ways of life that are different, the geographical and temporal space where Mexican values are to appear begins to emerge.

This is so because the identity of an individual or

a group assumes the "otherness" of the individuals and groups that surround them. The world is incredibly rich and complex: we can find our place in it only after acknowledging its thousand faces. As Paz puts it in his words of acceptance of the Neustadt International Prize for 1982:

> In esthetic terms, Plurality is a richness of voices, accents, manners, ideas and visions; in moral terms, Plurality signifies tolerance of diversity, renunciation of dogmatism and recognition of the unique and singular value of each work and every personality. Plurality is Universality, and Universality is the acknowledging of the admirable diversity of man and his works. . . . To acknowledge the variety of visions and sensibilities is to preserve the richness of life and thus to ensure its continuity.

Paz knows by instinct what German philosophers of the romantic era—Fichte, Schelling, Hegel—found out through arduous reasoning and what in our own time Martin Buber has restated successfully: there is no *I* without a *Thou;* there is no individuality without an "otherness," a plurality. We know everything, we are everything and everybody if, and only if and when, we acknowledge our diversity, engage in a dialogue with everybody else, create bridges between human beings and their own past, their traditions and hopes. A dialogue between ourselves and nature, between human history and the history of the cosmos.

It goes without saying that when a poet invades the realm of philosophy, the impact is bound to be strong and enduring. Philosophers deal with questions that we all care about, but they often are clumsy and obscure in the way they state them and in the way they make their conclusions explicit. Few philosophers are forceful writers. So few, in fact, that their lack of expertise about language and communication is perhaps the major factor that has brought philosophy into disarray and ineffectiveness in our time. Plato was a first-rate writer; so were Nietzsche, Bergson, Ortega y Gasset.

A concern with language, a concern about language, is what poets and philosophers have most in common. Modern philosophy from Descartes to the present has paid constant attention to the tools that have helped us reach toward knowledge, and foremost among these tools is language, which brings us knowledge in such a grasping, intimate way that we receive both knowledge and language at the same time, closely intertwined. Young Emerson points out in his journals, "The progress of metaphysics may be found to consist in nothing else than the progressive introduction of apposite metaphors."

Paz is committed to language, not only because he is a poet, but also because as a thinking man he sees in language a meeting place of space and time, essence and existence. "The word is man himself. We are made of

words. They are our only reality, or at least, the only testimony of our reality," Paz assures us in *The Bow and the Lyre.* Moreover, as Paz writes in *Alternating Current,* "The problem of meaning in poetry becomes clear as soon as we notice that the meaning is not to be found outside, but rather inside the poem; it is not to be found in what the words have to say, but rather in what the words *have to say to each other*" (". . . en aquello que *se dicen entre ellas*").

It is perhaps in *Blanco,* a long poem published in 1966, that Paz reaches his highest level as a philosophical poet. *Blanco* is a text that unfolds in several ways. We can read it as a whole, from beginning to end, or we can read first the central column, which deals with the birth of words, the birth of language. To the left of this central column is another column, a poem in itself if we choose to read it as such, an erotic poem divided into four sections which stand for the four elements in the physical world. To the right of the central column we find another column, another poem, also divided into four parts: it deals with sensation, perception, imagination and understanding. Read as a whole, *Blanco* can be baffling and exasperating if we do not understand that it is the interaction of the different parts across time (the time it takes to read the poem) and space (the printed page with its white spaces surrounding the texts as silence surrounds our words) that conveys the message. Language cannot be born, Paz seems to say in this poem, unless we combine into one single unit space, time, sensuousness, passion and silence.

It is through language that we can approach the world around us, Paz seems to tell us, and each new word created by us enriches us with a new treasure—with the joy which this victory produces we find new strength to go on and invent new words. This is the way he describes the creation of the word *sunflower:*

> Survivor
> Among taciturn confusions,
> 				It ascends
> On a copper stalk
> 			Dissolved
> In a foliage of clarity,
> 				Refuge
> Of fallen realities.
> 			Asleep
> Or extinct,
> 			High on its pole
> (Head on a pike)
> 			A sunflower
> Already carbonized light
> 				Above a glass
> Of shadow.
> 			In the palm of a hand
> Fictitious,
> 			Flower
> Neither seen nor thought:
> 				Heard,

It appears
>Yellow

Calyx of consonants and vowels
All burning.

Flashes of light and color, metaphors, images, synesthesia precede and follow the word *sunflower* (*girasol*), helping in its birth, reinforcing its presence and its meaning. Everything begins and ends in words. Words, on the other hand, need us, need our senses, our passion, in order to be born. In an audacious reverse movement similar to the flight of a boomerang, Paz compels poetic language to turn around and examine itself, examine words and sentences, in order to seize the second in which a sensation becomes a word.

As Ricardo Gullón has stated, "Paz, like André Breton, understands that the language of passion and the passion of language are on good terms with one another, that they are the recto and verso page of the same attitude. Moreover, language is where song happens. There is no song without words, even though a song can be diminished to a susurration or concealed in a number." Poetry, language, passion: these are key words for anyone approaching Paz's texts. It is the way he relates and combines them that makes his message a universal one, no matter how closely related many of his poems and essays are to the Mexican soil and culture that shaped him. By approaching language through poetry and passion he deals with a universal fact—there is no culture without language, and language belongs to all of us—through feelings (sensuousness, sexual passion) that are also our common heritage. An intellectual and philosophical quest has been carried out through experiences that can be shared by all. Can there be a greater achievement for a philosopher-poet? (pp. 591-94)

Manuel Durán, "Octavio Paz: The Poet as Philosopher," in *World Literature Today*, Vol. 56, No. 4, Autumn, 1982, pp. 591-94.

JOHN M. FEIN

(essay date 1986)

[Fein is an American educator and critic. In the following excerpt, taken from his *Toward Octavio Paz: A Reading of His Major Poems, 1957-1976* (1986), he provides an overview of the predominant characteristics of Paz's poetry.]

[Every] great writer we study is to some degree unattainable, no matter how clear or moving his literary creation may be. This incompleteness, which is perhaps more the reader's than the author's, is particularly applicable in the case of Octavio Paz, whose poetic goal is the expression of what he feels to be basically incommunicable. The reader, therefore, can only approach the author's work and accept with mystery, frustration, or pleasure the realization that his comprehension will be imperfect.

The undisputed intellectual leadership of Paz, not only in Mexico but throughout Spanish America, rests on a dichotomy of achievements. In the field of the essay, he is the author of twenty-five books on subjects whose diversity—esthetics, politics, Surrealist art, the Mexican character, cultural anthropology, and Eastern philosophy, to cite only a few—is dazzling. In twenty-one books of poetry spanning more than fifty years, his creativity has increased in vigor as he has explored the numerous possibilities opened to Hispanic poets from many different sources. His success in diversified fields is heightened by the ways in which his essays and his poetry are complementary: the core of his creativity is a concern for language in general and for the poetic process in particular.

Like most intellectuals, Paz is more the result of his rigorous inquiry and self-discipline than of an educational system. The family into which he was born in Mexico City in 1914 represented, in its combination of indigenous and Spanish heritage and of Catholicism and nonbelief, and in its impoverishment after the Revolution, the history of his country. As a child he led a rather solitary life in a crumbling mansion and attended a French religious school, having been tutored in that language by an aunt. He had access to his grandfather's library, which introduced him to Latin, Greek, and Spanish classics, nineteenth-century French authors, and writers in Spanish who were popular around the turn of the century.

At fourteen he showed the dedication to poetry and the autodidacticism that were to shape his life. Although his family persuaded him to attend the schools of Arts and Letters and Law at the university, he did not receive a degree. His enthusiasm for poetry turned to the Spanish generation of 1927; only later did he discover their predecessors of the post-modernist period. At nineteen, when he published his first book of poems, *Luna silvestre*, Paz was an active member of literary groups, a contributor to literary reviews, and the founder of two. He was in the center of a productive and eclectic activity that introduced the most innovative French, English, and Spanish writers to Mexico.

A key event in Paz's life was the invitation, at the suggestion of Pablo Neruda, to attend a congress of anti-fascist writers in Spain in 1937. At the height of the Civil War, he met not only the leading Spanish writers (Cernuda, Alberti, Altolaguirre, Antonio Machado), but also Spanish Americans (Neruda, Huidobro, Vallejo). An even more important result of the experience in Spain was the feeling of solidarity, which Paz was to call, in another context, "communion."

He continued to express that feeling in his work on behalf of Spanish Republicans, particularly those in exile in Mexico, and in his collaboration in *El popular,* a politically oriented newspaper sponsored by Mexican workers. In 1940 he broke with *El popular* and with Neruda as a result of the Russian-German pact. His literary prestige grew through his contributions to three literary journals (*Taller,* 1938; *Tierra nueva,* 1940; and *El hijo pródigo,* 1943) and his role in the introduction of Surrealism to Mexico.

With the support of a Guggenheim grant in 1944, Paz visited the United States, where he began the brilliant essay on Mexican character, *El laberinto de la soledad (The Labyrinth of Solitude),* that was to attract international attention when it was published in 1950. The first edition of his collected poetry, *Libertad bajo palabra,* appeared in 1949. His appointment to the diplomatic service took him to Paris, where he strengthened his knowledge of, and connection with, French writers, particularly Breton and the Surrealists. (pp. 1-3)

Paz's numerous books of essays offer ample evidence of his productivity as a thinker. Just as the meaning of history underlies his analyses of society, so does the significance of language connect his numerous essays on Hispanic and French poetry and art. Ranging from *El arco y la lira* (1956)—a brilliant interpretation of poetry as language, process, and social phenomenon—to his broad history of the evolution of modern poetry, *Los hijos del limo: Del romanticismo a la vanguardia* (1974) (*Children of the Mire: Modern Poetry from Romanticism to the Avant-Garde*), he views the distillation of language not as an adornment of mankind but as a key to its comprehension. His seminal study of the French artist, *Marcel Duchamp o el castillo de la pureza* (1968) (*Marcel Duchamp, or the Castle of Purity*), provides insights into contemporary hermetic expression, including his own work. The massive *Sor Juana Inés de la Cruz, o, Las trampas de la fe* (1982) is equally revolutionary in its scholarship on the remarkable philosopher, scientist, and authoress, and in its intellectual history of the Colonial period.

Paz's poetry and prose represent two aspects of a concern for the predicament of modern man, whom he is not unique in viewing as fragmented and mutilated. In fact, all of his work is unified by a utopian wish for the fulfillment of man's wholeness in individual creativity and in the building of society, offering an ennobling vision of man to an uneasy world. This vision underlies his attempts to reconcile opposites, especially those of passion and reason, linear and circular time, society and the individual, and word and meaning. (pp. 3-4)

There are two major characteristics of Paz's work that are particularly challenging to his critics. The first is his relationship to the Surrealists, among whom French poets figure more significantly than their Hispanic counterparts. It is obvious that Paz, who is trilingual in Spanish, English, and French, feels a great affinity with French culture and history of ideas. His veneration of André Breton, for example, clearly delineated in Jason Wilson's excellent book, suggests that his affiliation with Surrealism is part of the origin of his hermeticism. The difficulties for the critic are obvious: how can one define the theme of a poem that is so intensely personal that its ultimate definition rests within the text itself? How can one assume a common response from readers when the poem in fact invites multiple responses, each of which is justifiable and may conflict with, if not exclude, the alternate readings?

Another significant critical problem is posed by Paz's concept of poetry, which has developed over the period of many years and can be seen most clearly in his essays. These, as has often been observed, are the basis for comparing him to the late Alfonso Reyes, not only in their breadth and brilliance, but particularly in their contribution to critical theory and to an understanding of the role of poetry in society. Paz's first effort in this field, **"Poesía de communión y poesía de soledad,"** is as meaningful today as when it first appeared in *El hijo pródigo* in 1943. Some of the ideas outlined there were the nucleus for the best developed and most readable volume on poetic theory that Latin America has produced, *El arco y la lira* (1956). The observation of Paz's evolution as a critic is in itself an educational process. Paz himself is the first to note rectifications and clarifications (see Rodríguez Monegal's article on the differences between the editions of *El arco y la lira*), but the concepts underlying his theories remain basically unchanged. Central to his critical thought are the desire to make poetry more meaningful to man and the conviction that poetry must go beyond the text to (and through) the individual's response. The essence of the poem, he believes, is unwritten, and therefore silent. It is analogous to the pauses in musical composition that express as much meaning as the sounds. If the poem ends in silence, the critic is reluctant to intrude with his own interpretation of meaning.

The constants of Paz's concept of poetry can be stated in a series of paradoxes. The poet writes only for himself but must communicate to an audience. The poem is a mystery whose creation can never be accurately described, yet man cannot receive it without thinking about the process that created it. Language is a defective but indispensable instrument for conveying what is incommunicable. Poetry is an ecstasy that both denies and transforms reality; although it cannot be grasped, it is essential to man's concept of himself and to the functioning of society.

Perhaps the most troublesome of Paz's paradoxes is his rejection of analysis as an aid to understanding contemporary poetry. Even his notes to *Ladera este,* limited to geographical and historical explanations, are regarded by Paz with reluctance and suspicion:

> Since in some passages there appear words and allusions to people, ideas, and things that might puzzle the reader who is not familiar with that part of the world, several friends advised me to include at the end of this volume a few notes to clear up those difficulties—and others not less superfluous. I accede to them with the fear (hope?) that these notes, far from dissipating the enigmas, will increase them.

It is significant that the notes are omitted in the collected poetry of *Poemas*. A more important distrust of critical interpretation appears in Paz's essay **"Hablar y decir,"** in which he supports Maistre's observation that thought and word are synonymous and Breton's similar belief that poetry is the perfect equivalence between sound and meaning, rendering any further statement superfluous. It is, Paz maintains, meaningless to ask what a poem means: "Poems cannot be explained or interpreted; in them the sign stops signifying: it is." The clearest summary of Paz's anticritical stance is the conclusion of his introduction to *Poesía en movimiento:* "The meaning of poetry, if it has any, is neither in the judgments of the critic nor in the opinions of the poet. The meaning is changing and momentary: it comes from the encounter between the poem and the reader."

The diminishment, if not the elimination, of criticism's role in understanding poetry results in increased responsibilities for the reader. In the same way that contemporary drama experiments with the location of the stage and with the distinction between actors and audience to abolish the latter's passivity, so does Paz seek to enable the reader not only to respond to the poem, but to assist in its creation. His objective is to reduce the differences between poet and reader, so that the two can work together in a common purpose. He is aware, of course, of the paradoxical nature of his mission: just as to reach ultimate expression he must abolish words, so must the reader and poet communicate by transcending the poem. As early as 1938, Paz referred to "the reader of poetry who is more and more a true re-constructor of it." In recent years he has developed this concept to its logical conclusion, transforming the reader into a poet by confronting him with demanding literature: "According to this view of reader participation, the interpretive act becomes synonymous with the creative process itself."

In her very perceptive essay, Ruth Needleman traces the origin of Paz's concept of the reader to the fundamental change in his view of language that took place between the two editions of *El arco y la lira* in 1956 and 1967. In the first he denied the possibility of separating language from its human context. In the second he notes the loss of that context and the substitution of a multiplicity of meanings: "Coherence, as a re-sult, has ceded its place to fragmentation, so that the meaning, no longer immanent, resides in the very search for meaning." The poem, consequently, becomes variable according to the experience and the capacity of the reader: "The meanings are inherent in the poem, and the reader realizes them by rendering them conscious." Whether the average person can measure up to this responsibility is a serious question that Needleman answers indirectly.

Paz's poetry is consistent with his theories in the multiple possibilities it presents for interpretation. The reader who is not acquainted with those theories may feel that the poems are inconclusive, or even unconcluded, presented as sketches or notes. If he persists, however, he will understand that the poet invites him to feel his own version of the poem. Brotherston's statement in *Latin American Poetry* that Paz is "a poet of movement, defined by successive moments" succinctly classifies not the end of the reader's response but the beginning. Paz's description of Duchamp's work as the bridge between the polarities of the absence of meaning and the necessity of meaning is helpful in comprehending his own intentions. Perhaps more clearly than any other critic, Gabriel Zaid has urged us to have new objectives:

> When one examines it carefully, the work of Octavio Paz does not yield ultimate meanings. It is not a work derived from ultimate demands, but originating at the source of the ultimate demands. The final meaning of Paz's work is not a meaning but a living act: to move itself and to move us to the place of the final meanings.

In addition to the constants noted by critics (the desire for transcendence, the symbolism of the paradox, the quest for origins, and the polarities of solitude and communion), there is one less documented constant: Paz's attempts to shape through his poetry a more sensitive, independent, and enlightened reader. This is an additional goal for a poet who assigns a high priority to forging a new—or at least clearer—medium of communication. One feels that in Paz the order of urgency is, if not reversed, simultaneous. He would not be satisfied to write a different kind of poetry unless he had the hope that it would create a reader with a different set of expectations. (pp. 5-10)

John M. Fein, in his *Toward Octavio Paz: A Reading of His Major Poems, 1957-1976,* The University Press of Kentucky, 1986, 189 p.

EDWIN WILLIAMSON
(essay date 1989)

[In the following essay, Williamson examines how Paz's development as a poet is evidenced in *The Collected Poems of Octavio Paz, 1957-1987* (1988).]

Octavio Paz occupies a unique position in the Spanish-speaking world. He is the foremost living poet of the language as well as being one of the most authoritative interpreters of the Hispanic situation, a *pensador* in the tradition of Unamuno, Ortega y Gasset, Rodo and Mariategui. Poetry, however, has always been the vital source of his ideas. His work as cultural historian, political essayist and editor of *Vuelta,* the most influential journal in Latin America today, is rooted in his belief that the poetic conscience must be brought to bear on the central issues of contemporary history. The *Collected Poems* brings together for the first time Paz's mature work in a splendidly produced bilingual edition. Over half of the poems have not been rendered into English before and it is very gratifying to find here the most recent collection, the superb *A Tree Within,* which came out in 1987. . . .

The collection begins appropriately with *Sunstone,* an extended reverie which incorporates the sum of his poetic experience until 1957. The title refers to an Aztec calendar stone whose cycle of 584 days is reflected in the number of lines of the poem. This correlation evinces Paz's perennial concern to escape contingency by looking for a mythic dimension to personal experience. The Surrealist influence—his friendship with André Breton in the late Forties left an indelible mark on his poetry—is evident in the visionary intensity of the language. But despite its oneiric strangeness, the poem describes a purposeful quest for a fullness of being which time routinely denies the poet except for intermittent epiphanies granted him in the love of woman, the universal 'other'. The poem undulates through successive states of consciousness, interweaving memories of war and atrocity with personal recollections of people, places and events. Impelled by its own inner momentum, its flow is punctuated by sudden spasms of joy until it eventually finds its way back to the beginning:

> a course of a river that turns, moves on,
> doubles back, and comes full circle,
> forever arriving:

These lines repeat the opening sequence of metaphors and, ending with a colon, trace an image of history as eternal recurrence, though 'forever arriving', lacking the final spurting rhythm of *y llega siempre,* fails to capture the narrowness of this victory over the contingent and the terminal.

Salvation for history through love and poetry was to remain the romantic heart of Paz's enterprise. From 1959, when he returned to live in Paris, the search for pure being was extended under the influence of Mallarmé, from whom he derived a metaphysics of the poetic word as a primal reality buried under layers of dead language. The desire to cleanse the word from the slime of functional usage led to experiments with phonic resonance—intensive punning and internal rhyme—and typographical layout: spaced-out lines, stanzas suspended in mid-page, counterpointed islets of text, with the odd word exiled to a margin. Such experiments can be seen at their most radical in *Topoemas* (1968), a cross between Apollinaire's *calligrammes* and oriental ideograms.

Though the linear text remained the norm, Paz would continue to break up or displace lines to allow white spaces to show through, creating a pleasing effect of airiness which corresponded graphically to his belief in the transcendent potential of poetic language. Indeed, at their best, Paz's disjointed texts read with the freshness of a breeze: words appear to have been swept up by a wave of air and relieved of their burden of reference, to circulate in some undetermined space between the material world and whatever might lie beyond it. When they fail to come off, such poems are like arrested mobiles, with inert images hanging off a predictable set of ideas.

The mystical strain was more fully developed after 1962, when Paz became Mexican Ambassador in India for six years. His reactions to a new landscape and a new human reality are recorded in *East Slope* (1962-1968), a miscellany ranging from snapshots of nature or ironic sketches of social types to long meditations prompted by monuments and places where, surprisingly, as in **'Happiness in Herat'**, the quietism of Hindu mysticism is rejected for a more dynamic vision of a natural world transfigured into the 'perfection of the finite'. In the East, Paz recognises the Europeanness of his heritage as a Mexican: he refuses to discount material reality in the quest for plentitude of being.

Perhaps for this reason, he was drawn to the sacred eroticism of Tantric rites. The major works of his Indian interlude are indeed love poems. It was in India that he met his second wife and there that he most fully deployed his extraordinary powers of evoking sexual union in language that fuses exhilarated sensuality with religious awe. Eroticism and Mallarméan experimentation are combined in *Blanco* (1966), the most ambitious poem of this period. Conceived as a sort of verbal kaleidoscope, it consists of 14 texts that can be read separately or in a variety of interlocking permutations.

The aim is to generate a changing interplay of images and rhythms that will figure forth the oppositions and polarities that divide consciousness, and whose reconciliation is achieved only in the ecstatic moment of erotic fulfillment:

> No and Yes
> together
> two syllables in love

Blanco now seems to be too beholden to the vapid spirituality of the Sixties to convince in its entirety. But the headiness of the Indian years did not distract Paz from the grim realities of history. In 1968 he resigned his post as ambassador in protest at the massacre by government troops of several hundred student demonstrators at Tlatelolco before the Olympic Games were due to open in Mexico City.

Back in Mexico, he began his intellectual journey to discover a new political ethic for Latin America. *Return* (1969-1975) contains poems of terrible desolation:

> the blind in combat beneath the noon sun
> thirst panting anger
> beating each other with rocks
> the blind are beating each other
> the men are crushing
> the stones are crushing
> within there is a water we drink
> bitter water
> water whetting thirst
> where is the other water?

In this harsh wasteland the poet must find the resources to avoid becoming a 'gardener of epitaphs'. The two masterpieces of these years are **'San Ildefonso Nocturne'** and *A Draft of Shadows* (1974). Both reflect upon his own childhood—a new preoccupation—and on the ghastly proliferation of Mexico City, which had devoured the village where he was born and raised. Paz is forced back into an inner world:

> I close my eyes
> I hear in my skull
> the footsteps of my blood,
> I hear
> time pass through my temples.
> I am still alive.

Sheltering in that last redoubt, yet perturbed by the strange allure of death, he finally submits to the 'errant clarity' of the Moon, and contemplating his sleeping wife ('she too is a moon'), brings his poem to an end by placing his trust in the woman's 'quiet flowing'. Attenuated now from what it was in *Sunstone,* his faith in woman as the saving 'other' still serves to overcome despair and the obliteration of the cherished landmarks of childhood.

A Draft of Shadows, one of his most moving compositions, begins by alluding once more to those 'footsteps in the mind' which tread

> the path of echoes
> that memory invents and erases.

A long complex poem about the substance of personal identity, it has none of the attitudinising which sometimes mars the earlier works. There are intimations of a divine presence, a 'bodiless god' who refuses to be named in 'the language of the body'. This realisation cuts the poet down to size: his poem is nothing but

> air that sculpts itself and dissolves,
> a fleeting allegory of true names.

Yet if this is all that can be expected of poetry, it is also the sum of what can be salvaged from the ruin of time, for the self is simply 'the shadow my words cast'. Released now from his anxiety to be a hierophantic visionary, Paz accepts the humbler calling of a mere boxer of shadow-words. His reward is the discovery of a new voice.

In **"A Tree Within"**, the brief but charming title-poem of his latest collection (1976-1987), the poet tells how he felt a tree growing inside him, lighting up his whole body. Paz's new voice is gentler, more accepting of the world as it is, yet suffused with the roguish humour of a man entering old age who has come across a garden, not of epitaphs, but of images and sensations that repeat the 'great exclamation with which the world begins each day'. He now writes in a well-modulated, unforced, surrealist manner, with graceful clarity and no perceptible loss of the power to strike beautiful images, as in the surprisingly coltish **'The Dryad War'**, with its sparkling stream of fancies, or in the unerring metaphors of **'A Fable of Joan Miro'**. The advent of death is contemplated with a serenity that commands respect. In **"A Small Variation"** his last moment is imagined as one of those instants of communion which have formed the axes of his life as a poet, an instant which

> opens under my feet
> and closes over me and is pure time.

(p.20)

Edwin Williamson, "Spanish Practices," in *London Review of Books,* Vol. 11, No. 10, May 18, 1989, pp. 20-2.

SOURCES FOR FURTHER STUDY

Chantikian, Kosrof, ed. *Octavio Paz: Homage to the Poet.* San Francisco, Calif.: Kosmos, 1980, 248 p.

> Collection of critical and interpretive essays on Paz.

Chiles, Frances. *Octavio Paz: The Mythic Dimension.* American University Studies, Series II, Romance Languages and Literature, Vol. 6. New York: Peter Lang, 1987, 224 p.

> Examines Paz's conception of myth and its relation to his poetry.

Guibert, Rita. "Octavio Paz." In her *Seven Voices: Seven Latin American Writers Talk to Rita Guibert,* pp. 183-275. Translated by Francis Partridge. New York: Alfred A. Knopf, Inc., 1973.

> In-depth conversation in which Paz discusses his life and career.

Ivask, Ivar, ed. *The Perpetual Present: The Poetry and Prose of Octavio Paz.* Norman: University of Oklahoma Press, 1973, 160 p.

> Collection of lectures and essays originally presented at a Paz symposium held at the University of Oklahoma. Includes a brief bibliography and works by such critics as Manuel Durán, G. Sucre, and A. W. Phillips.

Phillips, Rachel. *The Poetic Modes of Octavio Paz.* London: Oxford University Press, 1972, 168 p.

> Critical overview.

"Homage to Octavio Paz: Our 1982 Neustadt Laureate." *World Literature Today* 56, No. 4 (Autumn 1982): 589-643.

> Contains encomiums and critical essays on Paz, including pieces by Jorge Guillén, Ivar Ivask, and José Miguel Ortega.

Samuel Pepys

1633-1703

English diarist, historian, and letter writer.

INTRODUCTION

*P*epys is recognized as one of the greatest diarists in the English language. As a highly placed civil servant and tireless man-about-town in Restoration London, he observed and recorded the goings-on of his age, providing a unique record of what it was like to be alive in the early years of the reign of Charles II. His *Diary* is therefore valued as a historical document of incomparable import. Strikingly candid and replete with anecdote and incident, the *Diary* is also esteemed as an original and finely crafted literary work.

Pepys was born in London in 1633 and remained a Londoner all his life. His father, John Pepys, was a tailor and first cousin of Edward Mountagu, first Earl of Sandwich, who was to become Samuel's close friend and patron. His mother, Margaret Kite, was the sister of a Whitechapel butcher. Pepys began school in Huntingdonshire, where his paternal family had lived for centuries as reeves, farmers, and minor landholders. He was then sent to St. Paul's School in London. In 1649 he saw Charles I beheaded: the beginning of the Commonwealth. The next year he went as a sizar to Magdalene College, Cambridge, where he took his B. A. degree in March 1654. In 1655, at twenty-two, Pepys married fifteen-year old Elizabeth Marchant de St. Michel, the beautiful but penniless daughter of a Huguenot refugee of good family. The couple moved into Mountagu's lodgings in Whitehall Palace, where Pepys was working as a secretary and domestic steward.

1660 was a watershed year for Pepys. Now living in Axe Yard, Westminster, he began the *Diary* on 1 January. He noted in a brief preface to the first entry: "My own private condition very handsome; and esteemed rich, but endeed very poor, besides my goods of my house and my office, which at present is somewhat uncertain." Uncertainty and poverty, however, in time gave way to undreamt of stability and riches. On 9

March Pepys was made Admiral's secretary by Mountagu, and two months later he accompanied Mountagu's fleet to Holland to bring over Charles II for the Restoration. These events, like so many that touched Pepys's life during the remainder of the decade, are treated fully in the *Diary*. On 28 June Pepys resigned his clerkship in the Exchequer. The next day he was appointed Clerk of the Acts to the Navy Board. During the next few years Pepys flourished. He took on the duties of justice of the peace, oversaw naval victualling, was admitted as a Younger Brother of Trinity House, the principal maritime corporation, and was appointed to the Tangier Committee. During the Second Dutch War of 1665-67, he served the Royal Navy faithfully, courageously remaining at his post in London during the Great Plague of 1665 and helping save the Navy Office from destruction in the Great Fire of London in 1666. On 31 May 1669, Pepys closed the *Diary* for good, mistakenly believing himself on the verge of blindness: "And so I betake myself that course which [is] almost as much as to see myself go into my grave—for which, and all the discomforts that will accompany my being blind, the good God prepare me." Henceforth, though he prospered mightily and kept extensive business memoranda, Pepys never again attempted to lay bare his life in diary form.

Following the death of Elizabeth in 1669, Pepys threw himself into business with astonishing fervor. With the resignation of the Duke of York as Lord High Admiral of the Navy in 1673, He was made Secretary to the Admiralty Commission, becoming, in effect, administrative head of the naval department. Later in the year, he was elected member of parliament for Castle Rising, Norfolk, where he proved an active and effective legislator and tireless spokesman for the navy. In 1679 Pepys was implicated in the Popish Plot. He was detained in the Tower of London for nearly two months, but the proceedings against him were abandoned when it became clear that the "evidence" against him had been fabricated by a malefactor. He retired in 1689, shortly after James II was succeeded by William of Orange in the Glorious Revolution. Free from the stresses of office, Pepys spent the remainder of his life in a comfortable house in York Buildings, London, writing the only work he saw published, *Memoires relating to the State of the Royal Navy of England* (1690), and perfecting and arranging the private library he ultimately left to Magdalene College.

Pepys's *Diary* covers the period 1 January 1660 to 31 May 1669: slightly less than ten years in a professional career that lasted nearly thirty-five. Except for proper names and occasional words in longhand, it is written in a somewhat modified form of the shorthand invented by Thomas Shelton and described in the 1635 edition of his *Tachygraphy*. The system has raised problems of transcription for editors, but the difficulties are generally minor, and very little of the text is obscure or invites interpretation. Pepys developed his own lingua franca for selected passages, chiefly those of an overtly erotic or especially sensitive nature, based on Spanish but containing a smattering of French, Italian, Dutch, English, Latin, and Greek. It is usually clear how these passages should be transcribed and rendered, but not always; the meaning of a few such entries is therefore not really evident.

The *Diary* is considered one of the most valuable English documents of the Restoration age. According to William Matthews, who coedited the most complete edition of the text, "the diary is one of the principal source-books for many aspects of the history of its period. It is also a repertory of the familiar language of its time, and therefore an important source for historians of the English language. Most importantly, it is one of the great classics of literature." Pepys conceived the *Diary* as a personal journal, a record of his day-to-day comings and goings, but it also served as a quotidian chronicle of public affairs and the men and women behind them. Thus it is both a history of Pepys himself and a history of his country. "The diary serves therefore not only as a mirror but also as a private window giving on to a broad and varied external view—on to court politics and naval administration, or (at the other extreme) on to the simple domesticities of a London household," Robert Latham has written. In the *Diary* Pepys aimed at objectiveness in his reporting. Whatever he judged worth recording, he recorded, cramming his entries with detail and concealing nothing for the sake of decorum or in the interest of self-deceit. The entries, written apparently within days of the events they describe if not hours, are therefore markedly factual in content and immediate in tone Pepys treated high and low themes with equal dignity and interest: all manner of men and women talked, and Pepys listened. Church affairs, navy business, court intrigues, political gossip, diplomatic doings, the activities of the Royal Society, the proceedings of the Privy Council, the Second Dutch War—all figure strongly in the pages of the *Diary*. Equally, Pepys's public, private, and domestic lives are described fully. He enthusiastically chronicled his growing fortune, making much use of figures and statistics; noted the contents of his increasingly elaborate and expensive wardrobe while confessing his private pleasure in outdressing his peers; recorded the countless meals taken outside the house: venue, company present, food served, ales, beers, wines, and spirits consumed; complained about servant problems; and variously heralded and lamented the changing state of his relationship with his wife. Moreover, Pepys graphically chronicled the two great London catastrophes of the 1660s—the 1665 Great Plague and the 1666 Fire—and the greatest spectacle of the age, the splendid coronation of Charles II. His account of the Plague is grimly chilling and grisly, amplified by horrifying tales of individual tragedies, while his description of the Fire is enhanced by his having pushed to the rear of the retreating panicky masses to view the devastation at close range. "A most horrid malicious bloody flame," he noted in the entry for 2 September 1666.

The *Diary* is particularly valued by students of drama and music. Pepys was an insatiable playgoer—he considered his fondness for the theater practically an addiction and even took steps to "cure" himself of it—and commented freely on what he liked and disliked. He paid special attention to the acting, believing that a good performance could improve even a mediocre play, and made notes on theater architecture, scenery, lighting, and the general state, mood, and appearance of the audience. He saw new plays and revivals alike, taking his cues from the ever-changing signboards. Thus he commented on the works of Shakespeare as well as many of the chief dramatists of the Restoration. For some plays, in fact, Pepys's comments are the only known contemporary criticism. Pepys also frequented musical performances. He was a musician himself and a keen and knowledgeable music critic. His music criticism is therefore valued both for its insight and fullness and as a rare record of musical tastes not otherwise especially well documented.

At Pepys's death in 1703, the *Diary* passed with his library to his nephew John Jackson and from him to Cambridge in 1724. There it lay, essentially undisturbed, for nearly one hundred years until edited by Richard Neville (later Lord Braybrooke) from a transcript made by a Cambridge undergraduate, John Smith. *Memoirs of Samuel Pepys, Esq. F. R. S.* was published in two volumes in 1825. Only a selection from the *Diary* was printed, the editor's aim being "to omit nothing of public interest." The *Memoirs* was received with practically unbridled enthusiasm. A new edition of the *Diary*, "Considerably Enlarged," appeared in 1848-49, but it was not until the publication in 1893-99 of an only slightly abridged version, edited by H. B. Wheatley, that the text was made available in a form that approximated the original.

Soon commentators began exploring the *Diary* for evidence concerning the development of the English language, the progress of the Restoration drama, and English narrative technique in the late seventeenth century. Others read it simply for the good stories it contains. At the same time, students of the *Diary* sought to reveal Pepys's apparent motive in keeping a journal, his method of composition, and his intended audience. The full text of the *Diary* was not published until 1983, the year Matthews and Latham completed the 11-volume *Diary of Samuel Pepys: A New and Complete Transcription*. Volume One, published in 1970, offered for the first time a close, careful examination of the manuscript. Matthews wrote: "[The] manuscript makes it fairly certain that Pepys's way of writing was more complex than is usually assumed, and consequently that his great diary is no simple product of nature, thrown together at the end of each succeeding day. In part at least, it is a product fashioned with some care, both in its matter and its style." This statement, questioning the common assumption that the *Diary* is artful more by accident than design, threw new light on Pepys as litterateur. Thus Matthews could add, "Pepys is probably the only diarist who has contributed verbal formulae to the bloodstream of English."

Pepys's *Diary* is the record of a man and his age, a mirror of soul and state. Between the daily "up betimes" and the familiar peroration "and so to bed," Pepys displayed his tremendous appetite for life—his love of things old and new, common and curious—in words both evocative and informative. As Ollard has stated: "The *Diary* is a great work, as literature, as history, as a psychological document and as a key to what has been known as the English character in an age of national cultures perhaps soon to become extinct. It is thus almost impossible to exaggerate its value and importance."

(For further information about Pepys's life and works, see *Dictionary of Literary Biography*, Vol. 101: *British Prose Writers, 1660 to 1800* and *Literature Criticism from 1400 to 1800*, Vol. 11.)

CRITICAL COMMENTARY

CHARLES WHIBLEY

(essay date 1896)

[Whibley was a prolific English critic and reviewer. In the following excerpt from an essay originally published in 1896, he studies Pepys's introspection in the *Diary*.]

[Above all, Pepys] is the frankest man in history: he is frank even to himself. The veriest fool, the commonest knave can cultivate an appearance of frankness to the

Principal Works

Memoires relating to the State of the Royal Navy of England, for Ten Years, Determin'd December 1688 (memoirs) 1690

Memoirs of Samuel Pepys, Esq. F.R. S., Secretary to the Admiralty in the Reigns of Charles II and James II, Comprising His Diary from 1659 to 1669. Deciphered by the Rev. John Smith, A. B. of St. John's College, Cambridge, from the Original Short-Hand MS. in the Pepysian Library, and a Selection from His Private Correspondence. 2 vols. (diary and letters) 1825; revised editions 1848-49, 1854

The Life, Journals and Correspondences of Samuel Pepys. 2 vols. (diaries and letters) 1841

The Diary of Samuel Pepys, M. A., F. R. S., Clerk of the Acts and Secretary to the Admiralty. 10 vols. (diary) 1893-99

Private Correspondence and Miscellaneous Papers of Samuel Pepys, 1679-1703, in the Possession of J. Pepys Cockerell (letters and prose) 1926

Samuel Pepys's Naval Minutes (prose) 1926

Further Correspondence of Samuel Pepys, 1662-79, from the Family Papers in the Possession of J. Pepys Cockerell (letters) 1929

Letters and the Second Diary of Samuel Pepys (diary and letters) 1933

Shorthand Letters of Samuel Pepys, from a Volume Entitled S. Pepys's Official Correspondence, 1662-1679 (letters) 1933

The Tangier Papers of Samuel Pepys (diary and prose) 1935

The Letters of Samuel Pepys and His Family Circle (letters) 1955

Charles II's Escape from Worcester: A Collection of Narratives Assembled by Samuel Pepys (prose) 1966

The Diary of Samuel Pepys: A New and Complete Transcription. 11 vols. (diary) 1970-83

The Shorter Pepys (diary) 1985

---

world. But Pepys's achievement was far higher and less simple. He looked at himself with absolute straightforwardness, and could understand his own vanities—could measure his own vices without difficulty. He never seeks a fantastic motive; he never excuses the grossest wantonness. He extenuates nothing—not even the faults of his friends. Here, then, is the one man we have been permitted to know, as we shall never know ourselves. Let us, then, make the most of him: let us do homage to the one master of self-revelation that history can furnish forth.

A lust of being and moving, of exercising his senses to their utmost, governed his existence. Unnumbered and innumerable are his crowded hours of glorious life. The man who "is with child to see any strange thing" is neither cynic nor Philistine. Nothing came amiss to him. He was as pleased with Sir George Ent's discourse upon "Respiration" as he was with the peerless beauty of Lady Castlemaine. Only he must always be doing, or hearing, or seeing some new thing. To-day he is singing with Knipp, and listening with a hungry ear to the praise of his famous song, "Beauty, Retire;" to-morrow he is discussing with Dr. Whistler whether masts should be kept dry or damp. Now he goes to Will's to meet "Dryden the poet (I knew at Cambridge)"; now he is chaffering for cloves with some poor seamen in a "blind alehouse." And all the while he is drinking in life at its abundant source. His zest is almost too violent, and you wonder how he could have sustained, through many years of suffering, this ferocious energy of enjoyment; how he remained firm in

this dogged determination to miss no minute of lapsing time. But to his industry no transition seemed abrupt: he turned from his mistress to his accounts without weariness or regret, and no sooner had he found an end of his figures than he was ready to play again with all the spirit of a released schoolboy. His philosophy was the most arrogant that ever a man about town imagined. "Read every book," he said in effect, "see every play, empty every wine-cup, kiss every woman." And when he died, in all piety he might have owned that he never missed an opportunity. Alexander conquered the world; but Pepys, with a keener, more selfish understanding of life, conquered a world for every sense. He could not take a boat without singing to the "skuller"; he could not meet a Dutch bellman without taking his clapper in his hand, without noting that "it is just like the clapper that our boys frighten the birds away from the corn with in summer time in England."

But in all his research, in all his desire to penetrate the mysteries of science, there is no touch of pedantry. He was not one to encumber himself with the impediments of useless knowledge. He learnt all that he could with the lightest heart and the merriest smile. For he had but two motives in his life: pleasure and self-advancement. Mr. R. L. Stevenson, the most valiant champion of Pepys and his *Diary*, wrote, maybe in a moment of morbid self-consciousness, that he was happy but once. Samuel Pepys knew only the briefest interludes of displeasure. For ten years he screamed aloud with happiness, in so confident a tone that you wonder that he was not always trying to dodge the nemesis of his own pleasures. "In this humour we sat till about ten at night," he writes, of himself, and Evelyn, and Sir J. Minnes, and my Lord Bruncker—"and so my Lord and his mistress home, and we to bed, it being one of the times of my life wherein I was the fullest of true sense of joy." "True sense of joy"—is it not magnificent? And the phrase may be matched upon every page. Yet says the professional historian of literature: "Pepys lacked enthusiasm"!

Nor was it part of his creed to put off till tomorrow what might be enjoyed to-day. His was the Epicureanism of Horace. *"Carpe diem"* he shouted in his joyous voice. "I do indulge myself a little the more in pleasure," said he by way of excuse to himself, "knowing that this is the proper age of my life to do it; and out of my observation that most men that do thrive in the world, do forget to take pleasure during the time that they are getting their estate, but reserve that till they have got one, and then it is too late for them to enjoy it with any pleasure." So Pepys let not an hour pass unchallenged, and by a youth of pleasure prepared an old age of happiness.

He loved the amenities of life: art, music, a new coat, the songs of birds, the river, the open air were his perpetual delight. But before all things he loved a pretty woman. At the outset he was but a modest wooer. He once—it was on his return from Delft—sat side by side with "a pretty sober Dutch lass," and "I could not fasten any discourse upon her," he declares in a bland confession of failure. During the same journey to Holland he found "a pretty Dutch woman in bed alone," and, "though he had a month's mind, he had not the boldness to go to her." But in a year's space his boldness was invincible. And the *Diary* . . . is a paean to the triumph of love. He might have said with truth that he never saw a pretty woman that he did not salute. A bright eye lit up for him the darkest sermon. The austerity of Church was but an occasion for the ogling of beauty. For every woman he has a magnificent phrase. "Our noble, brave, fat lady," he calls Madame Lethulier, when he saw her at church. Not even his bitterest enemy could call his patriotism in question, and yet hot upon the defeat of the Dutch fleet he writes: "that which pleased me as much as the newes was to have the fair Mrs. Middleton at our church, who indeed is a very beautiful lady." Two qualities only did he abhor in woman: avarice and that immodesty which sets no barriers in the path of love. So he hated Mrs. Lane with a freely expressed cordiality. For not only was she a too easy mistress, but she borrowed £5 upon the firm security of £4 10s. in gold—a transaction whereat the business habits of the excellent Pepys most properly revolted.

To kiss and tell is righteously esteemed the unpardonable sin. Yet Pepys kissed every day, and confided the exploit to his *Diary.* But by the wittiest inspiration of genius he made this ultimate confidence, not in bald English, but in an infantile jargon, wherein French and Spanish and Latin are unequally blended. And you think that he employed this artifice, lest the secret journal, conscious of his shame, should change its ink to a blushing scarlet. Nowhere else does he reveal so openly the master frailty of his temperament. The record was (let us assume) for himself alone. His vanity insisted that he should remind himself that he passed the evening with Mrs. Bagwell or with Mrs. Martin; his honour whispered that it was monstrous to tell the truth, intended only for his single eye, in plain English. Wherefore he invented a lingo of his own to salve a callous conscience. The contradiction is exquisite and characteristic. In these poor phrases of illegitimate French, you seem to catch the cunning casuistical brain of Samuel Pepys in perfect action. Upon every page he reveals himself with obvious intent; here he lays bare his conscience with an inadvertent subtlety. And the effect is almost too acute. You are not merely looking over his shoulder; you seem to be guiding the hand that writes.

By his own account a more general lover never lived. He made his conquests on the highway or in the kitchen. That he may dally with the wife, he sends the husband forth to purchase wine, and presently offers him a purser's place. When his sister Pall would marry, he recommends Mr. Harman, the upholsterer, "to whom I have a great love, and did heretofore love his former wife." But to be found out was in his eyes a cardinal sin. And when Creed disgraced himself at Oxford, Pepys was the first to condemn his indiscretion. Now and again a wave of penitence swept over the golden sands of his complacency. "Musique and women," he acknowledges, with regret, "I cannot but give way to, whatever my business is." And again: "I observe the folly of my mind that cannot refrain from pleasure." Even his good resolutions are made but to be broken. "I have made an oathe," says he one day, "for the drinking of no wine, & c., on such penalties till I have passed my accounts and cleared all." And in a week he confesses that he has broken his oath "without pleasure." "Without pleasure"—that is the one phrase in the book that one is persuaded to mistrust. For the first and last time Pepys seems to be posing, to be cutting an antic before a mirror. Had he said the wine was bad, you had understood him. But were the wine good, you know that, oath or no oath, Pepys would have delighted in it.

Yet amidst all the frivolity and selfishness of his time, Pepys remained a patriot. While the Dutch were threatening our coasts, the Secretary's mind was troubled the more if it rained, "to think what the sailors would do on board in all this weather." When the Plague drove all save heroes and paupers from London, Pepys remained at his post in the very best of good humours, serving his country with unbated zeal. In a hopelessly corrupt age, he took no more commissions than should satisfy his necessities; and the glory of the British fleet overcame in his regard the plumpest check, the most provoking eye. (pp. 115-21)

Was Pepys an artist? This is the question which has grimly agitated the critics. Yet the answer seems easy: assuredly he was. He understood the art of life incomparably well. He never opposed his absorbing greed of sensation; he bent all the sterner considerations of time to the full enjoyment of the moment. And the severest critic will hardly detect a single fault in the interpretation of his wishes. He was an artist also in frankness, in that rare quality which, despite (or on account of) its simplicity, is far more difficult of attainment than the highest heaven. The artistic result of which is that he has given us such a picture of a man as is approached nowhere else than in Boswell's *Life of Johnson.* Once it was fashionable to believe, with Macaulay, that Boswell's was an idiot grinning through a horse-collar. It is still popular to assert that Pepys is a garrulous braggart, who has amused the nineteenth century by accident. But in the world of art accidents do not happen, and the peculiar excellence of the *Diary* is as firmly intentioned as a play by Shakespeare or a lyric by Tennyson.

Pepys set out to give himself a finished record of his life, and while his modesty shrank from immediate publication, he doubtless intended posterity to enjoy the fruit of his ceaseless labour. That the manuscript, with its cipher explained, should have been carefully and generously bequeathed to Magdalene College is proof positive that Pepys had a certain conscious respect for his own work. Had the journal been the idle, lazy vapourings of an amiable loafer, it would have been destroyed before its indiscretions could have annoyed a wondering world. But the journal was the one, long, deliberate effort of Pepys's life, and it is idle to deny the title of artist to the man who has drawn the living portrait of a living man.

Even by his style, Samuel Pepys may claim the august title. For its very looseness is perfectly appropriate. He had already made an experiment in literature when, at Cambridge, he began his romance *Love a Cheate.* And if, as he said, he had lost one vein, most assuredly he found another. His mannerisms, his monotony, his constant use of the stereotyped phrases of the day, give to his *Diary* an air of reality which a more deliberate method would have missed. (pp. 121-23)

Charles Whibley, "The Real Pepys," in his *The Pageantry of Life,* William Heinemann, 1900, pp. 107-23.

ARTHUR PONSONBY
(essay date 1928)

[Ponsonby was an English miscellaneous writer. In the following excerpt, he examines the style and substance of the *Diary.*]

[What] are the chief merits which give [*The Diary of Samuel Pepys*] its unique position among all diaries? First and foremost, Pepys did not write for disciplinary reasons nor . . . for any special reader. He wrote because he enjoyed writing. In this he resembles another very eminent diarist, Sir Walter Scott. Not till he was fifty-six did Scott begin "journalizing", but the obvious enjoyment with which he wrote is the very element which makes his journal such delightful reading. "I am enamoured of my journal," he says, and again, "I think this journal will suit me well".

Nothing is more difficult than the comparison of diaries. Depending as they do on the individuality of the writer, they may be good for very different reasons. A fault in one may amount almost to a merit in another where the treatment is slightly different. Introspection, for instance, can be irritating when it is accompanied by excessive self-depreciation, yet the introspective note is what makes diaries like those of Marie Bashkirtseff and Barbellion specially interesting. Even these, however, are self-conscious and lacking in honesty. Pepys was not introspective and therefore does not suffer from these faults. Amiel was scientific in his self-analysis and quite honest, but no one reads Amiel's journal for entertainment. In the haze of his abnormal analytical self-dissection the atmosphere of his private life is smothered. Learning does not improve a diary. In spite of Evelyn's scholarship his *Diary* is on a very much lower level than that of his friend. This is partly due to his having written it up and epitomised periods. One feels that he registers only what he wanted to be known publicly. It would be interesting to know if in the course of their conversation together either of them had suggested to the other that diary writing was a desirable habit.

Fanny Burney's power of narration is of a higher order than that of Pepys and her capacity of reporting conversations unequalled. But the writer of fiction too often gets the upper hand over the recorder of facts and in the latter part of her diary she becomes diffuse and long-winded. Charles Greville, also an official, confines himself very nearly exclusively to a record of the political history of his day, and, important as his journal is, the colour of individuality is comparatively faint. On the other hand, Benjamin Haydon's diary, one of the most remarkable of English diaries, is charged with his personality. He carries his reader along in amusement at his unrestrained tirades and violent polemics and in amazement at his brilliant pen-portraits of his contemporaries. Known to his friends as a bad painter, a mad eccentric, and an importunate beggar, he was discovered by posterity to be in the midst of all his craziness a very shrewd observer and skilful recorder of the events of his life. But his egotism is excessive, his invective tiring, and his supplications unreadable. The long diary of Lord Shaftesbury gives the man's full life-story; his public spirit and his austerity penetrate in almost every entry. Full and honest as it is, there is no light touch, no entertainment, no observation of the trivialities which give colour and ornament to life, and it is therefore difficult to read. In a lighter vein is Tom Moore's diary. But his pleasant intimate gossip was written for publication.

In some of the diaries of more obscure people we find elements of naïveté and charm which are lacking in the records of those who have had to deal with greater events and have lived among eminent people. Thomas Turner, the Sussex storekeeper, and William Jones, the Vicar of Broxbourne, had special *flair* for diary writing. We get personality and atmosphere, spontaneity and humour unspoiled by any intention of publication. Dr. Edward Dale's few entries of Court life and descriptions of the Princesses Mary and Anne (afterwards Queens) are too scrappy to merit very much attention, but he undoubtedly had something of the Pepysian touch in his gossip. Swift has a witty sparkle, and Byron in his brief attempts an amusing, indiscreet recklessness. Both, however, had readers in view. There is a suggestion of playing to the gallery. In humour and certainly in candour Pepys is their superior.

Pepys in fact can hold his own and surpass all diarists by merits which some of the others have and by merits which none of the others have. . . . [He] was a regular daily writer and his impressions are therefore fresh; his candour is a proof of his honesty, and he had no thought of publication. The genius appears in his power of selecting the incidents and epitomising situations, in the casual jotting of humorous opinions, the marvellous observation of intriguing situations, the restraint in handling the larger events, and the delicacy in which he can lighten them by a whimsical word or phrase, the keen enjoyment in which he reports his good fortune, the optimism and joy which always chases away the gloom of despondency, and the introduction of the intimate, the secret, nay, even the obscene in their proper place with disarming ingenuousness. We laugh with him, we laugh at him, and we are always entertained.

Whether Pepys was moral, scrupulous, learned, or clever has nothing whatever to do with the excellence of his *Diary.* We find all this out when we read it because he tells us everything.

A full and sincere diary is to some extent a revelation. It may be the revelation of expected and characteristic thoughts and opinions; it may be the revelation of unsuspected thoughts and deeds; it may also be the revelation of hitherto unknown qualities, the fact of them being unknown redounding very much to the credit of the diarist. Because of its completeness Pepys's *Diary* is too often judged, so far as he personally is concerned, as a revelation of the weaknesses and moral lapses which were not observed by his contemporaries. But in order to be fair, this nosing out of unsavoury passages and chuckling over his follies and faults must be balanced by the observation of excellent qualities to which he only refers incidentally. He may have been timid and nervous physically; several occasions on which he was frightened are entered perfectly honestly. But in the far more important sphere of moral courage and in kindness to the unfortunate he is shown up in the *Diary* in a very favourable light. For instance when Lord Brouncker, who was no favourite with Pepys, fell into disfavour, Pepys walked with him in Westminster Hall although he "was almost troubled to be seen" with him. He considered him wrongly accused, and declares he is "able to justify him in all that he is under so much scandal for". It was a bold act for a subordinate official to send "a great letter of reproof " to his chief. When Pepys sent his well-reasoned but severe letter to Lord Sandwich on November 18, 1663, he confesses he is "afeard of what the consequences may be". But in discharging what he considered to be an important public duty he had no hesitation.

Again in 1669, when there was question of dismissing officers of the Navy, Pepys writes:

> I have not a mind indeed at this time to be put out of my office if I can make shift that is honourable to keep it; but I will not do it by deserting the Duke of York.

When his cousin Joyce drowned himself Pepys quite unostentatiously took very great trouble to help his widow. He goes and comforts her, "though I can find she can, as all other women, cry, and yet talk of other things all in a breath". At a time when he was under grave suspicion of being a Roman Catholic he almost quixotically invited Cesare Morelli the singer to stay with him as his guest, although Morelli's membership of the Church of Rome told against the Secretary of the Admiralty, who was accused of harbouring a priest.

Other instances could be found, but they must be searched for, because they are never stressed. Pepys was incapable of writing for effect. When he was moved his rapid shorthand correctly conveys his emotion. The description of Sir Christopher Mings's funeral which he attended with Sir W. Coventry is very striking. He gives verbatim the tribute paid to their dead commander by "a dozen able, lusty, proper men" who came to their coach side; and then he adds his own:

> Sir Christopher Mings was a very stout man, and a man of great parts and most excellent tongue among ordinary men. . . . He had brought his family into a way of being great; but dying at this time, his memory and name will be quite forgot in a few months as if it had never been, nor any of his name be the better for it; he having not had time to will any estate, but is dead poor rather than rich.

The self-conscious writer would have ended there, saying to himself, "I won't spoil that by recording anything else to-day". But Pepys went on. He reports a far from innocent visit to Mrs. Bagwell, and ends up his entry, "In my way home I called on a fisherman and bought three eeles which cost me three shillings". Is it too much to say that the value of what is serious when it occurs is greatly enhanced by a writer who also can admit his incorrigible frivolity?

A sentence in an entry can be very eloquent. An entry of pages may tell you nothing. The length of Pepys's entries varies according to his mood; unlike the over-methodical diarist, he does not confine his report of the day's doings to an equally measured space of page. He writes at some length when in the vein and when events prompt him. But even his short entries reflect his mood and are wonderfully informing. Here is the brief and very comprehensive record of April 10, 1668:

> All the morning at Office. At noon with W. Pen, to Duke of York and attended Council. So to Duck Lane and there kissed bookseller's wife and bought legend. So home, coach, Sailor. Mrs Hannam dead. News of peace. Conning my gamut.

Pepys reflects his mood by the length or brevity of his entries and by the style of his narrative rather than by any deliberate confessions of depression or elation. Often we can picture him writing as when he tells us the candle is going out, "which makes me write thus slobberingly". Or again: "I staid up till the bellman came by with his bell under my window, as I was writing of this very line, and cried 'Past one of the clock, and a cold, frosty, windy morning'"; and could the suggestion of depression be better indicated than it is by the simple word "and" in the concluding sentence on October 9, 1664? "To bed without prayers it being cold and to-morrow washing day."

When he writes at length he is never wearisome. His Sunday outing on Epsom Downs on July 14, 1667, is described at great length. This was purely because he enjoyed it so much, not because anything of importance occurred. As it is one of the prettiest passages in the *Diary,* and as it shows us Pepys not as an official nor as a frivolous townsman, but as an appreciator of simple beauty, a couple of extracts may be given:

> . . .the women and W. Hewer and I walked upon the Downes where a flock of sheep was; and the most pleasant and innocent sight that ever I saw in my life—we find a shepherd and his little boy reading, far from any houses or sight of people, the Bible to him; so I made the boy read to me which he did with the forced tone that children do usually read, that was mighty pretty, and then I did give him something, and went to the father and talked with him; and I find he had been a servant in my cozen Pepys's house, and told me what was become of their own servants. He did content himself mightily in my liking his boy's reading, and did bless God for him, the most like one of the old patriarchs that ever I saw in my life and it brought those thoughts of the old age of the world in my mind for two or three days after. We took notice of his woolen stockings of two colours mixed and of his shoes shod with iron shoes both at the toe and heels and with great nails in the soles of his feet which was mighty pretty. . . . took coach, it being about seven at night, and passed and saw the people walking with their wives and children to take the ayre, and we set out for home, the sun by and by going down, and we in the cool of the evening all the way with much pleasure home talking and pleasing ourselves with the pleasure of this day's work. . . . Anon it grew dark, and as it grew dark we had the pleasure to see several glow-worms which was mighty pretty.

A close scrutiniser of diaries will find words in the earlier part of this entry which show that it was not written on the day. They are the words, "for two or three days after". The next two entries are unquestionably written on the day and the explanation comes on the third day, when he writes that he goes to his chamber "to set down my Journall of Sunday last with much pleasure". This shows—and there may be other occasions which cannot so easily be detected—that when he had something very special he reserved the writing of it for a time when he had plenty of leisure, going on meanwhile with the ordinary daily entries.

Another excellent long description of an entirely different scene is the entry on January 1, 1667/68, in which he minutely pictures a gambling scene at "the Groome-Porter's", where all the different types of people and different manners of winning and losing are described. (pp. 81-9)

While the noting of trivialities gives colour to a diary, they can be and are in the case of some diaries insignificant and pointless. With Pepys the trivial note nearly always gives spice and character to his entry. When he meets Sir J. Lawson and has a very short talk with him, this would appear to be an incident not worth recording. But Pepys gives us the reason, "his

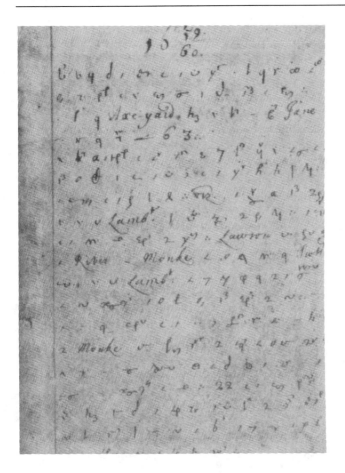

The opening page of the *Diary* manuscript. It begins: "Blessed be God, at the end of the last year I was in very good health."

hickup not being gone could have little discourse with him".

The *Diary* has suffered, as was inevitable, from the extraction of plums, the quotation of snippets, and the abbreviation of entries. Those who have read the full version are better able to judge the painstaking and methodical industry of the man. The full flavour and humanity of a diary can be appreciated only by reading consecutive entries, even though some of them may be devoid of historical interest or even of individual peculiarities. His meticulous recital of the seemingly unimportant has to be studied daily in order that the living man may be clearly discerned. But it is important to remember in attempting to estimate the man from the pages of his *Diary* that we can examine only nine and a half years of the seventy that he lived.

The entries contain no long philosophic or even political disquisitions—just a skilful recital of events. There are no elaborate character sketches with biographical details, but he hits off people in two or three lines certainly without a moment's hesitation as he wrote. A few of these passing comments may be quoted.

(Major Waters); a deaf and most amourous melancholy gentleman who is under a despayr in love . . . which makes him bad company though a most good natured man.

(Aunt James); a poor religious well meaning, good soul talking of nothing but God Almighty and that with so much innocence that mightily pleased me.

(Mr. Case); a dull fellow in his talk and all in the Presbyterian manner; a great deal of noise and a kind of religious tone but very dull.

(Mrs. Horsefield); one of the veriest citizen's wives in the world, so full of little silly talk and now and then a little sillily bawdy.

One can learn a great deal about a man from his observation of other people. Three of these descriptions taken at random from among the many show that he was pleased with simplicity, intolerant of pomposity, and put off by pretentious coarseness. Many fine shades of character may be detected in diary entries always provided that the writer is spontaneous and not consciously describing himself.

Perhaps Pepys's style is not what is called literary; his grammar may be faulty—it often is—his phrasing clumsy. All this does not matter in the smallest degree in diary writing. There are excellent diaries in which phrasing, and even grammar, spelling, and punctuation are all execrable. Charles Russell (1898), a foreman riveter, shows in an unpublished diary that he had no conception of grammar or of spelling, but his lively narrative of his adventures in Africa could not be improved. Your literary man who thinks about his English, his style, his balance, and his epigrams is very unlikely to be a good diarist. There are indeed not many literary men even who are capable of the terse powers of lucid expression sometimes displayed by Pepys. Without sententious epigram he can epitomise an event, a situation, or a character in phrases which would be spoilt by the alteration of a single word. Mother wit often counts more than education.

If diaries are to be classed as literature—and they most certainly ought to be—we must in considering them broaden our judgements and canons of taste with regard to style.

When a man can give you a vivid picture of events and personalities and convey to you his sense of living through his life with all his passing hopes and misgivings, joys and sorrows, petty irritations and high aspirations, and at the same time never weary you but invariably entertain you, his style must have some supreme merit however much it may violate the orthodox standards to which writers are supposed to conform.

There is sometimes a tendency to adopt towards the *Diary* an attitude of patronising amusement, to regard it merely as the effusions of an entertaining scribbler. Such critics seem to suggest that we could all write diaries of this sort if we wanted to or if we tried, and that after a couple of hundred years our records would be read with as much interest and amusement as we find in reading Pepys.

Let anyone try! Many have tried within the last two or three hundred years, and how few in their efforts come within any measurable distance of comparison with Pepys! To write regularly requires discipline. Not all are capable of this to begin with. Always to feel inclination requires a peculiar sort of effort. To epitomise your day so as to give a true picture of it requires special discrimination and power of selection. By power of selection we mean the choice of incident. A mere recital of consecutive incidents is not enough. Certain thoughts and deeds must be detached which may be trivial and not immediately relevant, but they may reflect the outward atmosphere and inward mood and make a reader feel present. This requires skill. After all, every minute of everyone's day is filled. Strother, the York shop assistant, endeavoured to write down *everything* that happened in the day. Of course it was impossible, and he gave up the attempt after two or three days. A sentence or two would have given him in his old age just as vivid an impression of those days as his laborious and almost unreadable effort. But selection, which is perhaps the most important element in a diarist's outfit, cannot be learned. No hard work, preparation, or study will make a man into a good diarist. It is not a matter of conforming to recognised standards. There are none. A good diarist *nascitur non fit.* There is no question of taking advice or of thinking out and cultivating an ingenious method. It all rests with the attitude of mind, the disposition and the instinctive inclination of the writer. Although almost every effort at diary writing has peculiar interest, success depends more on temperament than equipment.

On the other hand, the opposite tendency to regard Pepys as an outstanding extraordinary man and a great wit and observer is equally wide of the mark. As the earlier chapters have shown, he was quite an ordinary man, in no other way exceptionally talented, and as a writer in the literary sense he may quite justifiably be rather severely criticised.

Yet another opinion put forward by those who rightly appreciated Pepys's official pre-eminence is that the *Diary* is a "by-product" of no particular account; that there is nothing remarkable about his writing the *Diary,* that his claim to fame is that he was the "right hand of the Navy", and that such a man should write such a *Diary* if anything detracts from his greatness. There have, however, been many equally admirable, and indeed more admirable, Civil Servants than Pepys whose names are forgotten, whereas in his capacity as a diarist he stands alone. That official work is infinitely more important than writing a diary is a contention

that need not be disputed. However, to be merely noteworthy in the one but supreme in the other alters the balance of the comparison.

But in all of these views the central point of interest is missed, a point which is perhaps more psychological than intellectual or literary. It is that an average man, inconspicuous and, although assiduous in his work, by no means specially gifted, should have been able, unsuspected by his contemporaries and even by himself, to perpetrate a work of undoubted genius in a realm which about twenty-five per cent of educated people have privately explored without, except in a very few instances, approaching anywhere near the same result.

So much has been said of the side-lights thrown by Pepys on the events of his day, on the manners, customs, and fashions, and on his own domestic life. But too little has been said of the unsurpassed efficacy of the method in diary writing which his genius adopted and of his temperamental fitness for this self-imposed task.

Pepys's claim to be placed among Men of Letters must rest alone on the *Diary.* The remainder of his literary output is entirely negligible. The claim is well founded, and a by no means inferior position among the immortals has readily been accorded to him. (pp. 90-5)

Arthur Ponsonby, in his *Samuel Pepys,* The Macmillan Company, 1928, 160 p.

CHAUNCEY BREWSTER TINKER
(essay date 1934)

[Tinker was an esteemed educator and literary historian. In the following excerpt, he evaluates the literary and historical merits of the *Diary.*]

I remember to have read somewhere in the pages of Mark Twain the account of a youthful attempt to keep a diary, the result of which was the endless repetition of the simple sentence, 'Got up, washed; went to bed.' I forget what the anecdote was meant to illustrate—the fact that there was nothing in a boy's life worth recording, or the fact that the diarist's art is a difficult one. In either case, I submit modestly but firmly that Mark Twain was wrong. A true diarist will be interesting about anything and about everything; whether the dog has ruined the carpet or a king been seated on his ancestral throne, the true journalist is never dull. The Creator has dispensed him from boring his audience.

Take, for instance, the three incidents of the day recited above: one gets up, one washes, and one goes to bed, all processes sufficiently common—even washing—to seem useless to the literary artist; yet who would spare them from the pages of Samuel Pepys? 'Up and to my office' . . . 'Up betimes, and to St. James's' . . . 'Lay in bed, it being Lord's Day, all the morning, talking with my wife; then up.' I find that I resent the entries in his *Diary* that lack this familiar beginning, as though something essential had been omitted. As for the companion phrase, consecrated to the close of day, it has in our own time achieved such popularity that it bids fair to be permanently enshrined in the daily speech of men, and cease to be recognized as a quotation: 'And so to bed. . . . ' Sentiment will ultimately make an epitaph of it, like 'Say not good-night,' or 'Good-bye, proud world.'

As for bathing, that may be the most exciting of events, as the poets know: 'the cool silver shock of the plunge,' whether it be into the 'pool's living water' or into the chilly waters of the domestic tub. 'One clear, nice, cool squirt of water o'er your bust.'

> Up, and to the office . . . where busy till noon, and then my wife being busy in going with her woman to a hothouse to bathe herself, after her long being within doors in the dirt, so that she now pretends to a resolution of being hereafter very clean. How long it will hold I can guess.

> 22nd. Lay last night alone, my wife after her bathinge lying alone in another bed. So cold all night.

> 25th. Thence home to the office, where dispatched much business; at night, late home, and to clean myself with warm water; my wife will have me, because she do herself, and so to bed.

Verily, nothing that is human is alien to the diarist. For him life contains nothing that is common or dull. Let him tell us what he ate for dinner, or how cold he was in bed, or how a duchess smiled on him, or what is his balance at the bank, or how he has lost his faith in God, or regained it, or been snubbed by a rival, or cursed his enemy in his heart, or cast eyes of desire upon the parlor maid—all is grist to his mill. How near is grandeur to our dust! How easily does this mortal put on immortality!

But immortality is bought at a price, even by the diarist. It is a razor edge, as the Mohammedan tells us, across which the aspirant to Heaven must make his way. And the diarist, like the rest of us, is in perpetual danger of damnation for his sins. He may make much of them in his journals, and even delight us by his own delight in them: but he must not take pride in displaying them. He would do well to set down naught in the hope of admiration or in the fear of derision. Thus, if a genuine diarist records that he was cold in bed, he does so with a childlike simplicity, as a grievance, as a count against his wife, or as a humble, human fact; but

the gods forbid him to enjoy the sensation of being clever at his work. As soon as he becomes clever, attending to his style and aspiring to smart phrase and graceful posture, he is a self-conscious artist, a skillful operative. He may, with luck, become Shaw or Mencken, but he will never be a Samuel Pepys. The artist seeks, properly enough, success and applause; but the diarist is not concerned with such matters. He is not permitted to anticipate or even to desire them. When once his record is complete, he may realize, I suppose, in some dim fashion that he has prevailed over oblivion, so that he cannot destroy his work, even though he may, so far as the outward and surface part of him is concerned, be unwilling that any eye save his own should ever see what he has written. (pp. 153-54)

Perhaps the most recent diary published is that of the Yorkshire parson, the Reverend Benjamin Newton, a typical sporting clergyman of the early nineteenth century, who was interested in everything about him, except perhaps the souls of his flock. Like Pepys, he was acutely susceptible to the charms of the other sex, and listed handsome women in numerical order, according to their beauty of (*a*) face and (*b*) figure. He is perpetually entertaining because of his unfailing vivacity. This is the quality which endears Pepys to his readers:—

> I home to set my journall for these four days in order, they being four days of as great content and honour and pleasure to me as ever I hope to live or desire, or think any body else can live. For methinks if a man would but reflect upon this, and think that all these things are ordered by God Almighty to make me contented . . . in my life and matter of mirth, methinks it should make one mightily more satisfied in the world than he is.

Neither syntax nor theology here is beyond criticism, but what vitality it reveals, what sincerity, what contentment! I like to think that the gratitude of young Mr. Pepys was acceptable to his Creator.

> So dispatched all my business, having assurance of . . . all hearty love from Sir W. Coventry, and so we staid and saw the King and Queene set out toward Salisbury, and after them the Duke and Duchesse, whose hands I did kiss. And it was the first time I did ever, or did see any body else, kiss her hand, and it was a most fine white and fat hand. But it was pretty to see the young pretty ladies dressed like men, in velvet coats, caps with ribbands and with laced bands, just like men. Only the Duchesse herself it did not become. They gone, we with great content took coach again, and hungry come to Clapham about one o'clock, and Creed there too before us, where a good dinner . . . and so to walk up and down in the gardens, mighty pleasant. By and by comes by promise to me Sir G. Carteret, and viewed the house above and below, and sat and drank there, and I had a little opportunity to kiss and

spend some time with the ladies above, his daughter, a buxom lass, and his sister Fissant, a serious lady, and a little daughter of hers that begins to sing prettily. Thence with mighty pleasure, with Sir G. Carteret by coach, with great discourse of kindnesse, with him to my Lord Sandwich, and to me also; and I every day see more good by the alliance. Almost at Deptford I 'light and walked over to Half-way House, and so home, in my way being shown my cozen Patience's house, which seems, at distance, a pretty house. At home met the weekly Bill, where above 1,000 encreased in the Bill, and of them in all about 1,700 of the plague, which hath made the officers this day resolve of sitting at Deptford, which puts me to some consideration what to do. Therefore home to think and consider of every thing about it, and without determining anything, eat a little supper, and to bed, full of the pleasure of these 6 or 7 last days.

All this mighty pleasure in the midst of a plague-stricken city! Terror hangs over the world like an ever-blackening cloud, but the diarist's appetite for existence endures undiminished. And so it remains to the end of the journal, when, with the dread of blindness descending upon him and faced with the necessity of closing his *Diary,* he can still record:—

Dined at home, and in the afternoon by water to White Hall, calling by the way at Michell's where I have not been many a day till just the other day, and now I met her mother there, and knew her husband to be out of town. And here je did baiser elle, but had not opportunity para hazer some with her as I would have offered if je had had it. And thence had another meeting with the Duke of York, at White Hall, on yesterday's work, and made a good advance: and so, being called by my wife, we to the Park, Mary Batelier and a Dutch gentleman, a friend of hers being with me. Thence to 'The World's End,' a drinking-house by the Park; and there merry, and so home late.

No trace is here of gloom or apprehension; yet the sentences speed forward to the most pathetic utterances of the great *Diary.* Even as he prays for mercy in the blindness which he believes to be coming on him, he does not forget his 'amours to Deb' and all 'other pleasures' which his eyesight now compels him to resign.

This very quality in which Pepys excels was well described by another great writer of journals:—

The minds of some men are like a dark cellar—their knowledge lies concealed; while the minds of others are all sunshine and mirror, and reflect all that they read or hear in a lively manner.

These are the words of James Boswell, a man who, quantitatively at least, rivals Pepys as a diarist. Pepys covers but nine years; Boswell, who had no trouble with his visual organs, remained an inveterate journal-ist to the end, and, no doubt, presented himself at the gate of Heaven notebook in hand. Now Boswell was a vastly less healthy person than Pepys; he suffered through life from a recurrent melancholia which introduces the strangest lights and shadows into his journals; but in his happier hours he had to a very high degree indeed the passion of which I have been speaking. Johnson himself described Boswell's fondness for the metropolis as a '*gust* for London.' And there are other powers which Pepys and Boswell share.

Both, for instance, were collectors. Both belong to that hungry set who save things, who gather relics and preserve souvenirs, who love long rows of well-filled shelves and all the paraphernalia of a library. These men leave treasures to posterity.

There is an intimate connection between this mania and the relish of existence which both men display so noticeably. It is because of his gusto that the diarist attempts to preserve some memorial of it, however inadequate. He cannot bear to think that experiences so rich should perish without leaving a rack behind, and he therefore enters into mortal combat with oblivion. The closer his record to the event itself, the more nearly satisfied he will be. Boswell provides many amusing examples of this desire for verisimilitude. Once when he sent his friend Temple as a sort of ambassador to the young lady with whom he was, or thought he was, in love, he provided him with a long series of detailed directions, the most pointed of which is the command, 'Take notes.' By taking notes, you see, the ambassador may hope to preserve not only the *ipsissima verba* of the interview, but even the very atmosphere and tone of it. The incident will be preserved, as book collectors say, 'in the original condition.' As long as the scenes of one's past are dear to the heart, so long will a man try to prepare for his future nostalgia by the writing of diaries and the preservation of relics. A true diarist is like a great portrait painter who takes his own likeness. The *Diary* of Mr. Pepys is, in a way, the greatest *Selbstbildnis* ever painted. 'A man loves to review his own mind,' said Johnson to Mrs. Thrale; 'that is the use of a diary or journal.' To whom Lord Trimlestown, who was present, said, 'True, Sir. As the ladies love to see themselves in a glass, so a man likes to see himself in his journal.' (pp. 155-57)

[There] is no carelessness or inaccuracy, or rhetoric, no heightening and coloring, in Pepys or Boswell. Both men were professionally concerned with recording facts: Pepys was engaged in filing records for the Naval Office—lists of battleships, with their tonnage and personnel, their movements and their whereabouts, and thousands upon thousands of similar details of no special interest to posterity. Boswell, as a Scotch lawyer, had to present his cases to the court in written form. Such work begets in a man a sense of fact, and a respect for the moving finger of time. He is not likely to date an important letter 'Wednesday.'

Much of our pleasure in reading Pepys springs from our conviction of its authenticity. It is this that sweeps us along, page after page, over the names of persons of whom we know nothing. But we do know that they are real, like the persons whom we pass in the street, even though we can tell nothing whatever about them. Some of them are acquainted with Pepys, and we are acquainted with him—that is sufficient. With a few of them we, too, become better acquainted as we read on, so that, if we persevere, we find our pleasure constantly mounting, since our knowledge of what is going on is gradually clarified. We shall never come to a perfect vision of it all—even the most painstaking research will never attain to that—but life as it was three hundred years ago, and Samuel Pepys in his habit as he lived, these we may come to know.

Let us not mistake. Pepys is not great merely because he brings us into contact with the exciting events of his time. True, he lived through the *annus mirabilis* of 1666, and so had intimate personal knowledge of the defeat of the Dutch fleet, the great plague that swept over the city, and the Great Fire which swept over it in a more literal sense. These are important events, as are a thousand others with which Pepys brings us in contact, and so the *Diary* is an invaluable source book for historians. But this is not the reason that Pepys has the devotion of his readers.

The fact is that the man had the fine art of making his record sparkle with vitality. I cannot analyze that gift. I have never met anybody who could. Most essays on Pepys—and there are many delightful ones—rely for their charm on liberal quotations from the *Diary*. The more quotations, the more charm. The essayist usually contents himself, as in the present instance, with a characterization of the man, not with a critical analysis of his style. How shall one show the component parts of anything so artless?

Yet Pepys was an artist, and I believe that he knew it. It would be more accurate to say that he came in time to know it. It seems to me preposterous to try to believe that a man who has produced a vast work of genius should be unaware of what he has done. He may very well have been ignorant of its largest relations and of its permanent value to mankind; but that he should have had no intimation of its pictorial and panoramic quality, no realization of the fact that it plumbs the depths of human nature—this is to me beyond belief. I should as soon expect the builder of the pyramids to be unaware of the shape which he had erected.

And I believe, furthermore, that it was this knowledge of what he had done that prevented Pepys from destroying or ordering the destruction of the *Diary*. He could not do it, nor do I think that another man who had created such a thing (if we may tolerate such an assumption) could bring himself to destroy it. For Pepys it would have been a kind of suicide.

He was aware, of course, that it could be readily decoded,—was not the same code used in his office?— and, indeed, a cipher that cannot be decoded, if such there be, would be simply a form of oblivion. And yet there was a certain protection in it. A cipher does furnish a screen against casual observation; a long diary, like that of Pepys, might hope to survive many years unread. After a lapse of a couple of generations, secrecy was no longer of consequence. This was perhaps, consciously or subconsciously, what Pepys wished. He wanted privacy—protection, that is, from the inquisitiveness and derision of his neighbors; and this the cipher afforded, and would probably continue to afford as long as any of his contemporaries remained alive. To most of us posterity hardly matters. The genial soul of Pepys may very well have been content to meet it, and entrust his reputation to it. I cannot see why any man should shrink from that. It is one's neighbors and relatives whom one wishes to elude. In the masquerade of life a man does not care to give himself away. It is a world in which we are all making a plucky pretense. One takes conscious pride in 'getting away' with one's pose, and none more so than Pepys in public life. But there is solid comfort in making a clean breast of it, whether one is purging the stuffed bosom of the perilous stuff that weighs upon the heart or merely setting down the various devices by which he has succeeded in snatching the pleasures of existence as they fly. But it is so hard to get a hearing and to utter all that one would like to say! Confessors, I have been told, find some difficulty in persuading their penitents to abridge the tale of their sins. 'No excuses, please; no details,' they must be always hinting. But the diarist feels no such restraint, and hears no such monitor. He may go on forever.

And as for being read by posterity, is there not a certain pleasure in that, even though everything has to come out? It is certainly no worse than dying and meeting the Recording Angel, which is the experience that awaits us all. But, thanks be to God, it is an angel, and not our neighbors, our wives, or our professors whom we have to meet. Perhaps it will not be so bad after all. Who knows but there may be a solid satisfaction in it, upon getting a hearing at last? The angel will probably do the best he can for us. It is the way of angels.

Posterity has been friendly to Pepys. Not even an angel, I imagine, could have been more indulgently kind. Where is there an author more beloved by his readers? Boswell is still despised by multitudes, Walpole is disliked, Cowper pitied, and Rousseau distrusted. But Pepys is like Lamb, loved by everybody. I have encountered but one sneer at Pepys, and that was from the pen of a Communist, writing for the *New Masses,* one Michael Gold:—

> Samuel Pepys is esteemed by bourgeois readers because he did the things they do, or want to do: he accepted bribes, he dodged his taxes, he was unfaithful . . . to his wife, he beat his servants.

In the new world of Communism there will, I suppose, be none of these dreadful things, for sin and the knowledge of it will have been abolished (by law), and nobody will care whether he is loved by posterity or not. (pp. 157-59)

Chauncey Brewster Tinker, "The Great Diarist," in *The Atlantic Monthly,* Vol. 153, No. 2, February, 1934, pp. 153-59.

PERCIVAL HUNT
(essay date 1958)

[In the excerpt below, Hunt reviews the major themes and subjects of the *Diary*, noting especially the merits of Pepys's prose style.]

[In the *Diary*] Pepys wrote of his daily affairs. He did not write for the future, or to show wonders and himself to lesser people, or, it seems, even for his own re-reading. He wrote a chronicle day by day, a log of his actions, thoughts, and feelings, a direct account of his life, with not many sweeps of philosophy or abstraction. He did philosophize but not usually. He philosophized on his having got his position by favor, on the need that words of a song be left in the language in which they were written, on his lack of lasting sorrow when his brother died, on the conduct of the King and Court ("God knows what will be the end of it!"); on London after the Fire and after the Plague. He wrote of his childhood at Ashted when he went back there at thirty; and he wrote a tremendously effective and self-forgetful account of the Fire. But philosophizing is not the main recurring substance of the *Diary;* it is in the *Diary* because it was part of some day in his life.

Pepys had the luck or the instinct or the determination to be in important places at important times, often in places he has no business to be. Once there, he shoved his way, quite unashamed, to the front. Possibly what he wrote made up for his elbowing. At sixteen he stood close by the scaffold when Charles I was beheaded on a cold January afternoon; and at twenty-six, time having changed his fortune and opinion, he went to see General Harrison, who had signed the King's death-warrant, hanged and drawn and quartered—"a bloody day." He was in London when Oliver Cromwell died; and when Richard Cromwell gave up his ineffec-

tual rule; and while Parliament and the Army struggled; and he watched, one morning in February, 1660, "it being a most pleasant morning and sunshine," General Monk march his men into control of the City ("all his forces . . . in very good plight and stout officers"). He was secretary to the Admiral on the "Royal Charles," which brought Charles II back to England, and he saw him land at Dover and ride away to London "in a stately coach." At the coronation he pushed into the Abbey among the followers of the King's Surveyor-General and from a seat high up under the roof of the North Transept he saw and heard what he could. (At the next coronation, as a baron of the Cinque Ports, he walked close by the King.) When the new Queen (September 21, 1662), whom everybody was curious about, heard her first mass in her Chapel of St. James's, he crowded close up to the altar and to the Queen; and since his cousin was the ambassador and admiral whose ship carried the Queen from Portugal, Pepys heard much about her. He was in London during the Plague, and he watched almost hour by hour the Great Fire. He knew the King, the Duke of York, the Court, and some of the King's ladies. He saw the Established Church return with the Restoration, and the playhouses open, and the old ways come in again, though changed. He had part in the humiliations and triumphs of the endless, intermittent, vital Dutch Wars, and he lived a long time shadowed by the Popish Plot and by the Titus Oates and his like. He had part in the coronation of James II, and four years after that he saw James deposed and William III come. He knew London intimately, places and people, and the quiet English country beyond, and the villages, and the farmlands. He was familiar with workingmen in the City, and the men who kept the little shops and taverns, and their clerks, and the great merchants, and the banker-goldsmiths. He had been at Cambridge with Dryden; for years he talked and often ate with Thomas Fuller of the *Worthies;* he became a friend of "that miracle of a youth Christopher Wren" and of the noble Mr. John Evelyn, and of many such; and he corresponded with Sir Isaac Newton, Sir Hans Sloane, Sir Godfrey Kneller, the Duchess of Newcastle, the Duke of York, and masters and dons at Oxford and Cambridge, and other learned and humane men. Most of them he wrote of in the *Diary.* (pp. 4-6)

Music is a constant topic in the *Diary.* Often for awhile the *Diary* lets music lie unseen below what is told of acts and personalities, yet it soon comes again into expression, for Pepys's interest in music never ended. He writes of his own singing and composing and playing; of listening to the singing and playing of others; of choosing a servant partly because he had a good voice or read music or played the lute; of teaching his wife and his friends and his servants to sing; of studying the science of music—its structure, theory, mathe-

Pepys's private library in London.

matics; of speculating whether music-charts and other like inventions—were ever a help in composition; of going to hear good music and of his delight when he was surprised by good music heard unexpectedly. At home early and late, and at his friends'; at sea and on the Thames going down to inspect a Shipyard; in his own or in somebody else's garden; at church; at inns and taverns; and in coaches as he traveled on business; in almost every place and in most conditions of mind, Pepys sang or played or heard music, or he talked of it, or read or thought of it. He himself had a pleasant, well-trained voice, and played with skill the flageolet, the lute, and the treble viol. One June evening "it being very hot weather I took my flageolette and played upon the leads [the flat roof of his house] in the garden, where Sir. W. Pen came out in his shirt onto his leads, and there we staid talking and singing, and drinking great drafts of claret, and eating botargo [fish roe "to promote drinking"] and bread and butter till twelve at night, it being moonshine; and so to bed, very near fuddled" (June 5, 1661). There are many such entries, with variations. (p. 119)

Almost nothing has been written about the music in Pepys's prose, about its style. The prose of the *Diary*

is admirable. Rhythms (accents heavy and light, and pauses), the sounds of vowels and consonants in the phrasing, the variety and length and arrangement of phrases and sentences and words, all mingle into a fluid whole as the different ideas and feelings follow one another. The reader, unless he is an analyst, does not notice what makes the effect nor does it seem to him that Pepys ever was consciously after an effect. Indeed, Pepys wrote spontaneously; he wrote as he did because he thought and felt as he did and had a great literary gift. Pepys—to put it another way—was absorbed by the facts and by his feelings about them, and he could write prose that carried the facts and the implications, the suggestion, the experience which the facts had for him. His prose has the resonance of his temperament, his character, his abilities. His prose is his personality expressing itself in words.

When he tells a matter dull for him, it becomes dull stuff from the style of telling; when he tells a happy matter, his writing gets the happiness. His Navy Office summaries are sharply business-like; his excitement about a good play carries excitement.

The first Sunday he went to Saint Olave's after the Plague, Pepys walked through the churchyard (326 dead from the Plague, were buried there and in the church). "It frighted me indeed . . . more than I thought it could have done, to see so [many] graves lie so high upon the churchyards where people have been buried of the plague . . . I . . . do not think to go through it again a good while" (January 30, 1666).

In the evening, September 2, 1666, the first day of the Great Fire, Pepys, watching from

> a little ale-house on the Bankside . . . saw the fire grow . . . more and more . . . , in corners and upon steeples, and between churches and houses, as far as we could see up the hill of the City, in a most horrid malicious bloody flame, not like the fine flame of an ordinary fire . . . , it made me weep to see it. The churches, houses, and all on fire and flaming at once, and a horrid noise the flames made, and the cracking of houses at their ruins.

In both these, Pepys tells of his fear. The first holds an ominous, almost unlocalised feeling of horror, which Pepys implies but does not name; the second tells his specific terror of the Fire, with specific terms. In the first, the phrases are longer and slower-moving, and heavy with m's and n's and lagging ld's, d's, k's, and t's. The second has shorter phrases and sharper, higher sounds which run on faster.

One meal which Pepys had with the Duke of Albermarle, he did not enjoy: "I find the Duke of Albermarle at dinner with sorry company, some of his officers of the Army; dirty dishes, and a nasty wife at table, and bad meat, at which I made but an ill dinner" (4 April, 1667). In one sentence, three lines of the Diary, Pepys makes the facts quite clear. He gives, too, his feeling, by jagged phrases chopped into short lengths, by omitting many "and's," by the sound of the words "sorry," "dirty," "nasty," by strong alliteration of sharp "t's" and "d's." Pepys had been irritated by this dinner and still was irritated as he wrote those uncomfortable rhythms and the jangled sounds.

Sunday, June 11, 1665, Pepys had quite another sort of meal: "In the evening comes Mr. Andrews and his wife and Mr. Hill, and stayed and played, and sung and supped, most excellent pretty company, so pleasant, ingenious, and harmless, I cannot desire better. They gone we to bed, my mind in great present ease." Mr. Andrews was Pepys's friend before the *Diary* starts, and Mr. Hill he met in 1664 and kept as a good friend long after the *Diary* ends. What he says of the supper has a pervading sense of ease and comfort and rest among old friends, stated in clear facts and sustained in the simplest kind of sentence built upon parallel phrases linked in many "and's." The writing never rises to any sharp description. It flows slowly, yet it never drags because it has in it clear open vowels and liquid consonants—l, m, n, r—and alliteration, and almost rhyming words. Toward the end of the first sen-

tence, the words become longer and more homely; they move on slowly: "excellent pretty company, so pleasant, ingenious, and harmless." The second sentence, which ends the account, is contrastingly short. It shows two moods. The first phrases of five words—bare, short, clipped—tells that the evening is done: "They gone we to bed." The rhythm and sound of the next six words—the last six—carry the earlier mood.

One afternoon, May 22, when he was thirty, he walked with John Creed, secretary of the Tangier Commission, from Greenwich to Woolwich, down along the river, four miles or so. He wrote " . . . by water to Greenwich, and [after] calling at the little alehouse at the end of the town to wrap a rag about my little left toe, [it] being new sore with walking, we walked pleasantly to Woolwich, in our way hearing the nightingales sing." He seems to have written this off-hand. In the half-sentence he gives, quite completely and quite without strain, the tone of the pleasure he had on the walk. He uses short words, innocently actual details, barely two adjectives, a child-like directness of phrasing, and the nightingale for poetry and wonder.

Two long quotations, one from the *Diary*, the other from a letter, are fair examples of wholly different tones in Pepys's writing. The first was written when he was about thirty-two:

> . . . To the 'Change after office, and received my watch from the watch-maker, and a very fine [one] it is, given me by Briggs, the Scrivener. . . . But, Lord! to see how much of my old folly and childishnesse hangs upon me still that I cannot forbear carrying my watch in my hand in the coach all this afternoon, and seeing what o'clock it is one hundred times, and am apt to think with myself, how could I be so long without one; though I remember since, I had one, and found it a trouble, and resolved to carry one no more about me while I lived. So home to supper and to bed [May 13, 1665].

The second is from a letter to Evelyn, written when Pepys was sixty-seven and living in leisure at Clapham.

> I have no herds to mind, nor will my Doctor allow me any books here. What, then, . . . you say, . . . are you doing? Why, truly, nothing that will bear naming, and yet I am not, I think, idle; for who can, that has so much of past and to come to think on, as I have? And thinking, I take it, is working, though many forms beneath what my Lady and you are doing. But pray remember what o'clock it is with you and me; and be not now, by overstirring, too bold with your present complaint, any more that I dare be with mine, which, too, has been no less kind in giving me my warning, than the other to you, and to neither of us, I hope, and, through God's mercy, dare say, either unlooked for or unwelcome. I wish, nevertheless, that I were able to administer any thing towards the lengthening that precious rest of

life which God has thus long blessed you, and, in you, mankind, with; but I have always been too little regardful of my own health, to be a prescriber to others. . . . [Chapham, 7 August, 1700].

(pp. 120-23)

The *Diary* was written in an age of great prose. Within, roughly, the hundred and fifty years after 1550, the Book of Common Prayer (1549, 1552) and the King James Bible were published, and North's Plutarch (1579), Donne's devotional prose, Shakespeare, Bacon's *Essays,* Sir Thomas Browne's *Religio Medici,* and much of Milton and Dryden and Fuller and Izaak Walton and Bunyan and others. This English prose had pungency and exactness and comprehensibility, color and beauty and surprise. Unlike earlier writing in English it gave no implied or open apology for not being Latin or Greek. The new science, too, thought English a good language. In 1667 the Royal Society, which Pepys had become a member of in 1665, urged that writers and speakers reject all "swellings of style" that they aim at "a close, naked, natural way of speaking . . . a native ease," and, above all, that they use the speech of common men.

Pepys knew the classics, and much of the best writing of the closer past and of his own time. He valued the older, established writers. Contemporary writing he judged as he did any other sort of work by men he knew. He went to many plays of Dryden ("Dryden the poet I knew at Cambridge"; February 3, 1662), who was about his own age, some of which he cared for not at all and some of which, he wrote, "pleased me mightily." And he read Dryden's prose and did not hesitate to give his opinions of it. "I bought the Mayden Queen, a play newly printed which I like, at the King's house so well. . . . Mr. Dryden, . . . he himself, in his preface, seems to brag of [it] and indeed it is a good play" (January 18, 1668). He suggested to Dryden putting Chaucer's *Poor Person* into contemporary verse. Thomas Fuller, twenty-five years older than Pepys, he knew so well that when he "met with Dr. Thomas Fuller" he "took him to The Dog, where he did tell me of his last and great book which is coming out; that is, his History of all the Families in England; and he could tell me more of my own than I knew myself " (January 22, 1661). Once he had a long talk with Fuller about ways of writing, and another time he heard Fuller preach. It was "a dry sermon." Pepys looked at Dryden and Fuller and

other writers of his time with a level eye, seeing them not magnified or lessened by distance and accumulated criticism.

The two books Pepys read and heard and valued most were the King James Bible and the Book of Common Prayer. The *Diary* shows this all through it, in big things and little. The Bible, with the Prayer Book, has changing and suitable rhythms, gained it seemed unconsciously; it uses exact and simple words; it prefers to be specific rather than to generalize; and the subject is always clearly dominant, made all the more so by being written of in prose beautifully suited to express it. Such prose, the seventeenth century at its best valued and wrote; and so, at its best, seventeenth century prose has force and clearness and luminous suggestion. Izaak Walton and Sir Thomas Browne and John Bunyan and Pepys, in different styles, wrote that sort of prose. Browne, in the *Religio Medici,* quite individually wrote: "There is surely a piece of divinity in us, something that was before the elements, and owes no homage to the sun." And "We carry within us the wonders we seek without us; There is all Africa and her prodigies in us." And "We see by an invisible sun within us." Half way through "The Fourth Day" of the *Complete Angler* Walton wrote: "No life, my honest scholar, no life so happy and so pleasant as the life of a well-governed angler; for while the lawyer is swallowed up with business, and the statesman is preventing or contriving plots, then we sit on cowslip banks, hear the birds sing, and possess ourselves in as much quietness as those silent silver streams, which we now see glide so quietly by us." Bunyan, telling the death of Mr. Valiant-for-Truth, ended: "And so he passed over and all the trumpets sounded for him on the other side." "And the Pilgrim they laid in an upper chamber, whose windows opened toward the sun-rising: the name of the chamber was Peace; where he slept till break of day, and then he arose and sang." Browne, Walton, and Bunyan, each speaks in his own way, yet the Bible and the Prayer Book have a part in them all; as the two books have in the quite different writing of the *Diary.* (pp. 123-25)

Percival Hunt, in his *Samuel Pepys in the Diary,* University of Pittsburgh Press, 1958, 178 p.

SOURCES FOR FURTHER STUDY

Abernathy, Cecil. *Mr. Pepys of Seething Lane.* New York: McGraw-Hill Book Co., 1957, 384 p.

Comprehensive biography.

Bradford, Gamaliel. *The Soul of Samuel Pepys.* Boston: Hougton Mifflin Co., 1924, 262 p.

Character study of Pepys, with scattered comments on the aesthetic merits of the *Diary*.

Bryant, Arthur. *Samuel Pepys*. 3 vols. Cambridge: Cambridge University Press, 1933-38.

Well-documented biography of Pepys.

Drinkwater, John. *Pepys: His Life and Character*. Garden City, N.Y.: Doubleday Doran & Co., 1930, 374 p.

Biography aimed at the general reader.

Latham, Robert. Introduction to *The Shorter Pepys,* by Samuel Pepys, edited by Robert Latham, pp. xxi-xxxix. London: Bell & Hyman, 1985.

General critical introduction to the *Diary,* praising it as the most evocative and informative English document of its kind.

Ollard, Richard. *Pepys: A Biography*. London: Sinclair Stevenson, 1991, 411 p.

Excellent illustrated overview of Pepys's life and career, with extensive commentary on the *Diary*.

Summers, Montague. *The Playhouse of Pepys*. London: Kegan Paul, Trench, Trubner & Co., 1935, 485 p.

Survey of the English Restoration theater based on dramatic criticism in the *Diary*.

Harold Pinter

1930-

English dramatist, scriptwriter, short story writer, novelist, and poet.

INTRODUCTION

A major figure in contemporary drama, Pinter is best known for his enigmatic plays which blend absurdism and realism to illustrate the isolation and violence in modern society. Such topics as the ambiguity and subjectiveness of reality, the failure of interpersonal communication, and the primacy of power in human relationships figure prominently in Pinter's ominous yet humorous works. Central to Pinter's exploration of these concerns is a dramatic tension often attributed to the conflict between the meticulously preserved social pretenses of his characters and the subconscious desires or neuroses they repress. While some commentators have derided Pinter's style as confusing and unintelligible, most laud his synthesis of fabrication, interrogation, confession, and silence as among the most original and perceptive expressions of communication in the contemporary theater.

Pinter's early plays are often described as "comedies of menace" in which mysterious strangers threaten the inhabitants of an insulated, seemingly secure environment. In Pinter's first production, the one-act play *The Room* (1957), a blind man invades the comfortable flat of sixty-year-old Rose, entreating her to come home even though she vehemently denies knowing him. Her husband later discovers the visitor and savagely beats him in front of Rose, who is then struck blind. Pinter's subsequent work, the full-length drama *The Birthday Party* (1958), focuses upon Stanley, a pianist living in a shabby seaside hotel, whose birthday celebration is transformed into a torturous interrogation by two strangers. Initially demoralizing Stanley with a litany of serious and absurd charges, the pair take him away to an undisclosed location for a "rest cure." Reviewers, daunted by the cryptic plots of *The Room* and *The Birthday Party*, generally dismissed these dramas as nonsensical, an epithet subsequently applied to *The Dumb Waiter* (1960). In this play, assassins Gus and Ben, waiting for instructions in the basement kitchen of an abandoned restaurant, willingly fill meal orders transported via a dumb waiter. When Gus leaves momentarily, the machine brings a new message, directing Ben to murder the next person who enters the room. The play ends as he confronts his returning partner, gun in hand.

During the time Pinter produced these plays, the British theater was dominated in part by the "Angry Young Men," a group of writers whose portrayal of disillusioned, working-class characters in bleak, mundane surroundings reflected the heightened social consciousness of the post-World War II era. This period also gave rise to the Theater of the Absurd, an experimental dramatic style typified by the works of Samuel Beckett and Eugène Ionesco, which replaced the traditional formulas of plot, action, and denouement with such elements as contradiction, indecipherable dialogue, and bizarre images and situations. While Pinter's early plays have much in common with these theatrical trends, critics emphasize that a combination of elements from these two movements distinguishes his work. *The Hothouse* (1980), written in 1958 but not produced until 1980, exemplifies such a synthesis. A satiric, surrealistic portrayal of a government-run mental hospital and its sadistic, incompetent staff, this drama is often regarded as an implicit condemnation of modern bureaucratic institutions.

Following his radio plays *A Slight Ache* (1959) and *A Night Out* (1960), Pinter produced *The Caretaker* (1960), his first critical and popular success, which delineates a more recognizably realistic situation. Aston, a former mental patient, brings Davies, an opportunistic vagrant, to the house owned by his domineering younger brother, Mick. While Aston enthusiastically recommends the hiring of Davies as caretaker, Mick immediately detects the derelict's selfish motivations and abusively cross-examines him. Ultimately driven to distraction, Davies leaves, speaking incoherently about retrieving "his papers" in a London suburb. Critics discerned that *The Caretaker* differs from Pinter's earlier plays in that the atmosphere of menace arises not from a mysterious source but from the struggle for dominance between Mick and Davies. Later commentators also noted that *The Caretaker* introduces several themes developed by Pinter in his more recent work, including the subjects of reality and verbal communication. Daniel Salem stated that the reality of Pinter's characters "is double and always experienced on two levels. On the one hand there is a surface reality that everyone is led to believe in when trying to be guided by appearances. On the other hand, there is the hidden reality of secret emotions which contradicts surface reality, alters it, and gives each character his psychological depth."

In Pinter's teleplays *The Collection* (1961), *The Lover* (1963), and *Tea Party* (1963), those vying for power are spouses and family members rather than strangers. Similarly, Pinter's third full-length stage drama, *The Homecoming* (1965), concentrates on the exploitative relationships within a working-class London family. Regarded as one of Pinter's most effective works, this play centers upon the return from the United States of the eldest son and his attempt to dominate his depraved father and brothers. The son is rejected, however, in favor of his coolly detached wife, who gains control of the household, as the mother had, by agreeing to become a prostitute. Katherine H. Burkman asserted: "The men, on the whole, in Pinter's family plays are trapped in their ambivalent family relationships. Several of the women, though, who as whores seem to betray all that is sacred in the family, tend to find their way to freedom and to an authentic voice that is still a family one. . . . [They] find their way to a self-possession in which they accept their multiple roles as wife, mother, and whore, belonging to themselves and thereby offering new life to the family."

Pinter's subsequent dramas focus increasingly upon the subjectivity of memory. *Landscape* and *Silence,* two one-act plays produced together in 1969, feature exchanges of monologues in which intimately related yet isolated characters recall disparate versions of common events. Memory also plays a pivotal role in *Old Times* (1970), Pinter's next full-length drama. In this play, Anna welcomes Kate, her one-time roommate and, it is implied, her former lover, to the house she shares with her husband, Deeley. Apparently hoping to resume their affair, Kate competes with Deeley for possession of Anna by selectively recalling past events concerning his wife that will substantiate or negate their present claims upon her. Although Anna ultimately asserts her preference for Deeley by envisioning Kate as long dead, the trio prove to be inextricably bound by the past. In a review of this work, Harold Clurman observed that for Pinter "memory merges much of what has happened to us into things which we only imagined or dreamed as having happened. The reality of the past fades and memory transforms real events into shadowy remnants of experience which are no more substantial than reveries."

Pinter's recent plays, while still dramatically complex, are often considered more accessible than his earlier works. Critics generally contend that *Betrayal* (1978), for example, differs from other dramatic treatments of marital infidelity only in its reversal of chronological order. *Family Voices* (1981), which stylistically resembles *Landscape* and *Silence* in its use of alternating monologues, examines the repressive relationship between a mother and her son, who lives in a dissolute boarding house. *Family Voices* and the one-act dramas *Victoria Station,* which concerns the bizarre alliance between a taxi dispatcher and an uncooperative driver, and *A Kind of Alaska*, based on actual case histories of sleeping sickness victims who were revived after spending decades in comas, were combined to form a trilogy entitled *Other Voices* (1983). *One for the Road* (1984), which replaced *Family Voices* in later productions of *Other Voices*, reflects Pinter's growing concern for political and human rights in its realistic portrayal of the interrogation and torture of a family by a decorous government representative. *Mountain Language* (1988) also examines political repression. Based upon the alleged attempts of the Turkish government to eradicate the language and culture of its Kurdish minority, this work focuses upon a group of women waiting to visit loved ones in prison who are forbidden by guards to speak their own "mountain language."

In addition to his highly regarded original dramas, Pinter has won acclaim for his screen adaptations of such works as Marcel Proust's *A la recherche du temps perdu*, entitled *The Proust Screenplay* (1977), John Fowles's *The French Lieutenant's Woman* (1981), Margaret Atwood's *The Handmaid's Tale* (1990), and Ian McEwan's *The Comfort of Strangers* (1991).

(For further information about Pinter's life and works, see *Contemporary Authors*, Vols. 5-8; *Contemporary Authors New Revision Series*, Vol. 33; *Contemporary Literary Criticism*, Vols. 1, 3, 6, 9, 11, 15, 27, 58; and *Dictionary of Literary Biography*, Vol. 13: *British Dramatists Since World War II*.)

CRITICAL COMMENTARY

BERT O. STATES
(essay date 1968)

[States is an American critic and playwright whose works include *Irony and Drama: A Poetics* (1971) and *The Shape of Paradox: An Essay on "Waiting for Godot"* (1978). In the following excerpt from an essay that first appeared in *The Hudson Review* in 1968, he contends that *The Homecoming* presents a unique reality that effectively defies conventional mythic or psychological interpretations.]

[We] explain [*The Homecoming*] as a study in psychic ambiguity: under the banal surface a massive Oedipal syndrome (like the part of the iceberg you can't see) bumps its way to grisly fulfillment. Or, beneath Freud lurks Jung and the archetypal: the father-sons "contest," the "fertility rite" on the sofa, the Earth Mother "sacrifice," the tribal sharing of her body (a Sparagmos for sure), the cyclical "return," and so on. But before the play is any or all of these things, it seems to be something much different and much simpler.

Perhaps the best way to pin it down is to try to say why psychology and myth seem unsatisfactory as explanations. The trouble with them is that they bring to the fore a purposiveness which seems at odds with the nature of the imagination we are dealing with. They assume that the play is *about* these things, whereas I think they come much closer to being by-products, as we would be dealing with by-products of, say, a story by Poe in the themes of crime-does-not-pay, or man-is-evil, or even in the mythic structure which I am sure

there are plenty of in Poe, as there always are in tales of victimization. As for the psychological drives themselves, one somehow doubts that Pinter's characters, deep down, are any more troubled by appetites of the sexual kind than Dostoevsky's people are troubled by finding suitable jobs. They seem far more interested in manipulating the idea of sexuality, for its effect on others, than in their own performance. As for the mythic elements, it is simply hard to see what they prove, other than that Pinter deals in some pretty raw urges, hardly a distinction these days. To be "primitive" is not to be Pinteresque.

I suggest that it is in the peculiar way the story is told and in the liberties it takes with the reality it posits. For instance, if we reduce the play to its main turns of plot we have something like this: a son and his wife return to the family home on a visit abroad. Almost immediately, the father and brothers make open advances on the wife. She seems to tolerate, if not encourage, them and the husband makes no effort to protect his interests. In fact, it is the husband in the end who makes the family's proposal to the wife that she stay on as mother, mistress to everybody, and as prostitute. She accepts (!) and he goes back to their three children. We anticipate that it will be the wife who now controls the family.

It would be hard to conceive an action, in modern "family" terms, which violates so many of our moral scruples with so little effort and so little interest in making itself credible. . . . [The] reaction one has to the play comes nowhere near Pity and Fear, or any of

Principal Works

The Room (drama) 1957

The Birthday Party (drama) 1958

A Slight Ache (drama) 1959

The Caretaker (drama) 1960

The Dumb Waiter (drama) 1960

The Dwarfs (drama) 1960

A Night Out (drama) 1960

Night School (drama) 1960

The Collection (drama) 1961

The Lover (drama) 1963

The Homecoming (drama) 1965

Tea Party (drama) 1965

The Basement (drama) 1967

Landscape (drama) 1968

Night (drama) 1968

Silence (drama) 1968

Old Times (drama) 1971

Monologue (drama) 1973

No Man's Land (drama) 1975

Betrayal (drama) 1978

*Family Voices (drama) 1980

*A Kind of Alaska (drama) 1983

*Victoria Station (drama) 1983

*One for the Road (drama) 1984

Mountain Language (drama) 1988

*Performed together under the title Other Voices.

their weaker derivatives, but is better described as *astonishment at the elaboration*. And it is precisely this quality of astonishment that is apt to disappear from any thematically oriented recovery of the play. (pp. 149-50)

The Homecoming may be about homecomings of all kinds but it is not ultimately about ours. We witness it, it even coaxes us to grope for connections among our own realities (and find them), but it does not, as its primary artistic mission, refer us back to a cluster of moral or existential issues we care very much about. What astonishes about the play is its taking of an extraordinarily brutal action, passing it through what is perhaps the most unobtrusive and "objective" medium since Chekhov's, and using it as the host for a peculiar activity of mind. We have invented special words for this activity ("Pintercourse," "Pinterism," "Pinterotic," etc.), which Pinter understandably detests, but it seems we have needed them as semantic consolation for his having hidden from us the thing they refer to. (p. 150)

[The] source of our consternation and fascination with Pinter [is] our quest for the lost superiority of knowing more than the characters who now know

more than we do, the very reverse of the familiar "dramatic" irony in which *we* know but they don't. To put it crudely, it is the goal of the Pinter character, as agent of his author's grand strategy, to stay ahead of the audience by "inventing" his drama out of the sometimes slender life afforded him (glasses of water, newspapers, cheese-rolls, etc.). His motto, in fact, might well be Renan's remark (which I . . . crib from Chevalier [in his book on Anatole France]): "The universe is a spectacle that God offers himself; let us serve the intentions of the great choreogus by contributing to render the spectacle as brilliant, as varied as possible." To this end, he becomes, as it were, a little Pinter, an author of irony, sent into his incredible breathing world scarce half made-up, morally, to work on the proper business of his author's trade—to "trump" life, to go it one better by going it one worse. (pp. 151-52)

I feel obliged to put Pinter into the context he deserves most and that amounts to considering him as a craftsman rather than a thinker, a maker of theatre out of "accepted" materials. [For example], I find the question of whether he sees the world as "essentially violent" about as interesting and relevant to his art as whether, let us say, John Constable sees the world as essentially peaceful. (p. 157)

Terence Martin . . . makes a case for Poe's "play habit," the "desire to astonish by boundless exaggeration or confusion of proportions." He is "our one author," says Mr. Martin, "who makes an absolute commitment to the imagination—who releases the imagination into a realm of its own where, with nothing to play *with*, it must play *at* our destruction. He shows us insistently that the imagination at his kind of play is not only anti-social but anti-human. To do justice to his contemporaries, perhaps we should say that what Poe undertook was not to be looked at without blinking."

That is more or less how I feel about Harold Pinter. In fact, with just a little transposing, we could probably derive most of the old Gothic essentials from our play: the nightmare setting, the double vision of the real and the superreal, the lurking fatality and inexplicable tyranny, the mysterious inspecificity and yet *utter* relevance of everything. Even—allowing for an unfortunate degeneration in our heroine—the central Gothic theme of the pale and lovely maiden *dominated* by the inscrutable sadist of the "nameless vice." This is not intended as a dismissal of either Pinter or Gothicism. If anything, it is a plug for art which produces reactions other than the shock of recognition, art in which the very limitedness of the artist to relatively outré kinds of experience and his ability to arouse the precise *sense* of that experience are the things to be praised. To me, Pinter falls brilliantly into this category and it is with considerable respect for him that I subscribe to his own evaluation of himself as "overblown tremendously" by people who "tend to make too much of a meal." This is not at all to deny the good chance that he may come out in the end as the Poe or Huysmans of the Absurdist theatre—a better fate, perhaps, than the one in store for some of our sterner moralists. (pp. 159-60)

Bert O. States, "Pinter's 'Homecoming': The Shock of Nonrecognition," in *Pinter: A Collection of Critical Essays,* edited by Arthur Ganz, Prentice-Hall, 1972, pp. 147-60.

JOHN RUSSELL TAYLOR
(essay date 1969)

[Taylor is a British film and theater critic whose works include *Cinema Eye, Cinema Ear* (1964) and *The Rise and Fall of the Well Made Play* (1967). In the following excerpt from his critical study *Anger and After: A Guide to the New British Dramatists,* he traces the development of Pinter's dramatic style from his early "comedies of menace" to his more realistic plays such as *The Birthday Party* and *The Caretaker.*]

The technique of casting doubt upon everything by matching each apparently clear and unequivocal statement with an equally clear and unequivocal statement of its contrary—used rather crudely in some parts of [his first play, *The Room*]— . . . is one which we shall find used constantly in Pinter's plays to create an air of mystery and uncertainty. The situations involved are always very simple and basic, the language which the characters use is an almost uncannily accurate reproduction of everyday speech (indeed, in this respect Pinter, far from being the least realistic dramatist of his generation, is arguably the most realistic), and yet in these ordinary surroundings lurk mysterious terrors and uncertainties—and by extension, the whole external world of everyday realities is thrown into question. Can we ever know the truth about anybody or anything? Is there any absolute truth to be known?

However, this is to anticipate. In *The Room* the hand is not yet entirely sure and the mystifications are often too calculated, too heavily underlined. The suppression of motives, for example, which in later plays comes to seem inevitable, because no one, not even the man who acts, can know precisely what impels him to act, here often looks merely an arbitrary device: it is not that the motives are unknowable, but simply that the author will not permit *us* to know them. So, too, the melodramatic finale. . . . [Rose, in this play], belongs to that group of characteristic Pinter figures from his first phase (that in which he wrote 'comedies of menace'), those who simply fear the world outside. The plays of this group—*The Room, The Dumb Waiter, The*

Birthday Party, and *A Slight Ache*—all take place in confined surroundings, in one room in fact, which represents for their protagonists at least a temporary refuge from the others (it is tempting, but not really necessary, to see it in terms of Freudian symbolism as a womb-substitute), something they have shored up against their ruins. The menace comes from outside, from the intruder whose arrival unsettles the warm, comfortable world bounded by four walls, and any intrusion can be menacing, because the element of uncertainty and unpredictability the intruder brings with him is in itself menacing. And the menace is effective almost in inverse proportion to its degree of particularization, the extent to which it involves overt physical violence or direct threats. We can all fear an unexpected knock at the door, a summons away from our safe, known world of normal domesticities on unspecified business (it is surely not entirely without significance that Pinter, himself a Jew, grew up during the war, precisely the time when the menace inherent in such a situation would have been, through the medium of the cinema or of radio, most imaginatively present to any child, and particularly perhaps a Jewish child). But the more particularized the threat is, the less it is likely to apply to our own case and the less we are able to read our own semiconscious fears into it. (pp. 235-36)

[In *The Birthday Party*], the element of external violence has not altogether disappeared, but the heavy (if cloudy) symbolism of *The Room* has vanished, and instead we get a real comedy of menace which is funny and menacing primarily in relation to the unrelieved ordinariness of its background. The very fact that Stanley, Meg, and her husband Peter are believable figures living in a believable real world intensifies the horror of Stanley's situation when the intruders come to break into his comfortable humdrum life and take him away. But, it might be said, the arrival of McCann and Goldberg takes it out of the real everyday reality: whatever we may have done in our lives, it is unlikely to be anything so terrible and extraordinary that two professional killers would be hired to deal with us. The answer to that is that this might well be so if Stanley's offence were ever named, or the source of his punishment explained. But this is not the case: the menace of McCann and Goldberg is exactly the nameless menace with which Stanley cruelly teases Meg before they arrive. . . . Just as she can be terrified by this nameless threat of retribution for unknown crimes, so we can be terrified when the same fate actually overtakes Stanley. With his habitual dexterity in such matters Pinter manages to rig the scene of Stanley's breakdown in such a way that we never know what the guilt to which he finally succumbs may be: every conceivable accusation is thrown at him, one way and another. . . . Something for everyone, in fact: somewhere, the author seems to be telling his audience, you have done something—think hard and you may remember what it is—which will one day catch you out. (pp. 237-38)

The ambiguity, then, not only creates an unnerving atmosphere of doubt and uncertainty, but also helps to generalize and universalize the fears and tensions to which Pinter's characters are subject. The more doubt there is about the exact nature of the menace, the exact provocation which has brought it into being, the less chance there is of anyone in the audience feeling that anyway it could not happen to him. The kinship with Kafka, particularly *The Trial,* is obvious. . . . Pinter has not omitted to provide a footnote to *The Birthday Party* in a one-act play he wrote immediately afterwards, *The Dumb Waiter.* In *The Birthday Party* the hired killers (if they are hired killers) appear as all-powerful and inscrutable: where Stanley is the menaced, they are menace personified, invulnerable beings, one might suppose, from another world, emissaries of death. But no, *The Dumb Waiter* assures us, hired killers are just men like anyone else; they only obey orders, and while menacing others they themselves can also be menaced. (pp. 238-39)

The fact that the people being menaced [in *The Dumb Waiter*] are precisely those whose business it is usually to menace others, hired killers, offers an extra twist of irony, but does not make any essential difference to their situation. It does, however . . . [cast] doubts on the safety and integrity of the room itself. Without any physical intrusion whatever, the menace may be lurking already inside the room . . . ; it is no good simply keeping our minds closed to outside influence, for even inside there the seeds of destruction may already be planted. (pp. 239-40)

[*A Slight Ache*] marks the end of the 'comedy of menace' phase in Pinter's work, though ironically just when he was moving out of it the phrase was coined and has become almost unavoidable in discussion of Pinter, though generally applied to work which does nothing to merit the title. For these early plays, however, the description is admirably exact. Menace is unmistakenly present: the central characters . . . are all prey to unknown dangers, unspoken threats, and finally an unpleasant fate (all the more sinister for remaining undefined) overtakes them all. But comedy is present, too, usually in the earlier scenes, but nearly all through in *The Dumb Waiter.* Evidently, on one level at least, Pinter has learnt a lot from the master of controlled horror, Hitchcock, many of whose bravura effects are achieved in precisely this way, from making some horrible reality emerge out of a piece of light and apparently irrelevant comedy. But Pinter's comedy rarely even seems irrelevant: it is 'about' the same things as his scenes of terror, the inability, or he has implied, the unwillingness of human beings to communicate, to make contact with each other. If it is terrifying to open the door to a strange knock, it is equally terrifying to open your mind to someone else, for once he is in you never know what he may do. . . . Consequently, in ordinary conversation Pinter's characters twist and turn, profoundly distrustful of any direct communication, and even when they attempt it are generally constitutionally incapable of achieving it: hardly ever in his work does one encounter two people of the same level of intelligence in conversation—there is nearly always one leaping ahead in the exchange while another stumbles confusedly along behind—except at the lowest end of the scale, where both are so stupid that communication is virtually impossible anyway. And out of these confusions and conversational impasses Pinter creates his characteristic forms of comedy. . . . (pp. 241-42)

[If his revue sketches] are plays in miniature, they are plays with many differences from what has gone before. There is no menace, no battle between the light and warmth of the room and the invading forces of darkness and disruption from outside. . . . They are just tiny cameos in which two or more characters are put into relation with each other and allowed simply to interact; they are all, in a sense, about failures of communication, or more properly perhaps the unwillingness to communicate. . . . (p. 243)

[Later,] the emphasis in his work comes to be placed much more squarely on the relationships between characters, their attempts to live together without giving up too much of themselves. (It might be remarked, parenthetically, that if no character really wants to communicate with the others in Pinter's plays he nearly always wants the other to communicate with him, and much of the tension in the dialogue comes from the constant evasions, the slight revelations and drawings back involved in this endless skirmishing on the threshold of communication, with each character determined to find out more than he tells.) . . . [Though] the earlier plays are certainly not tied to a moral of any sort, they are slightly impeded in the presentation of people just being, existing, by the exigencies of plot, which require them to be menaced and to succumb. . . . [But in *A Night Out* and *The Caretaker*], the characters, the one mysterious external menace removed, can get on with precisely the job this statement envisages for them: just existing.

It is, in fact, tempting to see Pinter's progression from the earlier plays to the later in terms of a closer and closer approach to realism. In the early plays the quiet, often wryly comic tone of the opening scenes is gradually replaced by something much more intense and horrific, and something considerably farther away from mundane considerations of likelihood. The probability of what happens, indeed, is never at issue: it is clear from the outset that this is a private world we have been permitted to enter, and as such, whatever relations with any outside world of objective reality we may imagine we perceive, it has its own consistency and carries its own conviction. . . . Menace, [in *The Birthday Party*], is a matter of situation: it does not come from extraordinary, sinister people, but from ordinary people like you and me; it is all a matter of circumstances whether at some point I suddenly become the menace in your life or you the menace in mine, and not anything inherent in either of us. . . . [In] *The Dumb Waiter* he comes closer still [to reality] by elaborating the point about the normality of those who menace when they are outside the context in which their menace is exerted, and by leaving the violence implied in the final tableau instead of having it directly enacted on the stage. From here it is a short step to *A Slight Ache,* in which the nominal menace is completely passive and the real disruptive force exists in the mind of the menaced. There is no violence here at all, because no violence is needed.

The point at which this gradual change seems to crystallize in a single decision is in *The Caretaker,* where again we have the room, but no outside menace, simply a clash of personalities on the inside, and again we have to have one of the inhabitants displaced by another. (pp. 244-46)

[In *The Caretaker*] for the first time psychological realism overtly won out; these . . . are people existing, making their own decisions, creating the circumstances of their own lives, and not in any sense the puppets of fate, as were in many respects the characters of *The Room, The Birthday Party,* and *The Dumb Waiter. The Caretaker* still works completely in terms of a private myth, as they did, but it gains in richness and complexity by also working completely, as they did not, on the quite different level at which comprehensible motivation comes into play: for the first time we can sensibly consider (if we want to) why the characters do what they do as well as, more obscurely, why what happens has the effect it does on us. (p. 246)

[The] style of *The Caretaker* is much more direct than that of Pinter's earlier plays. Everything that Aston says—suitably enough, considering his mental condition—is perfectly clear and unequivocal. And though Mick's mental processes are devious the intention behind everything he says is clear, even when he is talking apparently at random just to unsettle the old man. . . . Only Davies is subject in his conversation to the characteristic Pinter ambiguity, and this is here symptomatic not of the general unknowability of things, but of a specific intention on the character's part to cover his tracks and keep people guessing about himself. . . . (pp. 247-48)

In fact, [*The Caretaker*] seems to be built upon a proposition new in Pinter's work, one which he has expressed as 'simple truth can often be something much more terrifying than ambiguity and doubt'. (p. 249)

Little by little the desire for verification has shifted from the audience into the play they are watching; instead of watching with a degree of mystification the manoeuvres of a group of characters who seem perfectly to understand what they are doing but simply offer us no means of sharing that understanding, we are now required to watch understandingly the manoeuvres of people who do not understand their situation but are trying laboriously to establish the truth about it. And this truth goes beyond the mere verification of single facts (except, perhaps, in the comedies) to a quest for the how and the why, the who and the what, at a deeper level than demonstrable fact. This involves a new preoccupation with the means of communication, since the question comes back, will people tell the truth about themselves, and if they will, can they? (pp. 257-58)

Significantly, the only people in Pinter's plays who appear to tell the whole truth, into whose minds indeed we are permitted to look, are madmen. . . . Between *The Room* and *The Dwarfs* we have in effect run the complete dramatic gamut from total objectivity to total subjectivity, and discovered in the process that there are no clear-cut explanations of anything. At one end of the scale no motives are explained and everything remains mysterious; at the other as many motives as possible are expounded for us, and if anything the result is more mystifying than before. It is only from a middle distance, as in *The Caretaker* and *A Night Out,* that we can see a picture simple enough to hold out the possibility that we may understand it, that we are given enough in the way of motive to reach some provisional conclusions on the characters and their actions. It is a perfect demonstration of the conspiracy on which normal human intercourse relies, and incidentally of the knife-edge on which dramatic 'realism' rests: if we were told a little less about what is going on it would be incomprehensible, but if we were told a little more the difficulty of establishing any single coherent truth would be just as great.

In fact, the great paradox of Pinter's career, by the normal standards of the theatre, is that the more 'realistic' he is, the less real. With most dramatists the sort of compromise by selection which permits us to feel we have a sufficient understanding of the characters and motives in *The Caretaker* and *A Night Out* is the nearest they get to reality; it seems like reality because in life we often assume much the same (generally on quite insufficient evidence) and anyway the idea that we can safely make such assumptions is reassuring. But in his other works Pinter has, to our great discomfort, stripped these illusions from us: we cannot understand other people; we cannot even understand ourselves; and the truth of any situation is almost always beyond our grasp. If this is true in life, why should it not be true in the theatre? (pp. 258-59)

A scene from the 1975 London production of *No Man's Land* with John Gielgud (left) as Spooner and Ralph Richardson as Hirst.

[Instead] of regarding Pinter as the purveyor of dramatic fantasy he is usually taken for, we might equally regard him as the stage's most ruthless and uncompromising naturalist. The structure of his characters' conversations, and even the very forms of expression they use, are meticulously exact in their notation of the way people really speak (and this is as true of his best-educated characters as of his least . . .), while in his minutely detailed study there is seldom room for the easy generalization, even in his most explicit plays, *The Caretaker* and *A Night Out.* But to label him simply as a naturalist so truthful that his audiences have refused to recognize themselves in the mirror leaves several important elements in his drama out of account.

First, there is his mastery of construction, which is anything but naturalistic—life never shapes itself so neatly. Not only can he handle to perfection the one-act form, working up little by little to one decisive climax, but he can also sustain a three-act drama with complete mastery. . . . [This] is not to say that he writes what we usually mean by the 'well-made play',

with its formal expositions, confrontations, and last-act revelations; for him much of the point of life is that we usually do come in half-way through a story and never quite catch up, that the two vitally concerned parties never do meet, that letter which will explain all and round things off neatly is probably never opened. And so instead his plays are usually built on lines easier to explain in musical terms. They are, one might say, rhapsodic rather than symphonic, being held together by a series of internal tensions, one of the most frequent being the tension between two opposing tonalities (notably the comic versus the horrific, the light or known versus the dark or unknown) or two contrasted tempi (in duologue there is usually one character considerably quicker than the other in understanding, so that he is several steps ahead while the other lags painfully behind). The resolution of these tensions used to be in a bout of violence, when one key would at last establish an unmistakable ascendancy (usually the horrific would vanquish the comic, the forces of disruption establish a new order in place of the old), but in the later works Pinter has shown new skill and resourcefulness in reconciling the warring elements or ending more subtly and equally convincingly on a teasingly unresolved discord.

This musical analogy points also to the other element in his drama which effectively removes it from the naturalistic norm; what, for want of a better word, we might call his orchestration. Studying the unsupported line of the dialogue bit by bit we might well conclude that it is an exact reproduction of everyday speech, and so, bit by bit, it is. But it is 'orchestrated' with overtones and reminiscences, with unexpected resonances from what has gone before, so that the result is a tightly knit and intricate texture of which the 'naturalistic' words being spoken at any given moment are only the top line, supported by elusive and intricate harmonies, or appearing sometimes in counterpoint with another theme from earlier in the play. It is this which gives Pinter's work its unusual and at first glance inexplicable weight and density; until we understand the process we are unable to account reasonably for the obsessive fascination the most apparently banal exchanges exert in his plays.

If Pinter's plays are the most 'musical' of the New British drama, however, it follows that they are the most poetic, because what else is music in words but poetry? . . . [His] works are the true poetic drama of our time, for he alone has fully understood that poetry in the theatre is not achieved merely by couching ordinary sentiments in an elaborately artificial poetic diction, . . . or writing what is formally verse but not appreciable to the unwarned ear as anything but prose. . . . Instead he has looked at life so closely that, seeing it through his eyes, we discover the strange sublunary poetry which lies in the most ordinary objects at the other end of a microscope. At this stage all question of realism or fantasy, naturalism or artifice becomes irrelevant, and indeed completely meaningless: whatever we think of his plays, whether we accept or reject them, they are monumentally and inescapably there, the artifact triumphantly separated from the artist, self-contained and self-supporting. Because he has achieved this, and he alone among British dramatists of our day, the conclusion seems inescapable that even if others may be more likeable, more approachable, more sympathetic to one's own personal tastes and convictions, in the long run he is likely to turn out the greatest of them all. (pp. 259-61)

John Russell Taylor, "A Room and Some Views," in his *The Angry Theatre: New British Drama,* revised edition, Hill and Wang, 1969, pp. 233-61.

ALAN JENKINS
(essay date 1981)

[Jenkins is a British critic, novelist, and biographer. In the following review of *Family Voices*, he praises the play as an unsettling yet effective rendering of exploitative personal relationships.]

Somewhere "in this enormous city" a young man thinks of his mother, who languishes somewhere on the south coast and thinks of her son. [In *Family Voices,* these] thoughts, formulated but not transmitted (their content tells us as much), mother and son address to each other in an unspecified mode, its ambiguities exploited to the full between unspoken monologue and unwritten letter. There is no suggestion of contact made, response secured, but only an overwhelming sense of solitary, echoless speaking. Harold Pinter's latest work is a play for two voices—and, at the end, a third voice, that of the young man's father—and for those voices' tones of voice. The young man tells himself entertaining, even exciting stories of his new "family", while the abandoned, widowed mother lives in her memories of the old. . . .

[*Family Voices*] is an exquisitely funny and plangent piece of theatre. . . . Much of it recalls "classic" Pinter—the writer of *The Homecoming* or *No Man's Land*—but refined almost to disappearing (we do not actually see, or hear, the grotesques in this play). . . .

Initially the boy is self-justifyingly, jauntily defensive about his move away from the nest; the mother anguished, plaintive, fondling memories as lovingly as she once dried the boy's hair, "so gently with my soft towel". Gradually, almost imperceptibly, a shift in emphasis occurs, the tone and burden of the utterances

change direction. The mother grows accusing, embittered; the boy, regretful and increasingly doubtful about his substitute family/landlords, the Witherses, contemplates with joy the prospect of a return and a reunion. No home, for this writer, can fail to be charged with uncertainty or terror; no family can be without its private dreads, its history of pain and miserable struggles for domination or independence. In *Family Voices* these are complicated by a departure from home and the discovery of a new, very different "home"; all the horrors are present, ready to come home to roost, though conveyed indirectly, both through the shifts and contradictions of the touching/terrible picture that emerges of the boy's "real family", and through the more startling and comic dislocatedness of his reports or fantasies as regards Mrs Withers ("I was a right titbit, she said. I was like a piece of plum duff "), Lady Withers ("She asked me to call her Lally"), the alarming Jane and unspeakable menfolk.

The elements of puzzle and inconsistency, the circumambient sexual ambiguousness, the pervasive overtones of menace and perversion—there are no prizes for noticing these in any play by Pinter. But they are distilled in this short piece into some fine flashes of sinister and fantastic double-talk.

Pinter's verbal touch, at its surest on the boundary between politeness and derangement, the genteel and the thuggish, and his marvellous ear for the self-revealing phrase, for the detail or cadence that renders acute embarrassment or conjures a world of social posturing, is put to deft effect. "I had never seen so many buns. One quick glance told me they were perched on cakestands all over the room . . . "

The father's last words from the grave, "I have so much to say to you. What I have to say to you will never be said", do not contain within themselves the possibility of the hoped-for communion. They entertain the possibility only of final, irrevocable separation, a kind of unending poignancy, and unbreakable silence. Inevitably, given all that we have heard these family voices say; yet Pinter's inventiveness is so grimly and constantly surprising, his language so rich for all its economy and simplicity, and his best moments are so memorable, that it almost seems like the price we have to pay—not for lip-service to "realism" or a "view of human nature" but for fidelity to a governing shape and feeling, and for what a critic once attributed to Samuel Beckett, "the dramatist's equivalent of perfect pitch".

Alan Jenkins, "No Man's Homecoming," in *The Times Literary Supplement,* No. 4069, March 27, 1981, p. 336.

BERNARD F. DUKORE
(essay date 1982)

[Dukore is an American educator, editor, and critic who has published numerous works on the theater, including *Seventeen Plays: Sophocles to Baraka* (1976) *and Money and Politics in Ibsen, Shaw, and Brecht* (1980). In the following excerpt from his *Harold Pinter*, he provides an overview of Pinter's career.]

Frequently Pinter's plays begin comically but turn to physical, psychological, or potential violence— sometimes, in varying sequences, to all three. Terror inheres in a statement in *The Room* that the onstage room, which is occupied, is to let. Although the play turns comic again, it ends on a note of physical violence.

In the early plays menace lurks outside, but it also has psychological roots. The titular room—in which the heroine lives, fearful of an outside force she does not specify—is dark. In *The Birthday Party* the sheltered young man fears visitors. In *The Dumb Waiter* outside forces menace a questioning killer. In *A Slight Ache* a psychologically disturbed man fears a man he invites inside. While menace may take the shape of particular characters, it is usually unspecified or unexplained—therefore, more ominous.

Partly because realistic explanations are absent, disturbing questions arise. One is unsure why characters visit others, why they commit inexplicable actions, why the others fear them. Frustrated reviewers or readers accuse Pinter of wilful obfuscation. Yet before he began to write plays, he had acted in conventional works with clear exposition and pat conclusions. The fact that his own, unconventional plays contain neither should alert one to the possibility that other dramatic aspects are more important, that Pinter's refusal to focus on answers to 'Who' and 'Why?' is a deliberate effort to focus on answers to 'What?' and 'How?' To put the matter another way, present activities, interrelationships, and stratagems are more dramatically important than past actions. His drama is not a matter of They have been, therefore they are; but rather, They do, therefore they are.

These early plays conform to the characteristics of the Theatre of the Absurd. . . . Their effective unsettling quality, with its fusion of realism and nonrealism, distinguishes Pinter's artistic signature from those of other writers of this genre. Because events and actions are unexplained, and apparently illogical or unmotivated, the world seems capricious or malevolent. One can

rely upon nothing. What is apparently secure is not secure. A haven does not protect. A weapon vanishes without warning. Linguistic absurdity may suggest the absurdity of the human condition. Fear of a menace may suggest the universal trauma of man in the universe. (pp. 24-5)

The title *A Night Out* would seem to herald a departure from the interiors of Pinter's first five plays. With the benefit of hindsight, however, the departure probably derives from the medium for which he wrote the work, radio, which permits an easier flow through different locales than the stage does. When writing a play for the stage, in contrast to writing one for another theatrical medium . . . , Pinter usually thinks in terms of a clearly delineated space. The chief exceptions are the lyric *Silence*, whose dramaturgy is unique in the Pinter canon, and the multi-scene *Betrayal*, whose structure may derive partly from his cinema experience. Furthermore the intrinsic quality of *A Night Out* suggests an emphasis not on the last word of the title but on the first two. Departure is temporary.

Nevertheless this play, like the two that follow [*The Caretaker* and *Night School*], is less enigmatic, mysterious, or unrealistic than Pinter's earlier work. (p. 46)

While the trio of plays . . . are to some extent enigmatic, their enigmas differ in kind from those of the earlier works. The nature of what is undefined is more specific and whatever mysterious qualities it may possess, the unreal is not among them. In short, these plays move toward greater realism. (p. 47)

In *The Room* and *The Birthday Party* characters who hope they have sanctuary try to defend themselves from intruders; in *A Night Out* a character tries to break out of his soul-stultifying haven. In contrast to all, a character in *The Caretaker* aims to find sanctuary. Unlike *The Room, The Birthday Party*, and *The Hothouse*, no unrealistic elements erupt in *The Caretaker;* yet, as in *The Hothouse*, electro-shock treatment in a mental institution figures prominently in it; and, as in *A Night Out*, its realistic mode is unbroken. (p. 48)

As in *The Collection*, infidelity is a subject of *The Homecoming*. As in *The Lover*, an unanticipated sexual arrangement concludes its action. As in *The Basement*, a woman's sexual allegiance shifts. As in *Tea Party*, a character who is unable to cope collapses. As in all these plays, but more savagely, characters in *The Homecoming* vie for positions of power, don protective masks, and both flippantly and abrasively mock each other.

To an all-male household—Max, a former butcher, his chauffeur brother Sam, and his sons Lenny and Joey, a pimp and a part-time boxer—the oldest son Teddy returns after six years in America, where he teaches philosophy, with his wife Ruth—a surprise to the family who did not know he had married or that he has three sons. At the end of the play the family proposes that Ruth stay, service them, and become a prostitute. After blurting out that Max's late wife Jessie committed adultery with his best friend, Sam collapses. Teddy leaves for America. Ruth remains. (p. 75)

The play disorients. A butcher cooks what one of his sons calls dog food. A young fighter is knocked down by his old father. A philosopher refuses to philosophise. A chauffeur is unable to drive. A pimp takes orders from his whore. The whore does not go all the way with a man. Words disorient, as when Lenny says of Teddy, 'And my goodness we are proud of him here, I can tell you. Doctor of Philosophy and all that . . . leaves quite an impression'. . . . The first phrase appropriate to an old woman not a young man, the triteness of the phrase that ends the first sentence, 'and all that' belittling the advanced degree—these disorient, thereby conveying the impression that what is said is not what is meant.

During the opening dialogue Lenny reads the racing section of a newspaper while Max asks for scissors and a cigarette. Although Max wants them, what underlies his requests is a demand for acknowledgement and attention. Lenny's indifference to his reminiscences, questions, insults, and threats indicates that the exchange is commonplace. Usually Lenny says nothing, a suggestion of his superior status (indeed, if he were not dominant, Max would not behave as he does). When Lenny speaks, it is often to assert a prerogative or to silence Max. When he initiates a subject (horseracing), it is to re-establish his status by contradicting Max, and when Max continues on it, Lenny's only response is to request a change of subject. Lenny takes the mickey out of Max who understands what Lenny is doing. When Max loses his temper and threatens to hit Lenny with his walking stick, Lenny mocks him by talking in a childlike manner. Beneath and through the dialogue they struggle for power—demanding recognition of status and self. (pp. 75-6)

In their frequently vicious struggles for power, no character is clearly victorious. Does Teddy intend at the start to let the nature of his family take its course and claim Ruth? If so, or if not, he does not leave the London house unscarred. Is Ruth at the end in the position of Queen Bee? If so, she may for specified periods of time become a worker who supports the drones. (p. 84)

In most of Pinter's plays the past is unclear: Stanley's transgression (*The Birthday Party*), Aston's experience in the mental asylum (*The Caretaker*), adultery (*The Collection*), and so forth. More prominently than before, however, [*Landscape, Silence, Night,* and *Old Times*] focus on the past. Usually they are called memory plays.

Landscape has two characters, Beth and Duff, who live in the house of their former employer, apparently deceased. They reminisce. Her memories include the sea, the beach, and a man lying on a sand dune; his, a dog, a park, and a pub. Her memories are gentle and fragile; his, frequently vulgar and aggressive. They do not converse with each other.

Like a painting, *Landscape* contains no movement. The characters do not leave their chairs, which a kitchen table separates; and they are separated from their background, which is dim. Figuratively the stage picture is an immobile landscape. The vista is distant, in that the audience is unable to penetrate beneath the facades of the reminiscing characters. Despite the clarity of the figures in the foreground, the sketch is faint and shadowy.

What happens, what the audience perceives, is two characters, physically and emotionally separated from each other and their environment, dwelling on their memories. (pp. 85-6)

Two incompatible people, once loving, are isolated from each other, implicitly rejecting each other, uncommunicative in an unchanging landscape. The play's final line, spoken by Beth, is ambiguous. 'Oh my true love I said' . . . apparently tender, but invoking a past love and thereby rejecting the man presently near her, as his verbal rape had just demeaned her.

As in *Landscape*, the noncomic *Silence* situates each of its characters in a chair in a distinct area of the stage—visually symbolic of isolation. Unlike *Landscape,* a character occasionally moves to another character. What the three personae of *Silence* remember occurred when Rumsey was forty, Bates in his mid-thirties, and Ellen in her twenties—their ages as they appear on stage. (p. 87)

All three characters, having chosen solitary lives, remember the past when they were together. Silences often separate their mnemonic monologues that decreasingly dovetail each other, until after a long silence that concludes the play, memory seems to fade with the fading lights. Like *Landscape, Silence* is a verbal construct with minimal action and character interrelations—a recited piece, more poetic than dramatic.

Much shorter than either is *Night,* another memory play with no movement but, unlike the others, with a conventional story. Also unlike them, it is generally comic and unlike other Pinter plays has a celebratory conclusion. A married couple, both in their forties, have conflicting memories of their first stroll together. . . . 'Gentle' and 'sweet' are adjectives one does not usually apply to Pinter's plays, but both befit the lovely *Night,* wherein the past brings nostalgia, not dread. Pinter goes gently into *Night.*

These atypical works, however, seem to be experiments in craft and strengthenings of thematic concepts to be employed in a major work in which memory is prominent. Pinter's next play is that work, *Old Times,* written six years after *The Homecoming,* his last previous full-length play. (pp. 88-9)

In *Old Times,* Deeley and Kate, married, live on the seacoast. Anna, a former roommate of Kate's, visits them. The women reminisce. Later, Deeley and Anna say they met each other twenty years before. Their rivalry over Kate intensifies. Kate, asserting her dominant position, terminates their sparring. As terms like rivalry and sparring suggest, the stratagems, taunts, and power struggles that characterise plays like *The Collection* and *The Homecoming,* where the past is also important, are major factors in this play. (pp. 89-90)

Like *Landscape* and *Silence, Old Times* is a memory play, but unlike these plays, *Old Times* portrays, in terms of dramatic conflict, the past's influence on the present. Unlike *Night,* which also contains conflict, the resolution of *Old Times* is devastating—akin, in this respect, to that of the other full-length plays thus far analysed. (p. 98)

[In certain respects], Pinter's most recent plays recapitulate earlier themes and techniques. In other respects . . . , they move—sometimes provisionally, sometimes boldly—in new directions. With *Monologue* and *No Man's Land,* the familiar terrain is more obvious than the new; with *Betrayal,* the reverse. (p. 99)

Monologue is a monologue. Its meaning inheres in its title. In drama, a monologue refers to a solitary person speaking, but not to himself, as in a soliloquy, and it differs from dialogue. In *Monologue,* a solitary character talks, but not to himself. The title is also apt in that the play is about isolation, its speaker is alone from start to finish, and no dialogue or response is possible. Because Pinter employs the visual as well as the verbal, *Monologue* can be effective only when an audience sees the play, not simply hears it recited: the speaker talks to an empty chair. Whereas Eugene Ionesco uses many chairs, in his play *The Chairs,* to embody nothingness and to suggest the metaphysical void, Pinter in *Monologue* employs one empty chair to embody absence and to suggest the isolation and loneliness of the play's sole character. The stage picture—a man addressing an empty chair—is a concrete, theatrical metaphor of the subject.

The play's ambience is the subtle, tragicomic movement from friendship to loneliness, as the speaker increasingly reveals the depths of his affection for the man and love for the woman. In losing her, he also lost him, and he pleads for their friendship, offering to die for their children, if they have children. But an empty chair cannot respond. At the end of the play, he fully reveals his true isolation and loneliness. (pp. 99-100)

Although *No Man's Land* contains more than one character, its opening is almost a monologue by the garrulous Spooner, a down-at-heel, self-styled poet whom

Hirst, a famous, prosperous writer, meets and brings home for a drink. Spooner attempts to ingratiate himself with his host and thereby to install himself in Hirst's home, replacing Foster and Briggs who are employed to protect Hirst from outside encroachment. Spooner's efforts fail. (p. 102)

No Man's Land may be the end of a phase in Pinter's writing, for it echoes many of his previous works. The ambience of menace recalls the early plays, and some of the menace is comic. Struggles for power between Spooner and Hirst's aides recall the works that focus on this theme, and as in those plays mockery is sometimes funny, sometimes threatening. (p. 104)

In *Betrayal* the backward movement, dramatic not narrative, is toward disillusion; the audience, having witnessed the end of the affair and its aftermath, understands how transitory are the lovers' feelings toward each other during the early time of the affair. The forward movement, more intermittent, is toward such revelations as how the husband deals with his friend after he has discovered his wife's infidelity with him. When the affair is about to begin, the audience has already seen how it ends. . . . [The] beginning that ends *Betrayal* is clear, and it fixes in art its retrieval of time lost.

The title is what the play is about, its pervading ambience, what happens in every scene. (pp. 107-08)

Despite the different dramaturgy of *Betrayal,* it uses familiar techniques and themes. Robert, for example, takes the piss out of Jerry, who is unaware of what lies beneath the surface. . . . Betrayal is also a theme of other plays by Pinter, including *The Collection* and *The Basement.* Furthermore, the last/chronologically first scene of *Betrayal* can be described in terms of the image Pinter employed for his first play: two people are alone in a room.

In such matters *Betrayal* recapitulates previous plays by Pinter. More important than similarities are major differences. In *Betrayal* Pinter provides what he refused to provide in earlier plays: verification. Also *Betrayal* is his only play in which the audience knows more than the characters do—excepting the first two scenes. *Betrayal* may be his most accessible play since it provides insight into his distinctive techniques. Because we know what happened or what the characters know before it happens or before they know it, we can perceive their manoeuvres as they evade, don masks, and mock each other. When Robert slyly taunts Jerry by asserting his own greater physical fitness, we understand (as Emma does and Jerry does not) his reference to his knowledge of her affair. When he refers to his folly as a publisher, we understand (as Jerry does not) his allusion to his folly as a trusting husband and friend. Because Pinter verifies actions and motivations, we can attend, without bafflement about the past, to the dramatic present.

Although Pinter has been writing plays for almost a quarter of a century, it seems likely from these recent works that his inventiveness is far from exhausted. To the contrary, he appears to be renewing himself, finding fresh areas and means to express his changing dramatic vision. Extending himself, he also maintains his footing on familiar terrain. His fresh starts are from fixed points, which provide solid technical bases for his dramatic departures. What the unmasked face of *Monologue,* the personal subject of *No Man's Land,* or the major dramaturgical departure of *Betrayal* may forecast is impossible to predict. One looks forward to the next Pinter play with the same eagerness one did ten or twenty years ago. A comparable statement can be made of few other contemporary dramatists. (pp. 114-15)

Bernard F. Dukore, in his *Harold Pinter,* Grove Press, 1982, 139 p.

BENEDICT NIGHTINGALE

(essay date 1984)

[In the excerpt below, Nightingale favorably compares the short plays of *Other Places* to Pinter's earlier work.]

Harold Pinter writes so seldom for the stage nowadays that he'd only have to trace a line of dialogue in the dirt with his big toe for the world's theatrical scholars to jet in with cameras, spades and preservative; and [the short plays *Victoria Station, One for the Road,* and *A Kind of Alaska*] offer more to dig into than that. *Victoria Station,* about a taxi dispatcher first puzzled, then infuriated and finally converted to a sort of crazed camaraderie by an amiably uncooperative driver, may seem little more than an anecdote, a nostalgic throwback to the revue sketches its author wrote 20, 25 years ago. Yet it injects a strangeness, an unease, a distinctive Pinterishness into the kind of disembodied banalities every passenger must have heard bleated from office to taxi and back again. It leaves you wondering if you aren't hearing the two survivors of some unmentionable disaster playing out their last rituals in an empty, airless city. And the other two components of the triple-bill Pinter has called *Other Places* are certainly much more than anecdotal.

One for the Road, which has only just opened in London, also risks being categorized as a throwback. It has something in common with the early *Birthday Party,* in which the vengeful representatives of an un-

named "organization" reduced a seemingly harmless young man to a walking vegetable, and something with the only slightly later *Hothouse,* which recorded a similar piece of mental destruction, this time in a Kafkaesque asylum run by incompetents and sadists. Both plays clearly had political implications and reverberations. Indeed, there's much in Pinter's work as a whole to call into question the commonly held view that he's the most apolitical of contemporary British dramatists. Don't several of his plays involve more or less malign intruders invading more or less private spaces? Wasn't it Pinter himself who pointed out that the appearance of sinister strangers at the front door, with or without raincoats, search warrants and oversized dogs, hasn't exactly been an unusual experience in Europe over the past 50 years?

But *One for the Road* is altogether less guarded about its intentions. One might conceivable choose to interpret it as an allegory about a cruel and tyrannical Old Testament deity, a grim little gloss on Beckett's *Waiting for Godot,* but it's much easier to see it as what it appears to be, a study of political brutality and oppression, Pinter's version of Beckett's *Catastrophe.* A burly English apparatchik . . . quizzes a captive family: tortured father, bloodied mother, and their 7-year-old son, who has committed the only offense anyone mentions, kicking and spitting at some God-fearing dictatorship's legionnaires. Some of the menace is smiling and oblique, as so often in Pinter: "I'm terribly pleased to meet you," "Everybody here has fallen in love with your wife." Some is unwontedly direct: "How many times have you been raped?" By the end, when it becomes apparent that the little boy won't be accompanying his ruined parents back into the world outside, you've felt something unique in Pinter: indignation about the abuse of human rights guilelessly steaming off the stage.

This impassioned piece of propaganda . . . may not, of course, be to the taste of those who like their Pinter more artful or their drama less ugly. . . . [Yet] the last play, *A Kind of Alaska,* is quieter, gentler and unique in quite another way. Throughout his career Pinter has concentrated on the dark intestinal drives, giving the impression that the human animal was governed exclusively by a triple hunger for territory, power and sex. In *Alaska* and *Alaska* alone, he admits to the existence of something that could be dignified as selfless devotion.

The play was inspired by Oliver Sacks's *Awakenings,* a series of studies of patients struck down by Encephalitis Lethargica in earlier decades and reactivated in the late 1960's by the drug L-Dope. Rose R, for instance, dreamed at age 21 she was a statue imprisoned in a castle, became precisely that for the next 40 years, and, restored to reality one morning, could never entirely believe it wasn't 1926. Similarly, Pinter's Deborah has been mentally incarcerated in a vast series of glass halls, where she's alternately listened to faucets dripping and danced "in the most crushing spaces," for no less than 29 years. Now she must accept that her sister is an ample matron, her father blind, her mother dead, the clamor and bustle of adolescence long since over. . . . [This] gray-haired Sleeping Beauty squints and blinks from her bed, a 16-year-old consciousness incredulously, angrily, pluckily getting its bearings in a world way beyond anyone's emotional compass. She recites the few terrible facts she can grasp, and declares, with poignant dignity: "I think I have the matter in proportion. Thank you." . . .

[*A Kind of Alaska* is] a moving play, and maybe more than that. It might have been no more than a bizarre case-history from some spidery archive, appealing mainly to those morbidly fascinated by sensational medicine. It could conceivably have become a lurid horror-story from the locked ward. As it is, many will find something of themselves in Deborah, as she peers from the remote present into the vivid past, benignly watched by her sister and her sister's husband, the doctor who has given his life to tending her. There's loss and regret, the feeling that life has evaporated before it's been used. There's also courage and resilience and generosity, the generosity of others, those who care for us. Pinter sees the murk all right: witness *One for the Road.* The evidence of *A Kind of Alaska* is that he isn't altogether unaware of the light. (p. H3)

Benedict Nightingale, "Three Plays Illuminate the Range of Pinter," in *The New York Times,* April 22, 1984, pp. H3, H6.

DANIEL SALEM
(essay date 1986)

[In the following excerpt, Salem examines the major stylistic and thematic elements of Pinter's dramas.]

To make the audience more aware of subconscious reverberations, Pinter blurs the signs of conventional theatrical grammar. He breaks the rules to which the passive spectator is accustomed and transforms classical rational speech. Like the musicians of the serial school, he suppresses the privileged functions of certain fundamental chords. He establishes no distinction between dissonance and consonance. He creates a kind of tension which is no longer based, as in traditional musical writing, on successive starts, suspensions and pauses, but on the absence of consonant chords (the non sequiturs) and on the continual subconscious fluctuations of characters who, constantly and secretly, modify the dramatic situation. Like Anton Webern, in

particular, Pinter uses silence as an element of tension. . . . Like cricket players, his characters (in *No Man's Land,* they are even named after four champions) watch each other and react in abrupt, unexplained, sometimes threatening ways.

A Pinter character never analyzes himself lucidly. He never interprets psychologically what he feels. He lies and evades reality. . . . Like Beckett and Ionesco, Pinter renounces completely the heritage of rhetoric and perpetually underlines the ambiguity of words. Beckett encouraged him to express the human condition in its existential reality and to mock language. He showed him that a playwright shouldn't be afraid of disconcerting his audience. One finds in Pinter numerous elements which characterize Beckett's work: the absence of any real plot, the musical quality of the dialogue, memory games, the ability to charge words and silences with maximum meaning. Yet, unlike Beckett, Pinter doesn't deal with the theme of despair hidden behind the mask. His subject *is* the mask. Beckett expresses a truth. Pinter presents characters who experience it. Beckett doesn't encourage a willing suspension of disbelief. Pinter, on the contrary, plays upon fascination and suspense.

Pinter's characters are also different from Ionesco's. Pinter's art isn't based, like Ionesco's, mainly on exaggeration and caricature. It is founded above all on concentration and distillation. Martin Esslin was right in underlining that the dramatists of the "Theatre of the Absurd" have invented a new language—of rupture and distillation—to which Pinter is indebted. But the truth is that Pinter doesn't belong to such a theatre. The reality of his characters is quite different. It is double and is always experienced on two levels. On the one hand, there is a surface reality that everyone is led to believe in when trying to be guided by appearances. On the other hand, there is the hidden reality of secret emotions which contradicts surface reality, alters it, and gives each character his psychological depth.

Pinter is close to those dramatists who, like Strindberg, express the inner dialogue and watch for the moment when the obstacles of the subconscious are overcome and suddenly the truth of the matter is revealed. He is convinced that every perception is subjective: one doesn't perceive reality, reality is what one perceives. And there is total contradiction between what is said and what is felt. So in order to show reality, one has to show the mask and the distorted vision. Like the French writer Nathalie Sarraute, Pinter is interested in the exploration of imperceptible palpitations. He respects the complexity and variety of human emotions. He tries to catch the slightest intonation expressing the secret impulses, all the subjacent and complicated movements which propel language.

What makes Pinter's style different, "Pinteresque," is the fact that he says nothing explicitly. He finds people and things enigmatic. His presentation of an enigma therefore remains an enigma. Any meaning in his work must be guessed, grasped intuitively, read between the lines. His hermetic writing resembles the cabalistic style that seeks to generate an "obscure flame." Rather than explain truth directly, Pinter exposes the lies that the spectator believes to be the truth. He shows that these lies are contradictory and reveals indirectly that they *are* lies, so that the spectator can finally discover *by himself* that the characters are lying. To those who refuse the truth, Pinter shows just how contradictory the lies are that are accepted. Such an approach is a call for more lucidity. As Arthur Koestler explains: "The intention is not to obscure the message, but to make it more luminous by compelling the recipient to work it out by himself—to recreate it. Hence the message must be handed to him in implied form—and implied means 'folded in'. To make it unfold, he must fill in the gaps, complete the hint, see through the symbolic disguise."

The emotional repercussions of a Pinter play are all the greater as the audience witnesses the development of an ambiguous situation and must rely on clues in order to understand it. Each play puts the spectator in the position of a voyeur and asks him to relive subconscious conflicts. The meaning of the dialogue can be grasped only if the public is able to add to the words, the pauses and the silences a series of echoes, connotations, and undertones.

Pinter's work mirrors anguished confusion and belongs to a specific period—the era of suspicion. It calls upon a forewarned audience capable of distinguishing a play's oneiric elements. It brings a new awareness to spectators who are in connivance with the dramatist, who don't take words literally and who mistrust characters. Such work can't please an audience that requires entertaining "well-made" plays, that seeks only an amusing, conventional, and reassuring social game. On the contrary, Pinter's work is shocking and provocative. It has the power to disturb. This is why the spectator's reaction is often resistance, embarrassment, and fear. He refuses a secret reality which refers to something that he has experienced but also repressed.

By dealing with the subconscious, Pinter touches directly upon something essential and generates deep-seated emotions. His dialogue seems to be based on conventional phrases and innocuous non sequiturs. But as soon as the cues are exchanged in a given situation, the spectator guesses what happens behind the masks. A latent content contradicts appearances and preconceived ideas about what should and what shouldn't be revealed. In the name of morality, prudence, and modesty, members of the audience may condemn the illumination of the innermost recesses of the psyche. Sensing that the behaviour of Pinter's characters secretly alludes to their own repression, they fear the flashes of lucidity in which they might see themselves naked. Incapable of accepting the truth objectively, they resort to defence mechanisms which allow them to avoid the uneasiness generated by the dialogue and particularly by the silences.

An audience which, unexpectedly and abruptly, discovers the repression process immediately divides itself. Spontaneously, it chooses between humour (which consists in including oneself among the accused) and incriminating irony, mockery, or indignation. Humour allows acceptance, while irony is a form of impotence. It is guilt transformed into intellectual vanity in order to allow oneself to laugh at others and thus be excluded from the situation.

We can distinguish three types of psychological reactions. First there is *adapted behaviour*. It is based on a lucid perception of the global reality expressed in the play, including what is revealed without being explicit: the spectator controls his emotions while grasping the meaning of the work. Then there is *blind behaviour*, based on repression: the spectator's perception is distorted by lack of empathy, by prejudice. Truth is denied, suppressed, because it is too unpleasant to be acknowledged. Finally, there is *uncontrolled behaviour*, based on panic: the spectator's perception is distorted by excessive emotional involvement. He reacts excitedly, angrily.

To meet with incomprehension and indignation is inevitable when certain conventional beliefs are threatened. *The Homecoming* is particularly disturbing because the family is preeminently the experience from which all feelings of love and hatred originate. As he shows all the ugliness of an embittered family, Pinter incites strong opposition. The spectator is embarrassed, nay frightened. . . . Without taking into consideration the spectator's feelings, the dramatist confronts him with a painful truth. Therefore a self-protection mechanism is at work. Touched subconsciously, attacked, the spectator feels repulsion and protests against someone who shows him images that shake his innermost defences.

Blind behaviour is also linked to the deep-seated belief that it is always possible to perceive one's motives clearly. It is in the name of such conviction that Pinter is often taken to task for his obscurity. The spectator who admires only order, harmony, and beauty will reject anything diseased or adulterated because he will feel that it debases his taste. He will insist on being entertained and charmed and will refuse any sudden awareness of reality.

He will also be put off by Pinter's comedy as it is a comedy of deception that raises a grim laughter. Pinter is interested in tragicomic situations, in situations which are both funny and painful because they are experienced in a state of anxiety. His characters are tragic but their suffering is caused by their own vanity. They encounter laughable obstacles (a disconnected gas-cooker, a wasp) and, making mountains out of mole-hills, they become ridiculous. Pinter shows how tragic it is always to be forced to put on an act in order to save appearances. His comedy is not a comedy of situation but *the comedy of exposed repression.* Such comedy is aggressive and embarrassing because it reveals the characters' subconscious distress.

Pinter's comedy corresponds to Jewish humour, a desperate humour that often helps make bearable the unbearable. When Spooner, in *No Man's Land,* embarks on a long monologue to blow his own trumpet in the hope that Hirst will hire him as private secretary, the situation is tragicomic, because it is hopeless. Lost in his frozen world, Hirst doesn't listen. . . . (pp. 71-5)

Pinter's plays generate two kinds of laughter: *a liberating laughter,* i.e., a lucid laughter conscious of the pain which is constantly mixed with the foolishness, and *a sneering laughter,* i.e., a blind laughter which considers the characters not as persons but rather as caricatures. It is a defensive laughter that Pinter defines thus:

> . . . where the comic and the tragic (for want of a better word) are closely interwoven, certain members of an audience will always give emphasis to the comic as opposed to the other, for by so doing they rationalise the other out of existence. . . . This indiscriminate mirth . . . represents a cheerful patronage of the characters on the part of the merrymakers, and thus participation is avoided. This laughter is in fact a mode of precaution, a smokescreen, a refusal to accept what is happening as recognisable (which I think it is). . . .

In so far as the spectator guesses, recognizes, and accepts the masks that the characters wear, he laughs because the absurdity of their self-justifications is suddenly exposed. He laughs at self-delusion. Tragicomedy derives from the distance between the character as he really is and the false image he tries to make other people believe. The greater that distance, the more it reveals the character's vanity, the more he looks ridiculous. On the contrary, the shorter the distance between his real self and what he believes he is, the more he shows his guilt and pain, the more he looks pitiful. Then laughter stops short. The spectator intuitively senses the character's suffering and the scene becomes tragic. Laughter stops whenever anguish appears. It stops in front of any tormented character seeking help and showing his subconscious open wound.

One rarely finds in Pinter the dramatic irony which allows the spectator to know more than the characters. Sometimes he even knows less than they do. He is confronted with characters who never display any true sense of humour, who never accept smilingly other people's limitations as well as their own. So when a character is unmasked, the spectator inevitably becomes conscious of the repression process. He can't avoid the subconscious depths. A Pinter play will never be a pleasant game as it invites the spectator to laugh at repression and denounces both the ridiculous and tragic aspects of vanity. Comedy is always closely linked to the intuitive knowledge that repression is mixed with pain.

Such is Pinter's relation with his audience. He refers the spectator to his innermost repressed feelings. If the spectator is too weak to tolerate that confrontation, he is petrified. If, on the contrary, he is able to acknowledge his own weaknesses, he will laugh at the revelation of what is behind the mask. He will be pleased with the breaking of the tacit pact of repression. He won't find it indiscrete or inopportune. The revelation of the subconscious will generate a liberating laughter.

Pinter's audience is finally divided in three groups: those who laugh lucidly, those who laugh blindly and those who are embarrassed, who do not laugh, who even sometimes can't stand other people's laughter. The performance of a Pinter play involves an exchange between two subconscious minds. At such a hidden level, depending on our own individual degree of maturity, on our ability to understand and recognize our own obscure thoughts and feelings, Pinter's work can be interpreted as either a series of painful and ironical grimaces or a series of intelligible images of reality. Each understanding is personal and unique. Some spectators immediately reject a Pinter play. It is a matter of self-protection. In order to preserve a precarious balance, they refuse to hear what transpires throughout the play. They shut themselves off from any experience liable to awaken their own guilt. Often, they counterattack by blaming Pinter. A dramatist, they say, shouldn't be wily, intent on showing "sick" people and, at the same time, refuse to pass judgement on them. Indeed, Pinter explores his characters' subconscious (without realizing that he is projecting his own guilt) but never clearly commits himself morally. He expresses what he sees and feels without any profession of faith.

Pinter's work is often rejected or misunderstood not only by the public but also by the actors and directors themselves. Any spectator feels the fundamental need to be able to penetrate the secret of the characters. As this need is never fully satisfied in Pinter's plays, the temptation for the director and actors to fill that "void" is strong. Unfortunately, whenever they yield to it, it is always at the expense of the central truth of the play.

The actor is often wrongly convinced that he has *to speak* the text, that he must help "clarify" it. Yet Pinter's writing is never accidental. As a dramatist, he carefully orchestrates words and silences so that his plays may shape an image as complex as his own experience of reality. (pp. 75-8)

Pinter's dialogues cover up a "subconversation." . . . Words carry the weight of a whole underground world. They must be considered as nets through which the meanings may slip and get lost each time a useless gesture or intonation blurs the form that the dramatist has carefully chiselled. The underground world over which Pinter's words are fixed like boards is the characters' secret motivation. It can be detected only by studying the mood of the scene. If one refuses to make the effort of discovering and respecting it, one distorts the underlying meaning of the lines, the confrontation behind the words. What is important is not so much what is being said as the way it has to be said. Above all, it is *the right rhythm* which has to be found, a rhythm which fits the characters' secret emotions. . . .

The intentionality hidden under the characters' words is revealed by the subtle way in which those words are spoken, *without removing the mask.* (p. 78)

The opaque clue offered by silence is particularly significant. Pinter asks the spectators to supplement his dialogue with an immediate meaning, grasped intuitively. He asks them to decipher what is implicit in the words and to do it according to their individual reactions to those words. A recognizable current of intentionality circulates through and between the words. Each spectator vaguely identifies it since he also carries it within himself. Pinter's work is intelligible only because of the fugitive introspection we all constantly undertake, more or less unconsciously. (p. 79)

Pinter isn't committed to any particular political struggle. The image of society that he gives is favourable neither to the established ideology nor to one class as opposed to another. The complexity of life, in Pinter's opinion, can't fit into a political theory. His commitment is expressed through his work on language, the different levels of which he recreates to the point of parody. The slyness of characters such as Goldberg, Edward, Harry, Willy, Spooner, Hirst, and Robert is, in his eyes, a form of violence, a masquerade, which effectively denounces the mystifications of abstract language and the use of labels and stereotypes in order to devalue people and exclude them.

In Pinter's plays, language is more often than not a means to an end which is domination. Instead of communicating, language subjugates. Evasion and deceit lie hidden under the disguise of logical discourse. Conscious of the incantatory, "Hitlerite" power of words, Pinter shows how they can become instruments of cruelty or be replaced significantly by drum beats, nervous giggles, or inarticulate sounds. (pp. 79-80)

Pinter doesn't show political or social conflicts. But he does allude to the secret motives which engender inhibition and aggressiveness. He doesn't divide society into guilty oppressors and innocent victims. But he does divide it into individuals, couples, families, whose behaviour constitutes society. In his work, only individuals and their reactions, their friction, provocation, resentment and fury, exist. Pinter believes that social violence is due to resentment. So when showing the mask, the game of conventional repression, he is showing a diseased society where angry accusations unleash social conflict, revolution, and war in the same way as they devastate individual lives. And society grants him leave to speak just as princes and kings allowed their jesters to amuse them in the past.

Not always, though. It isn't surprising that in the U.S.S.R., where psychoanalysis is rejected, Pinter's plays are banned. They are officially considered as *too pessimistic.* In October 1976, an amateur performance of *The Caretaker* in Moscow was called off by the authorities at the last minute. True, Pinter *is* pessimistic. He is a gifted, talented dramatist who only expresses the darker side of life. His work is the testimony of a truncated vision. He shows the frightening results of subconscious deformation but ignores the joy which rewards conscious elucidation. His work lacks an essential dimension: the contrast between the pain of perversion and the joy of mastered suffering. (pp. 80-81)

Pinter can only point at vanity without being able to fight it. Quite understandably, the reality that he recreates seems unrelenting, disappointing, and difficult to endure.

Pinter's vision of life is, indeed, pessimistic. Yet it isn't desperate. When Pinter shows that the inner life of his characters is unhealthy, he shows at the same time that it might be made healthier. A clear vision of mental illness helps to cure or at least check that illness. A writer like Pinter has no theory about his work. He follows his intuition about people and the pain they inflict on themselves and one another. He must be judged according to the degree of responsibility he displays in his understanding and expression of that pain. Pinter is pitiless because he is convinced that discretion can only prolong the pain. To him, sentimentality is only a cover-up for brutality. Everything happens as a result of reactions that are camouflaged by language. Words prove to be highly dangerous when used to dominate, to assert one's superiority, to produce theories cut off from reality, windmills working on a lot of hot air. Pinter is an intellectual answering Marguerite Yourcenar's definition: "Every intellectual is limited by his temperament and the resources of his own intellect. The image of reality he offers may be partly inaccurate or false but it is the sincerity of his effort, rather than the result, that counts."

Pinter's work expresses a reality he has experienced and it meets with a powerful response. By focusing attention on subconscious mechanisms, it is both moving and thought-provoking. In a subtle way, it helps clarify human relations and encourages the progress from intuition to analysis. By giving an embarrassing image of men, it acquires a subversive power. It contributes to the shaking of stereotypes. It generates suspicion about an alienating language. It favours a different consciousness. The images in Pinter's work are indeed oppressive but they may free from anguish those who accept and recognize them. Similar to the images in dreams, they open "inner eyes" and verify the existence of a subconscious reality. It isn't the verification of such a reality which is traumatic but the ignorance of it.

The effort of understanding required by Pinter's work also leads to a beneficial awareness of the importance of symbolic language. The misunderstanding of Pinter's plays is often based on the confusion of oneiric images and realism, on the mistake which consists in reading the text literally without translating its symbolic data, without interpreting the characters' psychopathic symptoms. A misunderstanding is inevitable if the spectator forgets that the characters' behaviour, like any human behaviour, isn't a direct reaction to a stimulus but a symbolic reaction, a transformed reaction, worked out unconsciously.

The deciphering of Pinter's work reveals the essential human problem—the fight between lucidity and blinding affectivity. Pinter's whole work deals with repressed anguish. To analyze his characters is to become conscious of the harm they do to themselves. It is to understand the psychological meaning of their symptoms. Such a diagnosis allows a better knowledge of the vicious circle of repression and helps to avoid it.

Pinter is no guide. He mirrors our subconscious. Yet his work is fuelled by a moral effort, inspired by an appeal to patience. If it has the power to move us, the merit of alerting us, it is because it expresses not only a dramatist's inner life but also the life of each one of us, recognizable by all. By obstinately revealing the truth about our secret pains, by helping us feel the immanent justice of life, Pinter's work awakens our ethical responsibility. It makes us reflect on our own errors and urges us on to fresh efforts of self-control. It represents a salutary landmark in our slow evolutionary ascent to higher levels of consciousness and lucidity. (pp. 81-2)

Daniel Salem, "The Impact of Pinter's Work," in *Ariel: A Review of International English Literature,* Vol. 17, No. 1, January, 1986, pp. 71-83.

SOURCES FOR FURTHER STUDY

Dukore, Bernard F. *Where Laughter Stops: Pinter's Tragicomedy.* Columbia: University of Missouri Press, 1976, 74 p.

> Regards "the movement of a funny play to a point where it is no longer funny" as the keynote of Pinter's dramaturgy.

Gale, Steven H., ed. *Harold Pinter: Critical Approaches.* Rutherford, N. J.: Fairleigh Dickinson University Press, 1986, 232 p.

> Collection of original essays that includes several appraisals of individual plays by Pinter as well as an overview of his career by Bernard F. Dukore.

Gordon, Lois, ed. *Harold Pinter: A Casebook.* New York: Garland Publishing, 1990, 278 p.

> Gathers a wide range of original essays on Pinter's works as well as previously unpublished photographs of him as a young actor with the McMaster Company in the early 1950s.

Hinchliffe, Arnold P. *Harold Pinter.* Boston: Twayne Publishers, 1981, 177 p.

> Surveys Pinter's life and career.

Sakellaridou, Elizabeth. *Pinter's Female Portraits: A Study of Female Characters in the Plays of Harold Pinter.* London: Macmillan Press, 1988, 235 p.

> Traces the development of Pinter's female characters from the stereotyped "mothers and whores" of his early plays to the complex women of *Betrayal* and *A Kind of Alaska.*

Thompson, David T. *Pinter: The Player's Playwright.* New York: Schocken Books, 1985, 152 p.

> Examines how Pinter's experiences as an actor influenced his writing.

Luigi Pirandello

1867-1936

Italian dramatist, short story writer, novelist, critic, and poet.

INTRODUCTION

*O*ne of the most important dramatists of the twentieth century, Pirandello prompted a reevaluation of traditional stagecraft through his innovative use of philosophical themes and experimentation with dramatic structure. Obsessed by the relationship of reality to appearances and of sanity to madness, he often portrayed characters who adopt multiple identities, or "masks," in an effort to reconcile social demands with personal needs. He was closely associated with the Theater of the Grotesque, a dramatic school that stressed the paradoxes and contradictions of life, and was also deeply concerned with making literature a more truthful and effective means for conveying human experience. Toward this end he developed the aesthetic theory of "humorism," which he defined as a mingling of comedy and tragedy to produce simultaneous emotional awareness of both of these aspects of the human condition.

Pirandello was born in Sicily to a prosperous sulphur merchant. Although his father initially sent him to study commerce at the local technical institute, Pirandello lacked interest in the subject and transferred to an academic secondary school, where he excelled in oratory and literature. He began writing at a young age, and by the time he was twelve had produced his first play, *Barbaro*, with siblings and friends. He also wrote poetry and fiction, publishing his first poem in 1883 and his first story a year later. After graduation, Pirandello attended universities in Palermo, Rome, and finally Bonn, where he earned a doctorate in Romance philology. He then returned to Rome, living on a remittance from his father while trying to establish himself as a writer. After his father arranged Pirandello's marriage to Antonietta Portulano, the daughter of a business partner, the couple settled together in Rome and had three children. To support his family, Pirandello was forced to increase his literary output and to take a position as professor at a women's normal school. In 1904 he realized his first critical success with the novel *Il fu Mattia Pascal* (1904; *The Late Mattia Pascal*), but this was overshadowed when his father's sulphur mines, in which Pirandello was heavily invested, were destroyed in a flood. All of Pirandello's wealth, including his wife's dowry, was wiped out. Upon hearing the news, Antonietta suffered an emotional collapse; she subsequently became obsessively jealous and delusional. Although subjected to relentless accusations and abuse, Pirandello refused to have his wife committed; instead, he took refuge in his study, where he lost himself in writing short stories, novels, and essays. He also wrote several plays, but was unable to get them produced.

The stress under which Pirandello lived was exacerbated when Italy entered World War I and his son was imprisoned in an Austrian POW camp. At the same time, Pirandello's wife became increasingly hostile and threatening, until at last he was forced to have her institutionalized. More than ever Pirandello turned to his writing for consolation. His biographer Gaspare Giudice wrote that "the sudden awareness that his own distress coincided with the laceration of the world outside, the correspondence of the absurd public agony with his own private pain, the confirmation that everything was vain and iniquitous" led Pirandello to produce the plays on which his fame would later rest. This period of intense creativity lasted from 1916 to 1922 and culminated in the production of his two greatest works: the dramas *Sei personaggi in cerca d'autore* (1921; *Six Characters in Search of an Author*) and *Enrico IV* (1922; *Henry IV*). Pirandello quickly went from being an author with a respectable but modest reputation to being one of the major literary figures in Italy. He took advantage of this public prominence to help Benito Mussolini and his Fascist Party endure a desperate crisis. In 1924 a leading member of the opposition, Giacomo Matteotti, was brutally assassinated by supporters of Mussolini. The Fascist Party was discredited, and Mussolini was nearly forced to resign, when Pirandello chose to join the Party as ostentatiously as he could. In a letter to the pro-Fascist paper *L'imperio,* he asked to join the Party and pledged his "humble obedience" to Mussolini. Mussolini, showing his appreciation for the gesture of support, provided funds for the Arts Theater that Pirandello had established. Pirandello, as producer and director, saw many of his plays first performed in this theater, and he took his company on tour throughout the world. However, the Arts Theater never achieved financial success and was dissolved in 1928. Frustrated by the failure of his theater, by his unsuccessful attempts to establish a government-sponsored National Theater in Rome, and by the decreasing popularity of his plays, Pirandello lived in self-imposed exile for the next five years. In 1934 he was awarded the Nobel Prize in literature, which he donated a year later to support the Italian invasion of Ethiopia. He continued to write as his health gradually deteriorated, and he died in December 1936.

Pirandello's early works were strongly influenced by verism, an Italian naturalist movement led by Giovanni Verga. Writing in his native Sicilian dialect, Pirandello skillfully described the landscape and inhabitants of Sicily. While his first successful novel, *The Late Mattia Pascal,* displays a naturalistic style, it also suggests the philosophical themes of his later work. Portraying a man who assumes a false identity in order to escape the circumstances of his life, *The Late Mattia Pascal* deals with the relationship of personal identity to the social definition of an individual. Pirandello's last novel, *Uno, nessuno e centomila* (1926; *One, None, and a Hundred Thousand*), expands upon this theme by examining Vitangelo Moscarda's efforts to free himself from the restrictions of his social identity. Unlike Mattia Pascal, who after abandoning his social identity painfully realizes that it is impossible to establish a new one, Moscarda seeks to rid himself permanently of those characteristics by which others have identified him. Pirandello's techniques of characterization parallel the struggles of his protagonists to deconstruct their superficial identities: instead of constructing a coherent character through a cumulative revelation of detail, Pirandello first described a character in superficial terms and then later contradicted what he had written. In his essay *L'umorismo* (1908; *On Humor*), which he dedicated "To the Memory of Mattia Pascal, Librarian," Pirandello articulated the major aesthetic principle that guided his work. Pirandello's theory of humorism is based upon his vision of the conflict between surface appearances and deeper realities. According to Pirandello, when an opposition exists between a character's situation and an audience's expectations, the audience gains an "awareness" of this opposition, and the situation appears comic. When the audience additionally recognizes a character's suffering beneath the comic appearance, the audience gains a "sentiment" or "feeling" of this opposition. Catharsis occurs when, through a combination of opposing reactions, the audience achieves both a compassionate understanding of the character's situation in the fictional world and a deeper insight into the real world. Pirandello was thus more interested in the audience's direct emotional experience of the theater than in the purely abstract and philosophical aspects of his plays.

Pirandello described his dramatic works as a "theater of mirrors" in which the audience sees what passes on stage as a reflection of their own lives: when his characters doubt their own perceptions of themselves, the audience experiences a simultaneous crisis of self-perception. In questioning the distinction between sanity and madness, Pirandello attacked abstract models of objective reality and theories of a static human personality. For these reasons, many critics have labelled him a pessimist and a relativist; others, noting the strong sense of compassion that Pirandello conveys for his characters, contend that Pirandello is not preaching a definable ideology, but is simply expressing his acute consciousness of the absurdities and paradoxes of human life. As Pirandello explained: "My works are born from live images which are the perennial source of art, but these images pass through a veil of concepts which have taken hold of me. My works of art are never concepts trying to express themselves through images. On the contrary. They *are* images, often very vivid images of life, which, fostered by the labors of my mind, assume universal significance quite on their own, through the formal unity of art."

In his most famous play, *Six Characters in Search of an Author,* Pirandello described the plight of six characters who interrupt the rehearsal of another Pirandello play to demand that their stories be acted out. His acknowledgement of the stage as the location of a theatrical performance—a place where life is only simulated—startled audiences and critics alike and heralded the self-conscious use of the theater that is a hallmark of modernist drama. Summarizing the effect of Pirandello's play, Antonio Illiano has written that the "sudden and unexpected appearance of live characters, who claimed to belong to the stage and could actually be seen and heard, was like a bombshell that blew out the last and weary residues of the old realistic drama." At the first performance of the play in Rome, the audience was so infuriated that a general riot broke out that lasted well into the night. The play was next performed several months later in Milan, but after the notoriety of the play's earlier performance, as well as the intervening publication of the text, the audience came knowing what to expect and the performance was a triumphant success which soon spread to theaters throughout the world. Pirandello's new technique created an ironic parallel between the relationship of the six characters to the stage manager and actors on the one hand, and the relationship of the performance of *Six Characters* to the actual audience on the other. When the characters argue that they are more real than the stage manager because their lives are fixed and unchanging in the roles that they eternally relive, they are actually challenging the audience's belief in the stable reality of their own personalities. Pirandello followed the success of *Six Characters* with *Henry IV,* which many critics consider his greatest work. Written four years after he had his wife committed, *Henry IV* is the last and most eloquent expression of the theme of madness that had been prevalent in Pirandello's personal life and in his art. It uses none of the modernistic dramatic techniques of *Six Characters* and instead draws upon and enriches classical dramatic patterns; the influence of *Hamlet* is especially evident. The play depicts a man who, as the result of an injury suffered at the hands of a rival, believes he is Henry IV. Eventually, he regains his sanity but in a fit of rage kills his rival, so that he must feign continued madness if he wants to avoid the consequences of his deed. Considered an apology for madness, *Henry IV* examines the practical reasons that make insanity and the construction of illusions the only logical response to a reality that is too painful to bear.

After writing *Henry IV,* Pirandello read a discussion of his plays in Adriano Tilgher's *Studi sul teatro contemporaneo* (1923), and the remainder of his career as a playwright was influenced by this critic's perception of his work. Tilgher saw in Pirandello's dramas a consistent and compelling philosophical formula which explained the often confusing and contradictory elements of these works. Tilgher wrote: "The philosophy implicit in Pirandello's art revolved round the fundamental dualism of Life and Form: Life, perpetually mobile and fluid, which cannot help developing into a form, although it deeply resents all form; and Form which determines Life, by giving it rigid and precise borders, and freezes it, suppressing its restless motion." Pirandello was pleased by the academic authority that Tilgher's essay gave to his dramas, and he was stimulated to approach more intently the life-form dichotomy in his works. Many critics blamed this objective for the decline in the quality of Pirandello's later plays, which were viewed as overly intellectual, obscure, and lacking emotional vitality. Tilgher himself later wrote that "it would have been better if Pirandello had never read my essay. It is never good for a writer to be too conscious of his inner world, and my essay fixed Pirandello's world in such clear and well-defined terms that Pirandello must have felt imprisoned in it, hence his protests that he was an artist and not a philosopher . . . and hence his attempts to escape. But the more he tried to escape from the critical pigeon-holes into which I had placed him the more he shut himself into them." Pirandello was bitterly disappointed by the critical and popular failure of his later dramas, a disappointment only partially mitigated by the Nobel Prize. However, after his death critics began to question the utility and appropriateness of the life-form dichotomy as the principal critical approach to Pirandello's works, and the rise of existentialist theory and of the Theater of the Absurd did much to alter the context of the debate on Pirandello.

Pirandello is today viewed with a more sophisticated appreciation for his philosophical themes and with near universal esteem for all his works, including his later dramas. What was previously scorned as overly intellectual and incoherent is now respected for its provocative treatment of relativism and antirationalism. Pirandello foresaw the abatement of the critical controversy that he inspired during his lifetime, and looked to that time when his works would be judged according to the artistic terms in which they were created: "The commotion aroused almost everywhere [by my work] is not the ideal environment for it. For me it is no more than a pledge for the future. Before it is attacked, as every human creation inevitably is, the meaningless clamour around it must be silenced; and there will be

a moment when, in the first lull it will come to life . . . clear as it once was in my mind when I contemplated it in its finished form and, for an instant, thought it perfect."

(For further information about Pirandello's life and works, see *Contemporary Authors*, Vol. 104 and *Twentieth-Century Literary Criticism*, Vols. 4, 29.)

CRITICAL COMMENTARY

ADRIANO TILGHER
(essay date 1923)

[Tilgher was an Italian philosopher and critic whose analysis of Pirandello's works in *Studi sul teatro contemporaneo* (1923) established the main tradition of Pirandello criticism and influenced Pirandello's own writing. In the following excerpt from that work, Tilgher examines Pirandello's worldview as it is presented in his writings.]

What, in Pirandello's view, distinguishes man from the other beings of nature? This, and only this: that man lives and feels himself live, while the other beings of nature just live, live purely and simply. The tree, for instance, lives completely immersed in its own vital sense; its existence equals the slow and dark succession of vital vicissitudes in it; sun, moon, wind and earth surround it, but it sees and knows nothing of them: it senses them, of course, but only insofar as they become states of its own being, from which it fails to distinguish itself. Since it knows nothing of anything else, the tree knows nothing of itself as different from anything else.

But in man, no matter how uncouth, life splits in two: even to the most uncouth of men it is essential to be and to know that he is, to live and to know that he lives. In man, life has projected and detached from itself as its own opposite something that Pirandello calls the feeling of life and that I would call, in philosophically stricter terms, consciousness, reflection, thought. In such detachment, with the attendant delusion of assuming as objectively and externally existing reality this mutable inner feeling of life, there lies the first cause of human misery. For once it has detached itself from life, the feeling of life (or consciousness as we may call it) by filtering through the brain tends to cool off, to clarify and idealize itself; from the particular, changeable, ephemeral state it was, it will eventually crystallize into a general, abstract idea (see Pirandello's essay *L'umorismo*.)

Having risen through logical abstraction to its own second power, having become reflective thought, the feeling of life tends to confine life within fixed boundaries, to channel it between chosen banks, to pour it into stiff, definitive molds: the concepts and ideals of our spirit, the conventions, mores, traditions, and laws of society. That causes a basic dualism. On the one hand, blind, dumb Life will keep darkly flowing in eternal restlessness through each moment's renewals. On the other hand, a world of crystallized Forms, a system of constructions, will strive to dam up and compress that ever-flowing turmoil. "Everything, every object, every life carries with it the penalty of its form, the pain of being so and never otherwise, until it crumbles into ashes" (see the short story **"Candelora"** [**"Candlemas"**]). "Every form is death. We are all beings caught in a trap, detached from the unceasing flux, and fixed to death" (see the short story **"La trappola"** [**"The Trap"**]).

Most men live within those frozen forms, without even so much as surmising that a dark, furious ocean may stir under them. But in some men, thought, that very activity which, lightning-like in its mystery, has split life asunder, separates from the forms into which life's hot flux has clotted and perceives them for what they really are: merely ephemeral constructions, under which the tide of life roars unconstrained by any human illusion. In the man who has achieved this deliverance from the forms of life, any human construction arouses a sense of contrast which topples it under his very eyes. There is something comical and grievous at the same time in that crash. The crash is comical because it lays bare the intrinsic unreality of human constructions, but grievous too, because, however flimsy, the demolished structure did afford man a shelter from the mad storm of life.

In such intimate mixture of laughter and tears, of comedy and sadness, is humor as Pirandello feels it to be and defines it. "I see something like a labyrinth, where through so many crisscrossing paths our soul

Principal Works

Mal giocondo (poetry) 1889

Amori senza amore (short stories) 1894

Beffe della morte e della vita (short stories) 1902

Bianche e nere (short stories) 1904

Il fu Mattia Pascal (novel) 1904
  [The Late Mattia Pascal, 1923]

Erma bifronte (short stories) 1906

L'esclusa (novel) 1908
  [The Outcast, 1925]

L'umorismo (essay) 1908
  [On Humor, 1974]

I vecchi e i giovani (novel) 1913
  [The Old and the Young, 1928]

Liolà (drama) 1916
  [Liolà published in Naked Masks, 1952]

Si gira (novel) 1916
  [Shoot! The Notebooks of Serafino Gubbio, Cinemato-
  graph Operator, 1926]

Così è (se vi pare) (drama) 1917
  [Right You Are! (If You Think So) published in Three
  Plays, 1922]

Il piacere dell'onestà (drama) 1917
  [The Pleasure of Honesty published in Each in His Own
  Way, and Two Other Plays, 1923]

Il carnevale dei morti (short stories) 1919

L'uomo, la bestia e la virtù (drama) 1919

Sei personaggi in cerca d'autore (drama) 1921
  [Six Characters in Search of an Author published in
  Three Plays, 1922]

Enrico IV (drama) 1922

[Henry IV published in Three Plays, 1922]

Novelle per un anno.15 vols. (short stories) 1922-37

Vestire gli ignudi (drama) 1922
  [Naked published in Each in His Own Way, and Two
  Other Plays, 1923]

Ciascuno a suo modo (drama) 1924
  [Each in His Own Way published in Each in His Own
  Way, and Two Other Plays, 1923]

Uno, nessuno e centomila (novel) 1926
  [One, None, and a Hundred Thousand, 1933]

Come tu mi vuoi (drama) 1930
  [As You Desire Me, 1931]

Maschere nude. 10 vols. (dramas) 1930-38

Questa sera si recita a soggetto (drama) 1930
  [Tonight We Improvise, 1932]

*Horse in the Moon (short stories) 1932

*Better Think Twice about It, and Twelve Other Stories
  (short stories) 1933

*The Naked Truth, and Eleven Other Stories (short sto-
  ries) 1934

I giganti della montagna (drama) 1937
  [The Mountain Giants published in The Mountain Giants, and Other Plays, 1958]

*The Medals, and Other Stories (short stories) 1939

Short Stories (short stories) 1959

Short Stories (short stories) 1965

*These stories have been selected from the series Novel-
le per un anno.

rambles without ever finding a way out. And in this labyrinth I see a double herma which laughs from one face and weeps from the other, laughs indeed from one face at the weeping of the twin, opposite one" (see *Erma bifronte* [*Two-faced Herma*], preface). Since humor is the attitude of the man whose thought, having attained self-consciousness, has broken through the screens of conceptual constructions to look out on life's abysmal tide of tumultuous incoherence, it has to be an essentially cerebral state of mind. Humor and cerebralism: all of Pirandello's art is summarized in these two words.

Therefore, antithesis is the basic law of his art. The customary relationships of human existence are triumphantly subverted. Among the comedies, *Pensaci, Giacomino!* (*Think It Over, Giacomino!*) features a husband intentionally forcing the (to him only too well known) young lover of his wife to come back to her, while *L'uomo, la bestia e la virtù* (*Man, Beast and Vir-*

tue) shows a lover dragging the betrayed husband back to the marriage bed. *Ma non è una cosa seria* (*It Can't Be Serious*) deals with marriage as an antidote against the danger of marriage. Of the short stories, **"Da sé"** (**"By Himself"**) presents the supposedly dead man who traipses to the graveyard thereby enjoying many things which are lost on quick and dead alike. **"Nené e Niní"** (**"Nené and Niní"**) acquaints us with two little orphans who bring ruin to a whole series of stepfathers and stepmothers. **"Canta l'epistola"** (**"Sing the Epistle"**) develops the motif of a mortal duel caused by the plucking of a leaf of grass. **"Il dovere del medico"** (**"The Physician's Duty"**) tells the story of a doctor who, from sheer sense of duty, lets his patient bleed to death, then in **"Prima notte"** (**"First Wedding Night"**) we see two newlyweds spend their first wedding night weeping respectively on the grave of her fiancé and of his first wife; finally, **"L'illustre estinto"** (**"The Illustrious Deceased"**) (to put an end to our practically inexhaustible examples) is the tale of an illustrious deceased who gets a hidden burial by night, like a dog, while a perfect nobody receives honors and gifts in his place.

Dualism of Life and Form (or Construction); the necessity for Life to sink into a Form without possibly ever being exhausted by it: here is the fundamental motif underlying all of Pirandello's work in such a way as to organize it into a strict unity of vision. That suffices to show the remarkable modern relevance of this writer of ours. All of modern philosophy, from Kant on, rises from this deep insight into the dualism between absolutely spontaneous Life, which in its perennial upsurge of freedom keeps creating the new, and the constructed Forms or molds which tend to imprison that upsurge, with the result that Life every time shatters those molds to dissolve them and go beyond in its tireless creativity. The whole history of modern philosophy is the progressive deepening of this basic intuition into self-possessed clarity. To the eyes of an artist like Pirandello, who lives on just such an intuition, reality will appear dramatic at its very roots, the essence of drama lying in the struggle between Life's primal nakedness and the garments or masks with which men must by all means insist on clothing it. *La vita nuda* (*Naked Life*), *Maschere nude* (*Naked Masks*). The very titles of his works are telling.

To enjoy Life in its infinite nakedness and freedom, outside all constructed forms into which society, history, and the events of each individual existence have channeled its course, is impossible. Mattia Pascal tried that, who, palming himself off as dead and changing name and aspect, believed he could start a new life, in the enthusiasm of a boundless liberty. He learned at his own expense that, having cut himself off from all social forms and conventions, he was only allowed to witness other people's life as a foreign spectator, without any further possibility to mingle with it and enjoy its fullness. Since he had estranged himself from the forms of Life, it now no longer conceded itself to him except superficially, externally. And when, surrendering to its call, he deluded himself that he could plunge again into the river of Life to be enveloped by its waves, that river rejected him, and again at his own expense he learned that it is not possible to act as living and dead at the same time. Thus in despair he resolved to stage a resurrection—too late to sit down again at the banquet of existence, in time only to see others partake of it (see the novel *Il fu Mattia Pascal* [*The Late Mattia Pascal*]). Of course it is possible to estrange oneself from the forms of Life, but only on condition that one gives up living.

To accept the Forms of constructions into which Life has been forced; to participate in them with heartfelt belief and yet avoid crystallizing oneself in one of them or in one of their systems, but to retain so much

spiritual fusion or fluidity that one's soul may go on from form to form without finally coagulating in any, without fearing the impurities it inevitably carries along in its ceaseless flow, since that very flowing will purify it: here is the practical wisdom of life. It is a wisdom of precarious value, far from insuring perfect happiness, since some form may always emerge to obstruct so firmly the soul streaming at white heat that the latter fails to melt the obstacle and finally subsides into it, stifled.

That is the case of Corrado Selmi of *I vecchi e i giovani* (*The Old and the Young*), in whom Pirandello has embodied this refreshing ideal of wisdom. Corrado has to commit suicide one day when certain past actions of his come to light, because these actions, for all the redeeming freshness of life he had put in them and the good he thus managed to spread around by their means or in their spite, do appear vile and dishonorable to society that looks at them from the outside.

But Selmi's idea of practical wisdom can only be achieved by a soul endowed with the strength to pass on from form to form without either being imprisoned in any one of them or losing in the passage the sustenance of its vital illusion. That means a soul capable of attaining in itself a balance between Life and Form and of dwelling there contentedly. But whoever radically lives by the Pirandellian insight that any Form must always be a limiting determination and therefore a denial of Life . . . will have only two choices left. Either (like the Vitangelo Moscarda of *Uno, nessuno e centomila* [*One, No One and a Hundred Thousand*]) he can try and live Life in its absolute primeval nakedness, beyond all forms and constructions, focusing on a vibrantly fleeting present, experiencing time moment by moment, without even thinking of time in the process for that would mean to construe it, to give it a form and thus limit and stifle it (This is an enactment of Bergson's intutionalism, with a timeless *pure present* substituted for *pure duration.* Such an ideal of life is, however, attainable at the limit, i.e., practically unattainable.);

or else, having discovered the provisional nature of Forms along with the impossibility to do without them, the ineluctable penalty one will eventually have to pay for the Form that Life donned or let itself be dressed in, one can renounce life: and that is the case of Don Cosmo Laurentano of *I vecchi e i giovani* (*The Old and the Young*).

"One thing only is said, my friends: to have seen through the game! I mean the game of this mocking devil who hides within each of us and has his fun projecting for us as external reality what, shortly after, he himself will expose as our own delusion, laughing at the pains we took for it and laughing also . . . at our failure to delude ourselves, since outside these delusions there is no reality left. . . . And so don't complain! Do trouble yourselves with your endeavors, without thinking that it all will lead to no conclusion. If it does not conclude, it means that it should not conclude, and that it is therefore useless to seek a conclusion. We must live, that is, we must delude ourselves; leave free play to the mocking devil within us. . . . "

• • • • •

Just because the Pirandellian Weltanschauung does not admit of one reason, of one logic, and of one law, but of as many as there are individuals, and indeed as many for the same individual as feeling creates in its endless variations, each character from his own viewpoint is right, and no such thing exists as one higher point of view from which to judge all others. Thus in the end Pirandello does not judge, absolve, or condemn any of his characters; rather, his judgment is implied in the portrayal he gives of them and of their actions' consequences. That makes for a firmly immanent morality, to the absolute exclusion of any reference to transcendent norms. For each one, the judgment is implicitly given by the results of his actions.

Thus, for instance, not one word of condemnation is ever uttered by Pirandello on his many fictive women, even though, personifying blind instinct unrestrained by reason and thought, they seem to be crazy, amoral, conscienceless creatures, addicted to orgies of sensual cerebralism as well as to hangover nausea and horror of it, with sudden yearnings for purity and motherhood. Such are Silia of *Il giuoco delle parti* (*Each in His Role*), Beatrice of *Il berretto a sonagli* (*Cap and Bells*), Fulvia of *Come prima, meglio di prima* (*As Well as Before, Better than Before*), the Stepdaughter of *Sei personaggi in cerca d'autore* (*Six Characters in Search of an Author*), the Murdered Woman of the "lay mystery" *All'uscita* (*At the Exit*), Ersilia of *Vestire gli ignudi* (*Naked*), all of them full of hatred against the man each confronts (respectively Leone, Ciampa, Silvio, the Father, the Fat Man) since he embodies what is directly contrary to them: order, reason, pondering calm, and prudence.

In the Pirandellian view of things, Life must needs give itself a Form and withal not exhaust itself therein. Also, in the human world the creator of Form is thought. Thus, while with other artists conscious thought only accompanies the unfolding of inner events from the outside, and throws on them a cold superficial light, so that drama is generated and consummated exclusively in the emotive sphere, the possible intervention of thought never being crucial, with Pirandello thought finds its way into every moment of psychological becoming.

His characters justify, condemn, criticize themselves in the very act of living through their torments; they don't just feel, they reason rightly or absurdly on their feelings, and in so doing transfer them from the level of mere emotionality to a level of higher, more truly human complexity. Man after all is not just feeling, but also and especially thought, and he reasons, whether rightly or absurdly, especially when he suffers. Feelings, passions, affections are always thrown into perspective by thought which colors and imbues them with itself, yet by the same token it, in turn, is colored by them and warmed by their flame. Thought here is life and drama, and takes shape gradually through ceaseless lacerations and contrasts. We thus have cerebralism, of course, but one and the same with the torment and passion of drama. Thinking thought, which is activity unfolding through continuous struggles and wounds, places itself at the center of art's world: with Pirandello, dialectic becomes poetry.

Pirandello's art, chronologically as well as ideally contemporary to the great idealist revolution that took place in Italy and Europe at the beginning of this century, carries over into art the anti-rationalism which fills modern philosophy and is now culminating into Relativism. Pirandello's art is anti-rationalist not because it denies or ignores thought to the total benefit of feeling, passion, and affections, but rather because it installs thought at the very center of the world as a live power fighting with the rebellious powers of Life. Anti-rationalist (or anti-intellectualist) do I call it, because it denies that a complete, self-contained and wholly determined order of truth preexists thought, as if the only thing left for thought itself to do were humbly to take notice of preordained truth and bow to it; yet it is a thought-affirming art, instinct with the drama of thinking thought. . . .

Thought actually leavens Life. Therefore, while for other writers reality is massively compact and monolithically rigid, given once for all, with Pirandello it flakes off into several levels which in turn then endlessly complicate one another. Not only what is commonly called real is such, but also, and with the same right, whatever appears to be real in the warmth of a feeling. A deeply dreamed dream (as in the short story **"La realtà del sogno"** [**"The Reality of Dream"**]), a memory (as in the short story **"Piuma"** [**"Feather"**]), or a fantasy (as in the short stories, **"Se . . . "** [**"If "**], **"Rimedio: La geografia"** [**"The Remedy: Geography"**], **"Il treno ha fischiato"** [**"The Train Whistled"**]) are as real to him who intensely lives them as this thick world of things and people to which alone we usually ascribe the name of reality. As a consequence, what is real to one person may not be to another, or may be real to still another in a different way, and what was reality to the same man fades off in his eyes once the engendering sentiment has failed. Jocularly, the short story **"Il pipistrello"** (**"The Bat"**) tells of one such clash between different levels of reality, and of the attendant troubles.

Two plays by Pirandello above all show this living dialectic of Spirit in action: *La ragione degli altri*

(*Other People's Point of View*) and *Sei personaggi in cerca d'autore* (*Six Characters in Search of an Author*). In *La ragione degli altri* a situation has arisen whose inner logic by its own unfolding determines the action's development and leads the characters to the only admissible end. The central character, Livia (who is fully aware of the situation's logic), has broken off with her husband Leonardo upon learning of a mistress, Elena, who has borne him a daughter. The weary mistress would like to send her husband back to her, and she is willing to forgive him, on one condition, however: that Elena surrenders to her the child to be raised as Livia's own daughter, in the comforts destitute Elena cannot give her. Elena took Leonardo away from her as a husband, and she is returning him as a father; well then, let the father either stay with his child's mother, or come back to his lawful wife, but with the child. To have him back only by half, a husband with herself and a father with the other woman, will never do. "Where the children are, there is the home!" and Leonardo had no children from Livia. "Two homes, that is out! I here and your daughter there, that is out!"

Such is the situation, of which Livia represents and interprets the inner logic, for her feeling has risen to the highest degree of rationality. Around her and the other characters move on different levels, all of them lower than Livia's: in all of them passion to some extent dominates reason. Each of them defends a particular right of his: Elena, as the mother she is, wants to send Leonardo back to Livia, but to keep the child; Guglielmo, as the father-in-law, regardless of the child, wants Leonardo to be reconciled to his daughter Livia, or else Livia to return to her parental home; Leonardo claims his right as a husband in love with his wife again and as a father who won't ever give up the child. The action is continuous dialectic, through which all these one-sided rights and reasons gradually become aware of their one-sidedness to yield finally to the right and reason of Livia, which contains them all and is therefore superior to all, for it interprets the good of the child, the strongest right and need. Livia is of course taking her mother away from the little girl, but she is giving her another, equally affectionate one, along with the father, and wealth and a name for good measure.

In *La ragione degli altri* (*Other People's Point of View*) we see a dialectic operate whereby a higher truth or reason conquers the lower ones. In *Sei personaggi in cerca d'autore* (*Six Characters in Search of an Author*) we see the very dialectic of truth of illusion taking shape. In this admirable play, which takes its cue from a motif outlined in the short story, **"La tragedia di un personaggio" ("The Tragedy of a Character"),** Pirandello wants to portray scenically the laboring process whereby the riot of phantoms born by the artist's imagination, throbbing with life as they no doubt are yet at first still confused, dark and chaotically unaccom-plished, aspires to a final composure in whose encompassing harmony what had initially flashed in the artist's mind as faintly distinguishable splotches of color may find the proper balance in an ample, luminous, well organized picture.

One is born a fictional character as one is born stone, plant, or animal, and if the really of the character is an illusion, any reality will likewise turn out to be an illusion once the animating feeling has changed. Who was born a character, then, has even more life than the so-called really existing men, for they change in every way from day to day, and pass and die, while the fictional character, instead, has his own incorruptible life, eternally fixed in his nature's unchangeable essential traits. "Nature uses the instrument of imagination to pursue its own creative work on a higher level." And once he is created, the character detaches himself from his author, lives by himself and imposes his will on the creator, who must follow and let him do as he pleases. One day six characters, whom their author had sketched and provisionally composed in an undeveloped, unfinished scenic plot, turn to a *stage manager* to propose that he allow them to act out onstage the drama irrepressibly stirring within them.

Not all of these characters are equally achieved. Two, the main ones (*Father and Stepdaughter*), are very close to accomplished artistic achievement, some other instead is little more than brute nature, blind impression of life (the *Mother*), still another (the *Son*) is lyrically achieved and rebels against a dramatic enactment. These six characters in search of an author do not, then, share the same level of consciousness: they are the scenic realization of the several levels of consciousness on which an artist's imagination has dwelt. Pirandello's play would realize in scenic terms the process of coalescence leading to the work of art, the transition from life to art, from impression to intuition and finally expression. The turmoil of scarcely sketched phaontoms who, full of an incoercible life the author gave them and cannot withdraw, play at overpowering one another, at securing each the center of the whole work and drawing to themselves all the interest of the *stage manager,* is very well rendered through a broken, panting dialogue. Pirandello has deeply seen that right here, in this *eccentricity* (literally meant), in this blind rushing to develop to the bitter end each separate seminal motif lies the whole essence of Nature or Life, what distinguishes it from Spirit, Art, which instead is coordination, synthesis, discipline, and thus choice and conscious sacrifice.

But this, which should be the play's central motif and indeed dominates it throughout Act I, finds no adequate development in Acts II and III, where we do not see, in scenic terms, the passage of characters from a lower to a higher level, for they fail to proceed from confusion to order, from chaos to artistic cosmos. Who was nature remains nature, who was realized only lyrically remains so. The play cannot come to light. Why? Because the *son* rebels against acting his role in the play, he is not cut out for scenes. The play fails, because instead of a coordinating spirit the characters meet a mediocre manager who tries to improvise it, and no work of art is to be improvised; it cannot be a mediocre manager, with no artistic experience or depth, a manager who sees only the so-called requirements of theater, to set up in a few hours a play needing no less than a painstaking elaboration. Yet this seems to me a particular reason, devoid of universal value and incapable of demonstrating anything. What universal meaning can be inferred from the fact that a tradesman of theater is unable to bring to fruition a theme left in its inchoate phase? To lead to complete expression of characters in whom whatever life was infused has not yet expressed itself ?

In Acts II and III the dominant motif of the play interweaves with the one of the distortion actual life undergoes when passing into the mirror of art (a motif which reappears in Act I of *Vestire gli ignudi* [*Naked*]). In Act II there operates again the evil mirror which sends back to the individual his own unrecognizable image. For when they see the actors, exclusively preoccupied with the scenic truth to be achieved, repeat their own gestures and those words they had uttered in the urgency of unstilled passion, the characters no longer recognize themselves, and in their bewilderment, they burst into laughter or despair. The mirror is in this case the art of the stage (though whatever is said of it can be said of art in general), and when it is reflected in it, actual life in the common sense of the word, the life of interest and passion, appears to itself distorted and false. But by dwelling at length on this theme, Pirandello unknowingly transforms his characters (who should be more or less achieved artistic phantoms) into real beings, and by thus transferring them from the level of imagination onto the level of actual life he splits the play at the seams.

But there is still a third motif which interferes with the others to the play's detriment. Of the six characters in search of an author, each one already knows what will happen to himself and to the others: they have the total vision of their destiny. For instance, whenever the *father* and the *stepdaughter* place themselves at a certain point of the story and try to pick its thread up from there, there is present to the scene the *mother* who already knows how it will end, and in her foreknowledge she is induced not to witness the action passively, but to implore that she be spared the horrible spectacle about to take place. Thus sentimental considerations may emerge to trouble, tentatively, the necessary architecture of a work of art, which has its own inner logic not to be disturbed by any regard for the spectators' tender hearts. But this motif should have been developed much more deeply and with greater emphasis. Besides, Act III after all only treads in the footsteps of Act II, and the end of the play is quite absurd; it's any old epilogue, stuck there just to wind things up and let the curtain fall.

Yet despite these structural faults the play does remain the strongest attempt in Europe so far to realize scenically a process of pure states of mind, by analyzing and projecting onto the stage the various levels and phases of one stream of consciousness. The attempt had already been made by others in Italy, but never with such violence and daring ambition. The drama the six characters carry inside without yet managing to express it . . . is typically Pirandellian. The hints we get of it, broken, uncorrelated and confused as they must needs be, since they constitute a sketch and not an accomplished work of art, still have as much tragic power as one can imagine.

The dangers such a theater incurs are intrinsic to its very nature, and the word *cerebralism* may sum them up (meaning, this time, arid intellectualistic contrivance). Of course it cannot be denied that Pirandello's characters look too much alike; rather than various characters, they seem one and the same character placed in ever different yet identical situations. Of course the progress of Pirandellian art moves not toward enrichment but toward the greater deepening of one and the same Weltanschauung. As all of Pirandello's work tends to the theater, so all his theater tends to one perfect work totally expressing the Pirandellian intuition of life, like a pyramid tending to one point into which everything underneath may converge and be resolved.

Often the play is the belabored and gray scenic dressing of an abstract reflection or of a situational device which preceded and replaced dramatic vision. Figures then become skeletal, frozen in a grimace, stuck in a mania which is the wooden covering of a set theme. Artistic value in those cases finds refuge entirely in the details of some scene. Words, circumscribed in their common meaning, are pale and deprived of imaginative radiance. The pattern will usually consist of a weird picturesque preparation serving to introduce abstract cogitations on a psychological or metaphysical truth.

But there are the plays born of a lively and powerful dramatic vision, to which abstract meditation is coeval and not preconceived: first of all, *Enrico IV* (*Henry IV*); then *Sei personaggi in cerca d'autore* (*Six Characters in Search of an Author*); *Il berretto a sonagli* (*Cap and Bells*); *Così è* (*se vi pare*) (*It Is So, if You Think So*); *Il piacere dell'onestà* (*The Pleasure of Honesty*); and, some notches down, *Pensaci, Giacomino!* (*Think It Over, Giacomino!*); *L'innesto* (*The Grafting*); *Come prima, meglio di prima* (*As Well as Before, Better than Before*); *Vestire gli ignudi* (*Naked*). Here whatever may be wooden or skeletal is a function of the peculiar dramatic insight, but under that deathly cold one senses the deep subterranean throb of life which finally breaks through; the frozen spasm will then melt into tears. Remaining always very simple (in fact the most sober and bare, the farthest from literary artifice, the most truly spoken idiom ever heard on our stages), the language of these plays is nimble, witty, juicy, bursting with vitality; dialogue is concise, detailed, unornate, and its fresh, relevant imagery admirably helps it to match the sinuosities of psychological becoming.

And all the art of this great writer seems to be caught in a magnificent ascending movement. It seems to me that he is gradually liberating himself from the biggest flaw of his first theatrical works: what I once called, in *Voci del tempo* (*Voices of Our Time*), the imbalance between the smallness of results, all steeped in the particular, and the metaphysical grandiosity of Pirandello's preliminary intentions. It's an imbalance between the grandeur of such intentions and the story which should have expressed them scenically, usually a story of hopelessly pathetic petty bourgeois creatures living in backwoods small towns, of little boardinghouse tenants, of people catering to village clubs, in a bleak, depressing atmosphere.

How on earth, for instance, can we recognize the universal drama of self-knowledge as death (*As Well as Before, Better than Before*) in the story of courtesan Fulvia who, after many years spent in shameful abjection away from her husband's home, returns there to contemplate herself in the image her daughter Livia has conceived of her through blessed ignorance of her real identity as a person or as a mother? Or, again, in the story of State Councillor Martino Lori, who after six years of unbelieveable gullibility wakes up to the fact that neither wife nor daughter were ever his own? The sorrow of the wretched man in Act III of *Tutto per bene* (*All for the Best*) is doubtless heartbreaking, but to share it we must postulate on his part an absolutely incredible, or at least unique blindness, which removes him from our compassion into a kind of estrangement.

Surely, even in these first plays, when the meaning Pirandello wants to squeeze from the story and the story itself succeed in finding their harmony we get actual masterpieces like *Il berretto a sonagli* (*Cap and Bells*). Where this harmony is not reached, beauty takes refuge in the details of some scene or character, mostly in the final scenes, when the mask drops and lays bare a sorrowing visage. But in *Six Characters* and in *Henry IV* the metaphysical urge shatters the puny frames which once throttled it, and it gets free play in ampler vicissitudes. The drama throbs with stronger life, its underlying metaphysical torment conquers an apter expression. The motifs are still the same, but tragedy unfolds in a higher, purer atmosphere. And Pirandello has not yet said his last word. He seems now to become increasingly aware of his original dramatic potential.

The first progress of the Sicilian artist took place when, having gone beyond the phase of the peasant short story in Verga's regional-naturalist mood, and beyond the subsequent phase of the ironic, skeptical short story based on manipulation of incident, and having passed from small- and large-scale fiction to the theater, he managed to integrate dramatically those motifs which in his earlier works of fiction lay side-to-side without substantial correlation, like gunpowder lacking a spark to fire it. In the production antedating *The Late Mattia Pascal* the synthesis of Pirandello's special humor is not yet really achieved. Pirandello endeavors to attain the artistic effect through a pessimistic narrative form in Verga's dramatic style, but intellectual negation prevents him from sharing wholeheartedly the anguish of his creatures. He would have us experience as drama what in his mind has been already overcome in a kind of philosophically resigned humor. In this phase of his art feeling and thought are juxtaposed rather than fused, and disturb each other.

This state of mind finds its most felicitous expression in *The Late Mattia Pascal*, where sorrow is overcome in the resigned acceptance of its absolute uselessness. After this novel, the art of Pirandello develops in such a way as to make ever more intimate the synthesis of its two basic elements, so that thought will be born along with feeling as its accompanying shadow. Live anguish gradually sheds any ironic felicity, any expressive indifference and intermediate nuance, to embody itself in ever leaner and more convulsed forms. That is when Pirandellian drama rises, from an intimate need. A second progress is now being made by the artist, who tends to clench the expression of his authentic dramatic center in all its purity and metaphysical universality. The progress made to date is the sure promise of the inevitably forthcoming masterpiece, in which Pirandello's vision of life will fully possess and express itself.

So far, one thing is sure: that with Pirandello for the first time Italian literature discovers how the spirit, far from being the simple, two-dimensional entity it once believed, is a chasm unfathomable by the eye, an unexplored region sounding with strange voices, streaked by phantasmagorias, peopled with monsters, where truth and error, reality and make-believe, wakefulness and dream, good and evil struggle forever tangling in the shadow of mystery. (pp. 20-34)

Adriano Tilgher, "Life versus Form," translated by Glauco Cambon, in *Pirandello: A Collection of Critical Essays,* edited by Glauco Cambon, Prentice-Hall, Inc., 1967, pp. 19-34.

BENJAMIN CRÉMIEUX
(essay date 1927)

[Crémieux was a French critic and friend of Pirandello who translated several of his plays into French. In the following essay, he introduces the theoretical basis and principal themes and techniques of Pirandello's works.]

The best critical study that has yet been printed on the work of Luigi Pirandello is undoubtedly that of Adriano Tilgher in his *Studi sul teatro contemporaneo.* He describes the rich content of Pirandello's work in an analysis with whose solidity and rigor no fault can be found. "Pirandellism" emerges from this volume systematized in the most coherent and complete way. But however interesting "Pirandellism" may be in itself it would be diminishing Pirandello's own literary stature to reduce him to a mere "ism." One may even ask whether this would not distort the significance of all his work.

"A theatre of ideas"—that was the theme on which French critics rang the changes after the first presentation in Paris of his play, *Six Characters in Search of an Author.* But we must return a negative reply to their suggestions. Pirandello's is, indeed, a theatre that makes you think, but it is not a "theatre of ideas." In the same way, there is no such thing as "Pirandellism" in Pirandello himself, and yet it is quite true that one can extract "Pirandellism" from Pirandello's work.

Pirandello himself has not changed for thirty years. To the people who used to ask him what he was he always replied that he was a "humorist," and one of his first works was indeed a study of humor, in which he set forth clearly those theories of art which he has since developed and deepened without fundamentally altering.

Humor, as Pirandello understands it, has nothing in common with the humor of our gay French authors. It is closer to English humorists of the eighteenth century, closer to the humor of a Stern or a Swift. Yet it does not wholly mingle with humor of this sort. Pirandello's humor is not an art form deliberately chosen by the writer as a result of his own character or personality, or chosen at random. No; genuine, profound, and thoroughgoing humor is a necessity to anyone who has a clear vision of the realities of human life. Most humorists confine themselves to exploiting the feelings of contradiction, to searching for the comic element that sorrow that lies just beneath tears and seeking the sorrow that lies beneath the comic, or else devote themselves to concealing their own keen sensitiveness beneath the ironic modesty of a smile.

True humor, according to Pirandello, takes its rise in man's consciousness of his own existence, in the fundamental truth that a man does not merely live his life but that he also *thinks* his life. Man is both spectator and actor at the same time. This is the one great difference between him and the rest of nature. A tree or an animal lives according to the law of its own existence—governed by the circumstances which affect it; but a man—even the most inferior—not only lives his life, but also has ideas about himself and about his life. The process of living flows ceaselessly on, changing from moment to moment. But the mind of man is not so swift as the process of life itself. Man's images of himself and of his own existence still appear to him to be faithful representations of the world outside, even at that very moment when life has already profoundly changed them. Hence arises a duality between life itself and man's image of it, between the Real and one's idea of the Real, for the latter is no more than the form in which man perceives Reality in order to be able to think it at all. Reality cannot be thought about except when it is given form by the human consciousness.

There are only two ways in which this duality can be done away with: one must either refuse to think about life at all and be content to live his life like a vegetable, or else he must refuse to heed any Reality outside his own mind. The latter attitude is suited to crazy men who pay attention only to their own fixed ideas, and it is suited also to heroes in literature—since they have been created by artists and are stable creatures who cannot change.

Each of these statements might be illustrated by one of Pirandello's plays or stories, and this is equally true of the statements that are to follow. Therefore the first feeling of duality which lies at the basis of humor is, for Pirandello, the basis for any true vision of human life, and so in becoming a humorist Pirandello is indulging in the strictest realism. He does not distort life, nor does he systematize it, as people pretend. He does nothing but keep human life as it is. *Bare Life* is the title of one of his recent collections of stories. *Bare Masques* is the general title that he gives to his plays. He does not condescend to dress up life or prettify it. He shows it as it really is—the perpetual duality between life and man's feeling of it.

The consequences of this never-ending duality are infinite. The four hundred short stories, the five novels, and the twenty-eight plays that Pirandello has written have no object except to illustrate the consequence of this principle; and in taking this course Pirandello, without being aware of it, has come in touch with Bergson's philosophy of change, with Freudianism, with Einstein's relativity, and with Marcel Proust. He has reached the bottom of the great problem which more or less disturbs the philosophers and writers of to-day—I mean the multiplicity of human personalities, the impossibility of communication between human beings, the difficulty of distinguishing between illusion and reality.

Adriano Tilgher has listed, with admirable skill, the principal themes employed by Pirandello. First of all there is a series of single themes to which we have already made allusion: the impossible attempt to live life as it really is, the renunciation of living, the impossibility of watching one's life, the nonexistence of personality, since each individual is a chaos of contradictory forces. After this comes a series of relationships of men among themselves: to be is only to seem, each individual is an island on which one can never land, men can never understand themselves. Third, there are the pieces which have as their fundamental thesis the abyss between the present and the past: man's desire to keep himself as he is while everything is changing around him and in him, the contradiction that exists between an individual man and the idea that other people have of him, the destruction of the mask with which man covers his own face, the acceptance of a mask which others impose by force (as in Pirandello's play about the man who is accused of being a gambler and who in the end has to become one and goes to court to ask for a gambler's license), the revolt of life itself against this mask (as in the third act of the *Pleasure of Honor*), and, finally, the triumph of the irrational.

Although it sometimes happens that dialectic and a kind of spirit of philosophic systematizing dominate some of Pirandello's stories or comedies and reduce them to mere jugglery,—full of skill, no doubt, but without anything genuinely stirring about them,—nevertheless the case is usually just the reverse. Pirandello looks to life itself for his first inspiration, no matter whether he is working on some strange but authentic occurrence, or whether he is deliberately inventing a plot. His plots are often extremely complex and yet so probable that oftentimes real life confirms them. Consider, for example, the adventure in *The Late Mathias Pascal*, which really happened some twenty years after Pirandello's novel had been published. On the bare materials furnished him by his imagination Pirandello works until he has transformed them to accord, not merely with his own personality, but also with each of his characters.

The realism with which Pirandello carefully reproduces the point of view of each of his characters results in extreme unevenness in the course of the dialogue in a story or a play. Remarks whose significance scarcely exceeds the ordinary observations of the entertainers in *La Vie Parisienne* stand side by side with passages whose unexpected quality, keenness, and depth make Pirandello the equal of a Stendhal, a Dostoevskii, or a Proust. Properly considered, this proves that Pirandello is not a dealer in ideas alone, not a mere philosopher, but a creator. He writes at the dictation of his own characters, and he does not endeavor to arrange or clarify what his heroes dictate to him. He simply transcribes faithfully. Hence arises a certain heaviness, sometimes a certain slowness and repetitiousness, but at the same time an extraordinary feeling of life.

The variety of Pirandello's subjects and heroes is amazing. When you have read some twenty or thirty of his ill-matched stories, a sudden crystallization takes place in your mind, and you see the Italy of the days before the war,—all of it,—Italy as it existed from the disaster of Adowa to the gallant entry into the great World War. No one has painted the middle classes of the Italian capital and provinces with more vigor and more truth in all that remarkable mingling of finesse, credulity, passion, positivism, poetry, and pharisaism which makes the Italian one of the most complex and strangest of all the peoples of the new Europe.

There is no need for haste in judging Pirandello. He scorns advertising and allurement. He knows that he is bitter and unpleasant reading, but he knows also how great a lesson of force and of goodness is contained in his work. He knows that he is not merely a destroyer. This life which flees from us without ceasing and which deceives those who think that they have pinned it down once for all—this life a man worthy of the name must bravely construct minute by minute as fair and fine as he can make it for himself and for others. In a large measure the misfortune of mankind is made by man's own intellectual and moral inertia. The territory over which man can exercise his power is very limited: the past is his no longer, the future is not yet his; but he can model the present to suit himself, provided he conforms to the requirements of life—life, which perpetually changes. A gleam of hope and optimism in the midst of ruins. (pp. 123-26)

Benjamin Crémieux, "Luigi Pirandello and His Writings," in *The Living Age,* Vol. CCCXVIII, No. 4122, July 7, 1927, pp. 123-26.

JOHN GASSNER
(essay date 1954)

[Gassner, a Hungarian-born American scholar, was a great promoter of American theater, particularly the work of Tennessee Williams and Arthur Miller. In the following excerpt, he surveys Pirandello's drama.]

Luigi Pirandello . . . became an important figure in the modern drama by dint of applying a fine intellect to the negativism of his colleagues. His was a highly modern mind replete with the relativism philosophy and psychiatric science of the twentieth century. In addition, he possessed an original inquiring spirit which after pondering acutely on the relation between the drama and subjective life did not hesitate to break down the last formalities of dramatic structure. The social and political realities which had forced themselves into the modern theatre received scant attention from him, and the situations which he most favored are remote from the cardinal conflicts of the age. Nevertheless, both his disillusionment and his psychology stamp him as an ultra-modern.

Pirandello achieved structure because his temperament, training and private life blended so completely with the "grotesque" dispensation. Born in 1867, in Girgenti, he was a native son of Sicily, the homeland of irascible temperaments and animal passions. Even his able apologist Domenico Vitorini declares, "I should not say that Pirandello is a kindly person." Naturalism flourished on Sicilian soil when Verga and others set down its primitive life. A streak of naturalism appeared in Pirandello in his early works and it is present even in many of his most cerebral efforts, since these also present sordid situations and deal with ele-

Pirandello as a student in Bonn.

mental passions. Incest, prostitution, and suicide appear liberally in *Six Characters in Search of an Author,* for example. Early in life he became violently anti-d'Annunzian. Living in a land of simple peasants over whom hung a "pall of inertia broken by sudden outbursts of jealousy and crime," he could have little patience with d'Annunzio's rococo sentiments and superman-worship. For Pirandello, as for the naturalists, all men were little specks of sensitive flesh, and these specks lived passively in a world over which they could exercise little authority. (pp. 435-36)

[Pirandello] was essentially an anarchist who had no use for society, and above all a pessimist.

He sometimes denied that he was one. But his explanations were exceedingly tenuous. Although he struck a comic note in most of his plays, and called them comedies, his vision was fundamentally tragic. He himself once stated, "I see life as tragedy," and it is not only the tragic content of such plays as *Six Characters in Search of an Author* that confirms this admission. In a foreword to a book about himself he wrote: "I have tried to tell something to other men, without any ambition, except perhaps that of avenging myself for having been born."

His humor throughout is ironic and saturnine; its brilliance owes everything to these attributes. It might be argued that anyone as cerebral as Pirandello, whose plays are full of logistic contortions, is essentially anti-tragic. His characters are the puppets of perverse syllogisms and Stark Young has rightly stressed the fact that they are theatrical abstractions. According to the latter, Pirandello has "transferred to the mind the legs and antics and the inexhaustible vivacity and loneliness and abstraction of the *commedia dell' arte.*" A writer who plays with such abstractions would indeed seem to be far removed from the field of tragedy. But had not Pirandello's spiritual parent Chiarelli already made a distinction between "the mask and the face"? Behind Pirandello's defensive *commedia dell' arte* mask it is easy to detect a face contorted with pain and a sense of futility. Did he not himself write in his thirty-fifth year: "Ask the poet what is the saddest sight and he will reply 'It is laughter on the face of a man'." Did he not add, "Who laughs does not know."

Pirandello is, however, an exception to his own axiom: He laughed because he "knew." He "knew" that life is absurd. If, like a Talmudist or a medieval theologian, he took delight in subtle dialectics for its own sake (in Rome and Milan people rioted and fought duels over him on this score), he was also expressing a conviction that nothing in life is certain except its uncertainty. Life possesses only the reality that the mind creates for itself; and the mind creates this reality—a man, to use his phrase, "builds himself up"—in order to defend itself against personal defeat. (pp. 436-37)

Among his early naturalistic sketches is the folk comedy *In a Sanctuary* revolving around a rustic quarrel concerning the intelligence of pigs, and *The Other Son* represents the heartache of a destitute old mother whose son has emigrated from Sicily. *The Patent* is a delightful farce about a poor fellow who is harassed by his neighbors because they consider him a sorcerer. He sues for libel and refuses to be placated by a patient, Pirandellian judge. An accident to the judge's goldfish in open court, however, confirms his reputation as a sorcerer. And by then the desperate and pathetic victim of rumor has decided to capitalize his notoriety. He will make the townspeople pay him to plague their competitors or to ward off evil from themselves by removing himself from their presence. *Sicilian Limes,* written in 1910, is a tender little play. A humble piccolo player who enabled a poor rustic girl to achieve fame as a concert singer visits her in northern Italy in the hope of winning her love. But he departs a painfully disillusioned man when he finds her morally corrupted by her sophisticated circle. A number of other effective pieces in Pirandello's early vein mark him a near master of the one-act form.

However, Pirandello achieved his mark in radically different work, which he anticipated in 1904 with his novel *The Late Mattia Pascal,* the story of a librarian who escapes an unpleasant domestic life by pretending death by drowning and assumes a burdensome new personality. True to his custom of dramatizing his short stories, he wrote *Pensaci, Giacomino! (Think of It, Giacomino!)* in 1914, and many characteristics of his art first came to the fore in this play. It possesses saturnine humor, a perverse character, and logic defensively pursued to extravagant lengths by this person. Old Professor Toti revenges himself upon the school system by marrying a pregnant young girl; now the authorities will have to pay a pension to his widow long after his death! He remains a husband only in appearance, however, while she enjoys the boyish love of young Giacomino. In fact, the husband expects to be betrayed since this marriage is unnatural—"Otherwise, how could I, poor old man that I am, have any peace." He does not mind the gossip of the town, is fond of her lover, and actually forces him to remain true to her. And he is satisfied, despite the laughter of the multitude, since he has saved a girl from prostitution and misery by his behavior. Here already we have Pirandello turning the conventions topsy-turvy, and proving that the socially incorrect view may be the better and more humane one.

The Pleasure of Honesty, in the same year, is another sardonic chuckle. A woman who is distressed by her daughter's unmarried state sanctions her liaison with a Marquis. But Agata becomes pregnant and needs the cloak of honesty which only a husband can supply. A husband is found for her in the person of a lonely and strange individual who agrees to screen the lovers for a consideration because he has no illusions regarding honesty. Yet once the mask of honesty is assumed, he insists that the mummers wear it forever. He insists on the utmost honesty after the marriage, and this cynic succeeds so well in upholding the principle of "honor" that he wins his wife's love and society's esteem.

Cap and Bells in 1915 marked a further step in Pirandellian satire. Men "build themselves up," says Pirandello, and cannot forgive anyone who destroys the role they are playing. "We are all puppets," one of the characters declares, but "we all add another puppet to that one; the puppet that each of us believes himself to be." And everyone wants that second puppet to be inviolable—that is, he wants everyone to respect it. In *Cap and Bells,* the grotesquely ugly bookkeeper Ciampa is not troubled by the knowledge that his wife is betraying him with his employer; why shouldn't she, since he is so ugly, so long as others do not suspect the situation and laugh at him! But when the employer's jealous wife exposes the intrigue and has her husband arrested at Ciampa's house, the situation is impossible not only for this woman who will now have to leave her husband but for Ciampa who is furious at having his "puppet" destroyed. Thereupon he hits upon a solution:—the jealous woman, who is already repenting her hasty deed, must allow herself to be declared insane. Then when the case against her husband is dismissed and Ciampa's honor is saved, she can return from the asylum—"cured." She doesn't fancy the idea, but Ciampa gets his way, and she is carried out of the house shrieking while Ciampa grins contentedly.

From *Cap and Bells* to *Right You Are, if You Think You Are* the way leads to the meaning of truth. After having maintained in *Cap and Bells* that each man creates a suitable mask for himself, Pirandello declared in his new play that we are incapable of penetrating the mystery of another person's identity. This means that we must exercise tolerance toward others; that is, we must respect their deepest fabrications because we cannot really know the truth about them. Suppose that all records were destroyed by an accident like the earthquake referred to in *Right You Are,* we would then have no way of verifying that people are what they claim to be. To demonstrate this point Pirandello concocted an extravaganza in which the élite of a provincial town are set at loggerheads because Signor Prola does not allow his wife's supposed mother to see her. He claims that the old woman is his mother-in-law only by a first marriage and that she is laboring under the illusion that her daughter is still alive. She, in turn, claims that Signor Prola is suffering from the delusion that his wife died and that the woman he is living with now is his second wife. Prola and his mother-in-law are, however, kind to each other and comparatively happy until the town begins to buzz with scandal. Nor can the town discover the truth since Signora Prola is willing to be a second wife to her husband and a daughter to the old lady. The point is not only that we cannot discover the identity of Signora Prola, but that it is unnecessary to do so. Illusion is a bitter necessity to at least one of the principals of this play, and it must be respected. The town is consequently satirized for its idle curiosity. Judged by realistic standards, *Right You Are* is of course preposterous, but accepted as a philosophical extravaganza it is neatly pointed, and it comes close to Aristophanic humor. Its real shortcoming is the thinness of the plot.

Thereafter many of Pirandello's plays were only comic or serious variations on the relativity of reality or the "drama of being and seeming," as Vittorini calls it. Dual personality is the theme of *Signora Morli One and Two,* in which a woman reveals different features to the gay husband who abandoned her and to the grave lawyer who protected and made her his wife in all but name. Dualism also appears in *As You Desire Me.* Here the characters alternately defend and accuse a woman who was responsible for a friend's suicide, and since each disputant wins his opponent over to the opposite position the woman's guilt can never be determined. Such is the value of men's opinions of each other or even of themselves.

In *Naked* a pathetic creature clothes herself with illusions in the hope of concealing her frustrations and inner poverty. The nurse Ersilia who has made what she believes to be a successful attempt at suicide tells a newspaper reporter that she is dying for love because she wants to be interesting to herself before the end. She recovers, however, and upon being wooed by the repentant lover who had abandoned her she confesses that he means nothing to her; she did not try to commit suicide for him and she will have nothing to do with him. These and other revelations culminate in everybody attacking her. She had only wished to die clothed in a beautiful romance which had been beyond her reach in life, but now she is accused of immorality and imposture. Stripped "naked" by others who fail to comprehend the complexity of human motives and finding herself forced back into the colorless reality from which she had tried to escape, she attempts suicide for a second time and dies.

The ultimate in self-delusion, however, is insanity, and it is with good reason that Pirandello put much of his best dramatic talent into his treatment of that theme. *Henry IV* is the tragedy of a complex and painful character who lost his mind after falling from his horse at the conclusion of a masquerade. A wealthy relative coddles his illusion that he is the medieval German emperor Henry IV and surrounds him with a grotesque retinue. After twelve years he recovers sanity but pretends insanity because the real world, in which he found so much perfidy and lost the woman he loved, is a poor substitute for the illusory one. When this woman and his rival, who had caused his fall out of jealousy, appear together, "Henry IV" wounds him mortally. Now, however, the pretence of madness is more imperative than ever if he is to escape the legal consequences of his vengeance, and he must remain Henry IV for the rest of his life. The challenge of the play lies in its hero's deliberate renunciation of reality as something too painful to bear. Without this nihilistic animus, *Henry IV* would be an inexcusably contrived melodrama. With it, the play is still contrived—but for a purpose. This is hardly sufficient to place it among the world's major plays, but owing to its bitter intensity and unique background it is one of the most powerful of Pirandello's work.

Finally Pirandello's foray into mirrors through which even Carroll's Alice did not venture also led him to question the adequacy of art. He devoted several plays to the problem and provided contradictory answers. *When One Is Somebody* is the tragedy of a famous writer who is compelled to remain in the mold which he created for himself by his works. Although a noble love rejuvenates him to the extent of giving him a new literary style and a fresh vitality which no one would have associated with him, society will not allow him to leave the prison walls of his fame. He must not violate the style which made him famous! In *Trovarsi* a famous actress cannot surrender her stage personality; she loses her lover, who resents the similarity between her public and her intimate behavior, but gains the seemingly greater gratification of remaining an artist.

As a rule, moreover, Pirandello expressed a strong dissatisfaction with art, complaining that it fell so short of the truth. In this he was not, however, echoing the complaint of the naturalists against those writers who failed to photograph factual reality. He was indeed genuinely displeased with conventional theatricality and satirized it mercilessly. But his basic disaffection arose from the fact that life, which is constantly changing, is invariably distorted or killed when presented on the stage. Human motives, too, are multifarious and cannot be reduced to a simple formula for a public impatient with subtleties. Pirandello, therefore, either denies the validity of all drama or calls upon it to become as fragmentary, relative and fluid as life itself.

In *Tonight We Improvise,* which describes a play in the making, he contrasts the intense aliveness of the characters with the artificiality to which the stage reduces them. Here the actors lose themselves in their role so completely that they crack the mold into which a fussy stage director tries to place them. Pirandello, who had a penchant for unconventional dramatic devices and prided himself on the ingenuity of his plots, found ample opportunity to exercise this talent in his critiques of the drama. He reached the peak of dramatic originality and critical profundity in the well-known *Six Characters in Search of an Author.*

Here the characters lead an independent life because their author failed to complete their story. They invade a rehearsal of another Pirandellian play and insist upon playing out the life that is theirs. Constantly interrupting the stage manager and the actors, disapproving narrow stage interpretations and insisting upon explaining themselves, they break down the structure of the play until it becomes a series of alternately comic and tragic fragments. Here Pirandello has, so to speak, written a play to end all plays. And all this from the fact that life, with its subjective complexity and irrationality, defies the glib interpretations of the stage and its actors.

One character protests to the director and the actors: "Of my nausea, of all the reasons, one crueler and viler than another, which have made this of me, have made me just as I am, you would like to make a sentimental, romantic concoction." No naturalist could have made a severer charge against formal dramaturgy. Moreover, the *dramatis personae* are "characters"—that is, they are stamped with certain characteristics which create their own situations regardless of the intentions of their creator: When a character is born he acquires immediately such an independence from his author that we can all imagine him in situations in which the author never thought of placing him, and he assumes of his own initiative a significance that his author never dreamt of lending him.

The drama which the six characters insist upon acting out in defiance of all the contrivances favored by the ordinary theatre is a nightmare of sordid situations and self-torment. The Father, who came to believe that his gentle wife was more in rapport with his humble secretary than with himself, set up a home for them. The family does not credit this motive and suspects that he wanted to rid himself of his wife; and no doubt his motivation was more complex than he can possibly understand or acknowledge. He kept the Son for himself, and the latter grew up into a lonely, embittered youth. After the clerk's death the Mother, who bore him three children, disappeared with her new family, and the Father met his Stepdaughter only years later in a disreputable establishment. He was prevented from committing incest only because his wife who saw the Father and the Stepdaughter together warned them. The Father took the family back with him, but since then their hearts have been consumed with shame, sorrow, and exasperation. The legitimate Son resents the presence of the Mother's illegitimate children, the Mother is passively miserable, her adolescent Boy broods upon suicide, the Father is constantly apologizing, and the Stepdaughter cannot ever forgive him or overcome her disgust. Ultimately the Mother's youngest child is drowned, the Boy shoots himself, and the characters run off the stage in confusion.

Try to make a neat little play out of all this, Pirandello seems to say! This is life! The tragedy of the six characters can never be completely dramatized because their motives are so mixed; because some of them—the Mother and the Son—do not explain themselves sufficiently; because others—the youngest child and the Boy—are inarticulate. Moreover, some of them are too passionately eager to justify themselves and are too bedeviled to stay within the playwright's frame. Many of the tendencies of the twentieth century—its impatience with formal art, its investigation of the nebulous but explosive unconscious, and its relativist philosophy—are caught in this work. *Six Characters in Search of an Author* is as important as a monument to the intellectual activity of an age as it is original and harrowing. And it is harrowing despite comic details because Pirandello's puppets are intensely, if fragmentarily, alive. Only in some unnecessarily metaphysical passages which produce more confusion than profundity can the play be said to fall short of complete realization.

Pirandello reached his high point with this work, written in 1921. Numerous other variations on his favorite themes merely displayed his ingenuity, and a few full-length dramas of womanhood (*As Well as Before, Either of One or of No One, Other People's Point of View,* and *The Wives' Friend*) are in the main only conventionally affecting. He repeated himself, lapsed into sterile cerebration, and generally missed the attribute of living characterization which distinguishes the work of most masters of the drama. His sardonic viewpoint too often evoked puppets and snarled his plots until both became mere contrivances. Only the power of his intellect set him above the mere artificers of the theatre. (pp. 438-44)

His work remains a monument to the questioning and self-tormenting human intellect which is at war not only with the world, the flesh and the devil but with its own limitations. Once the intellect has conquered problem after problem without solving the greatest question of all—namely, whether it is real itself rather than illusory—it reaches an impasse. Pirandello is the poet of that impasse. He is also the culmination of centuries of intellectual progress which have failed to make life basically more reasonable or satisfactory. He ends with a question mark. (pp. 444-45)

John Gassner, "Latin Postscripts—Benavente and Pirandello," in his *Masters of the Drama,* third revised edition, Dover Publications, Inc., 1954, pp. 424-45.

ANTONIO ILLIANO

(essay date 1967)

[Illiano is an Italian-born American educator and critic and the translator of Pirandello's *L'umorismo* into English. In the following excerpt, he addresses thematic elements of *Six Characters in Search of an Author*.]

A little less than half a century ago there appeared on stage in Rome one of the most brilliant pieces of deviltry in modern literature, Pirandello's *Six Characters in Search of an Author.* It created such a stir that in less than three years it was translated in many languages and performed all over Europe and in New York.

The sudden and unexpected appearance of live characters, who claimed to belong on the stage and could actually be seen and heard, was like a bombshell that blew out the last and weary residues of the old realistic drama. It took everybody by surprise—and confused, as it still does today, both audiences and critics. But the novelty of the invention is so stimulating, and its great inherent theatricality so skillfully handled, that the play seldom fails to provide even the most sophisticated audiences with a fresh, though not easily definable, type of cathartic experience. (p. 1)

Now who are these six characters and where do they come from? They appear on a stage where a company is about to begin rehearsals for a new play, Pirandello's *Il giuoco delle parti.* They interrupt, claiming that they are really six most interesting characters, side-tracked, however, in the sense that their original author first conceived them "alive," and then *did not want* or was no longer able materially to write them down in a work of art. They repeatedly assert that they are more real than the actors themselves, since, having been created, they now have a reality of their own, independent of their author. Consequently, they are now looking for a writer willing to put them into a book, and for a company of actors who will actualize and materialize their drama.

This extremely explosive beginning sets off a most complex series of chain reactions, developing in all directions, all intricately woven in a spinning rhapsody of polemics, contrasts, misunderstandings, disquisitions, and heated feelings; a rhapsody ending in true agreement with Hegel's theory of the drama, that is, not ending at all. (p. 2)

After being exposed to such an elaborate treatment, the listener or spectator cannot help feeling that he has just been taken for a most intriguing ride, and

deposited exactly where he started out. The next thing that comes to mind is the concern—critical and methodological—that unless one is extremely cautious about it all, the very same excursion is bound to start all over again. Clearly, the play has several meanings, several layers of reality adding up to an unconcluded and unconcluding plurality. In spite of a seemingly philosophical surface, it does not try to preach any moral or philosophy, not excluding skepticism. A definition of the *Six Characters,* if it were at all possible, must take into account the fact that the play is, first and foremost, a highly sophisticated and artistic re-enactment of relativism-in-the-making. It is, therefore, amusing to see how many critics, lured by Pirandello's deceitful disorder, either plunge into it and drown, or somehow skirt about on a slippery edge—and in both cases, missing the point, that the play, like life itself, is a many colored thing which refuses to be neatly pigeonholed. (pp. 2-3)

To understand the complex machinery of the *Six Characters* we must adopt a new critical perspective, a perspective that may enable us to face directly Pirandello's *forma mentis,* the inner generator of the energy and life of his art. A few questions concerning the so-called reality and autonomy of the characters may come in very handy at this point, to start us on our new itinerary.

First of all, is it true that the characters are more real than the actors, as they claim to be throughout the play? At this point perhaps we should briefly clarify the meaning and function of the actors as Pirandello uses them in this play. Obviously, they represent here the people of flesh and blood, physical life. As such—though fictitious figures themselves, in so far as they were conceived by the playwright for the story line of his comedy—we tend to see them in terms of a non-mythical world, and accept them not merely as plausible symbols but as real and actual human beings.

But in the case of Pirandello's characters, who are presented as neither the people conceived by the author for his play, nor as actors representing people, what shall we say about *them?* How can we describe or classify them? Again, is it true that these characters are more real than the actors?

The answer to this question will vary according to the meaning we attribute to the adjective *reale.* If we take *reale* to refer to that which is "physical, having a body," the answer is obviously negative. Here only the actors have physical substance, possess bodies, and are, therefore, real. If, on the other hand, we interpret *reale* in the philosophical sense of "pertinent to the *res* itself," and therefore substantial and everlasting, then the answer is affirmative; the characters *are* more real than the actors.

Now, this duplicity of *reale* is definitely no mere

coincidence. It is, on the contrary, cleverly used with ambivalent purpose, and becomes one of the main sources of ambiguity in the comedy. In fact, if we switch the question around and ask, "are the actors more real than the characters?," we stumble on the same horns of the dilemma, but in reverse. We answer with an affirmative in the sense that the actors refer to people endowed with physical consistency; and we answer in the negative because people are changeable and perishable. It is an insoluble dichotomy, and one that can turn into a most perplexing predicament; so that many observers and readers become easy prey to Pirandello's mix-up, and instinctively pose the question, "but then what is more real than what?" In utter seriousness, they consequently start looking for an answer that does not exist, without realizing that the author is asking the very same moot question, but for artistic purposes. They then take for granted that the characters are the symbols of art, and conclude that, when Pirandello says that they are more real than the actors, he actually means that art is superior to life.

Seen in the varied *spectrum* of meanings which the *Six Characters in Search of an Author* implies, this last interpretation is not an impossible one, provided it does not become too rigid and exclusive. As many writers have been fond of quoting, "life is brief and art is long." Life has one kind of reality, a transient one—since man is mortal, but art has another kind, since it can outlast its creation, and achieve a permanence we call perennial.

The main reason why it is difficult to wrap up the *Six Characters* in one sweeping generalization is that the characters themselves were not meant to be symbols. The actors, yes, may be taken to represent human nature with all its predicaments. But the characters were conceived, to use Pirandello's own definition of them, as *realtà create,* that is, as concepts stripped of all symbolizing vestment, as bare concepts and not personages symbolizing concepts. One may here indulge in a bit of sophistry and go so far as to say that they are indeed symbols, but symbols symbolizing lack of symbolism, nakedness. But we should rather stick with Ortega y Gasset's clear and articulate formulation, that "the traditional playwright expects us to take his personages for persons and their gestures for indications of a 'human' drama. Whereas here [in the *Six Characters*] our interest is aroused by some personages as such—that is, as ideas or pure patterns."

A very important question now arises as to what happens to these concepts, once they have been created; how does the playwright handle them?

Pirandello says that the creatures of his inspiration, once conceived, achieve a complete autonomy. We could agree with his pretense if we equate this alleged independence with its aesthetic value, that is, if we take the autonomy of the characters to mean their artistic liveliness and effectiveness. To be sure, clean-cut detachment between creator and creature is a Utopian mirage, one that has always attracted the naive idealist. Giving characters an independent kind of realism is an extremely refined device in literature, one we may say began with Cervantes, with whom Pirandello was quite familiar, and a device easily recognized in the work of many writers since. Here is, for instance, what some of them have said about it: "My notion always is that, when I have made people play out the play, it is, as it were, their business to do it and not mine." (Dickens) "Often my characters astonish me by doing or saying things I had not expected—yes, they can sometimes turn my original scheme upside down, the devils!" (Ibsen) "There is always a regular army of people in my brain begging to be summoned forth, and only waiting for the word to be given." (Chekhov) Or take Turgenev, who once said that an author must cut the navel-string between himself and the offspring of his imagination.

But it is one thing to talk about creative theories and another to actualize them on the artistic plane. And no other writer has brought this technique into the open and made it serve so successfully, as both Unamuno in the novel and Pirandello in the theatre. To be sure, in both these two authors there is an epistemological and ontological preoccupation, in so far as the question "Who and what are the characters?" is another way of asking "Who and what am I?," "Who and what are you?" etc. And, in both of them, the personages involved in their stories are involved in nothing more nor less than a stubborn and hopeless attempt to escape being dominated by their authors. . . . As for the desperate lot of the *Six Characters,* one needs only to survey their existence briefly.

It all started one day when Fantasy, the "maidservant" of Pirandello's art, inexplicably gave birth to six characters. It is not hard to accept this basic fact. These figures, however, have a very peculiar birth defect— one not readily seen. They are deprived of the consciousness of their true paternity: they know they are characters, they know they are rejected characters, they believe they were created and then deserted by some author, but they are completely unaware of the most crucial truth of all, namely, that their blood is truly Pirandellian. Once deprived of their identity, it is easy for the author to have them do whatever he likes. So he has them knock at his door and persistently beg him to write them down, in a play or novel. Not a chance. For a while, he argues he has to find a meaning for them, a meaning that would justify their artistic existence. Till finally, he has another spark of genius: Why not represent them just as they are, as rejected and unfinished: *This* may well be their meaning! So he grants them a fake passport, so to speak, and makes them believe that they are free to go and search for their promised land. So the six fools walk onto a stage, eager and desperate to achieve what they don't realize is unattainable, that is, what has *a priori* been decreed as such by their creator. On that stage, which the author has purposely chosen for them, because it is totally unprepared to receive them, they come to face with a most exasperating failure. But this is not all. Not by any means. Where is the author, while both actors and characters engage in a dialogue or cross purposes? Hiding and unseen, the author is watching all of them perform, and writing down his own play: The *Six Characters in Search of an Author.* It turns out that the poor stooges, while trying to enact their own suffering drama, have been used for a completely different purpose, one they do not and cannot suspect.

Are we still to speak of "autonomy" of the characters? Indeed, if we insisted in doing so, we would not only yield to easy and idle labelling, but, what is more relevant, we would dangerously hinder our penetration and understanding of the tragic *substratum* of the play.

To a large extent, the Pirandello touch here is romantic irony straight from the books of Heine, Tieck, Jean Paul Richter and F. Schlegel, to mention but a few of the German Romantics with whom Pirandello was well acquainted. To get closer to the truth, we should say that it is romantic irony highly tinged with Kleist's *Marionettentheater.* In Pirandello, however, the romantic view disintegrates through multiplicity, contradiction and ambiguity, as has happened with other writers in the same tradition. One of the first to attain a lucid perception of Pirandello's modernity was Yeats, who, grouping him together with Pound, Eliot and Joyce, once said that they " . . . break up the logical processes of thought, by flooding them with associated ideas or words that seem to drift into the mind by chance," and even more brilliantly remarked that in them "there is hatred of the abstract. . . . The intellect turns upon itself."

Pirandello's work, however, is not only the product of a literary tradition aware of the spiritual crisis faced in a modern culture, but indeed reflects what must be regarded as the peculiarly original structure of his mind, namely, the motivations which make him acutely conscious and perceptive of the absurdities and paradoxes of human tragicomedy. We said at the beginning that the reader or spectator experiences an uneasy sense of repetition and uncertainty. Now this feeling cannot be explained away in terms of romantic irony alone.

Romantic irony may be illustrated by the author who first creates and then deflates or destroys his creation. Whereas in Pirandello, once the process has started, it remains open to further dialectical developments. So that we have not only inversion or reversion, but also inversion of inversion, reversion of reversion.

Yeats sharply intuited the extent and importance of this phenomenon, when he spoke of the intellect that turns upon itself, and it is regrettable that he did not elaborate on this statement. An essay attempting to show in what way the intellect turns upon itself in Joyce, Eliot, Pound and Pirandello, could prove to be a most challenging study in comparative literature. Here one can only outline how the creative intellect, conscious of its powers, becomes a witness to itself in Pirandello's mind. There, in Pirandello's mind, the inversion in the creative process takes place as a work of reflection, an active and vigilant force which is at the basis of Pirandello's art and of his theory of humor.

In 1908, long before he became famous as a playwright, he had written a very important essay called *L'umorismo,* an exposition of his *poetica* and of his *Weltanschauung,* on which he was to build most of his future work. Any serious attempt to penetrate Pirandello's world should necessarily begin with an attentive and thorough study of this essay. (pp. 3-9)

"Humor" has a particular meaning and value for Pirandello. With him, the comic view may have the most serious of undertones. What seems humorous on the surface is revealed as a matter of sorrow and pain, and far from comic, underneath. To support this view, Pirandello gives us a striking example in an old lady with dyed hair, dressed like a young girl and wearing heavy make-up. At first sight she makes people laugh because she does not look as an old lady is supposed to: comedy consists of this awareness of the contrary. At this point, however, Pirandello's reflection interferes to tell us that the old lady is aware of being ridiculous, but is willing to deceive herself, by believing that the artifice of appearance will help her keep the affections of a younger husband. Well, if reflection comes to suggest all this, then there is nothing left to laugh about; on the contrary, the picture becomes quite sad. "From that *awareness of the contrary,* [reflection] has made me shift to the *sentimento del contrario.*" Here we finally hit the mark of Pirandello's *forma mentis:* the sentiment of the contrary. This is the essence of true humor. Human beings do not accept reality as animals do; they question it, but cannot find a clear purpose and explanation. So . . . they invent fictions that may give life some meaning, vain and illusory as it may be. Humor is like a restless little devil who comes to break them to pieces, so that we can see how, behind the Vanity Fair, *panta rei,* everything flows, in a steady uninterrupted stream.

This sentiment of the contrary was inborn in Pirandello. We can trace it as far back as his childhood, but in order to realize what a deep and moving force it was, we need only glance at a few of his titles. The very first Pirandellian published work is a collection of poems in his early youth called *Mal giocondo,* which reminds one of Heine's tortured wit. Years later other works came out with titles like *Fuori di chiave, Il fu*

Mattia Pascal, Erma bifronte, Maschere nude, etc. And what about the play here discussed, the *Six Characters in Search of an Author,* in which, beginning with the title, there is nothing that cannot be inverted or reversed? It should perhaps be clearer now what it is that Pirandello means when, in the *Preface,* he defines this drama as "a mixture of tragic and comic, fantastic and realistic, in a humoristic situation quite new and infinitely complex."

Many critics are attracted by the plentiful philosophical disquisitions scattered throughout his work and to the idea that the true nature of Pirandello is that of a philosopher. On this assumption they then proceed to reconstruct and reorganize his *Weltanschauung* into a well wrought and neatly chiselled system. Nothing could be more erroneous and impractical. Like all great artists, Pirandello has the qualities of a thinker, though not a completely original one. Actually, his thought is asystematic *a priori,* based on analysis and not synthesis, on fracture and multiplicity and not on unity; and his thinking is not separable from the process of artistic creation.

Finally, Pirandello's constant reflection and analytic drive should not be mistaken as motivated by sheer cerebrality. They are, instead, the product of deep suffering and overwhelming compassion for mankind's uneviable lot in a world of flux and misery. Speaking of himself and of his art, Pirandello once said: "To live before a looking glass is not possible. Try to look at yourself in a mirror while you are crying for your deepest sorrow, or while you are laughing for your merriest joy and your tears and your laughter will stop suddenly." And then he added polemically: " . . . only a few—not entirely dazzled by the shining of that mirror—have so far succeeded in seeing the amount of real sorrow and of human suffering which this 'overbrained humorist' has succeeded in putting into his dramas and comedies." (pp. 9-11)

Antonio Illiano, "Pirandello's 'Six Characters in Search of an Author': A Comedy in the Making," in *Italica,* Vol. XLIV, No. 1, March, 1967, pp. 1-12.

SOURCES FOR FURTHER STUDY

Bassnett-McGuire, Susan. *Luigi Pirandello.* New York: Grove Press, 1983, 190 p.

Thematic exploration of Pirandello's drama.

Bentley, Eric. *The Pirandello Commentaries.* Evanston: Northwestern University Press, 1986, 119 p.

Includes ten essays written between 1946 and 1986 by a prominent critic and translator of Pirandello's works.

Cambon, Glauco, ed. *Pirandello: A Collection of Critical Essays.* Englewood Cliffs, N.J.: Prentice-Hall, 1967, 182 p.

Contains thirteen essays by prominent critics. Included are an abridged English translation of Adriano Tilgher's important essay in *Studi sul teatro contemporaneo;* "The Techniques of the Unseizable," by Auréliu Weiss; and "Pirandello's Drama of Revolt," by Robert Brustein.

Giudice, Gaspare. *Pirandello: A Biography,* translated by Alastair Hamilton. Oxford: Oxford University Press, 1975, 221 p.

Abridged translation of the standard critical biography.

Radcliff-Umstead, Douglas. *The Mirror of Our Anguish: A Study of Luigi Pirandello's Narrative Writings.* London: Associated University Press, 1978, 329 p.

Examines the major themes and techniques of Pirandello's fiction.

Sogliuzzo, A. Richard. *Luigi Pirandello, Director: The Playwright in the Theatre.* Metuchen, N.J.: Scarecrow Press, 1982, 274 p.

Describes how Pirandello's consciousness of the demands of theatrical production influenced the creation of his plays.

Sylvia Plath

1932-1963

(Also wrote under the pseudonym Victoria Lucas)
American poet, novelist, short story writer, essayist, memoirist, and scriptwriter.

INTRODUCTION

Considered an important poet of the post-World War II era, Plath became widely known following her suicide in 1963 and the posthumous publication of *Ariel* (1965), a collection containing her most startling and acclaimed verse. Through bold metaphors and stark, often violent and unsettling imagery, Plath's works evoke some of the mythic qualities of nature and human experience. Her vivid, intense poems explore such topics as personal identity, individual suffering and oppression, and the inevitability of death. Deeply informed by autobiographical elements, Plath's writings poignantly reflect her struggles with despair and mental illness. Her efforts to assert a strong female identity and to balance familial, marital, and career aspirations have established her as a representative voice for feminist concerns. While Plath is frequently linked with confessional poets Robert Lowell, Anne Sexton, and John Berryman, all of whom directly express personal torments and anguish in their work, critics have noted that many of Plath's poems are dramatic monologues voiced by a character who is not necessarily autobiographical. Although sometimes faulted as self-indulgent and preoccupied with death and psychological suffering, Plath continues to be read widely, and her work has generated numerous scholarly studies.

Born in Jamaica Plain, Massachusetts, Plath enjoyed an idyllic early childhood near the sea. Her father, a German immigrant, was a professor of entomology who was especially interested in the study of bees. His sudden death from diabetes mellitus in 1940 devastated the eight-year-old Plath, and many critics note the significance of this traumatic experience in interpreting her poetry, which frequently contains both brutal and reverential images of her father as well as sea imagery and allusions to bees. Plath began publishing poetry at an early age in such periodicals as *Seventeen* and the

Christian Science Monitor, and in 1950 she earned a scholarship to Smith College. After spending a month during the summer of her junior year in New York City as a guest editor for *Mademoiselle* magazine, Plath suffered a mental collapse which resulted in her attempted suicide and subsequent institutionalization. Plath later chronicled the circumstances and consequences of this breakdown in her best-selling novel, *The Bell Jar* (1963). Following her recovery, Plath returned to Smith and graduated summa cum laude. After winning a Fulbright fellowship to study at Cambridge University, Plath met and soon married Ted Hughes, an English poet. The eventual failure of their marriage during the early 1960s and the ensuing struggles with severe depression that led to her suicide are considered crucial elements of Plath's most critically acclaimed poetry.

Plath's verse is represented in several volumes. *The Colossus* (1960), the only book of her poems published during her lifetime, collects pieces dating from the mid- to late 1950s; *Ariel* contains poems selected by Hughes from among the many works Plath composed during the final months before her death; *Winter Trees* (1971) collects several more of the *Ariel* poems and reflects Hughes's plan to publish Plath's later works in intervals; *Crossing the Water: Transitional Poems* (1971) reprints most of her post-*Colossus* and pre-*Ariel* verse; and *The Collected Poems* (1981), which won a Pulitzer Prize in 1982, features all of her verse, including juvenilia and several previously unpublished pieces in order of composition. Critics often maintain that during her brief career, Plath's verse evolved from a somewhat derivative early style to that of a unique and accomplished poetic voice. Katha Pollitt commented: "Plath's was one of those rare poetic careers—Keats's was another—that moved consistently and with gathering rapidity and assurance to an ever greater daring and individuality."

Plath's early verse reflects various poetic influences, evoking the mythic qualities of the works of William Butler Yeats and Ted Hughes, the diverse experiments with form and language of Gerard Manley Hopkins and W. H. Auden, and the focus on personal concerns that dominates the verse of Robert Lowell and Theodore Roethke. Most of her early poems are formal, meticulously crafted, and feature elaborate syntax and well-developed metaphors, as Plath employed such forms as the ode, the villanelle, and the pastoral lyric to examine art, love, nature, and personal themes. These pieces are more subdued than the later work for which she would become renowned. Critics generally believe that some of the later poems in *The Colossus* heralded a new phase in Plath's career. Marjorie Perloff commented: "[When], in the last two years of her life, [Plath] finally came into her own, the adopted voices merely evaporated, and a new harsh, demonic,

devastating self, only partially prefigured in such poems as 'The Thin People' (1957) and 'The Stones' (1959), came into being."

Plath's later work displays the increasing frustration of her aspirations. Her ambitions of finding happiness through work, marriage, and family were thwarted by such events as hospital stays for a miscarriage and an appendectomy, the breakup of her marriage, and fluctuating moods in which she felt vulnerable to male domination and threatening natural forces, particularly death. After the dissolution of her marriage, Plath moved with her two children from the Devon countryside to a London flat, where Irish poet William Butler Yeats once resided, and wrote feverishly from the summer of 1962 until her death in February of the following year. Many of her best-known poems, including "Daddy," "Lady Lazarus," "Lesbos," "Purdah," and "Edge," were composed during this period and form the nucleus of the *Ariel* collection. These pieces, which reflect her increasing anger, bitterness, and despair toward life, feature intense, rhythmic language that blends terse statements, sing-song passages, repetitive phrasing, and sudden violent images, metaphors, and declarations. For example, in "Daddy," perhaps her most frequently discussed and anthologized work, Plath denounces her father's dominance over her life and, among other allusions, associates him with nazism and herself with Jewish victims of the Holocaust: "I have always been scared of *you* / With your Luftwaffe, your gobbledygoo. / And your neat moustache / And your Aryan eye, bright blue. / Panzer-man, panzer-man, O You—." Plath explained in a radio broadcast that the poem's narrator is "a girl with an Electra complex. Her father died while she thought he was God." Response to "Daddy" reflects the general critical opinion toward much of her later work. Some critics contend that Plath's jarring effects are extravagant, and many object to her equation of personal sufferings with such horrors as those experienced by victims of Nazi genocide. Others praise the passion and formal structure of her later poems, through which she confronts her tensions and conflicts. Stanley Plumly stated that "behind the separate masks, all the masks of [Plath's] good poems, there is a unity, an integrity, and an integrating of imagination—that whatever the hammer-splittings of the self, behind the sad mask of the woman is the mind and heart of someone making transcendent poems."

Plath published *The Bell Jar,* which appeared shortly before her death, under the pseudonym of Victoria Lucas. She was unsure of the quality of the work and feared that it might offend those people, particularly her mother, on whom the characters are based. This novel details a college student's disappointing adventures during a summer month in New York City as a guest editor for a fashion magazine, her despair upon returning home, her attempted suicide, and the electroshock treatments and institutionalization she undergoes to "cure" her of depression and lethargy. The narrator of *The Bell Jar* encounters many of the pressures and problems Plath examined in her verse: her attempts to establish her identity are consistently undermined, she projects an ambivalent attitude toward men, society remains indifferent to her sensitivity, vulnerability, and artistic ambitions, and she is haunted by events from her past, particularly the death of her father. Although critical reception to *The Bell Jar* was mixed, reviewers praised the novel's satiric portrait of American society and its poignant study of the growing disillusionment of a talented young woman.

The posthumous publication of Plath's writings in other genres, many of which were edited by Ted Hughes, reflects the continuing interest in her work. *Three Women: A Monologue for Three Voices* (1968) is a verse play originally presented on British radio in 1962 in which three women discuss pregnancy. *Letters Home: Correspondence, 1950-1963* (1975) reveals Plath's reactions to pivotal events in her adult life through the publication of letters she exchanged with her mother. *Johnny Panic and the Bible of Dreams, and Other Prose Writings* (1977) collects short stories and excerpts from her diaries in which Plath reworked the personal experiences, themes, and topics she frequently explored in her verse. *The Journals of Sylvia Plath* (1982), which includes most of the extensive diary entries Plath compiled during her lifetime, received substantial critical attention. Katha Pollitt described this collection as "a storehouse of ideas for stories, novels, and poems; of stray phrases and incidents that would turn up, sometimes years later, in her finished work. They are the place, too, where she chronicled an almost unbroken parade of depressions, blocks, and visits of the 'Panic Bird,' and where she urged herself, over and over, year after dragging year, to throw herself into writing."

(For further information about Plath's life and works, see *Concise Dictionary of American Literary Biography, 1941-1968; Contemporary Authors*, Vols. 17-20; *Contemporary Authors Permanent Series*, Vol. 2; *Contemporary Literary Criticism*, Vols. 1, 2, 3, 5, 9, 11, 14, 17, 50, 51, 62; *Dictionary of Literary Biography*, Vols. 5, 6; and *Poetry Criticism*, Vol. 1.)

CRITICAL COMMENTARY

STAN SMITH

(essay date 1975)

[Smith is an English literary historian, critic, biographer, and poet. In the following excerpt, he addresses themes of "authentic selfhood and public image" in *The Bell Jar*.]

In *The Bell Jar*, Sylvia Plath uses the psychological alienation of the heroine, Esther Greenwood, to reinforce . . . *aesthetic* alienation. Esther's 'madness' offers her an increasingly 'objective', exterior view of the 'eating customs, jurisprudence, and love life' [in Bertolt Brecht's words] of the culture she has inherited. 'Manners', provide an important motif of the book. Using the finger-bowl at a special lunch, Esther, for example, 'thought what a long way [she] had come' . . . , and recalls that in her first encounter with a finger-bowl, she drank the water and the cherry blossoms in it because 'I thought it must be some clear sort of Japanese after-dinner soup'. Esther's 'oddity' is here revealed as, in origin, no more than a social disjunction, between her own learnt expectations and the codes of manners within which she comes increasingly to move. A clue to the process at work is revealed in her memory of a poet who in 'do[ing] something incorrect at table with a certain arrogance', 'made eating salad with your fingers seem to be the only natural and sensible thing to do'. . . . The poet, significantly, had been talking about 'the antithesis of nature and art'. Esther's perception of the fictive nature of 'manners' spills over into an attitude which evacuated the world of all spontaneous content. There are no such things as 'natural' responses, no intrinsic values in things, all are equally arbitrary and artificial, and all are viewed with the same cynical-naïve eye. Collapsing the 'antithesis of nature and art', Esther comes to view her own life as an aesthetic construct, a perpetual self-manipulation. . . . (p. 248)

Esther's paranoia penetrates the bland benevolent surfaces of other people's motives to discover their inner and unconscious significance. The first psychiatrist she visits, for example, is far less perceptive about her than she is about him. . . . What Esther observes here—and it is a recurring note throughout the book—is the artificiality, the *artifice*, of Dr. Gordon's identity. He is an image presented to the world, acting a conventional role. (p. 249)

Principal Works

*The Colossus (poetry) 1960

The Bell Jar [as Victoria Lucas] (novel) 1963; also published as The Bell Jar [as Sylvia Plath], 1966

*Ariel (poetry) 1965

*Crossing the Water (poetry) 1971

*Winter Trees (poetry) 1971

Letters Home: Correspondence, 1950-1963 (letters) 1975

Johnny Panic and the Bible of Dreams, and Other Prose Writings (prose) 1977; also published as Johnny Panic and the Bible of Dreams: Short Stories, Prose and Diary Excerpts [enlarged edition], 1979

The Collected Poems (poems) 1981

The Journals of Sylvia Plath (journals) 1982

*Each of these volumes, which were originally published in England, were published in the United States with an alternate selection of poems as The Colossus, and Other Poems (1962), Ariel (1966), Crossing the Water: Transitional Poems (1971); and Winter Trees (1972).

Esther's stance towards her own self is graphically depicted in a sequence in the Public Gardens where, watching children riding a swanboat, she recalls her own manipulated childhood. . . . She continually assumes the role of an aesthetic voyeur towards her own past and present experience. . . . Omniscience is redefined as a pose assumed to evade the suspicion of callowness and ignorance.

This fastidious aesthetic distance extends, too, to the apparently 'cured' and regenerate Esther who is the imputed author of *The Bell Jar.* The book itself supposedly fulfils that ambition to write a novel whose frustration contributed to the breakdown it records. If the younger Esther stands in schizoid relation to her own experiences, retrospectively analysing and interpreting them, endlessly turning them over in her mind in some kind of Proustian *recherche,* Esther the narrator assumes the same kind of stance to her past, seen as an initiation rite to be scrupulously and objectively tabulated. Plath, the actual author, seems to be manipulating a continuous and ironic parallel between the condition of schizophrenic self-alienation and the familiar devices of narrative technique. Esther's narrative distance from the recounted facts of her own previous life has a peculiar, antiseptic quality, presenting the most harrowing and intimate experiences with a dispassionateness which tends to endorse her own doubts about the extent of her cure. The hard-boiled narrative tone suggests a narrator herself numbed in some significant way, left cold by her own past. . . . Esther the narrator seems preoccupied with insulating her own past self under the bell jar of a retrospective fiction. Plath not only enables us to see the pathological honesty of vision which accompanies and in part causes the younger Esther's breakdown; she also suggests that the assurance embodied in the posture of the disinterested narrator may itself have more profound social significance, and closer analogies with the schizophrenic's experience, and with the self-alienation of a world that dismisses that experience as mere delusion, than we appreciate. This double 'estrangement effect' acts as a critical, ironic dimension in the novel.

One way in which the character Esther tries to reject the role to which she has been assigned and assume a manipulative power over others, is to invent a surrogate identity. It is clear that, initially, she sees it as a kind of authorial intervention in the plot of her own life, that gives her the opportunity to dissociate herself from the actions she commits, as the novelist employs a *persona* to establish a critical distance between himself and his narrative. (pp. 249-50)

Her actual identity becomes no more than the negative source of her positive image (Elly). Equipped with this *persona,* she assumes the heightened acuity of Stephen Dedalus's artist, 'like the God of creation, invisible, refined out of existence, indifferent, paring his finger-nails', in *The Portrait of the Artist as a Young Man.* (p. 251)

Recurrently, the desire to be a disinterested narrator comes up against the obstructive reality of a world of others who can reduce the rebellious self to 'a small black dot'. . . .

The sense of being a character in someone else's fiction intensifies with Esther's return home to Boston. (p. 253)

In revolt, she decides to spend the summer writing a novel. . . .

Yet her motives for writing the novel are impure, as her comment—'That would fix a lot of people'—suggests. In part, she is interested in revenge; she will elicit from them the respect they should have given her before by "fixing" them (perhaps there is a lurking photographic pun here) as characters in a scenario over which she will have complete mastery. For the novel is to be explicitly and directly autobiographical. Its protagonist 'Elaine', is another surrogate—'Elly Higginbottom', possibly, endowed with the dignity of her full Christian name. 'Elaine' is explicitly a self-projection. . . . Esther, however, lacks the critical distance from her character that both the imputed and the actual author of *The Bell Jar* possess. She is altogether absorbed in her heroine, unable to do more than transcribe her own actual experience at the moment of writing. And yet even to do this she is forced to stand back from herself in a way which heightens her self-estrangement, spying upon herself. . . . (p. 254)

[If] 'Elaine' stands in dependent relation to her author, Esther in turn feels herself the puppet of powers she cannot comprehend, as if she too were a character in a novel (Plath's further irony is that of course she is). But the 'narrator' of this 'novel'—Esther's life—is a whole matrix of social forces, of conventions and norms represented by her mother's authorial manipulations, which have converged to make Esther precisely the person she is. (p. 255)

Esther's most intense perception of the extent to which individuals are the manipulated dummies of a puppet-master society occurs on her visit to Dr. Gordon's mental hospital. . . . [The] place is a parody of normality, an ensemble of isolated vignettes which together act as an ironic commentary upon the 'normal' world. Most significant is the sense of display. . . . It is only their apparent immobility that distinguishes these people, as if their abnormality lies simply in the isolation and endless repetition of any one of a number of 'normal' actions. 'Insanity' is merely a still copy of sanity, isolating and exposing its strangeness. The 'schizoid' character parodies the process by which 'normal' identity is learnt from the imitation of images, assimilating not only the content but the form of the image, acquiring the stillness of the photograph which is a *leitmotif* of the book. Madness aspires to the condition of art. . . . (pp. 255-56)

The *leitmotifs* of photograph and puppet converge when Esther is expected, as part of her *Ladies' Day* commitment, to be photographed 'with props to show what we wanted to be'. . . . Reluctantly, she offers 'poet' as her self-definition, and is equipped with a rose for the part. . . . The photograph propagates a cult of individualism while actually negating it. For it is not the actual Esther but the cliché image that can be made from her which matters. She has become no more than a cipher in the life-process of a mass-circulation magazine, plucked momentarily out of anonymity to be invested with the fraudulent charisma of 'celebrity' whose image then returns to its place of origin divested and purified of circumstantial history. Significantly, in the mental asylum later, she refuses to admit that a picture in a magazine may be of her. . . . (pp. 256-57)

Esther sees suicide not so much as self-destruction as a theatrical ritual which will free her from her 'factitious' identity and restore her to singularity. It is her 'image' that she wishes to murder, the fraudulent twin which is her public *persona*, a shamming and artificial 'dybbuk'. . . . If the mirror-image here, like 'Elly Higginbottom' and 'Elaine', is a fictitious twin, the book also has its quota of real-life 'twins'. Joan Gilling, an old rival for Esther's boyfriend, is admitted to the same mental hospital where Esther is recovering from a later, almost successful suicide at-

tempt. As Esther had attempted to imitate a starlet's suicide described in the newspapers so Joan in turn had imitated her. . . . (p. 258)

But Esther learns to distinguish the mythic image from the more complex reality; to distinguish between copy and imitation, sameness and similarity; and to see that there is a crucial failure of discrimination in confusing another person with one's own projected image. . . . [If Esther's] rebuff in part accounts for Joan's eventual suicide, it is not something for which Esther can take responsibility. In a sense, she *has* invented her, but only because Joan chose to identify with that newspaper image of Esther which Esther herself disclaimed. . . . Structurally, Joan's suicide and Esther's recovery are arranged in an inverse ratio, to the extent that Esther is left wondering, at Joan's funeral, just what she thinks she is burying, the 'wry black image' of her madness, or the 'beaming double of [her] old best self'. In a sense, the suicide of this surrogate is Esther's rebirth.

The book has abounded in images of ropes and cords and strings of various kinds that share this ambiguity. . . . This ambiguity persists into the very last paragraph, when Esther faces the interviewing committee that is to decide on her release. The equivocal close opens a new putative future outside the bell jar of this story:

> The eyes and the faces all turned themselves towards me, and guiding myself by them, as if by a magical thread, I stepped into the room. . . .
>
> (pp. 258-59)

The thread could lead the redeemed heroine out of the 'familiar labyrinth of shovelled asylum paths' . . . ; or it could be 'the thread that might lead me back to my old, bright salesmanship' spoken of earlier . . . , that makes the puppet dance in the eyes of others. For, if Esther seems at last in control of her own life, she is 'guiding [her]self' back on to a public stage, where her future will be decided by the impression she makes on others. The novel closes on a deliberately unresolved upbeat note which never finally clarifies the tension between authentic selfhood and public image, between life as self-articulation and as ritual performance—between, ultimately, 'life' itself, and those 'attitudes', no matter how deeply assimilated and accredited, which merely counterfeit it. (pp. 259-60)

Stan Smith, "Attitudes Counterfeiting Life: The Irony of Artifice in Sylvia Plath's 'The Bell Jar'," in *Critical Quarterly*, Vol. 17, No. 3, Autumn, 1975, pp. 247-60.

JUDITH KROLL
(essay date 1976)

[Kroll is an American poet and critic. In the excerpt below, she argues that in Plath's works, "the personal concerns and everyday role are transmuted into something impersonal, by being absorbed into a timeless mythic system."]

The reading of [Plath's] work has been entangled in a fascination with her suicide and the broken marriage which preceded it, and such misreading is as widespread among her admirers as among her detractors: she has become for both a convenient symbol. To approach Plath as a poet rather than to use her as an image of a poet one must confront her work in its own terms, which is to say, as literature. In these terms, the fact, for example, that she killed herself is irrelevant to the consideration of the meaning of her work; as literature, her poems would mean what they do even if she had not attempted suicide.

Among the current classifications in literary criticism, Plath is usually assigned the category of 'confessional' poet. That view is facilitated by the obviously autobiographical element in her work and by the apparent accessibility of many of her best-known poems, in which the 'confessional' surface is sensational enough to divert the reader from seeing deeper meanings. One might even prefer to read many of her poems as one might view the bloodstains at the site of a murder, as residues of real events—for example, **"Daddy"** and **"Lady Lazarus"** as the expression by the actual Sylvia Plath of a supremely venomous attitude toward her father. The thrill this provides might easily be lessened when the more impersonal dimensions of such poems are considered. But the very accessible confessional aspect of her work is so powerfully affecting that the thought that there might be something more, and quite different in nature, hardly arises. Nevertheless, her poetry is not primarily literal and confessional. It is, rather, the articulation of a mythic system which integrates all aspects of her work, and into which autobiographical or confessional details are shaped and absorbed, greatly qualifying how such elements ought to be viewed. (pp. 1-2)

In a great deal of the work of Robert Lowell and Anne Sexton, often considered the paradigm 'confessional' poets, the voice—intensely personal and almost journalistic—is the direct voice of the author in an everyday role. In Plath the personal concerns and everyday role are transmuted into something impersonal, by being absorbed into a timeless mythic system. The po-

etry of Lowell and Sexton relates their narratives; in Plath—although many narrative details of her mythic system are drawn from her life—the emphasis is more on expressing the structure of her state of being. 'Confessional' poetry usually comprises a plurality of concerns—politics, the writing of poetry, marriage, aging, fame, and so on—that remain relatively independent. But in Plath's poetry, there is one overriding concern: the problem of rebirth or transcendence; and nearly everything in her poetry contributes either to the statement or to the envisioned resolution of this problem.

Because a mythic system accommodates the personal element, the voice of her poetry is detached from the personal in a sense that it is not in 'confessional' poets, whose strategy depends partly upon convincing the reader of a lack of such detachment. For them mundane life overflows into art, but with Plath it is just the opposite.

She has a vision which is complete, self-contained, and whole, a vision of a mythic totality, which such poets as Lowell and Sexton do not have. Much of the vitality in her poetry arises from the very incompleteness of the vision; from a sense that there exist possibilities of discovery and change; from the interest and pleasure one may have in observing the self in encounters whose outcome is not foreclosed; from confronting a future which is open-ended. Plath's late poems, on the other hand, convey the sense that no substantial change can be occasioned by experience, and that only rebirth or transcendence of self would be a resolution. . . . (pp. 2-3)

If her poetry is understood as constituting a system of symbols that expresses a unified mythic vision, her images may be seen to be emblems of that myth. Red, white, and black, for example, the characteristic colors in her late poetry, function as mythic emblems of her state of being much as they do in the mythologies which she drew upon. A great many other particulars of her poetry are similarly determined by her system, and personal and historical details as well are subordinate to it. While a confessional poet might alter certain details to make them more fitting . . . Plath's alteration of details has a deeper significance. Her protagonist in **"Daddy"** says, "I was ten when they buried you," but Plath was only eight when her father died. A magical "one year in every ten" cycle, however, conveys the mythic inevitability necessary to define her state of being. It is precisely such details of confessional literalness that Plath most frequently alters or eliminates, when they are not sufficiently mythic. . . .

The subordination of details, in Plath's poetry, to her mythic vision, goes beyond alterations of matters of fact, for the significance even of apparently 'occasional' poems about small events—such as cutting her thumb (**"Cut"**) or seeing red flowers (**"Poppies in October"**)—lies in their evocation of her pre-existing primary concerns. While the details in 'confessional' poems stand on their own, frequently unified only to the extent that they occur within a single consciousness, there is hardly a detail in Plath's poetry that is not connected with and does not intimate her entire vision.

To a reader unaware of this unity, Plath's poetry will seem to contain a collection of brilliant and fortuitous images, bearing more or less the significance they do for us in daily life. . . . (p. 4)

Without [the awareness of a mythic dimension in Plath's poetry], the elements of suffering, violence, death, and decay will generally be seen as aspects of a self-indulgent stance that is merely—albeit brilliantly—nasty, morbid, and decadent, the extremist exhibitionism. Were she a 'confessional' poet, this might be the case. But her poetry is of a different order, and these details are absorbed into a broader system of concerns. To see the autobiographical details only as such is to regard Plath's vision of suffering and death as morbid, but to appreciate the deeper significance of her poetry is to understand her fascination with death as connected with and transformed into a broader concern with the themes of rebirth and transcendence. . . . (p. 5)

To deal with the structure of Plath's poetry is primarily to deal with the voices, landscape, characters, images, emblems, and motifs which articulate a mythic drama having something of the eternal necessity of Greek tragedy. The myth has its basis in her biography, but it in turn exercises a selective function on her biography and determines within it an increasingly restricted context of relevance as her work becomes more symbolic and archetypal. . . .

All of Sylvia Plath's late poems, including even the few that seem to be out of the mainstream, can best be understood in terms of her underlying system, as can her characteristic and effortless skills—the arrestingly exact images; the language that is at once colloquial and charged with extraordinary intensity; the ritualistic and prophetic tone; the shifting perspectives, masks, and other devices—these all evolve from the same basic concerns and necessities. . . . (p. 6)

The crucial motifs of Sylvia Plath's myth can be identified as three sets of polarities: the male as 'god' and as 'devil,' the false self and the true self, and death-in-life and life-in-death (or death and rebirth). The motif of a dominant male figure includes the heroine's father, and other male figures—identified as husband, but sometimes as lover or bridegroom. This dominant male may appear in godlike guise as a colossus, "bag full of God," or "Lord of the mirrors," or in the guise of a "devil," Nazi, or "vampire." The protagonist, rejected by her personal 'god,' characteristically attempts to resolve the resultant death-in-life by transforming him into (or exposing him as) a devil or similar figure as a basis for rejecting him.

The motif of false and true selves derives from the heroine's relation to the male figure, from which her true self has been alienated, thus giving rise to a false self. Either the false self or the male (or both) must be killed to allow rebirth of the true self. The motif of death and rebirth also provides the terms of conflict and resolution in this matter: life lived by the false self is death-in-life, while the rebirth of the true self promises life-in-death, expressed in the poetry in images of purgation, purification, and transcendence.

The central motifs of Sylvia Plath's myth are so closely parallel to motifs that occur universally in the history of myth, religion, and literature . . . , that they might be identified as archetypes. It is not surprising that this should be the case, given Plath's personal and poetic history. In respect to the theme of the father as 'god' or 'devil,' for example, one might point out that Plath was, after all, writing about an elemental relationship, in her case made critical by the fact of her father's untimely death; one would expect such a relationship to be prefigured in universal structures of meaning. Further, she was familiar with literary and psychoanalytic archetypes and symbols. . . . [The] multitude of similarities between universal archetypes and the major motifs of her work helps to explain the power of her late poems. . . . (pp. 12-13)

[There] is no real temporal development in the late poems; for since the objects in these poems function as 'releasers' of a predetermined meaning, there is no real openness to possibilities (though there is sometimes an apparent temporal development, as in **"Kindness"** or **"The Bee Meeting,"** for the sake of drama). The object encountered by the persona does not have the potential for determining an outcome, and therefore a certain tension between object and subject is lacking. The tension in Plath's poetry is located instead in the pre-existing oppositions constituting the state of being which is 'released' by certain objects and situations through their inherent relevance to it, in a reenactment of her timeless myth. . . . (p. 19)

Plath's poetry reflects that she came to consider success in altering the terms of her being as the "only alternative" to "disintegration on a massive scale" (to use [Herbert] Fingarette's phrase). The terms of this conflict are inherently religious, as they are in the recognition of selfhood as a stigma even while remaining at its mercy, and as they are in the attempt to integrate experiences of selfless ecstasy into mundane life. With this in mind, it should be clear that her suicide cannot be construed as the end of a morbid, tortured, death-loving woman (and, as is clear in comparing her to a poet such as Anne Sexton, the speaker of the late poems does not present herself as sick or neurotic, but as a heroine trapped in "the illusion of a Greek necessity"); it is rather the mark of failure to achieve wholeness in circumstances which made this achievement a matter of life and death. It might be mentioned in this context that her last two poems, both dated February 5, 1963, were **"Balloons"** and **"Edge"**: in one of these a mother plays with her two children in a realistic domestic setting; the other presents a dead mother and her dead children in a stark symbolic manner.

Toward the end of her life, Plath underwent a religious crisis, undoubtedly precipitated by her domestic crisis, but also quite distinct from it. Although the breakup of her marriage probably made the problem of overcoming the "stigma of selfhood" an urgent one, the need to transcend personal history in a way more radical than that expressed in her poetry as mythic rebirth had long been implicit in her work. Anyone preoccupied with the limitations and apparent inescapability of personal history (concerns evident in **"The Disquieting Muses"** and **"Electra on Azalea Path,"** and in still earlier poems such as **"Lament"** and **"Full Fathom Five"**) has a very good chance of coming to be interested in entirely transcending personal history and the self which is its subject.

She had come to consider selfhood a problem; and she had experienced or imagined various states (reflected in **"Ariel," "Mystic," "Paralytic"**) in which a confining selfhood is dissolved in an ecstatic apprehension of a larger identity. Yet while such experiences offer insights, they do not in themselves constitute a way of life that will permanently integrate these insights. This is the problem of the 'dark night of the soul,' acknowledged directly in **"Mystic"** and implied in **"Ariel"** and **"Paralytic,"** where the ecstatic experience clearly has no future and will not itself be the state in which the speaker continues to live.

Had Plath survived, it seems likely, given the nature of her concerns at the end of her life, that she would have further developed and further explored the overtly religious themes of some of the last poems, coming more and more to realize her power of what Ted Hughes calls her "free and controlled access to depths formerly reserved to the primitive ecstatic priests, shamans and Holy men . . . "; and, as in the case of her mythology, evolving a sensibility shaped by several traditions, but with a voice unmistakably her own. The unflinchingness of her gaze, her refusal to compromise the truth, her precision, her intelligence, and her passion—all of these would have qualified her uniquely, in the discovery of her wholeness, to convince us that the achievement is possible. (pp. 209-11)

Judith Kroll, in her *Chapters in a Mythology: The Poetry of Sylvia Plath,* Harper & Row, 1976, 303 p.

M. D. UROFF
(essay date 1977)

[Uroff is an American critic and editor. In the following excerpt, she examines Plath's assigned position as a confessional poet.]

When M. L. Rosenthal first used the term, confessional poetry [in his *The New Poets*], he had in mind a phase in Robert Lowell's career when Lowell turned to themes of sexual guilt, alcoholism, confinement in a mental hospital, and developed them in the first person in a way that intended, in Rosenthal's view, to point to the poet himself. Rosenthal was careful to limit the possibilities of the mode but he did name Sylvia Plath a confessional poet as well because, he said, she put the speaker herself at the center of her poems in such a way as to make her psychological vulnerability and shame an embodiment of her civilization. Rosenthal's widely accepted estimation was challenged first by Ted Hughes who pointed out that Plath uses autobiographical details in her poetry in a more emblematic way than Lowell, and more recently by Marjorie Perloff who claims that Plath's poetry lacks the realistic detail of Lowell's work. If Hughes and Perloff are right, and I think they are, then we should reconsider the nature of the speaker in Plath's poems, her relationship to the poet, and the extent to which the poems are confessional.

What distinguishes Plath's poems from Lowell's is precisely the kind of person in the poem. With Lowell, according to Rosenthal, it is the literal self. Lowell himself has said that while he invented some of his autobiography, he nonetheless wants the reader to feel it is true, that he is getting the real Robert Lowell. The literal self in Lowell's poetry is to be sure a literary self, but fairly consistently developed as a self-deprecating, modest, comic figure with identifiable parents, summer homes, experiences at particular addresses. When he discloses under these circumstances his weaknesses, his ineptitude, his misery, his inflicting of pain on others, he is in fact revealing information that is humiliating or prejudicial to himself. In this sense, the person in the poem is making an act of confession, and, although we as readers have no power to forgive, Lowell's self-accusatory manner makes it impossible to judge. We are not outraged but chastened by such revelations. With Plath, it is otherwise. The person in her poem calls certain people father or mother but her characters lack the particularity of Commander and Mrs. Lowell. They are generalized figures not real-life people, types that Plath manipulates dramatically in order to reveal their limitations. Precisely because they are such types, the information that Plath reveals about them is necessarily prejudicial and has consequently misled some readers who react with hostility to what she has to reveal. Elizabeth Hardwick calls her lacerating and claims that Plath has the distinction of never being in her poems a nice person. While niceness is not a perfect standard for judging a person in a poem, Hardwick's reaction and that of many other critics who follow her reveal the particular way in which Plath's revelations are prejudicial to her. Plath's outraged speakers do not confess their misery so much as they vent it, and this attitude, unlike that of Lowell's characters, makes them susceptible to rather severe critical judgments. However, if we look at the strategy of the poems, we might arrive at a more accurate estimate of the person in them and of her relationship to the poet. (pp. 104-05)

[Lowell] says that when he started writing the poems in *Life Studies* he had been doing a number of readings on the West Coast and found that he was simplifying his poems, breaking the meter, making impromptu changes as he read. He claimed that poets had become proficient in forms and needed to make a "breakthrough back into life." *Life Studies* may be read as that repossession of his own life, and its mode is properly confessional because both in the poems and the prose of that volume the suffering and victimizing speaker searches through his own pain in order to perceive some truth about the nature of his experience. Plath's speakers make no such search. They are anxious to contain rather than to understand their situation. When Lowell's speaker in "Skunk Hour" says, "My mind's not right," he expresses some kind of desolate self-knowledge. By contrast, Plath calls the maddened woman in **"Miss Drake Proceeds to Supper,"** "No novice / In those elaborate rituals / Which allay the malice / Of knotted table and crooked chair." Both characters may be mad but their strategies differ. Where Lowell's character confesses his weakness, Plath's character employs all her energies in maintaining a ritualistic defense against her situation. She seems in a perverse way to act out the program of the poet whose informed and intelligent mind must manipulate its terrifying experiences. There is in fact a strange correspondence between Miss Drake's methods and those of her creator. Miss Drake is superbly sensitive, wildly inventive in objectifying her fears, and skilled at controlling them. But there is also a vast distance between Miss Drake and the poet, a distance that may be measured by the techniques of parody, caricature, hyperbole that Plath employs in characterizing her. There is something perversely comical about Miss Drake who "can see in the nick of time / How perilous needles grain the floorboards." If Miss Drake's rigid efforts are not quite ridiculed, it is fair to say that she does not engage our sympathies in the way that Lowell's speaker

in "Skunk Hour" (who may also be ridiculous) does. She has been distanced from us by the poet who sees her as a grotesque reflection of herself, employing the manipulative strategies of the uninformed mind against an undefined terror, channeling what might have been creative energy into pointless rituals.

"Miss Drake Proceeds to Supper" is an early poem but it reveals the way in which Plath controlled her own terrifying experiences in her poetry. She did so by creating characters and later speakers who demonstrate the way in which the embattled mind operates. Far from speaking for the poet, they stage crazy performances which are parodic versions of the imaginative act. Through them, Plath shows how terror may grip the mind and render it rigid. Through her speaker's projective fantasies, she projects her own understanding of hysterical control and the darker knowledge of its perilous subversion of the imagination. While Miss Drake's elaborate rituals are designed to hold off her fears, the poet who created her is handling in the act of the poem, however indirectly, her own frightening knowledge of madness. What for the mad woman is a means of avoiding experience becomes for the poet a means of controlling it. The poems, unlike the speakers in them, reveal Plath's terrifying self-knowledge.

In her poems, Plath is not concerned with the nature of her experience, rather she is engaged in demonstrating the way in which the mind deals with extreme circumstances or circumstances to which it responds with excessive sensitivity. The typical strategy of her speakers is to heighten or exaggerate ordinary experience and at the same time to intensify the mind's manipulative skills so that fathers become Fascists and the mind that must deal with the image it has conjured up becomes rigidly ritualistic. In her early poems, Plath stands outside and judges her characters, drawing caricatures not only of madness but of its counterpart, hysterical sanity. As she continued to write however, she began to let the characters speak for themselves in caricature, parody, and hyperbole which they use not as vehicles of judgment but as inevitable methods of their performances. When the mind that must deal with terror stiffens and rigidifies, parody will become its natural means of expression.

Between **"Miss Drake Proceeds to Supper"** and her late poems, however, Plath explored another way in which the mind responds to its terrors. In what has been called her middle period, Plath became interested in a kind of character who had been exhausted by her fears and could not control experience. For example, the insomniac of **"Zoo Keeper's Wife"** lies awake at night thinking over her grievances and the particular horrors of her husband's zoo full of "wolf-headed fruit bats" and the "bird-eating spider." Her response to her husband is as hyperbolic as the hysterical spinster's disdain for love's slovenliness in an early Plath poem, but she has no rituals with which to deal with it nor barricades to hide behind. Rather, she says, "I can't get it out of my mind." All she can do is "flog apes owls bears sheep / Over their iron stile" and still she can't sleep. Again, in **"Insomniac,"** the mind cannot handle memories that "jostle each other for face-room like obsolete film stars." The speaker's "head is a little interior of grey mirrors. / Each gesture flees immediately down an alley / Of diminishing perspectives, and its significance / Drains like water out the hole at the far end." It is in these poems and others like them of this period that Plath's speakers sound most like Lowell's in his more exhausted and despairing moods yet even here Plath focuses on the function or nonfunction of the mind rather than on the meaning of the experience.

As Plath turned into her later period in a poem such as **"Tulips"** the speaker of her poem seems to welcome the loss of control that had harried the insomniacs. As she goes into the hospital in this poem, she claims to be learning peacefulness, and she hands herself over to the hospital attendants to be propped up and tended to. The nurses bring her numbness in "bright needles," and, as she succumbs to the anethesia, she claims that she only wanted to be utterly empty. However, she does not rest in that attitude very long before she comes out of the operating room and its anesthetized state and begins reluctantly to confront her pain. Her first response is to complain that the tulips hurt her, watch her, that they eat up her oxygen. But, when the speaker claims a correspondence between the tulips' redness and her own wound, her manipulative mind begins to function again, first in negative ways, tormenting itself by objectifying its pain. Then, in a brief but alarming reversal, the speaker associates the tulips not only with the pain but with the heart so that the outside threat and power are not only overcome but subsumed. Because the speaker here has so exaggerated her own emptiness and the tulips' violence and vitality, she must then accept in herself the attributes she has cast onto the tulips which now return to her. The heart blooms. Here, for once, the manipulative mind works its own cure. If the supersensitive mind can turn tulips into explosions, it can also reverse the process and turn dangerous animals into blooming hearts. What it cannot do, despite the speaker's claim, is accept utter emptiness. It cannot refuse to be excited by the flowers that it does not want.

"Tulips" is an unusual poem in Plath's work not because it demonstrates how the mind may generate hyperboles to torture itself (which is a common strategy of Plath's poems) but because it shows how this generative faculty may have a positive as well as a negative function. **"Tulips"** is not a cheerful poem, but it does move from cold to warmth, from numbness to love, from empty whiteness to vivid redness, a process manipulated by the associative imagination. The

speaker herself seems surprised by her own gifts and ends the poem on a tentative note, moving toward the faraway country of health. Despite this possibly hopeful ending, however, the body of the poem demonstrates the way in which the mind may intensify its pain by objectifying it.

What takes place in **"Tulips"** in a private meditation (and perhaps the privacy accounts for the mind's pliancy) is given a much more ferocious treatment in the public performances of Plath's late poems. It is in fact the sense of being on public display that calls forth the rage of the speakers in these late poems. Forced to perform, they develop elaborate rituals. Their manipulative powers become a curse not a cure. In **"The Tour,"** the speaker, caught "in slippers and housedress with no lipstick," greets with mock hospitality her maiden aunt who wants "to be shown about": "Do step into the hall," "Yes, yes, this is my address. / Not a patch on *your* place, I guess." Instead of refusing to become a victim of the aunt's meddlesome curiosity, the speaker readily assents to it. After apologizing for the mess, she leads her aunt right into it, showing her the frost-box that bites, the furnace that exploded, the sink that ate "seven maids and a plumber." With mock concern, she warns the aunt, "O I shouldn't put my finger on *that*," "O I shouldn't dip my hankie in, it *hurts!*" "I am bitter? I'm averse?" she asks, dropping for a second her polite mask but resuming it immediately in her refrain, "Toddle on home to tea now." The speaker manipulates the aunt's curiosity, turning it back on itself by maintaining a tone of insistent courtesy and forced intimacy that is designed to jeeringly protect the aunt from the brazen exhibition of the open house of horrors. She appears to contrast her own dreary domestic appliances to her aunt's exotic possessions (the gecko she wears a costume jewelry, her Javanese geese and monkey trees); but actually her machines are "wild," she says, and in a different way unlike her aunt's tamed decorations. However, when she calls herself "creepy-creepy," she seems to have assumed her aunt's gecko-like qualities. The staginess of this speaker, her insistent rhyming, exclamatory sentences, italicized words, all provide not only a grotesque reflection of the aunt's alarm, but also suggest a kind of hysterical control. The speaker's ability to manipulate the aunt is matched by a more sinister ability to manipulate her own horrors, to locate them in furnace and stove, and there to give them a separate identity. Her mind, like Miss Drake's, is extremely skilled at objectifying her fears. The poet who felt that the intelligent mind must manipulate its most terrifying experiences also knew that the deranged mind could operate in such a way as to hold off its terror, separate itself from the agony it suffered, and the speaker here exemplifies that process. When at the end she warns the aunt not to trip over the nurse-midwife who "can bring the dead to life," she points to the source of her misery, the creative principle that has itself assumed an objective identity and become part of the mess. The midwife, like a poet, delivers life with "wiggly fingers," and she has in fact been very active in endowing dead household appliances with a lively if destructive energy; but now she too has been cast out.

In this speaker who can not only caricature her aunt with the "specs" and "flat hat" but also her own creepiness as well as her "awfully nice" creative faculties, Plath presents a damning portrait of the too inventive mind that exults in self-laceration. It is not quite accurate to say that this speaker is unaware of her own strategies because she is supremely self-conscious; but she is trapped by them. Where others have been devoured or repelled, she lives on, neither despairing nor shocked but charged with a hysterical energy that she deploys finally against herself. Her nurse-midwife is eyeless. She too can only see herself now as others see her. Her ability to manipulate her own suffering is a subversion of the poet's creative powers; it becomes a means of holding off rather than exploring her situation.

A quite different manipulator is the speaker in **"The Applicant"** who appears to be a comic figure, reveling in her machinations. Unlike the woman in **"The Tour,"** she seems to speak for others not for herself. She starts out with the characteristic question of the convention-loving woman, "First, are you our sort of person?" What interests her, she reveals, is not what we might expect from someone who would ask that question, the social qualities of her marriage applicant, but rather her physical parts. "Our sort of person" has no glass eyes, false teeth, rubber breasts, stitches to show something's missing. Once having assured herself on that score, she presents her applicant's hand in marriage, promising not only the traditional services that it will "bring teacups and roll away headaches" but that at the end it will even "dissolve of sorrow." Then, as if this "guaranteed" emotion might be too much for the man, she confides, "We make new stock from the salt." Such economy, such efficiency, this marriage broker seems to cluck. The woman "willing" "to do whatever you tell it" can be easily recycled. Next the speaker turns to the man who like the woman is "stark naked." Instead of putting him through the same examination of parts, she quickly offers him a wedding suit, "Black and stiff," that he can reuse as a funeral shroud. She adopts the familiar tone of the tailor ("How about this suit—" "Believe me, they'll bury you in it.") that shades into that of the mortician. Suddenly the suit, the girl, the deadly convention of marriage are all one, like a tomb, equally "waterproof, shatterproof, proof / Against fire and bombs through the roof." The subversive excess of her promises here is hastily passed over as her sales pitch continues: "Now your head, excuse me, is empty. / I have the ticket for that. / Come

here, sweetie, out of the closet." What she presents is "A living doll" whose value will increase with each anniversary, paper at first but silver in 25 years and gold at 50 years.

It might be argued that **"The Applicant"** does not properly belong to those poems in which Plath exposes the mind's manipulation of terrifying experiences. After all, marriage—and especially the marriage contracted here—is a conventional arrangement which should not affect the fears or passions or emotions of either the man or the woman. In addition, the speaker here appears safely removed from the situation she directs. These facts, however, do not explain the tone of the poem which comes through in the insistent refrain, "Will you marry it?" This speaker who has "the ticket" for everything seems, despite her all-knowing and consoling comic pose, very anxious to have her question answered. Again, as in the other poems we have discussed, the nature of the speaker in **"The Applicant"** deserves more attention than it has received. What she says is obvious enough but why does she say it? I have called her a woman although her sex is nowhere identified partly because of her language (she calls the woman "sweetie" and the man "My boy") and partly because of her claim that her applicant can sew, cook and "talk, talk, talk" (no man, I believe, would have considered that last feature a selling point) but chiefly because she seems to be extremely concerned for the successful outcome of her applicant. She is like the applicant herself willing to make any claim and to accede to any demands in order to strike a bargain. Hers is a pose of course, but it is the pose of the compliant woman. Like the patient in **"Tulips"** who accepts the gift of flowers that torment her and the niece in **"The Tour"** who responds to her aunt's detested visit, the speaker here insists on participating in a situation the demands of which she finds abhorrent. Her only recourse for dealing with it is a mode at which she is particularly skilled, burlesque. Yet behind the scorn and the scoffing is another feeling, something like hysteria, that expresses itself in her repeated question. She seems trapped by the sexual stereotypes she parodies. The ventriloquism of this poem hides the fact that this is an internal debate. The sexual fear that has driven the "sweetie" into the closet and the boy to his last resort also propels the manipulations of this shrewd if too agreeable woman. Here again is the controlling mind using its powers to compartmentalize rather than explore its situation.

"The Applicant" has been given serious consideration as Plath's statement on marriage yet it does not point to the poet herself in the same way that, for example, Robert Lowell's "Man and Wife" does. Its characters are unparticularized and unconnected to any specific event in Plath's experience. Its sexual stereotypes (the girl willing to do anything in order to be married and the boy only willing to marry if he can be convinced that he will get a worthwhile product) are manipulated by a speaker whose tension-filled control reveals not only their power over her but the terror that informs them. This speaker can manage, but she cannot escape her situation.

The relationship between poet and speaker in two other late poems, **"Lady Lazarus"** and **"Daddy,"** is somewhat more complicated because these poems do call upon specific incidents in Plath's biography, her suicide attempts and her father's death. Yet to associate the poet with the speaker directly, as many critics have done, does not account for the fact that Plath employs here as before the techniques of caricature, hyperbole, and parody that serve both to distance the speaker from the poet and at the same time to project onto the speaker a subversive variety of the poet's own strategies. In **"Lady Lazarus,"** the nature of the speaker is peculiar and defies our ordinary notions of someone prone to attempt suicide. Suicide is not a joyous act, and yet there is something of triumph in the speaker's assertion that she has done it again. The person recovering from a suicide attempt, as this speaker says she is, cannot possibly be so confident at the very moment of her recovery that her sour breath will vanish in a day and that she will soon be a smiling woman. Nor could she have the presence of mind to characterize those who surround her as a "peanut-crunching crowd" and her rescuers as enemies. And finally it seems psychologically impossible for the suicide victim to have the energy to rise at all against other people, much less to threaten to "eat men like air." The person who speaks here does so not to explore her situation but to control it. She is first of all a performer, and, although she adopts many different roles, she is chiefly remarkable for her control not only of herself but of the effects she wishes to work on those who surround her. She speaks of herself in hyperboles, calling herself a "walking miracle," boasting that she has "nine times to die," exclaiming that dying is an art she does "exceptionally well," asserting that "the theatrical / Comeback in broad day" knocks her out. Her treatment of suicide in such buoyant terms amounts to a parody of her own act. When she compares her suicide to the victimization of the Jews and later on when she claims there is a charge for a piece of her hair or clothes and thus compares her rescued self to the crucified Christ or martyred saint, she is engaging in self-parody. She employs these techniques partly to defy the crowd with its "brute / Amused shout: / 'A miracle!' " and partly to taunt her rescuers, "Herr Doktor" "Herr Enemy," who regard her as their "opus." She is neither a miracle nor an opus, and she fends off those who would regard her in this way. But the techniques have another function as well; they display the extent to which she can objectify herself, ritualize her fears, manipulate her own terror. Her extreme

control in fact is intimately entwined with her suicidal tendencies. The suicide is her own victim, can control her own fate. If she is not to succumb to this desire, she must engage in the elaborate ritual which goes on all the time in the mind of the would-be suicide by which she allays her persistent wish to destroy herself. Her act is the only means of dealing with a situation she cannot face. Her control is not sane but hysterical. When the speaker assures the crowd that she is "the same, identical woman" after her rescue, she is in fact telling them her inmost fear that she could and probably will do it again. What the crowd takes for a return to health, the speaker sees as a return to the perilous conditions that have driven her three times to suicide. By making a spectacle out of herself and by locating the victimizer outside herself in the doctor and the crowd, she is casting out her terrors so that she can control them. When she says at the end that she will rise and eat men like air, she is projecting (and again perhaps she is only boasting) her destruction outward. That last stanza of defiance is in fact an effort of the mind to triumph over terror, to rise and not to succumb to its own victimization.

The speaker's tone is hysterical, triumphant, defiant. Only once does she drop this tone to admit the despair that underlies it when she says, "What a trash / To annihilate each decade." Otherwise she maintains her rigid self-control in accents that range from frenzied gaiety to spiteful threats. Although her situation is much more extreme than those social occasions of **"Tulips," "The Tour," "The Applicant,"** it is, like them, not of her own making. She has been rescued when she wanted to die. Her response is perverse. She does not welcome her rescuers, nor does she examine the condition that forced her death wish; instead she accepts her fate and presents herself as in complete control. The effort of her act which comes through in her tone is intense yet necessary because without it she would have to face the fact that she is not in control. Her performance is a defense against utter desolation. Here again is the mind manipulating its own terrors. Plath was no stranger to this method, as we have said before, but while she works here with a parallel between hysterical control and creative control she presents the first as a mad reflection of the second. The speaker like Miss Drake is "No novice / In those elaborate rituals" that allay her terror yet her tremendous energies are so absorbed in maintaining them that she has no reserve with which to understand why she performs as she does. When she sees herself as a victimized Jew or Christ, she may be engaging in self-parody but the extremity of her circumstances does not allow her to realize it. The poet behind the poem is not caricaturing Lady Lazarus as she had Miss Drake; she is rather allowing Lady Lazarus to caricature herself and thus demonstrating the way in which the mind turns ritualistic against horror. Despite the fact that "Lady Lazarus" draws on Plath's own suicide attempt, the poem tells us little more than a newspaper account of the actual event. It is not a personal confession. What it does reveal is Plath's understanding of the way the suicidal person thinks.

"Daddy" is an even more complicated treatment of the same process. The poem opens with the daughter's assertion that "You do not do, you do not do." But if Daddy will not do, neither will he not not do, and we find this speaker in the characteristic Plath trap, forcing herself to deal with a situation she finds unacceptable. "Daddy" is not so much an account of a true-life situation as a demonstration of the mind confronting its own suffering and trying to control that by which it feels controlled. The simplistic, insistent rhythm is one form of control, the obsessive rhyming and repeated short phrases are others, means by which she attempts to charm and hold off the evil spirits. But the speaker is even more crafty than this technical expertise demonstrates. She is skilled at image-making like a poet and she can manipulate her images with extreme facility. The images themselves are important for what they tell us of her sense of being victimized and victimizer but more significant than the actual image is the swift ease with which she can turn it to various uses. For example, she starts out imagining herself as a prisoner living like a foot in the black shoe of her father. Then she casts her father in her own role and he becomes "one grey toe / Big as a Frisco seal" and then quickly she is looking for his foot, his root. Next he reverts to his original boot identity, and she is the one with "The boot in the face." And immediately he returns with "A cleft in your chin instead of your foot." At the end, she sees the villagers stamping on him. Thus she moves from booted to booter as her father reverses the direction. The mind that works in this way is neither logical nor psychologically penetrating; it is simply extremely adept at juggling images. In fact, the speaker is caught in her own strategies. She can control her terrors by forcing them into images, but she seems to have no understanding of the confusion her wild image-making betrays. When she identifies herself as a foot, she suggests that she is trapped, but when she calls her father a foot the associations break down. In the same way, when she caricatures her father as a Fascist and herself as a Jew, she develops associations of torture which are not exactly reversed when she reverses the identification and calls herself the killer of her vampire-father. The speaker here can categorize and manipulate her feelings in name-calling, in rituals, in images, but these are only techniques, and her frenzied use of them suggests that they are methods she employs in the absence of any other. When she says, "Daddy, I have had to kill you," she seems to realize the necessity of the exorcism and to understand the ritual she performs, but the fran-

tic pitch of the language and the swift switches of images do not confirm any self-understanding. The pace of the poem reveals its speaker as one driven by a hysterical need for complete control, a need that stems from the fear that without such control she will be destroyed. Her simple, incantatory monologue is the perfect vehicle of expression for the orderly disordered mind.

In talking to A. Alvarez, Plath called these poems "light verse." "Daddy" does not seem to fall easily into that category despite its nonsense rhymes and rhythms, its quickly flicking images. It is neither decorous nor playful. On the other hand, given its subject, neither is it ponderous or solemn. Above all it offers no insight into the speaker, no mitigating evidence, no justification. Plath's classification is clear perhaps only if we consider her speaker a parodic version of the poet. The speaker manipulates her terror in singsong language and thus delivers herself in "light verse" that employs its craft in holding off its subject. For all the frankness of this poem, the name-calling and blaming, the dark feeling that pervades it is undefined, held back rather than revealed by the technique. The poet who has created this speaker knows the speaker's strategies because they are a perverted version of her own, and that is the distinction between the speaker's "light verse" and the poet's serious poem.

From her earliest madwomen and hysterical virgins to the late suicides and father-killers, Plath portrays characters whose stagey performances are subversions of the creative act. Absorbed in their rituals, they confess nothing. They are not anxious to make a breakthrough back into life. In fact, their energies are engaged in erecting a barricade against self-revelation. Plath's fascination with this parodic image of the creative artist stems from a deep knowledge of the machinations of the mind. If she reveals herself in these poems, she does so in the grotesque mirror of parody. If these poems come out of her own emotional experiences, as she said they did, they are not uninformed cries from the heart. Rather, she chose to deal with her experience by creating characters who could not deal with theirs and through their rituals demonstrate their failure. These poems, like the speakers in them, are superbly controlled; but the poet behind the poem uses her immense technical control to manipulate the tone, the rhythm, the rhyme, the pace of the speakers' language in order to reveal truths about the speakers that their obsessive assertions deny. (pp. 105-15)

M. D. Uroff, "Sylvia Plath and Confessional Poetry: A Reconsideration," in The Iowa Review, Vol. 8, No. 1, Winter, 1977, pp. 104-15.

abandoning adulthood, provide the dynamic basis for Plath's poetry. . . .

Her poems dramatize a struggle for existence as the personality lives through repeated encounters with death.

Plath's poetry thus can be viewed not as a direct transcript of inner pathological states but as a ritual action that defines the roles that the poet may play. Essentially, the symbolic settings that Plath chooses for her dramas and the images that structure her ritual journeys compose a poetry of initiation in which the self and body are transformed through a succession of profound changes. The initiatory character of Plath's work emerges most clearly when we see how closely she follows the structural pattern and imagery of initiation in archaic societies. (p. 22)

According to [historian of religions Mircea Eliade] archaic man places a positive value on death through the initiation rite during which he simulates his own dying. . . . The pattern of death-and-rebirth is so common in ritual practices and in the literature of all cultures that Eliade feels free to call initiation the fundamental method that men have developed in order to deal with dying. (pp. 22-3)

If we adapt Eliade's perceptions about initiation to Plath's work, it becomes clear that her poems frequently perceive of death not as a suicidal ending but as the path to a transformed identity. This point is of particular importance, since the common critical tendency is to view Plath solely as a poet of suicide. Actually, the imagery and characteristic movement of her poems dramatize a death-and-rebirth pattern in much the same way that her novel *The Bell Jar* narrates a psychic death followed by personal regeneration. In a central group of poems, including **"The Stones," "Lady Lazarus," "Ariel,"** and **"Fever 103°,"** the transformation of death into life follows the three-part structure that most students of myth see as basic to initiation rites: entry into darkness, ritual death, and rebirth. Most of Plath's late poems dramatize only one or two of these aspects of initiatory structure, but almost all of them use the setting and imagery of ritual action. The dominant pattern of Plath's work—the journey to a black space where all opposites become one—merges at key moments into the larger action of initiation. (p. 23)

The first stage in the initiatory process involves the transformation of the external setting of the poem—landscape, seascape, domestic or hospital scene—into a symbolic landscape of death. In **"Tulips,"** for example, the monologue is spoken by a woman in a hospital bed. Recovering from surgery, she thinks of her hospital room as a white sea of death in which her body is a pebble. The monologue substitutes the metaphoric reality of water, pebbles, and cargo

JON ROSENBLATT
(essay date 1979)

[Rosenblatt is an American critic. In the following excerpt, he examines Plath's poetry, focusing on "a dramatic conflict between universal agencies in which the self must use ritual and magical methods in order to free itself."]

More successfully than any other recent American poet, Sylvia Plath dramatized those moments of crisis during which the self must choose between life and death. By using intensely personal material, she gave concrete form to an action involving violent self-transformation and initiatory change. Yet it is unfortunate that her poems, which embody a coherent and self-sufficient action, have been understood almost exclusively as confessional documents. (p. 21)

Instead of looking at the lyrics in *Ariel* and *Winter Trees* as confessional outpourings of self-pity and grief, we can see that they play out the dramatic conflict between opposed external forces on the field of the poet's body and self. Life and death operate in Plath's poetic world as tangible powers: they appear as dramatic agents embodied in people, trees, houses, colors, and animals. And they proceed to control the self's actions and desires, its present and its future. . . . The poetry focuses on a dramatic conflict between universal agencies in which the self must use ritual and magical methods in order to free itself.

Using these methods, Plath dramatizes a ritual confrontation with a powerful enemy force that may be death and its symbolic agents or life and its harsh demands for self-negation and painful individuation. This meeting between self and destructive other occurs frequently in Plath's work in a symbolic space that is often reached through a journey or voyage. In this central place, those aspects of existence that consciousness normally separates and opposes come together as one. Death and birth, self and other, good and evil, merge in a kind of darkness. Frequently, Plath compares this darkness to that of the womb, suggesting that she wishes to simulate the condition of unity that existed before the differentiation of consciousness took place in childhood. (pp. 21-2)

As might be expected, two possibilities are created as a result of the journey backward and inward to the beginning of life. The darkness into which the poet enters may be the prelude to her own death or it may be the means for her to gain a more vivid and intense existence. These two alternatives, which result from boats for the actuality of the hospital. The initial stage of change in **"Tulips,"** then, places the self in a water space where it can die. (pp. 23-4)

In the second stage of transformation, the self undergoes drastic forms of self-transformation in order to escape from the violence of the death-world. Paradoxically, this escape takes the form of physical destruction, including self-mutilation, dismemberment, or symbolic annihilation. . . . This process may be experienced as either pleasurable or painful, depending on the psychic motive that accompanies the particular image or action. Plath often switches from a horrified awareness of disintegration to an intense longing for it. (pp. 24-5)

These opposed reactions to death are actually aspects of the same ritual descent into darkness. In poems like **"Lady Lazarus"** and **"Fever 103°,"** which dramatize the complete destruction of personality and body, Plath expresses both attitudes. The speakers are simultaneously terrified by their annihilation and exalted by it. By bringing death and birth into the closest possible proximity, the process of initiation releases within the individual profoundly contradictory feelings toward existence. . . . Evidently, the ritual strategy is to use the death impulses in order to generate a renewed desire to live.

The characteristic imagery of this second stage in Plath's poems centers on physical dissolution and dismemberment. Her poems frequently employ images of knives, operations, amputations, blood, and lost limbs. Often she imagines herself being absorbed or "eaten" by some powerful forces external to her, usually the darkness of the sky or water or God. These images and processes point, of course, to the characteristic elements of initiation, with their bloodletting, incisions, and symbolic deaths. . . . Plath never presents an image that has only a single emotional charge or value. The imagery of disintegration is both fascinating and horrifying. In **"Totem"** the universe appears as a voracious mouth that consumes its own body: the railroad track "eaten" by the engine; the pigs and hares eaten by the farmers; men roped in and eaten by the spider Death. Absorption is the frightening prospect in **"Totem."** But in **"Poppies in July,"** images of the mouth and of eating indicate a desirable state of being. . . . Death can be either self-laceration or salvation, agony or peacefulness.

The final stage of Plath's initiatory scenario occurs only when the body has been cleansed through its own annihilation or effacement. In **"Face Lift"** the operation on the persona culminates in the replacement of her old, hated face with a new one. Symbolically, the speaker gains a new self. . . . She has been able to perform the magical act of self-generation, which is the true goal of Plath's scenarios. (pp. 25-6)

Imagery that is associated with the infant naturally revolves around birth and children. Embryological and obstetric metaphors predominate in poems that dramatize the rebirth of the self. (p. 26)

We can hardly read **"Getting There,"** or any of the other late poems about life and death, without feeling Plath's immense terror of biological reality. . . . Plath links death and birth so closely that they are virtually indistinguishable. The final image of **"A Birthday Present"** combines images of cutting and of birth. The speaker has been asking for an appropriate "birthday" gift—her death: "And the knife not carve but enter / Pure and clean as the cry of a baby, . . . ". . . . The deadly irony of the punning title suggests that only death could satisfy the speaker, but the final image gives another dimension to the death wish: Plath wants to go back to the purity of infancy as an alternative to the agonizing present. (pp. 26-7)

The persistence and depth of the initiatory images and structures in Plath's works point to the archaic nature of her beliefs, particularly her faith in spirit life and animism. Animals, insects, and vegetation in her poetry are aware of their roles and take on characteristics that are normally reserved for human beings: a bull rises up against a kingdom (**"The Bull of Bendylaw"**); bees take revenge against their keepers (**"Stings"**); flowers suffer or feel pleasure (**"Poppies in July"**). "The world is blood-hot and personal . . . " . . . , Plath says, in a phrase that could stand as the motto for all her poetry. All organic life, it appears to Plath, lives and dies aware of the violence or victimization that is part of nature.

The "personal" nature of the world thus imposes on all sentient beings the constant burden of suffering and death. Each encounter between beings and the world is a ritual confrontation with death that is repeated on all levels of existence and in all activities. For Plath death is a kind of spirit or god who incarnates himself in the objects and forms of the world. . . . At every turn death appears to frighten and to seduce animal and man.

It is not surprising, then, that blood becomes Plath's symbol both for animate beings and for a poetry that would be faithful to the nature of life. "The blood-jet," she says in a late poem, "is poetry." . . . Poems spring from the same life-consciousness or blood-consciousness that exists at the root of all natural and animal beings. Men, animals, and vegetative life exist as one in a universe that absorbs them into its blackness and nothingness; and poetry must give expression to the simultaneous destructiveness and creativity inherent in existence. (p. 33)

Within [the] context of a deathly, black exterior world and a blood-red, animate existence initiation appears as the means of transcendence to another condition of being. In many of Plath's full-scale initiatory dramas, the self attains a superhuman condition. In **"Fever 103°,"** the speaker becomes the Virgin, ascending to Heaven; in **"Lady Lazarus,"** she is a red-haired demon; in **"Ariel,"** an arrow shot to the sun; in **"Stopped Dead,"** a woman who can live off air; in **"Purdah,"** a fierce lioness. Alternately, she is magically reborn as a baby without the tormented consciousness of the adult, as in **"Face Lift," "The Stones,"** and **"Getting There."** . . . In a cosmos that is alternately persecutory and inert, the poet summons the courage to face the death-forces by undergoing, through the ritual journey, a descent into blackness. When the descent stops in the midst of the blackness, the poetry seems to mirror the inertness and passivity of nonbeing: poems like **"Edge"** and **"Words"** offer no resistance to the death-world. But in much of *Ariel* and *Winter Trees,* Plath rushes into sun, sky, or water in order to be reborn. (pp. 34-5)

What her poems reveal again and again is her tremendously violent struggle to gain control of the psyche. Each of Plath's poems portrays in different but parallel settings a momentary ordering of the symbols of life and death. (p. 35)

Jon Rosenblatt, "Sylvia Plath: The Drama of Initiation," in *Twentieth Century Literature,* Vol. 25, No. 1, Spring, 1979, pp. 21-36.

SOURCES FOR FURTHER STUDY

Bloom, Harold, ed. *Sylvia Plath.* New York: Chelsea House, 1989, 179 p.

Collects criticism of Plath's works. Includes an introduction by critic Harold Bloom.

Broe, Mary Lynn. *Protean Poetic: The Poetry of Sylvia Plath.* Columbia and London: University of Missouri Press, 1980, 226 p.

Chronological approach to Plath's career.

Butscher, Edward. *Sylvia Plath: Method and Madness.* New York: Seabury Press, 1976, 378 p.

Psychological study of Plath's life and work.

Holbrook, David. *Sylvia Plath: Poetry and Existence.* London: Athlone Press, University of London, 1976, 308 p.

Examination of Plath's life and poetry from a psychological perspective.

Steiner, Nancy Hunter. *A Closer Look at Ariel: A Memory of Sylvia Plath.* New York: Harper's Magazine Press, 1973, 83 p.

Memoir by Plath's college roommate.

Stevenson, Anne. *Bitter Fame: A Life of Sylvia Plath.* Boston: Houghton Mifflin Co., 1989, 413 p.

Well-regarded, thorough biography.

Edgar Allan Poe

1809-1849

American short story writer, novelist, poet, critic, and essayist.

INTRODUCTION

*P*oe's stature as a major figure in world literature is primarily based on his ingenious and profound short stories, poems, and critical theories, which established a highly influential rationale for the short form in both poetry and fiction. Regarded in literary histories and handbooks as the architect of the modern short story, Poe was also the principal forerunner of the "art for art's sake" movement in nineteenth-century European literature. Whereas earlier critics predominantly concerned themselves with moral or ideological generalities, Poe focused his criticism on the specifics of style and construction that contributed to a work's effectiveness or failure. In his own work, he demonstrated a brilliant command of language and technique as well as an inspired and original imagination. Poe's poetry and short stories greatly influenced the French Symbolists of the late nineteenth century, who in turn altered the direction of modern literature. It is this philosophical and artistic transaction that accounts for much of Poe's importance in literary history.

Poe's father and mother were professional actors who at the time of his birth were members of a repertory company in Boston. Before Poe was three years old both of his parents died, and he was raised in the home of John Allan, a prosperous exporter from Richmond, Virginia, who never legally adopted his foster son. As a boy, Poe attended the best schools available, and was admitted to the University of Virginia at Charlottesville in 1825. While there he distinguished himself academically but was forced to leave after less than a year because of bad debts and inadequate financial support from Allan. Poe's relationship with Allan disintegrated upon his return to Richmond in 1827, and soon after Poe left for Boston, where he enlisted in the army and also published his first poetry collection, *Tamerlane, and Other Poems.* The volume went unnoticed by readers and reviewers, and a second collection, *Al Aaraaf, Tamerlane, and Minor Poems,* received only slightly more attention when it appeared in 1829. That same year Poe was honorably discharged from the army, having attained the rank of regimental sergeant major, and was then admitted to the United States Military Academy at West Point. However, because Allan would neither provide his foster son with sufficient funds to maintain himself as a cadet nor give the consent necessary to resign from the Academy, Poe gained a dismissal by ignoring his duties and violating regulations. He subsequently went to New York City, where *Poems,* his third collection of verse, was published in 1831, and then to Baltimore, where he lived at the home of his aunt, Mrs. Maria Clemm.

Over the next few years Poe's first short stories appeared in the Philadelphia *Saturday Courier* and his "MS. Found in a Bottle" won a cash prize for best story in the Baltimore *Saturday Visitor.* Nevertheless, Poe was still not earning enough to live independently, nor did Allan's death in 1834 provide him with a legacy. The following year, however, his financial problems were temporarily alleviated when he accepted an editorship at *The Southern Literary Messenger* in Richmond, bringing with him his aunt and his twelve-year-old cousin Virginia, whom he married in 1836. *The Southern Literary Messenger* was the first of several journals Poe would direct over the next ten years and through which he rose to prominence as a leading man of letters in America. Poe made himself known not only as a superlative author of poetry and fiction, but also as a literary critic whose level of imagination and insight had hitherto been unapproached in American literature. While Poe's writings gained attention in the late 1830s and early 1840s, the profits from his work remained meager, and he supported himself by editing *Burton's Gentleman's Magazine* and *Graham's Magazine* in Philadelphia and the *Broadway Journal* in New York City. After his wife's death from tuberculosis in 1847, Poe became involved in a number of romantic affairs. It was while he prepared for his second marriage that Poe, for reasons unknown, arrived in Baltimore in late September of 1849. On October 3, he was discovered in a state of semi-consciousness; he died four days later without regaining the necessary lucidity to explain what had happened during the last days of his life.

Poe's most conspicuous contribution to world literature derives from the analytical method he practiced both as a creative author and as a critic of the works of his contemporaries. His self-declared intention was to formulate strictly artistic ideals in a milieu that he thought overly concerned with the utilitarian value of literature, a tendency he termed the "heresy of the Didactic." While Poe's position includes the chief requisites of pure aestheticism, his emphasis on literary formalism was directly linked to his philosophical ideals: through the calculated use of language one may express, though always imperfectly, a vision of truth and the essential condition of human existence. Poe's theory of literary creation is noted for two central points: first, a work must create a unity of effect on the reader to be considered successful; second, the production of this single effect should not be left to the hazards of accident or inspiration, but should to the minutest detail of style and subject be the result of rational deliberation on the part of the author. In poetry, this single effect must arouse the reader's sense of beauty, an ideal that Poe closely associated with sadness, strangeness, and loss; in prose, the effect should be one revelatory of some truth, as in "tales of ratiocination" or works evoking "terror, or passion, or horror."

Aside from a common theoretical basis, there is a psychological intensity that is characteristic of Poe's writings, especially the tales of horror that comprise his best and best-known works. These stories—which include "The Black Cat," "The Cask of Amontillado," and "The Tell-Tale Heart"—are often told by a first-person narrator, and through this voice Poe probes the workings of a character's psyche. This technique foreshadows the psychological explorations of Fyodor Dostoyevsky and the school of psychological realism. In his Gothic tales, Poe also employed an essentially symbolic, almost allegorical method which gives such works as "The Fall of the House of Usher," "The Masque of the Red Death," and "Ligeia" an enigmatic quality that accounts for their enduring interest and also links them with the symbolical works of Nathaniel Hawthorne and Herman Melville. The influence of Poe's tales may be seen in the work of later writers, including Ambrose Bierce and H. P. Lovecraft, who belong to a distinct tradition of horror literature initiated by Poe. In addition to his achievement as creator of the modern horror tale, Poe is also credited with parenting two other popular genres: science fiction and the detective story. In such works as "The Unparalleled Adventure of Hans Pfaall" and "Von Kempelen and His Discovery," Poe took advantage of the fascination for science and technology that emerged in the early nineteenth century to produce speculative and fantastic narratives which anticipate a type of literature that did not become widely practiced until the twentieth century. Similarly, Poe's three tales of ratiocination—"The Murders in the Rue Morgue," "The Purloined Letter," and "The Mystery of Marie Rogêt"—are recognized as the models which established the major characters and literary conventions of detective fiction, specifically the amateur sleuth who solves a crime that has confounded the authorities and whose feats of deductive reasoning are documented by an admiring associate. Just as Poe influenced many succeeding authors and is regarded as an ancestor of such major literary movements as Symbolism and Surrealism, he was also influenced by earlier literary figures and movements. In his use of the demonic and the grotesque, Poe evidenced the impact of the stories of E. T. A. Hoffman and the Gothic novels of Ann Radcliffe, while the despair and melancholy in much of his writing reflects an affinity with the Romantic movement of the early nineteenth century. It was Poe's particular genius that in his work he gave consummate artistic form both to his personal obsessions and those of previous literary generations, at the same time creating new forms which provided a means of expression for future artists.

While Poe is most often remembered for his short fiction, his first love as a writer was poetry, which he began writing during his adolescence. His early verse reflects the influence of such English romantics as Lord Byron, John Keats, and Percy Bysshe Shelley, yet foreshadows his later poetry which demonstrates a subjective outlook and surreal, mystic vision. "Tamerlane" and "Al Aaraaf " exemplify Poe's evolution from the portrayal of Byronic heroes to the depiction of journeys within his own imagination and subconscious. The former piece, reminiscent of Byron's "Childe Harold's Pilgrimage," recounts the life and adventures of a fourteenth-century Mongol conqueror; the latter poem portrays a dreamworld where neither good nor evil permanently reside and where absolute beauty can be directly discerned. In other poems—"To Helen," "Lenore," and "The Raven" in particular—Poe investigates the loss of ideal beauty and the difficulty in regaining it. These pieces are usually narrated by a young man who laments the untimely death of his beloved. "To Helen" is a three stanza lyric that has been called one of the most beautiful love poems in the English language. The subject of the work is a woman who becomes, in the eyes of the narrator, a personification of the classical beauty of ancient Greece and Rome. "Lenore" presents ways in which the dead are best remembered, either by mourning or celebrating life beyond earthly boundaries. In "The Raven," Poe successfully unites his philosophical and aesthetic ideals. In this psychological piece, a young scholar is emotionally tormented by a raven's ominous repetition of "Nevermore" in answer to his question about the probability of an afterlife with his deceased lover. Charles Baudelaire noted in his introduction to the French edition of "The Raven": "It is indeed the poem of the sleeplessness of despair; it lacks nothing: neither the fever of ideas, nor the violence of colors, nor sickly reasoning, nor drivelling terror, nor even the bizarre gaiety of suffering which makes it more terrible." Poe also wrote poems that were intended to be read aloud. Experimenting with combinations of sound and rhythm, he employed such technical devices as repetition, parallelism, internal rhyme, alliteration, and assonance to produce works

that are unique in American poetry for their haunting, musical quality. In "The Bells," for example, the repetition of the word "bells" in various structures accentuates the unique tonality of the different types of bells described in the poem.

While his works were not conspicuously acclaimed during his lifetime, Poe did earn due respect as a gifted fiction writer, poet, and man of letters, and occasionally he achieved a measure of popular success, especially following the appearance of "The Raven." After his death, however, the history of his critical reception becomes one of dramatically uneven judgments and interpretations. This state of affairs was initiated by Poe's one-time friend and literary executor R. W. Griswold, who, in a libelous obituary notice in the *New York Tribune* bearing the byline "Ludwig," attributed the depravity and psychological aberrations of many of the characters in Poe's fiction to Poe himself. In retrospect, Griswold's vilifications seem ultimately to have elicited as much sympathy as censure with respect to Poe and his work, leading subsequent biographers of the late nineteenth century to defend, sometimes too devotedly, Poe's name. It was not until the 1941 biography by A. H. Quinn that a balanced view was provided of Poe, his work, and the relationship between the author's life and his imagination. Nevertheless, the identification of Poe with the murderers and madmen of his works survived and flourished in the twentieth century, most prominently in the form of psychoanalytical studies such as those of Marie Bonaparte and Joseph Wood Krutch. Added to the controversy over the sanity, or at best the maturity of Poe (Paul Elmer More called him "the poet of unripe boys and unsound men"), was the question of the value of Poe's works as serious literature. At the forefront of Poe's detractors were such eminent figures as Henry James, Aldous Huxley, and T. S. Eliot, who dismissed Poe's works as juvenile, vulgar, and artistically debased; in contrast, these same works have been judged to be of the highest literary merit by such writers as Bernard Shaw and William Carlos Williams. Complementing Poe's erratic reputation among English and American critics is the more stable, and generally more elevated opinion of critics elsewhere in the world, particularly in France. Following the extensive translations and commentaries of Charles Baudelaire in the 1850s, Poe's works were received with a peculiar esteem by French writers, most profoundly those associated with the late nineteenth-century movement of Symbolism, who admired Poe's transcendent aspirations as a poet; the twentieth-century movement of Surrealism, which valued Poe's bizarre and apparently unruled imagination; and such figures as Paul Valéry, who found in Poe's theories and thought an ideal of supreme rationalism. In other countries, Poe's works have enjoyed a similar regard, and numerous studies have been written tracing the influence of the American author on the international literary scene, especially in Russia, Japan, Scandinavia, and Latin America.

Today, Poe is recognized as one of the foremost progenitors of modern literature, both in its popular forms, such as horror and detective fiction, and in its more complex and self-conscious forms, which represent the essential artistic manner of the twentieth century. In contrast to earlier critics who viewed the man and his works as one, criticism of the past twenty-five years has developed a view of Poe as a detached artist who was more concerned with displaying his virtuosity than with expressing his "soul," and who maintained an ironic rather than an autobiographical relationship to his writings. While at one time critics such as Yvor Winters wished to remove Poe from literary history, his works remain integral to any conception of modernism

in world literature. Herbert Marshall McLuhan wrote in an essay entitled "Edgar Poe's Tradition": "While the New England dons primly turned the pages of Plato and Buddha beside a tea-cozy, and while Browning and Tennyson were creating a parochial fog for the English mind to relax in, Poe never lost contact with the terrible pathos of his time. Coevally with Baudelaire, and long before Conrad and Eliot, he explored the heart of darkness."

(For further information about Poe's life and works, see *Concise Dictionary of American Literary Biography, 1640-1865; Dictionary of Literary Biography,* Vols. *3, 59, 73, 74; Nineteenth-Century Literature Criticism,* Vols. *1, 16; Poetry Criticism,* Vol. *1; Short Story Criticism,* Vol. *1;* and *Something about the Author,* Vol. 23.)

CRITICAL COMMENTARY

H. P. LOVECRAFT
(essay date 1927)

[Lovecraft is one of the foremost authors of supernatural horror fiction. His *Supernatural Horror in Literature,* originally published in 1927, is one of the earliest and most comprehensive studies of this genre. In the following excerpt from that work, Lovecraft praises Poe's achievement as the creator of the modern horror story.]

Poe's fame has been subject to curious undulations, and it is now a fashion amongst the "advanced intelligentsia" to minimize his importance both as an artist and as an influence; but it would be hard for any mature and reflective critic to deny the tremendous value of his work and the persuasive potency of his mind as an opener of artistic vistas. True, his type of outlook may have been anticipated; but it was he who first realized its possibilities and gave it supreme form and systematic expression. True also, that subsequent writers may have produced greater single tales than his; but again we must comprehend that it was only he who taught them by example and precept the art which they, having the way cleared for them and given an explicit guide, were perhaps able to carry to greater lengths. Whatever his limitations, Poe did that which no one else ever did or could have done; and to him we owe the modern horror-story in its final and perfected state.

Before Poe the bulk of weird writers had worked largely in the dark; without an understanding of the psychological basis of the horror appeal, and hampered

by more or less of conformity to certain empty literary conventions such as the happy ending, virtue rewarded, and in general a hollow moral didacticism, acceptance of popular standards and values, and striving of the author to obtrude his own emotions into the story and take sides with the partisans of the majority's artificial ideas. Poe, on the other hand, perceived the essential impersonality of the real artist; and knew that the function of creative fiction is merely to express and interpret events and sensations as they are, regardless of how they tend or what they prove—good or evil, attractive or repulsive, stimulating or depressing, with the author always acting as a vivid and detached chronicler rather than as a teacher, sympathizer, or vendor of opinion. He saw clearly that all phases of life and thought are equally eligible as subject matter for the artist, and being inclined by temperament to strangeness and gloom, decided to be the interpreter of those powerful feelings and frequent happenings which attend pain rather than pleasure, decay rather than growth, terror rather than tranquility, and which are fundamentally either adverse or indifferent to the tastes and traditional outward sentiments of mankind, and to the health, sanity, and normal expansive welfare of the species.

Poe's spectres thus acquired a convincing malignity possessed by none of their predecessors, and established a new standard of realism in the annals of literary horror. The impersonal and artistic intent, moreover, was aided by a scientific attitude not often found before; whereby Poe studied the human mind rather

Principal Works

Tamerlane, and Other Poems (poetry) 1827

Al Aaraaf, Tamerlane, and Minor Poems (poetry) 1829

Poems (poetry) 1831

The Narrative of Arthur Gordon Pym (novel) 1838

Tales of the Grotesque and Arabesque (short stories) 1840

The Raven, and Other Poems (poetry) 1845

Tales by Edgar A. Poe (short stories) 1845

Eureka: A Prose Poem (essay) 1848

The Literati: Some Honest Opinions about Authorial Merits and Demerits, with Occasional Words of Personality (criticism) 1850

than the usages of Gothic fiction, and worked with an analytical knowledge of terror's true sources which doubled the force of his narratives and emancipated him from all the absurdities inherent in merely conventional shudder-coining. This example having been set, later authors were naturally forced to conform to it in order to compete at all; so that in this way a definite change began to affect the main stream of macabre writing. Poe, too, set a fashion in consummate craftsmanship; and although today some of his own work seems slightly melodramatic and unsophisticated, we can constantly trace his influence in such things as the maintenance of a single mood and achievement of a single impression in a tale, and the rigorous paring down of incidents to such as have a direct bearing on the plot and will figure prominently in the climax. Truly may it be said that Poe invented the short story in its present form. His elevation of disease, perversity, and decay to the level of artistically expressible themes was likewise infinitely far-reaching in effect; for avidly seized, sponsored, and intensified by his eminent French admirer Charles Pierre Baudelaire, it became the nucleus of the principal aesthetic movements in France, thus making Poe in a sense the father of the Decadents and the Symbolists. (pp. 52-4)

Poe's tales, of course, fall into several classes; some of which contain a purer essence of spiritual horror than others. The tales of logic and ratiocination, forerunners of the modern detective story, are not to be included at all in weird literature; whilst certain others, probably influenced considerably by Hoffmann, possess an extravagance which relegates them to the borderline of the grotesque. Still a third group deal with abnormal psychology and monomania in such a way as to express terror but not weirdness. A substantial residuum, however, represent the literature of supernatural horror in its acutest form; and give their author a permanent and unassailable place as deity and fountain-

head of all modern diabolic fiction. Who can forget the terrible swollen ship poised on the billow-chasm's edge in **"MS. Found in a Bottle"**—the dark intimations of her unhallowed age and monstrous growth, her sinister crew of unseeing greybeards, and her frightful southward rush under full sail through the ice of the Antarctic night, sucked onward by some resistless devil-current toward a vortex of eldritch enlightenment which must end in destruction?

Then there is the unutterable M. Valdemar [from **"The Facts in the Case of M. Valdemar"**], kept together by hypnotism for seven months after his death, and uttering frantic sounds but a moment before the breaking of the spell leaves him "a nearly liquid mass of loathsome, of detestable putrescence." In the *Narrative of Arthur Gordon Pym* the voyagers reach first a strange south polar land of murderous savages where nothing is white and where vast rocky ravines have the form of titanic Egyptian letters spelling terrible primal arcana of earth; and thereafter a still more mysterious realm where everything is white, and where shrouded giants and snowy-plumed birds guard a cryptic cataract of mist which empties from immeasurable celestial heights into a torrid milky sea. **"Metzengerstein"** horrifies with its malign hints of a monstrous metempsychosis—the mad nobleman who burns the stable of his hereditary foe; the colossal unknown horse that issues from the blazing building after the owner has perished therein; the vanishing bit of ancient tapestry where was shown the giant horse of the victim's ancestor in the Crusades; the madman's wild and constant riding on the great horse, and his fear and hatred of the steed; the meaningless prophecies that brood obscurely over the warring horses; and finally, the burning of the madman's palace and the death therein of the owner, borne helpless into the flames and up the vast staircase astride the beast he has ridden so strangely. Afterward the rising smoke of the ruins takes the form of a gigantic horse. **"The Man of the Crowd,"** telling of one who roams day and night to mingle with streams of people as if afraid to be alone, has quieter effects, but implies nothing less of cosmic fear. Poe's mind was never far from terror and decay, and we see in every tale, poem, and philosophical dialogue a tense eagerness to fathom unplumbed wells of night, to pierce the veil of death, and to reign in fancy as lord of the frightful mysteries of time and space.

Certain of Poe's tales possess an almost absolute perfection of artistic form which makes them veritable beacon-lights in the province of the short story. Poe could, when he wished, give to his prose a richly poetic cast; employing that archaic and Orientalised style with jeweled phrase, quasi-Biblical repetition, and recurrent burthen so successfully used by later writers like Oscar Wilde and Lord Dunsany; and in the cases where he has done this we have an effect of lyrical phantasy almost narcotic in essence—an opium pageant of dream in the language of dream, with every unnatural colour and grotesque image bodied forth in a symphony of corresponding sound. **"The Masque of the Red Death," "Silence, a Fable,"** and **"Shadow, a Parable,"** are assuredly poems in every sense of the word save the metrical one, and owe as much of their power to aural cadence as to visual imagery. But it is in two of the less openly poetic tales, **"Ligeia"** and **"The Fall of the House of Usher"**—especially the latter—that one finds those very summits of artistry whereby Poe takes his place at the head of fictional miniaturists. Simple and straightforward in plot, both of these tales owe their supreme magic to the cunning development which appears in the selection and collocation of every least incident. **"Ligeia"** tells of a first wife of lofty and mysterious origin, who after death returns through a preternatural force of will to take possession of the body of a second wife; imposing even her physical appearance on the temporary reanimated corpse of her victim at the last moment. Despite a suspicion of prolixity and topheaviness, the narrative reaches its terrific climax with relentless power. **"The Fall of the House of Usher,"** whose superiority in detail and proportion is very marked, hints shudderingly of obscure life in inorganic things, and displays an abnormally linked trinity of entities at the end of a long and isolated family history—a brother, his twin sister, and their incredibly ancient house all sharing a single soul and meeting one common dissolution at the same moment.

These bizarre conceptions, so awkward in unskilful hands, become under Poe's spell living and convincing terrors to haunt our nights; and all because the author understood so perfectly the very mechanics and physiology of fear and strangeness—the essential details to emphasise, the precise incongruities and conceits to select as preliminaries or concomitants to horror, the exact incidents and allusions to throw out innocently in advance as symbols or prefigurings of each major step toward the hideous denouement to come, the nice adjustments of cumulative force and the unerring accuracy in linkage of parts which make for faultless unity throughout and thunderous effectiveness at the climactic moment, the delicate nuances of scenic and landscape value to select in establishing and sustaining the desired mood and vitalising the desired illusion—principles of this kind, and dozens of obscurer ones too elusive to be described or even fully comprehended by any ordinary commentator. Melodrama and unsophistication there may be—we are told of one fastidious Frenchman who could not bear to read Poe except in Baudelaire's urbane and Gallically modulated translation—but all traces of such things are wholly overshadowed by a potent and inborn sense of the spectral, the morbid, and the horrible which gushed forth from every cell of the artist's creative mentality and stamped his macabre work with the ineffaceable mark of supreme genius. Poe's weird tales are *alive* in a manner that few others can ever hope to be. (pp. 55-9)

H. P. Lovecraft, "Edgar Allan Poe," in his *Supernatural Horror in Literature,* Ben Abramson Publisher, 1945, pp. 52-9.

PATRICK F. QUINN
(essay date 1960)

[In the following excerpt, Quinn examines some of the problems confronting critics of Poe's stories.]

No simple statement will define the particular kind of experience we may have when reading Poe. It is not enough—certainly for literary criticism it is not enough—to call his stories, strange, extraordinary, fantastic. These words are useful only in a general or introductory way. They mainly serve to help set up the problem, the problem being: What is the content of Poe's strangeness? To be sure, his stories are extraordinary and fantastic; but in what special way are they so?

In trying to answer these questions we must keep several things in mind. First among them is a remark made by Poe himself. In his discussion of Hawthorne's stories, Poe says that the goal or aim of poetry is Beauty; whereas, in prose fiction, the goal or aim is Truth. Immediately we are puzzled. What did he mean by these terms Beauty and Truth? Consider the extreme but instructive instance of **"The Conqueror Worm."** In this poem we find a distinctively Poe-esque vision of mortality. The poem is a kind of allegorical scenario, with human beings as puppets or actors on the stage of life, enacting a drama that is meaningless to them, a drama made with "much of Madness, and more of Sin / And Horror the soul of the plot." The climax of the drama, and of the poem, occurs with the entrance on the stage of an enormous red and writhing worm, which with "vermin fangs" feeds on "human gore," and so brings the play, and life, to an end. For the play, writes Poe, is the tragedy "Man," and its hero the Conqueror Worm.

Whatever else can be said about this poem, it cannot be said to involve the contemplation of Beauty. And yet Poe repeatedly made it clear that, in his opinion such contemplation—or the aspiration towards it—was the sole province and justification of poetry. Between this opinion and the poem I have cited there is a sharp contradiction.

Similarly, we wonder what Poe had in mind when he said, in the second half of the remark alluded to, that "Truth is often, and in very great degree, the aim of the tale." His own tales, beyond argument, are strange, fantastic, and the like. What have they to do with Truth? What meaning did this word have for him?

The answer seems to be that he saw two different meanings in this word: the truth of logic and fact, on the one hand, and the truth of insight and imagination, on the other. Almost everyone who has written about Poe has emphasized or at least referred to some kind of *dualism* as characteristic of his mind and his writing. Thus, for example, among the characters he created, he seems to resemble most the doomed dreamer Roderick Usher. But he also resembles Legrand, the successful empiricist who is the hero of **"The Gold Bug."** We find something of Poe in the obsessed criminal whose story of defeat is **"The Black Cat."** But Poe is also recognizable in the analytical criminologist, the detective-hero Dupin. If we say that Poe's world is a nightmare world, we must add that his world is also one of facts and figures and logical inferences. The "people" we encounter in his stories are dream-figures, phantoms; yet at the same time they are firmly sketched and carefully studied. Or, as a final instance, *The Narrative of Arthur Gordon Pym* is the story of an imaginary voyage. Only if read in this way can it become intelligible. However, in spite of its inwardness, *Gordon Pym* is crammed with data about the actual and outward world. How, then, should we understand Poe's remark that Truth is the aim of the tale when the tale is that of Gordon Pym?

Another difficulty we should be aware of, also in relation to the same remark, is that Poe seldom if ever identifies the nature of the truth conveyed in his stories. We know that he disliked didactic poetry. Apparently this distaste for didacticism was carried over from his poetic theory into his practice as a writer of fiction, for it is hard to recall any important story of his which is clearly, self-evidently, didactic. And this is probably why the objection is sometimes made that Poe's stories are empty of significance because they have no themes. For Poe almost never states his theme. He only dramatizes it. In the final lines of **"The Conqueror Worm"** he does clarify his gruesome allegory, as we saw. In a story that somewhat resembles that poem, in **"The Masque of the Red Death,"** we find no such clarification of meaning. No key to interpretation is presented. Instead, the meaning of the story is left latent within the details of the story itself. This is Poe's usual procedure.

The curious fact to take note of here is that he does provide a key to the interpretation of his poem **"The Conqueror Worm,"** but he does not normally do this in his stories. And yet Poe's doctrine was that stories, and not poems, have Truth for their province or goal. It would be consistent with this principle if the stories stated their thematic point. But this rarely happens. If the stories "aim at Truth," they do so indirectly, by suggestion rather than by statement.

Poe, then, is a symbolist writer, and a symbolist writer of a certain kind. He belonged to no school or tradition, nor did he devise for himself a theory and method of literary symbolism. This is one way in which Poe differs from another great symbolist writer, James Joyce. Poe's stories, many of them, are symbolical, but not in the way Joyce's are. If we accept the thorough *explications de texte* that have been made of the stories in *Dubliners,* we must conclude that Joyce was able to invest multiple significance in almost every detail he used, no matter how trivial the detail might at first appear. The details chosen are graphically real; they convey a sense of actuality almost painful in its acuteness. And yet almost every time these details are there, for the reader who will study them, to bring in associations and reverberations that could never be summoned by merely realistic exactitude. Poe's stories cannot be successfully read, or rather studied, in this fashion. Details in his writing sometimes have a symbolic overtone, and sometimes they do not. For example, the narrator of **"MS. Found in a Bottle"** mentions that at one stage in his adventures he and a Swedish sailor were the only survivors of a tempest at sea. To ask the question: Why a *Swedish* sailor?—this is to assume, in effect, that Joyce rather than Poe wrote the story. Even in the final pages, when the narrator describes his experiences aboard an ancient and enormous ship, manned by a silent, aged, and infirm crew, even here, although we know how far behind us have been left the assumptions and criteria of realism, it is still hazardous to attempt particular symbolic identifications, to say that this detail represents one thing, and that other detail another. Usually in a story by Poe the details, the individual parts, resist what is called "symbol-hunting." Nevertheless, these parts do cohere in a totality—a *gestalt* or configuration—that does impress us as having symbolic force. It is as if the whole proves to be more than the sum of its parts. For this reason Poe's stories are difficult to analyze. In an effort to account for what is *felt* as their overall symbolic significance, we turn back, in analysis, to individual details. And these, we usually find, are lacking in symbolic resonance.

In other words, Poe's stories resist a direct gaze. The literal-minded reader will find them empty of meaning. The opposite kind of reader, who expects Poe to speak always in a consistently symbolic language, is also disappointed. The stories should be read obliquely, in accordance with the method, to call it that, used by Gordon Pym. After many days of confinement in the dark hold of the ship on which he had secretly taken passage, Pym came upon a message from the only other person on board who knew of his presence. In describing his attempt to read this message, Pym says: "The white slip of paper could barely be discerned, and not even that when I looked at it directly; by turning the exterior portions of the retina towards it,—that is to say, by surveying it slightly askance, I found that it became in some measure perceptible." By analogy, Poe's stories, too, become perceptible and intelligible if they are surveyed "slightly askance," if they are read, that is, indirectly and obliquely. So much for a *theory* as to how Poe should be read.

Practically, one can find no better introduction to Poe, no more effective way of getting to know the nature of his writing, than the story of Gordon Pym in its entirety. For in this, the longest of his stories, we find Poe's imagination at work on a large scale, and so we are given a larger opportunity than usual to study it and respond to it. *Arthur Gordon Pym* is a romance of the sea, a narrative of storm, shipwreck and other disasters on the oceans between Massachusetts and the South Pole. Some of the pages in this work are among the very best to be found in Poe. But if it is read only as an adventure story it is found to be unsatisfactory. A reader who expects to find a recital of adventures undergone by "real" people in realistic settings soon finds himself bored and puzzled by *Gordon Pym.* Although the prose is conventional, straightforward, and clear, and although the story begins on a solidly realistic basis, most of the experiences in Pym's narrative are inward rather than outward. Interior, imaginary, emotional disasters are translated, or projected outward, into the form of adventures at sea. To be aware only of this form, to notice only the dramatic events of the story, is to miss their interior meaning, where the essence of their life is.

To the question, therefore, What is *Gordon Pym* about? or What is Poe trying to say? one valid answer is probably this: The story is a graphic and dramatic representation of what it feels like to have the temperament of Gordon Pym. And what kind of temperament is that? Pym is the kind of person for whom the values of stability and security are meaningless, for whom everything that exists is deceptive and finally hostile. He is the kind of person who wants to sustain no firm link with the real world, the natural and the human environment, and who instead converts his life into a frenzied pursuit of death. For him, death is not to be feared but rather to be sought. *It* is the goal. But there are no goals worth finding in the course of normal life. In Poe's extended metaphor of the sea-voyage, life is represented as a long and agonizing journey to nowhere. This is one meaning, and the major one, of the whole story.

The most important lesson to be learned through a study of *Gordon Pym* is the one indicated earlier: Poe's true subject matter is not made of the incidents he writes about. These incidents, forming the action or plot, are his ways of getting at the subject. If we confine our attention only to the external details—to what is in effect the scaffolding—of the story, we can hardly claim to have read it.

For another example, **"The Fall of the House of Usher"** has been interpreted in various ways, even as a kind of political allegory of the relationship between England and Ireland. Such an interpretation is absurd, of course. Yet whoever thought of it was more responsive to the idiom of Poe than is someone who can find only the plot, and for whom **"The Fall of the House of Usher"** is only the story of a murder, the story of how Roderick killed his sister Madeline. To assume that the Ushers are meant to serve as representations of real people and that the events of the story might actually have happened, this is to set the story in an altogether misleading perspective.

"The Fall of the House of Usher" is not the story of a murder case. It is rather a representation of the experience of dread. As Poe understood this feeling, it was not equivalent to anxiety or fear. To some extent, dread contains both those feelings. But, in addition, as its distinctive characteristic, it also involves their opposite: the feeling of desire. Thus there results an explosive combination of antipathy and sympathy. Thus, what Usher feared was the death of his sister, and yet he killed her precisely because he at the same time longed for what he feared.

It is possible to say that the story of Usher dramatizes this insight into the complexity of the feeling of dread, that this insight is the basic subject and significant content of the story. But there is more to it than that. Roderick Usher is related to Gordon Pym in that for both of them the term *reality* in its commonsense, everyday meaning is meaningless. The reality they want is a dreamed reality, beyond the dimensions of time and space, and hence a nirvana attainable only through death. Pym's story concerns a quest for this nirvana, and so too, though less obviously, the story of Usher. Both stories are further alike in a still more fundamental way. They are written out of Poe's conviction that reality, consciousness, the "human condition," is false and limited. He refuses to accept it. Ultimately, what is conveyed in both stories is Poe's hatred of reality.

Hatred may seem an extravagant word, perhaps a wrong word. But I think it can be justified. It is true that in many of his stories Poe begins with the world of reality, the public world we all can recognize, and he writes about the specific actualities of this world with precision and care. Indeed, he seems at times almost too much interested in concrete particulars, as every reader of *Gordon Pym* can testify, and as is illustrated nicely in an early paragraph from **"MS. Found in a Bottle"**:

Our vessel was a beautiful ship of about four hundred tons, copper fastened, and built at Bombay of Malabar teak. She was freighted with cotton-wool and oil, from the Lachadive islands. We had also on board coir, jaggeree, ghee, cocoa-nuts, and a few cases of opium. The stowage was clumsily done, and the vessel consequently crank.

However, as we go on reading we find that Poe's care and precision remain, but the real world does not. It has been dissolved into a dream or nightmare world. What we experience when we read is this process of transformation, dissolution, dislocation. Natural facts are alluded to, but they no longer retain their factual quality. Thus the streams of water in the final section of *Gordon Pym* are recognizable as streams of water, but in Poe's description they more resemble colorless streams of blood. This is typical of what he does; as is also, in **"The Oval Portrait,"** the way in which the creative power of art is made over into its opposite, the power to destroy. Poe himself, in his own art, works in a similar way.

If we return now to the remark quoted a while ago—Poe's remark that poetry has Beauty as its aim, whereas prose fiction aims at Truth—we find it less puzzling than we did before. Beauty, for Poe, was a transcendental, present in a realm above and beyond the realm of the real, the realm of Truth. While on earth and living in time, we can attain "to but brief and indeterminate glimpses" of the "divine and rapturous joys" that belong to the realm of Beauty. Such glimpses are afforded by poetry and music. But [it] is only when we are "beyond the grave" that Beauty can be apprehended in its fullness. Meantime we are living in the realm of actuality, of reality, of Truth. For Poe this was a kind of prison in which he felt himself trapped. His fear of and abhorrence for this prison are the recurrent sensations conveyed by his stories, which, in this way, and in Poe's own terms, *are* concerned with the realm of Truth. Accordingly, a major theme of the stories is that to know this realm for what it is is to loathe and reject it. In one of the most perceptive studies ever written about Poe, a study based on the pervasive presence in Poe's writing of images of imprisonment, encirclement, and circumscribed space, Georges Poulet reaches this conclusion, among others: "L'homme est pour lui un enterré vivant qui a pour mission d'explorer les surfaces intérieures de sa chambre." This one sentence of Poulet's is the best statement that can be made to define Poe's view of reality and actual human life. (pp. 140-44)

For him, to advance in the direction of one's dreams is to leave real life behind. No foundations on earth can be put under Poe's castles, for these castles—like the ones in **"The City in the Sea"** and the House of Usher—are destined to fade from sight in the water that reflects them. . . . And for him the perfect future existed somewhere "out of this world." . . . (p. 145)

Poe's few attempts—in some of his poems and in the prose poem **"The Domain of Arnheim"**—to go somewhere out of this world and reconnoitre the su-

pernal realm of Essence are interesting attempts. But they failed. His imaginative powers in this respect fell far short of the task he set them. For that task was nothing less than to equal or surpass the achievement of Dante in the *Paradiso*. This he could not possibly do; and that Poe was aware of his inability is evidenced by the very limited number of poems he wrote.

Where Poe's imagination was successfully employed was along what may be referred to as the negative line of his argument, his hatred for and repudiation of the real, existential world. In the year before his death he gave this attitude its maximum expression in the most ambitious of all his writings, his treatise on the cosmos, *Eureka.* What we find as the conclusion of all the guesses and demonstrations in *Eureka* is that all of creation, all of reality, is unstable; that the entire universe is in a state of progressive collapse; and that this drive towards collapse is the one meaningful fact in the constitution of reality. In greater or less degree almost all of Poe's important writings may be read as individual variations on this, his paramount theme. (p. 146)

Patrick F. Quinn, "Four Views of Edgar Poe," in *Jahrbuch Für Amerikastudien*, Vol. 5, 1960, pp. 128-46.

FLOYD STOVALL

(essay date 1965)

[In the following excerpt from his introduction to *The Poems of Edgar Allan Poe*, Stovall discusses Poe's poetic achievement.]

Poe's poems, like his tales, are notable for their original conceptions and for the technical perfection of their execution. His ear was excellent; such irregularities of meter and discordant collocations as may be found in the late poems were intentional and served a purpose more important, at the moment, than pleasing the senses. But Poe could write mellifluous verse in his later as well as in his early years, as witness **"The Bells"** and **"Annabel Lee."** Like Coleridge, he found music essential to poetry, and in the "Letter to B——," the prefatory essay to *Poems*, 1831, which was his earliest venture in prose criticism, he defined poetry as music combined with a pleasurable idea. There is no question as to the musical quality of his poetry. Some critics, however, have complained of the absence of ideas. In 1909 W. C. Brownell said [in his *American Prose Masters*] of all Poe's writings: "They lack substance. Literature is more than an art." In our time, T. S. Eliot [in his *From Poe to Valéry* (1948)] has called Poe a gifted adolescent, and Allen Tate has said [in his *The Forlorn Demon* (1953)] that his perceptual powers remained undeveloped. There is a certain amount of truth in all of these opinions; but the faults they adduce, if they exist, should be seen in the proper perspective. This perspective is provided by Poe's theory of the nature of poetry and of the function of the poet. The poet's truth is an intuition, an excitement of the soul that he called the Poetic Sentiment, and it is the product not of rational thought but of the contemplation of beauty. The only substance of beauty is form. A rational construction, such as his prose poem *Eureka* or his tales of ratiocination, may have beauty, but that beauty subsists in the consistency, the harmonious relationship, of the ideas, not in the ideas themselves.

Poe's poems can be said to lack substance only if the theory which they exemplify is wrong. If his theory is right, or if we accept that part of it which concerns the relation of beauty and truth, we must admit that his poems have the true substance of art in their power of inducing intuitions of truth in the responsive reader. Such truths are untranslatable—they cannot be expressed in terms of the intellect or of the moral sense—but they are nonetheless real to all who accept truth and beauty as of one essence. Although exponents of the doctrine of "art for art" cannot rightly claim Poe as their prophet, they may well find comfort in his poetry as in his poetic theory. Some modern poets might, in all candor, confess a greater indebtedness to Poe than they have been inclined to do. Poe was surely among the first theorists to affirm that a poem's primary value is in itself, not in what it tells us about something, whether that something be a moral or intellectual truth or some revelation of the poet himself. A poem is not a document, but a total creation; it is not a part of a world only, but a world in itself. When these matters are better understood, Poe's poetry may be more highly estimated.

Of all American writers, critics have found Poe the most difficult to categorize in a phrase. Longfellow has been depreciated as a genial sentimentalist, Emerson tolerated as a hopeful idealist, Hawthorne appreciated as a physician of souls, and Whitman hailed as a prophet of the new Eden. But Poe was neither genial nor hopeful, and he grew to look skeptically on Edens here or hereafter. In his high regard for art he was akin to Hawthorne, and in his speculative intellect he had something in common with Melville; but where in nineteenth-century America will one meet with the equal of his critical acumen, his disciplined narrative skill, or his sure feeling for verbal sounds and rhythms? On the other hand, no other American writer of the first rank lent his talent to weaker performances than some of his carping book reviews or his more grotesque attempts at humor. Three or four of his poems addressed to literary ladies do but slight credit to their author. His late poems, with their ingenious and compli-

cated structure, have been said to "smell of the lamp." But Poe should be judged objectively on positive, not negative, evidence; in the final reckoning, his weaknesses should not be charged against his strength. One does not arrive at the true worth of a literary artist by taking an average of his work.

Perhaps Poe's greatest single literary virtue is his originality. Each of his best poems and tales, as I have said, is unique in its kind. He was not an assembly-line creator. And though his critical ideas may be largely derivative, he made them his own, enlarged them, and used them well to his own purposes. He wrote a dozen poems and nearly as many tales that approach artistic perfection. His tales, however contrived, are vivid, and the strange beauty of his poems is inimitable. Wherein lies his true genius? That would be hard to say with conviction. Any just estimate of his work must take into account his total achievement in the three fields of criticism, fiction, and poetry. In his own mind, and in the minds of a good many, though probably a minority, of his critics, he was a poet first of all and above all else. It is possible that he made his most enduring contribution to literature in the creation of a few unforgettable poems. (pp. xxxvi-xxxvii)

Floyd Stovall, in an introduction to *The Poems of Edgar Allan Poe* by Edgar Allan Poe, edited by Floyd Stovall, The University Press of Virginia, 1965, pp. xv-xxxvii.

KENNETH GRAHAM
(essay date 1967)

[In the following excerpt from his introduction to a collection of Poe's tales, Graham surveys their unifying characteristics.]

Poe's narrations are all, like the one found in a bottle ["MS. **Found in a Bottle**"], manuscripts sent back from the edge of nothingness. With unique singlemindedness and intensity they probe into a spirit world, at times dark, at times beautiful, that underlies and destroys all the material phenomena of life, a world of the whirlpool, of the pit and the grave, of consciousness-after-death, of mystically alluring eyes, of torture, of the desire to kill, of guilt, madness, and, in the end, utter silence. They may be narrowly obsessive and joyless, but their continuing power is founded on one recognizable and even familiar vision of life: that an awareness of death is the starting-point of knowledge, and that reality is not solid and reasonable but a flux, a maelström like the Norwegian fisherman's that contains within it some destructive promise of eternity. Yet Poe is at the same time incorrigibly reasonable.

Again like the fisherman lost in the maelström, his mind acts like a scientist's even as he perceives the inadequacy of science to attain Truth. A part of his creating imagination always clings to the solid and the rational, in a continual tension with the part that envisages the annihilation of the external world and the final loss of the self. And out of this conflict come the controlled energy and excitement that are the distinguishing marks of Poe's art.

Poe was first of all—in time, if not perhaps in quality of achievement—a poet, and in his poetry the same general themes displayed themselves. The poet pursues his vision of ideal love, beauty, and poetic inspiration that dwells in 'the regions which / Are Holy-Land' (**"To Helen"**)—the eternal world of spirit—but he is perpetually reduced to melancholy by the inescapable facts of material existence and human mortality. 'Our flowers are merely—flowers', is his regret (**"Israfel"**). Yet in the fact of death, and in the tone of melancholy, lie the poet's imaginative salvation and his point of closest connexion with the infinite. Death takes on the fascinating lineaments, not here of the reborn Ligeia, but of the dead Annabel Lee, joined soul to soul with her lover in her 'sepulchre . . . by the sea'—or of the buried Ulalume, whose memory haunts the poet like a succubus and draws him towards the death which, however horrifying in human terms, is the only means of fidelity to his vision. (pp. vii-viii)

The poetry, however, lacks the elements of reasoning and of realism that balances the spiritual and metaphysical concerns in the tales: the strict, perhaps excessive, formality of metre and rhyme-scheme alone represent this element, and in consequence many of the poems tend to dissolve too readily into their own moonbeams. If the ultimate aim of both his poetry and his tales was to destroy the outer shell of things and reveal and create a new world behind, it was the more earth-bound nature of the prose tale that allowed Poe to give proper value to the toughness and tangibility of that outer shell even as he struggled to break through it. The tales are very akin to the poems, but persuade us more effectively, more dramatically, more humanly, of the reality of their nightmares.

A nightmare of a different kind, which must be mentioned here for the light it casts on the tales, is Poe's *Eureka,* the self-styled 'prose poem' which he published in 1848, the year before his death, and which he seems to have regarded as his ultimate achievement ('I have no desire to live since I have done *Eureka.* I could accomplish nothing more.'). Arguing intensely, abstractly, and only at times poetically, Poe's point is simply—and far from humbly—that he has discovered the secret of the Universe: the secret of creation, of present life, and of the future. *'In the Original Unity of the First Thing lies the Secondary Cause of All Things, with the Germ of their Inevitable Annihilation.'* Creation began by God, the

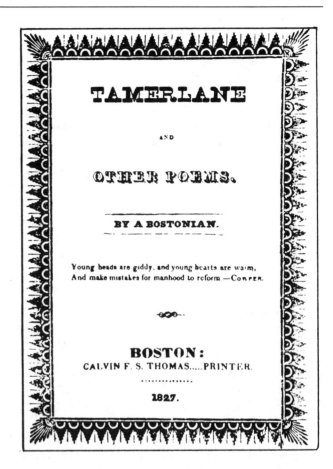

Front wrapper of *Tamerlane* (1827), Poe's first book.

One, diffusing himself in radiating waves of atoms; all these atoms have a perpetual tendency to coalesce again, as witness the force of gravity; and the Universe will end when this centripetal tendency comes to predominate, when the galaxies will whirl towards a common centre, and 'the tribe of Stars flash at length into a common embrace'—into the Oneness that Is God. Despite its obscurity and its *longueurs, Eureka* remains a fascinating map to the contours of Poe's imagination: a cosmological manifesto which the tales (and the poems) enacted in more concrete terms. The idea of cosmic unity that it celebrates is the magnified projection of Poe's famous aesthetic doctrine of the unity of plot and tone in the short story ('The Universe is a plot of God'). His narrators' many descents into maelströms, pits, tombs, and vaults are a symbolic enactment of what he describes in *Eureka* as the inborn tendency of the human mind to recognize the coming destruction of the world in the 'gyrating or vortical movements' of the galaxies. The *desire* of these narrators for destruction is part of the 'poetical nature' of man's mind, which, in its search for the artistic symmetry that is identical with Consistency, or Truth, yearns to know and be at one with the God who waits in the centre of the final vortex. That is, to create imaginatively is also to destroy. The powers of attraction and gravity are the sign and premonition of annihilation in *Eureka*—the atoms of all matter will come together in a fatal embrace, like Roderick and Madeline Usher, like all Poe's homicidal yet inseparable lovers (e.g. **"Berenice"** and **"Morella"**); like his murderers who love their victims (e.g. **"The Tell-Tale Heart"** and **"The Black Cat"**); like his split personalities (**"William Wilson"** and **"The Man of the Crowd"**); like those who secretly long to plunge downwards to their destruction (**"The Imp of the Perverse"**, **"MS. Found in a Bottle"**, and **"A Descent into the Maelström"**). If Time is the destroyer of all things material, so, too, is the Pendulum the destroyer in the Pit, and the ebony clock in **"The Masque of the Red Death"**. And if all things are atoms of God, it follows that matter and spirit are one, and that *'The Body and The Soul walk hand in hand'*—as they do so terrifyingly through the whole animistic universe of the tales.

When we read Poe's stories in the context of his total *oeuvre* in this way, we can see how even the most particularized and concrete of them take on suggestions of the widest reference. **"The Facts in the Case of M. Valdemar"**, for example, with its careful Defoe-like air of documentation and pedantry (so successful that it fooled many readers at the time into believing it true), only half-conceals Poe's preoccupation with the maelström and with the tantalizing order of existence that lies beyond death. And the latter part of **"The Colloquy of Monos and Una"**, by its sheer vividness of detailed reporting, goes a stage further. It dispenses with the dead-alive Valdemar and takes us into the very experience of personal annihilation, the reversion to Primal Unity which (in this case at least) is accompanied by a retention of a kind of consciousness.

The symbolism of Poe's voyagers—his explorers of the mind and the senses, as well as of the sea—is much richer, and more explicit. The teller of **"MS. Found in a Bottle"** and the fisherman in **"A Descent into the Maelström"** are both Ancient Mariners—the latter looks as strange as a 'traveller from the spirit-land'—with the vital difference from Coleridge that the Life-in-Death each endures is not shown as a punishment or as a flaw in Nature, but as the only road to the secret of existence and a total experience of the Universe. The seastorms and suffering which the teller of the first tale endures on his Ship of the Ages are the manifestation of a power that is the unknown side of life itself, the unconscious, poetry, divinity, the mad rush of self-destroying atoms that here takes the form of an irresistible South-bound current, culminating in a universal whirlpool. The Norwegian Maelström, similarly, is made almost explicitly more than a mere maelström by the motto to the tale, which links it with the depths of God's mystery. And to escape from it, as the fisherman does, is the sad anticlimax of most human lives, tantalized and ruined by their brief glimpses of eternity.

For Poe, the most notable glimpse of eternity available to man is in the beauty of woman, always ephemeral, always melancholic; and hence, 'the death . . . of a beautiful woman is unquestionably the most poetical topic in the world'. The shadow of the dying Fay, in **"The Island of the Fay"**, is gradually absorbed into the 'dark water', an image which, as so often in Poe, symbolizes the origin and the end of all things, the serene gloom of the death-dealing 'Spirit Divine'. But the fate of Berenice, Morella, and Ligeia is regarded in tones far less serene, and is allowed the full horror with which death is unavoidably regarded from the ordinary human—as opposed to the divine—standpoint. Yet Poe's complete immersion in this horror for its own sake goes far beyond the ordinary human reaction. It is deliberately evoked as a *positive* human faculty, a perverse excitement of the soul (fictionally, in the characters, as well as aesthetically, in the reader) that, by Poe's theory, is one approach to immortality. Thus, Egaeus the visionary—the poet? the writer of tales?—destroys Berenice, as he can destroy the most trivial objects, with the intensity of his monomaniac gaze, transmuting matter (her teeth) into abstraction (*'des idées'*), and affects us not as a unique psychopath but as an exaggerated representation of a fatal force that is everywhere—like gravity—at work. The woman is the visionary in **"Morella"**, welcoming death as a development, not an end, of consciousness (as in **"Monos and Una"**), and, from her abyss beyond the grave, haunting her earth-bound husband into an earth-bound terror: a Belle Dame Sans Merci whose vampirism breaks down her husband's sanity, and makes us question the very nature and value of our own sanity and reality. And in **"Ligeia"** the beautiful and learned witch-figure is shown to be so close to the world of spirit from the very beginning—her eyes full of the suggestion of water, stars, and mystery—that her God-like victory over mere human, physical death becomes the victory of a whole metaphysical principle, and a horrified initiation into supernatural wisdom for the husband who follows her progress—another of Poe's voyagers, victims, and artists.

Art itself is shown explicitly in two other tales as an angel of destruction. In **"The Oval Portrait"** the wife of the painter is caught in the vortex of the artistic imagination that portrays her: her death is tragic, but, like the absorption of the Fay into the dark water, it has its inevitability and even (especially in the tale's early version) its consolations. Prospero is the artist of **"The Masque of the Red Death"**, and the nightmare figure of the Red Death which he so fatally pursues through the coloured chambers of his own distorted imagination might even be seen, in part, as the grotesque principle that has inspired his own Gothic creations. The imagination, the faculty by which the Romantic approaches God, turns in, suicidally, upon itself.

Roderick Usher follows the same path, in the tale that is Poe's climactic study of the terror that accompanies, and causes, the utter breakdown of man's sense of reality—symbolized here in the destructive fissure that runs through the fabric of the House, and of Usher's sanity, and, by implication, of all concepts of the materiality of existence. The mysterious vapour, the reflection in the tarn, the wasting-away of Madeline (Usher's Berenice), the carefully nurtured terror of the narrator, the other-worldly décor of the rooms, the hyperaesthesia, gloom, and abstract painting of Usher himself, all are the emanation of an inhuman spirituality, like the flame that destroys the world in **"Eiros and Charmion"**, like the voice of the dark shape in **"Shadow"**, like the utter stillness which is the final victory for the Demon of the tomb over stoic humanity in **"Silence"**. The fall of the House of Usher, and the silent closing over it of the black waters of the tarn, are the clearest emblem of Poe's eschatological concerns, and of his art of catastrophe.

So many cosmic implications are only rendered through the immediate particular situation of each tale; and in certain of the tales the abyss in the nature of things is stressed less than its related abyss in the individual psyche. This is the case above all in Poe's tales of crime and guilt, in which we are taken, with claustrophobic intensity, into the experience of one doomed and damned figure. The irrational urge to kill, which proceeds out of an inborn sense of fear and blends into the urge to suicide, becomes our own, as we are imprisoned within the soliloquizing voice of **"The Tell-Tale Heart"** and **"The Black Cat"**. In the former the killer loves the old man and can imagine himself in the old man's place; while in the latter the narrator hangs the cat *because* it loves him (the influence of 'the Fiend intemperance' is really an irrelevance). The 'Spirit of Perverseness' drives the soul to do injury to itself, to commit sin *because* it is sin, or to confess unnecessarily to a perfect crime, in the same way as men are overcome by the irrational desire to jump when they find themselves on a precipice: the plunge into the depths once again, damned, apocalyptic, and seen as a necessary demon, personal and universal, that all men bear within them, like the seeds of their own death (**"The Imp of the Perverse"**). Even the Prisoner in **"The Pit and the Pendulum"** is a self-slayer and masochist, analysing his own sufferings (including his swoon, which is like 'a mad rushing descent') with the same fascination as the Inquisitors who watch through the roof. Suffering, like burial alive, is the self's half-eager, half-loathing submission to its own powers of annihilation—to which the French army's intervention in the last paragraph is an anti-climax more bathetic than the Norwegian fisherman's invocation of Archimedes. (It is as though a bricklayer had arrived just in time to save the House of Usher.)

These deep urges which force the individual to the brink of the pit—the admiring Baudelaire identified them as the *goût du néant*—are also revealed in the sense of guilt which haunts William Wilson and the Man of the Crowd: a guilt which by implication transcends anything attributable to the moral conscience. Though Poe tends to trivialize Wilson's *alter ego* into a mere Good Angel, the essential guilt, we are made to feel, is less that of moral transgression than an inborn guilt that sets the self fatally at war with itself: another sign of the current that drives humanity towards its Antarctica. This is the 'old fever in my system'—the Original Sin, the Gulf—that drives the second narrator with 'a craving desire' in the footsteps of the guilt-ridden Man of the Crowd: the Man who in his turn seeks to escape his own self-torments by drowning himself in the busy movement of the streets. Beyond the end of the tale (rather unsatisfactorily), and around the next corner, awaits the same mutual recognition that destroys the divided, disordered self of William Wilson. The whirlpool can so easily take the form of a mirror.

The experience of guilt itself, rather than its moral cause, is Poe's interest: he is as little intent on moral judgement as on normal human motives in a universe where all conventions are cast in doubt. That we should share the experience of Montresor's horrifying revenge in **"The Cask of Amontillado"** is more important than that we should know his reasons for carrying it out. Poe makes us explore the sadism that lurks in all of us; but after the demonstration there is no judgement. Hop-Frog's revenge is dramatically in excess of the offence given, and it is the excitement and distaste its execution arouses in the reader that are the centre of the tale. But as we have seen, in the tales considered as a whole the effect of horror is not just an effect-in-itself that ends there—a cheap thrill—but becomes one meaningful element in Poe's total view of existence.

The scientific aspect of Poe's mind may seem to have been lost sight of in this explication of his themes; but its operation is evident throughout, in points of detail. For example, most of his heroes, even at their most mad, have all the cold logic and lucidity of the sane: no one is more horrifyingly calm than Montresor. And a strain of pedantry, a passion for exactness, distinguishes them all, from the prosaic cargo-list in **"MS. Found in a Bottle"** to the various historical accounts of the Maelström. The ratiocinative Poe is most clearly shown, of course, in the cryptogram of **"The Gold-Bug"** (Poe was an inveterate setter and solver of cryptograms), and in the elaborate scientific detail of Hans Pfaall's balloon-journey, which is so much more convincing than the tiresome (and typical) burlesque-humour that encloses it and so unfairly betrays it. But even Hans Pfaall's mind wanders, in moments of reverie, among fantastic symbolic landscapes; and this alternation—or combination—is a characteristic of many tales. The let-down of the scientific explanation at the end of **"The Sphinx"**, for example, is not enough to exorcize the *fear* of the narrator's experience: a fear that is as easily evoked, as innate, and as universal as guilt. Or again, the narrator of **"MS. Found in a Bottle"** is a sceptical scientist, yet a 'nervous restlessness' haunts him 'as a fiend'; and even Rodrick Usher, at his guitar, shows an 'intense mental collectedness and concentration'. Dupin, the detective of **"The Murders in the Rue Morgue"** and **"The Purloined Letter"**, is the most famous instance of the fusion of the faculties, in his 'Bi-part soul'. His intellectual analysis in the highest degree of abstraction is vaguely linked, in some high realm of 'ideality', with the poetic imagination, so that there is no disparity between his fervid immersion in lurid dreams and his cold powers of reflection. In his ability to identify himself with and possess the minds of others, and in his 'excited or perhaps . . . diseased intelligence', Dupin is paradoxically akin to the obsessed criminals of the other tales, and is himself a voyager into preternatural knowledge and insight.

These, then, are some of the main patterns that unite [Poe's tales]. . . . With their detailed merits and demerits as art there is no space to deal. Perhaps the merits speak for themselves in his dramatic powers of compelling our participation in his people and events; in the excited and artificial rhetoric that is not always ornamental, but can serve to create the apposite tone of frenzy and disorder; in the details of colour and décor, themselves violent, inhuman, suggestive of feverish movement or strangeness beneath familiar objects (for example, his moving curtains); and in his clever use of intermediate narrators, themselves terrorized by what they describe, to double our own terror (as in **"A Descent into the Maelström"** and **"The Fall of the House of Usher"**). Despite his many flaws of anti-climax and absurdity, and despite his all-too-common sugary vulgarity, Poe at his best manages to achieve a unity between the language and the events of his tales that is the best imaginative justification for that philosophical concept of unity which is, at the deepest level, their dominant idea and inspiration. And in the end, the themes and patterns of ideas of any artist can only properly exist in terms of effective literary action. (pp. viii-xvi)

Kenneth Graham, in an introduction to *Selected Tales* by Edgar Allan Poe, Oxford University Press, Oxford, 1967, pp. vii-xxii.

BETTINA L. KNAPP
(essay date 1984)

[In the following excerpt from her critical study of Poe, Knapp investigates Poe's poetic theory as expressed in his essay "The Poetic Principle" and demonstrated throughout his poetic canon.]

"I am young—not yet twenty—*am* a poet—if deep worship of beauty can make me one," Poe wrote. "I would give the world to embody one half the ideas afloat in my imagination." Already he was the author of *Tamerlane and Other Poems* (1827) and *Al Aaraaf, Tamerlane, and Minor Poems* (1829) and the future creator of *Poems* (1831) and *The Raven and Other Poems* (1845), works which Poe was to revise many times in his perpetual search to perfect idea, form, and tonal music.

Poe began writing poetry while still a schoolboy. **"O, Tempora! O Mores!"** written in 1825, for example, is redolent with the gusto and fervor of youth. Poetry was to remain a passion with him always, a raison d'être, a means of expressing his innermost feelings as well as a way of satisfying his own aesthetic needs. Influenced by such British romantics as Coleridge, Byron, Shelley, Keats, and Thomas Moore, Poe added his own subjective outlook and poetic style, his own very distinctive brand of mystical vision. Nevertheless, . . . he was also in many ways very much a late eighteenth-century man, benefiting from the scientific disciplines of the Enlightenment. Inspiration, he felt, was not enough for any poet who seeks to create a work of lasting value. Discipline and control are a requisite part of the poetic process. A poem must be thought out; it must be sequentially organized, with each emotion and idea logically proceeding from its predecessor, the whole forming an intricate network of unified construction like the Parthenon in its architectural form, remaining indelibly in the memory. Poetry must be shaped, fashioned, and polished like an organic substance. Poe leaned in his aesthetics toward classical concepts that emphasized symmetry, simplicity, and harmony. This was the goal of the Parnassian poets, those practitioners of art for art's sake: Théophile Gautier, Leconte de Lisle, and later in England Walter Pater. They believed that art and aesthetics were in themselves creative acts, one of the goals of life, and suggested that order, discipline, restraint, and craftsmanship were vital factors in all such endeavors. A work of art must be simple, objective, and impersonal so that it may become the common property of all humanity. The French symbolist poets—Baudelaire, who translated so much of Poe into French, and Mallarmé, who dedicated poems and prose works to this "renegade" American—were drawn to him because of the refinement of his verbal feasts and the hermeticism of his thought. Poe both practiced and advocated a poetics devoid of political and moral connotations, based rather on aesthetic considerations, on cool, distanced observations of the subject, using nuanced and glittering tonal modulations.

Intuitive by nature, Poe discovered and explored realms that lie beyond the visible sphere, beyond the dimensions of time and space. In these supernal spheres he experienced an exaltation of the senses that enabled him to penetrate the very heart of mystery. There he probed and questioned, glimpsed visions sparkling with gentle or iridescent luminosity, strange and elusive outlines, shifting opalescent and crystalline light. He perceived both sonorous and inaudible voices, long moments of silences followed by the emergence of outer-worldly harmonies. The writing of poetry excited and tantalized Poe.

It also satisfied an emotional need in him, allowing him to explore the pain of his isolation and loneliness, the feelings of alienation with which his orphaned childhood had left him: "I have many occasional dealings with Adversity—but the want of parental affection has been the heaviest of my trials." Yet in good Parnassian and symbolist tradition, he never directly portrayed his sense of bereavement and affliction in a personal way, expressing his feelings always by means of symbols, analogies, metaphors, and other indirect stylistic means and methods. His inner emotions were encompassed in the mood he created, in the music of the words, the imagery in which he couched his Platonic essences, his visions of ideality and beauty. Poe's verses were depersonalized, filtered through the poetic process, rid of the dross of the outside world, the imperfections that cling to matter. Like the alchemist of old, Poe bathed his images in supernal waters, cleansing and triturating them until they gleamed in inner and outer resplendence, their unvitiated luminosity concentrated in one singularly magnetic unity. (pp. 43-6)

The concept of ideal beauty was basic to Poe's *ars poetica.* Beauty is the core and essence of the poem, its universality, and its meaning. "I designate beauty as the province of the poem," he wrote in his essay **"The Philosophy of Composition,"** published in 1846. "The *tone* of its highest manifestation" is one of "sadness." As beauty evolves in the written work, it "excites the sensitive soul to tears," thereby ushering into the poem a mood of melancholy, a whole emotional dimension. For Poe, melancholy "is the most legitimate of all poetical tones"; soundings of melancholy reverberating around death, the grief he had known as an orphan and when he lost his "ideal" love, Mrs. Stanard, his "moth-

er" figure, Mrs. Allan, and of course, grief over his wife, Virginia, who was so soon to die.

Of all the melancholy topics, what, according to the Universal understanding of mankind, is the *most* melancholy? Death which is also the most poetical: "When it most closely allies itself to beauty; the death, then, of a beautiful woman" is the most poetical theme.

Although death, implicit in the temporal world, is equated in Poe's poetic universe with the idea of metempsychosis (passing of a soul into another body after death), it also entails change, disruption, chaos, severing of the ties between loved one and lover, the agonizing, wrenching separation that rends every fiber of being: "Death is the painful metamorphosis. The worm becomes the butterfly—but the butterfly is still material—of a matter, however, which cannot be recognized by our rudimental organs."

Such a view as Poe's is timeless; it is Platonic and Apollonian, not Dionysisan, in character. It consists in "the excitement, or pleasurable elevation of the soul," in the delectation of the purest of pleasures life can offer: "the contemplation of the beautiful." Such an appreciation of beauty or of the sense of the beautiful exists "deep within the spirit of man" and is considered by Poe as "an immortal instinct," experienced at its most acute and refined state in the creative artist, the poet.

Poe defines beauty as a transpersonal or archetypal entity that exists over and beyond the chronological, personal, mortal sphere in that fourth dimension of the mystic that no longer bears the impress of the living person grounded in earthly needs. As envisaged by Poe, beauty is divorced from human wants and needs. Like the work of art, it exists in eternal domains.

It is no mere appreciation of the beauty before us— but wild effort to reach the beauty above. Inspired by an ecstatic prescience of the glories beyond the grave, we struggle, by multiform combinations among the things and thoughts of Time, to attain a portion of that loveliness whose very elements, perhaps, appertain to eternity alone.

Supernal beauty can be grasped during instances of ecstatic intuition, when the poet glimpses the pleasures that come with spiritual ascent and his whole being is infused with rapture. During these glimmerings, in some inexplicable way, the unconscious seems to become open to cosmic vibrations; it grasps, mixes, blends, sorts, and rearranges images, feelings, and sounds—conglomerates of infinite particles—into a new awareness.

Intuition for Poe was the great unifying principle that not only nourished but also reoriented the psyche. The poet, Poe suggests in his prose poem *Eureka,* must be both a Kepler and a Newton. "Kepler *guessed*—that is to say, he *imagined*" [intuited] the laws of gravitation. Later, Newton proved them logically and reasonably. It is during and after experiencing this very special condition of heightened awareness, Poe argues, that the poet is in a position to acquire direct knowledge. Expressed in mystical terms, the intellect knows, taste feels, and the moral notions oblige. Both rational and intuitive faculties function together. One does not block the other; on the contrary, each flows into and interrelates with the other in a most positive and satisfactory way. The mind therefore functions according to its own laws and logical processes—inductive, deductive, and reductive; taste operates through association of ideas and plays on both imagination and fancy. The great poet, Poe suggested, is endowed with vast intuitive powers, acute intellectual faculties, and a high order of taste. When these function at their best, the apprehension of beauty is possible.

The pleasurable feelings engendered by beauty, as Poe views them, are vastly different from the rapturous passion described by the romantic poets. Passion of an earthly kind, Poe believed, "degrades"; it hampers the poet's ascent to ethereal realms, impedes his visionary moments, distracts him from his obligations, "the contemplation of the Beautiful." Earthly passion undermines the serenity needed for the creation of pure beauty in the poems, the true and real love that is noble and altruistic.

In the search for supernal beauty, the poet must abandon reliance on the logic of overly rational processes, which only bog down the visionary zeal, limit the discovery of extraterrestrial realms, and obstruct the paths leading to unknown heights, those limitless vistas the poet must make his own if his voyage is to extend outside the three-dimensional sphere. Only in the world beyond the known can the poet experience this pure, giddying enchantment. Paradoxically, once the vision of ethereal essences is grasped firmly in the mind's eye, the poet can return to the mundane world and concretize the vistas opened to him, embedding his new feelings and fresh sensations into multiple rhythms and tonal harmonies. Ideal beauty then can be translated into a language comprehensible to others, with the poet imbuing the symbols and analogies, metaphors, and onomatopeias (words imitating natural sounds) into apocalyptic phantasms.

In each of Poe's poems he sought to express the ideality of his vision; although he realized, as did Coleridge, whom he admired and by whom he was greatly influenced, that the mind is unable to know any realm beyond that of its own understanding or realization. Yet Poe wrote, the poet must endow his work with "the Faculty of Ideality," which "is the sentiment of Poesy." (pp. 47-50)

Ideality for Poe is linked closely to imagination and intuition. It implies a kind of vision that titilates the senses and excites the mind's desire to know, to become a source of ideas, to enhance its power to communicate so that it may apprehend relationships, forms, feelings, and ideas. The road leading to ideality, which calls imagination and intuition into play, is disorganized, a confused mass. To reach such a goal, poetic or otherwise, implies for the mystic the destruction and re-creation of old but worn forms. When, for example, the poet seeks to pierce through the world of matter into a realm beyond, into supernal spheres, he must do away with all earthly, pedestrian, and well-worn paths. Visual and auditory images must take on fresh meanings and tonalities.

The ascension or descent—for the mystic they are the same—of the soul into the Platonic world of ideality allows the poet to appreciate life in both its transpersonal and its personal aspects, resulting in the unification of the universal and the particular. But the fire of inspiration that is known during the moments of poetic creation is not to be sustained, Poe maintained, for long periods of time.

For this reason, a poem must of necessity be brief. One should be able to read it at a "single sitting." If it is longer, intensity flags, interest falters, and the sublime realm is reduced to the paltry and banal. Even such great epics as *Paradise Lost* and the *Iliad,* Poe suggests, are made up of a "succession of brief " poems connected by prose passages. Everything existing in the temporal human sphere is transient and finite, including the creative process. The poet who is unaware that he is destined to fail—in the sense that he cannot know all—is doomed to "sorrow" and to "tears" because his desire will never be assuaged, his imagination being insatiable.

Imagination, Poe maintained, knows no bounds; it energizes the soul's power of ascent and is basic to the poetic process.

The pure Imagination chooses, from either *beauty* or *deformity,* only the most combinable things hitherto uncombined;—the compound as a general rule, partaking in character, of sublimity or beauty, in the ratio of the respective sublimity of the things combined—which are themselves still to be considered as atomic—that is to say, as previous combinations. But as often analogously happens in physical chemistry, so not unfrequently does it occur in this chemistry of the intellect, that the admixture of two elements will result in a something that shall have nothing of the quality of one of them—or even nothing of the qualities of either. The range of the Imagination is therefore, unlimited. Its materials extend throughout the Universe. Even out of deformities it fabricates that *Beauty* which is at once its sole object and its inevitable test.

"Music," Poe wrote, "is the perfection of the soul,

or idea, of Poetry" and is an essential factor in the creative process. Music, like poetry, is endowed with meter and rhythm, accented and unaccented beat. Both music and sound are mathematically connected. Poe's understanding of music may be likened to that of Pythagoras, the Greek mathematician and metaphysician.

For Pythagoras and for Poe sounds are based on numbers, with a correspondence existing between them since they are physical phenomena as well as abstract concepts. The harmonies inhabiting the cosmos, which Pythagoras called the music of the spheres, endow numbers with intelligible and sensible plenitude. Both heavenly bodies moving about in our earthly orbit and those in distant galaxies produce sounds, Pythagoras suggested. The musical consonances emanating from the various speeds of these bodies cannot always be heard by the human ear simply because of its physical limitations. They are perceptible, however, to other forms of life—and so is silence. Poe added:

> The sentiments deducible from the conception of sweet sound simply are out of reach of analysis—although referable, possibly, in their last result, to that merely mathematical recognition of equality which seems to be the root of all beauty.

Poe frequently used mathematical analogies when defining his aesthetic and philosophical concepts. "It is *Music,* perhaps, that the soul most nearly attains the great end for which, when inspired by the poetic Sentiment, it struggles—the creation of supernal beauty." The sounds of the harp, which Virginia played, or the flute, on which Poe enjoyed practicing, reverberate through increasingly rarefied matter, and only at certain frequencies can they be perceived by the human ear. As sonorities rise through the infinite particles filling the atmosphere, they are carried through space and light by electromagnetic waves until they reach that "unparticled matter permeating and impelling, all things" which Poe defined as God, Unity, One.

When the poet brings forth his work, inculcating it with beauty and sublimity, he is reflecting God's design in His created universe. The tonalities of the words, rhythms, silences, and pauses in the verse are experienced by nature as a whole, not only by the human ear but by flowers, grasses, valleys, rivers, forests, celestial gleamings and forms, each apprehended and mysteriously influenced by the poet's multiple ideographic exhalations and inhalations.

The poet is visionary and musician, a craftsman and a master of verbal incantations, a spiritual and aesthetic guide—a prophet. For the poet, patience and perseverance are not only necessities but obligations if ideality of the vision is to emerge with any sort of brilliance and clarity. Although "ecstatic intuition" and "a species of fine frenzy" are requirements during the stage of initial inspiration, afterward work must proceed "step by step, to its completion with the precision and rigid consequences of a mathematical problem."

The poet must work long hours to enforce the truth of his intuitive images, to express what he wants "in severity rather than efflorescence of language." A poet must be "cool, calm, unimpassioned," analytical, in control of idea, logic, grammar, syntax, and form. He must be ever vigilant that each word, thought, and image be depersonalized and universalized divested of those subjective and personal aspects that particularize, stultify, and mortalize what must be endowed with the eternal.

A poem should never be didactic or moralize; it must be simple and precise, an aspiration in all senses of the word, reminiscent in vision of Shelley's "Hymn to Intellectual Beauty" and his quest for the absolute meaning of life. It must be lyrical and pure in its imaginative course, like the work of Tennyson, whom Poe considered "the noblest poet that ever lived." He continued:

> I call him, and *think* him the noblest of poets—*not* because the impressions he produces are, at *all* times, the most profound—*not* because the poetical excitement which he induces is, at *all* times, the most intense—but because it *is,* at all times, the most ethereal—in other words, the most elevating and the most pure.

Poetry should be lyrical, as Shelley's "If ever poet sang (as a bird sings)—impulsively—earnestly—with utter abandonment—to himself solely—and for the mere joy of his own song—that poet [wrote Poe] was the author of 'The Sensitive Plant.' " Keats is the "sole British poet who has never erred in his themes. Beauty is always his aim," Poe added.

Poetry likewise must not be overburdened with aesthetic and metaphysical theories; it was this flaw that did so much to limit Coleridge's poetic élan, although Poe nevertheless admired him deeply. "Of Coleridge I cannot speak but with reverence. His towering intellect! His gigantic power!" When reading poetry, Poe wrote, "I tremble like one who stands upon a volcano, conscious, from the very darkness bursting from the crater, of the fire and the light that are weltering below." Veracity, not realism, is important. The "willing suspension of disbelief," as Coleridge termed it, must absorb the reader as the poet pours forth his music, having distilled his words, whittled away his emotions, and made manifest his reasoned constructs with their glimmering emanations in keeping with the preestablished design ordered by supernal beauty. Poe's poetry is mystery incarnate. (pp. 50-5)

Bettina L. Knapp, in her *Edgar Allan Poe,* Frederick Ungar Publishing Co., 1984, 226 p.

SOURCES FOR FURTHER STUDY

Bloom, Harold, ed. *Edgar Allan Poe: Modern Critical Views.* New York: Chelsea House Publishers, 1985, 155 p.

Collects major critical essays, including studies by Paul Valéry, D. H. Lawrence, Allen Tate, and Richard Wilbur.

Carlson, Eric W., ed. *The Recognition of Edgar Allan Poe: Selected Criticism since 1829.* Ann Arbor: The University of Michigan Press, 1970, 316 p.

Selected criticism organized into three periods: 1829-1899, 1900-1948, and 1949 to the present. These seminal writings on Poe include commentary by Fyodor Dostoyevsky, A. C. Swinburne, Henry James, T. S. Eliot, and W. H. Auden.

———. *Critical Essays on Edgar Allan Poe.* Boston: G. K. Hall & Co., 1987, 223 p.

Collection of thirty reviews and essays that chronicle Poe's literary reputation.

Howarth, William L., ed. *Twentieth Century Interpretations of Poe's Tales: A Collection of Critical Essays.* Twentieth Century Interpretations, edited by Maynard Mack. Englewood Cliffs, N.J.: Prentice-Hall, Spectrum Books, 1971, 116 p.

Includes essays by Clark Griffith, Donald Barlow Stauffer, James Gargano, Robert Daniel, and William Carlos Williams.

Kesterton, David B., ed. *Critics on Poe.* Readings in Literary Criticism, no. 22. Coral Gables, Fla.: University of Miami Press, 1973, 128 p.

Divided into four sections of selected excerpts and essays: (1) Critics on Poe: 1845-1940 (2) Critics on Poe since 1940 (3) General Critical Evaluations (4) Critics on Specific Works.

Quinn, Arthur Hobson. *Edgar Allan Poe: A Critical Biography.* New York: D. Appleton-Century Co., 1941, 804 p.

Complete and authoritative biography.

ISBN 0-8103-8365-9